UMI ANNUAL SUNDAY SCHOOL LESSON COMMENTARY

PRECEPTS FOR LIVING

1999-2000

UMI ANNUAL SUNDAY SCHOOL LESSON COMMENTARY

PRECEPTS FOR LIVING

1999-2000

International Sunday School Lessons

published by

URBAN MINISTRIES, INC.

A. Okechukwu Ogbonnaya, Ph.D., Editor

Dr. Melvin E. Banks, Sr., Litt.D., *Chairman*
Carl Jeffrey Wright, J.D., *President*
A. Okechukwu Ogbonnaya, Ph.D., *Vice President of Editorial*
Kathryn Hall, *Managing Editor*

VOLUME 2

Urban Ministries, Inc.
The African American Christian Publishing & Communications Co.
1551 Regency Court, Calumet City, IL 60409

CONTRIBUTORS

Vice President of Editorial
A. Okechukwu Ogbonnaya, Ph.D.

Layout & Design
*Larry Taylor, Vice President of
Creative Services*

Bible Illustrations
Fred Carter

Editorial Staff
Kathryn Hall, Managing Editor
Kim Brooks, Publications Assistant
Cheryl Wilson, Publications Assistant

Contributing Writers
Essays
*Deborah Branker-Harrod
Cheryl P. Clementson, Ph.D.
Rev. Dr. Odis Fentry
Carlyle Fielding-Stewart, III, Ph.D.
Dr. Carl E. King
Rev. Carol Mcllwain-Edwards
Jeanne Porter, Ph.D.
Samira E. Robinson
Judith St.Clair-Hull
Rev. Eric Wallace
Rev. Brian K. Woodson*

Bible Study Guides
Olivia Cloud
Evangeline Carey
Robert Dulin
Victoria Johnson
Michelle Obleton
A. Okechukwu Ogbonnaya, Ph.D.
Kathy Steward
Raedorah Stewart-Dodd
Diane Turner

More Light On The Text
Pamela Anderson
Koala Jones
James Mutayoba
A. Okechukwu Ogbonnaya, Ph.D.
Michelle Taylor
Rev. Alajemba Reuben Unaegbu

Unless otherwise indicated, all Scripture references are taken from the Authorized King James Version of the Bible.

A LETTER FROM THE EDITOR

Dear Brothers and Sisters in Christ,

We here at UMI are in the business of spreading the gospel of Jesus Christ and equipping the church for an effective ministry in the world. We are especially concerned with providing relevant tools to the church which will make her Divine witness to the Lord among God's children of African descent more effective. We believe that it is through the knowledge of the Word that God's people can be healed and restored to their true place in the heart of God.

PRECEPTS FOR LIVING is one of the tools which we believe will help Christians to become more effective communicators of the Word of God. This is the first Sunday School Lesson Commentary written from an African American perspective. In this we continue the UMI tradition of giving relevant gifts to the body of Christ as it seeks to reach the people of African descent for our Lord.

This Sunday School annual commentary is unique. One unique contribution of this work has already been stated, the fact that it is written from an African-American Christian perspective. Second, it provides deep analysis of scriptural passages in both the IN DEPTH section and in the new and unique feature appropriately titled MORE LIGHT ON THE TEXT. The more light on the text section is linguistic and cultural exposition of the text. It takes the passages verse by verse and comments on them from the perspective of the original language and culture. Another important aspect of the work is that the TEACHING TIPS section precedes each lesson. This section is important for those in the church who teach Sunday School and bible studies. It gives direction and suggests activities which may help you as you teach God's Word.

PRECEPTS FOR LIVING is a useful tool for Pastors in sermon preparation and Bible study tips, Church School Teachers, Sunday school superintendents and all Christians who are interested in a deeper understanding of the Word of God. We here at UMI have put much prayer into this Sunday School Annual. We know that God will use it to bless you in your walk.

Peace be with you.

A. Okechukwu Ogbonnaya, Ph.D.
Vice President, Editorial

TABLE OF CONTENTS

Fall Quarter, 1999

FROM SLAVERY TO PROMISED LAND

LESSONS
Unit 1: Liberation and Covenant
September

Unit 2: Wilderness Wanderings
October

Unit 3: Entering the Promised Land
November

Winter Quarter, 1999, 2000

STUDIES IN MATTHEW

LESSONS
Unit 1: Beginnings: Birth and Ministry
December

Unit 2: Jesus' Teachings and Ministry
January

Unit 3: Fulfillment of Jesus' Mission
February

Spring Quarter, 2000

Summer Quarter, 2000

CYCLE OF 1998-2004

Arrangement of Quarters According to the

Church School Year, September through August

	1998 - 1999	1999 - 2000	2000 - 2001	2001- 2002	2002- 2003	2003- 2004
Sep Oct Nov	God Calls a People to Faithful Living (Old Testament Survey) (13)	From Slavery to Conquest (Exodus, Leviticus, Numbers, Deuteronomy, Joshua) (13)	The Emerging Nation (Judges, 1,2, Samuel [1 Chronicles], 1 Kings 1-11 [2 Chronicles 1-9]) (13)	Jesus' Ministry (Parables, Miracles Sermon on the Mount) (13)	Judgment and Exile (2 Kings 18-25 [2 Chronicles 29-36] Jeremiah, Lamentations, Ezekiel, Habakkuk, Zephaniah) (13)	Faith Faces the World (James, 1,2, 2 Peter, 1,2,3, John, Jude) (13)
Dec Jan Feb	God Calls Anew in Jesus Christ (New Testament Survey) Christmas Sun. (12/20) (13)	Emmanuel: God with Us (Gospel of Matthew) Christmas Sun. (12/19) (13)	Good News of Jesus (Gospel of Luke) Christmas Sun. (12/24) (13)	Light for All People (Isaiah 9:1-7, 11:1-9; 40-66; Ruth, Jonah, Naham) Christmas Sun.. (12/23) (13)	Portraits of Faith (Personalities in the New Testament) Christmas Sun. (12/22) (13)	A Child is Given (4) (Samuel, John the Baptist, Jesus [2]) Lessons from Life (9) (Esther, Job, Ecclesiastes, Song of Solomon) Christmas Sun. (12/21)
Mar Apr May	That You May Believe (Gospel of John) Easter (4/4) (13	Helping a Church Confront Crisis (1, 2 Corinthians) Easter (4/23) (13)	Continuing Jesus's Work (Acts) Easter (4/15) (13)	The Power of the Gospel (Romans, Galatians) Easter (3/31) (13)	Jesus: God's Power in Action (Gospel of Mark) Easter (4/20) (13)	Jesus Fulfills His Mission (6) (Passion Narratives) Living Expectantly (7) (1,2 Thessalonians, Revelation) Easter (4/11)
Jun Jul Aug	Genesis: Beginnings (Genesis) (13)	New Life in Christ (Ephesians, Philippians, Colossians, Philemon) (13)	Division and Decline (1 Kings 1-17, [2 Chroni-cles 10-28], Isaiah 1-39, Amos, Hosea, Micah) (13)	Worship and Wisdom for Living (Psalms, Proverbs) (13)	God Restores a Remnant (Ezra, Nehemiah, Daniel, Joel, Obadiah, Haggai, Zechariah, Malachi) (14)	Hold Fast to the Faith (8) (Hebrews) Guidelines for the Church's Ministry (5) (1,2 Timothy, Titus)

* Parenthetical numerals indicate number of sessions.

For My People

Calm, calm, calm
the eye of the storm
propelling the movement of the wind
discerning the rising tides' ebb and flow
overturning a faithless ease and lax
envisioning a new world in the vanish-
ing terrain
ne'er has it been more clear
divine newness arises out of the ash

Peace, peace, peace
in the center of the tumult
echoes the Master's soothing voice
sweeter than Helena's siren song
blanket of blue ice over the restless sea
undulating promise of splendor
ne'er has it been more clear
a crystal fountain rises here

Strength, valor and confidence
holding back the rising flood
in the flow of the divine blood
as the Spirit in power broods
to undo hell's nimbus shroud
mahogany, tis not mere wood that
builds heaven's gate
ne'er has it been so clear,
a great mighty oak grows here

Rock, stone, rock
the waters of the ages beat
Rock, stone, rock
firmly planted in the Master's heart
Stone, though small and rough
yet, hid within the Rock of ages
ne'er has it been more clear
within the Rock a Jewel is formed.

A. Okechukwu Ogbonnaya

INTRODUCTION TO THE SEPTEMBER 1999 QUARTER

Units for Our Inspiration

This quarter covers the history of God's people from the Exodus through entry into the Promised Land. The study focuses on God's salvation of Israel from slavery. Within the body of these lessons, we will study how God cut a covenant with the people of Israel and examine the fulfillment of the divine promise of a land for the people. These lessons also focus on key passages from four biblical books customarily called the book of Moses: Exodus, Leviticus, Numbers, Deuteronomy including the book of Joshua. The method for examining the Scriptures follows a thematic process. The lessons focus on such themes as freedom, covenant, obedience, and faithfulness.

The Quarter at-a-Glance

FROM SLAVERY TO PROMISED LAND

UNIT 1. LIBERATION AND COVENANT

Liberation is a core theme of the Scriptures. God, from the beginning has intended for human beings to live as liberated beings. Our God is a liberator and protector of those whom He chooses. But these lessons go further than just the liberation of humans; it offers us liberation as divine activity. Thus, the unit combines liberation and covenant. True liberation is grounded in the nature and character of the God we serve. Therefore the combination of both themes serves to remind the reader that there must be an intentional relationship with God for there to be true liberation.

Within this unit, we look at God's liberative power in the life of the nation of Israel. Since Exodus serves as one of the paradigmatic themes of liberation within the Scripture, begin by looking at that single great act. These lessons will help you reconnect or keep in remembrance the power of God to liberate you from your circumstances. The unit consists of four lessons that survey the Exodus and the making of the covenant at Mount Sinai. Lesson one considers the call of Moses. Lesson two details the crossing of the Red Sea. Lesson three reports the making of the covenant at Mount Sinai. Lesson four describes the tabernacle and God's call for obedience.

LESSON 1: September 5
God Calls Moses
Exodus 3:1-12

This lesson emphasizes the visionary experience of Moses, which led him to follow God's call to liberation. Here in this lesson we walk with Moses while he tends sheep near Horeb. We follow him as he sees the Divine presence in the burning bush that was not consumed. We see how Moses is drawn to this unusual occurrence and in that process hears God call to him. We will learn how Moses responded. This lesson shows that it is not always easy to be chosen as one of the instruments of God's liberative power. The reader will also see how the Lord assured Moses that the Divine Spirit would be with him and would bring him and the Israelites to this mountain to worship. The lesson is not only designed to let you know that God uses frail human instrumentation to affect liberation, but to let you know that the Lord knew the plight of the people and wanted to liberate them from their oppression in Egypt.

Important for the study of this lesson is the fact that God has called us into a liberated existence so that we can be obedient.

LESSON 2: September 12
Crossing the Red Sea
Exodus 13:17-22—14:26-31

Biblically, this lesson directs us to consider how God led the Israelites out of Egypt. Within the lesson we see how God took them through the wilderness to avoid war with the Philistines, for whom they were not yet ready. We also learn how and why the children of Israel, in keeping with an oath between the Israelites and Joseph, took with them the bones of Joseph. We also see how God provided the people with guidance on their way to full liberation. Also, you will see that this liberating power led the people of God to a greater reverence, which in turn led to faith in God's power for those who choose, like Moses, to trust.

Hopefully, studying this lesson will help you deal with the anxiety that accompanies movement from the old and familiar to the new and promising. The lesson also shows how, during their difficult times, the Children of Israel received visible signs that helped to give them guidance and direction.

LESSON 3: September 19
The Covenant
Exodus 19:3-6; 20:2-4, 7-8, 12-17

The contents of this lesson concentrate on the Divine encounter on Mount Sinai. In this lesson we will see the Lord telling Moses to remind the Israelites how Yahweh liberated them out of slavery in Egypt. We see that not only does God remind them that it was divine power that liberated them, but also that God offers to make Israel a treasured nation, set apart for Divine service.

As you study this lesson, remember that the redemptive call is a call to live in covenant with God and with one another. This lesson will challenge you to act independently when others walk against the Lord God, make commitments and serve others unselfishly when directed by the Spirit to do so. As you study this lesson hopefully you will find new ways to deal with your struggle to maintain priorities. Particularly, the lesson reinforces what many of the readers already know: that God deserves first place in all that we as liberated people do.

LESSON 4: September 26
The Tabernacle and Obedience
Exodus 40:1-9; Leviticus 26:2-6, 11-13

The biblical contents of this lesson direct us to consider the Lord's instructions to Moses in setting up of the tabernacle meeting on the first day of the first month. Within the tabernacle was placed the ark of the covenant (screened by a curtain), the table, the lamp-stand and lamps, the altar for incense, the screen for the entrance, the altar of burnt offering, and the basin of water. Within this lesson you will come to terms with the call to obedience. The passage also deals with the Lord's promise to fulfill the covenant and to dwell among the people as their God. Not only was the tabernacle a sign of obedience from the people, it was the symbolic presence of the fact that now God dwelt among the people. The lesson leads us to places where we find comfort in the promise of God's presence.

This lesson is designed to guide the learner into affirming the divine moral authority, which is greater than the self. In this lesson we learn that while others in our world may resist the imposition of rules, we, as redeemed people, cannot ignore living by divine guidelines.

UNIT 2. WILDERNESS WANDERINGS

Unit 2 focuses on Israel's wandering in the wilderness and consists of five lessons. In this unit we will study God's leadership of the covenant people in the wilderness. While indeed, God does lead; many times the people of God chose not to follow that leadership. Thus in lesson two we see how the people's rebellion determined who would enter the Promised Land. We then examine the people's attempt to enter the land against God's direct command. This refusal to walk in obedience to God led to 40 years of additional wanderings in the dessert. In lesson four the commandment to love God with all one's heart, soul, and might is the focus. This lesson deals with one of the major obstacles to living within the covenant. Often, when people get prosperous, they tend to forget God. It is easy to credit the source of our prosperity to self rather than to God. To help deal with this issue lesson five relates a warning to the people not to forget God in prosperity.

LESSON 5: October 3
The Cloud and the Fire
Exodus 40:34-38; Numbers 9:15-19, 22-23

God was with the Children of Israel during the journey using a variety of means to show the Divine presence. Before the eyes of all the house of Israel, at each stage of their journey, God's presence was manifested by a cloud in the day and fire at night. In this lesson emphasis is placed on the instructions God gave to Moses after he set up the tabernacle. Our life concerns should lead us to seek spiritual guidance daily. We learn that the only consistent and dependable source of information to help us plan for the future is God's Word. Hopefully within this lesson you learn to depend on God for security and realize that though you may not know what to expect, God knows where you are going because the Lord your God is there.

LESSON 6: October 10
The People Rebel
Numbers 13:1-3, 32—14:4, 20-24

In this lesson we will see God giving the Children of Israel an opportunity to view the Promised Land. In obedience to God's command, Moses sent a leader from each of the 12 tribes to spy on the land of Canaan. With the exception of Joshua and Caleb, the spies brought back an unfavorable report. Because of the report the Israelites were disheartened and demanded to return to their former bondage in Egypt.

This lesson is directed to the concern that some of us find it easy to return to old ways when faced with difficulties. It also deals with the common lack of self-confidence and withdrawal from challenges in life. Hopefully, as you study this lesson you will gain the spiritual insight to avoid being influenced by the opinions of others who lead you to disobey the will of God. You will also come to terms with the fact that God understands and cares about your situations and feelings. Prayerfully, through this lesson you will be more willing to face uncertainty, placing your hope within the heart of the eternal God for the promise of a better life.

LESSON 7: October 17
The Desert Years
Deuteronomy 1:41—2:8a

The Scripture text for this lesson begins with a warning and ends with the promise of blessings. We see how refusal to listen, trust, and obey led to Israel's defeat by the Amorites. The lesson concentrates on God's care for people in times of need and the human tendency to act impetuously and regret it later. Hopefully we learn in this lesson, that avoiding one mistake now may save us a thousand heartaches later. This lesson should encourage you to recognize God's presence even in times of difficulty.

LESSON 8: **October 24**
The Great Commandment
Deuteronomy 6:1-9, 20-24

In this lesson, speaking through Moses God gave the people of Israel a set of laws to guide and bless their lives in a new land. In order to survive and enjoy the land of their new heritage, the people were continually to keep the laws in their hearts and minds, to recite them to their children, and post reminders of them on their person and in their households. In order to accomplish this task Moses mapped out instructions for them to follow to keep the Law prevalent in their minds.

This lesson will encourage you to teach your children well. People of God must seek to pass on their values and beliefs to their children. In this way, we help the next generation to understand the importance of loving God above all else.

LESSON 9: **October 31**
A Warning
Deuteronomy 8:7-20

In this lesson Israel is warned to take care not to forget the Lord God. The Biblical text for this lesson begins with the assumptions that people may be led to forget God because of their blessings and abundance. Within the lesson we will examine Moses' advice to the people to enjoy the good land the Lord was giving them and to bless God for the gift.

As you study this lesson you will be reminded not to lose your godly perspective because of material concerns, and remember that your actions have consequences. Finally, as you study this lesson, by the grace of God, you will not take credit for the accomplishments of others or receive glory that belongs to God.

UNIT 3. ENTERING THE PROMISED LAND

Unit 3 consists of four lessons that deal with Israel's entrance into the land of Canaan. Here again we find God bringing life out of what may have seemed a dead end. In these lessons you examine how God, in divine wisdom and power, deals with the various obstacles that the Children of Israel encountered as they entered the Promised Land.

In lesson one we see the death of Moses and the transition of leadership to Joshua. As the unit progresses lesson two reports the crossing of the Jordan River. Lesson three details the battle of Jericho and lesson four deals with the renewal of the covenant under Joshua's leadership.

LESSON 10: **November 7**
Joshua Succeeds Moses
Deuteronomy 31:1-8; 34:5-8a, 9

This lesson deals with several issues such as: divine guidance, divine presence, divine succor, and divine peace and security. The biblical content of this lesson emphasizes the fact that Moses informed the people of Israel that he would not enter the Promised Land with them. Moses assured Israel that the Lord would bring them into the new land, under new leadership, and give them victory. Having received the mantle of leadership from Moses, Joshua displayed the spirit of wisdom, and the Israelites followed him.

This lesson teaches us that even in chaotic times, many find comfort and courage in God's leadership.

LESSON 11: **November 14**
Israel Crosses the Jordan River
Joshua 3:7-17

When God calls us to be leaders in any capacity, this call also includes a promise of divine assurance. As you study this lesson you will hear God telling Joshua to be strong and courageous. Thus, the Biblical content of the lesson emphasizes God's promise to establish Joshua's leadership; it moves from God's promise to Joshua's action.

The question that this lesson seeks to address is: how can we go forward in faith? This lesson is geared to help you seek and value guidance from the Lord through your "unknown territory." Throughout this lesson you will learn not to become dismayed when God calls you to venture into the unknown. You will be called to have the faith to take risks for God and have a sense of divine providence as you step out on faith. Hopefully as you study this lesson you will learn how to discern God's voice and presence in your journey.

LESSON 12: **November 21**
The Destruction of Jericho
Joshua 6:1-5, 15-20

Here we observe, through the Scriptures, how the Lord gave Joshua a plan for taking the city of Jericho. Although the plan may have seemed a little foolish, Israel did as God commanded and through obedience and patience won the victory. This lesson tells us that we can win significant victories if we are courageous and cooperate with God and those whom God sends to help us. If we trust God we will be willing to follow His command, even when the command seems strange. Our trust will ultimately result in breakthrough.

LESSON 13: **November 28**
Choosing to Serve the Lord
Joshua 24:1-2, 14-22, 25

The scriptural passage from which this lesson is taken deals with a challenge to the Children of Israel to follow God. Here we see the Children of Israel gathered at Shechem as Joshua presents them with a challenge to choose between the Lord and other gods. Upon hearing Joshua's commitment to serve the Lord, the people decide they, too, will serve the Lord.

This lesson drives home the fact that we must all make fundamental choices in life. This lesson calls us to seriously consider the consequences that result from broken contracts and agreements. As the children of Israel, we must consider the weight of promises made to serve God and seek to fulfill our obligations, not just to man but to God as well.

EDUCATING THE CHILDREN

How many languages do you know? Do you know the languages of childhood? On the Day of Pentecost, the disciples learned the importance of speaking the languages of those we desire to teach. Preschoolers speak the language of fantasy. They like to play super-hero, listen to make-believe stories, and they want to believe in Santa Claus no matter what you tell them. They cannot distinguish truth from "just pretend." When they tell you they did not break the lamp, they are not really lying. They are telling you what they wish to be true. Very young preschoolers will believe that a hand puppet is alive even if you show them your hand inside the puppet.

Preschoolers are learning to recognize colors and can identify broad categories of skin color; although they do not yet understand the concept of race. When Black preschoolers comment on skin color, speak positively about their color. Explain that God made all colors of skin and He loves each one.

We can speak the fantasy language of preschoolers when we tell them Bible stories. They will believe all the wonderful, miraculous stories of our all-powerful God, His Son Jesus, and all that Jesus did. We can tell preschoolers that Jesus is always with them, even though they cannot see Him. Jesus is here, but He is invisible. He is so big and so strong that He created everything of beauty in our world just by saying the words. We tell preschoolers make-believe stories, and they hear too many untrue things on TV. But they will soon learn to tell the difference between our fantastic God and the world of fantasy. They can tell what things are true by sensing our faith in what cannot be seen but is the absolute truth. On the Day of Pentecost, people of many languages were astonished to hear the disciples declaring the wonders of God in their own tongues (Acts 2:11). God is able to help us speak the language of preschoolers to communicate God's wonders to them.

Primaries are learning a new language. They are very interested in categorizing what is real and what is just pretend. When they discover that Santa Claus is make-believe, they want to know if the Easter Bunny and the Tooth Fairy are make believe as well.

The language of primaries is the language of laws. Primaries know that there are rules to games, even if they do not want to follow them. They know that when Mama and Daddy are not with them, they must obey their rules. They realize that disobedience must be punished. Primaries are learning that God has rules and we must not break them. They can be sorry when they disobey God's laws. And so they can be introduced to God's provision for our salvation. We tell primaries that God is so holy and so wonderful that He cannot stand to have anyone with sin in His presence. All of us have sinned. Maybe we have talked back to our mothers or hurt a friend or taken something that did not belong to us. All of these things are sin and God cannot let anyone who has sinned into His heaven. But God loves us! And so He sent His Son Jesus to die on the Cross to take the punishment for our sins. God wants us to believe that Jesus took the punishment for our sins. All we have to do is believe and receive the Lord Jesus (John 1:12).

Is this too simplistic an explanation of salvation? Perhaps it is. But not for primaries. They are children of God's grace. The connection between salvation by faith and the need for commitment is not clear to primaries, although they can surely understand that God demands our obedience. At the Day of Pentecost, Peter quoted the prophet Joel as saying, "Everyone who calls on the name of the Lord will be saved" (Acts 2:21). We can learn to speak the language of the primary child to bring

Judith St.Clair Hull, Ph.D.

interaction with one another, they will come to believe in Jesus Christ.

The members of the team are committed to one another. Sunday School teachers and other leaders of the Christian education program need to provide an atmosphere of trust and community within their classrooms that extends beyond one hour on Sundays to the lives of juniors. Scripture tells us that the result of the Day of Pentecost was that "All the believers were together" (Acts 2:44, NIV). Juniors who have been saved can be challenged to commit their lives to Christ. Others can ask for salvation as they sign up to join God's team. Such commitments will be remembered the rest of their lives, even though not every commitment will be honored in the days to come.

Juniors are beginning to understand abstract truth. The symbolism of the bread and the cup of the Lord's Supper can be grasped by many juniors, so this may be a good age to begin participation in Communion. The unity with one another and with Christ symbolized by the Lord's Supper is the unity that will truly satisfy juniors.

Juniors are beginning to understand the concept of skin color as forming the bond of race. They can appreciate the heroes and heroines of their own people. African American juniors are part of the race of proud Black people created by God. This, too, is a team commitment. They can take pride in their own heritage and at the same time learn to appreciate the achievements of other people.

Can you learn the languages of childhood? Paul said, "When I was a child, I talked like a child, I thought like a child, I reasoned like a child," (from 1 Corinthians 13:11). Immerse yourself in the culture of children. Listen to how they express themselves. Observe them as they interact with one another. Read what other educators are saying about the various stages of development. And ask the Lord to help you to learn to communicate effectively with children. We need to learn how children think and what words will effectively communicate the Gospel to them.

him or her to faith in Christ.

Primaries cannot understand the language of symbolism. That is for the next stage of childhood. Primaries understand everything in a realistic sense. If we tell primaries to ask Jesus into their hearts, they will wonder how He can be so little as to fit inside of them—and if Jesus is inside of each one, how many "Jesuses" are there? We do not talk about our sins being washed away by the blood of the Lamb. Primaries do not understand this abstract language. Think very carefully how you express religious truth to primaries. Their interpretation is often not the same as that of adults.

Juniors speak the language of the team. Juniors have been known to cry when their favorite professional sports teams lose. This is the age when gangs begin their recruitment. Juniors want to be a part of the team. The unity with their peers that they seek is not unlike the union that Jesus says should be true of believers. Christian educators should be challenged to create the team camaraderie that Scripture describes as the body of Christ. The Bible says that believers are like the hands, feet, eyes, ears, and other body parts of one another. We help one another and need each other. Our unity is supposed to be such that when unbelievers see our

THEMATIC ESSAY

FROM SLAVERY TO CONQUEST

The story of the beginning of the nation of Israel is similar to the creation of the world. Both were created out of virtually nothing. The heavens and Earth were made through a primordial mixture of water and darkness called *chaos*, while the Children of Israel were produced through the loins of an elderly couple whom God enabled to have a child. Once Abraham's wife gave birth to Isaac, the child of promise, he is told to offer Isaac up as a sacrifice. God intervenes and spares Isaac's life. Isaac's wife later bears twins, one of whom is a liar and a deceiver named Jacob. Jacob, subsequently has 12 children who turn out to be liars and murderers. Ultimately, God took this chaotic family and made a nation out of it.

These creation stories establish the sovereignty of God. They establish among those who are able to hear and, in Israel's case, *see* that God alone is to be worshipped and served. The creation of the universe establishes God's sovereignty in the heavens. The creation and use of Israel establishes Divine sovereignty in the affairs of human kind. Israel will be the Almighty God's testimony to all the nations, especially Egypt.

In this story, we see success and failure, faithfulness and faithlessness, liberation and bondage, and victory and defeat. Yet God somehow gets the glory and honor. As Israel settled in the land of promise she found that her adventure was not over, but rather had just begun. The same is true in our lives. A covenant relationship with God (eternal salvation) does not mean that life will be a bed of ease. There will be obstacles along the way. We will all go through a wilderness experience where, even though we know God is present, we sometimes wonder where He is. Our faith will be tested by the obstacles or "giants in the land." We will be challenged to believe God's Word and face those "giants," or turn and run in disbelief.

God's promise to Abraham includes two tangible things (among others), progeny and land. Abraham is the father of many nations through the descendants of his children. Progeny is also fulfilled during Israel's sojourn in Egypt. It is also fulfilled through the other children of Abraham...the promise of land was soon to be realized. The story of Joseph in the book of Genesis sets the stage for Israel to leave Egypt in search of the land of promise.

In the Book of Exodus, God shows Himself to be a compassionate God who sees the affliction of His people, hears their groaning, remembers His covenant with Abraham and is moved to come down and deliver them from bondage. In this story we see Him use nature (hailstorms, pestilence and animals), and people (Moses, Aaron and Pharaoh) to accomplish His purpose. These miracles are to be signs to Israel as well as Egypt that God is sovereign. At the Red Sea, we see God fight for Israel, make a way where their was no way, and destroy her enemies. The Red Sea, the manna, the provision of water and quail were all proof that God was able to supply Israel's need.

At Mount Sinai we see God as a God of covenant relationships. He has never been a God who stands afar. God has intimate knowledge of and genuine concern for His covenant people. He set the rules for relationship interaction. The law became God's communication to Israel of His love and concern. He makes His will known. He is not a God of ambiguity.

The Book of Leviticus gives details on the ceremonial practices of worship in the various offices (priest, High Priest) and on the issues of cleanliness. It also establishes the way in which Israel will relate to a holy, righteous God. It explains how this people called by God will demonstrate their loyalty and love in their covenant relationship with God.

Reverend Eric Wallace

The Book of Numbers records the encampment of the people in the wilderness of Sinai and their travel to Moab. The numbering of the people in chapters 1—4 and chapter 26 brackets the main event in this book, the sending of the spies into Canaan and the reaction of the people to their report. The Book of Numbers records the failure of a generation and the hope of one to come. The story of the spies sent into the Promised land is one of faith and failure. Where in the Garden of Eden, Adam and Eve had to make a choice whether to listen to God's Word or that of the serpent, Israel is put to the same test. The people had to decide whether they would believe the report of the spies or the report of the Lord, which was confirmed by Joshua and Caleb. The sin in the garden was that of disobeying a prohibition. The sin in the wilderness was that of disobeying God's command to take possession of the land. In each case there was the punishment of death. The first generation would wander in the wilderness until all those over 20 years old had died. Chapter 26 recounts the numbering of the new generation that would possess the land.

The Book of Deuteronomy recounts the giving of the Law to the new generation. Within this book Moses makes three speeches. His first speech, in general, recounts to the new generation what took place in the wilderness, (Deuteronomy 1—4). His second speech (Deuteronomy 4:44-28:68) recounts the law, the Ten Commandments—along with the results of obedience or disobedience to the law. In his third and final speech, Moses exhorts the people to be committed to God—choosing life and not death.

Deuteronomy involves Moses' preparing the new generation to enter into the Promised Land, a land that he will not be able to enter along with them. Therefore it serves as a teaching session to remind the new generation of what happened to the old generation. Deuteronomy exhorts the new generation that God has not abandoned them, but has made His covenant with them. Therefore, they will be blessed if they are faithful and cursed if they are disobedient.

In chapter 31:14-23, we see the change in command. Moses hands over the leadership of Israel to Joshua in preparation for the conquest of Canaan. The people of Israel have been given their pep talk like a sports team before the big game. They are given a new leader with updated instructions to take the land. Poised on the east side of the Jordan river, they are ready to take possession of the promised land.

The Book of Joshua is the beginning of the fulfillment of the promise God made to Abraham concerning land. Abraham was told that he would have many children and that they would inherit the land of Canaan. The first promise was fulfilled in the magnitude of the people of Israel. The second has begun its fulfillment as the Children of Israel cross the Jordan river. The completion of this promise will not be fully realized until the reigns of David and Solomon, where Israel has firm control over all of Palestine. But the beginning of the end for the inhabitants of Canaan has begun.

The Children of Israel will now become a nation, a people with a homeland. And out of this homeland will come many more stories of faith, triumph, agony, and defeat. The Lord will raise up kings and sit them down. He will judge the nations by His prophets and bring judgment upon many. He will use Israel as His witness in blessing and in punishment. He will raise up mighty men and women who, through faith, will perform miracles and acts of bravery. And out of this tiny nation, small and fragile at times, He will bring forth the child of a virgin who will save man from his sins. The King of Glory will come forth a thousand years later to set up another kingdom not of this world. He will build a city not made with hands. And He will call 12 ordinary men of varying backgrounds to follow Him. He will make them fishers of men. With these men He will challenge a nation and then the world to make a decision to follow Christ or reject Him.

AFRICAN-AMERICAN CHRISTIAN WORSHIP

African-American Christian worship has been the source of spiritual vitality and spiritual power for Africans since the beginning of time. Corporate worship has historically been a reference point for clarity, sanity, transformation and wholeness for Africans in the midst of continuing racial holocaust.

Moreover, worship for African-Americans is not only a celebration of their relationship with Christ and the victories they have won both individually and collectively, but it is a corporate expression of hope, faith and renewal.

Worship provides a context in which the African-American community recalls its tragic and triumphal sojourn in this strange land and creates an arena for the perfection and ceremonial practice of the ritual dramas of Black life. Facilitating the discovery, cultivation and reinforcement of systems of meaning and value, it also helps the community embrace and celebrate a "God of our weary years and a God of our silent tears who has brought us thus far along this way."

I have stated in my book, *African-American Church Growth*, that three hallmarks of Black worship are: celebration, invitation, and information. This means that African-American Christian worship should unapologetically celebrate the risen and living Christ through the nuances of Black culture. Melva Wilson-Costen reminds us that African-American Christian worship helps African-Americans establish solid belief systems in response to a culture that has marginalized them. We should then, celebrate the trials we've endured, the mountains we've climbed and the obstacles we've overcome. Who but God could have brought us through the agony and ecstasy, the terror and tumult of our American odyssey? The unique culture and ethos created by the Black experience in America is celebrated in the worship experience. This culture also becomes the primary aesthetic for the idioms of Black worship.

Invitation means giving people an opportunity to belong to a caring fellowship of believers by enabling them to participate in the worship experience and in the total life of the church. Something in worship should compel the stranger back to Christ and the church. Inviting people to serve, witness and belong to the community of believers are important aspects of the African-American church's code of hospitality. Often the worship experience will be the first and only contact a visitor has with a particular church. If nothing in worship invites them to belong and participate, incites their interest or kindles their enthusiasm for the church, they may not return.

Equally significant is information. How does the worship experience inform worshipers of a living, loving, liberating Christ? What vehicles of information have we established within worship that will reach people where they are, transform and touch them at the core of their ultimate concerns? Preaching, teaching and outreaching through proclamation, music, witnessing, testimonials and other idioms are also important venues. Is the information provided in the worship experience, spiritually and intellectually challenging, inspiring and motivating? Does it prompt people to seek God, transform their lives and be transforming witnesses for Christ? Do we tell the stories in ways that are culturally, spiritually and relationally relevant to the real needs of the people we serve? Worship gives us a chance to not only learn about God but to receive vital information about ourselves, about our possibilities and disabilities thereby unlocking

Carlyle Fielding Stewart, III Ph.D.

life's most inscrutable mysteries.

Celebration, invitation and information should be accompanied by what I call the three c's of worship. African-American Christian worship should provide a theater for comforting the afflicted, creatively confronting sin and the evil of this world and clarifying blacks as people of God in their quest for hope, redemption and spiritual vitality.

A saving element of African-American Christian worship has been the way in which a people dehumanized, ravaged and oppressed by slavery and racism have found comfort, hope and joy in Christ through the worship experience. When the world despised and rejected them, the Word of God comforted them. When the outer Anglo community ostracized them, the inner community of Black believers embraced them.

Black worship has always had a therapeutic or medicinal value because Blacks have often been healed in the experience of worship. The pharmaceutical value of Black worship cannot be undervalued for we observe the forms of therapy, catharsis and healing in everything from the Sunday morning shout, to passionate preaching and singing, to the time of witnessing and testimonials. These elements of worship have always brought a measure of comfort to Blacks who could not access other forms of mental or physical health care in the larger society. In fact, these were the predominant forms of spiritual health care in African-American communities. If you couldn't go to the psychiatrist you could shout it out on Sunday morning and find a similar sweet relief from the sorrow and pain of this life.

Creative confrontation of evil and sin is also an essential part of Black worship. This means confronting the corporate and individual sin of white racism as well as the sin of personal omission and commission. The primary motivation for such confrontation is love of God, others, and self, and a fervent desire to bring healing and justice to self and community. Confronting evil openly and honestly helps the healing process and calling evil out is a vital proclamatory component in African-American Christian worship.

The Black preacher thus becomes the personification of power in his capacity to tell the devil off in the name of Jesus, which galvanizes the poor sin-

ner in the pew to put his armor on and do similar battle. The ability to confront individual and corporate sin openly in worship helps the individual to confront sin in the personal realm. What the slave could not say to "massa" personally could be verbalized to Satan by the preacher in the worship experience and thus some measure of resolution was achieved.

The same is true today. What is not expressed to evil doers directly is voiced vicariously through the Black preacher who is the symbol of power and authority in the Black community. Worship also emboldens believers to confront evil themselves head on, to tell the devil off personally or speak the truth against sin generally, and not live obliquely through the preacher as an emblem of liberation and justice.

Finally, clarification is an important dimension of African-American Christian worship. In a society that has perpetually exploited, dehumanized and devalued their worth, African-Americans have needed consistent clarification that they were people of inherent value. To counteract the juggernaut of racial denigration, Black people had to cultivate a forum to be clarified individually and collectively. Worship provided an opportunity where the person who was nobody during the week could become somebody on Sunday morning. The soul that was devalued in the eyes of White community could be revalued in the eyes of God and other sojourners in Christ. Where one couldn't find freedom of expression in the larger society, one could freely express oneself as a whole person in the worship experience. Whatever humanity denied Blacks could be reaffirmed and clarified within the celebration of worship. "You are ok. You are a child of God. God loves you when nobody else does....you are not niggers...." are words that clarify a person's value and worth theologically and spiritually and help them over the "humps" of dehumanization.

Celebration, invitation and information as well as clarification, comfort and creative confrontation have been great strengths of African-American Christian worship and continue to be cohesive structures binding the African-American community in its struggle for freedom, wholeness and vitality. This is simply one point of view.

WILLIAM STILL
(1821-1902)
Leader of the Underground Railroad and Reformer

One of the legendary leaders of the Underground Railroad was a freeborn black man named William Still. His father, Levin Steel, was a former slave from Maryland. After buying his freedom, he went to New Jersey and waited for his wife Sidney to join him. After her second attempt to escape, Sidney managed to join her husband with all but two of their children. To avoid recapture, the family changed its name to Still, and the mother's name to Charity. Later, William was born, the youngest of eighteen children.

As a boy, William helped his father on the family farm. In his early twenties' he left the farm and a few years later went on to Philadelphia, arriving with but five dollars in his pocket. Having had very few educational opportunities as a boy, he taught himself to read and write.

In 1847 he married Letitia George with whom he later had four children, two boys and two girls. In 1847 he also became secretary of the Pennsylvania Society for the Abolition of Slavery. At that time the Society consisted of a few white members who had little experience with the practical needs of runaway slaves. William, remembering his family's struggles to become free, became such a helpful member of the Society that in 1851 he was elected its chairman. He later became director of the General Vigilance Committee of Philadelphia, managing its finances and funding Harriet Tubman's numerous raids. He established a network of safe houses from the upper part of the South to Canada. He kept a careful record of each fugitive so that family and friends could later locate them in their new-found freedom. For awhile, he hid his records in a cemetery, publishing them in a book, *The Underground Railroad* in 1872.

As a leading conductor of the Underground Railroad, William used his large house as a station. He kept it stocked with food and clothing for the frightened runaways for fourteen years. About 649 slaves were helped in their escape to freedom. He even helped John Brown's widow and daughter when they passed through Philadelphia. In his classic book, he accounts for about 800 escaped slaves, including 60 children, who were helped during an eight year period. Black churches offered extensive aid, and while some few white churches offered help, most were hostile to runaways. Unfortunately, spies of both races were often present, looking for an opportunity to sell out escaped slaves for money. Even so, the system worked so well, that the slave hunters came up with the term "Underground Railroad." Often, while pursuing slaves, the trackers would loose all trace of the runaways. In their frustration and bewilderment, some suggested there must be an underground railroad the fugitives were escaping to; and although it was spoken in bitter sarcasm, the term came into popular use.

As runaways arrived at underground railroad stations in his network, William Still personally interviewed them. His meticulous records, along with the accounts of other observers of the runaway phenomenon, show that thousands of slaves vanished daily from the plantations as the numbers of field workers steadily dwindled. He helped dispel the notion that runaway slaves were aided chiefly by white abolitionists and Quakers by documenting the aid that black churches, institutions, and especially ex-runaways gave to themselves and each other.

A very dramatic example of the courage and creativity of those wanting to flee slavery is that of Henry "Box" Brown. Henry was sealed in a box with water and biscuits for sustenance. It took two days by steamboat, wagon and rail before he arrived at William Still's office. After emerging from the box, he sang a psalm, "I waited patiently for the Lord, and He heard my prayer."

The story of Margaret Garner is another illustration of dramatic uncertainties which often confronted fugitives. One snowy night, Margaret, with her husband, their four children and eleven other slaves from various plantations, crowded into a sled drawn by two horses taken from one of the slave holders. In the morning, they reached a small town and split up into smaller groups. One group was led to safe hiding places, until nightfall, when they were conducted to the Underground Railroad and escaped to Canada. Unfortunately, Margaret's group was discovered. Margaret, who had vowed never to be returned to slavery, immediately grabbed a sharp knife and killed her youngest baby. She would have killed her other children and herself had she not been stopped by the slave trackers. After a trial, Margaret, her husband and the next youngest child, were ordered back to their owners. While on a boat returning them to the plantation, Margaret and her baby fell over board. The baby drowned and two years later Margaret died of typhoid fever, asking her husband to wait for his freedom before marrying again. She believed black people would one day be free.

William Still also found time to help organize an association to collect data on black people. He set up an orphanage for the children of black soldiers and sailors in Philadelphia, and helped organize the first Y.M.C.A. for black men. He went into the stove and later the coal business and obtained a modest fortune. He remained active in helping his people develop their potential and gain more civil rights until his death in 1902.

Sources: Russell L. Adams, *Great Negroes Past and Present* (Afro-Am Publishing Co., Inc., Chicago, 1969), p. 31; Wm. Still Underground R. R. Foundation, Inc., 1998; Charles L. Blockson, *The Underground Railroad* (Prentice Hall Press, New York, 19870, pp. 217, 229, 233, 135; Dumas Malone, *Dictionary of American Biography (Charles Scribner's Sons, New York, 1936), Vol. 9, Part 2, pp. 22-23.*

SEPTEMBER 5
Bible Study Guide 1

1. Words You Should Know

A. Taskmaster (3:7)—Oppressors appointed as overseers of forced labor groups which were employed or enslaved by kings for large public works projects.

B. Affliction (3:7)—A state of being hurt or distressed by oppressors. As many as seven Hebrew words can be translated as affliction. The two primary words mean "to lower, humble, or deny," and "depressed."

2. Teacher Preparation

Read the background Scripture for this lesson. Find out more about Moses' background and about the wilderness region in which he lived.

3. Starting the Lesson

A. Separate the class into smaller groups of two to five persons. Ask each group to come up with a definition of a "call," as we understand it in the biblical sense. Allow each group to share the results of their discussion. Ask class members to share individual experiences concerning their own calling. Ask them whether they believe God calls everyone to a task or just deacons, ministers, and other church leaders.

B. Read the IN FOCUS story about Jerome. What are the qualifications for deacon in your church. Discuss why Jerome may make a good deacon. Could Jerome be a deacon at your church?

4. Getting into the Lesson

Ask class members to briefly review the story of Moses in Exodus 2. Also look at the excuses Moses gave God in chapter 3. Moses was by no means perfect. Discuss whether a man like Moses would be chosen for a leadership position in your church today? Name some unlikely leaders from your church, city, and beyond who came from an unsavory beginning yet reached great heights.

5. Relating the Lesson to Life

A. Review the information about Mount Sinai and the role of fire in the Bible from THE PEOPLE, PLACES, AND TIMES article. Think of some other instances in the Bible where God used fire to show His power. Spend some time discussing the biblical significance of Mount Sinai.

B. Give students an opportunity to answer the questions in SEARCH THE SCRIPTURES.

C. DISCUSS THE MEANING addresses fears which may hinder acceptance of a divine call. Allow students to share some of their personal fears. Also discuss how Moses was molded and shaped into a great leader in the process of doing God's will.

D. The LESSON IN OUR SOCIETY focuses on the person of Moses. Spend some time talking about who he was based on the information given in the Bible. Discuss what communities can do to help lift up and empower those who have gone astray to do great things for the Lord.

6. Arousing Action

A. Discuss how those who are reluctant to take on a task often make good leaders. Was Moses reluctant because he understood fully what God was commanding him to do, or did he simply think he was not capable of such a task?

B. Allow time for members to create a spiritual growth recipe as directed in MAKE IT HAPPEN. Give each class member a pencil and paper.

C. Give class members an opportunity to complete FOLLOW THE SPIRIT and REMEMBER YOUR THOUGHTS.

WORSHIP GUIDE

For the Superintendent or Teacher
Theme: God Calls Moses
Theme Song: Where He Leads Me
Scripture: Exodus 6:2-8
Song: I Want to Be Ready
**Meditation: Lord, help me to grow
into the person You would have me to
be so that I may do Your will.**

GOD CALLS MOSES

Bible Background • EXODUS 3
Printed Text • EXODUS 3:1-12
Devotional Reading • EXODUS 6:2-8

LESSON AIM

After studying today's lesson, students should realize that God may choose to use anyone to do great things.

KEEP IN MIND

"And God said unto Moses, I AM THAT I AM: and he said, Thus shalt thou say unto the children of Israel, I AM hath sent me unto you" (Exodus 3:14).

FOCAL VERSES

EXODUS 3:1 Now Moses kept the flock of Jethro his father-in-law, the priest of Midian: and he led the flock to the backside of the desert, and came to the mountain of God, even to Horeb.

2 And the angel of the LORD appeared unto him in a flame of fire out of the midst of a bush: and he looked, and, behold, the bush burned with fire, and the bush was not consumed.

3 And Moses said, I will now turn aside, and see this great sight, why the bush is not burnt.

4 And when the LORD saw that he turned aside to see, God called unto him out of the midst of the bush, and said, Moses, Moses. And he said, Here am I.

5 And he said, Draw not nigh hither: put off thy shoes from off thy feet, for the place whereon thou standest is holy ground.

6 Moreover he said, I am the God of thy father, the God of Abraham, the God of Isaac, and the God of Jacob. And Moses hid his face; for he was afraid to look upon God.

7 And the LORD said, I have surely seen the afflic-

LESSON OVERVIEW

LESSON AIM
KEEP IN MIND
FOCAL VERSES
IN FOCUS
THE PEOPLE, PLACES, AND
TIMES
BACKGROUND
AT-A-GLANCE
IN DEPTH
SEARCH THE SCRIPTURES
DISCUSS THE MEANING
LESSON IN OUR SOCIETY
MAKE IT HAPPEN
FOLLOW THE SPIRIT
REMEMBER YOUR THOUGHTS
MORE LIGHT ON THE TEXT
DAILY BIBLE READINGS

tion of my people which are in Egypt, and have heard their cry by reason of their taskmasters; for I know their sorrows;

8 And I am come down to deliver them out of the hand of the Egyptians, and to bring them up out of that land unto a good land and a large, unto a land flowing with milk and honey; unto the place of the Canaanites, and the Hittites, and the Amorites, and the Perizzites, and the Hivites, and the Jebusites.

9 Now therefore, behold, the cry of the children of Israel is come unto me: and I have also seen the oppression wherewith the Egyptians oppress them.

10 Come now therefore, and I will send thee unto Pharaoh, that thou mayest bring forth my people the children of Israel out of Egypt.

11 And Moses said unto God, Who am I, that I should go unto Pharaoh, and that I should bring forth the children of Israel out of Egypt?

12 And he said, Certainly I will be with thee; and this shall be a token unto thee, that I have sent thee: When thou hast brought forth the people out of Egypt, ye shall serve God upon this mountain.

IN FOCUS

As Jerome sat in Rev. Wilson's office, he never thought that he would be having such a conversation. Rev. Wilson wanted Jerome to consider becoming a deacon!

Jerome was filled with doubt. He didn't know if he

was qualified to be a deacon. "But, Reverend," he said, "you know that I used to be an alcoholic. Shouldn't a deacon be someone who hasn't struggled with this sort of a problem?"

Rev. Wilson assured him that no one on the deacon board is perfect.

Despite Rev. Wilson's assurances, Jerome continued to protest. "I don't know if I'm old enough yet. I have only been in the church for five years. Plus, I don't think I'm holy enough to be a deacon."

"Well, to be honest," Rev. Wilson said, "I see certain qualities in you that I believe the Lord can use for His kingdom. Why don't you pray and let the Lord decide whether or not you are qualified to be a deacon?"

THE PEOPLE, PLACES, AND TIMES

HOREB. Also known as Mount Sinai, this famous mountain is located in the south central part of a peninsula in the northwestern part of Arabia.

The term *Horeb* means "waste" or "wilderness area." It is possible that the word *Horeb* was used as the general term for the area and Sinai was the specific peak where God revealed Himself to Moses.

The meaning of the name *Sinai* is unclear, but probably means "shining." The root word for *Sinai* is probably derived from the word "sin," which is a Babylonian moon god. Some have suggested that the name means "clay-like," but that word does not fit the nature of the terrain. Yahweh made many revelations of Himself and His purposes to Israel on Sinai.

Based on information from *Holman Bible Dictionary*, Trent Butler, general editor. Nashville: Broadman & Holman Publishers, 1991, pp. 991-992.

FIRE. A flame is a consistent element in God's relationship with Israel. Biblically, it is often used as an instrument of God's power, either as approval or destruction. Fire was a part of the Abramic covenant (Genesis 15:17-18) as well as the burning bush (Exodus 3:2-3). God provided a pillar of fire by night to lead the Israelites to the Promised Land (Exodus 13:21-22). God also appeared in fire on Mount Sinai (Exodus 19:18; 24:17).

Fire is often used as a symbol of holiness. God is compared to fire to illustrate Divine holiness and anger against sin (Isaiah 10:17; Hebrews 12:29).

Based on information from *Holman Bible Dictionary*, pp. 493.

BACKGROUND

When God is preparing to redeem a people, God first calls someone to declare a prophetic word. God called Moses to speak a word from heaven to Pharaoh.

At the time of his calling, Moses was a fugitive hiding in the safety of shepherding his father-in-law's sheep in the wilderness. But even the wilderness is no hiding place for the one whom God wants to fulfill a special purpose.

The scenario at the burning bush is consistent with the model for the calling of a biblical prophet. The passage emphasizes God speaking to the fledgling prophet amid a vision and Moses' reluctance to heed the call. God called Moses, and other prophets, to return to society to be God's spokesman, despite personal shortcomings and perceived obstacles.

In the thirteenth chapter of Exodus, Moses refuses to accept God's call five times. Each time God countered his objections. Four of those times God assured Moses of Divine presence.

AT-A-GLANCE

1. God Calls Moses
(Exodus 3:1-6)
2. God Sends Moses Out
(vv. 7-12)

IN DEPTH

1. God Calls Moses (Exodus 3:1-6)

By the time God got Moses' attention on Mount Horeb, he probably thought of Egypt simply as part of his past. He probably did not entertain the thought of going back there. The life he now led as a shepherd was quiet and relatively uneventful. Far different from his life in Egypt, the wilderness surrounding Mount Horeb was a place of reflection and contemplation.

During his years of relative solitude as a herdsman, God was preparing Moses to do great things.

His time of shepherding was the incubation period for his soul to grow and prepare to do God's work. Often when it seems that there is "nothing" going on in our lives, God is using that time to knead us like dough. It is during those periods of seeming inactivity that God is preparing us for spiritual expansion.

In that quiet place, Moses could not help but notice the bush that was burning on Horeb, God's mountain. In the heat of the desert, an enflamed bush was not a rarity. In this case, Moses' curiosity was heightened by the fact that, although the bush was on fire, it was not burned. What Moses could not have known at that moment was that God's messenger was fueling the fire. A flame or fire is used in various places in the Bible to indicate the presence of God.

Moses stood in awe of the burning bush, but he was also receptive to its mystery. Perhaps this was one of the qualities of Moses which suited him for the task which lay ahead. When God saw that Moses was intrigued enough to investigate, God called him toward the bush. Upon hearing his name, Moses readily responded, "Here I am."

As Moses approached the designated spot, the Lord instructed him to remove his shoes. This act is a sign of reverence for the holy ground on which he was standing. This is the Old Testament's first use of the word *holy*.

God's introduction to Moses is as the God of his father—the God of Abraham, Isaac, and Jacob. This was a God who had a history with Moses' people. The One who spoke to Moses was a deity who had continued and endured through the generations of Hebrews. Therefore, when Moses came to deliver the people of Israel from bondage, he would not do so with an unknown god. Moses was commissioned and empowered by the same God of their forebears who was now choosing to be revealed more fully to them.

As Moses stood at the spot, the distance between God and humanity was shortened. Moses stood in the presence of Power. Moses realized this and hid his face in fear. He was afraid to look at God whose power was too awesome. As the holiness of God shines upon us, we are reminded of our lowly status and Divine greatness.

After God was made known to Moses, the second movement was to reveal God's plan and to assign Moses his role in that plan.

2. God Sends Moses Out (vv. 7-12)

Israel did not have to call on God to deliver them. The Lord heard before they called. God had seen their misery. The Lord heard their crying out because of their oppression. God was concerned about their suffering.

Because He cared for them, God came to deliver the Children of Israel from their suffering. God already had a plan for their future. This plan was far greater than release from bondage. They had no real homeland, but God had already chosen a place for them. God did not choose just any land or region for this chosen people. The Lord chose a land flowing with milk and honey. God could not sit idly by and let this people continue to suffer. By Divine grace and for godly purposes, the Lord had already given Israel the land they were to claim.

After Moses heard God's plan, he must have begun to wonder how he was going to accomplish all of this. He probably could not imagine himself taking on the mighty Pharaoh. A shepherd would dare not give orders to the ruler of a nation! Instead of looking to Almighty God to make the Exodus happen, at first Moses looked to himself and naturally was filled with doubts.

Moses questioned his own worthiness and ability to lead such a movement. He protested by referring to himself as a nobody. God responded with a promise to be with him through the entire ordeal. God even offered a sign to show Moses that this was from heaven. After Moses brought the people out of Egypt, they would worship the Lord on the very mountain where Moses now stood. God had to take Moses through a time of instruction before he could serve. Moses had to be told what to do in Egypt. But more important, Moses needed to learn the nature and depth of his relationship with the Lord.

SEARCH THE SCRIPTURES

1. What kind of work did Moses do before God called Him? (v. 1).

2. Name the place where Moses led his flock? (v. 1)

3. In what form did God's messenger appear to Moses? (v. 2)

4. What did Moses notice about the burning bush? (v. 2)

5. How did Moses react to the burning bush? (v. 3)

6. How did Moses respond when God called his name? (v. 4)

7. What did God instruct Moses to do as he stood before the bush? (v. 5)

8. How was God introduced to Moses? (v. 6)

9. How did Moses respond to the presence of God? (v. 6)

10. What did God say concerning the Israelites? (v. 7)

11. Why did God come down? (v. 8)

12. Where did God intend to lead the Hebrew people? (v. 8)

13. What was Moses supposed to tell Pharaoh? (v. 10)

14. What was Moses' initial response to God's call? (v. 11)

15. What assurance did God give Moses? (v. 12)

DISCUSS THE MEANING

1. Often we are slow to accept God's call because we are afraid. What are some common fears that may serve as barriers to accepting a divine call?

2. By the time Moses led his people to the land God had promised them, he had come a long way from that day at the burning bush. How are believers molded and shaped in the process of doing God's will?

LESSON IN OUR SOCIETY

The story of Moses' spiritual journey is a subplot in the powerful story of the Exodus. God took a fugitive from justice and used him for God's glory. Moses began his journey with God having little understanding of God's power. As he grew in the Lord and became an old man, he was able to perform mighty acts in God's service.

When we encounter persons who have strayed from the path of righteousness, we cannot determine whether God will still use that person to do great things. Often when a person who has led less than a sterling lifestyle accepts God's call, people are quick to recall that person's shaded past. The proper Christian response would be to celebrate the new direction to which God has called that person.

If we stand back in awe rather than judgment, we can see what God can do in the lives of men and women, and witness many of God's wondrous works.

MAKE IT HAPPEN

Think of someone you know whose life has really been turned around at the hand of God. What happened in that person's life to change him/her? Can you identify a series of growth stages for that individual? In other words, if you had to create a recipe for spiritual growth, what ingredients would be used and how would they be combined, step by step?

FOLLOW THE SPIRIT

What God wants me to do:

_____

_____

REMEMBER YOUR THOUGHTS

Special insights you learned:

_____

_____

MORE LIGHT ON THE TEXT
EXODUS 3:1-12

Exodus is a book of records of God's redemptive acts. It records God's deliverance of Israel from the bondage of slavery in Egypt to a covenant relationship with Himself. The book is a continuation of Genesis as we can see from the first chapter. It begins with the conjunction "Now" and lists the names of the children of Israel who came into Egypt, and it serves as a transition from the previous story. In the August 29, 1999 study, we learned how Joseph dramatically revealed himself to his brothers (Genesis 45:1-7). He then orders them to go and bring their entire family to Egypt, where they dwelled until the death of Jacob, Joseph, and their generation (Exodus 1:6). While in Egypt, the Children of Israel prospered and multiplied greatly, and became strong. Then a new king that never knew about Joseph comes into power, and starts to afflict the Children of Israel with hard labor and extermination. By an extraordinary act of wisdom and deliverance, God raises a leader whom He would use to redeem Israel from the bondage of Egypt. His name is Moses.

Chapter 2 gives us brief history of Moses' birth, his exile to Midian for killing an Egyptian to defend a Hebrew, his marriage to Zipporah, the birth of their children, and his occupation as a shepherd for the flock of his father-in-law Jethro in Midian. Chapter 3:1-12 records the account of the call of Moses to a different kind of shepherding—instead of animals, he is to lead his people.

3:1 Now Moses kept the flock of Jethro his father in law, the priest of Midian: and he led the flock to the backside of the desert, and came to the mountain of God, even to Horeb.

With conjunction "now," the writer resumes his account of the life of Moses after the interlude of 2:23-25. Moses has taken over the work of Jethro's daughters as a shepherd to their father's flock (2:16, 19), now his father-in-law. Watching sheep was a common daily work and probably a common occupation of the time (Genesis 37:2). Jacob also served as a shepherd to his father-in-law, Laban, and in return married his daughters (Genesis 29:15ff; 30:25ff).

While carrying out his daily work, Moses takes his flock to the "backside of the desert" and comes to a mountain side called "Horeb," also known as the "the mountain of God." Horeb was synonymous with Sinai. Why it is called the mountain of God is not revealed in the passage. Some suggest that it was a holy hill to the Midians, but unknown to Moses; others suggest that it was called the mountain of God after God's revelation to Moses there. The clause "he led the flock to the backside of the desert," suggests that Moses in this particular day went off his normal grazing area. Why did he go to the backside of the desert? We can only speculate here. The word *desert* is the Hebrew word *midbar*, which means a wilderness or pasture. It refers to an uninhabited land. Deserts are usually dry and sandy, and sometimes contain patches of oasis, as in the African Sahara Desert in the north or the Kalahari Desert in east Africa. It is common to see some green shrubs at the foot of a hill or mountain in desert or dry areas. Often, this land also becomes over-used and barren. When the little grasses are all gone, Moses goes in search of a greener pasture. It is not uncommon for shepherds to take their flocks long distances from home for weeks and months in search for fertile grounds. In Nigeria, the Hausa and Fulani cattle rearers in the north can walk hundreds of miles and live as nomads for months as they travel from the north to the south to find pasture and market for their cattle. This still occurs in Nigeria even today. Providentially, we can assume that the Spirit of God led Moses to the backside of the desert for a definite purpose that would soon unfold itself.

2 And the angel of the Lord appeared unto him in a flame of fire out of the midst of a bush: and he looked, and, behold, the bush burned with fire, and the bush was not consumed. 3 And Moses said, I will now turn aside, and see this great sight, why the bush is not burnt.

In the following verses, the Lord appears to Moses in an unusual way—in a flame of fire, through an angel. *Angel* is a translation of the Hebrew word *malech* pronounced **mal-awk',** whose root meaning is "to dispatch as a deputy." It literally means "messenger" or "ambassador"; it also means "king." *Mal'ak* as the "messenger" is one who is dispatched by an individual, a prince, a leader, or community with a message, order, or request and so on. Messengers usually have close relationships with the sender; they are the sender's spokespersons and representatives. Ambassadors to foreign countries serve this purpose for their countries' leaders, and sometimes these messengers are addressed as if they are the senders themselves (Judges 11:13; 2 Samuel 3:12f. etc.).

Just as we have messengers or representatives, God has His own heavenly emissaries. The Lord also uses humans in this function (Isaiah 44:26; Malachi 2:7; Ecclesiastes 5:5). Moses is the messenger of God in verse 10; Paul says we are ambassadors of the Lord charged with the message of reconciliation (2 Corinthians 5:18-20). God communicates through messengers, and reveals Divine truth through various media as we see here—in the flame of fire. The Old Testament does not say much about the form in which the angel appeared. The "Angel of the Lord appeared" to him in the flame either means that he saw an image (Daniel 3:25) or that the flame represented the appearance of the divine. Whatever the case, as he approaches the mountain, Moses sees a strange sight. Among the shrubs or bushes is one with flame burning.

Bush fires are common sights in deserts. Because of the dryness, most desert areas easily catch fire through lightning, human activities, or negligence (Exodus 22:5). Moses must have seen a lot of bush fires during his 40 years as shepherd in the land of Midian. However there is something strange about this one that attracted his attention: "The bush burned with fire, and the bush was not consumed." Astounded at the sight, Moses is curious and proceeds to watch the strange phenomenon and wonder why the bush is on fire but does not burn up. There have been some interesting explanations for this unusual event. The simplest one is that it is a miracle. However, some suggest that it is an electrical phenomenon in the clear dry sky of the desert or in the mountain. Others propose that the bush had reddish

branches and was full of red berries, so when the bright sun of the desert shone on it, it seemed as it were on fire. Another explanation is that a volcanic vapor arose, which from a distance might seem to come from a bush on the mountain. Others explain it scientifically as an optical illusion. But the Bible says that it is the presence of God, and leaves us either to speculate on how this could happen without reaching a conclusion, or to accept the fact God works in ways that are both mysterious and beyond our comprehension. It reveals the loftiness of God and the limitations of human understanding of the nature and mind of God. God's wisdom and knowledge are far beyond ours, and that is one of many things which distinguishes God from humankind.

4 And when the Lord saw that he turned aside to see, God called unto him out of the midst of the bush, and said, Moses, Moses. And he said, Here am I.

As Moses goes closer to investigate this unusual occurrence, God calls to him from the burning bush.

We read in verse 1 that "an angel" of the Lord appeared to him. Here it is the Lord God speaking to Moses from the flame. Theologians for years have debated about the identity of the angel in verse 1 and its relationship to God calling out of the burning bush in verse 4. In some passages, the Scriptures present the angel as different from God (Exodus 23:20-23; Numbers 22:22; Judges 5:23; 2 Samuel 24:16; Zechariah 1:12-13). In other passages, God and the Angel of the Lord are analogous and sometimes interchangeable (Genesis 16:7-13; 22:11-12; 48:15-16; Judges 2:1, etc.). In Mark 12:26, some New Testament writers identify the angel as God Himself (cf. Acts 7:30-35). Jesus simply says God spoke to Moses from the bush. The best explanation here is to understand the "Angel of the Lord" as a visible manifestation of God, known in the Old Testament as "theophanies," which means an appearance of God. They often occur in the midst of natural phenomena: in fire, Exodus 3:2; in a cloud, 13:21; in a whirlwind, Job 38:1; and in an earthquake, 1 Kings 19:11. Angels also can appear in the form of human beings

(Exodus 33:21-23; Isaiah 6:1; Genesis 18; Ezekiel 1:26-27). It is interesting to note that theophanies do not occur in the New Testament, probably because the ultimate appearance of God came in bodily human form as the incarnate Lord Jesus Christ, the Word who became "flesh, and dwelt among us" (John 1:14). The question of why God chose to reveal himself through the fire at this point is extraneous. God can use any method He likes to call our attention or to reveal Himself. What matters here is that Moses experienced God's presence and God speaks to him, and he speaks to God. As Moses approaches the sight, God calls out "Moses, Moses," and Moses answers "Here am I."

Here the writer uses the personal name of Lord *YAHWEH* or *Yehovah* the self-existent, eternal, Jehovah, the existing One. It is the proper name of the one true God and was never pronounced by the Jews in reverence to God. The personal name of God was treated with such awe that the scribes changed their writing material when they came to the name of God. They never wrote God's name with the same pen they used for other words in the passage. They also washed their hands each time they copied the personal name of God. The Bible also uses the general name *elohiym* (pronounced **el-o-heem'**) always in plural form. In ordinary usage, it is translated "gods," but specifically refers to the supreme God.

The use of both names makes the call authentic, and separates the God of the Hebrews from the gods of Egypt and other nations. "God called unto him" i.e., in Hebrew *qara'*, to utter a loud sound, to summon. The doubling of the name of Moses shows emphasis and a solicitation for definite and undivided attention of the person called. A similar doubling of the names occurs both in the Old and New Testament, e.g., Abraham—Genesis 22:11; Jacob—Genesis 46:2; Samuel—1 Samuel 3:10; Lord—Matthew 7:21-22; 23:37; Mark 15:34; Luke 10:41; 22:31; Acts 9:4. Here it signifies a state of urgency for Moses to halt instantly and not take one more step because of the holiness of the place (Exodus 3:5). Moses' response: "Here am I" (Hebrew *hineeny*) literally means "Behold me"; an expression that is found frequently in the Old Testament, which expresses attentiveness to a call and readiness to obey (cf. Abraham in Genesis 22:1, Samuel in 1 Samuel 3:4, and Isaiah in Isaiah 6:8). We notice here that God called Moses by name. God reminds Israel through Prophet Isaiah, "But now thus saith the Lord that created thee, O Jacob, and he that formed thee, O Israel, Fear not: for I have redeemed thee, I have called thee by thy name; thou art mine" (Isaiah 43:1). God, therefore, knows each and everyone of us by name, and it shows God's intimate relationship with those whom are His.

5 And he said, Draw not nigh hither: put off thy shoes from off thy feet, for the place whereon thou standest is holy ground.

After getting Moses' attention, God lets him know the type of place on which he (Moses) is standing— it's holy ground, therefore he should not come too close, and he has to take off his shoes. The phrase "Draw not nigh hither" *qarab* (pronounced **kaw-rab'**) means not to approach or to come near, and "holy ground" (*'adamah qodesh*) means a sacred or consecrated ground or place. The word *qodesh* can also be translated as "dedicated" or "hallowed." It is used to identify a place set apart for religious or sacred purposes like worship and sacrifices as in the Old Testament (e.g., the temple, the tabernacle and synagogue). Here God says to Moses, because this place or ground has been consecrated "you take off your shoes." The word `adamah* is rendered "ground," "land," "country," or "earth." The use of this word can be restricted to the very ground where the bush is burning, or it can include the whole Horeb Mountain. One is inclined to believe that God was speaking about the whole mountain area since He promises Moses that when He brings the Children of Israel out of Egypt, they would worship in "this mountain" (v. 12). The removing of shoes probably is a mark of reverence and respect to the Lord. It gives a sense of awe for the Almighty and a sense of humility to the worshiper. John the Baptist said that He who is coming after him is so great that he (John) is not even worthy to untie His shoe straps (John 1:27).

It is a customary practice in the oriental traditions to remove their shoes in the home and at all places of worship. This act of shoe removal is gaining grounds in many western homes, not because of the sacredness of the homes, but to avoid carrying dirt onto the carpets or rugs in the homes. In other traditions, such as in Africa where wearing of hats is common, people remove their hats as a sign of respect and reverence when they approach a king, an elder person, or a sacred place of worship. This traditional act of removing the hat is carried over into the African Christian community, more as a local tradition than as a biblical instruction. However, removal of shoes before entering a place of worship is practiced in many churches in Africa such as the Aladura Churches in Nigeria. They not only remove their shoes, but also wash their feet before they enter the church for worship. When we come into a place to worship, whether in a private home, a Cathedral or a church building, we are in the presence of God, the ground whereon we stand is holy; we should take off our shoes, physically and spiritually that is humble ourselves. There is something mystical about it that gives a sense of reverence and awe, and prepares us spiritually to meet our Creator.

6 Moreover he said, I am the God of thy father, the God of Abraham, the God of Isaac, and the God of Jacob. And Moses hid his face; for he was afraid to look upon God.

After reminding Moses that he is standing on a holy ground, God now identifies Himself so Moses will know that he (Moses) is not meeting an unknown God. The God who is speaking is the God of "thy father, the God of Abraham, the God of Isaac, and the God of Jacob." The phrase "I am the God of thy father" refers to Moses' immediate father, Amram (Exodus 6:13-20). During the early years of Moses' life before he was adopted into the house of Pharaoh, Amram probably introduced Moses to the Lord and instructed him in the ways of the God of their ancestors Abraham, Isaac, and Jacob. Amram must have carried out the biblical instruction, "Train up a child in the way he should go: and when he is old, he will not depart from it" (Proverbs 22:6). Moses' age before he is taken to the Pharaoh's daughter is not stated. He has not grown enough to understand his heritage and the difference between the true God of Israel and false gods of Egypt. He is fully weaned as Isaac was in Genesis 21:8, and Samuel was when he was taken into the house of God (1 Samuel 1:24ff). If Moses was weaned then he was old enough to start his education as the son of Pharaoh's daughter. Growing, Moses is conscious of the sufferings of the people of Israel in Egypt and wants to help, and his actions land him in exile (Exodus 2:11ff).

Moses has a clear knowledge of God, hence God

identifies Himself as the personal God of Moses' ancestors and his own father. Being aware of the majesty and sovereignty of God, upon hearing God's identity, "Moses hid his face; for he was afraid to look upon God." Apart from the awe of the glory of God as revealed through the burning bush, Moses hides his face because of the belief that if any one saw God he would die (Genesis 32:30). When Isaiah saw the glory and holiness of God in the temple, he became frightened because it revealed his own sinfulness, he cried "Woe is me! for I am undone; because I am a man of unclean lips, and I dwell in the midst of a people of unclean lips: for mine eyes have seen the King, the LORD of hosts" (Isaiah 6:5). Ezekiel fell to the ground face down when he saw "the appearance of the likeness of the glory of the LORD" (Ezekiel 1:28). Moses has the same reaction and hides his face.

7 And the Lord said, I have surely seen the affliction of my people which are in Egypt, and have heard their cry by reason of their taskmasters; for I know their sorrows; 8 And I am come down to deliver them out of the hand of the Egyptians, and to bring them up out of that land unto a good land and a large, unto a land flowing with milk and honey; unto the place of the Canaanites, and the Hittites, and the Amorites, and the Perizzites, and the Hivites, and the Jebusites.

Verses 7 and 8 introduce the reason for God's revelation to Moses: to deliver the Children of Israel from Egypt. In verse 7, Moses is informed that God is completely aware of the sufferings of Israel in Egypt, and in verse 8, God tells him what is going to be done about it. God uses three different verbs for sensory perceptions to describe Divine awareness of the plight of the people in Egypt: 1) *ra'ah* to see (their affliction `oniy or misery), 2) *shama* to hear (their cry *tsa` aqah*), and 3) *yada* to know (their sorrows *mak'ob* anguish or pain). The use of this variety of verbs brings out the fact in a very strong sense that God is in every way familiar with Israel's problem. The word *surely* or *ra'ah* (interpreted "behold," "see," or "certainly") adds emphasis to God's knowledge of the situation. Nothing is hidden. No aspect of the suffering has escaped God's attention. In other words, the Lord has been watching and observing the situation. This emphasizes the fact that God knows everything, and sees all things. There is nothing that happens without God's knowledge. This is a comfort for those who put their trust in the Lord.

The writer of Hebrews says that we have a High Priest who is touched by our infirmities, and to whom we can always go with our problems. Here, the first of 17 times in this book, God refers to Israel as "my people," which shows the personal and intimate relationship that exists between God and Israel. This relationship, established first with Abraham, and continued through Isaac and Jacob, is perpetuated unto this day. As an Israelites, Moses obviously knows that such relationship exists between Israel and YAHWEH.

The next verse (v. 8) tells us that God is not only aware of the terrible situation to which Israel is subjected to, but has compassion and has decided to deliver them out the land of Egypt into freedom. It is one thing to be aware of the circumstance, it another thing to do something about it. Here we see God's character of compassion in action. He comes down in person to liberate them from the bondage of Egypt and lead them into a better and prosperous land. This is one of the many instances of God coming down to be among men. The ultimate appearance of the Lord is in the person of Our Lord and Saviour Jesus Christ, who came to redeem the world from another type of slavery—slavery to sin. John the Baptist crying out and pointing says "Behold the Lamb God, which taketh away the sin of the world" (John. 1:29).

God tells Moses of the plan to deliver them from the land of the Egypt characterized by suffering and want and to take them into the land of Canaan described as "a good land and a large . . . a land flowing with milk and honey." The verb *to deliver* used here is the Hebrew word *natsal* which literally means "to snatch away," whether in a good or a bad sense, "to pluck" or "rescue." It implies the use of force. The description of the land into which God is going to take them signifies something better and larger than what they have in Egypt. The Israelites had occupied the land of Goshen and there "they had possessions therein, and grew, and multiplied exceedingly" (Genesis 45:10; 47:27). Probably this land was no longer large enough, and so God promised to give them the larger land of Canaan. This new land is already occupied by different people: the Hittites, Amorites, Perizzites, Hivites, and the Jebusites. The

presence of these people means that taking possession of the land will require hard work. Some people argue that it was unfair for God to give them other people's land. However, it ought to be noted that God is just returning them to the land from which God took them to Egypt, and fulfilling the covenant with Abraham (Genesis 17:8; 46:6 etc.). God is not just taking something away from someone and giving it to another. God is giving back what was originally theirs. Christ's redemption brings us back to our home from where we have, through sin, wandered away.

9 Now therefore, behold, the cry of the children of Israel is come unto me: and I have also seen the oppression wherewith the Egyptians oppress them. 10 Come now therefore, and I will send thee unto Pharaoh, that thou mayest bring forth my people the children of Israel out of Egypt.

After explaining His plan for Israel to Moses, God now invites him to be a part of the rescue team. By repeating God's awareness of the condition of the people of Israel in verse 9, the Lord emphasizes the urgency of the matter, which requires action. Although God has come to rescue the people, He also plans to use Moses as an agent or instrument to carry out this mission. With the conjunction "therefore" (Hebrew `attah), which means "in view of this" (i.e., the suffering, verses 7, 9), God extends the call to Moses thus: "I will send thee unto Pharaoh, that thou mayest bring forth my people the children of Israel out of Egypt." Here God involves Moses, as is done in numerous instances in the Bible, in His plan of redemption. Although it is God who does the work, human instruments are often used (Joshua 1:1-9; Isaiah 6:8-9, Jeremiah 1:1). God still calls people today as co-regents to carry out His redemptive plan. Are we willing to answer the call when it comes, or do we give excuses as Moses did in the next verse?

11 And Moses said unto God, Who am I, that I should go unto Pharaoh, and that I should bring forth the children of Israel out of Egypt?

In response to God's invitation, Moses makes a series of excuses (cf. Exodus 3:11—4:17), and in each case God counters them with His assurance. The first one that is within the perimeter of our present study is that he is unfit for such a task. Moses presents his excuse as a rhetorical question "Who am I . . .?" Moses has experienced failure before (2:11-15), which must have affected his self-confidence; he is a fugitive who is wanted in Egypt by Pharaoh. How can he face the same Pharaoh who banished him from Egypt? Moreover, Pharaoh's authority and army is so strong, that nothing can challenge them. The confidence of his youth is gone (Moses is now 80 years old), and the awesome task to which he is being called is overwhelming. Moses could see from the mention of the nations occupying Canaan (v. 8) the greatness of the mission, and probably thought that it was "mission impossible." All these things must have gone through Moses' mind and he poses the question to God, "Who am I, that I should go unto Pharaoh, and that I should bring forth the children of Israel out of Egypt?" In other words, it seems that he is saying to God, "You know me very well. I am not capable to do this task. It requires more than a simple fugitive shepherd, or weak old man as myself to deliver this people from the mighty hand of Pharaoh of Egypt." However, the Bible does not give us the reason why Moses feels unworthy for the task.

The Bible contains a number of other instances where people objected to the call of God for special assignments. Gideon gives his modest up bringing and youthful age as excuse (Judges 6:15); King Saul points to his poor family background (1 Samuel 9:21); Solomon gives his young age (1 Kings 3:7); Jeremiah complains about his young age and lack of eloquence (Jeremiah 1:6).

12 And he said, Certainly I will be with thee; and this shall be a token unto thee, that I have sent thee: When thou hast brought forth the people out of Egypt, ye shall serve God upon this mountain.

Nothing on earth could restore and inspire confidence to perform such a difficult task more than the backing of God himself; no better promise could be given than God's assurance that, "I will certainly be with you." What more could one ask for than the presence of God? The promise of His presence is echoed throughout the Scriptures (Genesis 28:15; Joshua 1:5; Jeremiah 1:8; Haggai 1:13; Matthew 28:20). Following the context, "And he said," refers to God's response. The assurance of God's presence is given to Gideon (Judges 6:6), and to Jeremiah (Jeremiah 1:8, 19). In the New Testament God's assurance can also be found in greetings and benedictions (Luke 1:28; 2 Corinthians 13:14); in the Great Commission (Matthew 28:20); and in Acts 10:38. The promise is fully realized and personified in the coming of the *Emmanuel (Immanuel)*, which means "God with us" (Isaiah 7:14; 8:8 cf.' Matthew 1:23).

God's promise to Moses, "I will certainly be with you," assures Moses that God would be close to him to protect, support, and strengthen him in the enormous task ahead. God knows the difficulties ahead, but His presence is a guarantee that Moses will succeed. With this promise, God seems to say to Moses: "Your objection is baseless. Who you are does not matter and even your lack of abilities does not count. What matters is My involvement, and My presence with you along the way." Similarly, God assures Jehoshaphat when confronted with great battle, "Be not afraid nor dismayed by reason of this great multitude; for the battle is not yours, but God's" (2 Chronicles 20:15). After assuring Moses of His presence, God backs it up with another guarantee when He says, "And this shall be a sign to you that I have sent you: When you have brought the people out of Egypt, you shall serve God on this mountain" (Exodus 3:12, NKJV).

DAILY BIBLE READING

M: Birth and Youth of Moses
Exodus 2:1-10

T: Moses Flees to Midian
Exodus 2:11-15

W: Moses Settles in Midian
Exodus 2:16-25

T: Moses at the Burning Bush
Exodus 3:1-12

F: Moses Called to Deliver Israel
Exodus 3:13-22

S: Moses Empowered by God
Exodus 4:1-9

S: Moses Responds to God's Call
Exodus 4:10-20

TEACHING TIPS

September 12
Bible Study Guide 2

1. Words You Should Know

A. Peradventure (3:17)—(used in KJV) chance, doubt or uncertainty; it may be possibly or perhaps.

B. Joseph (3:19)—one of the two sons of Israel (Jacob). He was Jacob's favorite son, having been born when his father was an old man. Joseph was sold into slavery in Egypt by his brothers. While there, he accurately interpreted Pharaoh's dream and spared the nation of Egypt and other countries as well. Pharaoh rewarded Joseph by making him second in command to the throne. The pharaoh who enslaved the Hebrews "knew" nothing of Joseph in a political or historical sense.

2. Teacher Preparation

Read the background Scripture for this lesson. Find out more about the Exodus experience in order to prepare for this lessons and the other lessons in this quarter.

3. Starting the Lesson

A. Ask class members whether they have ever questioned a decision made on their behalf by someone else, including an employer, a pastor, a spouse, a judge, and so forth.

B. Read the IN FOCUS story about Cynthia. Encourage class members to share personal stories of God's deliverance from seemingly hopeless situations.

4. Getting into the Lesson

Ask class members to think of persons and groups who have been oppressed. How was the situation resolved? In what way could the hand of God be seen working in that situation? Israel probably thought Pharaoh was more powerful than anything on earth. Discuss how oppressed people can be brainwashed into believing an oppressor is more powerful than God.

5. Relating the Lesson to Life

A. Review the information about Egyptian pharaohs from THE PEOPLE, PLACES, AND TIMES article. Find some additional information about the pharaohs of Egypt and share it with your class.

B. Give students an opportunity to answer the questions in SEARCH THE SCRIPTURES.

C. DISCUSS THE MEANING addresses human doubt in the face of God's awesome displays of power. Talk about how people allow themselves to forget God's power (like the Hebrews) or how they ignore His power and try to fight Him (like Pharaoh).

D. The LESSON IN OUR SOCIETY focuses on the similarities in the Hebrew community and the African American slave community. Spend some time discussing the ways in which God has moved in the history of both groups of people.

6. Arousing Action

A. Give each class member an index card. Ask members to write down anything they feel God cannot do on one side. On the other side, they should write what they feel are some things God will not do. (Side one should be blank.)

B. Allow members time to complete the MAKE IT HAPPEN activity. Give each class member a pencil and paper. Then ask them to compare what was written there with what they placed on the index card. Given what they believe about God, should anyone ever doubt what God can do?

C. Give class members an opportunity to complete FOLLOW THE SPIRIT and REMEMBER YOUR THOUGHTS.

WORSHIP GUIDE

For the Superintendent or Teacher
Theme: Crossing the Red Sea
Theme Song: My Heavenly Father Watches Over Me
Scripture: Psalm 106:1-12
Song: I Will Trust in the Lord
Meditation: Oh, God, teach me to trust in You always and to remember Your mighty acts on behalf of your people.

CROSSING THE RED SEA

Bible Background • EXODUS 13:17—14:31
Printed Text • EXODUS 13:17-22; 14:26-31
Devotional Reading • PSALM 106:1-12

LESSON AIM

After studying today's lesson, students should understand the depth of God's providence.

KEEP IN MIND

"And Moses said unto the people, Fear ye not, stand still, and see the salvation of the LORD, which he will shew to you to day: for the Egyptians whom ye have seen to day, ye shall see them again no more for ever" (Exodus 14:13).

FOCAL VERSES

EXODUS 13:17 And it came to pass, when Pharaoh had let the people go, that God led them not through the way of the land of the Philistines, although that was near; for God said, Lest peradventure the people repent when they see war, and they return to Egypt:

18 But God led the people about, through the way of the wilderness of the Red sea: and the children of Israel went up harnessed out of the land of Egypt.

19 And Moses took the bones of Joseph with him: for he had straitly sworn the children of Israel, saying, God will surely visit you; and ye shall carry up my bones away hence with you.

20 And they took their journey from Succoth, and encamped in Etham, in the edge of the wilderness.

21 And the LORD went before them by day in a pillar of a cloud, to lead them the way; and by night in a pillar of fire, to give them light; to go by day and night:

22 He took not away the pillar of the cloud by day, nor the pillar of fire by night, from before the people.

LESSON OVERVIEW

LESSON AIM
KEEP IN MIND
FOCAL VERSES
IN FOCUS
THE PEOPLE, PLACES, AND TIMES
BACKGROUND
AT-A-GLANCE
IN DEPTH
SEARCH THE SCRIPTURES
DISCUSS THE MEANING
LESSON IN OUR SOCIETY
MAKE IT HAPPEN
FOLLOW THE SPIRIT
REMEMBER YOUR THOUGHTS
MORE LIGHT ON THE TEXT
DAILY BIBLE READINGS

14:26 And the LORD said unto Moses, Stretch out thine hand over the sea, that the waters may come again upon the Egyptians, upon their chariots, and upon their horsemen.

27 And Moses stretched forth his hand over the sea, and the sea returned to his strength when the morning appeared; and the Egyptians fled against it; and the LORD overthrew the Egyptians in the midst of the sea.

28 And the waters returned, and covered the chariots, and the horsemen, and all the host of Pharaoh that came into the sea after them; there remained not so much as one of them.

29 But the children of Israel walked upon dry land in the midst of the sea; and the waters were a wall unto them on their right hand, and on their left.

30 Thus the LORD saved Israel that day out of the hand of the Egyptians; and Israel saw the Egyptians dead upon the sea shore.

31 And Israel saw that great work which the LORD did upon the Egyptians: and the people feared the LORD, and believed the LORD, and his servant Moses.

IN FOCUS

Cynthia walked down the aisle at church for the altar prayer. As she made her way down, she knew she had a lot to thank the Lord for. For the last two years, it had seemed like her life was being controlled by someone else. She recalled the day when she got the notice in the mail that she was being sued. To make matters worse, she had been named in a lawsuit because of something that really had nothing to do with her. It took two years to get a ruling on the case.

Cynthia had spent the last three years wondering if she was going to lose everything she had worked for all of her life. She didn't want to buy anything or even make any extra money because she feared losing that, too.

As if the suit wasn't bad enough, her business had suffered because people had heard about the legal action on the local news and had stopped patronizing her. Some months, there was not enough money to pay the bills.

By the time Cynthia reached the altar, she was crying. She realized that she had not missed a meal, she still had a roof over her head, and she had been vindicated from the vicious lies told in the lawsuit. God had provided for her and sustained her during what had been the lowest point of her life.

THE PEOPLE, PLACES, AND TIMES

PHILISTINES. A rival group that the Israelites faced as they settled in Canaan, the Promised Land. The word *Philistine* refers a group of people who occupied the southwest part of Palestine and gave that region their name. They were descendants of Egyptians who were descendants of Ham, whose name means "black" or "burnt faced."

The Philistines were experts in metallurgy, which is the skill of processing metals. Politically, they had a highly organized city-state system comprised of five towns in southwest Palestine: Ashdod, Gaza, Ashkelon, Gath, and Ekron. Each city-state was ruled by a "lord" who was a king-like ruler. They also had a highly trained military organization. The Philistines are also known for their distinctive types of pottery.

Based on information from *Holman Bible Dictionary*, Trent Butler, general editor. Nashville: Broadman & Holman Publishers, 1991, pp. 1108-1109.

PHARAOH. A title which means "great house," used to designate the ancient kings of Egypt. Each pharaoh of ancient Egypt had five "great names" which he assumed on the day he became ruler of the nation. It was not considered proper to use one of the five powerful names in a direct fashion, therefore, their ruler came to be addressed simply as Pharaoh.

In ancient Egypt, the pharaoh was an absolute ruler, commander of the armies, chief justice of the royal court, and high priest of all religions. Justice was defined in terms of "what Pharaoh loves" and wrongdoing was determined according to "what Pharaoh hates."

The term *pharaoh* was used to designate the king of Egypt from about 1500 B.C. until the Persian domination in about 550 B.C.

Based on information from *Holman Bible Dictionary*, p. 1103.

BACKGROUND

At last Pharaoh had relented and allowed the Israelites to leave Egypt, having discovered that his gods were no match for theirs. But the victory is not complete as they are still within Pharaoh's grasp.

God had taken care of everything. All the people needed to do was be willing to follow their Lord. Moses had given the people the Lord's instructions. God had already determined their route of exit.

God's plan and provision for the great Exodus from Egypt reveals the depth of divine understanding of the chosen people. God knew their weaknesses and led them out by way of a detour. The Lord knew that this people, if given the chance, would choose bondage over war.

Upon their departure, Pharaoh had a change of heart. He decided to use his mighty army and their chariots to return the Hebrews to Egypt so they could continue to live in bondage. Pharaoh's military strategy would prove to be no match for the strategy of the Almighty God.

AT-A-GLANCE

1. Victory and Freedom through God's Providence (Exodus 13:17-22)
2. Pharaoh's Army Destroyed (14:26-29)
3. Israel Serves the Lord (vv. 30-31)

IN DEPTH

1. Victory and Freedom through God's Providence (Exodus 13:17-22)

Despite the fact that going through "Philistine

country" was more direct, the Lord led Israel on a winding route to their destination. The Lord did not move them along the coast of the Mediterranean Sea because they would have encountered numerous Egyptian fortifications as this was the traditional route between Egypt and other regions of the fertile crescent. Another reason for the indirect route was because the Lord had instructed Moses to lead the people to God's mountain.

God knew the nature of the people. It was clear that they were afraid and were not strong enough to fight. Perhaps their years of involuntary servitude and no leader of their own had diminished their sense of their own abilities. God knew this people, but the people did not know God. They had not yet learned the true extent of Divine greatness. God led the Israelites through the wilderness toward the Red Sea.

Hundreds of years before the Exodus, Joseph had seen this day coming. As they departed, Israel took the mummified body of Joseph out of the land which had held them captive. Joseph's desire was to be taken with his people when they departed from the land. He was carried out of Egypt on the shoulders of a new generation. The God of Abraham, Isaac, and Jacob is faithful and dependable. The Lord kept the promise made to Joseph and to all of Abraham's descendants.

As Israel journeyed toward the land of promise, God's providence continued. The Lord went before the people by day with a pillar of cloud which protected them from the sun's scorching heat. By night, the Lord provided a pillar of fire to give them light. Bible scholars believe that the pillar of fire was a volcano. God did not release His people from bondage in Egypt and abandon them.

Israel was embarking upon a new journey. They needed reassurance. The pillars of cloud and fire were visible signs that God was with them both day and night. God's presence was constantly before Israel, revealing compassion and dealing with their fears and anxieties. They were continually provided for. The cloud and the pillar of fire did not leave them. God's divine presence overshadows and protects people of every generation, through every wilderness.

2. Pharaoh's Army Destroyed (14:26-29)

God had already done many miracles on behalf of Israel. Divine providence was generally quiet and

constant, but at times was dramatically vivid. At the Red Sea, Israel appeared to be facing an impasse. The vast sea was in front of them and Pharaoh's army was closing in behind them. The people flew into a panic and began to blame Moses for having taken them out of Egypt in the first place (14:11-12). In their panic-stricken state, they imagined that God had brought them out of Egypt simply to destroy them.

Moses answered them with a word of hope. If they would stand firm, they would soon see what the Lord would do. After that day, never again would they see the Egyptians. In an awesome demonstration of God's power, Moses stretched out his hand and the waters of the sea were divided. The Israelites went through the sea on dry ground, with a wall of water on both sides.

The Egyptians pursued them. All of Pharaoh's army—horses, chariots, and horsemen—followed the Israelites into the sea. God then looked down from the pillar of fire and threw the Egyptian army into a fit of confusion, causing the wheels of their chariots to come off so they could not drive easily. They realized that they were no match for Israel's God and wanted to flee at that moment. But the worst for them was not over. God's plans cannot be defeated by human effort.

The Lord told Moses to stretch his hand back over the sea so that the water would flow back over the Egyptian army. Moses did as God instructed him and, at daybreak, the sea had gone back to its place. The Lord routed the Egyptians into the midst of the sea. Once the waters returned to their normal place, the entire army of Pharaoh that had followed Israel into the sea was consumed. Not one of them survived. As the Egyptians drowned, the Israelites passed on to safety on dry land.

Apparently there were some soldiers, however, who had not entered the water. It was they who returned to spread the word about Yahweh, Israel's Commander. It is not certain whether Pharaoh drowned with his army. It is possible that he waited along the shoreline.

The drowning of Pharaoh's army certainly did not alter the stability of the Egyptian empire. The destruction of the Egyptian army was not the most important fact. What was most important in this event is the victory of the Lord on behalf of His people.

3. Israel Serves the Lord (vv. 30-31)

At the same time that the walls of water fell upon the Egyptian army, the walls continued to stand for Israel. They passed through the sea on dry ground. The people were convinced that the Lord saved them from the hands of the Egyptians on that day. They saw the Egyptians lying on the shore dead.

Having witnessed the power of God firsthand against the Egyptians, they were filled with reverence. Their God was more powerful than Pharaoh and his army! They put their trust in the Lord and in God's servant, Moses. Their physical deliverance at the hands of the Egyptians paralleled their spiritual transformation. They now believed in the Lord; they did not believe at the beginning of their adventure. Clearly God was the One who had done this great work, Moses was simply the vehicle through which God's work was done. In recognition of God's power, the people broke in song (Exodus 15).

SEARCH THE SCRIPTURES

1. Why did God lead Israel away from Egypt by an indirect route? (Exodus 3:17)

2. Where did God lead Israel? (v. 18)

3. Whose bones did Moses take with them? (v. 19)

4. Why did they take the bones? (v.19)

5. What provisions did the Lord make so that the Israelites could travel by day or night? (v. 21)

6. How long did the pillars of cloud and fire stay with Israel? (v. 21)

7. Why did the Lord tell Moses to stretch out his hand? (14:26)

8. At what time of day did the sea cover the Egyptians? (v. 27)

9. Who was killed when the sea came back together? (v. 28)

10. How did Israel react to what the Lord had done? (v. 31)

DISCUSS THE MEANING

1. Why did Israel continue to doubt the power of God, especially after the Lord had sent the 10 plagues and had provided the pillars of cloud and fire. Why did Israel never seem to have enough evidence of God's power to satisfy them?

2. Why did Pharaoh have a change of heart and attempt to recapture the Hebrews? Why did he feel he could defeat them after God had already performed powerful acts on Israel's behalf?

LESSON IN OUR SOCIETY

The story of the enslaved Hebrew community has often been compared to the experience of slavery among Blacks in this country. African Americans who lived through periods of terrible racial discrimination can easily attest that "God has brought us a mighty long way."

If we truly believe this, why do so may African Americans continue to doubt the power of God? Why do we turn to other things for consolation? Our Lord is a proven God who can provide for all of our needs. God has acted on our behalf many times. Surely a God who can part the waters of the sea can supply all of our needs, too.

MAKE IT HAPPEN

Think of times in your life when you felt as though there were no more options and all hope was gone. How did God intervene in that situation for you? How can you use those incidences to strengthen your faith for difficult times you may face in the future?

FOLLOW THE SPIRIT

What God wants me to do:

_____

_____

REMEMBER YOUR THOUGHTS

Special insights you learned:

_____

_____

MORE LIGHT ON THE TEXT
EXODUS 13:17-22; 14:26-31

After long and difficult confrontations with the Lord, Pharaoh finally allows the Children of Israel to leave. This begins the long journey that takes some 40 years, and it is the beginning of the fulfilling of God's promises and covenant with His people, Israel.

13:17 And it came to pass, when Pharaoh had let the people go, that God led them not through the way of the land of the Philistines, although that was near; for God said, Lest peradventure the people repent when they see war, and they return to Egypt:

18 But God led the people about, through the way of the wilderness of the Red sea: and the children of Israel went up harnessed out of the land of Egypt.

The people of Israel left Egypt to journey towards the Promised Land. God promised in the third chapter that they would be led out to inhabit a new land. The Scripture passage tells how the journey starts and the events that would take place on the way. The nearest route to Canaan is through the northeast via the land of the Philistines. However, God leads them down southeast towards the Red Sea into the wilderness, which is a longer route. This verse explains the reason why God decides to lead them through the long route. God, who knows the heart and thoughts of everyone, knows that Pharaoh would pursue them to recapture them, and perhaps the Philistines would help to fight them. With war on every side so soon after leaving Egypt, the Israelites would possibly regret leaving Egypt and would prefer to return. Their will to resist any aggression has already been weakened by the long period of slavery and suffering in Egypt, and they would not be prepared to face any military action. In addition, although they might be have been militarily equipped for war (v. 18), they were not emotionally prepared. God therefore does not direct them to take the easier way, but rather the longer route in order to avoid any possible military campaign on the very onset of the journey.

Another reason for taking the longer route is implicitly obvious from 3:12 where God says that they would worship the Lord in the mountain as a sign of His deliverance. If God had led them via the route of the Mediterranean sea coast through Gaza in Philistine, they would have missed Mount Horeb (Sinai). This would have raised some doubts in the minds of both Moses and the people, and would have affected their trust in the Lord's leadership. When God gave His guarantee in chapter 3, it was clear that it would not make sense to the ordinary mind for them to take the long route, rather than the shorter and direct route of the Mediterranean. The phrase "the children of Israel went up harnessed out of the land of Egypt" means that they were armed. Harnessed, (Hebrew *chamush* pronounced **ka-mush**) is translated "armed" (Joshua 1:14; 4:12; Judges 7:11); i.e., arrayed for battle by fives. There is no report that the Egyptians disarmed the Israelites when they left Egypt. Since the Israelites lived in the frontiers of Egypt, it is suggested that they might have helped protect Egypt from invading nomads.

Therefore, when they left, they went militarily well-equipped.

19 And Moses took the bones of Joseph with him: for he had straitly sworn the children of Israel, saying, God will surely visit you; and ye shall carry up my bones away hence with you.

In keeping with the oath made between the Children of Israel and Joseph (Genesis 50:25), Moses carries with him the bones of Joseph. Compare the account in Joshua 24:32: "And the bones of Joseph, which the children of Israel brought up out of Egypt, buried they in Shechem, in a parcel of ground which Jacob bought of the sons of Hamor the father of Shechem for an hundred pieces of silver: and it became the inheritance of the children of Joseph."

The account in Acts 7:15-16 suggests that the bones of the father were also taken from Egypt. The writer of the book of Hebrews confirms this when writes: "By faith Joseph, when he died, made mention of the departing of the children of Israel; and gave commandment concerning his bones" (Hebrews 11:22). Carrying the bones of Joseph along was not only a performance of the oath their fathers had sworn to Joseph, but an acknowledgment of the fulfillment of God's promise to visit them and bring them out of the land of Egypt. It also serves as an encouragement to their faith and hope that God would fulfill the other part of the promise, which was to bring them to Canaan. According to African culture, an African is never buried in a foreign land. When an African dies, his or her corpse is carried to his or her home town (village) for burial, even if one died in a another town or in another tribe in the same country.

20 And they took their journey from Succoth, and encamped in Etham, in the edge of the wilderness. 21 And the Lord went before them by day in a pillar of a cloud, to lead them the way; and by night in a pillar of fire, to give them light; to go by day and night: 22 He took not away the pillar of the cloud by day, nor the pillar of fire by night, from before the people.

The writer continues to tell the direction of their journey. After they left Egypt through Rameses, it seems their first stop was at Succoth (Exodus 12:37). The name means "tents or booths," probably a name given by Jacob where he built booths or tents for his cattle as he journeyed to Canaan (Genesis 33:17-18). When they left Succoth, they encamped at Etham which is at the edge of the wilderness. Exodus 13, verses 21 and 22 introduce the presence of the Lord as their guide, symbolized by the pillar of cloud during the day and pillar of fire during the night. When this visible presence of the Lord appeared as stated, probably immediately they left Rameses. It led them all the way day and night from Egypt to Canaan. The cloud probably protected them from the scorching heat of the desert sun during the day, and the fire gave light in all the camp during the night (Psalm 105:39; Numbers 9:16-18). This appearance of the presence of the Lord is called *theophany*, the self-disclosure of God. (3:2ff.). Chapter 14:19 calls him "the angel of God," while he is referred as the Lord (YHWH) here (compare 14:21-25, 31; cf. 3:2; 4ff).

Chapter 14, verses 1-25 tell the story of the miraculous deliverance of Israel from the pursuit of the Egyptians. As the Israelites left Egypt and camped at Etham, God instructs them to camp Pihahiroth by the sea, and predicted that Pharaoh and his army would think that they are trapped and would come after them (vv. 1-4).

Surely, the prediction came through. Pharaoh assembles his army and pursues them (vv. 5-9). As the army draws close, the Israelites begin to panic and complain against Moses and his leadership. This is the second of the 12 complaints recorded in the book against Moses. In response to their murmuring, Moses gives them assurance of God's deliverance: ". . . Fear ye not, stand still, and see the salvation of the Lord, which he will shew to you to day: for the Egyptians whom ye have seen to day, ye shall see them again no more for ever. The Lord shall fight for you, and ye shall hold your peace" (vv. 13-14). The pillar of cloud that went before them, went behind to protect them from the Egyptians (vv. 19-20). The Lord then instructs Moses to strike the sea with his rod. The sea divides into two parts, making walls on the either side, and dries up in the middle. The Israelites walk across, and the whole of the Egyptian army, with their chariots, pursues them into the middle of the sea. The Lord dismantles their chariots' wheels so that they could not move fast enough to catch up with the Israelites (vv. 21-25).

14:26 And the Lord said unto Moses, Stretch out thine hand over the sea, that the waters may come again upon the Egyptians, upon their chariots, and upon their horse-

men. 27 And Moses stretched forth his hand over the sea, and the sea returned to his strength when the morning appeared; and the Egyptians fled against it; and the Lord overthrew the Egyptians in the midst of the sea. 28 And the waters returned, and covered the chariots, and the horsemen, and all the host of Pharaoh that came into the sea after them; there remained not so much as one of them. 29 But the children of Israel walked upon dry land in the midst of the sea; and the waters were a wall unto them on their right hand, and on their left.

The Egyptians are trapped in the middle of the sea. They are neither able to move further nor retreat because the Lord took off their chariot wheels. God commands Moses again to "stretch out thine hand over the sea" so that the waters of the sea would return to cover the Egyptians. To stretch out (*natah*) his hand means "to extend" or "to let down." Some people would think that Moses would strike the water with some force, however the wording seems to suggest a gentle touch of the water with Moses' shepherd rod. Miracles are not based on how much force we exert or how loudly we shout, but on how obedient and faithful we are to the commands of God. Often times, God may ask us to do things that are nonsensical to the human eyes, but our trust in the faithfulness of God and obedience to His word will make it sensible and accomplish His desire for us. To touch the waters of a mighty sea with an ordinary rod in order to divide it or to return it to its normal place does not make sense to the ordinary human rationale. However, Moses only needed to obey the orders of the Lord for them to "see the salvation of the Lord, which he will" show them. As Moses touched the water again the second time, water begins to return. The Egyptians, seeing the walls of water coming down upon them tried to flee, but it was too late for them. The water covered all the host of the Egyptian army the pursued Israel, and not even one person escaped, probably including Pharaoh. This fulfills the prophecies of Exodus 14:3-4; 17, 26.

People throughout the ages have tried to explain away what happened that day on the Red Sea. Some, who refute the power of God over creation, say that the dividing of the sea was not a strange phenomenon but a natural course of events. They attribute the miracle to a high tide. That means, according to their argument, the sea was on high tide while the Israelites crossed, but the tide returned when the Egyptians were in the midst.

According to the biblical statistics, the number of the Children of Israel that left Egypt was "about six hundred thousand on foot that were men, beside children" and "a mixed multitude went up also with them; and flocks, and herds, even very much cattle" (12:37-38). The men mentioned here are 20 years old and older (Exodus 38:26), it does not include women. The mixed multitude includes all non-Hebrews who decided to go with them. It is suggested that the number (600,000) does not include the Levites, the priests or ordinary men, but soldiers. The number of the women, children (ages 19 and under) and the mixed multitude is not given in the Bible. In Israel, polygamy was a legal practice and having a large family (with many children) was common. Like most African communities, Israel was an agricultural community where the men married many wives in order to have many children who would help on the farm. It is therefore difficult and almost impossible to correctly estimate the number of people that left Egypt. Some suggest 6,000,000 people in total, which is about 10 people per family. This is a very conservative number.

Israel went out of Egypt in orderly companies (12:51). If they went 5 abreast as some versions suggest and there were around 6,000,000 people, there was a line of marching Israelites approximately 680 miles long, allowing 3 feet each for the 1,200,000 rows. If they went 50 abreast, there would be a lines of 68 miles; if 100 abreast, a line of 34 miles; if 200, then 17 miles; and if 400, a line of 8.5 miles. Allowing 3 feet to a person, 400 abreast would mean that a path was made through the solid ice of the Red Sea about 1,200 feet wide (15:8). This would vary, more or less, according to the column width of the march. It would take hours to cross. For the high tide to last until all the Israelites crossed to safety and all the Egyptian army was in the midst of the sea was nothing but a miracle. Others argue that the Israelites crossed at the shallowest end of the sea and that there was no dividing of the sea. Then it was even a greater miracle that the shallow sea drowned the strong Egyptian hosts, while even the old and weak Israelites walked across safely.

30 Thus the Lord saved Israel that day out of the hand of the Egyptians; and Israel saw the Egyptians dead upon the sea shore. 31 And Israel saw that great work which the Lord did upon the Egyptians: and the people feared the Lord, and believed the Lord, and his servant Moses.

Whatever the argument might be, the facts are that the Lord saved the Israelites from the Egyptians that day and Israel saw the Egyptians lying dead on the banks of the Red Sea as Moses prophesied (Exodus 14:13, 30). They saw God miraculously make a path through the sea and close it again after they were safe. The result of the miracle are: 1) the people feared the Lord; 2) the people believed the Lord; and 3) they believed Moses. Fear is the Hebrew word *yare'* (pronounced yaw-ray'), which means "to be afraid, to revere, or to frighten." Here it is used to indicate both fear and reverence. The Israelites were afraid of God because of the strange occurrence and as a result they revered or honored the Lord. They were astonished and they "believed" (Hebrew *'aman*), i.e., trusted the Lord and His servant. This miraculous deliverance created confidence in the leadership of *YAHWEH* and His servant, Moses. Centuries later, Isaiah could still boast of the mighty deeds of God and assure Judah of God's continuous intervention and deliverance (Isaiah 43:15-19).

DAILY BIBLE READING

M: The Festival of Unleavened Bread
Exodus 13:3-10

T: Led by Pillars of Cloud and Fire
Exodus 13:17-22

W: Caught Between Pharaoh and the Sea
Exodus 14:1-9

T: Going Forward at God's Command
Exodus 14:10-18

F: Israel Crosses the Read Sea
Exodus 14:19-25

S: God Saves Israel from the Egyptians
Exodus 14:26-31

S: Moses Sings of God's Victory
Exodus 15:1-13

TEACHING TIPS

September 19
Bible Study Guide 3

1. Words You Should Know

A. Peculiar (19:5)—(used in KJV) special or valued.

B. Covet (20:17)—(used in KJV) to have an excessive or unnatural desire for.

2. Teacher Preparation

Read the background Scripture for this lesson. Do some additional study and learn more about what it means to have a covenant relationship with God.

3. Starting the Lesson

A. Make a list of various types of covenant relationships, including marriage, legal agreements, and so forth. What causes those relationships to become strained or broken? How can both parties work to preserve and strengthen those covenant relationships. Discuss whether covenant agreements are viewed with the same importance as they were in biblical days.

B. Read the IN FOCUS story about Darryl. Ask class members to share how they view the Ten Commandments and how they keep themselves true to these commands.

4. Getting into the Lesson

Discuss how the first four commandments deal with our relationship to God and the last six address our relationship to one another. Talk with class members about why we must have a proper relationship with the Lord before we can have a proper relationship with one another.

5. Relating the Lesson to Life

A. Review the information about the significance of the Sabbath in THE PEOPLE, PLACES, AND TIMES article. Do Christians give their Sabbath the same degree of reverence as the Hebrew community? Spend some time talking about modern day idols.

B. Give students an opportunity to answer the questions in SEARCH THE SCRIPTURES.

C. DISCUSS THE MEANING addresses proper use and reverence of God's name. Talk about whether people take God's name seriously. List some of the more common ways that the Lord's name is taken in vain.

D. The LESSON IN OUR SOCIETY deals with the value of the Ten Commandments as a guideline for living. Discuss how different our world might be if everyone lived according to these commandments.

6. Arousing Action

A. Ask class members to name all of the Ten Commandments without looking at them. Allow class members to share which commandments come to mind most often in their daily lives.

B. Allow members time to complete the MAKE IT HAPPEN activity. Give each class member a pencil and paper to determine the degree to which they adhere to the Commandments.

C. Give class members an opportunity to complete FOLLOW THE SPIRIT and REMEMBER YOUR THOUGHTS.

WORSHIP GUIDE

For the Superintendent or Teacher
Theme: The Covenant
Theme Song: Is Your All on the Altar?
Scripture: Deuteronomy 4:32-40
Song: We've Come This Far by Faith
Meditation: My God, strengthen me to obey Your commands always. May I love Your laws and live by them daily.

THE COVENANT

Bible Background • EXODUS 19:1-20:21
Printed Text • EXODUS 19:3-6; 20:2-4, 7-8, 12-17
Devotional Reading • DEUTERONOMY 4:32-40

LESSON AIM

After studying today's lesson, students should know that God has set His people apart and expects them to live according to His commandments.

KEEP IN MIND

"Now therefore, if ye will obey my voice indeed, and keep my covenant, then ye shall be a peculiar treasure unto me above all people: for all the earth is mine" (Exodus 19:5).

FOCAL VERSES

EXODUS 19:3 And Moses went up unto God, and the LORD called unto him out of the mountain, saying, Thus shalt thou say to the house of Jacob, and tell the children of Israel;

4 Ye have seen what I did unto the Egyptians, and how I bare you on eagles' wings, and brought you unto myself.

5 Now therefore, if ye will obey my voice indeed, and keep my covenant, then ye shall be a peculiar treasure unto me above all people: for all the earth is mine:

6 And ye shall be unto me a kingdom of priests, and an holy nation. These are the words which thou shalt speak unto the children of Israel.

20:2 I am the LORD thy God, which have brought thee out of the land of Egypt, out of the house of bondage.

3 Thou shalt have no other gods before me.

4 Thou shalt not make unto thee any graven image, or any likeness of any thing that is in heaven above, or that is in the earth beneath, or that is in the water under the earth:

7 Thou shalt not take the name of the LORD thy

LESSON OVERVIEW

LESSON AIM
KEEP IN MIND
FOCAL VERSES
IN FOCUS
THE PEOPLE, PLACES, AND TIMES
BACKGROUND
AT-A-GLANCE
IN DEPTH
SEARCH THE SCRIPTURES
DISCUSS THE MEANING
LESSON IN OUR SOCIETY
MAKE IT HAPPEN
FOLLOW THE SPIRIT
REMEMBER YOUR THOUGHTS
MORE LIGHT ON THE TEXT
DAILY BIBLE READINGS

God in vain; for the LORD will not hold him guiltless that taketh his name in vain.

8 Remember the sabbath day, to keep it holy.

12 Honour thy father and thy mother: that thy days may be long upon the land which the LORD thy God giveth thee.

13 Thou shalt not kill.

14 Thou shalt not commit adultery.

15 Thou shalt not steal.

16 Thou shalt not bear false witness against thy neighbour.

17 Thou shalt not covet thy neighbour's house, thou shalt not covet thy neighbour's wife, nor his manservant, nor his maidservant, nor his ox, nor his ass, nor any thing that is thy neighbour's.

IN FOCUS

Darryl was helping the twins to memorize the Ten Commandments for the children's Bible knowledge contest at church. They could recite the first nine with no problem. Darryl was smiling and patting himself on the back somewhat as they went through them.

"Well," he thought, "I think I'm doing pretty good on this Commandments thing. I haven't murdered anybody. I've been faithful to my wife. I'm honest. I respect my parents."

Just at that moment, little Zena broke his train of thought. "Daddy, what's coveting mean?"

Darryl got out a dictionary and said, "Well, let's just see exactly what it means."

Zeus began reading the definition, "to desire another's possession or attribute inordinately." With a curious look on his face, Zeus asked, "Daddy, what's 'in-or-din-ately'?"

Before Darryl could answer his son's question, his mind had begun to drift to Herb Crawford's Mercedes Benz. He remembered wondering how Herb could afford such an expensive car and wishing he could afford one, too.

When he first saw Herb's car, Darryl couldn't even compliment him. Darryl was filled with envy that Herb had actually bought the car that he wanted! Darryl had even smiled, thinking, "Yeah, he's looking good now, but I'll bet he won't be able to keep up the payments."

As he thought about Herb's car, Darryl also thought about other times when he had desired something that someone else had. He had even tried to mimic Curtis Foster because he wanted to be able to speak as well as Curtis.

Darryl had to be honest and admit he had a problem with coveting what belonged to others. "I guess the Ten Commandments aren't just for kids," he thought.

THE PEOPLE, PLACES, AND TIMES

IDOL. An image or symbol used as an object of worship, replacing the one, true God. The Bible uses various terms to refer to idols or idolatry: a graven, cast or carved "image," a "statue," or an "abomination." Both the Old and New Testaments condemn idols and idolatry, but they are more of a concern in the Old Testament.

Idols were a part of everyday life for ancient Hebrews. The Egyptians represented their deities in the form of various animal-human images. Many of the Mesopotamian cultures, as well as the Hittites of ancient Asia Minor, used idols to represent their deities. The greatest threats to Hebrew worship, however, were the Canaanite gods Baal and Asherah, which were fertility images.

The first Hebrew rebellion centered around the golden calf made under Aaron's leadership in the wilderness (Exodus 32). Many Bible scholars believe that the threat of idolatry in the Jewish community was greatly reduced after the Babylonian Exile and continued to lessen throughout New Testament times.

Based on information from *Holman Bible Dictionary,* Trent Butler, general editor. Nashville: Broadman & Holman Publishers, 1991, p. 686.

SABBATH. The day of rest which is considered holy to God because of His rest on the seventh day after creation. It was viewed as a sign of the covenant relationship between God and His people and the eternal rest which He promised them.

The word *Sabbath* is derived from the Hebrew word *shabbat,* which means to "cease" or "desist." The primary meaning of the Sabbath is that all work ceases on that day. The Hebrew Sabbath was celebrated every seven days and became a fundamental part of the worship of the God of creation and redemption.

The Mosaic laws feature a number of regulations concerning the Sabbath. The Ten Commandments stipulate that the Sabbath belonged to the Lord. This was for two reasons. First, God rested on the seventh day after creation, and blessed the day and made it holy. The second reason was that it served as a reminder of Israel's deliverance from slavery in Egypt. The Sabbath became a day of sacred assembly and worship, a token of their covenant with God.

Jesus tended to observe the Sabbath as a day of worship in the synagogues. However, His failure to comply with tedious restrictions of Judaism often caused friction.

In the early days, Christians met on the Sabbath with the Jews in the synagogues to proclaim Christ (Acts 13:14). The Christian holy day was observed on the first day of the week, the day of the resurrection.

Based on information from *Holman Bible Dictionary,* p. 1216.

BACKGROUND

Central to Israel's existence was their commitment with the Lord. The covenant which sealed that commitment was the binding force which held them together during the early days. At the core of the Sinaitic covenant were the stipulations known as "the ten words" or "Decalogue."

The Ten Commandments (Decalogue) was a major influence in shaping God's people for His purposes. The Lord gave the Law to Moses on Mount Sinai as His divine standard of right. These Laws constituted God's covenant to be kept by current and future generations of Israelites. This covenant became the cornerstone by which the world would recognize God's people. It was the foundation of covenant life. The Law served as a net over God's people, insuring that they were within the bounds of covenant fellowship.

AT-A-GLANCE

1. The Call to Covenant Life (Exodus 19:3-6)

2. Proper Relationship with God (20:2-8)

3. Proper Relationship with Each Other (vv. 12-17)

IN DEPTH

1. The Call to Covenant Life
(Exodus 19:3-6)

The nineteenth chapter of Exodus begins to establish Yahweh's lordship over humanity. The God of Israel is sovereign Lord of all creation. He triumphed over the Egyptians' gods. Even the sea and the wilderness yielded to the power of the God of Israel.

The events which surround these verses were probably used in Israel's worship. The historic acts of God relative to Israel's faith were often recreated in worship. Years before, God had told Moses that one day Israel would serve the Divine Majesty on the very mountain where Moses had first encountered the Lord. True to God's word, that day had now come. Yahweh summoned Moses and extended an invitation to Israel to obey the voice from heaven and to enter into a covenant relationship with God as their father Abraham did. God gave Moses instructions for Israel. Moses was first to remind the people of all Yahweh had done for them.

God continued to claim Israel even through difficult times. God held true to the promises which were made to Abraham, Isaac, and Jacob. God extended the covenant at Sinai to those who had been delivered from bondage. God promised to make this people a very special treasure, a kingdom of priests, and a holy nation (Exodus 19:6). The term *holy* means that they were set apart for service.

God desires that all people be God's people. Still, none is forced into covenant with the Lord. God allows them to choose to become a divine people.

2. Proper Relationship with God (20:2-8)

God was very clear in outlining the expectations of this covenant to His people. Israel was not to worship nor give allegiance to any other god. In this first commandment, the Lord is identified and what the Lord as God had done for His people is restated. It was God who brought them out of slavery in Egypt. Yahweh was not timid in declaring sovereignty as the God of Israel, and not simply one of the many gods of Egypt. Israel's faith was to be completely in the God "who brought you out of the land of slavery." This great and miraculous feat can be attributed to no other deity.

God gave a total of ten commandments to the people. The first four commandments focus on Israel's relationship with God. The final six laws command Israel deal with how to be in right relationship with one another. But before they could treat others right, they had to have their relationship with God in order.

God's first commandment to Israel was not to worship any other god nor observe their rituals. Throughout Israel's history, the Lord had to warn them repeatedly about the sin of idolatry. They were always straying away from Yahweh to worship other gods, often the gods of the Canaanites. When their kings married women who were from other lands, the wives often brought the worship of their idol gods with them. Israel's rebellious and idolatrous behavior often wrought spiritual decay on the nation and God's wrath upon them. No gods, in fact nothing, could be more important to them than Yahweh.

In verse 4, the word *idol* literally means "a carved sculpture." God forbade the Israelites to carve or sculpt any objects that would be used as a representation of Divine essence. The Lord warned that Israel is not to make images of worship out of anything that was in the heavens above, beneath the earth, or beneath the waters.

The danger of creating images of God is that they often become the object of worship instead of God. This is what happened to Jereboam when he made images of God to prevent the people of the Northern Kingdom from going to Jerusalem (1 Kings 13:1—14:20).

No image or likeness can truly represent the essence of God. The essence of Yahweh is greater than any image can express; therefore, God cannot be limited to an icon, statue or linguistic category. The worship of images or things in nature dishonors the God who is Creator of the world. God's punishment of such idolatry would extend unto the third and fourth generation of those who disobeyed Him, yet the Lord would show mercy unto all those who loved and kept the commandments (Exodus 20:5-6).

The third commandment forbids the idle or empty use of God's name. God's name expresses His essential character and nature. Any irreverent use of the Lord's name renders us guilty of using it in vain. The Lord will punish or not hold guiltless, anyone who uses His name in vain.

The family patriarch was responsible for fulfilling the fourth commandment. The full meaning of this commandment must be understood in the context of Jewish society. For the devout Jew, the Sabbath, was to be used as a day of rest, prayer, and reading the Scriptures. No work of any kind was to be done by anyone, including slaves and servants. The Jewish Sabbath begins on Friday evening and ends on Sunday morning.

3. Proper Relationship with Each Other (20:12-17)

The Lord wanted to govern the daily relationships of the chosen people. A right relationship with God will result in right relationships with others.

The family unit in Jewish life was a source of strength and communal unity. Jewish children were expected to obey their parents and heed their advice. The word *honor* in verse 12 means that one "prefers" or holds his parents "in high esteem." This commandment is the first in which God promises to bless those who obey with "prolonged" days or long life on earth (Ephesians 6:2).

The sixth commandment calls for God's people to respect and protect human life in Israel's community. A stable society is built upon respect for life and for that which God has created. Killing other humans in cases of dispute, vengeance, and hatred was strictly forbidden. However, the Lord did not forbid the slaying of animals for food and clothes, or the killing of enemies in times of lawful war. Nevertheless, God's gift of life to every individual must be held in highest regard.

Adultery is betrayal or infidelity which defiles the holy estate of marriage. This word denotes one who

has unlawful intercourse with the spouse of another. God's seventh commandment forbids adultery because it mocks and cheapens God's ideal for marriage.

Stealing is taking something that belongs to another person, whether by force or deceit. The eighth commandment highlights the sacredness of property, that which God has given to someone else. Those who are idle and wayward must not take the rewards of those diligent and prudent.

The sin of lying is built on deceit, which corrupts the person who tells the lie and can do psychological and spiritual damage to the one who has been lied about. Although this ninth commandment has reference to falsely accusing one's neighbor in a court of law, the Bible warns believers of the importance of "speaking the truth in love" (Ephesians 4:15) in all areas of life.

In the biblical sense, the word *covet* almost always refers to a lustful desire to obtain or gain something. The evil of covetousness is that it leads to greed and lust. Covetousness is acted out in envy and jealousy toward another. An obsessive desire for another person's spouse, property, or even their talents and abilities takes our focus off God as the One who can supply all our needs.

Obedience to God is an indication of our love for Him. Our Lord Jesus summarized the Ten Commandments when He told the Pharisees that the greatest commandment of the Law is to "love the Lord your God, with all your heart, and with all your heart, and with all your mind" and to "love your neighbor as yourself" (Matthew 22:37-39, NIV).

SEARCH THE SCRIPTURES

1. Why did God summon Moses to the mountain? (Exodus 19:3)

2. What are some of the things God had done for Israel? (v. 4)

3. What promise did God give to Israel if they chose to be His people? (v. 6)

4. How did God introduce Himself before giving the commandments? (20:2)

5. What is the first commandment? (v. 3)

6. What punishment and for how long would the Israelites suffer if they made any idols? (v. 4)

7. Who was not to do any work on the Sabbath? (v. 11)

8. What is the first commandment having a promise attached to it? (v. 12)

9. What are the three short, but distinct, commandments concerning the behavior of God's people? (vv. 13-15)

10. What things did God forbid His people to covet? (v. 17)

DISCUSS THE MEANING

1. God clearly tells us not to misuse His name. People often associate taking God's name in vain with profanity. However, if we utter the words, "Oh, God," whenever we face unpleasantness, have we misused His name?

2. If everyone followed the Ten Commandments, would it still be necessary to have additional laws and/or rules? In other words, are they any conditions or situations that are not covered under the Commandments?

LESSON IN OUR SOCIETY

Some teachers of ethics and society are now teaching the Ten Commandments in their classes. They are not being taught as religion. Rather, they are taught as a decent way for people to live and relate to others.

God's design for people to live in peace and prosperity are timeless. The rules for conduct toward God and toward one another are just as valid today as they were when He issued them on Mount Sinai. God's Laws provide the foundation for a code of right conduct for all of humanity.

MAKE IT HAPPEN

List all of the Ten Commandments in one column on a sheet of paper. In another column, write down whether you adhere to this commandment: (a) strictly; (b) most of the time, but not strictly; (c) occasionally obey the commandment, but often fall short; or (d) rarely devote yourself to obeying this commandment as God intended. Please be honest with yourself. You do not have to share your answers with anyone else.

FOLLOW THE SPIRIT

What God wants me to do:

_____

_____

REMEMBER YOUR THOUGHTS

Special insights you learned:

_____

_____

MORE LIGHT ON THE TEXT
EXODUS 19:3-6; 20:2-4, 7-8, 12-17

Scholars have often regarded Exodus chapters 19 through 24 as the most important passages of the Old Testament. This passage records the account of the covenant God made with Israel at Mount Sinai. This covenant forms the pivotal part of God's relationship with Israel. The covenant was conditioned upon Israel's obedience to God's laws, which were given to the people at Sinai. The rest of the Old Testament centers mainly on Israel's response to this covenant relationship.

Three months have passed since the Children of Israel left Egypt. They arrive at the Sinai desert and camp at the foot of the mountain (Exodus 19:1-2). Here God is about to make an agreement with them. In the following passages of study, we shall look at the Lord's covenant relationship as explained through the famous Ten Commandments.

19:3 And Moses went up unto God, and the Lord called unto him out of the mountain, saying, Thus shalt thou say to the house of Jacob, and tell the children of Israel; 4 Ye have seen what I did unto the Egyptians, and how I bare you on eagles' wings, and brought you unto myself.

When God confronted Moses in the burning bush and called him to deliver the Children of Israel out of bondage, Moses was assured of God's presence. God said to him, "I will certainly be with you. And this shall be a sign to you that I have sent you: When you have brought the people out of Egypt, you will worship God on this mountain" (Exodus 3:12, NIV). God kept this promise, and the sign is now manifested.

Immediately upon arriving, Moses goes up to the top of the mountain. From there, the Lord asks Moses to remind the Children of Israel how the Lord had delivered them out of slavery in Egypt. The phrase "Moses went up unto God" means that he left the group and climbed up the mountain. Moses probably went up by himself to worship God, and while he was praying, God speaks to him. Some people say that God called him to the top of the mountain to speak him. However, it seems that Moses, cognizant of God's faithfulness in keeping promises, climbs to the top of the mountain to worship. Mountains are symbolically referred as the dwelling place of the Lord. When the Psalmist says, "I will lift up my eyes to the mountains; from whence shall my help come? My help comes from the LORD, who made heaven and earth" (Psalm 121:1-2, NAS), he refers to the symbolic use of the mountain as the dwelling place of God.

The Lord tells Moses to remind the Israelites of the miraculous way in which God "snatched" them out of the hand of the Egyptians. What God "did to the Egyptians" includes all the plagues (Exodus 6:7— 12:30) and the Red Sea event in which he destroyed Pharaoh's army (14:26-31).

God describes the process of their deliverance metaphorically thus "I bare you on eagles' wings, and brought you unto myself." This is one of the most beautiful pictures, describing symbolically God's marvelous grace to His people. The eagle (Hebrew *nesher*) is a strong bird of prey used here to describe the strong and loving care of God for His people. The Scriptures often use the eagle as a symbol for God and deity. In the book of Ezekiel, the beings surrounding the throne are represented by the face of an eagle (Ezekiel 1:10; 10:14). The eagle is known for its beauty, strength, swiftness (Deuteronomy 28:49), and its ability to soar to the heights. For these reason it is called, in the African tradition, the king of birds. It does not prey on small birds, but bigger birds, and it can carry its prey, sometimes as heavy as itself into the heights. Job says, "They pass by like swift ships, like an eagle swooping on its prey" (Job 9:26, NKJV). Isaiah says, "But they that wait upon the LORD shall renew their strength; they shall mount up with wings as eagles; they shall run, and not be weary; and they shall walk, and not faint" (Isaiah 40:31). It is said that while other birds carry their young ones in their claws, the eagle carries her own upon her wings, so the archers who shoot flying birds cannot hurt the young ones, unless they first shoot through the mother.

This beautiful metaphor describes how God had cared for Israel, has born them as it were on eagle's wings, held them high by almighty power, and carried them safely out of reach of the hands of death in Egypt. This event is recorded and rehearsed again by Israel years later in the song of Moses (Deuteronomy 32:10-47). The Lord not only brought them out to safety in the wilderness, He brought them out to serve as God's priests. That means God's main purpose in bringing them out of bondage is to establish a love covenant relationship with them—to have communion with them. This covenant is defined in the following passage.

5 Now therefore, if ye will obey my voice indeed, and keep my covenant, then ye shall be a peculiar treasure unto me above all people: for all the earth is mine: 6 And ye shall be unto me a kingdom of priests, and an holy nation. These are the words which thou shalt speak unto the children of Israel.

The Lord then makes one of the most remarkable utterances in all of Scripture: "ye shall be a peculiar treasure unto me above all people." This offer is conditioned by Israel's positive response of obedience. This response is described in two ways: 1) they are to obey God's voice, and 2) they are to keep His covenant. These conditions are introduced by the conjunction "Now therefore," which qualifies the foregoing facts: God's swift and powerful deliverance, of which they are reminded through Moses. This is how God's grace works; it is initiated by God. God cares for and delivers the Israelites not because of what they have done, or because Israel is better than any other nation, but because God chose to bless them.

The word *covenant* is the Hebrew word *beriyth*, which literally means "to cut," and in this context "to make an agreement." However, a covenant is slightly different from an agreement or contract between two people. Covenant, in the biblical sense, is a permanent arrangement. In contrast, a contract or an agreement always has an ending date or a time limit, which is usually between two equal partners. Generally, in the case of a covenant the superior tends to commit himself to the lesser in the context of mutual loyalty. A covenant agreement almost always follows a set pattern: with a promise, obligation, and reciprocal responsibilities (though not always in that order). Another difference is that a contract generally involves only one part of a person, such as a skill, while a covenant covers a person's total being. The pattern here is consistent with a formula of treaty contemporary with the time of the Exodus, which begins with a preamble in which the parties are identified, and contains a historical prologue of previous relationship between the parties. This pattern establishes proper framework for the up-coming arrangement.

In verse 5, the Lord says that if the people would listen and keep the conditions of the covenant, they shall be "a peculiar treasure . . . above all people." The term "peculiar treasure" (Hebrew *cegullah*) means a "valuable" or "special treasure" like that of a jewel. It means that God had chosen to love the Israelites unconditionally, and they are special to Him above all other nations. The Israelites are reminded of this special status over and over throughout their history (Deuteronomy 7:6; 14:2; 26:18; Psalm 135:4; Malachi 3:17; compare 1 Peter 2:9).

The phrase "for all the earth" underscores the fact that God is both the Creator and Controller of creation-the earth (*eret*) i.e., the world and all that is in it belongs to Him—and God has the right to do whatever He desires. Israel's relationship to God is set within the perimeter of God's sovereignty. David declares: "The earth is the Lord's, and the fulness thereof; the world, and they that dwell therein" (Psalm 24:1; cf. 50:12).

The Israelites are not only special people to God, they are "a kingdom of priests" and "a holy nation." To be a kingdom of priest implies some responsibility. Just as the members of the tribe of Levi were priests (God's representatives) to all the other tribes of Israel, Israel is to be a nation of priests to all other nations. The people are to be a people who live wholly to serve the Lord, and each one having the responsibility of being a mediator, or bridge, between God and other nations. Isaiah says, "But you shall be named the priests of the LORD, they shall call you the servants of our God . . ." (Isaiah 61:6, NKJV). Later in the New Testament, Peter the apostle includes all believers as the priests unto God through the redemption by the blood of Jesus Christ, and proclaims the praises of God "who called (us) out of darkness into His marvelous light" (1 Peter 2:9). This so-called "priesthood of believers" started at the Sinai mountain and not in the New Testament.

Therefore, as God's special treasure, Israel is to express themselves first, as priests to God and other nations, and second as a "holy nation" (Hebrew *gadowsh* pronounced **ka-dow-sh**). To be holy here means that they are to be separate, set apart unto God from all other nations. It implies a lifestyle which reflects the very nature and character of God. It is not living a perfect life, for Christ says that no one but

God is perfect, but living a life of trust in God, a life that is honoring to the Lord. Holiness is a theme that runs throughout the Scriptures. The Lord called on the Israelites several times in the Old Testament to sanctify themselves and be holy for God Himself is holy (Leviticus 11:44). Christ says that we should live in such a way that others may see our good works and glorify God (Matthew 5:16), and Paul says that God chose believers to "be holy and without blame before him in love" (Ephesians 1:4).

It is interesting to note that the choice of Israel by God is not contingent upon their commitment. They had already been chosen. Why God chose Israel instead of another nation like Egypt, remains a mystery. It only emphasizes God's grace and sovereignty. The Israelites are reminded of this grace as they journey to the promised land: "The Lord did not set His love on you nor choose you because you were more in number than any other people, for you were the least of all peoples; but because the Lord loves you, and because He would keep the oath which He swore to your fathers, the LORD has brought you out with a mighty hand, and redeemed you from the house of bondage, from the hand of Pharaoh king of Egypt" (Deuteronomy 7:7-80, NKJV). Therefore, there is no reason for boasting. Paul echoes this important truth when he says that we are saved only by grace through faith, not because of what we have done, rather it is a gift (Ephesians 2:8), and this nullifies any boasting. Paul writes in the fourth chapter of Romans that Abraham's righteousness is work of grace and not a reward of good deeds.

Moses returns from the mountain and relates the terms of the covenant to the Children of Israel, and they unanimously agreed to the proposal and said "All that the Lord has spoken we will do" (v. 8). The Lord then comes down in the form of cloud and fire to speak directly with the people (vv. 9-25).

20:2 I am the Lord thy God, which have brought thee out of the land of Egypt, out of the house of bondage.

Exodus 20:1 introduces the spoken words of the Lord to the people, in the form of the most significant document that has influenced both western civil and religious circles for centuries: the Ten Commandments. The civil laws of most countries, especially the Western culture, are rooted in the Ten Commandments. This "covenant law of God" is the one composition of religious principles that the Jews (Judaism), Roman Catholics, and Protestants hold in common. It contains the principles and guidelines for correctly relating both to God and to others. These commandments are summarized later in both the Old and New Testaments as loving the Lord and our neighbor (Deuteronomy 6:4-5; Leviticus 19:18; Mark 12:29-31). It is noteworthy that the first four of the Ten Commandments deal primarily with our relationship with God (vertical), while the remaining six deal with our relationship to one another (horizontal). Scripture reminds us, implicitly here and explicitly as stated by Jesus in the Mark passage referred to above, that neither of these relationships should be ignored nor should one be emphasized to the exclusion of the other. The Ten Commandments give divine direction for living the way God wants us to live.

God starts by self-identification as *YAHWEH* (Jehovah) their God, as opposed to any god; the Lord is God, the very one who brought them out of the land of Egypt, and from the house of bondage. Why did God submit this self-identification? "I am YHWH thy Elohim—i.e., I am the Eternal thy Creator" shows how important the words that would soon follow are; they are from the Lord who has established personal relationship with them. These words are from the very God who is both eternal and the creator, and who has just delivered them out of bondage in Egypt with such swiftness and power that it seemed that He carried them out on wings as the eagle's (Exodus 19:4) and brought them unto Divine abundance. This remarkable deliverance is still very fresh in their minds, therefore they listen and obey. By self-identification, God wants to authenticate the commandments and the authority behind them: they are from the true Eternal God, not from the false gods of Egypt.

3 Thou shalt have no other gods before me. 4 Thou shalt not make unto thee any graven image, or any likeness of any thing that is in heaven above, or that is in the earth beneath, or that is in the water under the earth:

On the basis of God's established relationship with Israel and His act of deliverance, God requires that they cling totally and unreservedly to Him. Here, stating negatively "Thou shalt have no other gods before me," God says I am the only true God, there-

fore you should have no relationship with other gods God issues a call for their undivided loyalty and devotion. This first commandment, the belief in one God (known as monotheism), is one thing that distinguishes the religion of Israel from all other religions of the Ancient Near East. The phrase "before me," translated from a Hebrew compound word `al- paniym, literally means "against my face," or "above me." God claims absolute ownership of Israel as their God. This is also the universal God who declares "all the earth is mine" (19:5). Here God also offers Divine intimacy with them. God is saying to the Children of Israel, and consequently to all who will accept Him, "I am your personal God, you don't need any other god. I am available to you. I desire to maintain an intimate and exclusive relationship with you." This is a love relationship, and God demonstrates love by delivering the Children of Israel from Egypt. How can we maintain our love relationship with God? It is through worship. Therefore, God forbids the worship of other gods, and demands absolute worship from the people whom He loves.

The first commandment (v. 3) forbids the worship of any other god but YAHWEH; the second forbids the worship of the true God using false representations or graven images (v. 4). While the first commandment is a law against polytheism (worship of many gods), the second is law against idolatry—worshiping the true God in a wrong way. Here God says, "You don't need any representation of Me in your worship." This commandment forbids making any kind of image or idol, and forbids all kinds of idolatry. The word translated as graven image is *pecel* from *pesel*, which means "hewn," "engraving" or "sculpture." This instruction is probably given because idols and images, such as the golden calf, which the Israelites were soon to imitate, represent the Egyptian's pantheons. The instruction forbids using anything created in heaven, which would include angels or heavenly bodies; on earth including human or animal images, wood, or stone carvings; or in the waters, which includes fishes or any other sea creature as an idol.

The Bible gives numerous examples of the things that are forbidden (Deuteronomy 4:15-19; Romans 1:23; cf. 2 Kings 17:16; 21:3; 2 Chronicles 33:3; Ezekiel 8:16). The question that arises here concerns the strictness of the instruction. Does this also forbid having paintings in churches, which some claim to be graven images (that serve as visual aids to remind and support us in our worship of God)? When do the symbols that aid us to visualize the Almighty become idols of worship? Do we need to see something in order to worship God? There is a caution here. We must be careful that with all the decorations and paintings, even the flowers we put in churches, the Cross, the very symbol that reminds us of the ultimate redemptive sacrifice, and yes, the Bible (that houses the very word of God), our church buildings and cathedrals do not become storehouses for graven images of worship rather than the places for true spiritual worship that they were meant to be. The Lord Jesus says to the woman at the well that God is to be worshiped sincerely in spirit and truth (John 4:23-24). Idolatry is anything that usurps the place of God in our lives; this includes people, money, possessions, even our marriage relationship. Verses 5 and 6 expand on this and pronounce the consequences of both obeying and disobeying the Law.

7 Thou shalt not take the name of the Lord thy God in vain; for the Lord will not hold him guiltless that taketh his name in vain. 8 Remember the sabbath day, to keep it holy.

The third law dealing with our relationship with the Father, is what some call the "law against profanity." "Thou shalt not take the name of thy God in vain," means we are to honor the name of the Lord. In previous studies we have learned the importance of names in the Hebrew culture. For them, the name is inseparable from the reality; it describes the very being and essence of the person whom the name identifies. The words *in vain* (Hebrew *shav'* or *shav*) mean "emptiness, vanity, falsehood, worthlessness and lying." Therefore this commandment forbids false swearing, blasphemy, and all profane, irreverent use of God's name in ordinary life. It also includes using the Lord's name in false religions, such as witchcraft and magic.

We disobey this commandment when we claim to believe in God and yet do not take Divine things seriously; or when we say things that are not from God, and falsely attribute those comments to heaven. Many times people use the phrase, "the Lord told me" just to make a point or make others believe in what they are saying. Several years ago a well-known preacher went on the air waves and said that God

told him that if he did not raise a certain amount of money for his work at a given time, that he would die. As the day was fast approaching, he literally went on television daily crying until one of his friends bailed him out of the embarrassment by giving him the money, but not without some friendly advice. I wonder how much wealth some preachers have acquired by extortion and false pretenses while claiming to do the work and will of God. This is a clear example of taking the name of the Lord in vain. One of the clearest examples, which carries a death penalty in the Old Testament, is when a prophet prophesies falsehood using the name of the Lord. This is the climax of taking the name of God in vain. However, the rightful use of the name of the Lord is confined to prayer, and praise, prophecy, teaching the true word of God, communion and worship (Malachi 3:16). The penalty for violation of this commandment, though not explicitly stated here, are well understood by the clause "for the Lord will not hold him guiltless that taketh his name in vain." However, other parts of the Bible clearly specify a death penalty (Leviticus 24:10-16, 23; Numbers 15:30-31).

The fourth and last commandment that relates to God, is one of the two that are stated positively. It begins with word "Remember," (Hebrew *zakar*), meaning "to recall," "to call to mind," or "to keep in remembrance," as in "remember the sabbath . . . keep it holy." This is an imperative, a call to be mindful to observe the day of rest, which evidently is the meaning of "sabbath" (Hebrew *shabath*) "to repose," i.e., "desist from exertion," "to cease," "celebrate," "rest," etc. This word does not mean "seven" as we often think. The commandment here (first given in Exodus 16:22-26, not in Genesis 2:2-3 as some suppose) is for the children of Israel to observe a day of rest, unto the Lord; a day set apart to rest on God. In Deuteronomy 5:12, the word "remember" is replaced with "keep" or "observe." As someone correctly noted, there is a twofold principle behind this commandment.

The first is that life must have a rhythm: a rhythm of work and rest, and a rhythm of worship in which we stand aside from our busy life, and recline in the arms of the Creator. The second principle, which is closely linked with the first, is the acknowledgment that all days belong to God, and one of the seven days in the week should be set apart as a special day for the Lord to commune with Him. It serves to remind us of God's deeds in creation and salvation. The day of the week is non-consequential. To the majority of Christians, Sunday is the Sabbath, in commemoration of the resurrection of Christ and the new creation. Keeping the Sabbath has been a point of contention; agreeing upon its original intent and which day of the week it is observed has been a problem in religious worship through the centuries. Christ addressed this subject in Matthew 12, and Paul talked about it in the Romans 14:5-6.

12 Honour thy father and thy mother: that thy days may be long upon the land which the Lord thy God giveth thee.

Verses 12 to 17 contain the last six of the Ten Commandments. We have already noted that the first four deal with our relationship with God, the remaining six deal with our relationship to one another. The fifth commandment begins with our relationship at home—the family. That puts the family where it rightly belongs, the point where all other horizontal relationships begin. Just as the saying goes, "charity begins at home," if we do not learn to live peacefully together at home, it is unlikely that we will learn to get along with anybody anywhere. There two other points to note here, 1) this commandment is the second of the two that give a positive instruction: "Honour thy father and thy mother," and 2) it is the first and only commandment of the Ten that promise a reward of blessing. All these make this commandment important. The family is the center of the society for both the Jews and Africans. The family is also the core of purposeful living. Take away the family system from an African, and his or her life is worth nothing. In the western culture, the family nucleus is the immediate parents, father and mother and the child or children (usually two). To the African, the family includes the father and mother, the siblings, grandparents (and great grandparents), the uncles and aunts, nieces and nephews. All these form the family.

The family structure gives a sense of order and identity, where one derives strength and discipline. The crux of this family structure is respect and reverence for parents, and a high regard and esteem for the older members of the family. The command here is more than mere obedience to our parents, we are to honor them. The word *honor* comes from the Hebrew word, *kabad*, meaning "to be heavy, to make

heavy, to make glorious," etc. It is the root word for glory. A dictionary definition includes "esteem; respect and reverence." The verse could be translated "dignify your father and your mother," make them heavy with honor in the literal sense of the word. What does it imply? It implies lovingly caring for them and preserving their dignity even in their old age. Caring for them is more than dumping them into senior group homes for our own convenience, and transferring our family responsibility to others. When we put away our elderly with this purpose in mind, we are dishonoring them. When circumstances make it impossible for our aging ones to live with us and receive the attention and care they deserve, and we put them in nursing, retirement, or convalescent homes, we can still honor them by well-planned, frequent and regular visits. We need to bring family values back to our homes and reeducate our children in the importance of respect and reverence for their parents. Parents, on the other hand, need to show respect to their children by paying attention to them and making them feel important, special, and appreciated. The family is where everyone is given an extravagant measure of attention because every person is counted as precious as someone beautifully puts it. A reward of keeping this commandment, as we have already said, is God's promise of long life (cf. Ephesians 5—6).

13 Thou shalt not kill.

The sixth commandment God gave to the Children of Israel prohibits murder. The foundation of this law is probably from the creation story in the Genesis in which God created human beings in his own image and likeness. This places an infinite value on human life. Jews value human life above anything else. To what extent does this law apply? The Bible does not seem to prohibit all killings, such as the death penalty for crimes like murder or adultery (Genesis 9:6, Leviticus 20:10) or killing in times of war (1 Samuel 15:3). However, it prohibits the malicious, premeditated, and willful destruction of a human being who was made in the image of God. The term *murder* includes all violence (Exodus 21:12), assault and battering (21:18), hatred and anger (Leviticus 19:14,17), and vengeance (Leviticus 19:18). In the Sermon on the Mount, Christ redefines and expands the meaning of this commandment (Matthew 5:21-22, 38-44) and includes indifference

to human needs, exploitation of other people, and destroying others' reputations as forms of killing.

14 Thou shalt not commit adultery.

This commandment prohibits all illicit sexual relationships and upholds the sanctity and sacredness of marriage for the propagation of and multiplication of the human race. The word *adultery* is a translation of the Hebrew word *na'aph*. It is the violation of the marriage vow, and the major cause of divorces and breakup of families. The Bible views the sin of adultery seriously and pronounces death to anyone caught in the act: "If a man be found lying with a woman married to an husband, then they shall both of them die, both the man that lay with the woman, and the woman: so shalt thou put away evil from Israel" (Deuteronomy 22:22). Jesus includes any lustful look at another woman as violation of this law. Paul says that adultery (including fornication) is also sin against oneself. "Flee sexual immorality. Every sin that a man does is outside the body, but he who commits sexual immorality sins against his own body" (1 Corinthians 6:18, NKJV)

15 Thou shalt not steal.

The simplest definition of stealing is "depriving people of what is rightfully theirs," or "someone taking what is not rightfully his or her own." It includes withholding from others, groups, or a body what belongs to them. Stealing is one of the most common sins committed in our society. It can take many forms and can be done in very subtle ways. I remember a few years ago, I bought some groceries from a corner store. I don't usually look at my receipts, but this particular day I did. To my surprise, I found that the store clerk had added some money (45¢) before she keyed in the right price. When questioned, she had no genuine explanation to give and refunded the extra money. I wondered how many other times this had happened to me, and how much people make each day through this dishonest means. That is one reason why the Bible warns that we should not envy the rich, because we don't know how they acquire their wealth. While there are many others who steal by force, such as purse snatching, break-ins (as of this day of March 13, 1998, Canada has the highest rate of break-ins in the western world, and Vancouver, is rated the highest per capita according to the survey), however, many more people steal by the stroke of the pen. Our society tends to forgive the rich and famous when they steal and punish the poor. Thousands of poor people are wasting away in prisons today for stealing things like cars, or household properties, because they can't afford to hire a good lawyer. While some executives and officers of big corporations, who have been found guilty of manipulating stocks, sit in their posh offices and board rooms.

Stealing is stealing, whether you do it with a pen or gun. Stealing can ruin both the victim and the thief, bankrupt a business, and destroy a country. Most of the African countries today are suffering economically, not because of lack of natural resources, but because of government corruption and stealing of public funds by those entrusted with such funds. Nigeria is a prime example. The Bible condemns stealing and often calls for double or more restitution (Exodus 22:7-10). Withholding a person's wages or not paying adequately is also a form of stealing. Over estimating or over charging for work done is a form of stealing, just as not giving an employer a full day's work for the pay received is stealing. The Bible says that we steal from God when we do not pay our tithes and offerings (Malachi 3:8-10). The Old Testament condemns stealing both property and people.

16 Thou shalt not bear false witness against thy neighbour.

The next sin which commonly occurs in our society is that of bearing false witness, or simply put, misrepresentation of others and of self. The ninth commandment prohibits false testimony in courts of justice, or perjury. It prohibits the circulation of false reports or rumors, "You shall not circulate a false report" (Exodus 23:1, NKJV). Bearing false witness also includes refusing to give evidence when one has evidence to give: "If a person sins in hearing the utterance of an oath, and is a witness, whether he has seen or known of the matter—if he does not tell it, he bears guilt (Leviticus 5:1, NKJV) There are various forms of bearing false witness. Lying, concealing the truth, false boasting or pride for self-promotion, and giving a false image of oneself are all forms of falsehood. However, the emphasis here is on relationships with others and has carries the idea that malicious lies, gossip, and the wrong use of the tongue against another person are forms of bearing false witness. James 3:5-6 deals with the wrongful use of this small member of the body. Bearing false witness surely can and does destroy. The Jews had to find false witnesses who helped to condemn Jesus to death. Many innocent people are dying in prisons all over the world today. Some have been wrongly executed because someone has committed perjury by giving a false witness, withholding the truth, or refusing to give helpful information by providing evidence that would save them. Bearing false witness is a serious matter, and the Bible condemns it (Deuteronomy 19:16ff).

17 Thou shalt not covet thy neighbour's house, thou shalt not covet thy neighbour's wife, nor his manservant, nor his maidservant, nor his ox, nor his ass, nor any thing that is thy neighbour's.

The last of the Ten Commandments deals with covetousness. The verb to *covet* is a translation of the Hebrew word *chamad*, which means "to greatly desire, to take pleasure in, to delight in," or "to lust." This commandment prohibits the inward and selfish desire of the heart to have or acquire anything that belongs to another. Many times, instead of rejoicing that others have been blessed, we wish that we were the recipients of the blessings; this is pure covetousness and therefore a sin. When we compare ourselves to others, or imagine how happy we would be if we were in some other person's shoes, we are definitely falling into the trap of covetousness. "To desire" or "take pleasure in," something is not all together wrong. However, when the desire is wrongly directed for selfish purposes, i.e., when we selfishly desire to have something that belongs to another person—that is covetousness. Paul encourages us to sincerely desire the best gifts (1 Corinthians 12:31). "I covet your prayers" has become a common saying among believers. That is a right use of the word. The cure for a covetous spirit is contentment (Hebrews 13:5); Paul says, "godliness with contentment is great gain" (1 Timothy 6:6ff). If unchecked, covetousness can leads to all sorts of evil including stealing or killing in order to have. It can destroy friendships and families as well as obstruct our relationship with the Father. James says: "Where do wars and fights come from among you? Do they not come from your desires for pleasure that war in your members? You lust and do not have. You murder and covet and cannot obtain. You fight and war. Yet you do not have because you do not ask. You ask and do not receive, because you ask amiss, that you may spend it on your pleasures" (James 4:1-3, NKJV).

DAILY BIBLE READING

M: Israel Camps at Mount Sinai
Exodus 19:1-9
T: Israel Meets God at Mount Sinai
Exodus 19:16-25
W: Honor God and Keep the Sabbath
Exodus 20:1-11
T: Commandments for Life in Community
Exodus 20:12-21
F: Observe God's Statutes and Ordinances
Deuteronomy 4:1-8
S: Teach Obedience to Generations that Follow
Deuteronomy 4:9-14
S: Commandments, A Gift of God's Love
Deuteronomy 4:32-40

TEACHING TIPS

September 26
Bible Study Guide 4

1. Words You Should Know

A. Laver (Exodus 40:7)—(used in KJV) a basin.

B. Anoint (v. 9)—a procedure in which a person or object is rubbed or smeared, usually with oil. The biblical purpose of anointing is generally to heal, to set apart, or to embalm.

2. Teacher Preparation

Read the background Scripture for this lesson. Do some additional study and learn more about the tabernacle or tent of meeting.

3. Starting the Lesson

A. Use a chalkboard to list the things in your church which are considered special or are set apart for special times or occasions. Without telling the class why you have written the objects down, ask them what the items have in common.

B. Read the IN FOCUS story about Paul and Carmelita. Engage class members in a discussion to compare the teaching of rules to children with our own struggle to learn and obey God's rules.

4. Getting into the Lesson

As you study today's lesson, talk about how modern-day believers can be more concerned with the beauty of the sanctuary than they are the sacredness of it. How often do we consider whether our houses of worship are pleasing to the Lord?

5. Relating the Lesson to Life

A. Review the information about the significance of the tent of meeting and the Ark of the Testimony (Covenant) in THE PEOPLE, PLACES, AND TIMES article. Discuss why the presence of the ark was essential to Israel's well-being.

B. Give students an opportunity to answer the questions in SEARCH THE SCRIPTURES.

C. DISCUSS THE MEANING addresses the relationship between being obedient to the Lord and receiving His blessings. Ask class members to share how they relate obedience to blessings in their own walk with the Lord.

D. The LESSON IN OUR SOCIETY highlights the benefits of obedience to God's laws. Discuss how God established these laws for the benefit of His people so that every generation would live in health and prosperity.

6. Arousing Action

A. Think of some of the laws of your city, state, and nation which parallel the laws of God in Leviticus 18—26. List them and compare their benefits for whole society.

B. Allow time for members to complete the MAKE IT HAPPEN activity. Ask the members to form small groups. Give each group a pencil and paper. Ask them to complete the exercise as a group and share their responses with the rest of the class.

C. Give class members an opportunity to complete FOLLOW THE SPIRIT and REMEMBER YOUR THOUGHTS.

WORSHIP GUIDE

For the Superintendent or Teacher
Theme: The Tabernacle and Obedience
Theme Song: Trust and Obey
Scripture: Psalm 84
Song: We've Come This Far by Faith
Meditation: Dear Lord, teach me to delight in Your laws. Help me to revere Your sanctuary as I come there to worship You. Remind me to only offer the best to You in Your house of worship.

41

THE TABERNACLE AND OBEDIENCE

Bible Background • EXODUS 40:1-33; LEVITICUS 26
Printed Text • EXODUS 40:1-9; LEVITICUS 26:2-6, 11-13
Devotional Reading • PSALM 84

LESSON AIM

After studying today's lesson, students should understand that God has established law for His people to live by and He has promised a good life for those who obey Him.

KEEP IN MIND

"Ye shall keep my sabbaths, and reverence my sanctuary: I am the LORD" (Leviticus 26:2).

FOCAL VERSES

EXODUS 40:1 And the LORD spake unto Moses, saying,

2 On the first day of the first month shalt thou set up the tabernacle of the tent of the congregation.

3 And thou shalt put therein the ark of the testimony, and cover the ark with the veil.

4 And thou shalt bring in the table, and set in order the things that are to be set in order upon it; and thou shalt bring in the candlestick, and light the lamps thereof.

5 And thou shalt set the altar of gold for the incense before the ark of the testimony, and put the hanging of the door to the tabernacle.

6 And thou shalt set the altar of the burnt offering before the door of the tabernacle of the tent of the congregation.

7 And thou shalt set the laver between the tent of the congregation and the altar, and shalt put water therein.

8 And thou shalt set up the court round about, and hang up the hanging at the court gate.

9 And thou shalt take the anointing oil, and anoint the tabernacle, and all that is therein, and shalt hallow it, and all the vessels thereof: and it shall be holy.

LEVITICUS 26:2 Ye shall keep my sabbaths, and reverence my sanctuary: I am the LORD.

LESSON OVERVIEW

LESSON AIM
KEEP IN MIND
FOCAL VERSES
IN FOCUS
THE PEOPLE, PLACES, AND TIMES
BACKGROUND
AT-A-GLANCE
IN DEPTH
SEARCH THE SCRIPTURES
DISCUSS THE MEANING
LESSON IN OUR SOCIETY
MAKE IT HAPPEN
FOLLOW THE SPIRIT
REMEMBER YOUR THOUGHTS
MORE LIGHT ON THE TEXT
DAILY BIBLE READINGS

3 If ye walk in my statutes, and keep my commandments, and do them;

4 Then I will give you rain in due season, and the land shall yield her increase, and the trees of the field shall yield their fruit.

5 And your threshing shall reach unto the vintage, and the vintage shall reach unto the sowing time: and ye shall eat your bread to the full, and dwell in your land safely.

6 And I will give peace in the land, and ye shall lie down, and none shall make you afraid: and I will rid evil beasts out of the land, neither shall the sword go through your land.

11 And I will set my tabernacle among you: and my soul shall not abhor you.

12 And I will walk among you, and will be your God, and ye shall be my people.

13 I am the LORD your God, which brought you forth out of the land of Egypt, that ye should not be their bondmen; and I have broken the bands of your yoke, and made you go upright.

IN FOCUS

Carmelita was having such a hard time getting their children to follow the rules of their home. It seemed to be harder since her husband Paul got this job that requires him to be on the road so much.

When Paul got home later that week, the two of them sat down and discussed how the children should have respect for their things and for their home. After all, the two of them worked hard to give them that home.

They decided to establish a reward system for the children. They would receive certain benefits and privileges for obeying the house rules.

"They've also got to understand that there are consequences for disobeying the house rules," said Paul.

"I know that's true," Carmelita responded. "But it's just so hard to stay on top of *everything* these days."

Paul acknowledged that he had been on the road too much to really help Carmelita. "Hopefully, after my first evaluation," he said, "I won't have to travel so much. That way we can both work to make sure our system of reward and punishment is used to benefit our children."

THE PEOPLE, PLACES, AND TIMES

TENT OF MEETING. Also known as the tabernacle, it was a sacred tent which served as a portable and provisional sanctuary where God met His people. Tents were dwelling places for nomads.

The original tent of meeting was a provisional structure where God met with the Children of Israel. It is believed that, at first, only Moses actually entered the tent to meet with God. Joshua protected and cared for the tent. After the Hebrews made the golden calf, God refused to acknowledge them as His people and would no longer dwell in their midst. Because there was now distance between God and the people, Moses moved the tent of meeting outside the camp. Ultimately, God promised to once again do great things in the midst of Israel (Exodus 34:10).

Moses called it the tent of meeting because it was the place of revelation. God met His people there when the pillar of cloud descended to the doorway of the tent (Exodus 34:9).

Based on information from *Holman Bible Dictionary*, Trent Butler, general editor. Nashville: Broadman & Holman Publishers, 1991, p. 1316-1317.

ARK OF THE TESTIMONY. Also known as the Ark of the Covenant; the ark is the container for the Ten Commandments and the key symbol of God's presence with the people of Israel.

The ark of ancient Israel has many names, all of which convey the holy sense of God's presence. The Hebrew word for *ark* means "box" or "coffin." The word *covenant* in the name, Ark of Covenant, defines the ark based on its original purpose, which was a container for the stone tablets on which the Ten Commandments were written. The ark dates back to Moses at Mount Sinai, but its origin is mysterious. There are contrasting accounts of how the ark was made in the Pentateuch (the first five books of the Bible). After the people sinned by worshiping the golden calf and

the original Decalogue tablets were broken, Moses made a plain box of acacia wood as a container to receive the new tables of the Law.

The ark is also known by several names, including "the ark of God," the more elaborate name, "the ark of the Lord," and "the ark of the covenant of the Lord of hosts (Yahweh Sabaoth) who is enthroned on the cherubim."

Based on information from *Holman Bible Dictionary*, pp. 98-99.

BACKGROUND

God had begun the process of directing Israel in the proper ways of life and worship. Once the tabernacle (or tent of meeting) was built, everything in it had to be consecrated. God gave Moses clear specifications concerning how the tabernacle was to be erected.

God's people were also to be dedicated for a purpose. Israel was to be a kingdom of priests and a holy nation (Exodus 19:6). Israel is to be holy in all things. Chapters 18—26 of Leviticus contain laws concerning right or holy conduct. Thus, this portion of Leviticus is known as the Holiness Code. It is a table of laws for those who were in covenant with God.

Unfortunately, Israel eventually began a cycle of rebellion and disobedience, which resulted in punishment by God. When their suffering became more than they felt they could withstand, they pleaded for God's mercy and returned to worshiping Him and obeying His laws. When they were once again comfortable with His blessings, Israel would fall back into a pattern of sinful behavior.

AT-A-GLANCE

1. Consecration of the Tabernacle (Exodus 40:1-9)
2. Rewards for Obedience (Leviticus 26:2-6; 11-13)

IN DEPTH

1. Consecration of the Tabernacle (Exodus 40:1-9)

God's requirement was that the tabernacle, all its contents, and Aaron and his sons be ceremonially consecrated and declared holy in service to the Lord. Nothing profane could be used in worshiping God. Moses was to anoint everything, thereby symbolizing that they were set apart for the service of the Lord. It was important that everything in the tabernacle be consecrated because it was more than a place of worship. The "tent of meeting" was the place to meet God. God was present at that place. God cannot be associated with anything that is unholy.

God's command was that the tabernacle be set up on the first day of the year. This was about one year after the Exodus and about eight and one-half months after their arrival at Sinai. God chose a special time to institute His special place of worship and the people and objects that were a part of that worship. This was not an insignificant matter. God commanded where every piece of furniture should be placed.

Two words figure prominently in God's instructions on erecting the Tabernacle: *hallow* and *anoint*. Each word occurs eight times in various forms. The major emphasis here is not the building itself, rather, it is on its dedication for a purpose.

2. Rewards for Obedience
(Leviticus 26:2-6; 11-13)

Leviticus 26 follows a pattern which is common to treaties in the ancient Near East—it provides blessings for remaining loyal to God and curses for rejecting Him. This chapter is built upon the idea that human beings have the capacity to affect their own fate through their obedience or disobedience to God.

The conclusion to the Holiness Code (Leviticus 18—26) is a final appeal on the part of Yahweh which outlines the rewards which will result from Israel's obedience to God's law as well as the punishment which will result from disobedience. It is likely that during Israel's religious festivals, the laws of the covenant between God and the nation were publicly proclaimed in an act of worship.

Because God's laws were themselves considered a part of God's blessing, the section which addresses reward is shorter than the section which addresses punishment. God wants the best life for the people. Divine covenantal regulations established a way of life which promised providence, security, and peace. The essential blessings are that God's presence will remain with His people and that the promises of the covenant with Abraham will be fulfilled.

The list of rewards for obedience concentrates on two primary aspects of life. One reward is the fertility of the fields and the abundance of its crops. A fruitful harvest was essential to life, longevity, and stability. If they could not produce enough food to eat, Israel would be dependent upon other nations for food. What a sad commentary that would have been upon God's people!

God controls all of nature. The promise was not mainly for a sufficient crop, but an abundant crop. They would not be able to finish this year's crop before it was time to harvest the next year's. Their key to abundant crops was simple—obey God's laws. Because they were God's people, God would take care of them and bless them. But, how could they claim to be God's people if they would not obey? God's people obey God's commands!

The second reward is deliverance in times of war. Here war is addressed in terms of the maintenance of national peace and security rather than military aggression or expansion. God was going to establish His people in a land flowing with milk and honey. Such a land would be a desirous place to dwell. No doubt, other nations would look upon Israel and try to figure out ways to take what God had given them.

As God promised, throughout Israel's history, as long as they were obedient to Yahweh and did not serve other gods, they enjoyed peace as a nation. When they allowed themselves to be influenced by the gods of their neighbors, Israel nearly always faced military aggression.

It was to Israel's advantage to obey God. From the outset, Israel was not a nation of warriors. Israel did not have an aggressive spirit. They did not thrive on war or conflict. In fact, they often tended to be rather cowardly. The Hebrews attacked Moses because they faced uncertainty at the Red Sea. They were reticent to enter Canaan because the land was already inhabited. They needed God's protection in order to preserve peace, yet because of their disobedience, they would often find themselves vulnerable to attack.

God's challenge was issued to a nation, not to individuals. Therefore, it was up to the nation of Israel to remain loyal to God. No few group of priests or faithful followers could keep God's law and expect that to satisfy the Lord. God wanted this for all the people. The covenant was made with a nation. God's promises of both blessings and curses likewise were made to a nation.

SEARCH THE SCRIPTURES

1. When did God command Moses to set up the tabernacle of the tent of meeting? (Exodus 40:2)

2. What was the first thing God told Moses to place inside the tabernacle? (v. 3)

3. Name at least three other items that God told Moses to put inside of the tabernacle. (vv. 4-7)

4. What item was Moses to place at the entrance of the courtyard? (v. 8)

5. What was Moses to do with the anointing oil? (v. 9)

6. What did God command the people to do regarding the Sabbath and the sanctuary? (Leviticus 26:2)

7. What was the first promise God made to Israel in exchange for their obedience? (v. 3)

8. What kind of harvest did God promise the chosen people if they were obedient? (v. 5)

9. What promise did God make to Israel concerning the land? (v. 6)

10. What did God promise concerning Divine presence among the people? (vv. 11-13)

DISCUSS THE MEANING

1. Do God's promises concerning blessings for obedience still hold true today? Does God automatically punish people when they disobey Divine laws today?

2. When persons who have been obedient and faithful to the Lord experience trouble, such as hunger or tribulation, how can they deal with their troubles in light of God's promises?

3. When we suffer the consequences of disobeying God's laws, do we suffer because God is punishing us or because our suffering is simply a natural consequence of our disobedience?

LESSON IN OUR SOCIETY

God's laws made sense for living. They were not simply a group of rules that God established to keep people in submission. The laws of the Holiness Code were partly for the people's own health and safety. The Code also helped people to maintain proper reverence in their relationship with God and with those called out for service.

The laws of God are not an outmoded code of conduct. God's laws are directives for healthy living and relating to one another. Many of the laws may seem irrelevant to our time. Perhaps advances in medicine and technology have eliminated the need for certain restrictions. The fact remains that God's law is designed to maintain people in health and prosperity in every age.

MAKE IT HAPPEN

Read through Leviticus chapters 18—26. List at least 10 laws which have helped to guide your life. Describe how adherence to those laws blessed and enhanced your life. Then list 10 laws which are largely not observed today. How has disobedience to those laws hindered or crippled our society in some way? (You may cite specific laws or general categories of God's law.)

FOLLOW THE SPIRIT

What God wants me to do:

_____

_____

REMEMBER YOUR THOUGHTS

Special insights you learned:

_____

_____

MORE LIGHT ON THE TEXT
EXODUS 40:1-9; LEVITICUS 26:2-6, 11-13

Exodus 35—40 covers the Lord's instruction for the preparation and erection of the tabernacle. Here God gives Moses the specifications for the tabernacle, the directions for worship and instructions for the consecration of Aaron and his children as the lineage for the priesthood. The main theme of this passage is the obedience of Moses, which is an example for the Children of Israel and for all who believe in God.

EXODUS 40:1 And the Lord spake unto Moses, saying, 2 On the first day of the first month shalt thou set up the tabernacle of the tent of the congregation.

This section of Scripture starts with God's detailed instructions to Moses concerning the erection of the tabernacle of the tent of the congregation of Israel, and the placing of its equipment, including the ark, in the tabernacle. God sets the date when the instruction is to be carried out. The tabernacle has been completed, and the people are probably anxious for its opening or dedication. God gives Moses the best time for its opening, the first day of the first month, which is the is beginning of the year.

The first month seems to be important to God in His relationship with Israel because it is also when He instituted the Passover feasts (12:2ff). It was in the first month that God unleashed the last plague against Egypt in which the all of the first born of Egypt were killed, but He passed over all the household of Israel that had the blood of the Passover lamb on their door lintels. God therefore instituted the first month for a memorial to the Children of Israel. To Moses, the Lord says "And this day shall be unto you for a memorial; and ye shall keep it as a feast to the LORD throughout your generations; ye shall keep it as a feast by an everlasting ordinance" (12:14). The first day of the year is also significant because it expresses a new beginning, and is easy to remember in worship of the Lord. The first day of year is usually an important day to all peoples. Many people make resolutions and new plans for the coming year at the beginning of the year.

The word *tabernacle* (Hebrew *mishkan*) means "dwelling place, habitation, tent, a residence." The tabernacle in the biblical sense represents the visible abode for the Lord, where the Israel congregated to worship the Lord. The temple later replaced the tabernacle after Israel had settled in the promise land. During the wilderness wandering, the tabernacle was moved from place to place. The closest idea today is the tents used by evangelists for tent meeting and crusades, which are carried from one location to another for evangelism.

3 And thou shalt put therein the ark of the testimony, and cover the ark with the veil. 4 And thou shalt bring in the table, and set in order the things that are to be set in order upon it; and thou shalt bring in the candlestick, and light the lamps thereof.

After erecting the tabernacle, the Lord orders Moses to put the Ark of the Testimony in the tabernacle and cover it with the veil (curtain). The veil probably is used to partition the inner part of the tabernacle where the ark is placed from the rest of the tabernacle, called the tent of the congregation (v. 1). The "ark" (*arown*), generally known as the "Ark of the Covenant," is also called "Ark of the Lord," "Ark of God," "Ark of the Covenant of the Lord" (Deuteronomy 10:8) and is referred to here as the "ark of testimony." The ark is said to be a rectangular box made from acacia wood with a lid of gold which is called the "mercy-seat." The ark is carried on two poles inserted at the four lower corners. The ark housed the two tablets of the Decalogue or Ten Commandments of the Lord ("the written law" cf. Exodus 20; 25:16, 21; Deuteronomy 10:1-5), the pot of manna, and the rod of Aaron (Hebrews 9:4-5). It also served as the place of meeting in the inner sanctuary where the Lord disclosed His will to His servants, Moses (Exodus 25:22, 30, 36), Aaron (Leviticus 16:2), and Joshua (Joshua 7:6). The ark was a symbol of the presence of the Lord. The ark would play a leading role in the life of the children of Israel, e.g., in the crossing of the Jordan (Joshua 3—5), the fall of the walls of Jericho (Joshua 6), etc. It also played major roles during the time of the judges and kings of Israel (cf. Judges 2:1; 20:27; 2 Samuel 5—7:2; 2 Samuel 6 etc.).

The Lord further instructs Moses to set the table, probably for the showbread, and set in order all the things upon it, and to set the candlesticks and light the lamps. The candlesticks were to burn constantly according to the instruction of God, "And thou shalt command the children of Israel, that they bring thee pure oil olive beaten for the light, to cause the lamp to burn always. In the tabernacle of the congregation without the veil, which is before the testimony, Aaron and his sons shall order it from evening to morn-

ing before the LORD: it shall be a statute for ever unto their generations on the behalf of the children of Israel" (Exodus 27:20-21, KJV). This represents the perpetual presence of the Lord Himself with the Children of Israel. In New Testament, Jesus says that He is the light that gives light to the world, and whoever believes in him will never walk in darkness. In 30:7 Aaron is given the responsibility to trim the lamps and "Aaron shall burn thereon sweet incense every morning: when he dresseth the lamps, he shall burn incense upon it."

5 And thou shalt set the altar of gold for the incense before the ark of the testimony, and put the hanging of the door to the tabernacle. 6 And thou shalt set the altar of the burnt offering before the door of the tabernacle of the tent of the congregation.

The next instructions were the placing of the altars in the tabernacle. Verses 5 and 6 indicate that there were two types of altars to be placed in the tabernacle. The first was the golden altar for incense. The people are to set this altar in front of the ark, just before the curtain inside the tabernacle that separated the most holy place from the rest of the worship area (Exodus 30:1-10; 40:26-27). Here priests burned incense everyday so its fragrance would fill the tabernacle when the sacrificial blood was sprinkled on the altar of burnt offering. The second type was the altar of burnt offering (27:1-8), which Moses was ordered to place in front of the entrance to the tabernacle (40:6). This altar (*mizbeach* meaning "a place of slaughter or sacrifice") was a table or an elevated place in the tabernacle or temple made of acacia wood and coated with bronze on which priests offered sacrifices to God. It was used for the daily burnt and meal offerings. According to *Nelson's Illustrated Dictionary*, this altar declared that entry into the presence of God must be preceded by sacrificial atonement for sin. This was a major or central part of Israel's worship and was carried into the New Testament with some modifications. Noah built the first altar after the flood (Genesis 8:20); Abraham built a number of altars for worship to the Lord (Genesis 12:7, 8; 13:18; 22:9, etc.). The altar played various roles in the life of the Israelites apart from being a place for sacrifice or burning of incense. For example, it served as place of refuge for the Children of Israel (1 Kings 1:50-51; 2:28), and during the times of Joshua the altar was a reminder of Israel's heritage (Joshua 22:26-29). Altars were not unique to Israel for the worship of God, but were common among other pagan nations who built altars for their gods. We read in

wash their hands and feet before offering sacrifices. The laver was made from bronze mirrors (38:8). We read in 1 Kings 7:27-39 that Hiram made ten lavers for Solomon's temple. Biblical record shows that each of the lavers rested on a bronze cart, and each cart was erected on two pairs of wheels; the panels of the carts were decorated with lions, oxen, and cherubim. However, we have no record of the specifications of the laver in the Exodus account, but the Lord commanded that it be kept throughout the Jewish generations (30:18ff). The next part to be set up round about the tabernacle was the court (*chatser*), which means "a courtyard" or "an enclosure." It can also mean "a settled abode, a settlement, a village, or a town." It is an open space or courtyard enclosed by walls. The tabernacle stood in a large courtyard approximately 100 cubits and 50 cubits wide. The dimensions of the court have been estimated by scholars at about 44 meters (146 feet) long and 22 meters (73 feet) wide (Exodus 27:9-19). A linen screen formed the sides of the courtyard with an opening for a gate. This pattern was duplicated in the construction of Solomon's temple. Solomon's temple had an inner and outer courts (1 Kings 6:36; Ezekiel 10:5), and Herod's temple had courts for Gentiles, women, Jewish men, and priests.

the Acts of the Apostles of the altar in Athens that was dedicated "TO THE UNKNOWN GOD" (Acts 17:23). There was no physical Christian altar mentioned in the New Testament, and the statement in Hebrews 13:10, "we have an altar" refers to the sacrifice of the Christ. The mention of the altar of incense in Revelation 8:3 is used only figuratively since there is no need for sacrifices in heaven, because the atonement for our sins is now complete through the death of Jesus Christ.

7 And thou shalt set the laver between the tent of the congregation and the altar, and shalt put water therein. 8 And thou shalt set up the court round about, and hang up the hanging at the court gate.

After placing the altars of incense and offering in their places within the tabernacle, a laver is to be placed between the altar and the tent of the congregation. The *laver* (Hebrew *kiyowr*) is a container or a basin in which the priests washed their hands for purification purposes when they were officiating at the altar of the tabernacle or the temple. In Exodus 30:18-21, Moses was instructed by God to make the basin so that Aaron and the priests would

9 And thou shalt take the anointing oil, and anoint the tabernacle, and all that is therein, and shalt hallow it, and all the vessels thereof: and it shall be holy.

The final instruction to Moses by God was the consecration of the tabernacle and the things in it. This forms the most important part of the tabernacle construction. To *anoint*, (*mashach* in Hebrew) means "to rub with oil," "to consecrate," and "to paint." When a person or thing is consecrated as symbolized by pouring or rubbing of oil, that person or thing is set apart for a specific assignment or use. The thing becomes holy unto God and belongs to God in a special sense. As we see here and throughout the Old Testament, oil is generally used for this purpose. The anointing of a person, a priest, a king, or a prophet signifies authority for a particular work or service (Isaiah 61:1).

The anointed person becomes God's emissary and spokesperson. King Saul (1 Samuel 26:9, 11), David (2 Samuel 22:51), and Solomon (2 Chronicles 6:42) were referred to by the following phrases "the Lord's anointed," "God's anointed," "my anointed," "your anointed," or "his anointed."

In the New Testament, believers are said to be anointed; they belong to God and are commissioned for service (2 Corinthians 1:21). The anointing of the tabernacle and all the furnishings signifies that they are dedicated and holy to God for worship, and therefore should be treated with reverence and awe. The dedication of an altar or place of worship was common among the dwellers of Canaan, and Elijah's encounter with false prophets of Baal suggests that they were familiar with and practiced the ritual. In the African traditional religion, the same ritual is common.

As in the Jewish tradition, most African religions set aside worship sites, and dedicate priests who represent the people before God. They have altars or shrines where they sacrifice animals, and (in the very early ages of the history) human beings, especially those who commit crimes. Human sacrifice became so rampant that a group of African people was targeted for extermination. In order to prevent this, the people were consecrated to the gods for their protection. As a result, they were considered holy and belonged to the gods. They were not to be harmed lest the anger of the gods would be evoked. Therefore, this group was regarded as sacred and "untouchable." As they multiplied they became known as the *Nso or Osu* among the Igbos.

LEVITICUS 26:2 Ye shall keep my sabbaths, and reverence my sanctuary: I am the Lord. 3 If ye walk in my statutes, and keep my commandments, and do them;

The Children of Israel were still in the wilderness, wandering towards the Promised Land. In this chapter of Leviticus the Lord reminds them of His covenant with them and promises a reward of blessing if they keep His commandments. In verse 1, the Lord reiterates the commandment against idolatry—making graven images or idols of worship. They were to be fully committed to the Lord alone without wavering and should strictly adhere to the conviction that God alone deserves the right to be called God and be worshiped. In the second verse, the Lord also reminds them of the fourth commandment (Exodus 20:8), which deals with the keeping of the Sabbath. As we saw in the previous study, the Sabbath law is very important in the Jewish relationship with the Lord; and keeping this law serves here as a condition to receiving the blessings of the Lord in the land. In our previous study, we understand that the Sabbath (*shabbath*) means rest; it is a day purposely set aside for rest from our daily "hustling and bustling" of life and dedication to the Lord in contemplation and worship.

Just as the tabernacle is a place hallowed for the worship of the Almighty, the Sabbath is a day consecrated to honor God in worship. Here the Lord equates the two and commands the people "Observe my Sabbaths and have reverence for my sanctuary." The tabernacle is referred to as the sanctuary (*miqdash*) meaning "a consecrated thing or place," especially "a palace." Keeping the Sabbath definitely goes together with reverencing the sanctuary since worship was carried out only in the tabernacle. The sanctuary (the tabernacle or temple) was meant to be used solely for honoring God. Jesus drove the traders out of the temple because of their misuse of it; He reminded them again of God's purpose. "It is written," He said "My house shall be called the house of prayer; but ye have made it a den of thieves" (Matthew 21:13; Mark 11:17; Luke 19:47, cf. Isaiah 56:7).

After giving the commandment, God now identifies the consequences of obeying the commandment. There is a three-fold condition here, 1) they should walk in God's statutes or laws, 2) they should keep God's commandment, and 3) do them. Then they would be blessed in the land. This blessing requires complete obedience to the commandments of the Lord, which includes the ones above and those given on the mountain of Sinai (Exodus 20:1ff).

4 Then I will give you rain in due season, and the land shall yield her increase, and the trees of the field shall yield their fruit. 5 And your threshing shall reach unto the vintage, and the vintage shall reach unto the sowing time: and ye shall eat your bread to the full, and dwell in your land safely. 6 And I will give peace in the land, and ye shall lie down, and none shall make you afraid: . . .

Verse 4 and the verses that follow describe in detail all the blessings the God will give to the Israelites if they keep the commandments. The first blessing was that of the rain, which is the "life-line" of the people, since their main occupation was farming. Unlike the Nile river in Egypt, there was no major river in Canaan which supplied much of the water for irrigation, therefore rain was essential for agricultural purposes. Without rain, the land of Canaan would be hard to cultivate (1 Kings 17:1). The Lord not only promises the rain, but promises to send it at the proper time "in its season." The word used here for rain is the noun *geshem* from the verb *gasham*, which means "to shower or rain violently." The idea here speaks of abundance. God promises to give them an abundance of rain (no stinginess) and the rain will come at its proper time. The granting of rain at the proper time will allow the land to produce to its capacity, and there would be an abundant harvest. The Bible talks about the first or the former rain and the latter rain (Deuteronomy 11:14; Jeremiah 5:24; Hosea 6:3). However, drought would mean famine and misery. If Israel would obey the Lord's commands, the grain would yield to its maximum and fruit trees would yield their fruit. The harvest would so plentiful that the threshing would run into the period of the vintage (*batsiyr*, i.e., the clipping of the grape), and the vintage of the grape would continue until the next sowing season. The laborer would be busy year round, and there would enough food throughout the year. The idea here is the same as that associated with God's promise in Amos 9:13, "Behold, the days come, saith the Lord, that the plowman shall overtake the reaper, and the treader of grapes him that soweth seed; and the mountains shall drop sweet wine, and all the hills shall melt." The people would also live in the land in safety (Hebrew *betach*), meaning "in confidence or assurance," or "without care." Because they have enough food, they would be worry free. This is a confirmation of Leviticus 25:19: "And the land shall yield her fruit, and ye shall eat your fill, and dwell therein in safety." Jesus advised His hearers to "seek ye first the kingdom of God, and his righteousness; and all these things shall be added unto you" (Matthew 6:33). Besides the agricultural abundance, the Lord promises them peace and protection from plunderers. They would enjoy both peace of mind, freedom from anxiety, and peace among the people or enemies—"ye shall lie down, and none shall make you afraid: . . .," says the Lord.

Verses 7 to 10 give further details of God's promises of protection and prosperity. He assures them of complete victory against any invaders to their land. In the next three verses, God promises them His continuous presence.

11 And I will set my tabernacle among you: and my soul shall not abhor you. 12 And I will walk among you, and will be your God, and ye shall be my people. 13 I am the Lord your God, which brought you forth out of the land of Egypt, that ye should not be their bondmen; and I have broken the bands of your yoke, and made you go upright.

"I will set my tabernacle among you," literally means that God would pitch the Divine tent among them; i.e., The Lord would make a dwelling place in their midst and He would live among the people. The Lord would walk among them just as in the Garden of Eden, and restore the relationship that was broken in the Garden. John 1:14 says that "the Word was made flesh, and dwelt among us, (and we beheld his glory, the glory as of the only begotten of the Father,) full of grace and truth." The purpose of God would be manifested, and Yahweh would be their God and they would be His people (Exodus 6:7; 25:8; 29:45-46), and the Lord would have no reason to "abhor" the people of Israel. To abhor (*ga`al*) means "to reject" (Leviticus 26:30, 43-44; cp. Jeremiah 14:19ff). The psalmist says, "For the LORD will not cast off his people, neither will he forsake his inheritance" (Psalm 94:14, KJV).

To assure them of this promise, and that He is the one speaking to them, the Lord identifies Himself once more, *Aniy Yahweh 'Eloheeykem* (I am the Lord your God), the very one who performed those remarkable things during your bondage in Egypt. He reminds them that He is the same God who brought them out of Egypt and set them free so that they should no longer be slaves. He broke the bars of their yoke and made them walk with their heads high. If they only would obey the commandments of God by not subjecting themselves to idol worship (Leviticus 26:1) and by keeping the Lord's Sabbaths and the sanctuary holy unto the Lord, then Israel would enjoy the freedom that belongs to the children of God.

DAILY BIBLE READING

M: God's Command Regarding the Tabernacle and Priests
Exodus 40:1-15

T: Building the Tabernacle
Exodus 40:16-23

W: Equipping the Tabernacle
Exodus 40:24-33

T: Rewards for Obedience
Leviticus 26:1-13

F: Consequences of Disobedience
Leviticus 26:14-22

S: God Either/Or
Leviticus 26:27-39

S: Confession Will Bring Renewal
Leviticus 26:40-46

TEACHING TIPS

October 3
Bible Study Guide 5

1. Words You Should Know

A. Glory of the Lord (Exodus 40:34)—the presence of the Lord. A visible perception of God's presence. The appearance of the Lord in all of His glory was so overwhelming that Moses could not approach it. In Hebrew, the appearance of His glory is sometimes called the *Shekinah* or *Shekinah glory*, meaning "to dwell."

B. Kept Charge of the Lord (Numbers 9:19)—(used in KJV) obeyed the Lord's command.

2. Teacher Preparation

Read the background Scripture for this lesson. Learn about other ways the Lord has made His presence known throughout the Bible.

3. Starting the Lesson

A. Create several road signs from construction paper. Show the signs to your class and ask them to explain what each sign means. Ask someone to share a time they did not see or did not heed a road sign.

B. Read the IN FOCUS story about Pastor Hendricks and Sister Campbell. Discuss how our journey with the Lord through ups and downs helps us to learn to depend on Him.

4. Getting into the Lesson

As you study the lesson, talk about how different our churches might be if each congregation were to notice a visible symbol of God's presence, such as the cloud.

5. Relating the Lesson to Life

A. Review the information about the significance of the cloud in biblical terms. Also, discuss the personality of Moses, according to THE PEOPLE, PLACES, AND TIMES article.

B. Give students an opportunity to answer the questions in SEARCH THE SCRIPTURES.

C. DISCUSS THE MEANING focuses on having a visible sign of God's presence. In our untrusting, highly-technical society, are we liable to be more suspicious than believing of such a sign?

D. The LESSON IN OUR SOCIETY addresses the preoccupation of our modern society due to "information overload." Discuss ways your class members can make themselves more receptive to signs and messages which come from the Lord.

6. Arousing Action

A. Ask class members who are in a leadership role (at church, work, home, school, social, political, and so forth) to share times when they have found it difficult to get others to follow. Ask them if being a leader has made them a better follower of God.

B. Allow members to complete the MAKE IT HAPPEN activity. Ask them to assess their personal readiness to follow God's directives.

C. Give class members an opportunity to complete FOLLOW THE SPIRIT and REMEMBER YOUR THOUGHTS.

WORSHIP GUIDE

For the Superintendent or Teacher
Theme: The Cloud and Fire
Theme Song: Lead Me, Guide Me
Scripture: Psalm 107:1-9
Song: Where He Leads Me
Meditation: Dear Lord, grant me the desire to do Your will always.

THE CLOUD AND THE FIRE

Bible Background • EXODUS 40:34-38; NUMBERS 9:15-23
Printed Text • EXODUS 40:34-38; NUMBERS 9:15-19, 22-23
Devotional Reading • PSALM 107:1-9

LESSON AIM

After studying today's lesson, students will understand and believe that God can be trusted to guide them through every day of their lives.

KEEP IN MIND

"For the cloud of the LORD was upon the tabernacle by day, and fire was on it by night, in the sight of all the house of Israel, throughout all their journeys" (Exodus 40:38).

FOCAL VERSES

EXODUS 40:34 Then a cloud covered the tent of the congregation, and the glory of the LORD filled the tabernacle.

35 And Moses was not able to enter into the tent of the congregation, because the cloud abode thereon, and the glory of the LORD filled the tabernacle.

36 And when the cloud was taken up from over the tabernacle, the children of Israel went onward in all their journeys:

37 But if the cloud were not taken up, then they journeyed not till the day that it was taken up.

38 For the cloud of the LORD was upon the tabernacle by day, and fire was on it by night, in the sight of all the house of Israel, throughout all their journeys.

NUMBERS 9:15 And on the day that the tabernacle was reared up the cloud covered the tabernacle, namely, the tent of the testimony: and at even there was upon the tabernacle as it were the appearance of fire, until the morning.

16 So it was always: the cloud covered it by day, and the appearance of fire by night.

17 And when the cloud was taken up from the taber-

LESSON OVERVIEW

LESSON AIM
KEEP IN MIND
FOCAL VERSES
IN FOCUS
THE PEOPLE, PLACES, AND TIMES
BACKGROUND
AT-A-GLANCE
IN DEPTH
SEARCH THE SCRIPTURES
DISCUSS THE MEANING
LESSON IN OUR SOCIETY
MAKE IT HAPPEN
FOLLOW THE SPIRIT
REMEMBER YOUR THOUGHTS
MORE LIGHT ON THE TEXT
DAILY BIBLE READINGS

---

nacle, then after that the children of Israel journeyed: and in the place where the cloud abode, there the children of Israel pitched their tents.

18 At the commandment of the LORD the children of Israel journeyed, and at the commandment of the LORD they pitched: as long as the cloud abode upon the tabernacle they rested in their tents.

19 And when the cloud tarried long upon the tabernacle many days, then the children of Israel kept the charge of the LORD, and journeyed not.

22 Or whether it were two days, or a month, or a year, that the cloud tarried upon the tabernacle, remaining thereon, the children of Israel abode in their tents, and journeyed not: but when it was taken up, they journeyed.

23 At the commandment of the LORD they rested in the tents, and at the commandment of the LORD they journeyed: they kept the charge of the LORD, at the commandment of the LORD by the hand of Moses.

OCT
3RD

IN FOCUS

Pastor Hendricks smiled as he saw everyone scurrying around taking care of last minute details. Tomorrow was their big day! They would officially enter their new worship center.

Suddenly, a voice behind him said, "Well, Pastor, there were times when I thought this day would never come."

Rev. Hendricks turned around to see Sister Campbell, one of the matriarchs of the church.

"You read my thoughts, Sister Campbell," he said. "The Lord has led us step by step, day by day. At every turn, He was there to guide us."

"I'm sure the good Lord had to fix it that way," said Sister Campbell. "I 'spect we needed to know that He was doing the building, not us."

She added with a laugh, "You know, Pastor, we have some fine young folks in this church. But, so many of them that got those big jobs think they can do anything, including tellin' God how He ought to run things!"

Pastor Hendricks joined in her laughter. "Yes, Sister Campbell, I think you're right. But I can't be too hard on them. I had to lean on the Lord through some tough times before I learned what it means to trust day by day."

"I know it, Pastor," Sister Campbell chimed in. "And won't He take care of it, too?"

THE PEOPLE, PLACES, AND TIMES

CLOUD. The pillar of cloud is the means by which God led Israel through the wilderness with His presence. The pillar also hid God's face from the people while it protected them. God also came down to speak to Israel in the cloud during times of crisis. God came to the tabernacle in the cloud and spoke to Moses.

Clouds demonstrate the power of God, the Creator of all things. Clouds have also been used in the Bible to accompany God's revelation. In the Old Testament, clouds have been used to both conceal and reveal the secrets of God. The Lord often came to Israel in a cloud.

Based on information from *Holman Bible Dictionary*, Trent Butler, general editor. Nashville: Broadman & Holman Publishers, 1991, p. 272.

MOSES. Servant of the Lord whose name means, "drawn out of the water." Moses served as leader of the Israelites from the time of their Exodus from slavery in Egypt through their journey in the wilderness. The Lord spoke to His people through Moses.

Because of his sin (Numbers 20), Moses was not allowed to enter the Promised Land with the people he had led for so many years. Yet, God remained with him and cared for him even at his death.

Based on information from *Holman Bible Dictionary*, p. 988-990.

BACKGROUND

Moses completed the tabernacle according to the Lord's commands. As promised, the Lord dwelled there. On a number of occasions in the Bible, ceremonies dedicating a House of God are followed by the observance of one of the three Hebrew pilgrimage festivals: Passover, Weeks *(Shavuot)*, and Booths *(Sukkot)*. It would seem natural to link a sacred space with a sacred time. The tabernacle was dedicated at the second Passover.

At the entrance of the tabernacle was a cloud, which changed to a fiery cloud by night. The cloud served to remind Israel of God's enduring presence among them. God was with them continually and the people learned to lean on Divine providence.

Usually, a cloud is associated with confusion or a lack of clarity. The wilderness is also generally considered a place which breeds confusion. God did not want His people to be confused. The cloud was a providential blessing for Israel. Through Moses, the Lord gave commands to the people. God was with them all the time, providing the leadership they so desperately needed to get from the wilderness to the Promised Land.

AT-A-GLANCE

**1. The Glory of the Lord
(Exodus 40:34-38)
2. The Cloud above the
Tabernacle
(Numbers 9:15-19, 22-23)**

IN DEPTH

1. The Glory of the Lord (Exodus 40:34-38)

From the first day that the tabernacle was completed, the cloud which signaled the presence of the Lord was present, also. It was as though God had placed the stamp of divine approval upon the work of Moses and the people.

The glory of the Lord filled the tabernacle. This not only assured Israel of Yahweh's continued presence, it served as assurance that the work they had done was approved.

Israel knew that the presence of the cloud was a divine phenomenon. When God had appeared to them at Sinai, the people were afraid. Now they were rejoicing over the cloud which symbolized the presence of the Lord. Israel was discovering that their God was not simply a God of the mountain. Yahweh was more than an angry God who showed His anger at their sin at Sinai. Yahweh was a God of love and providence who looked after their needs in unexpected and miraculous ways. The cloud was just one form of God's continued providence. At times, the cloud filled the tabernacle. At other times, the cloud hovered above the tent.

The glory of the Lord filled the tabernacle in such a magnificent way that Moses was unable to enter. As a member of the tribe of Levi, Moses was qualified to perform priestly functions until the responsibility was given to Aaron and his sons.

Through the presence of the cloud, God led Israel. As long as the cloud remained in and around the tent, Israel remained at rest from her journey. When the cloud rose above the tabernacle, it served as a signal to Israel that the time had come to move forward. They never knew when the Lord would determine it was time to move ahead. Israel did not have to concern themselves with the when and how of their journey. All they had to do was watch for the Lord's instructions and obey them.

By night, the cloud contained fire which probably served as a symbol of the glory of God in His burning, fiery presence. The Lord whom Israel had met at Sinai would not be left behind there. The Holy presence of the Lord continued among them, guiding them through the wilderness.

The Lord abides with the covenant people. God's people were never abandoned to the chaos of the wilderness. Day and night, this chosen people had visible assurance of God's presence among them.

2. The Cloud above the Tabernacle (Numbers 9:15-19, 22-23)

The cloud above the tabernacle had practical, as well as divine, significance for Israel. In the wilderness, there is very little shelter. The desert heat caused by the sun can be devastating. Therefore, the presence of the clouds was even more important. The cloud shaded the tabernacle and served as a shield. The Arabic word for cloud ('ana'n) means something which obstructs or intervenes. The cloud obstructed the sun's searing rays. The cloud which shaded the tabernacle was probably not a defined, lone cloud, but a mist or cloudy sky.

Nomadic people were trained at an early age to take advantage of natural elements. They refrained from traveling in the scorching sun. The wilderness travelers did not have the advantage of a meteorologist on the evening news who could explain changing in clouds and weather systems. Nomads learned to read the skies.

They followed the natural shelter God provided for them.

At night, the appearance of the cloud above Israel was like fire. It covered the tabernacle in the center of their encampment. Earlier in Exodus, the pillar of fire stood above Israel providing light for travel by night. The fiery cloud mentioned here hovered over the tabernacle. But God's people needed more than a natural cloud or fire to lead them. The presence of the cloud was a symbol of divine traveling orders. Israel moved at God's command as evidenced by the presence of the cloud. This cloud was a sign of God's presence.

During this period of their history, Israel was obedient to the Lord. God's people wanted to get to the Promised Land. They watched every Divine movement in order to get a little closer to that place. No matter how long the cloud stayed up—two days, a month or a year (v. 22)—the people stayed close. They allowed God to determine their destiny. Because they obeyed, God used wilderness experiences to teach them how to lean on Divine providence. A spiritual wilderness, like a physical wilderness, can be a frightening place because we may feel lost, not knowing which way to go. In times of dwelling in a spiritual wilderness, we must be like Israel and look to God to give us the signal to move. In the spiritual wilderness experiences of our lives, we should not make a move that God does not direct. God's presence will guide us through the desert. Our Lord requires us to walk by faith, not by sight.

SEARCH THE SCRIPTURES

1. What occurred at the tent of meeting? (Exodus 40:34)

2. Why couldn't Moses enter the tent of meeting? (v. 35)

3. How did Israel know that it was time for them to resume their journey? (v. 36)

4. What did the people do if the cloud did not lift? (v. 37)

5. What happened to the cloud at night? (v. 38)

6. How long did the cloud look like fire? (Numbers 9:16)

7. How would Israel know when to settle and make camp? (v. 17)

8. How long would the cloud remain over the tabernacle? (v. 22)

9. At what signal did Israel set up camp? (v. 23)

10. Through whom did God give His commands? (v. 23)

DISCUSS THE MEANING

1. Imagine that a divine phenomenon such as the cloud appeared over your church today. How many people in your church would trust the cloud as a sign of God's direction? How many would want to establish a committee to see how to get rid of the cloud? How many would want to fire the pastor for teaching that the cloud represented God's presence and wanting the congregation to follow it?

2. God proved willing and able to care for Israel on many occasions. Why did they still rebel against Divine instructions on other occasions? Why would they think that there was more to be gained by serving other gods?

LESSON IN OUR SOCIETY

It may be difficult for the modern mind to comprehend the cloud which signified the presence of the Lord. A simple object of nature served to guide God's people. So many times, we miss what God is telling us because we are looking for the Lord to speak through fireworks and fanfare. Often the Lord uses the simple things of life to cue and direct us. How many times have we missed God's cue because we are looking in the wrong direction? Take for example how god used a lay woman, Rosa Parks, to speak to the nation about freedom.

Sometimes we are too preoccupied to notice God speaking to us. We live in a world filled with distractions. Our urban areas are filled with activity. We live in the age of "information overload." People are bombarded with messages. How can we hear God if we are too distracted by other voices speaking to us?

Satan likes to keep our heads filled with messages and activities so that the voice of God will be lost to our hearing. Satan wants us to think we should rely on technology and societal rules to guide us. Often we place more trust in things than in God.

Many of us have learned to trust in the devices of our time to direct and guide us. Most of us trust our alarm clocks, giving little or no thought to the fact that the alarm will only work if the God we serve awakens us that day. Others of us follow a certain career track for success because it is expected of us, giving little or no thought to whether that is God's chosen direction for us.

MAKE IT HAPPEN

We should follow God's leadership day by day, ready to move at any moment. Take an assessment of your personal readiness to follow God's direction. If God issued a call for you to move in a certain direction today, would you go without question as Abraham did? Would you first want to know where you were going? Would you try to get out of it as Moses did at first? Would you give God your service or your excuses? Use a sheet of paper, if necessary, to determine your personal level of trust in God's leadership of your life. As you evaluate these questions, determine whether it would be easier for you to follow an "unexpected" directive from God as a single adult. In other words, is it more frightening to follow God's call when you are responsible for providing for a family?

FOLLOW THE SPIRIT

What God wants me to do:

_____

_____

REMEMBER YOUR THOUGHTS

Special insights you learned:

_____

_____

MORE LIGHT ON THE TEXT

EXODUS 40:34-38; NUMBERS 9:15-19, 22-23

Moses has set the tabernacle according to the instruction of the Lord with all the specifications, including placing the ark in the most holy place (Exodus 40:20-21; cf. 26:33-34), and all the furnishings in their proper places and the erection of the courtyard (40:22-33). Verse 33 concludes, "So Moses finished the work."

EXODUS 40:34 Then a cloud covered the tent of the congregation, and the glory of the Lord filled the tabernacle. 35 And Moses was not able to enter into the tent of the congregation, because the cloud abode thereon, and the glory of the Lord filled the tabernacle.

Everything is now set in order; Moses and the Children of Israel have finished the work and have fully carried out the instruction of the Lord. Now God descends and remains with them throughout their journey in the form of cloud and fire. Using the conjunction "then"—which indicates a sequence of event—the writer continues with his prose and details what happens from then. That is after Moses had completed the setting up of the tabernacle "a cloud covered" it. Cloud (`anan`) is generally defined in the dictionary as a visible mass of fine droplets of water or

particles of ice suspended above the earth's surface. Clouds are symbolic of many things in the Bible, especially the presence of God. As in this passage, the cloud symbolizes the visible presence of God. It is God coming to "tabernacle among them," i.e., to dwell in their midst (Leviticus 26:11-13). In Exodus 13:21-22 we have the account of God leading them out of Egypt in a pillar of cloud by day, and pillar of fire by night (cf. 30:43). Probably in these previous passages, the cloud appeared around the camp in the air, but now the cloud was seen in the tabernacle, which symbolizes God presence. The word *covered (kacah)* here simply means that the cloud engulfed the tent. The narrator further identifies the cloud as "the glory *(kabowd)* of the Lord." The word *kabowd* literally means "weight," but is used figuratively as "splendor" or "copiousness," and "honor." To glorify or honor literally means to "make weight." Therefore the glory, or the "weight," of the Lord was overwhelming; so overwhelming Moses could not enter the tent, because of God's presence—for "the cloud abode thereon, and the glory of the LORD filled the tabernacle." A similar glory of the Lord appeared when Solomon finished the building the temple (1 Kings 8:10-11). The word *abode (shakan)* means "to settle down, to reside or permanently stay." Hence this supernatural appearance of the cloud and light in the mercy seat of the tabernacle is known as the *Shekinah* (Leviticus 16:2; 2

Samuel 6:2; 1 Kings 8:11; 2 Chronicles 5:13; Psalm 80:1; Ezekiel 9:3; etc.). This sign confirms God's earlier promise to be with Moses and the people throughout their journey (Exodus 3:12). The idea here is not being with them in an abstract sense, but God comes to dwell among them in the tabernacle and leads them in the real sense in the form of cloud.

36 And when the cloud was taken up from over the tabernacle, the children of Israel went onward in all their journeys: 37 But if the cloud were not taken up, then they journeyed not till the day that it was taken up. 38 For the cloud of the Lord was upon the tabernacle by day, and fire was on it by night, in the sight of all the house of Israel, throughout all their journeys.

Besides symbolizing the presence of God, the cloud was the sign for Israel either to move or to encamp in their journey. Whenever the cloud moved from the tabernacle, the Children of Israel were to break up their camp and move with God. It is obvious that the moving of the cloud signified that God has moved and they should follow. Consequently, when the fire settled in the camp by night, the Children of Israel stayed put; and when it moved, the people followed. In fact, this was the same process God used to lead them in the Promised Land. He guided them with a cloud during the day and the fire during the night. Verse 38b says that "fire was over it by night, in the sight of all the house of Israel, throughout all their journeys." That means that there was physical fire (i.e., *'esh* which means "burning or fiery, fire, flaming, hot") seen by all in the camp of the Children of Israel throughout the journey. The fire here, besides serving as guiding light, lit the camp during the night, and probably supplied warmth during the cold nights of their journey.

It is interesting to note that the Israelites and other ancient cultures placed great value on fire. They used it for many things: to provide light, cook food, heat their houses, and fashion their tools and weapons. As the cloud was a symbol of God's presence, fire was also a symbol of God's mystical presence, as well as His power and judgment. The Bible refers to the Lord as a consuming fire, (Deuteronomy 4:24; 9:3; Hebrew 12:29). God instructed the Israelites to keep fire burning continuously on the altars of burnt offerings (Leviticus 6:13), and God consumed the people's offerings with flame as an assurance that He had accepted the people's sacrifices (Judges 6:21; 1 Kings 18:38).

NUMBERS 9:15 And on the day that the tabernacle was reared up the cloud covered the tabernacle, namely, the tent of the testimony: and at even there was upon the tabernacle as it were the appearance of fire, until the morning. 16 So it was alway: the cloud covered it by day, and the appearance of fire by night.

The account of God's presence, symbolized by the cloud and fire, and His leading is continued in the Book of Numbers. Here the whole process is described in some detail including how long the cloud stayed on the tabernacle before they moved and how long they traveled before it stopped again. On the day the tabernacle was erected, i.e., the first day of the first month (Numbers 9:15a; cf. Exodus 33:3; 40:2), the cloud engulfed the tabernacle. Here the tense is in perfect past, which shows that a single, unique time, definite historical event that took place, i.e., the settling of the cloud on the tabernacle, especially on the tent of the testimony. Inside the tent of the testimony, as we have already noted, was the Ark of the Covenant, which housed the written law God handed down to Moses on Mount Sinai. It seems that the "tent of the testimony" (17:22f; 2 Chronicles 24:6), the "tabernacle of the testimony" (Exodus 38:21; Numbers 1:50, 53; 10:11), and the "the testimony" (Numbers 17:10) are terms which are used interchangeably to refer to the same thing. The covering of the cloud seemed to have taken place in the day. But in the evening (Numbers 9:15b), there was an appearance like "a fiery fire" on the tabernacle and this fire remained until the next morning. The fiery fire signifies, as explained above, the presence in the tabernacle of the glory of the Lord (Exodus 40:34f). The same Hebrew word is used here and in Exodus 40:38 meaning "a devouring fire." Numbers 9:15 seems to describe the one time phenomenon, which becomes a pattern in the verses following. Verse 16 confirms this assumption: "That is how it continued to be; the cloud covered it, and at night it looked like fire" (NIV).

17 And when the cloud was taken up from the tabernacle, then after that the children of Israel journeyed: and in the place where the cloud abode, there the children of Israel pitched their tents.

The pattern set on the day that Moses and the people erected the tabernacle, and the cloud dwelled on the tabernacle, was that the cloud controlled the movement of the people. During the day when the cloud moved or "was taken up from the tabernacle," this became a sign that they should move. Accordingly, the Children of Israel would break camp and continue the journey. The word *journeyed* (Hebrew *naca*, pronounced **naw-sah'**) means "to pull up, especially the tent-pins, and frequently rendered departed, removed or set forward or march forward." The idea here is that as soon as the cloud lifts from the tabernacle, the people unplug their tent-pins, fold their tents, and march forward towards Canaan. The people would journey until the cloud descended on the tabernacle again, and "where the cloud abode" *(shakan*—see Exodus 40:35 above) the people would pitch their tents again.

18 At the commandment of the Lord the children of Israel journeyed, and at the commandment of the Lord they pitched: as long as the cloud abode upon the tabernacle they rested in their tents. 19 And when the cloud tarried long upon the tabernacle many days, then the children of Israel kept the charge of the Lord, and journeyed not.

Verses 18 and 23 seems to define further, how the process worked—through a direct commandment of the Lord. Verse 18 is therefore more than another way

of restating verse 17, and Exodus 40:36-38; their order to march forward was not merely signaled by the actions of the cloud on the tent of the testimony, it was a commandment communicated through Moses (v. 23b). Before they reached Sinai, the people of Israel traveled when the Lord commanded them (Exodus 17:1); they still required a definite oral direction. They stayed in the same place as long as the cloud abode *(schechinized)* upon the tabernacle. "They rested in their tents" suggests that the cloud stopped to give them rest, and showed how concerned the Lord was for their welfare. The people showed great patience and obedience to the commandment of the Lord, even when their stay at one place seemed too long.

22 Or whether it were two days, or a month, or a year, that the cloud tarried upon the tabernacle, remaining thereon, the children of Israel abode in their tents, and journeyed not: but when it was taken up, they journeyed. 23 At the commandment of the Lord they rested in the tents, and at the commandment of the Lord they journeyed: they kept the charge of the Lord, at the commandment of the Lord by the hand of Moses.

From these verses, we understand that the journey was divinely regulated, and the people strictly followed the will of God. Their stay at different stations varied; in places they stayed two days, some a month, and in other places they stayed over a year. It is believed that at one time they rested for over 18 years at one point before they resumed their journey. The reason for this irregularity is not made known in the passage, but obviously they were continuously governed and guarded by the infinite divine wisdom from on high, because God communicated to, with, and through through Moses His servant. The encampments and removals of the tent, and the wilderness wanderings typify the varied experiences of Lord's people in their life-journey through the world. The longer or shorter stops at various stations is typical of the diversity of stages God's pilgrims go through as they pass through to the eternal Promised Land. Just as the Children of Israel "kept the charge of the Lord, at the commandment of the Lord by the hand of Moses," we also need to keep in step with the will and plan of God in our lives. Sometimes the charge may sound unreasonable or the waiting may seem too long, but we can always rest in our tents as we listen to the commandment of Yahweh and follow His leading.

TEACHING TIPS

October 10
Bible Study Guide 6

1. Words You Should Know

Sons of Anak (13:33)—giants who were part of the Nephilim. They lived in Hebron and the hill country before being destroyed by Joshua.

2. Teacher Preparation

Read the background Scripture about the land of Canaan, the Promised Land.

3. Starting the Lesson

A. Bring a painting, or a vase, or some other object to class. Ask for two volunteers to look carefully at the object. Then ask one of the students to leave the room. Ask the remaining student to describe the object without looking at it. Then invite the other student to come back in, and ask him/her to describe the object. See how the two descriptions of the object differ. Talk about how two people can witness the same event and bring a different report. Ask someone to share a time when someone's version of a story differed from their own.

B. Read the IN FOCUS story about Alfred and Yvonne. Discuss with class members how some members in the church are more willing to take risks than others. How can the church exist in harmony and continue the ministry and balance the needs of both conservative and visionary members?

4. Getting into the Lesson

Ask volunteers to serve on one of two debate teams. One team should be on the side of Caleb and Joshua. The other team should be on the side of the other 10 spies. Try to help students understand that it is not always easy to take on a challenge—even for God's people.

5. Relating the Lesson to Life

A. Review the information about the giant peo-

ple of Nephilim from THE PEOPLE, PLACES, AND TIMES. Discuss how God can help His people overcome any obstacle, no matter how large.

B. Give students an opportunity to answer the questions in SEARCH THE SCRIPTURES.

C. DISCUSS THE MEANING focuses on Moses' leadership. Spend some time talking about Moses' leadership style. Engage the class in a discussion about why Moses had to convince God not to destroy His people.

D. The LESSON IN OUR SOCIETY addresses the price that has been paid for "progress" in the African American community. Discuss whether the price the Black community is paying is worth it.

6. Arousing Action

A. Use this time to share biographies about risk-takers who have taken a leap of faith to complete a task which others said was impossible.

B. Allow time to complete the MAKE IT HAPPEN activity. Ask members to share some of their experiences in making major life decisions.

C. Give class members an opportunity to complete FOLLOW THE SPIRIT and REMEMBER YOUR THOUGHTS.

WORSHIP GUIDE

For the Superintendent or Teacher
Theme: The People Rebel
Theme Song: God Never Fails
Scripture: Numbers 14:5-19
Song: God Will Take Care of You
Meditation: O Lord, grant me the strength to step out on faith and do the things that You have called me to do.

THE PEOPLE REBEL

Bible Background • NUMBERS 12:1—14:25
Printed Text • NUMBERS 13:1-3, 32—14:4, 20-24
Devotional Reading • NUMBERS 14:5-19

LESSON AIM

After studying today's lesson, students should know that God expects His people to trust Him completely because He has proven Himself over and over.

KEEP IN MIND

"If the LORD delight in us, then he will bring us into this land, and give it us; a land which floweth with milk and honey. Only rebel not ye against the LORD, neither fear ye the people of the land; for they are bread for us: their defence is departed from them, and the LORD is with us: fear them not" (Numbers 14:8-9).

FOCAL VERSES

NUMBERS 13:1 And the LORD spake unto Moses, saying,

2 Send thou men, that they may search the land of Canaan, which I give unto the children of Israel: of every tribe of their fathers shall ye send a man, every one a ruler among them.

3 And Moses by the commandment of the LORD sent them from the wilderness of Paran: all those men were heads of the children of Israel.

32 And they brought up an evil report of the land which they had searched unto the children of Israel, saying, The land, through which we have gone to search it, is a land that eateth up the inhabitants thereof; and all the people that we saw in it are men of a great stature.

33 And there we saw the giants, the sons of Anak, which come of the giants: and we were in our own sight as grasshoppers, and so we were in their sight.

14:1 And all the congregation lifted up their voice, and cried; and the people wept that night.

2 And all the children of Israel murmured against

LESSON OVERVIEW

LESSON AIM
KEEP IN MIND
FOCAL VERSES
IN FOCUS
THE PEOPLE, PLACES, AND TIMES
BACKGROUND
AT-A-GLANCE
IN DEPTH
SEARCH THE SCRIPTURES
DISCUSS THE MEANING
LESSON IN OUR SOCIETY
MAKE IT HAPPEN
FOLLOW THE SPIRIT
REMEMBER YOUR THOUGHTS
MORE LIGHT ON THE TEXT
DAILY BIBLE READINGS

Moses and against Aaron: and the whole congregation said unto them, Would God that we had died in the land of Egypt! or would God we had died in this wilderness!

3 And wherefore hath the LORD brought us unto this land, to fall by the sword, that our wives and our children should be a prey? were it not better for us to return into Egypt?

4 And they said one to another, Let us make a captain, and let us return into Egypt.

20 And the LORD said, I have pardoned according to thy word:

21 But as truly as I live, all the earth shall be filled with the glory of the LORD.

22 Because all those men which have seen my glory, and my miracles, which I did in Egypt and in the wilderness, and have tempted me now these ten times, and have not hearkened to my voice;

23 Surely they shall not see the land which I sware unto their fathers, neither shall any of them that provoked me see it:

24 But my servant Caleb, because he had another spirit with him, and hath followed me fully, him will I bring into the land whereinto he went; and his seed shall possess it.

IN FOCUS

Alfred and Yvonne were members of a growing church that had not yet secured a building. As part of the search committee, they were excited about the beautiful building they had found on the city's west side. It needed some work but it had everything a growing church needed. The people who owned the property were practically giving it away so the building fund could be used for renovation.

They were sharing their find with the other members of the committee. Suddenly, Frank Pierce said, "Man, I don't know about that neighborhood. They got people doing all kinds of stuff around there."

Another member chimed in, "Yeah, I want to be in the suburbs where it's nice."

Yvonne could feel Alfred's anger beginning to rise. She said, "Well, we're always talking about what needs to be done in the Black communities of our cities. How is anything ever going to change unless Black people like us decide to do something about it?"

Alfred had regained control of his emotions himself and said, "How are those streets ever going to change unless we show the love of Christ and do something to help change what's going on there?"

Someone else said, "Have we really asked the Lord where He wants us to be? Maybe He wants us in that neighborhood. If He does, are we willing to go?"

"Well," Frank said, "the Lord may want this church down there, but if that's the case, I'm finding me and my family another church!"

Nothing got settled in the building search committee meeting that night. When they left, however, it was obvious that the building committee and the church needed to get a clear understanding of the kind of church the Lord was calling them to be.

THE PEOPLE, PLACES, AND TIMES

DESERT OF PARAN. Wilderness area south of Judah, north of Sinai, and west of Edom. Israel camped there after leaving Sinai during the Exodus and sent spies to scout out the Promised Land from Kadesh. Through this very wide wilderness, the Israelites wandered in irregular lines of march.

Based on information from *Holman Bible Dictionary*, Trent Butler, general editor. Nashville: Broadman & Holman Publishers, 1991, p. 1074.

NEPHILIM. The term is probably from the root word meaning "to fall" and probably means "the fallen ones" or "ones who fall [violently] upon others." In the Old Testament (Genesis 6:4), the term designates ancient heroes who, according to most interpreters, are the products of a sexual union of heavenly beings and human women. God intervened to reestablish limits inherent in creation.

In the Book of Numbers, Nephilim designates a race of giants who descended from Anak against whom the Israelites appeared as grasshoppers.

Based on information from *Holman Bible Dictionary*, pp. 988-990.

CANAAN. A region west of the Jordan River and the Mediterranean Sea. This is the land which God promised the descendants of Abraham, the Children of Israel. The people of this region were descendants of Ham whose name means "black" (Genesis 10:15). Prior to the time when they inhabited the land, the country was probably organized around major cities, creating small principalities. There was no central organization for the purpose of defending the land—this made it easier for Israel to inhabit the land. Some stories in the Book of Joshua indicate that during emergencies, the kings of the independent city-states formed defense coalitions, but none had the power to unite all of Canaan against Israel. By the end of King David's rule, the Israelites and the Canaanites had melded together.

Based on information from *Holman Bible Dictionary*, pp. 226-228.

BACKGROUND

Israel had followed the Lord to the places where He led them. They were very near the land which they had been promised. It was a glorious work at the hand of the Lord. Still, the people were not without complaints and discontentment.

They were not content to be free from bondage. They began to complain about other things while they were in the wilderness. They complained about their misfortune. It appears that there was much more discontentment than thankfulness in the wilderness.

The Israelites also complained about Moses' leadership. Moses had the difficult task of leading God's people through the wilderness toward an unknown land. Moses even had to contend with criticism from his own family members. At times, he grew frustrated and went to God out of frustration and doubt.

In spite of all of the ups and downs, God was faithful to His people. As Israel drew near to the Promised Land, God wanted them to scout the land they were about to enter.

Perhaps because God had promised the land to them, they expected to just walk into the land with little or no effort on their part. What they discovered was that even though God intended for Israel to inhabit the land, they still had to act in faith in order to acquire the land.

IN DEPTH

1. God Sends Scouts to Canaan (Numbers 13:1-3)

The Lord commanded Moses to send spies to the land of Canaan to search it out. According to God's instructions, Moses sent a representative leader from each of the 12 tribes to spy out the land of Canaan which the people were preparing to enter. Each tribe would be duly represented. He gave all 12 men the same instructions.

Essentially, the men were instructed to bring back reports about the land and the way the land was built up and cultivated. Part of their report was to include whether those who were already inhabiting the land were strong and numerous or weak and few in number. For 40 days the men wandered over then entire land. Although they had received the same instructions, the men came back with radically different interpretations of Canaan.

2. Israel Received a Bad Report (13:32—14:4)

It is amazing that 12 men would have the same experience and yet view that experience in a totally different way. The men brought back evidence of the bounty of the land which, as God had promised, was flowing with milk and honey. It was indeed a glorious land filled with luscious fruits.

What overwhelmed and frightened the men was that the land's inhabitants were a stronger people than the Israelites. Most of the men who had gone into Canaan feared Israel could not overpower its inhabitants. They determined to give Israel an evil report about the land God had promised them.

The people heard two reports—a majority report and a minority report. Caleb and Joshua presented the minority report. They were the only ones who spoke in favor of taking on the challenge of possessing the land. Caleb and Joshua knew that even the various troops which inhabited Canaan were no match for Yahweh's power. With great confidence in victory, Caleb called for immediate mobilization.

But Caleb's counterparts argued by giving a bad report. They told the people things about the land that were not true, evil things. The lies they told were evil because they were directed against what God had provided for them. In spite of the fact that they returned to Israel with luscious fruits, they told the people that Canaan could not produce enough food to sustain life properly. They told the people that the land God had promised them devours its inhabitants.

They also reported that there were giants in the land. The men claimed to have spied the Nephilim, legendary giants who brought terror to people who were smaller in stature. They claimed that the inhabitants of Canaan were so big that the men of Israel looked like grasshoppers by comparison. In summary, Israel did not stand a chance against them.

When the assembly heard both reports, they turned against Moses and Aaron. The people wept. They made the same complaint that they had made previously about danger, hunger, and thirst. They determined that it would be better to be back in Egypt or the desert. They proposed among themselves to appoint a new leader to take them back where they came from. What they neglected to remember was that God had placed Moses over Israel and only God could remove him and choose another leader for them.

Human nature almost always causes us to choose the familiar over the unknown. As Israel cried out to return to Egypt, they had put out of their memory the truth of the horrible conditions of slavery. Somehow they felt that it was better than what they were facing now. Every time a sacrifice was demanded of the people, Israel began to long for Egypt.

The people wanted to reach the Promised Land, but they did not want to pay a price to get there. God had called for His people to move forward. What Israel did not want to acknowledge was that there is a price to be paid for progress in God's kingdom. That price is not always paid willingly by His people.

3. God's Judgment (14:20-24)

Israel's actions, which were fueled by their faithlessness and disobedience, did not sit well with God. The glory of the Lord appeared at the tent of meeting. The Lord asked Moses how long Israel would be against Him. In spite of all that God had done for them, they still did not believe in Him. He had proven Himself to Israel over and over again. They had witnessed His glory in signs, as well as the fire and cloud, the quail, and the manna. Despite all they had seen, Israel was choosing the oppression of Pharaoh over faith in God and moving into the land flowing with milk and honey which He had promised them. As a result, God told Moses He would cause plagues to come upon them and destroy them.

Moses intervened and asked God what would happen once Egypt heard about how He had destroyed Israel. Moses prayed for the Lord to protect His honor and reputation in the world. Although they did not deserve it, Moses sought forgiveness on their behalf. His intervention on Israel's behalf led God to forgive the nation but still punish the guilty generation, thus delaying fulfillment of His promise. The unbelieving spies who brought back an evil report were punished. All the spies, except Joshua and Caleb, were killed by a plague.

The faithless generation would not be allowed to enter the Promised Land. Because of their disobedience, they wandered in the wilderness for 40 years, until all from the faithless generation had died. Joshua and Caleb were exempted. Caleb had a different spirit from the others, therefore, he was allowed to possess the land.

SEARCH THE SCRIPTURES

1. Why did God command Moses to send out a group of men? (Numbers 13:2)

2. How was Moses to select the men? (v. 2)

3. What kind of report did the spies bring back to Israel? (v. 32)

4. Who spoke out in favor of the land? (v. 30)

5. What did the spies claim to have seen? (v. 33)

6. What did the people complain about? (Numbers 14:2)

7. What plan of action did the men of Israel decide to take concerning a leader? (v. 4)

8. Why was the Lord upset with Israel? (vv. 20-21)

9. What was God's punishment against Israel? (vv. 22-23)

10. Who was exempted from God's punishment? (v. 24)

DISCUSS THE MEANING

1. Israel sought to get rid of Moses because his lead-ership no longer suited them. Do churches often decide to change leaders for political or personal reasons, giving little thought or prayer to whether that leader is God's choice for that time?

2. Why would God question Moses about how long the people would rebel against Him? Why did Moses have to convince God not to destroy Israel?

LESSON IN OUR SOCIETY

Progress always comes at a price. Or, as the old saying goes, "nothing worth having comes easily." In our world of convenience, so many of us have come to expect things to come to us with little or no effort. Our children often see the fruits of our labor, yet expect that harvest to continue with no output on their part. African Americans have struggled greatly. Sometimes, in our efforts not to repeat the past, we go overboard in trying to grant ourselves and our children a life of ease.

It is a sadly interesting fact that the suicide rate among young Blacks is at an all-time high. A couple of decades ago, suicide among Black teens was virtually unheard of. Now it is highest among middle class Black teens. Could it be that the older generation has offered too much and asked for too little in return?

When human beings pay too little for what they have achieved, it usually results in little regard for the fruits of that achievement, even if that achievement is life itself.

MAKE IT HAPPEN

Think over the major decisions you have made in life. Did you ever choose less than what God intended for you based on your fear that you could not attain what you really desired? In other words, how often have you made choices based on fear, not faith? Perhaps you may chose a career path based on fear that you could not make it in your desired field. Maybe you married someone because you were afraid no one else would come along. Have you ever taken less than what God intended for you? How have such choices affected your life? How can you tell when your personal actions and choices are based on fear and not faith?

FOLLOW THE SPIRIT

What God wants me to do:

_____

_____

REMEMBER YOUR THOUGHTS

Special insights you learned:

MORE LIGHT ON THE TEXT
NUMBERS 13:1-3; 32—14:4, 20-24

The Lord led the Children of Israel systematically through the barren wilderness to their destination Canaan. It is now about two years since they departed from Egypt. They have now reached the wilderness of Paran, and encamped at Kadesh, which borders the southern part of Canaan—a few days journey to the Promised Land. It is here that the course of the journey changes because of Israel's rebellion and faithlessness.

13:1 And the Lord spake unto Moses, saying, 2 Send thou men, that they may search the land of Canaan, which I give unto the children of Israel: of every tribe of their fathers shall ye send a man, every one a ruler among them. 3 And Moses by the commandment of the Lord sent them from the wilderness of Paran: all those men were heads of the children of Israel.

Israel followed the Lord's leading into the wilderness of Paran and camped at Kadesh. Here the Lord orders Moses to send out men to go and spy the land of Canaan. The phrase *to search* (Hebrew *tuwr*) means literally "to spy," or "to explore." We are told here that God commanded Moses to dispatch 12 men, one from each of the 12 tribes of Israel to go and make a preliminary survey of the land and bring back reports. Why was this necessary? Why would God require people to go and survey the land ahead while He has led them so far without any help from the people? Was Moses pressured into it or was it his own decision? An answer to these questions is made possible when we compare this passage with Moses' account of this event in Deuteronomy 1:19-24:

And when we departed from Horeb, we went through all that great and terrible wilderness, which ye saw by the way of the mountain of the Amorites, as the Lord our God commanded us; and we came to Kadesh-barnea. 20 And I said unto you, Ye are come unto the mountain of the Amorites, which the Lord our God doth give unto us. 21 Behold, the Lord thy God hath set the land before thee: go up and possess it, as the Lord God of thy fathers hath said unto thee; fear not, neither be discouraged. 22 And ye came near unto me every one of you, and said, We will send men before us, and they shall search us out the land, and bring us word again by what way we must go up, and into what cities we shall come. 23 and the say-

ing pleased me well: and I took twelve men of you, one of a tribe: 24 And they turned and went up into the mountain, and came unto the valley of Eshcol, and searched it out.

From this account, it is clear that the motion to explore the land never originated from the Lord or from Moses, but from the people. It appears from this narrative that Moses spoke with confidence and trust, recognized the Lord's great deeds of the past and what God is capable of doing, and exhorted the people to march forward and take possession of the promised inheritance. He met with rebellion and unbelief as he had many times before along the way up to this point. It seems that Moses then approached the Lord with this problem, and God commanded him to do the wish of the people. This act of rebellion is tantamount to rejection of the leadership of Yahweh and is comparable to their demand for a king in rejection of Samuel's leadership and the Lord's rule over Israel years later (1 Samuel 8:4ff). This rebellious act, as we shall see later, not only cost them 40 years of prolonged wandering in the wilderness, but cost them the Promised Land. The anger of the Lord against this rebellion is also expressed years later through the prophet. In Ezekiel 20:6, God says that He spied the land before they left Egypt. It was therefore unnecessary venture to send spies, but God hearkened to their wish.

The Lord instructs Moses to choose 12 men among the 12 tribes to go and search out the land. Moses obeys the Lord and sends the men into the land. The phrase: "Every one a ruler among them" (Numbers 13:2) and "All those men were heads of the children of Israel" (v. 3) are synonymous, meaning that Moses selected the leaders of each tribe (cf. 1:4). They were probably people with reputation to whom the people would listen. They probably belonged to the ruling class, those referred to in Exodus 18:25 as "heads of the people" or the council, which represented different groups, thousands, hundreds, and fifties. This group was however different from the group that conducted the census (cp. Numbers 1:5-17; 13:4-16). Although it was not God's perfect will, He directed Moses to choose the rulers or leaders, people of character, authority, and prudence who would be "credible" in their report to the people. Alas, how they failed! Numbers 13:4-16 list the names of the groups, and verses 17-25 narrate how the search went and the outcome. Why did God ask Moses to choose the 12 men? The obvious answer is that each of them was to represent each of the 12 tribes of Israel. The other answer probably was for each to choose a land for his tribe. The Lord has promised the give to them every land their foot stepped (14:24 30; cf. Joshua 14:1; 22:13). Numbers 13:26-31 is an account of the report the 12 brought back to the people.

32 And they brought up an evil report of the land which they had searched unto the children of Israel, saying, The land, through which we have gone to search it, is a land that eateth up the inhabitants thereof; and all the people that we saw in it are men of a great stature. 33 And there we saw the giants, the sons of Anak, which come of the giants: and we were in our own sight as grasshoppers, and so we were in their sight.

The people return and bring an "evil report" (Hebrew *dibbah*), a defaming report, or slander as in Proverbs 10:18. A brief look at the preceding verses (26-31) is necessary to understand how slanderous the report was. In verses 26 and 27, the 12 report how great the land was, just as the Lord had promised them, and confirmed that the land "truly flows with milk and honey" (v. 27b, NKJV; cf. Exodus 3:8). They even brought some of the fruits as evidence of the bounty of the land. "And this is its fruit," they reported. The fruits included a cluster of grapes that was so heavy that two men had to carry it on a pole, some pomegranates, and figs (v. 23). The report seemed to raise some high optimism among the people thus far. This high hope, occasioned by such positive report of the land, as evidenced by the visible fruits brought home, is soon to be destroyed by their report concerning the inhabitants of the land (vv. 28-29). Here is the summary of the report of 10 of the spies:

1. The land is as God has said, one that flows with milk and honey. The fruit we have brought is a proof of it (vv. 26-27).

2. The people that dwell in the cities and in the land are strong (v. 28).

3. The cities are walled, fortified, and very great, and they are impossible to penetrate.

4. Giants occupy the land. We are like grasshoppers in their sight (vv. 28-29, 32-33).

5. We not able to go against those people, for they are stronger than we are (v. 31).

Although Caleb tried to change the report and to encourage the people to take possession of the land, the other 10 hushed him down and overshadowed his report. In verse 30, Caleb seems to say, "We agree to all

the reports concerning the fruitfulness of the land, the strength of the walled cities, and stature of the inhabitants of the land. However, we disagree with the report of our inability to go up against these giants. '"Let us go up at once, and possess it; for we are well able to overcome it."' The people re-emphasized the evil report to contradict Caleb's report and said, "We be not able to go up against the people; for they are stronger than we... The land . . . is a land that eateth up the inhabitants thereof; and all the people that we saw in it are men of a great stature." What did they mean by "a land that eateth up the inhabitants thereof"? To eat up (*'akal*) means "to burn up, consume, devour," and is used figuratively here. The suggestion that the land was lacking fertility and so devours its inhabitants by famine is incorrect, since they had already confirmed that it was "a land flowing with milk and honey" (v. 26); and the suggestion of bad climate has no basis because of the same reason. The other suggestion by scholars was that a plague was destroying the people. This is not probable since there nothing in the Scriptures to support it. The most probable meaning, which we are most inclined to adopt, is the wars which raged among the inhabitants of the land and their adjacent neighbors (cf. Numbers 21:26; Deuteronomy 2:18-23; cp. Ezekiel 36:13-15). The land not only devours its inhabitants, there were also giants or *nephiyl* (or nephil; nephlim plu.) a bully or tyrant. The term refers to the giants recorded in Genesis 6:4 before the flood; people of great stature who were known for their wickedness, oppression, and cruelty. They were from the descendants of the Anak. They were so tall and huge that the spies felt like grasshoppers (*chagab* or "locusts") before them. This shows a sense of helplessness and faithlessness before the Lord who had brought them so far, with unusual miracles.

14:1 And all the congregation lifted up their voice, and cried; and the people wept that night.

On hearing this evil report, people became disheartened and very hurt in spirit, and started to lament and complain, and wished that they were dead in Egypt. They lifted their voice, i.e., they cried aloud, or wailing in unison, and wept throughout the night. "And cried" means "they gave their voice or they set the voice" which refers to a loud noise or cry; that is to yell." The expression shows that not only did they cry in self pity for what was befalling them, they yelled, probably shouting verbal insults about Moses and his leadership. "They gave Moses their tongue" as the expression goes. As the Igbo say: "Ha enye ya onu," literally meaning "They gave him their mouth." This made explicit in the next verse (v. 2) when they murmured against Moses, Aaron, and implicitly against God. They not only lifted their voices loudly, causing uproar within the camp and laying insults upon Moses and Aaron, they sobbed, i.e., wept (Hebrew *bakah*, meaning to "make lamentation, generally to bemoan,") throughout the night. Instead of lifting up themselves courageously and resolving to march forward and possess the land of promise, they sat down in despair as already wounded and defeated people, frightened and resorted to sobs and complaints.

2 And all the children of Israel murmured against Moses and against Aaron: and the whole congregation said unto them, Would God that we had died in the land of Egypt! or would God we had died in this wilderness!

The clauses "all the children of Israel murmured" and "the whole of the congregation,"signifies a total rebellion and anarchy within the camp. Probably apart from Caleb and Joshua, who spoke favorably of the power of God to deliver the land to them, (13:30; 14:6ff.) the rest of the people rebelled and murmured (Hebrew *luwn* i.e., "to grumble, or to complain") against Moses. By murmuring against the leadership of Aaron and Moses, they murmured against God that appointed them. The statements, "Would God that we had died in the land of Egypt! or would God we had died in this wilderness!" mean that they wished that they had either died in Egypt under the strong arm of their taskmasters, or had been slain together with the first-born of the Egyptians. Moreover, they thought it would have been better for them to have died with plagues in the wilderness than to run the risk of going into Canaan and die at the hands of the inhabitants.

3 And wherefore hath the Lord brought us unto this land, to fall by the sword, that our wives and our children should be a prey? were it not better for us to return into Egypt? 4 And they said one to another, Let us make a captain, and let us return into Egypt.

The people not only murmured against Aaron and Moses, but they accused God of bringing them out to the land purposely to annihilate them with their fami-

lies, wives, and children under the sword of the Canaan giants. Stated as a question, "Why has the LORD brought us to this land to fall by the sword, that our wives and children should become victims?" (NKJV) they charged the all-loving Yahweh of the worst animosity, and the all-truthful God of the meanest hypocrisy. They questioned the Lord's motive, as if God had something to gain by their death in the wilderness. This question suggests that all the kind things God had promised and done for them up to this point were all a cover up intended to lure them out of Egypt to destroy them. This charge or complaint against God is even more explicitly stated in Deuteronomy 1:27, "And ye murmured in your tents, and said, Because the Lord hated us, he hath brought us forth out of the land of Egypt, to deliver us into the hand of the Amorites, to destroy us." After accusing the Lord maliciously, they asked rhetorically, probably among themselves, or possibly to God "Would it not be better for us to return to Egypt?" (cp. Joshua 7:7). They were, of course, not asking for God's opinion, but stating the decision which they had already made and were soon to carry out (v. 4). They conspired to overthrow the leadership of Moses and appoint another leader or "captain" (Hebrew *ro'sh* which means "head, company or band") to lead them back to Egypt. A later account of this incidence in Nehemiah 9:16-17 suggests that they actually carried out this threat. However, just the thought of it and the conspiracy to effect a change of leadership was, in the divine judgment, as good as if they had in fact done it. According to an Igbo adage, "A child who says to his father, 'I will slap you' has already committed the act." It is equivalent to what Jesus said, ". . . out of the abundance of the heart, the mouth speaketh" (Matthew 12:34). This conspiracy amounted to a total rebellion against the Lord, and renunciation of Yahweh's authority and leadership.

In their rebelliousness and resolve to return to Egypt, they never considered the consequences and difficulties they would encounter with their new chosen leader without the Lord. For example, could they expect the pillar of light and cloud to lead? Could they expect a supply of manna from heaven again? Would God divide the Red Sea for them? How peacefully would they be allowed to pass through the nations? If they succeeded in going into Egypt, would the inhabitants receive them with a fanfare? Would the Egyptians have soon forgotten the tragic death of their first-born, or the death of their fathers, husbands, children, and brothers that had perished in the Red Sea while pursuing them? With hearts full of evil and fear, they never counted the cost of their venture to return to the evil from which they were delivered. They were only bent on rebellion and had forgotten the mighty acts of the Lord all along these two years of departure from Egypt. Their rebellion resulted in God's fury, and he decides to destroy the entire nation (Numbers 14:11-12) but Moses intervenes on their behalf and asks for God's forgiveness (vv. 13-19).

20 And the Lord said, I have pardoned according to thy word: 21 But as truly as I live, all the earth shall be filled with the glory of the Lord.

The Lord grants Moses' prayer and forgives the people, but not without some consequences for their insurrection and faithlessness. "I have pardoned according to thy word," that is God spares them of the punishment He has pronounced on them (vv. 11-12; Exodus 32:7-14). This forgiveness is recorded in the Psalm of David, "Therefore he (the Lord) said that he would destroy them, had not Moses his chosen stood before him in the breach, to turn away his wrath, lest he should destroy them" (Psalm 106:23). However, the Lord promised to punish only those (the present generation) who grossly rebelled against Him, leaving their descendants to inherit the Promised Land. "But as truly as I live . . ." or "As surely as I live . . ." is a form of an oath appropriated by the Almighty, which signifies the seriousness and importance of the matter (Ezekiel 13:3; 20:33; 5:11) and the determination or resolve of God to do what He plans to do, either positively or negatively (cp. Jeremiah 4:2; Isaiah 45:23). The Lord declares that His glory would continue to fill the earth as far He exists. The meaning of this declaration or why it is made is not immediately obvious. However, from Numbers 14:21, one can deduce that the divine glory would fill the earth because of the punishment of the men who did not listen to God's voice or those who rebelled against the Lord. Although the consequence of their action is negative, it would produce honor to the Lord. In what way? On one hand, when people see the hand of God punishing the people for their sin, they would fear or reverence the Lord. This punishment would induce people to refrain from doing the same thing the other people did to incur the wrath of God, thereby God is glorified. On the other hand, while those rebellious people would be punished, God would still lead their posterity into the Promised Land. Either way, God's name would be honored all over the earth—people would hear of His miraculous deeds and glorify Him. As one writer says, the earth would be filled with the report of the glorious and righteous acts of God in punishing the offenders and crowning the remnant with His mercy. We see in the Scriptures that the glory of the Lord is seen in the revelation of His powerful acts in history.

The Psalmist says: "His name shall endure forever; his name shall continue as long as the sun. And men shall be blessed in Him; all nations shall call Him blessed. Blessed be the LORD God, the God of Israel, who only does wondrous things! And blessed be His glorious name forever! And let the whole earth be filled with His glory. Amen and Amen" (Psalm 72:17-19).

22 Because all those men which have seen my glory, and my miracles, which I did Egypt and in the wilderness, and have tempted me now these ten times, and have not hearkened to my voice; 23 Surely they shall not see the land which I sware unto their fathers, neither shall any of them that provoked me see it:

Verses 22 and 23 declare the reason why the punishment is coming upon them, and then pronounces the punishment—i.e., all those who have rebelled against Him would "not see the land which I sware unto their fathers." First God presents, as if He were in a court of law, His charges against the Children of Israel. Although, they had seen His glory evidenced by the miraculous works that He had performed both in Egypt and in the wilderness, yet they continued to tempt Him. This, according to God, was the tenth time they had tempted the Lord since they left Egypt. The definite number probably shows the frequency of their rebelliousness, which would warrant the type of punishment that was coming upon them. The word *tempted* is the Hebrew word, *nacah* pronounced **naw-saw'**, which means to "test, prove, tempt, to try." God sees their refusal to obey or listen to Him as testing Him, to see how He would react. It is also to be understood in relation to God's commandment as the trying of God's patience. The sin of Israel recorded here consisted of losing their faith in the Lord when presented with the evil and discouraging report of the 10 spies, and putting God to test after He had repeatedly demonstrated His power and goodwill toward them on several occasions. Because of their sin, God vowed that they would not see the Promised Land. "Surely they shall not see the land" rendered in Hebrew as "If (*'im* i.e., surely) they shall see," which is equivalent to a divine oath (v. 21). David said in the Psalms: "Unto whom I sware in my wrath that they should not enter into my rest" (Psalm 95:11; cf. Hebrew 3:18). It means, "definitely they will not see land," i.e., not enjoy the land, which God promised with an oath to their fathers. This divine declaration includes all those who provoked (na'ats) the Lord. It means those who "despised" or "abhorred" the Lord. It is the same word which is translated "to scorn" or "to blaspheme" the Lord. It also has the idea of ridicule. So, by their lack of faith in God and fear of the people in the land, they ridicule the Lord and bring contempt to His name. Therefore, they will not see the land, much less enter into it.

24 But my servant Caleb, because he had another spirit with him, and hath followed me fully, him will I bring into the land whereinto he went; and his seed shall possess it.

Just as God punishes rebellion and unfaithfulness, He also rewards obedience and faithfulness. While the rest of Israel panicked, distrusted the Lord's power, and had no confidence in God's leading, one man, Caleb, singled out himself from the statute quo, and God rewarded him accordingly. While God saw a spirit of cowardice and weakness in the rest of the people, He saw another spirit of boldness, courage, and resolution in Caleb. For that reason, God promised to take him to the land and give him and his seed that part of the land which he had spied out, i.e., the land of Hebron (Joshua 14:6-15; Judges 1:20). Although only Caleb is mentioned here, Joshua (v. 30; 32:12) and the priests (Joshua 14:1; 22:13) also were rewarded with entering and receiving the Promised Land. The type of spirit resident in Caleb is spirit of obedience, which the Lord acknowledges by "and (he) hath followed me fully." This phrase expresses Caleb's full and total resolute and constant obedience and faithfulness in following God. There was no turning aside or doubts in his walk with the Lord. He never faltered in his faith in the Lord God of Israel and God's power to accomplish what He promised, even in the presence of the giants of Anak (Numbers 14: 6-9; cf. 13:30). Nor did Caleb fall short in following or complying with the commands of the Lord. The same expression is made concerning Joshua (Numbers 32:12; Deuteronomy 1:36), who later led the people to the land of Canaan. Forty-five years later, probably five years after they had entered the land, Caleb, at the age of 85, could go to Joshua to claim the promise:

"Forty years old was I when Moses the servant of the LORD sent me from Kadesh-barnea to espy out the land; and I brought him word again as it was in mine heart. Nevertheless, my brethren that went up with me made the heart of the people melt: but I wholly followed the LORD my God. And Moses sware on that day, saying, Surely the land whereon thy feet have trodden shall be thine inheritance, and thy children's for ever, because thou hast wholly followed the LORD my God. And now, behold, the LORD hath kept me alive, as he said, these forty and five years, even since the LORD spake this word unto Moses, while the children of Israel wandered in the wilderness: and now, lo, I am this day fourscore and five years old. As yet I am as strong this day as I was in the day that Moses sent me: as my strength was then, even so is my strength now, for war, both to go out, and to come in. Now therefore give me this mountain, whereof the LORD spake in that day; for thou heardest in that day how the Anakims were there, and that the cities were great and fenced: if so be the LORD will be with me, then I shall be able to drive them out, as the LORD said" (Joshua 14:7-12, KJV).

DAILY BIBLE READING

M: Aaron and Miriam Jealous of Moses
Numbers 12:1-9

T: Miriam Punished with Leprosy
Numbers 12:10-15

W: Twelve Sent to Spy Out Canaan
Numbers 13:1-16

T: The Spies Carry Out Moses' Orders
Numbers 13:17-24

F: Fearful Spies and a Negative Report
Numbers 13:25-33

S: Israel Rebels Against Moses and Aaron
Numbers 14:1-12

S: Moses Intercedes for Israel
Numbers 14:13-25

TEACHING TIPS

October 17
Bible Study Guide 7

1. Words You Should Know

A. Hormah (v. 44)—a place meaning "split rock" or "cursed for destruction." It was the city which marked the limit of the Canaanite route of Israel after their failed effort to invade Canaan following the evil report of the spies. The exact location of Hormah is not known.

B. Kadesh (v. 46)—(also known as Kadesh-Barnea) the name of a place which means "consecrated." It is the place where the Hebrews dwelled for most of the 38 years after leaving Mount Sinai but before entering the Promised Land. Moses sent the 12 spies into Canaan from Kadesh-Barnea. This is the place from which the Hebrews attempted their ill-fated penetration into southern Canaan.

2. Teacher Preparation

Read the background Scripture for this lesson. Learn more about deserts so that you can share the information with your students.

3. Starting the Lesson

A. Bring a box of sand to class. Grab a handful of sand and sprinkle it back into the box. Help your students to see how difficult it would be to survive in a desert surrounded by dry sand such as this. Remind class members that God provided for His people in the midst of a dry desert land.

B. Read the IN FOCUS story about Terrell. Ask class members to share experiences in which God guided them out of a spiritual wilderness. Spend some time discussing how people get trapped in a spiritual wilderness and then how they may step out of it.

4. Getting into the Lesson

Ask class members to use their Bibles and Sunday School books to review some of the things God did for Israel during their wilderness years, such as manna from heaven, pillar of cloud and fire, parting the Red Sea, and so forth. Remind class members of how God provided for His people even when they were disobedient.

5. Relating the Lesson to Life

A. Review the information about Esau and the land God provided for his descendants from THE PEOPLE, PLACES, AND TIMES. Discuss how God provided for Esau's descendants just as He provided for Jacob's descendants. If time permits, review the story of Jacob and Esau. Speculate on how the Hebrew experience might have been different had Jacob not taken Esau's birthright.

B. Give students an opportunity to answer the questions in SEARCH THE SCRIPTURES.

C. DISCUSS THE MEANING highlights Israel's complaints, even though God had not ceased to bless them. Discuss why people are so often prone to be discontented in spite of rich blessings from on high.

D. The LESSON IN OUR SOCIETY features the importance of being given a second chance. Discuss the importance of second chances. Then discuss why Christians are often reluctant to grant second chances to others.

6. Arousing Action

A. Engage the class in a dialogue about people who have made a come back after a terrible mistake or some other tragedy. How were these persons able to bounce back from adversity when many people do not?

B. Allow time to complete the MAKE IT HAPPEN activity. Remind them that their responses to this activity can remain confidential.

C. Give class members an opportunity to complete FOLLOW THE SPIRIT and REMEMBER YOUR THOUGHTS.

WORSHIP GUIDE

For the Superintendent or Teacher
Theme: The Desert Years
Theme Song: We've Come a Long Way
Scripture: Isaiah 35
Song: Hold to God's Unchanging Hand
Meditation: O Lord, I thank You that You are always there to receive me upon my repentance. Thank You for being a loving God who will give His imperfect people another chance.

THE DESERT YEARS

Bible Background • DEUTERONOMY 1:41—2:25
Printed Text • DEUTERONOMY 1:41—2:8
Devotional Reading • ISAIAH 35

LESSON AIM

After studying today's lesson, students should see that God always makes a way for His people to do His will.

KEEP IN MIND

"For the LORD thy God hath blessed thee in all the works of thy hand: he knoweth thy walking through this great wilderness: these forty years the LORD thy God hath been with thee; thou hast lacked nothing" (Deuteronomy 2:7).

FOCAL VERSES

DEUTERONOMY 1:41

Then ye answered and said unto me, We have sinned against the LORD, we will go up and fight, according to all that the LORD our God commanded us. And when ye had girded on every man his weapons of war, ye were ready to go up into the hill.

42 And the LORD said unto me, Say unto them, Go not up, neither fight; for I am not among you; lest ye be smitten before your enemies.

43 So I spake unto you; and ye would not hear, but rebelled against the commandment of the LORD, and went presumptuously up into the hill.

44 And the Amorites, which dwelt in that mountain, came out against you, and chased you, as bees do, and destroyed you in Seir, even unto Hormah.

45 And ye returned and wept before the LORD; but the LORD would not hearken to your voice, nor give ear unto you.

46 So ye abode in Kadesh many days, according unto the days that ye abode there.

2:1 Then we turned, and took our journey into the wilderness by the way of the Red sea, as the LORD spake

unto me: and we compassed mount Seir many days.

2 And the LORD spake unto me, saying,

3 Ye have compassed this mountain long enough: turn you northward.

4 And command thou the people, saying, Ye are to pass through the coast of your brethren the children of Esau, which dwell in Seir; and they shall be afraid of you: take ye good heed unto yourselves therefore:

5 Meddle not with them; for I will not give you of their land, no, not so much as a footbreadth; because I have given mount Seir unto Esau for a possession.

6 Ye shall buy meat of them for money, that ye may eat; and ye shall also buy water of them for money, that ye may drink.

7 For the LORD thy God hath blessed thee in all the works of thy hand: he knoweth thy walking through this great wilderness: these forty years the LORD thy God hath been with thee; thou hast lacked nothing.

8 And when we passed by from our brethren the children of Esau, which dwelt in Seir, through the way of the plain from Elath, and from Ezion-geber, we turned and passed by the way of the wilderness of Moab.

OCT 17TH

IN FOCUS

Terrell walked down 28th Avenue and noticed all the young men who were just kinda hanging around with nothing to do. "What a waste!" he thought, "Those young brothers could be accountants, or plumbers, or mechanics, or computer programmers, or who knows what?"

Terrell then thought about all the years he wasted hanging around on street corners. Sometimes he committed petty crimes just to make a little cash. Most of the time, though, he was just hanging around doing nothing. He probably would have kept on doing nothing if it weren't for Harold.

One day Harold just asked him, "Man, did you ever think about the fact that God has something for you to do?"

The question had really made Terrell think about some things. He had never really thought about what plans God might have for him. He only thought about his plans for himself.

Then Terrell tried to put the question out of his mind. But it kept coming back to him. "What does God have for me to do?" When he realized how God had blessed him during all those years he gave nothing in return, it filled him with gratitude.

Those years were like living in the wilderness. Even though Terrell prided himself on looking and acting cool, he was really very confused on the inside. He was just wandering, looking for direction. At first, Terrell did not want to do things God's way. After a time of trying to do things his own way, he decided to give in to the Lord.

That was six years ago. Now Terrell knew what God wanted him to do. He spent two evenings a week talking with young men like those on the corner, asking them that same question, "Did you ever think about the fact that God has something for you to do?"

THE PEOPLE, PLACES, AND TIMES

SEIR. A mountain range which runs the length of Edom. Sometimes Edom and Seir are equated. Parts of the range are almost impassable. The name *Seir* means, "hairy," which is understood to be "thicket" or "small forested region." This region was home to Esau and his descendants.

Based on information from *Holman Bible Dictionary*, Trent Butler, general editor. Nashville: Broadman & Holman Publishers, 1991, p. 1242.

ESAU. Son of Isaac and Rebekah and elder twin brother of Jacob. Esau is father of the Edomite nation. Esau is best known for having traded his birthright to his brother in exchange for something to eat. The twins were estranged for many years but later met again and reconciled. Their descendants continue to struggle against one another to this day.

Based on information from *Holman Bible Dictionary*, p. 432.

BACKGROUND

Israel was paying the price for their disobedience to God 40 years in the wilderness. Yet, they wanted to take short-cuts around God's wisdom and judgment.

In spite of the fact they could not bring themselves out of Egypt, they repeatedly refused to ignore God's sovereign ability to lead and guide them. They had gone against God on more than one occasion and paid the price.

In today's lesson, Moses reminds Israel of the consequences of going against the will of God. Even though God had punished them, out of His mercy He still provided for them mightily so that they lacked nothing.

AT-A-GLANCE

**1. The Consequences of Disobedience (Deuteronomy 1:41-45)
2. Journey through the Wilderness (Deuteronomy 1:46—2:1-6)
3. God's Providence in the Wilderness (Deuteronomy 2:7-8)**

IN DEPTH

1. The Consequences of Disobedience (Deuteronomy 1:41-45)

When they were first given the opportunity, Israel was reluctant to go in and claim the land God had given them at Canaan. Out of fear, based on the spies' report, they began to long for Egypt. God's anger rose against Israel for their faithlessness. He chose to punish the faithless generation by refusing them entrance into the Promised Land.

Apparently, Israel then had a change of heart. They confessed their sin against God and perhaps decided that was sufficient to correct what they had done. Without consulting the Lord first, they decided to make up for their earlier cowardice by going in to attack the Amorites. God told Moses to warn them not to go. He told them He would not be with them if they took such action. God's warning was clear: the consequences of their attack would be their own defeat.

Even though Israel had just finished confessing their disobedience, they once again went against God. Instead of heeding the Lord's command, they chose to go and fight anyway. They must have presumed they would win the battle simply because God had promised the land to them. Yet they failed to acknowledge all that had taken place since the promise. Rather than victory, the Amorites who lived in the hill country came out against Israel and chased them like bees. Israel's soldiers experienced bitter defeat at the hands of the Amorites because the Lord was not with them.

When the defeated warriors came back to their camp, they cried before the Lord but He would not hear them. They had been duly warned. God's judgment had been issued. They should have known they would be defeated because the Lord had already told them victory would not be theirs.

2. Journey through the Wilderness (Deuteronomy 1:46—2:6)

The progress of Israel's journey through the wilderness was halted due to their long stay at Kadesh. God has determined that Israel's probationary period has passed and He is now ready to use them. God's work must wait on the readiness of His people. His doors of opportunity open when men and women have been shaped and fashioned to be fit for the task.

After their defeat, the Israelites then turned back in the direction from which they came. Their journey took them through Edom, which belonged to the descendants of Esau. Through Moses, God warned them not to attempt invasion nor any other act of aggression against the people of Edom.

It is ironic to think that any group of people would be afraid of Israel given their previous displays of cowardice. But Israel was now aware that God was preparing them to enter the Promised Land. This might have given them a sense of bravado, fueling feelings of aggression, especially toward the Edomites.

The Edomites are regarded as the "brothers" of Israel because the Edomites descended from Esau and the Israelites descended from his twin brother, Jacob. This region was off limits to the Israelites because God had given that land to Esau as a possession.

God's goodness and providence extended beyond the people of Israel. He had promised another region of land to Esau and his descendants. God honors and keeps His promises. Because God had promised this land to Esau, no one else could possess that land. Additionally, God had another land in mind for Israel. In the mean time, they were to pass through the Edomites' land and pay them for the time they were there. Israel did not have a right to go through a region which belonged to someone else and use their resources without paying for what they had used.

It is beneficial for all of God's people to remember that His abundance is sufficient to meet the needs of all His people. There was no need for God's people to clamor and fight over a homeland. God had chosen a homeland for them all.

The same sentiment can apply to any and all of God's blessings. What God has given to one person should not be coveted by another. Too often, people become fearful and think that the only way they can obtain the thing they desire is by taking it from someone else. It is never necessary for God's people to do this. No child of God should ever plot to steal anything—possessions, a talent or gift, authority or position—that God has given to someone else.

3. God's Providence in the Wilderness (Deuteronomy 2:7-8)

For 40 years, God blessed Israel with everything she needed to sustain life in the desert. In spite of their unfaithfulness, God provided and cared for them. God blessed the work they did. They did not lack anything. The Lord did all of this in spite of their disobedience. God still cared about them when they did not believe in Him. Israel had often grumbled and complained about the way God was providing for them during their time in the wilderness, but God continued to bless them with His goodness.

Because God had provided for them abundantly, there was no need to aggravate the Edomites by trying to steal from them. They were able to pass peacefully through the region which belonged to the Edomites. God's chosen are to journey as peacefully as possible in pursuit of His promises. A potentially hostile situation was averted because the people did as the Lord commanded.

SEARCH THE SCRIPTURES

1. What did Israel decide to do after they had sinned against God? (Deuteronomy 1:41)

2. What did the Lord tell Israel to do? (v. 42)

3. What did the people do instead of following God's advice? (v. 43)

4. Who defeated the Israelites? (v. 44)

5. What did Israel do after they were defeated? (v. 45)

6. Where did Israel go after their defeat? (Deuteronomy 2:1)

7. Through what territory did Israel pass? (v. 4)

8. How was Israel to treat the descendants of Esau? (v. 5)

9. How was Israel to pay them? (v. 6)

10. How long had the Lord watched over Israel in the wilderness? (v. 7)

DISCUSS THE MEANING

1. Israel often complained about being in the wilderness, even though God provided for them every step of the way. Why did they continue to complain even though God had done so much for them? Why do people complain in the face of God's blessings today?

2. God explicitly told Israel not to bother the Edomites' land? Do we sometimes want to take something that belongs to someone else because the blessing God has for us has not yet manifested?

LESSON IN OUR SOCIETY

No one is immune from making mistakes. Sometimes, however, people want to keep others living in the memory of their faults. It is not our place to judge. Only a loving, righteous God can judge the actions of humanity.

God showed mercy to Israel, even when they disobeyed Him. He kept on giving them another chance. God is a God of second chances. As God's people, we should be a people of second chances. We should be eager to extend to others the same grace and mercy that has been extended to us. By giving a second chance to someone who has made a mistake, we have an opportunity to show God's love to someone who may need it badly.

MAKE IT HAPPEN

Think about an area of your life in which God has given you a second, or perhaps even a third chance. How did you handle things differently once you obtained another chance?

Now think about an area in your life in which you would like another chance. If God were to grant you another chance, what would you do differently. How has this time away from that which you lost helped you to grow closer to God?

FOLLOW THE SPIRIT

What God wants me to do:

_____

_____

REMEMBER YOUR THOUGHTS

Special insights you learned:

_____

_____

MORE LIGHT ON THE TEXT
DEUTERONOMY 1:41—2:8

The people of Israel had journeyed from Horeb (Mount Sinai where God gave them the written covenant) into the oasis of Kadesh Barnea, an 11-day journey. The land of Canaan is now in sight and only a few days journey within reach. But the people ask Moses to send some people ahead to spy out the land. He sends 12 people, heads of the different tribes of Israel. On their return, they bring news of the goodness of the land and its inhabitants. Ten of them give a demoralizing and discouraging report. Two, Caleb and Joshua, give an encouraging report and try to spur the people to march forward to possess the land. Unfortunately, the people listen to the evil report of the 10 and revolt against Moses and his leadership, thereby provoking the Lord to anger. Consequently, the Lord punishes them (Numbers 13—14 see last week's study) and turns a few days journey into 38 years of wilderness wandering. In this first chapter of Deuteronomy, Moses reminds them of the incident, their reaction, their subsequent rebellions, and the consequences.

1:41 Then ye answered and said unto me, We have sinned against the Lord, we will go up and fight, according to all that the Lord our God commanded us. And when ye had girded on every man his weapons of war, ye were ready to go up into the hill. 42 And the Lord said unto me, Say unto them, Go not up, neither fight; for I am not among you; lest ye be smitten before your enemies.

Moses continues the story of their dealing with Lord and their reaction to the punishment of the Lord. He reminds them of how they repented and asked for forgiveness, and their resolve to go and fight for the land and to do whatever the Lord commands them to do. They seemed not to be afraid anymore, but enthusiastically wanted to go fight for the land. They equipped themselves in military regalia, armed with weapons of war, and prepared to go to the hills for battle. All this was against the will of God, since the Lord had told them to "turn around and set out toward the desert along the route to the Red Sea" (v. 40, NIV). This was part of the punishment, but the people probably thought that going to fight would appease the Lord and cause Him to change His mind. Their enthusiasm for battle did not constitute real atonement for their earlier sin. They thought they could manipulate the all-knowing God. As they prepare to set out for battle, the Lord asks Moses to warn them not to go because the Lord is "among you." The Lord strictly warned that if they went, they would "be smitten (nagaph), or defeated, before your enemies."

43 So I spake unto you; and ye would not hear, but rebelled against the commandment of the Lord, and went presumptuously up into the hill. 44 And the Amorites, which dwelt in that mountain, came out against you, and chased you, as bees do, and destroyed you in Seir, even unto Hormah.

Moses warns them as the Lord commanded, but the people do not listen. The phrase "ye would not hear" (Hebrew *shama'tem*) suggests that they purposely would not listen to the word of the Lord. They never paid attention but became defiant to God's warning through Moses—they deliberately ignored the warning. This is made clear in the next phrase "but rebelled against the commandment of the Lord." Contrary to Moses' advice, they went to war against the Amorites. They presumptuously (Hebrew *zuwd*, i.e., "to boil up, to act proudly or arrogantly, or to be arrogantly proud") went up to the hill to fight. They defied the orders of the Lord and the result is obvious (v. 44). Their defeat is described metaphorically, "chased you, as bees do, and destroyed you. . . ." This shows a total annihilation. It also probably refers to the great number of the Amorites that attacked the fewer number of the Israelite who arrogantly went to fight despite the warning from God. It could also refer to the deadly blow the Amorites inflicted upon them, which is comparable to the deadly sting of the bee.

Bees are such little creatures that one can easily crush one of them between the fingers; but when they come in great number, or when they are disturbed in their hives, they are known to have been so dangerous as to kill bigger animals such as dogs, cats, or horses. Bees can chase a whole village away, and their sting is known to kill people, especially those who are allergic to it.

Verses 43 and 44 show how stubborn the older generation of Israelites was. God faithfully and definitely commanded them not to go up and warned them of the consequence—defeat, but they went and were defeated as predicted. They rebelled when God asked them to go up (Numbers 13:26—14:35), and they rebelled when God warned them not to go up (Deuteronomy 1:42-43).

45 And ye returned and wept before the Lord; but the Lord would not hearken to your voice, nor give ear unto you. 46 So ye abode in Kadesh many days, according unto the days that ye abode there.

After their defeat by the Amorites, they returned and wept before the Lord. Their weeping here does not indicate repentance or that they are brought to obedience, rather it seems they weep because of their humiliation at the hands of the Amorites. The statement, "the Lord would not hear-

ken to your voice, nor give ear unto you," signifies that the Lord's patience has grown thin because of their constant rebellion. He would not listen to them. As already mentioned above, their going to up to fight for the land was aimed at changing the mind of God to allow them enter the Promised Land. Their cry after their defeat was also to make God retract that decision. Their cry does not move God anymore; God has endured their disobedience long enough and has resolved to do away with that generation (Numbers 14:23-35). Verse 46 indicates that they stayed at Kadesh for a long time before going into wilderness wandering.

2:1 Then we turned, and took our journey into the wilderness by the way of the Red sea, as the Lord spake unto me: and we compassed mount Seir many days.

With the conjunction "then," Moses continues his narrative, and changes his language, from using the second person pronoun plural "you" to first person pronoun plural "we." He uses the second person plural when describing the rebellious attitude of the people, and changes to the first person plural when he talks about their movement. "Then," that is after many days at Kadesh, which could mean months or even years, they turned back to the wilderness, towards the Red Sea, i.e., southward. They camped at Mount Seir as the Lord commanded Moses. Mount Seir is said to be a range of mountains, rather than a single mountain. This mountain range covers approximately an area of 70 miles north and south and 30 miles east and west. Here they "compassed" the area "many days." To compass *cabab* means "to revolve, to encircle, or to go round in a circle." This phrase seems to indicate that the people pitched their tents at different times and sites on the mountain range long before (ca. 38 years) they came to the Red Sea, at Eziongader and Elath or the gulf of Akabah (v. 8; cp. 1 Kings 9:26). Numbers 33:18-35 indicates that they camped in over 18 places before reaching the Red Sea. The reason for their long stay is obviously a chastisement for their murmuring, and in keeping of God's word that the generation that distrusted the Lord would be purged from the new generation (Numbers 14:23-35). It was also to prepare Israel to enter into the Promised Land. Afterwards, they came back to Kadesh before their final trips through Moab and Edom into Canaan. It is suggested that they spent over 38 years on this journey.

2 And the Lord spake unto me, saying, 3 Ye have compassed this mountain long enough: turn you northward. 4 And command thou the people, saying, Ye are to pass through the coast of your

brethren the children of Esau, which dwell in Seir; and they shall be afraid of you: take ye good heed unto yourselves therefore: 5 Meddle not with them; for I will not give you of their land, no, not so much as a footbreadth; because I have given mount Seir unto Esau for a possession.

After the Israelites had wandered around the wilderness of Seir long enough, the Lord directed them to move again northward. Probably after all the old generation that left Egypt passed away, except Caleb and Joshua, the Lord now gives the order for continuation of the trip. Although God's anger may last for a while, He does not contend forever in His anger. Our unbelief may slow the realization of the Lord's promises for us, but it will not delay it forever. God's Word will always come through irrespective of our sin. He will always keep His Word, even if not directly to the people with whom He made the promise. Israel's long-awaited deliverance would come at last. God not only commands them to set off again towards their destination through the north, He also gives them instructions on how to conduct themselves along the way and how to deal with the inhabitants of the lands through which they would pass.

The Lord gives specific instruction concerning the Edomites (i.e., the descendants of Esau). The Israelites should be careful not to take advantage of their weakness because "they shall be afraid of you." Using an imperative "Meddle not" or "Do not meddle" from the Hebrew word, *garah*, (i.e., "to cause strife, to stir up, to contend") the Lord commands the Israelites not to wage war against the children of Esau. The reasons are clear: 1) it was not in God's plan to give them that land, "not so much as a foot"; 2) the Lord had given the land to Esau as his possession. The tone here is one of both command and warning. They dare not try to contend for the land around Mount Seir, and even if they did because of the fearfulness of the people, they would not succeed because God would not allow them to have it. The land It belonged to the children of Esau, therefore the Israelites should not use force against them when passing through their land.

6 Ye shall buy meat of them for money, that ye may eat; and ye shall also buy water of them for money, that ye may drink. 7 For the Lord thy God hath blessed thee in all the works of thy hand: he knoweth thy walking through this great wilderness: these forty years the Lord thy God hath been with thee; thou hast lacked nothing. 8 And when we passed by from our brethren the children of Esau, which dwelt in Seir.

Rather than fighting the Edomites, the Lord further instructs the Israelites to establish an amicable business rela-

tionship with the people. They are to buy food and water from them when they come to the land. Since the Lord has blessed them enormously and has rewarded them for their hard work, they must pay for whatever they needed from the people (v. 7). Here we suggest that God is warning them against plundering or taking the Edomites' belongings by force. These verses also imply that they were to maintain their integrity by not begging the Edomites for help because the Lord has continued to take care of them, "'These forty years the LORD your God has been with you; you have lacked nothing'" (v. 7). They should not be a burden to the people, or use any indirect methods for their provision, the Lord seems to say here. Rather they should rely on the divine providential care, which hitherto they have experienced throughout the 40 years of wandering. Therefore they should place their trust and confidence in God for the future.

The full account of their passage through Edom is recorded in Numbers 20:14-22. Although the Edomites denied them passage through their borders, the Israelites took a different route without forcing their way through in obedience to the Lord's commanded.

DAILY BIBLE READING

M: Moses Reminds Israel about Horeb
Deuteronomy 1:1-8

T: Tribal Leaders Were Appointed
Deuteronomy 1:9-18

W: Israel Refused to Obey God
Deuteronomy 1:19-33

T: Israel Was Punished for Disobedience
Deuteronomy 1:34-45

F: Israel Wandered in the Wilderness
Deuteronomy 1:46—2:13

S: A Generation of Warriors Passed Away
Deuteronomy 2:13-25

S: Israel Began the Conquest of Canaan
Deuteronomy 2:26-37

TEACHING TIPS

October 24
Bible Study Guide 8

1. Words You Should Know

A. Frontlet (v.8)—A small case made of leather which was affixed to the forehead of male Jews. It contains passages from the Law and was worn during morning prayer except on Sabbaths and during festivals.

B. Testimonies (v.20)—Divine commands given to God's people to teach them how God expected them to behave.

C. Statutes (v. 20)—The decrees, formal commands of God.

2. Teacher Preparation

A. Read the background Scripture for this lesson. Learn more about the way the Hebrew community concerned themselves with teaching their children the Law and culture. Learn some of the objects/devices they used as teaching/learning tools.

B. Make a list of some traditions that have been passed down in the Black community. For instance, how have African Americans preserved the legacy of Dr. Martin Luther King Jr. and the Civil Rights Movement? How have many of the traditions and songs of the church been preserved? Remind your class that most, if not all, cultures make provisions to retain certain cultural values and traditions.

3. Starting the Lesson

Read the IN FOCUS story about Melissa and her daughter Jasmine. Ask class members to share their experiences with trying to teach children important religious and spiritual values.

4. Getting into the Lesson

As you discuss today's lesson, talk about Jesus' statement in Matthew 22:36-40. How can following that simple command eliminate the need for laws, contracts, and other devices which help to ensure honesty and integrity among persons?

5. Relating the Lesson to Life

A. Review the information about phylacteries (frontlets) and the Shema from THE PEOPLE, PLACES, AND TIMES. Discuss how these things helped the Hebrew community maintain their relationship with the Lord throughout the generations.

B. Give students an opportunity to answer the questions in SEARCH THE SCRIPTURES.

C. DISCUSS THE MEANING focuses on the definition of love according to the Book of Deuteronomy. Discuss how this definition differs radically from our modern notion of love.

D. The LESSON IN OUR SOCIETY highlights the importance of parental and family involvement in Christian education. How can churches and parents reasonably balance their responsibility to future generations?

6. Arousing Action

A. Create a list, in ranking order, detailing who is responsible for teaching children about God and for ensuring that the tenets of faith will be passed down from generation to generation. Be sure the list includes actions to be taken by each party responsible.

B. Allow time to complete the MAKE IT HAPPEN activity. Allow class members to discuss these questions as a group. This may also be an opportunity for some parents to air their frustrations in trying to religiously educate their children.

C. Give class members an opportunity to complete FOLLOW THE SPIRIT and REMEMBER YOUR THOUGHTS.

OCT 24TH

THE GREAT COMMANDMENT

Bible Background • DEUTERONOMY 6
Printed Text • DEUTERONOMY 6:1-9, 20-24
Devotional Reading • DEUTERONOMY 30:11-20

LESSON AIM

After studying this lesson, students should realize that God expects the family to play a key role in religious education.

KEEP IN MIND

"Hear, O Israel: The LORD our God is one LORD: And thou shalt love the LORD thy God with all thine heart, and with all thy soul, and with all thy might" (Deuteronomy 6:4-5).

FOCAL VERSES

DEUTERONOMY 6:1 Now these are the commandments, the statutes, and the judgments, which the LORD your God commanded to teach you, that ye might do them in the land whither ye go to possess it:

2 That thou mightest fear the LORD thy God, to keep all his statutes and his commandments, which I command thee, thou, and thy son, and thy son's son, all the days of thy life; and that thy days may be prolonged.

3 Hear therefore, O Israel, and observe to do it; that it may be well with thee, and that ye may increase mightily, as the LORD God of thy fathers hath promised thee, in the land that floweth with milk and honey.

4 Hear, O Israel: The LORD our God is one LORD:

5 And thou shalt love the LORD thy God with all thine heart, and with all thy soul, and with all thy might.

6 And these words, which I command thee this day, shall be in thine heart:

7 And thou shalt teach them diligently unto thy children, and shalt talk of them when thou sittest in thine house, and when thou walkest by the way, and when thou liest down, and when thou risest up.

LESSON OVERVIEW

LESSON AIM
KEEP IN MIND
FOCAL VERSES
IN FOCUS
THE PEOPLE, PLACES, AND
TIMES
BACKGROUND
AT-A-GLANCE
IN DEPTH
SEARCH THE SCRIPTURES
DISCUSS THE MEANING
LESSON IN OUR SOCIETY
MAKE IT HAPPEN
FOLLOW THE SPIRIT
REMEMBER YOUR THOUGHTS
MORE LIGHT ON THE TEXT
DAILY BIBLE READINGS

8 And thou shalt bind them for a sign upon thine hand, and they shall be as frontlets between thine eyes.

9 And thou shalt write them upon the posts of thy house, and on thy gates.

20 And when thy son asketh thee in time to come, saying, What mean the testimonies, and the statutes, and the judgments, which the LORD our God hath commanded you?

21 Then thou shalt say unto thy son, We were Pharaoh's bondmen in Egypt; and the LORD brought us out of Egypt with a mighty hand:

22 And the LORD shewed signs and wonders, great and sore, upon Egypt, upon Pharaoh, and upon all his household, before our eyes:

23 And he brought us out from thence, that he might bring us in, to give us the land which he sware unto our fathers.

24 And the LORD commanded us to do all these statutes, to fear the LORD our God, for our good always, that he might preserve us alive, as it is at this day.

IN FOCUS

Jasmine was sitting outside talking with her friends. Her mother, Melissa, stood inside watching from the kitchen window. She smiled as she noticed that their conversation was about Jesus.

All the girls started telling the things they knew about Jesus. After a while, it was Jasmine's turn. After a moment, Melissa's smile turned flat. Jasmine was telling "facts" about Jesus that were totally unlike anything her six-year-old daughter would have learned in Sunday School.

After her friends had gone home, Melissa asked Jasmine, "Where did you learn those things you were saying about Jesus."

"Oh," said Jasmine calmly, "from this really cool movie that was on TV the other night."

Melissa realized that she needed to spend more time teaching her child the truth about Jesus Christ. That incident let her see how dangerous it is to assume that her child would learn everything she needed to know simply by attending church school. Melissa was beginning to understand that, as a parent, it was her responsibility to give her child a proper foundation for religious education.

THE PEOPLE, PLACES, AND TIMES

PHYLACTERY (Frontlets). Objects which contain Scripture passages and are worn on the forehand and between the eyes, especially at prayer times. Jews followed scriptural commands literally, writing Exodus 13:1-10, 11-16; Deuteronomy 6:4-9; 11:13-21 on small scrolls and placing them in leather containers which were then placed on the forehead and left arm.

By New Testament times, the frontlets were known as phylacteries (see Matthew 23:5). Jesus criticized those who called attention to themselves by wearing phylacteries that were larger than usual.

Phylacteries generally were bound to the forehead with thongs; however, some were worn on the upper arm so that when a person crossed his arms, the Scriptures contained in the phylactery would be close to the heart.

Based on information from *Holman Bible Dictionary*, Trent Butler, general editor. Nashville: Broadman & Holman Publishers, 1991, p. 516.

SHEMA. Transliteration of a Hebrew word meaning "hear." Taken from Deuteronomy 6:4 and applied in 6:4-9 as the basic statement of Jewish law. For the people of God, the Shema became a confession of faith by which they acknowledged the one true God and His commandments for them. In later worship practices, Deuteronomy 6:4-9; 11:13-21; and Numbers 15:37-41 were combined into the larger confession which summarized the Jewish confession.

In the New Testament, when Jesus was asked to name the "greatest commandment," He answered by quoting the Shema (Mark 12:29).

Based on information from *Holman Bible Dictionary*, p. 1261.

BACKGROUND

A portion of the text for today's lessons includes what is known as the *Shema*. The sixth chapter of Deuteronomy is regarded by Bible scholars as a sermon on the first commandment, which forbids Israel to have any gods besides Yahweh.

As the time to enter the Promised Land drew near, Israel received further commands from the Lord concerning their conduct. The Lord knew that, with each succeeding generation, there was a great possibility that Israel would forget how they got to Canaan and all that the Lord had done for them by taking them from bondage in Egypt to the Promised Land. God wanted every generation to remember the experience of slavery in Egypt. They needed to remember the trying behavior of their ancestors in the wilderness. Above all, future generations needed to know of God's constant grace which rescued His people time after time.

God's desire was that Israel would have constant reminders of the covenant. This became the staple of the practice of Jewish rituals, from the early education of their children in the biblical text to the *mezuza*, a small box on the doorpost containing passages from Deuteronomy.

AT-A-GLANCE

**1. Obedience Commanded
(Deuteronomy 6:1-3)
2. Love and Fear the Lord
(vv. 4-9)
3. Teach Your Children
(vv. 20-24)**

IN DEPTH

1. Obedience Commanded
(Deuteronomy 6:1-3)

God wanted His people to be in the right moral condition upon entering the Promised Land. Moses began to fulfill the task which the Lord assigned. He gave them practical instruction to prepare them for life in Canaan. Moses described certain situations to them and told them how they should respond. He gave Israel the charge which had been given to him at Horeb.

The worship of idol gods was quite prevalent in Canaan. The Lord did not want to turn His people loose in that environment without a firm foundation. Israel was to bear witness to the fact that Yahweh is the only true God. Israel must know their God and serve Him only. They needed to love Him and fear Him so that they would not be tempted to worship other gods. The Lord's expectation of His people was that every generation would learn to revere Him in such a way that it would yield their obedience to Him.

The reward for obedience to God was not immortality, but prolonged life on earth. In ancient Judaism, life beyond death in the dismal, cavernous Sheol offered no attraction. Conversely, long life on earth was much more enticing. Long life and prosperity were symbols of God's favor and blessings in ancient Judaism.

2. Love and Fear the Lord (vv. 4-9)

The Shema stands above all other commandments in Judaism. It is the symbol of faith to the Jew. It opens the service at the synagogue. It is written on parchment. It is worn in the phylacteries. It is inscribed on the doorpost. Originally it was designed to distinguish Yahweh from the various Canaanite gods such as Baal. It later came to serve as a confession of faith for Judaism.

In Matthew 22:36-40, when Jesus replied to the Pharisee's question by quoting the Shema together with the law of neighborly love (Leviticus 19:18), the Master called it the "greatest" commandment.

In verse 4, Israel is called to attention, after which Yahweh, Israel's God, is presented. When used in the context of Jewish worship, it was read: "Yahweh, our God—one Yahweh." Jews later avoided speaking the name YHWH for fear of profaning it. Later the term, "the Lord" was adopted.

The term "one Lord" expresses a great deal more than the concept of one God. In addition to complementing the first commandment, "one Lord" also addresses the singleness of God's purpose. He is one and His will is one. There is no escaping Yahweh or His will. The Shema calls for Israel to concentrate her undivided attention on Yahweh alone. Only He—the single and unique God—is worthy of their full devotion.

Because God is one, His people are to love Him and teach His commandments. Love, as interpreted here, was more than the feeling of warmth and caring often associated with love in the western world. Love, in the context in which the Shema was written, included demonstrations of loyalty and obedience.

Loving God, however, is not the most common response to Him in Scripture. For example, Hosea often spoke of God's love for Israel, but not Israel's love for God.

In Deuteronomy, love is precisely the response Israel is to have. Throughout the book, that love is evidenced through obedience to God's law. No other book of the Old Testament places love for Yahweh in such a central position.

Deuteronomy does not relate love in terms of a parent to child nor in terms of marriage. Love, in Deuteronomy, is a love that can be directed by God. It is a kind of love that is intimately related to both fear and reverence. In essence, to love God is to be loyal to Him, to keep His commandments, to heed His voice, to serve Him, and to walk in His ways. Love for God, in Deuteronomy, is a covenantal love.

In the Shema, this love for God must be expressed through singleness of purpose and absolute, undivided devotion and allegiance to Him. Every part of one's being is attached to that love. Love for God is to be total, complete, and unending.

3. Teach Your Children (vv. 20-24)

The day would come when those who had experienced the Exodus and the wilderness would be no more. The day would come when children who knew nothing of Israel's history would become curious and ask questions about the faith of their fathers. It was important that the message of Yahweh be kept alive. It was the duty of every father to teach his children why Israel is faithful to Yahweh. There were some essential facts that were not to be forgotten. God had brought Israel out of bondage in Egypt. God had provided for Israel in miraculous ways during the wilderness years. God had successfully guided Israel to the land of promise.

This information was not to be passed down as sterile data or a mechanical code. The story of Yahweh's goodness to Israel and why Israel is obedient to Him should be told instinctively. Instead of confessing belief in abstract terms, Israel's children were taught the old story of God's redemption and grace, which included the Exodus and the Promised Land.

This same God gave Israel these commandments, decrees, and laws so that they might enjoy long life. God's gift of the law was not a type of burden or punishment for Israel to bear. Instead, it was an extension of His grace and providence so that His chosen nation might have the abundant life. The provision in these verses allow for the religion to begin anew with each child born into the world. Loyalty to Yahweh would not be automatic. It needed to be taught.

The final verses of Deuteronomy chapter 6 seek to show that in Israel, both being alive and possessing righteousness depended on whether or not one observes the requirements of God's covenant with Israel. This is proved by first citing the historical acts of God which Israel can be called upon to give witness to because these things happened before their eyes. Israel did not have to use hearsay to tell of God's goodness. They knew personally. They had their own stories to tell about God.

SEARCH THE SCRIPTURES

1. Why was Israel to know the laws of God? (Deuteronomy 6:2)

2. Why was Israel to obey God? (v. 3)

3. How was Israel to relate to God? (vv. 4-5)

4. Where was Israel supposed to keep God's commandments? (v. 6)

5. At what times was Israel to teach their children about God's commandments? (v. 7)

6. How were the Israelites supposed to display the commandments of God? (vv. 8-9)

7. What question could Hebrew fathers expect their sons to ask? (v. 20)

8. How were fathers supposed to answer their sons? (v. 21)

9. What deeds had Yahweh done? (vv. 22-23)

10. Why did the Lord command His people to obey all the decrees He had given them? (vv. 24)

DISCUSS THE MEANING

1. Love, as defined in Deuteronomy, is characterized by series of actions—loyalty, devotion, allegiance. God has proven Himself capable of this kind of love. Are human beings ever able to return this type of love to Him?

2. Why have we shifted the responsibility for teaching our children about God to the church instead of the home? Who bears the greatest responsibility for providing religious education to our children—the family or the church?

LESSON IN OUR SOCIETY

Many of our churches have erected extensive complexes to aid Christian education and have built massive family life centers to enable the church to minister to the total person.

With the emergence of all of our elaborate buildings, programs, and staff, we must be careful that we do not shift too much responsibility to the church for the religious education of our children. The church's responsibility is to facilitate the family in spiritual development and Christian education, not the other way around.

Parents must be careful that they do not relinquish their duties in this area, thinking that it is the church's responsi-

bility. Conversely, the church must not think too highly of its own role in being the provider of religious education. Primarily, the church can expect to reinforce and undergird what is taught in the home. Parents cannot expect the church to successfully teach what is not being taught at home. Neither can parents expect the church to impart a standard of righteousness which is not being lived out in the home.

MAKE IT HAPPEN

If you have children, how much have you really impacted their religious education and spiritual growth through your teaching and your living?

If a child were to ask you "Why are we supposed to serve Jesus and give our life to Him?" how would you respond? Perhaps you still have this question in your own mind. Take a sheet of paper and list some basic things your child should know about the Christ we serve.

FOLLOW THE SPIRIT

What God wants me to do:

_____

_____

REMEMBER YOUR THOUGHTS

Special insights you learned:

_____

_____

MORE LIGHT ON THE TEXT
DEUTERONOMY 6:1-9, 20-24

In the preceding chapter (chapter 5), Moses rehearses the Sinai law for the Children of Israel and the circumstances under which it was initially given. He urges them to always keep the law of God so that they can reap the benefit, which is long life in the land that Lord had promised them. The next nine verses define the law, how the people are to keep it, and to what extent they should keep it in order for them to reap the benefits that come with it. They are to preserve the law by teaching it to their generations to come. The portion under discussion constitutes the Shema of Israel's religion, and the basis for the Christian belief in the "One Eternal God."

6:1 Now these are the commandments, the statutes, and the judgments, which the Lord your God commanded to teach you, that ye might do them in the land whither ye go to possess it: 2 That thou mightest fear the Lord thy God, to keep

tory of Israel. The reward for keeping the law is that they, their children, and future generations would live long. To live long refers not necessarily to an individual long life, which probably is included, but rather to the long life of Israel as a nation. Here it means if they "keep all His statutes and His commandments," they would possess the land for a long time; conversely if they fail to fear the Lord and keep His commandments, they would disinherit the land. Israel's captivity by Persia and Judah's exile to Babylon are consequences of their failure to keep the law of the Lord. Therefore, as each generation remembers to obey the commandments, they enjoy the benefits of the land, and their days would be prolonged. The law is intended for their well-being so that Israel could enjoy life to the full, for it is "given that it may go well with you" (5:33; cf. 6:18; 12:28).

all his statutes and his commandments, which I command thee, thou, and thy son, and thy son's son, all the days of thy life; and that thy days may be prolonged.

Using the conjunction "now these," or *wazo't* from the word *zo'th*, which can also be translated as "this, or this . . . that, or here is," Moses continues his thoughts from Deuteronomy chapter 5. The phrase, "Now these are the commandments, the statutes, and the judgments," includes all the commandments Moses has rehearsed with them in the previous chapter and the ones that are soon to follow (6:1ff). The Lord, Moses says, has ordered him to teach them or to remind them of the law, which they would keep when they possess the land. The purpose of this rehearsal of the law in their hearing is so that they will remember to obey and fear the Lord. The fear of the Lord, which means reverence in one's heart for God, is the most powerful force for obedience. Proverbs describes the fear of the Lord as "the beginning of wisdom: and the knowledge of the holy is understanding" (9:10). The kind of "fear," (*yare'*) used here is not to be afraid of God as if he were a dreadful and vengeful Being standing over people ready to punish them for the smallest infraction of His law. It speaks of more of respecting or revering God as the "Our Father" who deserves to be honored and respected. It also teaches that men (generically used) ought to learn to respect God both as the law giver and as a just and righteous judge, bearing in mind His justice as well as His mercy and long-suffering. Moses uses two Hebrew words, which are synonymous, *chuqqah*, translated "statutes," and *mitsvah* rendered "commandment" by KJV ("decrees and commands" in NIV). These words emphasize the importance of keeping the law of God. The law is to be perpetuated throughout the his-

3 Hear therefore, O Israel, and observe to do it; that it may be well with thee, and that ye may increase mightily, as the Lord God of thy fathers hath promised thee, in the land that floweth with milk and honey.

"Hear therefore," that is in view of the benefits, Moses urges them, as if pleading with them, to listen (hear) and obey (observe) the law of the Lord. If they will endeavor to keep the commandments, things will go well with them, they will multiply numerically in keeping with the promise the Lord made to their fathers. That promise includes living in the land which flows with milk and honey, which describes the fertility and productivity of the land.

4 Hear, O Israel: The Lord our God is one Lord: 5 And thou shalt love the Lord thy God with all thine heart, and with all thy soul, and with all thy might.

Verses 4-9, with 11:1-21, and Numbers 13:37-41 constitutes the Shema or creed of Israel in the Hebrew liturgy, which pious Jews recite twice daily in their worship. It expresses the heart of Israel's confession of faith, and confirms firstly, the unity of God ("the Lord is one," NIV), and secondly the covenant relationship between Israel ("the Lord our God"). The word translated "one" is the Hebrew word *echad* from *achad*, which means "to unify; collect; to be united as one" (Genesis 2:24; 3:22; 11:1, 6 etc). Here, Moses implicitly declares the uniqueness of God of Israel, namely that Yahweh is the One God, and He is not a pantheon of many gods that are worshiped by the surrounding nations. Moses begins this declaration by calling for the whole congregation of the people of Israel, "Hear, O

Israel," (*Shama` Yisaa'eel*) to pay attention to this important information, namely the uniqueness of God, and their response to Him. Moses invites the people to give Yahweh their complete allegiance by loving Him with the totality of their being: "with all thine heart, and with all thy soul, and with all thy might." Yahweh is to be Israel's sole object of worship and affection, and not other gods.

Verse 4 has been regarded as the positive way of expressing the negative commands of the first commandments of the decalogue (5:7-10; cf. Exodus 20:2-4). In the New Testament, Christ, responding to the inquiry of the young lawyer, adds the phrase "with all your mind," and describes these two verses (vv. 4-5) as "the first and great commandment" (Matthew 22:37-38; Mark 12:29-30; Luke 10:27). This type of love requires total surrender of the whole being to God, who has given Himself completely, without reservation, and unconditionally to love the people of Israel. He therefore deserves and expects them to reciprocate with the same unreserved and total love for Him. This command to love the Lord is found frequently in Deuteronomy and expresses the response God expects from His people (10:12; 11:1, 13, 22; 12:3; 19:9; 30:6, 16, 20 etc.); it is also found in the covenant renewal of Joshua (Joshua 22:5; 23:11). The Scripture often links the command to love with the command to obey. Jesus says to his disciples, "If ye love me, keep my commandments" (John 14:15); "He that hath my commandments, and keepeth them, he it is that loveth me: and he that loveth me shall be loved of my Father, and I will love him, and will manifest myself to him"(John 14:21); and "If a man love me, he will keep my words: and my Father will love him, and we will come unto him, and make our abode with him" (John 14:23).

6 And these words, which I command thee this day, shall be in thine heart: 7 And thou shalt teach them diligently unto thy children, and shalt talk of them when thou sittest in thine house, and when thou walkest by the way, and when thou liest down, and when thou risest up.

"And these words, which I command thee this day," includes all the commandments in the previous chapter, the declarations in this chapter, and the ones following. These commandments are to be stored in their heart, where nothing can touch them. The word *heart* (Hebrew *lebab*) used also in verse 5 refers to the seat of understanding, intellect, and intention. It is where we do our thinking, and where our character is formed. The heart represents the nucleus of the human being, in which decisions and moral choices,

both good and bad, are made. True love, worship, and holy principles emanate from within the heart, as do the evil issues of life (Mark 7:19-21). The heart is also the seat of consciousness, therefore, to store the commandment in our heart is to keep it in our consciousness as long as we live. In other words, God's commandments should become a part of our being, and we are to be conscious of them all the days our lives. This is made explicit in the command that parents teach the commandments to their children diligently. The phrase "thou shalt teach them diligently" translates the Hebrew word, *Asinine*, which has an idea of "to sharpen, or to pierce." Moses instructs them of their parental duties. They are to teach the children the law constantly, and systematically, formally and informally, until these words of the commandments pierce through to (penetrate) their hearts. The commandments should be the center of daily life, in conversation at home, or on the road, at bedtime, and when they rise up. They should go to bed at night, and arise in the morning with the law of the Lord embedded in their hearts so that they would not forget it. The Lord commanded Joshua: "Do not let this Book of the Law depart from your mouth; meditate on it day and night, so that you may be careful to do everything written in it. Then you will be prosperous and successful" (Joshua 1:8, NIV). The Israelites are to teach the commandments to their children not only to instruct them in the ways of the Lord at an early age (Proverbs 22:6), but also perhaps to help preserve the law and their heritage for generations (v. 20ff) should any thing happen to the written law.

8 And thou shalt bind them for a sign upon thine hand, and they shall be as frontlets between thine eyes. 9 And thou shalt write them upon the posts of thy house, and on thy gates.

To make the law a visible and permanent part of their life, the Israelites are to bind them upon their hands as a constant reminder of their allegiance to Yahweh and the law, and post it on their forehead and on the lintels of their houses. Binding them on their hands is probably a figurative expression of how diligent their allegiance to the law should be shown. The imagery is also used in the Jewish rituals of the Passover (Exodus 13:9), in the sacrifice of the first-born animals, and the redemption of the first-born sons (Exodus 13:16). The same idea is expressed in a number of the Proverbs regarding mercy and truth (3:3), obedience to parental commandments (6:21), and keeping God's law (7:3). The Jews later interpreted it literally and enclosed some written portions of the law in small cases, which are called phylacteries (cf. Matthew 23:5), and bound them on their hands and foreheads. The significance of these instructions is well understood, and that is to keep them conscious of God, by a visible and constant reminder of the law.

20 And when thy son asketh thee in time to come, saying, What mean the testimonies, and the statutes, and the judgments, which the Lord our God hath commanded you? 21 Then thou shalt say unto thy son, We were Pharaoh's bondmen in Egypt; and the Lord brought us out of Egypt with a mighty hand: 22 And the Lord shewed signs and wonders, great and sore, upon Egypt, upon Pharaoh, and upon all his household, before our eyes: 23 And he brought us out from thence, that he might bring us in, to give us the land which he sware unto our fathers.

An African adage says that when an old man dies in a village or tribe, it is as if an entire library is burned or destroyed. A whole history or heritage of a village or family would be lost if it were not passed to the next generation. To preserve the legacy of the people, there is a need to tell stories to the children at a young age about the family, the village, or the tribe where they have been, and how they got to that moment of their journey of life. This was how the Africans preserved their history before the art of writing was introduced. This is the same instruction Moses gives in these verses. Apart from the formal teaching of the law to the new generation (v. 6), the parents have the obligation to tell stories about their heritage, the mighty deliverance God gave them from the land of Egypt and from the hand of Pharaoh, and how God led them through the wilderness into the land of promise.

Here are two methods of education: formal (didactic, v. 6) and informal, telling stories (inductive, v. 20ff) through question and answer. The children's questions offer opportunities for explanation and teaching. Such questions and opportunities are, of course, made possible if the parents themselves are clearly keeping the law so as to raise some curiosity in the minds of their children. The question "What mean the..." can be reworded thus: "What is the real significance of the law. . .?" "Why do we have to keep the law?" By answering this question, the father rehearses the historical basis of the law, how it originated, and the benefits of observing it. Rather than giving a simple answer, the Lord demands the parents to tell the full story of the acts of God in redemption from bondage, which is the basis of the law. This redemptive story of God's mighty deeds would instill spirit of gratitude and loving obedience to the Lord; it would generate worship and reverence for God in the minds of the people. Keeping the law demonstrates our love for the Lord.

24 And the Lord commanded us to do all these statutes, to fear the Lord our God, for our good always, that he might preserve us alive, as it is at this day.

Added to the historical basis of the law in redemption (vv. 21-23), the reason for keeping the law is that they might fear (honor) the Lord, and enjoy the blessings and benefits of redemption "for our good always" (v. 24). It is also for their preservation in the land. It is not only necessary to keep or obey the law of God, it is also necessary, as Moses seems to intimate here, that the children know whole story behind what they do, why they worship the Lord and not the other gods. Therefore, the law would be meaningless and ineffective without the story behind it—i.e., the redemptive story from Egypt to the Promised Land. Likewise, the Christian life or the creed will have no meaning without the story behind it—the redemptive story of the death and resurrection of the Lord and Saviour Jesus Christ. Taking our children to church is not enough, we are to teach them diligently, and tell them constantly the story about the Saviour and significance of His death, and its benefit to us. We should always heed to Peter's admonition, ". . . sanctify the Lord God in your hearts: and be ready always to give an answer to every man that asketh you a reason of the hope that is in you with meekness and fear" (1 Peter 3:15).

DAILY BIBLE READING

M: God's Great Commandment to Israel
Deuteronomy 6:1-9

T: Do Not Follow Other gods!
Deuteronomy 6:10-15

W: Tell of God's Mighty Acts!
Deuteronomy 6:16-25

T: Chosen by God's Love and Grace
Deuteronomy 7:7-11

F: Blessing of Obedience
Deuteronomy 10:12-22

S: A Land of Milk and Honey
Deuteronomy 11:8-12

S: Love God and Teach Your Children
Deuteronomy 11:13-21

TEACHING TIPS

October 31
Bible Study Guide 9

1. Words You Should Know

A. Water, fountains and depths (v. 7)—water was essential in a region surrounded by the desert. The Lord was providing His people with a land which had an abundant water supply.

B. Grains and fruits, olive oil and honey (v. 9)—just like the water, a land rich in fruits, grains, and other important staples were evidence of God's providence to His people. After their many years in the desert living on manna and other things which were available in the wilderness, a land which produced an abundant harvest was a blessing indeed.

2. Teacher Preparation

Read the background Scripture for this lesson. As you read today's lesson, keep in mind that Moses' words to Israel may seem repetitious, but apparently the repeated message was needed.

3. Starting the Lesson

A. Ask students to create a list of things and deeds that people (as groups or individuals) regularly take credit for— deeds for which credit should actually go to the Lord.

B. Read the IN FOCUS story about what Michael learned by watching Mr. Henderson. Why are we in danger when we begin to give ourselves too much credit for for the blessings we have received from the Lord?

4. Getting into the Lesson

As you discuss the lesson, examine some of the characteristics of Israel as a nation of people. Discuss whether any group of people would have needed to be reminded constantly of God's goodness, as Israel needed. Might other groups have responded differently? Would any group of people, under conditions similar to Israel's, soon have forgotten God's blessings and disobeyed Him as Israel did?

5. Relating the Lesson to Life

A. Review the information about manna from THE PEOPLE, PLACES, AND TIMES. Discuss how waiting to receive manna from heaven daily should have helped the Israelites learn to lean on and trust in the Lord.

B. Give students an opportunity to answer the questions in SEARCH THE SCRIPTURES.

C. DISCUSS THE MEANING focuses on the kinds of resources people can start to rely on instead of God. How do these things interfere with our relationship with God?

D. The LESSON IN OUR SOCIETY highlights the importance of balance among Christians. How do we have healthy self-esteem without discounting our Lord? How do we avoid the trap of assuming that we are the sole supplier of our own success?

6. Arousing Action

A. Ask class members the following questions: What are some warning signs which the Christian community should heed about our teens? What are some signs within the African American community?

B. Allow time to complete the MAKE IT HAPPEN activity. Allow class members to conduct a personal (and if necessary, private) assessment of themselves and how they relate to the Lord.

C. Give class members an opportunity to complete FOLLOW THE SPIRIT and REMEMBER YOUR THOUGHTS.

OCT 31ST

A WARNING

Bible Background • DEUTERONOMY 8
Printed Text • DEUTERONOMY 8:7-20
Devotional Reading • PSALM 85

LESSON AIM

After studying this lesson, students should recognize that the Lord is the Source of all the blessings that His people receive.

KEEP IN MIND

"Beware that thou forget not the LORD thy God, in not keeping his commandments, and his judgments, and his statutes, which I command thee this day" (Deuteronomy 8:11).

FOCAL VERSES

DEUTERONOMY 8:7 For the LORD thy God bringeth thee into a good land, a land of brooks of water, of fountains and depths that spring out of valleys and hills;

8 A land of wheat, and barley, and vines, and fig trees, and pomegranates; a land of oil olive, and honey;

9 A land wherein thou shalt eat bread without scarceness, thou shalt not lack any thing in it; a land whose stones are iron, and out of whose hills thou mayest dig brass.

10 When thou hast eaten and art full, then thou shalt bless the LORD thy God for the good land which he hath given thee.

11 Beware that thou forget not the LORD thy God, in not keeping his commandments, and his judgments, and his statutes, which I command thee this day:

12 Lest when thou hast eaten and art full, and hast built goodly houses, and dwelt therein;

13 And when thy herds and thy flocks multiply, and thy silver and thy gold is multiplied, and all that thou hast is multiplied;

14 Then thine heart be lifted up, and thou forget the LORD thy God, which brought thee forth out of the land

---

LESSON OVERVIEW

LESSON AIM
KEEP IN MIND
FOCAL VERSES
IN FOCUS
THE PEOPLE, PLACES, AND TIMES
BACKGROUND
AT-A-GLANCE
IN DEPTH
SEARCH THE SCRIPTURES
DISCUSS THE MEANING
LESSON IN OUR SOCIETY
MAKE IT HAPPEN
FOLLOW THE SPIRIT
REMEMBER YOUR THOUGHTS
MORE LIGHT ON THE TEXT
DAILY BIBLE READINGS

---

of Egypt, from the house of bondage;

15 Who led thee through that great and terrible wilderness, wherein were fiery serpents, and scorpions, and drought, where there was no water; who brought thee forth water out of the rock of flint;

16 Who fed thee in the wilderness with manna, which thy fathers knew not, that he might humble thee, and that he might prove thee, to do thee good at thy latter end;

17 And thou say in thine heart, My power and the might of mine hand hath gotten me this wealth.

18 But thou shalt remember the LORD thy God: for it is he that giveth thee power to get wealth, that he may establish his covenant which he sware unto thy fathers, as it is this day.

19 And it shall be, if thou do at all forget the LORD thy God, and walk after other gods, and serve them, and worship them, I testify against you this day that ye shall surely perish.

20 As the nations which the LORD destroyeth before your face, so shall ye perish; because ye would not be obedient unto the voice of the LORD your God.

IN FOCUS

As he stood outside his car at the gas station, Michael saw Mr. Henderson pull up at the next pump. "Now there's a sight I thought I'd never see," he thought, "Harold Henderson pumping his own gas."

Michael thought back to the time when everyone referred to him as "Hefty" Henderson because he had a lot of money. He once owned four furniture and appliance stores in the Black community.

As Michael drove off, he thought about the time he had

lunch at a table adjacent to Mr. Henderson. "Hefty" was talking to another man about how he became a success. Everything in his conversation was, "I. . . I. . . I. . . ." Even then Michael remembered thinking that Mr. Henderson was taking an awful lot of credit for the success of his stores.

Just a couple of years after that day at the restaurant, some large retailers opened some furniture and electronics stores that were able to offer lower prices than Mr. Henderson's. Plus, these stores had their own charge accounts, while Mr. Henderson no longer allowed purchases on credit.

Michael had heard that after he had to close all but one of his stores, Mr. Henderson got up in church and said he wondered why God allowed his business to go down.

"Humph," Michael said to himself as he turned into his driveway, "it's funny how Mr. Henderson gave no credit to God for his success, but he wanted to blame God for his downfall!"

THE PEOPLE, PLACES, AND TIMES

MANNA. Considered to be food from heaven, manna is a grain-like substance which sustained the Israelites during their years in the wilderness.

The small, round grains (or flakes) appeared around the Israelites' camp each morning with the dew. They were gathered, ground, and baked into cakes or boiled.

The name manna may have come from the question the Israelites must have asked when they first saw the grains: "What is it (*man hu*)?"

The Bible emphasizes that God caused manna to appear at the right time and place to meet their needs. Manna could not be stored and therefore was of little use to the Israelites beyond its immediate use. Therefore, Israel had to rely on God daily for their provision of manna.

Based on information from *Holman Bible Dictionary*, Trent Butler, general editor. Nashville: Broadman & Holman Publishers, 1991, p. 916.

SCORPION. Small invertebrate animal which is known for the sting and accompanying venom which are released through its slender, segmented tail. While Israel was in the wilderness, God protected them from scorpions and snakes.

Based on information from *Holman Bible Dictionary*, p. 1237.

BACKGROUND

Today's lesson text is part of the third sermon which is related to the historical section in Deuteronomy 5. Like the

two previous sermons, it is based on the first commandment.

Israel is admonished to observe or be careful to follow the commandment of Yahweh. As in previous sections, obedience to the Lord is linked to blessings and prosperity. The people are again reminded of all that the Lord has done for them over the last 40 years. They are reminded of the wilderness years and God's providence during that time.

This sermon, like the others, focuses on the future years, when all of Israel's suffering and God's role in alleviating that suffering may be forgotten. Additionally, the lure of other gods would become more appealing as generations with no personal knowledge of the Exodus and succeeding events would become vulnerable to violating the first commandment.

God's people needed to understand that their blessings came by His hand. Their prosperity would be parallel with their obedience. The Lord knew His people. He knew that after many years of prosperity, Israel might well begin to credit themselves for their own prosperity and well-being. Despite repeated warnings, Israel did begin to disregard the presence of the Lord's directing hand in their history and their future.

AT-A-GLANCE

**1. Remember God's Blessings
(Deuteronomy 8:7-10)
2. Don't Become Proud and
Forget the Lord (vv. 11-20)**

IN DEPTH

1. Remember God's Blessings
(Deuteronomy 8:7-10)

God had provided for Israel in every aspect of their lives. They needed to remember the way through which the Lord had brought them. They needed to recall the times of prosperity, but they also needed to remember the bitter and difficult times. God had to humble Israel for a purpose.

God's purpose for Israel was knowledge—knowledge of their faith. The Lord first wanted to show what Israel was made of and tested them to that end. He also wanted them to know what was really important. The Lord was bringing them into a prosperous land. Moses was reminding Israel of what God had already done as well as what He promised to do.

It may be difficult for those in the Western world to understand the significance of the features of the Promised Land which are named in verses 7-8. Israel had spent 40 years as a nomadic culture. For such people, water is a precious resource, especially when much of the land is desert territory. Additionally, a people who have had no homeland would greatly treasure a land wherein there was plentiful water, grains, fruit trees, and honey.

They had come a long way from wandering in the desert. Israel would lack nothing in the land that God was giving them. Minerals were rich in the land—iron and brass (copper). They would be prosperous and contented and filled with thanksgiving to the Lord.

Moses gave repeated warnings from God to Israel, realizing that remembering God would prove to be difficult as the years of prosperity continued. They were God's people, however, and they were to receive His blessings with thanksgiving and humility, not pride. The Israelites needed to be a disciplined people who remained loyal to the commands and statutes of the Deliverer. God's chosen people were never to forget His loving acts of redemption on their behalf.

2. Don't Become Proud and Forget the Lord (vv. 11-20)

Living in a present state of prosperity is no guarantee against future suffering. The bounty of blessings that the Lord was about to heap on top of the blessings He had already given would be overwhelming. Israel was warned to remember the Source of their blessings. After 40 long years of living in the wilderness, Israel probably could easily begin to think that they had earned the right to live in the Promised Land. They needed to remember that it was only through God's goodness that they were about to enter the land flowing with milk and honey.

It is often a temptation to trust ourselves instead of the Lord. When the stomach is full, God often gets pushed to the sidelines. As Israel entered its years of prosperity, the people might forget the hundreds of years of slavery. They might forget how Pharaoh's army almost returned them to bondage. The memory of the wilderness years could become faint and dim.

Perhaps Moses understood this tendency of human nature from firsthand experience, having gone from a life of prosperity to living in the wilderness as a shepherd. Yet, in the wilderness he found the Lord and God nurtured Moses' spirit until it grew in the knowledge of God.

Moses cautioned Israel against claiming self-sufficiency, as they had on some occasions in the desert. Such an attitude always leads to downfall: "Pride goeth before destruction, and an haughty spirit before a fall" (Proverbs 16:18). A feeling of self-sufficiency can only exist when one has forgotten about the blessings of God.

Israel is admonished to remember that not only wealth, but the power and ability to gain that wealth is a gift from their God. The promise of prosperity had been made to their forebears and the Lord honors His promises. The blessings they received were not because of any goodness or merit on the part of the current generation.

The importance of keeping the first commandment is reiterated at the end of the sermon (vv. 19-20). In the bliss of prosperity, Israel must not forget that it was the Lord, Yahweh, who brought them to this point. The years in the wilderness served to humble them in readiness to assume the life of prosperity and plenty associated with residence in the Promised Land.

A final note of caution about potential sins is included in the sermon's close—specifically concerning forgetfulness and rebellion. If they forgot what God had done for them, they would be susceptible to rebellion against Him. Only sin could cause a breach in the covenant between God and His people. God wanted His people to know that disregarding Him brought serious consequences, just as obedience to Him brought His blessings and great responsibility.

Israel was unique from other nations. She was set apart by the Lord God Almighty. Forgetting about the God who brought them to the Promised Land would lead to destruction. Israel's distinction from other nations was that her people had heard and obeyed the voice of Yahweh. As God's chosen people if they no longer heeded His voice, they would lose their distinguishing characteristic and suffer a terrible fate.

SEARCH THE SCRIPTURES

1. Why was it important for Israel to remember it was God who blessed them?

2. Why did Moses feel it necessary to constantly remind Israel of the source of their blessings?

3. What is the gift from God that enables His people to gain wealth?

4. Moses cautioned God's people against the danger of forgetting God. Their forgetfulness could bring on what sin?

5. What was God's commandment to the people if they insisted on ignoring His servant Moses' warnings?

DISCUSS THE MEANING

1. Despite warnings and firsthand knowledge of God's blessings, Israel forsook the Lord and pursued other gods. That may seem strange to modern Christians until we examine our own use of horoscopes, psychic readings, and tarot cards. When we rely on such devices, are we forsaking the wisdom and direction of the Lord?

2. Why does human nature lead us to rely more on ourselves and less on God once we are in a state of economic comfort and security? Why do people begin to give themselves credit for their success and prosperity instead of thanking God?

LESSON IN OUR SOCIETY

Our modern society pushes us to have a favorable impression of ourselves, and that is good. In our push for self-affirmation, however, we often push God aside. In fact the word *ego* has been defined as "easing God out." The more we focus on self, the less we focus on God. This is a potential danger that lies within the self-help movement.

In the corporate world, people who have achieved economic success or have gone from "rags to riches" are often asked to share the secrets of their success with others. These persons often talk about market conditions, personal success tips, goal-setting, and positive thinking. Less often, do we hear successful people give credit to the Lord for giving them the ability to achieve that success.

In the African American community, gains in economic success has brought a legion of other problems. Studies show: middle class Blacks are more likely to suffer from low self-esteem; middle class Black women are more likely to suffer from eating disorders such as bulimia; and middle class teens are more likely to be suicidal than Black teens from lower income households. In light of these facts, we must question whether we are forgetting about God as our economic prosperity rises.

MAKE IT HAPPEN

List the things which sometimes block you from being a faithful servant of the Lord. Think of and list some times when you have devoted yourself to making money or economic success, rather than doing the work of the Lord.

Recall times when you may have credited yourself with results when the glory should have gone to the Lord. What happened to help you place your blessings in proper perspective?

FOLLOW THE SPIRIT

What God wants me to do:

REMEMBER YOUR THOUGHTS

Special insights you learned:

MORE LIGHT ON THE TEXT
DEUTERONOMY 8:7-20

In the first six verses of this chapter, Moses urges the people to remember to keep the commandments and reiterates the benefits of obeying them. He reminds them of the past, the 40 years of wandering and all the hardships and obstacles, which served to test and train them for their future relationship with the Lord as possessors of the new land. He also reminds them how God sustained them and supplied all their necessities, including food (both spiritual and physical) and clothing, along the way up to this point.

As we have noted in the previous studies, Israel is at the verge of entering the Promised Land. Moses is preparing them for the final stage of the journey. He is reminding them again of their responsibility and obligation towards God and His law, and how they should live in order to reap the benefits of the land.

8:7 For the Lord thy God bringeth thee into a good land, a land of brooks of water, of fountains and depths that spring out of valleys and hills; 8 A land of wheat, and barley, and vines, and fig trees, and pomegranates; a land of oil olive, and honey; 9 A land wherein thou shalt eat bread without scarceness, thou shalt not lack any thing in it; a land whose stones are iron, and out of whose hills thou mayest dig brass.

In verses 7 to 9, Moses describes Canaan, the Promised Land, as a land rich with natural resources. The land hitherto has always been described metaphorically as the "land flowing with milk and honey" (Exodus 3:8, 17; 13:5; 33:3), but here Moses explicitly details the riches of the land which God is about to give them. In these verses, Moses warns the people against laxity in their worship of the Lord or apostasy when they enjoy the riches of the land. The clause, "For the Lord thy God bringeth thee . . ." (KJV), rendered in most translations as "For the LORD your God is bringing you . . ." (NKJV, NIV, NAS), seems to have the idea that the promise is about to be fulfilled; therefore they have to behave themselves in an appropriate way. The understanding here is that "now that the Lord your God is taking you into the land, therefore. . . ." Alternatively, the preposition "for," (Hebrew *kiy*) in Deuteronomy 8:7 could be translated "when," as in 6:10. It can be rephrased thus: "when the Lord your God brings you. . . ." In that case, the sentence runs through to the end of verse 10, and then the warning in verse 11 begins. The understanding here is, "When God brings you into the good land and you settle to enjoy the goods of the land, and are satisfied, you praise the Lord, . . . then beware that you do not forget the LORD your God, (by) failing to observe his commands, his laws and his decrees that I am giving you this day" (NIV, cf. 6:10-12).

In contrast to the barren wilderness land which the Israelites have been used to for the past 40 years, the Lord is about to bring them into a good, and productive land with bountiful agricultural resources. This land is adorned with natural water reserves, brooks, fountains, and deep reservoirs of water that shoot out (*yatsa`*, or spring out) in the valleys and hills. These water resources would make the land fertile and assure abundance of crops and fruit production. The land is full of all types agricultural products, so full that they would have enough and there would be no scarcity. The word used here for *scarceness* is *mickenuth* (pronounced **'mis-kay-nooth'**), which means "poverty or misery." Moses emphasizes that God has supplied everything for their life ahead that they would lack nothing in food and natural mineral resources, such as iron and brass (*nechosheth*, which is better translated as copper since brass is made of a combination of zinc and other materials). It is said that ancient iron and copper mines have been discovered in recent years below the Dead Sea in the valleys of Arabah. Iron and copper ore has also been discovered in the nearby hills.

10 When thou hast eaten and art full, then thou shalt bless the Lord thy God for the good land which he hath given thee.

After describing in detail the richness of this good and productive land, Moses calls on the Israelites to enjoy the provision God has given them and remain thankful: "thou shalt bless the Lord thy God for the good land." "When thou hast eaten and art full," refers to the enjoyment of God's provision for them; it also carries the idea of giving thanks or saying the grace before and after meals, which is a Jewish tradition and is practiced in most Christian homes as well. Here we have the idea that there is nothing wrong with enjoying the natural things with which God has blessed us. It therefore annuls the fallacy that those who live according to the ordinances of the Lord should live joyless

and unhappy lives. However, such enjoyment should be anchored on a continuous spirit of gratitude to the Provider of all things. This is a prescription for the proper response of gratitude for the blessings God gives. However, the common response is forgetfulness in times of prosperity, which Moses warns against in the following verses.

11 Beware that thou forget not the Lord thy God, in not keeping his commandments, and his judgments, and his statutes, which I command thee this day:

In verse 11, Moses comes out with a strong and stern warning against forgetting the Lord and what He has done for them. They should not take God's blessings for granted, or give the glory to other gods or to themselves. The idea here can best be expressed with an Igbo idiom, which says *Nwa nza rijuo afo, ya ekwe chi ya mgba*. This literally means that when *nwa nza* (a very tiny bird, the tiniest bird found in the tropics) over-feeds himself, he challenges his *chi* (god, i.e., the one who has provided for him) to a wrestling match. Moses gives an accurate prediction of Israel's natural inclination to forget God in times of prosperity and success. This attitude is not unique to Israel. Man, especially those who "have made it" according to worldly standards, is generally prone to quickly forget the history behind his success, and the benefactor of his prosperity—God. How soon and how often we give lame excuses for not worshiping God (not attending church services). How common it is to seek the Lord and pray for His blessing when we are in need, worship him constantly by attending church, and then withdraw immediately after our prayers are answered. Time always takes the blame, especially our lack of it. Here Moses tells them, surely you are going into the land with abundance, but while you are basking in the abundance of the land, "Be careful that you do not forget the LORD your God," (NIV), who gave you all the good things. The second part of the verse defines how this can happen: and that is by "failing to observe his commands, his laws and his decrees that I am giving you this day" (v. 11b, NIV). The word *forget* (*shakach* or *shakeach*) is more than having a mental lapse about something or someone, it means "to ignore, to cease to care." Moses' warning here is that it is possible to enjoy the blessings of the Lord and ignore God Himself by failing to obey His laws. Disobedience demonstrates a lack of love for the Lord.

12 Lest when thou hast eaten and art full, and hast built goodly houses, and dwelt therein; 13 And when thy herds and thy flocks multiply, and

thy silver and thy gold is multiplied, and all that thou hast is multiplied;

The same train of thought and warning is continued in verses 12 and following. Indeed, verses 11-17 comprise a long, single sentence in Hebrew which details different and specific blessings that would come their way in the land. These blessings, if the Israelites were not careful, would cause them to ignore (forget) the Lord. Verse 11 here looks like a summary or headline, and the rest of the verses like the body and detailed speech of a sermon. Moses predicts prosperity in various things: they would have plenty to eat; they would build good homes to live in; their domestic animals will increase in abundance; they will be blessed monetarily, in gold and silver and in everything. Nevertheless, they should not allow these riches to go to their heads, or cause them to puff up with pride so as to forget the Lord.

14 Then thine heart be lifted up, and thou forget the Lord thy God, which brought thee forth out of the land of Egypt, from the house of bondage; 15 Who led thee through that great and terrible wilderness, wherein were fiery serpents, and scorpions, and drought, where there was no water; who brought thee forth water out of the rock of flint; 16 Who fed thee in the wilderness with manna, which thy fathers knew not, that he might humble thee, and that he might prove thee, to do thee good at thy latter end; 17 And thou say in thine heart, My power and the might of mine hand hath gotten me this wealth.

Continuing to warn against laxity in their reverence to God and pride as a result of the abundance of the land, Moses reminds them once more where they have come from, and what made it possible for them to have these riches. Moses tells them that they should bear in mind that there would have been no prosperity if God had not brought them out of the land of Egypt and cared for them throughout their wandering in the wilderness for the 40 years (vv.14-16). He lists the various ways God cared for them throughout their journey, up to that point. God brought them out from the house of bondage; He led them through the desert and saved them from dangerous and poisonous animals, such as fiery serpents (Numbers 21:6) and scorpions; He miraculously gave them water from the rock (Exodus 17; Numbers 20); He supplied their food daily throughout the 40 years of wandering. Someone has estimated the total number of days that God cared for Israel in the wilderness as 15,065, and a total of 41 years and 3 months as how long it took them to journey from Egypt to

Canaan. We learned that the estimated number that left Egypt was 6,100,800 people including children (Exodus 12:37). This number must have at least doubled before they got to this point, considering the births and deaths that occurred along the way. Therefore, to care for this number of people for such a long time, would be tremendous, and yet the Lord supplied all their necessities. Hence, there is no room whatsoever for them to arrogate themselves to say in their hearts, "My power and the might of mine hand hath gotten me this wealth" (v. 17). That would mean "challenging God to a wrestling match." The writer of Proverbs realized this danger when he wrote: "Remove far from me vanity and lies: give me neither poverty nor riches; feed me with food convenient for me: Lest I be full, and deny thee, and say, Who is the LORD? or lest I be poor, and steal, and take the name of my God in vain" (Proverbs 30:8-9). It is interesting to note that all this care and provision in the wilderness for 40 years served the same purpose as the difficulties and obstacles they encountered. That is as a test to humble them and to prove them so as to know their hearts whether they would love God and keep His laws (vv. 2-6, 16), and to prepare them for latter years in the land (v. 16).

18 But thou shalt remember the Lord thy God: for it is he that giveth thee power to get wealth, that he may establish his covenant which he sware unto thy fathers, as it is this day.

Instead of arrogating themselves and claiming that they have achieved their prosperity through their own power, Moses cautions them to "remember the thy God" because he is the one that gives you the power to acquire wealth. The word *Power* (Hebrew *koach*, i.e., "strength or might") is best translated *ability*. Hence, Israel is to remember that Yahweh alone gave them the ability to acquire wealth. Moreover, whatever wealth they enjoy is the result of His covenant with their forefathers, in keeping with His character of faithfulness. The lesson here is that God gives power and ability to get wealth, and so wealth in itself is not sin (v. 18). It becomes sin when it is used contrary to the will and law of the Lord, or when it is acquired by foul or illegal means. It also becomes sinful when we occupy our hearts and minds with our wealth rather than the Lord and His law; when we worship the wealth rather the Giver of all wealth. We must acknowledge the fundamental Biblical economic principle, which David clearly articulated in the Psalm (24:1), that the earth and all that is in it belong to God. That He has given it to man for his use (Psalm 115:16). James confirms that every good and perfect gift comes from the Father above (James 1:17). Therefore, man has an obligation to remember the Lord, by ascribing to Him all the glory and honor due him for all the blessings he bestows on His people.

19 And it shall be, if thou do at all forget the Lord thy God, and walk after other gods, and serve them, and worship them, I testify against you this day that ye shall surely perish. 20 As the nations which the Lord destroyeth before your face, so shall ye perish; because ye would not be obedient unto the voice of the Lord your God.

Verses 19 and 20 serve as the climax of the chapter and reinforce the thrust of the whole passage—warning against apostasy and rejection of Yahweh as the true God. Here, especially verse 19, Moses precisely defines what it means to "forget the Lord," and that is to "walk after other gods, and serve them, and worship them," which, in short, is disobeying of the first commandment (Exodus 20:2ff). While in the Book of Exodus the consequence of disobeying this commandment is not explicit, in this verse Moses clearly prescribes the punishment that awaits such rebellion. The phrase translated as "If thou do at all forget the Lord thy God," is a doubling of the Hebrew word for forget, rendered *shaakoach tishkach*, (literally, forget) which gives the emphasis and the seriousness of the warning. That is to say "if by any means" (i.e., after you have seen the great things and experienced the good things the Lord has done for you, from the bondage of Egypt to the bounty of the Promised Land (vv. 12-16), "you forget the Lord your God" by following other gods, "ye shall surely perish" (v. 19). In stating "Ye shall surely perish," Moses again applies a double Hebrew verb *'abad*, meaning "perish" but written thus: *'aabod to'beeduwn*, which is rendered "surely, or definitely die"; there is no way they could escape the punishment. God will definitely keep this negative part of the deal just as He is faithful to keep the positive part of blessing them

when they do well. Here there is no option of either following God or other gods, neither is there any place for following both the Lord and other gods. God's warning is clear and precise. Either they follow the Lord totally and live, or follow the other gods of the land, and perish. This punishment is consistent with God's character of justice. He is no respecter of persons. He promises to destroy Israel for the same reason he commanded the Israelites to ruthlessly exterminate the nations (Deuteronomy 7). We read in that chapter that the destruction of the inhabitants of Canaan was not arbitrary, but because of their idolatry, which is explicitly spelled out in the chapter 9. The gift of the land to Israel is therefore not just a sign of favoritism on His part, but a two-way deal that requires total allegiance to God if Israel is to enjoy the land permanently and to the fullest. Failure to obey the law results in the same punishment as meted out to the other nations. In spite of this chilling warning and threat, the sin of apostasy unfortunately plagued the Children of Israel throughout their history, especially throughout the time of the judges, and often led to their servitude and exile. The demand for an unflinching obedience to the law is effective for all nations at all times, and through His grace God has given us a way of escape through His Son. All that we need is to believe on Him, and we shall be saved from eternal damnation.

DAILY BIBLE READING

M: Don't Let Prosperity Spoil You
Deuteronomy 8:1-10
T: You Are Not Self-Made People
Deuteronomy 8:11-20
W: You Were a Stubborn Bunch
Deuteronomy 9:6-14
T: God Heard Moses on Your Behalf
Deuteronomy 9:15-21
F: Moses Interceded for Israel Again
Deuteronomy 9:25-29
S: Beware of False Prophets
Deuteronomy 13:1-5
S: Purge Those Who Worship False gods
Deuteronomy 13:6-11

TEACHING TIPS

November 7
Bible Study Guide 10

1. Words You Should Know

A. Beth-poer (34:6)—the place near where Moses died and was buried. The land belonged to the tribe of Reuben. The name means "house of Peor," and was named for the god Peor. It is believed the temple of Peor was once located there.

B. Sepulchre (34:7)—a tomb or grave; the word is translated from a Hebrew word describing a space carved out of a large rock wherein bodies were placed. In ancient Palestine, sepulchres were generally carved out of the walls of existing caves. Families were buried together on the carved slabs of stone. When a body had decayed to the skeleton, the remains were then placed in a hole farther back in the cave, allowing another body to be placed in the sepulchre.

2. Teacher Preparation

Read the background Scripture for this lesson. As you read today's lesson, pay careful attention to Moses' relationship to Joshua and his concern for what would take place even after his death.

3. Starting the Lesson

A. Ask class members to share a time when an older, wiser person gave them advice which gave them courage to face a difficult or challenging situation. Spend some time discussing how people often begin to see things differently when they grow older and have spent more time walking with the Lord.

B. Read the IN FOCUS story about Dr. Lewis and Rev. Powell and the transition of leadership in that church. Why are such transitions sometimes difficult?

4. Getting into the Lesson

As you discuss the lesson, examine some of the characteristics of Israel as a nation of people. Discuss whether any group of people would have needed to be reminded constantly of God's goodness, as Israel did. Might other groups have responded differently? Would any group of people, under conditions similar to Israel's, soon have forgotten God's blessings and disobeyed Him as Israel did?

5. Relating the Lesson to Life

A. Review the information about Joshua, Moab, and the Jordan River from THE PEOPLE, PLACES, AND TIMES. Guide class members toward learning more about the people and events which are a central part of the journey into the Promised Land.

B. Give students an opportunity to answer the questions in SEARCH THE SCRIPTURES.

C. Using information in DISCUSS THE MEANING, examine the various aspects of the transition in leadership and how the two men handled the situation. Think about how many modern-day churches can learn from the relationship between Moses and Joshua.

D. The LESSON IN OUR SOCIETY focuses on the qualities and character of a godly leader. Think of other leaders who have possessed qualities like Moses and Dr. King, especially leaders from your church, city, or region.

6. Arousing Action

A. Using the information on leadership from this study, encourage class members to debate the familiar question: Are good leaders born or made?

B. Allow members to complete the MAKE IT HAPPEN activity. Allow them to discuss seeds they might have sown which will benefit another generation or which they might not see harvested.

C. Give class members an opportunity to complete FOLLOW THE SPIRIT and REMEMBER YOUR THOUGHTS.

JOSHUA SUCCEEDS MOSES

Bible Background • DEUTERONOMY 31:1-8; 34
Printed Text • DEUTERONOMY 31:1-8; 34:5-8a, 9
Devotional Reading • NUMBERS 27:12-23

LESSON AIM

Today's lesson should help to strengthen students' understanding and interpretation of what it means to be a godly leader.

KEEP IN MIND

"And the LORD, he it is that doth go before thee; he will be with thee, he will not fail thee, neither forsake thee: fear not, neither be dismayed" (Deuteronomy 31:8).

FOCAL VERSES

DEUTERONOMY   31:1
And Moses went and spake these words unto all Israel.

2 And he said unto them, I am an hundred and twenty years old this day; I can no more go out and come in: also the LORD hath said unto me, Thou shalt not go over this Jordan.

3 The LORD thy God, he will go over before thee, and he will destroy these nations from before thee, and thou shalt possess them: and Joshua, he shall go over before thee, as the LORD hath said.

4 And the LORD shall do unto them as he did to Sihon and to Og, kings of the Amorites, and unto the land of them, whom he destroyed.

5 And the LORD shall give them up before your face, that ye may do unto them according unto all the commandments which I have commanded you.

6 Be strong and of a good courage, fear not, nor be afraid of them: for the LORD thy God, he it is that doth go with thee; he will not fail thee, nor forsake thee.

7 And Moses called unto Joshua, and said unto him in the sight of all Israel, Be strong and of a good courage: for thou must go with this people unto the land which the LORD hath sworn unto their fathers to give them; and thou

LESSON OVERVIEW

LESSON AIM
KEEP IN MIND
FOCAL VERSES
IN FOCUS
THE PEOPLE, PLACES, AND TIMES
BACKGROUND
AT-A-GLANCE
IN DEPTH
SEARCH THE SCRIPTURES
DISCUSS THE MEANING
LESSON IN OUR SOCIETY
MAKE IT HAPPEN
FOLLOW THE SPIRIT
REMEMBER YOUR THOUGHTS
MORE LIGHT ON THE TEXT
DAILY BIBLE READINGS

shalt cause them to inherit it.

8 And the LORD, he it is that doth go before thee; he will be with thee, he will not fail thee, neither forsake thee: fear not, neither be dismayed.

34:5 So Moses the servant of the LORD died there in the land of Moab, according to the word of the LORD.

6 And he buried him in a valley in the land of Moab, over against Beth-peor: but no man knoweth of his sepulchre unto this day.

7 And Moses was an hundred and twenty years old when he died: his eye was not dim, nor his natural force abated.

8 And the children of Israel wept for Moses in the plains of Moab thirty days:

9 And Joshua the son of Nun was full of the spirit of wisdom; for Moses had laid his hands upon him: and the children of Israel hearkened unto him, and did as the LORD commanded Moses.

IN FOCUS

Dr. Lewis breathed a sign of relief after a long day at church. His retirement service had gone well. They had even given him the honor of naming him pastor emeritus of the church.

Dr. Lewis knew he would miss being at the church on a daily basis, but he was also looking forward to helping a group of churches start a Bible college in their area. A school to train ministers was long overdue in their little neck of the woods.

He knew the church would be in good hands, though. Young Rev. Powell was a dynamic preacher who was full of the Holy Spirit and had a heart for the people. The two had labored together in the pulpit for the last three years. When Dr. Lewis knew that it was time for him to move on to another form of ministry, the church easily accepted the leadership of Rev. Powell.

As much as Dr. Lewis was looking forward to getting the Bible college started, he was also looking forward to going on a long awaited fishing trip!

THE PEOPLE, PLACES, AND TIMES

JOSHUA. Leader of the Israelites who initially took control of Canaan, the Promised Land. His name, which means "Yahweh delivered" is appropriate as it was he who led Israel into the Promised Land.

Born in Egypt during Israel's period of bondage there, he was a member of the tribe of Ephraim. Joshua served as Moses' servant. He was on the mountain with Moses when he received the commandments. Joshua was also one of the 12 spies sent out to investigate Canaan. Only he and Caleb returned with a favorable report.

Joshua was a capable administrator for his people and proved to be effective in maintaining harmony among people and groups.

Based on information from *Holman Bible Dictionary*, Trent Butler, general editor. Nashville: Broadman & Holman Publishers, 1991, p. 816.

MOAB. A narrow strip of land located directly east of the Dead Sea. The history of Moab is linked with that of Israel. The Moabites were regarded by the Israelites as close relatives (Genesis 19:30-38). There were times of peace and conflict between the two nations. The story of Ruth illustrates peaceful relationships with Moab. Conversely, Saul reportedly fought with the Moabites (1 Samuel 14:47).

Based on information from *Holman Bible Dictionary*, pp. 982-983.

JORDAN RIVER. The longest and most important river of Palestine. It rises from the foot of Mount Harmon and flows into the Dead Sea. Due to the twists and turns of its course, the Jordan is over 200 miles long. Through its descending course, the river passes through a variety of climates and terrains. The name means "the descender."

The Jordan River and Jordan Valley played an important role in a number of memorable events from both the Old and New Testaments. The first mention of the Jordan occurs in the story of Abram and Lot (Genesis 13:11). Under Joshua's leadership, Israel crossed the Jordan "on dry ground." The Jordan is also the featured site of many

of the miracles performed by Elijah and Elisha. In the New Testament, the most significant event occurring at the Jordan is the baptism of Jesus, performed by John the Baptist.

Based on information from *Holman Bible Dictionary*, pp. 813-814.

BACKGROUND

The time had drawn very near when Israel would cross the Jordan River to enter the Promised Land. Throughout their journey, including the 40 years in the wilderness, Moses had led his people according to the will of God. But because of the people's sin, God was angry with Moses and would not allow Him to enter the Promised Land (Deuteronomy 4:21-22; 31:2).

Heretofore, Moses has been preparing his people to enter the land, knowing he would not be there with them. A true leader, he continued to show concern for Israel, admonishing them in a series of sermons to obey Yahweh and not to forget the blessings He bestowed upon their forebears.

As their time together draws to a close, there were some practical considerations that needed to addressed for the good of the people. The torch of leadership had to be passed on. Moses appointed his successor at the holiest place of their encampment the Tent of Meeting.

AT-A-GLANCE

**1. Moses' Farewell to His People
(Deuteronomy 31:1-8)
2. The Death of Moses
(Deuteronomy 34:5-9)**

IN DEPTH

1. Moses' Farewell to His People
(Deuteronomy 31:1-8)

Moses' life can be broken down into three periods of 40 years. His first 40 years were spent in the house of Pharaoh. His second 40 years were spent with Jethro. Moses' final 40 years were spent with the Israelites on their way to Canaan. At age 120, Moses feels he can go on no longer.

In a farewell talk to Israel, Moses acknowledged his advanced age and his infirmity as part of the reason he would go no further on the journey with Israel. Moses also cites the fact that the Lord had already decided not to allow him to lead Israel's advance into Canaan. The Lord would

to Joshua. He must have felt confident that Joshua would be honest and do right by all the people of Israel. The new land would have to be divided equitably among the tribes. Such an important task could not be left to someone who could not be trusted to divide the land with equity, not showing favoritism to his own tribe. The Lord would assure Joshua of His divine presence.

Moses knew that his time of leadership was drawing to a close. He gave up leadership of his people to Joshua. He did not look for ways to fail Joshua. Instead, he gave words of encouragement to Joshua to help him be an even better leader to Israel.

Moses exhibited a high degree of confidence in both Joshua and Israel. The foundation was already laid. The people would be "strong and of a good courage." Everyone was prepared for what was about to take place.

2. The Death of Moses (Deuteronomy 34:5-9)

The Lord continued to care for Moses during and after his time of death. Moses died in the region of Moab and was buried in an undisclosed grave. His burial was taken care of by the Lord.

Even though Moses was 120 years old at the time of his death, he was not without strength. Apparently, he was still relatively agile in his advanced age. Moses was able to act on courage and faith to say, "not my will, but thine, O Lord."

Verse 7 reveals Moses' physical and mental condition at the time of his death. Apparently, for a man his age, Moses was in relative good health. His eyesight was still good and his mental functioning was still vibrant. The Hebrew phrase which is translated as *nor his natural force abated*, only occurs here in the Old Testament. The Hebrew word for *fled* is understood to mean "moist" or "fresh." It is generally used to describe trees, wood, and fruit which is new or green, not dried. In some nonbiblical documents the word has been used as "life force," apparently to depict strength as the time of death drew near. Therefore, even at the end of his life, the Lord blessed Moses with a strong mind and an energized spirit.

In order to fully equip Joshua to assume to his role as Israel's leader, the Spirit of wisdom came upon Joshua because Moses had laid his hands on Joshua. The Spirit gave him the gift of wisdom, which would serve to guide Joshua through the many difficult decisions he would have to make.

The gift of the Spirit is a gift of empowerment. God does not want weak leaders directing His people. Joshua needed resources which were far beyond the human ability in order to successfully lead God's people. Moses laid

personally lead Israel into the Promised Land.

Moses relays this information to Israel with calm assurance and objectivity. In spite of the fact that he will not enter the Promised Land, Moses was still concerned for Israel's future. But with God leading them, their success was certain.

Moses assured Israel that the Lord would go before Israel to defeat the nations and possess the land. The Lord would destroy Israel's enemies just has He had destroyed other armies. Their enemies would be destroyed right before their eyes. The Lord was going to deliver Israel's enemies to them to assure their victory.

Then, in a public show of unity and continuity, Moses summoned Joshua to come before all of Israel. Before the assembly, Moses charged Joshua to be strong and courageous. Moses passed the torch to his faithful assistant. As Israel's new leader, Joshua had the responsibility to go with Israel into the Promised Land.

Obviously, Joshua was a man of high integrity. Moses appeared to have no reservation in transferring the reigns hands on him, perhaps in an official ceremony, to demonstrate to all of Israel that Joshua had been consecrated to assume the office of Israel's leader.

Yet, no matter how fully and ably equipped Israel was to enter Canaan, the loss of Moses cut a deep wound. As a free people, they had known no leader but him. It was Moses who single-handedly took a group of former slaves loosely linked by religion and blood and bonded them together as a nation. For their sake, Moses was willing to be kept from the land he had labored so hard to bring his people to.

His complete devotion and dedication to Yahweh had inspired Israel to perform acts they previously had not thought possible. From the time he approached the burning bush at Horeb to the leading of the ceremonials at Moab, Moses gave himself in service to the Lord. He was God's instrument.

Moses has been depicted by some scholars as a "guilt offering" to God on Israel's behalf. He bore the sins of his people and pleaded for their forgiveness. At the very least, Moses provided Israel with a new opportunity and mercy for their sins.

SEARCH THE SCRIPTURES

1. How old was Moses when he told Israel he would not go into the Promised Land with them? (Deuteronomy 31:2)

2. Who was going to go with them to destroy the nations they would face? (v. 3)

3. Who would become their new leader? (v. 3)

4. What did Moses say the Lord would do for Israel? (vv. 4-5)

5. What were Moses' last instructions to Israel? (31:6)

6. Who did Moses affirm as the new leader of Israel? (v. 7)

7. What advice did Moses give to Joshua? (v. 8)

8. After Moses wrote the law, where did he put it? (v. 9)

9. Name the land where Moses died. (Deuteronomy 34:5)

10. Who buried Moses' body? (v. 6)

11. What was Moses' physical and mental condition at the time of his death? (v. 7)

12. How long did Israel mourn Moses' death? (v. 8)

DISCUSS THE MEANING

1. What could have happened if Moses had been rebellious and disobedient and decided to resist giving up the reigns?

2. Why was Moses required to stay behind because of the sins of his people? Do you think God's decision was "fair" to Moses? Why can we not use the human measure of fairness to try and understand the ways of God?

3. How do you think Joshua was impacted by Moses' example and leadership style?

LESSON IN OUR SOCIETY

Every person cannot serve as one of God's leaders. A servant who possesses the character and commitment to God's call as Moses did is rare. Occasionally, we are able to witness such a servant of God in action. Not every leader is willing to work tirelessly to help those following to reach their goal. Leaders who are willing to work tirelessly knowing they will never partake of the fruit of the harvest are even more rare.

Dr. Martin Luther King, Jr. was that caliber of leader. He labored for an effort he knew he would never see come to fruition. Israel prospered in the land to which Moses guided them. Similarly, African Americans and persons of various races, religions, creeds, colors, and incomes have a foundation on which to build a prosperous life, partly because of the efforts of Dr. King.

Every leader should be willing to lead an effort, even if he or she will never benefit from that effort personally.

MAKE IT HAPPEN

Have you avoided participating in or leading a project or movement because you believe you will never see any benefit from your labor.

Keeping the following quotation in mind, write down some work you have left undone: "Judge each day, not by the harvest you reap, but by the seeds you sow."

Think about seeds you have sown which are still producing a harvest or which may not produce a harvest in your lifetime.

FOLLOW THE SPIRIT

What God wants me to do:

_____

_____

REMEMBER YOUR THOUGHTS

Special insights you learned:

_____

_____

MORE LIGHT ON THE TEXT
DEUTERONOMY 31:1-8; 34:5-8

The Children of Israel are at the final stage of their 40 years journey to the Promised Land under the leadership of Moses. The covenant God made with their forefathers is about to become a reality. Moses has accomplished his assignment, and he is to transfer leadership to Joshua. Joshua will be leading the people in the final phase of the trip. They have now reached the outskirts of Canaan on the plains of Moab by the Jordan River. Moses summons the people's attention, gives them his final counsel, and introduces their new leader, Joshua. This speech is, however, a continuation of the final address he started at the beginning of the book.

31:1 And Moses went and spake these words unto all Israel. 2 And he said unto them, I am an hundred and twenty years old this day; I can no more go out and come in: also the Lord hath said unto me, Thou shalt not go over this Jordan.

Here begins the last counsel and blessing of Moses to the Children of Israel—his farewell speech, his charge and official transfer of leadership authority to Joshua. Moses begins first by addressing the people, and encouraging them to be strong and resolute in their trust in the leadership of Yahweh, who will never fail or abandon them, for He is the real leader (vv. 1-7). Second, he addresses Joshua and commissions him for the task ahead, encouraging him to be strong and courageous in the Lord's leadership (vv. 7-8). Verse 1 reads literally that "Moses went and spake these words (things) to Israel." Some scholars interpret this as, "When Moses had finished speaking all these words, to all the children of Israel, he said to the. . . ." The idea in this interpretation is that when he had ceased talking to them for some time, he later came again and began speaking again. Others see it as a continuation of the address which he started at the beginning of the book. Although there is a division among scholars on this issue, the main point should not be forgotten, and that is the importance of the address. It seems that Moses has been giving them charges regarding the law and their relationship with Lord, and how they are to comport themselves in obedience to the law of God when they enter the land. Now he addresses them concerning the threat of the Canaanites and the obstacles they are going to face. Although he is not going to be with them any more, God is still with them to go before them. These first verses serve as a transition from a former topic to something new—the immediate challenges they are about to face, including the change in leadership. Therefore, although it is probably a continuation of his final address, the verse also contains an introduction to a new but an important topic which requires the people's attention. Like changing gears when driving, Moses turns to another point in a speech.

Moses begins by reminding them of his age and his limitation for leadership. He tells them, "I am an hundred and twenty years old this day," and that his leadership is about to end. He follows with a number of reasons why he could no longer lead them to the Promised Land. First, "I can no more go out and come in," seems to suggest physical frailty and inability to carry on his leadership duties. However, the account in 34:7, as we shall see later, does not seem to support this idea, for it clearly states that "his eye was not dim, nor his natural force abated" when he died. The reason he could no longer go out and come in was more likely because of the divine decree that he should die that very day (34:1-8). He knows that his mission, by divine revelation, is ending and he knows he would soon die. The spirit of leadership has left him. After this day, he is no longer able to lead them across the Jordan. The second reason, which is very much related to the first, is that the Lord has told him, "Thou shalt not go over this Jordan" (3:23-29; 32:50-52; cf. Numbers 20:11-12). The Jordan was therefore the boundary of his life's journey, and he is quite aware of it. It is therefore not a surprise to him, hence he calls his people to give them the last charge and advice, like an old man at the point of death who gathers his family and relations to give them the last counsel before he passes on.

3 The Lord thy God, he will go over before thee, and he will destroy these nations from before thee, and thou shalt possess them: and Joshua, he shall go over before thee, as the Lord hath said.

God will continue to be the leader of Israel as He has been from the beginning, Moses assures them. Even when Moses was at the helm, it is God who was leading (Exodus 3:8) and used Moses to carry out His plans (Exodus 3:10). This fact is not going to change when Moses passes on. Yahweh will still go before them to the land of promise. "He will go over before thee," here suggests that the Lord Himself will cross over ahead of them to the land (Deuteronomy 31:3a), and probably means the crossing of the Jordan. He will not only go before them to overcome the natural obstacle, the river Jordan, the Lord will victoriously fight their battles and destroy the nations before them, the human obstacle to their possession of the land. Then they would take over the land. He has earlier assured them of Yahweh's presence and victory over the nations:

"Understand therefore this day, that the LORD thy God is he which goeth over before thee; as a consuming fire he shall destroy them, and he shall bring them down before thy face: so shalt thou drive them out, and destroy them quickly, as the LORD hath said unto thee" *(Deuteronomy 9:3).*

Although Yahweh will accomplish these things for them, He will use Joshua as His instrument. Joshua will be the human leader—God's representative and co-regent. The appointment of Joshua has been made known to them before this time (1:37-38; 3:28). Therefore, it should not be news to them, but a reassurance of God's plan and purpose. There is, therefore, no reason for panic or anxiety. The Lord will neither withdraw His divine leadership after the death of Moses, nor leave them without a human leader like Moses. The leadership qualities of Joshua have already been proven when he led the battle against the Amalekites (Exodus 17:8-13).

4 And the Lord shall do unto them as he did to Sihon and to Og, kings of the Amorites, and unto the land of them, whom he destroyed. 5 And the Lord shall give them up before your face, that ye may do unto them according unto all the commandments which I have commanded you. 6 Be strong and of a good courage, fear not, nor be afraid of them: for the Lord thy God, he it is that doth go with thee; he will not fail thee, nor forsake thee.

As reassurance of the Lord's leading, Moses tells them that the Lord would overthrow the inhabitants of the land as He had done to the kings of the Amorites—Sihon and Og (Numbers 21:34; 32:33; Deuteronomy 1:4; 2:24ff; 3:2ff; 4:46-47). The inhabitants of Amon under Sihon and Og resisted the passage of the Israelites, and the Lord overthrew them and gave the land to Israel, to the tribes of Reuben, Gad, and Manasseh as their possession (Deuteronomy 29:7-8). As the Lord has given these people to you, so shall He deliver the rest of the nations to you "that ye may do unto them according unto all the commandments which I have commanded you." The command is to destroy the inhabitants of Canaan (7:2). In the light of God's promise and His leadership, Moses uses two sets of four strong Hebrews words (two positively and two negatively) to encourage them to be resolute and strong as they face the immediate future. The first set are positive and almost synonymous: "Be strong" (Hebrew *chazaq*), i.e., to fasten upon, to take hold, to be courageous, to stand firm; and "of good courage" (*'amats*), i.e., to be alert, brave, bold or to be determined. The second set, which are expressed negatively and identical in meaning are "fear not, nor be afraid of them" literally "do not" (*'al*) "fear" (*yare*) and "do not" (*'al*) "be afraid" (*'arats*) (*aw-rats*), i.e., to be dreadful, to be frightened, or to be terrified, "of them." Moses probably thinks that this reassurance and encouragement is nec-

essary in view of their past experience. Their forefathers, frightened on hearing the report of the spies, rebelled against the Lord and it caused them to miss the Promised Land, and 40 years delay in the wilderness (cf. Numbers 13—14; see our October 10, 1999 study). In essence, Moses says to them, although there may be giants in the land, which cause panic, be resolute, bold, and hold fast to the Lord's leadership, for "He will go over before thee, and He will destroy these nations from before thee" (cf. Deuteronomy 31:3). God is not going to "fail" (*raphah*) or disappoint you, and He is not going to "forsake you." The picture is that of children abandoned by their parents without anyone to care. This tragedy is common place in many war-torn areas of the world where both the parents abandon their children in flight for their lives, or where the parents are killed and children are left without parents to care for them. Here the Lord, through Moses, assures the people that He would not leave them as orphans, He will always be with them. There is no greater assurance than the promise of the divine presence and the constancy of Yahweh with those who trust in Him (4:31; Joshua 1:5; Isaiah 41:17; 42:16; 44:21; etc.).

7 And Moses called unto Joshua, and said unto him in the sight of all Israel, Be strong and of a good courage: for thou must go with this people unto the land which the Lord hath sworn unto their fathers to give them; and thou shalt cause them to inherit it. 8 And the Lord, he it is that doth go before thee; he will be with thee, he will not fail thee, neither forsake thee: fear not, neither be dismayed.

Moses gives the same assurance and encouragement to Joshua and commissions him to go and lead the people to inherit the land according to the covenant of the Lord with their forefathers. The phrase "for thou must go with this people unto the land" leaves no room for choice. It is a divine order that must be obeyed, Moses seems to tell him. Although the Lord has commissioned Joshua, the real leader is Yahweh Himself. He uses Joshua only as a human instrument. As the people are charged to trust strongly and boldly in God, Joshua is to also look on the Lord for leadership. Using exactly the same words, Moses bids him to be strong and resolute promising him God's divine presence and care. He, however, added another word translated as "don't be dismayed" (*chathath*), which is synonymous with "fear" (*yare*) and "afraid" (*'arats*) (v. 6), to admonish Joshua not to be broken (in spirit or in heart), or to faint or become discouraged (i.e., to be shattered).

34:5 So Moses the servant of the Lord died there in the land of Moab, according to the word of the Lord. 6 And he buried him in a valley in the land of Moab, over against Beth-peor: but no man knoweth of his sepulchre unto this day.

The following verses give the account of the death of Moses in the land of Moab. Earlier in this chapter (vv. 1-4), we learn that Moses went up Mount Nebo to the mountain summit of Pisgah, and there the Lord shows him the Promised Land. There he dies. Here we have one of the 18 times Moses is described as the servant of the Lord in the Bible (Joshua 1:1, 13, 15; 8:31, 33; 11:12; etc.). The phrase "according to the word of the Lord" refers to God's command that he would only see the land, but would not enter it (v. 4b; 3:27). The pronoun "he" in the phrase "he buried him in a valley in the land of Moab" is generally assumed to refer to Yahweh as the one who buried Moses. The context supports this. Some scholars suggest that, although Yahweh buried Moses, He used agents, some companions with Moses. If that is true, then the next phrase, "but no man knoweth of his sepulchre unto this day" would be contradictory. There is nothing to support the assumption. Indeed, there seems to be no reason why the names of the people who buried him should be omitted here. There is need to speculate here, other than to accept what the Bible informs us. Since no one knew where he was buried, we can only assume that he went to the top of the mountain alone (vv. 1-4) and never returned, or was taken out the sight of the people. However, according to this record, "he is buried." Why was his burial place kept a secret? The most likely reason is that the Lord kept it secret so that Israel would not pay him homage (like other religions) or worship Moses as a god like the pagans do.

7 And Moses was an hundred and twenty years old when he died: his eye was not dim, nor his natural force abated. 8 And the children of Israel wept for Moses in the plains of Moab thirty days . . .

Verse 7 gives us the actual age of Moses at his death. According to biblical records, Moses died the youngest of his kindred at age 120. Levi his great great-grandfather died at the age of 137 years; his great-grandfather Kohath was 133 years; his father Amram was 137; Aaron his brother died at age 123 (Exodus 6:16ff; Numbers 33:39). His sister Miriam was 126 or more when she died (Numbers 20:1). The state of Moses' health is described here as healthy because "his eye was not dim" (*kahah* i.e., weak, or dull) "nor his natural force abated" (*leach* i.e., the

freshness of unimpaired). Therefore, his vision was sound and his physical strength never diminished (see the discussion on v. 2 above). The Children of Israel gave him a full burial rite according to their custom (cf. Numbers 20:29 for Aaron) by mourning 30 days for him.

9 And Joshua the son of Nun was full of the spirit of wisdom; for Moses had laid his hands upon him: and the children of Israel hearkened unto him, and did as the Lord commanded Moses.

After the death of Moses, the reins of leadership fall on the shoulders of Joshua, and this is authenticated by the gift of wisdom. The divine gift of wisdom is required by every one of Israel's leaders to be able to lead or govern the whole nation (e.g., Solomon). Moses had laid his hand upon him, which symbolizes imparting of grace and authority, and transfer of leadership (Numbers 27:1-23; cf. Numbers 8:10; Acts 6:6; 1 Timothy 4:14; 2 Timothy 1:6). God gives the gift of wisdom for needed work.

The people listened to Joshua and did all that the Lord had commanded through Moses.

DAILY BIBLE READING

M: God Will Lead Israel Across Jordan
Deuteronomy 31:1-6

T: Read and Obey the Law
Deuteronomy 31:7-13

W: Joshua Is Commissioned to Succeed Moses
Deuteronomy 31:14-23

T: Death of Moses in Moab
Deuteronomy 34:1-7

F: Moses Is Mourned and Remembered
Deuteronomy 34:8-12

S: God's Promise and Command to Joshua
Joshua 1:1-9

S: Israel Prepared to Cross the Jordan
Joshua 1:10-16

TEACHING TIPS

November 14
Bible Study Guide 11

1. Words You Should Know

A. Cubit (v. 4)—a unit of measure of approximately 18 inches. The general measure of a cubit was the interpreted as the span from the elbow to the tip of the middle finger. The amount of space to be maintained between the Israelites and the ark was 2,000 cubits.

B. Sanctify (v. 5)—purify or set apart. Israel needed to be ready for the battle ahead.

2. Teacher Preparation

Read the background Scripture for this lesson. As you read today's lesson, try to empathize with Joshua's fear and concern in taking on the huge responsibility of becoming Israel's new leader.

3. Starting the Lesson

Read the IN FOCUS story about Kim and Juanita. Discuss why people often try to discourage others from taking risks—even when the decision to go forward is rooted in faith.

4. Getting into the Lesson

As you discuss today's lesson, review some symbols of the Christian faith that are generally displayed in our churches and homes. Discuss how those objects can strengthen us as they often serve as reminders of God's presence.

5. Relating the Lesson to Life

A. Review the information about the Levites and the other people who were so much a part of Israel's life as they entered Canaan from THE PEOPLE, PLACES, AND TIMES. Help class members understand why the other cultures who inhabited Canaan often had a negative influence on Israel.

B. Give students an opportunity to answer the questions in SEARCH THE SCRIPTURES.

C. Using information in DISCUSS THE MEANING, examine the methods God used to fulfill His promise to His people. Does the modern day Christian understanding differ from the Old Testament Jewish understanding of how God provides for us and delivers us?

D. The LESSON IN OUR SOCIETY relates the difficulty people often face when embarking upon a new experience. Discuss why faith and trust in God are especially important to us during those periods.

6. Arousing Action

A. Ask for a volunteer to share a time when God gave him or her assurance of His presence during an uncertain or difficult time.

B. Allow time to complete the MAKE IT HAPPEN activity. Allow class members to discuss feelings they may have that God is leading them to move into a new stage or vocation in life.

C. Give class members and opportunity to complete FOLLOW THE SPIRIT and REMEMBER YOUR THOUGHTS.

ISRAEL CROSSES THE JORDAN RIVER

Bible Background • JOSHUA 3
Printed Text • JOSHUA 3:7-17
Devotional Reading • JOSHUA 4:15-24

LESSON AIM

Today's lesson should help students to know that God requires His people to step out on faith and trust in Him to accomplish His goals.

KEEP IN MIND

"Have not I commanded thee? Be strong and of a good courage; be not afraid, neither be thou dismayed: for the LORD thy God is with thee whithersoever thou goest" (Joshua 1:9).

FOCAL VERSES

JOSHUA 3:3 And they commanded the people, saying, When ye see the ark of the covenant of the LORD your God, and the priests the Levites bearing it, then ye shall remove from your place, and go after it.

4 Yet there shall be a space between you and it, about two thousand cubits by measure: come not near unto it, that ye may know the way by which ye must go: for ye have not passed this way heretofore.

5 And Joshua said unto the people, Sanctify yourselves: for tomorrow the LORD will do wonders among you.

6 And Joshua spake unto the priests, saying, Take up the ark of the covenant, and pass over before the people. And they took up the ark of the covenant, and went before the people.

7 And the LORD said unto Joshua, This day will I begin to magnify thee in the sight of all Israel, that they may know that, as I was with Moses, so I will be with thee.

8 And thou shalt command the priests that bear the ark of the covenant, saying, When ye are come to the brink of

LESSON OVERVIEW

LESSON AIM
KEEP IN MIND
FOCAL VERSES
IN FOCUS
THE PEOPLE, PLACES, AND TIMES
BACKGROUND
AT-A-GLANCE
IN DEPTH
SEARCH THE SCRIPTURES
DISCUSS THE MEANING
LESSON IN OUR SOCIETY
MAKE IT HAPPEN
FOLLOW THE SPIRIT
REMEMBER YOUR THOUGHTS
MORE LIGHT ON THE TEXT
DAILY BIBLE READINGS

the water of Jordan, ye shall stand still in Jordan.

9 And Joshua said unto the children of Israel, Come hither, and hear the words of the LORD your God.

10 And Joshua said, Hereby ye shall know that the living God is among you, and that he will without fail drive out from before you the Canaanites, and the Hittites, and the Hivites, and the Perizzites, and the Girgashites, and the Amorites, and the Jebusites.

11 Behold, the ark of the covenant of the Lord of all the earth passeth over before you into Jordan.

12 Now therefore take you twelve men out of the tribes of Israel, out of every tribe a man.

13 And it shall come to pass, as soon as the soles of the feet of the priests that bear the ark of the LORD, the Lord of all the earth, shall rest in the waters of Jordan, that the waters of Jordan shall be cut off from the waters that come down from above; and they shall stand upon an heap.

14 And it came to pass, when the people removed from their tents, to pass over Jordan, and the priests bearing the ark of the covenant before the people;

15 And as they that bare the ark were come unto Jordan, and the feet of the priests that bare the ark were dipped in the brim of the water, (for Jordan overfloweth all his banks all the time of harvest,)

16 That the waters which came down from above stood and rose up upon an heap very far from the city Adam, that is beside Zaretan: and those that came down toward the sea of the plain, even the salt sea, failed, and were cut off: and the people passed over right against Jericho.

17 And the priests that bare the ark of the covenant of the LORD stood firm on dry ground in the midst of Jordan, and all the Israelites passed over on dry ground, until all the people were passed clean over Jordan.

IN FOCUS

Kim and her mother, Juanita were sitting at the kitchen table going over the fourth quarter's receipts from their consignment shop for children's clothing. When they opened a year ago, so many people had predicted they would not stay open more than a few months. Instead of folding, they had made over four times what they projected for the first year.

People had told them that no one in their neighborhood would support a consignment shop. There were so many naysayers that after a while, Kim began to have her doubts. But Juanita was undeterred. She explained to Kim, "I know this is what we are supposed to do. The Lord showed me that a store like this is needed, not just to help us make money, but to help hard-working parents get quality, affordable clothes for their children."

A few months after they opened, a couple of other people tried to open similar shops, but they did not stay open more than a couple of months. Kim told Juanita that she believed they had been successful because they looked at their store as a type of ministry which helped parents stretch their dollars. After every season, Juanita and Kim decided to give the clothes that didn't sell to the women and children's shelter.

"It just goes to prove," Juanita said, "If the Lord tells you to do something, you should go forward in faith and not pay attention to other folks' negative talk!"

THE PEOPLE, PLACES, AND TIMES

LEVITES. This is the lowest of three orders of Israelite priesthood. God chose the tribe of Levi to carry out the responsibilities of the priesthood. Originally, Israel's priests and temple personnel where selected from the firstborn male of every family in Israel. The tribe of Levi was appointed because they were the only group who stood against those Israelites who worshiped the golden calf at Horeb.

The tribe of Levi was not given a parcel of land as inheritance in Canaan because the Lord was their inheritance. The Levites were placed in 48 Levitical cities throughout the land. A portion of the tithe from the remaining tribes was given to support the Levites' needs. Because the Levites were dependent on the generosity of

others to meet their needs, families were encouraged to invite Levites to join them during meals and during the celebration of national festivals.

Levites were to be totally dedicated to the Lord and not concerned with the things of the earth or a prosperous lifestyle. The Levites were consecrated to God and given to Israel as a gift from God in order to perform the duties at the tabernacle. Because of them, the holiness of the temple was maintained and the glory of the Lord dwelled in Israel.

Based on information from *Holman Bible Dictionary*, Trent Butler, general editor. Nashville: Broadman & Holman Publishers, 1991, pp. 975-976.

CANAANITES, HITTITES, HIVITES, PERIZZITES, GIRGASHITES, AMORITES, and JEBUSITES. These were the various ethnic groups that occupied Canaan when Israel came there. All of them were descendants of Ham, whose name means "black" (See Genesis 10:6-20). During the time when Israel entered Canaan, the Hittites, Jebusites, and Amorites occupied the hill country. The Canaanites were concentrated along the Mediterranean coast and the Jordan Valley. The Hittites suffered a great degree of displacement when Israel moved into the Promised Land. Most of them resisted Israeli occupation of the land.

Eventually, many of these groups became involved in the affairs of the Israelites, including business and trade. Some of the Israelite men married women from these groups. When this happened, a great deal of idol worship came into Israel.

BACKGROUND

After the death of Moses, Joshua assumed the reigns of leadership for all of Israel. Moses had already given Joshua his blessing. At the beginning of the Book of Joshua, the Lord commissions Israel's new leader. At the time of Moses' death, Israel was camped east of the Jordan across from Jericho. The Lord told Joshua and Israel that the time had come to cross the Jordan and enter into the land which he had promised Moses.

Before they could assume the land, however, they would have to go into battle. But the Lord promised victory to Joshua. As their leader, Joshua commanded the people to mobilize and prepare to cross the river. Then he solicited the assistance of the tribes with whom Israel was already allied.

Joshua's next step was to send two spies to Jericho to investigate the territory. The two entered Jericho and found refuge in the household of Rahab. In exchange for her silence, the two spies agree to spare her life when the city is destroyed. Because of her help, the two spies were able to leave Jericho without harm.

Once they had spied the land, they were ready to cross the Jordan. After Joshua led the people to the banks of the river, they slept there before crossing over to the other side. He gave the people their final instructions, which included to sanctify themselves. Israel had a big day ahead!

AT-A-GLANCE

1. God Instructs Joshua (Joshua 3:7-13)
2. The People Cross on Dry Land (vv. 14-17)

IN DEPTH

1. God Instructs Joshua (Joshua 3:7-13)

The Lord made plain what He intended to do for Joshua. Israel was about to take the step for which they had been preparing for 40 years. They would have to have complete trust in Joshua and be willing to follow his direction without reservation. The Lord promised to lift up (magnify) Joshua before Israel. God wanted them to know that He was with Joshua, just as He had been with Moses. The promises which had been made in the first chapter (vv. 1, 15) would now come to pass.

God then gave instructions to Joshua which he, in turn would give to Israel. First, Joshua was to assemble the priests who were responsible for the Ark of the Covenant. The priests were to simply stand at the edge of the Jordan River. Joshua assembled the people to hear what God was about to do. Because of Yahweh's mighty acts, they would know beyond the shadow of a doubt that He is the living God. He is a God who has proven His ability to command both nature and history. Israel knew God by what He did, not by who He was. God is an active Power in the lives of those He rules. The other nations worshiped idol gods. Israel's God was alive and participating in their lives in a tangible way.

As they crossed the Jordan, they would know that the living God was among them. He would not fail to drive out Israel's enemies that were occupying the land. Typically, seven groups are listed as occupants of Canaan at the time of Israel's arrival: the Canaanites, Hittites, Hivites, Perizzites, Girgashites, Amorites, and Jebusites. The

Canaanites and the Amorites, two other Semitic groups, constituted the majority of people occupying Canaan.

The Lord commanded that His ark go before Israel as they crossed the river. As soon as the priests who were carrying the ark reached the banks and set foot in the river, the waters flowing downstream would be cut off and rise like a pile. This event brings to mind the miraculous crossing of the Red Sea. In this instance, however, the Ark of the Covenant—the symbol of God's presence—led the way. When the ark was carried to the waters of the Jordan, the waters parted and gave way so that God's people could cross over into the Promised Land on dry ground.

When the water receded and the people were able to go over into the Promised Land on dry ground, they were reassured that the living God would be with them in the monumental task they were about to face—conquering enemy territory. God demonstrated that He can use the forces of nature to reveal Himself and bring forth salvation.

2. The People Cross on Dry Land (vv. 14-17)

The people broke camp to cross the Jordan and the priests carried the Ark of the Covenant in front of them. The time of Israel's crossing occurred during harvest season, which occurred in April in the lower Jordan Valley. The harvest season was also the time during which the snow melted from Mount Hermon, causing the Jordan to flood. Because of the time of year in the Jordan Valley, the fact that God miraculously held the waters back for Israel to cross was all the more impressive.

As the priests' who were bearing the ark dipped their feet in the brim of the flooding river, the waters from upstream stood and rose into a heap. Downstream, toward the Dead (Salt) Sea, the Jordan ran dry and Israel crossed over into the Promised Land on dry ground.

The place where the waters were dammed up was far off, at Adam, the city beside Zarethan. Adam, which was located about 16 miles upstream from Jericho near the Jabbok, flowed with the Jordan. Historically, the Jordan has been blocked on several occasions in the vicinity named in verse 16. The west bank of the river, located near Adam, is made up of elevated sections of land and cliffs of marly clay. Earthquakes, which are frequent in the Jordan Valley, and undercutting by high waters have, at times, caused these cliffs and mounds of clay to collapse across the Jordan and dam it up. God used a phenomena of nature to manifest His purposes.

Our Lord completes what He starts. He leaves no unfinished business or loose ends. Ultimately, His purposes are always fulfilled. Israel grew weary at times. It took them 40 years and the death of a generation of people to be ready to possess the land God had promised. But His plans were completed and His promises kept and fulfilled.

SEARCH THE SCRIPTURES

1. What did the Lord promise to Joshua? (Joshua 3:7)

2. What command did the Lord give to Joshua for Israel? (v. 8)

3. What amount of space was to be kept between the people and the ark? (v. 4)

4. Through what act would Israel know that the living God was among them? (v. 10)

5. How many men per tribe were to be taken out? (v. 12)

6. What would happen as soon as the soles of the priests' feet stepped into the Jordan? (v. 13)

7. What happened when the people broke camp? (v. 14)

8. What was the status of the Jordan River during the harvest season? (v. 15)

9. From which direction did the river's water stop flowing? (v. 16)

10. Where did the priests carrying the ark stand as the nation passed on dry ground? (v. 17)

DISCUSS THE MEANING

1. Why would God promise a land to His people which was already occupied by other nations? Must God's people, on occasion, fight for something God has already promised them?

2. Why do many years sometimes have to pass before God's promises are fulfilled?

LESSON IN OUR SOCIETY

Going into unknown territory can be frightening. For believers, it is always an act of faith. Sometimes we find ourselves unable to venture into something unknown, even if we feel certain God is leading us there. When we cannot go where God has told us, it is because we are putting the emphasis on ourselves and not on the Lord. If Moses had continued to focus on his own shortcomings at the burning bush that day, he would never have witnessed the miraculous acts of God. A new venture always requires us to take a step of faith.

Many African Americans have made great strides in this nation because they were willing to be "the first" and venture into unknown, sometimes hostile territory. If all of our forebears had been afraid to step out on faith and venture into the unknown, what would be the condition of our people today?

MAKE IT HAPPEN

Think about something you feel God is leading you to do, yet you have not ventured into it because you feared the unknown—perhaps a move, a career change, a new relationship or friendship, a new area of ministry service, or some other action. Think of the journeys of three biblical characters who went into the unknown with only their faith in God. Pray for the courage to do God's will just as the Bible personalities did. Pray for a spirit that causes you to celebrate every new adventure with the Lord.

FOLLOW THE SPIRIT

What God wants me to do:

_____

_____

REMEMBER YOUR THOUGHTS

Special insights you learned:

_____

_____

MORE LIGHT ON THE TEXT
JOSHUA 3:7-17

The Book of Joshua continues the narrative where Deuteronomy left off, and takes the Israelies from the fringes of the wilderness near the banks of the Jordan to Canaan—the Promised Land. It describes in detail the process and preparation of the entrance, conquest, and occupation of the land of Canaan. Joshua the son of Nun (1:1) is commissioned and charged by God for the task ahead, being reassured of the divine presence all through (1:1-9). Joshua now takes over as Israel's new human leader, and he calls on the people for cooperation (vv. 10-18). In chapter 2, spies are sent into the land, and they bring back encouraging reports to Joshua and the people. Chapters 3 and 4 record the miracle of crossing the Jordan River. The first six verses of chapter 3 contain definite instructions by Joshua to the people in their preparation for the final trip through the Jordan. He calls on the people to sanctify themselves (v. 5) and orders the priests to take up the Ark of the Covenant and go before the people (v. 6). Taking up the ark here, as in Numbers 10:39, is tantamount to Yahweh arising and going before them.

3:7 And the Lord said unto Joshua, This day will I begin to magnify thee in the sight of all Israel, that they may know that, as I was with Moses, so I will be with thee. 8 And thou shalt command the priests that bear

the ark of the covenant, saying, When ye are come to the brink of the water of Jordan, ye shall stand still in Jordan.

As they are set for the journey, the Lord speaks to Joshua to reconfirm him as God's chosen leader before the people. Here the Lord promises Joshua that on that very day, He (the Lord) would begin to magnify (*gadal*) Joshua in the presence of the people. *Gadal* means "to make great, to become important or to exalt." The exaltation of Joshua is not only through the immediate event that is about to take place the of the crossing of the River Jordan (a one time event)—but through many other miracles and acts of God in conquering the nations and occupying the land. The immediate event is however the beginning of wonders to come, which will authenticate Joshua as leader. The wonders will confirm and assure the people that Yahweh is with Joshua just as he was with Moses. The people would acknowledge Joshua's leadership and respect him as they did Moses when he parted the Red Sea, "Israel saw that great work which the LORD did upon the Egyptians: and the people feared the LORD, and believed the LORD, and his servant Moses" (Exodus 14:31).

In addition to the promise, the Lord asks Joshua to give direction to the priests that bear the ark. The special instruction for the priest is necessary since they will lead the way as the people follow. Indeed, the priests will go 2000 cubit (c. 3000 ft) ahead of the people (v. 4) to show the way. Here they are to "stand still in Jordan" as they come to the bank of the river. However, we are not told what would happen. The narrator leaves the reader in suspense. The fact that Joshua gave the order to the priests is assumed. It is omitted here probably to avoid needless repetition. This is consistent with the style of Old Testament narratives which often take for granted that God's commands are passed on as directed (Exodus 14:15; Deuteronomy 31:14, 28). It is interesting to note here that while Moses was directly involved in the parting of the Red Sea by dipping his shepherd's rod in the waters (Exodus 14:16, 21), Joshua is only to give orders. We have already noted that the ark symbolizes the presence of God, and plays a role during Joshua's time, but it was not yet instituted at the time of Israel's crossing of the Red Sea. Hence, Moses used his rod. Both Elijah and Elisha parted the Jordan in the Old Testament in two other instances (2 Kings 2:8-15). The reaction of the people watching Elisha perform this miracle was respect for Elisha. Their prostration before him served the same purpose meant here—to exalt. Jesus prayed often in the New Testament for God to glorify Him (John 16:14, 17:1, 5).

9 And Joshua said unto the children of Israel, Come hither, and hear the words of the Lord your God. 10 And Joshua said, Hereby ye shall know that the living God is among you, and that he will without fail drive out from before you the Canaanites, and the Hittites, and the Hivites, and the Perizzites, and the Girgashites, and the Amorites, and the Jebusites.

Joshua now summons the people to come and hear what the Lord is about to do, and to know that the Lord is with them. Here Joshua calls the people's attention to an important announcement he is about to make. One wonders how Joshua could get the attention of such a large number of people at once. We assume, and probably correctly, that there were no sophisticated public address systems as we have today. However, Israel is known for their use of the rams' horn for announcements and to sound a warning during emergencies (cf. Joshua 6:4-5). They probably used the same method, which is used in most African villages, to summon people to the village arena for important announcements or meetings. In a typical Igbo village, one or two people would go around the villages with *ekwe* (a wooden gong) to announce important declarations from the village head or council. Alternatively, the *Ikoro* (a big *ekwe* carved from a tree trunk with hollow inside) is sounded to summon the people to the "village square" when the village head has an important announcement or information to give the people, or during an emergency.

After summoning the people together, Joshua tells them that the Lord is about to do something miraculous which they should come and hear about. The coming miracle, Joshua tells them would make the people "know that the living God is among you." The word "know" (Hebrew *yada'*) is experiential and means "to recognize, to discover or acknowledge" that the Lord is really among them. Joshua qualifies this God as the living God, who stands opposed to and different from the gods of the nations. "Living" (Hebrew *chay*) can be translated as "strong or active." Unlike the gods of the nations, which are dormant and lifeless and unable to act or save (Psalm 96:5; 115:3-7), Yahweh the God of Israel is not only living and active, he is lively and powerful to save. He demonstrates Himself through miracles and signs. Knowing that the living God is present among them would inspire worship and trust. Joshua now qualifies this declaration by detailing what God would do to show that He is both living and active, and present among them. He certainly will drive out all the present inhabitants of Canaan from before them. "Without fail drive out" (Hebrew *yarash*) is doubled (called "infinitive absolute") to emphasize the certainty of the action, and can be translated as "certainly or definitely" the Lord will drive the people away. That means nothing will stop the living God from doing what He has promised to do, i.e., drive away all the peoples of the land (Exodus 33:2). The use of the infinitive absolute is intended to give them confidence and trust to march on in obedience to Lord's command and to listen to Joshua as their leader.

Joshua then enumerates the nations and calls them by name.

11 Behold, the ark of the covenant of the Lord of all the earth passeth over before you into Jordan. 12 Now therefore take you twelve men out of the tribes of Israel, out of every tribe a man.

After assuring the people of God's presence and the miracles that will happen, Joshua calls their attention to the Ark of the Covenant of Lord. Probably the priests bearing the ark have already started marching forward toward the bank of Jordan, then Joshua pointing to them says, "Behold (*hinneh*, i.e., "see, lo, or look"), the ark of the covenant of the Lord of all the earth is crossing over ahead of you into the Jordan" (NAS). The statement here is tantamount to saying that the Lord, the Creator of all things, the Omnipotent God has already gone before them to the Jordan (refer to the October 3, 1999 study). We have already noted that the ark represents the presence of God in physical form (see Numbers 10:35). The phrase, which refers to the sovereignty of God over the earth, is also found in Micah 4:13; Zechariah 4:14 and 6:5, and it gives Israel both the right and confidence to claim the land God is giving them. The tone of Joshua 3:11-12 seems urgent since the ark is already ahead of the people. They are to select 12 men, one from each tribe, to represent the whole nation. The beginning of this verse "now therefore" seems to indicate that the appointment of the 12 should be done before the crossing of the river. The function of the 12 is not disclosed until Joshua 4:2-5.

13 And it shall come to pass, as soon as the soles of the feet of the priests that bear the ark of the Lord, the Lord of all the earth, shall rest in the waters of Jordan, that the waters of Jordan shall be cut off from the waters that come down from above; and they shall stand upon an heap.

Verse 13 forms the climax of the narrative. Here Joshua picks up where he stopped in verse 11. The climax is the dividing of the Jordan, which begins the fulfillment of Lord's promise to Joshua (v. 7). Joshua gives the details of the miracle, i.e., the water parts as soon as the priests carrying the ark step into the river. Although critics use natural causes to explain the phenomenon soon to happen, the fact that it is announced ahead confirms the miracle. They may call it coincidence; however, everything depends on "the ark of the Lord, the Lord of all the earth." Nothing would happen until "the soles of the feet of the priests that bear the ark of the Lord. . . shall rest in the waters of Jordan." Here we see that it takes both faith and obedience to achieve a desired result. On the one hand, the waters of the Jordan would not part if the priests carrying the ark did not step into the river. This is faith at work. On the other hand,

if they go into the Jordan without carrying the ark, thus partially obeying the direction of the Lord, nothing would happen. It is the Lord who performs the miracle, but He always involves humans in achieving His purpose. Joshua announces that as soon as the priests set their feet on the shores of the river, the water flowing up stream will cease, pile up in a heap, and stay place as a solid wall. Thus a path would be created for passage, and naturally the water downstream would flow off down to the Dead Sea. This miracle is similar to of the Red Sea miracle under the leadership of Moses (Exodus 15:8). Reminiscing on the goodness and greatness of the Lord and calling for His praise, the psalmist declares, "He divided the sea, and caused them to pass through; and he made the waters to stand as an heap" (Psalm 78:13). Thus both miracles are closely related and show the sovereignty of Yahweh over the whole creation. The phrase "shall be cut off," The word in Hebrew which is used here to describe this event is *karath*. It has the idea of chopping off a body part, like cutting off the head from the rest of the body. The picture here is like an invisible wall with limitless height is instantly erected as the priests step into the water, and it ceases to flow across. The next few verses give the historical details of the event, which Joshua announces to the people.

14 And it came to pass, when the people removed from their tents, to pass over Jordan, and the priests bearing the ark of the covenant before the people; 15 And as they that bare the ark were come unto Jordan, and the feet of the priests that bare the ark were dipped in the brim of the water, (for Jordan overfloweth all his banks all the time of harvest,)

The writer now describes in detail what happened as the people obeyed the instructions given to them through Joshua. The promise of verse 7 is fulfilled. The anti-climax of the story is reached. The faithfulness of God in keeping His word is realized. Verse 14 starts with the description of the movement of the people. The priests that bear the ark have moved ahead of the people towards the banks of the Jordan (v. 11). When the people see them, then they "removed from their tents" and follow them. The NIV translation seems to imply that the people decamped, and then the ark bearers went ahead of them. However, everyone is probably decamped and ready to go, but the priests with the Ark of Covenant move ahead first (c. 3000 ft., cf. v. 4), and all eyes are on them. Then the people start their own movement. The narrator, who all the while has been building anticipation and suspense, continues to employ them in verse 15. We are taken to the banks of the river, we see the feet of the priests dip "in the brim (*qatseh*, i.e., edge) of the water," then comes another delay in the form of a long parenthesis (v. 15b). Here the writer describes the condition of the river at the time Israel arrives at the water bank. It is harvest time, when the riverbanks are flooded, probably the spring. During the spring, the rains and melting snows from the mountains cause the rivers to overflow their banks. God must have chosen this period purposely to further confirm that the miracle was His own doing, and to reassure the Israelites of His presence, and to give them a sign that He would overthrow the nations of Canaan for them (vv. 9-13). Could it be that God chose this period humorously with those critics and agnostics who would dismiss the miracle with a humanistic and rational point of view in mind?

16 That the waters which came down from above stood and rose up upon an heap very far from the city Adam, that is beside Zaretan: and those that came down toward the sea of the plain, even the salt sea, failed, and were cut off: and the people passed over right against Jericho.

After the parenthesis, which gives us the season in which Israel arrived at the bank, the writer resumes his narrative in verse 16. Without the parenthesis, the story will read thus:

"As soon as the priests stepped into the river, the water stopped flowing and piled up, far upstream at Adam, the city beside Zarethan. The flow downstream to the Dead Sea was completely cut off, and the people were able to cross over near Jericho" (Joshua 3:15-16).

Verse 16a tends to indicate that the waters continue to build up as a heap-like dam as far as Adam, a city near Zaretan, probably in the land of Manasseh, as suggested by some scholars. The city of Zaretan is only mentioned again in 1 Kings 7:46. The location of the ancient city of Adam is not clearly identifiable, however sources indicate it was about 20 to 30 miles north of Jericho. The Israelites' thoroughfare in the water was at Jericho, a city a few miles north of the Dead Sea. That means the water flow from upstream backed up 20 to 30 miles, and flooded the whole land. To bring out the magnitude of this miracle, it is said that between the Sea of Galilee and the Dead Sea, the Jordan contains a number of rapids and cascades. In spring season, the rain and melting snow cause the water to flow swifter. These conditions make the Jordan impracticable for foot passage. The swift current makes it difficult and dangerous even for expert swimmers. In recent years, we have seen the damage that flooding has caused in different parts of the world, e.g., in California, Quebec, Canada, etc. Currents from flood waters can wash off roads, tear down trees and houses, and destroy whatever is in its path. This is the picture portrayed in verse 16a. It shows the greatness of this miracle. Verse 16b makes the narrative even more remarkable. From the point where the Children of Israel cross down to the delta at the Dead Sea, the water "failed"

(Hebrew *tamam*), i.e., literally "to cease," or "to be gone." This means that either the water downstream also ceased to flow making a wall as in Exodus 14:15, or the entire Jordan River dried up from that point to the mouth where it enters the Dead Sea so there was a wide passage of several miles.

17 And the priests that bare the ark of the covenant of the Lord stood firm on dry ground in the midst of Jordan, and all the Israelites passed over on dry ground, until all the people were passed clean over Jordan.

After the climax of this story, the writer summarizes his narrative and tells the conclusion. In obedience to God's command in verse 8, "the priests that bare the Ark of the Covenant of the Lord" remain standing in the middle of the Jordan. The river bed and the banks where the water has been overflowing become dry—neither wet nor muddy. Their stock, wagons, children, and everything are able to cross on the firm ground without being trapped in mud or sand. The priests stand and are not allowed to move until "all the people were passed clean over Jordan." "Clean" translates from the Hebrew word *tamam* rendered "failed" in the verse 16. Here it means "complete or finished." That is the priests remain stationary in the middle of the river until the last person crosses the Jordan completely.

DAILY BIBLE READING

M: Spies Are Sent to Jericho
Joshua 2:1-7
T: Rehab Seeks Assurance of God's Protection
Joshua 2:8-14
W: Rahab Helps the Spies Escape
Joshua 2:15-24
T: Israel Follows Ark of the Covenant
Joshua 3:1-6
F: Israel at Jordan's Banks
Joshua 3:7-13
S: Israel Crosses the Jordan
Joshua 3:14—4:3
S: Twelve Memorial Stones Placed in Jordan
Joshua 4:4-14

TEACHING TIPS

November 21
Bible Study Guide 12

1. Words You Should Know

A. Straitly (v. 1)—(used in KJV) completely or totally.

B. Ram's horns (v. 4)—the animal's horns were used as instruments. Having been in the wilderness for 40 years, Israel had not owned objects such as horns of brass. Also known as a shophar, the horn was blown on the Day of Atonement in the jubilee years to announce the release of slaves and debt. It was also used as the Israelite's trumpet of war.

2. Teacher Preparation

A. Read the background Scripture for this lesson. Study additional material about the region of Jericho, including the earthquakes which were frequent occurrences.

B. Before class, find some examples of a great work being completed which initially may have seemed impossible. You may even share sports events in which the "underdog" pulled off a stunning victory. Encourage class members to share personal examples of victory in situations which seemed impossible.

3. Starting the Lesson

Read the IN FOCUS story about Thomas' promotion. Ask class members why it is sometimes important for people to stay on course and follow their dream and/or calling, even though others may not be very encouraging.

4. Getting into the Lesson

As you review today's lesson, discuss the importance of having a strategy for victory when engaged in battle—whether physical or spiritual. Spend some class time exploring the possibility that Israel intended to intimidate Jericho by encircling the walls. Also discuss how fear can paralyze people, assuring victory to the opponent. If time permits, explore how Satan uses fear to defeat believers.

5. Relating the Lesson to Life

A. Review the information about the region of Jericho, the story of Rahab's family, Jericho's only survivors, and the biblical significance of the number seven as outlined in THE PEOPLE, PLACES, AND TIMES. Search the New Testament to find instances where the number seven or seventy is used.

B. Give students an opportunity to answer the questions in SEARCH THE SCRIPTURES.

C. Using information in DISCUSS THE MEANING, explore class members' understanding of destruction for the sake of eliminating spiritual contaminants. Discuss how some people have used such biblical examples to justify their own acts of violence against other groups of whom they do not approve.

D. The LESSON IN OUR SOCIETY relates the experiences of our enslaved ancestors to that of the Hebrews. Why is it important for African Americans to continue to sing the songs which gave hope and courage to our forebears?

6. Arousing Action

A. Ask for a volunteer to share a time when he or she was paralyzed by fear, only to discover that God already had the situation under control.

B. Allow members to complete the MAKE IT HAPPEN activity. Encourage them to engage in a period of self-examination for the purpose of discovering personal obstacles or barriers to spiritual growth.

C. Give class members an opportunity to complete FOLLOW THE SPIRIT and REMEMBER YOUR THOUGHTS.

NOV 21ST

107

THE DESTRUCTION OF JERICHO

Bible Background • JOSHUA 6
Printed Text • JOSHUA 6:1-5, 15-20
Devotional Reading • PSALM 47

LESSON AIM

Today's lesson should help students to understand and appreciate what it means to have the power of the Lord on their side.

KEEP IN MIND

"And it came to pass at the seventh time, when the priests blew with the trumpets, Joshua said unto the people, Shout; for the LORD hath given you the city" (Joshua 6:16).

FOCAL VERSES

JOSHUA 6:1 Now Jericho was straitly shut up because of the children of Israel: none went out, and none came in.

2 And the LORD said unto Joshua, See, I have given into thine hand Jericho, and the king thereof, and the mighty men of valour.

3 And ye shall compass the city, all ye men of war, and go round about the city once. Thus shalt thou do six days.

4 And seven priests shall bear before the ark seven trumpets of rams' horns: and the seventh day ye shall compass the city seven times, and the priests shall blow with the trumpets.

5 And it shall come to pass, that when they make a long blast with the ram's horn, and when ye hear the sound of the trumpet, all the people shall shout with a great shout; and the wall of the city shall fall down flat, and the people shall ascend up every man straight before him.

15 And it came to pass on the seventh day, that they rose early about the dawning of the day, and compassed the city after the same manner seven times: only on that day they compassed the city seven times.

16 And it came to pass at the seventh time, when the priests blew with the trumpets, Joshua said unto the people, Shout; for the LORD hath given you the city.

LESSON OVERVIEW

LESSON AIM
KEEP IN MIND
FOCAL VERSES
IN FOCUS
THE PEOPLE, PLACES, AND TIMES
BACKGROUND
AT-A-GLANCE
IN DEPTH
SEARCH THE SCRIPTURES
DISCUSS THE MEANING
LESSON IN OUR SOCIETY
MAKE IT HAPPEN
FOLLOW THE SPIRIT
REMEMBER YOUR THOUGHTS
MORE LIGHT ON THE TEXT
DAILY BIBLE READINGS

17 And the city shall be accursed, even it, and all that are therein, to the LORD: only Rahab the harlot shall live, she and all that are with her in the house, because she hid the messengers that we sent.

18 And ye, in any wise keep yourselves from the accursed thing, lest ye make yourselves accursed, when ye take of the accursed thing, and make the camp of Israel a curse, and trouble it.

19 But all the silver, and gold, and vessels of brass and iron, are consecrated unto the LORD: they shall come into the treasury of the LORD.

20 So the people shouted when the priests blew with the trumpets: and it came to pass, when the people heard the sound of the trumpet, and the people shouted with a great shout, that the wall fell down flat, so that the people went up into the city, every man straight before him, and they took the city.

IN FOCUS

Thomas had been told by a lot of people, mostly Black, that he would never become a "DM," district manager at his company. "They don't give those kinds of jobs to Black folk," one guy told him. Thomas thought it was strange, but sad, that the people who were most discouraging were other Black people.

In the seven years Thomas had worked there, his sales team had performed consistently in the top three percent. Thomas had given his best on the job, and he had earned the right to a promotion. When people told him he'd never get the job because he's Black, Thomas simply replied, "Well, the final decision is really in God's hands."

What Thomas and many others had no way of knowing was that the company wanted to increase their visibility in the African American community. To do this, they would have to have more Blacks in high level positions.

Thomas received his promotion, and became the first Black "DM" at his company. One of the vice presidents shared with him that the company wanted to reach the Black community. Thomas said to himself, "Yeah, that might have been the company's reason for promoting me, but I know that God already had His plan in mind."

THE PEOPLE, PLACES, AND TIMES

JERICHO. The name Jericho means "moon." It is believed to be the oldest city in the world and was the first city Israel conquered under Joshua's leadership. Jericho is located along the lower Jordan Valley.

Jericho was a popular place because it was an oasis situated in a hot plain, isolated from other major settlements. Over the life of the city, Jericho has served as both a busy urban center and a small campsite. As early as 8,000 B.C., Jericho was a walled town of about 10 acres. Jericho came to have solid defense ramparts and walls. By Joshua's time, the walls of Jericho, which had been built thousands of years ago, were still being used for defense of the settlement.

Based on information from *Holman Bible Dictionary*, Trent Butler, general editor. Nashville: Broadman & Holman Publishers, 1991, pp. 759-761.

RAHAB. A prostitute who lived in Jericho whose name means "broad." She hid two Hebrew spies who had been sent by Joshua. When the king of Jericho discovered their presence, he sent men to arrest them. Rahab outsmarted the king by hiding the men on her roof. She sent the men who had come to arrest him on a bogus chase toward the Jordan River. In exchange for her aid, Joshua spared her life and that of her family when the Hebrews destroyed Jericho.

Rahab is listed in the genealogy of Jesus. In Hebrews 11, she is listed among the faith heroes.

Based on information from *Holman Bible Dictionary*, p. 1163.

SEVEN. A number used to represent completeness or perfection. During the time of the siege on Jericho, the number seven was sacred to the Hebrews as well as other Eastern cultures.

God's creation work was both perfect and complete in seven days. The seven-day week reflected God's first creative activity. Seven was also important in other cultic matters. For example, major festivals, such as Passover and Tabernacles (Booths) lasted for seven days, as did wedding feasts. In the Pharaoh's dream which was interpreted by Joseph, seven good years were followed by seven years of famine. Jacob worked a cycle of seven years for both Rachel and Leah.

Similar use of the number seven can be found in the New Testament, including the seven churches of Asia Minor.

Based on information from *Holman Bible Dictionary*, pp. 1029-1030.

BACKGROUND

Once the Hebrews had safely crossed the Jordan, they commemorated the event by taking 12 stones from the riverbed and placing them at the next night's camp site. One man from each tribe was to select a stone. The stones were to serve as a memorial for instructing future generations of Hebrews about the Lord's intervention at the Jordan River. Other memorials were established as well. Teaching children about the faith through the use of memorials was an established Hebrew practice.

After they crossed the Jordan, the manna which had fallen from heaven each day ceased. Since Israel had reached the land of promise, the daily provision of manna was no longer necessary.

Prior to the siege of Jericho, Joshua had an encounter that was similar to Moses at the burning bush. Joshua saw a man standing in front of him with his sword drawn. Joshua asked the man whether he was an enemy or an ally.

"Neither," the man replied (5:14). The man identified himself as the commander of the army of the Lord. Upon hearing this, Joshua fell to the ground face down in reverence. Joshua then asked what message the Lord had for him. He was then told to take off his shoes as the place where he was standing was holy.

AT-A-GLANCE

1. The Plan to Conquer Jericho (Joshua 6:1-7)
2. Jericho's Wall Comes Down (vv. 15-20)

IN DEPTH

1. The Plan to Conquer Jericho (Joshua 6:1-7)

Israel's conquest of Canaan occurred in three military campaigns: (1) the central highlands; (2) southern Canaan; and (3) the northern region of Galilee. This first campaign, which included the cities of Jericho and Ai, was designed to divide and conquer.

Jericho was a well-fortified city. The residents of the walled city had already anticipated an attack and had closed and barred their gates. They were afraid of Israel's might. However, the walls primarily served to keep the inhabitants of Jericho inside for judgment. The city was closed so that no one was permitted to go in or come out. The information contained in verse 1 is somewhat parenthetical to Joshua's experience before the Lord's messenger (5:15) and the Lord's instructions to Joshua (6:2).

In giving Joshua his instructions, the Lord assured him that the victory has already been won. Jericho, its king, and its soldiers would be handed over to Israel's army. God's destruction of Jericho for Israel was a sign of God's power to fulfill His promises.

The Lord instructed Joshua to march Israel's soldiers around the city once a day for six days. The march was to be led by a company of seven priests who blew seven trumpets made of rams' horns. These seven men also escorted the ark which symbolized God's presence. The ark went before Israel when they went into battle. In essence, the Lord went before Israel in every battle, as evidenced by the presence of the ark.

The number seven is emphasized a great deal here. Because the number seven was significant for other cultures besides the Hebrews, marching around the walls seven times may have served as a form of psychological warfare. The people of Jericho were already afraid of engaging an enemy who had the living God going before them. With each successive march, the fear mounted inside the walls of Jericho. They didn't know what to expect. Jericho's enemy marched around the city walls in silence for six consecutive days. On the seventh day, they were to march around the walls of the city seven times, after which the priests would blow their trumpets.

The loud blast of the trumpet was the people's signal to shout the battle cry. The dual purpose of the battle cry was to inspire the troops as it intimidated the enemy. The shout also had religious significance as it was associated with the ark in the rites of holy war (1 Samuel 4:5-8). At the sound of the shout, the city's wall would fall down.

Some may try to find physical reasons or evidence of the fallen wall at Jericho. Other students of the Bible believe the walls lowered into the ground like an elevator, allowing Israel to enter the city by walking across the tops of the wall. Some believe the Lord might have used an earthquake to bring about His purpose. Still others think the tramping and vibrations might have weakened the walls causing them to tumble. No matter how the incident is interpreted, to the Israelites, the fall of Jericho's walls served to demonstrate God's power over nature.

2. Jericho's Wall Comes Down (vv. 15-20)

For six days, the men had marched and nothing had happened. It may have begun to seem that their efforts had been wasted. On the seventh day, the procession began their daily march sequence. This time, however, they marched around the city wall seven times. At the seventh turn, the priests blew their trumpets and Joshua gave the command for the people to shout because the Lord had given them the city. It was Israel's obedience to the Lord's commands which won them the victory, not their military might.

Because of her willingness to help the Israelite spies, Rahab and her household were spared from destruction. Every other living thing in Jericho was destroyed. Human fortifications cannot withstand the power of God. The entire city was *accursed* destined for destruction. The root translation of the word denotes "something set apart from common use and devoted to the divine."

It was a common practice for Semitic cultures to isolate an enemy population for complete destruction. A great deal of moral perversion was known to exist in Canaan. Although this practice may seem cruel by modern estimates, Semites believed that anything which might compromise or contaminate the life and religion of the people needed to be destroyed. They understood the contagious nature of sin. The religion of Yahweh had to be maintained in a purified state at all costs. No measure was considered too drastic. Israel was given clear instructions to keep themselves away from everything that was marked for destruction, lest they themselves become corrupted.

There were a few exceptions, however. Only Rahab and her household and some specific articles were designated to be spared. Additionally, all of "the silver, gold, and vessels of brass and iron" were to be given to the treasury of the Lord.

The people did as God told them. When the priests blew the trumpets, they "shouted with a great shout." The wall of Jericho fell down flat. The people were able to walk into the city and take it over.

As long as God's people were obedient to Him, they were witnesses to His mighty power exhibited on their behalf. The wall of Jericho was but one of a series of battles which the Lord fought on Israel's behalf.

SEARCH THE SCRIPTURES

1. Why was Jericho closed off? (Joshua 6:1)

2. What did the Lord tell Joshua that He had done? (v. 2)

3. How many days did the Lord tell Joshua to encompass the city? (v. 3)

4. How many priests were to be there? (v. 4)

5. How many times were they to circle the city on the seventh day? (v. 4)

6. What were the people supposed to do when they heard the horn blow? (v. 5)

7. What did the people do on the seventh day? (v. 15)

8. Whose was the only household saved in Jericho? (v. 17)

9. What were the Lord's instructions concerning those things which were to be destroyed? (v. 18)

10. Which things were to be consecrated to the Lord? (v. 19)

DISCUSS THE MEANING

1. Why do you think it was necessary for the city of Jericho and its inhabitants to be completely destroyed?

2. If a group of people destroyed a city today and claimed that God told them to do it, how would you respond? Does God require us to destroy things today?

LESSON IN OUR SOCIETY

Miraculous stories such as the fall of the wall of Jericho are sometimes difficult for modern-day readers to believe. In fact, that may be the precise reason such events do not occur in our time.

To our forebearers, stories such as the fall of the wall at Jericho were a stronghold of their faith. As a group of oppressed people, they found strength in a God of deliverance a God who could destroy anything that stood in the way of righteousness. The Old Negro spiritual, "Joshua Fit De Battle of Jericho," told the story of God's assurance of victory in battle against the enemies of His people.

Although we are no longer enslaved, we still need to know that God is a God of deliverance and power.

MAKE IT HAPPEN

You may have encountered walls in your Christian walk which need to be destroyed so that you will allow the Lord to come in. Make a list of the obstacles you have overcome. Look at each item on your list and say a prayer of thanksgiving that God has enabled you to overcome. Then make a list of the obstacles you have yet to overcome. Say a prayer of petition. Ask God to shape you in whatever way necessary to help you overcome each of those obstacles.

FOLLOW THE SPIRIT

What God wants me to do:

_____

_____

REMEMBER YOUR THOUGHTS

Special insights you learned:

_____

_____

MORE LIGHT ON THE TEXT
JOSHUA 6:1-5, 15-20

The Israelites have successfully and miraculously crossed the Jordan, and are now set to possess the land. The news of this and other acts of God has spread all around the regions of Canaan, and their inhabitants are afraid of the Israelites (5:1). The Lord appears to Joshua in the form a man set for battle and instructs him on how to go about possessing the land. The first battle would be against the Jericho, which is the first city on the west of the Jordan. The conquest and destruction of this land will be the subject of our study for today.

6:1 Now Jericho was straitly shut up because of the children of Israel: none went out, and none came in.

The first verse of this chapter describes the seemingly hopeless, and almost impossible situation that confronts the Israelites as they approach Jericho. This difficulty is much like other obstacles they have overcome along the way, such as crossing the Red Sea and the Jordan River. The difference in this case is that city has prepared for war by fortifying their city walls. The verse starts by telling the state of mind of the inhabitants of Jericho when the people of Israel arrive at their borders. "Now Jericho was straitly shut up." The double usage of the word *cagar* is employed here to describe shutting in of the people of the land. Literally the phrase reads "Jericho was shutting up shut," which means that the city was sealed so that no one was able to go in or go out of the city. They were shut within the walls because they were fearful of the Israelites' coming attack (2:10-11; 5:1).

2 And the Lord said unto Joshua, See, I have given into thine hand Jericho, and the king thereof, and the mighty men of valour.

It is important to note that verse 1 is inserted parenthetically here, then the narrator continues the thought which he began in 5:13. The chapter division in 5:15 somewhat misleadingly creates the impression that the Lord's theophany and speech with Joshua ended there. However, the Lord's conversation with him continues (6:2-5) with detailed war plans against Jericho. Joshua and the Children of Israel are at the wall of Jericho, probably gazing at the wall and contemplating how to overcome such a formidable barrier. According to some archaeological sources, the wall of Jericho is a pear-shaped mound 366 meters (400 yards) in length from the north to the south, 183 meters (200 yards) in width, and about 67 meters (70 yards) high.

As Joshua is gazing at this impenetrable wall the Lord appears in military regalia (5:13-15) and speaks to him. The Lord assures Joshua that He has given him the city of Jericho. "See" (Hebrew *ra'ah*), the Lord said, "I have given (*nathan*) into your hand Jericho" with their king and their army. The language here indicates a completed action. In other words, the Lord seems to say to Joshua, "There is no cause for alarm or worry. I have already won battle for you. I have already handed the land over to you as I have promised" (1:3). "It is as good as done, and what is required is faith to appropriate it" (Hebrews 11:30). The Lord's specific mention of the king and his army, not only implies total victory, but also indicates and confirms that the inhab-

itants of Jericho have planned to attack Israel. They are ready to defend their city. The Lord then assures Joshua of victory.

3 And ye shall compass the city, all ye men of war, and go round about the city once. Thus shalt thou do six days. 4 And seven priests shall bear before the ark seven trumpets of rams' horns: and the seventh day ye shall compass the city seven times, and the priests shall blow with the trumpets. 5 And it shall come to pass, that when they make a long blast with the ram's horn, and when ye hear the sound of the trumpet, all the people shall shout with a great shout; and the wall of the city shall fall down flat, and the people shall ascend up every man straight before him.

In verses 3-5, the Lord gives direction how this battle, which has already been won in the spiritual realm (as well as psychologically), is to be won physically. The Lord then gives Joshua the battle strategy to convey to all the Children of Israel. The instructions are clear, and can be listed thus:

1. The people, led by the men of war (soldiers), are to march round the city of Jericho once each day for six days. The word compass used here is the Hebrew (*cabab*), which means "to surround or circle round." The idea is not to march as in military parade, but go around the walls of the city once a day (v. 3).

2. Seven priests with seven rams' horns (trumpet) shall go in front of the Ark of the Covenant around the city each day. Here the priests with trumpets will lead the way around the city (v. 4).

3. The people are to circle the city seven times on the 7th day (v. 4).

4. At the end of the 7th time, the priests shall blow a long blast of the rams' horn, the people are to "shout with a great shout" (v. 5). The phrase, "shout with a great shout" are two synonymous Hebrew words, *ruwa'*, which means "to sound an alarm, make a joyful noise," and *teruw'ah* which is "an acclamation of joy or battle cry." The cry is for both the intimidation of the enemy and the encouragement of the friendly forces (Numbers 10:9; 23:21). Shouting is frequently associated in many instances with the Ark of the Covenant (1 Samuel 4:5; 2 Samuel 6:15; cf. Numbers 29:1; Psalm 33:3).

The people are to march straight in to take possession of the land (v. 5). There is no need to look for the spiritual significance of the use of the number seven in this passage, however it is interesting to take note of that. It is also noticeable that the priests are to lead the people in wars and take an active part in the affairs of Israel. Ministers of the Lord are to be in the forefront in accomplishing the commands of the Lord (cf. v. 4-6; 3:3, 8, 13-17; 4:3; see also last Sunday's study). The result of obeying all these instructions is that the wall of Jericho will "fall down flat" i.e., completely. That means total destruction. It will give way and the people of Israel (everyone) will march straight in to take possession of the land.

15 And it came to pass on the seventh day, that they rose early about the dawning of the day, and compassed the city after the same manner seven times: only on that day they compassed the city seven times. 16 And it came to pass at the seventh time, when the priests blew with the trumpets, Joshua said unto the people, Shout; for the Lord hath given you the city.

Verses 1-5 are God's instructions to Joshua regarding the taking of the city of Jericho, which Joshua is to order the people of Israel. Verses 6-14 contain Joshua's instruction to the people and the description of the actual procession (the encircling) of the city from the first day to the sixth day. The narrator now takes us to the events of the seventh day. The Children of Israel have obeyed the Lord and have done everything according to the instruction of Joshua to them. Then early in the morning of the seventh day, which we can refer to here as their "D-Day," the people start early to circle the city. Their starting "early about the dawning of the day" as mentioned here, is important in view the special instruction regarding the seventh day (v. 4b). Since it would take them longer to march around the city seven times in one day, they need to start early. On this eventful day, the people circle the city just as they have been doing for the past six days, silently with seven priests carrying rams' horns leading the way, followed by those carrying the Ark of the Covenant and the soldiers, and then the people (vv. 8-14). Each march must be completely around the city. To do that seven times on the last day, and then march in to capture the city afterward would take hard work and faith.

Imagine the reaction and attitude of the people (both the Israelites and the inhabitants of the Jericho) as Israel goes round the city. To the Canaanites, who have been anticipating and fearful of the inversion of their city for a long time after hearing what the Lord has been doing (2:10-11; 5:1), marching around the city in silence must be a strange way to fight. It must have provided a spectacle and an entertaining sight for them to watch this number of people going around the city day after day, for seven days, in silence. There is no effort to break or to scale the wall, no weapons of war are used, not even war chants are heard, except on the seventh day. The inhabitants of Jericho had not seen or heard such a seemingly dumb war strategy before. As they watch, probably in utter amazement, they wait strategically for the time when the walk would wear out the people, and they would attack. To the Israelites as well, this method looks very strange and foolish, but they act in strict obedience to the Lord, who uses the things that seem foolish to the world to put to shame the wise, and the weak things to defeat the mighty (1 Corinthians 1:27-28). Moreover, they have seen enough of God's mighty deeds along the way especially in the most recent time (Joshua 3—4), that they have to trust and obey Him.

Verse 16 relates the fulfillment of the God's promises and the result of total faith in and obedience to the word of God even when it sounds silly and irrational. The people have completed the procession according to the instructions of the Lord. After the priests have sounded the trumpets, Joshua announces to the people to shout (*rua'*) for joy because the "Lord has given you the city," which reminds them of God's promise to give them the city (v. 2; cp. 8:1, 18; Judges 3:28; 4:7, etc.).

17 And the city shall be accursed, even it, and all that are therein, to the Lord: only Rahab the harlot shall live, she and all that are with her in the house, because she hid the messengers that we sent.

Joshua instructs the people what to do when they enter to take possession of the land. The city of Jericho, Joshua says is "accursed" (Hebrew *cherem*). The word *cherem* means "a thing dedicated, consecrated" or devoted for destruction." The curse means that the thing or person has been sentenced to total and irrevocable destruction" (Leviticus 27:28-29; Deuteronomy 13:16). When such a curse is pronounced on a city, as we see here (v. 17), all the people, animals, the spoils which the people would ordinarily keep, are completely burned, destroyed, or consecrated for the sanctuary (vv. 19, 24; cf Deuteronomy 20:10; 1 Samuel 15:3). Why such a severe banishment against Jericho? The curse is justified partly because they are part of a people whose cup of iniquity is full (Genesis 15:16), and because other surrounding nations have conspired to defend the city against Israel (Joshua 24:11). It would also serve as an example to other nations, and paralyze their attempt to resist the onslaught of the Israelites.

In keeping with the promise of the two spies and their covenant with Rahab "the harlot" in chapter 2, Joshua commands that she and all her household should be spared (vv. 22-23). Here, God's goodness and mercy is extended to a Gentile, who was a member of the Canaanites whose destruction has been foretold as early as Genesis 15:16. The reason she is spared is that "she hid the spies," which were sent to spy the land. However, the actual reason is her trust in and fear of the living God which was indicated by her confession. The writer of Hebrews says that it is her faith, (Hebrew 11:31) that worked to "justify" her (James 2:25). It is worthy of note that through her one act of kindness, inspired by her faith in the living God of Israel (2:9-11), her entire family is saved, and exempted from the curse and destruction (vv. 22-23).

18 And ye, in any wise keep yourselves from the accursed thing, lest ye make yourselves accursed, when ye take of the accursed thing, and make the camp of Israel a curse, and trouble it. 19 But all the silver, and gold, and vessels of brass and iron, are consecrated unto the Lord: they shall come into the treasury of the Lord.

Joshua then warns against taking the booty of the land. The people are to keep themselves clean from the accursed things from the land. That means that they should not take anything from the land for their own individual use. The consequence for defiance of this order is clear. Anyone who breaks the law would be subject to a curse and thus cause trouble in the camp. This prohibition does not only apply to their occupation of the Jericho, but to the entire region of Canaan (cf. Joshua 7). However, there are certain things that are to be kept from destruction, and instead are to be devoted to God and for His service—"all the silver, and gold, and vessels of brass and iron." These materials are to be set apart (Hebrew *qodesh*, which means "hallowed, make holy") and stored away in the treasury of the Yahweh.

20 So the people shouted when the priests blew with the trumpets: and it came to pass, when the people heard the sound of the trumpet, and the people shouted with a great shout, that the wall fell down flat, so that the people went up into the city, every man straight before him, and they took the city.

Here, the narrator gives us the climax of this interesting and astounding feat of God's victory over the city of Jericho. "So," i.e., recalling the reader's attention to the event in verse 16, Israel obeys Joshua's instruction. When they heard the sound of the trumpet, "the people shouted with a great shout" per the instruction given in verses 5-6.

At the long blast of the rams' horns, coupled with Joshua's signal, the people raise the battle cry of triumph. As they are shouting, probably in excitement and in obedience to the word of Yahweh, the wall of Jericho starts to crumble. As the wall falls flat, the people of Israel move in, "every man straight before him, and they took the city." The falling wall must have crushed to death many of the inhabitants, the armed men on top of the wall guarding the city, and the spectators that crowded about the wall watching (and mocking) the Israelites as they match round the city. Others probably were crushed by the stampede of people in running for their lives and in a state of astonishment at the strange phenomenon that is happening. 1 Kings 20:30 records, "But the rest fled to Aphek, into the city; and there a wall fell upon twenty and seven thousand of the men that were left . . . ." The wall, meant for their defense, became a weapon for their destruction. In the words of Matthew Henry:

"The sudden fall of the wall, no doubt, put the inhabitants into such a consternation that they had no strength nor spirit to make any resistance, but they became an easy prey to the sword of Israel, and saw to how little purpose it was to shut their gates against a people that had the Lord on the head of them" (Micah 2:13, paraphrased). (From *Matthew Henry's Commentary*, PC Study Bible, Biblesoft, 1993-1996.)

DAILY BIBLE READING

M: The Passover Celebrated at Gilgal
Joshua 5:10-15

T: Israel Begins Conquest of Jericho
Joshua 6:1-7

W: Six-Day March Around Jericho's Walls
Joshua 6:8-14

T: Destruction of Jericho By Israel
Joshua 6:15-20

F: Rahab and Her Family Are Spared
Joshua 6:22-25, 27

S: Joshua Renews the Covenant
Joshua 8:30-35

S: A Sacred Song of Remembrance
Psalm 44:1-8

TEACHING TIPS

November 28
Bible Study Guide 13

1. Words You Should Know

A. The flood (v. 2)—(used in KJV) another term to designate the river, specifically, the Euphrates River.

B. House of bondage (v. 17)—(used in KJV) the land of slavery, which was another designation for Egypt, the place where the Hebrew's ancestors had been slaves.

2. Teacher Preparation

Read the background Scripture for this lesson. Read ahead also to find out how long Israel remained faithful to the Lord before they fell into idol worship and disobedience.

3. Starting the Lesson

A. Use a chalkboard or tear sheet to list some things that people in our society are prone to choose over service to the Lord. Ask class members to help you determine reasons why each action or object may at times appear more appealing than serving the Lord.

B. Read the IN FOCUS story about how more and more people in this society appear to be less and less inclined to commit themselves to a cause a relationship, or a belief.

4. Getting into the Lesson

As you discuss today's lesson, research some of the gods of the other inhabitants of Canaan, which Israel later came to worship. Provide your class members with a list of the names of idol gods such as Baal, Mot, Anat, Astarte, and Ashtoreth (Ashtorah), Hadad, Molech, Horon, and Respeph.

5. Relating the Lesson to Life

A. Review the information about Terah, father of Abraham as contained in THE PEOPLE, PLACES, AND TIMES. Help class members understand the lineage and the events which took place from the days of Terah until the time when Israel reached the Promised Land. Use this information to reinforce class members'

understanding of how God can use a simple act to lead to great and powerful things.

B. Give students an opportunity to answer the questions in SEARCH THE SCRIPTURES.

C. Using information in DISCUSS THE MEANING, to discuss God's love, grace and mercy. Engage class members in a dialogue about how God never breaks His promises nor abandons His commitments/covenants.

D. The LESSON IN OUR SOCIETY emphasizes the need for leaders and others to be willing to take a stand for the Lord.

6. Arousing Action

A. Ask for a volunteer to share a time when he or she took a stand, where they were in the minority. Some members may recall instances in which others pledged support initially but later retreated into inactivity or nonchalance.

B. Allow time to complete the MAKE IT HAPPEN activity. Allow class members an opportunity to examine ways in which they have betrayed the Lord.

C. Give class members an opportunity to complete FOLLOW THE SPIRIT and REMEMBER YOUR THOUGHTS.

NOV 28TH

115

CHOOSING TO SERVE THE LORD

Bible Background • JOSHUA 24
Printed Text • JOSHUA 24:1-2, 14-22, 25
Devotional Reading • JOSHUA 24:14-24

LESSON AIM

Today's lesson should help students to understand that serving the Lord is a choice that God gives each of us.

KEEP IN MIND

"And the people said unto Joshua, The LORD our God will we serve, and his voice will we obey" (Joshua 24:24).

FOCAL VERSES

JOSHUA 24:1 And Joshua gathered all the tribes of Israel to Shechem, and called for the elders of Israel, and for their heads, and for their judges, and for their officers; and they presented themselves before God.

2 And Joshua said unto all the people, Thus saith the LORD God of Israel, Your fathers dwelt on the other side of the flood in old time, even Terah, the father of Abraham, and the father of Nachor: and they served other gods.

14 Now therefore fear the LORD, and serve him in sincerity and in truth: and put away the gods which your fathers served on the other side of the flood, and in Egypt; and serve ye the LORD.

15 And if it seem evil unto you to serve the LORD, choose you this day whom ye will serve; whether the gods which your fathers served that were on the other side of the flood, or the gods of the Amorites, in whose land ye dwell: but as for me and my house, we will serve the LORD.

16 And the people answered and said, God forbid that we should forsake the LORD, to serve other gods;

17 For the LORD our God, he it is that brought us up and our fathers out of the land of Egypt, from the house of bondage, and which did those great signs in our sight, and

preserved us in all the way wherein we went, and among all the people through whom we passed:

18 And the LORD drave out from before us all the people, even the Amorites which dwelt in the land: therefore will we also serve the LORD; for he is our God.

19 And Joshua said unto the people, Ye cannot serve the LORD: for he is an holy God; he is a jealous God; he will not forgive your transgressions nor your sins.

20 If ye forsake the LORD, and serve strange gods, then he will turn and do you hurt, and consume you, after that he hath done you good.

21 And the people said unto Joshua, Nay; but we will serve the LORD.

22 And Joshua said unto the people, Ye are witnesses against yourselves that ye have chosen you the LORD, to serve him. And they said, We are witnesses.

25 So Joshua made a covenant with the people that day, and set them a statute and an ordinance in Shechem.

IN FOCUS

Our society is increasingly becoming one in which people do not commit themselves very often or for very long. People can often be overheard explaining that their lack of commitment is due to their needs not being met in a particular situation.

Today, fewer people are loyal to a particular denomination. Some studies have shown that younger generations tend to choose a church, not a denomination, nor do they necessarily stay with the denomination of their childhood.

About half of all marriages in this country end in divorce.

It is not unusual for some people to marry three, four, or more times.

Some people have even adopted a lifestyle of incurring debt and filing for bankruptcy every 7 to 10 years. They are not committed to paying the bills they pledged to pay when they signed for the merchandise, product, or services they have received.

Manufacturers are discovering that people are not necessarily brand loyal. Growing numbers of consumers have grown accustomed to having more and more options.

It is no wonder that living in such a society has rendered some people unwilling to commit to a relationship with God.

THE PEOPLE, PLACES, AND TIMES

SHECHEM. Name of a place meaning "shoulder, back." Both a district and a city in the hill country of Ephraim in northern Palestine.

Shechem was the first capital of the Northern Kingdom of Israel. Rehoboam, successor to King Solomon, went to Shechem to be crowned king over all of Israel. Samaria eventually became the permanent capital of the Northern Kingdom.

It was at Shechem that Jesus visited with the Samaritan woman at Jacob's Well.

Based on information from *Holman Bible Dictionary*, Trent Butler, general editor. Nashville: Broadman & Holman Publishers, 1991, pp. 1258-1259.

TERAH. The father of Abraham, Nahor, and Haran. Terah, along with a group of the people from Ur of the Chaldees, moved his family along the Euphrates River to Haran. He intended to go on from Haran to Canaan, but died in Mesopotamia. He was 205 years old.

Based on information from *Holman Bible Dictionary*, p. 1334.

BACKGROUND

Like his predecessor, Joshua had come to the time when his work was done. He had some things to share with Israel before he left them.

Joshua gathered all the tribes of Israel together and gave them words from the Lord. He reminded them of all of God's gracious acts. Joshua reminded them of where their ancestors had come from how God moved Abraham from a land along the Euphrates into Canaan. He told how the Lord gave Abraham progeny. The Lord helped each generation after Abraham.

After telling about Abraham, Joshua reminded them of how God sent them Moses and Aaron and how the plagues came upon Egypt until Pharaoh let the Hebrews go. He told the tribes how God allowed their forebears to cross the Red Sea.

Now that they were safely settled into the Promised Land, the Lord did not want them to forget the One who made it all possible. The Lord had performed many mighty and miraculous acts on behalf of His people.

IN DEPTH

1. Joshua Exhorts Israel to Serve the Lord (Joshua 24:1-2, 14-15)

Joshua called together all of the 12 tribes of Israel at the ancient cult-shrine of Shechem, located at the east end of the valley between Mount. Ebal and Mount Gerizim. According to the Lord's instructions, Joshua reminded them of some things which the Lord had done on their behalf. Their obligation to Him, in return for all of His benefits, was to be loyal to Him.

Joshua's purpose was to exhort all those present to serve Yahweh exclusively. Israel has a choice in the matter, however. In spite of all that Yahweh has done for Israel, they still had the right to reject Him as their God. They are free to reject His covenant as well. Therefore, Joshua challenged them to reach a decision. Israel had to decide whether they would serve the God who had been with them and provided for them throughout their history or the Mesopotamian ancestral gods. Joshua left no doubt in their minds what he and those in his household would do—they would serve Yahweh.

At this point in Israel's limited exposure, the gods of other peoples might have appeared more exciting than Yahweh. Serving the other gods probably seemed less restrictive. But Israel had made a covenant with Yahweh. They were bound to keep that covenant. Yet some of them probably considered rejecting Yahweh now that He had victoriously ushered them into the Promised Land. Perhaps some of them began to think they no longer had need of

Yahweh because they perceived He had done for them all that He could.

God had proven Himself time and time again through His mighty acts. It was now Israel's decision whether to choose the God who had exhibited such power on their behalf throughout history. Even after all God had done for them, He still allowed them to choose. God did not demand their loyalty. He wanted them to give Him their love, which is understood as loyalty and obedience, willingly.

The same is true for us today. God's desire is that we want to follow Him. The choice between God and another way might be understood in terms of a choosing a factory second, imperfect model over a first quality, name brand model.

2. Israel Declares Its Loyalty (vv. 16-22, 25)

Israel recognized that indeed Yahweh has done great and mighty acts on their behalf and readily affirmed their loyalty to God. They would not worship other gods because it was the Lord who had proven Himself to them. They recalled many of His miraculous acts. The Lord had done many miracles right before their eyes. The Lord had protected and cared for Israel everywhere they went. He had even driven out their enemies from the land so that they could inhabit it. They acknowledged their continued dependence upon Him. Therefore, they agreed that they, too, would serve the Lord and give total allegiance to Him.

Perhaps Joshua felt they had declared loyalty to the Lord too quickly. He wanted to discourage them from making rash promises that they could not sustain once the assembly had gone home. Joshua may have thought that a pledge of allegiance made so quickly might also be broken just as quickly. Once again he confronted them with the nature of the decision they had made. He demonstrated some reservations about their commitment to the task.

In his effort to help Israel understand the full impact of their statement of allegiance, Joshua painted a stark picture of a God who demands uncompromising loyalty. He is a God who would not tolerate transgressions against the covenant they had made with Him. Since they were free to choose or reject the Lord, if they chose to serve Him, they were expected to be loyal to Him. If they did not want to serve the Lord and obey His commands, they were free to reject Him and serve whomever they pleased. Perhaps Israel wanted the benefits of serving the Lord without having to sacrifice anything in return.

A commitment to serve the Lord had to be total and absolute. Israel could not serve Yahweh and other gods, too.

They could not simply give lip service in a public setting. The good feelings generated that day at Shechem would not be enough to sustain their commitment to the Lord. The people needed to give themselves fully to the Lord. Yahweh is a jealous God who will not tolerate competition. There was no room for compromise or middle ground—they either had to serve God or serve the gods of those around them.

Joshua understood the all-consuming nature of Israel's covenant with Yahweh. As their leader, he had seen evidence of their weakness concerning their commitment to the Lord. Joshua knew, as the Lord knew, that Israel remained weak, immature, and unsure in their devotion to God. In spite of all that had happened, Israel could not be trusted to worship God alone. The covenant was not a fleeting or "fly-by-night" sort of agreement subject to compromise or amendment.

As a leader and as a follower of the Lord, Joshua is to be commended. No matter what the nation of Israel chose to do, he and all of those in his household were going to serve the Lord. He was not interested in winning their approval or acceptance. Joshua remained a leader until the very end. He wanted Israel to serve Yahweh and presented them with the facts and reasons as to why they should. Knowing they had a choice, Joshua informed them of his plans for himself and his household. He was not willing for his family to chase after other gods who had done nothing for him or his family. He remained faithful to the God who had been faithful to him.

SEARCH THE SCRIPTURES

1. What did the Lord promise to Joshua? (Joshua 24:7)

2. What command did the Lord give to Joshua for Israel? (v. 8)

3. What amount of space was to be kept between the people and the ark? (v. 4)

4. Through what act would Israel know that the living God was among them? (v. 10)

5. How many men per tribe were to be taken out? (v. 12)

6. What would happen as soon as the soles of the priests' feet stepped into the Jordan? (v. 13)

7. What happened when the people broke camp? (v. 14)

8. What was the status of the Jordan River during the harvest season? (v. 15)

9. From which direction did the river's water stop flowing? (v. 16)

10. Where did the priests who carried the ark stand as the nation passed on dry ground? (v. 17)

DISCUSS THE MEANING

1. Why would God choose such a weak and immature people like Israel to claim as His own?

2. Is it possible that the people of Israel were sincere at the time their commitment to Yahweh was made? How could they have been lured by other gods who had not proven themselves?

LESSON IN OUR SOCIETY

It seems that fewer people today are willing to take a stand, as Joshua did, no matter what others decide to do. Even believers are not always eager to take a stand for the Lord. Some of us are concerned about our standing the community or among our friends. Some of us fear suffering repercussions on the job or even within our own home. Others are afraid of being labeled as "Jesus freaks."

In Matthew 16:24, Jesus told His disciples, "If any man will come after me, let him deny himself, and take up his cross, and follow me."

In times of crisis, it is not our social standing which will see us through. Our social standing is often fickle and fleeting. Many people who were once highly celebrated later fell into obscurity. It is not our position or employer who will stand firm for us when all else fails. Millions of people have been the victims of corporate downsizing and layoffs. A lot of those people thought they were indispensable in their jobs. We cannot even count on our family and loved ones to always stand by us during difficult times. Only "God's unchanging hand" will still be there for us to hold on to no matter what. He deserves our every effort to try to return to Him what He has given to us.

MAKE IT HAPPEN

God had proven Himself to Israel over and over again, yet they continued to worship other gods. In what ways has God proven Himself to you by performing marvelous acts in your life? How have you betrayed Him by going against Him, giving your love and your loyalty to another object of worship?

FOLLOW THE SPIRIT

What God wants me to do:

_____

_____

REMEMBER YOUR THOUGHTS

Special insights you learned:

_____

_____

MORE LIGHT ON THE TEXT
JOSHUA 24:1-2, 14, 22, 25

Israel has conquered all the lands as the Lord promised. She is now settled for "the Lord had given (them) rest . . . from all their enemies round about" (23:1). A few years later, some suggest about 25 to 30 years after their entrance to the land, Joshua is now about 110 years old (13:1; 24:29). He knows that both his life and leadership will soon end. He gathers all the tribes of Israel to address. He reminds them of all that the Lord has done for them and charges them to maintain a good relationship with Yahweh by keeping "all that is written in the book of the law of Moses, that ye turn not aside therefrom to the right hand or to the left" (23:6). This is the first of two such gatherings Joshua calls before he dies.

24:1 And Joshua gathered all the tribes of Israel to Shechem, and called for the elders of Israel, and for their heads, and for their judges, and for their officers; and they presented themselves before God. 2 And Joshua said unto all the people . . . .

Although some scholars suggest that the gathering in chapter 24 is a continuation of the gathering in chapter 23, one is strongly inclined to believe that they are two separate occasions. While the location of the gathering of chapter 23 is not mentioned, Shechem is mentioned as the place for the gathering of chapter 24. The meeting in Joshua 23 must have taken place in Shiloh, which served as the religious headquarters where the Ark of the Covenant was located (18:1; 19:51). Shechem is believed to be the home of Joshua (vv. 30-32; cf. 19:49-51), about eight miles from Shiloh. Since the gathering is not a religious one, such as a feast, and being very old he knows that he would soon pass on, it is reasonable for Joshua to be closer to home for his final address as leader.

The other reason for choosing Shechem for this solemn gathering can be understood from the patriarchal tradition. Shechem is an ancient city. Abraham is believed to have built an altar at Shechem (Genesis 12:6) when he arrived in Canaan; Jacob bought a piece of ground and built an altar for the Lord here (Genesis 33:18-20; cf. Joshua 24:32). Shechem is one of the cities consecrated as a city of refuge for anyone who mistakenly kills another (20:7-9; 21:21). For all these reasons, Shechem is a sacred place for such an important meeting, it is also called a sanctuary (24:25-26).

The chapter starts with the conjunction "and" which can be better rendered, "afterwards." That means after Joshua's first address to the Children of Israel at Shiloh

(Joshua 23), within a period of few days or even months, he summons them again at Shechem and gives them his final farewell address (Joshua. 24). The word for "to gather" is the Hebrew verb *'acaph* and that is "to assemble, to bring together." It has the idea of summoning them for an important occasion. Joshua summons all the tribes of Israel with her elders, heads, judges, and officers, to this sacred site. The clause, "and they presented themselves before God," seems to suggest that God initiated the assembly through a divine revelation to Joshua. From verse 2 to 13 is Joshua's address, which details the historical redemptive acts of God for Israel. Speaking on God's behalf ("thus says the Lord" v. 2), Joshua summarizes the story of Israel from the time of Abraham to the very point of their existence, including how the Lord has been with them providentially in all situations, and how He has loved and blessed them unconditionally. The Lord says, "I have given you a land for which you did not labor, and cities which you did not build, and you dwell in them; you eat of the vineyards and olive groves which you did not plant" (v.13).

14 Now therefore fear the Lord, and serve him in sincerity and in truth: and put away the gods which your fathers served on the other side of the flood, and in Egypt; and serve ye the Lord.

In verses 2-13, Joshua served as God's prophetic spokesman. Using an adverbial conjunction `attah*, translated here as "now therefore," Joshua begins his final personal exhortation to the Children of Israel. That is, in view of the Lord's acts in history, Israel is to maintain a good and God-fearing relationship with Yahweh.

First, they are to fear the Lord, i.e., to have an attitude of reverence, respect, and honor towards God as the Hebrew word *yare* implies. It is in this sense that the word "fear" is used here; in contrast to being afraid of the Lord, as if God were a terror or cruel judge waiting to pounce on His subject for any mistake or wrong doing. The fear of the Lord is an attitude of awe produced by the majesty, love, and goodness of God shown to His people. The Bible speaks often of the fear of God (Deuteronomy 4:10; 6:2, 13, 24; Psalm 130:4). Proverbs says that fear of the Lord is the beginning or foundation of wisdom and knowledge (1:7; 9:10). Second, Israel is to serve the Lord in sincerity and in truth. To serve (Hebrew `abad) the Lord means to worship Him. The word for sincerity, *tamiym* in Hebrew, suggests "fullness, complete, integrity or without blemish or spot." The word *'emeth* means "trustworthiness, faithfulness," etc.. To worship the Lord thus, is the only way to serve Him. It should be devoid of hypocrisy and fallacy, for God hates

such (2 Corinthians 1:12; Ephesians 6:24; Titus 2:7). Jesus tells the woman at the well in Samaria that "the true worshipers shall worship the Father in spirit and in truth: for the Father seeketh such to worship him" (John 4:23-24). In his response to the woman's argument that their forefathers worshiped on the mountains of Samaria (John 4:21, i.e., in Shechem), Jesus quotes what Joshua declares here to the people of Israel. Worshiping God sincerely and faithfully is an outgrowth of a heart that fears or is in awe of God. It is a heart the serves Him completely with no reservation.

Such sincere and unreserved service of the Lord is to be exclusive, and has no room for other gods. Therefore, the people are to "put away the gods which your fathers served" (v. 2; Genesis 11:31). Jacob made the same demand on his household in Genesis 35:2; Samuel also called on the whole of Israel to "put away strange gods and Ashtaroth from among you, and prepare your hearts unto the LORD, and serve him only" (1 Samuel 7:3). The gods from whom the Israelites are to disassociate themselves include, not only those beyond the Euphrates (the other side of the flood), but also those in Egypt. This indicates that Israel served the gods of Egypt while they were there. Egypt is identified earlier in this chapter (vv. 2-13) as the place where the people cried out to God and were delivered, giving us a general sense that Israel was innocent while they lived in Egypt. However, this verse, with other Old Testament passages, presents a different picture of the situation. For example, Ezekiel 20:7; 23:3-8 indicates that Israel played the harlot while in Egypt. The making and worship of the molten calf in the Sinai desert is an indication that they worshiped the Egyptian's gods (Exodus 32). Then Joshua calls on them to put away these other gods, and serve only the Lord.

15 And if it seem evil unto you to serve the Lord, choose you this day whom ye will serve; whether the gods which your fathers served that were on the other side of the flood, or the gods of the Amorites, in whose land ye dwell: but as for me and my house, we will serve the Lord.

Joshua now speaks to their conscience. After reviewing the redemptive acts of God in history and challenging them to do away with other gods, and serve only the Lord, Joshua leaves room for them to make their choice. The possibilities are clear. Either they choose to worship the Lord (v. 14) or serve the gods of their forefathers or the gods of the Amorites whose land they now occupy. "And if it seem evil unto you to serve the Lord . . ." can be reworded thus, "but if you feel that serving the Lord is not good for you, then choose for yourselves whom you want to serve." Choosing

to serve other gods is not a real smart choice, but a possible option. Joshua wants them to think for themselves and make an honest and voluntary choice. He is not offering an alternative, but is seeking for a confession of faith in Yahweh from them; this he gets in verses 16-20. Without waiting for them to reply, Joshua declares his resolve to worship the Lord with his household "but as for me and my house, we will serve the Lord."

16 And the people answered and said, God forbid that we should forsake the Lord, to serve other gods;

In response to the challenge and demand of Joshua, the people declare a total allegiance to the Lord. "God forbid" (Hebrew *chaliylah*) i.e., far be it from me (us), let it not be, that we should forsake the Lord to serve other gods. The Hebrew term "forsake" (`azab*) means "to loosen" and is in contrast to Joshua's demand for the people in 23:8 to "cleave" or "cling" (*dabaq*) unto to the Lord (cf. Deuteronomy 28:20; 31:16; Judges 2:12-13; 10:6-10). Forsaking the Lord is termed as an abomination. So the people's response here can be reworded thus: "May it be an abomination before that we should forsake Him and serve other gods." We must cling to Him, and not to other gods, they imply. In other words, it is not evil for us to serve the Lord.

17 For the Lord our God, he it is that brought us up and our fathers out of the land of Egypt, from the house of bondage, and which did those great signs in our sight, and preserved us in all the way wherein we went, and among all the people through whom we passed: 18 And the Lord drave out from before us all the people, even the Amorites which dwelt in the land: therefore will we also serve the Lord; for he is our God.

Giving the reasons why they are resolved in their hearts to serve the Lord (vv. 17-18), they declare:

1. Jehovah is the God that has brought us and our fathers up out of the Egyptian bondage.

2. He is the one who did great signs in our sight.

3. He is the one who preserved us alive throughout our journey and among all the nations (peoples) we passed on our way.

4. He is the one who drove out all the inhabitants of the land in which we now dwell, including the Amorites.

Therefore, with all these reasons, the people declare their loyalty to the Lord. They do not want to be less loyal to the Lord than Joshua has pledged to be (v. 15). They, likewise, will serve the Lord for He is their God.

19 And Joshua said unto the people, Ye cannot serve the Lord: for he is an holy God; he is a jealous God; he will not forgive your transgressions nor your sins. 20 If ye forsake the Lord, and serve strange gods, then he will turn and do you hurt, and consume you, after that he hath done you good.

Joshua's response, "Ye cannot serve the Lord," rings with a note of seriousness. It is intended to confront Israel with the magnitude of the pledge she has just made. It should not be taken in its pure sense. Joshua is saying it is a serious matter to serve the Lord, therefore it requires a thoughtful consideration. It is not a thing to be decided hastily or on impulse. Two things should be taken into consideration before such pledge is made. First, God is holy, and second He is jealous. God's holiness (Hebrew *qodesh*) is what makes him unique, incomparable to, and separate from the other gods (1 Samuel 2:2). He therefore demands that the entire life of His people bear the stamp of holiness, a demand He makes of them during their wilderness wandering (Leviticus 20:7; 1 Peter 1:15, 16). No one can serve the Lord unless they sanctify themself and put away their idols (v. 14; Leviticus 20:7), less they provoke the Lord because He is "jealous." "Jealous"should be translated here as "zealous" rather than "angry" as the Hebrew word *qan-now'* tends to denote. The zeal of the Lord is seen in His love relationship with Israel and demonstrated by his redemptive acts in history. This type of jealousy can be likened to a husband and wife relationship, in which both are zealously in love (madly in love) with each other, and trust each other. If such love and trust is betrayed, through unfaithfulness (adultery), it results in disappointment and anger (*qannow*). It is usually hard to forgive such betrayal. The Lord has established such a jealous relationship with Israel that if they become unfaithful by following idols (other gods), they make Him angry and will consequently be punished (Exodus 20:5; 34:14; Deuteronomy 5:9). Joshua warns that the Lord will not forgive your transgressions nor your sins, i.e., He will not condone their iniquities, or overlook them. Two words are used here for sin: "transgressions" (*pesha'*), which means "revolt (national or religious), rebellion," and "sin" (*het*) which is more common and designates the sinful act of missing the mark.

The consequences of their rebellion is that the Lord will turn the covenant of blessings promised to them for obeying the law into the covenant of curses meant for disobedience. Turning to other gods and serving them, thereby forsaking the Lord will constitute a breach of this covenant. Therefore, the Lord will invoke the penalty for breaking the covenant (23:15; cf. Leviticus 26; Deuteronomy 28). The sin of serving the strange gods will cause God to "turn and bring disaster on you and make an end of you, after he has been good to you" (NIV). The passage here does not fully represent the character of God that includes forgiveness for those who repent and come to God and turn away the strange gods. This is left for other parts of Scripture (cf. Leviticus 26:41-42; 2 Chronicles 7:14; 30:9; Nehemiah 1:9; Isaiah 55:7, etc.). For the moment, Israel is left to ponder the weight of her decision and commitment to serving the Lord.

21 And the people said unto Joshua, Nay; but we will serve the Lord. 22 And Joshua said unto the people, Ye are witnesses against yourselves that ye have chosen you the Lord, to serve him. And they said, We are witnesses.

In spite of Joshua's words in verse 20, the people reconfirm their pledge unequivocally to serve the Lord. The picture here is that of a shout of "No!" (*lo'*) in unison, "We will serve the LORD!" Joshua's seemingly negativity and threat of punishment for disobeidence never discourage nor deter them from reaffirming their pledge to God for the second time (cf. v. 18). In his response to their reaffirmation of faith

in the Lord, Joshua holds them accountable and responsible to their pledge (cf. Ecclesiastes 5:4). Using a judicial language, Joshua calls them witnesses to their vow to serve the Lord. Again, in unison, they reply, "We are witnesses!" In verses 23 and 24, Joshua charges them again to put away all the strange gods that are in their midst, and turn fully to serving the Lord and the people again pledge their loyalty to Yahweh.

25 So Joshua made a covenant with the people that day, and set them a statute and an ordinance in Shechem.

Based on the repeated commitment and declarations that Israel has made to serving the Lord, Joshua makes a covenant "with the people" or "for the people." The Hebrew used here allows for both translations (see KJV, NKJV, and NIV). It is however better translated as "with" since Joshua represents, not the people, but rather the Lord. The statute (*choq*) and ordinance (*mishpat*) that is set for the people that day at Shechem are not new "decrees" and "laws," but a reminder of the Lord's already existing requirements for Israel. The ceremony can rightly be referred as "covenant renewal" (cf. Deuteronomy 29:1).

DAILY BIBLE READING

M: Joshua Summons Israel to Remember God
Joshua 23:1-5
T: Israel Exhorted to Love and Obey God
Joshua 23:6-10
W: Joshua Warns against Unfaithfulness to God
Joshua 23:11-16
T: Joshua Rehearses Israel's History
Joshua 24:1-7
F: Israel Promises to Be Faithful
Joshua 24:14-18
S: Israel Renews the Covenant
Joshua 24:19-24
S: Death of Joshua and Eleazar
Joshua 24:25-31

NOTES

NOTES

INTRODUCTION TO THE DECEMBER 1999 - 2000 QUARTER

This study of Matthew's Gospel focuses on the life and ministry of Jesus. Most sessions depict a certain aspect of His ministry and how He was received by those to whom He ministered. The book of Matthew is expressly called "the book . . . of Jesus Christ." This study in Matthew is meant to show the power of Jesus' ministry and to explore His example for those who will spread the Gospel throughout all the world in His name. In this quarter we study the saga of the birth of the Lord to the point of His ascension as He delegates his authority to His followers.

In this quarter we will examine the various sections of His teachings. As you study these lessons you will come to see why Matthew is recognized by scholars as the book of the teachings of Jesus. The three units in this quarter deal with: Jesus' birth and ministry; specific teachings of Jesus; and the fulfillment of Jesus' mission to the world.

The Quarter at-a-Glance

STUDIES IN MATTHEW

UNIT 1. BEGINNINGS: BIRTH AND MINISTRY

This unit consists of four sessions that emphasize the birth of Jesus. Here we see the Israelite tradition of naming the lineage whenever the person being introduced is considered of great importance. Genealogies also point to the fact that there was about to be a radical transition in the storyline. In this unit we skip the genealogy and go directly to the herald of the king. A herald in many parts of the world, such as African and traditional Oriental cultures, sent announcers before royalty and other important persons. The first lesson introduces John the Baptist as the herald of Jesus' coming. Here again we see a traditional pattern; every king must prove himself in battle. Jesus' temptation was that initiation into battle with the archenemy of heaven. Lesson two recounts Jesus' temptations. Lesson three is the account of Jesus' birth. The final lesson covers the visit of the wise men.

LESSON 1: December 5
King's Herald and Baptism
Matthew 3:1-8, 11-17

This lesson begins with the verse in which John declares that he baptizes with water, mainly for repentance, while Jesus is more powerful and will baptize with the Holy Spirit and fire. Several components of Biblical content are presented: one of which is John the Baptist's message of repentance and his announcement of the coming of the Lord. Here we study the various people who came to hear John and to be baptized by him. The study also leads us to consider the attitudes and wrong intentions with which some of them came, such as the Pharisees and Sadducees. In another component we are encouraged to look ahead to the One who would baptize with the Holy Spirit and fire and would separate the wheat from the chaff. We see Jesus insisting on being baptized by John to fulfill all righteousness. Finally, to affirm the nature of the Lord Jesus, we examine what happened when Jesus came up from the water—the Spirit of God descending upon Jesus like a dove, and a voice from heaven confirming His Sonship.

As you study this lesson you will be led to examine the importance of taking time to prepare for the mission that God has for your life. By looking at John's message you will be able to face the feelings of guilt for having done wrong. The lesson will also help you move from guilt to the experience of forgiveness.

LESSON 2: December 12
Temptations and Ministry
Matthew 4:1-14

The Biblical content of this lesson relates to the initiation of Jesus into spiritual battle with the enemy. We study how Jesus, having been led by the Spirit into the wilderness to be tempted, fasted for 40 days and nights. We also see how this spiritual exercise led to temptation to satisfy His hunger by turning stones to bread. We learn how Jesus overcame temptation by using Scripture to rebuke Satan. We also examine the temptation in which the devil placed Jesus on the pinnacle of the temple and suggested that He jump, but Jesus again rebuked Satan using Scripture that affirmed people are not to put God to the test. Finally we look at the temptation in which the devil promised Jesus the kingdoms of the world if He would worship him. Then we see Jesus rebuke

Satan using Scripture about worshiping God alone. Our study leads to the point where the devil left Jesus, and the angels ministered to Him. Finally, we come to the temptation to scare Jesus from His mission by casting John into jail. Jesus deals with this by moving to Galilee and continuing His mission of fulfilling the Word of the Lord.

As you study this lesson remember that as one is called to do the will of the Lord there shall be times of testing. If your time of testing is now or comes in the future, by examining again the victory of Jesus over the devil, you can have faith in your own victory through the power of Christ.

LESSON 3: December 19
Birth of Jesus
Matthew 1:1-6, 18-25

The content of this lesson focuses on Jesus Christ as a descendant from Abraham and David, a family line that includes several women who were not daughters of Israel. Within this lesson we shall examine the reaction of Joseph when he discovered that Mary, to whom he was engaged, was with child. We shall also consider the implication of his decision to quietly end their relationship. Within the lesson we see how the heavenly dimension interrupts human thought and redirects it to the purpose of the Lord. The text in which this lesson is grounded connects what is happening here with what God has been doing all along. The writer tells us that these events fulfilled Isaiah's prophecy that a virgin would bear a son named Emmanuel, which means "God is with us." The key to the story of the birth of Jesus is that Joseph, being fully convicted by the angel's words, obeyed and married Mary, and when the child was born, they named Him Jesus. Thus we can say that Jesus was born out of obedience into obedience.

LESSON 4: December 26
Coming of the Wise Men
Matthew 2:1-12

This lesson deals with the events that took place after Jesus' birth. Wise men came searching for the newborn king. Upon hearing this news, a frightened King Herod asked the religious leaders to find out where the Messiah was to be born and return to tell him where they found the child. Herod sent them to Bethlehem, where Micah had prophesied the Messiah would be born. The wise men followed the star and joyfully found the place where Jesus lay. They knelt before Jesus and gave Him valuable gifts. Warned in a dream not to return to Herod, the wise men returned to their own country by another route.

Hopefully as you study this lesson you will be led to a place of true worship. Our life on earth should be concerned

with a deeper worship of God, which then gives us the ability to discern the will of God from the superficiality of the world. In this lesson, like the wise men, we should learn not to take the world and its opinion at face value, but rather to seek the face of the Lord through worship.

UNIT 2. JESUS' TEACHINGS AND MINISTRY

"Jesus' Teaching and Ministry," is a five-session unit that includes the calling of the twelve disciples, teachings on prayer, examples of Jesus' miracles of compassion, growing opposition to Jesus, and the parable of the laborers in the vineyard.

LESSON 5: January 2
The Twelve Disciples
Matthew 4:18-22; 9:9-12; 10:1-4

The focus of this lesson emphasizes the call of the twelve disciples. First, we see two sets of brothers (Peter and Andrew, James and John) who were called by Jesus and obeyed the call to leave their vocation of fishing to follow Jesus. Second, we see Matthew, a tax collector who responded to Jesus' call by leaving his business to follow Jesus. We also see that when Jesus calls someone, no amount of human criticism changes the fact of that calling. Within the text we see the Pharisees criticizing Jesus for eating with sinners. Jesus reminds them that He spends His time with those who need Him most. Furthermore, we see that not only did Jesus call the twelve disciples to follow Him, He empowered them to cast out unclean spirits and heal the sick.

This lesson is meant to help the student think about commitment, and the life concerns appropriate to such commitments that we make to the Divine. Some of us may be required to make vocational changes in obedience under the direction of the Holy Spirit that may have some personal and social costs. By studying the lesson it is hoped that the Spirit will create within our innermost being a willingness to make the necessary sacrifices to fulfill the call of Christ.

LESSON 6: January 9
Teachings on Prayer
Matthew 6:1-15

The purpose of this lesson is to emphasize that prayer is an essential part of the Christian life. Here we learn that prayer is not just what we say, but how we live out our commitment in the world. In this lesson you will study how Jesus cautioned against practicing piety, especially in prayer, to impress others. Because giving should be the direct result of our devotion, Jesus taught that giving alms should be done confidentially, just as prayer should be done. The lesson leads to Jesus' teaching that prayer should be a personal and private matter. In teaching about the content of prayer, Jesus taught that one should not use empty phrases in prayer because God knows what we need before we ask Him. This lesson also examines what is commonly referred to as the Lord's prayer.

As you study this lesson it will challenge your thinking about prayer and its effectiveness. Finally, the lesson calls us to learn to forgive those who have wronged us so that our prayers may be received in the heavenly realm. As Christians, prayer should be one of our major life concerns.

LESSON 7: **January 16**
Miracles of Compassion
Matthew 9:18-31, 35-36

In this lesson we see Jesus expressing divine compassion for the lost sheep of the house of Israel. We shall traverse such terrain as Jesus restoring life to the daughter of a synagogue leader. We further see Jesus' compassion revealed in His healing of the woman who suffered from hemorrhages for 12 years. Here a simple touch of Jesus' cloak and basic faith released compassion and healing. This journey of divine compassion reaches two blind men who believed in His power. Jesus so touched these men that though He ordered them not to tell anyone, they went away and spread the news. It was the same compassion that caused Jesus to go about teaching, healing, and proclaiming the Good News. By the time you finish this lesson you will experience the depth of Jesus' compassion for you and those around you as well as His willingness to meet all your needs.

Hopefully this lesson will lead you to think about the wholeness that is offered to you in Jesus. As you study, begin to recognize God as the source of healing and understand that this God can give you help, comfort, and power for the problems that you face.

LESSON 8: **January 23**
Opposition to Jesus
Matthew 12:22-32, 38-40

Just because we are doing the will of God does not mean that we will be immune to opposition from those around us. The emphasis of this lesson goes to the heart of the problem of antagonism that is directed to those who do the will of God in a God-defying world. This lesson takes us through the healing of a demoniac who was blind and mute and the result of the act of healing. Instead of turning to praise and adoration, the crowd began to ask whether Jesus was truly the Messiah or a messenger of Satan. The Pharisees said that Jesus performed His miracles in the power of Beelzebul,

the ruler of the demons. We see how Jesus, in His divine wisdom, showed the folly of the Pharisees' accusation by casting out the demons by the Spirit of God. Jesus states that whoever is not in agreement with His methods is against Him, and whoever does not gather with Him scatters. It is a fact that those who opposed the work of Jesus were really fighting against the work of God. Jesus warned this kind of opposition is blasphemy against the Holy Spirit, which will never be forgiven. Not only does opposition to the work of Christ show itself by denying the power of God at work, it shows itself by defiantly asking Jesus for a sign as the Pharisees did.

This lesson is meant to make those who study it reflect on the power of Jesus and to base our faith and view of Christianity on the good that He does. Instead of demanding proof before you cast your faith upon the Lord, this lesson calls us to see the good in our life and in the lives of the people around us as evidence of Jesus' supernatural power. This lesson calls one to look at what Jesus did and who He is and to commit to Him.

LESSON 9: **January 30**
Laborers in the Vineyard
Matthew 20:1-16

This lesson concentrates on the parable of the laborers in the vineyard. Jesus told this parable to illustrate how in God's kingdom the last will be first, and the first will be last. The parable shows the tendency humans have to feel superior to one another.

This lesson also addresses rewards that are deserved and the grace that is showed to those who may not deserve it. As human beings, we want jobs with clearly defined terms of work and remuneration. In fact, many people who work are distrustful of their employers. It is okay to be upset with perceived inequities in the workplace and even to be critical when others are treated with generosity and you are not. But problems arise when you think that you deserve to be treated better than someone else by God because you have been keeping account of the good things that you have done, or how long you have been a Christian. Here we see that God's grace is shown even to those who may be considered late-bloomers in the kingdom of God.

UNIT 3. FULFILLMENT OF JESUS' MISSION

Unit three, "Fulfillment of Jesus' Mission," is a four-session unit. Session one is about Jesus' triumphant entry into Jerusalem. Session two relates to being prepared for Christ's return. Session three focuses on Jesus' death, and session four on His Resurrection and the commission to His followers.

LESSON 10: **February 6**
Coming to Jerusalem
Matthew 21:1-13

"Tell ye the daughter of Sion, Behold, thy King cometh unto thee, meek, and sitting upon an ass, and a colt the foal of an ass" (21:5), reads the key verse of this lesson. To fulfill this prophetic prediction from the Book of Zechariah Jesus sent two disciples to secure a donkey to ride into Jerusalem. The passage states that as Jesus entered Jerusalem, the crowd threw down their coats and branches along the road and shouted praises to Him. You will see how instead of letting these accolades go to His head, Jesus was still concerned about doing the will of the Father who sent Him. It is at this time that Jesus entered the temple and overturned the money changers' tables, declaring, "My house shall be called a house of prayer; but you have made it a den of robbers" (v. 13).

Rather than being guided by the rave reviews of the people Jesus was guided by the Word. Our life's concern as Christians is to carry out the divine assignment that may seem unreasonable to others. Surely many people would have thought the Lord foolish for messing up His political opportunity by overturning the money-changers' tables. But this lesson calls us to be willing to give of our resources both internal and external, for such a worthy cause as the Gospel of Jesus Christ. If you are one of those who think Christians are primarily interested in money, think again. For according to Jesus in this passage, we are about the work of prayer. Also this lesson should urge you to follow the lead of Jesus and not be so eager to follow the crowd.

LESSON 11: **February 13**
Watching for Christ's Return
Matthew 24:45—25:13

Are you keeping awake? Are you watching and praying? The Biblical content of this lesson seeks to move you to deal with these questions by examining Jesus' parables about faithful and unfaithful servants. In the parable about the five wise and the five foolish bridesmaids, Jesus illustrates the importance of being prepared for His return. The importance of being awake and ready for the coming of the Lord is powerfully illustrated as the five bridesmaids return asking that the door be opened only to hear that they were not known.

This lesson calls you to consider the joy of being prepared at the coming of the Lord. But at the same time, Christians are warned against taking a nonchalant attitude in our spiritual wakefulness. We must be attuned to the spiritual dimensions, always living as though the Lord is physically present.

LESSON 12: **February 20**
Death of Jesus
Matthew 27:38-54

This lesson calls us to examine once more the death of Jesus on our behalf. Many people were quick to turn on Jesus because they saw His death as shameful and spineless. It proves how quickly human beings can turn on their friends and leaders. We examine the fact that Jesus was crucified between two bandits. The people, chief priests, scribes, and the bandits mocked Him. We also see the other miraculous events that took place at that time. These are replete with significant symbolism regarding the nature and identity of this man called Jesus.

This lesson should encourage us to look to Jesus and to keep our faith even when people misunderstand our stance. Though people misunderstood Jesus and this misunderstanding led to His death, He knew that His experience of death would cause many to get a clearer view of who they are and who God is for them. This death was not a mere martyrdom, but a redeeming death for all.

LESSON 13: **February 27**
Resurrection and Commission
Matthew 28:1-10, 16-20

To what imperative does the Resurrection of Jesus respond? Jesus' Resurrection gave birth to the Great Commission. The Scriptural text deals with the encounter of Mary Magdalene and the other Mary at Jesus' tomb, the earthquake, the angel who opened the tomb, and the guards who became like dead men. It is in this text we hear the first proclamation of the Resurrection event. The angel told the women that Jesus had been raised and instructed them to tell the disciples to meet Him at Galilee. When the eleven disciples saw Jesus in Galilee, they worshiped Him, though some doubted. Jesus declared that He had been given all authority in heaven and earth. Based on that truth, now Jesus commissioned His followers to go and make disciples of all nations and baptize them in the name of the Father, Son, and Holy Spirit, and He assured them of His eternal presence.

This lesson is meant to give insight into the basis of our authority as believers. Just as the women who went to the tomb came back bearing good news, be ready as you read this lesson to share the Good News of His Resurrection with your loved ones and others who need this hope. Even when you experience doubt remember the power of Jesus upon which your own authority is now based and keep moving in faith. We can attempt spiritually difficult tasks because we are assured of assistance from our resurrected Lord. Finally, as you study this lesson, know that the final report for Christians can never be bad news, but good news because Jesus is alive!

MODES OF LEARNING

Do you remember grade school? I remember. I remember thick oak doors that looked so heavy that they would not budge. Somehow though, polished golden doorknobs made them to yield to a small child's hand. I remember rooms that smelled of contraband candies, slightly sour milk and the crisp autumn air that clung to our clothes from the walk to school. I remember desks evenly spaced in neat rows, facing the blackboard as if ready for learning to commence. I remember cavernous windows that made our relatively small, somewhat cramped rooms seem larger. I remember sitting at my desk, usually in the front of the classroom. I remember peering through those windows and finding that the clarity of the sky offered me a clean slate to ponder the ideas that my teachers were introducing. I remember how it felt when a new idea started to make sense to me and become a part of my thinking.

Back then, my teachers always seemed to introduce ideas by writing them on the blackboard. As a teacher wrote an idea on the board and discussed it, it was as if she wrote the idea on a slate in my head and as if my brain recorded a summary of what she was saying. I could see the words with my mind's eye and as the idea played across the TV screen of my brain, I could hear my teacher articulate the idea in my head. It was as if my brain were a VCR that had been programmed to record the images and sounds that were the focus of the day's lesson. The new idea caused me to think of other ideas that I had stored in my memory. Staring out into the clean, clear sky helped me to discover how the new idea was connected to my old ones. As my gaze fell upon the nearest window, I could see in my mind's eye both the new and the old ideas. I would enter into a dialogue with myself to determine how the old and new were linked. I would pose questions to myself that would help me to examine the connection between old and new. My answers to these questions would often lead to more questions and subsequently more answers until, finally, I understood how the new idea was connected to my old ideas. Pondering the link between the new and the old felt like trying to match the pieces of a puzzle that when put together formed a clear picture. When I had pieced together my ideas, it was clear to me that the new idea was no longer something strange and unfamiliar that stood apart from my old ideas. In fact, there ceased to be a new idea and some old ideas. Now, there was a seamless body of knowledge that my mind had constructed as a result of seeing and hearing a new idea. As a child, I always absorbed ideas best when I could see and hear them. I still learn best through these modes of learning. I am a visual and an auditory learner.

Modes of learning are the unique ways in which individuals intercept new ideas that they will ponder and blend into their stores of knowledge. Specifically, we use our senses of sight, hearing, touch, smell and taste to take in new ideas. Each of us uses these senses on a daily basis and, as a result, we learn things. Clearly, our sight allows us to take in new ideas as we glance at billboards while driving along the highway. Our hearing allows us to learn the tune to a song that a passerby hums. Our sense of touch allows us to perceive the heat of a pot that should be handled with an oven mitt. Our sense of smell allows us to detect the aroma of freshly baked cookies. Our taste buds allow us to sample the sweetness of those cookies. Therefore, our senses allow us to absorb new ideas in the world around us all the time, even when we are not actively pursuing knowledge.

When we are trying to pursue knowledge, however, one (or more) of our senses instinctively works to

Deborah Branker Harrod

harness the new ideas. For example, when I am attempting to learn a new hobby, I seek to hear and see the concepts that I need to know to master this new interest. While I could probably learn by assimilating ideas through my senses of touch, smell or taste (either singly or in combination), taking in ideas through visual and auditory means is natural to me. It is like breathing. My senses of sight and hearing comprise my dominant modes of learning, and each of us has our own modes of learning, which are our natural ways of taking in ideas. Those of us who are visual learners take in new ideas by reading or writing the ideas or seeing visual representations of them. Ideas can be written or read in the form of poems, songs, fiction or non-fiction. Film, television, video, museum exhibits and cultural tours can provide visual representations of ideas. Watching people interact with one another during the course of a day can also furnish visual representations of ideas. Auditory learners take in new ideas by hearing themselves or others discuss the ideas. Ideas can be heard when listening to songs, poetry, debates, sermons, lectures or casual conversations.

Tactile learners rely on their sense of touch to absorb new ideas. They often need to manipulate physical representations of an idea to take it in. Young tactile learners thrive in "touch and feel" museums, which are usually designed for children between the ages of 3 and 10. They give children a chance to learn about something through hands-on exploration of it. For example, one museum that I frequent with my daughter has a six-foot replica of the human ear for children to climb on, run through and play in. The children learn about the ear by touching this huge model of it. Those devoted to culinary pursuits, such as chefs, use their sense of taste and smell as receptors of new information. Newborn infants also rely on their sense of smell and taste (and also touch) to take in new information about the world around them because their other senses are not fully developed at birth. Lastly, chemists who design perfumes and florists use their sense of smell to take in new ideas that relate to the world of nature.

Our modes of learning seem to automatically kick in to help us master leisurely pursuits such as a new dance, the lyrics to a popular song or how to cook a new dish. They should also kick in when we are trying to master the subject matter taught in academic settings. In formal learning situations, teachers can provide students with the opportunity to use their unique ways of learning. They can do so by designing lesson plans that support a variety of learning styles. For example, a church schoolteacher wants his second grade students to understand some of the lessons held in the story of Noah and the ark (Genesis 6:9-22; 7—9:17). Some of those lessons are: (1) all living things on Earth are supposed to obey God, (2) disobeying God without repenting can result in death, (3) God works to cleanse the Earth of evil and (4) God sticks to His promises.

To help his students understand these abstract concepts, the teacher would have the class examine the setting and important symbols in the story using their senses of sight, touch, hearing, taste and smell. Given that the ark is central to the story, it would be the symbol that the class studies. To help visual learners understand what an ark is, the teacher would show the class pictures of one. To reinforce the visual learners' understanding of the ark, he would ask each student in the class to draw or paint his/her own ark, and then he would provide the chance for each ark to be viewed by each member of the class. To assist tactile learners in comprehending what an ark is, the teacher would allow the class to touch and study a small-scale model of an ark. To solidify the tactile learners' understanding of an ark's structure, the teacher would allow the members of the class to build their own arks (from ice cream sticks, perhaps) and then ask them to show their creations to one another. The students would be allowed to touch each other's arks. To aid auditory learners in comprehending what an ark is, the teacher would state the components of an ark aloud (maybe in the form of a rap or a poem) and then have the members of the class discuss whether their drawings and models included these components. The students would also discuss why God told Noah to build an ark and not some other buoyant structure and what the ark symbolizes in the story.

In order to support the learning of the students who learn through the senses of taste and smell, the class would study the setting of the story. To help those students who learn by tasting, the teacher would have the class prepare and taste some of the types of foods consumed by those who perished in the flood, the types of food that may have sustained Noah and the inhabitants of the ark, and the food consumed after the flood. This exercise would give the class insight into the behaviors that prompted the flood, life on the ark, and life after the flood. The members of the class would then prepare a meal in which they would share modern-day foods that represent the prevailing attitudes before the flood, the feeling that reigned in the ark, and the spirit that surfaced after the flood. A class discussion of attitudes before, during, and after the flood would accompany the sharing of food. To help those students with keen senses of smell to learn, the teacher would have the class stand about and smell the air of a humid (early summer) day and describe it. Then he would ask then to smell the air after a long, hard rain and to compare how the air smelled on the two days. Following this activity, he would ask the class to imagine how the air on Earth smelled before Noah entered the ark and after he emerged from it. This exercise can give the class insight into the notion that evil permeated the very air that the people breathed before the flood and that a spirit of renewal flowed through the air after the flood. Class discussion would accompany this exercise.

Clearly, the activities outlined above are designed to help children with all of the different learning styles to understand the importance of the ark and the setting of the story. Activities such as these help the teacher, as well as the students, to learn. By designing and frequently executing lessons such as these, the teacher gets to observe and discover each child's learning style. Those students who seem consistently excited and particularly engaged by the visual representations of an idea might be visual learners. Those who often seem mesmerized by lecture or discussion of an idea are probably auditory learners. Those who seem enthralled by examining physical representations of ideas are usually tactile learners. Those intrigued and riveted by learning through tasting or smelling might learn best through those respective modes of learning. When teachers know the learning styles of their students, they can make the learning process more engaging, personally relevant and effective for each individual student. Likewise, students become more enthusiastic and confident learners when their modes of learning inform the design of the curriculum. Students learn more when they feel respected by their teachers and peers and when they are excited about the course of study. A classroom where learners are engaged and respected is a classroom where ideas flourish. Ideas are exchanged, and the lives of the members of this learning community are enriched as a result. The ideas are like the essence of God Himself inhabiting us and motivating us to act in ways that sustain life

and honor Him. The ideas come from our minds, which God formed from the same soil He used to form our hands, our feet and our hearts. In shaping our minds, God shaped the manner in which we take in new ideas. When breathing the breath of life into us, He molded us into visual learners, auditory learners or individuals who learn by touching, tasting or smelling. The many different ways in which we take in ideas reflect the complexity of our Maker. God is one entity with infinite dimensions. Likewise, human beings are one people with many unique ways of learning. We are truly made in God's image.

Yet some educators do not see diverse ways of intercepting ideas as a reflection of the complex beauty of God. They fail to celebrate the fact that God has allowed humankind many different ways of perceiving and appreciating His Creation. Instead, these individuals favor a single mode of learning in their classrooms. For example, some of these educators may be visual learners themselves, and they may create classroom environments which encourage only visual learning. Such classrooms have lots of educational materials that can be read or viewed such as posters, books and videotapes. Yet, they do not have a lot of materials to support the learning of students who learn using their other four senses. Continually forcing students to adopt a favored mode of learning is asking them to ignore the beauty of their own God-given brilliance. It is asking them to extinguish what is Godly in them. It is denying the world the ideas and the goodness that could have come from that God-inspired brilliance.

When we extinguish the lights of others, we become the architects of a world that breeds self-loathing, apathy and chaos. When we stand idly by and witness others' lights being extinguished, our passiveness fosters the emergence of a world without the beauty and grace of God. So often, we comment that we are in search of the Lord to rid the world of its ills. Yet in our search for a larger than life God who will make everything better overnight, we fail to see Him as He presents Himself to us every day. Perhaps if we saw evidence of God's creativity in each other, our world and our lives would make sense again. If we saw the diving design of God that resides in all living things, we would not want for the Lord's comfort, guidance and mercy. They would be with us always. Imagine a world where each little light could shine. Imagine a world where we allow ourselves to be as brilliant as God knows we are.

EMMANUEL, IS GOD WITH US?

Can we ever be truly successful in an attempt to prove the existence of God? In Scripture, the Lord reveals that He is Emmanuel, also known as Jehovah, Elohim, Yahweh, Adonai, and God, to provide just a few names. Each name carries a special meaning that is associated or attached to it. In times past, names were indicative of the character of the person. As a society, we have moved away from really giving attention to the meaning behind the names that we give to our children, family, and friends. When we look at this name of God, Emmanuel, we are introduced to its meaning in Matthew 1:23 as "God with us." In a word study of the Hebrew term, Emmanuel means "mighty, the Almighty" and "with." The picture presented is the presence of the "Almighty with" us. Therefore, one who knows and loves the Saviour would desperately want to share the Word of God in such a way that we prove His existence. The bottom line is that we are not called to authenticate Emmanuel's presence; He will do that. We are called to be living testimonies of God's presence in us.

One day several years ago, as I was carpooling, the driver gave his explanation of the presence of God. He said, "Good took the world after Creation, wound it up like a clock, cast it into the cosmos, and said, 'Now there, make it on your own.' As a result of God distancing Himself, we are left with the havoc that we are experiencing today." There are many theories to explain why we are left with the questions that plague our society today. In essence, where is God? Is Emmanuel with us in this present day? Philosopher Soren Kierkegaard advised, "It is so impossible for the world to exist without God, that if God should forget it, it would immediately cease to be" (David Manning White, *The Search For God*, New York: Macmillan, 1983).

There are a number of reasons why we sometimes question the presence of Emmanuel. Some of these issues relate to our own human limitations. For instance, because of our increasing dependency on our senses, we develop a need to see or touch our Lord. We are in a society in which visualization and audio are at a premium. Our senses of sight and hearing are constantly being stimulated and, are therefore, becoming increasingly demanding. Faith is being knocked out of the picture. If we are not careful we can become the antithesis of 2 Corinthians 5:7—a people walking by sight and not by faith.

Then there are the issues created by our limited perception of God, such as being silent, slow, and separate. We consider Him to be silent because of a need for some kind of audible influence. We look for a word, whether in the church or in society, and we are constantly trying to determine if God will speak in a way that we can hear. We consider Him to be slow because we are influenced by a world that hurries up to wait, but becomes very impatient at the prospect of waiting. Years ago, televisions had to warm up before they would work. Today, however, we live in a microwave society that has instant grits, fast food restaurants, 15-minute oil lubes, weekend colleges, and transportation that can get us from one destination to the other in a matter of hours, as opposed to days. So when it comes to our God, we are expecting fast results according to the way the world has trained us to respond. Then the seeming aloofness of God causes us to see Him as separate from our day to day actions and responsibilities.

In the Old Testament prophecy about Emmanuel, it tells of One who will be with us. As we study the name, a story begins, and by the very nature of the question there is the presumption that God did start out with us. Since He started, when did He ever leave us? The passage in the Book of Joshua, chapter 1 specifically states the promise of God's presence to the new leader of the nation of Israel (v. 9). Even though there is the natural human tendency to worry and even become frightened by the responsibilities before us, we can rest assured that God would never leave us nor forsake us. This was the promise of a Heavenly Father who will be a protector and a provider for a called people.

We are introduced in Numbers 14:19 to the concept of "the Lord is with us" as the Children of Israel are at the border of Canaan. After the 12 spies returned with their report concerning the exploration, the community begins to weep. Their raised voices were against Moses and Aaron. In

Dr. Carl E. King

133

Using the Old Testament war stories as a comparison, we can glean that there often is preparation for some kind of battle. This New Testament battle is between our Saviour and the evil one Satan. We are to be encouraged even though it might seem that we are out numbered or about to be over-powered by the enemy, our God is with us.

Jesus Christ won the victory in the ultimate battle occurred at the Cross. Every other battle from the previous Scripture passages was just a prototype of the battle that Christ would endure for His chosen ones. In each of the Old Testament passages, we see that the promise was given to those who in some way had committed themselves to obedience. Even though there will always be those who are faithful and those who are unfaithful, or the presence of the "wheat and the tares" it will be God that does the separating. Sometimes those who wrestle with the concept of His presence will have a negative influence on those who believe and are willing to fight on, as with the Children of Israel at the borders of Canaan. The first generation did not go in, but the next generation enjoyed the benefits of obedience.

At times, we need to remember that God is with us as we face the prospect of being out-numbered two to one, and as we struggle with a "grasshopper versus a giant" perception. We need to remember "Emmanuel," and hold on to His assessment of our circumstances and change our evaluation of ourselves. Or maybe our need is to be reminded of Yahweh-Shammah, and think not on just preparing for battle, but that the battle was already fought and won. Jesus said, "it is finished" while He was on the Cross. This simply means that the enemy had done his worst, and the counsel and the commandment of the Father concerning His sufferings was fulfilled. It means that every detail concerning the redemption of man was complete—that reconciliation was now possible, that the dominion and power that was given away to Satan has been taken back by God through Jesus Christ; that Emmanuel has delivered the final blow to Satan, and it is finished! We are more than conquerors in this battle of life!

We must maintain the position of righteousness to which our Heavenly Father has called us until the day in which He calls us to our eternal home. We will be called to a city that forever will be known in Hebrew as *Yahweh-Shammah*, "the Lord is there." This is maybe a word play on *Yerushalayim*, the Hebrew pronunciation of Jerusalem (see Ezekiel 48:35, *NIV Study Bible* comments).

To answer the question "Is Emmanuel with us?" is to respond that **He is with us** and has **never left us** (Hebrews 13:5, 6; Matthew 28:20). Emmanuel, our God with us, will eventually take us to a city that is named to emphasize His presence for an eternity.

response Joshua, one of the 12, challenged the people to believe in their success by reminding them, " . . . the Lord is with us. Don't be discouraged about the immensity of the battle nor the size of your abilities" (vv. 8-9, paraphrased).

We see a similiar passage in 2 Chronicles 13:12, recounting King Abijah's sermon on Mount Zemaraim reminding Judah before they went to battle against Jeroboam and Israel that "God is with us; he is our leader." And in Psalm 46:11, the psalmist tells a nation preparing for the onslaught of the enemy that there should be this undying faith, that victory would be theirs because of the presence of "the Lord Almighty." In Isaiah 7:2, we find Ahaz seeking to comfort the people of Judah when they thought that they were outnumbered and experiencing difficulty fighting against Jerusalem. The people were shaken "as the trees of the forest are shaken by the wind" (NIV).

In each Bible story, the people of God face odds that seem insurmountable. Each time they were preparing for some sort of battle; and in each case God uses a believer to share a word of faith, hope, or encouragement with the disgruntled, discouraged, disadvantaged, and distraught. For each of the different situations, the message is the same. Even though the name Emmanuel is not being used, the essence of the name is evident. These are the Old Testament examples. We are also introduced to this name in the New Testament as the representative of God Himself.

AFRICAN-AMERICAN SPIRITUALITY: HAVING CHURCH

"It is important for the Church of God to tell the people of God, "Hey, hey, hey!' Our God sees. Our God hears. Our God knows and our God will come down and deliver us." Dessmond TuTu

Having church is a familiar idea within the African-American community. Customarily, wherever African-Americans gathered there was a chance you would hear a call to have church. The call to have church indicates that church is not only a place but an event, a happening. In the earlier years of African-American history, from slavery to integration, church included all of life. Wherever African-Americans gathered, church happened because God was present. We often lift up family, school and church as institutions that held the African-American community together and where God was most present. There were other institutions within the African-American community where people gathered to have church. We gathered at night clubs, the hairdresser or beauty salon, barber shops, pool halls, and gambling halls. These places are not classified as institutions nor places where God's presence could be experienced. African-Americans were formed spiritually by these gathering places as well as by the church family and school. When we gathered in the "club," it was not just for entertainment but to tell the story that in ways we were not allowed to tell in the house of worship. In the club people could dance and sing the blues that reached deep down into the soul and expressed the pain, sorrow, grief and joy we experience as African-American people living in America. The hairdresser or beauty salon, barber shops and pool halls were places where people gathered—not only to attend to their outer appearances but to tell stories, to discuss the Bible, and to pass on news of who was sick, who had died, married, divorced, separated and needed help. These were places where outreach ministry happened and offerings were taken to aid those in need, and to help families who were not able to bury their love ones. These were places where people who were hurting, grieving or sorrowful could go for comfort.

Integration destroyed many of these places of gathering and scattered African-American people throughout America. The African-American family was fragmented and the extended family of grandparents, aunts and uncles, who were the "backbone" of the African-American family, were separated by distance because of increased mobility of African-Americans in the society. Today we gather in the same places, as well as new places, but we tell different stories. In earlier times when we gathered to have church, we praised God, called upon God's name, gave thanks to Him for His goodness and asked Him to watch over us. All that happened the past week was gathered up on Sunday morning and lifted to God so that He might bless us, judge us, and call us to repentance, so that we might draw closer to and be empowered by the Holy Spirit to go forth into the world and proclaim the Good News. After we praised the Lord through song, gave thanks through testimonies, called on God's name and sought His blessings through prayer, the Black preacher came forward to tell the story. The story is similar to the story of the Israelites. We were enslaved in America. We cried out and God heard our cries. God delivered us from slavery, segregation, and discrimination into the promised land of freedom.

Like the Israelites, we quickly took on the ways of the enslavers and over time we became alienated from having church. We still gather in familiar places, places that we have created or that have been created for us. When we gather, however, we tell or listen to a different story. The story now told is that we are descendants of queens and kings. Our ancestors lived and created a highly-advanced civilization that history, in most instances, does not include. We tell this story to correct history and build self-esteem, particularly

Reverend Dr. Odis Fentry

God we survived. The Black preacher told these stories of Exodus, the Exile, David and Goliath, Shadrach, Meshach and Abednego in the fiery furnace, and many others. He didn't tell them to diminish the self-esteem of the people; white folk had already crushed the self-esteem of Blacks. The Black preacher knew and the people knew that the point of the stories were not enslavement, suffering, humiliation, pain and death. The point of all of these stories is restoration. Regardless of our condition, God will hear our cries and restore us to new life.

Today, more than ever, the African-American community needs to hear the whole story. We have become alienated from the whole story, and the guilt that alienation produces prevents us from telling or hearing the whole story. But we continue to gather to hear the stories, to have church. As Walter Brueggeman says in his book *Finally Comes the Poet*, "It is the resilience of the yearning that causes people to dress up in their heaviness and present themselves for the drama one more time. Sunday morning is, for some, a last desperate hope that life need not be lived in alienation. We need not dwell on the sin that produces alienation." To avoid or rid ourselves of this alienation, African-Americans must develop a new model of having church. We must allow all of who we are, both consciously and subconsciously, to be brought to the places where we gather to have church. When we gather to have church, whether in small prayer groups, spiritual growth groups, Bible study groups or on Sunday morning, let the good, bad and ugly be lifted up to God. God can handle it. We may not be able to articulate what's happening, but the poet (the preacher) among us will step forward and speak for all of us and by God's grace we will be restored, made whole and transformed until we are rightly related to ourselves, to God, to one another and to the environment in which we live.

It is no accident that African-Americans chose to hear the Word of God, not only through our African heritage but also through the Hebrew Scriptures. Both look at life holistically. Death, destruction, evil, deception, beauty and joy are all part of life under the providence of God.

among our people. However, we might be guilty of ignoring a strand of African history that completes the story of our African heritage.

Many of the Desert Abbas and Ammas were African. They were people of prayer, and wisdom, and were great thinkers and theologians revered for their contribution to the whole church. Some of these persons are well known, such as Augustine, Tertullian and others. There are others, however, who were well known in their day such as Abba Moses, better known as Black Moses. They taught us how to pray, love, suffer, and endure.

If we do not tell the whole story, we cannot have church. The whole story is that we are descendants of people who were kings and queens, and people who created a highly-advanced civilization. We inherited a rich religious tradition from Africa, which was in touch with Christianity long before White people discovered it and exploited it for their own purpose. For African-American spirituality, the core stories are those of enslavement, suffering, humiliation, and restoration. These are stories that tell us that people tried to eliminate us from the face of the earth, but by the grace of

Aleksandr Sergeyevich Pushkin

(1799-1837)

Aleksandr Sergeyevich Pushkin was a Russian poet and author, creator of the Cyrillic alphabet which Russians use today, and creator of the Russian classical literature with its lyric and epic poems, novels, plays, and short stories.

Aleksandr Pushkin was born June 6, 1799, in Moscow, into a well-to-do and noble family. He was extremely proud of his great-grandfather Abram Hannibal, a black general who served under Peter the Great. Pushkin's gift for poetry was noticed early in life. Pushkin was formally educated at the Imperial Lyceum at Tsarkoye Selo. In 1817, at the age of 18, Aleksandr joined the social whirl of the capital in the ministry of foreign affairs and joined an underground revolutionary group. In 1820, he was exiled to the Caucasus because of a poem he wrote entitled Ode to Liberty, but he continued to hold government offices. The poem reflected Pushkin's distaste for bondage and servanthood. He cried for freedom and was the spokesman for poor and oppressed people. He was later pardoned and allowed to return to St. Petersburg. His passion for poor and oppressed people surely was influenced by his childhood nurse.

> # The Russian language had been considered too primitive for literature.

His nurse provided a neglected Pushkin with affection, she taught him Russian folklore, and gave him first-hand descriptions of the history and conditions of poor people in Russia.

Pushkin's most famous work, *Eugene Onegin*, was begun in 1823 and wasn't completed until 1831. It was described as the first of the great Russian novels in spite of the fact that it was in verse. Aleksandr Pushkin provided Russia with a literary heritage. The Russian language had been considered too primitive for literature. Pushkin not only created the Cyrillic alphabet, but was the "Daniel Webster" of his day, putting together a usable dictionary of the Russian language.

Aleksandr died February 10, 1837, from wounds that he suffered in a duel fought in St. Petersburg. One hundred years after his death, the Soviet government published the complete works of Pushkin in The Literary Heritage of Pushkin.

Some of his other works are *The Prisoner of the Caucasus, The Fountain of Bakhchisarai, The Gypsies, Boris Godunov, Poltava, The Bronze Horsemen, The Fisherman and the Fish, The Golden Cockerel* and *The Captain's Daughter.*

TEACHING TIPS

December 5
Bible Study Guide 1

1. Words You Should Know

A. Sin. (Matthew 3:6) Greek *poneros*—evil, denotes a rebellion against God and a transgression against His standards.

B. Repentance. (v. 2) Greek *metanoia*—denotes a change of mind and *metamelomai*—a change of attitude. It is an invitation for people to turn from their sins unto the grace of God.

C. Kingdom of Heaven or **Kingdom of God.** (v. 2)—Refers to the spiritual rule of Christ within the heart of those who are saved.

2. Teacher Preparation

A. Begin preparing for this quarter by reading the UNIT INTRODUCTION in the Bible Study Guide.

B. Prepare for Unit 1 by reading the UNIT 1 INTRODUCTION. Then read Matthew 3:1-8, 11-17.

C. Now, carefully study the FOCAL VERSES by reading them at least three times using a different version for each reading.

D. Materials needed: Bibles, paper, pens or pencils, board, and chalk, the *Teacher Manual* and the *Teaching Success Kit* item for Lesson 1.

3. Starting the Lesson

A. Before the class enters, write the AT-A-GLANCE outline and the words "Sin," "Repentance," and "Kingdom of Heaven" on the board.

B. After the students have entered and settled, lead the class in prayer emphasizing the LESSON AIM. Then, have a volunteer read the IN FOCUS poem.

C. Before beginning the lesson, explain the focus of Unit 1 using the UNIT 1 INTRODUCTION.

4. Getting into the Lesson

A. Pass out paper and a pencil or pen to your students. Ask them to write their definition of "sin," "repentance," and the "Kingdom of heaven." Then, ask for volunteers to read their definitions.

B. Share the definitions of "sin," "repentance," and "the kingdom of heaven" from the WORDS YOU SHOULD KNOW and allow for discussion.

C. To help the students understand the context of today's lesson, read the BACKGROUND information. Then ask for volunteers to read the FOCAL VERSES according to the AT-A-GLANCE outline. After the students

have read each segment, ask the corresponding SEARCH THE SCRIPTURES questions.

5. Relating the Lesson to Life

A. Direct the students to read the DISCUSS THE MEANING questions and allow them to discuss and compare definitions. This will help them to see how the lesson applies to their personal life.

B. Next read the LESSON IN OUR SOCIETY article and allow for class discussion. The students should be able to see how the lesson applies to our modern-day society.

6. Arousing Action

A. Direct the students' attention to the MAKE IT HAPPEN suggestion. Challenge them to seriously examine their own life to be sure of their own salvation. You may ask if anyone would like to accept Christ as their personal Saviour. You may lead them in a prayer of repentance at that time or after class. Also have them speak with your pastor about their commitment.

B. Next, encourage your students to read the DAILY BIBLE READING. This will also help them to become astute in God's Word.

C. Solicit prayer requests. Have students also write down requests and put them in a closed container. Each class session, pray over these written requests as well as the spoken ones. Remind your students to share with the class when prayers are answered so that you may rejoice together.

KING'S HERALD AND BAPTISM

Bible Background • MATTHEW 3
Printed Text • MATTHEW 3:1-8, 11-17
Devotional Reading • MATTHEW 21:23-27

LESSON AIM

By the end of the lesson, students will be able to recognize that now is the time to prepare for eternity—where they will spend life after death. They will also be able to explain how John the Baptist prepared the way for Jesus to come to save us all from our sins.

KEEP IN MIND

"I indeed baptize you with water unto repentance: but he that cometh after me is mightier than I, whose shoes I am not worthy to bear: he shall baptize you with the Holy Ghost, and with fire:" (Matthew 3:11).

FOCAL VERSES

MATTHEW 3:1 In those days came John the Baptist, preaching in the wilderness of Judaea,

2 And saying, Repent ye: for the kingdom of heaven is at hand.

3 For this is he that was spoken of by the prophet Esaias, saying, The voice of one crying in the wilderness, Prepare ye the way of the Lord, make his paths straight.

4 And the same John had his raiment of camel's hair, and a leathern girdle about his loins; and his meat was locusts and wild honey.

5 Then went out to him Jerusalem, and all Judaea, and all the region round about Jordan,

6 And were baptized of him in Jordan, confessing their sins.

7 But when he saw many of the Pharisees and Sadducees come to his baptism, he said unto them, O generation of vipers, who hath warned you to flee from the wrath to come?

LESSON OVERVIEW

LESSON AIM
KEEP IN MIND
FOCAL VERSES
IN FOCUS
THE PEOPLE, PLACES, AND TIMES
BACKGROUND
AT-A-GLANCE
IN DEPTH
SEARCH THE SCRIPTURES
DISCUSS THE MEANING
LESSON IN OUR SOCIETY
MAKE IT HAPPEN
FOLLOW THE SPIRIT
REMEMBER YOUR THOUGHTS
MORE LIGHT ON THE TEXT
DAILY BIBLE READINGS

8 Bring forth therefore fruits meet for repentance:

11 I indeed baptize you with water unto repentance: but he that cometh after me is mightier than I, whose shoes I am not worthy to bear: he shall baptize you with the Holy Ghost, and with fire:

12 Whose fan is in his hand, and he will throughly purge his floor, and gather his wheat into the garner; but he will burn up the chaff with unquenchable fire.

13 Then cometh Jesus from Galilee to Jordan unto John, to be baptized of him.

14 But John forbad him, saying, I have need to be baptized of thee, and comest thou to me?

15 And Jesus answering said unto him, Suffer it to be so now: for thus it becometh us to fulfil all righteousness. Then he suffered him.

16 And Jesus, when he was baptized, went up straightway out of the water: and, lo, the heavens were opened unto him, and he saw the Spirit of God descending like a dove, and lighting upon him:

17 And lo a voice from heaven, saying, This is my beloved Son, in whom I am well pleased.

IN FOCUS

A Christian writer, wrote the following poem that denotes why we need to spread the Good News that Jesus Christ is still saving souls so that we might have eternal life. The Gospel of Jesus Christ is still making a positive difference as we live out our lives here on earth as well.

THE EYES OF PAIN

I saw those eyes on so many city streets
as I hurriedly passed by.
They were filled with many unshed tears,
Oh, the pain one couldn't deny!
Sometimes they stood gazing into the wind,
or even peering into the sky,
questioning and wondering what went wrong,
oh, seeking the reason why!
Those eyes exposed a broken human spirit
whose vision long ago took flight,
and the battle wounds they bore
embraced a countenance as dark as night.
Oh yes, I saw those same eyes
on many who could not cope,
and their today was a constant fight for survival
and the future possessed such little hope.
In fact, those eyes stirred my very soul
and caused me to ponder life,
and question how a mere mortal could reform
a world of trouble and strife.
But then, a little voice so deep within
spoke quite sure and fast,
"Only God can heal the broken spirit,
and grant a peace that lasts!"

(*The Eyes of Pain*, Copyright by Evangeline Carey. Reprinted by permission.
All rights reserved).

People are crying out all around us—turning to drugs, alcohol, and sexual immorality because they are looking for a peace that last. This peace is not found in these things. The peace that surpasses all understanding, the joy that the world cannot give can only be found in a personal relationship with Jesus Christ.

Today's lesson focuses on the beginning of Christ's ministry to a lost and dying world. John the Baptist heralded, or announced Christ's coming. He told the Jews of his day, and through God's Word as well, to "Repent, for the kingdom of heaven is near" (v. 2, NIV).

THE PEOPLE, PLACES, AND TIMES

THE TIMES. It was a time of peril and expectation. The people of Israel had been waiting centuries for a deliverer, a king, a leader to free them from their Roman oppressors. They waited for someone who would rescue them and set up an earthly kingdom where justice would prevail. However, Jesus did not fit the bill. He came preaching about a heavenly kingdom where people lived by the stan-dards of God. This kingdom was established in people's heart. He came to die for all mankind so that those who believed on Him would have eternal life. Therefore, Jesus was presented to the nation of Israel, but was rejected by them.

JESUS CHRIST. Jesus Christ is God and man all in one. He is God's one and only Son sent to save mankind from their sins. He came to die so that we can live forever with a Holy God. Jesus came to be our Messiah, our Saviour, our Lord, our Master, the King of our life. He is the second person of the God-head (God, the Father, *God, the Son*, God, the Holy Spirit). We enter His kingdom by faith—faith in His blood shed for the remission of our sins. Jesus came to show us the way. We can follow Him by studying and obeying His Holy Word.

BACKGROUND

Matthew, one of the original twelve disciples, wrote this Gospel to prove to the Jews that indeed Jesus was the Messiah or the "Anointed One" who came to be their Saviour. All they needed to do, of course, was accept Him as so. The Jews, however, were looking for a king who would set up his kingdom here on earth and free them from Roman oppression. They were not expecting a suffering Saviour who would be tried, found guilty, thrown in jail, and crucified as well. They were not looking for a King whose kingdom was established in man's heart.

Matthew had been a hated Jewish tax collector before Jesus came into his life. Ordinarily, these tax collectors stole from their own people to pad their pockets as well as the government's. When Matthew became a follower of Christ, he could no longer have this dishonest profession. Indeed, Jesus prepared Matthew for both eternal life with God and right living with his fellow man here on earth.

AT-A-GLANCE

1. John the Baptist Prepares the Way for Jesus by Preaching and Baptizing (Matthew 3:1-6)
2. John Addresses the Pharisees and Sadducees (vv. 7-8)
3. John Baptizes and Announces Jesus' Coming (vv. 11-12)
4. The Baptism of Jesus (vv. 13-17)

IN DEPTH

1. John the Baptist Prepares the Way for Jesus by Preaching and Baptizing (Matthew 3:1-6)

John the Baptist was an uncompromising, God-appointed messenger who spoke with authority of the coming Messiah who would save His people from their sins. Even though John was considered odd or unique because of his hermit-like, wilderness life style, his clothes woven from camel hair, and the locust food he ate (v.4), his message was clear: "Repent" (v. 2).

John exhorted his fellow Jews to turn from their sins and turn to God because the kingdom of God or heaven was near (v. 2). People came from all over Jerusalem and Judea to hear this man of God (v. 5). In fact, Isaiah the prophet had spoken of John and called him "a voice crying in the wilderness." (Isaiah 40:3). John knew that the people needed to make a 180-degree turn—turning from their self-centered lifestyles characterized by lying, cheating, stealing, murdering, sexual immorality, abuse, etc., to God-centered lives characterized by obedience to God's edicts as spelled out in His Word.

2. John Addresses the Pharisees and Sadducees (vv. 7-8)

The Jewish religion of that day was divided into several groups of which the Pharisees and Sadducees were the two most prominent. The Sadducees were descendants mainly from priestly nobility and therefore proudly considered themselves descendants of Abraham. The Pharisees were descendants from all classes of people. Although these two groups disliked each other, both were critical, legalistic, and hypocritical as they dwelled on the letter of the law when it came to other people, and not the intent of the law. John the Baptist denounced them for their hypocrisy (v. 7). He challenged them to prove by the way they lived that they had really made that 180-degree turn of true repentance from sin (v. 8). He challenged them to prove by their actions that their hearts had been changed. John knew that there is no respect of persons with God, even religious leaders like the Sadducees and Pharisees needed to repent from sin or they too were in danger of hell fire (v. 10).

3. John Baptizes and Announces Jesus' Coming (vv. 11-12)

John baptized people as an outward sign that they had asked God to forgive their sins and would be obedient to His Word. By being baptized, they were declaring their commitment to doing the will of God. In verse 11, John lets the people know that he (John) is not Jesus the coming Messiah. John was just heralding the arrival of Jesus and the beginning of His ministry. Therefore, John was willing to decrease in the sight of the people. He knew that God would not share His glory with any man. John made sure that the people knew where Jesus fit in the hierarchy of things. In fact, he emphasized that he (John) was baptizing with water, but Jesus would come and baptize with the Holy Spirit and with fire. In verse 12, John warns them of God's judgment where God will separate believers from unbelievers. Unrepentant people will be judged and thrown into the lake of fire for eternity because they rejected the only one who could save them, Jesus.

4. The Baptism of Jesus (vv. 13-17)

John the Baptist had the privilege of baptizing Jesus Christ, the Son of the Most High God, Saviour of the World, Himself (v. 13). What an honor! What a privilege!

Even though Jesus had not sinned, He was baptized to support John's work, and to advance the work of the kingdom of heaven. He was our example. He was being obedient to the Father, and God was well pleased (vv. 16-17).

SEARCH THE SCRIPTURES

1. Where did John the Baptist preach? (Matthew 3:1)

2. What did John preach? (v. 2)

3. What prophet had spoken of John long before he came on the scene? (v. 3)

4. How did John feel about the Pharisees and Sadducees? Why? (vv. 7-10)

5. When Jesus was baptized by John, what did a voice from heaven say? (v. 17)

DISCUSS THE MEANING

1. Sometimes people confuse salvation and baptism. When they are asked if they are saved, they say, "Yes! I got baptized." Discuss the difference between the two.

2. John the Baptist called the Pharisees and Sadducees "vipers" in verse 7. From John's discussion with these religious leaders, what lesson can we draw about leaders who mislead God's people? Can you be saved by trying to keep the letter of the law instead of believing on the Lord, Jesus Christ?

LESSON IN OUR SOCIETY

In 1998, our President was caught up in a sexual scandal in the White House. The sordid details were blasted over the air ways and in the newspapers for months. Many people were embarrassed to even discuss the facts. Many Christians asked themselves, "How can we afford to trust a

President who says he's a Christian but does not uphold God's Word by his conduct?"

Even the President needs to listen to John the Baptist's challenging call to repentance. Indeed, we each must seriously consider the state of our spiritual life. Is yours in order? Do your actions show that you have accepted Jesus Christ as your personal Saviour?

MAKE IT HAPPEN

If you are already saved, when was the last time that you talked to a friend, co-worker, or relative about their salvation? Commit yourself this day to winning a lost soul to the kingdom of God.

FOLLOW THE SPIRIT

What God wants me to do:

_____

_____

REMEMBER YOUR THOUGHTS

Special insights you learned:

_____

_____

MORE LIGHT ON THE TEXT
MATTHEW 3:1-8; 11-17

1 In those days came John the Baptist, preaching in the wilderness of Judea,

In this verse, we see the introduction of John the Baptist's ministry. John the Baptist was a prophet of the house of Israel with his own message and disciples. Christians refer to John as "the forerunner" of Jesus, the Messiah. Unlike Luke, Matthew does not give the family lineage of John the Baptist. In the Gospel of Matthew, John the Baptist makes an abrupt appearance. Matthew just begins with "in those days" (Greek *en tais hemerais ekenais*). This phrase should be viewed in the context of the social/political condition described by Matthew in chapters 1 and 2. What were those days like? Israel was under oppression; Herod had usurped the throne of Israel and was ruthless in his dealings with the people. The phrase has a certain prophetic mood to it. It is a word of expectation. The phrase is like breathing a sigh of relief. "In those days, those horrible days, those painful days, those days of despair."

The Greek word *hemera* (pronounced **hay-mer'-ah**) may literally refer to the time span between dawn and dark or the chronological day as measured by a clock. Here it is used figuratively to refer to a period. In a sense it characterizes the mood of the age, especially when the reference is made by someone who has an intense feeling about the age, negatively or positively. The sentence continues "came John the Baptist." The Greek reads, *paraginetai ioannes ho baptistetes*. The key word here is "came" or *paraginetai* (pronounced **pa-ra-gee-nay-tay**), taken from the Greek word *paraginomai* (pronounced **par-ag-in'-om-ahee**). This word is a combination of two Greek words *para* and *ginomai*. Translated, it means "to become near" or "to make an earnest approach to one's destination." In other words, John the Baptist had finally arrived.

In verse 1, Matthew tells us when John appeared, at what location John drew near to the people of Israel, and what he did when he came. John the Baptist came "preaching" (Greek *kerusso*, pronounced **kay-ru-s'-so**), which simply means that he came as a herald or a town crier. This word is specifically related to the declaration of divinely-ordained truth. In the New Testament, it is used mainly in reference to the proclamation of the Gospel. We could say that John the Baptist published a message. For the word *kerusso* could also mean publish. The word "publish" has the same root as the word "public." We are also told that John came preaching "in the wilderness of Judea." The Greek translation is the word *eremos*, (pronounced **er'-ay-mos**) and refers to a lonesome place—a wasteland. John came from the natural desert preaching to people who, at that time, were in a spiritual wasteland.

2 And saying, Repent ye: for the kingdom of heaven is at hand.

The content of John the Baptist's proclamation, according to this verse, is repentance. John's first words of warning are, "Repent ye" (Greek *metanoeite*, **met-an-o-ehi- te**). The phrase is derived from the Greek word *metanoeo* (pronounced **met-an-o-eh'-o**), which is a combination of *meta* meaning "beyond" and *noieo* meaning "mind," especially as it affects one's thought process. The content of John's message addressed the minds of the people. What John was saying required them to think differently or reconsider their mental outlook. The doctrine he preached was repentance; "Repent ye" implies a total alteration of the mind, a change in judgment, disposition, and affections to another and a better bias of the soul. In other words, "Consider your ways; change your mind; you have thought amiss; think again, and think aright." A change of mind produces a change of behavior. It combines abstraction and a sense of existential compunction. John is calling people to examine their moral feelings. He challenges them to start thinking and feeling differently. It is interesting that John uses the imperative or command. By stating it this way, John implied that there is a reward for listening and a consequence for not listening and acting in accordance with this imperative. You may want to picture John pointing to the crowd and saying "You, Repent!"

The next phrase which follows John's call to repentance is a natural response to the questions that were raised in the mind of the people. "Why should we change our minds? We like the way we have been thinking. Why should we transform our feelings? We feel fine. What makes this repentance necessary?" John's response is: "for the kingdom of heaven is at hand" (Greek *eengiken gar he basileia ton ouranon*). The key word here is *basileia*, pronounced **bas-il-I'-yah** which means "royalty." This reminds one of the practice among some African peoples. It is said that when the chief or the king was riding into town someone went ahead of him shouting, "The king is near; the king is near; prepare the way for the king."

To say that "the kingdom of heaven is at hand" is to imply that what was abstract is now being made concrete. What seems afar off is now brought near. That is the Gospel, which flows from the sight of Christ, from a sense of His love, and from hopes of pardon and forgiveness through Him. It is a great encouragement for us to repent—repent, for your sins shall be pardoned upon your repentance. Return to God in a way of duty, and He will, through Christ, return unto you in the way of mercy. It is still just as necessary to repent and humble ourselves, to prepare the way of the Lord, as it was then. There is a great deal to be done, to make way for Christ to enter a soul. Nothing is more needful than the discovery of sin, and a conviction that we cannot be saved by our own righteousness. The way of sin and Satan is a crooked way; but to prepare a way for Christ, the paths must be made straight. Those whose business it is to call others to mourn for sin, and to mortify it, ought themselves to live a serious life—a life of self-denial and contempt of the world. By giving others this example, John made way for Christ.

There may be many forward hearers, where there are few true believers. Curiosity and love for novelty and variety may bring many to attend good preaching and to be affected for a while who never are subject to the power of it. Those who received John's doctrine, testified of their repentance by confessing their sins. Similarly, those who are ready to receive Jesus Christ as their righteousness, are brought with sorrow and shame to own their guilt. The benefits of the kingdom of heaven, now at hand, were thereupon sealed to them by baptism. John washed them with water, in token that God would cleanse them from all their iniquities. By nature and practice all were polluted, and could not be accepted as children of God unless washed from their sins in the fountain Christ was to open (Zechariah 13:1).

3 For this is he that was spoken of by the prophet Isaiah, saying, The voice of one crying in the wilderness, Prepare ye the way of the Lord, make his path straight.

The phrase "For this is he that was spoken" is a common phrase by which Hebrew writers called up authoritative traditions. Matthew is fond of this type of reference to the Hebrew Old Testament. The word for "spoken" is the Greek word *reetheis* taken from the word *rheo* (**hreh'o**), which is derived from the idea of pouring forth out of the fullness of one's heart. In this case, it refers to that which was uttered by an anointed person through the fullness of the Holy Spirit. From its sound, it refers to speech that involves breathing. It can also mean "what is commanded." Ordinarily, it means simply "to speak" but here it refers to the divine dynamism which influences prophetic utterances.

Where do we go to find the identity of this man who came to the wasteland preaching a change of mind? For Matthew, John's identity can be found in the prophetic utterance of the prophet Isaiah. The Greek word *prophetes* (pronounced **prof-eh'-tace**) comes from a combination of the Greek words *pro* which could mean "forward" or "towards" and the Greek word *phemi*, which means a "foreteller" (prophet); by analogy, an "inspired speaker;" by extension "a poet." The Judea-Christian belief system and the religious movement within it argues that God speaks and that this speech gives insight to human beings. Thus when we read, "this is that which was spoken," we are immediately placed in the inspirational action of God by which insight is given to human beings. It is a way of saying, "this is that insight which came to Isaiah." Here is one of the miraculous connections between the New Testament and the Old Testament: the thread of prophetic insight runs through both.

What insight was given to Isaiah the Prophet? The very character of someone who will live at least 700 years after Isaiah was unknown in the physical realm. Isaiah says, "the voice of one crying in the wilderness." The meaning of the Greek word for "*voice*," pronounced **fo-nay'**) includes both the sound and the medium through which ideas come to disclosure. It may be said that here John is one who carries the tune, that is, the divine tune. It could also be read "as one who addresses the people on behalf of another." There was a language heard in the wilderness; it was the language of God. The noise Isaiah hears in the wilderness is one of deep, divine intent. "Voice" is not just the mechanism by which we form speech. There is a perception in which our voice is an embodiment of us. It is the means whereby one is able to mobilize and to engage the world. Our voice is our moral authority. Therefore, it can be said, that this voice in the wilderness was a moral clarion.

Note also that the voice was "crying" (Greek *boao*, say **bo-ah'-o**), possibly meaning a continuous call for help that derives from a primary need. It may also mean to make a show of force, as in shouting for help in such a way that one creates a scene. Here the prophet calls this voice a crying voice; Its purpose is to get attention. Also remarkable is the context in which this voice cries. The voice cries in the wilderness; it cries in the desert (Greek *eremos*, pronounced **er'-ay-mos**). The voice is heard in a place of uncertainty. In places where people have lost their affinity with God and with themselves, there God's voice is heard through His servants.

A lone voice is crying in a lonesome place for a lonesome people. The voice cries out in a place of waste. It cries out from a desolate and solitary land into the lives of those who hear it. What does this voice say? First it cries out for preparation, "prepare the way of the Lord . . . ." The Greek word *hetoimazate* (pronounced **het-oy-mad-sate**) is taken from the word *hetoimazo* (pronounced **het-oy-mad'-zo**) which means to prepare. More importantly it also means to make provision for or to make ready. It brings to mind the thorough preparation that is made for Holy days such as the Day of Atonement. It refers here not only to the external alertness which is demanded of one in holy convocations, but also to spiritual fitness of the person or the environment in which the convocation is to take place. So the voice is crying out, "construct, build, or raise up a fitting structure for the Lord."

Again, one is reminded of the tremendous preparation which King David and his son Solomon put into the building of the temple. However, this preparation was not related to physical building construction, but the building up of the people as the habitation of the Lord. Thus he says, "Prepare ye the way of the Lord." The purpose of this preparation is to make themselves ready for the everlasting God, who is their refuge, to come into their lives. Does God have a way? Lest you and I should misunderstand this cry for preparation and think that all we have to say is "I'm prepared," the prophet adds, "make his path straight." This preparation is a call for action. God knows our tendency to regard the act of preparation as a valid reason not engage the world.

Preparation is needful, but sometimes Christians use this preparation as an excuse to avoid dealing with the world. "Prepare ye the way of the Lord" does not mean to become inactive or do nothing. For Jesus Himself tells us to, "occupy till I come." The Greek word *poieo*, pronounced **poy-eh'-o** and translated to "make" or "do," means to directly apply one's preparation. It means to bring together or plan an action; to band together; to bring forth into reality that which one has in one's mind. Therefore, we cast out the attitude that separates thinking from action or puts a wedge between prayer and action. Planning is good, but at some point we must commit. Outlining is good, but at some point one must develop the content. Bargaining is good, but at some point one must close the deal. The sense here is that one is to commit without delay, to execute the will of God in the world. One is to act vigorously to fulfill the will of God. One is to move beyond just looking at the map, and begin the journey. "Make his path straight" implies that we must keep and observe God's ordained path; we ought to be committed to perform the will of God—make His path straight. The word "straight" is the translation of the Greek word *euthus* (pronounced **yoo-thoos'**) which literally means straight or level. In addition, it can also mean to be true. The word "straight" carries with it a sense of urgency that is similar to the word "immediately." This emphasizes the urgency of the call to the Messiah's way.

4 And the same John had his raiment of camel's hair, and a leathern girdle about his loins; and his meat was locusts and wild honey.

John's rugged way of dressing is significant in that it may have served to remind the religious Jews of the prophecies of Elijah and Amos. His appearance reached into the history of Israel reminding them of the archetypal prophetic outlook. (See Zechariah 13:4 and 1 Samuel 28:14.) John's attire was not particularly good for the humid and dusty desert in which he lived. This style of dress probably made him sweaty, smelly, and added to his discomfort. However, it was not a fashion statement, but a statement of religious significance. It was not that John did not have access to proper attire. In fact, he could probably afford to wear fine clothes; his father was the priest of the people. His appearance emphasized the intensity of his message and marked John as a man of simplicity. His simplicity reached into every area of his life—his food, his clothing, and his dwelling.

5 Then went out to him Jerusalem, and all Judaea, and all the region round about Jordan,

The appearance of John must have made him something to behold. This verse begins with "then went out to him." The word "went" comes from the Greek word *ekporeuomai* (pronounced **ek-por-yoo'-om-ahee**) which means to depart, as in traveling to a new location. They departed from one place and proceeded to another with a certain intention. They were undertaking a project. It is almost as if they had an issue waiting to be resolved. Indeed, the coming of the Messiah has been part of the religious psyche of the people of Israel from the days when Moses said, "the Lord your God would raise another prophet like me" (Deuteronomy 18:18, NIV).

Therefore, it is not surprising that the people would go out to get to know this strange looking man. We read that Jerusalem, and all Judea, and all the region around went to see him. The Greek word *pas* includes all kinds of people. His fame spread throughout the region. The Greek tells us that his fame reached *pas perichoros* throughout the region. The close proximity of the people who lived in Jerusalem and the surrounding vicinity made it easy for rumors to travel. The fact that the people came to Jerusalem to worship on various festivals may have also given notoriety to John. People traveling to Jerusalem could come into the city bearing news of this strange man who wandered in the wilderness, thus prompting others to go in search of him. In addition, the fact that people were always on the lookout for a Messiah fueled John's fame as well. It would also seem that it was not just residents of Judea who sought out this ascetic, but people from the beyond the Jordan as well.

6 And were baptized of him in Jordan, confessing their sins.

Clearly they came for a purpose—to become a part of a movement. They came to be baptized. The concept of being washed was not a Johanine novelty. Washing for ritual purposes was commonly practiced in various parts of Africa and used in initiation ceremonies. Africans went so far as to practice the ritual of washing one's face every morning before looking into the sun; a symbol of cleansing oneself before entering into the presence of God. For people of Israel, washing was just as important. The word "baptism" comes from the Greek word *baptizo*. It is a derivative of Greek word *bapto* which means to saturate or to overwhelm something in such away that it looks different, or to be fully wet.

Ceremonially, it is an act which signals the transference of status from an outsider or a foreigner to an insider or a citizen. It is a physical affirmation of a spiritual event. In the tradition of Israel, the idea of *rachat* was intrinsically linked to being clean before God. In some African cultures it was considered insulting to come before the presence of dignitaries unwashed. So, the call to baptism by John is connected with the idea that the reign of God is near. If God is the ultimate King and ruler, our Father and eternal parent, it would be insulting for God's children to come into His presence without washing.

7 But when he saw many of the Pharisees and Sadducees come to his baptism, he said unto them, O generation of vipers, who hath warned you to flee from the wrath to come?

In the days of John, there were different religious parties, among whom the most familiar were the Pharisees, Sadducees, Zealots, and Herodians. We encounter the Pharisees, Sadducees, Herodians, and Zealots in New Testament Scripture. However, scholars have identified another sect called the Essenes, and some have speculated that John (and possibly Jesus) was part of this radical egalitarian group.

In verse 7 we are told the Pharisees were among those who came to John for baptism. The word "Pharisee" means separated one. The Pharisees were probably the most popular and powerful religious group. They were renowned teachers and rabbis who went around the world teaching the people about Judaism. They seem to be the originators of the synagogue, which was the precursor of the Christian church. The Apostle Paul claimed that he was a Pharisee prior to his conversion to the way of the Messiah (Philippians 3:5). According to Josephus, their power was disproportionate to their number. For they were not more than 6,000, yet they controlled the synagogues and had political clout with the masses of Israel. The fact that they came to John is significant because they were very discriminatory regarding the company they kept.

We are told that the Sadducees also came to be baptized by John. The Sadducees were leaders of their time. In Israel, without a king, the high priest would act in place of the king. Because the Sadducees could trace their descendants to high priestly families, they saw themselves as natural leaders of Israel. Historically, they were in charge of the rituals and protocols of the temple. Some of them even claimed to be direct heirs to the priests who served in the first temple built by Solomon. They may have come to John the Baptist because he was the son of Zacharias, the priest. But John's radical views probably disturbed them deeply. His simplicity was an affront upon their opulence. His scathing remarks to the Sadducees show that he was deeply disappointed with this people who, in many respects, were his relatives.

We read that "he saw them come to his baptism." Here Matthew does not say that they came to ask questions as John says, but that they came to participate in the spiritual revolution that was going on; or did they? In John the Baptist's opinion, they did not come to experience the power of the movement. The phrase *genneemata echidnoon* (children of vipers) is meant to show double motives on the part of the seekers. The second part "who warned you to flee from the wrath to come?" was directed specifically to the Sadducees who did not believe in the future judgment of God or in the possibility of a heaven and hell.

Thus the question is, "If you do not believe in the final judgment, why are you running?" It is as if John were saying, "I thought you did not believe in these type of things." The Greek word for "flee" is *pheugo* (pronounced **fyoo'-go**) which speaks of their desire to literally run away. Their teachings had placed Israel under the judgment of God and now they sought refuge in the word of a new prophet, hoping that the chaos they had created would pass them by. Having spent all their lives ignoring the call of God, now they thought that by an outward show they could avoid the coming judgment of God. They taught, like many Christians, they could live their lives as they wanted and

then "hocus pocus," they would vanish before trouble comes. But God is not mocked, whatsoever a person continuously sows is what he or she shall reap (Galatians 6:7).

8 Bring forth therefore fruits meet for repentance:

John the Baptist emphasizes his point. He says, "Okay, let me give you the benefit of the doubt. Let's say you are coming with the right motive. Let's assume that you are truly repentant. Then bring forth fruit worthy of the repentance." Remember however, that as "vipers" they must go through a fundamental change of nature. Simply put, "You want to be in? You must stop being a snake and become a lamb." In the Greek, verse 8 reads *Poieesate oun karpon axion teese metanoias*. Literally translated it says, "Bring forth therefore fruits meet for repentance." The word translated as "bring" is the Greek word *poieesate* (pronounced **poyi- sa-th**) which entails a prolonged form of action, that is, continue to bring forth—keep making, doing, and applying directly to your life that which agrees with what God has appointed.

It can also mean to connect one thing to another in order to produce a result. The Pharisees and Sadducees were to bear fruit or let the Word of God impregnate them and to travail like a mother with her child until they brought forth what God intended for their lives. For them to stop being children of vipers and become children of God they truly must commit to the content of John's message. They are not allowed to commit merely in pious phrases, rather they must continue to deal with it in earnest. The word "bring" as used here also carries the idea that they must engage in this fruit-bearing task without any delay. If they truly intend to "flee from the wrath to come," they must execute judgment and exercise righteousness.

For them to move from one species of people (vipers) to another (righteous) they must fulfill the law of the Lord God in their bodies. Coming to John the Baptist does not in any way absolve them from the struggle that is part of the journey into the New Promised Land. They must now immediately lighten their ship by casting out all the excess weight created by their self-righteousness. These fruits which they must continually bear John says, "are fruits worthy of *metanoia,*or repentance. *Metanoia* (pronounced **met-an'-oy-ah**) means that they must allow themselves to feel compunction and come to terms with their guilt as well as incline their hearts and lives to reformation. They must make a reversal and turn or repent from their ways.

11 I indeed baptize you with water unto repentance: but he that cometh after me is mightier

than I, whose shoes I am not worthy to bear: he shall baptize you with the Holy Ghost, and with fire:

Now John begins to explain why they must come to his baptism with the intention to change. John's baptism was ritualistic in that it followed the Israelite tradition of *mitsva* (law). The primary focus of the baptism of John is preparatory. It indicated acknowledgment and repentance from sin and the personal commitment of the recipient to follow the lifestyle ordained by the God of Israel instead of the Greek or gentile style of living. This baptism calls to question one's former way of doing things. Indeed, as is so often the case, the Sadducees and the Pharisees compounded their problems by making promises they never intended to keep.

John's call to radical transformation may have seemed intense, but he seems to be saying, "If you think that I am assertive and radical, think again. There is one that is coming after me who is even stronger." When John the Baptist says, "But he that cometh after me is mightier than I, whose shoes I am not worthy to bear," he moves from himself to the person of Jesus. John speaks here of what is about to happen in the immediate future. He places himself and his activities in contrast to One who is about to appear. The Greek phrase *Ho de opiso mu erchomenos* literally means, "he who after me is coming." The word *erchomai* (pronounced **er'-khom-ahee**) indicates that something or someone that must be supplied by another is needed for the completion of an action or an idea.

Thus, John refers to his work as being only a prelude to the real thing. This does not mean that Jesus accompanied John, as some have insisted, but that John was expecting the Messiah. In fact, John makes it clear that he does not know, the person who is to follow. However, he understands the power that accompanies his appearance; John knows what the appearance of the "one" who is coming is going to bring. This person will follow after John not in power or in nature but in sequential appearance. One could understand the word for "after," *opisthen*, to mean priority with regard to direction. So in a sense the one who is coming is in back of John, as is characteristic of the shepherds of the old.

As one who is sent, John goes ahead and announces the coming of the One. So this phrase "coming after me" should be connected to idea of John being a messenger who goes ahead of the Messiah. Here again, we find the cultural metaphor of leaders coming behind their criers. Therefore, when John says, "he who is coming after me is mightier than I," this statement must be understood in line with the prophesied Messiah as the king coming behind. So

indeed, figuratively and literally, Jesus shows Himself to be mightier than John. The word translated as "mightier" or "greater" comes from the Greek word *ischuroteros* (pronounced **is-khu row-tey-ros).** This word is derived from the word *ischuros*, which represents force, as in power. It also could mean boisterous, which leads us to John's statement in verse 12. The Messiah is coming as a powerful wind to blow away the chaff.

To underscore the contrast, John the Baptist uses another cultural example. They all knew that unlatching the shoe of another is the lowest task in society, left for the servants of servants. Yet John says, "whose shoe latchet I am not worthy to carry" (Greek: *hou ouk eimi hikanos ta hupodeemata bastasai*). The Greek word *hupodema* (pronounced **hoop-od'-ay-mah**) represented that which was under one's feet. So John might as well have said, "I am not fit to place my hand under his feet." John uses the negative *ou* before the Greek word *hikanos* (pronounced **hik-an-os'**) to describe himself; it denotes competency. In a sense, John is stating that he has not come into sufficient authority or age, nor has he had ample preparation in character, to be able to perform even this little task for the Master. His statement reveals his humility. Another way to view this phrase is that John is saying he will be content enough just to touch the sole of the Master's feet. He is "not worthy" to perform such work for the Lord, but considers his assignment an honor. Also interesting is the use of the Greek word *bastazo* (pronounced **bas-tad'-zo**) meaning to carry or lift up.

Finally, John declares what the one to come (Jesus) will do for them. He tells them, "he will baptize you with the Holy Spirit and with fire" (Greek *autos humas baptisei en pneumati hagioo kai puri*). The one who is coming will saturate them with the Holy Spirit. It must be remembered that the Holy Spirit can only come from God. John did not pretend to give them the Holy Spirit, but he does say that the one who is coming will baptize them with the Holy Spirit and fire. Most of the metaphors used by John the Baptist in relation to Jesus have to do with purification. He will cut down the trees that do not bear fruit; he will blow away the chaff; and now he will baptize with the Holy Spirit and fire. Wow! But John is just beginning to describe this incredible person who is coming behind him.

12 Whose fan is in his hand, and he will throughly purge his floor, and gather his wheat into the garner; but he will burn up the chaff with unquenchable fire.

In verse 12, Jesus is represented as a farmer at the end of the harvest period, gathering and preparing the harvested grain for preservation. To say, "his fan is in his hand" is Hebraic way of declaring power. As in verse 10, where the axe in his hand represents power to cut down and to plant, the fan in his hand here represents power to cleanse and chase away clutter. It is important that we note the use of the word "purge" from the Greek word *diakatharizo* (pronounced **dee-ak-ath-ar-id'-zo**) which comes from the term *katharizo* and is connected to the removal of the criminal by judgment. Here the term is used to convey the idea of complete cleansing. In certain parts of the world, people still clear the brushes and set fire to them in order to prepare the land for the planting season. The same concept is being expressed here. The three things that this *One* will perform upon His appearance are clearing, gathering and burning. Here God's divine cleansing, embracing, and purificative judgment is revealed.

13 Then cometh Jesus from Galilee to Jordan unto John, to be baptized of him.

In the midst of all this, Jesus shows up to be baptized. Since we assume that John did not know who the Messiah will be, the use of the word *paraginomai*, translated in the King James as "cometh" should really mean "suddenly appears." He arrived. We could say, by implication, this was His first true public appearance and declaration of who He understood Himself to be. Remember, John and Jesus were cousins. So the word "Jesus cometh or appeared," should not deceive us in its simplicity. It is replete with significance, for at this moment John's eyes are opened. This is revelation to him and to the people who were gathered with him at the Jordan.

Jesus came from Galilee (*Galilaia*, **gal-il-ah'-yah**) which probably is a name of Hebrew origin for a region of northern Palestine that was not near to the Lord. It was the hills of the heathen. This coming from Galilee may have contributed to the use of the term "he appeared." For most people did not believe that good things could come from that region. Jesus appeared to be baptized. Amazingly, He who created water was now to be washed by water.

14 But John forbade him, saying, I have need to be baptized of thee, and comest thou to me?

John was not prepared to subject this Great One, whose coming he had declared, to the same cleansing ritual used for unworthy sinners. We read in the Greek: *ho de ioannes diekooluen autou* which indicates that John strongly resisted the idea of baptizing Jesus, even to the degree that he sought to hinder this altogether. How could he baptize the One that he had just described in such powerful and glowing terms?

He would have utterly prohibited it had Jesus not insisted. But the opinion of humanity is far removed from the wisdom of God. John acknowledges that he was the one in need. He uses the Greek word *chreia* (pronounced **khri'-ah**) which is a way of saying, "This is not my task it is yours." In John's opinion, this occasion demanded that Jesus show forth His glory by baptizing others and miraculously removing their sins and doing all that John had been telling them. By stating that he needed to be baptized by Jesus, John acknowledges his own destitution and lack. He wanted Jesus to fill his own need and satisfy his desire for spiritual fulfillment.

15 And Jesus answering said unto him, Suffer it to be so now: for thus it becometh us to fulfil all righteousness. Then he suffered him.

Jesus' response to John deals with the fact that this was John's time to work. The Greek term for "answering" *apokrinomai* (**ap-ok-ree'-nom-ahee**) is a combination of two terms, *apo* and *krino*, meaning to conclude for oneself. In order words, Jesus gave a decisive response to John. John was trying to enter into a debate with Jesus as Peter would later do. Jesus responds to John in the Hebraic fashion which affirms His authority. Jesus goes on to say that He knows that this will be hard, but that John should be able to suffer this little inconvenience for the fulfillment of the Scriptures or as Matthew says, "of all righteousness." The Greek word translated "suffer," *aphiemi* (**af-ee'-ay-mee**) is meant to remind John that he was a messenger, not the author of the drama which was about to unfold.

John the Baptist was sent forth to help reveal the Messiah. Therefore, John could cry as loud as he wanted against this process; however, he must perform the act of revelation. Furthermore, this word *aphiemi* also means forgive. Was John getting angry that Jesus would come to him? Was he insulted by the fact that his understanding of the role of the Messiah was now being challenged? Was he confused by the fact that the Messiah, instead of commanding authority, was now asking him, a mere messenger, to baptize Him? The implication in Jesus' response is that John must forsake, lay aside, or let go of his preconceived notions of the Messiah.

Think of it, how difficult would it be for you to yield your point of view if you have spent your whole life believing and convincing others of a certain perspective? The word "suffer" is really meant to remind John of the simplicity which has been a part of his life and his ministry. The addition of the word "now" (*arti*) is meant to compare his past mentality with what should be his present mindset.

In this moment of encounter, he was being told to suspend his paradigm—not forever, but just for now. Why? The passage suggests that what God was about to do would soon become apparent. For the purpose of making something clear, Jesus came to John for this act.

The idea is one of trying to set up a conspicuous tower which will be suitable, proper, and fit. So far what John has established or built is partial. For the work to be completed (Greek *pleroo*, **play-ro'-o**), John the Baptist must step outside of his own paradigm and do that which the Lord bids him do. The word "fulfill" here suggests a sense of stuffing something to the brim. How was John's work going to be "leveled up?" John had been building the house, however this act would be the finishing touch. How was righteousness going to be executed and John's word verified? Jesus says that this act fulfilled all righteousness. By doing this it would seem that John's word now coincides with his prediction. If Jesus was who John said He was, then why is John arguing with him?

16 And Jesus, when he was baptized, went up straightway out of the water: and, lo, the heavens were opened unto him, and he saw the Spirit of God descending like a dove, and lighting upon him:

John did baptize Jesus. Now it is up to God to show the rest. First, Jesus **"went up straight** out of the water." This phrase is significant. There is a sense of urgency in the way Jesus is shown here, leaving the waters of Baptism. The use of the Greek word "straightway," *euthus*, (**yoo-thoos'**) suggests that Jesus left at once. This divine immediacy and redemptive urgency will continue as Jesus embarks on His ministry. The next phrase is equally forceful. It literally begins with "and see" (Greek: *kai idou*) and is used as an impersonal declaration of "lo! behold! see!"

What are we commanded to behold? In confirmation, "the heavens were open unto him." this divine revelation is directed to Jesus Himself. Note the phrase "see" and "he sees" which is the Hebrew expression of revelation, also proverbial among certain Africans. For example, the Igbos say, *ney ahum* or "look I see,"—an expression often connected with prophetic insight. Jesus saw two things: (1) the heavens opening, and (2) the descending of the dove. Matthew implies that these particular confirmations were private, in that they were directed to Jesus.

17 And lo a voice from heaven, saying, This is my beloved Son, in whom I am well pleased.

This verse deals with the Divine declaration of the identity of Jesus. John had addressed the people on behalf of the Messiah; now it was God's turn. Here God speaks in a language they could understand. He says, *houos estin ho huios mou ho agapeetos* translated, this phrase is like saying, "this one," "this specific one" is my beloved Son. The concept of "Son" (Greek *huios*, **hwee-os'**) shows a primary relationship between the One who is speaking and of the One who was spoken. The voice does not say "this is a son" but "this is my Son." The voice uses a personal possessive pronoun to describe this relationship. God says here, "this is my beloved." It must be remembered here that one can be loved because of a fundamental relationship that exists between one and another; this type of love is derived from kinship.

However, the voice proceeds further and says, "in whom I am well pleased." Does God love? The answer is an unequivocal, "yes." But is God pleased with all that God loves? The response is not always yes. For God to say here, "in whom I am well pleased" (Greek: *en hoo eudeekesa*) is to say more than "I love him." The Greek translation of "well pleased" is the word *eudeekesa* derived from the root word *eudokeo* (pronounced **yoo-dok-eh'-o**) meaning to think well of someone or approve of someone's action. This is not just a matter of good will, but a matter of commending one's lifestyle as worthy of emulation.

DAILY BIBLE READING

M: John Preaches and Baptizes
Matthew 3:1-6
T: John Proclaims Jesus' Coming
Matthew 3:7-12
W: Jesus is Baptized by John
Matthew 3:13-17
T: John Sends Messengers to Question Jesus
Matthew 11:2-6
F: Jesus Praises John the Baptist
Matthew 11:7-11
S: Jesus Admonishes the Crowd
Matthew 11:12-19
S: John the Baptist Is Executed
Matthew 14:1-12

TEACHING TIPS

December 12
Bible Study Guide 2

1. Words You Should Know

A. Desert. (Matthew 4:1) Greek *eremos* ---an uninhabited, lonely, deserted, abandoned place.

B. Worship. (v. 10) Greek *proskyneo*—to prostrate oneself, do obeisance to another. We worship by giving praises and adoration to God.

2. Teacher Preparation

A. To gain a better understanding of the context for today's lesson and Jesus' mission here on earth, read Matthew 4:1-17 and Luke 4:14-21.

B. Study the FOCAL VERSES. Understand that Satan was trying to get Jesus to sin and what temptations he used in order to carry out his ploy. Contrast what was done to Jesus with the temptations he uses on God's people.

C. Record your answers to the SEARCH THE SCRIPTURES and DISCUSS THE MEANING questions.

D. Materials needed: a board, chalk, a Bible.

3. Starting the Lesson

A. Before the students arrive, write the title of today's lesson and the AT-A-GLANCE outline on the board.

B. After the students are seated and settled, take prayer requests, pray a prayer of thanksgiving, pray for the requests, say a word of prayer over the lesson and ask that the aim for that lesson be understood.

C. Then, ask your students to define "a desert experience" and "worship of God." After this discussion, tell them that today they will learn about faith under pressure or faith under fire.

D. Read the IN FOCUS story, stressing the theme of temptation and ministry.

4. Getting into the Lesson

A. Have volunteers to read the BACKGROUND and THE PEOPLE, PLACES, AND TIMES sections. Have them discuss what they read.

B. Ask volunteers to read the FOCAL VERSES. Occasionally, you might want to pause and emphasize a verse or explain it so that your students can get a feel of what was happening to Jesus, how He felt, and what Satan was trying to do.

C. Allow students to share their understanding of the Scriptures so that you can see if they are indeed getting the message of today's lesson.

5. Relating the Lesson to Life

Direct the students' attention to the LESSON IN OUR SOCIETY section and discuss it. Compare and contrast this lesson with the FOCAL VERSES. Encourage the students to consider how the lesson applies to them personally.

6. Arousing Action

A. Direct the students to the MAKE IT HAPPEN suggestion and discuss some of the ways that Satan tries to tempt believers. Challenge students to remember some pointers for surviving tests of faith: prayer, staying in the Word, relying on God's promises, and standing on His Word.

B. Encourage students to do their DAILY BIBLE READING as a part of their daily devotion and to apply these principles when their faith challenged.

C. Close with prayer.

TEMPTATIONS AND MINISTRY

Bible Background • MATTHEW 4:1-17
Printed Text • MATTHEW 4:1-14
Devotional Reading • LUKE 4:14-21

LESSON AIM

By the end of the lesson, students will know that Satan is a very real adversary, and not only did he tempt Jesus, but he also tries to tempt the children of God daily. He wants to destroy our faith and destroy our testimony.

KEEP IN MIND

"Then saith Jesus unto him, Get thee hence, Satan: for it is written, Thou shalt worship the Lord thy God, and him only shalt thou serve" (Matthew 4:10).

FOCAL VERSES

MATTHEW 4:1 Then was Jesus led up of the Spirit into the wilderness to be tempted of the devil.

2 And when he had fasted forty days and forty nights, he was afterward an hungred.

3 And when the tempter came to him, he said, If thou be the Son of God, command that these stones be made bread.

4 But he answered and said, It is written, Man shall not live by bread alone, but by every word that proceedeth out of the mouth of God.

5 Then the devil taketh him up into the holy city, and setteth him on a pinnacle of the temple,

6 And saith unto him, If thou be the Son of God, cast thyself down: for it is written, He shall give his angels charge concerning thee: and in their hands they shall bear thee up, lest at any time thou dash thy foot against a stone.

7 Jesus said unto him, It is written again, Thou shalt not tempt the Lord thy God.

LESSON OVERVIEW

LESSON AIM
KEEP IN MIND
FOCAL VERSES
IN FOCUS
THE PEOPLE, PLACES, AND TIMES
BACKGROUND
AT-A-GLANCE
IN DEPTH
SEARCH THE SCRIPTURES
DISCUSS THE MEANING
LESSON IN OUR SOCIETY
MAKE IT HAPPEN
FOLLOW THE SPIRIT
REMEMBER YOUR THOUGHTS
MORE LIGHT ON THE TEXT
DAILY BIBLE READINGS

8 Again, the devil taketh him up into an exceeding high mountain, and sheweth him all the kingdoms of the world, and the glory of them;

9 And saith unto him, All these things will I give thee, if thou wilt fall down and worship me.

10 Then saith Jesus unto him, Get thee hence, Satan: for it is written, Thou shalt worship the Lord thy God, and him only shalt thou serve.

11 Then the devil leaveth him, and, behold, angels came and ministered unto him.

12 Now when Jesus had heard that John was cast into prison, he departed into Galilee;

13 And leaving Nazareth, he came and dwelt in Capernaum, which is upon the sea coast, in the borders of Zabulon and Nephthalim:

14 That it might be fulfilled which was spoken by Esaias the prophet, saying,

IN FOCUS

Never did I feel and see the attacks of Satan on my family and myself as when I began to truly delve into God's Word, teach an adult Sunday School class, and write Sunday School and Bible School curriculum. God had called me to these ministries. I knew it without a doubt. I felt His anointing. I knew it in my heart. These times of testing of my faith came through attacks on my own body in the form of cancer, my husband's body in several different forms including ulcers, and rebellion of children that grieved my very spirit. Often times, the attacks were so fierce that I thought that I should give up teaching and writing. In fact, Satan suggested to me in my spirit that I do so.

Yet, I dove into the Scriptures even more and sought God in intense prayer, fasting, and study of His Word. Many times, I did not feel God's presence or see Him working in my circumstances.

The spiritual battle was fierce in my mind where Satan kept accusing me and telling me that I was not worthy to teach or write God's Word. Yet, I knew that Satan was trying to deter my ministry. Many times as I taught at seminars and spoke, I did so in tears and heartache. In fact, my heart felt as if it was being torn asunder—just ripped apart.

Through searching the Scriptures and reading the works of other authors who had experienced similar testing, I learned how to fight in spiritual warfare. I learned how to completely rely on God to deliver not only my family, but myself as well. I became completely dependent on Him for my deliverance.

The battle went on for several years, but I kept before God. In fact, He sent other Christians to minister to my needs. Sometimes when I felt I could go no further, a card would come in the mail or a friend would call encouraging me to hang in and continue to rely on God. In tears, I pressed on!

God did answer my prayers. Satan tried to hinder my ministry just as he did Jesus' in today's lesson, but he is a liar and a thief. Just a few Sundays ago, my baby daughter got saved . . . living proof that God had heard me and listened to my many groanings and prayers before Him. In fact, she will be baptized on next Sunday.

What A Mighty God We Serve!

THE PEOPLE, PLACES, AND TIMES

THE ISRAELITES—JEWS. Descendants of Abraham who had been waiting for the Messiah, "the Anointed One," for hundreds of years. Due to their own sins, forsaking the commandments of God and turning to idolatry, found themselves in bondage to their enemies. God kept His promises to them, but the Israelites often broke theirs. Although they were God's chosen people, they intermarried with foreign women, who led them to worship false gods. In today's lesson, the Israelites fall under Roman oppression.

Matthew wrote his Gospel to prove to the Israelites that Jesus was indeed the Messiah. He was the one they had been looking for so long. However, many Jews would not accept Jesus as Messiah, just as today many refuse to accept Jesus as Saviour and Lord.

BACKGROUND

In today's lesson, Jesus is ready to begin His ministry. In Matthew chapter 3, He was baptized by John the Baptist and heard God Himself say that He was well pleased (v. 17). Now, the Holy Spirit leads Him into a desert place or wilderness to be tested.

Jesus' time of testing comes after he had been fasting for 40 days and nights. He is hungry and vulnerable. In His humanity, Jesus experiences human needs and frailties, human emotions, and even human testing as Satan appears to tempt Him. Satan wants to abort Jesus' mission. He wants Jesus to fail—to sin. However, Satan underestimates Jesus. Jesus is determined to do the will of God, the Father. He quotes the Word of God and refused each temptation to sin.

In the wilderness setting, Jesus setting, Jesus demonstrates how we, too, should deal with Satan when we are tempted. We must remember that Satan is a very real adversary and that we are no match for him on our own. We are dependent upon the power of God and His Word to get us through. We must learn to use the Word as our spiritual sword just as Jesus used the Word. Jesus' time of testing, the temptations that Satan brought, and Jesus' victory teaches us an important lesson: our God can surely save and deliver.

AT-A-GLANCE

1. Jesus Is Led by the Holy Spirit at the Time of Testing (Matthew 4:1-2)
2. How Jesus Overcomes Temptation (vv. 3-10)
3. Jesus Ministered to Others (vv. 12-14)

IN DEPTH

1. Jesus Is Led by the Holy Spirit at the Time of Testing (Matthew 4:1-2)

After spending precious time with the Father through 40 days of fasting and praying, Jesus was on a spiritual high, sharing spiritual matters with the Father. Yet, He was hungry. It is common for human beings to be hungry after fasting or going without food for this long.

Mark 2:12-13 and Luke 4:1-13 give this same account of Satan tempting Jesus right after Jesus' baptism. These

Scriptures show us who Jesus really is: the Son of the Most High God, and we can overcome Satan's attacks or temptations.

Note that it was not Satan, himself, who led Jesus into the wilderness to be tested, it was the Holy Spirit. This should let us know as well that Satan cannot do anything that God does not allow. He has to get permission from God. Satan is powerful and we're no match for him in our humanity, but he is not all powerful. **Only God is.**

Scripture is very clear that Satan is "the tempter." He is crafty and cunning, and seeks to get believers to fall to continue in sin. It is Satan who tries to defeat us, not God. God **never** tempts us. (James 1:13). In 1 Thesssalonians 3:5 Paul warns the Thessalonian church that Satan was trying to defeat their mission of helping the Christians at Thessalonica. Ephesians 6:11 also tells us to put on the whole armor of God before taking our stand against the devil's schemes. This armor includes: truth, the gospel of peace, faith, salvation, the Lord, and praying in the Spirit. Again, God is preparing us for spiritual battle against the enemy.

2. How Jesus Overcomes Temptation (vv. 3-10)

Satan, the tempter, appeals to Jesus' physical needs and desires. He knew that Jesus was hungry and weak after 40 days and nights of fasting, so he tempted Jesus to turn stones to bread. The sin was not in turning the stones to bread. Satan had hidden motives—a hidden agenda. He wanted Jesus to obey him. He wanted to abort Jesus' mission to save all mankind from their sin. Jesus served only one master and He is God. It would have been wrong and a division of loyalties for Jesus to obey Satan.

Jesus' answer to Satan was that, "It is written, Man does not live on bread alone, but on every word that proceedth out of the mouth of God" (v. 4). The operative words are: **It is written.** Jesus used the Word of God on Satan. You see, Satan knows the Word, and he knows that man also needs spiritual food for the soul. Therefore, to gain physical food by any means necessary and thereby lose one's soul, destroys the inner man. Remember Satan wants to kill the inner man by sending your soul to hell.

Satan's second scheme was to tempt Jesus by appealing to His power. "If you are the Son," he said, "throw yourself down. For it is written …" Again, Satan knows the Word of God. He, too, can quote Scriptures. There was no doubt that God could command angels to save Jesus. Again, Satan's motives were evil, wrong, cunning, and crafty. God does not have to bow down to Satan or prove anything to him.

Jesus answered in verse 7 that, "It is also written: Do not put the Lord your God to the test." Jesus knew Scriptures also, and He knew how to use and obey them. Jesus was not going to disobey God's Word and test God over the schemes of Satan. He had spiritual discernment and recognized Satan's motives.

Satan's third scheme appealed to Jesus' humanity through His pride and desires (vv. 8-9). Satan offers Jesus the kingdoms of the world if Jesus would bow down and worship him. Again, Jesus was well aware of Satan's schemes and did not yield to the temptation. Yielding to temptation is sin. Experiencing temptation is not sin; it is common to humankind.

Jesus' answer to this third temptation was sharp and to the point (vv. 10-11). He was tired of Satan's harassment. Therefore, Jesus rebuked Satan, told him to get away from Him. Jesus resisted Satan and passed this test of faith, again by using the Word and obeying it. When Satan knew that he was defeated, he left Jesus. Afterwards, the angels ministered to Jesus.

3. Jesus Ministered to Others (vv. 12-14).

After Jesus passed His test of faith and put Satan in his place, He went His Father's business, ministering to lost souls and preaching the Word in Galilee and Capernaum. He preached as John the Baptist had—to repent because the kingdom of heaven was near. It was time for Him to fulfill His mission on earth. He would be deterred no longer.

SEARCH THE SCRIPTURES

1. What was Jesus' answer when Satan told Him to turn the stones into bread? (Matthew 4:4)

2. What was Jesus' answer when Satan told Him to throw Himself down from the highest point of the temple? (v. 7)

3. What was Jesus' answer when Satan told Jesus that He would gain all the kingdoms of the world if He would bow down and worship Satan? (v. 10)

4. What did Satan do when Jesus resisted him the final time? (v. 11)

DISCUSS THE MEANING

1. Why do you think that Jesus fasted and prayed? What does fasting and praying do for the believer?

2. Each time that Jesus answered Satan, He used the words, "It is written" (vv. 4, 7, 10). Where is "it" written and what points were Jesus making when He said these words?

LESSON IN OUR SOCIETY

The news that the casino boats were coming to our immediate area traveled fast. Excitement filled many in a city already plagued by high unemployment, crime, lost hope, and loss of faith. Some churches, however, viewed this news with trepidation because they knew that gambling destroyed homes, families, and communities, encouraged the growth of organized crime, and caused people to depend on anything but God for economical survival.

Some churches began prayer vigils, while others tried to petition legislators to refuse to pass the bill which proposed to bring gambling boats to the community. However, some ministers supported the legislation because they felt that this was the answer to many people's prayers.

A few years later, the casino boats are alive and well. Sure enough, the cost is high. Some mothers have lost their welfare checks on these boats; some elderly have lost their pensions; and still others have lost their homes as they gambled away their money for the mortgage. Satan has also tempted some Christians to go to the boats, under the disguise that it is "gaming" and not "gambling." Non-believers see them and feel that it must be all right because Christians are doing it. Satan is surely smiling as these Christians live out this poor testimony before a dying, lost world.

MAKE IT HAPPEN

If you have yielded to Satan's temptations to do something that you know is wrong, ask God to forgive you and commit today to turn your life around. If it is a habit, then pray that God will take away the desire to do what He has commanded you not to do. Ask Him to help you live out a testimony that glorifies Him.

FOLLOW THE SPIRIT

What God wants me to do:

_____

_____

REMEMBER YOUR THOUGHTS

Special insights you learned:

_____

_____

MORE LIGHT ON THE TEXT
MATTHEW 4:1-14

This chapter focuses on the temptation of Christ. Observe that directly after He was declared to be the Son of God and the Saviour of the world, Jesus was tempted. Great privileges and special tokens of divine favor will not shield us from temptation. However, if the Holy Spirit is a witness to our adoption as children of God, that will answer all the suggestions of the evil spirit. When we rely upon our own strength, God will not intervene when the devil tempts us. "But every man is tempted, when he is drawn away of his own lust, and enticed" (James 1:14), but our Lord Jesus had no corrupt nature, therefore He could only be tempted by the devil.

From the temptation of Christ, it appears that our enemy is subtle, spiteful, and very daring, but he can be resisted. It is a comfort to know that Christ suffered being tempted, for it means that our temptations, if not yielded to, are not sins but afflictions only. Satan aimed, in all his temptations, to make Jesus sin against the Father. Christ was succored after the temptation. He knew, by experience, what it was to suffer being tempted. We may expect, not only will Jesus feel compassion for His tempted people, but He will come to them with relief.

4:1 Then was Jesus led up of the Spirit into the wilderness to be tempted of the devil.

This verse begins with the leadership of the Spirit. While Matthew says, "Jesus was led up into the wilderness by the Spirit to be tempted by the devil," Mark 1:12 states that the Spirit "drives" (*ekballei*) Christ into the wilderness. It was a strong urging by the Holy Spirit that led Jesus into the wilderness to think through the full significance of the great step that He had now taken. That step opened the door for the devil and involved inevitable conflict with the slanderer (*tou diabolou*). The words "led up" used here by Matthew are translated from the Greek word *anago* (pronounced **an-ag'-o**) which means to lead up—probably referring to the fact that Jesus was coming from the Jordan valley into the wilderness. But the term means more than that; it means to extend or to bring something out.

Jesus has been hidden from the enemy until now. When He was a child the devil sought to destroy Him, but God hid Him. One could speculate that the devil did not know who the Messiah would be. But now the identity of the Messiah has been brought into the open. It could also mean that His ministry had now been launched into a new frontier as the God-man. However, this obviously is the time when Jesus must face the archenemy of humanity in order to prove Himself worthy of our trust.

The leadership of the Holy Spirit is important on several counts. First, it underscores the fact that Jesus was not in the habit of running into temptation. Note the use of the

Greek word for "spirit," *pneuma* (**pnyoo'-mah**). This word could mean the current of air or blast of breeze. This reminds one of the story of Elijah being caught in the whirlwind. It is by analogy that this word comes to mean spirit. This could be translated to mean that Jesus was led in His rational soul or that He was in His right mind when He went to the wilderness, or His mental disposition was not sluggish. Note also that the word could be used for an angel or a demon, but in the New Testament it usually refers the truth that God is Spirit or to the Spirit of Christ—hence the translation Holy Spirit.

However, we must also note that the Greek here does not say the Holy Spirit, but simply "spirit" (*pneumatos*). Second, it suggests that because this encounter was initiated by the Spirit and not out of vanity that victory was all but certain. We continue to read that the Spirit led Him "into the wilderness," indicating that He entered into a particular place in a specific time. This entails that there was a purpose and an end result. The wilderness is an uncertain place in which we find none with whom we have affinity. It is a lonesome place, and by implication a place of waste. Usually the feelings of desertion, desolation, and aloneness created by the wilderness experience are enough to drive one into mental and spiritual confusion.

We read further and find the explanation for this journey, "to be tempted of the devil" (*peirasthenai hupo tou diabolou*). Notice how Matthew avoids any implication that the Spirit is part of the temptation. The Greek word *peirazo* (**pi-rad'-zo**) means to become an object of test; the idea is that of a test of endurance. The word "tempt" used here (*peirazo*) and in Matthew 4:3 means originally to test, to try. That is its usual meaning in the ancient Greek and in the Septuagint. Here it comes to mean, as often in the New Testament, to solicit to sin. The evil sense comes from its use for an evil purpose. Jesus' inner motives and resolve were now to be scrutinized.

Note also that the word can mean disciplinary training in which one must prove their character for the task ahead. But this testing is done by the adversary for which the Greek word *diabolos* (**dee-ab'-ol-os**) is used. This term is used to refer specifically to Satan. Jesus is tested by the falsifier, the one who accuses and slanders for the purpose of unnerving the tested. Note also that Matthew locates the temptation at a definite time, "then" (*tote*) and place, "into the wilderness" (*eis ten eremon*). This testing or temptation occurs probably in the same location where John was preaching. It is not surprising that Jesus was tempted by the devil immediately after His baptism, which signified the formal entrance into the Messianic work. That is a common experience with ministers who step out into the open for Christ. Judas has this term applied to him. There are those today who do not believe that a personal devil exists, but they do not offer an adequate explanation of the existence and presence of sin in the world. Certainly Jesus did not discount or deny the reality of the devil's presence.

2 And when he had fasted forty days and forty nights, he was afterward an hungered.

Note that the effect of the temptation was not felt until He was physically ripe for the temptation. We read "when he had fasted." Note also the use of the 40 days, denoting the reenacting of the actions of Moses and Elijah in the height of their ministry. Jesus begins where Moses and Elijah were at their height, showing once more that He is greater than Moses and Elijah. One could also say that He spent 40 days in the wilderness, 1 day for each year that Israel spent in the wilderness. The Greek word *nesteuo* (**nace-tyoo'-o**) indicates that He abstained from food for religious reason. This was not a hunger strike, it was a fast as demanded by Isaiah (Isaiah 58).

The Greek word *hemera* (**hay-mer'-ah**) meaning "day" has been used to suggest that He fasted mainly in the day. But, in fact, it may used to refer to the whole 24 hours. To eliminate any misunderstanding, Matthew adds "and night" using the Greek word *nux* (**noox**) for "night," literally not a figurative darkness. To say "he was afterward an hungered," if we take the meaning of the word "afterward" or *husteron*, may refer to late that evening of the 40th day. One could also understand it to say "after 40 days of fasting he was eventually hungry." The Greek word translated as "hungry" is *peinao*, (**pi-nah'-o**) which actually means that He literally felt the pinching of hunger. It could also mean that He toiled or that He was literally pinning away from hunger. He was absolutely famished. He craved sustenance. There is nothing sinful about being hungry.

3 And when the tempter came to him, he said, If thou be the Son of God, command that these stones be made bread.

In this verse, we encounter the temptation to give up on goodness and to distrust divine care and provision. Trying to take advantage of Jesus' outward condition, the tempter draws His attention to the fact that He was hungry and that God His Father does not seem to care. It is as if Satan is implying that Jesus is about to die from starvation (Greek *nesteutic*), while the angels are in heaven rejoicing. This temptation involved much more that the idea of bread; it was a double attack on Jesus' connection to the goodness of God

read "in that you are the son of God." Another possibility is to see the tempter as saying "though you are the son of God." This interpretation implies that there was a tacit acknowledgment that he was in the presence of the Divine One.

The word "if" was followed by the phrase "you are the son of God." The word for "son" is the Greek word *huios* (**hwee-os'**). The use of this word refers to the immediate, remote, or figurative kinship to a person. So what the enemy seems to be saying here is "if you are still the son of God, the one by whom all things were created." In other words, "Are you the same Word? I don't remember you looking so tattered and ragged. The person I knew when I was in heaven could have turned up this desert and created a feast." This reminder of His relationship to Deity was meant to cause Jesus to misuse His power. We find also the devil's real motive for tempting Jesus. He in effect does not suggest this to Jesus, he rather says to Him imperatively, "command that these stones be made bread." The word from which "command" is translated is the Greek *epo* (pronounced **ep'-o**) meaning command or grant; it also means tell.

It is as though the tempter is saying to the Lord, "These stones are ready to obey your every wish. They would gladly grant your request. All you have to do is tell them what to do." The use of the Greek word for "these" *houtos* (**hoo'-tos**) may suggest that the tempter was moving Jesus to imagine that the stones were indeed alive and ready to transform themselves. The word "stone" here translated from the Greek word *lithos* (**lee'-thos**) is different from *petra* meaning rock. The Greek word, *ginomai* (pronounced **ghin'-om-ahee**), or to become, affirms what has just been said. It suggests the possibility of immediate transformation, not through a prolonged process.

Jesus was being asked to use His creative power to *"gen"*-erate. He was being asked to be reflexive and not reflective. He was being asked to subvert the very nature which He Himself had put in place by doing something mainly for the purpose of proving who He was. He was to assemble food from the stones and ask that it be brought. The tense of the word used here can also mean to continue. The tempter may have wanted this to be a continual display of Jesus' power. So if Jesus did it once, He was more likely to

as well as on His power. Note the use of the Greek *peirazon* (**pi-rad'-zon**) meaning the tempting one. We read here that "the tempter came to him . . ." meaning that the tempter approached Jesus. The enemy came near to visit in the hour of His vulnerability. This word could also mean that the tempter worshiped, thus assenting to the fact that Jesus was Lord. Watch the progression here. First, the enemy draws close to Jesus and even worships Him. Second the enemy speaks. The Greek word *epo* (**ep'-o**) suggests not only the idea of speaking, but answering a question which may be nagging.

Could it be that Jesus in that moment thought of the glories and provision in the heavenly places which are rightly His? Could it be that He was asking Himself why He had to do this for a people who probably would never appreciate it. This could also mean that the tempter called himself bringing a welcomed word to Jesus. The contradiction of the tempter is obvious here since our reading of the Greek shows that he has already acknowledged the Lordship of the Lord Jesus. For the tempter now to say "if" suggests that the tempter is challenging or taunting Him by saying "forasmuch as you are the son of God." It could also do it again and again and again. He was asked to change the nature of the stone because of His own pain of hunger. The word *ginomai* can also mean fall or to be finished. Thus, we find that this was also a temptation to short-circuit the divine process and to follow in the footsteps of the enemy.

What was the one goal for this magical proposal? Bread. The Greek *artos* (**ar'-tos**) which comes from the word *airo* means bread as well as that which raises itself. Everything here points to the perpetuation of an act independent of the rules set by God.

4 But he answered and said, It is written, Man shall not live by bread alone, but by every word that proceedeth out of the mouth of God.

In this verse, we find the first response of Jesus to the tempter. We read "but he (Jesus) answered and said." The use of both "answer and said" is vital. The word "answer" is from the Greek word *apokrinomai* (pronounced **ap-ok-ree'-nom-ahee**) which is a combination of *apo* and *krino*. It can mean to conclude for oneself or to judge for oneself. Jesus did not let the word of the enemy be the last word; He judged for Himself. He came to His own conclusion independent of the statement by the tempter. We could interpret this to mean that since Jesus is the Word of God and He responded from the Word God, He indeed did conclude for Himself because He is the very source of the Word He now begins to speak.

From His essential divinity, He now addresses the expectation of the enemy. His answer is based on the word "written" from the Greek *grapho* (**graf'-o**) which literally means to engrave—as God did upon the stone tablet on Mount Sinai for Moses. That writing from which He quotes is the Holy Writ which He Himself as the Angel of the Lord's presence gave to the people in order to guide them through the desert in which He now finds Himself. What was it that was written in relation to this confrontational context? It had to do with what it means to be a human being. Jesus' reply, "man shall not live by bread alone" speaks not to what it means to be Divine, for He knew what it means to be Divine; He now had to learn how to be human. The word *anthropos* (**anth'-ro-pos**) or "man" speaks to the formation of human countenance as the enlightening manifestation of an inner radiance.

Thus, we could read this to say that the frame of the countenance shall not be determined by bread alone. Or we could say that being human does not consist of eating or consumption alone. The Greek word *zao* (**dzah'-o**), translated "live," does not just refer to literal animal life but to the figurative or spiritual effervescence from God's very own being which follows a human being throughout a lifetime. It is what quickens the human being. This essential aliveness does not derive from a loaf of bread or that which is the result of human labor. The technical prowess of which humanity is so proud, alone cannot secure a person from the stinging cosmologically insatiable craving for wholeness.

Note also the use of the Greek word *monos* (**mon'-os**) or "alone" underscoring the fact that God has so ordered the universe that humanity shall live by its fruits but this alone does not constitute the basis of human wholeness. Some Greek scholars have stated that the word *mono* takes its root form *meno* which means remaining. Lets assume that this is the case for one sentence. It would mean that human beings cannot remain long in human form if all they have to live for is the materiality of their surroundings. But it is better to see this to mean that while it is necessary for human beings to eat and to possess various means for material needs, this is not the sole means or the singular form for their sustenance.

Another way to read this text is to see Jesus as saying to the tempter, "Mere bread is not sufficient reason to subvert the order of God." It could be said that human beings cannot survive by themselves. Then Jesus puts in the clincher, "but by every word" placing emphasis on "every" which is the Greek word *pas* (**pas**) indicating that life is inclusive of all that God has to say. To live, one must take hold of the whole Word of God—it does not matter in what manner or means. In fact, it can mean by the daily Word of God. In this sense, it may mean that human beings can truly live only by taking hold of as much of God's counsels as one can lay one's heart upon. Note the term Jesus uses here for "word" is not *logos* but the Greek word *rhema* (**ray'-mah**), referring to an utterance or collective guidance and sometimes to a special communication of the Divine Spirit in a particular situation.

One must consider every matter or topic with specific reference to narrative that describes the interaction between God and the world. The word *rhema* denotes Divine communication for particular purpose. The next phrase says "that proceedeth out of the mouth of God." The idea is that *rhema* is a critical and creative word that "comes" (Greek *ekporeuomai*, **ek-por-yoo'-om-ahee**) from one with power. It has the sense of something that departs from the speaker as messenger. It is a word discharged for a specific project. But it can also mean that which issues out of the abundance of one's being, as a baby comes from the completed term of pregnancy. Note that it says "the mouth of God." the Greek word for "mouth," *stoma* (**stom'-a**), simply means an opening and by extension an opening in the human face. It can also mean the edge of a weapon. Thus ends the first encounter with the tester.

5 Then the devil taketh him up into the holy city, and setteth him on a pinnacle of the temple,

In this second temptation, Satan tempted Jesus to pressure God to use Divine power to protect Him. One of God's promises is that of power and protection to keep the chosen safe. This sort of presumption is especially common to people who are sensitive to spiritual processes. Note also that Satan took Him to a holy place and there sought to assault him. We must watch and pray, even in holy places. We remain on our guard because sometimes it is in the most unlikely places that the tester seems to have great advantage, for it is in these places that we often become prideful and presumptuous. Here again we encounter the word *diabolos* (**dee-ab'-ol-os**) referring to Satan, but it is more than demonic suggestion because we also read "the devil taketh him up." The Greek word *paralambano* (**par-al-am-ban'-o**) for "to take" means to receive one near. It can also mean that the devil associated with Him.

Instead of making a suggestion, the devil now becomes familiar and intimate and approaches to enter into a relationship. Actually the devil assumed an office of emissary of goodwill. It is also interesting here to note that this word can mean to learn. The devil takes time to learn what it is that can bring us down, and then he works overtime to see that it happens. The tempter did not only show Him the place, but "took him into" it, indicating that Jesus entered a place in a specific time for a specific purpose. It can also mean to be among. In another sense, it can mean that the tempter caused Him continually to look into the city in a far more exceeding way that would allow Him to see the riches and the power within it. The tempter caused Jesus to look into it with reflective intent.

Into what did the enemy take Jesus? We are told "the holy city." This word *hagios* (**hag'-ee-os**) means he took Jesus into the sacred, or physically pure, or ceremonially consecrated city. Many believe that this was Jerusalem. The question that arises is whether these temptations all occurred in the wilderness, or whether this one took place in the city. There may be two ways to look at this. In that Jesus was the Son of God and the devil is also a spirit and given what we believe about spirits, it is not impossible that both of them had the capacity to reach the holy city in a way that we do not yet understand. The Greek word for "city" is the word *polis* (**pol'-is**).

Further we read, "and setteth him," Greek *histemi* (**his'-tay-mee**), meaning that the tempter caused him to stay there for a prolonged time. The devil was making sure that He saw the city which God had appointed as the capital of the new earth. This also implies the idea of covenant and established order. To set Him up here means that he upheld Jesus and presented the city before Him as He stood. The tempter placed Him on a "pinnacle." This can mean that he took Jesus to an extreme corner of the temple. The word used here for "temple" is the Greek word *hieron* (**hee-er-on**') meaning sacred place, denoting the central Temple at Jerusalem. See how the devil would have killed Jesus and also desecrated the temple in the process?

6 And saith unto him, If thou be the Son of God, cast thyself down: for it is written, He shall give his angels charge concerning thee: and in their hands they shall bear thee up, lest at any time thou dash thy foot against a stone.

In the third temptation, the tempter continued to lay forth his scheme for turning Jesus from His call. The attempt here is to relate to Jesus in systematic discourse, appealing to His emotions as well as His intellect. Again the tempter continues his conditional argument, whether or not you are the Son of God can only be known if you do this or that and the result is this or that. For in as much as the primary connection between Jesus and the Father can be made to remain in the realm of possibility and reality, the enemy believes he can get Jesus to act in ways unbecoming His status as the Son of God. To prove that He is the Son of God, the tempter suggested that Jesus, "cast thyself down." Note he does not say "God says cast thyself down." Interestingly, the Greek word for "cast" is *ballo* (**bal'-lo**) from which we probably get the word for ball. It means to throw in a violent or intense way. It can also mean that the tempter wanted Him to strike Himself down.

It must be remembered that suicide was one of the most grievous sins, even in Israel. In many African villages, one who commits suicide is not even buried by their relatives. Thus by doing this, the enemy was telling Jesus to sever the connection between Himself and God and make sure that God cannot look upon Him. The next word is *kato*, for "cast" which is comparative of *katotero* (**kat-o-ter'-o**) which means to move progressively downward. In fact, the enemy wanted Him to do something that was beneath Divine dignity. The word can also mean bottom. While literally Jesus would have fallen to the bottom of the building, spiritually He would have fallen into the bottom where the devil himself lived if He chose to cast Himself down.

While the passage does not say this, since the word can

also mean under, could it be that this was also the tempter's way of stating that Jesus needed to be under his authority? The tempter now joins Jesus in quoting the Scripture. Quoting Psalm 91, the devil says "he shall give his angels charge over you." The word *aggelos* (**ang'-el-os**) means to bring tidings. But what kind of tidings will the angels of the Lord bring to Jesus if He were to cast Himself down? The same message that the devil heard when he fell into hell. The tempter's use of the word *entellomai* here is translated "give charge" and means to enjoin as in the command of the military captain who commands his or her troops to enjoin another army. While the Old Testament uses this passage to talk about God's protection, "to give charge" should be read in terms of God entering into battle with His Son.

If Jesus were to give in, this thing would have been all over. It is true that God will protect those who trust Him and will work on their behalf and keep company with them. It is also accurate that God's concern for us is thorough. Here the tempter attempts to convince Jesus that God's power as reflected in the hands (Greek *cheir*, **khire**) of the angels will work for Him even when He chooses to side with the devil; but the devil is a liar. The verse further reads "bear thee up." The key word in that phrase is *airo* (**ah'ee-ro**) which simply means to lift. So here Jesus was being told that the angels of the Lord will take Him away before He suffers any harm. Figuratively, this word can mean to raise or to keep in suspension. This suggests that the enemy was trying to use the possibility of Jesus' own resurrection to cause Him to sin against God.

Note that this word is connected with the Hebrew word *nasa'* which means to expiate sin. So what the devil was saying to Jesus is "I know that doing what I'm asking you to is sin, but God will expiate your sin. You are the Saviour of the world, why should He not forgive you?" The enemy continues, "How do I know that God will lift you up?" Referring to Psalm 91:11, he says, "Peradventure you dash your foot against the rock." The Greek word translated in KJV as "lest at any time," *mepote* (**may'-pot-eh**), really means that you will not ever. Can you hear God saying you will never dash your feet? Note the use of the word "strike" or "dash" from the Greek *poskopto* (**pros-kop'-to**) which means to surge against like water or to trip up literally or spiritually. The tempter proceeds to propose that Jesus move in a direction which would not draw Jesus nearer to God but create direct conflict between Him and God. Thus, though Jesus may be saved from dashing his feet against a stone, He would literally become His own stumbling stone.

7 Jesus said unto him, It is written again, Thou shalt not tempt the Lord thy God.

In this verse, Matthew narrates Jesus' response to this temptation to throw Himself down from the pinnacle of the temple. Matthew's crafting of the narrative is interesting. In verse 4, Matthew uses the Greek *Ho de apokitheys eipen* "He (Jesus) answered and said." In verse 6, Matthew uses the Greek *legei*, from the word *logos* and here he uses the Greek *phemi* (**fay-mee'**) which comes from the same Greek word as *phos* rooted in the concept of light. This word "said" as used here carries with it the idea to show or make known one's thoughts. Thus it is more than just speaking. It is equivalent to the phrase "make it plain." It can also mean that here Jesus affirms what God says rather than what the enemy was saying.

From another perspective, it can mean that Jesus affirms the Word which the tempter quotes as coming from God but proceeds to say "it is written again." The idea is that God engraved the Word not just once but more than once. Note the use of the word "again." It is not Matthew using the word to denote that Jesus again says that it is written, rather it is Jesus saying "it is written again." This word is meant to point the enemy to the deceptive *eisegesis* which has thus far characterized his desire to sway Jesus. The Greek word *palin* (**pal'-in**) translated as "again" could mean that Jesus was pointing the enemy to the fact that before this verse from the psalm, something else has been said. It can also mean once more. Thus Jesus is saying to the enemy "You missed the foundation on which that quote stands. Devil, there is a principle without which your take on the Psalm means nothing—one's relationship with God." This word can also mean on the other hand, pointing to the fact that in order to use the Scriptures effectively once must look at all of Scripture, not just to that which seems to fit one's emotional whims.

What is the other Scripture which must serve as the foundation for Jesus' actions? "Thou shall not tempt the Lord thy God." What is spoken of here as suggested by the use of the Greek word for "tempt," *ekpeirazo* (**ek-pi-rad'-zo**) carries the idea of extremity. You must not "test thoroughly" your God. This is the idea of extreme. Jumping from the pinnacle is a human extreme. You must not remove the boundary of life that God has placed in hopes that God will deliver you. Simply put, you must live in obedience to the divine imperative if you expect to be kept. Putting the Lord to the test is making oneself the master of the Lord. This of course is a cardinal principle which connects us to God. We respect the boundaries that God has set for us. The use of the word "lord" denotes that God is the supreme authority, the controller of the universe. To put God to the test by sheer foolishness will only result in our destruction.

8 Again, the devil taketh him up into an exceeding high mountain, and showeth him all the kingdoms of the world, and the glory of them;

Satan tempted Christ to idolatry with the offer of the kingdoms of the world, and the glory of them. The glory of the world is the most attractive temptation to the unthinking and unwary; by it, men are most easily imposed upon. Christ was tempted to worship Satan. He rejected the proposal with abhorrence. Saying, "Get thee hence, Satan!" Some temptations are openly wicked; they are not merely to be opposed, but rejected at once. It is good to be quick and firm in resisting temptation. If we resist the devil, he will flee from us. But the soul that deliberates is almost always overcome. We find but few who can decidedly reject such baits as Satan offers; yet what is a man profited if he gain the whole world, and lose his own soul?

I love the way Matthew begins this verse, "again the devil took him" in Greek *palin, paralambano auton ho diabolos*. Think of how you would respond if somebody keeps doing the same thing over and over again. Think of the response "Again?" which accompanies the repeated offense. That seems to be the idea here. The tempter began his temptation anew. In a sense, the devil returned to try once more where he had failed. The enemy thought that he had learned something of the strategy of the Lord so he would try once more. In verse 5, he takes Jesus to the extremity of the temple, hoping to trip Him to His death.

Matthew tells us that the tempter took Him to the pinnacle which was the highest part of the temple. In this verse, we read that he took Jesus to the highest mountain. The word here for "exceeding" is the Greek word *lian* (**lee'-an**) which is a comparative term referring to the height of the temple pinnacle. Thus compared to the temple, this place was much higher. The word *lian* really means exceeding great or the chiefest. It might be worth noting that in traditional African cultures, as well as in the traditions of Israel, the places of spiritual power are described by concepts of height.

The next word used is the word "high" translated from the Greek word *hupselos* (**hoop-say-los'**) which means lofty. This word also describes not only the physical feature of a place but the character or esteem of someone, someplace or something. The Greek word for "mountain" here is the word *oros* (**or'-os**) which means to rise, thus by analogy means mountain or place of lifting. In this place, the devil "showed" (Greek *deiknuo*, pronounced **dike-noo'-o**) which indicates a prolonged view which was intended to cause Jesus to see mainly from an abstract perspective and not from the Divine or realistic perspective. The tempter abstracted everything from its flesh and blood reality and showed Him, Matthew says, "all the kingdoms of the world and the glory of them."

The idea that he showed Jesus all the kingdoms of the world can only be understood in terms of Jesus' nature as the Divine One who can see all things at once. The use of the word "all" (Greek *pas*) may suggest that what Jesus saw was included all forms of worldly glories. This word can also mean "any," which may mean that Jesus was showed everything His heart desired within the kingdoms of the world. This word also implies that the devil suggested the means whereby Jesus could be like of the kings of the world. One cannot help but wonder if the devil thought that Jesus did not know who He was. The idea that the King and Creator of the universe would be so impressed by worldly royal pomposity abstracted from divine rule suggests that devil is not as smart as he has made himself out to be.

The idea that the eternal framer of all realms would leave it to come to reign in one part of the earthly dirt does not seem far fetched to the tempter. The tempter uses "the world, and the glory" which translated in Greek is *tow kosmow* referring to the orderly arrangement and decoration of the world. What was the tempter going to show the Son of God who is the One from whose infinite being all the adorning beauty in the wide or narrow sense—including that which adorns the devil himself—derives? But show Him and then try to tell Him, the enemy did. Temptation does not have to make sense, it just has to offer a half-baked satisfaction. Furthermore, the tempter told of the glories of the world—Greek *doxa* (**dox'-ah**) which means dignity, honor, praise, and worship.

9 And saith unto him, All these things will I give thee, if thou wilt fall down and worship me.

In this verse, we come face to face with the cost of all the power which the enemy claims to have. The enemy boastfully lays forth his claim to fame in ways which any human being can relate. In doing so, the devil uses the phrase "I will" which got him into trouble with God in the first place. The tempter says "I will give to you" all of these, referring to the world. It must be remembered that for any member of the house of Israel this promise of power would have been tempting. You see every one who had power over them had chosen to use it against the people of God. Note also that in the Greek wording of the phrase "all these" one can literally read "all these things." Thus, the very heart of the temptation is for the Lord to make the getting and keeping of things His main aim for coming into the world.

Note also the use of the word "give" translated from the Greek word *didomi* (**did'-o-mee**) which suggests the sense of adventure. The devil seems to be saying "Jesus you have the ability to have a great adventure; forget about this call thing." Here the devil is really offering to deliver up the world to Jesus as if it belonged to him. The idea is that he will gladly minister and suffer demotion. The devil has always been a liar.

Then comes the cost: "if only thou will fall down and worship." Can you believe the enemy who had just said that he "will give" now placing a condition on this offer? Of course in this case, the tempter is not making a definite or certain promise. Is it not interesting that the devil says "if you will fall?" The Greek word for "fall" can also mean to fail to come down or to make something light. The second part of the offer is also interesting. It is not the falling that is the problem, it is what one is doing in the falling. The devil says to Jesus, "worship" or "fail by worshiping me." The Greek word for "worship *proskuneo* (**pros-koo-neh'-o**) can mean to kiss like a dog licking his master's hand. The enemy wanted Jesus to prostrate Himself before him. This act would require that Jesus give up His divinity and acknowledge that the devil is greater that the Lord God.

10 Then saith Jesus unto him, Get thee hence, Satan: for it is written, Thou shalt worship the Lord thy God, and him only shalt thou serve.

Matthew uses the Greek word *lego* to introduce Jesus' response. Remember that this word is akin to the name John uses to identify Jesus as the artificer of the cosmic system. Here instead of beginning with the Scripture, Jesus uses His authority for the first time in this conversation. It is an imperative command in Greek *hupage satana* translated as "Get thee hence." The word *hupago* (pronounced **hoop-ag'-o**) means to lead oneself—hence "show yourself out." It could also mean "under," thus meaning that Jesus was sending Satan back to the underworld. This is like a king saying "leave me." From the way Jesus speaks here, it is obvious that the conversation is over. Since Jesus is the Son of God, this word must have caused the devil to sink out of sight.

After telling Satan to depart, Jesus tells him why: "For it is written, thou shall worship the Lord thy God and Him only shall thou serve." Satan knew better. Worship derives from reverence. It is connected to the divine image within

human beings. But not even God requires that we come to Him like a dog licking a master's hand. There is no creature before which a human being must crouch or prostrate in homage, reverence, or adoration. God, and God only, deserves worship. For our God alone is supreme in all ways, authority, and power.

Here we find that Jesus uses the Hebraic mode of speaking about God; when there is need to declare divine absoluteness, He uses God and Lord. The Lord thy God is expression of the ultimacy of God. To worship would be to acknowledge that Satan was now His father. What affinity does Jesus have with the pretender to deity? The passage which Jesus uses the Greek word *monos* (**mon'-os**) to state how one should relate to this supreme being whose authority the devil seemed to want to take. The word can mean "only" but it also means "remaining." This then speaks to the fact that when everything is gone, including the devil, the one thing that shall remain is the Lord thy God. One must serve that which will remain.

The supremacy of this One whom Jesus calls here "the Lord thy God" is what makes Him the sole recipient of worship from every creature. Not only does this quotation which Jesus takes from the Hebrew Scripture say that we worship God alone, but even our service (Greek *latreuo*, **lat-ryoo'-o**), our most menial labor, must be done with this God in mind. We are to minister to God alone. Jesus was on this earth to render religious homage and to serve God; anything short of that would have been problematic.

11 Then the devil leaveth him, and, behold, angels came and ministered unto him.

After the rebuke in the previous verse, we read here that the devil left Him. The devil could now find nothing with which to accuse or slander Jesus. Jesus has resisted the devil, and now the devil flees from Him. The use of the Greek word *aphiemi* (**af-ee'-ay-mee**) translated "leaveth" can mean to send. It can also mean to cry. What if this defeat caused the enemy to cry? The word also implies that the devil now forsakes Jesus. The enemy laid aside his present strategy. In this wrestling match, the devil yields to Jesus. Then we read that when the enemy left, "behold." This "behold" is a Hebraic form of expression carried into the Greek. It is meant to express the suddenness and the excitement which accompanies revelation.

Because Jesus has conquered Satan, the angels now come to minster to Him. In some African villages where wrestling is practiced, the winner receives service from his or her relatives after victory. The Greek suggested that after this encounter, the angels came to Him. Would they have come near to Him if He had given in to the tempter? The word used here to denote "came" suggests that they approached Him; literally, they come near Him. It can also mean that they worshiped Him and assented to Him. But they did not only come to Him, they also served Him. Note the combination of worship and service in what the angels did. This is the same act that Jesus says must be done to God alone. Note also that Jesus got what the devil was promising to give Him. Here He was being attended and waited upon by a host of angels as a friend. By the way, this word can also mean friend. It is the word from which get our word "deacon." Jesus has succeeded in His initiation into the battle of the ages as a human being. Now there had to be celebration, which follows initiation in African cultures.

12 Now when Jesus had heard that John was cast into prison, he departed into Galilee;

In verse 11, we read that the devil left Jesus. Having failed to confound Jesus, the devil reaches out to someone who was dear to Him. This verse begins with the Greek word *de* (**deh**) which means "but." Thus we can read it to say, "but Jesus heard that John was cast into prison." We can also read it as saying, "moreover Jesus heard that John was cast into prison." These two readings will connect the verse to the continuous attack of the enemy to challenge the resolve of Jesus to do the will of God. Jesus "heard" (Greek *akouo*, **ak-oo'-o**) which means to hear. Jesus heard the noise or report that His cousin had been cast into jail. John had been given over to jail or surrendered to jailors. This could also mean that John was betrayed into prison. Jesus' response was to withdraw from the area.

13 And leaving Nazareth, he came and dwelt in Capernaum, which is upon the sea coast, in the borders of Zabulon and Nephthalim:

This verse suggests that Jesus was now leaving behind anything that might hinder His call. He simply abandons whatever of the world that He had remaining in order to reserve Himself totally for God's work. Jesus went to stay at Nazareth. *Strong's Concordance* says that the word Nazareth is of uncertain derivative (*Strong's Concordance* sec. 4, p. 59); but it would seem that given the context in Numbers 6:2, where we first find the word Nazarene, in Hebrew it means to be consecrated (sec. 3., p. 92). This town must have had some connection to the vow of being Nazarene or set apart; since people in that part of the world made every move based on its spiritual significance. Matthew even tells us that it is written that He shall be called a Nazarene (2:23).

Leaving the place of separation, Jesus went to Capernum. There the Greek tells us that He "dwelt" *katoikeo* (**kat-oy-keh'-o**) meaning He built a house. At Capernum, Jesus had a permanent residence, and thus became an inhabitant of the city. He lived by the sea shore as the Greek word *parathalassios* (**par-ath-al-as'-see-os**) will suggest, in accordance with the division of the land by Moses among the tribes of Israel.

14 That it might be fulfilled which was spoken by Esaias the prophet, saying,

Jesus did everything to make sure Scripture is fulfilled. It is interesting to note that the Greek word *pleroo* (**play-ro'-o**) translated "fulfilled," means that the prophecy of Isaiah 40:3-5 came up to level ground where people could now understand what was meant. He executed what Isaiah had seen. He is the verification, the accomplishment, and the perfection of all Messianic prophesies. Whatever God commanded through Isaiah regarding the Messiah, Jesus now fulfills by moving to the land of Naphtali and Zebulun. Not only does Jesus fulfill Isaiah's word, He realizes the significance of Isaiah's name which means "Jah has saved." Isaiah was the foreteller; Jesus is the fulfillment of what was told. Isaiah was the inspired speaker; this One who is now come to Zebulun is the inspirer and the speaker. Isaiah was the arranger of Divine poetry; here comes the poet and lyric.

DAILY BIBLE READING

M: Jesus Is Tempted by the Devil
Matthew 3:1-11
T: Jesus Begins His Ministry in Galilee
Matthew 4:12-17
W: Jesus in the Synagogue at Nazareth
Luke 4:14-19
T: Jesus Is Rejected in Nazareth
Luke 4:20-30
F: Jesus Casts out a Demonic Spirit
Luke 4:31-37
S: Jesus Heals and Preaches
Luke 4:38-44
S: Jesus Heals a Man with Leprosy
Luke 5:12-16

TEACHING TIPS

December 19
Bible Study Guide 3

1. Words You Should Know

A. Righteous. (Matthew 1:19) Greek *dikaiosyne*—the biblical concept denoting what is right; the straight, smooth way according to *Wycliffe Bible Dictionary*, Charles F. Pfeiffer, Howard F. Vos, John Rea, Massachusetts: Hendrickson Publishers, Inc., 1998, pp. 1471-1472.

B. Emmanuel. (Matthew 1:23) Greek—the prophetic announcement of the virgin birth of Christ. It means, "God with us."

2. Teacher Preparation

A. To gain a better understanding of why mankind needed a Saviour, read the story of Adam and Eve's sin in Genesis 3:1-19. You will see how humankind fell from grace through the first Adam and needed a second Adam to restore us. This could only be done through the shed blood of Jesus Christ for the remission of our sins.

B. Next, study the FOCAL VERSES. Understand what kind of man Joseph was, and why God used him to be Jesus' legal and earthly father. Also, examine the times in which they lived and how becoming pregnant before marriage had grave implications for Mary.

C. Write down the answers to the SEARCH THE SCRIPTURES and DISCUSS THE MEANING questions.

D. Materials needed: a board, chalk, a Bible.

3. Starting the Lesson

A. Before the students arrive, write the title of the lesson and the AT-A-GLANCE outline on the board.

B. After the students are seated and settled, ask for prayer requests, and start your session with prayer by taking the requests before God and concentrating on the LESSON AIM. Then, ask them to define the words, "righteous," and "Emmanuel," in the context of today's lesson.

C. Read the IN FOCUS story.

4. Getting into the Lesson

A. Have volunteers read the BACKGROUND information and THE PEOPLE, PLACES, AND TIMES section. You may want to explain some of the significant points found in these sections.

B. Ask for volunteers to read the FOCAL VERSES according to the AT-A-GLANCE outline.

C. You may want to explain and discuss each verse after it is read or have an over-all discussion after the entire passage is read.

5. Relating the Lesson to Life

A. Direct the students' attention to the LESSON IN OUR SOCIETY section and encourage discussion.

B. Review and discuss the DISCUSS THE MEANING questions. Help the students to see how the lesson applies to their own life.

6. Arousing Action

A. Direct the students to the MAKE IT HAPPEN suggestion, and challenge them to put the suggestion into practice during the week.

B. Encourage them to read the DAILY BIBLE READING.

C. Finally, pray and ask God to prepare your hearts.

WORSHIP GUIDE

For the Superintendent or Teacher
Theme: Birth of Jesus
Theme Song: "O Come, O Come Emmanuel"
Scripture: Matthew 1:1-6, 18-25
Song: "I Surrender All"
Devotional Thought: May our Lord and Saviour Jesus Christ become so real in our hearts, that we will know without a doubt that He is truly the Son of God, who came to die for us so that we might have eternal life.

BIRTH OF JESUS

Bible Background • MATTHEW 1
Printed Text • MATTHEW 1:1-6, 18-25
Devotional Reading • JOHN 1:1-14

LESSON AIM

By the end of the lesson, students should know without a doubt that Jesus is the one and only Son of God, and that He came into the world for one purpose—to die for the salvation of all believers. They should know that Jesus is God-man. He is God, who lived as a man. Therefore, He fully understands all our experiences and the struggles we go through.

KEEP IN MIND

"And she shall bring forth a son, and thou shalt call his name JESUS: for he shall save his people from their sins" (Matthew 1:21).

FOCAL VERSES

MATTHEW 1:1 The book of the generation of Jesus Christ, the son of David, the son of Abraham.

2 Abraham begat Isaac; and Isaac begat Jacob; and Jacob begat Judas and his brethren;

3 And Judas begat Phares and Zara of Thamar; and Phares begat Esrom; and Esrom begat Aram;

4 And Aram begat Aminadab; and Aminadab begat Naasson; and Naasson begat Salmon;

5 And Salmon begat Booz of Rachab; and Booz begat Obed of Ruth; and Obed begat Jesse;

6 And Jesse begat David the king; and David the king begat Solomon of her that had been the wife of Urias;

18 Now the birth of Jesus Christ was on this wise: When as his mother Mary was espoused to Joseph, before they came together, she was found with child of the Holy Ghost.

19 Then Joseph her husband, being a just man, and not willing to make her a publick example, was minded to put her away privily.

20 But while he thought on these things, behold, the angel of the Lord appeared unto him in a dream, saying,

LESSON OVERVIEW

LESSON AIM
KEEP IN MIND
FOCAL VERSES
IN FOCUS
THE PEOPLE, PLACES, AND TIMES
BACKGROUND
AT-A-GLANCE
IN DEPTH
SEARCH THE SCRIPTURES
DISCUSS THE MEANING
LESSON IN OUR SOCIETY
MAKE IT HAPPEN
FOLLOW THE SPIRIT
REMEMBER YOUR THOUGHTS
MORE LIGHT ON THE TEXT
DAILY BIBLE READINGS

Joseph, thou son of David, fear not to take unto thee Mary thy wife: for that which is conceived in her is of the Holy Ghost.

21 And she shall bring forth a son, and thou shalt call his name JESUS: for he shall save his people from their sins.

22 Now all this was done, that it might be fulfilled which was spoken of the Lord by the prophet, saying,

23 Behold, a virgin shall be with child, and shall bring forth a son, and they shall call his name Emmanuel, which being interpreted is, God with us.

24 Then Joseph being raised from sleep did as the angel of the Lord had bidden him, and took unto him his wife:

25 And knew her not till she had brought forth her firstborn son: and he called his name JESUS.

IN FOCUS

Marva raised her son, George, in the church environment. In fact, as a very small tyke, he went to Sunday School, children's church, revivals, Vacation Bible School, and later, Youth Fellowship. However, when George got into junior high and especially into high school, Marva noticed a drastic change in behavior. It was on the negative down-slide. Peer pressures were more pronounced, and George was having a hard time saying, "No," to some of their demands.

Marva had always prayed for George—that God would save him, keep him, and cover him with the blood of Jesus. She knew she had trained him up in the way he should go, but Satan was definitely attacking her child.

Not only did Marva continue to pray, but she began to fast and she had others to do so as well. They prayed that God would give George a change of heart, and that the Holy Spirit would remind him of God's Word and point his way back to God's righteousness.

Years passed; George was a junior in college and Marva found herself still praying . . . still claiming George's salvation. One Sunday as Marva sat in church worshiping God, she looked up and George walked into church. He seemed focused, purposeful, and determined.

When the pastor gave the altar call, George went to the altar and gave his heart to The Lord. Indeed, it was a time of rejoicing! Jesus Christ was born in George's heart. The prayers of the righteous had availed much. They had won a soul to Christ.

THE PEOPLE, PLACES, AND TIMES

JOSEPH. A descendant of King David. He was Jesus' earthly and legal father, who was engaged to Mary (Jesus' mother) when Jesus was conceived by the Holy Ghost. The Word calls him a man of integrity and He believed God's Word. Joseph was not swayed from his stand by public opinion, but stood firm on the Word and did what was right. Therefore, he had spiritual discernment and was sensitive to the guidance of the Lord, regardless of the consequences.

MARY. The mother of Jesus, chosen by God, Himself. She was the first and only human being who ever had an Immaculate Conception or conceived a child who was without sin. Her cousin was Elizabeth, the mother of John the Baptist, as the forerunner of Jesus prepared the way for Him. Mary was engaged to Joseph when she conceived Jesus and later married him. Mary was also a descendant of King David and later had other children.

BACKGROUND

Matthew wrote his Gospel to the Jews especially to prove that Jesus was indeed the long-awaited Messiah. He wrote to show that the prophecies of the Old Testament had been fulfilled in the New Testament. The promised Saviour, the promised Deliverer was Jesus Christ, Himself.

It had been more than 400 years since the last Old Testament prophets told of Christ's coming. Now the Jews were oppressed by Roman rule.

Therefore, they looked for a king who would set up his kingdom here on earth. That king would, then, establish justice in his kingdom. When Jesus came as a suffering Saviour, who was accused by the religious leaders, tried, convicted, and crucified, many Jews would not accept Him as Messiah. In fact, Jesus came talking about a heavenly kingdom established in the heart of one who believes on the Lord Jesus Christ and receives salvation. He came serving rather than being served. Jesus definitely did not fit the bill of the Israelites' expected Messiah.

AT-A-GLANCE

1. The Genealogy of Jesus (Matthew 1:1-6)
2. From Confusion to Divine Clarity (vv. 18-23)
3. From Divine Clarity to Human Obedience (vv. 24-25)

IN DEPTH

1. The Genealogy of Jesus (Matthew 1:1-6)

Matthew began his Gospel with Jesus' genealogy to show the royal lineage of Jesus. One's family background was very important in Israel. This blood line proved whether or not a person was one of God's chosen people. Remember the Israelites were God's chosen. The Messiah needed to be an Israelite in all respects. For Jesus to be the Messiah He had to fit in the "Who's Who," of Israelite history. To appeal to the people of Israel, He needed to meet the genealogical criteria, and Matthew set out to prove that he did.

Matthew's task was not so much to prove that the Messiah was divine, but to show that He was connected to the promise of God as it relates to the house of Israel from the days of Abraham. Israelites believed that the Messiah must be genealogically traceable to Abraham, Isaac and Jacob. But more significantly, He must be traceable to the beloved king of Israel, David. As Divine, the Messiah is intimately connected to God. But as a human, He is intimately connected to the best of the spiritual and prophetic tradition of Israel. If the Messiah was to rule over Israel and as the Hebrew Testament teaches: "There shall not fail to sit upon the throne of Israel one from the house of David" then it is easy to understand why Matthew takes this Davidic connection so seriously.

But the Messiah was not just to serve Israel, He was slated to be the Saviour and King of the nations. Thus, in this genealogy Matthew includes some members of Jesus' lineage who, in those days, may not have been considered nobility. As you read the genealogy, it reads like the "who's who" of faith and failure. Look at the father Abraham, a man of unprecedented faith, who in some instances showed a clearly human flaw through his willingness to let his wife pass as his sister, thus exposing her to assault. Take Jacob, so deeply religious yet terribly deceitful in his dealings with other people. Matthew's genealogy of Jesus interweaves outsiders and insiders. Take Tamar who was a stranger in Israel, yet through divine providence became one of the ancestors of the Messiah. Take also Rahab, an outsider and one marginalized even among her own people yet through faith became partaker of the covenant. Also included in this pageant of messianic "who's who" is Ruth, a Moabite. The Moabites were a people Israel quarreled with many times. Also look at King David the beloved king of Israel, a man after God's own heart, yet in many ways flawed. All these people, with their faith and flaws, insiders and outsiders, Israelites as well as Gentiles, form the thread that weaves the humanity of Jesus. Just as Jesus, in his manifestation on earth, brings God and humanity together, in this genealogy we see Him bringing Jews and Gentiles together. In his own body, as indicated within Matthew's account, Jesus breaks down the barriers of ethnicity, gender, and even religion. In spite of all their faults, the one thing all these people had in common was their faith and their willingness to place their lives in God's hand and trust Him.

2. From Confusion to Divine Clarity (vv. 18-23)

How did the particular process leading to the birth of the Messiah begin? Having laid out the background of the Messiah's birth, it must be remembered that Matthew was showing that Jesus in His humanity was connected to the best of Israelite tradition. But here, instead of continuing as would be expected in speaking of an ordinary human person, Matthew introduces something else. When Matthew says, "Mary had been engaged to Joseph" his Jewish audience would have nodded their heads in affirmation. When he says that "before they lived together she was found to be with child," they could have accepted that because in the tradition of Israel they were technically married. But when he says, "she was found to be with a child from the Holy Spirit" he introduces a problem to their mind—for to them the Messiah was nothing more that a human being. By stating it this way, Matthew sets the stage to argue that this human being was and indeed is equal to the eternal One of Israel. This would have posed a great intellectual and theological problem for an Israelite.

This problem is exemplified in the way God deals with Joseph. Joseph here represents the religious tendency of the people of Israel. First, Joseph is described as a righteous man. This righteousness exceeded the legal code. For as we read, this righteousness made him unwilling to expose Mary to disgrace. Unlike the Pharisees who throughout the life of Jesus would show themselves unwilling to be compassionate, Joseph showed that he understood the compassion of the Lord. While he may not have wanted to disgrace her, he could not have married her without breaking the law. So he resolved to put her away in secret.

In his confusion, God sent an angel to dispel his confusion. Note also that in all of Israel's history whenever a great

one was to be born who would impact the direction of the nation—Isaac, Jacob, Samson, Samuel—there was divine manifestation. In this case the angel came to Joseph as a representative sign that God will wipe away all the confusion that he faced when seeking to do His divine will. God spoke to him in connection to the divine acts in history. By calling Joseph a "son of David" God intended for Joseph to consider several things. First, what God has done in history as it relates to the people. Second, God sought to help Joseph look at the situation in broader perspective rather than concentrate on the shame which he and Mary would endure. Third, God wanted to take away the spirit of fear that had overtaken Joseph because of his confusion. Fear was going to make him do exactly what he wanted to avoid, which was expose his wife to ridicule. But God says, "be not afraid to take Mary as your wife." This speech by God clarified the relationship that Joseph was to have with his spouse. It also clarified what his perception of whose the child should be. Furthermore, it helped to clarify the event to the people of Israel; who for so long had awaited deliverance from the Lord. Now Joseph must see the God of Israel in this child, and see this event as a God-event. When God speaks into our situation we see more clearly, and our relationships are put in the right perspective.

God also clarifies the situation by pointing us back to the Scripture. Here Matthew says all this can be related to what God had said. This reference to the past may seem to us mere appendage, but for Israel this is of great significance. This prophetic utterance helps to point out to Joseph and to those of us who believe, that we are not living within human wishful thinking. Rather our belief as well as Joseph's acceptance of Mary is grounded in the prophetic insight that comes directly from the Lord God. If Joseph was confused and he heard Isaiah 7:14, his heart would have leaped. He would have thought, *Look the very one who takes away our human confusion is in my house. The wisdom of God, the insight of the holy, the light that chases the human night is in my house there is no need to be afraid.* Can you envision the angel calling to this confused brother saying "a virgin shall conceive and bear a son" and referring back to him and the Israelites of Joseph's day, "and they shall call his name Emmanuel" (v. 23), which means "God with us"? Can you imagine how the clouds were lifted from his befuddled mind? Can you see him as he literally wakes up, wipes his eyes, and says, "Now I can see"?

3. From Divine Clarity to Human Obedience (vv. 24-25)

Once God clarifies the events to Joseph and how this was God's work, Joseph set aside his personal feelings and worked with respect to the clarified Word spoken to him.

Divine clarification must lead to practical application of God's Word. God reveals things to us so that we might act in concert with the movement of His Spirit in the world. Insights are not given to us so that we harbor them and hoard them for self-promotion, but to create within ourselves a motion to action. Not just any action, such clarifications ought to lead to action that is consistent with the character of God. God can use you to preserve and to unfold the Divine will as Joseph was to be used of God. All you need to do is listen to the Divine that speaks to you in your heart and in the Word of God. Too many of us spend time fighting with God when we should take our lesson from Joseph and stop worrying about who agrees or disagrees with our Divine insight and just do what God reveals to us to do. God would only command us to do something that is consistent with the Word of God. God told Joseph what to do, and human opinion no longer mattered. Instead he chose instead to please the One who was in charge of his soul. God's approval meant more to Him than man's. We thank God that Joseph allowed God to clarify his vision as it relates to the birth of the Saviour.

SEARCH THE SCRIPTURES

1. Who was Zerah's mother? (Matthew 1:3)
2. Who was Obed's mother? (v. 5)
3. Who was King David's father? (v. 6)
4. How did the angel of the Lord appear to Joseph? (v. 20)
5. In times past, God had given His message through whom? (v. 22)

DISCUSS THE MEANING

1. Jesus came into the world fulfilling prophecy and God's plan of salvation. What is His plan?
2. God knew the stigma in the Jewish society of a woman having a baby before she was married. Why do you think God chose to use Mary to conceive Jesus?

LESSON IN OUR SOCIETY

You and I cannot save ourselves from our own sins. This truth is evident in the direction of our society today. The crime, drug usage, alcohol usage, rise in unwanted pregnancies, abortions, teens putting their babies in trash cans, and wars and rumors of wars tell us that people are in desperate situations and feeling hopeless. Government programs and laws have not remedied these situations.

In many of our cities, there are churches on every corner. Yet, the ills of mankind have become even more grave. People are spiritually lost. They have either heard the Good News and have become discontented or disillusioned by church leaders who only lead to be served instead of serving God's people, or have not heard the Good News of salvation at all. Indeed, the fields are ready for harvest, but the laborers are few.

We each need to believe on the Lord Jesus Christ as our personal Saviour and be saved not only from sin, but ourselves as well. God's Word tells us that God knows how to direct and guide our lives better than we do. We make big messes of our life and only God can forgive us and cleanse us from sin. Only Jesus can set us free from the power and guilt of sin. We can be forgiven through believing on Jesus and what He did for us when He laid down His life. The living God wants us to turn from our sins and believe the Good News!

MAKE IT HAPPEN

There are so many people who do not understand the Good News of salvation and what it means for them. Their eyes are on people and their miss-steps and mistakes instead of on Jesus Christ. Let these people see Jesus in you this day and everyday. Pray and ask God to help you walk the walk as well as talk the talk of a Christian because you are saved. Witness to someone this week.

FOLLOW THE SPIRIT

What God wants me to do:

_____

_____

REMEMBER YOUR THOUGHTS

Special insights you learned:

_____

_____

MORE LIGHT ON THE TEXT
MATTHEW 1:1-6, 18-25

1:1 The book of the generation of Jesus Christ, the son of David, the son of Abraham.

This introductory verse is exclusive to the Book of Matthew. Matthew, in recording this account of the genealogy of Jesus, attempts to show Jesus as the "Christ," the one who is the "Son of David" and the "Son of Abraham." This is meant to connect Jesus, who was born to Mary and Joseph, as the One who will fulfill the promise made to Abraham and David. Note that this verse begins with the word "generation," a translation of the Greek word *genesis*, which as we all know is the name of the first book of the Bible meaning beginning or the nativity of someone or something. Figuratively, it means the nature of something.

2 Abraham begat Isaac; and Isaac begat Jacob; and Jacob begat Judas and his brethren;

The genealogy begins with Abraham, to whom the promise of blessing to all nations was made. The importance of Abraham to the life of the Messiah cannot be overstated. He was declared by God to be the father of a multitude and called by God for the specific purpose of blessing the world (Genesis 12:2-3, 7). The promise made to him was both immediate and perpetual—material and spiritual. The heart of his call and blessing was that he would be the ancestor of the great Deliverer, whose coming had been declared by God in Genesis 3:15. Abraham's part in the genealogy of the Messiah is exemplified by the fact that he, himself, had one son of promise—Isaac, whom he offered to God as a sacrifice on Mount Moriah. As the ancestor of Messiah in the flesh, Abraham exemplified faith that stands the test of circumstances and time (Hebrews 11:17-19).

It is fitting for the story of the Messiah to start with Abraham at the helm. He is called "the friend of God" (James 2:23), "faithful" (Galatians 3:9), and he is regarded as "the father of us all" (Romans 4:16). His son Isaac, whose name means laughter, is named after his mother. Isaac is a type of Christ by virtue of the fact that he was a child of promise. One of Isaac's sons, Jacob, (later renamed Israel) though full of deceit, became the heir of the promise.

3 And Judas begat Phares and Zara of Thamar; and Phares begat Esrom; and Esrom begat Aram;

The name Judah (Judas) is of Hebrew origin unlike Abram and Abraham which are of Chaldee-hamitic origin. The name *Yehuwdah* (pronounced **Jehudah**) became the name of one of the 12 tribes of Israel. Judah means praise. Judah was the fourth son of Jacob and Leah. He was the son of a woman who was rejected by her husband Jacob, because she supposedly was not comely. The name is the result of Leah's praise to the Lord because of the relief she felt at his birth. Seeing that her husband could no longer ignore her, she sings, "Now will I praise Jehovah (Hebrew *hodeh adonai*), and she called his name Yehudah" (Genesis 29:35).

Judah was enigmatic. He participated in the plot to kill his brother Joseph, and then intervened to save his life by selling him into slavery instead (Genesis 37:26-27). He took a lead in the affairs of the family, and "prevailed above his brethren" (Genesis 43:3-10; 44:14, 16-34; 46:28; 1 Chronicles 5:2). We know that Judah resided among the Canaanites at Adullam for a time, and that he married a Canaanite woman. He was given a blessing of leadership by his father Jacob in Genesis 49:8-12. Judah's eldest son Er, was married to a Canaanite woman named Thamar or Tamar. Er died prematurely (Genesis 38:1-7), and through Tamar's trickery she got Judah to father twin sons, one of whom became an ancestor of the Messiah.

Tamar is one of four Gentile women mentioned in Matthew's genealogy of Jesus. The twin sons born to Tamar were named Phares and Zara. Zara, (pronounced **dzar-ah'**) is of Canaanite not Hebrew origin and possibly means "to answer." Given the fact that Tamar was denied a husband and as a result of tricking Judah, her prayer was answered by having twins sons. Zara is not tied to the line of the Messiah; however, it is interesting that he is mentioned with his brother. It would seem that the Israelites had a special regard for twins. But note here, unlike the case of Jacob and Esau where the youngest takes over, it is the oldest son, Phares, who becomes bearer of the covenant.

4 And Aram begat Aminadab; and Aminadab begat Naasson; and Naasson begat Salmon;

Aram is the only name to appear in the genealogy of Jesus for a span of approximately 400 years. Aram was the name of Abraham's ancestors. The name appears in numerous places in the Hebrew Testament. Aram was the father of Aminadab (pronounced **uhm'min'uh'dahb**). The name means "my people give freely." This was the name of Aaron's father-in-law (Exodus 6:23). The use of the name goes back to the stay of Israel in Africa. For we find that one of the leaders of Israel in the wilderness bore the name as well (see Numbers 1:7). We also find the name in David's proto-genealogy found in Ruth 4:19. The name Aram is specifically mentioned in connection to the Messiah in Matthew 1:4 and Luke 3:33. Aram was also the father of another wilderness leader, Naason or Nashon (pronounced in Hebrew **Nay'-ahsh-ahn**). This is the same person mentioned in Exodus 6:23. It is interesting that the personal name Nashon means "serpent," and he was a member of the tribe of Judah from which our Lord comes (if you wish to learn more about this person see Numbers 1:7; 2:3; 7:12; 17; 10:14). His son was Salmon.

5 And Salmon begat Boaz of Rachab; and Boaz begat Obed of Ruth; and Obed begat Jesse;

Salmon is another among the Israelites who married outside of his tribe. It is important that we do not confuse the fact that this woman was not picked because she had a different skin color from the general population of Israelites. Most Israelites coming from Africa would have been dark-skinned. Therefore, the issue is not color, but tribal and religious affiliations. Salmon, for whose name we really cannot find a Hebrew definition, became the father of Boaz through another Gentile woman.

This Gentile woman named Rachab or Rahab assisted Joshua in his conquest of Jericho (Joshua 2-6). Rachab, pronounced **Ray'-hahb** is a Canaanite name meaning, "broad." Probably referring to her willingness to take on strangers. She was called a prostitute. Yet, also remember, this could mean she was not married or that she was an independent woman. Because women were expected to be married in those days, if she was not married people thought something was wrong with her. Her faith and willingness to take risks for what she believed led her to hide two Hebrew spies whom Joshua sent to Jericho to determine the strength of the city (Joshua 2:1). Rahab's brilliance is seen in her ability to outsmart the king and create a strategic alliance which helped her and family. In return for her help Joshua spared her and her clan when the Hebrews destroyed Jericho (Joshua 6:17-25). In this verse, Rachab is named as the mother of Boaz and regarded as one of the heroes of faith in Hebrews 11:31.

The son born to Salmon and Rachab was named Boaz. Boaz's name (pronounced **Bo'-az**) means "lively" or "quickness." This lively hero can be found in the Book of Ruth. He was a wealthy relative of Naomi's deceased husband. Having just migrated to Israel after the death of her husband, Ruth had to glean grain in the fields to sustain her mother-in-law and herself. In the process, she met Boaz and was invited to remain as his guest. The news of Ruth's goodness and loyalty to Naomi was not lost on the family. It was a typical Israelite custom for blessings to be pronounced upon one who has shown good character.

Boaz pronounced a blessing on Ruth because of her dedication to her mother-in-law, Naomi. In the process of the relationship, Ruth was instructed by her mother-in-law to lay down at the feet of Boaz. This was the traditional way of showing that Boaz was responsible for her care. However, according to the custom of Levitical law, a widow must be married to the nearest male relative of her deceased husband. Boaz fell in love with Ruth and made the nearest relative an offer he could not refuse; thus allowing Boaz to marry Ruth. From the union of yet another outsider came a son named Obed. His name means "serving." Obed was David's grandfather, and an ancestor of Christ (Matthew 1:5; Luke 3:32). Obed fathered Jesse.

6 And Jesse begat David the king; and David the king begat Solomon of her that had been the wife of Urias;

Some scholars say that the name Jesse means "man" or "manly," but it would seem that the prefix "Je" should stand for God as in Jeshua or "Jeremiah." This name could, therefore, mean "God's man" or "man of God." Jesse was

the father of David the king (1 Samuel 16:1) and was Ben Yehudah (son of Judah) whose homestead was in Bethlehem. As the grandson of Boaz and Ruth, he was probably marked for something special indicated by his name (1 Samuel 16:1; Ruth 4:17). Jessie had eight sons and two daughters. We are not told David was the youngest child, but we do know that he was the youngest boy. Though Jesse was a good man, he was short-sighted in his view of the future of Israel when it came to selecting a king from among his children. He seemed to have underestimated the gift of David either because of his size or his age. He is also mentioned in the genealogies of Jesus in the Gospels of Matthew and Luke.

David is a personal name meaning "favorite" or "beloved." David was the first king to unite Israel and Judah and the first to receive the promise of a royal Messiah in his lineage. David was pictured as the ideal king of God's people. He ruled from about 1005 to 965 B.C.

The last of these four Gentile women is Bathsheba, the wife of Uriah, the Hittite. Although Bathsheba is an Israelite, because she married a Gentile, rabbinic law considers her a Gentile, thereby making her offspring Gentile as well. Bathsheba later becomes the wife of King David, and to their union Solomon is born (2 Samuel 12:24).

18 Now the birth of Jesus Christ was on this wise: When as his mother Mary was espoused to Joseph, before they came together, she was found with child of the Holy Ghost.

The phraseologies here suggest that the author is about to change the direction of his thought. It is almost like saying "be that as it may." The word "now" (Greek *dè*) is a primary particle which tells us that the writer is about to recommence with a broken thought. The beginning of this verse resumes the story announced in Matthew 1:1. The second half of this verse, 18b, introduces Mary and Joseph who are the main characters in the narrative to follow. It also presents the plot of the story: Mary is engaged to Joseph. They have not engaged in premarital sexual relations. Yet, Mary is pregnant by the Holy Ghost. The writer tells us, in the Greek, that this section is about the genesis of Jesus Christ. The use of the word "birth" (Greek *genesis*) speaks directly to the present condition of natal revelation, and not His ancestry.

The King James Version of the Bible reads, "was on this wise" meaning "it was like this." Note the use of the Greek word *houto* (pronounced **hoo'-to**) which means "in this way or in this manner." Matthew's goal here seems to show the uniqueness of the birth of Jesus as opposed to the birth of those persons mentioned in the genealogy.

The writer proceeds to tell us the condition under which

Mary found herself. We read, "when as his mother Mary was espoused to Joseph." The key word here is "espoused," translated in the Greek *mnesteutheisis* (pronounced **mnes-tyoo-thay -sis**) derived from the Greek word *mnesteuo* (pronounced **mnace-tyoo'-o**). It means the act of giving a woman over to a man for a wife. It really refers to something precious which is given at the time of one's engagement. The word *mnaomai* points to the idea of fixing one's mind or mentally grasping something or someone. In this case, Mary was fixed in the mind of Joseph; she was precious in the mind of another.

Having described the mental connection between Mary and Joseph's mind the writer now says, "before they came together" and in the Greek reads, *prin sunelthein autous*. This term means more than coming together in same vicinity. The word from which we derive the phrase "come together" is the Greek word *sunerchomai* (pronounced **soon-er'-khom-ahee**), which means "to convene" such as what happens in wedding parties. In this case, the phrase could mean, before Mary departed into the company of her husband-to-be, or before there was any conjugal cohabitation.

Matthew says all this in preparation of the uniqueness of this birth. We read further that Mary was "found" (Greek *heurethe*, pronounced **hyoo-rethe**) taken from the Greek word *heurisko* (pronounced **hyoo-ris'-ko**). The use of this word suggests that it may have been a while before she was "found." What was Mary found with? She literally is seen as one who, according to the Greek, was *en gastri*. Simply stated, she was found with the stomach, with matrix, or with belly, a euphemism for being with child or pregnant. However, Matthew does not stop there. He states that Mary's being with child is not a result of an act of Joseph, but from the Holy Spirit.

The Greek word *hagios* (**hag'-ee-os**) translated as "holy" means that the condition of being pregnant resulted from something sacred, physically pure, morally blameless, religiously righteous, and ceremonially clean. It would have been simple for Matthew to stop there. However, he said it was not merely something ceremonially clean that caused Mary's condition, but rather the *pneuma* (pronounced **pnyoo'-mah**) or Holy Ghost. Thus, he insisted, that which is currently in the womb of this "found" woman was the breath of God, the very breeze of holiness. This child was the result of a vital principle and mental disposition of something superhuman. In the context of Israel, this Being could only be God.

19 Then Joseph her husband, being a just man, and not willing to make her a public example, was minded to put her away privily.

Note here that Joseph is referred to as the husband of

Mary, nothing less—nothing more. The word husband (Greek *aner*, pronounced **an'-ayr**) primarily refers to an individual male—specifically the husband. In truth if Mary was Joseph's wife, the tradition of Israel demanded that she should be killed for conceiving a child by another person. But we read that Joseph is a just man. However, unlike the King James Version of the Bible, the Greek does not say "just man." Rather, the Greek simply reads, "being righteous" (Greek *own dikaios*). It means that Joseph was equitable in character and act. It implies that he was innocent and holy. Of course here we are dealing with relative innocence. The fact that he was "a just man," could mean that he lived by the laws of the God of Israel.

Mary is pregnant, her conception is by the Holy Spirit, but Joseph does not know this. By law he has the right to divorce her or to kill her. Yet, he decides to privately dissolve the marriage. We read further that Joseph was "not willing to make her a public example" (Greek *mee theloon autees deigmatisan*). His just nature would not allow him to act in a certain way. This again will throw light on the word translated "just." It does not mean justice in terms of giving someone what they deserve, but connotes a sense of mercy and compassion. The idea of his unwillingness to make Mary a public example implies that he acted otherwise, apparently strengthened by something beyond the law.

What made Joseph "just" was the fact that he was determined to take a different position from that of the crowd. Rather than let the law take its course, he refused to be passive and chose mercy over the rules of law. To "will" something is to be inclined, or gladly to do a thing. In the Hebrew language, the concept of "will" (*thelo*, pronounced **thel'-o**) is tied to having delight in some thing or action. "Just" people do not delight or desire to see others hurt even when they are wrong. The Greek word translated into the phrase "make her a public spectacle" is *deigmatisan* (pronounced **dig-ma-tis-an**), which is connected to the word *paradeigmatizo*, (say **par-ad-igue-mat-id'-zo**) meaning to show the public or to expose to infamy. It also means to put to an open shame.

We also read in the same verse that he "was minded to put her away privily" (Greek *eboulethe lathra apolusai aute*). The Greek word *eboulethe* is translated in the King James Version as the word "minded" and "want to" in the NIV. It is derived from the Greek word *boulomai* (pronounced **boo'-lom-ahee**) which denotes a reflective disposition. It is comparable to the word used in the first part of the verse translated "willing," i.e., "not willing to expose her to public shame." Here again we see Joseph not only as a naively innocent man, but as a deeply religious man whose profound reflection on Divine things led him to act in ways that set him apart from his generation.

20 But while he thought on these things, behold, the angel of the Lord appeared unto him in a dream, saying, Joseph, thou son of David, fear not to take unto thee Mary thy wife: for that which is conceived in her is of the Holy Ghost.

The line of thought we have followed from verse 19 that reflects the character of Joseph is further confirmed in verse 20 as we encounter the Greek word *enthumeomai* (pronounced **en-thoo-meh'-om-ahee**) in the phrase "while he thought." This word is a combination of the Greek terms *en* and *thumos* which together mean to be inspired or to ponder by spiritual animation. So here we see how deeply Joseph's thoughts went. Here was a man whose sense of justice did not blind his ability to think. His contemplation paid off, for in the next phrase we read, "Behold, the angel of the Lord appeared unto him in dream." This phrase reflects Matthew's Hebraism of the Old Testament. We find a divine messenger bringing tidings to many of God's people in times of confusion. In Joseph's confusion, he went into contemplation and in the middle of his contemplation a heavenly messenger was sent. This messenger is meant to lead him into the proper way to act. God send this messenger to bring clarity and to drive away the confusion. We are told that the angel of the Lord appeared. The use of the Greek word *phaino* (pronounced **fah'ee-no**) shows that in the midst of his confusion came a light to show him the way—to effect a transition literally and figuratively from ignorance and confusion to wisdom and understanding. The appearance of the angel is revelation.

Next we read, "Joseph son of David . . ." the first revelation was to remind Joseph of who he really is. The connection between him and David reminded him immediately of the promise given to his ancestor David regarding the coming Messiah. We read further, "fear not to take unto thee Mary thy wife . . . ." The angel then addresses the issue at hand. The angel speaks to the psychological situation of fear that was keeping Joseph from doing what he knew was right. In addressing the present situation, the angel did not avoid the fact that Mary was pregnant, but assured Joseph that the child was of Divinity.

21 And she shall bring forth a son, and thou shalt call his name JESUS: for he shall save his people from their sins.

In this verse, the angel announces to Joseph that the child is to be named Jesus. After having an angel put his

life in historical perspective and explain what was going on in the present, Joseph was probably left with the question: What is the purpose of all this? First, the angel dealt with the immediate future: the child will be a son. Second, the child shall be named Jesus, (Hebrew "Yeshua" or "Joshua") which probably reminded Joseph of the great warrior conqueror who, by the power of God, delivered the Children of Israel from their enemies. Finally, the angel connects the name of the child with the future act of the child, "He shall *save* his people from their sins."

Note that salvation is an intrinsic part of the history of Israel. The use of the word "save" (Greek *sozo*, pronounced **sode'-zo**) from the root word *sos* which addresses the salvific view of the people of Israel. In fact, living in the midst of oppression, Joseph would have understood this term in relation to deliverance and protection. This term "save" also implies healing and preservation. In this period of "Israel's pain" this term also spoke to their need for well-being and wholeness.

22 Now all this was done, that it might be fulfilled which was spoken of the Lord by the prophet, saying,

Here again we see Matthew's deep entrenchment in the prophetic tradition of Israel as he points us back to the Old Testament. He tell us that everything that is happening here has been prophesied by the prophet. Isaiah prophesied, in a message to King Ahaz, about a virgin birth and a child who would save the people of God (Isaiah 7:10-16). A key term here is "fulfillment," Greek *pleroo* (pronounced **play-ro'-o**) which means to make replete, to make level a hollow or a valley. Thus, this experience furnishes Joseph with an explanation of the text in the Old Testament. In a sense, God inspired the word of the prophet with meaning for the reader. It also means that what has been promised is now being executed. Such fulfillment served to affirm the prophet for the generation.

23 Behold, a virgin shall be with child, and shall bring forth a son, and they shall call his name Emmanuel, which being interpreted is, God with us.

Matthew affirms that Jesus is the One who the prophet Isaiah spoke about in Isaiah 7:14. Jesus is Emmanuel, meaning God is with us—the promised deliverer. Here again we are told that his mother was a virgin. The word for "virgin" that is used here is the

Greek word *parthenos,* (**par-then'-os**) which as far as can be determined by scholars means a maiden, and by usage implies an unmarried daughter. In biblical times, females married at a very early age and the bride was expected to be virgin. Any interpretation must take into consideration that she did not know a man sexually. In fact, the Hebrew word `almah* (**al-maw'**) is the feminine form for a young person. Here it denotes the one who is still governed by parental authority, or one who is veiled. It also means a "damsel" or "virgin." It must be remembered that the law regarding virginity was strictly enforced in Israel, and breaking it resulted in death.

As a result, all interpretations of this passage must include the absence of sexual relationship. What was at stake here was not the fact that she was a virgin, but the fact that she was found with child. The context in which this prophecy occurs in Isaiah shows the Lord challenging the people and calling them to see God do a new thing. Verse 23 continues with "and they shall call his name Emmanuel." Here the name itself explains the nature of the child who is to be born. Emmanuel is a combination of *im,* which means "with" or "equal with," and *el,* which is short for *Elohim.* This term is often used to mean something that accompanies or something before or beside another. Here it can mean that He, Emmanuel, is the reason for which Elohim, the Creator of the universe, has come among us.

24 Then Joseph being raised from sleep did as the angel of the Lord had bidden him, and took unto him his wife:

"Being raised from sleep" has deep spiritual significance. Remember, Joseph was dreaming until this verse. Here we read "being raised" which implies that someone raised Joseph. The word translated "raise" is the Greek word *diegeiro,* (**dee-eg-I'-ro**) and is also a combination of two Greek words, *dia* and *egeiro,* meaning to be fully awake. It can also mean arise, awake, or stir up oneself.

We then read that Joseph "did as the angel of the Lord had bidden him." The word for "did" is the Greek word *eepoiesan,* taken from *poieo,* (pronounced **poy-eh'-o**) meaning "to make or do." It means to make application of ideas directly into life. It can also mean that Joseph agreed to the solution that the angel had proposed. It also implies that Joseph committed himself to continue to exercise himself fully in the Word of God revealed to him. What God had ordained was now going to be his

purpose. His reason for rising up was to not transgress the law, but to live out the revelation.

25 And knew her not till she had brought forth her firstborn son: and he called his name JESUS.

The phrase "knew her not" in the Greek reads *ouk eginosken autee* and suggests the absolute absence of knowledge. One possible meaning is that one is unaware of, or lacks, certain expressive feelings. In other words, one is resolved not to understand. In this case, the phrase means that Joseph had absolutely no sexual relation with her. The next word "till" suggests that Joseph continued in a state of abstinence until, or for as long as, Mary was pregnant. Actually he remained abstinent until she gave birth. The Greek word *eteken* taken from the word *tikto* (pronounced **tik'-to**) means to produce something from seed or to bring forth as a mother.

What did Mary bring forth? The Greek uses the word *prototokos* (pronounced **pro-tot-ok'-os**) to describe this event. It comes from the word *protos* and another form of the word *tikto* or firstborn, first-begotten. Note that this word is different from the word *monogenes* used to describe the relation between God the Father and the Son in John 3:16. Joseph names the child Jesus as the angel instructs him to. According to Matthew, Joseph is to name Jesus, which incorporated him into the Davidic line.

DAILY BIBLE READING

M: The Genealogy of Jesus the Messiah
Matthew 1:1-11

T: Jesus' Genealogy Completed
Matthew 1:12-17

W: The Birth of Jesus the Messiah
Matthew 1:18-25

T: Jesus Christ, God's Eternal Word
John 1:1-14

F: The Angel Gabriel Visits Mary
Luke 1:26-38

S: Mary Visits Her Cousin Elizabeth
Luke 1:39-45

S: Mary's Song of Praise
Luke 1:46-56

TEACHING TIPS

December 26
Bible Study Guide 4

1. Words You Should Know

A. Wise Men. (Matthew 2:1) Greek *magi*—royal astrologers; they were learned men who were experts in the science of their day and in interpretations of dreams.

B. Worship. (v. 2) Greek *proskyneo*—involves prostrating oneself before our Lord and Saviour, rendering thanksgiving and praises to God for being God. This does not include prayers of petition for our needs.

2. Teacher Preparation

A. Study the Devotional Reading (Psalm 98). Then read the Background Scripture (Matthew chapter 2).

B. Carefully re-read the FOCAL VERSES to get a feel for the actual setting of these Scriptures and to understand the political climate in which Jesus was born and the hate and fear King Herod had for the new King of the Jews.

C. Read Bible Study Guide 4, and answer the SEARCH THE SCRIPTURES and DISCUSS THE MEANING questions.

D. Materials needed: Bible, chalk board, and chalk.

3. Starting the Lesson

A. Before the students arrive, write the title of the lesson and the AT-A-GLANCE outline on the board. Now, write the words, "Magi," or "wise men," and "worship" on the board.

B. Begin the class session with prayer. Take prayer requests and ask God to bless the class time so that the aims of the lesson will be met.

C. Engage the class in a discussion of the terms "Magi," and "worship." Especially concentrate on the word, "worship" as many students do not understand what it means to truly worship the Lord. Stress that when we come to church, we should come in an attitude of worship.

D. Read the IN FOCUS story.

4. Getting into the Lesson

A. To help the students gain a better understanding of the context, ask for volunteers to read the BACKGROUND section and THE PEOPLE, PLACES, AND TIMES article.

B. As the students are reading, engage the class in discussion and analysis along the way for better understanding.

C. Review the SEARCH THE SCRIPTURES questions.

5. Relating the Lesson to Life

A. Direct the students' attention to the LESSON IN OUR SOCIETY article to help them understand how the lesson applies to their life. Allow time for discussion and debate.

B. Review the DISCUSS THE MEANING questions. Allow time for discussion and debate as well.

6. Arousing Action

A. Review the MAKE IT HAPPEN suggestion and challenge the students to put it into practice during the week.

B. Challenge the students to do the DAILY BIBLE READING to increase their understanding of the related lessons.

C. End the session with prayer.

WORSHIP GUIDE

For the Superintendent or Teacher
Theme: Coming of the Wise Men
Theme Song: "We Three Kings of Orient Are"
Scripture: Matthew 2:1-12
Song: "Heark! The Herald Angels Sing"
Prayer: As the wise men sought You Lord, help us always to seek You with all our heart. And when we find You, let us make You Lord and Saviour of our life daily.

COMING OF THE WISE MEN

Bible Background • MATTHEW 2
Printed Text • MATTHEW 2:1-12
Devotional Reading • PSALM 98

LESSON AIM

By the end of the lesson, students will recognize that if we want Jesus in our life, we must search for Him with all our heart as the wise men did when following the star. When we "find" Jesus, we must accept Him as Lord and Saviour and worship Him as so.

KEEP IN MIND

"Saying, Where is he that is born King of the Jews? for we have seen his star in the east, and are come to worship him" (Matthew 2:2).

FOCAL VERSES

MATTHEW 2:1 Now when Jesus was born in Bethlehem of Judaea in the days of Herod the king, behold, there came wise men from the east to Jerusalem,

2 Saying, Where is he that is born King of the Jews? for we have seen his star in the east, and are come to worship him.

3 When Herod the king had heard these things, he was troubled, and all Jerusalem with him.

4 And when he had gathered all the chief priests and scribes of the people together, he demanded of them where Christ should be born.

5 And they said unto him, In Bethlehem of Judaea: for thus it is written by the prophet,

6 And thou Bethlehem, in the land of Juda, art not the least among the princes of Judah: for out of thee shall come a Governor, that shall rule my people Israel.

7 Then Herod, when he had privily called the wise men, enquired of them diligently what time the star appeared.

8 And he sent them to Bethlehem, and said, Go and search diligently for the young child; and when ye have found him, bring me word again, that I may come and

LESSON OVERVIEW

LESSON AIM
KEEP IN MIND
FOCAL VERSES
IN FOCUS
THE PEOPLE, PLACES, AND TIMES
BACKGROUND
AT-A-GLANCE
IN DEPTH
SEARCH THE SCRIPTURES
DISCUSS THE MEANING
LESSON IN OUR SOCIETY
MAKE IT HAPPEN
FOLLOW THE SPIRIT
REMEMBER YOUR THOUGHTS
MORE LIGHT ON THE TEXT
DAILY BIBLE READINGS

worship him also.

9 When they had heard the king, they departed; and, lo, the star, which they saw in the east, went before them, till it came and stood over where the young child was.

10 When they saw the star, they rejoiced with exceeding great joy.

11 And when they were come into the house, they saw the young child with Mary his mother, and fell down, and worshipped him: and when they had opened their treasures, they presented unto him gifts; gold, and frankincense, and myrrh.

12 And being warned of God in a dream that they should not return to Herod, they departed into their own country another way.

IN FOCUS

Mark and Tom were best friends and were saved around the same time. Both had prestigious jobs in very large corporations. Yet, Mark noticed that Tom was growing by leaps and bounds as a Christian. He seemed to be leaving Mark very far behind in his Christian walk.

Mark noticed that Tom knew Scriptures, and seemed to be less stressed than he. Even though both of their daily schedules placed them dead center on the "fast track," Tom seemed to rise above the pressures. Mark had to know how and why Tom's Christian experience was so much different from his own.

One Sunday after church, Tom and Mark engaged in a long chat. Tom shared with Mark some eye-opening, as well as heart-opening, lessons. "I seek God the first thing in the mornings," he declared. "I know that I need Him to order my day. Therefore, God takes a lot of stress out of my job and life."

Mark had often heard the preacher speak on seeking

God the first thing in the morning, but he had not personally tried it himself. The very next morning, Mark did just that. He got up an hour earlier and had a private devotion before his day started. At the end of the day, he was not as tired or stressed.

Tom also shared with Mark how he (Tom) listened to Christian music and teaching tapes on the way to and from work. Mark tried these things as well, and found that when He sought God's will with all his heart, God came to him and brought much needed order.

THE PEOPLE, PLACES, AND TIMES

THE WISE MEN. These men were not commoners. They were from the elite class in society and known as astrologers as they studied the stars. Some theologians believe that they could have been from different lands representing the entire world coming to bow to or honor Jesus as King of kings; while others believe that they came from Babylon or near there. Either way, they were King Herod's link to the whereabouts of the Baby Jesus. Their sole purpose in coming to find Him was to worship—not to ask Him or His people for anything. They brought gifts that were very valuable to them signifying that Jesus was indeed the King of The Jews and deserves our very best.

KING HEROD. A mere man who thought that he could destroy the God-man, Jesus Christ. He was powerful by man's standards, but was no match for the Almighty God. He was ruthless, cunning, a liar, and a murderer. When he could not find out where the Baby Jesus was, he had all the male babies killed in his land. Herod was crowned, "King of the Jews," by the Roman captors, but was not accepted by the Jews because He was not of the Davidic line and was not a full Jew.

BACKGROUND

The Jews had been waiting on the promised king for centuries. They waited in great anticipation, confident in the knowledge that the who was coming would establish his kingdom here on earth and bring justice once and for all. They knew that he would deliver them from bondage and from their enemies. (Now it was the Romans who were their oppressors).

Old Testament prophets predicted that he would come; he would come to save his people. Yet the Israelites, God's chosen people, did not truly understand who this Messiah, this "Anointed One," was. He was Jesus, the one and only Son of the Living God, who came to save them from their sins by establishing His kingdom in their heart. His kingdom was not earthly at all.

Herod the Great was king over the four political districts and several lesser territories of Israel: Judea, Samaria, Galilee, and Idumea. The Messiah's birthplace had been prophesied as Bethlehem of Judea, which came under King Herod's rule. Therefore, he was quite disturbed over the arrival of this new King of the Jews. As he was not the rightful heir to the throne of David, the Jews did not readily accept him as their king anyway. Herod was not the one promised and talked about by Old Testament prophets. Therefore, while the Jews were excited and filled with anticipation, Herod's heart was filled with trepidation. He feared that Jesus could swing the balance of power away from Rome and away from him. His heart, then, was fixed on getting rid of Jesus. Herod knew that he was powerful, but he did not know that *Jesus was all powerful!*

AT-A-GLANCE

1. **The Wise Men Look for the Baby Jesus (Matthew 2:1-2)**
2. **King Herod Sought the Baby Jesus (vv. 3-8)**
3. **The Wise Men Find the Baby Jesus (vv. 9-11)**
4. **The Wise Men Obeyed God Rather than Man (v. 12)**

IN DEPTH

1. The Wise Men Look for the Baby Jesus (Matthew 2:1-2)

The wise men or Magi, in today's lesson were from the learned class and were advisors of kings. They were known for their study of the stars or occult learning, and had seen the star pointing the way to the birthplace of the new King of the Jews. In today's vernacular, they would be called astrologers.

In Christmas celebrations today, Christians celebrate the arrival of three wise men to see the Christ Child. However, it is not known how many there actually were. Theologians believe that they traveled in an entourage of hundreds because desert robbers made traveling alone very dangerous. Because of their high standing, they had access to Herod, the king. Theologians believed that they knew the Old Testament's predictions of a coming Messiah, and were probably studying the stars for some sign of His coming.

It is believed that these Magi saw the star leading to the

Baby Jesus at a time when Jesus was between 40 days and 2 years old (Matthew 2:16; Luke 2:22, 39). They, then, traveled thousands of miles to find this Baby. The journey took them many months, but they were determined. They searched for Him with all their heart, and they found Him.

The star they saw (v. 2) is believed to have been a supernatural light given by God to show the wise men the way to the Perfect Light—Jesus Christ, who was to light up a dark world stained with sin. You see, all this was in God's plan. It is obvious from Scripture, that God had these men to seek out Jesus. He was using them for His greater plan of supplying Mary and Joseph with funds to get them away from Herod who wanted to kill Jesus. God has a way of meeting His children's needs, even if He has to send someone traveling from thousands of miles, into another country, to do so.

2. King Herod Sought the Baby Jesus (vv. 3-8)

King Herod, an Idumean from the Edomite line of kings, became ruler over Judea shortly before Christ was born. History tells of his brutality, even the murder of his wife and two sons. He is said to not only have been cruel and cunning, but cold-blooded as well. It was his son, Herod Antipas, who ruled for 33 years and killed John the Baptist. (Mark 6:14-29).

King Herod sought the Baby Jesus for completely different reasons than the wise men. Whereas these men wanted to worship Jesus, Herod found Him to be a threat. He already knew that many Jews hated him (Herod) for being a usurper of King David's throne when he was not the rightful heir. He knew that if Jesus was truly the rightful heir, then trouble was on the horizon. Therefore, not only was Herod worried about his position, but he was worried that Jesus would cause the balance of power to swing away from Rome. He could not, therefore, sit idly by and let Jesus take over the throne. His ruthlessness would not allow it. His fear would not tolerate it.

Herod sent a private message to the wise men (vv. 8-9). The operative word is "private." He was lying and scheming again. He wanted the wise men to come and see him to elicit their help in his murderous plot. His words seemed innocent when he told them in verse 9 to go to Bethlehem and search for Jesus, and then come back and tell him so that he could worship Him too. He knew that he had no intention of worshiping Jesus. He had every intention of doing Him harm.

The religious leaders and priests of that day also knew the Scriptures and viewed Jesus as a threat. They knew of the prophecy Micah 5:2 and that the Jews were expecting a Messiah to be their great political and military deliverer. As a result, their standing in the community as interpreters of God's Word, even though they often did not live it, was in jeopardy. They believed in teaching and emphasizing the letter of the law without showing mercy. Jesus was coming on the scene to teach and show them a better way.

Even though the religious leaders were present when Jesus taught, they still did not accept Jesus as the Messiah. They often looked for ways to entrap Him or snare Him. Therefore, these men became Jesus' greatest enemy.

3. The Wise Men Find the Baby Jesus (vv. 9-11)

By the supernatural light of that star, the wise men found the Perfect Light, Jesus. It is believed that Jesus was probably one or two years old then. Mary and Joseph were married and living in a house in Bethlehem (Luke 2:39). The Magi brought their expensive gifts giving them to the King of kings, Lord of lords, Jesus Christ the Saviour of the world. The gold was symbolic of a gift fit for a king. frankincense or incense was a gift for a God or Deity, and the myrrh was a spice used to anoint a body before it was buried. They worshiped Jesus for who He was and not for what they could get from Him. They gave Him gifts that were valuable to them, as we should in our worship. We should all do as the wise men: find Jesus, accept Him as Lord and Saviour, and worship Him!

4. The Wise Men Obey God Rather than Man (v. 12)

These Magi were not listening to what King Herod told them to do. A higher authority spoke to them through a dream and told them not to return to Herod. Satan's evil attempt to murder Jesus was rendered unsuccessful. Even though Jesus would later die, be crucified, and rise again, God was not ready for this to happen. Jesus still had mission work to do first. God's plan of salvation would unfold in His own timing. No man can rush God. Therefore, these wise men went home another way. God warned them, and they obeyed His warning.

SEARCH THE SCRIPTURES

1. From what direction did the wise men come as they followed the star? (Matthew 2:1)

2. According to the chief priests and teachers of the law, in what city was Jesus to be born? (v. 5)

3. What did King Herod say he wanted to do to the Christ Child? (v. 8)

4. What did the wise men do when they saw the Child with His mother? (v. 11)

5. How did God warn the wise men about Herod's true plan for the Baby Jesus? (v. 12)

DISCUSS THE MEANING

1. In what ways can we seek God daily?

2. Jesus made the ultimate sacrifice for us. What kinds of sacrifices can we offer to show that we love God?

3. Is it necessary to prepare ourselves before we offer worship God? If so, how?

LESSON IN OUR SOCIETY

Jesus Christ has already come, died for our sins, rose again, and is coming back again. Indeed, it is the time to worship Him. However, too often Christians worship Him only when we feel like it or when all seems well in our little world. **Not So!!!** The time to worship our Risen Saviour is when we feel like it and when we do not. In other words, our hearts should always be in an attitude of praise and worship because God is good to us all the time.

His blessings are too numerous to count. Even though we may not have all that we want, He supplies all of our needs. In fact, God loved us so much that He sent Jesus Christ, His one and only Son because He knew that we needed Him in order to reconcile with a Holy God. He sent Jesus for one reason only and that was to die for us. Surely, this is the greatest love of all!

We can, therefore, worship God because we may not be where we hope to be in Him yet, but thank God that we are not where we once were — hopelessly lost in sin. Thank God for His wonderful salvation!

MAKE IT HAPPEN

Spend time this day and park of each day this week worshiping God. Put aside our requests and petitions. Forget about asking God for anything. Table that for now. Just thank Our Creator for being God and for all He has done already in your life.

FOLLOW THE SPIRIT

What God wants me to do:

_____

_____

REMEMBER YOUR THOUGHTS

Special insights you have learned:

_____

_____

MORE LIGHT ON THE TEXT
MATTHEW 2:1-12

1 Now when Jesus was born in Bethlehem of Judaea in the days of Herod the king, behold, there came wise men from the east to Jerusalem,

Matthew attempts to set the stage in this introductory verse by giving Bethlehem as the place, and identifying the time as the days of Herod the King. The Greek word *de* translated "now" is used primarily to inform the reader of the continuing conversation about Jesus which began in chapter 1. In a sense, the writer seems to be preparing the reader for more surprises. The first chapter began with a statement of genealogy or what one version of the Bible terms "generations." Chapter 2 continues by explaining the events that followed.

The use of the word "generation" (Greek *genneshentos*, pronounced **gen- ne- ten-tos**), from the Greek *gennao* as it relates to being born, has more to do with the birthing process than it does with the whole procreation. As used here, it refers specifically to the process undergone by the mother. In another sense, it can mean regeneration. However, we know this is not about regeneration unless, of course, one takes the theological route of considering the eternal generation of the Son which took place in eternity.

The word "born" means to beget. This term refers to a human bringing forth, the delivering of the son into human hands; or, as one might say here, the gendering of the Divine. This specific act of gendering the Divine happened in a specific historical context, Bethlehem. The name Bethlehem is a combination of the Hebrew words *Beyith* meaning house and *lechem*, a personal name with uncertain derivation. It may mean "house of bread."

"In the days of Herod" refers to the time period when Herod and his sons were in rulership over a section of Judea (Matthew 2:1-23). Herod the Great was the ruler in power when the Baby Jesus was born. He was the one who felt threatened by Jesus' birth and tried to kill Jesus. He had four sons who also ruled: Herod Phillip I, father of Agrippa I and grandfather of King Agrippa; Herod Agrippa II, known as King Agrippa; Herod Phillip II, who beheaded John the Baptist; and Herod Antipas, who condemned Jesus to die. The entire Herod family including the so-called Herod the Great were wicked and murderous. Herod's tyranny is obvious in history (see Luke 13:31-32; 23:6-12; 23:15; Acts 4:27).

The Greek word *hemera* (pronounced **hay-mer'-ah**) used to describe the reign of Herod means "to sit" or "to tame." Indeed, Herod the Great was used by the Romans in an attempt to tame the desire for freedom by the people of Israel. Herod as the king of Judea made sure that the people had no time or space to free themselves from the yoke of bondage imposed by foreign powers. By all accounts, this period was marked by political subjugation, religious interference, and conflict within the territories of Israel. We are told that he was king *basileus* (pronounced **bas-il-yooce'**), meaning that he was the foundation of power or sovereign. However, given the fact that he was not divinely appointed to rule Israel, nor was he a descendant of David, he was always seen as a usurper. Herod the Great was a psychologically troubled man who murdered everyone with any sense around him, even his own son and his beloved wife. He was extremely suspicious and paranoid.

This state of mind throws light on Matthew's next statement "behold, there came wise men from the east." In the midst of Herod's folly, wise men came. There were still people looking for the good. There were still human beings who were wise enough to seek out the good, not to kill and destroy, but to acknowledge good and give thanks. While Herod was pretending to be King of Judea and ignoring the rule of the God of Israel, "behold there came . . . ." The word used to describe their approach is the Greek word *paraginomai* (pronounced **par-ag-in'-om-ahee**), meaning to appear publicly. It is a combination of two words, *para* and *ginomai*, meaning to become near or to approach. In Africa, wisdom was a secret art. Therefore, the use of the word *paraginomai* is significant because it shows a break from their secrecy. The event had to be spectacular for them to come out in this way. Such people shunned the limelight and were rarely seen. Who were these wise men? The wise men (Greek *magos*, pronounced **mag'-os**) were men of rank and quality and more than likely had wealth in abundance because of their practice in wisdom. In those days, it was believed that these masters of the secret arts of the world, could by their predictions, bless or curse someone.

We are told that the wise men came from the east. The word east in the Greek is *anatole* (pronounced **an-at-ol-ay'**) and is misleading when used by a Hebrew-speaking Israelite such as Matthew. In Greek *anatole* refers only to the rising of light or the dawn. However, within the Hebrew usage from which Matthew was probably working, it means an ancient place. It can also mean the beginning of something as in "the dawn of human race." It can also mean the place of rising. It is only by implication that it is translated east. The Greek word *anatello* (pronounced **an-at-el'-lo**) means to cause to arise where something springs. We now know that Africa is the place of the springing up

of human beings, and in fact the most ancient place if we take the Hebrew meaning of the word "east" seriously.

2 Saying, Where is he that is born King of the Jews? For we have seen his star in the east, and are come to worship him.

These wise men (i.e., *Magos*) were usually knowledgeable in astrological analysis. We now know that African people were familiar with the constellations and that with knowledge came the ability to interpret the effect of what was happening in the solar systems. The Dogon and Ibos people of West Africa exemplify such knowledge among African peoples. Of course, the ancient Egyptians knew the movement of heavenly bodies as well.

Upon finding this new King they would worship and pay homage to Him. The verse reads, "saying, where is he. . . ." They did not come in silence. This is significant given the vow of secrecy that was characteristic among members of ancient African wisdom cultures. The word "saying" (Greek *lego*, pronounced **leg'-o**) is primarily the act of putting or laying forth, or to relate one's findings in words. Again, another characteristic of these groups (wise men) was communication in cryptic forms.

Having understood the birth of the Messiah, they now resort to a systematic method of discourse that anyone could understand. Even at His birth the Lord began to crack the veil of knowledge. However, this points to the idea that they were saying something specific and expressed it in a unique way. These men of mystery were breaking their silence. What were they about to say? They asked a question that changed the thought of many in history and brought the people of God out of their sleep walking. No longer would the people of Israel and their pretend king be able to avoid the divine interrogative. For by asking this question these wise ones were forcing them to think of the promise of the everlasting God.

The use of the word "where" translated in Greek as *pou* indicates the rising of an inquiry with deep implications. The question that they raised, "Where is he that is born King of the Jews?" is more than just wanting to know the physical locality of Jesus, but carries a strength and form that leaves one with no alternative but to accept that something great has happened. What stands out is the confidence with which they asked question. There was certainty in their question which could produce faith in the willing, and fear in the ungodly. The One whom they seek has already been born. Literally this child has been brought forth, delivered to the world by God. As much as the wise men may have thought of themselves, they were coming to honor this King.

The term "King of the Jews" (Greek *basileus toun Ioudaiov*) indicates that although the One they seek is newly born, He indeed is the base of the existence of Judah. Implying that in Him the nation finds its foundation of power. He is the true sovereign ruler of the people who are currently under the rule of Herod.

"We have seen his star in the east." In the Greek, the phrase reads *eidomen gar autou ton astera*. One of the key words is the word "seen" used primarily to refer to the act of seeing in the past tense. Remember that these were wise men with insight into hidden matters. By implication, the use of the word "seen" means "to know." They have come to know something special. It means to become aware and to consider something intently. It also means that they have perceived something beyond the mere physical appearance of whatever it is they had seen.

Think about it, they were foreigners and yet they were the first to understand that the Messiah had come—they had seen "His star." The Greek word for star is *aster* (pronounced **as-tare'**). However, it could mean seeing more than just a single stationary star, probably a prolonged form or manifestation. In fact, it represents something that is strewn over the sky, possibly a comet. In addition it can also mean, the enlightenment which comes from positing an idea.

Not only did they see, they came to worship Him. Remember that these men were deeply learned and not many things gave them a sense of awe. Consequently, we find them having gained insight into what was happening and coming to worship. The word *erchomai*, or "come," suggests that they each entered wholly into the light of knowledge carried within the star that was strewn across the sky. These wise men came to worship. With all their learning and all their wealth, they still came to worship. The word "worship" is the Greek word *proskuneo* (pronounced **pros-koo-neh'-o**) and is formed from the words *pros* and *kuneo* meaning to kiss and prostrate oneself in homage. They came to do reverence and to adore this newborn King.

3 When Herod the king had heard these things, he was troubled, and all Jerusalem with him.

Given the reputation of these keepers of secrets, Herod, who perceived himself to be the foundation of power and sovereignty in Judah, heard this news and was troubled. The Greek word *akouo* (pronounced **ak-oo'-o**) translated "to hear" has many meanings. As used here, it suggests that Herod gave audience to someone who brought this news to

his ears. Herod was given to listening to rumors, and this news would have agitated him. The implication here is that the news of a king of Israeli descent had been born to replace the mean, destructive ruler from Idumea.

Another possible meaning for *akouo* is to hear with understanding. When Herod understood what was being said, as a result of this hearing or understanding of the rumors, he "was troubled." The word translated "was troubled" is from the Greek word *tarasso* (pronounced **tar-as'-so**) which means to stir or to agitate. Simply stated, Herod was angry. This man who had worked so hard to be accepted by the people of Israel now saw a threat to his usurped rulership.

The irony of how human beings react to news of divine intervention is captured in the phrase "and all Jerusalem with him." Herod's fear resulted from what the Romans might do if they realized someone else was being called King without their permission. Why would the whole of Jerusalem be troubled at the news of the Messiah's entrance? While they expected a Messiah, it seems that by taking on Herod's fear they really did not believe that Israel's Saviour would come as God had promised their ancestors.

Note also that the Scripture does not say all of Judah, but all of Jerusalem (Hebrew *Yeruwshalaim Hierosolyma* or *Jerushalaäm*) which in Scripture is denoted as the seat of the great king. This is Zion, the chosen of the Lord, under the demonic grip of an earthly tyrant. This is a city of peace gripped in fear, not because of an army, but because God has just arrived in the flesh. Herod represents the resistance of the world to the divine kingship represented by Jesus; and the tendency of the people of God to let the fear of the world become their fear in the midst of the divine revelation.

4 And when he had gathered all the chief priests and scribes of the people together, he demanded of them where Christ should be born.

In this verse, we see Herod's strategy for dealing with his troubled heart. First, he called the very people who were guardians of the promise—the chief priests. Note that they were not the high priests. The idea here is that he gathered them together as God would have gathered them. They convened, however, not in response to what God was doing, but to be entertained in Herod's company. This was not a divine assembly of dedicated servants gathered together. Historically, those who gathered to inform Herod were referred to as Herodians, and they did so for Herod to bestow some favor on them.

We are told that he gathered all the chief priests. The word "all" (Greek *pas*) is inclusive of every group of priests that served in the temple. Even if all the chief priests did not go to his house, enough of them went to affect the whole group. The Greek word used to describe these priests is the word *achiereus* (pronounced **ar-khee-er-yuce'**) from the word *arche* meaning "first" or "high" and the word *hiereus* meaning "priest." Thus, the term can be translated "high-priest." The plural here (i.e., priests) suggests that it may represent a different category of priest from the high priest, for there could only be one high priest at a time. This refers more to the order of the priests initiated by Moses when he divided the children of Aaron. Another possibility is that Herod deposed the presiding Israelite high priest and set up another that would serve him. The people of Israel would not recognize Herod's appointed high priest, thereby making it possible that Herod called both high priests to conference with him.

We also read here that Herod brought together the scribes. The Greek word used here for "scribes" is the word *grammateus* (pronounced **gram-mat-yooce'**) meaning person vastly learned in linguistic and grammatical processes. They were also interpretive writers of divine proclamations who recorded various occurrences in relation to the Word of God. Scripture says they were "the scribes of the people." The Greek word *laos* simply means people. Note that the word "together" from the Greek word *sunago* means to lead together, and is used twice in this verse to denote the seriousness of this gathering.

Fear will lead enemies to come together against the work of God. What was the purpose of this gathering? We are told it was to "enquire of them where the Christ should be born." However, the Greek translation reads "where the Christ is being born." The word translated "he enquired" is the Greek word *epunthaneto* (pronounced **epu-tha-ne-to**) from the root word *punthanomai* (say **poon-than'-om-ahee**) which is to question or to make sure by inquiry. It is used mainly in the context of asking for the purpose of obtaining information.

The use of this word *epunthaneto* points to a fundamental flaw in Herod's character in relation to his use of authority. In actuality, Herod should have demanded to know the location of the "Christ" because it was his right to do so as the so-called king of Israel. However, the implication here is that he made a diligent search for something that was hidden. We could also interpret this to mean he had an urgent need to know. The issue was to find out where Christ was to "be born." Interestingly, Matthew uses the passive continuous tense of the word *gennao* or "be born" and implies that the birth of deity would take a long time. But here it probably comes from his sense that this king was probably still in the womb.

5 And they said unto him, In Bethlehem of Judaea: for thus it is written by the prophet,

The primary focus of this verse is to prepare us for the interpretive response of the leaders of Israel to the demand by Herod. The Greek word *eipan* used here represents "to speak or say by word or by writing." The word *houtos* refers to what precedes or follows. In another words, it could mean that they gave him an answer. One could read the Greek this way, "they answered him in this way" or "after that (referring to Herod's demand) they answered him in this manner." It refers to a particular fashion in which the response was made.

Again, we find Matthew using his signature phrase "thus it is written." The Greek word here is *gegraptai* (say **ge-graf-tay**) from the root word *grapho* meaning "to engrave." They were speaking of the oracle engraved by the prophets of Israel. The meaning seems to be "this is how the prophet describes it." The Israelites looked always at what God spoke through the prophets as the basis of what was happening in the present. This passage states, "the prophet," there is no name attached to it. For them, it was not the identity of the prophet that was important because the prophet simply acted as a foreteller. What is important to remember here is that they saw the Scripture as being inspired. To them, these things were not mere poetic revelings, but divine insight into the future.

6 And thou Bethlehem, in the land of Judah, art not the least among the princes of Judah: for out of thee shall come a Governor, that shall rule my people Israel.

Verse 6 is a paraphrase of Micah 5:2. This prophecy gave the religious leaders and the people hope that the promises made to their ancestors, via the prophets, would be fulfilled. They had no problem stating that the Messiah would be born in Bethlehem. Yet, all their belief, knowledge, and hope did not keep them from joining Herod in his paranoia. Remember, Bethlehem (which means house of bread) was the birthplace of their beloved king of Israel, David, who was the monarchial ancestor of the Messiah. The promise is made specifically to include the Israelites who were a part of Judah.

The word *ge* (Greek for "land") means "a special parcel of soil" as well as "the earth." We read, "art not the least among the princes of Judah." This is an affirmative statement linking Bethlehem among the king-makers of Israel. Because of this prophecy

God looked beyond the stature of David and anointed him king, so it will be with the city of Christ's birth.

The passage states that something substantial—someone of importance was going to come out of this city, someone considered to be a nobody will emerge as a chief among leaders. The Greek word used in this passage for "prince" is *hege-omai* (pronounced **hayg-em-ohn'**), which means prince. In other words, God is saying out of this dry place where nothing has happened, literally a person of power, a prince, will come forth. The passage addresses this person's inner strength; He will have authority.

Though Bethlehem has been labeled as a place of low esteem, this One who comes will cause them to think right about themselves and about God. No longer shall they think they are the least. No longer shall they think they are the dreg, the outcast, or the door mat of the arrogant. They shall now know that they are not the least among the people, they are highly-esteemed in God's sight. Verse 6 also describes what the leader will do. The Greek word used here is *poimaino* (pronounced **poy-mah'ee-no**), which means "to tend as a shepherd and to feed the sheep." His work is directed to all people not just to the people of Bethlehem.

many of the leaders believed that the Messiah would not only be born in Bethlehem, but that He was going to make His ministerial appearance from there as well.

In this verse we see a correlation to the story of the anointing of David as king. The Greek word *elachistos* (pronounced **el-akh'-is-tos**) is translated "least." It is the superlative form of the word *elachus* which means "short." It also means least in terms of size or quantity or to be less dignified. Again, recall that in 1 Samuel 16, David, who was considered the "least" was elected king, and this event took place in Bethlehem. Even the prophet was misled by David's size. Remember also that Saul stood head and shoulders above all the Israelite warriors. Thus, the people of Israel came to look upon size as the criteria for being used by God. In fact, this may have been because surrounding the Israelites were the Philistines and Amelekites who where people of great height and stature. Here the prophet is emphatic, "thou Bethlehem art the least."

Implicit is the understanding that people may have considered Bethlehem to be of no consequence just as David's father considered him to be of no consequence. Yet, in God's eyes neither David or Bethlehem was by any means "the least." Economially, Bethlehem did not have the power to rival that of Jerusalem, Bethel, or even Samaria. Yet God was about to do something great with it. Just as

7 Then Herod, when he had privily called the wise men, enquired of them diligently what time the star appeared.

Having discovered that this king would be born among a people he thought were inferior, Herod called the wise men unto him "privily." The Greek word translated as "private" is *lathra* (pronounced **lath'-rah**), meaning "secretly." Herod was probably relying on the fact that these wise men usually belonged to secret societies and that they would more than likely give him a straightforward answer if he asked them in secret.

We read further that he inquired of them when the child was to be born. The word "diligently" is translated from the Greek word *akriboo* (pronounced **ak-ree-bo'-o**) meaning that he wanted the wise men to provide the exact or specific time of the star's appearance. Note also that the word used here for "time" is the Greek word *chronos*, which refers to a sense of space and of time. This is distinguished from *kairos* which is interpreted as a divine moment of action. Herod was attempting to designate a fixed time which would allow him to control the events that have occurred. By so doing, he could possibly affect the events that took place between the birth of the Child and the fulfillment of the prophesies. The word *chronos* can also mean delay, which means that Herod was seeking to see how much time had passed since the event took place.

8 And he sent them to Bethlehem, and said, Go and search diligently for the young child; and when ye have found him, bring me word again, that I may come and worship him also.

In this verse, we see Herod's pretension. He is now going to use these men of wisdom to do his dirty work. He let them depart for the purpose of accomplishing an objective that is different from one he states. The use of the word "go" here denotes that he sent them away properly and orderly. He gave them his blessing saying, "go" (Greek *poreuomai*, pronounced **por-yoo'-om-ahee**), traverse the land; take a journey; find out where the child is; to remove all doubt of his birth.

Also used here is the word "search" (Greek *exetazo*, pronounced **ex-et-ad'-zo**) meaning "to examine and test thoroughly by deep questions until one has ascertained the facts." Note also that Herod wanted to get the child before he could be of any threat to him. Look how many times the Greek word *akribos* (diligent) appears in this passage. This clarifies the determination of those who seek to undermine the work of God as opposed to those who seek God's glory.

Another interesting word used here is "find." It is translated in the Greek as *heurisko* (pronounced **hyoo-ris'-ko**) meaning to find and to obtain what one is searching for. Not only did Herod tell them to search and to obtain the information, he told them "bring (Greek *apaggello*, pronounced **ap-ang-el'-lo**) me word again." He wanted to make certain they brought him the announcement. It is important to know that if these people were among the ancient wise men, it would go against their training to make a public announcement of their knowledge to someone who is not one of their own. Just by stating, "That I may come and worship him" does not qualify Herod to share in their knowledge of the child's whereabouts. The way the statement is phrased suggests that Herod probably intended to supply them with something they otherwise did not have.

To "come back" to Herod has a variety of connotations. Here, it suggests that they recognized the kingship of Herod as opposed to the King who had been divinely revealed to them. Herod explained that he intended to go and "worship the child." The Greek word for "worship" is *proskuneo* (pronounced **pros-koo-neh'-o**) which means to "kiss." The kiss is normally used in connection with friendship. Literally, it means to prostrate oneself in homage; to reverence or adore. Herod assumed that these wise men would worship the child and included himself among the worshipers by using the word "also" (Greek *kago*.).

9 When they had heard the king, they departed; and, lo, the star, which they saw in the east, went before them, till it came and stood over where the young child was.

The phrase "they heard," translated *akouo*, means that the wise men gave an audience and let Herod's pretense enter their ears. Given the meaning of the word, we could also say that what Herod said was a noise. This phrase implies that they understood what Herod meant, not merely what they heard.

The wise men did follow a number of the king's suggestions. They did indeed traverse the land. They removed themselves from Herod's presence. They did not stop their journey, they kept on walking in the light of the star. Note that as they started walking they again saw or "lo" (Greek *idou*); actually the word is an exclamation. While they were in Herod's company the light and the knowledge of the location of the star was hidden. But once they left Herod's presence they were able to turn their attention to the light—the light that rose within their mind. They were led by the light, not by their wisdom.

An important word here is the Greek word *proago* (pronounced **pro-ag'-o**) which is translated as "go before." The star is now seen as a princely messenger leading an audience into the presence of a powerful king. They were preceded by this divine messenger which announced to them the place where God, in meekness, now lays. The use of the word "till" (Greek *heos*) suggests the continuance of divine guidance.

Similarly, the light of God's Word will lead us until we come to the time and place where God intends for us to be. The light of God's presence will wait to take us as far as we need to go. We may tarry long in the night of Herod's house, but the light of the Lord keeps shining and will lead us out when we decide to undertake our journey.

God's light accompanied them along their journey and helped them to enter into the presence of the Son. This light kept them from falling away like leaves before their time. This passage could also represent the growth that occurs when we follow the light. We read that the star came and stood in the place where the Child lay. The Greek word *histemi* (pronounced **his'-tay-mee**) refers to the ability "to stand." Used here it can be interpreted that the light came to the place where Jesus lay and stopped. But think of this: the light came to where Jesus lay and could move no further for it had found its home. The Lord, from whom it derived its very essence, was here. We are told that "it came and stood over where the young child was." It is interesting that the Greek word for "above" or "over" is *epano*, and it can also be used to denote a place of rank.

10 When they saw the star, they rejoiced with exceeding great joy.

Here we read of the response of these wise men. As you recall, when they were talking with Herod, the star was hidden from their sight. In verse 10, we read that "they saw the star." The word here denotes a sense of certainty as it relates to an act of the past. This sight affirmed the experience they had back in their home town. Their knowledge was now being confirmed by seeing the star. We are told that they "rejoiced with exceeding great joy." The Greek reads, *hecharesan charan megalen sphodra*. The word "rejoice" comes from the Greek word *chairo* (pronounced **khah'ee-ro**) which means "to be cheerful or well-off."

Another key word here is the Greek word *sphodra* (pronounced **sfod'-rah**) translated in the King James Version as "exceeding." As used here, it really means violently or vehemently. They probably burst into ecstatic dancing. Not only does Matthew use the word *sphodra*, he adds another Greek word, *megas* which literally means big. Translated, they were high in the spirit or they became loud in a mighty way.

11 And when they were come into the house, they saw the young child with Mary his mother, and fell down, and worshiped him: and when they had opened their treasures, they presented unto him gifts; gold, and frankincense, and myrrh.

The Magi (wise men) came from the east. They followed the star as quoted in Micah 5:1-2 and 2 Samuel 5:2. The star guided them to the exact location in Bethlehem. They brought three gifts: gold, for Jesus as king; frankincense, for Jesus the divine (also used in worship); and myrrh, for Jesus the crucified Saviour (also used in embalming). In verse 11, we read of another "coming," the word "coming" here simply means that they arrived at their primary destination. For them this was personal. They had been through so many tense moments and now had come to the place for which they sighed.

They entered the house (Greek *oikia*, pronounced **oy-kee'-ah**), which means residence. Note that the wise men are not at the stable; they are in the abode of the family. The Greek word *heurisko* (pronounced **hyoo-ris'-ko**) is used here to indicate that they found what they were looking for. No wonder they were so ecstatic; these people were like the man Jesus described later in His ministry who found a field of great treasure and sold all that he had to obtain it. They had made sacrifices. They had left home, father, mother, friends, relatives, and their comfort in search of the Saviour. This event is a pre-attestation to Jesus' statement in Matthew 7:7, "seek and you and shall find."

They found the Child with Mary, which in the Hebrew is the same as Mariam, and more likely a name of Egyptian origin like Moses. From its pronunciation, (**Miryam**) it could probably have been taken for the Hebrew word *Mahir* or *Mahir* which means diligent. And *ya (m)* which refers to "God." The name comes to mean "my/our God is diligent." We also read, "and falling" (Greek *kai pesontes*) which could mean "to alight or to kneel." The next word, "worshiped" is the Greek word *proskuneo* translated "worship" and meaning "to kiss" or "to prostrate oneself in homage." This tells us the type of falling down expressed by the wise men. In the phrase "when they had opened their treasure," the keyword here is "open" which comes from the Greek *anoigo* (pronounced **an-oy'-go**).

Note that while they now physically opened their treasures, they would not have been opening up these treasures if they had not first opened their hearts to God's revelation. Note also that the Greek word for "treasure" is *thesauros* (pronounced **thay-sow-ros'**) from which we get our word "thesaurus." These wise ones had saved their treasures so they would able to give. In fact, the word could also mean a deposit of wealth. We are told that they offered gifts to Him. It is interesting that the word for "gifts" is *doron* (pronounced **do'-ron**) which refers to "a present," but specifically in the sense of making a sacrifice.

Much has been made of the symbolism of the gifts. Here let us look at the fact that the Greek word *chrusos* (pronounced **khroo-sos'**) translated "gold," speaks to the use which leaders made of precious metal. It was a sign of wealth and represented the king's or queen's ability to provide for his/her subjects. It was also used for religious ornamentation. But here the word can also mean coin. The word for "frankincense" (Greek *libanos*, pronounced **lib'-an-os**) is taken from the Hebrew *lebownah*, which refers to the incense tree. It is also used to refer to incense itself. Myrrh (Greek *smurna*, pronounced **smoor'-nah**) was an ointment used for burial in many African traditions. Again this word is probably one of the leftover Egyptian words which forms the Hebrew *mor*, adopted into the Greek language. Myrrh is perfumed oil or scented oil that is still used in many parts of Africa and Asia.

12 And being warned of God in a dream that they should not return to Herod, they departed into their own country another way.

This verse deals with intervention of the Lord into their lives to save them from serving as instruments for carrying out Herod's work. We are told that the Lord appeared and spoke to them in a dream (Greek *chrematizo*, pronounced **khray-mat-id'-zo**) which means that there was an utterance such as done in oracles. There was a divine intimation that gave them firmness to deal with the business. In a sense, it means after they had seen the Lord they could not bear to think of Herod and his request. Here the word means that they were called or admonished, or as the King James Version of the Bible puts it "warned." God revealed something to them. For the first time in all of these conversations and in their long journeying, God speaks to the wise ones. How did God speak to them? Through a dream. The Greek word for God's communication to them is *onar* (pronounced **on'-ar**); in the Old Testament, the Hebrew word for this phenomenon is *chalom* or *chelem*. It is interesting that the word which is translated "return" in the KJV and "not go back" in the NIV is the Greek word *automatos* (pronounced **ow-tom'-at-os**) which means to be self-moved. God was saying in this passage, do not automatically return to Herod because he is the king. Going back to Herod would have been appropriate according to human thought, it would have been in accord with their perception of themselves as men of honor. But God gave them a strict injunction that went against what they themselves may have wanted. It is important to know that since Herod was king, he may rewarded them immensely for their work.

God's instruction is in direct opposition to Herod's request and to their own feeling. "They departed," we read. The Greek word for "departed" *anachoreo* (pronounced **an-akh-o-reh'-o**) means that they turned aside from the way of Herod. They withdrew themselves from their commitment to Herod. Rather than go through the city to the palace, they probably went home through the woods. The Greek word *chora* (pronounced **kho'-rah**) suggests the idea of an empty expanse. They went back to the coast or to

their fields. The final phrase of this text is "another way." They did something different. The Greek word for "another," *allos* (pronounced **al'-los**), suggests that they forsook their primary way and took a different way.

Not only did they physically take another way, they began to think differently about the standard of the world which looked at royalty and the rich as being basically good and the poor basically bad. My, how God tends to shatter our stereotypical paradigms. God is not bound by one way of doing things, particularly when that way is grounded in human foolishness. The sentence ends with the word "way" (Greek *hodos*, pronounced **hod-os'**) suggests that God removed what they thought was their primary way to give them a new road.

By doing this, God gave them divine progress. They thought they knew the way; or they may have thought that the only way back was through Herod's house. But God shows them that there is always another way to get out of a deal with the devil. It also suggests that their mode of being in the world was in one swoop transformed by God. God gives another means for the journey. The way of Herod leads to the lower valleys of death. Here God opens their eyes and showed them the Divine highway leading to the will of God.

DAILY BIBLE READING

M: The Birth of Jesus
Luke 2:1-7
T: Jesus' Birth Announced to Shepherds
Luke 2:8-20
W: Jesus is Presented in the Temple
Luke 2:21-27
T: Simeon and Anna Praise God
Luke 2:28-38
F: Wise Men Inquire About Jesus' Birth
Matthew 2:1-6
S: Wise Men Visit and Honor Jesus
Matthew 2:7-12
S: Herod's Wrath Is Unleashed
Matthew 2:13-18

TEACHING TIPS

January 2
Bible Study Guide 5

1. Words You Should Know

A. Akolouthos. Greek for follow in the same way or likewise.

B. Halieus. Greek for fisherman.

C. Mathetes. Greek for disciple; a learner; a follower (of Jesus) or imitator of one's teaching.

D. Apostellein. Greek for one who shares the authority of the one who sends them; a representative.

2. Teacher Preparation

A. Begin preparing for this lesson by studying the Devotional Reading. Then read the Bible Background.

B. Now go back and carefully read the FOCAL VERSES for Lesson 5.

3. Starting the Lesson

A. Have students read the BACKGROUND.

B. Write the AT-A-GLANCE outline on the board. Introduce the terms in Words You Should Know and talk about how they relate to the lesson.

C. Have the class read IN DEPTH.

D. Explain each section allowing time for questions.

4. Getting into the Lesson

A. Have an individual read IN FOCUS and ask them if they or anyone they know have had a similar experience.

B. Read THE PEOPLE, PLACES, AND TIMES and discuss the person of Matthew his conversion, the things he wrote about Jesus, and his fellow disciples.

5. Relating the Lesson to Life

A. To help the students understand and apply the eternal truths of today's lesson, review the DISCUSS THE MEANING and LESSON IN OUR SOCIETY questions.

B. Ask the students to share any special insights they received from today's lesson.

6. Arousing Action

A. Remind students to read DAILY BIBLE READINGS and SEARCH THE SCRIPTURES during the week.

B. Discuss ways to MAKE IT HAPPEN during the week. Ask the students to report back on their progress next week.

C. End the session with prayer.

WORSHIP GUIDE

**For the Superintendent or Teacher
Theme: The Twelve Disciples
Theme Song: "I Want to Be a
Follower of Christ"
Scripture: Matthew 4:18-22; 9:9-12;
10:1-4
Song: "Jesus, The Name Above All
Names"
Meditation: Heavenly Father, thank
You for calling us to follow You and
for making us fishers of men.**

THE TWELVE DISCIPLES

Bible Background • MATTHEW 4:18-22; 9:9-12; 10:1-4
Printed Text • MATTHEW 4:18-22; 9:9-12; 10:1-4
Devotional Reading • MATTHEW 10:5-15

LESSON AIM

By the end of the lesson, students will understand the call from Jesus to discipleship; the commitment needed to become a disciple of Jesus; and the commission Jesus has given to each Christian to become fishers of men.

KEEP IN MIND

"And he saith unto them, Follow me, and I will make you fishers of men" (Matthew 4:19).

FOCAL VERSES

MATTHEW 4:18 And Jesus, walking by the sea of Galilee, saw two brethren, Simon called Peter, and Andrew his brother, casting a net into the sea: for they were fishers.

19 And he saith unto them, Follow me, and I will make you fishers of men.

20 And they straightway left their nets, and followed him.

21 And going on from thence, he saw other two brethren, James the son of Zebedee, and John his brother, in a ship with Zebedee their father, mending their nets; and he called them.

22 And they immediately left the ship and their father, and followed him.

9:9 And as Jesus passed forth from thence, he saw a man, named Matthew, sitting at the receipt of custom: and he saith unto him, Follow me. And he arose, and followed him.

10 And it came to pass, as Jesus sat at meat in the house, behold, many publicans and sinners came and sat down with him and his disciples.

11 And when the Pharisees saw it, they said unto his disciples, Why eateth your Master with publicans and sinners?

12 But when Jesus heard that, he said unto them, They

LESSON OVERVIEW

LESSON AIM
KEEP IN MIND
FOCAL VERSES
IN FOCUS
THE PEOPLE, PLACES, AND TIMES
BACKGROUND
AT-A-GLANCE
IN DEPTH
SEARCH THE SCRIPTURES
DISCUSS THE MEANING
LESSON IN OUR SOCIETY
MAKE IT HAPPEN
FOLLOW THE SPIRIT
REMEMBER YOUR THOUGHTS
MORE LIGHT ON THE TEXT
DAILY BIBLE READINGS

that be whole need not a physician, but they that are sick.

10:1 And when he had called unto him his twelve disciples, he gave them power against unclean spirits, to cast them out, and to heal all manner of sickness and all manner of disease.

2 Now the names of the twelve apostles are these; The first, Simon, who is called Peter, and Andrew his brother; James the son of Zebedee, and John his brother;

3 Philip, and Bartholomew; Thomas, and Matthew the publican; James the son of Alphaeus, and Lebbaeus, whose surname was Thaddaeus;

4 Simon the Canaanite, and Judas Iscariot, who also betrayed him.

IN FOCUS

Domitrese was in a state of shock. She couldn't believe that Pastor Johnson had called on her to be on the Pastor's Advisory Board. If she accepted the position, she would be the youngest person serving. To her knowledge, the membership had never changed. The church had the same programs conducted in the same way like a ritual, year after year. Domitrese could hear Mother West now, "We have always done it this way and the people haven't complained. We don't change a good thing." Mother West criticized every attempt to do something new or different.

There were older, wiser people on the board, and Domitrese wondered how she could possibly be of service. She also felt that it was an honor and a privilege to serve the Lord. "Whatever You ask of me, Lord, that's what I'll do," she prayed.

Today's lesson is about Jesus' twelve disciples. We will see the type of men He called to work for Him.

THE PEOPLE, PLACES, AND TIMES

MATTHEW. The author of this Gospel of Matthew. His names means "gift of Jehovah," and he is also known by his priestly tribal name, Levi (Mark 2:14). Matthew wrote the genealogy of Christ, and documents His claim to be Messiah. Matthew was a publican, a Jewish man employed by the conquering ancient Romans to collect taxes. He gained his wealth by lying, cheating, and extorting money from people. The Jewish people saw him as a traitor, and they despised him. After his conversion to Christ, his ministry was to preach mostly to the Jews. He made many referrals to Old Testament Scripture nearly 100 of them and he mentioned the phrase "kingdom of heaven" 32 times (13:1-53). Later when other disciples returned to their former occupations, Matthew never did. He was present at the ascension of Jesus.

BACKGROUND

Chapter 4 begins with Jesus' 40 day fast, His being led by the Holy Spirit to defeat Satan in the wilderness, and finally His moving to Galilee to begin His three-year ministry.

The first set of brothers Jesus called were Peter and Andrew as they fished (Matthew 4:18). "Follow me," Jesus said, "And I will make you fishers of men." Immediately they stopped what they were doing and followed Him.

The second set of brothers, James and John, the sons of Zebedee, were mending their nets when Jesus called. They too immediately followed him. Notice these men were already working, because God doesn't call them lazy and inactive. Jesus called them to a new vocation as fishers of men. Jesus chose brothers because they understood the importance of family unity and the harmony of working together.

When Jesus saw Matthew sitting at the tax office, He saw more than just a publican, and He summoned him. Jesus will use anyone who makes himself available to Him by allowing Him to be Lord over their lives. Matthew heard the call as a release from his bondage and immediately he

AT-A-GLANCE

1. The Call (Matthew 4:18-22)
2. The Commitment (9:9-12)
3. The Commission (10:1-4)

left everything behind and responded.

Having selected twelve disciples, Jesus empowered them to cast out unclean spirits and to heal illnesses (10:1-4). They were to take what they had personally learned as his students and evangelize the entire world.

IN DEPTH

1. The Call (Matthew 4:18-22)

Jesus did not go to the religious leaders in Jerusalem to choose His disciples. He was at least 100 miles away at Bethany beyond the Jordan River in Galilee on the seashore. There He found ordinary fisherman. *Halieus*, the Greek word for fisherman, suggests care, patience, and skill. Jesus was seeking industrious, responsive people who were fit for endurance and familiar with hard work.

The disciples, who demonstrated a willingness to let go of the past and submit themselves to Jesus, were carefully chosen for a new vocation. "You did not choose Me, but I chose you" (John 15:16). "So likewise, who ever of you does not forsake all that he has cannot be my disciple" (Luke 14:33, NIV).

Many adults are required to make vocational changes due to down-sizing or when business simply go out of business. Some people are even willing to make sacrifices. How far are you willing to go for the sake of the Gospel?

The first four men were hard at work when they were summoned. It was not just on any job, but part of a family unit with their brothers and fathers working together. They understood the importance of obedient and brotherly cooperation. James and John's father was referred to by name (Zebedee) and was perhaps better known than Peter and Andrew's father.

It was common in those days to be known by two names like Simon Peter, because one name was for friends and family, while the other was for the business community. Matthew, the Levite, was also called Levi (Mark 2:14; Luke 5:28).

2. The Commitment (9:9-12)

Jesus saw Matthew in every aspect mentally, physically, emotionally, and spiritually all in a glance. And when the Saviour called him, Matthew responded by immediately detaching himself from his occupation and attaching himself to Jesus. He made a lifetime commitment. When we accept Christ into our hearts and totally surrender our lives to Him, something happens. What's on the inside, shows up on the outside. People can see the difference.

To celebrate this momentous occasion Matthew threw a great house party with Jesus as the guest of honor. His friends, also tax collectors and sinners, all ate dinner with Jesus (9:10). When the Pharisees criticized Jesus for eating with sinners, Jesus overheard and quoted a proverb that showed He spent His time with those who needed Him most (9:11-12). Our actions change when we fall in love with Jesus, and we too should want to tell our sinful friends about the Saviour.

Elijah's servant Elisha put it best when he said, "As the Lord lives, and as your soul lives, I will not leave you!" (2 Kings 2:4). We should have the same commitment to Jesus.

3. The Commission (10:1-4)

Matthew gives a listing of the first twelve disciples. Twelve signifies the number of tribes of Israel.

We see Jesus in the role of teacher as He calls the disciples to instruct them before sending them out as His apostles. The Greek word, *apostellein*, means one who shares the authority of the one who sends them, a representative. The word is used only in this passage of Scripture, referring only to these twelve men.

Jesus empowered his disciples to cast out every unclean spirit and to heal every illness. They were sent in pairs to encourage and help one another. God is aware of what we need before we need it, and makes provisions for us.

Today, as ambassadors of Christ, we too are commissioned to "study to show ourselves approved to God, a worker who does not need to be ashamed, rightly dividing the word or truth" (2 Timothy 2:15). Before we go out witnessing to our friends, family, and the world, we must first have a personal relationship with Jesus for ourselves. Think what would happen if each of us were to disciple twelve people and send them out with the Gospel. What kind of impact would we make on our world?

SEARCH THE SCRIPTURES

1. Should a person wait until he has ample time to devote to the ministry before answering the call?

2. Can Jesus only use people who have lived exemplary lives for the purpose of the Gospel?

DISCUSS THE MEANING

1. What advantage would a person with a strong family background have over a person without one?

2. Why did Jesus organize/send the disciples out two-by-two for ministry?

LESSON IN OUR SOCIETY

In our society we are taught to be independent, self-motivated, and self-centered. Christ teaches us to bond together and to be interdependent. We could learn much from the way Christ organizes the disciples for ministry, two-by-two. We need each other and we need fellowship and encouragement from other Christians.

MAKE IT HAPPEN

There is always help needed in our local churches. Contact your pastor or administrator in your church and ask how you can be a blessing to the body of Christ. Consider it an honor to work for the Lord.

FOLLOW THE SPIRIT

What God wants me to do:

_____

_____

REMEMBER YOUR THOUGHTS

Special insights you learned:

_____

_____

MORE LIGHT ON THE TEXT
MATTHEW 4:18-22; 9:9-12; 10:1-4

4:18 And Jesus, walking by the Sea of Galilee, saw two brethren, Simon called Peter, and Andrew his brother, casting a net into the sea: for they were fishers.

In these verses, we see the power of Jesus' call and the type of obedience He desires. This passage is the only extended report, in the Gospel of Matthew, of how Jesus chose His disciples. There is a brief description of how Matthew, the tax collector, was called (Matthew 9:9). But there is no mention of the calling of the other seven disciples.

Peter and Andrew, two brothers, were described as men who were making a decent living as professional fishermen. They were, no doubt, good at what they were doing and felt confident in their abilities. They were about the business of fishing, casting their net into the sea, when Jesus appeared.

When Jesus arrives, our lives are never the same. The plans we have, the direction we think our lives are going, can suddenly take a very dramatic turn. It's exciting and a great adventure to meet Jesus and to hear His new plans for us, but it takes courage and faith to follow Him.

19 And He saith unto them, Follow me, and I will make you fishers of men.

Jesus found them at their trade and indicated to them that the same abilities they used to lure and catch fish, they would be able to use to bring people into the kingdom of God. Even though they may not have been as proficient and confident in their ability to do that, He assured them He would "make" them able to do the job. Jesus is the one who makes all of His followers able to do the good works they are called to do. He equips and prepares them and us.

He said to them, "Follow me." This is translated from the Greek word *deute* (pronounced **dyoo-teh**), which literally means "come." It is a command or exhortation. Jesus clearly expected them to obey and follow Him.

20 And they straightway left their nets and followed him.

They responded, the text says, "straightway," translated from the Greek word *eutheos* (pronounced **yoo-theh-os**) which means "immediately." They left their nets and followed Him.

Some Christians today are called to do exactly that, to leave their jobs and professions and follow Jesus' call into fulltime ministry. Seminaries are full of "second-career" students who have left lucrative positions in law, advertising, teaching, journalism, etc., to become fishers of people.

But even those Christians who are not called to leave everything behind and start over are called to follow Jesus' call in some way. We are all to be evangelists, drawing people into the kingdom, through the way we live, the way we serve, and the people we are.

And the type of obedience Jesus wants is just what these disciples immediately exemplified. Sometimes it is our human tendency to procrastinate until everything is right, but Jesus calls us to follow Him now, immediately. Our tendency is to wait or put it off, but we should choose to follow the Lord today---immediately, because tomorrow might be too late.

21 And going on from thence, he saw other two brethren, James the son of Zebedee, and John his brother, in a ship with Zebedee their father, mending their nets; and he called them. 22 And they immediately left the ship and their father and followed him.

Jesus went on, in these verses, to call two more disciples, James and John, the two who are commonly referred to as the Sons of Thunder (Mark 3:17). They, too, were in their boat, doing work related to their profession as fishermen. And they were accompanied by their father. But when Jesus called them, they too responded immediately and left the

boat. Matthew includes a specific mention of the fact that they left their father as well, and followed Jesus.

Here is an illustration of how following Jesus can sometimes cause stress in your family. Can you imagine how their father must have felt. He sat there as these two big strong men, who were probably responsible for doing much of the work, walked away from the family business. Though the text doesn't record it, he may have had some things to say to them which were not altogether positive. But still, they left. They did what they were called to do.

Many scholars have struggled, trying to figure out the meaning behind Jesus' words that He did not come to send peace, but a sword to set a man at variance against his father, and a daughter against her mother (Matthew 10:34-36). Or in Luke 14:26, which says that if you do not hate your mother and father and all your relatives, you are not fit to be a disciple of Jesus. Basically, scholars have agreed that what Jesus was doing was establishing a priority for the kingdom. This priority takes precedence, even over these all-important family relationships.

In the African-American community there is a great respect for elders and families, and this is a very good thing. We do want to love our families and give of ourselves to them. But nothing, or no one, should stand in the way of following Jesus. The Father, who we owe our greatest loyalty and obedience to, is our heavenly Father. Sometimes, like James and John, part of our call may mean leaving our family behind to do the work of the ministry.

9:9 And as Jesus passed forth from thence, he saw a man named Matthew, sitting at the receipt of custom: and he saith unto him, Follow me. And he arose, and followed him.

In this passage Jesus called one who was despised by many. The text says Matthew was sitting at the receipt of custom. This is where the taxes were collected. In our society today we have very negative feelings toward those who work for the Internal Revenue Service. In social settings, they are often reluctant to reveal what they do for a living. The Jewish attitude toward "tax-gatherers" was even worse than ours. Not only were they collecting high and sometimes unfair taxes, lining their own pockets with their greed and unscrupulous behavior they were working for a foreign, oppressive government.

For African-Americans it might be akin to seeing Jesus call a member of the Ku Klux Klan. Such a man might be considered despicable and it might be unthinkable that Jesus would call someone like this to become His disciple. And yet, He does call him, just like He calls others who are considered too corrupt or too far-gone to be helped. Jesus does look beyond our faults to see our need, and even a tax-gatherer can find new life in Him.

Like Peter and Andrew and James and John, this man, Matthew, obeyed the command Jesus gave him and followed Him immediately. He, again, sets an example for us.

10 And it came to pass, as Jesus sat at meat in the house, behold, many publicans and sinners came and sat down with him and his disciples. 11 And when the Pharisees saw it, they said unto his disciples, Why eateth your Master with publicans and sinners? 12 But when Jesus heard that, he said, unto them, They that be whole need not a physician, but they that are sick.

Apparently the first thing Matthew did after responding to the call, was to host a banquet for Jesus. Naturally Matthew's co-workers and fellow tax-gatherers were in attendance, as well as some other "sinners." The Pharisees were aghast at this. How could any decent Jew, no less a holy man, hang out with this low-life crowd? They pulled His disciples aside and confronted them over this unseemly behavior. And when Jesus heard about it, He responded by saying it was not the healthy (or those who think they were) but the sick who need Him.

It is a relief that Jesus does not expect us to be well and whole and perfect before He will accept us. We can come "just as we are" to Jesus from any path of life. We can come with any kind of past or history, having committed any kind of sin and find His love, His compassion, His forgiveness, and His salvation. He is the Great Physician and He stands ready to heal us of all our diseases of body, mind, and soul.

10:1 And when he had called unto him his twelve disciples, he gave them power against unclean spirits, to cast them out, and to heal all manner of sickness and all manner of disease.

Jesus assembled the twelve men who would be called His disciples. Twelve is a number that is rich in symbolism and meaning. It corresponds to the number of the tribes of Israel. These twelve disciples suggest the fulfillment of the hope of Israel and indicate that, indeed, the Christian church is the true Israel.

And Jesus gave them power. The word translated "power" is from the Greek word *exousia* (pronounced **ex-ou-si-ah**) which means "authority" or "capability." It's the kind of authority that could be associated with a government official, a legal right. Jesus empowered and equipped them to carry out the mission of the church, by bestowing this authority on them. Now they, too, had the power and the right to cast out unclean spirits and to heal every disease and malady. They were clearly sent to bring deliverance and new life to those who were sick in body, mind, and

heart.

2 Now, the names of the twelve apostles are these; The first, Simon, who is called Peter, and Andrew his brother; James, the son of Zebedee, and John his brother; 3 Philip, and Bartholomew; Thomas, and Matthew the publican; James the son of Alphaeus, and Lebbaeus, whose surname was Thaddaeus; 4 Simon the Canaanite, and Judas Iscariot, who also betrayed him.

This is the only place in the Gospel of Matthew where the twelve are referred to as "apostles" from the Greek *apostolos*, which means "one who is sent." Apostles share the authority of the one who sends them, as the person's representative. Matthew is the only Gospel writer to use this more formal term for the twelve.

Then he names them, two by two, which is how the Gospel of Mark describes them being sent out. And Judas' name is followed by the awful reminder that he was the one who betrayed Jesus.

These twelve were the beginning of a new movement of God. Their call and mission is also ours. We, who would be Jesus' disciples today, should know He gives us authority and empowers us. He sends us out, like these twelve, to do greater things than even He did (John 14:12), to liberate people and bring them the Good News of salvation.

DAILY BIBLE READING

M: Jesus Calls the First Disciples
Matthew 4:18-22
T: Jesus Calls Matthew
Matthew 9:9-13
W: Authority Conferred upon the Disciples
Matthew 10:1-4
T: The Twelve Proclaim God's Kingdom
Matthew 10:5-15
F: Disciples Told of Coming Persecutions
Matthew 10:16-25
S: The Disciples Told Not to Fear
Matthew 10:26-33
S: Not Peace, But a Sword
Matthew 10:34---11:1

TEACHING TIPS

January 9
Bible Study Guide 6

1. Words You Should Know

A. Alms. (Matthew 6:1) Greek *eleemosune*—a compassion of benefit towards the poor, giving.

B. Pray. (v. 6) Greek *euchomai*—to pray to God; make earnest supplication; worship.

C. Forgive. (v. 12) Greek *aphiem*—to send away or the remission of a punishment due to sinful conduct; the complete removal of the cause of the offense.

2. Teacher Preparation

A. Prior to the class, call your students and ask them if they have any prayer requests. If so, pray for the requests mentioned. If not, pray for them as the Holy Spirit leads.

B. Read the BACKGROUND.

C. Read DAILY BIBLE READING and note how God's people sought him in numerous situations.

D. Materials needed: 3x5 index cards, pencils, small receptacle to hold cards (perhaps a shoe box), dry board and markers.

3. Starting the Lesson

A. Ask at least three students to open in prayer.

B. Select one student to read the FOCAL VERSES 1-9, and a second student to read FOCAL VERSES 10-15.

C. Ask the class whether or not prayer is important today. Ask why it is or is not.

4. Getting into the Lesson

A. Ask the students to read IN FOCUS. Ask if anyone has found themselves in a similar situation. Spend no more than five minutes in discussion.

B. Ask a student to read the BACKGROUND and LESSON IN OUR SOCIETY and discuss what it is that God wants from us.

C. Select three students to read IN DEPTH.

5. Relating the Lesson to Life

A. After "Our Giving," ask if anyone has ever been in a position where they needed to receive, food, clothing, money, etc. How did it make them feel to receive what was needed?

B. After "Our Prayer," ask how they feel about being repetitious in their prayers. Spend no more than five minutes on discussion.

C. After "Our Forgiveness," ask for a moment of silence so everyone can search their hearts for unforgiveness.

6. Arousing Action

A. List on the board what the class considers to be the most important need for prayers for today.

B. Have each student write a prayer request on a 3x5 card, but do not put their name on the card. Place card in the small receptacle.

C. Have the students pair off and pray for one another.

D. Have each student select a 3x5 prayer request card from the receptacle (make sure it is not theirs) and each day during the week pray for that request.

E. Remind the students to finish the lesson in the private devotion. Close the class in prayer.

WORSHIP GUIDE

For the Superintendent or Teacher
Theme: Teachings on Prayer
Theme Song: "I'm Just One Prayer Away"
Scripture: Luke 18:1
Song: "I Will Call Upon the Lord"
Meditation: Dear Lord, what a pleasure and honor it is to pray. Please hear our prayers, O Lord, and deliver us from all unrighteousness.

TEACHINGS ON PRAYER

Bible Background • MATTHEW 6:1-15
Printed Text • MATTHEW 6:1-15
Devotional Reading •LUKE 11:1-13

LESSON AIM

By the conclusion of the lesson students will know the right motives in giving, the right model for prayer; and the promises and warnings for the right understanding in forgiveness.

KEEP IN MIND

"But thou, when thou prayest, enter into thy closet, and when thou hast shut thy door, pray to thy Father which is in secret; and thy Father which seeth in secret shall reward thee openly" (Matthew 6:6).

FOCAL VERSES

MATTHEW 6:1 Take heed that ye do not your alms before men, to be seen of them: otherwise ye have no reward of your Father which is in heaven.

2 Therefore when thou doest thine alms, do not sound a trumpet before thee, as the hypocrites do in the synagogues and in the streets, that they may have glory of men. Verily I say unto you, They have their reward.

3 But when thou doest alms, let not thy left hand know what thy right hand doeth:

4 That thine alms may be in secret: and thy Father which seeth in secret himself shall reward thee openly.

5 And when thou prayest, thou shalt not be as the hypocrites are: for they love to pray standing in the synagogues and in the corners of the streets, that they may be seen of men. Verily I say unto you, They have their reward.

6 But thou, when thou prayest, enter into thy closet, and when thou hast shut thy door, pray to thy Father which is in secret; and thy Father which seeth in secret shall reward thee openly.

7 But when ye pray, use not vain repetitions, as the heathen do: for they think that they shall be heard for their much speaking.

LESSON OVERVIEW

LESSON AIM
KEEP IN MIND
FOCAL VERSES
IN FOCUS
THE PEOPLE, PLACES, AND TIMES
BACKGROUND
AT-A-GLANCE
IN DEPTH
SEARCH THE SCRIPTURES
DISCUSS THE MEANING
LESSON IN OUR SOCIETY
MAKE IT HAPPEN
FOLLOW THE SPIRIT
REMEMBER YOUR THOUGHTS
MORE LIGHT ON THE TEXT
DAILY BIBLE READINGS

8 Be not ye therefore like unto them: for your Father knoweth what things ye have need of, before ye ask him.

9 After this manner therefore pray ye: Our Father which art in heaven, Hallowed be thy name.

10 Thy kingdom come. Thy will be done in earth, as it is in heaven.

11 Give us this day our daily bread.

12 And forgive us our debts, as we forgive our debtors.

13 And lead us not into temptation, but deliver us from evil: For thine is the kingdom, and the power, and the glory, for ever. Amen.

14 For if ye forgive men their trespasses, your heavenly Father will also forgive you:

15 But if ye forgive not men their trespasses, neither will your Father forgive your trespasses.

IN FOCUS

Virginia sat at her desk with her hands folded together, head bowed, and eyes closed. It was the lunch hour and she had decided to forgo her lunch in favor of prayers. She needed to hear from God. After nine years of employment at the university, it looked as if she was going to be fired! She had transferred into the position only seven months ago when her former job had been phased out. Up until now her work record had been impeccable. Now her new supervisor was telling her that her work was unsatisfactory. "Dear Lord," she prayed. "Please give me the strength to endure whatever comes my way and help me to have the right attitude, especially towards my supervisor. I trust in you and not the situation. Show me what to do Lord."

Have you ever had something to happen to you that was not in your control? Where did you turn? Today we want to examine God's teachings on prayer.

THE PEOPLE, PLACES, AND TIMES

PRAYER. The communication from the heart of man to the ear of God. Throughout the Old and New Testaments, we find God answering the prayers of those persons who needed Him. Abel's blood cried out from the dust of the earth and God heard him and avenged him (Genesis 4:10-12). The Hebrews, while in Egypt, cried out because of their hard taskmasters, and God sent Moses to deliver them (Exodus 3:1---4:17). David prayed for forgiveness and restoration after being caught in sin, and God heard his prayer (Psalm 51). Elisha prayed for his servant's eyes to be opened to see the army of the Lord, and God made it so (2 Kings 6:17). The disciples asked Jesus to teach them to pray after they had watched Him (Luke 11:2-4). Peter prayed and Tabitha woke up from the dead (Acts 9:40-41). Faith (Mark 11:24) and forgiveness (Mark 11:25) are needed in order for prayers to be answered.

BACKGROUND

Jesus taught that the true righteousness of the kingdom must be applied in the everyday activities of life. He cautioned against practicing piety to impress other people. Almsgiving was designed to be a display of mercy, but the Pharisees had distorted the showing of mercy by using it to demonstrate their devotion to religious duties in almsgiving and prayer. Giving without fanfare and quietly praying will receive its rewards.

Just as the Pharisees made a public display in giving, so they did in praying. They prayed in public places to be seen and heard by men. Jesus says they got their reward in the applause of the people. Instead of condemning prayer of this kind, the Lord purified the practice by directing us into a private place to be alone and pray to our Father. Jesus went on to give us an example of how to pray with certain guidelines.

AT-A-GLANCE

1. Our Giving (Matthew 6:1-4)
2. Our Praying (vv. 5-13)
3. Our Forgiving (vv. 14-15)

IN DEPTH

1. Our Giving (Matthew 6:1-4)

Jesus cautioned against practicing piety to impress other people. The righteousness of the Pharisees was insincere and dishonest. They practice their religion for the plaudits of the people. They were hypocrites, who deliberately used religion to promote their own gain. But true righteousness comes from within. We should not practice our giving for the applause of men but for the reward of God.

Giving to the poor, praying, and fasting were important traditions to the Pharisees. Jesus, however, warns that our hearts should have the right attitude when we practice our giving. If our motive is to gain the praise of men, we have the wrong attitude. But if our motive is to serve God in love and please Him, then we will give our gifts without calling attention to them. Though all giving doesn't necessarily have to be done anonymously, we should not use our giving to make people think we're more spiritual than we really are.

2. Our Praying (vv. 5-13)

Jesus gave instructions to guide us in our praying. He taught that prayer should be done confidentially. It is not wrong to pray in public, but it is not right to pray in public if you are not in the habit of praying in private. It is not wrong to seek God's help or bless our food. Our Lord prayed privately (Mark 1:35), so did Elisha (2 Kings 4:33) and Daniel (Daniel 6:10). We should pray sincerely (Matthew 6:7, 8), not using empty phrases, because God knows what we need before we ask. If we repeat our requests, that doesn't make it a vain repetition; it is when we babble without a sincere desire to seek and do God's will (Matthew 6:9-13). Jesus gave his followers a model prayer known as the Lord's Prayer. We should use this prayer as a pattern; Jesus said to pray after this manner. The purpose of prayer is to glorify God and these are the guidelines for prayer: (1) it should involve worship, reverence and magnify of our Father; (2) it should concern itself with the work God is engaged in, namely, the establishment of God's kingdom and His will being done on earth; (3) it should be concerned with daily needs; (4) it should contain confession and seek forgiveness; and finally (5) it should seek protection and deliverance from the evil one. Notice this model prayer begins with our Father. We put God's concerns first, then we can bring our own needs.

This is the God-appointed way of having our needs met, because prayer also prepares us for God's answer.

3. Our Forgiving (vv. 14-15)

We must pray having a forgiving spirit toward others. If you do not forgive repentant offenders, God will not forgive you. Christians must be prepared and willing to forgive the offenses of others; if we don't forgive, our prayers are to no avail. If God would answer the prayers of a person who is unforgiving, then He would be encouraging sin. Forgiveness puts you in right relationship with my brothers and sisters, and with God. You can pray effectively; therefore, forgiveness is an important part of prayer.

The basic concept of prayer is forgiveness. Forgive your brother and be forgiven. Refuse to forgive a repentant brother, and you shall not be forgiven. Forgiveness is to be released from all guilt and condemnation. We all need forgiveness. Forgiving means we should not be bitter or hostile, seeking revenge, or holding hard feelings against another person. We should not rejoice when others fall on hard times or experience trouble and trials in their lives. Blessed are the merciful, for they shall obtain mercy (Matthew 5:7).

SEARCH THE SCRIPTURES

1. Is giving for recognition by men rewarded by God? (Matthew 6:4)

2. To whom should we pray? (v. 6)

3. How is forgiveness connected to prayer? (v. 14)

DISCUSS THE MEANING

1. When a man does good and shows kindness, does it matter to God what his motive is? (Matthew 6:1)

2. If God knows what we have need of, why pray? (v. 8)

3. What is prayer? (v. 9)

LESSON IN OUR SOCIETY

The Pharisees wanted to be seen praying so that people would see how religious they were. They sought the approval of men. We see the same thing today in our churches and on our televisions. Yet more and more people seek answers through the Psychic Hotline because they do not want to spend the time developing a relationship with their Creator. If we really want answers to today's complex issues, we must ask God because He sees the complete picture from beginning to end.

MAKE IT HAPPEN

Prayer is needed more today than ever. This week set aside a specific time each day for prayer. Psalm 63:1 says, "Early will I seek Thee." Ask the Father to bring to your mind those people who have hurt you or persecuted you. Then ask Him to help you to forgive those people. If you can contact any of them, do so, and resolve whatever differences you may have. Remember, prayer changes things.

FOLLOW THE SPIRIT

What God wants me to do:

_____

_____

REMEMBER YOUR THOUGHTS

Special insights you learned:

_____

_____

MORE LIGHT ON THE TEXT
MATTHEW 6:1-15

In this passage, which is part of the Sermon on the Mount, Jesus talks about two important aspects of the Christian life: almsgiving and prayer. The overall theme is that these activities of righteousness should be done with the right motivation. If they are done for the benefit and admiration of others, then they accomplish nothing. In fact, those who do this are called hypocrites. They look pious and righteous, but they are seeking to glorify themselves and not God.

1 Take heed that ye do not your alms before men, to be seen of them: otherwise ye have no reward of your Father which is in heaven.

Verse 1 starts with a warning, "Take heed" ("be careful"), and then tells us not to bring our alms and seek the attention of others as we bring them. If we seek attention, that will be our reward, and we will have no reward from God.

2 Therefore when thou doest thine alms, do not sound a trumpet before thee, as the hypocrites do in the synagogues and in the streets that they may have glory of men. Verily I say unto you, They have their reward. 3 But when thou doest thine alms, let not thy left hand know what thy right hand doeth: 4That thine alms may be in secret: and thy Father which seeth in secret himself shall reward thee openly.

Jesus issued a more specific warning to those who would actually hire trumpeters to precede them as they marched into the temple to present their offerings. He said these are hypocrites and the immediate rush and attention they receive from the crowds are the extent of their reward.

Today we don't hire trumpeters, but sometimes we might find ourselves "blowing our own horn," so to speak, by naming the amounts and frequency of our donations. Also we might expect to be rewarded and acknowledged by those to whom we give. If so, our name on the pew or the offering plate, will be the extent of our reward. Jesus tells us that giving with an expectation of being noticed and rewarded by people, is to give with the wrong attitude.

In verse 3, Jesus tells us we should do our giving in secret, keeping secret what we are doing, even from ourselves to some extent. Because there is a human tendency to brag, even to ourselves sometimes, to tell ourselves what we can expect from God in response to our generosity. Verse 4 emphasizes the importance of "secrecy," which means we should give because it is the right thing to do, not because we will get something out of it. Even though this verse does assure us that if we do give out of the right motives and without seeking attention, God will see and reward us, openly.

5 And when thou prayest, thou shalt not be as the hypocrites are: for they love to pray standing in the synagogues and in the corners of the streets, that they may be seen of men. Verily I say unto you, They have their reward. 6 But thou, when thou prayest, enter into thy closet, and when thou hast shut thy door, pray to thy Father which is in secret; and thy Father which seeth in secret shall reward thee openly.

Verses 5-6 apply this same "secrecy" principle to prayer. Jesus declared that praying to impress others, makes people into hypocrites again. He described the hypocrites as those who found conspicuous places to stand and pray in the synagogue and even on the street corners. Their objective was to have everyone see them and admire their devotion and dedication. What should be done instead, was to go into a secret closet and even though no one else may know what we are doing, God will see and know and will reward us. This is not to say we should avoid praying in public, but we should not pray to show the public how pious and spiritual we are. Even in public, our motivation should be to glorify and seek God and God alone.

7 But when ye pray, use not vain repetitions as the heathen do: for they think that they shall be heard for their much speaking. 8 Be not ye therefore like unto them for your Father knoweth what things ye have need of, before ye ask him.

In verse 7, Jesus continued His instructions about prayer. Not only are we to avoid praying in order to be seen by others, but we are to avoid the practice that was common to the Gentiles of using lots of words to try to impress or manipulate God. The Gentiles had so many gods and so many names for them that they would try to list them all to make sure they included the right one. Also they would try to flatter the gods in order to convince them to answer the prayer. Jesus said, specifically, do not be like them. He assures us that God, our Father, the omniscient one, knows already what we need even before we ask. And God cannot be manipulated. God stands ready to answer our prayers and bless us because of the love He has for us.

Finally, in verses 9-15, He tells us how we should pray. Jesus gives us the model of prayer we commonly call the Lord's Prayer. It is also recorded in Luke 11:1-4. According to Luke's Gospel, Jesus gives this prayer in response to a request from one of the disciples (Luke 11:1). Matthew does not include this request, but he includes a longer and more developed version of the prayer. It was not intended to replace the corporate prayer in the synagogue, but to give His disciples a model for their own private prayer time. Books have been written analyzing this prayer. It is so rich in meaning and subject to various interpretations. Although it is short, it is a powerful model for the way

that we should pray in our own prayer closets.

9 After this manner therefore pray ye: Our Father which art in heaven, Hallowed be thy name.

Jesus started by affirming that God is the Father, the one in the heavens. This was typical of many formal Jewish prayers. We know that Jesus referred to God as "Abba" which is an affectionate, familiar term, similar to our current use of the term "daddy." It shows the kind of relationship He had with God the Father. We too should seek to have that same kind of closeness and intimacy in our relationship with God.

Fatherhood is a very sensitive and delicate issue in the African-American community. So many forces have conspired, from the lingering effects of slavery to the current evils of racism and other forms of oppression, against African-American men. The result is that many homes and families are headed by women. There are some negative feelings associated with the term "father" for this reason and others. So many theologians now are questioning whether we really should address God as Father, since it does evoke such powerfully negative feelings in so many.

But we cannot take away the fact that this is how Jesus addressed God as Father, Daddy. This picture of what the Father/son, Father/daughter relationship can be like, can guide us as we work to repair the damage and heal the pain in the African-American community. The seams of our families, can be mended and made strong by looking to God, the perfect Father, the all-loving all-caring Father, as a model.

After this opening address, the Lord's Prayer contains seven petitions. There are three "You" or God petitions, things we are praying God will do for His glory. These are followed by four "we" petitions. They are four things we want God to do for His children.

The first "You" petition, hallowed be thy name, would more accurately be stated, "Let thy name be hallowed." This means that God's name should be sanctified, revered, and considered holy. For Jewish people, the name of God was considered so holy it could not be spoken or even written in its entirety. The name of God was synonymous with God, for them. For us, the prayer is a request that in all the earth the name of God would speak of God's holiness and kingdom.

10 Thy kingdom come, Thy will be done in earth, as it is in heaven.

This phrase refers to the end times, when there will be fulfillment of all prophecies and expectations. At that time God's kingdom will prevail, and God will rule and reign on earth as God does in heaven. This is what we look forward to, as Christians, and we seek to make it a reality in our daily lives as we wait, in the meantime, for the kingdom of God to come in totality.

The second half of this verse continues with the desire for the coming of the kingdom, that is, God's ultimate will for the earth and humanity. As we pray these words, we have to consider what we are doing day to day, to bring the kingdom and God's will to fruition on earth. For this is our ultimate mission in life as God's people.

At this point the "we" petitions begin, as we request the things we need from God: sustenance, forgiveness, protection, and deliverance.

11 Give us this day our daily bread.

Some scholars have debated over whether this means literal bread in terms of our daily physical needs, or whether "daily bread" should be taken in the spiritual sense, or even in the understanding of what will be consumed at the heavenly banquet. The majority opinion seems to be when we pray for our daily bread, we are praying to have our physical needs to be met, as they arise, on a daily basis. It doesn't necessarily mean we will be able to build bigger barns to store it all, but we will have enough for the day.

12 And forgive us our debts, as we forgive our debtors.

Whether we use the word "debts," "trespasses," or "sins," it is pretty clear that we want to be forgiven for the wrong things we do. The flip side of the coin is that we, too, must be willing to forgive the wrongs done to us.

13 And lead us not into temptation, but deliver us from evil: For thine is the kingdom and the power and the glory, forever. Amen.

This is a difficult passage to understand, because it implies God actively "leads" us into temptation. The epistle of James cautions us never to say that God is tempting us (James 1:13-14). Most scholars agree that this means God doesn't allow us to be tempted or tested beyond our ability to persevere. There is a very popular saying people quote, especially in times of trial, "He won't put more on you than you can bear."

Then the prayer continues with a request to be delivered from evil. The more accurate translation of the Greek word *ponerou* (**po-ne-rou**) used here is "evil one." When times of testing do come, as they will, then we pray to be delivered from the evil one Satan. He comes only to steal, kill, and destroy (John 10:10). These two petitions go together.

Some people feel Christians should not undergo trials and temptations. But Jesus said we would have tribulations in the world (John 16:33). We should be of good cheer in the midst of them, however, because we know that He has overcome the world. So when we are tempted, when we suffer, when we are tossed and driven by the storms of life, we have to pray for the strength to bear it and to come through it and to be delivered from the evil one.

14 For if ye forgive men their trespasses your heavenly Father will also forgive you: 15 But if ye forgive not men their trespasses, neither will your Father forgive your trespasses.

Finally Jesus goes back to the subject of forgiveness in verses 14 and 15. These two verses are not part of the prayer, but are included again to emphasize the importance of forgiveness and the fact that in the life of the Christian, we must both forgive others and be forgiven ourselves for the misdeeds we do.

We sing and pray this prayer so often that it can become rote and lose its meaning for us. But when we look at it with fresh eyes it can come alive again and give us, as Jesus intended, clear instructions on how to pray effectively. How serious are we in wanting His kingdom to come and God's will to be done? Do we live as kingdom people, aware of who and whose we are? How easy or difficult is it for us to forgive others when they do something wrong to us? How satisfied are we with having just our daily needs met, as opposed to all our wants and our desires met? Are our wants and desires reflective of God's will for our lives? These are all questions which arise when we take time to really reflect and meditate on the Lord's Prayer.

DAILY BIBLE READING

M: A Call to Love Enemies
Matthew 5:43-48
T: Instructions about Alms and Prayer
Matthew 6:1-6
W: The Lord's Prayer
Matthew 6:7-15
T: Ask, Search, Knock: God Will Respond
Matthew 7:7-11
F: Persevere in Prayer
Luke 11:5-13
S: A Parable on Perseverance in Prayer
Luke 18:1-8
S: The Pharisee and the Tax Collector
Luke 18:9-14

TEACHING TIPS

January 16
Bible Study Guide 7

1. Words You Should Know

A. Compassion. *Splagchnon,* a Greek word meaning to have pity on or sympathy, inward affection, plus tender mercy.

B. Miracle. An extraordinary event taken to manifest the supernatural power of God fulfilling His purposes as described in the Gospels.

C. Faith. The act or state of wholeheartedly and steadfastly believing in the existence, power, and benevolence of God, of having confidence in His providential care, and of being loyal to His will as revealed or believed in.

2. Teacher Preparation

A. Pray for each of the students in your class during the week. Desperation is something that each person is apt to experience at one time or another. Ask your students if and when they ever felt desperate and what they did about it.

B. Familiarize yourself with the lesson by reading it at least three times before the class and review the LESSON AIM. Stress the importance of Jesus' teaching, preaching, and healing those who are fainting, confused, and scattered.

3. Starting the Lesson

A. Begin the lesson with prayer, asking God to allow His truth to penetrate every heart and to affirm the LESSON AIM in the lives of the students.

B. Individually and silently, have students work on the SEARCH THE SCRIPTURES questions, as an introduction for those who did not have the opportunity to study the lesson in advance and as a review for those who did. Assign the questions to each student as they enter the class. Pair off students so they can work together in answering the questions.

C. Have a student read the IN FOCUS section aloud. Ask the class whether or not they have ever been compassionate towards another person and ask them how they went about handling it.

4. Getting Into the Lesson

A. Review the AT-A-GLANCE outline to show the direction of the lesson and the hopelessness of each situation. Discuss the importance of faith for those involved.

B. Using the BACKGROUND section will help bring the lesson to life for the students.

5. Relating the Lesson to Life

Have the students read LESSON IN OUR SOCIETY and MAKE IT HAPPEN. Discuss ways we can make a difference.

6. Arousing Action

A. Ask two students to summarize what they have learned from this lesson. Have the students meditate on FOLLOW THE SPIRIT and list the REMEMBER YOUR THOUGHTS for special insights they learned to accomplish the LESSON AIM.

B. Close the class in prayer especially concentrating on arousing compassion for others.

JANUARY
16TH

WORSHIP GUIDE

For the Superintendent or Teacher
Theme: Miracles of Compassion
Theme Song: "Use Me"
Scripture: Isaiah 7:8
Song: "Send Me Lord, I'll Go"
Meditation: Precious Lord, fill me with compassion and love for Your people that I may be a blessing to You. Create in me a clean heart and renew the right spirit within me. Humbly I offer myself for Your use. Be Thou glorified, O Lord!

MIRACLES OF COMPASSION

Bible Background • MATTHEW 9:18-38
Printed Text • MATTHEW 9:18-31, 35-36
Devotional Reading • MATTHEW 11:2-6

LESSON AIM

By the end of the lesson students will understand that Christ was moved inwardly with mercy, pity, and affection; why they should express and demonstrate God's compassion to the hopeless and helpless; the importance of teaching, preaching and healing those who are fainting, confused, and scattered.

KEEP IN MIND

"But when he saw the multitudes, he was moved with compassion on them, because they fainted, and were scattered abroad, as sheep having no shepherd" (Matthew 9:36).

FOCAL VERSES

MATTHEW 9:18 While he spake these things unto them, behold, there came a certain ruler, and worshipped him, saying, My daughter is even now dead: but come and lay thy hand upon her, and she shall live.

19 And Jesus arose, and followed him, and so did his disciples.

20 And, behold, a woman, which was diseased with an issue of blood twelve years, came behind him, and touched the hem of his garment:

21 For she said within herself, If I may but touch his garment, I shall be whole.

22 But Jesus turned him about, and when he saw her, he said, Daughter, be of good comfort; thy faith hath made thee whole. And the woman was made whole from that hour.

23 And when Jesus came into the ruler's house, and saw the minstrels and the people making a noise,

24 He said unto them, Give place: for the maid is not dead, but sleepeth. And they laughed him to scorn.

25 But when the people were put forth, he went in, and took her by the hand, and the maid arose.

26 And the fame hereof went abroad into all that land.

27 And when Jesus departed thence, two blind men followed him, crying, and saying, Thou Son of David, have mercy on us.

28 And when he was come into the house, the blind men came to him: and Jesus saith unto them, Believe ye that I am able to do this? They said unto him, Yea, Lord.

29 Then touched he their eyes, saying, According to your faith be it unto you.

30 And their eyes were opened; and Jesus straitly charged them, saying, See that no man know it.

31 But they, when they were departed, spread abroad his fame in all that country.

35 And Jesus went about all the cities and villages, teaching in their synagogues, and preaching the gospel of the kingdom, and healing every sickness and every disease among the people.

36 But when he saw the multitudes, he was moved with compassion on them, because they fainted, and were scattered abroad, as sheep having no shepherd.

IN FOCUS

There was a young pastor, Oletha James, who volunteered for the prayer line at a local TV station. While answering the phones, she received a call from a young woman by the name of Sandra who was suicidal. Sandra began to tell the pastor a tale of abuse and how she consistently failed at everything she attempted. Pastor Oletha listened and was overwhelmed with compassion for Sandra and wept as she began to pray. She decided to personally follow-up on Sandra by phoning her, but when she received no answer she prayed that much harder. On her last try, Sandra answered. She told the pastor she was very depressed and wanted to commit suicide. She also mentioned she had told God, "If you are real, have someone call and pray for me." Because of her compassion, Pastor Oletha was able to bring Sandra to a decision for Christ.

In this week's lesson we will see how Jesus always responds to those who are desperate, who confess their hopelessness and helplessness. We will see how Jesus, being moved by compassion, restores life to Jairus' daughter, heals a hemorrhaging woman, gives sight to two blind men, and sanity and speech to a demon-possessed man.

THE PEOPLE, PLACES, AND TIMES

JAIRUS (he will awaken). The man who came on behalf of his beloved daughter. The Gospel of Luke tells us Jairus oversaw the administration of the synagogue at Capernaum. This was an elected position and a powerful one. Jairus was a devout Jew and leader. He was the father of a 12-year-old daughter whom he loved deeply. Jairus showed strong courage by going to Jesus who was hated by the religious elders. He was more than likely risking his job at the synagogue. Because of his deep love for his daughter and his belief in Jesus, he approached Christ with humility, worship, and faith.

BACKGROUND

Matthew writes a cluster of miracle narratives, one healing narrative inside the framework of another. Each story tells of desperation, and each one can stand independent from the others. These narratives demonstrate the authority, power, and compassion of Jesus. His fame had spread throughout the region, and thousands of people were following him because everywhere he went he cured every disease and sickness (Matthew 9:35).

First, there is the desperate cry of a synagogue ruler for the life of his daughter. Next, there is the hopelessness of a woman with a 12-year bleeding disorder. Finally, there is the unceasing cry of the two blind men for their sight. Jesus came to demonstrate the compassion of God to men.

Today there are many reasons why people follow Jesus, because it is what their friends are doing, or simply to receive blessing. The scribes and Pharisees (religious rulers), however, followed Jesus to test the validity of Him being the Son of David, the Messiah. Jesus was their king but they would not acknowledge Him. They were trying to discredit Him and find a reason to put Him to death. The Pharisees went so far as to say He casts demons out of people by the power of the ruler of demons (v. 34). But the peo-

ple were saying, "Never has anything like this been seen in Israel" (v. 32). Jesus is moved to deep compassion by what He sees people confused, leaderless, scattered, and dying in their sins!

IN DEPTH

1. Compassion for the Hopeless (Matthew 9:18-19)

Jairus, a leader from the synagogue, interrupted Jesus as He spoke. He fell down before Jesus and made a desperate request for Him to raise his 12-year-old daughter from the dead. He said, "But if you will come and lay your hands upon her, she shall live" (vv. 18-19). This is also the only reference in the book of Matthew regarding the laying on of hands. We see Jesus and His disciples immediately got up to follow Jairus (v. 19); God immediately responds to genuine faith because it is His desire we should trust and depend on Him. Jesus told Jairus, "Fear not, believe only and she shall be made whole" (Luke 8:50). Being interrupted and delayed by the ailing woman could have easily discouraged Jairus. But Jesus, knowing all things, said this to revive Jairus' faltering faith. Although the worst had happened, the Son of God had authority over death and the power to restore life. Jesus was touched by the faith Jairus displayed.

This is an example of how our leaders should approach Christ, in humility, worship, and faith. We have all experienced loved ones dying, so we can understand the desperation Jairus felt. But in times of hopelessness, do we ask Jesus for His touch? He knows what is best for us, and we must trust Him to touch our needs.

2. Compassion for the Helpless (vv. 20-22)

A woman with a chronic bleeding problem touches Jesus' clothing and is healed by her faith in Him (vv. 20-22). Matthew uses the phrase "And, behold," to interrupt the story about the dead girl to introduce the hemorrhaging woman. She was considered to be unclean, contaminated, and unworthy. According to the Mosaic law, she was to be cut off from the Jewish community and ostracized. The woman was desperate and unable to help herself. But she purposed in her heart that if she could just touch the hem, the fringe, the tassel of Jesus' garment, He would never know and she would be healed.

What do we need for Jesus to touch for us? Cancer? AIDS? Desperation and faith stirs Jesus to compassion, for He who knows all can help all! This poor woman had been cut off from society and family according to Jewish tradition. Jesus turned and saw her, for her faith had touched Him (Mark 5:32). Faith will never go unnoticed or ignored by Christ.

3. Compassion for the Blind (vv. 27-31)

Two blind men followed Jesus as He left Jairus' home crying out, "Thou Son of David, have mercy on us" (v. 27). The title Son of David refers to the day when signs of the presence of the messianic age would be seen (Isaiah 29:18). Although the men could not see with their eyes, they could spiritually discern that this Jesus had special power and authority. They could only hear what was happening; faith came by hearing and hearing by the Word of God (Romans 10:17). These two blind men followed Jesus and took the steps needed because they wanted God to have mercy on them. They uttered a cry for mercy because they believed He could help them. They were persistent in following Him, all the way to the house. He could have ignored them, but the Lord stands ready to help us.

Only in Matthew does Jesus ask them a question: "Believe ye I am able to do this?" (v. 28) Their response was "Yes, Lord," and they were healed because of their persistent faith. They were desperate and acknowledged their need. Jesus was touched by their faith and was moved by compassion to help them. Blindness can be viewed as spiritual ignorance and unbelief (Matthew 15:14) to the fact there is a Saviour, and we need not remain afflicted. Therefore, we must be born again to have spiritual sight (John 3:3). The blind men's faith in Jesus released the healing power. Men everywhere are lost and need a Saviour. Jesus' vision involves the changing of every human life on earth.

Jesus ordered them not to tell anyone, but they went away and spread the news to everybody (vv. 30-31). It was simply too good to be kept a secret! Those who walked in darkness received light (4:16), and the children of the kingdom are now themselves "the light of this world" (5:14-16).

Satan had us bound, but Jesus set us free by His shed blood. The scales of blindness fell from our eyes when we accepted Christ into our hearts. It is now our responsibility to lead others to Christ!

4. Compassion for the Multitude (vv. 35-36)

Jesus went to cities, villages, graveyards, seashores, mountaintops, synagogues, even to people's homes teaching, preaching, and healing people. He saw the multitude as lost sheep without a shepherd, but with a great spiritual need. The abundant sicknesses was not what caused Jesus' deep compassion, but the aimless existence and wandering of the people. There was no purpose or meaning to their lives.

No one escapes the eye or heart of Jesus. This is His ministry, His mission, His purpose, and it has not changed in over 2000 years. Jesus has overcome the world and still demonstrates His compassion towards us by meeting our spiritual, physical, and emotional needs. There is nothing too hard for Him to do, no situation too difficult for Him to handle, no place He cannot go to reach us.

SEARCH THE SCRIPTURES

1. What did the Jewish leader ask of Jesus? (Matthew 9:18)

2. The mourners reacted to Jesus with scorn. How did Jesus respond? (v. 25)

3. What instructions did Jesus give the blind men? (v. 30)

4. Why was Jesus moved with compassion when he saw the multitudes? (v. 36)

DISCUSS THE MEANING

1. Jesus' compassion is seen in His response to the Jewish leader, the hemorrhaging woman, the blind men, and the demon-possessed man. How should we respond to Jesus knowing He is full of compassion?

2. If Jesus demonstrated the compassion of God toward people, then everyone should have this same compassion for others. When we see men fainting, scattered and without purpose, should we not demonstrate this same compassion?

LESSON IN OUR SOCIETY

There are many in our society today who are hopeless, helpless, and desperate. Some are drug addicts, prostitutes, alcoholics, and some just homeless and dirty. Many believers avoid these people and have a difficult time ministering to them, because of fear and a lack of willingness to be compassionate. How do you think Jesus feels about this avoidance? Where would we be if God had not shown us His mercy?

MAKE IT HAPPEN

Almost every family is dealing with some form of substance abuse. Many organizations, such as hospitals, halfway houses, and soup kitchens, are in need of volunteers. Right in our own neighborhoods and communities, we can make a difference. This week make a special effort to show compassion to someone. Observe and study people and allow God to demonstrate his mercy through you for their physical and/or spiritual needs.

FOLLOW THE SPIRIT

What God wants me to do:

_____

_____

REMEMBER YOUR THOUGHTS

Special insights you learned:

_____

_____

MORE LIGHT ON THE TEXT
MATTHEW 9:18-31; 35-36

18 While he spake these things unto them, behold, there came a certain ruler, and worshipped him, saying, My daughter is even now dead: but come and lay thy hand upon her, and she shall live.

An official of the government came to Jesus and told him that his daughter had just died. He came in respect, taking time to bow and worship before Jesus, acknowledging who He was, before he made his request. He came in faith, clearly expecting Jesus would raise her from the dead. He went even so far as to tell Jesus how to do it: "Lay your hand on her," he said, "and she will live."

This man had lost his daughter! Research has shown that the loss of a child is the most devastating death to cope with. No parent ever expects to have to bury their own child. But this official doesn't come asking Jesus "why" his daughter died. This is the question we are all tempted to ask at times like these. We ask, but we usually get no answer, because the only answer is the one Jesus gives in John 16:33: In the world we will have tribulation.

19 And Jesus arose, and followed him, and so did his disciples.

Jesus responded to the official's faith. And He always responds. He loves the kind of faith that gives people the boldness to come and ask and to believe He is able to do something to remedy the situation. Jesus and His disciples began to follow the official to his house.

20 And behold, a woman, which was diseased with an issue of blood twelve years, came behind him and touched the hem of his garment: 21 For she said within herself, If I may but touch his garment, I shall be whole.

Jesus and the disciples didn't get very far before they encountered this woman, another person in need of healing from Jesus. She had been suffering with a hemorrhage for 12 years! It's easy to read that in black and white, but imagine going day after day for 12 years experiencing it. Somehow she had endured, until the day she saw Jesus coming toward her through the crowd.

Perhaps she didn't have the same boldness that made the official able to approach Jesus directly. And, of course, it was taboo for a menstruating woman to touch a man; she was considered unclean. So she had to overcome that barrier as she came up behind Him and touched the hem of His garment.

She had been convincing herself all the way, as she maneuvered through the crowd, "If I can just touch His garment, I shall get well." She had the same kind of dynamic faith as the official, faith that enabled her to believe, "Nothing shall be impossible" for Jesus (Matthew 17:20).

22 But Jesus turned him about, and when he saw her, he said, Daughter, be of good comfort, thy faith hath made thee whole. And the woman was made whole from that hour.

Jesus recognized, responded to, and rewarded that faith. He first told her to be of good comfort, recognizing how tired she was, being in that condition for so long. She was, as we often say, sick and tired of being sick and tired. He knew what she had been through and knew she needed comfort in the midst of her affliction. Then He gave her the joyous news that her disease had been cured. Her faith had made her well, from that very hour. It was almost as though she was raised from the dead; she certainly had new life after her encounter with Jesus.

And sometimes we have to come to Jesus just like this woman. We have to make our way through the crowd and other obstacles, perhaps crawling, getting to Him any way we can. We need to have the kind of faith that keeps us going, knowing if we can just touch the hem of His garment, we can be whole. No matter what our issue, Jesus brings healing and new life into our situations and circumstances.

23 And when Jesus came into the ruler's house, and saw the minstrels and the people making a noise,

When Jesus arrived at the official's house, He found they had already begun to mourn. The musicians had been hired and there was a crowd there loudly grieving the loss of this girl. In their minds, it was settled, the child was dead. There was nothing left to do but go through the motions of bereavement.

24 He said unto them, Give place: for the maid is not dead, but sleepeth. And they laughed him to scorn.

He began to speak the truth to them all, saying that the girl was not dead, but asleep. They laughed at Him, the text says, to scorn. It must have seemed ludicrous. This prophet coming into a house of death and saying these ridiculous things. It seemed just as ridiculous to them then, as it might to some today.

A pastor in Kenya told the story of how he was conducting a funeral service and some members of the family asked him to stop while they prayed for their loved one to be raised from the dead. Unfortunately they were not able to see this same kind of miracle. But it is easy to imagine people laughing and shaking their heads over the ridiculousness of it.

Sometimes the things we believe, by faith, might seem ridiculous to others. When we tell them what we are praying for, or believing in, they might laugh us to scorn. But faith in Jesus is no laughing matter. Laughter and disbelief cannot coexist with faith.

25 But when the people were put forth, he went in, and took her by the hand, and the maid arose.

The people who laughed were "put forth." They had to be removed from the house. Only then could Jesus perform the miracle; when unbelief was not present. He took the little girl by the hand and she arose.

There is surely a lot of sickness, and many accidents claim the lives of people we love, at all ages. It seems we can come to terms better with the loss of someone older, but no matter how young or old the person is, those left behind

experience a lot of pain and grief.

But we need to be aware that Jesus weeps with us, just as He wept at the tomb of Lazarus (John 11:35). Jesus knows and feels our pain. He is with us, to assure us, just as He assured Martha that He is the resurrection and the life (John 11:25). Jesus has won the victory over death. Because of that, we can know that our loved ones live on in His kingdom, and we can be reunited with them one day. So let us not grieve as those who have no hope (1 Thessalonians 4:13).

26 And the fame hereof went abroad into all that land.

The news about Jesus continued to spread. This is truly the Gospel, the Good News Jesus said He was anointed to preach, when He stood up in the temple, as recorded in the Gospel of Luke. He said that He had come to heal the brokenhearted, to preach deliverance to the captives and the recovering of sight to the blind, to set at liberty them that are bruised (Luke 4:18). It is the same Good News we should be spreading today.

27 And when Jesus departed thence, two blind men followed him, crying and saying, Thou son of David, have mercy on us. 28 And when he was

come into the house, the blind men came to him: and Jesus saith unto them, Believe ye that I am able to do this? They said unto him, Yea, Lord. 29 Then touched he their eyes, saying, According to your faith be it unto you. 30 And their eyes were opened; and Jesus straitly charged them, saying, See that no man know it. 31 But they, when they departed, spread abroad his fame in all that country.

This is one more miracle Jesus performed in response to faith. The blind men came to Him, seeking healing. They referred to Him as the Son of David which indicated that they viewed Him as the Messiah, the promised one (Ezekiel 34:23). Jesus tested their faith to see if they really believed He could do what they were asking Him to do. They answered that they did believe. And then, when he touched them, He emphasized again that it was being done to them, according to their faith. They were healed, their eyes were opened and they received their sight. Jesus sent word to John the Baptist that the blind were receiving their sight as evidence He was indeed the Messiah (Matthew 11:5). This miracle is evidence to us as well, that Jesus is the Messiah, the One who fulfills prophecy, the one who comes as Immanuel, God with us, and heals all our diseases.

And as we consider our faith, we might ask the same question of ourselves. Do we really believe Jesus is able to do what we are asking Him to do? Or do we have doubts swirling around in the back of our minds? The book of James tells us to have faith and not to doubt (James 1:6). This is not easy, sometimes. Faith has been described as a muscle; the more we use it, the stronger it gets and the heavier the load it can lift. We need to constantly work to strengthen and increase our faith.

The words of the hymn, Amazing Grace, "I once was blind, but now I see," express the reality of our experience many times. Blindness can affect more than the body; it can also be the state of our soul. When we are in need of salvation, we are blind. Sometimes the circumstances of our lives blind us to the goodness of God and the way out of our troubles. Whatever the cause of our blindness, we can cry out, with faith, like these men. And Jesus will have mercy on us, touch us, and enable us to see.

Jesus cautioned them not to tell anyone about what they had experienced. But the news was too good for them to keep to themselves. They added to the fame that Jesus was gaining around the country.

35 And Jesus went about all the cities and vil- lages, teaching in their synagogues, and preaching the gospel of the kingdom, and healing every sickness and every disease among the people. 36 But when he saw the multitudes, he was moved with compassion on them, because they fainted, and were scattered abroad, as sheep having no shepherd.

Jesus continued to teach, and preach the Gospel and to heal. He did it all with compassion. The Greek word that is translated "compassion" is *splagchnizomai* (pronounced **splangkh-nid-zo-mai**), which is a strong word meaning pity and compassion that comes from deep within a person's being. Jesus was greatly moved, touched, and affected by the plight of the persons he observed. He saw their struggles; He felt their pain and frustration; He knew how lost they were. The writer of Matthew says He saw them in a scattered and pitiful state, as sheep without a shepherd.

He knows about our struggles too, and continues to be moved with compassion for our plight. He wants to be our shepherd; He has already laid down his life for us (John 10:11). All we have to do is accept Him and respond to the Good News of the Gospel. Then the benefits and blessings of the kingdom will be ours, both now and forever.

DAILY BIBLE READING

M: Jesus Continues His Healing Word
Matthew 8:1-13
T: Jesus Heals the Gadarene Demoniacs
Matthew 8:28 9:1
W: Jesus Heals a Paralytic
Matthew 9:2-8
T: Jesus Gives Life and Healing
Matthew 9:18-26
F: Jesus Heals the Blind and Mute
Matthew 9:27-38
S: Jesus Heals a Man's Withered Hand
Matthew 12:9-14
S: The Faith of a Canaanite Woman
Matthew 15:21-31

TEACHING TIPS

January 23
Bible Study Guide 8

1. Words You Should Know

A. Blasphemy. The Greek word *blasphemos*, refers to a person who sees with his own eyes the power of the Lord and declares it to be Satanic. This represents the condition of the heart to be beyond divine illumination and therefore hopeless.

B. Condemnation. To disapprove of strongly; the act of declaring guilty; convicted; infliction of a penalty. Since the Pharisees did not believe Jesus to be the Messiah and accused Him of working miracles through the prince of demons, they were condemned to be judged by their followers.

C. Confirmation. Validating by formal approval; to prove to be true; verification. The Pharisees wanted Jesus to prove Himself to be the Messiah by validating it to be true.

2. Teacher Preparation

A. Begin preparing for the class by reading the Devotional Reading.

B. Listen to a Bible audio tape of the entire Book of Matthew to gain an overview. Then read the BACKGROUND.

3. Starting the Lesson

A. Open the class with prayer.

B. If possible, divide the class into five sections. Give each group one of the AT-A-GLANCE segments.

4. Getting into the lesson

A. Ask students from each section to read from the FOCAL VERSES.

B. Ask one student to read the LESSON AIM to the entire class.

C. Allow each group to study their portion of the IN DEPTH section for at least 15 minutes.

D. Have the class come back together.

5. Relating the lesson to life

A. Ask the class whether or not they have experienced opposition.

B. Discuss how Jesus handled His opposition. Relate how we should handle opposition in our lives.

C. Read the KEEP IN MIND verse.

6. Arousing action

A. Ask students to find ways during the week to deal with situations of opposition and report back next week on the outcome.

B. Assign MAKE IT HAPPEN and SEARCH THE SCRIPTURES to the class as homework.

C. Close the class with prayer.

OPPOSITION TO JESUS

Bible Background • MATTHEW 12:22-45
Printed Text • MATTHEW 12:22-32, 38-40
Devotional Reading • MATTHEW 12:1-14

LESSON AIM

By the end of the lesson students will understand that a person either stands with Christ believing and trusting in Him, or else a person stands against Him in unbelief and distrust.

KEEP IN MIND

"He that is not with me is against me; and he that gathereth not with me scattereth abroad" (Matthew 12:30).

FOCAL VERSES

MATTHEW 12:22 Then was brought unto him one possessed with a devil, blind, and dumb: and he healed him, insomuch that the blind and dumb both spake and saw.

23 And all the people were amazed, and said, Is not this the son of David?

24 But when the Pharisees heard it, they said, This fellow doth not cast out devils, but by Beelzebub the prince of the devils.

25 And Jesus knew their thoughts, and said unto them, Every kingdom divided against itself is brought to desolation; and every city or house divided against itself shall not stand:

26 And if Satan cast out Satan, he is divided against himself; how shall then his kingdom stand?

27 And if I by Beelzebub cast out devils, by whom do your children cast them out? therefore they shall be your judges.

28 But if I cast out devils by the Spirit of God, then the kingdom of God is come unto you.

29 Or else how can one enter into a strong man's house, and spoil his goods, except he first bind the strong man? and then he will spoil his house.

30 He that is not with me is against me; and he that gathereth not with me scattereth abroad.

LESSON OVERVIEW

LESSON AIM
KEEP IN MIND
FOCAL VERSES
IN FOCUS
THE PEOPLE, PLACES, AND TIMES
BACKGROUND
AT-A-GLANCE
IN DEPTH
SEARCH THE SCRIPTURES
DISCUSS THE MEANING
LESSON IN OUR SOCIETY
MAKE IT HAPPEN
FOLLOW THE SPIRIT
REMEMBER YOUR THOUGHTS
MORE LIGHT ON THE TEXT
DAILY BIBLE READINGS

31 Wherefore I say unto you, All manner of sin and blasphemy shall be forgiven unto men: but the blasphemy against the Holy Ghost shall not be forgiven unto men.

32 And whosoever speaketh a word against the Son of man, it shall be forgiven him: but whosoever speaketh against the Holy Ghost, it shall not be forgiven him, neither in this world, neither in the world to come.

38 Then certain of the scribes and of the Pharisees answered, saying, Master, we would see a sign from thee.

39 But he answered and said unto them, An evil and adulterous generation seeketh after a sign; and there shall no sign be given to it, but the sign of the prophet Jonas:

40 For as Jonas was three days and three nights in the whale's belly; so shall the Son of man be three days and three nights in the heart of the earth.

IN FOCUS

Elder Johnson was finally getting that needed rest. Of course, it was not exactly how he had pictured it, because he was in the cardiac section of the hospital. The doctors said he had suffered a mild heart attack and put him on complete bed rest. From his bed, Elder Johnson reflected on the circumstances leading up to his hospitalization. He had wanted to see the church increase in members by conducting mid-week Bible study, street evangelism, and Friday night fellowships. Unfortunately, the church board did not see it that way. In fact, they were quite clear in what they wanted. "We don't believe in all that running around the street stuff," they had said. "We hired you to preach on Sunday mornings and that's all!" But Elder Johnson knew God wanted him to do much more than conduct Sunday morning services, so he continued to stress the importance of reaching the lost souls for Christ. Arguments had broken out among the members; some agreed with Elder Johnson, while others agreed with the board. The last straw came after Sunday morning service when the board members asked him to resign his post. The stress simply became too much, and his wife rushed him to the hospital.

God sent His Son into the world equipped to handle opposition from religious leaders. Today's lesson teaches us how Jesus dealt with opposition.

THE PEOPLE, PLACES, AND TIMES

BLASPHEMY. The Greek word *blasphemos* means to speak evil toward God; the cursing or reviling of God; contemptuous or irreverent speech about God or things regarded as sacred; a transliteration of a Greek word meaning literally "to speak harm" in the Biblical context. Blasphemy is an attitude of disrespect that finds expression in an act directed against the character of God. In the Old Testament, the punishment for the crime of blasphemy against the name of God was meted out by the community who took the offender outside of the city and stoned him to death (Leviticus 24:14). The third commandment states we must not take the name of the Lord our God in vain (Exodus 20:7).

BEELZEBUB. The Greek word *beezeboul* is a name given by the Jewish people for Satan, the prince of demons, perhaps derived from Baal-Zebub, god of the Philistine city Ekron (2 Kings 1:2). Baal means "lord," and Baal-Zebub means "lord of the fly" which was worshiped by the Philistines as the producer of flies with the ability to defend the people against the pests.

BACKGROUND

Jesus was no longer welcome to teach in the synagogues. There was rising opposition to Christ both from the religious (Matthew 12:1-45) and his own family (vv. 46-50). Jesus, King of the Jews, was being rejected by the religious rulers because He claimed to be the Messiah. But the people were amazed by His works and began to question whether or not He was the Son of David spoken of by the prophet Isaiah who would come and open blinded eyes (Isaiah 29:18-19). Never had such a thing been seen in Israel (Matthew 9:33). The Pharisees were growing increasingly agitated by Jesus' miracles, which they could not perform. Large crowds were following Jesus, and the Pharisees were terrified of losing their position as religious leaders with power over the people. They plotted on how they might destroy Him (12:14).

IN DEPTH

1. The Act and the Accusation (Matthew 12:22-24)

Jesus proved His messianic power with a man who was demon-possessed, blind, and mute by healing him so that he both spoke and saw (v. 22). This was the only time someone was healed of both blindness and muteness. The people were amazed and said, "Is not this the son of David, the promised Messiah?" (v. 23). It was believed the man's demon possession was the cause of his maladies. Although the Pharisees practiced exorcism of demonic spirits, they could not heal the blind and the mute. The author, Matthew says Jesus healed the man immediately without speaking to him as He had done when He caused the spirits to enter into swine which ultimately drowned (8:28-34).

Jesus has been given all power over all things by the Father. There is nothing so binding us that Jesus cannot free us. No drugs, no alcohol, no perversion. Everything that Jesus did is too numerous to be recorded in the Bible, but by faith we can experience them. For example, a marriage that appears to be completely over can be restored by asking Jesus to fix it and then obeying Him while He does. There is nothing that He cannot do if we only have faith.

The Pharisees denied Christ and said He was of the devil. When they saw the people turning to Christ, they purposed to shatter the people's hope and belief for fear of losing their positions of religious authority and possibly their control of the people. They charged Jesus with being from the devil and working through the power of the devil (v. 24).

2. The Explanation (vv. 25-26)

Jesus remained level headed, calm, and proceeded to prove He was of God and the true Messiah. He answered the charges of the Pharisees with logical, irrefutable reasoning. Jesus stated that a kingdom divided destroys itself. If Satan casts out Satan, he is divided against himself. "How shall then his kingdom stand?" (v. 26) The evidence of supernatural power was clearly seen and admitted by

Christ's enemies. People were being healed and miracles performed by some force other than human power.

The Pharisees charged His power was evil and not from God. In other words, Christ was sent to deceive people and lead them away from traditional religion and beliefs. Jesus' argument was Satan is not going to empower anyone to deliver people from evil, like Jesus was doing time after time. His works and power had to be of God. His works were too numerous, too immense, too good, too virtuous, and too effective to be from any source other than God.

Christ's very purpose for coming to earth was to conquer Satan and break his power. You are either for Him or against Him.

3. The Condemnation (vv. 27-30)

Jesus addressed the Pharisees' question directly, "If I cast out demons by Beelzebub, by whom do your followers cast them out?" The Pharisees knew their exorcism of evil spirits was done by the power of God. In fact, exorcism of evil spirits by the power of Satan is an impossibility. Jesus pointed out the folly of their accusations by explaining that no house or kingdom divided against itself could stand. Therefore, by condemning Jesus' exorcism by the power of God, they were condemning themselves by opposing the works of God and their followers would be their judges (v. 27).

If Jesus cast our demons by the power of God, then the kingdom of God was directly present with the people. The people believed it because of the miracles they witnessed, but the religious leaders denied it because of their rituals and traditions.

A strong man has to be bound before his property can be taken (v. 29). Satan is the strong man, and Christ invaded Satan's house and his property was taken. Jesus has bound Satan. He enters Satan's house to free those who are imprisoned and takes Satan's (human) goods. He is turning men from darkness to light, and from the power of Satan to God, that they may receive forgiveness of sins, and everlasting life.

Jesus bound Satan during His temptation in the wilderness. For the first time in history, Satan confronted a man whom he could not lead away from God. Jesus bound Satan as He resisted temptation after temptation and then stood fast. Each time He overcame a test and trial, Satan was bound a little more. At the Garden of Gethsemane, Christ could have avoided the cross, but chose to obey God. At the cross, He secured perfect righteousness. He had never sinned, for God had made Him, who knew no sin, to be sin for us, that we might be made the righteousness of God in Him (2 Corinthians 5:21). Satan's domain of evil and sin was broken. Christ, as the perfect man, stood for an

embrace all men who would place their lives into His keeping. You are either for Him or against Him. No straddling the fence!

With Christ or against Christ, "He that is not with me is against me; and he that gathereth not with me scattereth abroad" (v. 30). This could be a picture of a shepherd or a farmer. Each is involved in gathering; one gathers sheep, and the other gathers crops. There is the possibility that each could be guilty of scattering. Christ pulls no punches when He states you are either with Him or against Him. A person either believes and trusts Christ or stands against Him in unbelief and distrust. A person works with Him in gathering others, or else works against Him by scattering others. There is no demilitarized zone! There are two sides, with Christ or against Christ.

Refraining or abstaining from evil is not enough. We must gather together with Christ. We must consistently do good. If we do not gather together with Christ, we scatter. You either are for Him or against Him.

4. The Eternal Separation (vv. 31-32)

The Pharisees had ascribed the works Jesus did to the devil, but, in fact, His works were a sign of God's Spirit rested upon Him. Attributing the works of the Holy Spirit, which worked through Jesus, to be from the devil was the unpardonable sin. Frequently we hear the name of God and Jesus Christ being blasphemed. It does not mean the Holy Spirit is more important than God or His Son Jesus Christ.

This situation existed only while Christ was ministering here on earth and appearing just as any other Jewish man. Evil spoken against the Holy Spirit was evil coming from the heart directed to God, the final authority. However, after the day of Pentecost, when Jesus was proven to be God's Christ, to reject Jesus Christ became the unpardonable sin. So it is today. We have all known people who have lived sinful, depraved lives for years and later repented and given their lives to Jesus. They are now living for God. Jesus made it clear that all sins can be forgiven. But God cannot forgive the rejection of His Son. It is the Spirit that bears witness to Christ and convicts the lost sinner. The Spirit regenerates the heart of man that he may understand and accept the ways and will of God. You are either with Him or against Him.

5. No Confirmation (vv. 38-40)

When some scribes and Pharisees asked Jesus for a sign, He responded that the only sign would be that of Jonah. The Jews required a sign; they always required signs for any prophet or messenger who claimed to be sent from God. They wanted more than the signs of miracles. They wanted something spectacular, such as an event occurring in the sky appearing upon Jesus command. "For the Jews require a sign, and the Greeks seek after wisdom" (1 Corinthians 1:22).

Jesus called them an evil generation and there shall no sign be given except the sign of the prophet Jonas (Matthew 12:39). They wanted Jesus to prove His Messianship by some spectacular sign so they could believe. They were unwilling to believe because they were apostates, who went after signs and works instead of seeking the God of faith and love. Jesus stated they would receive only the sign of Jonas, the prophet, which points to the resurrection of Christ from the dead. The resurrection is the great proof that Jesus is the Messiah. You either believe He was resurrected from the dead or you do not. You are either with Him or against Him.

SEARCH THE SCRIPTURES

1. Jesus healed a _____ _____ man who was both _____ and mute (Matthew 12:22).

2. The Pharisees accused Jesus of casting out devils by the power of _____ (v. 24).

3. Jesus explained to the Pharisees that a kingdom divided against itself cannot _____ (v. 25).

4. All manner of sin and _____ shall be forgiven men, except the _____ against the Holy Spirit (v. 31).

5. Jesus answered by saying, "And there shall no _____ be given to it" (v. 39).

DISCUSS THE MEANING

1. Why did the Pharisees accuse Jesus of healing the demon-possessed, blind, and mute man by the power of Beelzebub?

2. What does it mean to blaspheme the Holy Spirit?

3. What does it mean to blaspheme Jesus?

LESSON IN OUR SOCIETY

Today in our society, profanity and sex have become very commonplace. We are bombarded with it on television, young children curse, and teens are involved in many types of immoral sex acts. But they who know their God will do great exploits (Daniel 11:32). Christ came doing those things which He saw His Father do. Since we are in the world but not of the world, one of the greatest exploits we can perform is showing the world the love of Christ by the way we live our lives. This week be challenged. Do not act like the world; ask Jesus to deliver you from the spirit of profanity and lust. Then refrain from using any form of

profanity, or watching sex scenes on television or video.

MAKE IT HAPPEN

Most people run into opposition at one time or another, because people do not agree with us about everything. Jesus said He was the Messiah, but the Pharisees opposed this by accusing Him of being a blasphemer. As Christians, we are frequently accused of not behaving like servants of God. This week make a list of those things about yourself that you know are not pleasing to God. From the list, choose one particular behavior that you know is most unpleasing and write down what you believe to be a good solution. Before the class meets next week, find a situation where you may begin on working to improve your behavior. Example: When people do not agree with you, you snap at them or talk about them behind their backs. Solution: This week buy a scriptural card of encouragement and personally give it to them.

FOLLOW THE SPIRIT

What God wants me to do:

_____

_____

REMEMBER YOUR THOUGHTS

Special insights you have learned:

_____

_____

MORE LIGHT ON THE TEXT
MATTHEW 12:22-32, 38-40

22 Then was brought to Him one possessed with a devil, blind, and dumb: and he healed him, insomuch that the blind and dumb man both spake and saw.

Jesus continued to demonstrate His authority over demons and His power to heal all kinds of illnesses and diseases. Jesus can heal us and set us free as well, from whatever binds us and keeps us from seeing and speaking. No weapon formed against us shall prosper (Isaiah 54:17).

23 And all the people were amazed, and said, Is not this the son of David?

A demonstration of God's supernatural ability, is always amazing. This miracle caused the multitudes to begin to wonder whether Jesus might really be the Son of David, the Messiah, the promised one (Ezekiel 34:23). The two blind men had already referred to Jesus by this title (Matthew 9:27); now it was being accepted by the multitudes.

24 But when the Pharisees heard it, they said, This fellow doth not cast out devils but by Beelzebub the prince of the devils.

This was too much for the Pharisees. They considered it impossible. They had already made up their minds that Jesus could not possibly be the Messiah. So they decided to accuse Him of being in league with Beelzebub, another name for Satan. They were, in essence, accusing Him of magic and sorcery which was punishable by death.

When presented by a truth that is threatening to our "already-made-up-minds," we sometimes react this same way. Even in the face of overwhelming evidence, we dig in our heels and refuse to be open to the reality that is staring us in the face.

25 And Jesus knew their thoughts, and said unto them, Every kingdom divided against itself is brought to desolation and every city or house divided against itself shall not stand: 26 And if Satan cast out Satan, he is divided against himself: how shall then his kingdom stand?

Jesus, who knew their thoughts immediately, was quick to point out how ludicrous and ridiculous their accusation was. He used basic logic, saying any kingdom, city, or house, divided against itself, shall not stand. Even the stubborn Pharisees had to admit this was true and their assertion, itself, could not stand.

27 And if I by Beelzebub cast out devils, by whom do your children cast them out? therefore they shall be your judges.

Jesus went on, to strengthen His rebuttal, by saying that if He was truly casting out demons by the power of Beelzebub, then all those who are associated with the Pharisees (here referred to figuratively as their "children") could be casting out demons by this same power. Of course, the Pharisees would not want to link their own people to this demonic source of power. To do so might bring down on them the anger and judgment of those others, who indeed did do exorcisms by the power of God. Jesus had cleverly painted them into a corner, through His brilliant reasoning.

28 But if I cast out devils by the Spirit of God, then the kingdom of God is come unto you.

Jesus made a very clear statement here, that He was doing exorcisms through power of the Spirit of God. He pointed out this was evidence that the kingdom of God had arrived. It was present then to the people of Israel, as it is present for us today. We live in that mystical tension of knowing the kingdom is already here, but not yet here in its

fullness. But we should live knowing we are children of the King, and His kingdom has all authority and power over demons, sickness, and sin.

29 Or else how can one enter into a strong man s house, and spoil his goods, except he first bind the strong man? and then he will spoil his house.

The strong man in this verse is Beelzebub, or Satan. Jesus asserts that although Satan is strong, Jesus is stronger and has the power to bind him. Once Satan is bound, then his property, those he has held captive, can be released and set free. Again this applies to all people, who are bound by the power of the enemy. Jesus has the power to set them free, as He stated, He is anointed to preach deliverance to the captives and set at liberty those who are bruised (Luke 4:18). As His disciples, we have the power and authority to bind the strong man and set the captives free in Jesus' name.

30 He that is not with me is against me: and he that gathereth not with me scattereth abroad.

This verse speaks strongly to those who say they can be "spiritual" without being Christian. Jesus was drawing a line and saying if we are not firmly "for" Him, we are "against" Him. There is no middle ground or point of neutrality. Those who are lukewarm, God spews out of His mouth (Revelation 3:16).

Many have said they believe in Jesus as a great teacher or prophet, but they do not believe that He is the Saviour. This verse speaks to them saying that if they are not "for" Him, acknowledging all He has revealed Himself to be, then they are against Him. This verse says if they are not gathering people into the kingdom, then they are actually scattering them. This is a strong warning.

31 Wherefore I say unto you, All manner of sin and blasphemy shall be forgiven unto men: but the blasphemy against the Holy Ghost shall not be forgiven unto men. 32 And whosoever speaketh a word against the Son of man, it shall be forgiven him: but whosoever speaketh against the Holy Ghost, it shall not be forgiven him, neither in this world, neither in the world to come.

The key to understanding this very difficult passage is to recognize that it is tied into the preceding verses. Jesus was still addressing those who have attributed the deliverance He had performed by the power of the Spirit to Satan. This was a very serious charge. He says to slander another human being, or even Him, could be forgiven. But this was a sin against the Holy Spirit, an unforgivable sin! It is unforgivable because attributing God's work to Satan leaves no room for salvation. It is a rejection of God s plan of salvation and amounts to apostasy, or walking away from the faith.

Jesus' whole mission and ministry is based on the power of the Holy Spirit to carry it forward. Those who would see the evidence of this power and how it works for good, and still stand stubbornly and attribute it to Satan or evil, cannot be forgiven.

This verse has troubled many, who come to their pastors, seeking counseling, afraid they have committed this unpardonable, unforgivable sin. But, as many commentators have said, those who worry they have committed the unpardonable sin, cannot be guilty of it. As long as people are concerned about whether they have offended the holiness and righteousness of God through their actions, as long as they recognize that the Holy Spirit is the power behind the healing and miracles they have witnessed, as long as they don t attribute God s power and goodness to Satan, they have not committed the unforgivable sin.

38 Then certain of the scribes and of the Pharisees answered, saying, Master, we would see a sign from thee.

A challenge, then, came forth from the scribes and Pharisees, asking for a sign they could see. They had seen numerous signs, in the miracles, deliverances, and healings Jesus had performed. But, as though they had seen nothing, they still asked for a sign. And this was the same group of people who had just accused Jesus of casting out demons in the name of Beelzebub. This was truly adding insult to injury! They were adamantly and stubbornly refusing to accept Jesus mission and ministry.

The term they use to refer to Jesus, translated "Master," is *didaskale* (pronounced **di-das-ka-le**) which means "teacher" in Greek. This is a formal term, which shows respect, equivalent to "Rabbi." But it is most often used in the Gospels by those who had not accepted Jesus. Those who were still resisting His message and refused to become His disciples referred to Jesus as Master.

Unbelievers today might be willing to admit Jesus is a great teacher, or prophet, but if they don't recognize Him as Immanuel, God with us, the Saviour, then they are still rejecting and resisting Him.

39 But he answered and said unto them, An evil and adulterous generation seeketh after a sign; and there shall no sign be given to it, but the sign of the prophet Jonas: 40 For as Jonas was three days and three nights in the whale s belly; so shall the Son of man be three days and three nights in the heart of the earth.

Jesus told them it is an evil and adulterous generation who asks for this type of confirmation. He is recorded as saying the same thing in Matthew 16:4 and Mark 8:12. He would never perform a miracle just to prove to someone who He is and what kind of power He has. Satan put Him to that kind of test in the wilderness and He resisted the temptation to use His power to prove who He was then (Matthew 4:3, 5).

Jesus told them they will only get one sign, that He, like Jonah, will be concealed inside the belly of the earth for three days and three nights. His death and resurrection would be the greatest sign pointing to who He is, but He knew they would still not believe, even when they saw it.

Today we can see so many signs: Creation, the Word of God (which contains fulfilled prophecy), miracles in people's lives, Jesus resurrection from the dead. But, amazingly, there are those who are not satisfied and still look for a sign. They want more proof that God exists, that Jesus is the way, the truth, and the life (John 14:6), that salvation and eternal life are real. They too are part of the evil and adulterous generation who are is caught up in seeking proof and being full of doubt that they miss the glorious gift Jesus came to give them.

DAILY BIBLE READING

M: Plucking Grain on the Sabbath
Matthew 12:1-8
T: Jesus Accused as Beelzebub's Man
Matthew 12:22-32
W: Understand the Signs of the Times!
Matthew 12:33-45
T: Jesus Is Rejected at Nazareth
Matthew 13:54-58
F: Confrontation between Jesus and the Pharisees
Matthew 15:1-9
S: Jesus' Enemies Demand a Sign
Matthew 16:1-12
S: Peter Declares that Jesus is Messiah
Matthew 16:13-20

TEACHING TIPS

January 30
Bible Study Guide 9

1. Words You Should Know

A. Laborer. Greek *ergo,* meaning to work or toil as in an occupation; doing labor or work; a person who works hard; an employee.

B. Wages. A pledge or payment, usually monetary remuneration, by an employer especially for labor or services according to contract and on an hourly, daily, or piecework basis.

2. Teacher Preparation

Call your students during the week before Sunday's lesson to pray for them. Ask them to read the upcoming lesson and think of ways they can work in God's kingdom and be prepared to share their answers in class on Sunday.

3. Starting the Lesson

A. Begin the lesson with prayer, asking the Lord to open our understanding. Ask students for testimonies of God's goodness.

B. Ask the students what it means to work in God's vineyard.

C. Have the class read the LESSON AIM and FOCAL VERSES.

4. Getting Into the Lesson

A. Choose someone to read the BACKGROUND.

B. The AT-A-GLANCE outline will help you to teach the lesson effectively, use it to point out the important principles of the lesson and IN DEPTH will add more insight.

C. SEARCH THE SCRIPTURE questions will help students to be aware of the context and content of this lesson.

5. Relating the Lesson to Life

A. Use the DISCUSS THE MEANING questions for thought-provoking discussion. But don't allow the class to become a debating session.

B. Sometimes students have difficulty believing that teachers and other leaders have areas in their lives where growth is necessary. Sharing your testimony will encourage students to be open and to share their experiences also.

6. Arousing Action

A. Ask the students to read LESSON IN OUR SOCIETY before sharing their list of ways to work in God's vineyard with the class.

B. Some of the student's ideas may be qualified as work in God's vineyard. Example: Call and pray with one of the elderly in the church. Offer to perform a task for them, such as clean a room or prepare a meal.

WORSHIP GUIDE

For the Superintendent or Teacher

JANUARY 30th

Theme: Laborers in the Vineyard
Theme Song: "Bringing in the Sheaves"
Scripture: Matthew 20:16
Song: "He Touched Me"

Meditation: Thank You, Dear Lord, for giving us a purpose for living. How wonderful it is to know that whether we come early or late to Your wonderful kingdom we are welcome. Help us not to grumble or complain about Your generosity towards others, but to be grateful for what You are doing in our lives.

LABORERS IN THE VINEYARD

Bible Background • MATTHEW 19:16—20:16
Printed Text • MATTHEW 20:1-16
Devotional Reading • MATTHEW 20:20-28

LESSON AIM

By the end of the lesson students will understand why Jesus used the parable of the laborers in the vineyard to teach His disciples, and the importance of having God's grace and generosity.

KEEP IN MIND

"So the last shall be first, and the first last: for many be called, but few chosen" (Matthew 20:16).

FOCAL VERSES

MATTHEW 20:1 For the kingdom of heaven is like unto a man that is an householder, which went out early in the morning to hire labourers into his vineyard.

2 And when he had agreed with the labourers for a penny a day, he sent them into his vineyard.

3 And he went out about the third hour, and saw others standing idle in the marketplace,

4 And said unto them; Go ye also into the vineyard, and whatsoever is right I will give you. And they went their way.

5 Again he went out about the sixth and ninth hour, and did likewise.

6 And about the eleventh hour he went out, and found others standing idle, and saith unto them, Why stand ye here all the day idle?

7 They say unto him, Because no man hath hired us. He saith unto them, Go ye also into the vineyard; and whatsoever is right, that shall ye receive.

8 So when even was come, the lord of the vineyard saith unto his steward, Call the labourers, and give them their hire, beginning from the last unto the first.

9 And when they came that were hired about the eleventh hour, they received every man a penny.

10 But when the first came, they supposed that they should have received more; and they likewise received every man a penny.

11 And when they had received it, they murmured against the goodman of the house,

12 Saying, These last have wrought but one hour, and thou hast made them equal unto us, which have borne the burden and heat of the day.

13 But he answered one of them, and said, Friend, I do thee no wrong: didst not thou agree with me for a penny?

14 Take that thine is, and go thy way: I will give unto this last, even as unto thee.

15 Is it not lawful for me to do what I will with mine own? Is thine eye evil, because I am good?

16 So the last shall be first, and the first last: for many be called, but few chosen.

IN FOCUS

"It just isn't fair!" thought Michael. "This is the second time that I've been asked to be acting supervisor in Phillip's absence. He may be the supervisor, but I am performing the job and everybody says I'm much better than he is. After Phillip's last lengthy illness he has not been in the office for a full pay period!"

Every time Michael thought about the money part of it, he got angry all over again. Company policy stated that when a supervisor was off on leave, the acting supervisor would assume the duties and receive supervisory pay. Upon the return of the supervisor, the acting supervisor would resume his old position and revert back to his former salary. Michael had made up his mind that whenever the supervisor returned, he would quit unless the company offered him the supervisory position on a permanent basis.

Today's lesson is on the right attitude for kingdom work.

THE PEOPLE, PLACES, AND TIMES

MONEY. Money is anything used as a medium of exchange including that which is authorized by governments. The word is first mentioned in the Bible by God when he told Abraham to use it to purchase servants. Before people ceased to roam the lands as nomads, animals, produce, and services were used for bargaining, but that became cumbersome. Nevertheless, as communities and cities were established, metals replaced the items traded. In Jesus' day a denarius, which is also known as a penny, was paid as a fair day's wage to the Roman soldier. Since it was difficult to transport the metals in their raw form, gold, silver, copper, and bronze were weighed, refined, imprinted with images and/or symbols, and stamped into coins. A person could easily transport coins in leather pouches or purses and carry them concealed on their person.

BACKGROUND

Jesus had just finished answering the question of a young man of wealth and position, presumably a ruler of a synagogue, on what good thing he could do to have eternal life. Jesus' response dealt with the riches of the world versus the kind of righteousness required to enter His kingdom. The young man, having confessed to keeping the law, knew that there was still something lacking in his life. Then Jesus told him to go and sell what he had, give it to the poor, and then follow Him. With sadness, the young man walked away.

Jesus explained to His disciples that it was easier for a camel to go through the eye of a needle than for a rich person to give up his possessions and enter the kingdom of heaven (Matthew 19:24). This amazed the disciples who had left all they had to follow Jesus. With man it was impossible, but with God all things are possible (v. 26). Peter wanted to know what reward they would receive by being obedient to Christ. And Jesus told them that they would sit on twelve thrones and judge the twelve tribes of Israel (v. 28).

However, the Lord detected a possible wrong motive in Peter's question. He warned the disciples that some who were first in their own eyesight would be last in the judg-

ment, and some who were last would end up first. This truth is magnified in the parable of the workers in the vineyard.

IN DEPTH

1. God's Grace in the Morning (Matthew 20:1-2)

This parable is recorded only by Matthew. The landowner hired laborers at the day's beginning to work for a contracted sum of a denarius, or a penny, for a days work (vv. 1-2). When the Lord appoint laborers for kingdom work, it will always be the right assignment for the right task, because God is sovereign and will always compensate a worker according to the services rendered. One hour of trustful, humble service is of greater value to God than a lifetime of self-serving zeal.

The landowner sought laborers early in the morning, about 6:00 a.m. The "early birds" who were earnest about being hired were already out. Most adults today want jobs with clearly defined terms of work and remuneration just as the landowner agreed with the laborers (v. 2). The penny offered for a day's work was the going rate for the day. When the landowner offered it, the laborers knew that they were being offered a good wage. Today, however, we are not very trustful of our employers. Whatever the going wage is, we feel that we are worth more, and the employer is getting over on us. The workers who were hired first served because they wanted a guaranteed wage and they were working for the temporal benefits only.

In the kingdom of God, many people seek the Lord early in their lives. This does not make them more spiritual than the people who come later, but it does allow for more years of serving the Lord. The disciples wanted to know what they would receive by giving up all to serve Christ. The right attitude for us is to be willing to trust the sovereignty of God's grace as we serve Him with our whole hearts. "Eye hath not seen, nor ear heard, neither have entered into the heart of man, the things which God hath prepared for them that love him" (1 Corinthians 2:9). The object here is to learn that we should not serve God because we expect a reward, nor insist on knowing what we shall receive. We must trust Him and believe that He will always give what is best.

2. God's Grace at Midday (vv. 3-5)

The landowner went out again at 9 a.m. to hire workers for the vineyard. God shows His infinite compassion in this parable towards His people. At the sixth and the ninth hours, the afternoon of a person's life, God seeks to draw them into His kingdom. Always, God is drawing His children to Him. In the midst of our mess, He is drawing us not by might or by power, but by His Spirit.

The young adults who seek God in our churches are far

---

too often ridiculed for their attire, their music, and their lifestyle. What about God's grace? When the young people sincerely accept Christ into their hearts, what is on the inside (Jesus) will show up on the outside! They must be loved, encouraged, and discipled shown how to live a right-eous life.

It is said that an idle mind is the devil's workshop. Without direction for our lives we will idle away God's gift of life and open up ourselves to the wiles of Satan. As others come into the kingdom, we must be careful not to claim ourselves to be super saints because we have been Christians longer. The Church does not belong to us, but to Jesus. There is always room at the Cross for newcomers. Although we cannot work our way into heaven, the Scriptures tell us, "Faith without works is dead" (James 2:20). Christians work in God's vineyard for the joy of serv-ing Him. Nevertheless, the person who comes early and the person who comes later, both receive the same welcome into the kingdom from God.

3. God's Grace in the Evening (vv. 6-7)

God never gives up on us. We cannot earn what God gives us nor can we put God in our debt. What God gives to us is by His grace. There are those who spend their younger years on self pleasure—hanging out with their friends and being the life of the party. When asked, "Why stand ye here all the day idle?" They say unto him, "Because no man hath hired us." You must be where the hiring is taking place. This answer was just an excuse for not being responsible. Have we encouraged others to feel that the church belongs to them too? Have we taken new believ-ers under our wing to disciple them, or are they standing around idle?

The Jews knew they were the chosen people and looked down on the Gentiles. Believing themselves to have already entered into God's kingdom, they felt that everyone else was unworthy to enter, especially the Gentiles. Usually they hated and despised the Gentiles and hoped for nothing but their destruction. When an elderly person comes to the Lord, it can be considered the "eleventh hour" of their lives. Those who come into the vineyard later in life some-times feel unworthy. But when they come, it is truly a glory to God since many elderly people are set in their ways, afraid to make changes and fearful of other people.

The eleventh hour is just before sunset, around 5:00 p.m., which leaves about an hour for laborers to work. In an individual's life, it means there is a short time left to work for God. Nevertheless, for the elderly, to trust the Word of God and accept salvation is wonderful.

"No man hath hired us," is a poor excuse to offer God. Yet God's grace extends to the willingness of a heart to work for Him and He tells them, "Go ye also into the vine-yard." The latecomers agree to "whatsoever is right, that

shall ye receive," trusting the landowner to reward them fairly. They are satisfied by being employed at all.

4. God as the Landowner (vv. 8-16)

In Matthew 19:27, Peter poses the question to Jesus, "We have left all and followed you. Therefore what shall we have?" The Lord detects a possible wrong motive in the question. We are to serve out of love and gratitude.

Imagine one of the workers who was hired first but paid last. After seeing the men who were hired last receive a full day's pay, they assumed they would receive much more, but the owner gave each man one penny each. They com-plained that these last men had worked only one hour and received the same wage as those who bore the heat of the day.

The danger of Peter's question becomes obvious here. We too often assume that we deserve more when we've done nothing to deserve it. The first were only willing to work if they had a contract. The owner gave what was agreed upon, and they were dissatisfied because they com-pared themselves with the other workers. Judge nothing before the time (1 Corinthians 4:5). We look at the person, but God looks at the heart. We must serve Him and believe He will always do what is best. Beware of being critical of God's generosity, as these men were. Instead of rejoicing for the other men who received a penny, they felt left out, even though they received what was agreed upon. Those hired first grumbled when they received the same wage as those hired later, even though they had worked longer in the heat (vv. 11-12). We should trust God and not serve Him simply for a reward, be it temporal or eternal.

The goodness of the owner, who was concerned and cared for all the men, was shown by his giving each man enough. The men who were hired first were jealous and complained. This shows the real nature of their hearts; they were selfish and should have repented. They had little or no compassion for their brethren, who also had families and needs. The lesson here is not to be over-confident when it comes to the rewards of God. If you have served for 20, 30, or 40 years does not mean you will receive more, because those first in their own eyes, and the eyes of others, may be last in the judgment. Likewise do not be discouraged, for those who consider themselves unprofitable servants may end up first. Thus "the last shall be first, and the first last."

SEARCH THE SCRIPTURES

1. How much were the laborers to receive when the landowner said "Whatever is right, I will give you?" (v. 4)

2. What is meant by the eleventh hour? (v. 6)

3. Why were the laborers who were hired first com-plaining? (vv. 11-12)

DISCUSS THE MEANING

1. Who is the landowner?
2. Does the landowner have the rights to determine how much he will pay a laborer?
3. What did Jesus mean when he said the last shall be first and the first shall be last?

LESSON IN OUR SOCIETY

In recent years, more and more businesses have gone from a six- to a seven-day work week. Companies such as Federal Express now deliver on Sundays, and beauty salons, cleaners, and even banks are also open for business. The nation is consumed with gaining more and more riches and this attitude has spilled over into the church. Many talented musicians once considered it a privilege to volunteer their services for the work of the Lord. Now they burden the churches with demands for exorbitant wages for their services. "What does it profit a man to gain the whole world and lose his soul?" (Matthew 16:26). How much of your time and talent do you donate to the work of the ministry? Do you have the same attitude as Peter who asked, "What do we get out of following Christ?" What is the price for salvation?

MAKE IT HAPPEN

God loves us in spite of our imperfections and flaws. He demonstrates that love by continually inviting us to come into the vineyard. It then becomes our responsibility to be witnesses to others of His love, grace, and goodness. This week make it a point to invite as many of your friends as you can to come to church on Sunday.

FOLLOW THE SPIRIT

What God wants me to do:

_____

_____

REMEMBER YOUR THOUGHTS

Special insights you have learned:

_____

_____

MORE LIGHT ON THE TEXT
MATTHEW 20:1-16

This passage of Scripture is a parable. Parables were one of Jesus' favorite teaching tools. He was able to communicate very effectively, and simply, through the use of these stories that reflect kingdom truths.

1 For the kingdom of heaven is like unto a man that is an householder, which went out early in the morning to hire labourers into his vineyard. 2 And when he had agreed with the labourers for a penny a day, he sent them into his vineyard.

Jesus established that the parable He was about to present to those who had ears to hear would teach them something about the kingdom of heaven. He stated the basic understanding between the householder and the laborers. The householder was the one who took the initiative to go out to them and make them an offer. He hired them early in the morning to work in the vineyard for the day and he agreed to pay them one penny. They apparently were satisfied with that payment and went into the vineyard to begin their work.

3 And he went out about the third hour, and saw others standing idle in the marketplace, 4 And said unto them; Go ye also into the vineyard, and whatsoever is right I will give you. And they went their way. 5 Again he went out about the sixth and ninth hour, and did likewise.

The householder hired more laborers at 9:00 a.m, at noon, and at 3:00 p.m. He didn t establish a fixed price with them, but just told them that he would pay them what is "right." They went out to join the others who had been working for hours already in the hot sun.

6 And about the eleventh hour he went out, and found others standing idle, and saith unto them, Why stand ye here all the day idle? 7 They say unto him, Because no man hath hired us. He saith unto them, Go ye also into the vineyard; and whatsoever is right, that shall ye receive.

When the day was almost over, at 5:00 p.m., the householder was still hiring laborers, those who had been standing around all day waiting to be chosen. He didn't consider it too late to put them to work. The other workers must have looked up in surprise when these latecomers joined them in the vineyard.

8 So when even was come, the lord of the vineyard saith unto his steward, Call the labourers, and give them their hire, beginning from the last unto the first. 9 And when they came that were hired about the eleventh hour, they received every man a penny.

One hour after "these johnny-come-latelys" had been hired, they were summoned to receive their pay---first, before those who had been working in the sun all day long. And they were paid the same amount that those first workers had been promised—one penny! How generous, to pay someone who had only worked for an hour, the full amount—one penny. The "first" group were surely thinking that they would be paid more.

10 But when the first came, they supposed that they should have received more; and they likewise received every man a penny. 11 And when they had received it, they murmured against the goodman of the house, 12 Saying, These last have wrought but one hour, and thou hast made them equal unto us, which have borne the burden and heat of the day.

They were outdone and disgusted, to think they would be paid the same amount as the one-hour group. It just did not seem fair to them, as they thought of the many hours they had sweated in the sun. How could they be paid equally, when they had not done an equal amount of work?

They felt that they had a lot to murmur and complain about, and they told the householder how they felt.

13 But he answered one of them, and said, Friend I do thee no wrong; didst not thou agree with me for a penny? 14 Take that thine is and go thy way: I will give unto this last, even as unto thee. 15 Is it not lawful for me to do what I will with mine own? Is thine eye evil, because I am good?

The householder responded by telling the spokesman that he had honored their agreement. He had paid them what he agreed to pay. He advised them to stop their murmuring, take their money, and move on. He reminded them it was his perogative to give to the one-hour workers what he wanted, even if it did not appear "fair" to them. He asked them if his goodness to the one-hour workers was making them evil.

16 So the last shall be first, and the first last: for many be called, but few chosen.

Jesus summed up the parable with these words. He reminded His hearers that the kingdom of heaven would be filled with those that no one may expect. It will happen here on earth, where we may see those coming to Christ who have lived a life of sin, out in the streets. They join the church and quickly take on a leadership role or a high visibility position. They might be elected president of the choir, or become the head of the usher board. Those who have been in church all their lives, may resent the fact that these folk are "earning" so much recognition and status. Our competitive "old man" (Romans 6:6) may rise up and begin to murmur and complain. Like the brother of the prodigal son, those who have remained with the Father for a long time may feel slighted and taken for granted. But they must realize that they have their reward. All that the Father has belongs to them (Luke 15:31).

The same principle applies to heaven and eternal life. The first person we see when we get there may be the "last" one we would expect. The first person into heaven may be the one who was converted on their deathbed after living a life of sin. Those who have tried to live a righteous life for years may be upset that those years haven't earned them a better place or a higher rank.

We need to learn that God does choose to do what God wants, with whom God wants. But the most important lesson we can learn from this parable is about the goodness, generosity, and grace of God. God goes out to humanity. God takes the initiative, just like this householder, and finds people where they are. Some may have been waiting for a long time, feeling useless and disgusted. They may have begun to despair of ever being called or chosen. Imagine how happy they must be, when they realize that God has come for them and has a plan for their lives. Begrudging them their happiness and their reward, because of petty jealousy, would surely be wrong.

God has been fair and generous to all of us, those who have labored all day and those who came in at the last hour. Truly, no one deserves what God so freely gives us through His grace and mercy. There is none righteous, no not one (Romans 3:10). So we should all celebrate together that we have a place in the kingdom and a share in eternal life.

DAILY BIBLE READING

M: The Rich Young Man and Jesus
Matthew 19:16-22

T: All Things Are Possible for God
Matthew 19:23-30

W: Hiring of Laborers for the Vineyard
Matthew 20:1-7

T: God's Grace Illustrated
Matthew 20:8-16

F: Jesus' Death and Resurrection Foretold
Matthew 20:17-23

S: Jesus Teaches about Servanthood
Matthew 20:24-28

S: Jesus Demonstrates Servanthood
John 13:1-15

TEACHING TIPS

February 6
Bible Study Guide 10

1. Words You Should Know

A. "Might be fulfilled." (Matthew 21:4) Greek *pleroo*—to finish (a period or task). The term refers to the prophecies and activities surrounding Christ's crucifixion and resurrection.

B. Prophet. (v. 11) Greek *prophetes*—a foreteller; by analogy an inspired speaker. Specifically, one the people had come to know by reputation.

2. Teacher Preparation

A. Read and meditate upon the Devotional Reading and the BACKGROUND.

B. Study the FOCAL VERSES in the most popular translations used by the church in corporate worship or by the students in individual study. Make a list of study notes and contemporary language.

3. Starting the Lesson

A. Write the AT-A-GLANCE outline on the board.

B. Entertain the student's definitions and understandings of prophets and prophecies.

4. Getting into the Lesson

A. Share "Words You Should Know" with students.

B. Read FOCAL VERSES and answer SEARCH THE SCRIPTURES as a group.

5. Relating the Lesson to Life

A. Allow students to break off into small groups and answer the DISCUSS THE MEANING questions.

B. Reconvene in the larger group and reflect on LESSON IN OUR SOCIETY.

6. Arousing Action

A. Examine rituals, routines, and traditions which dictate corporate and individual worship.

B. Explore new actions and attitudes to employ in corporate and individual worship.

C. Close the class with prayer.

COMING TO JERUSALEM

Bible Background • MATTHEW 21:1-17
Printed Text • MATTHEW 21:1-13
Devotional Reading • LUKE 19:29-44

LESSON AIM

By the end of the lesson, students will be able to tell the story of Jesus' triumphal entry into Jerusalem; understand Jesus' humility as central to His effectiveness; and determine to return the house of God into a house of prayer.

KEEP IN MIND

"Tell ye the daughter of Sion, Behold, thy King cometh unto thee, meek, and sitting upon an ass, and a colt the foal of an ass" (Matthew 21:5).

FOCAL VERSES

MATTHEW 21:1 And when they drew nigh unto Jerusalem, and were come to Bethphage, unto the mount of Olives, then sent Jesus two disciples,

2 Saying unto them, Go into the village over against you, and straightway ye shall find an ass tied, and a colt with her: loose them, and bring them unto me.

3 And if any man say ought unto you, ye shall say, The Lord hath need of them; and straightway he will send them.

4 All this was done, that it might be fulfilled which was spoken by the prophet, saying,

5 Tell ye the daughter of Sion, Behold, thy King cometh unto thee, meek, and sitting upon an ass, and a colt the foal of an ass.

6 And the disciples went, and did as Jesus commanded them,

7 And brought the ass, and the colt, and put on them their clothes, and they set him thereon.

8 And a very great multitude spread their garments in the way; others cut down branches from the trees, and strewed them in the way.

9 And the multitudes that went before, and that followed, cried, saying, Hosanna to the Son of David: Blessed is he

LESSON OVERVIEW

LESSON AIM
KEEP IN MIND
FOCAL VERSES
IN FOCUS
THE PEOPLE, PLACES, AND TIMES
BACKGROUND
AT-A-GLANCE
IN DEPTH
SEARCH THE SCRIPTURES
DISCUSS THE MEANING
LESSON IN OUR SOCIETY
MAKE IT HAPPEN
FOLLOW THE SPIRIT
REMEMBER YOUR THOUGHTS
MORE LIGHT ON THE TEXT
DAILY BIBLE READINGS

that cometh in the name of the Lord; Hosanna in the highest.

10 And when he was come into Jerusalem, all the city was moved, saying, Who is this?

11 And the multitude said, This is Jesus the prophet of Nazareth of Galilee.

12 And Jesus went into the temple of God, and cast out all them that sold and bought in the temple, and overthrew the tables of the moneychangers, and the seats of them that sold doves,

13 And said unto them, It is written, My house shall be called the house of prayer; but ye have made it a den of thieves.

IN FOCUS

As history cites, a member of the British Parliament, Neil Marten, was once giving a group of his constituents a guided tour of the Houses of Parliament. During the course of the visit, the group happened to meet Lord Hailsham, then lord chancellor, wearing all the regalia of his office. Hailsham recognized Marten among the group and cried, "Neil!" Not daring to question or disobey the command, the entire band of visitors promptly fell to their knees! (*Today in the Word*, July 30, 1993).

This true, but humorous story, illustrates what can occur when a group of people accustom themselves to commands of worship and honor. Without a moment's hesitation the group automatically bowed down before the head of state and did not consider the command "kneel" might be a homonym (two words which sound alike but have different meanings) for "Neil."

Comparatively, the crowd in today's lesson had grown accustomed to kingly and priestly representatives, and responded to this unusual King in like manner. For even though this King and Priest arrived in humble adornment and accompaniment, the crowd perceived His exceeding greatness. Today's lesson focuses on Jesus' final preparation for His crucifixion. A time believers have come to call His Triumphal Entry.

THE PEOPLE, PLACES, AND TIMES

MESSIAH. Transliteration of Hebrew word meaning "anointed one"; translated into Greek as *Christos* or "the Christ." Since apostolic times the name Christ has become the proper name of Jesus, the Person whom Christians recognize as the God-given Redeemer of Israel and the church's Lord. "Christ," or Messiah, is therefore a name admirably suited to express both the church's link with Israel through the Old Testament and the faith that sees in Jesus Christ the worldwide scope of the salvation in Him. Their Messiah was a warrior-prince who would expel the hated Romans from Israel and bring in a kingdom in which the Jews would be promoted to world dominion.

The people in the Dead Sea Scrolls were evidently able to combine a dual hope of two Messiahs, one priestly and the second a royal figure. The alternation between a kingly Messiah and a priestly figure is characteristic of the two centuries of early Judaism prior to the coming of Jesus.

MESSIAHSHIP IN JESUS' MINISTRY. A question posed in John 4:29 (compare 7:40-43) is: "Is not this the Christ (Messiah)?" It is evident that the issue of the Messiah's identity and role was one much debated among the Jews in the first century. In the Synoptic Gospels the way Jesus acted and spoke led naturally to the dialogue at Caesarea Philippi. Jesus asked His disciples, "Who do you say that I am?" It was a question to which Peter gave the reply, "Thou art the Christ (Messiah)" (Mark 8:29). Mark made it clear Jesus took an attitude of distinct reserve and caution to this title since it carried overtones of political power, especially in one strand of Jewish hope represented by the Psalms of Solomon. Jesus, therefore, accepted Peter's confession with great reluctance, especially in light of the disciple's objection when told that the Messiah must suffer (see Mark 8:32). For Peter, Messiah was a title of a glorious personage, both nationalistic and victorious in battle. Jesus, on the other hand, saw His destiny in terms of a suffering Son of man and a Servant of God (Mark 8:31-38; 9:31; 10:33-34). Hence He did not permit the demons to greet Him as Messiah (Luke 4:41) and downplayed all claims to privilege and overt majesty linked with the Jewish title.

During the course of Jesus' ministry, Jesus sought to wean the disciples away from the traditional notion of a warrior Messiah. Instead Jesus tried to instill in their minds the prospect that the road to His future glory was bound to the Cross, with its experience of rejection, suffering, and-humiliation. At the trial before His Jewish judges (Matthew 26:63-66), Jesus once more reinterpreted the title Messiah (Christ, KJV) contrary to the Son of man figure based on Daniel 7:13-14. This confession secured His condemnation, and He went to the Cross as a crucified Messiah because the Jewish leaders failed to perceive the nature of messiahship as Jesus understood it. Pilate sentenced Him as a messianic pretender who claimed (according to the false charges brought against Him) to be a rival to Caesar (Mark 15:9; Luke 23:2; John 19:14-15). It was only after the Resurrection that the disciples were in a position to see how Jesus was truly a Messiah, and Jesus then opened their minds to what true Messiahship meant (see Luke 24:45-46). The national title Messiah then took on a broader connotation, involving a kingly role which was to embrace all peoples (Luke 24:46-47). In Pauline thought, "Christ" is a richer term than "Messiah" could ever be. One indication of this is the fact that the early followers of the Messiah called themselves "Christians," Christ's people (Acts 11:26; 1 Peter 4:16), as a sign of their universal faith in a sovereign Lord.

(Adapted from "Messiah" by Ralph P. Martin; *Holman's Bible Dictionary for Windows, Version 1.0,* Parsons Technology, 1994.)

BACKGROUND

The significance of Jesus' entry into Jerusalem was so great, unlike other records of events and details cited in the other Gospels, all four New Testament Gospel writers make record of it. As it was time for the Passover, over 2 million inhabitants of the land made the annual exodus to Jerusalem for the feast and celebration. One could speculate this was the most excellent moment for the Messiah to make Himself known to so many of His people at one time. The symbolic focus of sacrifice was before them, and He would present Himself as the ultimate sacrifice. Matthew's record includes 41 prophetic quotes from the Old Testament which confirm Jesus as the Messiah.

The people had seen others who professed to be the messiah, the conqueror of the land, the warrior set to overthrow the ruling government. They were all too familiar with processions of great war-horses and armies entering the cities. They did not, however, expect such a humble entrance of a King riding on an animal that was a symbol of quietness, humility, and goodwill. Still they knew this was the Messiah and gave Him a King's welcome, replete with an unridden colt, a carpet of garments off their backs, a pathway of palm leaves, and shouts of praise which rang out into the streets. Throngs of people, already gathering in the city, turned their attention to the King.

Jesus, ushered in as a King, knew this was the end of His earthly life and the beginning of His eternal reign. Jesus, regarded as an agitator, faced the hostile religious leaders, knowing that before the festival was ended His blood would be on their hands. Jesus entered the town of His trial assured of His triumph!

1. Presence of the Prophet
(Matthew 21:1-7)
2. Procession of the People (vv. 8-11)
3. Purging the Place of Prayer
(vv. 12-13)

IN DEPTH

1. Presence of the Prophet (Matthew 21:1-7)

Jesus sent two disciples to secure a donkey to ride into Jerusalem, in order to fulfill the prophecy of Zechariah. It's possible that Jesus made arrangements beforehand to have a donkey and her colt ready for His use. It's possible that His reputation preceded Him. When the owner of the donkey and the colt learned that Jesus requested them, he gave them freely and joyfully. It's also possible that Jesus, in His divine knowledge, gave these instructions to the disciples. What is most significant is that Jesus chose a humble animal to ride into the city, not a mighty war-horse with sinewy muscles of great mass and strength leading a procession of highly-trained warriors armed with breastplates of brass and plans for battle. Jesus rode on a colt, a symbol of humility, which made His entry and crucifixion forever memorable. But the presence of a King on a colt did not keep the people from praising Him. They perceived the prophet among them, and greeted him as a King.

2. Procession of the People (vv. 8-11)

As Jesus entered Jerusalem, the crowd threw down their coats and branches along the road, and shouted praises to Him. Their actions honored Him, and they greeted Jesus with shouts and songs of the hallel psalms (Psalm 118:26) that were customary greetings to people journeying to Jerusalem for the Passover. However, the people knew Jesus was much more than just another traveler. They were honoring Him for the miracles they had seen Him perform.

The throngs of people, the furor that the Messiah had come, and the deafening shouts of praise created a momentum in the city that could be sensed, seen, and heard. Leading the procession were children, not soldiers, who sang His praises and shouted His glory. As the momentum grew, local religious leaders counseled Him to quiet the people. However, knowing His end was near, Jesus

told them, "If these become silent, the stones will cry out!" (Luke 19:40). This peculiar response indicated that Jesus' Kingship was not based on the recognition of the people, but on the foundations of the city and the temple which would declare His glory. Jesus was prophecy fulfilled, and no human proclamation could ultimately confirm or deny that truth.

The people of Jerusalem were excited and asked about Jesus' identity. Before this time, Jesus had not allowed anyone to publicly acknowledge Him as the Messiah. Most of Jesus' ministry had been done outside of Jerusalem to avoid agitating the Jewish leaders. But now these same people, to whom He had ministered, were leading the procession into the city, and the city dwellers wanted to know about this King who sat on a colt and not on a throne. The crowd replied that He was the prophet Jesus from Nazareth of Galilee. Some joined in the praise; others were disappointed when they saw Jesus enter the city without the majestic fanfare.

3. Purging the Place of Prayer (vv. 12-13)

Jesus entered the temple and overturned the money changers' tables, declaring, "My house shall be called a house of prayer; but you have made it a den of robbers." Like the record of His entry into Jerusalem, all four Gospels record the incident of Jesus cleansing the temple of the merchants and money changers. Since all four writers identify the incident, it must be critical to recounting Jesus' ministry.

When Jesus entered the temple, he witnessed a convenient service run by crooks. Birds and animals, suitable for sacrifice, were on sale in the temple courts. There was a currency exchange for persons who needed to exchange their regional currency to pay the temple tax.

The birds and animals on sale were necessary. Sacrificial animals had to be certified unblemished and acceptable by the temple priests. It was convenient for those traveling long distances to Jerusalem for the Passover to purchase animals within the temple gates, rather than risk having ones they brought be declared unacceptable. There was also a legitimate need for a currency exchange. Two million plus people, from all over the Roman empire, came with many different currencies. But the temple tax had to be paid in Jewish money. So the money changers and the merchants provided a legitimate, convenient service, but they were corrupt; they exploited people. They were motivated by greed and cheated people with unfair rates of exchange and exorbitant interest rates.

Jesus waged war, not on the politics of Roman rule as others had tried, but at the very core of the corruption money. It had been prophesied (Zechariah 14:21) that there would come a day when no merchant would do business in the house of God. Jesus' cleansing of the temple by over turning the tables became this prophecy fulfilled. Jesus was mad that the corruption of the government caused an interruption of the quality of worship in the temple.

SEARCH THE SCRIPTURES

1. How does the prophet Zechariah describe Jesus' "triumphal entry"? (Zechariah 9:9)

2. A grand entry into a city was common among those claiming to be the messiah. How did Jesus' entry differ from what the Jews had previously witnessed? (Matthew 21:1-7)

3. What did the people say and do as Jesus entered Jerusalem? What was the significance of their words and actions? (vv. 8-9)

4. What was the difference between the people of Jerusalem and the multitude who went before and after Jesus? (vv. 10-11)

5. The selling of unblemished animal sacrifices in the temple was a convenience to the people. Why did Jesus get mad and put the sellers out of business? (vv. 12-13)

DISCUSS THE MEANING

1. In fulfilling His mission, Jesus was careful to look and act different from others professing to be the messiah. What character element did Jesus possess that believers should imitate?

2. What did Jesus mean when He declared, "My house shall be called a house of prayer; but you have made it a den of robbers"? What other activities have believers allowed to take precedent over worship, specifically prayer, in the church?

LESSON IN OUR SOCIETY

History tells us of the Italian poet Dante Alighieri who one day was deeply immersed in meditation during a church service. Alighieri failed to kneel at the appropriate moment. His enemies hurried to the bishop and demanded that Dante be punished for his sacrilege. Dante defended himself by saying, "If those who accuse me had their eyes and minds on God, as I had, they too would have failed to notice events around them, and they most certainly would not have noticed what I was doing."

Alighieri's enemies sought to condemn him for not going along with the crowd, for not adhering to tradition. The charge lobbied against Alighieri boiled down to the fact that he forgot to be perfunctory in his praise. Instead he was caught up in the presence of the Almighty. Where are your eyes during worship?

MAKE IT HAPPEN

Examine your individual worship practices in the house of God. Does everything you do honor Him? Evaluate, but not judge, corporate worship practices of your congregation. What practices would you bring to the attention of the church leadership so that the church could look more like God's house?

FOLLOW THE SPIRIT

What God wants me to do:

_____

_____

REMEMBER YOUR THOUGHTS

Special insights you learned:

_____

_____

MORE LIGHT ON THE TEXT
MATTHEW 21:1-13

1 And when they drew nigh unto Jerusalem, and were come to Bethphage, unto the mount of Olives, then sent Jesus two disciples,

Though the Triumphal Entry is also told in Mark 11:1-10, Luke 19:29-38, and John 12:12-19, the Gospel of Matthew is plentifully endowed with the fulfillment of Old Testament prophecy. More prophets, also known as inspired speakers, are quoted in Matthew than in Mark, Luke, and John combined. Matthew's writing style is marked by his emphasis on the teaching ministry of Jesus. To understand this text, consider the context. Activities in the life of Jesus immediately before Matthew 21:1 includes Jesus' informing His disciples that He would be going to Jerusalem where the chief priest and scribes would mock, whip, and ultimately sentence Him to death.

Jesus assures His disciples, however, that God would raise Him to life on the third day (Matthew 20:18-19). While Jesus is sharing this grave news, Salome, the wife of Zebedee and mother of two of the disciples, James and John, is so preoccupied with her sons' successes that she misses, or ignores, the gravity of the inhuman intent of Jesus' enemies. Though there is evidence in Matthew 20:17 that Jesus and company were in motion, talking and walking away from Judea and going to Jerusalem, Jesus hears, questions, and answers Salome. He settles the indignation of the ten other disciples, a common reaction among the disciples toward women (Matthew 26:8) and children (Matthew 19:14). He also opened the eyes of two blind men sitting by the Jericho roadside.

Out of this context the text emerges. Jesus has expressed

the purpose of their departure from Judea (Matthew 19:1). Their destination is Jerusalem (a classroom without walls) and a place frequented by Jesus, the Mount of Olives (Matthew 21:1).

The Mount of Olives is mentioned once in the Old Testament (Zechariah 14:4) and 12 times in the New Testament. I could say that the 13 references to the Mount of Olives and the twelve disciples and Jesus make a case for the significance of the number 13, a number perceived to be unlucky in western society. This personal notation aside, the Mount of Olives is the place where Jesus agonizes and is betrayed, and it is also the suggested place of His second advent (Acts 1:9-12). Other references to the Mount of Olives can be found in Matthew 24:3; 26:30; Mark 11:1; 13:3; 14:26; Luke 19:29, 37; 21:37; 22:39; and John 8:1. The differences among the synoptic Gospels and John regarding the Mount of Olives are noteworthy. Both Matthew and Mark omit Jesus' descent from the Mount, and Matthew omits Bethany as a landmark along the way.

2 Saying unto them, Go into the village over against you, and straightway ye shall find an ass tied, and a colt with her: loose them, and bring them unto me.

"Saying unto them" is very common introductory language in the Gospel teachings. The phrase strongly suggests to the listener, "Pay attention, take note, and get ready for a word from the Lord." While in training for the military chaplain's corp, trainees quickly learned to become keenly mindful that something important is about to happen when they hear the words, "Attention on deck." "Saying unto them" has a comparable impact.

Jesus is still speaking today through His Holy Spirit, giving instructions through God's Holy Word, and bringing back to your remembrance the things which He has spoken. We are prohibited by Revelation 22:18-19 from adding to or taking away from *this* book, and while there is great debate to this day over the literal application of God's Word, Jesus is still saying unto us, "Go." As a matter of fact, this is the great commission, "Go" (Matthew 28:19). In the text, the Master is about to give instructions to His disciples. The instructions are related to the purpose, the destination, and the activities evolving around the Gospel's triumphal entry narrative.

The terminology "village over against you" differs among biblical versions. The New King James Version (NKJV) reads "village opposite," whereas the New Revised Standard (NRSV) and the New International Version (NIV) read "village ahead," clarifying the KJV's words "against you." Likewise with the word "straightway" which, in the previously stated versions, uses the word "immediately."

Bearing in mind that contemporary disciples can read the Holy Bible with forethought, you may raise the question, "How did Jesus know where to send the two unnamed disciples for the animals?" I am led to believe that either Jesus had already traveled the way He was sending the disciples and observed the animals, or this is another example, however slight, of Jesus' sovereignty. I choose to believe He is sovereign, and the disciples chose to follow His instructions, believing His words to be true and accurate. The disciples may have questioned this change in transportation. After all Jesus and the disciples had, up to now, walked everywhere. Now a new mode of transportation was called for in Jesus' ministry.

The Gospels of Mark and Luke give the exploring disciples a little extra assistance. Matthew writes, "Straightway ye shall find an ass tied, and a colt with her" (21:2). Mark adds, "And as soon as ye be entered into it, ye shall find a colt tied, whereon never man sat" (11:2) and Luke says, "In the which at your entering" (19:30). These minor details are important in the sense they give the two disciples a specific point of reference, namely, the city limits of the village across from the foot of the Mount of Olives.

It is also worthwhile to observe a common pattern in the number of disciples Jesus sent. In the Bible the number two is often given in an "either/or" way: two gates, two great lights, two eternal places, two masters, two debtors, two sons, etc. In these incidences, the Bible is teaching how to make choices by comparison. The number two is also given in an "both/and" way: Jesus sends two of His disciples to visit John the Baptist while he is imprisoned (Matthew 11:2); Jesus sends "forth the disciples by two's and gave them power over unclean spirits (Mark 6:7); Jesus sends the seventy (70) by two's into every city and place where Jesus would come (Luke 10:1) and Jesus walks with two on the Emmaus Road (Luke 24:13). In these references, as well as in the current text, Jesus alludes to camaraderie.

3 And if any man say ought unto you, ye shall say, The Lord hath need of them; and straightway he will send them.

In the New American Standard Bible (NASB), this verse reads, "And if anyone says something to you." These words are more inclusive than those used in the NKJV and take into account the unlikely event that the disciples may meet the owner's wife or child. Further, if the two disciples are questioned about fulfilling His command, Jesus instructs the disciples to use words of urgency. Jesus takes no chances of offending the owner of the animals as He prepares for His triumphal entry into Jerusalem. Jesus is confident the owner will respond positively to His need.

Again Jesus uses the word "straightway." The Greek word *eutheos* means at once. Jesus expects the owner to respond to the disciples immediately. Culturally speaking, in the words of Dr. Jeremiah A. Wright, Jr., Jesus expects the owner to send the animals "rat now." Thus the disciples are further instructed to say, "The Lord has need of them." How much do we, as believers, trust God to supply our every need? Hopefully, we can answer confidently by quoting Philippians 4:19, "But my God shall supply all your need according to his riches in glory by Christ Jesus."

4 All this was done, that it might be fulfilled which was spoken by the prophet, saying,

Verses 1-3 complete the plans for Jesus' triumphant entrance into Jerusalem. Matthew begins this verse with the word *all*, which means *whole*. As an adverb, it is used to mean altogether; in other words, verses 1, 2 and 3 fulfill prophecy to the letter. The Greek *ginomai* allows for using *performed*, *finished*, and *ended* as alternative words for *done*. Now that which was spoken by the prophet has come to fruition. The stage is now set to accomplish the prediction of the very next verse.

Modern psychic hotlines, in my opinion, are a mockery to the biblical prophets and prophetesses. The phrase "as spoken by the psychic" cannot be compared to the phrase "was spoken by the prophet." The prophets' words are foretell God's promise to redeem fallen humanity. The psychics' words flirt with the perils of fallen humanity; they toy with people's emotions. In 12 different places, the Bible denounces necromancy, witchcraft, forecasting, and divinations. The most striking reference is recorded in Acts 16:16-24. Here Paul is met by an innocent, young woman possessed with a spirit of divination. She had greatly increased her employers' wealth by soothsaying. She followed after Paul and others announcing, "These men are the servants of the most high God, which show unto us the way of salvation." Grieved by her intentions, Paul turns to her and commands the spirit of divination to come out of her in the name of Jesus Christ. The damsel's employers are enraged; their hopes for further gain are lost. Conversely, the prophets' profit is the fulfillment of God's promises to the benefit of God's people.

5 Tell ye the daughter of Sion, Behold, thy King cometh unto thee, meek, and sitting upon an ass, and a colt the foal of an ass.

The beginning word *tell* reminds me of the age-old oral tradition among God's people and prompts the question, "What is being told and to whom?" Beginning with the *whom*, the Greek word for daughter is *thugater* and means a female child. In Hebrew, it means descendant or inhabi-

tant. Taken as an entire phrase, "Tell ye the daughter of Sion" can be interpreted, "Say, speak, or announce to the descendants from the hill, a mountain, or the city of Jerusalem, Behold. . . ." This pronouncement of the coming King is a traffic stopper. Behold, *idou*, is a demonstrative particle in Greek and draws attention to the subject King and the beginning of the long awaited day of liberation of God's people.

Though the King is arriving, *erchomai*, He comes meekly. Historically, a king does not arrive without a legion of bodyguards, officers, property, housing, pomp, and circumstance. Instead of arriving on a beast of burden, kings approach their subjects in chariots carried by the palace entourage. Jesus, however, comes without a horde of attendants surrounding Him; He comes meekly and sitting on an ass, and a colt the foal of an ass, or beast of burden.

6 And the disciples went, and did as Jesus commanded them,

It is appropriate when God's children obey His voice without hesitation. "And the disciples went" strongly suggests an immediate response to Jesus command. Presumably Peter was not one of the two disciples Jesus sends. Peter is the disciple most likely to challenge Jesus (Matthew 15:15; 18:21; Mark 11:21; Luke 12:41), to speak too quickly or inappropriately (Mark 8:32). More than likely Jesus sent James and John, since they were bucking for a special seat in the kingdom. Whoever the two disciples were, they acted swiftly to do as the Lord commanded. Obedience is an important characteristic in the life of God's children. The action word in this verse of Scripture, *poieo*, means without delay.

7 And brought the ass, and the colt, and put on them their clothes, and they set him thereon.

In fulfillment of Zechariah 9:9, the Gospels describe the coming of the Christ in all meekness and mercy to effect salvation, not in His might and majesty. It was the opposite of envy, enterprise, and arrogance; Zion's King enters Jerusalem outwardly impoverished, representing the life of Zion's humble citizens. Indeed, that Jesus' entrance into Jerusalem can be compared with His birth. His nursery was borrowed, humble, and meager. Likewise, His triumphant entrance was on a borrowed means of transportation, humble, and meager.

Reading about the disciples putting their clothes on the animals is reminiscent of Jesus' instruction to the disciples in Matthew 5:40 and Luke 6:29. Here Jesus emphasizes the importance of freely giving up your cloak should anyone sue you for your coat. And in Matthew 6:28, Jesus de-emphasizes worrying about clothing, among other things.

Apparently the disciples have learned and accepted this lesson because they spread their clothes on the animals and set Jesus thereon. Two distinguishing features in this Scripture should be noted. First, the KJV and NKJV uses the term *clothes;* the NRSV and NIV uses the term *cloaks;* the NASB uses the term *garment,* and the Amplified and Living Bible uses the term *coat.* In actuality, the Greek word *himation* makes the words cloak, garment, clothes, raiment, robe, apparel, vesture, and coats interchangeable. Therefore, it can be assumed the disciples spread an array of clothing.

The second distinguishing feature related to this Scripture is the animals. Matthew fails to mention the animals had never been used for transporting humans. Mark and Luke, however, include the words "on which no one has ever sat." Again, we can draw comparisons between His life and His death. He was the first to be laid in that borrowed manger. He was the first to sit on that borrowed beast of burden. He was the first to hang upon that cruel cross. He was the first to be laid to rest in that borrowed tomb. Finally, He was the first to be raised from the dead by God.

8 And a very great multitude spread their garments in the way; others cut down branches from the trees, and strewed them in the way.

This was the week of Passover. Jerusalem and surrounding regions were crowded with travelers from the diaspora. The law required this migration on a number of occasions. Again, note the connection with Christ's birth. Joseph and Mary were traveling to Bethlehem to register for the census. Bethlehem was so crowded that all of the lodging places were filled. "No room in the inn" was common during the festivals, also called feasts in the English Bibles (particularly during the Feast of Passover, Pentecost, and the Day of Atonement).

During the Feast of Passover, a great multitude was available to spread their *himation* and to cut down branches from the trees. The branches allowed a softer and gentler ride against the uneven, stony, dirt roadway for the King of the Jews. Only in Mark does the crowd spread leafy branches along the way. And John alone uses the exclusive term "palms" (John 12:13). Mark does give us a hint to these leafy branches which John specifically identifies as palm trees.

9 And the multitudes that went before, and that followed, cried, saying, Hosanna to the son of David: Blessed is he that cometh in the name of the Lord; Hosanna in the highest.

For centuries, beginning with the fall of humankind (Genesis 3:6-7), God's people awaited the fulfilment of the Old Testament promise of the perfect King who would reign over His people. He was coming to establish a kingdom with laws written on the heart, a kingdom without taxation, a kingdom of love, joy, and peace. Psalms 45 and 110 give the promise of a Messiah yet to come. Daniel verbalizes his vision of one who is given dominion, glory, and a kingdom in which all would serve (7:13-14). Matthew and Luke magnify the King in His earthly ministry. And John reveals the culmination of this same theme with Christ seated on a throne; on His raiment are the words, "KING OF KINGS, AND LORD OF LORDS" (Revelation 19:16). It is because of these prophecies that the crowd proclaims Jesus as King during His triumphal entry during the feast of Passover, later to be called Palm Sunday.

"Hosanna" is the greeting used by the gathered community of faith on the occasion of Jesus' triumphal entrance into Jerusalem. From Psalm 118:25-26, the Hebrew word for this greeting is most closely translated as the following prayer: "Save now," or "Save, we beseech Thee." It should be noted at this point that the annual festival, called Passover, commemorated the final plague on Egypt when the firstborn of the Egyptians died, and the Israelites were spared because of the token of blood on the lintel and the two side posts at the door of the Israelites (Exodus 12:22). Jesus informed the disciples that He would be sacrificed, and His blood would be the last redeeming effort to save all believers everywhere Jews and Gentiles alike. The multitude cried out to be saved from military, political, and social oppression. Among the crowd are descendants of the great flood, the exodus, and the exiles. Among them are the faithful remnant who have observed the festivals, the Mosaic Law, the belief in the coming Messiah, and in the promise of the Lamb of God who takes away the sins of the world.

The word "Blessed" in it's Greek form, *eulogeo* or *yoologeho,* means to speak well of. Blessings are quite common in the Pentateuch. Patriarchs either blessed or preferred their firstborn. Such is the case with Isaac, who was deceived into blessing first his second-born, Jacob (Genesis 27). Laban was obligated to give his first daughter a matrimonial blessing over Rachel, the woman Jacob loved (Genesis 29:26-30). In the Hebrew *barak,* the patriarchs were performing an act of adoration and a pronouncement of family prophecy and inheritance.

Later in Matthew, Jesus blessed the gathered community with the Beatitudes during the Sermon on the Mount. The Living Bible (LB) uses the introductory word "happy" (Matthew 5:3-11). In the context of the Beatitudes, *makarios* is the Greek word for blessed and means fortunate and happy. The multitudes who witnessed Jesus' triumphal entry went before and behind Jesus speaking well of "he that cometh in the name of the Lord" (Matthew 21:9).

The name of the Lord is the Old Testament manifestation of Yahweh, according to the Yahwist or "Y" writers, whereas the Priestly or "P" writer, called Yahweh *God*. Generally, the writer would not write out the name *Yahweh*, but use the letters YHWH for the God of the covenant. The authors of the Gospels, though Jewish, use the Greek word *Adonay*, the Greek equivalent of *Kyrios*. In the New Testament, the title *Kyrios* means *Christ*, one who is supreme in authority; as a title, it means God, Lord. Whereas Luke omits the reference to David, he exclaims, "Peace in Heaven, and glory in the higest" (Luke 19:38). You cannot get any higher than highest. The highest is where God, angels, the great cloud of witness dwell, and where heaven in. Although the phrase "Son of David," is presented several times throughout Scripture, Jesus existed from the beginning, apriori David, and deserves the supreme title *Kyrios*.

10 And when he was come into Jerusalem, all the city was moved, saying, Who is this?

In my mind, living long enough to enter into the millennium is a moving experience. Here you are reading material that was written in 1998 with the year 2000 as a publication date. Jesus was the expected Redeemer, prepared from the foundation of the earth to enter into the appointed place at the appointed time. Before He appeared, all the shouts of *Kyrios* were of no consequence. Now they see God in the flesh and are challenged to the core of their own being. His spiritual power stirs up their vile affections and every fiber of their hearts are moved. The NRSV uses the words, "The whole city was in turmoil." The Greek *seir*, used in the KJV for "moved," means to agitate (Amplified Bible) or cause to tremble.

In verse 10, the inquiring minds are among a group of trouble-making opponents with ill-intent toward Jesus. Some of them who are saying, "Hosanna" now would later say, "Crucify Him."

Others would sing, "Pass me not, O gentle Savior."

11 And the multitude said, This is Jesus the prophet of Nazareth of Galilee.

What an affirming proclamation. Those who are speaking this affirmation are bearing witness to a tradition peculiar to prophets. This last drama in Jesus' ministry bears similar features to thedramatic actions of prophets in Israel's history. Ahijah, for instance, draped himself with a new garment and, then tore it into 12 pieces for the benefit of Jeroboam. His prophecy demonstrated that the nation of Israel was going to be torn apart and only two

tribes would stand with Solomon (1 Kings 11:29-32). Likewise, Jeremiah strapped himself in a yoke to express his displeasure with slavery (Jeremiah 27:1-6). In other words, when words would not suffice, Israel's prophets historically vented their messages in drama.

In contemporary society, the elders and mature worshipers sing of the approaching King, "Pass me not, O gentle Savior" or "All hail the power of Jesus' name." And so it is in the Gospel'sdrama as the multitude answers, "This *must* be the prophet."

Though Jesus is called rabbi (KJV) eight times, He is called prophet about a dozen times. Throughout the Gospels, many of these references to Jesus as a prophet are given as a reproach of His Galilean neighborhood (Matthew 13:57; Mark 6:4; Luke 4:24; John 4:44).

For the most part, the title prophet referred to an Old Testament character, and John the Baptist was a prophet quoting prophets and used prophetic words, "Prepare ye the way of the Lord." Of course, Jesus also quoted Old Testament prophets. It seems to me the New Testament is a book fulfilling the words spoken by prophets.

12 And Jesus went into the temple of God, and cast out all them that sold and bought in the temple, and overthrew the tables of the moneychangers, and the seats of them that sold doves,

In his commentary on Matthew, William Barclay gives two New Testament definitions for temple. The Greek word *naos*, characterizes a small structure where the High Priest enters both the Holy Place and the Holy of Holies on the festival Day of Atonement. Surrounding *naos* is a much larger area with escalating courtyards: the Court of the Gentiles was accessible to the public; the Court of the Women was used by the Israelites; the Court of the Israelites was where people gathered for temple services; and the Court of the Priest was specifically for the priest. The RSV distinguishes the entire area by the Greek word *hieron*. It is from the Court of the Gentiles that Jesus turned out the money-changers and turned over the seats and tables (called benches in the NIV and four-footed tables in the Amplified).

Contemporary churches often use this incident to prohibit, at worse, and discourage, at best, commercial activity within the church facility. If it were left up to some church leaders, many potluck dinners and car washes would be history, despite the fact that fund-raising is more palatable than tithing. In the current text, though, money changing had become a racket.

Think of the Festival of Passover as you think of April 15th. Just as you must reckon with the IRS on the 15th of April, Jews had to pay a temple tax during Passover. The tax was to be paid in certain currency and it was the function of money-changers to make the suitable conversions.

People who travel internationally understand the importance of fair and equitable conversions of currency. The shysters in the temple courts were cheating on the rate of exchange and exploiting the Jews from the diaspora. They were also in cahoots with town officials who used the kickbacks to repair roads, to purchase gold plates for the temple courts, and to pad the pockets of the temple treasury.

Peddling doves was the greatest offense, however, because the doves were often used in sacrifices, in the rite of purification for women after childbirth, and in certifying cured lepers. Any animal presented as a sacrifice had to be unblemished. This may not have been the case for the over-priced doves being sold in the courts of the temple. It was this and the blatant exploitation that caused the Saviour's anger. These actions show the mind of Jesus concerning the reverence He held for the Temple of God.

As if Israel's exile experiences were not enough, they allowed Jerusalem to be captured around 175 B.C. After this time, the Jewish culture was introduced to Greek life and worship, and this defiled the temple with its swine sacrifices to Zeus, among other things. Jesus may very well have entered the temple with the intent of symbolically cleansing it from its historical mire. Does not the judgment of God begin in the household of faith?

13 And said unto them, It is written, My house shall be called the house of prayer; but ye have made it a den of thieves.

Den of thieves, referred to as "den of robbers" in the NRSV, NIV, and the Amplified, may be an expression referring to the rocky caves where thieves and robbers hid in mountainous parts of Judaea. The possible connection between the mountain booty and the crude merchants is noteworthy.

These people were not only selling in the house of God, they probably had no intention of giving to God that which belongs to Him. Thus they are akin to the people described in the Book of Malachi as robbers. When God's people use His house, but refuse to give back to God; they have also made His house into a den of thieves. Dr. Wyatt T. Walker calls those who do not give back to God common thieves. It is a loathsome association with the outlaw and, raises the question of integrity within and among God's people who resort to such things.

Jesus proceeds to cleanse the temple. Jesus uses the word "temple" in reference to His body, and Paul uses it to refer to the believer's physical body. It would behoove each believer to guard against those points of the heart where

covetousness may enter.

The Synoptic Gospels differ slightly with John regarding this text. In Matthew, Jesus is called the prophet from Nazareth. In John, the text includes the phrase "for all nations." This should be interpreted to mean that the cleansing of the temple was symbolic for tearing it down in order to make way for the new generation. The merchants were not there out of devotion, to hear "what thus saith the Lord," or to pray to God.

Perhaps this is why Jesus did not condemn the entire temple. Though He turned the temple out, He also healed the lame and the blind within the courts of the temple. His wrath was specifically directed toward the money-hungry profiteers, not those who came to pay the temple tax, to offer genuine sacrifice, and to participate in the festival. God working through Jesus Christ did not, and does not, hold the pure in heart accountable for the mean-spirited, mammon-serving money-changers. However, woe unto those who make it hard for others to worship in God's house of prayer. Spirits of bitterness, strife, envy, etc., can grossly interfere with a worshipful atmosphere and steal the worship center's Holy Presence and its real purpose—to be a House of Prayer for all nations.

DAILY BIBLE READING

M: Jesus Sets His Face Toward Jerusalem
Luke 9:51-56

T: Jesus Enters Jerusalem Amid Hosannas
Matthew 21:1-11

W: Jesus Cleanses the Temple
Matthew 21:12-17

T: Chief Priests and Elders Resist Jesus
Matthew 21:23-27

F: Parable of the Wicked Tenants
Matthew 21:33-46

S: A Question about the Resurrection
Matthew 22:23-33

S: The Greatest Commandment of All
Matthew 22:34-46

TEACHING TIPS

February 13
Bible Study Guide 11

1. Words You Should Know

A. Blessed. (Matthew 25:46) Greek, *makarios*—supremely blessed or well off; particularly in light of Divine intervention.

B. Wise. (v. 2) Greek, *phronimos*—implying a cautious character. Surpasses the practical skill and training necessary to get the job done; the word emphasizes quality over qualifications.

2. Teacher Preparation

A. Read and meditate upon the Devotional Reading and the Bible Background.

B. Study the FOCAL VERSES in the most popular translations used by the church in corporate worship or by the students in individual study. Make a note of study notes and contemporary language.

C. Recruit students ahead of class to act out in mime (silent but exaggerated expression of events and emotions) the servants and the bridesmaids vignettes. You will need a narrator, two servants, a master, ten bridesmaids, a bridegroom, and a crowd (the rest of the class).

3. Starting the Lesson

A. Write the AT-A-GLANCE outline on the board.

B. Discuss personal habits of preparation and procrastination.

C. Read IN FOCUS as a centering devotional.

4. Getting into the Lesson

A. Share "Words You Should Know" with students as introduction to the lesson.

B. Allow students to act out lesson in mime and narration.

5. Relating the Lesson to Life

A. Review KEEP IN MIND Scripture.

B. Script and role play responses students would have to questions regarding the return of Christ.

6. Arousing Action

A. Reflect on LESSON IN OUR SOCIETY.

B. Lead a time of prayer for boldness and preparation as students face persecution and wait for the coming Lord.

WORSHIP GUIDE

For the Superintendent or Teacher
Theme: Watching for Christ's Return
Theme Song: "Yield Not to Temptation"
Scripture: Matthew 7:24-27
Song: "Lord, Help Me to Hold Out"
Meditation: Dear God, because only You know when Christ will return, fill me with your Holy Spirit that I might persevere in service and remain prepared for His return.

FEBRUARY 13TH

WATCHING FOR CHRIST'S RETURN

Bible Background • MATTHEW 24:1—25:13
Printed Text • MATTHEW 24:45—25:13
Devotional Reading • MATTHEW 24:36-44

LESSON AIM

By the end of the lesson, students will be able to tell the story of the wise and foolish bridesmaids; understand the importance of staying prepared for Jesus' return; and determine to shun procrastinating habits—today.

KEEP IN MIND

"Watch therefore, for ye know neither the day nor the hour wherein the Son of man cometh" (Matthew 25:13).

FOCAL VERSES

MATTHEW 24:45 Who then is a faithful and wise servant, whom his lord hath made ruler over his household, to give them meat in due season?

46 Blessed is that servant, whom his lord when he cometh shall find so doing.

47 Verily I say unto you, That he shall make him ruler over all his goods.

48 But and if that evil servant shall say in his heart, My lord delayeth his coming;

49 And shall begin to smite his fellowservants, and to eat and drink with the drunken;

50 The lord of that servant shall come in a day when he looketh not for him, and in an hour that he is not aware of,

51 And shall cut him asunder, and appoint him his portion with the hypocrites: there shall be weeping and gnashing of teeth.

25:1 Then shall the kingdom of heaven be likened unto ten virgins, which took their lamps, and went forth to meet the bridegroom.

2 And five of them were wise, and five were foolish.

LESSON OVERVIEW

LESSON AIM
KEEP IN MIND
FOCAL VERSES
IN FOCUS
THE PEOPLE, PLACES, AND TIMES
BACKGROUND
AT-A-GLANCE
IN DEPTH
SEARCH THE SCRIPTURES
DISCUSS THE MEANING
LESSON IN OUR SOCIETY
MAKE IT HAPPEN
FOLLOW THE SPIRIT
REMEMBER YOUR THOUGHTS
MORE LIGHT ON THE TEXT
DAILY BIBLE READINGS

---

3 They that were foolish took their lamps, and took no oil with them:

4 But the wise took oil in their vessels with their lamps.

5 While the bridegroom tarried, they all slumbered and slept.

6 And at midnight there was a cry made, Behold, the bridegroom cometh; go ye out to meet him.

7 Then all those virgins arose, and trimmed their lamps.

8 And the foolish said unto the wise, Give us of your oil; for our lamps are gone out.

9 But the wise answered, saying, Not so; lest there be not enough for us and you: but go ye rather to them that sell, and buy for yourselves.

10 And while they went to buy, the bridegroom came; and they that were ready went in with him to the marriage: and the door was shut.

11 Afterward came also the other virgins, saying, Lord, Lord, open to us.

12 But he answered and said, Verily I say unto you, I know you not.

13 Watch therefore, for ye know neither the day nor the hour wherein the Son of man cometh.

IN FOCUS

From the pages of history comes an incident from the American Revolution that illustrates how tragedy can result from procrastination. Colonel Rahl, commander of the British troops in Trenton, New Jersey, was playing cards when a courier brought an urgent message stating that General George Washington was crossing the Delaware River. Rahl put the message in his pocket and didn't bother to read it until the game was finished. Then, realizing the seriousness of the situation, he hurriedly tried to rally his men to meet the coming attack, but his procrastination was his undoing. He and many of his men were killed, and the rest of the regiment were captured. Nolbert Quayle said, "Only a few minutes' delay cost him his life, his honor, and the liberty of his soldiers. Earth's history is strewn with the wrecks of half-finished plans and unexecuted resolutions. 'Tomorrow' is the excuse of the lazy and refuge of the incompetent."

This true report bridges the historical gap between the Gospel story and the believer's life. As an American citizen, one has most likely heard this story from General Washington's perspective. However, one can speculate on the outcome had Colonel Rahl and his men been prepared and anticipated the approach of General Washington and his troops. It is evident that procrastination cost the British, perhaps a victory, or at least a fair fight.

THE PEOPLE, PLACES, AND TIMES

PARABLES. Stories, especially those of Jesus, told to provide a vision of life, especially life in God's kingdom. Parable means putting alongside for purposes of comparison and clarification. Parables utilize pictures such as metaphors or similes and frequently extend them into a brief story to make a point or disclosure.

Though Jesus perfected the oral art of telling parables, their background can be found in the Old Testament and in secular sources. The stories of Jesus are linked with the heritage of the prophetic parables in the Old Testament (Isaiah 28:23-29; 5:1-7; 1 Kings 20:39-43; Ecclesiastes 9:13-16; 2 Samuel 12:1-4).

Many of the parables grew out of conflict situations when Jesus answered His religious critics. These parables, usually for Pharisees and sinners simultaneously, expose and extol. Jesus exposed the self-righteousness of His critics and extolled the kingdom of God. When John the Baptist was accused for being too serious and Jesus of being too frivolous, Jesus came back with the parable of the playing children (Matthew 11:16-19; Luke 7:31-35) to expose the inconsistency of the criticism. In one of His most famous parables, He extolled the forgiving love of the father and exposed the hostile criticism of the unforgiving elder brother (Luke 15:11-32).

In fact, Jesus interpreted His ministry and its place in the history of salvation by means of a parable. He addressed different audiences such as the crowds, the disciples, and the critics with definite purposes. Indeed, the Storyteller, as well as the tale, is important; that is, the fact that Jesus was the author affects the meaning. As Jesus interpreted His min-

istry through parables, these sometimes have a "Christological penetration." Jesus Himself appears indirectly in the story (Mark 3:23-27). The parables are not merely clever stories but a proclamation of the Gospel. The listener must respond and is invited to make a decision about the kingdom and the King. The parable of the wicked tenants (Mark 12:1-12) represents a blatant confrontation.

These stories got Jesus in trouble as He made veiled claims of kingliness and exposed hypocrisy in the religious hierarchy. One of the reasons they crucified Jesus was because of His challenging parables and the claims of His kingdom. Some of the stories carry a pastoral and others a prophetic relevance. The parable of the mustard seed (Matthew 13:31-32) speaks pastorally about ending despair, and the parable of the persistent widow (Luke 18:1-8) encourages us to never give up. The parable of the barren fig tree (Luke 13:6-9) speaks prophetically concerning national priorities; the parable of the wicked tenants (Luke 20:9-19) accosts arrogant religious leaders; and the parable of the rich fool (Luke 12:16-21) confronts false confidence in materialism. Through the parable of the Pharisee and the tax collector (Luke 18:9-14), grace peers down on two people praying in the temple, and we see that appearances are deceiving. Grace shines on worship, and revelation happens!

(Adapted from "Parables" by Peter Rhea Jones, in *Holman's Bible Dictionary for Windows, Version 1.0*, Parsons Technology, 1994.)

BACKGROUND

As Jesus leaves the temple, having upset religious corruption, He predicts the ultimate physical and symbolic ruin of the temple. This surprises the disciples and is, to them, inconceivable; the presence of the temple was central to Jewish worship customs. Yet Jesus, having their rapt attention, seizes this teachable moment to warn the disciples of an influx of false prophets. He foretells extreme trouble and persecution of for Christians, and exhorts them

AT-A-GLANCE

1. Rumors of His Return (Matthew 24:45-51)

2. Response of the Righteous (25:1-9)

3. Realities of His Reign (vv. 9-13)

to prepare and remain prepared for His return.

The disciples ask Jesus two questions which set the stage for the events to follow: (1) When would the Temple be destroyed; (2) What would be the signs of His return? Jesus answered them: (1) The temple would be destroyed in their lifetime; (2) a great cosmic procession would make His return visible and obvious to all on earth. The former was confirmed in A.D. 70. The latter is known by no one except the Father.

IN DEPTH

1. Rumors of His Return (Matthew 24:45-51)

Jesus told a parable about faithful and unfaithful servants to illustrate the importance of being prepared for His return. This parable could be considered a clarion call to church leaders to prepare for His return. These servants are the overseers of all of the household servants in the master's absence. Although both are aware the master is gone and will eventually return, the contrast of how they fulfill their tasks are vivid. The wise servant deals judiciously and consistently with the other servants in attending to the master's business. He is least concerned for the time of the master's return, but attends instead to his call and his commitment of service. The foolish servant, however, takes advantage of the master's absence and uses the time to be slothful in his tasks and abusive to his subjects. Upon the master's unannounced return, the wise servant is delightfully rewarded, and the foolish servant is dreadfully punished.

2. Response of the Righteous (25:1-9)

These maidens are called virgins in the KJV and the NIV, bridesmaids in the LB, and maidens in the RSV. Each of these terms are associated with the Greek word *parthenos*, which means chaste and an unmarried daughter.

In a parable about five wise and five foolish maidens, Jesus emphasizes being prepared for His return. Lest believers conclude that He is only interested in leaders' responsibility for readiness, Jesus now turns His attention away from the leaders' to the individual's responsibility to prepare for His return. The setting of this parable is of a wedding. A wedding was the greatest festival of their culture; the people understood the significance of being a bridesmaid. When a wedding was going on, all other business stopped, and the entire town focused on the wedding and the wedding party. All eyes were on the maidens, those betrothed to a bridegroom. This betrothal indicates that the bridegroom was not seen; however, he was not absent, as his return was expected.

It is common knowledge to the bridesmaids that the bridegroom is coming. The bridesmaids, however, differed in how they perceived their roles. Five prepared for his return, expecting him at any moment, and five figured he would return eventually, but without urgency. Five of the bridesmaids came with extra oil for their lamps, and five did not. When the bridegroom came later than expected, the foolish bridesmaids had to go buy more oil. Five of them made provision above and beyond their need, while the other five figured that when he returned, whenever he returned, they would have time to get ready. Jesus' parable stresses the individual responsibility to be prepared. It is a responsibility that a group identity cannot fulfill.

3. Realities of His Reign (vv. 9-13)

While the five bridesmaids were gone the bridegroom came, and those who were ready went with him to the marriage feast and the door was closed. No one can explain the bridegroom's delay, or Christ's delay, in returning. What is important to the Church, however, is that knowledge of His return is not sufficient for entrance into His eternal reign. This knowledge must be accompanied with preparation. All of the bridesmaids knew the bridegroom would come for them, but the wise ones prepared for his return before they went to sleep. Jesus points out that even though all bridesmaids brought lamps, expecting a night return, five of them did not expect His return that night. All of the bridesmaids, grew tired of waiting and went to sleep, which in itself is no practical offense. Sleep, or rest, was needed by the physical body. The difference, however, was that five of the bridesmaids took care of business before going to bed.

At midnight there was a great awakening. Five of the bridesmaids awoke to great joy and five to great sadness. The prepared bridesmaids were joined with the bridegroom and the wedding festivities began. The foolish bridesmaids tried to get oil from the wise bridesmaids, but were refused. Their refusal, as first glance, seems harsh and indifferent. However, it was the wisest decision made. With the wedding taking place at night, if they had shared their oil, there would not have been enough oil and light to last throughout the festivities. The wise bridesmaids could not share their preparedness. Here Jesus stresses the importance to each of us to prepare for His return. It is not enough to live in the here and now, but it is equally important to prepare for the hereafter.

By the time the five bridesmaids returned to the place of the wedding festival, the door was shut; the opportunity to reign as brides was closed to them. Tragically, the bridegroom would not acknowledge a bridesmaid who did not prepare for his return while there was time.

Jesus declared that one should be ready at all times because no one knows the time of His return. This is an exhortation to focus on a Christian lifestyle, not cultural legalism, while awaiting the return of the Lord.

SEARCH THE SCRIPTURES

1. What are the contrasts between the faithful and wise servant and the evil servant? (Matthew 24:45-51)

2. What parallels are between the servants and the bridesmaids? (25:1-5)

3. In the time of crisis, how did the bridesmaids respond? (vv. 6-10)

4. What are the implications of the door being shut? (vv. 10-12)

5. What is the point of the parable? (v. 13)

DISCUSS THE MEANING

1. While waiting for the bridegroom, both the wise and the foolish maidens slept. However, what did the wise bridesmaids do before they waited?

2. Lamps without oil are useless. What other analogies can be given in the life of a believer, or in the work of the Church, that indicate ineffectiveness and unfulfilled purpose?

LESSON IN OUR SOCIETY

We are told when John Huss was arrested and informed he would be burned to death for his faith, he purposely practiced holding his hand over fire to prepare for his final test. He burned himself in preparation. He wanted to be faithful to the end.

Huss heard of his upcoming persecution, simply for believing and preaching Christ. Because he knew he would not denounce his faith in Jesus, he prepared for his fate at the stake. Although it is most unlikely that you will face being burned to death because of your faith in Jesus, what persecution do you face as a believer, and how do you prepare to face it?

MAKE IT HAPPEN

Scientist Nostradamus predicted that the end of the world would come time and time again. But it hasn't. Heaven's Gate cultists believed eternal life was obtained through poison pudding and a celestial escort by the Hale Bopp Comet. But it didn't. Televison psychics make confusing, illogical, and twisted predictions that seldom show any relevance to the events that actually come to pass.

The next time you overhear rumors of the end of the world or a way to eternal life, be bold and courageous; confess, as Christ did, "Watch therefore, for ye know neither the day nor the hour wherein the Son of man cometh" (Matthew 25:13). For the believer's hope is not in knowing when, but in knowing Christ will return and we should remain ready.

FOLLOW THE SPIRIT

What God wants me to do:

_____

_____

_____

REMEMBER YOUR THOUGHTS

Special insights you learned:

_____

_____

MORE LIGHT ON THE TEXT
MATTHEW 24:45—25:13

45 Who then is a faithful and wise servant, whom his lord hath made ruler over his household, to give them meat in due season?

Dr. Cain Hope Felder identifies a new theme in Matthew 24:36—25:30. He calls this new theme the Delayed Parousia. He defines the term *parousia* to mean "royal or official visitation." Unlike Mark and the end time theology of Paul, Matthew does not insist on the immediacy of Jesus' second advent. Therefore, verse 45 implies there is time to determine "who then is a faithful and wise servant."

The introductory phrase of verse 45 suggests there is some question about the faithfulness and the level of wisdom regarding the servant. The very first words "Who then" is interpreted from the Greek *tis ara* to mean interrogate with the idea of drawing a conclusion. The conclusion to be drawn about the faithful and wise servant has to do with his trustworthy character. The lord has left instructions and is concerned whether the servant will be "sensible;" NASB uses this word in place of *wise*. A look at the Living Bible (LB) verifies the interrogative nature of this verse. It reads, "Are you a wise and faithful servant of the Lord? Have I given you the task of managing my household, to feed my children day by day?" Not only does the Living Bible bring clarification, but also uses the upper case for Lord. This means that the instructions are issued by *Kurios*, the Greek word for God and Lord. Further, the Living Bible directs the question to all who read the verse. This approach takes the inquiry out of the confines of the first century and makes it eternally applicable.

The question I raise is this, "What are the characteristics of a faithful and wise servant?" Listing the characteristics of a faithful and wise servant is not enough to make a servant faithful or wise, as Isaiah says, "But we are all as an unclean thing, and all our righteousness are as filthy rags" (Isaiah 64:6). Nonetheless, a faithful servant must be sincere, reliable, and committed to the Lord's household, immersed in preparing the best spiritual food possible for God's family until the Lord returns. The Lord's absence does not permit laziness, apathy, or indifference among His people, like the behavior of the one who is given a talent and buries it. The household is to use their gifts to the max while they wait on the Lord.

46 Blessed is that servant, whom his lord when he cometh shall find so doing.

The one who is reliably preparing for the Lord until His appearing is rewarded with *makarios*, the Greek word for happiness. Notice the possessive pronoun HIS, referring to the servant's lord followed by the word WHEN. This third parable of Matthew uses definitive language, clearly avoiding the IF word, which certainly leaves out any doubt about the Lord's appearing.

The use of the word SHALL, denoting the inevitable, is a powerful word in the KJV. Notable scriptural references include Genesis 2:17, "But from the tree of the knowledge of good and evil you shall not eat, for in the day that you eat from it you SHALL surely die;" or Psalm 23, "surely goodness and mercy SHALL follow me all the days of my life." This same word is used when Abram's name is changed to Abraham (Genesis 17:5) and Sarai to Sarah (Genesis 17:15), improbable or impossible conceptions, and various resurrections from the dead. All in all, blessings will be bestowed upon all faithful servants who do not grow weary while they wait on their Lord.

47 Verily I say unto you, That he shall make him ruler over all his goods.

Another reward bestowed on a faithful servant is often a promotion. Matthew is unparalleled in recording God's rewards for people who are faithful. In Matthew 25:21 and 23, the master divides his money among his servants according to their abilities. The Master deals harshly with a servant who wastes time or talent. Only those who are reliable will be commended, "You are a good and faithful servant. You have been faithful over this small amount, so now I will give you much more" (LB). In the above, however, the master is even more generous. He puts the faithful servant

in charge of all his possessions. There is something to be said about responsible stewardship. As stated in the Living Bible, God gives us time, abilities, and resources, and God expects us to invest them wisely until Christ returns for His people. Clearly, the issue is not one of how much, but what we do with what we have.

48 But and if that evil servant shall say in his heart, My lord delayeth his coming;

Throughout Holy Writ, God consistently gives blessings and warnings. God gave Adam and Eve the garden and all its blessings. He gave them free reign over creation. God gave them a cholesterol- and trouble-free diet, and He provided them with living quarters most of us dream about and work hard to duplicate. But God also gave them a warning, "You may freely eat of every tree of the garden; but of the tree of the knowledge of good and evil and blessing and calamity you shall not eat, for in the day that you eat of it you shall surely die."

And so it has been throughout human history, blessings with warnings, including the unfolding drama in the above Scripture, "but and if." The Greek meaning of the word *ean* for "if""means "in case that." So the warning to the servant is to avoid the assumption that delay is denial.

There are those who turn away from God's agenda thinking they have time to return before the Lord appears. As we shall see later, being unprepared for His appearance is devastating to the foolish maidens. The Apostle Paul wrote to the church in Rome after the death and resurrection of the Lord. Though Paul writes urgently about the Lord's appearing, he may have made the reader aware of the peril of practicing cheep grace. That is to say, Paul may have asked the reader, "Are you to turn to sin because grace abounds or away from God and practice evil because of the delayed parousia? God forbid."

49 And shall begin to smite his fellowservants, and to eat and drink with the drunken;

As it is with grace that goes from glory to glory, so it is with evil. It goes from bad to worse. First, the servant thinks evil in his heart, and then with evil thoughts begins to smite others. The Greek word for "smite" used in this verse is *tupto*. This is a repetitive blow, over and over again. The servant who *tupto* or beats his fellow servants up, then drowns his conscience in alcohol. It is reported that modern society suffers from a number of woes including overeating and alcholism. It is also clear that modern society's pathology effects the oppressed and the oppressor.

50 The lord of that servant shall come in a day when he looketh not for him, and in an hour that he is not aware of,

By the time this lesson is published, the world will be within weeks of kissing the 20th Century farewell and will also be briskly approaching a new millennium. It could be the Lord shall come in the new millennium, but because of His delay, He'll find many of His servants otherwise occupied with folly. When Matthew penned the words of Jesus in chapter 24:45—25:1-13, the uppermost thought of the Lord was to be watchful. The crucifixion was at hand; Jesus had put the disciples on notice that God would raise Him from the grave three days after His death, and then He would ascend to His Father.

Only Luke records the ascension of Jesus. Luke writes in Acts 1:8 and following the agenda for servants of all times, until Jesus returns. Here Luke gives us a glimpse of the Christ leaving the realm of time and space where He had accomplished the redemption of fallen man and woman. As He returned to the infinite and eternal spirit realm, the two men who accompanied Him said to His disciples, "Men of Galilee, why do you stand looking into the sky? This Jesus, who has been taken up from you into heaven, will come in just the same way as you have watched Him go into heaven." Luke makes plain that if the Lord's servants are not watchfully looking for His appearing, they will be caught unaware when He comes.

Whenever the subject of death came up in my childhood household, my dad, the late Earnest Anderson, would say, "Don't die hungry." I would reply, "We don't know when we're going to die, how can we control whether we'll be hungry or not?" He would respond "Never get hungry." If we are to be ready when Jesus comes and since we know not the day nor the hour, we must never stop watching for Him, never stop expecting him, never stop preparing for Him. The old folks used to sing, "bread of heaven, feed me 'till I want no more." Hearing this song reminds me to add to it the words of my dad, "Never get hungry." To live without watchfulness and readiness invites a disastrous belief that there is unlimited time to put things right before the Lord comes.

51 And shall cut him asunder, and appoint him his portion with the hypocrites: there shall be weeping and gnashing of teeth.

We wrote earlier about blessings and warnings. These warnings are not designed to plant fear, guilt, or helplessness. God is just, righteous, and loving; therefore, the purpose of the warning is to make the servant aware there are rewards for the faithful and consequences for the faithless. The faithful servant is made ruler over all His possessions and the faithless servant is flogged severely, bisected (the Greek word in this verse *dichotomeo* applies to both cut and asunder), and judged with the hypocrites.

To paraphrase Finis Jennings Dake's definition of a hypocrite, one who makes a false profession, assumes characterizations other than the real one, and covers up his or her devising to gain credit for his or her virtues. Hypocrites hope to prosper through deceit. Hypocrites, those who are faithless (Matthew 8:12), those who do not acknowledge the marriage feast (Matthew 22:13), unprofitable servants (Matthew 25:30), and those who profess but do not confess (Luke 13:28), shall be relegated to a place where there shall be weeping and gnashing of teeth.

The Greek word for weeping is *klauthmos* and means wailing. From the phrase "there shall be weeping and gnashing of teeth," one could surmise Matthew's familiarity with the book referred to in Jewish tradition as *qinot* or Lamentations. This book is so named because of a series of calamities, including the destruction of Jerusalem, the slaughtering of Jewish people, the cannibalism practiced by starving mothers, the collapse of the Jewish system of worship, and the banishment of the Jews. To this day, Orthodox Jews customarily render a verbal recitation of the entire Lamentations on the 9th day of the Jewish month *Ab*, the recognized date of the destruction of Solomon's temple in 586 B.C. Lamentations is also read weekly at the Wailing Wall in Jerusalem.

It has been said that a picture is worth a thousand words. Picture in your mind a place where there is perpetual darkness. All you can hear is sorrowful, bitter, remorseful never ending weeping and the sound of grinding, grating teeth like fingernails across a chalkboard. While this picture may have a chilling effect in your mind, add to this a mechanism which repeats the sights and sounds endlessly, so that it completely engulfs your entire being.

It is commonly believed that a loving God could not relegate His children to a place of eternal separation and suffering. In the Bible study on the Antediluvian Dispensation of the Ages of Innocence and Conscience, we've discovered that Adam and Eve were expelled from the Garden of Eden. Though both of them blamed someone other than themselves for the expulsion, God was very precise about the one and only commandment in place for that time. There really is no one to blame for voluntary disregard for the Lord's agenda. The one thing God gives every living soul is choice. God could not relegate His children to a place of eternal separation and suffering, but His children can relegate themselves. The choices and their rewards or consequences are as clear today as in the day when Adam and Eve chose an agenda different from God's. Therefore, it behooves God's servant to be faithful over a few things and when the Lord comes, He will make them ruler over many, if not all His possessions.

Though Matthew 25:1-13 is the beginning of a new chapter, it is a continuation of the author's theme on the delayed *parousia* wherein he warns the participants to be watchful and prepared for the Lord's return. The characterization in this segment of Scripture, however, is of a bridegroom instead of a lord, and the players are two types of maidens instead of two types of servants.

25:1 Then shall the kingdom of heaven be likened unto ten virgins, which took their lamps, and went forth to meet the bridegroom.

Matthew begins this parable with the Greek word *tote* which is used seven times to mean *at that time* and two times to mean *from that time*. The parable of the faithful and wise servant, this parable, and the parable of the talents which follows are all a part of Matthew's delayed *parousia*. It can be surmised that all three parables identify individual and group responsibilities associated with watching one's time, talent or abilities until the Lord, or Bridegroom, returns. Upon His return, what will take place in His kingdom will be like a Palestinian wedding.

At this point in the Scripture, there is no clear distinction between the bride and the young ladies attending the bride. As this parable of the kingdom of heaven unfolds, you will see the bride's wedding party had significant differences. Initially, however, they were alike in the following ways: they had knowledge about the bridegroom; they desired to go with him and the bride to the banquet; they each had a lamp they would use if the bridegroom came at night; and they all grew weary and napped.

In many of Jesus' parables, the characters are initially without distinction. The two men who built houses, for example, initially used the same building materials: they may have used the same contractors; they may have built in the same neighborhood; they may have patterned their homes on the same plans, etc. But the character and steadfastness of the builders and the buildings is evident during the stormy season.

Unlike weddings in western nations where the wedding party plans for months and sometimes years for a one hour festival, Palestinian weddings were celebrated over a long period of time. The Palestinian maidens, usually ten of them, ironically, keep the bride company until the bride-

groom arrives. However, at the time of his arrival, Palestinian law requires a man to be sent along the streets shouting, "Behold! the bridegroom comes." Since this could happen at any time, persons on the streets at night had to have lighted lamps so that the community could get a glimpse of the bridegroom. Once he enters the bridal ceremony, the door must be closed, and those who come after are not allowed to enter.

2 And five of them were wise, and five were foolish.

In this verse, we begin to see the differences between the ten young lady friends of the bride. Equally divided, five of them are distinguished as wise. The Greek word for wise, *phronimos*, means "thoughtful." To be thoughtful implies these women counted the cost of saying yes to being in their girlfriend's wedding. Counting the cost must have meant to them the economic implications for clothing, time off from their duties, and the cost for their accessories (i.e., the lamps, oil, etc.). In order words, the wise women may have had an affinity for detailed preparations which included having a Plan B.

Conversely, the five labeled as foolish accepted the invitation to be in the wedding party, but were negligent in their preparations. The Greek word for foolish is *moros*. Strong's Concordance alludes to the probable meaning of the word *moros* to indicate, ironically enough, "as if shut up and heedless." Like their contemporaries, these ladies appear to be equal in their sincerity and commitment toward supporting the bride. But they fail Matthew's litmus test concerning watchfulness and preparedness.

3 They that were foolish took their lamps, and took no oil with them:

From outward appearances, the five that were foolish looked like genuine participants of the wedding party. Before we consider their hypocrisy, however, bear in mind that their regard for the bride and the bridegroom was similar to the five wise bridesmaids. These foolish ladies had also adjusted their schedules to accommodate the bridal party. They, too, felt some attachment to the bridegroom, a prototype of Christ. They started out being full participants, but proved to be inconstant. They knew the bridegroom would come at night, probably midnight, or sometime before sunrise, because it was a Jewish custom to start a wedding processional at the rise of the evening star. Therefore, there was no question that they would need oil. Though they had oil in their lamps, the scriptural phrase "they took no additional oil with them" shows they had no forethought. They had no Plan B to accommodate the possible delay of bridegroom.

Matthew Henry's Commentary does not allow the leeway provided by Strong's or the Apostle Matthew's theme. Henry calls these ladies hypocrites. When they agreed to be in the wedding, they also agreed to carry out their duties until the bridegroom appeared. The *Biblical Illustrator* suggests that there is a relationship between the foolish virgins and the seed that falls upon rocky ground (Matthew 13:5-6, 20-21). The implication is that these women had the desire to be in the wedding ceremony but lacked an understanding of the full extent of their commitment. Had the foolish maidens examined their vessels, they would have realized their need for more oil.

4 But the wise took oil in their vessels with their lamps.

Here we see a mindset that thinks about and covers all the bases to complete a task. Their wisdom is evident when they purchase extra oil for their vessels, called flasks in the NIV and jars in the LB.

The behavior of the wise women also speaks to their character. The store of oil relates to 2 Peter 1:5-9. Here the Apostle writes, "And beside this, giving all diligence, add to your faith virtue; and to virtue knowledge; and to knowledge temperance; and to temperance patience; and to patience godliness; and to godliness brotherly kindness; and to brotherly kindness charity. For if these things be in you, and abound, they make you that you shall neither be barren nor unfruitful in the knowledge of our Lord Jesus Christ. But he that lacketh these things is blind, and cannot see afar of." The wise answered the call of the bride and bridegroom in faith. Faith is one of many possible symbols for oil. Since faith alone is sufficient according to 2 Peter 1:5-9, these wise women will also add to their faith additional qualities to sustain them during the time they support the bride and watch for the bridegroom.

It is commonly said about Generation X that previous generations failed to transmit something they can fall back on. It appears they are using up all of their lives as they go along. This has also been said of us in the present age who fail to pass on the principles that have brought us along the way. When darkness falls or we come face-to-face with the dark side of the soul, what do we have to light the way or to fall back on if we've spent all and left nothing in reserve? Is this present age prepared to walk the extra mile in faith and, simultaneously, to watch for the coming Christ?

5 While the bridegroom tarried, they all slumbered and slept.

Who among us is ready to meet Jesus? Apparently, Matthew understands the need for His delay. Throughout his book, he writes words like Matthew 24:36, which reads, "But of the day and hour knoweth no man, no not the angels . . . but my Father only." In other words, the exact time of Christ's (Bridegroom's) coming is not the greatest concern for God's people. Instead, the greatest concern is to be prepared or watchful.

The Greek word for tarried is *chronizo* and means "to take time." The NASB uses the word "delaying." The Greek word for delay is *chronizw* which means "coming a long time." In the meantime, Matthew gives the bridesmaids and God's people time to prepare their souls for His appearing, because there will be no time to prepare when the call goes out, "Here He comes."

In this verse, we see the wise and the foolish women became fatigued. Many contemporary believers can also identify with spiritual battle fatigue, and sometimes we need to take better care of our physical needs. Proper eating, regular exercise, and systematic bed rest can do wonders for the soul, mind, and body.

There is no telling how long these women had been organizing for the wedding, checking banquet halls, negotiating prices with banquet hall owners, getting advanced notices posted, and a host of other projects to be completed before the bridegroom arrives. So it is with us. Until the Bridegroom (Christ) comes, those of us who have accepted the invitation to work will experience fatigue. Preparation in contemporary society corresponds to the work the women do, and this includes organizing evangelistic ministry, checking the worship facilities for space and stewardship efforts, negotiating through prayer and fasting for appropriate leadership, getting the word out that the church is a safe space for healing and hope, and a host of other projects before Jesus Christ comes for His Bride, the Church. The work of evangelism alone can be enervating.

Just as the wedding party had no idea when the bridegroom would come, our society has no specific time for the Lord's appearing. Anyone who has an instructor, teacher, or college professor noted for his or her unannounced, pop-quizzes is more likely to be prepared than not. If it were possible to know the exact hour of our Lord's return, the human condition might see more apathy, laziness, and folly than already exists. Not knowing that hour may very well keep the believer from becoming absorbed with earthly or worldly unreadiness. What we do have is the expectation and the divine appointment to prepare, watch, and work while we're waiting. If rest is needed, we should have a reserve supply of faith for when the call comes.

6 And at midnight there was a cry made, Behold, the bridegroom cometh; go ye out to meet him.

All over the world, most people are asleep in the middle of the night and unless there is a reason to listen out for someone or something, it takes more than one ring from the telephone, one knock on the door, or one call from a voice to awaken a sound sleeper. Though this Passage doesn't imply an Eastern wedding tradition, there is, in fact, more than one call announcing the bridegroom's arrival. In contemporary society, every groom has a best man. In Palestine, this man goes before the bridegroom and shouts repeatedly throughout the neighborhood, "The bridegroom is coming; the bridegroom is coming." In the Orient, it is the custom for a procession of people to walk through several streets of the town; the bridegroom is attended by a body of friends bearing torches so that he is in full view of the on-lookers.

The bridesmaids were responsible for preparing the bride to meet the bridegroom. In all likelihood, the bride was also asleep when the announcement went forth. There is the possibility the maidens and the bride were sleeping wisely, with their lamps burning like a modern day nightlight. They would only need a minimum amount of preparation before the bridegroom's actual appearance. As we will soon discover, the foolish maidens may have been sleeping in hopes that the morning would precede the bridegroom's arrival.

7 Then all those virgins arose, and trimmed their lamps.

As soon as the virgins heard the shout and the celebrations from the neighbors leaning out of their windows and peering from their doors, they got up and trimmed their lamps. The Greek word, *egeiro*, is akin to collecting one's faculties.

The Greek word for "trimmed" is *kosmeo* and means to put in proper order. Candle burners know how to keep the candle wick clear from debris, and persons with hand lamps know how to keep the wick slightly moist with oil and the globe free from soot. In the Jewish tradition, there was another type of lamp called *lampas*. This Greek word means torches.

Torches, a word used in the NIV, consisted of a long pole with oil-drenched rags at the top. The charred ends of

the rags were cut off and dipped in olive oil. The oil had to be replenished about every 15 to 20 minutes. It is more likely these were the *lampas* used by the processional wedding party and not by the maidens.

The lamp, at this point, is the pivotal detail in the parable. Lamps are used to light the way. David says, God's Word is a lamp unto our feet and a light unto our pathway (Psalm 119:105, paraphrased). The lamp in this verse is like the profession of Christianity and the light represents progress, duty, and comfort. Therefore, the trimming implies obtaining fresh oil. This may be the ideal place to recall two things: (1) the previous mention of the lamp was as a symbol of faith and, adding to this symbolism, knowledge and experience; (2) the characterization of the wise virgins applies to all believers.

It is important to note that while the lamp may be symbolic for faith, knowledge, and experience, the reader must bear in mind these three characterizations cannot be lent, borrowed, or bought. These characteristics are not for their own end but as a means to the end, a hard lesson for the unprepared to learn in time of need.

8 And the foolish said unto the wise, Give us of your oil; for our lamps are gone out.

Can you hear the panic in the foolish virgins' voices? Can you remember a time in your life when you missed a passing grade by one digit? Or maybe you arrived late for a job interview, even though you left home in plenty of time, because of a traffic jam or your car breaks down.

The foolish and the wise maidens started out in time. They all have the same title, that is, virgins; their attire for the wedding is the same; they have the same duty to meet the bridegroom; they all succumbed to fatigue; they all possessed the same equipment, a lamp and oil; and they all had the same invitation to the banquet. Based on outward appearances one could conclude there are no differences between the maidens. As I often tell my congregation, "If you can see it, it isn't faith." Until faith becomes sight, or external, however faith is an internal issue. Imagine a painting of a fire. It's easily identified as a fire; it looks like a flame; it looks hot, but when you need heat and light, the picture of a fire cannot give you either one. At this point in the Scripture, the foolish virgins are stuck in a traffic jam, or their car just broke down. So what do they do? They appeal to their prepared and prudent colleagues for help.

On his cassette tape *101 Ways to Transform Your Life*, Dr. Wayne W. Dyer has a cliche that is most appropriate for this situation; "Circumstances don't make a man, they reveal him." The extent of the virgin's resources reveals those with unfailing grace and faith in the task at hand; it also reveals those who deceive themselves and rely on external support.

9 But the wise answered, saying, Not so; lest there be not enough for us and you: but go ye rather to them that sell, and buy for yourselves.

It never ceases to amaze me that people with plenty, especially those mature citizens, are less likely to lend to others. Maybe that's why they have hefty reserves. Habitual readiness put the wise women in a position to enter into the joy that comes with internalism, as opposed to externalism. The wise women could no more give from their reserve than they could transfer their integrity, commitment, or their faith. These are qualities that must be developed from within, sustained by the Holy Spirit, and nurtured daily with discipline and prayer. Psalm 23 speaks of one's cup running over, from the inside out. It is from this internal reserve that the contemporary believer is able to respond to God's invitation, even if they have to wait for an unknown period of time.

The message to the foolish is they have to do more than to look the part, they have to commit to their part. It is not enough to do good, to believe, or to have faith, every believer must get into the habit of being good, believing, and living by faith. The lesson is, as it was with the faithful servant, be watchful and careful about nourishing the inner life and less comfortable with preserving outward appearances.

And so, the wise made a very practical choice. Taking no chances, they advised their colleagues to take the initiative for their own resources. There are many who think they may see Jesus based on the prayers of their mother, their father, or their preacher. But when Jesus comes, when the call goes out from heaven, "Behold, the Bridegroom comes," only those with reserve enough to go all the way will see Jesus for themselves.

We used to sing a little song in my hometown church, and it went something like this: "Give me oil in my lamp, keep it burning, burning burning, give me oil in my lamp I pray, hallelujah; give me oil in my lamp, keep it burning, burning, burning, keep it burning till the break of day."

The bottom line is this, the invitation goes out to those with ears to hear. The wise counted and paid the cost and expect the same from all others, especially the foolish. What's more important than investing in preparedness? It is commonly said, "It is better to have insurance and not need it, than to need it and not have it." That was the case in the Black Church and the American educational system during the post World War I and II era. The standard pol-

icy was built on the "what if" or "take it in case you need it" premise. That's one of the reasons males were encouraged, if not required, to take home economics and females took science. If you never need it, you're still prepared if something happens. If a life-changing experience required "it" and you don't have it, then what? Will you have time to acquire "it" before the opportunity permanently passes you buy?

When the 10 virgins went to sleep, their lamps were burning. When the announcement came, however, the Greek reads that the foolish virgins said, "Our lamps are going out."

There is never a good time to discover that your light is dim because of personal negligence to the things of God. There is real sadness in the heart which needs light and, upon seeking it, finds those prepared unwilling to take a chance lest they be found wanting themselves. How sad it must be to come so far and then be told you can go no further.

We know that the oil, in this reference, is not symbolic of the Holy Spirit because God's Spirit cannot be bought. What it most likely represents is guidance. When the evening falls and night looms over the canvas of the heavens, when sickness lingers or grief prevails, when the time comes to walk through the valley of the shadow of death, the soul needs loving guidance—guidance which leads you to your purpose, in this case, to meet the Bridegroom.

10 And while they went to buy, the bridegroom came; and they that were ready went in with him to the marriage: and the door was shut.

If there is such a thing as shopping at the wrong time, this is it. Clearly nothing and no one should have a greater priority to the committed heart than the Saviour. Though this particular parable has no parallel, there is some controversy as to whether the bridegroom is the Christ or representative of a newly married man. When the Bridegroom refers to the Christ He is connected with the bride, the Lamb's wife, and the Holy City (Revelation 21:2, 9, for example). There are numerous other references which refer to a newly married man (Psalm 19:5; Isaiah 61:10; 62:5; Jeremiah 7:34; 16:9; 25:10; 33:11; Joel 2:16; John 2:9; 3:29; Revelation 18:23).

As with most of Jesus' parables, this one is also directed against the chosen people, the Jews. Their whole history, and the sole purpose of the bridesmaids, was to prepare for the bridegroom's arrival. If no one else was ready to meet the bridegroom those who received a personal invitation should be. Woe to a church that fails, at every gathering of the community of faith, to extend an invitation to prepare for the Son of God's appearing. And woe to the believer who finds himself or herself displacing the number one priority for all believers—watch and prepare for the Lord's appearing.

How many blessings do believers miss by taking care of material things before setting spiritual things in order? Is this not a matter of stewardship? And what is the ultimate price for being unprepared?

The bridegroom comes and takes those who are ready with him to the wedding feast, and shuts the door. The door is a symbol of separation. In the spiritual world and in the natural world there is a seed-time and harvest time. Sowing seed at the wrong time means harvesting at the wrong time, if at all. For hundreds of years Noah planted the seed of warning regarding the great flood. The community thought he was completely crazy to build an ark in a land which knew no rain. But when all things were ready and the believers were in place, God shut and locked the door. Neither Noah, his family, nor the strongest of animals could open the door.

Both Greek words *kleiw* and *kleio* mean to lock. The door of repentance, religious opportunity, hope, grace, and mercy is eternally locked against the faithless, against unbelievers, and against those preoccupied with shopping at the wrong time.

11 Afterward came also the other virgins, saying, Lord, Lord, open to us.

Too often the world turns to the Lord when all else fails or when it becomes convenient. The writer of Ecclesiastes says, "Remember now your creator in the days of your youth while the evil days come not, nor the years draw nigh, when you shall say, I have no pleasure in them" (Ecclesiastes 12:1). In other words, prepare a place for the Lord in your heart, in your life, in your plans early on. Get

your heart fixed and your mind made up to serve the Lord before your reserves ebb from worldly wear and tear.

We live in the dispensation of grace wherein God gives us unmerited favor. Unfortunately, many take God and God's blessing and God's time for granted. Many assume God's mercy and loving-kindness gives license to procrastination, tardiness, and apathy towards preparedness. Many are under the impression there is little fun in Christ, so they continue to live in darkness, at worse, and mediocrity at best. Thank God, the Holy Spirit pricks at the conscience of humanity from time to time, and if we would but listen. We will not come to God after our lives are in a mess, after our finances are in disarray, after our marriages fall apart, after our bodies are wreaked with disease or pain, after we have developed a reprehensible relationship with God's family.

In Matthew 7 Jesus gives a similar word to His disciples. He says in verses 21-23, "Not every one that saith unto me, Lord, Lord, shall enter into the kingdom of heaven, but he that doeth the will of my Father which is in heaven. Many will say to me in that day, Lord, Lord, have we not prophesied in thy name? and in thy name have cast out devils? and in thy name done many wonderful works? And then will I profess unto them, 'I never knew you: depart from me, ye that work iniquity'" (Matthew 7:21-23).

One of the things Jesus is saying in this Scripture is that professing righteousness must be coupled with concrete faith in the gracious provision of God's salvation. Many can perform various religious works and many can talk about the kingdom of heaven. But like the old folk used to sing, "Everybody talkin 'bout heaven ain't goin' there."

In Matthew 7:23 and in 25:11, the author uses *Kurios*, the Greek word for Lord. Kurios means supreme in authority, or God. So whether the word bridegroom is capitalized or not, the person whom the virgins call "Lord" is God.

12 But he answered and said, Verily I say unto you, I know you not.

This answer is found in two other places in the New Testament. In Luke 13:25, the Jews are debating about the number of persons who will be saved when all is said and done. Most Jews had a strong dislike for Samaritans and Gentiles and didn't want them counted as redeemed. So they ask the Lord, "Are there just a few who are being saved?" (NASB). And Jesus answered "Strive to enter by the narrow door, for many I tell you, will seek to enter and will not be enabled." Luke 13:25 and 27 make the same point as Matthew 25:11 when Jesus says, "Once the head of the house gets up and shuts the door, and you begin to stand outside and knock on the door, saying, 'Lord, open up to us!' then He will say to you, 'I do not know where you are from.'"

Throughout Holy Writ, the Greek word for "know" is *eido* and *ginosko*. *Eido* means to be aware, perceive, be sure, and understand, whereas *ginosko* has a greater variety of applications, including sexual or emotional intimacy. Intimacy and understanding are two things that become activated in an individual's developmental relationship with God. As the relationship develops and the individual obeys God's will, the believer takes on recognizable, godly characteristics. In Luke 13: 25 and 27, Jesus is saying to the Jews (and to the delinquent maidens) that their behavior is unrecognizable or unrighteous. Matthew uses different words than Luke who quotes Jesus as saying, "Depart from me, all you evildoers." The results are the same; the door is locked, and the virgins are denied entrance.

What's worse? To be separated physically or emotionally from God? To have the door of salvation shut with the words, "I do not know you" or to hear the words from behind a shut door, "Depart from me, I never knew you?" These are questions every doubtful, watchless, procrastinating person must wrestle with and, hopefully, move away from their ineffectualness and towards preparing for the Lord's return.

Don't let it be said to you, "Too late."

13 Watch therefore, for ye know neither the day nor the hour wherein the Son of man cometh.

There is an old hymn that we don't hear very much anymore. We used to sing it in my hometown church and one of the verses reads: "There is awful danger in delay, be ready when he comes; will you cast your only hope away? Be ready when he comes."

Many things should cause humanity to look for and long for the Lord's coming. One of Satan's greatest tools for deception is love of the world. The world is neither waiting nor watching for the second Advent. It is for this reason that believers are in the world but advised to be not of the world. All ten virgins started out together with equal opportunity to sit at the same table with the Bridegroom (Christ) and the Bride (the Church), and half of them were totally prepared by focusing on the agenda. The other half ended up having to separate themselves from the fellowship. While they were having their needs satisfied by the world, the Lord came and shut (locked) the door. As good as their intentions were, they were shut up and unaware of their need for a reserve, and now they are shut out because they failed to fill up for the journey.

There is no question whether Jesus is coming back for His own. Therefore, "if" is an inappropriate reference. The heart of those who accept the invitation to *gregoreuo*, (the Greek word which means "be vigilant") must be prepared, focused, and wholly committed to Him.

My best friend and I were talking about a sermon where the preacher asked the gathered community "What is Satan's most effective tool of deception?" As the story goes, Satan became very disturbed about the number of persons giving their lives to God. So Satan called a meeting with the imps and asked them what they planned to do about this wave of new conversions. One imp replied, "I can tell them God is a liar." Satan responded, "There are too many scientists turning away from the theory of evolution and believing in a greater truth behind the wonder of creation. People who believe these scientists are too far gone."

Another imp said, "I can persuade the masses to believe that when you're dead your done." Satan said, "That only works for those who disbelieve the resurrection, which is the hope of the Church. What I want to do is stop or at least slow down the spiritual conversions." The last imp said, "I've got it. Together we can convince the masses that they have plenty of time." And Satan said, "that's it!" When Jesus comes, it is too late to acquire a relationship with God. The invitation is the Lord's, the RSVP is yours to be on the alert.

DAILY BIBLE READING

M: Signs of the End
Matthew 24:1-8
T: Jesus' Followers Will Be Persecuted
Matthew 24:9-14
W: Beware of False Messiahs
Matthew 24:15-28
T: Coming of the Son of Man
Matthew 24:29-35
F: Be Watchful and Expectant
Matthew 24:36-44
S: Call to Be Faithful Servants
Matthew 24:45-51
S: Parable of the Ten Bridesmaids
Matthew 25:1-13

TEACHING TIPS

February 20
Bible Study Guide 12

1. Words You Should Know

A. Cross. (Matthew 27:40) Greek—*stauros*, an instrument of capital punishment. It was reserved as the worst, most vengeful form of execution, usually for the most heinous crimes of robbery.

B. Resurrection. (v. 53) Greek, *egersis*—a resurgence from death. Implying that death was indeed certified; but that the one who is certified as dead is again alive.

2. Teacher Preparation

A. Read and meditate upon the Devotional Reading and Bible Background.

B. Study the FOCAL VERSES in the most popular translations used by the church in corporate worship or students in individual study. Make a note of study notes and contemporary language.

C. Write out answers to the SEARCH THE SCRIPTURES questions.

3. Starting the Lesson

A. Write the AT-A-GLANCE outline on the board.

B. Discuss "Words You Should Know," with particular emphasis on what a cross means in our culture as a symbol of fashion vs. faith.

C. Read IN FOCUS as a centering devotional and the LESSON AIM as a guide for discussion.

4. Getting into the Lesson

A. Have the students read silently, carefully, and deliberately THE PEOPLE, PLACES, AND TIMES.

B. Have them read it again aloud, with each student reading two to three sentences each.

C. Discuss former knowledge, present emotion, and impact of the harsh process of crucifixion as capital punishment.

5. Relating the Lesson to Life

A. Break off into small groups for DISCUSS THE MEANING questions.

B. Reconvene in larger group and share reflections and discoveries.

6. Arousing Action

A. Reflect on LESSON IN OUR SOCIETY.

B. Devise strategies to respond to MAKE IT HAPPEN.

C. Secure corporate commitment to meditate upon DAILY BIBLE READING this week.

D. Close the class with prayer.

DEATH OF JESUS

Bible Background • MATTHEW 27:32-61
Printed Text • MATTHEW 27:38-54
Devotional Reading • JOHN 19:16-30

LESSON AIM

By the end of this lesson, students will be able to tell the story of Jesus' last hours on the cross; understand how Jesus' stalwart faith in the face of mockery is a model for the believer in facing persecution; and be determined to be faithful to the call of God until death.

KEEP IN MIND

"Now when the centurion, and they that were with him, watching Jesus, saw the earthquake, and those things that were done, they feared greatly, saying, Truly this was the Son of God" (Matthew 27:54).

FOCAL VERSES

MATTHEW 27:38 Then were there two thieves crucified with him, one on the right hand, and another on the left.

39 And they that passed by reviled him, wagging their heads,

40 And saying, Thou that destroyest the temple, and buildest it in three days, save thyself. If thou be the Son of God, come down from the cross.

41 Likewise also the chief priests mocking him, with the scribes and elders, said,

42 He saved others; himself he cannot save. If he be the King of Israel, let him now come down from the cross, and we will believe him.

43 He trusted in God; let him deliver him now, if he will have him: for he said, I am the Son of God.

44 The thieves also, which were crucified with him, cast the same in his teeth.

45 Now from the sixth hour there was darkness over all the land unto the ninth hour.

46 And about the ninth hour Jesus cried with a loud voice, saying, Eli, Eli, lama sabachthani? that is to say, My

LESSON OVERVIEW

LESSON AIM
KEEP IN MIND
FOCAL VERSES
IN FOCUS
THE PEOPLE, PLACES, AND
TIMES
BACKGROUND
AT-A-GLANCE
IN DEPTH
SEARCH THE SCRIPTURES
DISCUSS THE MEANING
LESSON IN OUR SOCIETY
MAKE IT HAPPEN
FOLLOW THE SPIRIT
REMEMBER YOUR THOUGHTS
MORE LIGHT ON THE TEXT
DAILY BIBLE READINGS

God, my God, why hast thou forsaken me?

47 Some of them that stood there, when they heard that, said, This man calleth for Elias.

48 And straightway one of them ran, and took a sponge, and filled it with vinegar, and put it on a reed, and gave him to drink.

49 The rest said, Let be, let us see whether Elias will come to save him.

50 Jesus, when he had cried again with a loud voice, yielded up the ghost.

51 And, behold, the veil of the temple was rent in twain from the top to the bottom; and the earth did quake, and the rocks rent;

52 And the graves were opened; and many bodies of the saints which slept arose,

53 And came out of the graves after his resurrection, and went into the holy city, and appeared unto many.

54 Now when the centurion, and they that were with him, watching Jesus, saw the earthquake, and those things that were done, they feared greatly, saying, Truly this was the Son of God.

IN FOCUS

Several tough issues face every Christian who is called to be a leader. If one desires to follow the leadership modeled by Christ, one must be willing to stand alone and go against public opinion in order to promote one's convictions. While fear of failure may keep others from acting on their convictions, a Christian leader must be willing to risk failure in the eyes of the world. Paul encourages Christians to remain above reproach. Jesus' statement that we must be willing to take up our cross daily and follow Him is important. To follow Christ, one must be willing to sacrifice personal interest for the kingdom of God. While many may be satisfied with acceptance and mediocrity, the Christian leader must never be content with the average; he or she must always strive for the best, looking always to Jesus. A Christian leader cannot allow herself or himself to idolize things and use people.

Jesus' life, trials, and crucifixion typifies this leadership model. As we face life's challenges, we must consider instead that Jesus, Himself, created this leadership paradigm for Christian leaders to follow.

THE PEOPLE, PLACES, AND TIMES

CRUCIFIXION. A medical doctor provides a physical description of a cruxifixion: The cross is placed on the ground and the exhausted man is quickly thrown backwards with his shoulders against the wood. The legionnaire feels for the depression at the front of the wrist. He drives a heavy, square wrought-iron nail through the wrist and deep into the wood. Quickly he moves to the other side and repeats the action, being careful not to pull the arms too tightly, but to allow some flex and movement. The cross is then lifted into place. The left foot is pressed backward against the right foot, and with both feet extended, toes down, a nail is driven through the arch of each, leaving the knees flexed. The victim is now crucified. As he slowly sags down with more weight on the nails in the wrists, excruciating, fiery pain shoots along the fingers and up the arms to explode in the brain—the nails in the wrists are putting pressure on the median nerves. As he pushes himself upward to avoid this stretching torment, he places the full weight on the nail through his feet. Again he feels the searing agony of the nail tearing through the nerves between the bones of his feet. As the arms fatigue, cramps sweep through the muscles, knotting them in deep, relentless, throbbing pain. With these cramps comes the inability to push himself upward to breathe. Air can be drawn into the lungs but not exhaled. He fights to raise himself in order to get even one small breath. Finally carbon dioxide builds up in the lungs and in the blood stream, and the cramps partially subside. Spasmodically he is able to push himself upward to exhale and bring in life-giving oxygen. Hours of this limitless pain, cycles of twisting, joint-rending cramps, intermittent partial asphyxiation, searing pain as tissue is torn from his lacerated back as he moves up and down against the rough timber. Then another agony begins: a deep, crushing pain deep in the chest as the pericardium slowly fills with serum and begins to compress the heart. It is now almost over—the loss of tissue fluids has reached a critical level—the compressed heart is struggling to pump heavy, thick, sluggish blood into the tissues—the tortured lungs are making a frantic effort to gasp in small gulps of air. He can feel the chill of death creeping through his tissues … finally his body begins to die. The Bible records all of this with the simple words, "And they crucified Him" (Mark 15:24).

The people present fully understood the impact of this simple statement. Yet it is sometimes painfully obvious that people in the contemporary church suffer from too many degrees of historical and cultural separation to fully embrace the atrocity of crucifixion.

BACKGROUND

The Jewish leaders seize and accuse Jesus of breaking the law and present Him to Pilate for judgment and execution. Pilate, although unconvinced by the weak charges lobbied against Jesus, is too much the coward to release Him. Obviously Jesus did break the letter of the law, but not the spirit of the law. Instead, Pilate restores Jesus into the custody of the local religious leaders to do with Him as they will.

Jesus begins His final descent from His humanity and ascent into eternal Divinity through three distinct acts. First, He parts with His personal possessions. It was not uncommon that the clothes and personal possessions of a crucified man were given to, or divided among, those crucifying him as payment or reward. Second, He reassigns His affectionate relationship with His mother over to His favorite disciple, thereby meeting her earthly needs. Because a woman's identity was intrinsically tied to her identification to a male family member, Jesus executed the adoption of His mother and her new son. And finally, He breathes His last breath, gives up the ghost, and dies, thus fulfilling His earthly mission.

AT-A-GLANCE

**1. Cruel Mockery
(Matthew 27:38-44)
2. Crucified Agony (vv. 45-50)
3. Certain Identity (vv. 51-54)**

IN DEPTH

1. Cruel Mockery (Matthew 27:38-44)

When Jesus was crucified between two bandits, the people, the chief priests, the scribes, and even the bandits mocked Him. They compared Jesus with the two bandits who were crucified as customary punishment for robbery. Jesus had been known to associate with others who were considered abhorrent—tax collectors and sinners. Additionally, having upset their primary money making venture of the feast extortion in the temple—crucifixion was the preferred punishment to showcase their outrage and threat against anyone who might foster notions of doing the same.

Imagine the scene. A three-man crucifixion taking place, but business went on as usual. As the people passed by, denoting the habit or commonplace scene of crucifixions, they mocked Jesus as just another fool, thief, or low-life getting his due. And the religious leaders led the jeers against Jesus who had destroyed, not the physical temple where the people worshiped, but the material temple that mattered most to them, their money and their pride.

The ultimate mockery and insult came as they challenged Jesus' ability to save Himself, much like Satan's tempting of Jesus in the wilderness (Matthew 4:5-6). What a tragedy. They did not see that to save others Jesus literally could not come down from the cross and save Himself.

2. Crucified Agony (vv. 45-50)

At about 3 p.m., after three hours of darkness, Jesus cried out the words of Psalm 22:1, but bystanders misunderstood what He said. His crying out demonstrates the final vestiges of Jesus' humanity. Jesus knew the crucifixion was going as planned and would soon be over, but He found the separation from God temporarily intolerable. His cry proclaimed His faith, even as Jesus faced this certain, abhorrent death.

And Jesus' cry was misunderstood by those around. Some thought He was thirsty for drink, yet in reality, Jesus longed to be wholly reunited with the Father. Others, who knew of the Jewish belief that the prophet Elijah was taken up to heaven and did not die, thought Jesus was calling out for Elijah to save Him from this public humiliation and great distress. In response they offered Jesus an anesthetic, a drink to comfort Him in His great agony. But Jesus, knowing there was no remedy for His agony, cried out again and died.

As prophesied, Jesus' death came quicker than most. This was done most likely to prevent the breaking of His bones as was done to the two thieves to hasten death before sundown. Still, one could never accurately say the religious leaders actually killed Jesus against His will. Actually, Jesus willfully gave up His life because He chose to and when He

chose to do so. Jesus showed His ultimate control over His circumstances, control which neither the Jewish or Roman leaders never really possessed.

3. Certain Identity (vv. 51-54)

At Jesus' death, the curtain of the temple was torn from top to bottom, the earth shook, rocks were split tombs were opened, and many of the saints who had died were raised. At the instant Jesus died, His prophecy of the rending, or tearing, of the temple veil took place. At this point the usefulness of the temple was no more, as access to God and the Holy of Holies was given to everyone. Again, an earthquake indicated the violent, cataclysmic response to Jesus' death. And as the earth parted, tombs of others who believed were opened, and after Jesus' resurrection, they too were raised.

The centurion and his soldiers saw what took place and testified that Jesus was God's Son. How ironic, the very guards who crucified Him, cast lots for His clothes, and confirmed His death were also the first to confess Jesus as the Son of God! They realized, then, this Jesus was no ordinary man.

SEARCH THE SCRIPTURES

1. Who mocked Jesus while He was on the cross? (Matthew 27:38-44)

2. What did Jesus cry out the first time; and what was the response? (vv. 46-49)

3. What happened when Jesus cried out the second time? (v. 50)

4. What three unusual events took place when Jesus died? (v. 51)

5. Who were the first at the cross to confirm to Jesus' identity? (v. 54)

DISCUSS THE MEANING

1. Jesus was crucified between two thieves. What could be a reasonable explanation for His being identified with thieves?

2. Was Jesus killed by the Roman soldiers? Or did He voluntarily die to fulfill His mission? How can believers voluntarily die to fulfill God's purpose for our lives?

LESSON IN OUR SOCIETY

George Atley was killed while serving with the Central African mission. There were no witnesses, but the evidence indicates that Atley was confronted by a band of hostile tribesmen. He was carrying a fully loaded, 10-chamber Winchester rifle. He had two choices: (1) to shoot his attackers and risk negating the work of the mission in that area, or (2) refuse to defend himself and be killed. When his body was later found in a stream, it was evident that he had chosen the latter. Nearby lay his rifle all 10 chambers still loaded. He had made the supreme sacrifice, motivated by his burden for lost souls and his unswerving devotion to his Saviour. With the Apostle Paul, he wanted Christ to be magnified in his body "whether by life or by death."

MAKE IT HAPPEN

What do you do when you see God mocked in our culture? Do you remain silent or do you respond in righteous indignation? Discuss how you can respond to this mockery of Christianity so prevalent in media, politics and schools.

Share the process of death by crucifixion with another believer. Discuss with them the intense physical agony Jesus must have endured for our sins. Meditate on this scene throughout the week while prayerfully preparing to take communion.

FOLLOW THE SPIRIT

What God wants me to do:

_____

_____

REMEMBER YOUR THOUGHTS

Special insights you learned:

_____

_____

MORE LIGHT ON THE TEXT
MATTHEW 27:38-54

38 Then were there two thieves crucified with him, one on the right hand, and another on the left.

Tote, meaning at the time Jesus was crucified, two thieves were crucified also. Aside from the fact that Jesus came to this planet to bring us salvation, how did birds of a different feather end up dying the same death? So often we make the assumption that like-minded people who run together are of the same character. And nine times out of ten this is probably the case. But this one time, Jesus is unjustly equated with, and reduced to the same treatment as, a common thug.

There is something about the two words, *with him,* that gives the impression that all three of the men crucified on this day were somehow partners in crime. Like hearing the evening news broadcaster saying that the police have two of

the three suspects in custody and they're looking for the third one who was with them. Like the two servants, the ten virgins, and the two men who built houses (Matthew 7, 24, and 25), they all started out looking externally alike. Before the story is over, though, only those with internal differences were distinguished. So it is with the three who were crucified together. Outwardly, they were viewed by many to share a common crime worthy of crucifixion. One, however, greatly differed, internally speaking. The Amplified Bible, NASB, and NKJV capitalize the pronoun Him, giving the reader the first clue that Jesus was unlike any man who ever lived.

Jesus' center position in this scene strongly suggests that His suffering and death were not for, or peculiar to, one side of humanity or the other. Those who come to believe in Him, like the thief on His right side, and those who disbelieve in Him, like the thief on His left side (see Luke 23:39-43), will have occasion to suffer. Those who believe in Him, however, suffer only for a season, learn the lesson associated with their suffering, and never suffer alone.

In the end, the differences between the two thieves also become evident. The unrepentant thief is a classic example of how close someone can be with Jesus and still perish, and the repentant thief is a possible example of a death bed conversion experience. One must be cautious, however, when assuming someone can break the habit of sin if death comes a knockin' at their door. Like the unrepentant thief, there is the possibility that those who indulge in some relentless, unhealthy, unholy behavior may grow hardened and indifferent to the presence of God. The unrepentant thief's words make it pretty clear that such indulgence got the better of him.

39 And they that passed by reviled him, wagging their heads,

This passion narrative is also recorded in Mark, Luke, and John, each with various details. Both the KJV and the RSV uses the Greek word for passion to refer to the suffering which Jesus endured from the night He instituted the Lord's Supper until He breathed His last breath. The reviling and wagging of heads are two of many grueling experiences in the passion narrative. Prior to these immediate character defamations, Jesus has been betrayed by one of the twelve, has begged His Father for an alternative to the cross, has admonished His disciples to avoid violence, was denied by another disciple, was abandoned by the remaining disciples, and was sentenced to death by the world's government, among other things. And the worst expression of the human condition continues with the reviling and shameful wagging of human heads.

The word reviled comes from the Greek word *blasphemeo* and it means to speak evil. Amazingly, according to Luke, Jesus says from the cross, "Father forgive them for they know not what they do," referring to the crucifixion and the hurling abuses yet to come. Unlike preparations for a modern funeral processional, wherein people seek to say kind things about the decedent, the very ones who cried "Hosanna" earlier in the week were now speaking blasphemy. This does not become the unpardonable sin until they speak such things toward and about God's Holy Spirit.

40 And saying, Thou that destroyest the temple, and buildest it in three days, save thyself. If thou be the Son of God, come down from the cross.

In the frenzy of an intense situation, it is possible to forget one's history, hope, and home training. Sometimes deciding to be a part of a riotous crowd can be the wrong decision. Whether or not these were Jews or Romans jeering at Jesus about destroying and rebuilding the temple, they certainly heard, and maybe misunderstood, the words of Jesus when He compared His death and resurrection to the prophet Jonah's experience (see Matthew 12:40). You will remember that Jonah was in the belly of the great fish three days and after this time, Jonah was vomited out upon dry land (Jonah 2:10). This is also the only sign Jesus gives to those looking for confirmations to His astounding miracles.

Somehow the crowd misconstrues Jesus' ability to save Himself with being miraculously saved by God, and then they also forget the words of Jesus. According to John the beloved who record Jesus' own explanation, "For this [reason] the Father loves Me, because I lay down My [own] life to take it back again. No one takes it away from Me. On the contrary, I lay it down voluntarily. [I put it from Myself.] I am authorized and have power to take it back again. These are the instructions (orders) which I have received [as my charge] from My Father" (John 10:17-18, Amplified Version).

Later John writes, "Greater love hath no man than this, that a man lay down his life for his friends" (John 15:13). If Jesus had wanted to abort His purpose to save His people from their sins, He could have called on legions of angels to destroy the world and set Him free. Saving Himself was neither His, nor His Father's agenda. Their agenda was, and is, to save humanity. This agenda, however, is an internal work. The crowd was too quick to judge God's work from outward appearances.

Again we hear the "if" word being used by the doubters and bullies in the crowd. They are quoting their god, Satan, verbatim, saying "If thou be the Son of God. . . ." (Matthew 4:3).

Matthew 4:3-10 records the three temptations of Jesus. And in each temptation, the devil approaches Jesus saying, "If thou be the Son of God." Inherently, "if" implies the devil knows Jesus is truly God's Son and attempts to distract Jesus from His messianic mission.

The devil extends the invitation to Jesus in three forms: (1) with under-confidence, the devil appeals to Jesus' physical appetite and Jesus answers with Deuteronomy 8:3; (2) with over-confidence, the devil calls for Jesus to display His powers, and Jesus answers with Deuteronomy 6:16; and (3) with other-confidence, the devil addresses the issue of ambition and Jesus answers with Deuteronomy 6:13. On the cross, the children of the devil are tempting Jesus with non-confidence and Jesus answers by staying on the cross.

41 Likewise also the chief priests mocking him, with the scribes and elders, said,

One of the gloomiest moments in history occurs when representatives of the realm of God assent with the principalities of evil. Though Paul's words had not been recorded at this time, it behooves contemporary believers in Christ-centeredness to keep Ephesians 6:10-18 in mind—especially verse 12, "For we wrestle not against flesh and blood, but against principalities, against powers, against the rulers of the darkness of this world, against spiritual wickedness in high places." When humanity fails to understand this letter to the Ephesians, humanity fails. It is only when the righteousness of God's realm governs that a person and a people are exalted (Proverbs 14:34). Clearly, the fulfillment of prophecy must prevail. That is to say, Jesus was destined to die on the cross, but the act of the chief priests, in this case, is like pouring salt into an open wound.

42 He saved others; himself he cannot save. If he be the King of Israel, let him now come down from the cross, and we will believe him.

In actuality, Jesus continued to save others by staying on the cross. Neither His ministry nor His message included self-salvation. It wasn't that Jesus could not save Himself, Jesus would not abort His Father's will. We have heard it said, and we have sung the song with these words, "He **could** have called 10 thousand angel to destroy the world and set Him free. But He chose to die for you and me."

In Holy Writ, people commonly express their insatiable doubts through their "prove it" attitude. If Jesus had come down from the cross, it would not have been enough to satisfy their doubt or save their lives. In Luke 16:30-31, a doubter asks Abraham to send someone from the dead to warn his brothers about the reality of eternal destiny. Abraham reminds the doubter that his brothers have Moses and the prophets. If they do not believe these godly people, neither will they believe someone from the dead. Biblical and contemporary doubters look for miracles, occasions to control, and opportunities to impose their sense of "rightness" over righteousness. The allegiance of those who wanted Jesus to come down from the cross is one of control and self-righteousness.

Interestingly, the doubters were specific in their challenge. "If you are the king of Israel" addresses the unspoken confessions and hidden desires to trust God in the worst of situations. According to Matthew 5:11-12, when you are in God's will, you must be ready to rejoice, you must be reminded that without the Cross there is no crown of glory, and you must keep in view God's purpose for your life, no matter what others may say. Matthew distinguishes his writings from the others with the phraseology, "That it might be fulfilled as spoken by the prophet." The "nay-sayers" at the cross knew Jesus' lineage, identity, identification, purpose, and commitment to His Father. In this subject verse, they again attempt to break the king of Israel's spirit. Who would not ask himself, "If I am the king of Israel, why am I hanging here?" A king, lifted up on a cross and not on a throne? A king, stripped of his clothing and not robed in the finest of linen? A king, sharing a plot of ground on Golgotha's hill and not reigning over kingdoms?

43 He trusted in God; let him deliver him now, if he will have him: for he said, I am the Son of God.

A verse of Scripture often quoted in the form of a cliche, "God is the same yesterday, today, and tomorrow," refers to the fact that God's agenda is unchanged by the human condition, human opinion, and human circumstances. Though Matthew depicts Jesus hanging between two thieves, revilers wagging their heads, Scripture quoting mockers, doubting chief priests, heckling scribes, burlesquing elders, and proponents of the "if" word at the scene of the crime, none of these efforts changes God's agenda or breaks Jesus' will.

44 The thieves also, which were crucified with him, cast the same in his teeth.

Could the thieves have thought that by joining their voices with revilers beneath the cross, perhaps they would be pardoned and set free? Or is the blindness of evil and the hardness of heart unchanged at the point of death because of its grip in life? Matthew does not share the perspective of Luke that one thief saw the light and opened his heart to the reality of immortality and eternal life through Him who knew no sin. Here Matthew warns the sinner that there is such a thing as "too late" as was the case with the five foolish virgins.

45 Now from the sixth hour there was darkness over all the land unto the ninth hour.

Bearing in mind that the sixth hour and the ninth hour in Hebrew is 12 noon and 3 o'clock in the afternoon, respectively. Imagine what it could be like from 12 midnight to 3 a.m., worldwide, without the moon, the stars, and electricity. Now imagine the same phenomena in the middle of the day. This is beyond the darkness experienced during a total eclipse. This is a hundred midnight hours before sundown. This is also imagery of the magnitude of sin and a soul without God's light.

46 And about the ninth hour Jesus cried with a loud voice, saying, *Eli, Eli, lama sabachthani? that is to say, My God, my God, why hast thou forsaken me?*

In addition to being the words of the psalmist, this is the only place in recorded history where Jesus referred to His Father outside of the parent/son relationship. Could He have felt God's omnipresence and, simultaneously, His Father's hatred toward sin? I submit that Jesus could not lay claim to the depths of humanity's suffering without experiencing the same. In the life of men and women everywhere, there are times when we are immersed in circumstances beyond our wildest imagination, and sometimes a situation temporarily makes us feel that God is nowhere to be found. In 2 Corinthians 4:8-9 however, Paul writes, ". . . we are troubled on every side, yet not distressed; we are perplexed, but not in despair; persecuted, but **not forsaken;** cast down, but not destroyed."

It is rare for Jesus to refer to His Father as God and to have His words recorded in His native tongue; however, this is not how the drama ends. How many times does humanity give up because of their suffering, minutes before their breakthrough?

What others understood Jesus to say in His suffering or conclude in contemporary times of suffering is antithetical. As the antithesis relates to Jesus, some thought He was calling on the sun god Helie, a word closely associated with *helias*, the Greek word for Elijah. Others thought He was hallucinating images of Elijah. These and contemporary speculators, however, fall short of the Holy Spirit's power to interpret the moans and groans of God's suffering servant. It is a terrible thing to give up at the apparent breaking point of one's suffering. Thank God, Jesus neither came down from the cross nor gave up on God.

47 Some of them that stood there, when they heard that, said, This man calleth for Elias.

According to 1 Kings 17:1 and 2 Kings 2:18, Elijah was the greatest and most romantic character ever produced by Israel. He was a man of the desert who counseled kings, performed miracles, struggled against Baal, and will share the prophetic role in the second Advent that John the Baptist expressed immediately preceding the first Advent of the Christ.

48 And straightway one of them ran, and took a sponge, and filled it with vinegar, and put it on a reed, and gave him to drink.

In order to numb the pain from the nails driven into the hands of crucified criminals, Barclay refers to a drink of drugged wine laced with frankincense that was prepared by a group of wealthy, sympathetic, Jerusalem females. It was this form of sedation that was offered to Jesus. The Greek word for vinegar is *oxos* and it means sour wine.

49 The rest said, Let be, let us see whether Elias will come to save him.

Cynicism can be a dangerous thing. There were those among the number at the cross who knew of the miracles, parables, ministry, and mission of Jesus and, yet, had not come to a place in their experience where they would stand in support of Jesus. Prophets foretold His coming, the heavens announced His miraculous arrival, God responded to His prayer life, and the masses sought Him out for healing. It often appears as though the voice of the negative minority is heard above the voice of the positive majority. The negative minority in this Scripture are substituting what they are saying for what they know about God's history. They are also substituting their intellect for their spirituality, and their sight for their faith.

Not only have they misunderstood the words Jesus speaks from the cross, but also nurse their misunderstanding with the classical "wait and see" attitude. Such perspectives can and do cripple humanity's spiritual development with God. God is under no obligation to pull rabbits out of the proverbial magician's hat or cause a loved one to appear at the behest of disbelievers demanding signs and wonders. God requires faith, not cynicism.

50 Jesus, when he had cried again with a loud voice, yielded up the ghost.

While the Synoptic Gospels and John give their perspective on the passion narrative, only John adds to this particular reference a second shout from Jesus. After this great shout, Jesus says, "It is finished" (John 19:30), and then He gives up the ghost. The Greek word *tetelestai* renders the same message adding the emphasis on the victor's shout. The victor's shout is the proclamation of a man named Jesus who completed His task, fulfilled God's purpose for His life, and won the crown through the suffering and the struggles of betrayal, denial, abandonment, and the Cross.

51 And, behold, the veil of the temple was rent in twain from the top to the bottom; and the earth did quake, and the rocks rent;

The veil of the temple was a heavy piece of curtain draped in Jerusalem's temple and separating the Holy from the Holy of Holies. Only the high priest entered the Holy of Holies once a year on the Day of Atonement. This curtain symbolized the barrier between humanity and the way to God's presence. The death of Jesus, however, removed the hidden love of God and the way to God's presence. The tearing of this veil is also symbolic of the open access that all persons have to the eternal Sacrifice and the eternal High Priest, even Jesus Christ. Note that the direction of the renting is from top to bottom as opposed to from side to side. In other words, this is an act of God coming down to the lower level, the bottom, so that humanity may go up to the highest level in God through Jesus Christ.

52 And the graves were opened; and many bodies of the saints which slept arose,

Here we behold Jesus' power over the grave. Paul asked in 1 Corinthians 15:55-57: "O death, where is thy sting? O grave, where is thy victory? The sting of death is sin; and the strength of sin is the law. But thanks be to God, which giveth us the victory through our Lord Jesus Christ." The victory Paul writes about is given to everyone who believes in the Christ. Because of Him, the grave has no power. and death has no sting. For those who believe in Jesus' ministry, obedience, death, and resurrection, all fears about death and the grave are under His blood.

53 And came out of the graves after his resurrection, and went into the holy city, and appeared unto many.

Within theological and religious circles, the great debate about Matthew's parousia and Paul's eschatology continues. While Matthew is noted for delaying the parousia, also known as the Day of the Lord, some question whether or not the resurrected believers will be recognizable. This particular Scripture, however, affirms that those who came out of their graves after Christ's resurrection, appeared unto many during the next 40 days.

The Sadducees, who did not believe in resurrection (Matthew 22:23; Acts 23:8), challenged Jesus about this subject. Jesus answered the Sadducees with this question: "Have you not read that which was spoken unto you by God, saying, 'I am the God of Abraham, and the God of Isaac, and the God of Jacob? God is not the God of the dead, but of the living.'" This dialogue is paralleled in Mark 12 and Luke 20. In John 5:28-29, Jesus says, "Marvel not at this: for the hour is coming, in the which all that are in the graves shall hear his voice, and shall come forth; they that have done good, unto the resurrection of life; and they that have done evil, unto the resurrection of damnation."

In John 11:25, when Jesus called His friend Lazarus from the tomb, He said to Martha, "I am the resurrection, and the life: he that believeth in me, though he were dead, yet shall he live." In 1 Corinthians 15:13, Paul says outright, "if there is no resurrection of the dead, then is Christ not risen." His message to the Corinthian church and to contemporary believers is that the resurrection is central to the Christian faith.

The crowning reference by Paul regarding the resurrection is found in 1 Corinthians 15:51. Paul declares the hope of God's people when he writes, "We shall not all sleep, but we shall all be changed." Paul is referring to his belief that not all believers will die, or sleep, the Greek word used here is *koimao*. When Christ returns in the future, or Eschaton, the dead in Him will be raised and glorified. And those who remain alive and in Christ, shall behold the Bridegroom coming for His Bride. And both the risen in Christ and those who remain alive and in Christ shall be changed, in a moment, into incorruptible glorified bodies like the resurrected and recognizable body of our Lord (see 1 Thessolonians 4:14-17).

54 Now when the centurion, and they that were with him, watching Jesus, saw the earthquake, and those things that were done, they feared greatly, saying, Truly this was the Son of God.

The results of Christ's death—the renting of the veil, the earthquake, the hidden light of the sun, the resurrection of many—was powerful and effective. It was the centurion who, in all probability, participated in selecting Simon of Cyrene to carry the horizontal beam of Jesus Christ. It was the centurion who, in all likelihood, beat the back of Jesus until His flesh hung open, pressed the plated thorns onto the skin of His skull, stripped Him down to His loin cloth, and gambled for His garment. But there are some phenomena in life that can serve as a wake up call and bring you to a place of adoration to God for God's mercy and grace.

Like the serpent who was lifted up by Moses in the wilderness, Jesus is lifted up and draws the centurion to say, "Truly. . . ." Who else could love humanity so much that He would leave a heavenly throne, take on earthly clothing, put up with earthly life, yield to the cruelty of man, and suffer pain, loss of dignity, injury, and ultimately loss of life, so that we could take off earthly clothing and live in eternal glory? Only the true Son of God Jesus.

DAILY BIBLE READING

M: Jesus Delivered to Pilate; Judas' Suicide
Matthew 27:1-10
T: Jesus Before Pilate
Matthew 27:11-18
W: The Crowd Agitates for Barabbas' Release
Matthew 27:19-23
T: Jesus Is Handed Over for Crucifixion
Matthew 27:24-31
F: Jesus Is Crucified
Matthew 27:32-44
S: Jesus Dies
Matthew 27:45-56
S: Jesus Is Buried
Matthew 27:57-61

TEACHING TIPS

February 27
Bible Study Guide 13

1. Words You Should Know

A. Sepulcher. (Matthew 28:1) Greek—*taphos* the place of interment, or a tomb. Specifically, the place loved ones go to visit after the body has been placed there.

B. Name. (v. 19) Greek, *onoma*—authority, character. Emphasizing a proper noun to identify a person, as in "by name," this meaning stresses the power and nature of a person to accomplish a specific task.

2. Teacher Preparation

A. Read and meditate upon the Devotional Reading and the Bible Background.

B. Study the FOCAL VERSES in the most popular translations used by the church in corporate worship or students in individual study. Make a note of study notes and contemporary language.

C. Write out answers to the SEARCH THE SCRIPTURES questions and your personal responses to the DISCUSS THE MEANING questions.

3. Starting the Lesson

A. Write the AT-A-GLANCE outline on the board.

B. Read IN FOCUS as a centering devotional.

4. Getting into the Lesson

A. Break up into small groups to study the Scriptures and discover insights.

B. Reconvene into large group and share doctrinal insights and practices.

5. Relating the Lesson to Life

A. Read THE PEOPLE, PLACES, AND TIMES section.

B. Create student teams to present various positions concerning women in ministry, particularly the preaching ministry.

C. Explore areas of agreement and establish rules for tolerance in living with this dichotomy.

D. Reflect on the testimonial in LESSON IN OUR SOCIETY and make a corporate covenant to imitate Jesus' ministry to women, and with women.

6. Arousing Action

A. Discuss the MAKE IT HAPPEN survey results.

B. Brainstorm opportunities to fulfill the Commission.

C. Plan to present results of evangelistic efforts on next week.

D. End the class with prayer.

WORSHIP GUIDE

For the Superintendent or Teacher
Theme: Resurrection and Commission
Theme Song: "It's Real"
Scripture: 1 Corinthians 15:1-23
Song: "He Lives"
Devotional Thought/Prayer: Lord Jesus, I hear Your commission. By the power of the Holy Spirit, I commit to being a doer of Your Word also.

RESURRECTION AND COMMISSION

Bible Background • MATTHEW 27:62—28:20
Printed Text • MATTHEW 28:1-10, 16-20
Devotional Reading • JOHN 20:19-31

LESSON AIM

By the end of the lesson, students will be able to tell the chronology of events from Resurrection morning through the Great Commission; understand how mixed emotions may accompany the call to ministry; and determine to go, teach and baptize in the name of the Father, Son and Holy Spirit.

KEEP IN MIND

"Go ye therefore, and teach all nations, baptizing them in the name of the Father, and of the Son, and of the Holy Ghost: Teaching them to observe all things whatsoever I have commanded you: and, lo, I am with you always, even unto the end of the world. Amen" (Matthew 28:19-20).

FOCAL VERSES

MATTHEW 28:1 In the end of the sabbath, as it began to dawn toward the first day of the week, came Mary Magdalene and the other Mary to see the sepulchre.

2 And, behold, there was a great earthquake: for the angel of the Lord descended from heaven, and came and rolled back the stone from the door, and sat upon it.

3 His countenance was like lightning, and his raiment white as snow:

4 And for fear of him the keepers did shake, and became as dead men.

5 And the angel answered and said unto the women, Fear not ye: for I know that ye seek Jesus, which was crucified.

6 He is not here: for he is risen, as he said. Come, see the place where the Lord lay.

LESSON OVERVIEW

LESSON AIM
KEEP IN MIND
FOCAL VERSES
IN FOCUS
THE PEOPLE, PLACES, AND
TIMES
BACKGROUND
AT-A-GLANCE
IN DEPTH
SEARCH THE SCRIPTURES
DISCUSS THE MEANING
LESSON IN OUR SOCIETY
MAKE IT HAPPEN
FOLLOW THE SPIRIT
REMEMBER YOUR THOUGHTS
MORE LIGHT ON THE TEXT
DAILY BIBLE READINGS

7 And go quickly, and tell his disciples that he is risen from the dead; and, behold, he goeth before you into Galilee; there shall ye see him: lo, I have told you.

8 And they departed quickly from the sepulchre with fear and great joy; and did run to bring his disciples word.

9 And as they went to tell his disciples, behold, Jesus met them, saying, All hail. And they came and held him by the feet, and worshipped him.

10 Then said Jesus unto them, Be not afraid: go tell my brethren that they go into Galilee, and there shall they see me.

16 Then the eleven disciples went away into Galilee, into a mountain where Jesus had appointed them.

17 And when they saw him, they worshipped him: but some doubted.

18 And Jesus came and spake unto them, saying, All power is given unto me in heaven and in earth.

19 Go ye therefore, and teach all nations, baptizing them in the name of the Father, and of the Son, and of the Holy Ghost:

20 Teaching them to observe all things whatsoever I have commanded you: and, lo, I am with you always, even unto the end of the world. Amen.

IN FOCUS

Consider this wry, but sobering, illustration: "There ain't gonna be no Easter this year," a student remarked. "Why not?" his friend asked incredulously. "They found the body," the student replied. Despite his irreverent humor, the student displayed a measure of insight often not shared by modern theologians. Many theologians are perfectly willing to assert that Jesus died and rotted in the grave, but that the resurrection still has value as a symbol of "newness of life" or "new beginning," so that Christianity can go on quite nicely as though nothing changed. The student's joke implied that without the resurrection Christianity is worthless (William Craig, *Knowing the Truth About Resurrection, Our Response to the Empty Tomb*, p. 125).

If you read Paul's commentary on Jesus' resurrection in 1 Corinthians 15:14-19, this friend would be dead right. Paul, points out the distinctions of the Christian faith and stresses the kind of results one's faith in the resurrected Christ should have on us who believe.

THE PEOPLE, PLACES, AND TIMES

WOMAN. The picture of women revealed in the Bible is far from one-dimensional. Frequently subjected to the rule of her male counterpart, often adored for her beauty and purity, and occasionally praised for her leadership in times of crisis, women emerge from the pages of the Bible with as much complexity as men.

Women in biblical times lived in a patriarchal society. Both the Old and New Testament worlds normally restricted the role of women primarily to the sphere of home and family, although a few strong women emerged as leaders. In religious life she was subordinate to man. Fathers, husbands, and other male relatives gave protection and direction to women. Jesus raised the window for women. He paid attention to them. His manner was inclusive, and He acknowledged their place in the kingdom. By what He did, and what He said, He elevated the status of women. Paul also caught Jesus' vision. Although Paul saw the need to preserve order in the early church, he exclaimed in Galatians 3:28: "There is neither Jew nor Greek, there is neither bond nor free, there is neither male nor female: for ye are all one in Christ Jesus." The final barrier preventing women from fully participating in the kingdom of God toppled under Jesus' influence.

Jesus was able to retain the best in the Hebrew tradition and yet cut away some of the rigid structure that restricted it. He was able to do the same for women. Without radically changing their roles, Jesus enlarged and transformed women's possibilities for a full life. His manner and teachings elevated her status and gave her an identity and a cause. Jesus' manner in His interactions with women is at least as significant as His teachings about women. At the risk of censure from a male-oriented society, Jesus talked to women, responded to their touch, healed them, received

their emotional and financial support, and used them as main characters in His stories. Jesus saw women as persons. Martha wanted Jesus to make Mary help with the serving duties, but Jesus affirmed Mary's choice to learn as a disciple. Women of that day could not be disciples of rabbis, but Jesus recognized women's potential for intelligent thought and commitment (Luke 10:38-42).

Besides seeing women as persons, Jesus involved them in His earthly ministry. Luke mentioned a group of women who traveled with Jesus as He journeyed from town to town (Luke 8:1-3). Among them were Mary of Magdala, Joanna, and Susanna. These women provided financial support for Jesus and the twelve apostles. Women also proclaimed the Gospel. In His encounter with the Samaritan woman, Jesus revealed Himself as the Messiah. She immediately left and began telling people, "He told me everything I have ever done" (John 4:39, NRSV). Many Samaritans believed in Jesus because of this woman's testimony.

Women were the first at the tomb after the resurrection. As such, they were the first to broadcast His victory over death (Luke 23:55-24:11). Matthew, Mark, and Luke all called attention to the loyal women who participated in Jesus' Galilean ministry and followed Him all the way to the Cross and the grave. They received and shared the greatest news: "He is not here, but has risen" (Luke 24:6, NRSV).

As a master teacher, Jesus used parables to teach about the kingdom of God. He reached out to the women in His audience by telling stories about their life experiences. By capturing their attention and commitment through parables, He offered them a place in the kingdom.

Jesus' parable of the ten maidens, five foolish and five wise, hints at the way Jesus saw and dealt with woman (Matthew 25:1-13). He saw women as neither inferior nor superior, but simply as persons. He saw their potential, their sinfulness, their strengths, and their weaknesses, and He dealt with them directly. As a group, He elevated their status and strengthened their participation and influence in their world. But as individuals, He treated them as friends and disciples.

Women are the subject of many questions and controversies in the church today. Is she equal to man? Can she exercise the same spiritual gifts as man in the church? Should she be subject to her husband in all matters? As Christians turn to the Bible for guidance in responding to these questions, they must be careful not to focus on one verse or passage. The total impact and message of the Bible should become the guiding spirit in answering these and other questions.

The Old Testament clearly subjected women to the will and protection of her husband. She was extolled for performing her important roles as wife and mother. On occasion she rose above those roles and led the Jewish nation in times of crisis.

The New Testament brings a different picture of women into focus. Jesus, and later Paul, elevated the status of women so that she could be a full participant in the kingdom of God. However, she is urged to use her responsibility, as well as her freedom, to find her place in the body of Christ. The spirit of freedom and love in Christ belongs to women as well as men.

(Adapted from "Woman" by Kay W. Shurden, in *Holman's Bible Dictionary for Windows, Version 1.0*, Parsons Technology, 1994.)

BACKGROUND

Women witnessed Jesus' crucifixion, up close. Women, who had known His healing power, gathered at Jesus' feet in His finest and final hour. Motivated by gratitude, courage, and love, these women did not run away, hide, or deny the Christ. In spite of His public humiliation and grotesque execution, these women wanted to be identified with the crucified Messiah. Although they could not trade places with Him, or take Him down, these women were not watching out of helplessness or coincidence. They were witnesses to His crucifixion in preparation for their purpose of becoming messengers with the message of eternal faith: the Messiah had risen!

After Jesus died, his body was taken by the disciples and entombed. However, resonating among the religious leaders was Jesus' prophecy that He would be raised in three days. To insure that the disciples did not come back and steal the body and then fabricate a story of resurrection, a large boulder was set before the tomb and soldiers were assigned to stand guard. They did not perceive, even yet, His power.

AT-A-GLANCE

1. Women at the Tomb
(Matthew 28:1-8)
2. Worshipers at the Mountain
(vv. 9-18)
3. Witness in the Earth
(vv. 19-20)

IN DEPTH

1. Women at the Tomb (Matthew 28:1-8)

When Mary Magdalene and the other Mary went to Jesus' tomb, the earth quaked, an angel opened the tomb, and the guards became like dead men. It stands to reason that because there is no specifics given on the resurrection process, the most important point made is that the tomb was, and remains, empty. And so the story begins with the telling of the empty tomb. While the women were on their way to the tomb, laden with spices and hoping the guards would allow them to anoint Jesus' dead body in loving grief, there was an earthquake. But the earthquake did not deter the women. On the contrary, the guards, upon seeing the angel, were so afraid they fainted into a deep sleep, an act that would become for them a convenient alibi and lie to explain the empty tomb. Regretably, many Jews believe this lie even still.

But the women, instead of experiencing a teary-eyed, tragic scene at the sepulcher, they were met by an angel. The angel told the women that Jesus had been raised and instructed them to tell the disciples to meet Him in Galilee. Unlike the guards, the women's fear was not overwhelming, for they retained hope in the prophecies of a risen Messiah. Their fear was in seeing the unusual, but their fear was not immobilizing. Their fear was smothered by great joy as they listened to the angel, for their hope had been realized.

As the women joyfully hurried to tell the disciples, Jesus met them and encouraged them to tell the disciples to go to Galilee where they would see Him. The women were the first to know of the resurrected Messiah. Oh, what joy filled their souls! And on their way to deliver the message, lest they be accused of relaying hearsay, the women were graced with the very presence of the Lord. This was the Jesus they remembered, but He was now embodied in full divinity. Bowing to Jesus and grabbing His feet was a sign of ultimate reverence and submission.

2. Worshipers at the Mountain (vv. 9-18)

When the eleven disciples saw Jesus in Galilee, they worshiped Him, though some doubted. Jesus, repeating the angel's instructions, sent the women to call His disciples, whom He called brothers, so that He might appear to them also. It is significant to note that those He called brothers were the same who deserted Him in the final hours (except His beloved disciple John, who was given the responsibility to care for Jesus' mother). Although the disciples had failed Jesus, He demonstrated His deep love and total forgiveness and restored them to full brotherhood and partners in ministry.

As the disciples worshiped, it should be noted that some still struggled with doubt. This doubt, however, confirmed that Jesus knew His resurrection would not necessarily convince everyone (Luke 16:31). So the doubt of the disciples cannot entirely be held against them; it was an affirmation of Jesus' words.

Jesus declared that He had been given all authority in heaven and earth. This was to affirm Jesus' absolute power over things of earthly and of spiritual realms. This is the same authority and power that Jesus would transfer to the disciples in the following commission. It was by this declaration that Jesus declared His saving grace would be accessible to all nations, thus establishing the precedent for a world-wide church of believers.

3. Witness in the Earth (vv. 19-20)

Jesus commissioned His followers to go and make disciples of all nations and to baptize them in the name of the Father, Son, and Holy Spirit, and assured them of His eternal presence. The disciples' obedience assured them of Jesus' continued presence with them. So it is with us today as we do as commanded, to make disciples by baptizing and teaching. The disciples' authority, as it continues in believers today, would be accompanied by the risen Lord's promise to be with us to the very end of the age when He returns and we reign with Him forever. Jesus' presence remains in the person and is evident in the power of the Holy Spirit.

SEARCH THE SCRIPTURES

1. What natural phenomena heralded the supernatural resurrection? (Matthew 28:2)

2. Did the angel roll the stone away to let Jesus out or to let the women in? (vv. 5-6)

3. What four messages did the angel give the women? (vv. 5-7)

4. What emotions did the women express upon receiving the call to carry the Good News of the risen Lord a.k.a. to "preach the Gospel"? (v. 8)

5. What conflicting emotions were among the disciples upon seeing Jesus? (v. 17)

6. What is the three-fold commissioning given to the disciples of Christ? (v.19)

DISCUSS THE MEANING

1. There was an earthquake when Jesus was crucified. Why would an earthquake be an appropriate indicator of His resurrection?

2. The Scripture records that some of the disciples doubted that Jesus had risen. Did their doubt prevent Jesus from commissioning them? Do we need to be doubtless to be called to minister?

LESSON IN OUR SOCIETY

There is a common conflict within the church, one which is growing in momentum and in hostility, and this conflict centers on the role of women as preachers and as church leaders. Consider this Pastor's reflection:

"As a pastor, a husband, and a father, I have a dread of burying someone else's talents, particularly those bestowed on women. Accordingly, I have tried to scrutinize my views, the place of tradition, the thrust of theology and the force of my prejudices. Repeatedly, I have come back to this fact: If the Lord has given gifts, I had better be careful about denying freedom for their exercise. More than that, I need to ensure that the women in my life have every encouragement from me to be what He called and gifted them to be. A major part of my life must be spent as a man caring for, nurturing, encouraging, and developing gifted women because they aren't the only ones who will give account for their stewardship. As a man, in a male-oriented church, I may one day be asked about their gifts, too. I would like to be able to say I did considerably more than burying. A talent is a terrible thing to waste" (Stuart Briscoe, in "Homemade," February, 1985).

MAKE IT HAPPEN

Christ met unbelievers where they were. He realized what many Christians today still don't seem to understand. Cultivators have to get out in the field. According to one count, the Gospels record 132 contacts Jesus had with people. Six were in the temple, four in the synagogues, and 122 were out with the people in the mainstream of life.

When was the last time you told somebody about the crucified Christ and the risen Lord? Do you feel you lack opportunity? This week make a list of 10 people who you come in contact with daily. Make it a point to ask them if they know Jesus, and share the tenets of salvation with them.

As did the women, run and tell somebody that Jesus, the Christ, is risen!

FOLLOW THE SPIRIT

What God wants me to do:

_____

_____

REMEMBER YOUR THOUGHTS
Special insights you learned:

_____

_____

MORE LIGHT ON THE TEXT
MATTHEW 28:1-10,16-20

1 In the end of the sabbath, as it began to dawn toward the first day of the week, came Mary Magdalene and the other Mary to see the sepulchre.

For the record, the holiday called Easter is celebrated the first Sunday following the full moon closest to March 21. This spring festival is mentioned only in Acts 12:4. The Greek word for Easter is *pascha* and means "the special sacrifices connected with Passover."

In the New International Version (NIV), verse 1 begins, "After the Sabbath, at dawn on the first day of the week." The Living Bible (LB) begins it, "Early on Sunday morning, as the new day was dawning." There is much controversy even now regarding the Lord's Day and related questions: Which is the Sabbath Day? Is the Sabbath and the day of rest the same? Is Sunday the new Sabbath as well as the first day of the week? It is worthwhile to recall that the Jewish day ends at sundown or 6 p.m. and begins at sunrise. This knowledge accounts for the three days between Jesus' death and resurrection. He died and was buried before 6 p.m. on what we call Good Friday, that's day one. Saturday at 6 p.m. is the end of day two, and early Sunday morning, day three, God raised Jesus from the dead. Counting days in the Jewish tradition challenges the issue regarding Jesus being crucified on Thursday. It has also been said Jesus is the Sabbath and, therefore, we must worship Him daily. This, notwithstanding, the Bible says, as followers of Jesus, the disciples met on the first day of the week.

While Matthew acknowledges Mary Magdalene and the other Mary (Joses) going to the sepulcher, Mark adds, "Mary the mother of James, and Salome" (mother of James and John). Luke, on the other hand, gives no names. He simply writes, "they went to the tomb," while John names Mary Magdalene. These additions and omissions notwithstanding, Matthew gives birth to the Gospel of Jesus Christ through women. The first to carry the word is Mary and the first to carry the resurrection message are women. God chose women in the beginning of Matthew, and Christ sent women first, according to Matthew. And the message from God and Christ are, respectively, "Call Him Jesus for He will save people from their sins" and "Go and tell my disciples 'I am risen as I said.'"

2 And, behold, there was a great earthquake: for the angel of the Lord descended from heaven, and came and rolled back the stone from the door, and sat upon it.

Earthquakes occur 16 places in the Bible, including at the cross when Jesus committed Himself into God's hands (Matthew 27:51) and on Mount Sinai when God gave Moses the Ten Commandments (Exodus 19:18). Notice the association of these two earthquakes with liberation. The Hebrews had been delivered from Pharaoh and Jesus had been delivered from death. It was certainly among the phenomenal occurrences that brought the centurion to proclaim, "Surely, He was the Son of God." Whatever it takes to bring humanity to confess Jesus as Lord is worthwhile.

Celestial phenomena must also be considered. It is likely that the angel of the Lord's descent can be like the breaking of a woman's water when a child is about to be born. The metaphor for the earthquake, as it relates to the birth of a child, could be like a woman's labor pains. In travail, the earth prepares to dislodge and push out God's child from its belly. At various places in our lives, God shakes our consciences to awareness and our sinful selves to repentance, and great is the resurrection to renewed, revived, and revisioned hope in Jesus Christ.

In Matthew, an angel descended and sat upon the stone. In Mark, a young man sat in the tomb. In Luke, two men stood by the tomb. And in John, two angels sat in the tomb. You may be familiar with the tune, "All day, all night angels watching over me, my Lord." There should be little doubt that invisible, protective, heavenly, positive beings are all around us. They were also all around our Lord. They are there when we need help in holding back the darkness at the entrance of light.

3 His countenance was like lightning, and his raiment white as snow:

From the Greek word *eidea*, we learn that the angel's appearance was like the swift, untouchable, uncontainable, bright flash of lightning we see dancing across the heavens during an electrical storm. During the night or in a daytime storm, lightening illuminates a brilliance that dispels the evening shades and shines brighter than the day. Is this not what Jesus does when He shows up in our dreaded, dead, despairing situations? Are we able to contain His presence? When Moses asked God to show his face, God told Moses to stand in the cleft of a rock. As God's glory passed by, God's hand covered Moses and Moses could only see God's afterglow because God's glorious light was more than any human being can experience and live to talk about.

The people of Senegal, Muslims, and baptismal candidates worship in white, the color for purity. John the revealer writes, "After this I beheld, and, lo, a great multitude, which no man could number, of all nations, and kindreds, and people, and tongues, stood before the throne, and before the Lamb, clothed with white robes, and palms in their hands" (Revelation 7:9). These are they who have washed their robes in the blood of the Lamb, having come through the great tribulation.

It is fitting for the angel of the Lord to wear a bright, light colored robe, symbolizing the fact that Jesus has come through a great tribulation and now advises His people to be of good cheer. Not only because He has overcome the world, but also because our resurrected bodies will also bear the garment of light, the Greek word for *leukos*.

This particular subject verse gives us a glimpse of what it shall be like when we behold Him face to face and what we shall look like on that resurrection morning when all the dead in Christ shall rise.

4 And for fear of him the keepers did shake, and became as dead men.

Of all the Gospel writers, only Matthew includes this detail. What would make this feature important to a converted tax collector? Could it be that Matthew had encountered the grueling aftermath that families experience when settling inheritance tax issues? Or is he mindful of the games people play with tax lawyers and the advantages funeral directors can impose on the grief-stricken? Or, more closely related, does Matthew want to dramatize the fact that human brawn and governmental authority is no match for God?

5 And the angel answered and said unto the women, Fear not ye: for I know that ye seek Jesus, which was crucified.

In Holy Writ, writers have recorded "fear not" 365 times, one for each day of the year. These women had no reason to be *phobeo*, the Greek word for frightened. They were beloved by the Lord. It was Jesus who elevated women to their rightful position in a culturally biased society. It was Jesus who delivered Mary Magdalene from seven demons, spared the life of the woman caught in adultery, and equalized the sexes' responsibility to fidelity. It was Jesus who admonished the disciples for their sexism. It was Jesus who conversed with woman at the well who had been through multiple divorces, and He chastised the disciples for their

bigotry. And, in the end, it was the women who came to believe in themselves and in God's call in their lives through Jesus Christ. Therefore, the fears the angel addresses here has to do with the reason they cannot find Jesus in the tomb.

The reason these women had come to the tomb was to anoint Jesus' body with oil and spices. In the book of Mark, they raised the question, "Who will roll the stone away?" In Luke, they found the stone rolled away and went in, but did not find Jesus. In John, Mary Magdalene sees the stone rolled away and runs to tell Peter that "they" have taken Jesus' body away. It is this panic that the angel addresses. Jesus is not stolen, lost, or taken away to some unknown place, He is risen.

6 He is not here: for he is risen, as he said. Come, see the place where the Lord lay.

In both Matthew and Mark, the angel invites the women to enter the tomb and examine the place where Jesus was laid to rest. In John, the women are asked, "Why do you seek the living among the dead?" Isn't it true that the things in life you fear the most seldom come to fruition and when they do, they are rarely as bad as you originally thought?

The angel graciously extends an invitation to these women to believe God's Word. No matter what the circumstances are, believe and trust God. Understandably, these women had been through a lot and had cause to be concerned about the body of Jesus. They had witnessed the government's abusive treatment toward Jesus and watched in horror as Jesus was beaten, tortured, and forced to carry the old rugged cross. They were at Golgotha and heard the cruel accusations hurled at Jesus. The angel is assuring these women that it was God, not the government, not the culture, not the opinions of man, who had the last word and that "He is risen."

7 And go quickly, and tell his disciples that he is risen from the dead; and, behold, he goeth before you into Galilee; there shall ye see him: lo, I have told you.

The tone in this verse is just as urgent as the tone Matthew uses at Jesus' triumphal entry in chapter 21, "immediately and straightway." "Go quickly," is the command of the angel. There is no time for delay, apathy, or doubt. Jesus is not only risen, but also in route to the place where He devoted most of His earthly ministry---Galilee. It is also the major center of Judaism during the life of Jesus. There the women, the disciples, and others will see the Man from Galilee, their friend and resurrected Lord.

experienced no particular anxiety or struggle in getting out of them. And such is the case with eternal things. They shall come to pass in God's time and in God's way. The message of the resurrection is one of trusting in God. It also indicates His body had not been stolen.

John also speaks of himself in verse 8 as the one who saw these things and as a result, believed. Though he doesn't say, one could conclude, that he believed "Jesus is risen."

9 And as they went to tell his disciples, behold, Jesus met them, saying, All hail. And they came and held him by the feet, and worshipped him.

It is commonly believed God will not reveal a "next" step or show more light on the path until there is contiguous obedience. As the women obeyed the angel's instructions, Jesus meets and greets them. The Greek word used by Jesus, *chairo*, means, "be well, God speed, and rejoice."

The person who meets the risen Lord must live in the joy of His presence. There is no indication the women ever doubted Him, but those who did----Peter, Pharisaic Jews, and pious priests----would meet the risen Saviour and either worship Him, as Peter and the others did, or bribe the keepers of te Herod's appointed high priest, thereby making it possible that Herod called both high priests to conference with him.

We also read here that Herod brought together the scribes. The Greek word used here for "scribes" is the word *grammateus* (pronounced **gram-mat-yooce'**) meaning person vastly learned in linguistic and grammatical processes. They were also interpretive writers of divine proclamations who recorded various occurrences in relation to the Word of God. Scripture says they were "the us meets the women who visited the sepulcher; or, as in Luke, Jesus appears to two travelers on the road to Emmaus; or, as in John, Jesus appears to those disciples who were fishing; or, as in all four Gospels, Jesus shows up among the eleven, His presence will surely call forth some form of worship.

8 And they departed quickly from the sepulchre with fear and great joy; and did run to bring his disciples word.

Obedience and trust are flip sides of the same coin. When we trust God, we obey God without hesitation. The fear Matthew refers to here is from the Greek word *phobos* which includes respectful, reverence, and a sense of awe in its definition. In tandem with Matthew's reference to "great joy," it can be concluded this fear is not the same as being afraid.

Mark's account specifically directs the women to "go tell His disciples and Peter." Luke reads more casually, "And returning from the tomb they told all this to the eleven and to all the rest." There isn't the same intensity in Luke as there is in Matthew's and Mark's narration. John highlights the importance of the Gospel writer's message to Christ's disciples and Peter. You may remember that John, identified as the disciple whom Jesus loved, outran the others to the tomb upon hearing Mary Magdalene say, "They have taken away the Lord. . . and we know not where they have laid him" (John 20:2). Only John writes of the Jewish burial linen wrappings and their neatness, implying that Jesus

10 Then said Jesus unto them, Be not afraid: go tell my brethren that they go into Galilee, and there shall they see me.

Jesus calls the women to believe in the promise of God, to share the Good News, to rejoice at His appearing, and to be not afraid of others' disbelief. The brethren labeled these women foolish (Luke 24:11) and refused to believe them. They were preoccupied with the sad turn of events: their denial (Peter), their loss (Judas committed suicide), their fear (abandoning Jesus), and their grief (the death of their Rabbi). And yet, they have nothing to lose by going to the place where they first met the Lord.

There's an old camp meeting song popularized by Andre Crouch and the words read something like, "Take me back to the place where I first believed." Hearing the women tell the words of Jesus in this Scripture must have reminded them of the day Jesus called them by name and promised to make them fishers of men if they follow Him.

16 Then the eleven disciples went away into Galilee, into a mountain where Jesus had appointed them.

The eleven needed Jesus now more than ever. There are some situations in life that bring humanity so low that if we don't seek Jesus, life is unbearable. Sometimes humanity experiences its own Gethsemane, and believers experience their own crucifixion. But the hope for us all is that there is an appointed place to go to meet with Jesus.

In contemporary society, mountaintop experiences come through meditation on God's Word, inspirational literature, and prayer. The disciples went to meet Jesus carrying a very common burden in contemporary society. One of their own had betrayed one of their own, and unable to find solace from within, he violently killed himself. Drug infestation, immorality, death, crippling addictions, suicide, and crime have all increased drastically in the 90's. Every family in America has been affected by some form of devastation. And yet, every affected believer is of intimate interest to Him who bore our sins and conquered death. Jesus still calls God's children of faith to meet Him in the high places at the appointed times.

The Scripture doesn't say, but could the mountain meeting place have been the Mount of Olives? That's the place where Matthew begins the end of Jesus' earthly ministry. That is the place where Jesus descends and proceeds with His triumphal entry. That is the place where Jesus and His disciples visited a number of times for a number of reasons. Could it be that by ritual the disciples knew, without being told, where they would meet Jesus without Him saying? This is the beauty of a intimate relationship, words need not be spoken to know the heart of one another.

17 And when they saw him, they worshipped him: but some doubted.

When the disciples arrived, Jesus was already there. When contemporary believers purpose in their mind to exercise their faith, they see Jesus. Like His Father, He is also omnipresent and trustworthy. The test of your faith can be related to seeing what it will take to stop you from believing in God through Jesus Christ. Apparently, it does not take much to disbelieve. But it does take persistence to lay your doubts aside. In every age, generation, church, neighborhood, and circumstance, there are two types of people, those who believe and those who doubt. When your doubt keeps you from seeing Jesus, try your faith.

Thomas is counted among those who tried his faith. When Jesus appeared among the disciples in John 20:19-21, Thomas was absent. Upon his return, the disciples told him about their time with the risen Lord, and Thomas flat out refused to believe them. Jesus appears to Thomas a week later in John 20:26-29 and says these words for all who doubt, "Blessed are those who have not seen and yet have believed."

Those who doubt usually do so out of ignorance. This kind of doubt is different from denial. True doubt leads to inquiry and a search for information. At this point the inquiring mind must know that there is the thinker waiting to transform the human mind with truth. God is willing to reveal Himself in human affairs. That is what the Holy Bible is about, God revealing Himself.

18 And Jesus came and spake unto them, saying, All power is given unto me in heaven and in earth.

Although each is different, the Synoptic Gospels and John all end with Jesus making some reassuring pronouncement. Mark ends with a long litany of promises, namely, that the disciples would use the name of Jesus to cast out demons, speak in new tongues, pick up serpents, drink deadly things without harm, and lay their hands on and heal the sick. Luke ends with Jesus' promise of the Holy Spirit. And John ends with a threefold restoration of Peter. Matthew comes to a close with a word for humanity about the Messiah.

Matthew's Gospel gives humanity a claim: "all power …" The NASB, NIV, and LB use the phrase "all authority . . . ." Much of humanity uses authority to impose, oppress, and control others. There is no progress among ignorant, unfaithful, unmerciful, self-centered leadership in powerful positions. A classical example of this kind of power can be seen in the behavior of those who crucified our Lord. This is negative authority. They used their power to destroy, not realizing that Jesus uses His power to save. This is real authority. The Greek word for power and authority is *exousia* and means in the sense of ability, capacity, jurisdiction, and delegated influence. The power spoken of by Matthew is delegated to Christ. Humanity is safe in the hands of Him who is omnipotent.

19 Go ye therefore, and teach all nations, baptizing them in the name of the Father, and of the Son, and of the Holy Ghost:

The Great Commission addresses the task of conquering the world for Christ with the same intensity that Christ conquered death. This Commission to the church in every generation is God's plan of action put in motion by the simple phrase, "Go, teach, and baptize."

The Commission is boundless: reach all nations. The Commission has a goal: make disciples. The Commission has objectives: teaching and baptizing. The Commission has identity in the name of the Father, Son, and Holy Ghost. This divine nature is One, meaning there is no division in the Trinity. This Scripture does not read "in the names," but "in the name." While God is known by, and called by, many names, the Father, Son, and Holy Ghost remain one in holiness. Only as we come to God through the Son and by the Holy Spirit are we made holy. No man-made, hand-made, materialistic or mythical god will accomplish humanity's ultimate purpose: to be reconciled to God.

The Commission is a commandment, not a suggestion. No one is to be overlooked or left out of God's plan of salvation. Jesus died and God raised Him from the grave for everyone's benefit, not a remnant. This Commission is addressed to ancient, contemporary, and future disciples of Christ. Some scholars note that the proper interpretation of the Commission is "As you go, make disciples." In other words: As you go to work, make disciples; as you travel, make disciples; as you rear your children, make disciples, as you go shopping, make disciples; as you go to worship, make disciples; as you go to school, make disciples; in everything you do, make disciples.

The hymn of the ages encapsulates the intent of the Commission, and it reads, "Remember, only what you do for Christ will last."

20 Teaching them to observe all things whatsoever I have commanded you: and, lo, I am with you always, even unto the end of the world. Amen.

This verse clarifies what disciples of Christ are to teach.

Believers in Christ are to teach others to observe what Jesus commanded. When in doubt about a certain doctrine or dogma, the real question to ask is, "What did Jesus teach?" In the late 90's, the acronym (WWJD) for "What would Jesus do" has embossed on tee shirts, writing instruments, jewelry, books, billboards, and assorted memorabilia. And this is the answer to society's ills: do what Jesus commands.

Matthew ends with a word of reassurance, empowerment, and fulfilled prophecy through Him who came to this planet to be "God with us." In Acts 1:8, Luke informs us that God's Holy Spirit empowers us for the global task of making disciples as we go. The Saviour and the Spirit's twin presence are within the heart of all believers clearing the way to accomplish this Commission until we enter Christ's millennial reign.

Jesus is everywhere and with everyone always. He is never too busy. No concern is too small, and no challenge too big for Him. He promised, and we know by His Word that He keeps His promise, to be with us in life and in the life to come. At this point, Matthew signs off with the word "Amen," which means *and so be it.*

DAILY BIBLE READING

M: Pilate's Soldiers Guard Jesus' Tomb
Matthew 27:62-66
T: The Resurrection of Jesus
Matthew 28:1-10
W: Jesus Commissions His Disciples
Matthew 28:11-20
T: Jesus and Travelers on the Emmaus Road
Luke 24:13-27
F: The Travelers Recognize Jesus
Luke 24:28-35
S: Jesus Appears to His Disciples
Luke 24:36-43
S: Jesus Blesses the Disciples, and Ascends
Luke 24:44-53

NOTES

INTRODUCTION TO THE MARCH 2000 QUARTER

Units for Our Inspiration

Paul's two letters to the church at Corinth deal with matters that also confront the contemporary church community. This three-unit study, "Helping a Church Confront Crisis," provides a guide to seeking solutions for some of the problems we encounter in the church today.

The Quarter at-a-Glance

CONTINUING JESUS' WORK

UNIT 1. CHRIST THE BASIS OF UNITY

Unit 1 is a four-session study of 1 Corinthians. It begins with a lesson about Christian unity. Other lessons focus on the role of the Holy Spirit as teacher, the leaders of the church as servants of Christ, and the need for discipline in the church.

LESSON 1: March 5
Helping a Church Confront Crisis
1 Corinthians 1:2-17

Throughout history the name of Jesus has been used as a divisive tool, pitting Christian against Christian. The biblical emphasis of this lesson is on using the name of Jesus as a source of Christian unity rather than as a source of hate and division. Paul begins his letter by pronouncing a blessing on the saints in Corinth, affirming that they were one with all believers in Christ. We see Paul proceeding to thank God that the Corinthian believers' spiritual gifts demonstrated God's grace to them. Paul's next step was to pray that God, who is faithful, will strengthen those who are called. Finishing his preamble, Paul proceeded to make a special appeal, in the name of Christ, for agreement that would end the quarrels and divisions in the church.

In this lesson we see division often arises because many cannot distinguish between heeding the leader and idolizing him or her. Hopefully this lesson will urge us to desire unity and to seek it within the church.

LESSON 2: March 12
The Holy Spirit as Teacher
1 Corinthians 2:1-2, 4-13, 15-16

In this lesson we look at the fact that believers receive the Spirit that is from God, and that Spirit helps us understand the gifts bestowed on us by God. The lesson begins with Paul proclaiming Jesus Christ and Him crucified. Paul's proclamation rested on the demonstration of the Spirit and of power, declaring that the believer's faith rest not on human wisdom, but on the power of God.

The key here is the fact that the Holy Spirit is the originator of true wisdom which forms the basis of true Christian unity. Hopefully, as you study this lesson, you will resolve to rely on a demonstration of the Spirit rather than human words and wisdom.

LESSON 3: March 19
The Church and Its Leaders
1 Corinthians 4:1-13

This lesson emphasizes the role of the Christian leader as a steward of God's mysteries. In this lesson, we see that Paul asked that he and the other leaders be considered as servants of Christ and trustworthy stewards of God's mysteries. Paul used himself and Apollo as examples that the believers have no reason to boast because everything they have received is a gift.

One key fact of this lesson is that mature leadership leads to unity in Christ or enhances the spirit of unity. If you are a burgeoning Christian leader and are confused about what leadership style to practice, study this passage and you will begin to discern a direction of leadership style.

Some leaders in Corinth were in the habit of making others feel inferior through their gifts. Here we see Paul making decisions based on the best interests of the followers of Jesus and not on his own wishes. This lesson is meant to help you use your gifts to edify others, not belittle or tear down.

LESSON 4: March 26
The Need for Discipline in the Church
1 Corinthian 5:1-13

This lesson focuses on the need for discipline in the church regarding sexual relationships. Here we study how Paul reprimanded the Corinthians for failing to address a case of sexual immorality within their church.

Using the metaphor for dough preparation, Paul demanded that the person be put out of the church because a little yeast leavens the whole batch of dough. He insisted that the believers needed to get rid of malice and evil and live in sincerity and truth. Paul realized that believers would encounter sin in the world. He also told them not to recognize brothers and sisters in Christ who refused correction of their sin; he instructed the people of Corinth to enforce discipline in the church.

This lesson calls for both discipline and the willingness to forgive an offence and give a second chance to a penitent. At the heart of the discipline being studied here is the biblical recognition of sexual immorality, greed, and idolatry as sin.

UNIT 2. UNITY IN HUMAN RELATIONSHIPS

Unit 2 is a five-session study from 1 Corinthians. Each lesson deals with relationships: marriage, singleness, family, how to let love and knowledge work together, spiritual gifts, the Resurrection (Easter session), and the way to live by love.

LESSON 5: April 2
Counsel Concerning Marriage
1 Corinthians 7:1-5, 8-16

This passage of Scriptures is strictly speaking about responsibility in marriage and singleness. It deals with appropriate behavior in both of these contexts. The scriptural passage addresses conclusions, drawn by some, that sex is immoral or bad, and that a husband or wife may deprive one another of sexual intimacy. The Scripture clearly states that husbands and wives do not have authority over their own bodies, and are not to deprive one another of sexual intimacy, other than by mutual agreement for spiritual reasons.

Also found in the text is Paul's advice to the unmarried and widows to marry if they cannot maintain celibate lifestyles. On the issue of divorce Paul states neither husband nor wife should initiate separation or divorce. However, should the couple divorce, they should remain unmarried or be reconciled to each other.

The lesson seeks to make clear that sexual intimacy is appropriately expressed within marriage. The Scripture is our guide in the face of confusion about society's changing sexual mores. This lesson is not meant to be last word about all your struggles in dealing with sexual behavior but calls you to live according to the Word of God.

LESSON 6: April 9
Concerning Love and Knowledge
1 Corinthians 8

This lesson deals with the relationship between love and knowledge. When the church in Corinth raised the issue of Christians eating food sacrificed to idols, Paul stated that pride in intellectual superiority creates an arrogant sense of self-esteem while love creates a concern for others. Paul's demonstrates that eating meat offered to idols is not a sin, but destroying the faith of a weak follower is. Paul's decision is not to eat such meat out of concern for the less mature brothers and sisters.

This lesson is meant to keep us from letting our feelings of intellectual superiority cause us to wound others for whom Christ has died. This lesson calls you to allow loving consideration for others to guide your behavior. If you are indifferent to your influence on others, this lesson is meant to call you back to loving consideration.

LESSON 7: April 16
Spiritual Gifts
1 Corinthians 12:4-20, 26

This lesson deals with the varieties of gifts given to the church by the Spirit and the various activities resulting from God's generosity. The lesson emphasizes the reality of the variety of gifts, services, and activities and the fact that these all come from one God who is the source of all. Paul lists the various kinds of gifts the Spirit gives to believers for service and to glorify the church. The distribution of the gifts in the body of Christ reveals unity and diversity of the body in Christ. This principle of unity and diversity within the church is compared to the human body. Using the parts of the human body, Paul illustrates how each spiritual gift works in relationship to the others; there is one body with many parts. He then concludes the passage to show that spiritual gifts are meant to affirm our interconnection not our separateness. Since all members make up the body of Christ, if one member suffers, the whole body suffers; if one member is honored, all rejoice together.

This lesson emphasizes the fact that we have been given gifts to help us work together as members of the body of Christ. It is so easy for human beings not to accept that all members of the human family are of equal value. However, this lesson calls us to appreciate people who have strengths and abilities that are different from our own.

LESSON 8: April 23
Christ's Resurrection and Ours (Easter)
1 Corinthians 15:20-27, 35-44

In this passage of Scripture Paul makes the point that Christ rose from the dead as the "first fruits." The basic concern then of this lesson is to show that just as the human body of Christ, which was dead, came back to life by the energizing power of the Holy Spirit, so shall those of us who believe in Christ be energized by His Spirit to live again. Also key in this passage is the fact that just as death came through a human being, Adam, so will the Resurrection come through Christ, the second Adam. The lesson points to the fact that after Christ destroys every ruler, and every authority and power even death, the kingdom will be handed to God, the One who will again be the central focus of all who live.

LESSON 9: **April 30**
The Way of Love
1 Corinthians 12:31—13:13

Spiritual gifts and service have no value unless exercised in love. This lesson focuses on the meaning and power of Christian love. We see that real love is characterized by patience, kindness, trust, hope, and endurance. It is free of arrogance, selfishness, and ill will. Further, we see that when compared with other spiritual gifts; love supercedes them all.

Since we Christians speak often of love and the Corinthians mistook love as promiscuity, the question arises: "What is real love?" Christian love is more than inner orientation and greater than outward show. Christian love is grounded in the very nature of God, who loves us unconditionally, even so far as to send His Son Jesus to die on the cross.

UNIT 3. THE GLORY OF CHRISTIAN MINISTRY

Unit 3 is a four-session study of 2 Corinthians. Sessions one and two focus on the victory that Christians have through Christ in spite of trials and difficulties. Session three gives directions concerning Christian giving. Session four contains Paul's appeal to the Corinthians to live by the faith that they professed.

LESSON 10: **May 7**
The Christian March of Triumph
2 Corinthians 2:4-17

The main purpose of this lesson is to affirm the victory which Christ gives to those who are under his wings. The lesson begins with Paul's letter to the Corinthians reprimanding them for their behavior toward "one" who has sinned. Paul urged the church to forgive, and love the "one" who had caused pain, lest he despair. Paul asked the church to forgive the one who had sinned so that Satan could not have his way and cause division in the group resulting in loss of the offender. Here again he tells the Corinthians how the witness of Christians can lead

others to eternal life. Finally, he encourages them, as believers, to serve Christ with sincerity and integrity ensuring that they will live a victorious life in Christ.

LESSON 11: **May 14**
Trials and Triumphs of Christian Ministry
2 Corinthians 4:5-18

In this lesson we learn that we are afflicted in every way, but because we are God's children we will not be crushed. Our triumph is based on the fact that God, the creator of light, shines in the believers' heart to let others know the glory of God in Jesus Christ. Our power comes from God and not from ourselves. We experience many difficulties and trials, but through God's power we are not destroyed in order that Jesus may be made known. This lesson is meant to show you that the one who calls you is adequate.

If your life is in Christ, you will know triumph over difficult circumstances. Know that you are a person who has the capacity to move from suffering to triumph.

LESSON 12: **May 21**
The Collection for Jerusalem Christians
2 Corinthians 9:1-13

This lesson emphasizes the idea that principles of Christianity include giving generously, cheerfully, out of commitment, and without compulsion. It is based on the fact that God generously gives to us so that we may continue to share God's blessings with others. The lesson also reminds us that generous giving by believers results not only in meeting people's needs but also leads people to thank and glorify God.

This lesson is aimed at helping us move from reluctance to joyful giving. Christians are called to give generously to meet the needs of others. Through this study you will become aware of the blessings that come with giving.

LESSON 13: **May 28**
Living in the Faith
2 Corinthians 13:1-13

This lesson calls us to examine ourselves to see whether we are living in the faith. This self-examination is imperative to keep us from living in self-deception. Such self-examination helps us to realize that Jesus Christ is in us, calling us to reach for our divine ideal. We are exhorted like the Corinthians to examine our own lives for evidence of faith in Christ so that we ourselves do the right thing.

Our goal, as we study this lesson, is to become less like those who rebel against authority just to prove their own power. By examining yourself, you will learn of your weaknesses and by grace want to overcome them.

RELIGIOUS EDUCATION: THE CONTRIBUTIONS OF AFRICAN AMERICAN WOMEN

The preserving, teaching, reshaping, and creating within Christian education for African-American women is witnessed from historical, social, and spiritual perspectives. The lives and the work of African-American women in the field of Christian education are very much affected and connected to the political and religious milieu of their times. The contribution of African-American women is more than educating persons about the Bible. As we shall see, it includes learning about the religious journey of God's people from the past; its contemporary application; and future manifestations of God's Word in the lives of His people.

I believe that Christian education is the very fiber of the church. Christian education serves as the vehicle that leads people to discover or rediscover the truth about themselves, God, and the world around them. Such discovery is found in all aspects of the church. The aesthetics of the church, the foods we serve, the Bible classes we teach, the preached Word, and the Sunday School lessons we share, are all pieces of the fabric that Christian education weaves together. African-American women often have had to knit the pieces together with very little or weak thread.

Before slavery to contemporary times, African-American women have served in the forefront of religious education. Through preaching, teaching, writing, lecturing, and just plain living, African-American women have provided a powerful part of the cornerstone for struggling to keep God's Word alive.

Historically, religious education in the church has involved not only studying Scriptures and the moral values, but also basic academic skills, such as reading, writing, and mathematics. For example, a child could learn to identify numbers and sequential ordering of numbers as she or he discovered how to locate chapter 10 and verse 1,

2, and 3 of a particular book. Adults and children also develop oratorical skills through plays and other public speaking opportunities in church. Socially, religious education provides a forum to discuss the issues that have plagued our people and our society. Unlocking the Scriptures for ways to support and make God's Word a living reality has been the fight for many African-American women. Spiritually, religious education provides the conduit by which women, men, and youth learn to develop a personal and collective relationship with God, Christ, and the Holy Spirit. This can be accomplished through a variety of ways, including Bible lessons, arts and crafts, drama and other vehicles to create a means of illuminating God's Word in our souls and throughout our lives.

Religious education for people of color must always go beyond the traditional ways of proclaiming God's Word because of the historical, social, and spiritual dynamics that impact and shape our lives. Therefore, there must be a myriad of various personalities, styles, and a passion for God's Word to help pass on a new legacy of Christian education within our community and the world. We need persons such as Harriet Tubman and Sojourner Truth, who were not educated at the Harvard or Howard Universities of their time, yet still had fire and determination to the injustice of slavery and abises relating to women of color. Their strong, eternal belief in God allowed them to demonstrate what God can do through us if we are willing vessels. Tubman and Truth have contributed to Christian education by showing us that God's Word is not to bind us to a life of injustice.

The work of such persons as Amanda Smith, "evangelist and missionary;"[1] Mary McLeod Bethune, educator

[1] Marilyn Richardson, *Black Women and Religion - A Bibliography* (Boston: G. K Hall & Co., 1980), p. 66.

Cheryl P. Clemetson, Ph.D.

and social activist; and Nannie Helen Burroughs, educator, social activist, religious educator, and humanitarian; Julia Cooper, "feminist, educator, and writer,"[2] provided spiritual, social, and educational leadership for many. They preached the Gospel, lectured, and wrote for racial equality and the suffrage movement for black women in particular. Institutions of higher learning, such as the Bethune College, now known as Bethune-Cookman College in Daytona, Florida, were started by Mary McLeoud Bethune with $1.50. Nannie Helen Burroughs founded the institution now known as Nannie Helen Burroughs School in Washington, D.C., for women and girls. Later it became a co-ed elementary and middle school. Each of these women used the resources that were available to them to share knowledge and encourage others to fight for justice.

When we look at the contributions of African-American women today in the field of Christian education, the legacy of having the social, spiritual, and historical dimensions of Christian educators is still significant. We still have persons like Dorothy Height, a living legend for justice and equality of women and all humanity. We need our Sunday School teachers and religious education directors to reflect the images of doctors, lawyers, custodians, bakers, and computer programmers so that our children and our adults are exposed to various occupations and teaching experiences. There are more educational materials being written and illustrated by African-American women. Dr. Delores Carpenter, Professor of Christian Education at Howard Divinity School, is an educator, pastor, writer, and lecturer. Her contributions to Christian education include lessons and writings for children and adults. She is imaginative and insightful in her writings and preaching. Dr. Carpenter also addresses the issues of women. She emphasizes the importance of women in the church and the ministry. Dr. Carpenter is a role model for girls and women. Her talents and gifts in the ministry, as an activist, leader, teacher, and mother are genuine and uplifting.

If Christian education is to continue addressing God's Word in a way that is relevant and enlightening to others, then African-American women must work in the political, social, and spiritual facets that shape and affect our lives as a people and as women of God. Consequently, we need to hear and see the voices of Representative Maxine Waters and Representative Eleanor Holmes Norton as they address political and social issues. This will help us to illustrate the prophet Amos' words to "let justice roll on like a river," as we compare Amos' times to today (Amos 5:24, NIV). We need to hear the clarion and pastoral voice of Dr. Vashti McKenzie as her words from the Lord give direction and guidance.

In addition to our famous or better known persons, we should never forget the unsung "sheroes," such as our grandmothers, mothers, aunts, Sunday School teachers, church mothers, tough and loving baby-sitters who helped us to learn to say grace and to hold our hands to pray, and the African-American nuns who helped us understand what it means to "reverence the Lord." Please do not forget the importance of the neighborhood watch Mom before "Neighborhood Watch" became a nationally known community event. She helped us better understand what the omnipresence of God means because the neighborhood watch Mom always seemed to be watching you. We must remember our schoolteachers and principals who made us have a moment of silence to acknowledge and respect God in our cultures and who emphasized prayer. (Keep this quiet because the law said that we could not, but we did.)

The contributions of African-American women to Christian education are found in the stories and lesson that we write and share, the music that we teach and sing, the preaching that we preach on Sundays, and our involvement in voter registration, voting, and running for public office. Our contributions are found in our ability to tell the same story about the birth, life, death, and resurrection of Jesus Christ. Our contributions are reflected in being able to accept the role of Sunday School teacher, even when we know God has called us to preach. Yet, the church may still say, "God does not operate that way."

To paraphrase Maya Angelou, "we still keep rising"[3] and contributing to Christian education in the church and in the community. The contributions of African-American women to Christian education includes more inclusive language and illustrations. There are more women entering and completing seminary training in pastoral ministry and religious education. This means that the roles of women in the church are being stretched to new depths. The political and social changes and issues concerning women and girls are being lifted closer to the forefront. Issues concerning women and girls in the work of Christ that have either been overlooked or not emphasized are opening new avenues of understanding the ministry of Christ. As the Lord continues to pour out his spirit upon "all flesh" (Joel 2:28, KJV), and we receive this outpouring, change happens. The wheels of progress often turn slowly, but there are changes that demonstrate through women the power of God. Therefore, we will continue to benefit from the excellence of African-American women in the field of Christian education.

[2] Ibid., p. 67
[3] Maya Angelou, *Maya Angelou: Poems,* "And Still I Rise" (New York: Bantam Books, 1971), p. 154

HELPING A CHURCH CONFRONT CRISIS

The Lord has provided us with tools to help a church confront crisis. First, let us establish what the church is. The church is the bride of Christ and the Body of Christ of which Christ is the Head. The church is made up of individuals who come together corporately to worship and praise the Lord, preparing to meet Jesus in the air when He returns to receive us unto Himself.

Let us visit Matthew 16:13-19 to find out what truly makes us the church of Jesus Christ. Jesus asked his disciples, "Whom do men say that I the Son of man am?" And they said, "some say you are Elias: . . . Thou art John the Baptist. . ." Jesus then asked Peter, "But whom say ye that I am?" Peter answered and said, "Thou art the Christ, the Son of the living God." And Jesus answered and said unto him, "Blessed art thou Simon Barjona: for flesh and blood hath not revealed it unto thee, but my Father which is in heaven. Then Jesus said, "I say also unto thee that thou art Peter, and upon this rock (Peter's revelation of who Jesus is) I will build my Church and the gates of hell shall not prevail against it." Jesus also promised Peter something in verse 19, "And I will give unto thee the keys to the Kingdom of heaven: and whatsoever thou shalt bind on earth shall be bound in heaven and whatsoever thou shalt loose on earth shall be loosed in heaven."

We are the church, those of us who have received Jesus Christ as our personal Lord and Saviour and we must individually as well as corporately have the revelation that Jesus is the Christ, the Son of the living God. When we know this, we also will know that the gates of hell shall not prevail against the church, individually or corporately. And because Jesus died on the Cross for our sins, we have the victory! "Now thanks be unto God which always causeth us to triumph in Christ" (2 Corinthians 2:14).

The Word assures us that crises will come, the principalities of darkness will try to conquer, control, and take over our church, but they cannot overtake the church of Jesus Christ! Jesus warned us that perilous times would come in John 16:33, "In this world ye shall have tribulation: but be of good cheer I have overcome the world." The word "world" in this Scripture denotes the spiritual world and Satan is the god of this world.

The church is experiencing much deception and at times it appears that the church is losing, but it is not. Second Corinthians 5:7 says, "For we walk by faith, not by sight." All the enemy can do is hinder (frustrate, hamper) the church, but he shall not prevail! Hallelujah!

What is a crisis? A crisis by definition is a demonic attack that attempts to defeat the church. A crisis could be a personal disaster, strait or plight, etc. Or, it could be corporate—a controversy, dispute, dissension, contention or strife within the body. Remember, no matter what we're confronted with, the revelation of who Jesus is, is our solution!

Our archenemy, Satan, the devil, has a hierarchy of helpers. He is the prince of the power of the air. He has principalities and powers, rulers of the darkness of this world, spiritual wickedness in high places, demons and fallen angels at his beck and call to cause havoc and crises in the lives of God's people. When we study the Word of God, we are not ignorant of the devil's devices. We know that "the thief cometh not, but for to steal, but to kill and to destroy; but I (Jesus) am come that they might have life and that they might have it more abundantly" (John 10:10). Know this, that when crises come to the church, it is a sure sign of victory! The Word of God says in Matthew Chapter 16, ". . . the gates of hell shall not prevail against it." When we look at any crisis, we must look at it with our spiritual eyes. "The things that are seen are temporal, but the things are not seen are eternal (2 Corinthians 4:18).

God, in His infinite wisdom, has provided an organizational chart for the warriors in His church: a shepherd—the head and overseer of the church; church leaders; ". . . some apostles, and some prophets and evangelists; and some pastors and teachers for the perfecting of the saints, for the work of the ministry. For the edifying of the Body. . ." (Ephesians 4:8-13); intercessors

Rev. Carol McIlwain Edwards

and the body of Christ (i.e., fellow saints). We need not fear, but encourage ourselves because God has the answers to all crises.

God has not left His church without an arsenal and ammunition. The arsenal of weapons include the Holy Bible or the Word of God, Jesus—the Anointed One and His anointings, the precious Holy Spirit, faith, prayer in the name of Jesus, fasting, the whole armour of God, praise and worship, the keys to the Kingdom to bind the enemy and loose the solution, the baptism of the Holy Spirit, the prayer of agreement, etc. A crisis could come directly to the pastor, the leadership, or to one of the members of the church. The church should always be in prayer for itself, its members and the Body of Christ as a whole. However, the spirit behind the crisis can be readily identified by the intercessors who fast, pray and worship the Lord on a continual basis and close to the Lord. Prayer should be consistent and continuous until the answer comes. When we pray we must stand, believe and be persistent. We are told in Matthew 7:7-8, "Ask and it shall be given you; seek and ye shall find; knock, and it shall be opened unto you. For everyone that asketh receiveth; and he that seeketh findeth; and to him that knocketh, it shall be opened." The pastor has the power and the responsibility to initiate, participate and concentrate on the crisis at hand. When the answer to prayer does not come forth speedily, the church membership may be asked to pray for the situation (if it is shared corporately.) When referring to demons Deuteronomy 32:30 says, "one can chase a thousand and two can chase ten thousand. Imagine the number of demons the leadership can chase, not to mention the corporate church body.

Ministry is necessary to teach the Body of Christ spiritual warfare, how to identify the enemy and how to bind him and cast him to dry places. It is critical to teach that the church should have daily communication with the Lord, our Heavenly Father to thank Him for all of our blessings and to ask Him, according to His Word, for favor requested in the name of Jesus Christ. Jesus told us in Matthew 21:13: "It is written, my house shall be called the house of prayer." At times, prayer, fasting (Mark 9:29) and intensified praise and worship are necessary.

The people of God should be taught to locate Scriptures that will take care of the crisis at hand and pray, citing them. The main Scripture is, ". . . The gates of hell shall not prevail against our church!" The following are examples of crises/demonic attacks against the church coupled with Scriptures one can use in the fight to attack them:

Financial: Tithing—Malachi 3:10-12, "Bring ye all— the tithes to the storehouse, that there may be meat in mine house and prove me now herewith, saith the Lord of hosts, if I will not open you the windows of heaven, and pour you out a blessing, that there shall not be room enough to receive it. And I will rebuke the devourer for your sakes . . . . " Also, we can bind the spirit of lack, and loose the spirit of abundance from Heaven, in the name of Jesus (see Ecclesiastes 11:1; Philippians 4:19). Giving—Luke 6:38, "Give, and it shall be given unto you; good measure, pressed down, and shaken together, and running over, shall men give into your bosom."

Disunity: Matthew 12:25 " . . . Every kingdom divided against itself is brought to desolation; and every city or house divided against itself shall not stand" (see also Amos 3:3; Matthew 18:19; Acts 2:1).

Unhappy marriages: Ephesians 5:21, "Submitting yourselves one to another in the fear of God."

Problems raising children: Deuteronomy 6:4-7, "Hear, O Israel: The Lord our God is one Lord: And thou shalt love the Lord thy God with all thine heart, and with all thy soul, and with all thy might. And these words, which I command thee this day, shalt be in thine heart: And thou shalt teach them diligently unto thy children" (cf. Proverbs 22:6; Isaiah 54:13; Ephesians 6:1-4).

Loss of membership: Matthew 18:11-14, "For the Son of man is come to save that which was lost. How think ye? if a man have an hundred sheep, and one of them be gone astray, doth he not leave the ninety and nine, and goeth into the mountains, and seeketh that which is gone astray? And if so be that he find it, verily I say unto you, he rejoiceth more of that sheep, than of the ninety and nine which went not astray. Even so it is not the will of your Father which is in heaven, that one of these little ones should perish."

God has already given us answers to confront all our crises and it is up to us to seek them out in His Word and apply them. The church, individual or corporate, must have the revelation that Jesus is the Christ, the Son of the living God. Jesus built His church on the revelation Peter received directly from the Father. Troubled times will come, but we must believe, stay alert, stay in-tuned to the Holy Spirit and apply the Word of God to every situation in life. We have the keys to the kingdom, the power to bind and cast demons out of our church, and the gates of hell shall not prevail against it! We have the victory! Reign, Jesus, Reign!

POINT OF VIEW ON YOUTH EDUCATION

popular saying is, "It takes a village to rear a child." Yet, the primary responsibility for educating a child rests with his parents. As a matter of fact, education starts in the womb. Parents should read the Bible and sing praises unto the Lord every day. Pray aloud so the baby can hear you in the womb.

A baby can be compared to a blank sheet of paper waiting to be written upon. Writing can be synonymous with "imparting knowledge" so that the principles of the Lord can be inculcated into our children. Although it is a miracle within itself, a mother and father came together in answer to God's will and a baby was created. The baby is a gift from God (Psalm 127:3), loaned to the parents to care for, nurture, and prepare for return to God. The child must learn that God knew him before he was in his mother's womb and that God has called him for a specific purpose (Isaiah 44:2). He must get to know God as the Father

(Ephesians 4:4-6) and be made completely aware of his status as a child of God. He must also be made aware that he is an heir of God and a joint heir with Christ and that he has dominion over the world. He must be taught God's provisions of protection: the precious blood of Jesus Christ, the whole armour of God, Holy Angels watching over him, the prayer cover, the Hedge of Protection, and the precious Holy Spirit are available to lead and guide him into all truth and to comfort him. He should be taught that these blessings come about only if he receives Jesus Christ as Saviour and Lord of his life.

First let us look at the Scripture where Jesus states in Matthew 19:14, "Suffer (allow) little children, and forbid them not to come unto me: for of such is the kingdom of heaven." Jesus wants us to allow our children to come to Him so they will not perish (Matthew 18:14). When the children come to The Lord Jesus Christ, their true education begins.

Rev. Carol McIlwain Edwards

God loves children and He compares them to the following: Arrows (Psalm 127:4); seed (Psalm 112:1-3; Proverbs 11:21b); as well as olive plants (Psalm 128:3). The word "point," (i.e., point of view) reminds me of the word "arrows." Psalm 127:4 states, "As arrows are in the hands of a mighty man, so are the children of the youth." We (as adults), have to point the arrows (children), in the direction they should go so they will defeat the enemy and not miss the mark! Children have to know that Jesus is ". . . the way, the truth, and the life. No man cometh unto the Father but by Him" (John 14:6).

We must train children according to Proverbs 22:6, "Train up a child in the way that he should go: and when he is old he will not depart from it." Before we can teach and train our children with the Word of God, it is our obligation and responsibility to study the Word for ourselves!

Parents must stop being selfish and pay more attention to their children, spending more time teaching and training them according to the Word of God. Our youth are seed. God describes what happens to our seed when they have godly parents in Psalm 112:1-3. I believe the majority of parents look to the church to teach their children the Word of God and the public/private school to teach their children to read, etc. Some rely on the church and school to rear their children. This is not what the Lord commands.

It is not enough to bring our children to church, but it is essential to introduce them to Jesus and continue to teach them to hear God's voice (John 10:1-5). They need to be baptized in the Holy Spirit so that they can receive power to witness and to defeat the enemy with the Word of God! Luke 17:1, 2 warns us to be careful not to offend God's little ones (our youth).

David, Daniel, and Jeremiah are examples of youth who have been touched by God. The Lord wants to touch our children and for them to experience the anointing of the Holy Spirit. Mark 10:13 states, "they brought little children to [Jesus], that He might touch them." God wants youth to experience His presence, His anointing, His power. But in order for them to be touched by God, we must introduce Him in such a way that they can learn to hear and obey Him.

Somehow in our walk with the Lord, our children have been discouraged by negative forces within and without the church, because of society and members of the church not walking in the statutes of the Lord. We must teach them not to look at the things that are seen, but to look at the things that are not seen: for the things that are seen are temporal (subject to change), but the things that are not seen are eternal. (Hebrews 11:1, 2, paraphrased). We should teach them that no matter what they observe in the House of the Lord or in society, they should pray and not allow these things to turn them away from the Lord. Jesus never changes! He is the same yesterday, today and forever! You can trust God! Our youth should have the assurance that God will never leave or forsake them (Hebrews 13:5)!

The main obligation for educating our youth lies with parents and the church. The church provides the laboratory in order to produce a well-rounded, educated youth. It takes the dedication of parents, a secure home life, a church that values its youth and their promise, good schools and a good community. We must see to it that all these ingredients are in place to prepare our youth for today and tomorrow! Children are our future. The Bible has given instructions on what, why and how we are to teach them. Jesus said, "Suffer the little children to come unto me, for of such is the kingdom of heaven" (Mark 10:14). Heaven belongs to our children too!

The Lord tells us unless we become as little children, we can no wise enter into the Kingdom of Heaven (Matthew 18:3). Let us observe our children and learn to imitate their unfailing faith; observe and appreciate their uniqueness; affirm them and let them know that there's no one else on the earth exactly like them; that God created them for a special purpose to help all of His children! And above all, communicate with them where they are—on their level.

Yes, it does take a whole village to rear our children, but we know that the parents have the primary responsibility. What have we written on the blank sheet of paper (our youth)? Think about it! Have we written joy on this paper? Have we written an invitation for them to meet God as their Father? Have we written an invitation for them to receive Jesus Christ as their personal Lord and Saviour and that Jesus is the only way that they can get to God, our Father? Have we been writing positive things on this very valuable sheet of paper? Have you invited them to get to know the Holy Spirit—the one Who will lead and guide them into all truth; the One who will comfort them—empower them? Have you written on them who they are, how they are made and why they were made? Again, what have you written on your precious sheet of paper?

Phillis Wheatley
(1753-1784)

Phillis Wheatley overcame the adverse conditions of slavery to become a world renown poet. Ms. Wheatley was born in Africa, most sources say Senegal, around 1753. When she was about seven or eight years old, she was kidnapped and sold to John and Susannah Wheatley of Boston. She was sold for a cheap price on the Boston dock because the ship's captain didn't think she would live long.

The Wheatleys were impressed with the young slave girl's ability to learn quickly and taught her English, Latin, and Greek. She mastered the English language a short while after her arrival in America,

The Wheatleys were impressed with the young slave girl's ability to learn quickly and taught her English, Latin, and Greek.

poems. It was signed by a group of Boston citizens who examined the young Phillis. She was also granted her freedom from the Wheatleys in 1773.

The theme of salvation ran throughout many of Ms. Wheatley's works. She said every person, regardless of race, was in need of salvation. She connected Christian freedom and beliefs to racial freedom for Blacks. She wrote against the irony of Christians owning slaves and supporting the degrading institution of slavery. Ms. Wheatley included Biblical characters in many of her poems, such as *Goliath of Gath*. She wrote

and she was able to read the Bible and quickly comprehended its teachings. The Wheatley family was reportedly a Christian family and introduced Christ to their slave girl, who was given special attention and treated much like a family member.

The intelligent young girl, who was frail and sickly looking, received international attention and became famous when she wrote *On the Death of the Rev. Mr. George Whitefield, 1770*. The poem was an elegy for the evangelical preacher. The poem caught the attention of an English noblewoman and philanthropist, Selina Hastings of Huntingdon. The Countess supported Ms. Wheatley's work and helped fund her book *Poems on Various Subjects, Moral and Religious in 1773*. The book, a collection of 39 poems, contained an opening note certifying that a young Negro slave girl had written the

a poem that honored George Washington, who later met with her and commended her on her work.

Ms. Wheatley, named Phillis after the slave ship on which she arrived in Boston, married John Peters in 1778. Mr. Peters was a free Boston Black man. Their children died as babies, and Ms. Wheatley died while in her 30s. Despite her fame, she died in complete poverty.

However her work lived on. Abolitionists used her poetry and ideas to campaign against the institution of slavery, and she is now credited with beginning both the Black American writing tradition and the Black American women's writing tradition. She served as an example of how humans could overcome tragic life situations.

TEACHING TIPS

March 5
Bible Study Guide 1

1. Words You Should Know

A. Unity. Greek *henotes*—"one." Used in the Old Testament in the sense of togetherness of persons (Genesis 13:6), fellowship, and praise. Isaiah 11:6-7 tells of a future time when there will be a togetherness among animals. The New Testament speaks of the unity of faith that binds together the people of God (Ephesians 4:13).

B. Baptism. (v. 14) Greek *baptizo*—The rite or ordinance by which persons are admitted into the Church of Christ. It is the public profession of faith in Christ; a symbol of the washing of the soul from sin.

2. Teacher Preparation

A. Prayerfully Read 1 Corinthians in its entirety. Read all four lessons in this unit, then read the FOCAL VERSES for this week's lesson at least twice. Use a different version for each reading.

B. Familiarize yourself with the BACKGROUND material for the lesson.

C. Write the definitions for "unity" and "baptism" on the blackboard. Be prepared to discuss these definitions with students.

3. Starting the Lesson

A. Begin the lesson with prayer. Ask God to enrich your teaching and bless your students with understanding.

B. Ask students to read the IN FOCUS lesson. Ask them what they normally do when faced with conflict.

C. Preview the four lessons for this unit, tying in the theme for the unit, using the UNIT INTRODUCTION located in the *Student Manual*.

4. Getting into the Lesson

A. To help students understand today's lesson, have a volunteer read aloud the FOCAL VERSES and another read the BACKGROUND information.

B. Summarize key points from the IN DEPTH section and have students answer the SEARCH THE SCRIPTURES questions.

5. Relating the Lesson to Life

A. Use the DISCUSS THE MEANING questions to help students relate this lesson to their own lives.

B. Continue the discussion by reading aloud the LESSON IN OUR SOCIETY section. This will help students apply today's lesson to modern day society.

6. Arousing Action

A. Review the KEEP IN MIND verse and ask students how they can use this verse to guide them in their relationships both at church and at home.

B. Challenge the students to put the suggestion from the MAKE IT HAPPEN section into action in their daily living.

C. Encourage the students to read the DAILY BIBLE READINGS and to preview next week's lesson.

D. Solicit prayer requests and close the class with prayer.

WORSHIP GUIDE

For the Superintendent or Teacher
Theme: Helping A Church Confront Crisis
Theme Song: "We Are the Church"
Scripture: Matthew 12:25
Song: "One Bread, One Body"
Meditation: Eternal God, I thank You for Jesus Christ, in whom I am one with all who call on Him. Help me to keep my mind and my heart focused on You, so I can do Your will, Amen.

HELPING A CHURCH CONFRONT CRISIS

Bible Background • 1 CORINTHIANS 1:1-17
Printed Text • 1 CORINTHIANS 1:2-17
Devotional Reading • 1 CORINTHIANS 1:18-25

LESSON AIM

By the end of the lesson, students will: better understand their position as members of "the Body of Christ" and the need for unity within the church; learn how to resolve conflicts which may divide a church; and purpose themselves to be on one accord, united in service to the Lord.

KEEP IN MIND

"Now I beseech you, brethren, by the name of our Lord Jesus Christ, that ye all speak the same thing, and that there be no divisions among you; but that ye be perfectly joined together in the same mind and in the same judgment"(1 Corinthians 1:10).

FOCAL VERSES

1 CORINTHIANS 1:2 Unto the church of God which is at Corinth, to them that are sanctified in Christ Jesus, called to be saints, with all that in every place call upon the name of Jesus Christ our Lord, both theirs and ours:

3 Grace be unto you, and peace, from God our Father, and from the Lord Jesus Christ.

4 I thank my God always on your behalf, for the grace of God which is given you by Jesus Christ;

5 That in every thing ye are enriched by him, in all utterance, and in all knowledge;

6 Even as the testimony of Christ was confirmed in you:

7 So that ye come behind in no gift; waiting for the coming of our Lord Jesus Christ:

8 Who shall also confirm you unto the end, that ye may be blameless in the day of our Lord Jesus Christ.

9 God is faithful, by whom ye were called unto the fellowship of his Son Jesus Christ our Lord.

10 Now I beseech you, brethen, by the name of our Lord Jesus Christ, that ye all speak the same thing, and that there be no divisions among you; but that ye be perfectly joined together in the same mind and in the same judgment.

11 For it hath been declared unto me of you, my brethren, by them which are of the house of Chloe, that there are contentions among you.

12 Now this I say, that every one of you saith; I am of Paul; and I of Cephas; and I of Christ.

13 Is Christ divided? Was Paul crucified for you? Or were ye baptized in the name of Paul?

14 I thank God that I baptized none of you, but Crispus and Gaius;

15 Lest any should say that I had baptized in mine own name.

16 And I baptized also the household of Stephanas: besides, I know not whether I baptized any other.

17 For Christ sent me not to baptize, but to preach the gospel: not with the wisdom of words, lest the cross of Christ should be made of none effect.

LESSON OVERVIEW

LESSON AIM
KEEP IN MIND
FOCAL VERSES
IN FOCUS
THE PEOPLE, PLACES, AND TIMES
BACKGROUND
AT-A-GLANCE
IN DEPTH
SEARCH THE SCRIPTURES
DISCUSS THE MEANING
LESSON IN OUR SOCIETY
MAKE IT HAPPEN
FOLLOW THE SPIRIT
REMEMBER YOUR THOUGHTS
MORE LIGHT ON THE TEXT
DAILY BIBLE READINGS

IN FOCUS

Judge Lana Carter sat anguished in her chambers. She had been a juvenile court judge for 16 years and had never had a case this difficult to rule on.

271

Two couples, the Williams and the Toussaints, were fighting to adopt a little girl, Kia, to whom they had both been foster parents. Kia, who was now six, was taken from her natural mother at birth and was placed with the Williams, who remained her foster parents for three years. When Kia's mother moved to Ohio, Kia was placed with the Toussaints, who lived there, in hope that Kia would eventually be able to reunite with her natural mother. After three years, those hopes were lost when Kia's mother signed away all of her parental rights.

Learning of this, both the Williams and the Toussaints petitioned the court to adopt Kia. That is where the problem started. They were both perfectly qualified to adopt Kia. Both couples had been foster parents for several years. Both provided loving and nurturing homes for those in their care. Kia thrived in both environments and loved both couples. Both couples had been given recommendations from DCFS, as well as their church. Each had hired a psychologist who outlined why their client was well suited to become Kia's parents. In every way, the couples were equal. The couples even admitted that Kia would benefit living in either home. It was a deadlock.

As Judge Carter reviewed the petitions along with the supporting documentation, she wished this was one of her more routine cases, where a needy child was taken from an unfit home. The system was full of such children.

After hours of extensive review, she realized that the Williams and the Toussaints' shared the shame sentiment regarding Kia's well being. They both wanted what was best for Kia and, in spite of their fighting, they were honest enough to admit that either was capable of being good adoptive parents. This both eased Judge Carter's mind and helped provide the solution. She ruled in favor of the Williams, who had Kia first and was with her during her formative years with the stipulation that the Toussaints be allowed to visit Kia occasionally.

Sometimes, we have different views on how situations should be handled. This sometimes leads to conflict and division. If however, we share the same sentiment, conflicts can be resolved and easily avoided.

In today's lesson, we'll learn that the source for Christian unity and the resolution for division is Jesus Christ.

THE PEOPLE, PLACES, AND TIMES

APOSTLE PAUL. Born in Tarsus, Cilicia around 5 A.D. Paul (also known as Saul, his Jewish name) was born to Hebrew parents in a Gentile city. Paul's trade was a tentmaker before becoming an apostle. He was educated in Jerusalem under Gamaliel (Acts 22:3; 26:4-5). On his way to persecute Christians at Damascus, he was converted to Christianity (Acts 9: 22; 26).

Paul established the church of Corinth during his second missionary journey. He came to Corinth afraid, but was calmed by a heavenly vision. He is the author of at least 13 New Testament epistles. Paul was imprisoned two times in Rome, where he was eventually beheaded.

(Adapted from *Smith's Bible Dictionary*, Nashville: Thomas Nelson Publishers, pp. 487-494.)

CORINTH. A city of Greece, located about 40 miles west of Athens. Because of its ideal geographical location between Italy and Asia, Corinth was a hub of trade. It was a city renowned for its wealth and its arts. It was almost equally known for it vices and extravagances. As far as religion, the principle deity worshiped was Venus, the goddess of love, or licentious passion. In fact, the term "Corinthianize" was coined to signify a person who lived a sexually immoral life.

(Adapted from *Smith's Bible Dictionary*, Nashville: Thomas Nelson Publishers, pp. 123-124.)

UNITY. Used in the Old Testament in the sense of togetherness of persons (Genesis 13:6), fellowship, and praise. Isaiah 11:6-7 tells of a future time when there will be a togetherness among animals. The New Testament speaks of the unity of faith that binds together the people of God (Ephesians 4:13).

(Adapted from *Vines Expository Dictionary*, McLean: MacDonald Publishing, p. 1194.)

BACKGROUND

In A.D. 52, the Apostle Paul came to the city of Corinth—a city rich in wealth and vices—and through faith, much laboring, and diligent work he established a church there. This church was greatly blessed and favored as a result of their commitment to Christ. A few years after Paul left, he received word from the household of one of the members that the church was in spiritual trouble. It had divided into sects and fallen into sinful ways. Paul was deeply affected upon hearing this. In 54 A.D., Paul wrote to them, to admonish them to correct the ills that had befallen them, and to help them grow spiritually.

He wrote to the Corinthians for two reasons. The first was to address reports about the church that were not favorable (1 Corinthians 1:11; 5:1). The matters reported to him included: church divisions, a case of sexual immorality, lawsuits between church members, the abuse of Christian free-dom, and a report of general chaos. Second, he wrote to answers questions about marriage and single life, problems over food consecrated to idols and on social functions held at the temple, on the place of women in public meetings, on the matter of spiritual gifts, and on the meaning of the resurrection of the dead.

He began his letter to the church of Corinth by stating his qualification for the position of an apostle. His Apostolic status was being questioned by some in the Corinthian church. False leaders had risen, and Paul felt it necessary to address this. He did so not in a prideful, boasting manner, but in order to maintain his position as an authority figure. Paul was called as an apostle of Jesus Christ, through the will of God (1 Corinthians 1:1). His calling was a divine one. He was commissioned by God. He founded the church at Corinth on God's authority. It is on that authority that he addressed the church.

Paul's epistle not only reprimands the church, but is a testament on Christian unity, which is the focus of this unit. 1 Corinthians is just as useful today as a divine solution for church infighting, dissension, and turmoil. Its timeliness and truth is invaluable, as it addresses many difficulties which the church may face.

AT-A-GLANCE

**1. One Body in Christ
(1 Corinthians 1:2-9)
2. Unity in Christ (vv. 10-13)
3. Serving Christ (vv. 14-17)**

IN DEPTH

1. One Body in Christ (1 Corinthians 1:2-9)

Though the purpose of this epistle is to admonish the church of Corinth for allowing itself to become divided and getting into spiritual trouble, Apostle Paul begins by offering up his blessing to the saints of Corinth. His address is to all "sanctified in Christ Jesus, called to be saints" (v. 2). As Christians, we are set apart from men of the world by baptism and made holy. We are all one with those who believe in Christ. Unity in Christ is multi-cultural and multi-racial. We are one with any person, anywhere, who confesses Jesus Christ as his personal Saviour. Thus, as the universal body of Christ, we should "make every effort to keep the unity of the Spirit through the bond of peace. There is

one body and one Spirit" (Ephesians 4:3-4a, NIV).

Paul also offers up thanksgiving to the Lord on behalf of the church of Corinth for several reasons: 1) For His grace (v. 3). Once the church became united with Christ, they also became objects of divine favor. 2) For the abundance of spiritual gifts God had blessed them with (vv. 4-5). They had received as many gifts as any other church as a guarantee of Christ's testimony among them, and so that they could wait patiently for Christ (v. 7). Having received a great deal of spiritual gifts, they found themselves not wanting for anything. This allowed them to focus more earnestly on the second coming of Christ, which is one characteristic of being a Christian. God had provided for them incredibly, so that they had no reason not to be committed in their faith. For those that wait on Him shall be, "blameless in the day of our Lord Jesus Christ" (v. 8). Christ will, until the end, keep all of those who wait on Him.

God is faithful (v. 9). God loves us. This same God called us into fellowship with Jesus Christ, and if we commit our ways to the Lord, we know that He will keep His promises to provide for all our needs.

2. Unity in Christ (vv. 10-13)

The word "unity" is from the Greek word *henotes*, meaning "one." It is on this principle that Christianity lies. There is one Christ—one object of our worship. Paul enters into his subject by first appealing for unity (v. 10). Paul appealed to them in the name of Jesus, because 1) Christ is the head of the universal church. There is only one body of Christ and there should be no divisions. 2) Ephesians 3:15 states of Christ, "Of whom the whole family in heaven and earth is named." No one else is named, because there is no one else worthy to be named. Therefore, no other names should be lifted up in the church. 3) Christ commands the church to operate in unity and mutual love (John 13:34; 15:17).

That ye all speak the same thing. In terms of their religious opinions, believers in Christ should hold and express the same things. This is not suggesting that every opinion uttered from their lips be the exact same. This means that the church should agree on the basic teachings of Christianity, and they should express their opinions in biblical language. If there is disagreement, it should not be expressed in anger and ill will, but in good spirit.

That there be no divisions among you. The church is not to be broken into different parties or groups, or hold up different leaders. It is to be regarded as one. It should be able to withstand all and be indivisible.

That ye be perfectly joined together. Paul exhorts the church to promote harmony and fix all that needs to be fixed in order for unity to be restored. "Perfectly joined together," in this context is to correct moral evils and errors (Galatians 6:1). The church had to come together and settle all matters that were keeping them divided, then join together to work toward the same desires. Those desires should be centered on serving Christ, and following Him.

In the same mind. This phrase is not referring directly to intellect—since it is impossible, and not meant for everyone to have the exact same views or think the exact same way—but refers more to what is in the mind, including one's thoughts, opinions, and plans. The church should have an openness of mind towards each other, good will, and harmonious thoughts. This can be achieved when believers keep their minds on Christ and allow His Spirit to indwell within each of them.

And in the same judgment. The word "judgment," in this context, comes from the Greek *gnome*, meaning "purpose of mind," or "will." The church's sentiments should be the same. They should have kindness towards one another, love, and respect. A church can have all of these, even if they have different intellectual views. In other words, they didn't always have to see eye to eye, but underneath they should have a shared feeling of unity in spirit.

Paul received word of the division within the church at Corinth from the house of Chloe (v. 11). Paul had probably found all of this out from a church member who ran into him and told him what was going on. It seemed that a lot of the strife was caused by pride. Corinth was an artsy cosmopolitan city, and many of its citizens were educated. The teachers were all eloquent, each trying to gain distinction by being more eloquent than the next. In addressing them, he mentioned the names of familiar leaders. He mentioned Apollos (Acts 18:27-28) because Apollos was incredibly eloquent and many people probably wanted to imitate him. He also spoke of Peter (John 1:42), who was regarded as the apostle for the Jews.

He also reminded them of Christ (v. 12). There should have been no need to cite the supreme leader, but members of the church probably did so because they refused to profess that they were led by any other.

In order to show them the senselessness of their divisions, Paul asked them, "Is Christ divided?" (v. 13) Was anyone other than Christ crucified and offered up as a sacrifice for sin? Are believers baptized in the name of anyone other than Jesus Christ? The answer is no. There is only one Christ. Only one whose blood was good enough to be offered up as the price for the sins of the world. That fact alone should be the ultimate humbler. Christian unity could be realized if every

believer would stop and remind themselves that salvation for all men was paid for by the blood of but one, Jesus Christ. No man or woman, no matter how great they may be, is as great as Jesus Christ. Therefore, as Christians, we should be of one heart and one mind, following and worshiping the one and only Christ.

Paul urged them, then, to end all divisions among them in the name of Jesus. Because if we follow Jesus, we should all have the same purpose and be of the same mind. Our motives should be the same—to serve God—even if we don't always agree on how to do it. The church must end quarrels and unite simply because they are one in the body of Christ and should be of one mind.

3. Serving Christ (vv. 14-17)

In these verses, Paul humbles himself and accounts for his ministry. He "thanked God" that he didn't baptize very many (vv. 14-16) and says his true purpose was to preach the Gospel (v. 17). He does this in retrospect. The fact that he had baptized some may have led some to believe that he had set himself up as a leader or baptized in his own name. When you are baptized "into" someone, you become intimately connected to that person and devoted to him/her. By this act you promise to be governed by that person's authority. Paul was not trying to take Jesus' authority. In fact, he was trying to do the opposite: he was trying to restore it to the church of Corinth. He had baptized some (vv. 15-16), but he was sure he did not baptize any members in his own name. The reason for this, Paul states, is that "Christ sent me not to baptize, but to preach the gospel" (v. 17). Paul was called to deliver the message of the Gospel. His job was to deliver the Good News of salvation and to help bring souls to the Lord.

It is important to remember that no one should be put in Christ's place. People seem to get caught up by the person who baptized them instead of getting caught up in the Saviour and the Good News of their salvation. This again reasserts the point that there is only one Christ. No one should be put in Christ's place, even church leaders. Christ is the foundation, and all Christians, including leaders, must serve him whole-heartedly. Don't get caught up in human leaders. Embrace the message much more than the messenger.

When preaching, Paul came "not with wisdom of words, lest the cross of Christ should be made of none effect" (v. 17). He came without the eloquence and wisdom for which many of the leaders wanted to be known. He came with the doctrine of Christ, plain and simple. Paul knew Christ's doctrine was more than capable of standing on its own.

Christ died for the sins of men. If it took a verbally superior, well-executed speech to convey that message, then the actual message was not effective. The message is Christ crucified. In its most simple form, it is a far more powerful message than any renowned orator could give.

SEARCH THE SCRIPTURES

1. According to Paul, who belongs to the Church of God? (1 Corinthians 1:2)

2. In Christ, how have we been enriched? (v. 5)

3. What did Paul urge the church to do in order to end quarrels and division? (v. 10)

4. How did Paul know the church of Corinth was in spiritual trouble? (v. 11)

5. According to Paul, what did Christ send him to do? (v. 17)

DISCUSS THE MEANING

1. How can a church become "perfectly joined together in the same mind and in the same judgment? (v. 10)

2. What did Paul mean when he asked the church if Christ was divided? (v. 13)

LESSON IN OUR SOCIETY

Valerie Smith welcomed taking a new position at the firm where she had worked for six years. It would allow her to return to her home town and more importantly to her home church. Upon returning, Valerie noticed how much things had changed, especially how youth attendance had plummeted. She mentioned her concern to the pastor, who suggested she work with the youth director in an effort to increase attendance.

Valerie's hard work paid off. Within six months, youth attendance had almost doubled. This was due in large part to many new programs Valerie implemented, much to the dismay of the youth director. Though she was a hit with the youth and the members of the congregation who welcomed seeing their youth return, the youth director saw her as a threat, and rallied to have her removed from her position.

At the monthly church meeting, the request Valerie be removed caused quite a stir. The members quickly divided into sides, and a yelling match ensued. This greatly upset the pastor, who refused to take sides. Instead, he said to them all, "The issue is not whether Valerie should be removed, but how our church let a minor conflict divide us. Are we working for the same purpose, or are we each on separate missions?"

We live in a time when two of our most precious foundations, the home and church, are facing more and more inner turmoil and division. How can we begin to repair such divisions? What can we do to head off conflicts before they start?

MAKE IT HAPPEN

Volunteer to lead a "Unity Prayer" each day this week in your home, church, or anywhere else where you may face conflict. Pray for unity, strength and agreement in the name of Jesus Christ. Use today's KEEP IN MIND verse as a guide.

FOLLOW THE SPIRIT

What God wants me to do:

_____

_____

REMEMBER YOUR THOUGHTS

Special insights you learned:

_____

_____

MORE LIGHT ON TEXT
1 CORINTHIANS 1:2-17

1:2 To the church of God which is at Corinth, to them that are sanctified in Christ Jesus, called to be saints, with all that in every place call upon the name of Jesus Christ our Lord, both theirs and ours.

Paul addresses the church that is at Corinth as a church of God. This means that the church does not belong to Paul who started it but it belongs to God. Paul then sees this church as part of the larger church which is "in every place." Hence the church at Corinth is part of the *katholikos*, namely, the universal church. The church is sanctified, *hagiarimenoi*, by God. In the Old Testament, sanctification was done to persons and things. Sanctification means "setting apart as holy and for the Lord." To sanctify, *hagizein*, is the action of setting apart, and *hagiasmos* refers to a person who is set apart. God is holy; so is His temple, the temple vessels, and inner most part of the temple called the holy of holies (see Isaiah 48:2; 64:10; Exodus 3:5). Israel is a holy nation (Exodus 19:14; Leviticus 19:2; Isaiah 62:12). Being holy does not refer to outward piety but to the dedication of people and things to the Lord. For example, in some churches Christians dedicate church buildings, their children, and the like.

God had made Christ our sanctification (1 Corinthians 1:30). Paul uses this term to refer to the Corinthian believers' relationship to God. They are identified by what God had done to them, namely, electing and setting them apart. They have been dedicated to the Lord to serve and adore him (Romans 15:16; cf 6:22). Hence Paul says that they are "called to be holy" and to be "saints." For Paul holiness refers to observable conduct, i.e, to share in God's blessings of the kingdom (Daniel 7:18-27).

Paul addresses the whole church although there is division within. Here he uses the term *ekklesia*, to designate that the Corinthians are called *kalew* from outside, *ek-* i.e., from pagan religion by the Lord and thus sanctified for the Lord. The term *ekklesia* is used to designate early Christian communities or local congregations (see 5:1-5,: 11:18; 14:23; cf. Deuteronomy 4:10).

3 Grace be unto you, and peace, from God our Father, and from the Lord Jesus Christ.

Traditionally, *charein*, which means "rejoice," was a greeting. Paul has reduced this to *charis*, meaning "grace" and added the traditional Israelite *Shalom*, (Arabic *salaam*) from which the Swahili *Salamu* is adopted. All these terms refer to peace and tranquility. God grants us grace which is God's way of expressing His mercy to humanity. He does this through His Son whom He gave as a sacrifice for human sin. The composer of the Christian hymn "Amazing Grace" was overwhelmed by this fact of God giving His only begotten Son as to compose this wonderful hymn. Grace and peace are God's gifts which we are given freely as sinful humans.

4 I thank my God always on your behalf, for the grace of God which is given you Jesus Christ.

Paul once again calls attention to grace. He expresses his thanksgiving to God because God has been so generous to the Corinthians by granting them the kind of grace that is in Christ. The term "to thank," *eucharistein*, means the same as "blessing," *aulogetos* (2 Corinthians 1:3; Ephesians 1:3; 1 Peter 1:3).

The phrase "in Christ" refers to the Corinthians as part of the body of Christ. This unity has been brought about by Christ and bridges human relations with God and with other believers. It is a new existence that Christians enjoy throughout the world as children of God together with Christ. It is marked by baptism.

5 That in everything ye are enriched by him, in all utterance and in all knowledge.

Certainly the Corinthians and all who call upon the name of the Lord are enriched. Because of the abundance of charismatic gifts that God offers. We are enriched with *logos*, "speech" especially uttering in tongues. But *logos* refers also to God's word of salvation. Moreover, we are also blessed with *gnosis*, "knowledge." The most important gifts are love, faith, and hope (1 Corinthians 13:13). In Him, meaning in Christ, we are blessed like that. So the Corinthians, like all Christians are enriched rather than impoverished. Christ became poor that we may be rich (2 Corinthians 8:9). He also enriched Paul for his ministry (1 Corinthians 4:8-13; 2 Corinthians 6:10). For Paul, spiritual enrichment surpasses other riches. While the Corinthians were boasting of their eloquence in speech and their worldly knowledge, they were acting merely as human beings. Used well, the Corinthian gifts could build the church as the body of Christ.

6 Even as the testimony of Christ was confirmed in you.

Paul bore witness to the good news of Christ among Corinthians especially about the cross of Christ (1:18-25; 2:1-2) and His resurrection (15:1-11). God Himself guaranteed the truth of the message by enriching them with every kind of spiritual gift. The Corinthians lacked nothing.

7 So that ye come behind in no gift; waiting for the coming of our Lord Jesus Christ:

Paul's pleasure, like that of many pastors, is when the congregation bears fruit and they have no spiritual lack. In a broader sense, the blessing of redemption and the gifts of the Spirit always produce fruits. Because of these blessings of redemption and the resulting fruits they do not fear the coming of the Lord as they face the final judgment. For every Christian, that there will be final victory when we face God's judgment is what matters. So all believers await the second coming of the Lord, *parousia*, in glory to judge the world with hope and not fear.

8 Who shall also confirm you unto the end, that ye may be blameless in the day of our Lord Jesus Christ.

Repeating the emphasis on the Day of the Lord, or the Last Day, Paul knows that they will be found blameless before God's judgment seat. It is like a kind of prayer concerning our appearance before God. Pastors and church leaders must be even more ready to face God because the Lord has entrusted them with so many souls. Paul is concerned about the believers in Corinth and hence his own accounting before God. But he is sure that they "will be

found blameless" for Christ has given them His righteousness to win the race even on the Day of our Lord (cf. 1 Corinthians 3:13-15; 5:5 and 1 Thessalonians 5:2). Moreover, God has granted them forgiveness as one of the gifts of His grace.

9 God is faithful, by whom ye were called unto fellowship of his Son Jesus Christ our Lord.

Paul seems to be sure that the Corinthians, who hold fast to the Gospel, will be found guiltless in the Day of the Lord. The God of Israel is faithful and just. God's promises will be fulfilled. The Lord never fails anyone who believes. Based on this premise, Christians can hope for a favorable judgment. So Christians should remain strong in hope since they are already in fellowship with Christ in the Spirit (2 Corinthians 13:13; Philippians 2:1). Since God is faithful and God grants all good things through Christ, those who are in Christ are at an advantage. The faithfulness of God in this passage is connected to the calling of God through Jesus Christ. This faithfulness works for us in our fellowship with the Son of God. It is important to note the use of the Greek word "koinonia" which denotes such concepts as partnership, participation, and communion. Those of us who are connected to Christ's fellowship know that He will never fail us.

10 Now I beseech you, brethren, by the name

of our Lord Jesus Christ, that ye all speak the same thing, and that there be no divisions among you; but that ye be perfectly joined together in the same mind and in the same judgment.

The word *auto legein* means "to say the same thing." When used in relation to God it seems to imply that we must trust and affirm what God says about us. But when it is used about human relations, it deals with righteous consensus grounded, not in opinion, but on our understanding of God's will. Christians ought to have concord rather than divisions, debates, disagreements and the like. The Corinthians were divided although they were still one church. In America today, there are many things that divide God's people: race, color of the skin, economic status, career, gender, denomination, political agendas, parties, etc. Neighborhoods are also formed in the same way.

In Corinth, the church was divided into groups that followed different workers of the Lord who happened to serve there, including Paul as the founder, Peter, and Apollos. There was also a faction whose slogan was "we are of Christ."

Paul uses the term *schisma* (11:18; 12:25) to refer to the factions in the church. The verb *schizein* refers to "rending, tearing, or dividing." When Corinthians converted to Christianity they brought with them their old traditions (e.g., philosophical divisions, social and economic status, etc.). Paul notes that there was a *eiresis*, a rending (or tear) within the Christian social fabric which needed some repair. Parties were within the church, not torn from it (cf. John 7:43; 9:16; 10:19).

Paul is addressing the issue of a broken or torn apart community. He is exhorting the Corinthians to "adjust," "restore," or "put in order" (*katartizein*) the church. The term is used almost like a medical term denoting knitting broken bones together and putting dislocated joints into a natural position. In Mark 1:19, it refers to mending nets. Metaphorically it refers to resetting a church community whose human relations are at the breaking point. So, Paul is trying to repair this rend. In other words, Paul is trying to reconcile the divided parties. The term which means "be joined" or "be united," in "one mind," *nous*, or literally "sameness of mind," comes from the word *concordia* which is the name of the Greek goddess of reconciliation. In other words, the Corinthians must say the same thing, or have the same opinion, in Christ.

11 For it hath been declared unto me of you, by brethren, by them which are of the house of Chloe, that there are contentions among you.

Paul received the report of contentions from members of Chloe's household. Houses or homes of people were meeting places for churches in the first century (e.g., Stephanas', Achaicus', Crispus, and Fortunatus, cf. 16:15-17). Chloe was a rich woman who owned a house. In the ancient world there were no telephones or postal service. Messages were delivered by word of the mouth resulting in gossip or rumors. Corinth, as a market place of the world, was susceptible to rumors; the Christians picked up their habits from the world.

12 Now that I say, that every one of you saith, I am of Paul; and I of Apollos; and I of Cephas; and I of Christ. 13 Is Christ divided? Was Paul crucified for you? Or were ye baptized in the name of Paul?

Parties and divisions were listed in verses 12 and 13. The Corinthians were "puffed up" in favor of human leaders. Apollos, for example, was favored because of his eloquence. Cephas was followed because he was the Lord's disciple. Some were for Paul, the founder of that congregation, and others were simply calling themselves "of Christ." Paul argues in 2 Corinthians 3:5-9 that he planted, others watered, but God causes growth. How could some claim that they are of Christ and others were not because of who may or may not have baptized them? Was Christ divided? How could Christ be compared to human leaders? Clearly Paul seems to argue following their carnal logic.

Christ seems here to be divided as though in pieces. The rhetorical process here leads to the conclusion that Christ is not divided. Paul asks, "Was Paul crucified for you?" He is trying to water down their slogans by choosing his own name, rather than Peter's or Apollos'. Paul then discusses the baptism through which they were Christianized; he shows them what baptism should mean. Baptism in Christ is important for Christian faith. No one was baptized in the name of Paul or any of his co-workers. According to Acts 2:38; 8:16; 10:48; 19:5 (cf. Romans 6:3), early Christians were baptized in Jesus' name.

14 I thank God that I baptized none of you, but Crispus and Gaius; 15 Lest any should say that I had baptized in mine own name.

Paul here breaks into what is called a eucharistic prayer. The Greek reads *eucharisto To(e) Theo. Euchaustic* in the Greek could mean "meal" or "communion of praise." He acknowledges that he had baptized a few individuals in the name of Jesus. Many who considered themselves aligning with Paul also claimed to have been baptized in his name.

Thus from the days of Paul, baptism itself has been a divisive issue in the church. Paul did baptize Crispus, the leader of the synagogue (Acts 18:8), including Gaius, and Stephanas (16:16).

17 For Christ sent me not to baptize, but to preach the Gospel: not with wisdom of words, lest the cross of Christ should be made of none effect.

Paul makes it clear that he was sent to preach the Gospel. Christ himself "sent," *aposteilen*, Paul. So, Paul is an apostle, *apostolos*, "one sent." Paul is commissioned to preach the Gospel. Paul distinguishes between baptizing and preaching. Baptizing is a one-time action for almost all churches, but preaching is a life-long calling. It is the only way that people are brought to Christ. Preaching is like fishing. The Word is a hook. Salvation is not gained through human logic or human wisdom to effect change. Paul divided wisdom in two: human and divine wisdom. Paul does not see human wisdom as a driving force that captures humanity to conversion, rather it is God's power working in God's Word. To empty the power of the Word is not to preach the Cross. Literally, the cross is the instrument on which Christ was crucified. Figuratively, it represents the act of propitiation resulting from the death of the Lord.

DAILY BIBLE READING

M: **Paul Greets the Corinthian Christians**
1 Corinthians 1:1-9
T: **Divisions among Corinthian Christians**
1 Corinthians 1:10-17
W: **God's Power and Wisdom in Christ**
1 Corinthians 1:18-25
T: **Christ Jesus, the Source of Our Life**
1 Corinthians 1:26-31
F: **Paul Encourages Timothy**
2 Timothy 1:3-14
S: **Serve Jesus Christ Faithfully**
2 Timothy 2:1-13
S: **The Ways of God's Servant**
2 Timothy 2:14-26

March 12
Bible Study Guide 2

1. Words You Should Know

A. Wisdom. (1 Corinthians 2:1) Greek *sophia*—The insight into the true nature of things.

B. Eloquence. Greek *logios*—Denotes a man who was learned, skilled in literature and the arts. It was used frequently among the Greeks to denote one who was skilled in words. He could use his learning very convincingly.

C. Sanctify. Greek *hagiazo*—The setting apart of the believer for God. He is separated from the world in his behavior by the Father through the Word.

2. Teacher Preparation

A. Prayerfully re-read 1 Corinthians in its entirety. Read today's DEVOTIONAL READING and pray for guidance. Read today's lesson, studying the FOCAL VERSES for this week.

B. Familiarize yourself with the BACKGROUND material for the lesson. Be prepared to tell students the key points of the BACKGROUND material from memory.

C. Write definitions for "wisdom," "eloquence," and "sanctify" on the board.

3. Starting the Lesson

A. Begin the lesson with prayer. Ask God to fill your classroom with His Spirit so that He can enrich your teaching and guide your students toward understanding.

B. Ask students to read the IN FOCUS lesson. Afterwards, ask them to define "wisdom," "eloquence," and "sanctify" in their own words.

C. Have students give their answers to the definitions. Ask them whether one has to be eloquent in order to be wise. Discuss their answers.

D. Begin the lesson by telling them about the BACKGROUND material.

4. Getting into the Lesson

A. To help students understand the lesson, have a volunteer read the FOCAL VERSES aloud. Then have another read THE PEOPLE, PLACES, AND TIMES section.

B. Divide the class into three groups, and give each a section of the IN DEPTH commentary to study. Have the groups summarize the highlights of their sections for the class. Allow 15 minutes for this exercise.

C. At the expiration of 15 minutes, bring the groups back together and allow each spokesperson to discuss their highlights.

5. Relating the Lesson to Life

A. Use the DISCUSS THE MEANING questions to help students relate this lesson to their own lives.

B. Continue the discussion by going on to the LESSON IN OUR SOCIETY section.

6. Arousing Action

A. Challenge the students to put the suggestion from the MAKE IT HAPPEN section into action in their daily living. By show of hands, ask the students to agree to pray this week for the guidance of the Holy Spirit and really listen as He provides guidance.

B. Assign next week's lesson as homework. Encourage the students to read the DAILY BIBLE READINGS. Close the class with prayer.

WORSHIP GUIDE

For the Superintendent or Teacher
Theme: The Holy Spirit As Teacher
Theme Song: "Filled with the Spirit's Power"
Scripture: John 14
Song: "Christ from Whom All Blessings Flow"
Meditation: Father, I thank You for Your gift of the Holy Spirit, whom You sent to teach me of Your divine wisdom. Help me to receive the Spirit with an open heart, so that I may fully receive what You have given so freely, Amen.

THE HOLY SPIRIT AS TEACHER

Bible Background • 1 CORINTHIANS 2-3
Printed Text • 1 CORINTHIANS 2:1-2, 4-13, 15-16
Devotional Reading • 1 CORINTHIANS 3:1-9

LESSON AIM

In today's lesson, students will learn not to rely on human wisdom when it comes to matters of faith; and that true and divine wisdom comes from God, is communicated to us through the Holy Spirit, and brings unity with it.

KEEP IN MIND

"Now we have received, not the spirit of the world, but the spirit which is of God; that we might know the things that are freely given to us of God" (1 Corinthians 2:12).

FOCAL VERSES

1 CORINTHIANS 2:1 And I, brethren, when I came to you, came not with excellency of speech or of wisdom, declaring unto you the testimony of God.

2 For I determined not to know any thing among you, save Jesus Christ, and him crucified.

4 And my speech and my preaching was not with enticing words of man's wisdom, but in demonstration of the Spirit and of power:

5 That your faith should not stand in the wisdom of men, but in the power of God.

6 Howbeit we speak wisdom among them that are perfect: yet not the wisdom of this world, nor of the princes of this world, that come to nought:

7 But we speak the wisdom of God in a mystery, even the hidden wisdom, which God ordained before the world unto our glory:

8 Which none of the princes of this world knew: for had they known it, they would not have crucified the Lord of

LESSON OVERVIEW

LESSON AIM
KEEP IN MIND
FOCAL VERSES
IN FOCUS
THE PEOPLE, PLACES, AND TIMES
BACKGROUND
AT-A-GLANCE
IN DEPTH
SEARCH THE SCRIPTURES
DISCUSS THE MEANING
LESSON IN OUR SOCIETY
MAKE IT HAPPEN
FOLLOW THE SPIRIT
REMEMBER YOUR THOUGHTS
MORE LIGHT ON THE TEXT
DAILY BIBLE READINGS

glory.

9 But as it is written, Eye hath not seen, nor ear heard, neither have entered into the heart of man, the things which God hath prepared for them that love him.

10 But God hath revealed them unto us by his Spirit: for the Spirit searcheth all things, yea, the deep things of God.

11 For what man knoweth the things of a man, save the spirit of man which is in him? Even so the things of God knoweth no man, but the Spirit of God.

12 Now we have received, not the spirit of the world, but the spirit which is of God; that we might know the things that are freely given to us of God.

13 Which things also we speak, not in the words which man's wisdom teacheth, but which the Holy Ghost teacheth; comparing spiritual things with spiritual.

15 But he that is spiritual judgeth all things, yet he himself is judged of no man.

16 For who hath known the mind of the Lord, that he may instruct him? But we have the mind of Christ.

IN FOCUS

Margarite Lewis sat patiently on the crowded bench, waiting for the next bus to Atlanta. She had been saving the money she earned at her after-school job for six months in order to make this trip. Dr. Robert Calens, a renowned east coast professor, was giving a lecture at the state university on a new method he devised for mastering the SAT's. This particularly interested Margarite, who wanted so badly to go to an Ivy League college. She knew good SAT scores were necessary in order to achieve that goal.

On the bus, Margarite once again went over Dr. Calens' credentials: two Ph.D.'s, Rhodes Scholar, author of seven books, fluent in six languages—this professor was awesome! He *had* to know a sure-fire way to ace the SAT's, as wise as he was.

After several hours of travel, Margarite was finally sitting inside the auditorium. She took out her notebook and several pens eagerly awaiting Dr. Calens' entrance. Looking around, she noticed that the majority of the audience was much older. There weren't very many teens in attendance.

"Excuse me," Margarite said to a woman sitting next to her. "Can you tell me why there aren't many students here? I thought Dr. Calens was going to discuss methods for mastering the SAT's."

"He is," the lady replied." That's why so many educators are here. They want to see what he has to say."

Dr. Calens took the podium and began his lecture. Within minutes, Margarite was captivated. He was an incredible speaker. He had charts and graphs and tons of supplementary material to support his theories. Margarite scribbled furiously trying to keep up.

Four hours later, Margarite sat alone in the auditorium, trying to organize her notes. Once Dr. Calens stopped talking, she couldn't figure anything out! She thought she was keeping up, but now she was confused. It would take days, and probably reading Dr. Calens' book, which she would have to buy, in order to figure out this "foolproof" method.

Margarite didn't hear the lady she was talking to earlier come in. "Well?" She asked Margarite. "How did you enjoy Dr. Calens?"

"He was very impressive," Margarite responded.

"What did you learn?"

Margarite flushed. "Well, I learned that the secret for doing well on the SAT is to. . . ." She stopped, not knowing what to say next.

"Study and get a good night's sleep," the woman said.

"Excuse me?" Margarite was now really confused.

"Honey," the lady laughed. "Underneath all that fancy talk and big words all the man said was study and get some sleep."

Have you ever been in a position similar to Margarite? Have you ever gone to church and listened to a speaker who was so seemingly wise and eloquent? Did he have an extensive vocabulary and an ability to turn a phrase just so? Did you find yourself engrossed by the speaker, clapping in amazement at his wisdom? Were you moved, maybe even confused by his words? When all was said and done,

though, was your soul fed? Did you get the underlying message? Or was he just a bit too wise?

In today's lesson, the Apostle Paul spoke to the people of Corinth about two types of wisdom: human (natural) wisdom and divine (spiritual) wisdom, sent by the Holy Spirit.

THE PEOPLE, PLACES, AND TIMES

HOLY SPIRIT. Third member of the Godhead. He possesses attributes of deity, yet has functions distinct from the Father and Son. He came to earth at Pentecost (Acts 2:1-4; 1 Corinthians 12:13) to permanently indwell every believer. He inspires the Scriptures and speaks through them (Acts 1:16; 2 Peter 1:21). The Spirit guides, inspires, reveals, and continues the work and ministry of Jesus Christ (John 16:5-15). The Holy Spirit can be treated as a person: He can be lied to and tempted, resisted, grieved, and blasphemed against. He has a will and is capable of thought and love.

The Holy Spirit is the very presence of God in the world (Psalm 139:7). Through the Holy Spirit, God is actually here and working. In Isaiah 63:10, when the people "vex" the Spirit, God becomes their enemy; in 63:14 the work of the Spirit giving rest is parallel to the act of God leading His people.

The Greek word for spirit, *pneuma*, means "breath, or wind." Both wind and breath are symbols of the Holy Spirit (Genesis 2:7; Job 32:8). Other symbols of the Holy Spirit are the dove (Matthew 3:16); oil (Luke 4:18; Acts 10:38); fire for purification (Matthew 3:11: Luke 3:16); living water (Isaiah 44:3); and the guarantee of all that God has in store for us (2 Corinthians 1:22). In the Old Testament, the Holy Spirit appears from the beginning with God (Genesis 1:2) and comes on certain men for special purposes.

On the night of the Resurrection, Jesus "breathed on" the disciples and said to them, "Receive the Holy Spirit" (John 20:22, NIV). At Pentecost, with a mighty wind and tongues of fire, the disciples were all filled with the Holy Spirit and spoke in foreign languages (Acts 2:9-11). When the first Gentiles were converted, the Holy Spirit was poured out on them and they spoke in tongues (Acts 10:44-48). In addition, when Paul met a group of John the Baptist's disciples, the Holy Spirit came on them (Acts 19:1-7).

(Adapted from *The New International Dictionary of the Bible*, Grand Rapids: Zondervan Corporation, pp. 446-447.)

SANCTIFY. From Greek word hagiazo to dedicate, separate, set apart from the world, make holy. It is the process of being set apart into God by the Spirit to grow out of sin and more fully into Christ (2 Thessalonians 2:13; 1 Peter 1:2). To sanctify is to make the declaration of belonging to God. Sanctification is done through the redemptive work of Christ and through the indwelling of the Holy Spirit.

(Adapted from *Vines Expository Dictionary*, McLean: MacDonald Publishing Company, p. 999.)

BACKGROUND

The main message of 1 Corinthians is that unity is achieved when Christians come together in the name of Jesus Christ. In order to achieve unity, Apostle Paul asserts, the church must have true wisdom. For, "wisdom is supreme; therefore get wisdom" (Proverbs 4:7, NIV). True wisdom is a gift from God sent to us through the Holy Spirit and is much different than human wisdom. Everyone is not privy to the gifts of God or the Holy Spirit, nor does everyone know how to discern the teachings of the Spirit.

The crucifixion and resurrection is the wisdom of God. The gift of salvation, which God planned before creation was revealed and realized in Jesus. "Perfect" wisdom brings understanding of the mystery of Christ to the baptized faithful (1 Corinthians 1:5). Paul compares different types of men: *psychikoi*, or "natural" men, who use their natural faculties of knowledge and understanding; and *pneumatikoi*, or men who are "spiritual" men in whom the Holy Spirit dwells and acts. Beginners in spiritual life, "infants," received the Holy Spirit when they were baptized (Romans 8:23). They are not, though, treated as spiritual men because their behavior and thinking is still that of the flesh (1 Corinthians 3:1-13). They, in essence, still behave as infants. The Corinthians, who were boastful about their spirituality because of their charismatic gifts, were still in this spiritual "infancy" stage.

When it comes to faith, Christians shouldn't rely on human wisdom. Humans try to come up with answers for everything based on their natural or human wisdom. The more wisdom they amass, the more they think they can rattle off the answers to all of life's questions. As Christians, however, we know in many cases the answer is deeper than human knowledge can comprehend. The answer, simply stated, is: it's the power of God at work. We've all had a unique experience that was nothing more than God working on our hearts. Human wisdom couldn't explain it. Nor can human wisdom explain our joys or any of our emotions. It cannot explain the peace we feel in anticipation of heaven or in our love of God.

How is unity achieved through divine wisdom? To have divine wisdom is to have the Spirit of God. Having the Spirit of God is having Christ. Christ is the basis of all unity (Colossians 1:16-17; Hebrews 1:3). When we are wise spiritually, we have received a supernatural knowledge that is shared by others in the body of Christ. We are on level ground with them. No one tries to out do or be more intelligent than the other. We are of the same mind in Christ and His wisdom helps unite us by revealing to us all the gifts of the Gospel.

In today's lesson, we will learn about true wisdom, how it differs from human wisdom, how it is communicated, and how we can become receivers of it.

AT-A-GLANCE

1. Rely Not on Human Wisdom (1 Corinthians 2:1-5)
2. True and Divine Wisdom (vv. 6-9)
3. The Holy Spirit as Communicator of Wisdom (vv. 10-16)

IN DEPTH

1. Rely Not on Human Wisdom (1 Corinthians 2:1-5)

In verses 1-5, Paul lets the church of Corinth know that the message of the Gospel is pure and simple: Christ was crucified for the redemption of our sins. This message was what Paul needed to get across to the people. He didn't try to be distinguished because of eloquent speech. In fact, he said he came, "not with excellency of speech or wisdom" (v. 1). This was intentional. Paul wanted to show that the Gospel of Christ did not need human wisdom or eloquent speech in order to be effective. He was a spiritual leader who let the success of his message lie directly in the message, not in the delivery. In contrast, the Greek leaders of that time prided themselves on their eloquence and worldly wisdom.

Paul said he was "declaring . . . the testimony of God" (v. 1). He was bearing witness to God's plan of redemption through Jesus Christ. It was Jesus Christ, and only Jesus Christ, that Paul purposed himself to know. He "determined" to only know Christ (v. 2)—that is, he made a resolution that his focus would be solely on Jesus Christ. He purposely chose not to get involved in learning the Corinthian ways or taking in the temptations of such a beautiful, worldly city. He definitely resolved not to try to compare, or be like, any of the orators or philosophers of the city. He didn't try to acquaint himself with anything that was of interest to the Corinthians. He kept his focus on Christ, and the message of the Cross. This should be the focus of every Christian.

"And my speech and my preaching was not with enticing words of man's wisdom, but in demonstration of the Spirit and of power" (v. 4). Paul's style of preaching was simple. He preached his message without garnishing it with fancy words or phrases, which was common practice in Greece, and he let the Holy Spirit demonstrate its validity. The Holy Spirit provided the proof. It demonstrated that Paul's preaching had a divine origin. The Holy Spirit did this by the gifts of tongues and by sanctifying hearts (1 Corinthians 1:5-7; 14). He also came with "power." "Power" here refers to the divine power of God. God's power is demonstrated in the transformation of men's lives. This power can transform any man: the drunk, the thief, the mean-spirited man, even the blasphemer. Any sinner can be converted. God's power also provides peace and joy. There is no greater proof of the divine message. Every converted sinner provides proof of the power of the Gospel!

The message Paul was trying to convey is that our faith should not be dependent on human wisdom or reasoning (v. 5). Christian faith should rest on the nature and power of God. Faith leads us to believe that God loves us. By faith we consent that God has given us the gift of salvation through Jesus Christ. Through Jesus, the sinner is made anew. Humans cannot effect salvation. It is not in the power of human beings to take away sins or transform souls. Finite beings cannot explain or produce lasting joy and peace. The source of these is the eternal Christ.

2. True and Divine Wisdom (vv. 6-9)

In response to those who desired more from Paul's preaching, he asked, "Howbeit we speak wisdom among them that are perfect; yet not the wisdom of this world, nor of the princes of this world, that come to nought" (v. 6). What Paul was preaching to them was much more valuable than the entertainment of a fine speech. He was preaching the divine, true wisdom. The wisdom he was preaching could not have been delivered by the men of the world, as eloquent as they may have been. This was wisdom which:

"God ordained before the world unto our glory" (v. 7). God has a plan for us. This plan was mapped out in the beginning of time. It is His plan for salvation. Paul says it was "hidden." It was not known to the minds of men until it was revealed in the Gospel.

"None of the princes of this world knew" (v. 8). It is this "hidden" wisdom, Paul asserts, that the rulers of the age did not possess. If they had, they would not have crucified Jesus Christ. Jesus was crucified because the people didn't know Him. If those involved in His crucifixion knew of His excellency, of who He really was, they would not have killed Him. Not the Saviour! They were ignorant, and Jesus prayed, "Father, forgive them, for they know not what they do" (Luke 23:34).

"Eye hath not seen, nor ear heard, nor have entered into the heart of man, the things which God hath prepared for them that love him" (v. 9). This verse says basically that no one has really been able to fully understand the things that God has prepared for His people. It is outside of our realm of understanding. God has prepared things for those that love Him and wait on Him. Those things include the wisdom revealed in the Gospel and the mercy and happiness which the Gospel makes known to God's people. The wisdom of the Gospel includes the pardoning of sin, the atonement, the joy that comes with religion, and redemption from sin and death. These things are beyond man's comprehension, especially without the revelation of Christ. Also far outside of man's comprehension is what awaits God's people in heaven!

One evidence of our love of God is waiting patiently on Him. The wisdom of the plan of salvation, the love of God, and the gift of life in heaven is made available only to Christians; it is wisdom which is not possessed by the men of the world. Christians are fortunate to be blessed with divine wisdom, for it provides peace and comfort far beyond that available to a worldly man.

3. The Holy Spirit as Communicator of Wisdom (vv. 10-16)

How is divine wisdom delivered to the Christian? Through the Holy Spirit. The Holy Spirit was promised to us by Jesus Christ (John 14: 26). The Spirit was sent to "teach us all things." We are told the Spirit "searcheth all things; yea, the deep things of God" (v. 10). This lets us know two things: 1) The Holy Spirit knows God. He knows all of His plans and purposes. 2) He is divine. He knows God intimately. Nothing created knows God like that. The

bless us with His Son as our Redeemer, He also gave us His Spirit to help us fully appreciate His gifts (v. 12). We cannot do this naturally, neither can a man who is not enlightened with the Holy Spirit. The Holy Spirit sanctifies, enlightens, and comforts the minds of Christians; whereas, men of the world choose darkness and therefore do not understand, or even receive the teachings of the Holy Spirit.

These gifts, that were given by God, are what Paul and the other apostles speak of (v. 13). Man's elaborate words are not needed to convey the messages that the Holy Spirit teaches. Paul uses the phrase "comparing spiritual things with spiritual." In other words, one thing helps to illustrate the other. Trying to use human principles to explain spiritual things will prove impossible every time.

Can everyone receive the teachings of the Holy Spirit? No. The man who chooses to live in darkness and who is not sanctified doesn't receive the gifts of God (v. 14). Love of evil ways prevents the man from opening his mind to God. A man of the world, who relies on his own wisdom, receives nothing by faith. It is by faith that we receive Jesus Christ and the gifts of the Gospel. Until a corrupt man chooses to receive Christ, he will be without the gifts of God.

Those who do receive the Spirit, Paul states, have the mind of Christ. Believers are influenced by the Spirit (vv. 12-16).

Holy Spirit is *equal to and of* God. There is a union between the Holy Spirit and God. Paul parallels this union to our own souls (v. 11). No one in this world knows the innermost, deepest parts of a person—except that person's own soul. We can choose to reveal some parts of our being—but our souls know all. So too, did God choose to reveal parts of His inner self to us through the Holy Spirit.

Christians, through the Holy Spirit, have been privileged to the gifts and the wisdom of God. Not only did God

SEARCH THE SCRIPTURES

1. Why did Paul choose to keep his preaching simple and pointed? (vv. 4-5)

2. What will happen to the wisdom of this age? (v. 6)

3. What is "God's secret wisdom" that Paul refers to? (v. 7)

4. How intimate is the relationship between God and the Holy Spirit? (vv. 10-11)

5. How can we understand the gifts from God? (vv. 12-13)

DISCUSS THE MEANING

1. "The Spirit searches all things; even the deep things of God" (v. 10). Explain how this makes the Holy Spirit divine.

2. What did Paul mean when he said he resolved to know nothing except "Jesus Christ and Him crucified"? (v. 2)

LESSON IN SOCIETY

In order of priority, education ranks high on many people's list. As early as infancy, a great deal of importance is put on learning. Mother's are told to read to babies in the womb to get them on the proper learning track. We drill into our children's heads how important it is to listen to their teachers, do their homework, and work hard so they can go to college. In fact, many adults are returning to college, pursuing higher education for personal and professional benefit.

What priority do we give to our spiritual education? What value do we place on receiving divine wisdom? How can we make our thirst for God's divine wisdom equal to that of our thirst for human wisdom? What message should we be trying to give our children regarding this invaluable education?

MAKE IT HAPPEN

There is a song that asks the Holy Spirit to, "speak to my heart." If you haven't lately, ask the Spirit to speak to your heart. Make a commitment to listen to the Spirit, to let Him guide you, and enrich you. Remember: the Holy Spirit was given to us from God to dwell in us and to teach us. He wants you to call on Him for guidance.

FOLLOW THE SPIRIT

What God wants me to do:

_____

_____

REMEMBER YOUR THOUGHTS

Special insights you have learned:

_____

_____

MORE LIGHT ON THE TEXT
1 CORINTHIANS 2:1-2; 4-13; 15-16

2:1 And I, brethren, when I came to you, came not with excellency of speech or of wisdom, declaring unto you the testimony of God. 2 For I determined not to know any thing among you, save Jesus Christ, and him crucified.

Paul is reminding the Corinthians of the vitality of the Spirit. God has offered His Spirit in order that we may bear testimony of God. It is the Spirit who will enable us to preach, not in the wisdom of this world and the eloquence of speech, but the truth that testifies about God's grace.

The content of the message that God commissions Paul and others to preach is Christ and Him crucified. This is the essence of the church's preaching. Paul employs the term *logos*, meaning "message," or literally "word." The word of Cross is the central message of the church. It is the kernel of the Gospel: how God so loved the world that He gave His only son to die on the cross for human salvation (cf. John 3:16). Paul addresses the Corinthians as brethren whom he wants to understand and experience the blessing of God's offer through the cross of Christ. People may preach a social gospel, or a political message, or philanthropy. Paul determined to preach nothing but Jesus, and Him crucified. This is the summary of the entire Gospel. Paul offers no excuse. Though a whole Gospel demands we be concerned for the total welfare of persons, preachers ought not to compromise this message. Crucifixion entails blood, death, sacrifice, atonement, and reconciliation of humanity with God. Christ is the passover lamb given by God (5:7). So the cross must not be reduced to a human level for it is the power of God unto salvation (Romans 1:16). Paul preaches this Gospel message empowered by the Spirit.

4 And my speech and my preaching was not with enticing words of man's wisdom, but in demonstration of the Spirit and of power:

Paul refuses to use persuasive words or human wisdom. In preaching the Gospel, the Spirit of God suffices. Human wisdom entails faulty imaginations, fallacy, falseness, and fabrication of ideas. But Paul resolved to use the wisdom endowed to him by God through God's Spirit. It is this wisdom which embodies the divine power, or *dunamis*, which transforms human life.

5 That your faith should not stand in the wisdom of men, but in the power of God.

In verse 5, Paul is still comparing and contrasting God's

power and human wisdom. The Gospel owes nothing to human wisdom. Both the message of the Cross and the Messenger who brought it were despised by words of human wisdom. But God chose the despised vessel to bear power. It is Christ's saving power found in the Cross which Paul finds to be real wisdom.

6 Howbeit we speak wisdom among them that are perfect: yet not the wisdom of this world, nor of the princes of this world, that come to nought:

With relentless persistence, Paul points to human wisdom and the wisdom of God. He notes that preaching should be done to the "perfect," *teleioi*, i.e., the spiritually mature. Those who are able to understand the mysteries of God. The crucifixion as a saving event is a mystery. It requires God's wisdom to comprehend it. Human attempts, even by those whom the world considers to be "princes," cannot grasp it. Indeed the princes who crucified Jesus would not have done so if they had known that they were crucifying the Lord of glory (2:7). The understanding that salvation was purchased at the cross is the divine wisdom that comes through faith. The *teleioi* are those who have come to grips with the goal of crucifixion.

7 But we speak the wisdom of God in a mystery, even the hidden wisdom, which God ordained before the world unto our glory:

The word *musterion* or "mystery" does not mean a puzzle which humans cannot understand, rather it refers to the Gospel that God has revealed through Christ and its saving power. This mystery was before ages, but God has decided to reveal it through the Cross. It is only a spiritual attitude that can unlock this mystery. To unbelievers, such wisdom of knowing the saving power of the Cross is hidden. It is unveiled to believers so that it is not a matter of common knowledge. It was planned in the mind of God before the ages (cf. Ephesians 3:2-12). God has *proorizo*, "predestined" or ordained before hand. This means that God's plan has been in place "for our glory" before humanity was formed (1 Corinthians 2:7, NIV). "Glory" as used here refers to the state of humanity after the resurrection.

8 Which none of the princes of this world knew: for had they known it, they would not have crucified the Lord of glory.

As indicated in verse 8, the princes of this world (Acts 3:17; 4:25-28) were not informed that of God's predestining the cross for human salvation. They did not have the divine wisdom to understand it. Jesus is the Lord of glory

(cf. James 2:1). The expression "Lord of glory" is taken from wisdom literature, especially the Apocrypha Book of Enoch 22:14; 25:3; 27;3-4; 63:2; 75:3. The epithet "glory" is used for God the Father. Christ as Lord of glory refers to His exalted state where He will also bring the redeemed to "our glory" (1 Corinthians 2:7).

9 But as it is written, Eye hath not seen, nor ear heard, neither have entered into the heart of man, the things which God hath prepared for them that love him.

From the old, way back, people had not heard or beheld with their eyes anything like this. This mystery should not cause fear. But God has foreordained and prepared it for those who love the Lord. It had not entered the human heart (cf. 65:17) but still it was foreordained for them that wait God's mercy, i.e., the perfect, *teleioi*. All that God offers to us is the Gospel with its cross-centered message. It may not be perceived by the eye or the ear, indeed the heart of humanity may fail to comprehend it. That is why it stands "hidden" in "mystery." God alone can reveal it.

10 But God hath revealed them unto us by his Spirit: for the Spirit searcheth all things, yea, the deep things of God.

The expression "to us," *hemon*, refers to all humble Christians, including Paul and his co-workers and those who are making God known through Jesus. Originally God had hidden His plan of salvation, now it has been revealed. The term "to reveal," *phenoroo*, refers to God's initiative. God has removed the veil from what was hidden. This is done through the activity of the Spirit. The Spirit searches all things; He reveals and empowers. The Spirit penetrates all things even though unknown to us. The term *bathos* often refers to the depth of the sea. Here the Spirit is able to search even to that depth of the things of God and reveal them to those who love God. These depths are known to the Spirit and can be revealed to those who love God. The Spirit both reveals divine truth and guides Christians.

11 For what man knoweth the things of a man, save the spirit of man which is in him? even so the things of God knoweth no man, but the Spirit of God.

The Spirit of God knows the things of God, and the spirit of man knows simply the things of man. Nobody really can know what is going on in another person's mind except the person. Others can only guess from outside. In the same way, God's Spirit knows what takes place within the heart and mind of God. "Like is known by like." The Spirit knows God from inside. This means the Spirit is divine. So the revelation given by the Spirit to those who love God is authentic and reveals what is of God.

12 Now we have received, not the spirit of the world, but the spirit which is of God; that we might know the things that are freely given to us of God.

Once again "we" (i.e., the Christians) are contrasted with unbelievers. Christians are led by God's Spirit. The spirit of the world probably is Satan since Satan is the prince of this world (John 12:31; Ephesians 2:2). But it may also be the spirit of human reasoning which Paul calls human wisdom, or rationalization. What makes the world the world is unbelief.

We are of Christ and have received His Spirit who is from God (Galatians 3:2). The Spirit assures us that we have real knowledge. We are certain because we believe that God has freely given us His Spirit.

13 Which things also we speak, not in the words which man's wisdom teacheth, but which the Holy Ghost teacheth; comparing spiritual things with spiritual.

Believers must pass on their knowledge of Christ to other people. This is not done in "words taught by human wisdom" but through the Spirit of God. The Spirit extends to believers the spirit-inspired utterance which convicts people of their sin and brings them to repentance. "Spiritual things," *spneumatika*, should be "combined," *synkrinontes*, with spiritual truths. Spiritual truths must be communicated to spiritual people. This is in agreement with Jesus' word that one should not give children's food to dogs, or pearls to pigs for they will tramp on them (Matthew 7:6). Indeed the Spirit will teach spiritual people the things of God. For those who have the spirit of the world cannot receive the Spirit of God; there must be a spiritual regeneration within them.

15 But he that is spiritual judgeth all things, yet he himself is judged of no man.

The person who has God's Spirit within him can make spiritual judgments. When the Spirit of God empowers a person, everything changes. He or she is able to make spiritual judgments. The Spirit of God guides those who love Him because the Spirit reveals to them the secrets of life. Paul himself is an example in his ability to make right judg-

ments about all things. He has the Spirit of God which enables him to transcend natural judgments. A natural person, because they are merely natural, cannot judge spiritual people.

16 For who hath known the mind of the Lord, that he may instruct him? But we have the mind of Christ.

Certainly human beings cannot know the mind of God (Isaiah 40:13). There is that impossibility of knowing the "things of God" (1 Corinthians 2:11). Paul's concern was to show that the Spirit does indeed have complete knowledge of the "depth of God." The Spirit knows those depths which a natural man cannot know. No Christian can understand all of Christ's thoughts, but for those who have the indwelling Spirit within their hearts, there is a possibility to reveal the mind of Christ. The spiritual person understands these revelations through the Holy Spirit. So we who are recipients of God's Spirit have something wonderful to thank God for. The Lord has graciously revealed His mind to us. We have been blessed with the wisdom of God. To the Corinthians and to all that believe, Paul has assured us the divine wisdom of the Gospel of Jesus Christ.

DAILY BIBLE READING

M: Proclaiming Christ Crucified
1 Corinthians 2:1-5

T: The True Wisdom of God
1 Corinthians 2:6-16

W: Put Away Quarrels and Jealousies
1 Corinthians 3:1-9

T: Build on the Foundation of Jesus Christ
1 Corinthians 3:10-15

F: We Belong to God through Jesus Christ
1 Corinthians 3:16-23

S: Life in the Spirit
Romans 8:1-8

S: We Are Children of God
Romans 8:9-17

TEACHING TIPS

March 19
Bible Study Guide 3

1. Words You Should Know

A. Steward. (1 Corinthian 4:1) Greek *oikonomos* The word "steward" denotes the manager of a household or estate. Stewards were responsible for handling all of the affairs of a family and for providing for it.

B. Judgment. (v. 3) Greek *krima* The result of action signified by judging. A decision passed on the faults of others. Man is subject to divine judgment.

2. Teacher Preparation

A. Read the DAILY BIBLE READINGS for this week as part of your devotion.

B. Read the fourth chapter of 1 Corinthians as well as the DEVOTIONAL READING for preparation and insight into the lesson.

C. Study the FOCAL VERSES and the commentary for this lesson in the Bible Study Guide. Familiarize yourself with the BACKGROUND material for this lesson.

D. Materials Needed: Bible, board or newsprint, and the *Teaching Success Kit* for this lesson.

3. Starting the Lesson

A. Begin the lesson with prayer. Ask God to give you the wisdom to effectively lead this class and to bless your students with understanding.

B. Have students read the IN FOCUS lesson. Ask students to share their ideas of what the role of a church leader is.

4. Getting into the Lesson

A. Have the students read the BACKGROUND information. Solicit volunteers to read aloud the FOCAL VERSES.

B. Summarize key points from the IN DEPTH section and have students answer the SEARCH THE SCRIPTURES questions.

5. Relating the Lesson to Life

A. Read the KEEP IN MIND verse in unison, and ask the students to share what the verse means to them.

B. Use the DISCUSS THE MEANING questions to help students relate this lesson to their own lives.

C. Continue the discussion by going on to the LESSON IN OUR SOCIETY section.

6. Arousing Action

A. Allow the students time to silently read the MAKE IT HAPPEN suggestion. Ask them if they will commit themselves to serving God this week by following the suggested action.

B. Suggest the students preview next week's lesson and come prepared to discuss what they have learned. Also encourage them to read the DAILY BIBLE READINGS.

C. Close the class with prayer.

THE CHURCH AND ITS LEADERS

Bible Background • 1 CORINTHIANS 4:1-13
Printed Text • 1 CORINTHIANS 4:1-13
Devotional Reading • 1 PETER 5:1-11

MARCH 19TH

LESSON AIM

By the end of this lesson, students will understand that church leaders are stewards of God, that all judgment of church leaders and others should be reserved for God, and that mature church leaders bring unity to the church.

KEEP IN MIND

"Think of us in this way, as servants of Christ and stewards of God's mysteries" (1 Corinthians 4:1).

FOCAL VERSES

1 CORINTHIANS 4:1 Think of us in this way, as servants of Christ and stewards of God's mysteries.

2 Moreover it is required in stewards, that a man be found faithful.

3 But with me it is a very small thing that I should be judged of you, or of man's judgment: yea, I judge not mine own self.

4 For I know nothing by myself; yet am I not hereby justified: but he that judgeth me is the Lord.

5 Therefore judge nothing before the time, until the Lord come, who both will bring to light the hidden things of darkness, and will make manifest the counsels of the hearts: and then shall every man have praise of God.

6 And these things, brethren, I have in a figure transferred to myself and to Apollos for your sakes; that ye might learn in us not to think of men above that which is written, that no one of you be puffed up for one against another.

7 For who maketh thee to differ from another? and what hast thou that thou didst not receive? now if thou didst

LESSON OVERVIEW

LESSON AIM
KEEP IN MIND
FOCAL VERSES
IN FOCUS
THE PEOPLE, PLACES, AND TIMES
BACKGROUND
AT-A-GLANCE
IN DEPTH
SEARCH THE SCRIPTURES
DISCUSS THE MEANING
LESSON IN OUR SOCIETY
MAKE IT HAPPEN
FOLLOW THE SPIRIT
REMEMBER YOUR THOUGHTS
MORE LIGHT ON THE TEXT
DAILY BIBLE READINGS

receive it, why dost thou glory as if thou hadst not received it?

8 Now ye are full, now ye are rich, ye have reigned as kings without us: and I would to God ye did reign, that we also might reign with you.

9 For I think that God hath set forth us the apostles last, as it were appointed to death: for we are made a spectacle unto the world, and to angels, and to men.

10 We are fools for Christ's sake, but ye are wise in Christ; we are weak, but ye are strong; ye are honourable, but we are despised.

11 Even unto this present hour we both hunger, and thirst, and are naked, and are buffeted, and have no certain dwellingplace,

12 And labour, working with our own hands: being reviled, we bless; being persecuted, we suffer it;

13 Being defamed, we entreat: we are made as the filth of the world, and are the offscouring of all things unto this day.

IN FOCUS

Jim Jones was born in Lynd, Indiana on May 13, 1931. As a youngster, his mother felt that Jim was a messiah, and Jim eventually shared her feelings. In his twenties, he began serving as a minister, even though he had no former theological training. In 1955, he opened the Community Unity Church in Indianapolis, an integrated church. One year later, he bought a synagogue and founded his own church, named the People's Temple.

In 1964, Jim Jones was ordained by the Disciples of

Christ denomination. A bit later he moved his church to California and sponsored programs such as child care, job-training, and elderly care. He began to sever his ties and allegiance to Christianity and focus more on himself. In fact, he donned the title, "Dad," and demanded the total allegiance of his followers. In order to gain such submission, he beat, blackmailed, threatened, and even sexually abused some of his followers. It was required that the temple members turn over their property and life savings to him. A lot of the elderly members endorsed their monthly Social Security checks over to him.

Jim Jones was a scam artist and a corrupt person. He pretended to perform miracles on people, healing them of their sicknesses. He engaged in immoral sexual acts and was a drug addict. When details of his life and practices were made public, he left California and went, with his followers, to Guyana in South America, where he had previously purchased land. This land was renamed Jonestown, in honor of Jim Jones. The year was 1974, and for a while, Jim Jones was out of the spotlight.

However, in November of 1978, the U.S. received word that some members of the People's Temple were being held in Guyana by Jim Jones against their will. To investigate the claim, U.S. Representative Leo Ryan was sent to Guyana. As Mr. Ryan was leaving Guyana with some defecting members of the People's Temple, he was shot and killed along with four other people by members of Jim Jones' cult.

Following this, Jim Jones gathered all of his followers to put into action a mass suicide ritual that his community had been practicing for months. Jim Jones told them, "Everyone has to die. If you love me as I love you, we must all die or be destroyed from the outside." Jim Jones ordered them to drink a beverage which was laced with cyanide. Those who refused were either shot or injected with poison. Over 900 people died that night. Jim Jones also died, from a self-inflicted gunshot wound.

(Adapted from *World Book Encyclopedia*.)

In today's lesson, we focus on the role of the church and its leaders. Jim Jones is an example of one church leader who used his position for self-serving purposes. He quickly abandoned Christianity and its teachings in order to focus on a religion that uplifted him. The tragedy is that many people trusted in and followed him.

Church leaders are entrusted with a great responsibility, they are stewards for God, working to maintain the church

and deliver God's message of salvation. How, and to what extent we should regard these leaders is discussed today.

THE PEOPLE, PLACES, AND TIMES

APOSTLES. Greek *apostolos* is one sent forth. In the New Testament, the term originally was used as the name of the 12 disciples that Jesus chose to send forth to preach the Gospel and to be with Him while ministering on earth (Matthew 10:2-4). It was also used in a broader sense to denote Christian messengers and teachers.

One of the original qualifications of an apostle was that he be personally acquainted with the whole ministry of Jesus Christ, from the moment He was baptized by John until the time He was taken up to heaven. The apostles were chosen directly by Jesus Christ and had the power to perform miracles. Their main work was to found churches and uphold them with powers bestowed upon them specifically for that purpose.

The apostles were from low social backgrounds and mostly uneducated. Jesus sent them out in two's to preach repentance and to perform miracles in His name (Matthew 10). They traveled with Jesus, watching His works and listening to His addresses to the people. They recognized Him as Christ (Matthew 16:16; Luke 9:20) and ascribed to Him supernatural powers. However, in recognizing the mission and spiritual teaching of Christ, they were slow in progress. Even though Jesus Christ had been preparing the disciples for His removal from the earth, they were weak in their knowledge of Him (Luke 24:21). At the feast of Pentecost, the Holy Spirit came down on the church and the apostles changed. They began to testify of the life, death, and resurrection of Jesus with boldness, as He said they should (Luke 24:48; Acts 1:8, 22; 2:32).

(Adapted from *Smith's Bible Dictionary*, Nashville: Thomas Nelson Publishers, p. 46.)

DAY OF JUDGMENT. A day of punishment for God's people. John the Baptist says this day will fall on those who do not make ready the way of the Lord (Luke 3:9). One day, Jesus will come to judge both the living and the dead (Matthew 25:31). Judgment is an aspect of the deliverance of believers (Luke 18:1-8). In an effort for people to come to repentance, God is long-suffering when it comes to judgment. On the day of judgment, every resistance to God's power will be overthrown, including evil spiritual powers (1 Corinthians 6:2-3) and people (Matthew 25:31-46). The present world will be shaken and destroyed (Matthew 24:29, 35) and a new world will be established to replace the present one. The administration of final judgment has been given by God to His Son at His appearance in glory (Matthew 3:11-12).

BACKGROUND

This week, our passage of study focuses on the role of the church leaders as servants of Christ. After Paul left Corinth, the church broke into several factions, each of them proclaiming their own leader. Before actual physical church buildings were erected, people split into groups to meet in houses or halls. In Paul's letter, he mentioned three rival groups: followers of Paul, followers of Cephas (Peter), and followers of Apollos. Another group remained steadfast to Christ, refusing to lift up anyone else.

Cephas (Peter) was considered the leader of the twelve apostles. Peter's original name was Simon. Brought up as a fisherman, he and his brother Andrew were partners of John and James. At the time of his calling, Peter was probably between 30 or 40 years old. Peter, Andrew, John, and James were disciples of John the Baptist when he was called by the Lord. Jesus gave Peter the name Cephas, meaning "rock," or "stone." The designation of Peter and the other eleven apostles took place after Jesus' public ministering in Galilee, Decapolis, Peraea, and Judea (Matthew 10:2-4; Mark 3:13-19).

Peter is named first in every list of the apostles and Jesus addressed him as their representative. At one point, Peter rejected Jesus' prediction of suffering and humiliation, but at the Last Supper he was especially earnest in his request to have the traitor pointed out. Although he never visited Corinth, some, especially Jewish Christians, chose to follow Peter.

Apollos (1 Corinthians 1:12) was a very, very eloquent Jewish Christian. He was taught by disciples of John the Baptist on the way of the Lord, but during his travel to Ephesus, was taught better by Aquila and Priscilla. He became a preacher of the Gospel, first in Achaia and then in Corinth (Acts 18:27; 19:1). The different groups liked to compare Apollos to Paul—Apollos being the more eloquent of the two. Even with the comparisons, there was never a rivalry between them.

Paul, although a trained scholar, had trouble reaching the people in Corinth with his simple, unpolished speeches (Acts 18:9-10). The people of Corinth fancied themselves as thinkers and intellectual superiors, but Paul refused to get caught up in that. He pointed out that such an attitude kept them bound to man's way of thinking. And, it is evident that although intelligent, they were still in need of teaching—spiritual teaching. The people of Corinth needed to hear the Word of God. They needed a leader whose focus was God, who worked to build God's church.

Paul was such a leader. Titus 1:7-8 tells us the characteristics of a good leader, or "steward":

"Since an overseer is entrusted with God's work, he must be blameless—not overbearing, not quick tempered, not given to drunkenness, not violent, not pursuing dishonest gain. Rather he must be hospitable, one who loves what is good, who is self controlled, upright, holy and disciplined."

Such a steward upholds unity in the church. Unity is based on the profession of faith in the Lord Jesus. A steward who professes such faith and acts in an according manner, sets an example for his church. An earnest, mature leader cares greatly about how he builds on the foundation of Christ.

Paul and other preachers of the Gospel are *diakonoi*, or "servants" of God. God has chosen them as instruments to be used to call the people of Corinth to faith. God assigns each preacher a mission; the choice is not up to the preacher. Paul's mission was to found the church at Corinth. As founder, Paul felt it his obligation to address the role of the church leaders and to remind the church that its one and only object of worship is Christ, to whom all church leaders are servants.

AT-A-GLANCE

1. **Church Leaders As Servants of Christ (1 Corinthians 4:1-2)**
2. **Church Leaders Are Not to Be Judged (vv. 3-5)**
3. **Church Leaders As Vehicles for Unity (vv. 6-13)**

IN DEPTH

1. Church Leaders As Servants of Christ (1 Corinthians 4:1-2)

Apostle Paul begins this chapter by instructing the people of Corinth how they should regard church leaders. The word "servant" spells out the hierarchy: church leaders are subordinates; they are not heads. They are commissioned by God and report to Him. They are not to be lifted up as heads of a party. They are, though, due their respect as stewards for the Most High.

Paul referred to them as "stewards of the mysteries of God" (v. 1). The word "steward" denotes the manager of a

household or estate. Stewards were responsible for handling all of the affairs of a family, and for providing for it. Church leaders, therefore, are responsible for the maintaining of the church. They are to make the Gospel of Jesus Christ known. They are to give guidance and counsel to the members. They are to keep the church running for the Lord.

Unlike other stewards, church leaders have an even greater responsibility, for they were chosen by God and are entrusted with "the hidden mysteries of God." Those mysteries are the truths revealed in the Gospel. This is both an important position and an incredible honor.

Much is expected of the church leader. He is expected to be "faithful" (v. 2). God selected them as His delegates, to deliver the message of the Gospel and to save souls. They have to prove themselves faithful to Him. This is the most important requirement. The leader's full and complete loyalty must be to God.

The church leader has at his disposable the truths of the Gospel. He also has the trust of God. He could, if he wanted to, use them to his own selfish advantages, and not properly fulfill his obligation as a servant of God. That is why he must be devoted to the Lord. He must purpose himself to honor the trust that he is given and to always use his gifts for the fulfillment of the Gospel. He should strive to maintain the rules of faith and conduct demanded of Christians. He

also must continually grow in Him to become a mature leader.

A mature leader has a definite leadership style and does all work for the glory of God. He knows that his primary obligation is to Christ and he leads accordingly, not always pleasing everyone and sometimes making difficult, yet appropriate, decisions for the church he leads. This type of church leader unifies the church, keeping them disciplined, focused, and of the same mind. If he doesn't, he's in big trouble! Why? Because he was appointed by Jesus and entrusted with the welfare of His kingdom. He is going to be judged on his work. That is a mighty responsibility.

With that in mind, it is due reverence that we should give our church leaders. We should respect and follow them as leaders chosen by God. We should never, however, worship them.

2. Church Leaders Are Not to Be Judged (vv. 3-5)

Another thing we should not do is judge our church leaders, and they should not concern themselves with whether or not they are being judged (v. 3). Church leaders are in a position where they are continually judged by men. This is not to concern them (v. 4). Man is not the judge of man. God is. Church leaders, like every other man on earth is subject to judgment from God, only.

Having a good reputation is helpful in ministry, but it is not the most important thing. If human acceptance is the most important part of a church leader's ministry, then his motives are selfish and he is not being a faithful servant of God.

There are several reasons why we should not judge: 1) We are in no position to do so. No one is without sin and everyone falls short of the glory of God. 2) The only and ultimate judge of man is God. A time is coming when God will judge us and "bring to light the hidden things of darkness and make manifest the counsels of the heart" (v. 5). One day all of our secrets and hidden sins will be brought to light and we will be judged accordingly. 3) We are biased when we judge ourselves. We tend to be easy on our own selves, justifying our motives and conduct. Yet, we so quickly and harshly judge others. Were we a bit more humble and honest, we'd probably not be so rough on others. Because we are so inclined to judge others more harshly than ourselves, it is in our best interest to leave all judgment to God.

In the phrase " I judge not my own self" (v. 3), Paul is conscientious of his shortcomings and knows that he is not perfect. He also realizes that were he to judge himself he'd be far too lenient. God clearly sees all our imperfections. Paul knows this and realizes judgment is not the right of any man.

3. Church Leaders As Vehicles for Unity (vv. 6-13)

In verses 6-7, Paul warns the church not to "think of men above that which is written that no one be puffed up for one against another." We are not to boast or elevate our own or anyone else's importance, nor are we to demean and try to belittle others. As Christians, we are all part of the Body of Christ—united with the same purpose and mind. We are not divided into several factions. We are on level ground with all the saints and practicing this attitude will help to ensure that we remain a united body by not letting human pride get in the way.

No Christian should glory in men, claiming himself to be a disciple of a preacher. To do such a thing breaks the unity within the church. The preachers of the Gospel serve God to help the faithful. The faithful are not there for the preacher, but for the message of the Gospel. Apostles of Christ are in charge of preaching the message of the Gospel, not their own doctrines. They are a source for unity; their job is to keep the body of Christ united as one body.

Paul compared the suffering apostles with the Corinthians, who felt they were superior over other Christians. The Corinthians seemed to have forgotten that their gifts were given by God. Their actions seemed to indicate that they thought they were perfect, definitely above others. The apostles, on the other hand, suffered a great deal in an effort to establish churches (vv. 8-13). They faced persecution and defamation. They endured, though, following the example set by Christ. Christ died and shed His blood on the cross for us. The apostles were considered fools. It is this faithfulness and humility that today's church leaders should possess in order to assure unity remains in the church.

SEARCH THE SCRIPTURES

1. How should church leaders be regarded? (v. 1)

2. What must a church leader prove to be? (v. 2)

3. At the time of judgment, what will God do? (v. 5)

4. According to Paul, why shouldn't people boast? (v. 7)

5. In what position did Paul feel the apostles were placed? (v. 9)

DISCUSS THE MEANING

1. Paul, when defining his role as a church leader, noted that his conscience was clear, but he was not innocent (v. 4). What point was he trying to make about judgment?

2. Ephesians 4:12-13 states that God gave us apostles and church leaders "so that the body of Christ may be built up until we all reach unity in the faith and in knowledge of the son of God, and become mature, attaining to the whole measure of the fullness of Christ." What happens when a leader fails to meet such an obligation?

LESSON IN OUR SOCIETY

A prominent church leader was in the news recently for being under investigation by the State's Attorney's office. He was under investigation because church members accused him of running up their credit cards and not paying rent to one of the members he rented from. In addition, all of his financial affairs were in question because of his extravagances: a home worth well over half a million dollars; a car worth over eighty thousand dollars, and lots of expensive clothes and jewelry. In spite of all these luxuries, he hadn't paid any of his debts, nor was the church that he had collected a great deal of money for being built. As a result, his whole ministry is in question.

There are many "false leaders" out today, playing on a person's religious belief and faithfulness in an effort to gain something—in most cases personal wealth. Stories are in the newspapers daily of people who have given their life's savings away to a person they thought was a true spiritual leader. How can we avoid falling prey to "false leaders"? What can we do as Christians to welcome those who are searching for true spiritual leadership into our church?

MAKE IT HAPPEN

Commit yourself to helping your church leader deliver the message of Christ and salvation, by extending an invitation to church to at least one person every day this week. If needed, also offer to have transportation provided. Follow up each invitation with a telephone call.

FOLLOW THE SPIRIT

What God wants me to do:

_____

_____

REMEMBER YOUR THOUGHTS

Special insights you have learned:

_____

_____

MORE LIGHT ON THE TEXT
1 CORINTHIANS 4:1-13

Paul gives the servant model and shows how it relates to how the Corinthians are treating or mistreating him. He changes images from a garden to a building and insists he is God's servant, not theirs. So they may not judge him.

4:1 Think of us in this way, as servants of Christ and stewards of God's mysteries.

Paul is looking back to 1 Corinthians chapter 3 as shown in the introduction above (4:1). Paul, Apollos, and Peter are co-workers and servants of Christ. That's how Paul wants people to regard them. Pastors, bishops, and whosoever works in the church is a servant of Christ. *Hyperetai* and *oikonomos* are the terms used. They refer to a person who is entrusted with a certain service but accountable to his boss. Paul and his co-workers are *oikonomoi*, stewards (which refers to economy) entrusted with the work of spreading the Gospel, i.e, the *musteria*, "mysteries" or "secrets" of God. These are not God's puzzles, rather it is the word of the Cross: knowing Christ and Him crucified. This goes back to 2:7 where those who have the Spirit of God can discern God's plan of salvation which was long hidden from humanity and is now revealed through Christ for whom Paul, Cephas or Peter, and Apollos are "servants" and

"stewards." They do not own the Gospel. A steward can be entrusted to run a household for his boss. And *oikonome*, refers to a stable construction, peaceful maintenance, and improvement, in this case of the Corinthian congregation. So if the Corinthian church is divided, the servants are responsible for the situation. Their responsibilities are therefore political. The servants must unite the factions within the congregation and bring peace. They are trying to build up the temple of God in whom the Holy Spirit dwells (3:16-17). They are humble servants of Christ. They are like waiters who serve at a table. They are both entrusted and accountable to God (cf. 2:7; 13:2; 14:2) for the spread of the Gospel through preaching, baptism, sharing the Lord's Supper, and exercising charismatic gifts.

2 Moreover it is required in stewards, that a man be found faithful.

Stewardship means faithfulness and trustworthiness. God requires this of every Christian. This means absolute fidelity to the Gospel. Just as Paul received it, thus must he preach it. Faithfulness to oneself, faithfulness to the Gospel, and faithfulness to the Lord who commissions us (cf. 15:1-11) are marks of good stewardship.

3 But with me it is a very small thing that I should be judged of you, or of man's judgment: yea, I judge not mine own self. 4 For I know nothing by myself; yet am I not hereby justified: but he that judgeth me is the Lord.

Paul is complaining of having been judged by those he brought to richness rather than by God who sent him (cf. 2:5). In fact, they are even investigating him, bringing him before the jury. But the criterion should be faithfulness to the Gospel. Only God can judge any pastor and church worker fairly. This does not mean that Christians cannot take action against someone who does wrong (see Matthew 18:16-20; 1 Corinthians 5:1ff.).

Pastors may be criticized by some for taking a stand, for example preaching against divorce and the like. But they have been entrusted with the Word with its sharp edge though it may be bitter. Human judgments, be they of rulers or fellow Christians, are nothing. Only God's judgment matters. God justifies the one accused wrongly. He even recompenses. To be justified by God denotes a judicial relationship, either ethical or forensic, related to law courts, in this case to God (cf. Deuteronomy 25:1; Genesis 18:25). To be justified is to be acquitted or vindicated before a judge's tribunal (Exodus 23:7). God has justified Paul, hence has acquitted him of all charges. His conscience is clear so that personal evaluation is irrelevant.

5 Therefore judge nothing before the time, until the Lord come, who both will bring to light the hidden things of darkness, and will make manifest the counsels of the hearts: and then shall every man have praise of God.

Christians are discouraged to judge others before the appointed time. Stop reaching a verdict. Make no judgments for they lack God's eschatological perspective. It is the Lord, the Master of the household, who will pass the verdict and each one's secrets will be put to light and each one will receive their reward on the day of the Lord. [NB: This text refers to a particular situation in Corinth and cannot be generalized to represent every human situation].

However, the church cannot be self-confident. Churches make false judgments motivated by some political or social intrigue. Churches tend to be wrong. Churches may wrongly accuse their pastors. Paul reminds us that only faithfulness to God and to the Gospel matters, not success in adding members.

6 And these things, brethren, I have in a figure transferred to myself and to Apollos for your sakes; that ye might learn in us not to think of men above that which is written, that no one of you be puffed up for one against another.

Paul reveals that his teaching concerns the Gospel and the Corinthian situation following its abuse of God's servants of the Gospel (3:5—4:5). Christians tend to take pride in certain pastors or charismatic leaders and neglect the fact that even the minor characters are essential. (4:6-8,10). In fact, some Christians become puffed up just like the Corinthians were as they become divided about power and questions of leadership. The specific mention of Apollos indicates that the Corinthians were in disagreement and were partly in alignment with either Paul or Apollos. Divisions in any church disable the ministry and cripple the church.

7 For who maketh thee to differ from another? and what hast thou that thou didst not receive? now if thou didst receive it, why dost thou glory as if thou hadst not received it?

Everything God has given to Corinthians including servants of every kind like Paul and Apollos is God's free gift. They don't have to puff up. They should express humility before God. Every Christian must express the humility

before the God and His Gospel and in respect of our fellow Christians, even those with whom we do not agree. Christ Himself humbled Himself unto death on the cross. Christians should be imitators of Christ. The attitude of boasting seems to dominate the Corinthians just as it does with many Christians today. Puffing up because of economic success, a good home, neighborhood, and the like is common (cf. 3:21). 1 Corinthians 1:12; 3:4 refers to such boasting. In 1 Corinthians 1:31, Paul declares, "Let the one who boasts boast in the Lord." If the praise is from God (4:5), then no one should boast at all. Boasting is thus a divisive force in the community. The grouping of partisanship is rooted in such claims like *logos* (rhetoric) and *gnosis* (wisdom) found in verse 8.

8 Now ye are full, now ye are rich, ye have reigned as kings without us: and I would to God ye did reign, that we also might reign with you.

Paul begins a biting irony attacking the Corinthians' point of view. Indeed, according to 1 Corinthians 1:5 and 12:3, they have all drunk the Spirit and have been enriched with the spiritual gifts. Now they are even going beyond the basic principle of their salvation—beyond the cross which brings humility. They instead are proud and have a false sense of victory. They regard themselves as kings ruling in the spiritual world when indeed they are supposed to be servants. It hurts that the founder of their success has been reduced to nothing. They have forgotten where they came from. They regard themselves to have arrived in the heavenly setting. They think that they have all they want being "rich" *ploutoi* (cf. 1:5) "without us" i.e., Paul and his co-workers who planted the church in Corinth. Indeed Paul uses irony to mend the church. Paul sees their present boasting as tantamount. It must be remembered that "pride" was the first cause of human fall in Eden. Satan wished to be like God. In the like manner, the Corinthians think they have already made it to the next world even though they are still on earth. The servants who brought them there have no share, i.e., in the phrase "without us." So Paul ridicules them, "How I wish you had begun to reign!" It is a wishful thinking that some Christians tend to have when they compare the spiritual gifts they have to the gifts of others. This behavior demonstrates spiritual immaturity.

9 For I think that God hath set forth us the apostles last, as it were appointed to death: for we are made a spectacle unto the world, and to angels, and to men.

Paul and his co-workers and all that serve in the church are laborers employed by God and our Lord Jesus Christ.

And as Matthew notes, "the harvest is plenteous but the laborers are few" (Matthew 9:38). Even these few are being persecuted by those they serve. It is a common suffering that pastors have to endure (see 16:8; Acts 19:23ff.). But Paul accepts where God has put them. They are apostles, i.e., the ones sent to deliver the Good News. He hence owes his role to the divine action, *apedeixen*, that they are what they are.

The terrible suffering Paul and his co-workers are enduring can be equated with a *theatron* or "spectacle." By this Paul refers to the emperor wars where the victorious Roman emperor could stage a splendid parade of the conquered army and booty. At the end of the procession were captives of war who were condemned to die in the arena. These people were forced to fight with wild beasts (as gladiators) until they were torn apart by animals or made to kill one another. Paul regards himself to have similarly been made a spectacle (cf. 2 Corinthians 2:14). He is a spectacle to the world, to the angels, and humanity. This kind of dishonor has been suffered by some, who in their strong commitment, have shed their blood for this cause (Dr. Martin Luther King Jr., John Huss, etc.), suffering like Job for the sake of the Gospel.

10 We are fools for Christ's sake, but ye are wise in Christ; we are weak, but ye are strong; ye are honourable, but we are despised. 11 Even unto this present hour we both hunger, and thirst, and are naked, and are buffeted, and have no certain dwellingplace, 12 And labour, working with our own hands: being reviled, we bless; being persecuted, we suffer it: 13 Being defamed, we entreat: we are made as the filth of the world, and are the offscouring of all things unto this day.

All these verses can be summarized with one Greek term, *kolaphizo*, which means "brutality" or "ill-treatment." The verses present the irony that Paul wanted to reveal. The Corinthians are classified as "so wise" in Christ when in fact he means all together that they are missing Christ (2:6-16). Those in Christ should be sensible, or to use Paul's word *teleioi*, "perfect" or "mature." They should not follow the world but the kernel of the Gospel, i.e., humility. We know already that the "weakness of God" displayed in the Cross, is God's saving power to those who believe. So Paul is being ironic (cf. 1:26-28). We see how Paul continues with another reverse order in verses 11-13. Paul knows that many were not of "noble birth" (1:26) but he calls them "the honored." Ironically, it is self honor. In contrast, the apostles are at the end of the procession in a spectacle *theatron* and as "the dishonorable" go to their deaths. For both Paul and Peter, indeed, died a spectacular death for their faith in Christ. Paul gives a deliberate contrast between himself and the Corinthians.

Many times we claim to be what we are not either to mistreat others or to advance our own honor and esteem. We know for sure in the Beatitudes that the blessed are those who hunger, thirst, and suffer for the sake of righteousness. This seems to be what Paul is reflecting on. The Corinthians who regard themselves as "rich" have already been filled.

Indeed the question of homelessness is true since Paul was an itinerant evangelist with no permanent dwelling (Hebrews 11:13-16). He and his co-workers worked "with their own hands" as tent makers as they spread the Gospel. Thus, apostolic hardships are always clear in people's lives. Indeed, Paul and his co-workers are being ill-treated, but as the Sermon on the Mount teaches—when cursed, they blessed (cf. Luke 6:28; Romans 12:14). The teaching of the Sermon on the Mount is true for every Christian. So, Paul's suffering was also his "sacrifice" (Colossians 1:24) for the sake of the Gospel. The sufferings of Paul echoes the Isaianic servant songs in Isaiah 53:2-3. Serving the Lord entails fellowship in the sufferings of Christ (Romans 8:17; Philippians 13:10). Indeed, Christians like Paul and his friends must give their lives for the sake of the Gospel (Matthew 10:38-39). It is the kind of great suffering for Christ's sake. Though persecuted, they endure it not to seek self-honor but the glory of Christ.

DAILY BIBLE READING

M: Apollos and Paul, Servants of Christ
1 Corinthians 4:1-7

T: The Ministry of the Apostles
1 Corinthians 4:8-13

W: Paul's Fatherly Love for the Corinthians
1 Corinthians 4:14-21

T: Clothe Yourselves with Humility
1 Peter 5:1-5

F: Faithful Leaders Will Encounter Suffering
1 Peter 5:6-11

S: Do Not Judge One Another
Romans 14:1-12

S: Live in Harmony with One Another
Romans 15:1-6

TEACHING TIPS

March 26
Bible Study Guide 4

1. Words You Should Know

A. Discipline. Greek *sophronismos*—The admonishing or calling to soundness of mind or self-control; chastisement.

B. Excommunicate. The separation from the communion of the church. It was a spiritual punishment meant to punish the offender and keep the church protected from wickedness (2 Timothy 3:17). Those sentenced to excommunication were those who committed heresy or gross immoralities. In order to be restored to communion, the offender must be truly repentant. Once done, the sentence is publicly reversed, the same way as it was publicly ordered.

2. Teacher Preparation

A. Prayerfully read 1 Corinthians 5-6:11 and James 3:13-18 before studying this week's FOCAL VERSES. Be prepared to explain why discipline is needed in the church and how it keeps the church united.

B. Read the BACKGROUND material for the lesson. Be able to name and define some sins which still abound in the church, that should be subject to the church's discipline.

C. Write the definitions for "excommunicate" and "immorality" on the board.

3. Starting the Lesson

A. Open with prayer. Thank God for your class and pray that He enriches your teaching.

B. Ask students to read the IN FOCUS lesson and discuss why discipline is a necessary part of life.

C. Discuss the definitions of the words on the board. Ask the students to identify "immoral" behaviors.

4. Getting into the Lesson

A. The BACKGROUND section and THE PEOPLE, PLACES, AND TIMES section will give students a clearer understanding of today's lesson. Have a volunteer read each section aloud.

B. Have the students divide into groups and focus on one section of the IN DEPTH commentary. Have the students read their assigned section and prepare a summary to be presented to the class. After 15 minutes, have a spokesperson from each group present their summary. Then allow time for questions and answers.

5. Relating the Lesson to Life

A. Have the students write down the answers to the SEARCH THE SCRIPTURES exercise.

B. Have the students use the DISCUSS THE MEANING questions to help them further relate today's lesson to their lives.

C. Continue the discussion by going on to the LESSON IN OUR SOCIETY section.

6. Arousing Action

A. Review the KEEP IN MIND verse and ask students how they can use this verse to guide their actions and attitudes as members of the body of Christ?

B. Read the MAKE IT HAPPEN suggestion aloud. Challenge the students to put the suggestion from the MAKE IT HAPPEN section into action in their daily living.

C. Solicit prayer requests. Close the class with prayer.

WORSHIP GUIDE

For the Superintendent or Teacher
Theme: The Need for Discipline in the Church
Theme Song: "For the Unity of Christ's Body"
Scripture: Titus 2:12
Song: "For The Healing of the Nations"
Meditation: Dear Lord, I thank You for giving commands that govern my life. Help me to always ignore my own desires, so that I can keep my covenant relationship with You, Amen.

THE NEED FOR DISCIPLINE IN THE CHURCH

Bible Background • 1 CORINTHIANS 5—6:11
Printed Text • 1 CORINTHIANS 5:1-13
Devotional Reading • JAMES 3:13-18

LESSON AIM

By the end of the lesson, students will recognize that discipline in the church is necessary, that failure to enforce discipline is unhealthy to the church body, and will purpose themselves to avoid behaviors which would require discipline from the church.

KEEP IN MIND

"Therefore let us keep the feast, not with old leaven, neither with the leaven of malice and wickedness; but with the unleavened bread of sincerity and truth" (1 Corinthians 5:8).

FOCAL VERSES

1 CORINTHIANS 5:1 It is reported commonly that there is fornication among you, and such fornication as is not so much named among the Gentiles, that one should have his father's wife.

2 And ye are puffed up, and have not rather mourned, that he that hath done this deed might be taken away from among you.

3 For I verily, as absent in body, but present in spirit, have judged already, as though I were present, concerning him that hath so done this deed,

4 In the name of our Lord Jesus Christ, when ye are gathered together, and my spirit, with the power of our Lord Jesus Christ,

5 To deliver such an one unto Satan for the destruction of the flesh, that the spirit may be saved in the day of the Lord Jesus.

6 Your glorying is not good. Know ye not that a lit-

LESSON OVERVIEW

LESSON AIM
KEEP IN MIND
FOCAL VERSES
IN FOCUS
THE PEOPLE, PLACES, AND
TIMES
BACKGROUND
AT-A-GLANCE
IN DEPTH
SEARCH THE SCRIPTURES
DISCUSS THE MEANING
LESSON IN OUR SOCIETY
MAKE IT HAPPEN
FOLLOW THE SPIRIT
REMEMBER YOUR THOUGHTS
MORE LIGHT ON THE TEXT
DAILY BIBLE READINGS

tle leaven leaveneth the whole lump?

7 Purge out therefore the old leaven, that ye may be a new lump, as ye are unleavened. For even Christ our passover is sacrificed for us:

8 Therefore let us keep the feast, not with old leaven, neither with the leaven of malice and wickedness; but with the unleavened bread of sincerity and truth.

9 I wrote unto you in an epistle not to company with fornicators:

10 Yet not altogether with the fornicators of this world, or with the covetous, or extortioners, or with idolaters; for then must ye needs go out of the world.

11 But now I have written unto you not to keep company, if any that is called a brother be a fornicator, or covetous, or an idolater, or a railer, or a drunkard, or an extortioner; with such a one no not to eat.

12 For what have I to do to judge them also that are without? do not ye judge them that are within?

13 But them that are without God judgeth. Therefore put away from among yourselves that wicked person.

IN FOCUS

Several parents with their children were sitting in the waiting room of the neighborhood pediatrician when a woman came in screaming at a child to "get in here!" Minutes later a seven-year-old casually strolled in, going straight past his mother directly to the toy box. He snatched open the lid and began to throw the toys on the floor. Despite his mother's demands, he continued throwing. Repeatedly, but to no avail, his mother told him to pick the toys up until she finally went behind him and picked them up herself. She grabbed his arm and tried to lead him to a seat, but he kicked, wiggled, and fought until she let him go, back to the toy box to throw out more toys.

The small boy threw toys until something caught his eye. In the corner, another boy around the same age was playing with an action figure. The boy threw down the toy he was holding and went over to the child. He demanded, "Give me!" The other child said "no," and the little boy hit him with a balled fist. Seeing this, his mother went to him and demanded he apologize; he didn't. He jerked away from his mother and sat on the coffee table in the middle of the room.

When the nurse called for the little boy, he refused to move. He sat on the coffee table and kicked his feet. When his mother told him to come, he refused. His mother threatened him; he wasn't fazed. His mother said she was going to tell his father when he got home. The boy said, "so." Finally, the mother dug into her purse and pulled out some chocolate. The boy snatched the chocolate and ran back to the office where the doctor was. His mother smiled apologetically at the others in the waiting room and hurried behind him.

Two of the other parents shook their heads at each other and one remarked, "That child needs some serious discipline. If he belonged to me, he wouldn't dare get away with such behavior."

Like that little boy, some Christians may need to be disciplined in the church. In today's lesson, we'll address the need for discipline and how such discipline brings unity to the church.

THE PEOPLE, PLACES, AND TIMES

SATAN. The word "satan" (*satanas*) means "adversary" and is used as such in 1 Samuel 29; Numbers 22:22, 32; and Psalm 109:6. The existence of a spirit of evil is clearly revealed in the Scripture; the first appearance occurring with the serpent. In the Book of Job, the first actual mention of "Satan" occurs. Satan is spoken of as a "spirit" in Ephesians 2:2 and as "the prince of the demons" in Matthew 12:24. It is thought that Satan was once an archangel, with superhuman power, wisdom, and energy who fell from heaven. He is opposed to the things of God, including love, truth, and holiness.

Satan has power over souls. Directly, he is an evil nature which can possess a man's soul. He has a gang of evil spirits, for all of whom an "everlasting fire is pre-

pared" (Matthew 25:41). Not only considered the "prince of demons," Satan is also considered the "prince of this world" (John 12:31; 2 Corinthians 4:4; Ephesians 6:12). He tries to break communion between man and God, and the bonds of truth and love that bind men together. Every time a man sins, he becomes a "servant of sin." This creates a tendency for evil in man and helps further the work of Satan.

Satan is destined for destruction at the hands of the Lord, where he will be subject to eternal damnation.

(Adapted from *Smith's Bible Dictionary*, Nashville: Thomas Nelson Publishers, pp. 591-592.)

EXCOMMUNICATION. In the New Testament, excommunication was instituted by the Lord and practiced by Paul (1 Corinthians 5:11). Excommunication involves separation from the communion of the church. It was a spiritual punishment meant to benefit the offender and protect the church from wickedness (2 Timothy 3:17). Those sentenced to excommunication committed heresy or gross immoralities. In order to be restored to communion, the offender must be truly repentant. Once done, the sentence is publicly reversed, just as it was publicly ordered.

(Adapted from *The New International Dictionary of the Bible*, Grand Rapids: Zondervan Corporation, p. 330.)

BACKGROUND

This lesson stresses the need for discipline within the church. Proverbs 13:24 sums up the necessity of discipline: "He who spares the rod hates his son, but he who loves him is careful to discipline him." When you truly love someone, you realize that it is important to also discipline them. The Apostle Paul loved the church of Corinth, he was its founder and spiritual leader. When one of its members sinned, he knew it was necessary to discipline that member. If sin and acts of misconduct are allowed to exist without challenge, then the church would not function capably as a whole, nor would the church show love for its own.

The case that prompted Paul to write about discipline was a rumored act of sexual misconduct. This act, incestuous fornication, was so despised, it was even blasted among the "heathens," or those not associated with the church.

Sexual immorality is especially terrible because it is a sin committed directly against the body. Our bodies are not our own, but, "members of Christ himself" (Corinthians 6:15). Our "body is a temple of the Holy Spirit, who is in you, whom you have received from

God" (1 Corinthians 6:19). The human body is to be valued; we should honor God by honoring our bodies.

In response to such a vile rumor, the church at Corinth did nothing. It did not impose any discipline of the offender, nor was the church particularly upset by this offensive transgression. Instead, they remained "puffed up" (1 Corinthian 5:2) or filled with pride, even though they were embroiled in scandal. Because of this, Paul felt it necessary not only to address the specific act of which he had heard, but also to instruct the church on the necessity of maintaining and enforcing discipline.

Why is discipline needed in church? First of all, discipline of members and enforcement of God's law helps to keep sin from permeating the church. "Know ye not that the unrighteous shall not inherit the kingdom of God? Be not deceived: neither fornicators, nor idolaters, nor adulterers, nor effeminate, nor abusers of themselves with mankind, nor thieves, nor covetous, nor drunkards, nor revilers, nor extortioners, shall inherit the kingdom of God (1 Corinthians 6:9). The church has members who once may have fallen into one of those categories. But through baptism and sanctification, those sins were washed away. Enforcing discipline helps to ensure that no one falls back into such dark, sinful ways.

What were some of the sins Paul spoke of?

Fornication: *(porneia)* illicit sexual intercourse (John 8:41); includes adultery (Matthew 5:32; 19:9).

Idolatry: *(eidolon)* the worship of a visible deity. In early times, the sun and moon were selected as objects of idolatry. Idolatry was a serious crime in Israel. The offender was sentenced to destruction; his relatives were not only to denounce him and deliver him to punishment, but their hands were to render the first blows.

Covetous: *(epithumeo)* to fix one's desire on; to long for or lust for something or someone (Acts 20:33).

Extortion: *(harpage)* denotes pillage, plundering, robbery; to seize or carry off by force (Matthew 23:25; Luke 2:39).

Adultery: *(moichos)* the giving of one's self to someone other than the wife or husband. Spiritual adultery is used to express unfaithfulness to covenant vows to God, who is represented as the husband of His people (Luke 18:2; 1 Corinthians 6:9; Hebrew 13:4).

None of these sins, or others not mentioned, should be tolerated. This was especially hard in a city like Corinth, where vices and infractions were a way of life.

Second, a well-disciplined church is a united church. Christ is our source for unity. When we fall into sin, we fall out of the ways of the Lord, out of His grace. This separates us from those in the church who are still one in Christ. When discipline is enforced, the members are kept in line with the ways of the Lord. They are of the same mind and the same purpose. They are encouraged to "walk in the spirit and ye shall not fulfill the lust of the flesh" (Galatians 5:16). Quick, appropriate discipline from the church ensures that the church remains spiritually intact, and that the offender is given a chance at redemption and forgiveness.

AT-A-GLANCE

**1. A Call for Discipline
(1 Corinthians 5:1-2)
2. Administering Discipline (vv. 3-8)
3. Enforcing Discipline (vv. 9-13)**

IN DEPTH

1. A Call for Discipline (1 Corinthians 5:1-2)

Reports were spreading throughout Corinth that a despicable act of sexual misconduct had occurred in the church (v. 1). It is this act that Paul uses to illustrate the need for discipline in the church. The act, incestuous fornication (supposedly between a man's son and that man's wife) was so terrible that even the "heathens," or those not in the church, had heard of it and were commenting on it. It is these reports that Paul felt should have upset the church. They should have realized that rumors were circulating all over, and they should have felt it necessary to get to the bottom of those rumors. If they proved true, the church should have enforced some sort of disciplinary action.

Instead, though, Paul charges them with being "puffed up" or filled with pride (v. 2). He wasn't charging them with being proud of the specific act. He was charging that in spite of the offense and in spite of the fact that wickedness had permeated the church, they were still proud of their own wisdom. They should have been much more humbled. They should have mourned. They should have made removing the offender their priority. Men have a tendency to be proud at the wrong times.

2. Administering Discipline (vv. 3-8)

The word "mourn" gives us an idea of how discipline should be administered in the church. The Greek word *pentheo* means to have "sorrow" or "grief." Disciplinary acts within the church should be mourned or grieved. It should trouble the church that one of its own has fallen into wickedness, and that such wickedness has caused impurity to exist within the church. It should grieve the church that it has to impose discipline on one of its own. With that, the offender should be treated with compassion and tenderness, not with anger or bitterness. The need for the enforcement of discipline should be a time of deep sadness for the church. In such a time, there is little room for pride.

What was the actual discipline suggested for the offender? **Excommunication,** or removal from the church, is the suggested discipline. The offender should not be allowed to remain in the church as long as he was in a sinful state. Paul suggested that this sentence be passed. He was not physically present, but having established the church, his heart was there, and he gave advice as though he were present (v. 3). Paul's power to evoke such authority of opinion comes from Jesus Christ. He didn't mean "his" power, but the power of the church, assembling in the name of Jesus and doing whatever was necessary to promote Jesus' honor (v. 4).

"To deliver such an one unto Satan for the destruction of the flesh, that the spirit may be saved in the day of the Lord Jesus" (v. 5). The phrase "to deliver unto Satan" suggests that the punishment be the imposition of bodily diseases from Satan. Satan has been referred to as the author of bodily disease. The apostles were known to be able to inflict disease on criminals (Acts 13:11; 1 Corinthians 11:30). The motive behind such punishment is "destruction of the flesh." It is important that the imposed punishment be in line with the offense. The offender, in this case, committed a sin against his flesh, therefore, the punishment imposed was one against the flesh. The purpose was "that the spirit may be saved in the day of the Lord Jesus." Disciplining the offender was to his benefit. It would humble him and help reform him and lead him back to a righteous path. This had to be done if his soul were to be saved. If not, his soul would not be ready on Judgment Day when Jesus comes for His people.

Once Paul suggested what disciplinary measure should be imposed on the offender, he spoke to the church regarding their behavior during this crisis. He told them, "your glorying is not good" (v. 6).

Their "glorying," or "boasting," was inappropriate in light of everything that was going on. It is really never a good idea to be boastful—everything we have is a gift from God. In Corinth at that time, the people should have been especially humbled—sin was present in the church.

Paul compared this sin to leaven or "yeast" in dough. It just takes a small amount of yeast to work itself throughout the dough. So, too, does one sin or one act of spiritual impurity work its destructive way through the church. Paul tells the Corinthians they must "purge" out the old leaven (v. 7). They must put away or free themselves of all of their old "leaven," or vices, or anything capable of bringing impurity to the church. He is telling them to do this so they can be made "new," or free from the sins which once bound them. We want to be like Christ. Christ was the lamb sacrificed for our sins. His blood was pure and without blemish. He paid the price for all of the sins of the world so that we may be made holy. Since the ultimate sacrifice has already been made, we should put away all sin.

Verse 8 encourages us to "keep the feast." The "feast" symbolizes how the Jews, when celebrating the paschal supper on the sacrificing of the lamb, put away all leaven. They put away sin. "Keeping the feast" then refers to honoring and serving God by avoiding and putting away evil. How should the church "keep the feast"? "Not with the old leaven of malice and wickedness" (v. 8). They should not be influenced by their old ways and feelings and corruptions. They should put away all evil and sin. In its place, they should embrace characteristics we attribute to Christ: faithfulness, sincerity, and truth.

3. Enforcing Discipline (vv. 9-13)

The need for discipline in the church is necessary for the effective running of the church. While at church, the members have fellowship with those who share their sentiments and faithfulness to uplifting Christ. What about our day to day living with others in a world full of sin? To this, Paul says, "not to keep company with fornicators, the covetous, extortioners, or idolaters" (vv. 9-11, paraphrased). It is impossible to avoid interaction with men of the world—those who choose darkness. Some of them are right in our own families! This is not what Paul was suggesting. He was suggesting that a person should not consider such a person a brother or sister in Christ, nor should Christians be influenced or motivated by them. This spiritual disasso-

ciation is required even with those in church who have fallen into sinful ways.

When a faithful Christian does interact with those of the world: 1) He should make sure he doesn't conform to their ways. He should never have nor show approval for any of the ways, opinions, or fancies of the world; 2) He should never do or say anything that would place Christianity in a negative light. Instead, at all times the believer should work to win souls for Christ; 3) He should always do good and show kindness toward people of the world. Although they are not spiritual brothers, Christians should care deeply about their souls and should try to bring them to Christ.

This is where the need for discipline within the church is really emphasized. The world is full of sinners, and until each individual sinner chooses to accept Christ for himself, the church has no control over him (v. 12). The church does, however, have the authority to discipline their own (v. 13). It is one body and of one mind. It has to "walk like Jesus walked." Jesus was without sin. If a member of the church is ruled by fleshly desires, he is allowing an opening for disharmony in the church body. The church has every right to enforce discipline among its members who have sinned. The person should be excommunicated for the benefit of the church, and more importantly, that person's soul.

In this modern and "carefree" age, it is still important to recognize that behaviors like sexual immorality, greed and idolatry, among others, are still sins and such offenders with in the church have to be disciplined.

SEARCH THE SCRIPTURES

1. What were the rumors circulating around Corinth involving the church? What was the response of the church of Corinth amidst the rumors? (vv. 1-2)

2. What, according to Paul, is the prescribed disciplinary action for someone who has sinned against the church? (v. 2)

3. How should we "keep the feast"? (v. 8)

4. In what manner should Christians treat those who live in sin? (v. 11)

5. What should believers do to the "wicked person"? (v. 13)

DISCUSS THE MEANING

1. Explain the meaning of 1 Corinthians 5:5: "To deliver such an one unto Satan for the destruction of the flesh, that the spirit may be saved in the day of the Lord Jesus."

2. Paul made a reference to the effect of a "little leaven" in relation to the "whole lump." In terms of sin, what point was he trying to get across to the church? (v. 6)

LESSON IN SOCIETY

One of the biggest challenges that faces Christians and the church is that we live in a world where sin runs rampant. For every person who chooses right, there is one who chooses darkness. Apostle Paul realized that Christians had to live daily with sinful people, and told the church of Corinth "not to company" with them (v. 9). He didn't intend this to mean that Christians should snub them or not be personable towards them, for to do so would not be in keeping with our Christian character. We should, whenever possible, offer our own testimonies and evangelize sinners in hopes of winning souls for Christ.

One of the ways to win over those who choose darkness is to "sell" them on the greatness of God. This is done by being a walking example of the grace and gifts given by the Lord. Are you a walking example of the goodness of God? Can men of the world tell by your attitude and behavior that you are living for Christ?

MAKE IT HAPPEN

We have learned that the tiniest sin, just "a little leaven," has destructive powers. It is capable of working itself throughout the church bringing with it disharmony and division.

Do some introspection. Are you holding on to a sinful behavior that could eventually harm the church? Commit yourself this week to "purging" yourself of any vice or behavior that is not pleasing to the Lord.

FOLLOW THE SPIRIT

What God wants me to do:

_____

_____

REMEMBER YOUR THOUGHTS

Special insights you have learned:

_____

_____

MORE LIGHT ON THE TEXT
1 CORINTHIANS 5:1-13

5:1 It is reported commonly that there is fornication among you, and such fornication as is not so much named among the Gentiles, that one should have his father's wife.

Paul, like us, expresses dismay that a step-son could sleep with his step-mother. The nature of the problem is the sin of fornication or sexual immorality. The horror rests in how this sin has been published so that the entire Corinthian church was smeared with mud. Horror led Paul to decide to come "with a rod in hand" to punish them. A man committed an act of *porneia*, or "sexual immorality" (from which the English word *pornography* is derived). The sin was not only terrible before the Christian believers, it was also repulsive to non-believers. It brought division in the church. Paul contends that the sinner must be expelled from the community. A man sleeping with his father's wife was unheard of.

The term *porneia* appears in Paul's catalog of unwanted vices. It is a principle sin because it is committed in one's own body. A thief can return stolen property to the owner, but once sexual immorality is committed it puts an indelible mark on the person since it is committed within the person's body. The sad thing is that the Corinthians seem to condone the sinful acts since they had not taken disciplinary actions against the offender. Pagans would not condone it.

Too often in this country we hear of incest, of fathers sexually abusing their daughters, or of rape and other forms of sexual misconduct. How could a Christian do such a thing?

2 And ye are puffed up, and have not rather mourned, that he that hath done this deed might be taken away from among you.

Not only was the sinner puffed up for what he did,

but Paul also told the community *perysiomenoi este,* "you are puffed up." In verse 6 the term *kauchema* means that "boasting" was going on in praise of this sin. Instead of depending on Christ, the Corinthians were satisfying their bodily desires. They "should have rather mourned," *epenthesate,* for the sin and should have "cast out," *ekkballo,* the sinner.

Would this be too harsh? Certainly not. Mourning and throwing out the sinner "from their midst," *arethe ak mesou humon,* should be the proper response. Since they did not cast out the sinner from their midst that means that they adorned the sin. Casting out the sinner would be acknowledging God's holiness. In Isaiah 6, Isaiah who had not committed a sin like this, when he heard the chanting of "Holy, holy, holy" in the temple and beheld the glory of God, he was prompted to confess ". . . I am a sinful person living among sinful people" in response to God's holiness (cf. 2 Kings 23:4-5; 22:11; Zechariah 13:23; Ezra 10:3).

It is lack of sense to take pride in sin. It is to forget the theme of the Cross and the sufferings of our Lord. It is to crucify the Lord for the second time. For God has made Christ sin that we may be saved. Christ is our "righteousness," "wisdom," and "sanctification" (holiness, 1 Corinthians 1:30). Sinning boldly is proof that we lack "wisdom" and hence redemption (6:11). Christ died for our sins that we may lead a new life.

3 For I verily, as absent in body, but present in spirit, have judged already, as though I were present, concerning him that hath so done this deed, 4 In the name of our Lord Jesus Christ, when ye are gathered together, in my spirit, with the power of our Lord Jesus Christ, 5 To deliver such an one unto Satan for the destruction of the flesh, that the spirit may be saved in the day of the Lord Jesus.

It does not matter that Paul is not present in person to impose the necessary disciplinary action. In fact, Paul is present with them spiritually as they will take action against the offender. Each believer in Christ has received that Spirit so that he may be in one Spirit with the Lord (2:12-13). The Christian is a temple of God in whom the Holy Spirit dwells (6:19). Indeed, whenever the assembly of spiritual people gather, the Lord is also present in that spiritual gathering, i.e., the church. For Christ is the head of the church. Since nobody has even dared take action, Paul as their pastor decides for them. The sinner must be cast to Satan. In Matthew 18:16-

20, Jesus promised to be in the midst of the church when two or three gather in his name. So the casting out of the sinner is in the authority that the church has been given by the Lord. So, in the assembly, the Holy Spirit and the Lord will be present in decision making.

They will have to cast the sinner to Satan so that his flesh will be destroyed but his spirit will be saved. It is very hard to understand what Paul is talking about by separating the spirit from the body. Sin which is committed in the body affects the spirit and leads to God's judgment. To cast the man to Satan, in fact, means to excommunicate the sinner (1 Timothy 1:20). Moreover, the sinner who is already in Satan's camp must be cast there officially. It is anticipated that his spirit will be saved at last. This will involve total repentance. The verse emphasizes the danger of sin. Churches need to practice church discipline. There is no cheap grace. The reason for church discipline is remedial, loving, and redemptive where the power of Christ is at work.

6 Your glorying is not good. Know ye not that a little leaven leaveneth the whole lump? 7 Purge out therefore the old leaven, that ye may be a new lump, as ye are unleavened. For even Christ our passover is sacrificed for us:

They must get rid of the old leaven instead of taking pride in it. The Corinthians, like every Christian, are "a new batch without yeast." So what may contaminate the lot must be *ekkathairo* "cleaned out," in the sense of excommunicating the offender. That is the only remedy. The batch without yeast is the congregation that is clean before each other and before the Lord. The evil that has entered the church must be cast away.

The fact remains which makes all things new: "Christ our Passover has been sacrificed" (v. 7). The Passover *Pascha* refers to the Jewish Passover which required that the old batch be removed from the house. In Egypt, they had offered their sacrifice in order that the destroying angel might pass over them. The same analogy is used here with reference to getting rid of sexual immorality since Christ as our Passover lamb has been offered. Emphasis is on Christian emergence to new life in Christ, so that the symbolism of yeast makes an important emphasis (cf. Exodus 12:15; 13:7). This had to be done before the *Pascha* celebration. But Christ as our Passover lamb has already been sacrificed and sin is supposed to have been cast away.

8 Therefore let us keep the feast, not with

old leaven, neither with the leaven of malice and wickedness; but with the unleavened bread of sincerity and truth.

Since Christians have been washed and purified, the sinner must be excommunicated in order for them to stay uncontaminated. Every Christian must remain new. The old order must be reformed and a new one must emerge. So, it is necessary to excommunicate the incestuous offender. Christians must be a new loaf for the Passover meal. The sacrifice on the cross has already been completed. Christ died in order to recreate us into a new people.

9 I wrote unto you in an epistle not to company with fornicators: 10 Yet not altogether with the fornicators of this world, or with the covetous, or extortioners, or with idolaters; for then must ye needs go out of the world.

Paul reminds the Corinthians that he had warned them before in another letter. A pastor who fails to warn his\her members of the congregation about the danger of sin stands himself in jeopardy before God's judgment. Indeed, we cannot as Christians cut ourselves off from the world and its people. We meet them in our neighborhood, in stores where we purchase our necessities. But Christians ought to be light and salt in the world (Matthew 5:13-14). If not, we would have to leave the world altogether. In His high priestly prayer in John 17, Jesus prays that His disciples not be taken out of this world but be protected from the evil one. Indeed, the world is full of greedy people, swindlers, thieves, idolaters, and unbelievers. But Christians ought to enlighten the world's sinners with the Gospel.

11 But now I have written unto you not to keep company, if any that is called a brother be a fornicator, or covetous, or an idolater, or a railer, or a drunkard, or an extortioner; with such a one no not to eat.

Whoever belongs to the community, i.e., a brother or sister in Christ, should not practice such sins and proudly rejoice in them. Such a person should be excommunicated. The incestuous man has become what a Christian should never be. He must be cast out. Paul adds a few more vices that a Christian should not involve herself/himself into simply as examples, for there are many more than that (see Galatians 5:19ff). To commit sin boldly is to abide in the old self. With such a sinner, Christians should not even share a meal

(cf. 2 John 10). This does not refer to sharing the Lord's Supper but the ordinary table. Jesus ate with sinners and Paul sees that as permissible. What he forbids are those who are members of the community participating in the sins that they recanted during or before their baptism.

12 For what have I to do to judge them also that are without? Do not ye judge them that are within?

Christians can only discipline those who are insiders. Those who are not Christians cannot be disciplined by Christians. Therefore, the Christian offender, being an insider, must be judged for his\her irresponsibility

13 But them that are without God judgeth. Therefore put away from among yourselves that wicked person.

The scope has been limited to those who are insiders, those who belong to the church. Believers must face church discipline. God is responsible for those outside the church. We as Christians will not play the role of God. Paul summarizes with a note from Deuteronomy 17:7, that the offender must be expelled from the church. So the church must not tolerate bold sinners who take pride in sinful behavior.

DAILY BIBLE READING

M: Sexual Immorality Defiles the Church
1 Corinthians 5:1-8
T: Stay Away from Sexual Immorality
1 Corinthians 5:9-13
W: Resist Lawsuits among Believers
1 Corinthians 6:1-11
T: Watch Your Tongue!
James 3:1-12
F: Choose Wisdom that Is from Above
James 3:13-18
S: Submit to God's Will and Way
James 4:1-10
S: Seek Humility and Avoid Judging
James 4:11-17

TEACHING TIPS

April 2
Bible Study Guide 5

1. Words You Should Know

A. Good (1 Corinthians 7:1)—As used here, the word "good" means expedient, profitable, or advisable.

B. Sanctified (v. 14)—Its use here means to be set apart for special use, care, and attention.

2. Teacher Preparation

This lesson is about sexual intimacy and celibacy, marriage and remaining single, and divorce and remarriage. But you can handle it! Simply follow God's Word. Paul's counsel is not as complicated as it may first appear.

A. Begin your preparation with prayer. Ask God to give you freedom to talk about a subject that may at first be uncomfortable for some to talk about. Read the BACKGROUND section for today's lesson. Then read all of 1 Corinthians 7 at least three or four times. This should give you a real grasp of the issues involved in Paul's counsel.

3. Starting the Lesson

Review with your students the BACKGROUND section of their Student Manuals. Explain that Paul's counsel is best understood against this background material.

4. Getting into the Lesson

Outline the areas of concern to be discussed:

A. Advice to Married Persons about Sexual Intimacy (1 Corinthians 7:1-5)

B. Advice to Single Christians about Marrying or Remaining Single (vv. 8-9)

C. Advice to All Christians about Separation and Divorce (vv. 10-16)

5. Relating the Lesson to Life

Ask each of your students to share one question regarding each of the areas to be discussed in the outline above. List 10 or 15 of their questions on the chalkboard.

A. Read the printed text aloud and try to find answers to the questions your students have asked. This step can be accomplished in small groups.

B. Discuss any questions which you or your students feel were not answered in the printed text.

6. Arousing Action

Have your students to read the MAKE IT HAPPEN section of their Student Manuals. Encourage them to identify with one of the questions listed there and commit to doing something about it on the days of this coming week.

WORSHIP GUIDE

For the Superintendent or Teacher
Theme: Counsel Concerning Marriage
Theme Song: Doxology
Scripture: Psalm 8:3-5
Song: What a Fellowship
Devotional Thought: Thank You, O God, for creating me and for helping me to shape and manage my life.

COUNSEL CONCERNING MARRIAGE

Bible Background • 1 CORINTHIANS 6:12—7:16
Printed Text • 1 CORINTHIANS 7:1-5, 8-16
Devotional Reading • 1CORINTHIANS 7:25-35

LESSON AIM

To engage students in a dialogue about Christian marriage and about the Apostle Paul's counsel for handling specific problems related to marriage in an immoral society.

KEEP IN MIND

"What? know ye not that your body is the temple of the Holy Ghost which is in you, which ye have of God, and ye are not your own?" (1 Corinthians 6:19).

FOCAL VERSES

1 CORINTHIANS 7:1 Now concerning the things whereof ye wrote unto me: It is good for a man not to touch a woman.

2 Nevertheless, to avoid fornication, let every man have his own wife, and let every woman have her own husband.

3 Let the husband render unto the wife due benevolence: and likewise also the wife unto the husband.

4 The wife hath not power of her own body, but the husband: and likewise also the husband hath not power of his own body, but the wife.

5 Defraud ye not one the other, except it be with consent for a time, that ye may give yourselves to fasting and prayer; and come together again, that Satan tempt you not for your incontinency.

8 I say therefore to the unmarried and widows, It is good for them if they abide even as I.

9 But if they cannot contain, let them marry: for it is better to marry than to burn.

10 And unto the married I command, yet not I, but the Lord, Let not the wife depart from her husband:

LESSON OVERVIEW

LESSON AIM
KEEP IN MIND
FOCAL VERSES
IN FOCUS
THE PEOPLE, PLACES, AND TIMES
BACKGROUND
AT-A-GLANCE
IN DEPTH
SEARCH THE SCRIPTURES
DISCUSS THE MEANING
LESSON IN OUR SOCIETY
MAKE IT HAPPEN
FOLLOW THE SPIRIT
REMEMBER YOUR THOUGHTS
MORE LIGHT ON THE TEXT
DAILY BIBLE READINGS

11 But and if she depart, let her remain unmarried, or be reconciled to her husband: and let not the husband put away his wife.

12 But to the rest speak I, not the Lord: If any brother hath a wife that believeth not, and she be pleased to dwell with him, let him not put her away.

APRIL 2nd

13 And the woman which hath an husband that believeth not, and if he be pleased to dwell with her, let her not leave him.

14 For the unbelieving husband is sanctified by the wife, and the unbelieving wife is sanctified by the husband: else were your children unclean; but now are they holy.

15 But if the unbelieving depart, let him depart. A brother or a sister is not under bondage in such cases: but God hath called us to peace.

16 For what knowest thou, O wife, whether thou shalt save thy husband? or how knowest thou, O man, whether thou shalt save thy wife?

IN FOCUS

Questions about marriage, divorce and remarriage, sexual intimacy, and the advantages and disadvantages of the single life have been discussed since the beginning of humankind. Questions emerged during the Apostle Paul's day and guided by the revelation he had, he offered his counsel.

The issues in Paul's day often found him giving both a word from the Lord, as well as his own personal advice. Such is still the case. Many of the issues involving sexual intimacy, marriage, divorce, remarriage, and the single life continue to cry out for solutions. On some issues, God's Word is clear. On other issues, we are left to pursue conclusions reached after much prayer and counsel.

A careful study of 1 Corinthians should heighten one's appreciation for the Apostle Paul who dealt with some sticky issues without taking sides when he could have easily done so.

Paul saw good in both celibacy and in marriage. He correctly understood that just as some are gifted to be married, others are gifted to lead a single life. In either case, however, Paul reminded his audience that God calls all to peace, purity, and godliness. The need for all persons, single and married, to manage their sexual desires is important.

While we do not often think of the need for married persons to manage their sexual desires, the need is great. If this were not so, incest, sexual abuse, and adultery would not exist. Single persons are not the only ones called by God to manage their sexual desires. The call extends even to those who are married. Oftentimes single persons do a better job of managing their sexual desires than do those who are married.

Today's lesson gives us an opportunity to review what God's Word has to say about marriage and the single life in a sex-crazed world.

THE PEOPLE, PLACES, AND TIMES

The Gospel of Jesus Christ can positively impact every area of our lives; even our marriages, sexual desires, and relationships. There is perhaps no area of our lives that needs to be touched by the Gospel of Christ more than our marriages and sexual selves. Believers in every generation have need to know God's concept of marriage. Believers also have need to know what God had in mind when He gave us the gift of sexuality.

At a time in our history when one sexual encounter can result in HIV infection, it is critical that we review again and again God's will and plan for managing our marriages and sexual desires. What the Christian church has said for centuries and contemporary studies now affirm is that religion has the capacity to impact one's marriage and sexual habits for good.

Some students of human relationships have gone so far as to say that marriage and family is the primary spiritual community. It started with God and if it is to know good health it must continue with God. It still remains true, however, that all of the questions about marriage, divorce, and sexuality were not answered in Jesus' and Paul's day. The chances are very great that they all will not be answered in our day. As in Paul's day, advice will continue to be given in light of God's commands and the changing circumstances of the times.

Let us pray that God will continue to be gracious toward us while we seek to maximize the joys and blessing that can accrue to those who choose to lead a celibate or married life. Both can bring honor and glory to God and His kingdom.

BACKGROUND

There appears to have been some very vocal people in the Corinthian church who advocated celibacy for all Christians, including those who were married. This pro-celibacy faction made their position clear: "It is good," they said, "for a man not to marry" (1 Corinthians 7:1, NIV). Moreover, this group recommended divorce for those who could not remain celibate within marriage.

A survey of the sexual practices in Corinth will show that pro-celibacy was a radical reaction to rampant immorality. Corinth was one of the most immoral cities in the ancient world. Mention any kind of sexual deviation and it was openly practiced in Corinth. All aspects of Corinthian life were permeated with sexual immorality. "To live like a Corinthian" was the password for any reference to loose living.

Even the religion of Corinth revolved around sexual activity. Sex was the goddess of Corinth. The Greek goddess of love, Aphrodite, was at the center of worship in Corinth. A temple constructed and maintained in her honor housed 1,000 sacred prostitutes whose services were utilized by local residents, tourists, and traveling tradesmen from far and wide. Sex was so much a part of Corinthian life that decent people could not walk the streets without being accosted or eyed for involvement in some sexual activity. Those who write about life in ancient Greece refer to Corinth as the "cesspool of immorality."

There were those in Corinth, however, who wanted things to be different. They understood that sexual immorality was contrary to the ways and will of the Creator God. They believed that the God revealed in Jesus Christ called for a higher standard of living, one of purity and godliness. Therefore, in an effort to counteract immorality, the pendulum of their thought swung to the opposite extreme. In essence, they promoted celibacy for all as the best way to protect oneself against the enticements and temptations of sexual immorality. Their message was heard and believed by enough people in the church at Corinth to occasion some conflict with those of the church who were not in agreement with the pro-celibacy faction.

In an effort to bring closure to this dispute, the church wrote the Apostle Paul in hope that he could advise them about what the Lord taught concerning sexual intimacy and celibacy, marriage and remaining single, and divorce and remarriage. Thus, Paul's opening statement, "Now for the matters you wrote about" (1 Corinthians 7:1, NIV).

Like a wise pastoral counselor, Paul avoids allowing himself to be identified with either the pro-celibacy or the pro-marriage factions. Even though Paul was practicing celibacy, he does not take sides with those who favored celibacy. Nor does Paul allow his pro-marriage background in Judaism to push him to take up sides with those who favored marriage. Rather, Paul takes the high road and recognizes the strengths in both celibacy and marriage.

AT-A-GLANCE

1. Advice to Married Persons about Sexual Intimacy (1 Corinthians 7:1-5)
2. Advice to Single Christians about Marrying or Remaining Single (1 Corinthians 7:8-9)
3. Advice to All Christians about Separation and Divorce (1 Corinthians 7:10-16)

IN DEPTH

1. Advice to Married Persons about Sexual Intimacy (1 Corinthians 7:1-5)

Fully aware of the enticements of easy sex in Corinth, Paul counsels that, while it may be expedient and profitable in certain situations for a man not to marry (1 Corinthians 7:1b), marriage can be a helpful deterrent to immorality. Therefore, "each man should have his own wife, and each woman her own husband" (1 Corinthians 7:2). Paul recognizes that there are times when circumstances dictate that it is unwise to marry; i.e., times of persecution, war, disease, or sickness. On the other hand, because of rampant immorality everyone should have his or her own spouse.

Paul's counsel has double meaning. For to say that marriage can be a helpful deterrent to immorality is to imply that outside of marriage, a man and woman should not be sexually intimate. Paul's counsel is supported by the writer of Hebrews 13:4: "Marriage should be honored by all, and the marriage bed kept pure, for God will judge the adulterer and all the sexually immoral" (NIV).

Having affirmed both marriage and celibacy as viable options for a Christian lifestyle, Paul proceeds to help the Corinthians understand the role of sex in marriage. Paul is most direct in saying that each party in a marriage owes sex to his or her partner. Husbands and wives are responsible to help assure the sexual happiness of each other (1 Corinthians 7:3). It is incumbent upon married persons to be sexually intimate often enough so as not to frustrate or tempt either person in the relationship to cheat on the other. If health allows, husbands and wives should have free access to each other's bodies. Neither the husband nor the wife have complete authority over their own bodies (vv. 3-4). Each should extend to the other equal privileges of sexual intimacy.

Even though husbands and wives are not to deprive one another of sexual intimacy, Paul does allow for one exception. Where there is mutual consent and agreement to a limited time, it is both good and expected that husbands and wives will consent to abstain from sexual activity in order to give themselves more fully to prayer and to the Lord's work. Paul allows that spiritual reasons, including the need and time for fasting and prayer, should take precedence over sexual activity. This is not, however, to be forced upon one's spouse. Rather, it is done through mutual consent and for a mutually agreed upon period of time, lest Satan use the occasion to tempt either spouse due to "lack of self-control" (1 Corinthians 7:5b).

Paul's advice to married persons about sexual intimacy is both needed and relevant for our day. Like the society of ancient Corinth, ours is also a sex-crazed society. Believers have need to be reminded that the married couple is to cleave together, seeking always to fulfill the sexual hungers of each other. By mutual consent they should agree to avoid sexual activity with each other so that they may give themselves to fasting and prayer. This arrangement, however, should be for a reasonable period of time, lest either party to the marriage is tempted to seek sexual satisfaction through yielding to allurements outside one's own marriage.

2. Advice to Single Christians about Marrying or Remaining Single (1 Corinthians 7:8-9)

In his advice to single Christians, Paul again appeals to the advantages of both celibacy and marriage. Paul advocated that unmarried persons and widows remain single if they can practice celibacy. Otherwise, he advised, single persons should marry.

Paul's advice to remain single is offered on the assumption that "the present crisis" dictates that all persons should remain as they are. Moreover, he adds, "those who marry will face many troubles in this life, and I want to spare you this" (1 Corinthians 7:26, 28b). Paul further notes that to remain single affords one more time to give to the Lord's work (1 Corinthians 7:35b).

It is not clear what Paul has in mind when he refers to the "present crisis." One would think, however, that because of "the present crisis" those who remain single will also face many troubles in this life. It appears that the Corinthians were facing some severe distress and persecution. But the nature of that distress is not indicated. Some have suggested that the threat of persecution was an ever-present reality, which placed the Christians under constant pressure from a hostile world. In any event, Paul advises the unmarried and the widows to remain unmarried (1 Corinthians 7:8), providing they can practice celibacy (1 Corinthians 7:9). If single persons cannot practice celibacy, Paul's advice is that they should get married. It is better to risk marriage under "the present crisis," than to be consumed by one's own sexual passions (1 Corinthians 7:9b).

To remain single is an excellent course of action if one can remain pure and practice godliness. To remain single is a poor course of action if it results in sexual immorality. Again, Paul's counsel in this matter is useful in our day. To remain single has its advantages and disadvantages. To get married has its advantages and disadvantages. All persons would do well to seek counsel and advice when making such decisions.

3. Advice to All Christians about Separation and Divorce (1 Corinthians 7:10-16)

The counsel Paul gives regarding separation and divorce is not merely his personal advice. He notes from the beginning that his comments about separation and divorce are a command from the Lord. Where a Christian wife and husband are concerned, the "wife must not separate from her husband . . . husband must not divorce his wife" (1 Corinthians 7:10b, 11b). As believers, Paul asserted that neither the husband nor the wife should initiate separation or divorce. However, should separation or divorce occur, they should remain unmarried or be reconciled to each other (1 Corinthians 7:11a).

In reading verses 10-11, it should be noted that Paul uses the words separate and divorce interchangeably. However, if these words mean something different, it is because the woman was not legally entitled to divorce her husband. She could, however, simply move out, separate herself from her husband. In the society of Paul's day, only the man was legally entitled to seek a divorce from his wife.

In verses 12 through 16, Paul turns to give his personal advice, not the Lord's command, to believers married to unbelievers. In the case of marriage to an unbeliever, divorce is discouraged because the union may result in salvation for the unbeliever.

It is possible that some believers in Corinth feared that they might become defiled were they to have sexual relations with their unbelieving spouse. Paul disagrees and offers verse 14 as the basis for his disagreement: "For the unbelieving husband has been sanctified through his wife, and the unbelieving wife has been sanctified through her believing husband. Otherwise your children would be 'unclean,' but as it is, they are holy."

Paul's rationale, however, is not proof that the unbelieving spouse is or will be saved. To be sanctified in this context means that the unbelieving spouse and the marriage is set apart for special attention from God and the church. Paul's advice here is especially helpful in our day when so many in our churches are married to unbelievers. The church must find a way to relate with special deference to church members' unbelieving spouses. Special effort and priority attention should be given to their inclusion in the church's fellowship and outreach services. When this kind of interest and concern is shown, it encourages and supports the believing spouse to continue with the marriage.

However, Paul wisely adds in verse 15, "if the unbeliever leaves, let him/her do so. A believing man or woman is not bound in such circumstances; God has called us to live in peace." Moreover, "How do you know, wife, whether you will save your husband? Or, how do you know, husband, whether you will save your wife?" (1 Corinthians 7:16). With the adequate care and support of the faith community, the unbelieving spouse may be won to Christ through the faithful witness of the believing spouse.

SEARCH THE SCRIPTURES

1. Why does Paul encourage each man and woman to have his/her own spouse? (1 Corinthians 7:2)

2. When and under what conditions is it okay to deprive one's spouse of sexual intimacy? (vv. 5-6)

3. But if they cannot control themselves _____ _____ they should marry, for _____ _____ . (v. 9)

4. God has called us to _____ . (v. 15)

DISCUSS THE MEANING

1. What does it mean to live a celibate life?

2. In what sense is the unbelieving spouse sanctified by the believing spouse? (1 Corinthians 7:15)

3. What do you think Paul means by "the present crisis"? (v. 26)

LESSON IN OUR SOCIETY

How do you see applying Paul's counsel in your own life? Is his counsel realistic for our day? How can we best follow Paul's counsel in 1 Corinthians 7:10-11 when two believers, who should have never gotten married in the first place, are headed for a divorce?

Every pastor knows of situations where, if Paul's counsel had been followed, the end results would have been much more healthy. God is concerned about our peace. The centuries have shown that people can lead celibate lives and find fulfillment. People can also be married and find fulfillment. The secret in both has very much to do with how we manage our sexual desires. The managing of one's sexual desires is a task for both those who are single and those who are married.

MAKE IT HAPPEN

Each day of this week, take an inventory of your sexual health. If you are married, what is the level of peace in your relationship? Does your estimate of your relationship agree with that of your spouse? If you are single, are you pleased with your management of your sexual desires?

No, these are not easy questions to ponder, but in a sex-crazed society we have need to constantly attend to our sexual health and relationships. If you discover that things are not as they should be, seek help. God wants us to have peace in these intimate areas of our lives.

FOLLOW THE SPIRIT

What God wants me to do:

_____

_____

REMEMBER YOUR THOUGHTS

Special insights you gained:

_____

_____

MORE LIGHT ON THE TEXT
1 CORINTHIANS 7:1-5, 8-16

7:1 Now concerning the things whereof ye wrote unto me: It is good for a man not to touch a woman.

The Corinthian church had written to Paul seeking clarification about a few theological and practical matters that they struggled with. The first issue that Paul addressed was the issue of marriage and sexuality. Until this point in the letter Paul dealt with issues that they, in their spiritual immaturity, did not consider worth dealing with. The phrase *Peri de oon egrapsate*, means "about or concerning the things of which you wrote me," suggests that Paul was at a turning point in the epistle. This section concerns matters arising from every day interaction with others. Until now Paul appears to deal with the internal relationships between members of the ecclesiastical community. Beginning with verse 7:1 he starts dealing with the problems surfacing between Christians and the pagan world.

The first issue dealt with here relates to male/female relationships. The question in Greek reads, *Kalon anthropos gunaikos aptesthai*, meaning "it is good for a man not to touch a woman." The word translated "good" is the Greek word *Kalon* (pronounced **Ka-lon**) means beautiful, good, or virtuous. It has to do with appearance or what philosophers call "mores." Simply put, since Paul has insisted that the Corinthians should keep away from all appearance of evil, can a man have a relationship with a woman and still be a child of God? Is it unseemly for a man to touch a woman? Note also that Paul does not use the Greek word for the male gender; he uses the Greek word *anthropos*, which is the equivalent to the Hebrew *ha adam*. For the woman he uses the term *gunaikos* which specifically refers to wife. Thus, the question really is directed to the spiritual decency of marriage. In other words, is it okay for a man to touch his wife?

"It is well for a man not to touch a woman." This is the general thesis. The meaning of "touch" refers to sexual contact specifically, not just general physical contact. Paul states this general thesis, followed by a number of exceptions. Thus, this general statement should not be interpreted as Paul denouncing the institution of marriage. Paul applauds any man or woman who has enough control of his or her sexual desires to remain free of distraction from sexual pursuits and marital relationships (7:28-31). But if a man or woman does not have such self-control, then by all means they should marry.

Some of the Corinthians argued for an ascetic lifestyle, the complete abstinence from sex. This type of asceticism was not widely accepted, for the obligation to marry was quite strong. Girls were ready for marriage by age 15, boys by age 18. The economy was greatly dependent upon people who were entering into marriage, creating families, and establishing households. There was very little expectation that these young women and men would remain virgins all their lives. However, the acceptable context for sexual expression was within a marital relationship.

2 Nevertheless, to avoid fornication, let every man have his own wife, and let every woman have her own husband.

Here Paul uses the plural form of the word fornication (Greek *porneias*, translated as sexual immorality), to denote the common occurrence of a variety of sexual practices, including fornication (sex outside of marriage), adultery, prostitution, sodomy, homosexuality, incest, etc.

Paul understood the reality of the human condition, that most people are not called to a celibate lifestyle. Also prevalent was a lack of self-control with regard to sexual desires. Therefore, if self-control is lacking, marry a wife or husband and fulfill that desire within the marriage. The object of that sexual desire is to become one flesh (Genesis 24; 1 Corinthians 6:16). This oneness cannot be achieved while going from person to person.

3 Let the husband render unto the wife due benevolence: and likewise also the wife unto the husband.

The way Paul phrases this verse suggests that some in Corinth were refusing to enter into relationship with their spouse. Paul urges them to take the posture of continual mutuality. The Greek word *apodidotow* suggests an unbroken act of self-giving; connected to the Greek word *Ophellen* (pronounced **o-fey-len**) translates into the phrase "due benevolence" or "fellowship."

Both wife and husband equally share the rights to conjugal relations. It is part of the marital framework, which also includes mutual caring, economic provisions, a home, and the mutual working towards building a life together. Sexual rights cannot be demanded in isolation of these other components, which make up the marital relationship.

4 The wife hath not power of her own body, but the husband: and likewise also the husband hath not power of his own body, but the wife.

Neither spouse has the right to claim sole authority over their bodies, without consideration of the other, because marriage is an agreement to join oneself to another that these two may become one. By virtue of the marriage, neither husband nor wife, has sole consideration of his or her body. Mutual consideration should be maintained throughout the relationship.

5 Defraud ye not one the other, except it be with consent for a time, that ye may give yourselves to fasting and prayer; and come together again, that Satan tempt you not for your incontinency.

Paul allows for the possibility of sexual abstention being structured into a marriage, if it is by agreement for a specified period of time. Sexual desire is a strong drive and can be repressed more easily if one knows there is an end in sight. It is useful to set sex aside, at times, in order to devote oneself more fully to God. If a person's sexuality is out of control, this sex drive can become idolatrous, replacing any concern for devotion to God. On the other hand, many zealous religious practitioners place great strains on spouses and children by turning to their devotion to God and ignoring their worldly obligations. Paul identifies some parameters, which allow for balance, devotion to God, and fulfillment of the marriage. This does not preclude other conditions when abstinence may be necessary, e. g., during a fragile pregnancy or in the weeks following birth.

At the end of the agreed time, Paul warns that the couple should restore their intimate relations in order to avoid temptation. For the one with the least amount of self-control will eventually seek to fulfill that sexual desire somewhere else. This desire can become irrepressible, seeming to take on its own diabolical personality.

8 I say therefore to the unmarried and widows, It is good for them if they abide even as I.

The unmarried men, *agamos*, most likely refers to men who are no longer married as a result of divorce or death. It is possible to include men who are not yet married in the interpretation of *agamos*, but it is not likely given the importance of marriage to the culture. For those men and women who have done the marriage thing but now find themselves single, Paul encourages them to remain single, even as Paul himself does. But if they are not practicing self-control, they should marry. For it is better to marry than to be aflame.

Again Paul considers the reality that not everyone can exercise self-control, particularly over a long period of time. This level of self-control is to be considered a gift (see Matthew 19:10-12); not everyone can do it. Thus, rather than burn (some add "with passion"), it is better to go on and remarry. It is also possible to interpret "to burn" as burning in hell as a punishment for the sin of fornication, particularly in light of the close reference to Satan.

10 And unto the married I command, yet not I, but the Lord, Let not the wife depart from her husband:

For this next piece of advice, Paul draws upon the authority of the words of Jesus. Those who are married should not seek to dissolve their marriage. This is the statement of general principle. In Matthew 19, Jesus argued with the Pharisees that divorce was not permitted in the beginning, but was only allowed by Moses because of the hardness of people's hearts. They could not forgive. Divorce was permitted only when the wife was unchaste. Short of this, divorce was not permitted by Moses.

In Judaism, a woman was not allowed to initiate divorce at all, but could separate from her husband and return to her father's home. This could be done for a number of reasons such as abandonment, unchastity, poverty, abusiveness, or not meeting one's sexual obligations. Once she was gone for a period of time, it was up to the husband to come and win her heart back, or to divorce her. Much of this carried over into early Christianity as well.

11 But and if she depart, let her remain unmarried, or be reconciled to her husband: and let not the husband put away his wife.

M: Jesus Teaches about Divorce
Mark 10:1-9
T: Strive for Moral Purity
1 Corinthians 6:12-20
W: Be Faithful to Your Spouse
1 Corinthians 7:1-7
T: Directions for Single and
Married Life
1 Corinthians 7:8-16
F: Remain with God above All Else
1 Corinthians 7:17-24
S: Married or Not, the Time Is
Short
1 Corinthians 7:25-31
S: Does Marriage Hinder
Discipleship?
1 Corinthians 7:32-40

Continuing with the emphasis of Jesus' argument, the marriage should remain in tact. The husband should not divorce his wife. The wife should be open to reconciliation, but if that is not possible, then she should remain single. This was due to some concern that remarriage would be considered adultery, but it is not clear whether this is meant for the wife only or the husband as well.

12 But to the rest speak I, not the Lord: If any brother hath a wife that believeth not, and she be pleased to dwell with him, let him not put her away.

Paul makes a distinction between the Lord's command and his own interpretation of Jesus' words. "The rest" refers to the married persons whose spouses are not of the faith. If any brother, one who is a believer, has a wife who chooses not to become a believer, he should not seek to divorce her if she agrees to continue in the marriage. Christianity was not to make light of the marriage bond.

13 And the woman which hath an husband that believeth not, and if he be pleased to dwell with her, let her not leave him.

The context warrants that we understand the woman to be a Christian. If her husband chooses not to become a believer, she should not seek to separate from him if he con-

sents to continue in the marriage. The object was to keep the marriage intact, if both could agree to do so.

In the history of Judaism, a mixed-marriage across ethnic, but particularly across religious lines was at times viewed disdainfully, and at other times with neutrality (see Ezra, Nehemiah, Ruth, Genesis). The religious difference was thought to contaminate the person's religious convictions and affections. Thus, at times, one can find the prophets demanding that mixed marriages be severed. The difference between the practice of Judaism, and that of Christianity may lie in fact that, in Christianity, salvation was not dependent on the practitioner's deeds; wherein in Judaism it was tantamount.

14 For the unbelieving husband is sanctified by the wife, and the unbelieving wife is sanctified by the husband: else were your children unclean; but now are they holy.

The belief of one partner brings the other and their children into the circle of salvation.

15 But if the unbelieving depart, let him depart. A brother or a sister is not under bondage in such cases: but God hath called us to peace.

If the unbelieving partner cannot consent to remain in the marriage, because of the belief of the believing partner, then a divorce is to be granted to the unbeliever. The believer is no longer bound, and remarriage is possible. According to Paul's interpretation, it seems better to permit the divorce, than to try to force an unhappy and contentious situation to persist. But notice that the onus of the decision to separate is not upon the believer.

16 For what knowest thou, O wife, whether thou shalt save thy husband? or how knowest thou, O man, whether thou shalt save thy wife?

This statement seems to raise some doubt or place limitation on the meaning of sanctification. If on one hand the believer sanctifies the unbeliever, why is the saving in doubt?

This verse is alternately translated as: "Wife, for all you know, you might save your husband. Husband, for all you know you might save your wife." The question disputed in the translation of the prepositions *ei* and *ean* concerns whether their sense is affirmative or negative. Some argue that they imply neither, but the context provides the sense. This alternate translation is more affirmative, being rendered more as a positive statement, than a question at all.

TEACHING TIPS

April 9
Bible Study Guide 6

1. Words You Should Know

A. Knowledge. (used throughout the text)—Not limited to things intellectual, but rather refers also to information that produces results and leads to positive action. It is this understanding of knowledge that brings Paul to say in 1 Corinthians 13:2 that knowledge without love amounts to nothing.

B. Idols. (used throughout the text)—A material object or image to which one attributes deity and worships it as such.

C. Weak, or weak conscience. (vv. 7-12)—Used here it refers to the level of one's moral awareness and apparent inability to discriminate in matters of choice when intellect conflicts with emotions.

2. Teacher Preparation

A. In addition to reading 1 Corinthians 8, read also 1 Corinthians 10:25-30, and Romans 14:1—15:13. For a better understanding of these texts, read them several times from the Living Bible.

B. Next read IN FOCUS. On the basis of the biblical texts in section A above, ponder how you would answer the questions near the end of IN FOCUS. Identify a similar situation in your own life. Rehearse it sufficiently and open your teaching session by sharing it with your students.

C. Materials needed: Bibles (giving students different translations will help to enhance the overall quality of student participation). It would be helpful if a chalkboard is available.

3. Starting the Lesson

A. Remind the class of the aim of today's lesson; i.e., to identify and explore the principles that should guide our choices and the exercise of our freedom when the Bible gives no clear command. Ask students to identify some examples; e.g., drinking alcoholic beverages, wearing suggestive forms of dress, listening to certain kinds of music, playing games that sometimes involve gambling, engaging in premarital physical contact, buying lottery tickets that support worthy government projects, etc.

B. Share the example from your personal life which you identified above in the Teacher Preparation section.

C. Ask students to share what they would have done had they been in your situation. If you have no personal story to share, utilize the IN FOCUS story told above and have students discuss some of the questions listed near the end of IN FOCUS. Make sure you give yourself enough time to get into the biblical material and help students relate the lesson to real situations in their own lives.

4. Getting into the Lesson

A. Ask a student to read the BACKGROUND article aloud. Discuss the article only for purposes of clarity.

B. Based on this article, ask students to identify three or four problems they think should be addressed. List these on the chalkboard. Now read the biblical text, 1 Corinthians 8, and ask the students to indicate how the text responds to the problems they identified. Did they identify problems to which the text does not speak? If so, can love provide an answer?

5. Relating the Lesson to Life

A. Discuss why believers should be concerned about the impact of their behavior upon others.

B. Ask students to share what they learned from today's lesson.

6. Arousing Action

A. Review the MAKE IT HAPPEN suggestions and ask for a show of hands of those who will commit to doing what it outlines.

B. Close the session with prayer asking God to help them to deepen their spiritual lives in order that they might know better how to let love govern their conduct in relationships with others.

WORSHIP GUIDE

For the Superintendent or Teacher
Theme: Let Love Abound
Theme Song: "Bind Us Together"
Scripture: 1 Corinthians 10:23-32
Song: "Blest Be the Tie That Binds"
Devotional Thought: Grant that we might acknowledge You in all our ways, O God. Make our brothers and sisters our concern. May what we do and say strengthen and encourage them, for Christ's sake. Amen.

CONCERNING LOVE AND KNOWLEDGE

Bible Background • 1 CORINTHIANS 8
Printed Text • 1 CORINTHIANS 8
Devotional Reading • 1 CORINTHIANS 10:23—11:1

LESSON AIM

By the end of the lesson, students will identify and discuss what principles should guide their choices and the exercise of their freedom when the Bible gives no clear command.

KEEP IN MIND

"And if any man think that he knoweth any thing, he knoweth nothing yet as he ought to know. But if any man love God, the same is known of him" (1 Corinthians 8:2-3).

FOCAL VERSES

1 CORINTHIANS 8:1 Now as touching things offered unto idols, we know that we all have knowledge. Knowledge puffeth up, but charity edifieth.

2 And if any man think that he knoweth any thing, he knoweth nothing yet as he ought to know.

3 But if any man love God, the same is known of him.

4 As concerning therefore the eating of those things that are offered in sacrifice unto idols, we know that an idol is nothing in the world, and that there is none other God but one.

5 For though there be that are called gods, whether in heaven or in earth, (as there be gods many, and lords many,)

6 But to us there is but one God, the Father, of whom are all things, and we in him; and one Lord Jesus Christ, by whom are all things, and we by him.

7 Howbeit there is not in every man that knowledge: for some with conscience of the idol unto this hour eat it as a thing offered unto an idol; and their conscience being weak is defiled.

8 But meat commendeth us not to God: for neither, if we eat, are we the better; neither, if we eat not, are we the worse.

9 But take heed lest by any means this liberty of yours become a stumblingblock to them that are weak.

10 For if any man see thee which hast knowledge sit at meat in the idol's temple, shall not the conscience of him which is weak be emboldened to eat those things which are offered to idols;

11 And through thy knowledge shall the weak brother perish, for whom Christ died?

12 But when ye sin so against the brethren, and wound their weak conscience, ye sin against Christ.

13 Wherefore, if meat make my brother to offend, I will eat no flesh while the world standeth, lest I make my brother to offend.

IN FOCUS

Several years ago this writer was sitting in the family room of his home relaxing to the musical sounds of jazz and blues when my pastor dropped by for a visit. He chided me about my musical tastes and suggested that I should not fill my mind with the devil's music. Somewhat puzzled by his comments, I questioned, "What is wrong with my listening to jazz? The blues speak about life and its hardships, and jazz tends to help relax my mind. I enjoy listening to both art forms. They give me a reprieve from stressful distractions."

My pastor went on to tell me about his pre-Christian years when as a young man he spent time in the nightclubs of Chicago, Illinois. "Jazz and low-down-dirty blues," he said, "were the music of choice. In the night clubs," he continued, "wine and other alcoholic beverages flowed freely. Tobacco smoke filled the atmosphere. Men were present to pick-up women, and women were present hoping to be picked up. It was the place to go to let it all hang out. That life style," he said, "was me. However, when I gave my life to Jesus Christ and decided to be one of His followers, I left the night club life behind. But to this day," he added, "when I hear jazz and blues I cannot avoid associating it with my past night club experiences. So much of night club life, life I experienced," he noted, "was unsavory." It did not contribute to leading a Christian lifestyle. Nightclub life is a lifestyle to which I have vowed never to return."

I reminded my pastor that I knew nothing about nightclub life, and therefore, could not feel the depth of his internal struggle. However, I continue to appreciate his emotional honesty and candor. My inability to feel and to fully understand the depth of his struggle, however, does not exonerate me from the need to reevaluate the role and place in my life for these two musical art forms. I know and am convinced in my own mind and heart that listening to blues and jazz music are not sinful for me, nor do they conjure up any unsavory remembrances.

But where my pastor friend is concerned what should I do? Seek to convince him that he is wrong to attribute negative values to these musical art forms? Tell him that this is my house; I will listen to what I want to listen to in my house— even when you come to visit? Or should I stop listening to jazz and blues because my brother does not share my position and knowledge about these art forms? Should I go on listening to such music except in his presence, and if so am I being emotionally dishonest?

What should my pastor friend do? Ignore his conscience and listen to jazz and blues with me? Should he look down on me and judge me as being wrong in my thinking?

Can the Bible help us in this matter? Is there a commandment that says, "Thou shalt not listen to such music as jazz and blues?" In the absence of such a commandment, what principles should guide our thoughts and behavior?

Today's lesson is intended to help identify the principles that should guide one's behavior in the gray areas of life— those areas of life where the Bible gives no clear command and we are free and responsible to cultivate our own conscience, make our own decisions, and pursue our own course of action.

THE PEOPLE, PLACES, AND TIMES

1 Corinthians 8 is a reminder of the significant place of love in our homes, churches, and relationships. No one needed this reminder more than the members of the church in ancient Corinth.

The church in Corinth was an urban, multiracial, multicultural church located in the richest, most cosmopolitan, and most important city in Greece. No people were more gifted, talented, and industrious than the members of the church of God in Corinth (1 Corinthians 1:4-7). They had the best of teachers and preachers. The gifts of the Spirit were very much alive and in use. Anyone who had a spiritual gift could exercise their gift at the Corinthian church. This church could boast a 10-year association with the Apostle Paul who had served in their midst for about a year and a half (Acts 18:11).

Sometime after Paul's departure to organize churches in other cities, things got out of hand. The behavior of the saints in Corinth resulted in a misrepresentation of what life in Christ is all about. The gifts of the spirit were exercised without any controlling disciplines and as a result drew more attention to self than to God. Worship services became more electrifying than edifying (1 Corinthians 14). For a multiplicity of selfish reasons, the saints began to group themselves around selected teachers and preachers (1 Corinthians 1:11-12). Relationships broke down into liberals and conservatives, with the liberals exercising their freedom in ways that became stumbling blocks for the conservatives (1 Corinthians 8). The conservatives, thinking themselves more righteous than the liberals, began to judge the liberals as unchristian. Things got confusing and ugly (1 Corinthians 6). In the midst of the confusion and ugliness, Satan had a heyday causing some to grow apathetic toward the immorality of others (1 Corinthians 5).

Something had to be done. Something had to be said to bring righteous order and mature focus to a gifted people who were all too quickly losing their way. There was need to correct disruptive ways of thinking and to put relationships back into proper perspective. Judgmental attitudes and abusive behavior needed to be eradicated. The gifts of the Spirit needed to come under the control of the Spirit. Living examples were needed to model Christian management of personal rights and freedom. In short, a pastoral word was imperative. 1 Corinthians 8 is the Apostle Paul's inspired response to this need.

BACKGROUND

In the Roman cities of Paul's day, people could eat in a variety of places. Nearly every social and community function served meat that had been offered to idols. Certain social functions, such as weddings, business galas, and civic rallies were oftentimes held in pagan temples. Sometimes they were held in the homes of wealthy individuals who worshiped idol gods. At these gatherings, whether held in pagan temples or in homes owned by wealthy non-believers, a meat offering or sacrifice was usually made to invoke the blessings of the house's idol god.

Depending upon the nature and extent of one's social contacts, Christians were oftentimes invited to attend these friendly functions. But given the character of these social functions, what were Christians to do? Should they attend these events knowing that meat offered to idols would be served? If Christians chose not to attend these events, what repercussions might they incur? What if the Christian's employer sponsored the event? Would the Christian's absence affect job relationships? What about the employer's need for employees to network and develop social contacts for the sake of the business?

This situation posed a problem for the Christians of Paul's day. The problem spilled over into the believer's daily life, in that the meat used in temple sacrifices was put on the market for public purchase. Some Christians, particularly those of Jewish heritage, believed that it was wrong to purchase and to consume such meats. They were convinced in their own minds that meat offered to idols had been tainted through association with idol worship. Some argued that the blood had not been drained according to Levitical code and therefore was not to be eaten. While on the other hand, the Gentile Christians had no such scruples. They were convinced in their minds that it was okay to eat meat used in pagan sacrifices. Moreover, they had no problems going to any social function, whether held in pagan temples or in the homes of idol worshipers.

Obviously, this situation was fertile for attitudes to develop based on radical difference of opinion about one of life's gray areas—an area where there is no clear biblical command. Those who believed it was wrong to eat meat sacrificed to idols were frozen in their position and tended to judge those who ate meat offered to idols as unworthy to be called Christian. Those who believed it was not wrong to eat meat sacrificed to idols were frozen in their position and tended to feel superior in knowledge to those who believed it wrong to eat such meat. Their opinions drove their behavior as each side tried to outdo the other side. Attitudes flared, relationships were threatened as each side defended its opinion. Finally, the Corinthian church decided to write the Apostle Paul about the issue. Paul's response is what 1 Corinthians 8 is all about.

It should also be noted that Paul speaks more pointedly about this issue in 1 Corinthians 10:25-30. Here he emphasizes the freedom of those who have no scruples

about eating meat sacrificed to idols. While in Romans 14:1—15:13, Paul admonishes those who have scruples about eating meat sacrificed to idols not to accuse those who eat such meat of sin. In essence, where the gray areas of life are concerned, Paul places unity of relationships above unity of knowledge. Moreover, Paul counsels all to let love toward those for whom Christ died govern the expression of one's liberty, as well as to check one's tendency to judge the expression of another's liberty.

Today, when the selfish exercise of one's personal rights are often exalted above personal responsibility in relationships, Paul's pastoral limitations are an appropriate and much needed challenge.

AT-A-GLANCE

1. Unity of Relationships Supersedes Unity of Opinions (1 Corinthians 8:1-3)
2. There is But One God (vv. 4-8)
3. The Proper Exercise of Christian Liberty (vv. 9-11)
4. The Role of Love in Christian Conduct (vv. 12-13)

IN DEPTH

1. Unity of Relationships Supersedes Unity of Opinions (1 Corinthians 8:1-3)

The church in Corinth was disputing about several issues. Unable to come to closure on either, they wrote Paul and requested his counsel. This explains Paul's introductory comment, "Now about meat sacrificed to idols."

At least two opinions prevailed among the Corinthian Christians "about meat sacrificed to idols." Some were persuaded that their testimony for Christ would be compromised if they ate meat left over from pagan sacrifices. Moreover, they reasoned, to participate in activities where idol gods were worshiped and meat sacrificed to idols was served would make it appear that they were participants in pagan worship. Other believers, thinking and acting in the name of Christian liberty, did not feel this way. Additionally, persons in each camp rallied around a knowledge base aimed to defend their position and direct their behavior. Unfortunately, however, their opposing opinions gave rise to opposing attitudes that resulted in behavior which threatened Christian fellowship.

Here Paul writes to remind believers in both camps that, rather than promote Christian conduct, knowledge without love produces false pride. But knowledge tempered with love toward God builds up the church and advances the cause of Christ.

Christian fellowship is put at risk when our opinions and our knowledge become ends in themselves. Knowledge plus love is one of the primary means God uses to build up others and thereby enhance Christian relationships. In essence, love for God expressed through proper attitudes and actions toward others, and particularly toward fellow believers, is what true knowledge is all about.

2. There is But One God (vv. 4-8)

Having indicated that love and unity of relationships supersedes opinions and unity of knowledge, Paul proceeds to encourage the Corinthians to unite around four central truths:

A. idols are not real (v. 4b)

B. there is only one God (v. 4c)

C. God provides all things, including food (v. 6)

D. food, including meat, is neutral; i.e., it does not enhance or retard one's relationship with God (v. 8)

Paul recognizes, however, that although some of the Corinthians are intellectually convinced that there is one God, they have not yet internalized this conviction emotionally. Emotionally they continue to be informed by their former beliefs about idol gods. Thus, their conscience is weak, and they will be made to feel guilty if they eat meat knowing it has been sacrificed to an idol (v. 7).

Oftentimes, persons who are able to give intellectual consent to certain behaviors are not able to give emotional consent. In such case, if they pursue actions determined by their intellect while their emotions are not in harmony, they will have defiled their conscience. In the Apostle Paul's thought, one's conscience is "weak" when it does not keep pace with one's intellectual development. Genuine faith development occurs when there is equal concern for both one's intellectual and emotional selves. This is the unstated pastoral concern that informs Paul's counsel to the Corinthians.

3. The Proper Exercise of Christian Liberty (vv. 9-11)

Since food does not enhance or retard one's relationship to God, eating meat is a personal right to be exercised within the context of Christian liberty. Although the exercise of this right will not affect one's relationship to God, it may have consequences for one's brothers and sisters in Christ. Therefore, personal rights cannot be the measure for personal conduct. Christian liberty does not grant freedom to neglect the difficulties of the weak. Eating meat sacrificed to idols is not essential and therefore should not be allowed to "become a stumbling block to the weak" (verse 9).

In verses 10-11, Paul illustrates how even in the name of Christian liberty the careless exercise of one's rights can destroy the faith of the weak and lead them into sin. To curb this possibility, Paul pleads with those who feel drawn to exercise their liberty to first consider the potential consequences of their behavior for others. Paul is most adamant about this potential situation. He concludes that one sins against both the weak and against Christ, when the exercise of personal rights becomes a stumbling block wounding the conscience of the weak.

The proper exercise of Christian liberty is always tempered with love that seeks to help the weak and sees everyone as persons for whom Christ has died.

4. The Role of Love in Christian Conduct (vv. 12-13)

Where the welfare of our brothers and sisters are concerned, love makes us sensitive to the moral sensibilities of others. Love makes us sensitive to our influence upon others and guides our behavior. Love knows how to yield to the interests of others without compromising one's own personal integrity. Love seeks to build up others. "Love is not self-seeking" (1 Corinthians 13:5b, NIV). Love is not enamored with self-gain and self-gratification. Love does not insist on its own rights. Love shows respect for the conscience and convictions of one's fellow believers.

When the choice is between one's personal rights and the welfare of others, love will choose to serve the welfare of others. In the final analysis, love knows when not to eat the meat that causes others to fall into sin.

SEARCH THE SCRIPTURES

1. What can we do to build up people? (v. 1)

2. What is the value of an idol? (v. 4)

3. Some of the Corinthians continued to be affected by their past association with idols. In what ways were they affected? (v. 7)

4. In what sense can one's freedom become a stumbling block? (vv. 9-11)

5. When one sins against a fellow believer, one also sins against _____. (v. 12)

DISCUSS THE MEANING

1. Many adults are determined to do what they want to do even though doing so may be a stumbling block to others. Why should believers be concerned about the impact of their behavior upon others?

2. In what ways can we be more sensitive to our influence on others?

LESSON IN OUR SOCIETY

The "I gotta be me" and "out for self" syndrome has permeated our nation's collective psyche and is an ever present threat to Christian fellowship and behavior. There is too little concern for the inter-relatedness of our lives and behaviors. What we do and what we fail to do affects others in varying degrees.

The father who deals drugs tends to influence his sons to deal drugs either directly or indirectly. Behaviors are both taught and caught. Just as Timothy's grandmother Lois and his mother Eunice influenced him for good (2 Timothy 1:4-5), today's parents can influence their children for good. Church members can influence each other for good. We are both an influencer and influenceable. Therefore, when the Bible gives no clear command, what principles should guide our choices and the exercise of our freedom? In what ways can a church filled with differences of opinion about the gray areas of life maintain unity of purpose and fellowship?

What should church members do when they disagree on how they ought to live before God? How many differences of opinion can our relationships with one another accommodate without over-stressing the relationship? Is there a relational breaking point where matters of differing opinions are concerned? If so, how may we know this before the relationship is damaged?

MAKE IT HAPPEN

This week make a list of things which you and some significant other in your life disagree about. What feeds your differing opinions? Have you shared this information with each other? If not, would such sharing help each of you to better understand one another? In what ways can your love and concern for one another help each of you to manage your disagreements?

FOLLOW THE SPIRIT

What God wants me to do:

_____

_____

REMEMBER YOUR THOUGHTS

Special insights you have learned:

_____

_____

MORE LIGHT ON THE TEXT
1 CORINTHIANS 8:1

8:1 Now as touching things offered unto idols, we know that we all have knowledge. Knowledge puffeth up, but charity edifieth.

Idol meat/food is the second concern of the Corinthian church to which Paul responds. There were and are many religions which offer food to their god(s) for a variety of purposes. It is difficult to pinpoint the precise purpose for the offering without observing the ritual; even within a single ritual, individuals may experience the ritual differently. However, one may find three general purposes for food offerings: sacramental, communion, and celebration. As a sacrament, the participants symbolically consume the flesh and blood of the god, in order to take on the life energy or power of the god. As communion, the participants bring to memory some event or act upon which the faith of the believer depends. As a celebration, the community of believers shares a common meal, in which they might give recognition to their common belief or dependency upon the god in their lives.

When Paul states "We know that all of us possess knowledge," he levels any hierarchy that might exist in the minds of the reader. "I know as well as you do." This knowledge or *gnosis* may be thought of as revealed teachings which one may obtain through secret societies, through deep intellectual thought or study, or by some direct revelation from the divine. *Gnosis* was prized in hellenistic societies and was used to elevate one's status above others. The "we" that Paul refers to is probably the leadership or the teachers of the Corinthian church, who had obtained a greater level of *gnosis* regarding the Christian teachings than the average worshiper.

"Knowledge puffs up, but love builds." *Gnosis*, as personal knowledge, puffs up the ego of the individual, when compared to individuals who do not have this same *gnosis*. It only benefits the individual. By contrast, love builds up the community and is the standard which Christians ought to strive to obtain (see 1 Corinthians 5:6-8).

2 And if any man think that he knoweth any thing, he knoweth nothing yet as he ought to know.

"A little knowledge is a dangerous thing." This popular saying catches the spirit of Paul's challenge to the Corinthian leaders. The one who thinks he knows something has yet to realize how much more there is to know. The ego has become inflated, thus demonstrating that he has not yet arrived at a full knowledge. True knowledge humbles.

3 But if any man love God, the same is known of him.

Verse 3 gives Paul's main point in this excursus on *gnosis*. Human knowledge, even if it concerns God, is not as important as love for God. This love for God is demonstrated within the human community; it builds up the community, rather than puffing up the individual. It is more important to be known by God, for therein lies redemption and blessing. In 1 Corinthians 13:8, Paul says that love never ends, but knowledge passes away.

4 As concerning therefore the eating of those things that are offered in sacrifice unto idols, we know that an idol is nothing in the world, and that there is none other God but one.

One might wonder under what circumstances would a Christian have occasion to eat such food. It is known that the leftover meats from these sacrifices found their way into the public market. The parts that were not burned or consumed at a feast were sold in the marketplace. Thus, anyone who ate meat at all was at risk of getting this meat. Also, if the Christian was invited to the home of a non-Christian and was served a hospitality meal, it was quite possible that some of this meat would be served. Thus in order to avoid being defiled by the idol meat, many Christians became vegetarians.

Also there were occasions when persons of status or of particular affiliation would gather for festive occasions in the Greek temples. This might include Christians with social rank or family affiliation, regardless of their religious affiliation. At such events, one was certain to be served idol meat.

"We know that an idol has no real existence." In Deuteronomy 6:4, Moses pronounces the oneness of God to the Israelites. It is known as the *Shema*, because the first word in the command is "Hear!" This affirmation of sole devotion to and acknowledgment of the one God set the Israelites apart from the surrounding polytheistic (many gods) religions in the region. This fundamental tenet was also incorporated into Christianity from its earliest stages. This monotheistic view of the world meant that one God was responsible for the creation of the cosmos and for maintaining its order, rather than many gods battling with one another. The God of Israel and Christianity was not viewed as the strongest among many, but the only real God. With this knowledge, the Corinthian Christian could eat the idol meat with a clear conscience, because the idol was not real.

5 For though there be that are called gods, whether in heaven or in earth, (as there be gods many, and lords many,)

This statement is an acknowledgment of the circumstances of the pluralistic culture in which the Corinthian church found itself. The Greek pantheon consisted of many gods and demigods who were believed to exert control over the heavens, as well as human affairs. Even amongst the nobility, who ruled the earthly affairs, there were some who claimed divinity.

6 But to us there is but one God, the Father, of whom are all things, and we in him; and one Lord Jesus Christ, by whom are all things, and we by him.

For us, the Christians, trained in the teachings of Jesus, we know that there is only one God, who is the Father of creation. This encapsulates the so-called gods in heaven and earth. It is this Father from whom all things issued, and for whom we owe our existence. As for the many lords of the land, the Christian acknowledges Jesus Christ only. The understanding of the Lord as the one through whom creation took place sounds very much like the concept of the *logos* (the pre-existent and co-existent agent through whom the creation occurred) found in the first chapter of the Gospel of John.

7 Howbeit there is not in every man that knowledge: for some with conscience of the idol unto this hour eat it as a thing offered unto an idol; and their conscience being weak is defiled.

This knowledge of God the Father, and Jesus Christ the Lord, was not fully known or understood equally by all Christians. Those who had been accustomed to eating food offered to idols, because they had formerly worshiped those idol gods, sometimes found it difficult to re-think that experience. They may have heard the words, but the words did not sink deep into their consciences in order to transform their understanding. Therefore, in their consciences they felt defiled, because they had conflicting thoughts, while eating or seeing other Christians eat such meat.

The "weak" are the ones who do not "know." They are the counterpart to the "us" who know the teachings. Paul does not condemn them for being weak at all.

8 But meat commendeth us not to God: for neither, if we eat, are we the better; neither, if we eat not, are we the worse.

Those with understanding knew that the Christian would not gain any benefit from eating idol meat, because the idol had no real existence. But neither would the Christian be harmed if they did not eat the meat, for the same reason. So, the Christian had the liberty to choose for himself or herself whether to eat or not.

9 But take heed lest by any means this liberty of yours become a stumblingblock to them that are weak.

Having this knowledge, the Christian gained liberty to eat or abstain without consequence to his or her salvation. However, Paul warned that this liberty was not to be exercised without consideration of its impact upon the weak. Liberty is not absolute.

10 For if any man see thee which hast knowledge sit at meat in the idol's temple, shall not the conscience of him which is weak be emboldened to eat those things which are offered to idols;

This is the stumbling block: that the weak, seeing those who know more than they do eat idol meat, may feel pressured or encouraged to eat as well. But in the mind of the weak, he/she is violating his/her conscience. This may keep the weak from ever breaking away from their former understanding of eating idol meat.

11 And through thy knowledge shall the weak brother perish, for whom Christ died?

Thus the exercise of liberty may not only be a stumbling block, but may lead to the destruction of a weak believer. So the knowledge which puffs up, destroys one of those for whom Christ died.

12 But when ye sin so against the brethren, and wound their weak conscience, ye sin against Christ.

Now Paul's argument has come full circle. Yes, knowledge gives liberty, but that liberty should not be exercised if it would wound a weak believer. Destroying the weak is a sin against Christ himself. While eating idol food may have no consequence against one's soul, behavior that would destroy the Christian community does. Paul firmly states his position in his concluding statement.

13 Wherefore, if meat make my brother to offend, I will eat no flesh while the world standeth, lest I make my brother to offend.

Because love is greater than knowledge, Paul would gladly give up his liberty of eating idol meat, in order to build up the Christian community. Paul considers the relinquishing of meat an insignificant loss, compared to the loss of a soul.

DAILY BIBLE READING

M: Knowledge Puffs Up; Love Builds Up
1 Corinthians 8:1-6

T: Don't Cause Another to Stumble
1 Corinthians 8:7-13

W: Love Has Priority Over "Rights"
1 Corinthians 9:1-12

T: Preaching the Gospel Is Reward Enough
1 Corinthians 9:13-18

F: Do Whatever It Takes
1 Corinthians 9:19-27

S: Learn From Lessons of the Past
1 Corinthians 10:1-13

S: Flee from the Worship of Idols
1 Corinthians 10:14-22

TEACHING TIPS

April 16
Bible Study Guide 7

1. Words You Should Know

A. Manifestation. (1 Corinthians 12:7) Here it refers to a disclosure of the Spirit's activity.

B. The Gift of Faith. (1 Corinthians 12:9) While it is true that all believers have faith, the gift of faith is the ability to extend one's basic faith to serve the community of faith in extraordinary ways.

C. The Gift of Prophecy. (1 Corinthians 12:10) The ability to speak God's Word in ways that instruct, build others up, and encourage greater commitment to the will and purposes of God.

2. Teacher Preparation

Although the FOCAL VERSES for this lesson are limited to 1 Corinthians 12:4-20, 26, you would do well to read Romans 12:1-8, Ephesians 4:1-16, and 1 Peter 4:10-11. The more conversant you are with what the Bible has to say about spiritual gifts, the more confident you will be in your teaching.

Read the IN FOCUS and BACKGROUND and THE PEOPLE, PLACES, AND TIMES sections of this lesson. This will help you to put the FOCAL VERSES in their proper context. Your aim is not to explain each of the spiritual gifts. Rather, your aim is to help students to distinguish between the proper and improper use of spiritual gifts.

3. Starting the Lesson

Inform your students that today's lesson is about spiritual gifts. Then ask, "What is the purpose of spiritual gifts? Why does God give us spiritual gifts?" List student responses on the chalkboard. Except for clarification, these responses should not be discussed. Simply list them. Tell the class that you will come back to them near the end of the class session.

4. Getting into the Lesson

A. Summarize for your students the content of the IN FOCUS and BACKGROUND sections of this lesson. Then ask one of your students to read aloud for the class the FOCAL VERSES.

B. Have the students discuss what they think the Apostle Paul is saying to the Corinthian Christians. What three or four things does Paul want the Corinthians to know about spiritual gifts? List these on the chalkboard.

5. Relating the Lesson to Life

Given the list of things the Apostle Paul wants the Corinthians to know about spiritual gifts, how might this same list apply to our present-day understanding and use of spiritual gifts? Are gift glorification, projection, denigration, or individualization issues for us today? If so, in what sense? How can we correct our misuse of spiritual gifts?

6. Arousing Action

Have students read the MAKE IT HAPPEN section of their manuals. Ask them to follow the suggestions as their assignment for the week.

APRIL
16TH

SPIRITUAL GIFTS

Bible Background • 1 CORINTHIANS 12:1-30
Printed Text • 1CORINTHIANS 12:4-20, 26
Devotional Reading • ROMANS 12:1-8

LESSON AIM

By the end of the lesson, students will understand how using spiritual gifts in unspiritual ways affects Christian fellowship and explore the effect of spiritual gifts upon the fellowship and ministry of the church.

KEEP IN MIND

"Now there are diversities of gifts, but the same Spirit. And there are diversities of operations, but it is the same God which worketh all in all" (1 Corinthians 12:4, 6).

FOCAL VERSES

1 CORINTHIANS 12:4 Now there are diversities of gifts, but the same Spirit.

5 And there are differences of administrations, but the same Lord.

6 And there are diversities of operations, but it is the same God which worketh all in all.

7 But the manifestation of the Spirit is given to every man to profit withal.

8 For to one is given by the Spirit the word of wisdom; to another the word of knowledge by the same Spirit;

9 To another faith by the same Spirit; to another the gifts of healing by the same Spirit;

10 To another the working of miracles; to another prophecy; to another discerning of spirits; to another divers kinds of tongues; to another the interpretation of tongues:

11 But all these worketh that one and the selfsame Spirit, dividing to every man severally as he will.

12 For as the body is one, and hath many members, and all the members of that one body, being many, are one body: so also is Christ.

13 For by one Spirit are we all baptized into one body, whether we be Jews or Gentiles, whether we be bond or free;

and have been all made to drink into one Spirit.

14 For the body is not one member, but many.

15 If the foot shall say, Because I am not the hand, I am not of the body; is it therefore not of the body?

16 And if the ear shall say, Because I am not the eye, I am not of the body; is it therefore not of the body?

17 If the whole body were an eye, where were the hearing? If the whole were hearing, where were the smelling?

18 But now hath God set the members every one of them in the body, as it hath pleased him.

19 And if they were all one member, where were the body?

20 But now are they many members, yet but one body.

26 And whether one member suffer, all the members suffer with it; or one member be honoured, all the members rejoice with it.

IN FOCUS

During times when many are intently asking, "What is my gift?" today's lesson provides a needed corrective. The biblical approach to the quest for spiritual gifts ask, "What are the needs of the church?" Spiritual gifts are given to build up the body of Christ. Spiritual gifts are to be exercised for the good of the whole church so that it might be strong to do the work of ministry. Rather than to provide for individualistic pleasure and personal edification, spiritual gifts are to benefit the entire faith community. Therefore, those who "are eager to have spiritual gifts," should "try to excel in gifts that build up the church" (1 Corinthians 14:12).

Today's lesson is a clear reminder that God designs gifts to meet the ministry needs of His church. He distributes spiritual gifts according to His will. Rather than petition God for specific gifts, individual members would do well to align themselves with God's will to fulfill the church's ministry needs.

One of the greatest expressions of spirituality is to be available to work with God's Spirit to fulfill the church's ministry needs. Seeking to discover gifts within oneself is to put the cart before the horse. Those who would be spiritual will seek first to know the needs of the church. Upon discovering the church's needs, they will then seek to know how God wants to use them to meet identified needs. If one's attitude is right, and if one is committed to the diversity, unity, and mission of the church, God will give the appropriate gift at the right time.

One of the problems of the Corinthian church was that some of its members sought to develop their spirituality by seeking spiritual gifts. In other words, they were seeking and using spiritual gifts in unspiritual ways. The Apostle Paul's correction to this practice is a timely message in our day.

Spiritual gifts are given by God to be used in ways that build up the church. Individual members of the church are blessed and edified as they prayerfully work with God's Spirit to build up His church. When individual members are edified as a result of God's church being built up, then Christian unity is experienced, the church is empowered, and each member is rendered ready to feel and share both the pain and joy of all other members (1 Corinthians 12:26).

THE PEOPLE, PLACES, AND TIMES

This review of Paul's handling of the issues facing the Corinthian church reminds us of the continuing temptation of some to seek short cuts to enriching their faith and deepening their spirituality. The corridors of church history are strewn with the wreckage of individuals who opted to embellish what they assumed to be a spiritual gift, rather than to commit to labor lovingly with God and others over the long hall to build up His church.

Gift *glorification*, gift *projection*, gift *denigration*, and gift *individualization* are sure ways to abuse spiritual gifts. The Corinthians were using spiritual gifts to exalt certain believers above other believers. The *glorification* of spiritual gifts always leads to selfish pride in some and feelings of inferiority in others. The Apostle Paul was opposed to gift glorification in his day. The Scriptures are opposed to gift glorification in our day.

Gift *projection* is also an abusive use of spiritual gifts.

According to C. Peter Wagner, we engage in gift projection when we say, "'Here's what I do, and God blesses it. If you just do what I do, God will bless you in the same way.' People with a gift projection syndrome want the whole body to be an eye. They impose guilt and shame on fellow Christians."

We engage in gift *denigration* when we say, "I have no need of you" (1 Corinthians 12:21). The implication is that the gifts that God gives to some are unimportant. The reality is that the gifts God gives are the gifts His church needs. "Those parts of the body that seem to be weaker are indispensable, and the parts that we think are less honorable we treat with special honor" (1 Corinthians 12:22-23). This is God's way, and it enables us to "have equal concern for each other" (1 Corinthians 12:25b).

Gift *individualization* is also problematic in God's church. Spiritual gifts are misused when they are over-individualized. While gifts are given to individuals, they are exercised within and for the benefit of the community of faith. Spiritual gifts are not given for personal pleasure and edification. They are given to build up the church. Therefore, the community of faith is the controlling context for the use of spiritual gifts. The question ought always to be, "How can my exercise of this gift benefit the entire church?" Spiritual gifts are for the common good; for building up the church!

BACKGROUND

No church was more gifted than the church of God in Corinth. The Corinthian church did "not lack any spiritual gift" (1 Corinthians 1:7). How could such a spiritually gifted church have within its midst so many groups contending and quarreling among themselves? (1 Corinthians 1:11-12). Moreover, how could such a spiritually gifted church be so devoid of the capacity to deal redemptively with immorality (1 Corinthians 5:1-12), and to intervene in disputes requiring mediation? (1 Corinthians 6:1-11). How could the Corinthian's corporate worship experiences and Holy Communion services be so chaotic and divisive in nature? (1 Corinthians 11).

Spiritual gifts are given to unify and build up the body of Christ (Ephesians 4:12-13) "so that in all things God may be praised through Jesus Christ" (1 Peter 4:10-11). However, the Corinthians were seeking and using spiritual gifts in unspiritual ways. They desired spiritual gifts primarily for personal pleasure and edification. The problems the Apostle Paul addresses illustrate the Corinthian's self-seeking and disruptive use of certain gifts. It is from this perspective that we are to understand 1 Corinthians 12:31:

"But eagerly desire the greater gifts. And now I will show you the most excellent way" (NIV). In other words: "So you desire the best that there is! Let me show you what the best is." Then Paul proceeds in 1 Corinthians 13 to talk about how the exercise of all the spiritual gifts would be for nought without love.

In 1 Corinthians 14, Paul outlines the disciplines necessary for the proper exercise of the spiritual gift which so many of the Corinthians seemed to desire, namely the gift of tongues. Paul is concerned to show that the Corinthian's self-seeking individualistic view of spiritual gifts does nothing to build up the church. For example, in 1 Corinthians 14:1-5, Paul cites the gifts of prophecy and the interpretation of tongues as being more important than the gift of tongues because of their capacity to edify the whole church. Any use of spiritual gifts is primarily for the strengthening of the church (1 Corinthians 14:26) and not for personal pleasure and edification. It is when the church is built up that its members are edified and God is glorified.

The Apostle Paul wants the Corinthians to move away from their self-seeking posture; he wants the Corinthians to embrace God's will and to work with God's Spirit to build up the church. To do this, Paul believed, required a diligent quest to know the ministry needs of the church. To ask, "What is my spiritual gift?" before knowing the needs of the church tends to be self-seeking. To desire and to exercise spiritual gifts without a demonstrated commitment to serving the needs of the church results in a disruptive use of gifts. God gives a variety of spiritual gifts to enhance the diversity and well being of His church. When God's church is enhanced and built up, its members are blessed and edified.

**1. Many Gifts Given by One Lord
(1 Corinthians 12:4-6)
2. Many Gifts Activated by One Spirit
for the Common Good (vv. 7-11)
3. Many Gifts Exercised by One Body
(vv. 12-20)
4. Many Gifts Given, Activated,
Exercised with Equal Concern for
Each Member (v. 26)**

IN DEPTH

1. Many Gifts Given by One Lord
(1 Corinthians 12:4-6)

Here the Apostle Paul talks from three perspectives about the manifestation of spiritual gifts. First, God, through the grace of His Spirit, is the source and giver of a variety of spiritual gifts (v. 4). Second, the variety of gifts God gives are to be graciously used to render Christian service (v. 5). Third, the variety of gifts God gives individuals to render Christian service is expressions of His work (v. 6).

God is the source and giver of all spiritual gifts. God is ultimately the one who, through the gifts He gives, works all ministries and services through all believers.

2. Many Gifts Activated by One Spirit for the Common Good (vv. 7-11)

In verse 7, Paul's use of the phrase "the manifestation of the Spirit" is his way of summarizing the outworking of the variety of gifts referred to in verses 4-6. Paul is most emphatic in saying that the manifestation of the gifts God gives through the grace of His Spirit "are given for the common good." In other words, God activates a variety of spiritual gifts in a variety of believers for the purpose of serving the ministry needs of the entire church. Spiritual gifts are not the result of our seeking. Rather, they are the result of God's initiative. Spiritual gifts represent God's faithful response to our commitment to work with Him to build up His church by identifying and serving its ministry needs.

In verses 8-10, Paul lists the various kinds of gifts the Spirit gives to believers. The gifts listed are not exhaustive of all spiritual gifts. Paul lists enough, however, to demonstrate that there are a variety of gifts and ways in which they are manifested in the community of faith. For example, there are gifts through which instruction is given, i.e., wisdom and

knowledge. There are also gifts through which supernatural power is manifested, i.e., faith, healings, and miracles. Third, there are gifts through which inspired speech and utterance is given, i.e., prophecy, discerning prophecies, tongues, and the interpretation of tongues.

In listing these gifts, Paul is quick to emphasize that the manifestation of each gift is activated by the same Spirit. The believer's task is to seek to know and to do the will of God. Then God responds by giving us the gifts we need to most effectively do His will. In other words, "All these are the work of one and the same Spirit, and he gives them to each man, just as he determines" (1 Corinthians 12:11, NIV).

3. Many Gifts Exercised by One Body
(vv. 12-20)

Having said that God gives a variety of gifts to be used in a variety of ways to serve a single end, Paul now turns to affirm the oneness and unity of the church. Paul wants his readers to know that "different kinds of service" and "different kinds of working" conducted by a variety of believers need not result in congregational fragmentation and disharmony. God has structured His church so as to allow for both diversity and unity. According to the Apostle Paul, the unity and diversity of the church can be compared to the unity and diversity of the human body. There is one body with many parts. While all of the parts of the human body have different functions, the whole body functions as a cohesive unit. So it is with Christ's body, the church.

The church is made up of people from all walks of life and all ethnic and socioeconomic brackets. No two members are alike. Each is unique and contributes to congregational life out of the context of their individual uniqueness. But "we were all baptized by one Spirit into one body whether Jews or Greeks, slave or free and we were all given the one Spirit to drink" (1 Corinthians 12:13, NIV). Moreover, we continue to be watered with the one and the same Spirit. Our differences have been grafted into the one body where we are held together by one Spirit to serve the singular end of building up the body of Christ, the church.

Since God has placed and arranged these different parts in the body (1 Corinthians 12:18), we would be wise to accept the idea that it takes all kinds of parts to make the body function effectively. God has chosen to build up His church through the diversity that comes from specialization of function. Like the human body, the church is an organism. If the church were one giant organ, it could not carry out the many different and diverse functions of ministry. Just as it is necessary for each part of the human body to function in ways that complement other parts, even so it is necessary for each spiritual gift to work in a complementary relationship to all other gifts. All members of the church are important and essential to building up the church. Consequently, what one member feels we all feel. It cannot be avoided. That is the nature of the body. That is the nature of the church.

4. Many Gifts Given, Activated, Exercised with Equal Concern for Each Member (v. 26)

There should be no competition for, selfish seeking of, or clinging to spiritual gifts. For to do so is to demean and misuse the gifts of the Spirit. It can only result in exalting one gift over another. When spiritual gifts become the occasion for disruption in the church, we have lost sight of the Spirit's call to work with God to build up the church. The diversity of gifts which God gives and activates, at His initiative, are to be exercised with equal concern for each member. Just as every member is important, the exercise of every gift is important no matter whom God chooses to exercise the gift.

God has made us mutually interdependent. It is only when we bring a balanced perspective to the exercise of spiritual gifts that we understand that when one member suffers, the whole body suffers; when one member is honored, all rejoice together (1 Corinthians 12:26).

SEARCH THE SCRIPTURE

1. Who places and arranges spiritual gifts in the church? (1 Corinthians 12:18)

2. Why are spiritual gifts given? (v. 7)

3. "For we were all _____ by one _____ into one _____." (v. 13)

4. "The body is a_____, though it _____ parts; and though _____, they form one _____." (v. 12)

5. "As it is, there are many _____." (v. 20)

DISCUSS THE MEANING

1. What is meant by the phrase "The manifestation of the Spirit"?

2. In what sense is the church an organism?

LESSON IN OUR SOCIETY

Throughout the church's history people have tried to satisfy their spiritual hunger by seeking some spiritual gift. Others have sought to embellish their identity by claiming

certain gifts, "I have the gift of healing," or "I have the gift of discernment." However, spiritual gifts are not to be worn on our chest as badges of importance. Spiritual gifts are given to promote the common good. Spiritual gifts are given "to prepare God's people for works of service, so that the body of Christ may be built up until we all reach unity in the faith and in the knowledge of the Son of God and become mature, attaining the full measure of perfection found in Christ" (Ephesians 4:12-13, NIV).

MAKE IT HAPPEN

Take this week to pray for your church. Ask God to help you to help your church become the church God would have it to be. Ask your pastor or other church leaders to help you identify five or six ministry needs in your church. Once you have done these things, begin praying and talking with others in whom you have confidence about how you might get involved in helping to meet some of your church's ministry needs. In your praying, let the Lord know that you are willing to work with Him to better prepare yourself for Christian service. Then when an opportunity comes for you to serve, however small or large the task, dare to plunge in and take on the challenge. It just may be that God will gift you in some special way to do effectively for His honor what you thought you could never do. When He does, give Him the praise and thank Him that He counted you worthy to work with Him to build up His church.

FOLLOW THE SPIRIT

What God wants me to do:

_____

_____

REMEMBER YOUR THOUGHTS

Special insights you gained:

_____

_____

MORE LIGHT ON THE TEXT
1 CORINTHIANS 12:4-20, 26

12:4 Now there are diversities of gifts, but the same Spirit.

Paul was addressing a faction of the Corinthian church that believed the only true manifestation of the Holy Spirit was the ecstatic speaking in tongues and interpretation of tongues. Paul sought to show that the one Spirit manifests itself in a variety or diversity of gifts (*charismata*). All these gifts come from the same Spirit.

5 And there are differences of administrations, but the same Lord.

There are also numerous types of service (*diakonia*) which are rendered throughout the Christian community, but it is the one Lord in whose name this work is done.

6 And there are diversities of operations, but it is the same God which worketh all in all.

There are also varieties of activities (*energamata*), but it is the one God who causes them to activate in everyone. These *energamata* are performances of power, workings, and operations by God (such as miracles, healing, etc.).

Now Paul has pointed to the one Spirit, one Lord, and one God that we refer to as the Trinity. The Godhead is a unity composed of a diversity of three. Likewise, the church is one entity composed of a diversity of gifts, services, and activities that emanate from the one source.

7 But the manifestation of the Spirit is given to every man to profit withal.

To every individual is given some manifestation of the Spirit for the purpose of enhancing the common good. There is no cause for competition, or feelings of superiority, because all these are given for a common purpose. Paul follows these statements with examples of the diversity of these manifestations of gifts, services, and activities.

8 For to one is given by the Spirit the word of wisdom; to another the word of knowledge by the same Spirit;

This one Spirit is responsible for both the utterance of wisdom (*sophia*) and the utterance of knowledge (*gnosis*), but these are apportioned differently as the Spirit wills. The gifts of wisdom and knowledge have to do with the teaching role of the church. Some are more gifted at memorizing Scripture, while others are better able to apply passages to real life situations. Some can easily see connections between various parts of the Bible, while others know one part well. All of these are necessary aspects of teaching.

9 To another faith by the same Spirit; to another the gifts of healing by the same Spirit;

Some people have such an extraordinary faith that their presence inspires those who are weak in faith.

Others have the kind of faith that leads to healing of physical, emotional, mental, and spiritual ailments. It is the same Spirit who gives these gifts as He wills.

10 To another the working of miracles; to another prophecy; to another discerning of spirits; to another divers kinds of tongues; to another the interpretation of tongues:

Faith in the power of the Spirit enables some to perform miracles of all kinds. Another may be gifted with prophecy and insight. The Corinthians experienced prophecy by the ecstatic speaking in tongues. Therefore, it was necessary to have someone present to discern by what spirit a word of prophecy was given (there is true and false prophecy), as well as someone who could interpret the ecstatic speech. The gifts of speaking tongues and interpreting tongues do not always come together.

11 But all these worketh that one and the selfsame Spirit, dividing to every man severally as he will.

Again Paul emphasizes that it is the one Spirit, not many different spirits, who causes these gifts, services, and activities to exist in individuals. But even more than this, the Spirit allots them as He wills. All these

---

DAILY BIBLE READING

M: Understand the Source of
Spiritual Gifts
1 Corinthians 12:1-6
T: Many Spiritual Gifts, but One
Spirit
W: One Body, Many Members
1 Corinthians 12:12-19
T: We Need One Another
1 Corinthians 12:20-31
F: Transformed by New Life in
Christ
Romans 12:1-8
S: Marks of a Faithful Christian
Romans 12:9-15
S: Guidance for Living the
Christian Life
Romans 12:16-21

manifestations of the Holy Spirit are necessary for the common good.

12 For as the body is one, and hath many members, and all the members of that one body, being many, are one body: so also is Christ.

Paul now applies the analogy of the one consisting of many to the body of Christ (the church). The body is not the body because of its separateness; the body of Christ is one body because its diverse members operate as one.

13 For by one Spirit are we all baptized into one body, whether we be Jews or Gentiles, whether we be bond or free; and have been all made to drink into one Spirit.

Through the ritual of baptism, the Spirit draws together many diverse people into one body. Baptism symbolizes dying and rising into Christ's body. Afterward, one's experiences are viewed through Christ's perspective, not through the world's. So the worldly differences of nationality, race, and social status are of no consequence.

14 For the body is not one member, but many.

Everyone cannot have the same gift, the same service, or demonstration of power if the body of Christ is to operate effectively. The body must consist of many members with diverse gifts. The oneness of the body does not take away from the diversity of its members.

15 If the foot shall say, Because I am not the hand, I am not of the body; is it therefore not of the body?

In many cultures, the foot is regarded as being very lowly. To touch another person with one's foot would be considered disrespectful, if not insulting. But the touching of hands is considered a gesture of friendship. Thus, if the lowly foot did not wish to belong to the body, because it did not have the status of a hand, that would not in the slightest way change that fact that it is still a member of the body in reality.

16 And if the ear shall say, Because I am not the eye, I am not of the body; is it therefore not of the body?

The ear and the eye both occupy a position upon the head, so there is not as great a difference in status as was found between the foot and the hand. However, the difference lies in function. These two organs have distinct purposes, neither of which the body would gladly do without.

17 If the whole body were an eye, where were the hearing? If the whole were hearing, where were the smelling?

The body of Christ cannot function properly with prophecy only. There also must be healing, hospitality, teaching, etc. Paul's point is that if the whole consisted of one thing instead of a diversity of things, the body would suffer a great loss of function, if not its very existence.

18 But now hath God set the members every one of them in the body, as it hath pleased him.

Paul credits God with the divine will to have arranged by plan, each member of the body. It is organized for God's purpose.

19 And if they were all one member, where were the body? 20 But now are they many members, yet but one body.

There would not be a body, if all the members were the same. Diversity is necessary.

According to God's purpose, there are many diverse members that work together for the good of the whole body.

26 And whether one member suffer, all the members suffer with it; or one member be honoured, all the members rejoice with it.

With our physical bodies, an injury to any part is felt throughout the body. So it is with the body of Christ (the church). Yet if one member exercises his or her gift(s) for the glory of the Lord, the whole of the church is edified. This is attested to in the fact that the presence or absence of a single member in a church can make an enormous difference in the quality of worship, in the feeling of hospitality visitors receive, even in the effectiveness of the church's administrative functions.

TEACHING TIPS

April 23
Bible Study Guide 8

1. Words You Should Know

A. First fruits. (1 Corinthians 15:20, 23)—For background information, read Leviticus 23:10-11, 17, 20. Since God was the creator of all living things, all living things belong to Him. The offering of the first fruits was the Hebrew's way of affirming God's ownership and authority over the whole crop to be harvested. They were giving back to God a portion of what had been entrusted to their care.

B. Flesh. (1 Corinthians 15:39)—Flesh here does not mean sinful body. Here it refers to the body of various forms of animal life.

2. Teacher Preparation

A. To prepare to teach this lesson, read the entire chapter of 1 Corinthians 15 several times from different versions of the Bible. *The NIV Study Bible* will prove extremely helpful if you make use of its footnotes, and keep in mind its major topics. Read also Leviticus 23:9-21. Use a Bible dictionary to look up the term "first fruits" and become familiar with its definition and function in Israel's history. Pray for God's guidance and illumination.

B. Next, read the IN DEPTH section. Recognize that a lot of material is covered in 1 Corinthians 15. Your challenge will be to focus upon Christ's resurrection and ours. Avoid becoming sidetracked by all of Paul's references to the consequences of failure to believe in the resurrection. The IN DEPTH outline should help you to stay focused. Keep in mind that what you are reading about is something that God will do; God raised up Christ and at the right time and in like manner God will raise us up also.

C. In your own words, answer the two DISCUSS THE MEANING questions.

3. Starting the Lesson

A. Begin this class session by asking one of your students to read aloud to the class the IN FOCUS portion of the *Student Manual*. Depending upon the size of your class, you may want to divide into small groups of four or five and have students discuss their thoughts about the IN FOCUS story. Remind them that this is a true story. It actually happened the way it is told. Allow about 10 minutes for their small group discussions.

B. Following student's small group discussion, ask them how belief in the bodily resurrection of Christ can speak to the mother's situation.

4. Getting into the Lesson

A. Using the results of your prior preparation for this session, read the FOCAL VERSES to the students. Then using the IN DEPTH material, review Paul's response to those who said that there is no resurrection of the dead.

B. Remind your students that Christ's resurrection and ours is a mystery, and we remember that it is a work that God does.

C. Go on to remind your students that the power by which God raised Christ and will raise us is available for our daily living. This is our hope for living a victorious life.

5. Relating the Lesson to Life

A. Ask your students if they have any new insights on how they might speak to the mother in the IN FOCUS story.

B. Discuss how will they apply the insights of today's lesson in their daily lives.

C. Ask the students to answer the questions under DISCUSS THE MEANING.

6. Arousing Action

A. Have your students identify some situation where resurrection faith could help make a difference.

B. Encourage the students to seek God's guidance for how they might share their faith to help those in the situations they have identified in A above.

C. Close the session with prayer asking God to help all believers to appropriate more fully God's resurrection power, and to remember that when this life is over we are assured a new body.

APRIL 23RD

WORSHIP GUIDE

For the Superintendent or Teacher
Theme: Christ's Resurrection and Ours
Theme Song: "We Have A Hope"
Scripture: 1 Corinthians 15:12-19
Song: "He Lives!"
Devotional Thought: Thank You, O God, for the hope we have of a life beyond the grave. Thank You for the confidence we have of experiencing victory in this life.

CHRIST'S RESURRECTION AND OURS

Bible Background • 1 CORINTHIANS 15
Printed Text • 1 CORINTHIANS 15:20-27, 35-44
Devotional Reading • 1 CORINTHIANS 15:12-19, 50-57

LESSON AIM

By the end of the lesson, students will explore and discuss the meaning of the resurrection for one's daily life and relationships.

KEEP IN MIND

"But now is Christ risen from the dead, and become the firstfruits of them that slept. For as in Adam all die, even so in Christ shall all be made alive" (1 Corinthians 15:20, 22).

FOCAL VERSES

1 CORINTHIANS 15:20 But now is Christ risen from the dead, and become the firstfruits of them that slept.

21 For since by man came death, by man came also the resurrection of the dead.

22 For as in Adam all die, even so in Christ shall all be made alive.

23 But every man in his own order: Christ the firstfruits; afterward they that are Christ's at his coming.

24 Then cometh the end, when he shall have delivered up the kingdom to God, even the Father; when he shall have put down all rule and all authority and power.

25 For he must reign, till he hath put all enemies under his feet.

26 The last enemy that shall be destroyed is death.

27 For he hath put all things under his feet. But when he saith all things are put under him, it is manifest that he is excepted, which did put all things under him.

15:35 But some man will say, How are the dead raised up? and with what body do they come?

36 Thou fool, that which thou sowest is not quickened, except it die:

37 And that which thou sowest, thou sowest not that body that shall be, but bare grain, it may chance of wheat, or of some other grain:

38 But God giveth it a body as it hath pleased him, and to every seed his own body.

39 All flesh is not the same flesh: but there is one kind of flesh of men, another flesh of beasts, another of fishes, and another of birds.

40 There are also celestial bodies, and bodies terrestrial: but the glory of the celestial is one, and the glory of the terrestrial is another.

41 There is one glory of the sun, and another glory of the moon, and another glory of the stars: for one star differeth from another star in glory.

42 So also is the resurrection of the dead. It is sown in corruption; it is raised in incorruption:

43 It is sown in dishonour; it is raised in glory: it is sown in weakness; it is raised in power:

44 It is sown a natural body; it is raised a spiritual body. There is a natural body, and there is a spiritual body.

IN FOCUS

I remember conducting the funeral service for a 26-year-old African-American male. He was the fourth of five blood-related brothers to be gunned down over a period of two years as the result of drug-related disputes.

The funeral home's chapel was filled to capacity with young people, family, and friends of the deceased. The deceased's mother was present. The fifth brother was also

---

LESSON OVERVIEW

LESSON AIM
KEEP IN MIND
FOCAL VERSES
IN FOCUS
THE PEOPLE, PLACES, AND TIMES
BACKGROUND
AT-A-GLANCE
IN DEPTH
SEARCH THE SCRIPTURES
DISCUSS THE MEANING
LESSON IN OUR SOCIETY
MAKE IT HAPPEN
FOLLOW THE SPIRIT
REMEMBER YOUR THOUGHTS
MORE LIGHT ON THE TEXT
DAILY BIBLE READINGS

present, sobbing bitterly. I learned later that at the time of his brother's funeral he too was also actively involved in dealing drugs. The violent deaths of his other brothers, apparently, did not dissuade him from continued involvement in a lifestyle that brought much pain to himself and his mother. Now his fourth brother was dead, and he is his mother's only living child.

This mother pleaded with each of her sons to give up their involvement with drugs. The past two years were miserable years as she witnessed the dissipation of her own flesh and blood in a way of life that made no sense. Much to her grief, her pleas were not heard, or if heard, they were not heeded.

The funeral service was very emotional, especially for the many young people who had come to pay their respects to one of their peers. The mother of the deceased, however, sat stoned-faced through the entire service. Her facial expression never changed. She did not cry. She did not groan. She did not speak one word.

I escorted the family and close friends to the cemetery. The grave-side service was brief and cold. Most persons who accompanied the family to the cemetery seemed to take their cue for expressing grief from the deceased mother, who still showed no signs of outward emotion. As family and friends began to leave the grave site to get into their cars and go their separate ways, the mother spoke for the first time during these services. I overheard her say: "This is my fourth of my five sons to be killed dealing drugs. And I'll be so glad when the other one is gone, so that I can get on with my life."

Months of grief and pleading had turned this mother's heart to a heart of stone. All of her aspirations for her last son had died. She showed no signs of hope of ever seeing a better future for her remaining son. In fact, she seemed to imply that the improvement of her own future was somehow wrapped up in the anticipated—if not desired—death of her youngest son.

In what ways can the resurrection of Jesus Christ speak to this mother and her situation?

THE PEOPLE, PLACES, AND TIMES

Every generation has its share of skeptics. The Corinthians were not the last to question what God does. The idea of a bodily resurrection and of a tomorrow when the dead in Christ will be resurrected in new bodies capable of living in a renewed world with God forever is fertile ground for the skeptic.

Some of the Corinthians did not realize, nor do some in our day, that our resurrected body will be different from our present body. The resurrected body may look like our present body, but in substance it will be different. The resurrected body will be a thing of glory, perfected so as to reflect the grace and glory of God Himself.

This is a mystery, but people in every generation and in every place would do well to believe it. An additional word from the Apostle Paul may be helpful: "If only for this life we have hope in Christ, we are to be pitied more than all men. But Christ has indeed been raised from the dead, the firstfruits of those who have fallen asleep . . . For as in Adam all die, so in Christ all will be made alive" (1 Corinthians 15:19-20, 22, NIV).

BACKGROUND

The writing of 1 Corinthians 15 was occasioned by the need for a corrective response to some Corinthians who were saying "there is no resurrection of the dead" (1 Corinthians 15:12). While they believed in a spiritual resurrection, they challenged those who believed in a bodily resurrection. The idea of a decayed, maimed, decomposed body being recreated to healthy, functioning, flesh and blood status, they reasoned, was an impossibility. They put two critical questions to Paul and to those who, along with him, believed in a bodily resurrection: (1) How are the dead raised up? (2) With what body do they come? (1 Corinthians 15:35).

Paul was most disturbed, even shocked, that some of the Corinthians would pursue such a thought. Paul's response is simply that to say that there is no resurrection of the dead equals saying that Jesus Christ has not been raised. "And if Christ has not been raised, our preaching is useless and so is our faith" (1 Corinthians 15:14, NIV). Moreover, Paul argues, the bodily resurrection of Jesus establishes and proves the hope of the resurrection of our human bodies.

For any who would doubt the bodily resurrection of Jesus, Paul appeals to the host of eyewitnesses to the resurrection of Jesus Christ (1 Corinthians 15:5-7). Additionally, Paul offers his own experience as proof of the bodily resurrection of Jesus (1 Corinthians 15:8-11).

After giving considerable attention to the consequences of denying the resurrection of the body (1 Corinthians 15:12-19), Paul proceeds to write about (1) the hope of our bodily resurrection and (2) the reign of God (1 Corinthians 20-28). Finally, in 1 Corinthians 15:35-44, Paul (3) responds to two questions: "How are the dead raised up?" and "With what body do they come?" Today's lesson focuses upon these three areas of Paul's response to those Corinthians who first doubted the bodily resurrection of Jesus Christ.

IN DEPTH

1. We Have a Living Hope
(1 Corinthians 15:20-23)

Paul turns now to present his case for both the certain
hope of Christ's resurrection and ours. To do this, he uses
the Old Testament imagery of the "firstfruits," and the
Adam-Christ analogy. The law of the firstfruits (Leviticus
23:10-11, 17, 20) required that a sheaf of the firstfruits of
one's harvest be brought to the priest as an offering to the
Lord. This was done as a guarantee for the full harvest. In
other words, Christ's resurrection is the first part of the harvest "of those who have fallen asleep." Therefore, Christ's
resurrection is a guarantee that at His second coming the
rest of the harvest will come in; namely, our resurrection. In
this sense, Christ is the guarantee of our resurrection.

In the Adam-Christ analogy, both Adam and Christ are
understood to be the founders of a new humanity.
Therefore, since Adam was responsible for death entering
the world, Christ is responsible for the resurrection of the
dead. Just as all who were represented in Adam died, so also
shall all who are represented in Christ be made alive at the
resurrection. Since we know that God raised Christ from
the dead, we know also that Christ is the guarantee of our
resurrection.

What a living hope we have in Jesus Christ! He assures
us life and guarantees our resurrection. Christ has reversed
what Adam did. The sin of Adam brought death into the
world. The atonement of Christ brought life. The resurrection of Jesus Christ guarantees the resurrection of
believers. Christ's resurrection makes our resurrection necessary. Therefore, all who place their hope in Jesus Christ
can have newness of life in this world and in the world to
come.

2. We Have the Guarantee of God's Reign and
the End of Evil (vv. 24-27)

Because of what God has done for us through Christ, a
new age has been inaugurated. All things are currently

being subjected to God. This language points to the end of
time, as well as to the end of the world. There will come a
day when Jesus Christ shall have put everything, except
God the Father, under His feet—all sin and evil, violence
and abuse, crime and injustice. When this will be is not
given. Christ through the continuing work of the Holy
Spirit is still in process of redeeming the world so that in the
end Christ can present to God a world redeemed.

Since we are certain that God raised Jesus from the
dead, we can be certain that God through Jesus Christ will
one day bring a final end to evil and complete the establishment of His rule and kingdom. Then love and righteousness will reign and rule forever. All those who shall have
lived in communion with God shall also reign with God in
His eternal kingdom of love and righteousness.

3. We Have the Guarantee of a New Body
(vv. 35-44)

Having reviewed the certainty of Christ's bodily resurrection and ours, Paul now responds to some specific questions. Paul assumes that some of the Corinthians are still
not convinced of the idea of a bodily resurrection. Thus, he
anticipates their questions. How is the resurrection of a
dead and physical body to occur? Moreover, what kind of
body will it be?

Paul thinks such questions foolish, primarily because the
Corinthians have failed to take into account God's actions
and power. Even so, Paul proceeds with a response. Having
used the Adam-Christ analogy and the imagery of the firstfruits, Paul now uses other related analogies to the resurrection of the dead. Just as the Corinthians were familiar
with the imagery of the firstfruits, Paul also assumes their
familiarity with the organizational structure of other physical life forms. Paul uses the seed analogy to remind the
Corinthians that the seed which is planted does not come
to life unless it dies (v. 36). Moreover, the seed that is planted does not simply grow larger. Rather, God gives each kind
of planted seed its own new body (vv. 37-38). This transformation is something that God does.

A bodily resurrection is a miraculous event. It can
only be brought about as God wills and enables it.
Just as God causes seeds to die and then grow as new
plants, He also causes a bodily resurrection to occur.
Just as God gives each seed its own plant body and
life, He will also give each believer his or her own distinct resurrection body.

Paul's analogy also carries the thought that the
resurrection is not to occur in the same body that
dies and decays. The personality of the dead will

remain and be given over to a new body.

In verses 39-41, Paul explains his comments in verse 38. Paul wants his readers to know that God gives each seed its own kind of body. This has to be because all life forms differ. Mankind has one kind of flesh, animals another, birds another. Just as there are different kinds of earthly bodies, there are also different kinds of heavenly bodies. Each of the earthly and heavenly bodies have their own distinct splendor and beauty. Since this is God's doing, it is clear that God is able to take these differing life forms and cause them to serve His ends.

So it will be with our resurrection (v. 42). God will take our mortal bodies and do what He wills. Our mortal bodies made perishable, dishonored, weak, and totally humiliated by sin, God will make anew. Just as God provided appropriate life forms for all life, even so our resurrected bodies will be different but appropriate for their spiritual nature.

We have this guarantee: God will give all those who die in Christ new bodies. Our new bodies will be capable of living in the new world God has promised those who have faith in Christ and who in this life walk upright before Him.

SEARCH THE SCRIPTURE

1. "For He must reign until _____ _____ feet." (1 Corinthians 15:25)
2. "When you sow, you do not _____ _____, but just a seed, _____." (v. 37)
3. "If there is a natural body , _____ _____." (v. 44b)
4. "The body that is sown is perishable, _____ _____." (v. 42b)

DISCUSS THE MEANING

1. How are the dead raised?
2. With what kind of body will they come?

LESSON IN OUR SOCIETY

What difference does the resurrection of Jesus Christ make in our lives? Is there any hope for the mother we met in the IN FOCUS section of this lesson? Our concern about Christ's resurrection and ours is more than an after-life matter. The power of God that raised Jesus from the dead and that will resurrect our bodies at the end of time is available to us now. The power of God can alter a life gone astray. The power of God can breathe new life into any dead or decaying situation. The hope we have is a living hope.

MAKE IT HAPPEN

This week, identify two situations where you have witnessed God's power bring new life into some dying situation. Write down your findings, and thank God for what He is doing to bring resurrection life into the brokenness of our world.

Perhaps you know someone who has need to hear about the resurrection power that can be available to them. Share your hope with them and believe that God's Holy Spirit will intervene and make a difference.

FOLLOW THE SPIRIT

What God wants me to do:

_____

_____

REMEMBER YOUR THOUGHTS

Special insights you gained:

_____

_____

MORE LIGHT ON THE TEXT
1 CORINTHIANS 15:20-27, 35-44

15:20 But now is Christ risen from the dead, and become the firstfruits of them that slept.

In the previous verses of chapter 15, Paul reiterates to the Corinthians how important Christ's resurrection is to their faith, as well as to their own hope for the future. Now Paul begins to elaborate on why Christ's resurrection is crucial for the coming of God's kingdom.

The term *first fruits* is an expression which in the Old Testament literally meant "the first grain and fruit to ripen for harvest, even the firstborn among people and domesticated animals." At times it also meant the "choicest" among a group of things or persons. It was these first fruits that were offered to Yahweh for the redemption of the rest of the harvest and for the rest of the people. The first fruits were sanctified, in order that they might be acceptable to Yahweh. Then upon their acceptance, the nation was redeemed from its sins. This was done regularly by individuals and annually for the nation as a whole.

In the New Testament, this term is also used figuratively, meaning the first in a sequence. So if Christ was the first fruits of those who have died, then one could expect that more would also be raised from the dead. Now Paul did not

say the Christ was the first to be raised from the dead, for the miracle of Jesus raising Lazarus from the dead must have been known by many. But Lazarus' resurrection did not institute the beginning of the resurrection for humanity. The miracle of Lazarus' resurrection showed that death was not final, that there was a power greater than death, and that Jesus had command of that power.

Herein lies the difference. Christ as the first fruits, the choicest among humans, was the means of redemption and was resurrected in order to establish the possibility of resurrection for humanity. Christ became the redeemer of humanity, the resurrection of life.

21 For since by man came death, by man came also the resurrection of the dead.

Adam disobeyed God's command, which resulted in the introduction of death into the world. While Adam was not the first to die (physically), it was through Adam's loins that the first death came. His son Cain slew his other son Abel. This was the beginning of all the death and dying that followed.

Since it was through a human being that death came

into the world, likewise the resurrection of the dead had to come through a human being. This implies some intentionality on God's part, as well as some specialness in Adam and Christ. They were not simply human beings.

22 For as in Adam all die, even so in Christ shall all be made alive.

Here Paul establishes the parallel for Adam and Christ, which he later explained more thoroughly in Romans 5:12-21. Through one man's trespass all were condemned and die, likewise through one man's act of righteousness, all will be justified and will live.

23 But every man in his own order: Christ the firstfruits; afterward they that are Christ's at his coming.

There is an order to this plan, which Paul now begins to explain. First, Christ the first fruits (the redeemer) must resurrect; then when He arrives those who belong to Christ (the redeemed) shall be resurrected. The word order also carries the meaning of military ranking, like the ordering of troops for battle. The word *parousia* ("coming") was a term used to indicate the arrival, presence, or coming of an emperor. But was also used to indicate the appearance of God. Christ will become the King who sits at the right hand of God. His troops will be readied for battle against His foes. This imagery of the royal coronation is found in Psalm 100:1 and Acts 2:34-35.

24 Then cometh the end, when he shall have delivered up the kingdom to God, even the Father; when he shall have put down all rule and all authority and power.

Then comes the end (*telos*). This refers to the end or completion of Christ's reign, which began at His coming. Christ's reign is to be for a specified period; namely, until God has destroyed every ruler, authority, and power. God shall bring to an end anything or anyone who would serve as a substitute ruler, authority, and power for God. This includes any kingdom or nation, any authority (including religious authority), any evil power, which requires the devotion and submission of people to itself and away from God. Those enemies that sought to destroy Jesus Christ will be brought under His rule. Then the kingdom shall be turned over to God.

The Children of Israel had lived under the reign of God, at first, but rejected God's authority and reign, in favor of a human king. This rejection of God's authority led to all kinds of deplorable acts (see Judges 17-21). In Judges 8:22, the Israelites had asked Gideon to rule over them, but Gideon refused because he knew that it was God who had empowered him to defeat Israel's enemies. Gideon said, "I will not rule over you, and my son will not rule over you; the Lord will rule over you." Years later, in the time of the Prophet Samuel, Israel still asked for another king, so they could be like other nations. This time God, being rejected, permitted Samuel to appoint a king. They were willing to submit to the harshness of an earthly king, but were not willing to submit to the heavenly King.

But in the end, God's kingdom will be restored. There will be no ruler, authority, or power remaining which anyone could substitute for God's rule, authority, and power, not even God's Son. For Christ shall hand over the kingdom to God the Father. As Paul summarizes in verse 28, God will be everything to everyone.

25 For he must reign, till he hath put all enemies under his feet.

Christ's reign will continue until God has put all of Christ's enemies under His (Christ's) feet. The metaphor of "putting . . . under the feet" means that those enemies will

have been stripped of all power and authority. They will themselves be under subjection to Christ's rule, power, and authority. They will lie prostrate at Christ's feet.

26 The last enemy that shall be destroyed is death.

After all of God's other enemies have been destroyed, the last enemy, death (which was also the first), shall be destroyed. This will be the end of all God's enemies. Not even the fear of death shall keep people from full devotion to God.

27 For he hath put all things under his feet. But when he saith, all things are put under him, it is manifest that he is excepted, which did put all things under him.

Paul adds this statement for emphasis, so that there will be no question as to whose kingdom it is. God is the one who puts things under subjection, under the feet of Christ; even as God put all things under the feet of humans (Genesis 1:28f, Psalm 8:6). Having all things under Christ's feet does not include God. This rule is not ultimately for Christ, but is to be turned over to God in the end.

35 But some man will say, How are the dead raised up? and with what body do they come?

How are the dead, especially the long dead, to be raised when their bodies have decayed? This question reflects the literal thinking of some of the Corinthians. This brought doubt about the possibility of any resurrection of the body. If the body is decayed, what will be raised? This thinking was similar to that of Nicodemus the Pharisee, whom Jesus perplexed in John 3.

36 Thou fool, that which thou sowest is not quickened, except it die:

In order to show the foolishness of this kind of literal thinking, Paul responds with a literal and common metaphor of sowing and reaping. It is foolish to think that the dead will come back with the same body as before. Everyone knows that when you plant something, the thing planted must die before it can come to life again in a new form.

37 And that which thou sowest, thou sowest not that body that shall be, but bare grain, it may chance of wheat, or of some other grain:

Continuing his illustration, Paul shows how the form of the body initially planted is not the same as the form that is restored to life. No, only a kernel of grain is put in the ground, but what comes up is a glorious plant. The body that must die is not as glorious as the body that will be raised.

38 But God giveth it a body as it hath pleased him, and to every seed his own body.

The resurrected body will be a body of God's choosing. It will not be the same as that which has died, and not all that are raised will be alike. Even among seeds, each has a different form; the mustard seed differs from a peach seed, which differs from a fig seed. Likewise, their full-grown forms differ from one another.

39 All flesh is not the same flesh: but there is one kind of flesh of men, another flesh of beasts, another of fishes, and another of birds.

Moving from the example of seeds and plant life, Paul shows the diversity of types of flesh. God made different forms for humans, animals, birds, and fish.

40 There are also celestial bodies, and bodies terrestrial: but the glory of the celestial is one, and the glory of the terrestrial is another.

Paul expands his metaphor from vegetation, to flesh, and now to the stars and planets. The heavenly bodies (sun, moon, stars, and planets) are quite different than the bodies of the earthly beings in the previous example. These heavenly bodies have a greater glory or radiance than do the earthly bodies.

41 There is one glory of the sun, and another glory of the moon, and another glory of the stars: for one star differeth from another star in glory.

Even with the greatness in glory or radiance of heavenly bodies, they too differ from one another in glory. With all these varieties of bodies, how could anyone believe that the same body that died would be given again?

42 So also is the resurrection of the dead. It is sown in corruption; it is raised in incorruption:

At the resurrection, the raised persons shall be given a diversity of forms, with differing levels of glory, according to God's choosing. That which is sown or buried is perishable. It is subject to decay and destruction. But that which is raised is imperishable. It will be indestructible.

43 It is sown in dishonour; it is raised in glory: it is sown in weakness; it is raised in power:

The body may be buried in dishonor, as was Jesus' crucifixion and burial, but it will be raised in glory. There is no need to fear what kind of death or burial one receives, for there will be a glorious resurrection anyway. For many cultures, it was believed that one must have the appropriate kind of burial and rituals performed in order to achieve a good after-life. But Paul's statement alleviates all worry. It does not matter, if one's body is left in an unmarked grave, or not buried at all. When Christ comes, one will still receive a glorious new form. Though one may die in the weakness of old age, one will rise with power.

44 It is sown a natural body; it is raised a spiritual body. There is a natural body, and there is a spiritual body.

Paul has used many common images to illustrate the fact that a transformation must occur between death and resurrection. This is the final and most important difference that must take place, the change from the physical to the spiritual. The body to be raised will be a spiritual body, because flesh cannot inherit the kingdom of God.

DAILY BIBLE READING

M: The Resurrection of Christ the Lord
1 Corinthians 15:1-11
T: How Can You Deny the Resurrection?
1 Corinthians 15:12-19
W: The Resurrected Christ Destroys Death
1 Corinthians 15:20-28
T: The Dead Are Raised: Believe It
1 Corinthians 15:29-34
F: God Will Give the Glory
1 Corinthians 15:35-41
S: Raised a Spiritual Body
1 Corinthians 15:42-49
S: We Have Victory Through Jesus Christ!
1 Corinthians 15:50-58

TEACHING TIPS

April 30
Bible Study Guide 9

1. Words You Should Know

A. Tongues of men. (v. 1)—one's own language as well as foreign languages.

B. Tongues of angels. (v. 1)—angelic speech that communicates something intelligent and that is capable of being understood by the hearer.

C. Gift of prophecy. (v. 2)—the God-given ability to speak in ways that build up the community of faith.

D. See face to face. (v. 12)—suggests standing in the presence of God where and when all things will be seen and understood clearly.

2. Teacher Preparation

A. Read 1 Corinthians 13 from at least three different translations of the Bible. This will help familiarize you with the flow and meaning of the text.

B. Study the IN DEPTH material. It will give you a better grasp of the mature ways in which love behaves and acts toward other persons. As you study the IN DEPTH material, jot down any ideas or life situations that further illustrate the IN DEPTH material.

3. Starting the Lesson

A. Open the class session by asking the students to tell about the greatest display of love they have seen within the past week. After three or four students have shared, take a minute to guide the class in a prayer of thanksgiving for the gift of God's love.

B. Ask one of your students to read aloud 1 Corinthians 13.

4. Getting into the Lesson

A. Using the IN DEPTH material, summarize for the students how love gives value to our service (1 Corinthians 13:1-3).

B. If your class is large enough, break up into groups of three to five students, and have each group discuss how love gives maturity to our behavior toward others (1 Corinthians 13:4-7). You may want to assign certain verses to each of the small groups. For example, one group could discuss how love's

refusal to be rude is an expression of maturity, etc.

C. Following student discussions, summarize how love gives lasting stability to our life and relationships (1 Corinthians 13:8-12).

D. Then ask your students to discuss why they think love is the greatest thing in the world (1 Corinthians 13:13). Following their responses, have one of the students read the IN DEPTH section # 5. Help the students understand this portion of the IN DEPTH material.

5. Relating the Lesson to Life

Ask students to share any new insights or ideas they gained as a result of today's lesson. Have them think about how these ideas and insights will affect their behavior during the coming week.

6. Arousing Action

Direct your students' attention to the MAKE IT HAPPEN section of the student lesson. Remind them to be alert to how they behave and act under pressure during the coming week. Challenge them to keep a one-week diary of their experiences. Encourage them to let love and respect for others moderate their behavior.

APRIL 30TH

WORSHIP GUIDE

For the Superintendent or Teacher
Theme: The Way of Love
Theme Song: "Love Divine, All Loves Excelling"
Scripture: Psalm 136:1-9, 23-26
Devotional Thought: For the joy of receiving Your love, O God, we give You thanks. Help us to love one another with the love You so graciously extend to us.

339

THE WAY OF LOVE

Bible Background • 1 CORINTHIANS 12:31—13:13
Printed Text • 1 CORINTHIANS 12:31—13:13
Devotional Reading • 1 JOHN 4:7-21

LESSON AIM

By the end of the lesson, students will explore the various ways in which love behaves and affirm love as the most excellent way to live and to manage one's life and relationships.

KEEP IN MIND

"And now abideth faith, hope, charity, these three; but the greatest of these is charity" (1 Corinthians 13:13).

FOCAL VERSES

1 CORINTHIANS 12:31 But covet earnestly the best gifts: and yet shew I unto you a more excellent way.

13:1 Though I speak with the tongues of men and of angels, and have not charity, I am become as sounding brass, or a tinkling cymbal.

2 And though I have the gift of prophecy, and understand all mysteries, and all knowledge; and though I have all faith, so that I could remove mountains, and have not charity, I am nothing.

3 And though I bestow all my goods to feed the poor, and though I give my body to be burned, and have not charity, it profiteth me nothing.

4 Charity suffereth long, and is kind; charity envieth not; charity vaunteth not itself, is not puffed up,

5 Doth not behave itself unseemly, seeketh not her own, is not easily provoked, thinketh no evil;

6 Rejoiceth not in iniquity, but rejoiceth in the truth;

7 Beareth all things, believeth all things, hopeth all things, endureth all things.

8 Charity never faileth: but whether there be prophecies, they shall fail; whether there be tongues, they shall cease; whether there be knowledge, it shall vanish away.

LESSON OVERVIEW

LESSON AIM
KEEP IN MIND
FOCAL VERSES
IN FOCUS
THE PEOPLE, PLACES, AND
TIMES
BACKGROUND
AT-A-GLANCE
IN DEPTH
SEARCH THE SCRIPTURES
DISCUSS THE MEANING
LESSON IN OUR SOCIETY
MAKE IT HAPPEN
FOLLOW THE SPIRIT
REMEMBER YOUR THOUGHTS
MORE LIGHT ON THE TEXT
DAILY BIBLE READINGS

9 For we know in part, and we prophesy in part.

10 But when that which is perfect is come, then that which is in part shall be done away.

11 When I was a child, I spake as a child, I understood as a child, I thought as a child: but when I became a man, I put away childish things.

12 For now we see through a glass, darkly; but then face to face: now I know in part; but then shall I know even as also I am known.

13 And now abideth faith, hope, charity, these three; but the greatest of these is charity.

IN FOCUS

Sharing in the congregational life of an urban church for over 25 years provides many opportunities to see love in action. Consider, for example, the Sunday morning worship service when the pastor's offertory appeal focused upon a single parent female member of the church whose home was going into foreclosure. The appeal was made with exceptional sensitivity and love. No one was embarrassed. The donations given by concerned and loving members were overwhelming, even awesome.

On the next day, a couple of the church's financial officers accompanied this recently divorced mother to her mortgage company. The mortgage note was brought current and refinanced making the monthly note more manageable for this single working mother. Foreclosure proceedings were halted. The rest is history.

All this took place several years ago. This mother continues to retain ownership of a modest, but comfortable home on which she pays the note with faithful regularity.

Today, one of her three children is a university graduate. Her other two children are currently pursuing higher education at two of the nation's great universities. The church, along with individual members in the church, continues to give moral support and help with college tuition.

Consider another example. A young drug addict stumbled into the church's worship service one Easter Sunday morning. He requested financial help. It did not take several concerned and loving men of the church long to conclude that what this young man needed was not financial help. He needed what money cannot buy. He needed to know that his life mattered and that if he wanted to turn his life around he could.

The next several months were extremely difficult. The risks, setbacks, and disappointments were many. But thanks to the love of five Christian men, the services of an in residence rehab-center and the presence of God's Holy Spirit, the young man is now clean and leading a productive life.

Love continues to be the most excellent way to bring peace and harmony to any disruptive situation. Henry Drummond once wrote that love is the "greatest thing in the world." Love gives value to our service, maturity to our behavior toward others, and lasting stability to our life and relationships.

THE PEOPLE, PLACES, AND TIMES

Corinth was a prosperous and rich city. Located about 45 miles to the northeast of Athens, Corinth was also a commercial and military center. It served as a shipping town and was often referred to as "the bridge of the sea…" Corinth's geographical location made it an ideal exchange point for shipping merchants transporting cargo between Italy, Sicily, Spain, Asia Minor, Syria, Phoenicia, and Egypt.

By the time of Paul's ministry, Corinth had become the capital of the Roman province of Achaia. Seven miles east of Corinth was the Temple of Poseidon, the citadel of Greek luxury, entertainment, and profligacy. It was at the Temple of Poseidon that the Isthmian Games, one of the great national festivals of ancient Greece, were celebrated every two years. The Greek goddess of love and beauty, Aphrodite, was also worshiped at the Temple of Poseidon through the assistance of 1000 female prostitutes, According to the ancient Greek geographer and historian, Strabo, these temple prostitutes or priestesses attracted many people to Corinth, as well as much wealth.

Sexual immorality in Corinth was rampant. As a result, the saying "to live like a Corinthian" came to be a household phrase to describe those who led a "loose life." This was the Corinth that Paul knew when he came preaching the Gospel of Jesus Christ. "Paul stayed for a year and a half" in Corinth, "teaching . . . the word of God" (Acts 18:11). During that year and a half, Paul established the church of God in Corinth. Prior to their conversion, many of Paul's converts led loose lives. It is not unreasonable to think that some of Paul's converts may have been regular clients of the temple priestesses at Poseidon (1 Corinthians 6:9-11). The church of God in Corinth was truly an urban, multi-racial, multi-cultural church, made up mostly of Jews and Gentiles.

It is a testimony to the power of the Gospel and to Paul's ministry that a viable congregation was planted in such a city as Corinth. The problems that existed in the Corinthian church and which occasioned Paul's letter are duplicated in many urban churches today. Many church members came from having led loose lives, from having looked for love in all the wrong places. The human heart hungers for a love which cannot be found anywhere but in God through faith in Jesus Christ. Those who embrace God's love and who allow God's love to embrace them will be supplied with what is needed to manage church problems and congregational stress in ways that please God. Whatever pleases God helps build up healthy people, places, and times.

BACKGROUND

The Corinthian church was a very gifted church (1 Corinthians 1:5-7). Unfortunately, however, attitudes and misunderstandings about the use and purpose of spiritual gifts resulted in congregational disunity. What God had given the church, to help bring newness of life to individuals and promote community well-being, was lost in selfishness, envy, jealousy, arrogance, impatience, and cliquishness.

Rival teachers emerged and certain church members worked overtime to lobby their particular teacher into greater prominence and authority (1 Corinthians 13-17; see also 1 Corinthians 3). Important questions about doctrine, ethics, and church discipline arose. Responses to these questions clashed and hardened opposing factions' negative perception of each other. Division in the church was the order of the day. Moreover, the attitudes caused by these divisions rendered the church's leadership powerless to bring order and peace to a congregation that had so much to offer.

News of the Corinthian church's problems reached Paul, probably by way of Stephanas, Fortunatus, and Achaicus (1 Corinthians 16:15-18). 1 Corinthians is Paul's attempt to redirect energies in the Corinthian church and to embellish the unity God had given the church. In framing his letter, Paul was wise enough to know that nothing could be righted in the church at Corinth apart from a fresh awareness and rebirth of love.

No church can be spiritually alive, bring glory and encouragement to God's people apart from love. Love should permeate the vision and mission of every church. Love should be the church's ultimate goal. Thus, Paul's eagerness to show the Corinthians this most excellent way.

AT-A-GLANCE

**1. Love Gives Value to Our Service (1 Corinthians 13:1-3)
2. Love Gives Maturity to Our Behavior toward Others (vv. 4-7)
3. Love Gives Lasting Stability to Our Life and Relationships (vv. 8-12)
4. Love Is the Greatest Thing in the World (v. 13)**

IN DEPTH

1. Love Gives Value to Our Service (1 Corinthians 13:1-3)

When Paul uses the word love, he is not talking about a feeling. Rather, he is talking about the kind of action that puts service to others ahead of service to oneself. Love shows itself in behavior that puts others first and helps them. This kind of behavior and action is made possible only by the love that God pours into our hearts by the Holy Spirit (Romans 5:5).

Paul wants his readers to know that the action and behavior which love makes possible has value; it amounts to something and helps others. Paul illustrates this truth by contrasting the proper use of the Spirit's gifts with the way in which the Corinthians were using these gifts. The Corinthians were using their spiritual gifts for selfish ends. Paul wants them to know that spiritual gifts have no value when they are used to serve selfish ends. Spiritual gifts have value when they are used in the service of others. Only love for others makes such use of the Spirit's gifts possible. In other words, love gives value to our service.

Verses 1-3 illustrate this by citing the Corinthian's exercise of four different spiritual gifts; the gift of tongues in verse 1, the gifts of prophecy and faith in verse 2, and the gift of generosity in verse 3. However, one should not limit this truth to these four gifts. Paul has all the gifts of the Spirit in mind. Spiritual gifts have value only when love dictates their use. Love always dictates that the gifts of the Spirit be used in the service of others.

For example, in verse 1 if the spiritual gift of tongues is used and does not have the interests of others at heart, then what is said, even if it is heaven's language, will have no value to those who hear it. It is like an untrained person trying to make melody on instruments about which they know absolutely nothing. The meaning of the phrase, "I am only a resounding gong or a clanging cymbal" is meaningless noise.

It is God's love at work in our hearts that gives value to everything we say and do. Knowing that God's love gives value to our service, we have no need to use our service as a means to call attention to ourselves. Love, Paul will say later (1 Corinthians 13:5b), "is not self-seeking."

2. Love Gives Maturity to Our Behavior toward Others (vv. 4-7)

Verses 4-8 should not be treated as a definition of love. Rather, Paul describes in these verses how Christians are to behave in their relationships with others. Christians are to live, act, and behave in ways that are mature. Christians are to be mature in their behavior toward others, including their spouses, parents, brothers and sisters in Christ, employees, employer, unsaved friends, next door neighbors, or worst critic.

God's will for believers is that they be mature in their behavior toward others. Verses 4-8 demonstrate how love makes one's behavior mature. For example, love shows patience and kindness toward others (1 Corinthians 13:4a). Patience is the ability to put-up with the idiosyncratic or annoying behavior of others for a long time without resentment, anger, or a desire to seek revenge. Kindness is the ability to give generously of oneself to others without any thought of return.

Maturity in behavior is also characterized by what love refuses to do and be. **For example, love "does not envy"** (1 Corinthians 13:4b). It does not nurture jealous feelings against others because of what they have. To get bent out of shape because one does not have what someone else has is immature. Love gives maturity to behavior and rejoices in the recognition, possessions, popularity, abilities, and good fortunes of others. Proverbs 14:30 helps make the point: "A heart at peace gives life to the body, but envy rots the bones."

Second, love "does not boast." It does not behave as a braggart or as a self-centered person whose actions are always calling attention to themselves. Mature persons do nothing out of selfish ambition or vain conceit, but in humility consider others better than themselves (see Philippians 2:3).

Third, love "is not proud." It has no overtones of

arrogance. It is modest and humble. It refuses to behave in a manner that puts itself above others, for to do so demonstrates immaturity. Love gives one the maturity to refuse to put oneself above others.

Fourth, love "is not rude." It does not act in an unmannerly or disgraceful way. God's love gives maturity to one's behavior and makes mannerly and graceful conduct possible. Christian love cares too much about people to behave in immature and unseemly ways.

Fifth, love "is not self-seeking." It is not enamored with self-gain or self-justification. It does not insist on its own rights. In the context of 1 Corinthians, love knows when not to eat meat when eating meat is going to cause one's brother or sister to fall into sin. Moreover, it is very immature to exercise one's freedom in ways that show disregard for the conscience and convictions of one's fellow believers.

Sixth, love "is not easily angered." It has a long temper. The fact that love can become angry at all suggests that anger and love can coexist. Love can become angry; however, it is not easily angered. Love knows how to control its own emotions. It is the kind of love and maturity called for in Romans 12:18: "If it is possible, as far as depends on you, live at peace with everyone" (NIV). To know when to exercise loving anger requires a great deal of maturity. If love's temper is short, the chances are very great that one will express anger in very immature ways. The wisdom of Ecclesiastes 7:9 says, "Do not be quickly provoked in your spirit, for anger resides in the lap of fools" (NIV).

Seventh, love "keeps no record of wrongs." It absorbs the wrong done to it and forgets it. It has no motivation to be resentful or to hold a grudge. Nothing is more immature than to see a born again believer carrying a grudge against someone, unable to let by-gones be by-gones. Love grants freedom from the need to keep records of wrongs. Love gives maturity to one's behavior, makes sure that nobody pays back wrong for wrong, and always tries to be kind toward others (see 1 Thessalonians 5:15).

Eighth, "Love does not delight in evil but rejoices with the truth" (1 Corinthians 13:6, NIV). It is important to note that Paul makes evil and truth two sides of the same reality. In other words, it is not enough to refrain from taking pleasure in the sins and wrongs of others. One must go on and rejoice when others succeed and are recognized and promoted for who they are and for the good they have contributed. The refusal to take delight in evil and commitment to rejoice with the truth is evidence of maturity and a heart of love.

Ninth, love "always protects, always trusts, always hopes, always perseveres." Paul's repetitious

use of the word "always" suggests that in everything love always protects, trusts, hopes, and perseveres. The first and last of these four verbs (i.e., "protects" and "perseveres") deal with present circumstances. The second and third of these four verbs (i.e., "trusts" and "hopes") deal with circumstances in the future. When one links present circumstances with future circumstances, the intended meaning of this Scripture verse is clear; love can put up with everything. "There is nothing love cannot face" (1 Corinthians 13:7, NEB), neither in the present nor in the future. Buoyed by its trust and hope in the future, love can deal with any situation or hurdle any relational barrier. Love protects against threatening circumstances and enables one to persevere against life's challenges.

However, Paul's comment that love always trusts and hopes does not mean that love always believes the best about everything and about everyone. Rather, it means that love never ceases to have faith. It never loses hope. This is why love can endure. It "never fails" (1 Corinthians 13:8, NIV). Love always trusts God in the interest of the one loved. Love hopes to the end that God's mercy will prevail in every circumstance, both in the present and in the future.

3. Love Gives Lasting Stability to Our Life and Relationships (vv. 8-12)

Paul has already stated in verse 7 that there is nothing love cannot face. Now he concludes by saying, "Love never fails."

In what sense can it be said that love never fails? In view of all that Paul has said about love, believers know that this kind of love is possible only because of the indwelling presence of God's love. "We love because he first loved us" (1 John 4:19, NIV). This kind of love is not generated by human genius. It is made possible only by a continuing action of God within the believer.

Since God's work and love endures and lasts forever, His love at work within us never ceases. His love never vanishes. We can ignore, abuse, and refuse to accept God's love. But God's love will continue to dog our steps and hound our lives.

To further dramatize his point about the never ending, never failing, love of God, Paul goes on to say in verse 8b that there is no comparison between what we do and what God's love does. What God does is permanent and perfect. What we do is impermanent and imperfect. Our prophesying will cease. Our tongues will be stilled. Our knowledge will pass away. There is no permanence or perfection in what we do. What we do is child's play compared with the never failing love and activity of God.

Paul wants his Corinthian readers to know that the gifts

of the Spirit are only appropriate to the present life of the church. One day, death will bring an end to each believer's exercise of the Spirit's gifts. On that day, believers will need more than the gifts of the Spirit to see them across Jordan. They will want to know that God's love and mercy has laid eternal claim upon their lives.

Therefore, Paul invites the Corinthian and modern-day believers to join him in putting "childish ways behind" themselves. It is futile, infantile, and immature to feud about the Spirit's gifts. Rather, make love your aim. Wait with patience, kindness, and love toward one another until the day when we shall all see face-to-face and when we shall know fully, even as we are fully known (1 Corinthians 13:9-12).

When believers give love its proper place, what they do takes on a sense of the eternal and gives stability to their lives.

5. Love Is the Greatest Thing in the World (v. 13)

In conclusion and in contrast to the temporary gifts of the Spirit with which the Corinthians were selfishly preoccupied, "these three remain: faith, hope, and love. But the greatest of these is love." Love is the greatest in that it continues with the believer throughout all eternity. Like the gifts of the Spirit, faith and hope remain with us in this life. But God's love extends into eternity where we shall see clearly Him who is love (see 1 John 4:13-16).

SEARCH THE SCRIPTURES

1. What makes us able to love with the love of God? (Romans 5:5; see also 1 John 4:19)

2. In terms of 1 Corinthians 13, how are Christians to behave in their relationships with others? (1 Corinthians 13:4b-7)

3. What two characteristics of love help make our behavior mature? (1 Corinthians 13:4a)

4. A heart at peace gives _____ but _____.

5. What does love always do? (1 Corinthians 13:7)

DISCUSS THE MEANING

1. In what sense does love never fail?

2. What is meant by the phrase "Love always protects, trusts, hopes and perseveres"? (1 Corinthians 13:7) Does this mean that those who love must always trust everybody?

LESSON IN OUR SOCIETY

Ours is a highly competitive society, where compassion and consideration for other's concerns often get lost in the selfish pursuit of personal goals. Although, many of the problems in the church at Corinth were occasioned by misguided direction, they were accelerated by an absence of love and concern for others. It is usually not our disagreements that bring about family feuds, church disputes, and wars. Rather, it is our inability to exercise love and respect while working through our disagreements. Love + Respect + Commitment to Talk it Through tends to = Resolution of Difficult Problems.

This formula works in churches, families, and marriages. It works on school playgrounds and in the bargaining halls of labor and management. It also works between racial and ethnic groups. Wholesome competition that feeds our healthy needs for entertainment is good. But competition of any kind that is void of love and respect tends usually to occasion violent disputes and even wars. Love and respect for others is still our greatest means for handling potentially volatile situations with personal maturity. Disputes that show disregard for the well-being of others and that erupt into violence are expressive of aggressive immaturity.

God's will is that we be mature persons; always counting others better than ourselves.

MAKE IT HAPPEN

What is the measure of your maturity? Does love and respect control your behavior and dictate your actions? During this next week keep an emotional thermometer within your reach. Be alert to how you behave and act under pressure. Seek to let love and respect moderate your behavior.

FOLLOW THE SPIRIT

What God wants me to do:

_____

_____

REMEMBER YOUR THOUGHTS

Special insights you have learned:

_____

_____

MORE LIGHT ON THE TEXT
1 CORINTHIANS 12:31—13:13

12:31 But covet earnestly the best gifts: and yet shew I unto you a more excellent way.

In the previous chapter, Paul explained how the presence of diverse gifts in the church operated for a common purpose, and how such diversity is essential to the well being of the church. Although these gifts may differ, and some may be esteemed as better or more desirous than others, every gift is needed in order for the church body to function effectively.

Having said this, Paul moves to a deeper level of understanding: "Covet earnestly the best gifts." One should seek these gifts with zeal, not half-heartedly. The phrase "the best gifts" refers to the Corinthians' emphasis on the gifts of prophecy, speaking in tongues, and the working of miracles. One can attain all these gifts, but there is yet a more excellent way, a better way to conduct one's life.

31 Though I speak with the tongues of men and of angels, and have not charity, I am become as sounding brass, or a tinkling cymbal.

Speaking in tongues is one of those spiritual gifts which allows humans to experience the spiritual world. In a moment, a person can be so tuned-in to the spirit world that sounds involuntarily come forth, attempting to communicate to and from the spirit world. Those who experience this phenomenon may do so without the slightest cognitive understanding of what occurred. And thus, Paul compares the experience to the sounds of familiar instruments, whose clanging may be heard as bothersome, irritating noise when played without understanding. The sounds issue forth from the mouth, and no one may be able to interpret them into any meaningful thought. So much for the prized gift, if love is not the motivating factor.

The Greek word *iagapei* used to be translated as "charity" in older translations of the Bible. This was found to be inadequate, because of its connotations of class: the "haves" giving or acting on behalf of the "have-nots." This was usually a temporary, or one-time act. But *iagapei* implies a much greater, long-term commitment, as is described in verses 4-7. Thus the word "love" is better able to capture the significance of what is meant.

In what way does love make such a difference? Everyone has seen how mothers easily interpret the grunts and moans of their pre-verbal children into intelligible wants and wishes. Or even how verbally impaired adults struggle to form sounds and sentences that seem completely unintelligible to one person, but completely clear to another. The difference is whether or not the listener listens in love. Listening in love, the two make a mental and emotional connection that allows the listener to fill in the missing or mispronounced sounds. With love, sometimes speaking is not even necessary to communicate. Without love there are too many gaps to understand one another.

2 And though I have the gift of prophecy, and understand all mysteries, and all knowledge; and though I have all faith, so that I could remove mountains, and have not charity, I am nothing.

One would think that it would be impossible to have these gifts, particularly a strong faith, and not have love. But apparently it can happen. Without love, what would motivate someone with such gifts: fame, self-indulgence, or profit? People would probably view a person with such motivations and gifts as very dangerous. The prophet without love who delivers a message of destruction is experienced as an evil doomsday prophet, rather than a comrade who tries to turn his/her people back to salvation. A person with understanding of all mysteries and knowledge without love would be feared, because no one could trust their use of such knowledge. A person who has enough faith to perform wondrous acts but does not have love could not be depended on by those needing such miracles.

3 And though I bestow all my goods to feed the poor, and though I give my body to be burned, and have not charity, it profiteth me nothing.

These last two acts are examples of ultimate sacrifice. The giving of all one's goods for the sake of the poor is charity at its best. Human sacrifice was common in the early stages of many religions. Although human sacrifice was not condoned by Christianity in Paul's day, its significance was easily understood. These acts could quickly give one favor in the eyes of others, but the memory of such acts would fade much sooner than expected. If one performed these acts out of a sense of pride rather than love, or to gain immortality in the public's eye, one's immortality would be short-lived.

After summing up the emptiness of spiritual gifts without love, Paul goes on to explain the characteristics of love.

4 Charity suffereth long, and is kind; charity envieth not; charity vaunteth not itself, is not puffed up,

Love is patient and willing to endure discomfort over an extended period of time. Love is not in a hurry to get past the pain that comes in relationship with others. In kindness, love seeks to eliminate or reduce the misery of others. Love is not envious of what others have, it rejoices with them. Love does not seek to exalt itself, nor is it puffed up with pride.

5 Doth not behave itself unseemly, seeketh not her own, is not easily provoked, thinketh no evil;

Love does not make a public nuisance of itself. Love knows how to conduct itself, taking into account the feelings and aspirations of others. Love does not se own advantage at the expense of others. Love be easily provoked into injuring another (ph emotionally), because it is patient. Love does not plot out evil intentions. Love does not give the impression of patience, while waiting for a time to attack.

6 Rejoiceth not in iniquity, but rejoiceth in the truth;

Love does not rejoice in unrighteousness or injustice. The Greek word *iadikiai* covers a range of meanings from moral wrongfulness to legal injustice. Love does not rejoice in any acts that rob the poor, the elderly, widows, or orphans. Love rejoices when truth is revealed and when justice is done.

7 Beareth all things, believeth all things, hopeth all things, endureth all things.

Love is able to silently bear all things; it does not need to tell every slight to gain sympathy for itself. Love believes in the possibility of all things. Love hopes in the possibility of all things, and does not give into pessimism. Love is enduring, because it is steadfast.

8 Charity never faileth: but whether there be prophecies, they shall fail; whether there be tongues, they shall cease; whether there be knowledge, it shall vanish away.

The need for love will never come to an end. The prophecies of today will become hollow empty words tomorrow. Speaking between two worlds will one day come to an end; it will no longer be necessary. Even the knowledge we hold so dear today shall vanish, and become as dust in the wind. But still love will exist. God is love.

9 For we know in part, and we prophesy in part. 10 But when that which is perfect is come, then that which is in part shall be done away.

All of our knowledge and prophecy is incomplete, based upon fragments of revelation of reality. It is not always clear how these fragments fit together. It does not represent a total picture and thus must cease as more truth comes into clear view. When that which is perfect or whole comes into view, then all the fragmented parts shall be done away with. They will show themselves to be obsolete.

11 When I was a child, I spake as a child, I understood as a child, I thought as a child: but when I became a man, I put away childish things.

Our partial and fragmented knowledge is likened to the difference between a child's understanding and an adult's. The child only sees certain facts and processes them based upon that limited exposure and experience. But an adult sees and processes many more facts and thus has a broader understanding. Once one has gained an adult understanding, one cannot be a child anymore and puts away childish ways.

12 For now we see through a glass, darkly; but then face to face: now I know in part; but then shall I know even as also I am known. 13 And now abideth faith, hope, charity, these three; but the greatest of these is charity.

Now we are unable to see clearly into reality, into the face of God. But the time is coming when we shall see God face to face, without distortion. Now we have partial knowledge of what God is like. But in time we shall know of God, even as we are known by God. Paul dealt with this understanding of love and knowledge earlier in 1 Corinthians 8:3. There he emphasized how God comes to know us by the love we demonstrate to one another. And to be known by God was far better, than to possess all knowledge and understanding of the mysteries.

DAILY BIBLE READING

M: The Gift of Love
1 Corinthians 13:1-7
T: Love Is the Greatest Gift
1 Corinthians 13:8-13
W: Love: An Old New Commandment
1 John 2:7-17
T: Show Your Love for One Another
1 John 3:11-17
F: Believe in Jesus, and Love One Another
1 John 3:18-24
S: Let Us Love as God Loves
1 John 4:7-12
S: We Abide in God If We Love
1 John 4:13-21

TEACHING TIPS

May 7
Bible Study Guide 10

1. Words You Should Know

A. Distress. (2 Corinthians 2:3, 4)—Great suffering of body or mind; worry; anguish.

B. Overwhelmed. (2 Corinthians 2:7)—To overpower, crush.

C. Reaffirm. (2 Corinthians 2:8)—To assert positively.

D. Schemes. (2 Corinthians 2:11) A crafty plot; a systematic plan.

E. Peddle. (2 Corinthians 2:17)—To travel about with goods for sale; to sell from place to place.

2. Teacher Preparation

A. Prepare for this quarter by first reading the UNIT 3 INTRODUCTION. Then use the QUARTER-AT-A-GLANCE to overview the unit.

B. Now focus on Lesson 10. First read the DEVOTIONAL READING, then the BACKGROUND SCRIPTURE.

C. Carefully study the FOCAL VERSES. Read them at least three times using a different version each time.

D. Read the commentary in the IN DEPTH section.

E. Materials needed: Bible, 3x5 index cards, a board or newsprint.

3. Starting the Lesson

A. Before the class enters, draw a line down the middle of the board and on one side write: fear, rejection, loneliness, discrimination, lack of confidence. On the other side write words like: overcomer, victory, triumphant, trust, faith, delivered.

B. After the students have entered and settled, assign someone to read the IN FOCUS story. Ask the class if they see any correlation with the words on the board and the IN FOCUS story. Lead the class in prayer focusing on the LESSON AIM.

C. Before beginning the lesson, explain the focus of Unit 3 using the UNIT INTRODUCTION.

4. Getting into the Lesson

A. Ask the class to share some of their own personal situations where they had feelings from the left column of the board and how they dealt with them.

B. Read the verses where Paul shared his own personal feelings of being overwhelmed and grieved.

C. Guide the class into a discussion on how Paul gained victory as he focused on the only victory in his life. Have volunteers read the FOCAL VERSES according to the AT-A-GLANCE outline.

D. After the students have read each segment, ask the corresponding SEARCH THE SCRIPTURES questions.

5. Relating the Lesson to Life

A. Direct the students to the DISCUSS THE MEANING questions and encourage discussion and debate. This will help them to see how the lesson applies to them personally.

B. Next read the LESSON IN OUR SOCIETY article and allow for discussion. This will help the students to see how the lesson applies to our modern-day society.

6. Arousing Action

A. Direct the students' attention to the MAKE IT HAPPEN suggestion. You may want to ask for a show of hands of any who would like to answer God's call to salvation. If any students raise their hands, call them to the front of the class and lead them in a prayer of repentance. Remind the class that living for the Lord is a way of becoming a sweet savour or smell to God.

B. Remind the class that witnessing for our Lord to the lost is so important. Ask each one if there is someone that they can lead to the Lord this week. Close in prayer asking the Lord to speak to each student individually to show them someone they can lead to Christ.

WORSHIP GUIDE

For the Superintendent or Teacher
Theme: The Christian March of Triumph
Theme Song: "Where He Leads Me I Will Follow"
Scripture: 1 Corinthians 10:1-13
Song: "Lead Me"
Devotional Thought: Dear Lord, I am so glad that I can cross over from feelings of defeat and abandonment, to victory and Your eternal presence as I allow You to lead me all of my life.

MAY 7TH

THE CHRISTIAN MARCH OF TRIUMPH

Bible Background • 2 CORINTHIANS 1—2
Printed Text • 2 CORINTHIANS 2:4-17
Devotional Reading • 2 CORINTHIANS 1:3-11

LESSON AIM

By the end of the lesson, students will acknowledge that we will face many fears, disappointments, and misunderstandings in life. They will also understand that we can overcome these struggles and experience triumph as we go through them trusting God as the leader of our lives.

KEEP IN MIIND

"Now thanks be unto God, which always causeth us to triumph in Christ, and maketh manifest the savour of his knowledge by us in every place" (2 Corinthians 2:14).

FOCAL VERSES

2 CORINTHIANS 2:4 For out of much affliction and anguish of heart I wrote unto you with many tears; not that ye should be grieved, but that ye might know the love which I have more abundantly unto you.

5 But if any have caused grief, he hath not grieved me, but in part, that I may not overcharge you all.

6 Sufficient to such a man is this punishment, which was inflicted of many.

7 So that contrariwise ye ought rather to forgive him, and comfort him, lest perhaps such a one should be swallowed up with overmuch sorrow.

8 Wherefore I beseech you that ye would confirm your love toward him.

9 For to this end also did I write, that I might know the proof of you, whether ye be obedient in all things.

10 To whom ye forgive any thing, I forgive also: for if I forgave any thing, to whom I forgave it, for your sakes forgave I it in the person of Christ,

11 Lest Satan should get an advantage of us: for we are not ignorant of his devices.

LESSON OVERVIEW

LESSON AIM
KEEP IN MIND
FOCAL VERSES
IN FOCUS
THE PEOPLE, PLACES, AND TIMES
BACKGROUND
AT-A-GLANCE
IN DEPTH
SEARCH THE SCRIPTURES
DISCUSS THE MEANING
LESSON IN OUR SOCIETY
MAKE IT HAPPEN
FOLLOW THE SPIRIT
REMEMBER YOUR THOUGHTS
MORE LIGHT ON THE TEXT
DAILY BIBLE READINGS

12 Furthermore, when I came to Troas to preach Christ's gospel, and a door was opened unto me of the Lord,

13 I had no rest in my spirit, because I found not Titus, my brother: but taking my leave of them, I went from thence into Macedonia.

14 Now thanks be unto God which always causeth us to triumph in Christ, and maketh manifest the savour of his knowledge by us in every place.

15 For we are unto God a sweet savour of Christ, in them that are saved, and in them that perish:

16 To the one we are the savour of death unto death; and to the other, the savour of life unto life. And who is sufficient for these things?

17 For we are not as many, which corrupt the word of God: but as of sincerity, but as of God, in the sight of God speak we in Christ.

IN FOCUS

Nichelle Nichols played Uhura in the original Star Trek TV program and six Star Trek movies. She was one of the first Black women regularly featured on a weekly TV show. As such, she had obstacles to overcome. According to Steve Jones in *USA Today*, a few studio executives were hostile toward her character, which was often diminished by script rewrites, and the studio even withheld tons of her fan mail. After one year on the program, she was fed up. Nichols, who was also an extremely talented professional singer and dancer, told Gene Roddenberry she was going to quit and pursue her performing career.

Before she did, however, she went to a fund-raiser for the NAACP. There she happened to meet Dr. Martin Luther King, who urged her not to leave the show. She was a role model for many.

Says Nichols, "When you have a man like Dr. Martin

Luther King say you can't leave a show, it's daunting. It humbled my heart, and I couldn't leave. God had charged me with something more important than my own career."

The rest, as they say, is history. Not only did she become a fixture on Star Trek, she actually influenced NASA, challenging them to hire Blacks and women for their astronaut corps. She led a 1977 NASA recruitment drive that saw 1,600 women and 1,000 minorities apply within four months.

By giving up her plans to sing and dance, Nichols marched to a different drummer. She led a march that brought about triumph and victory to many people of color. Nichols found the defining role of her career as Lieutenant Uhura in one of the most popular TV shows ever and influenced a nation.

In today's lesson, Paul encourages believers going through struggles and painful circumstances to open their eyes and see how God can bring victory through the very circumstances that cause pain.

THE PEOPLE, PLACES, AND TIMES

No letter of Paul's is more personal and intimate in nature than 2 Corinthians. Paul bared his soul and professed his abiding love for the Corinthians. Such expressions were:

MUCH AFFLICTION AND ANGUISH OF HEART. "Pressures" or "distresses" are mentioned nine times by Paul in this letter (1:4 [twice], 8; 2:4; 4:17; 6:4; 7:4; 8:2, 13). Sometimes the word is translated "troubles" other times "hardships" or "harassed." Troubles are experienced by all Christians. The Apostle Paul probably endured more pressures than nearly all of his readers. Troubles, Paul said, helps Christians shift their perspective from the external and temporal to the internal and eternal (cf. 1:9; 4:17-18).

LEST SATAN SHOULD GET AN ADVANTAGE. One of Satan's schemes is to drive wedges between the saints of God. He uses a spirit of bitterness or unforgiveness to destroy relationships. Paul was keenly aware of how this destroyed relationships as well as churches. The church of Corinth had been dealing with an erring member who had apparently repented from wrong doings. Paul wanted the church to forgive this member and continue demonstrating love and devotion before Satan got involved.

TROAS. A city built by Antigonia Troas. It was located on the coast of Mysia, opposite the southeast island of Tenedos. Troas was a Roman colony, and one of the most important towns in the providence of Asia. Paul had planned to meet with Titus at Troas.

MACEDONIA. A large and celebrated country lying

north of Greece, between Greece and the Balkans. This region has a mountainous interior and a hardy population. Under noted kings, Philip and Alexander, its fertile plains and extensive seaboard exercised a surprising influence over the history of the world.

TRIUMPH IN CHRIST. A Roman military triumphal procession was one of the grandest spectacles of ancient times. In 2 Corinthians 2:14, Christ is referred to as the Great Conqueror, making public exhibition of the spoils of war. Paul is merely an instrument used for the accomplishment of His work. Thus, wherever he preached, Christ triumphed; and as in the Roman victories soldiers were profusely scattered around, so the knowledge of Christ was proclaimed everywhere by the apostles. In the Roman conquests, the fragrance which filled the air was inhaled by both the captives of war doomed to death and the people who by means of the victory were saved from a similar fate. Thus the Gospel is preached to all, but with different results; for the believer, salvation; to him who rejects, eternal death. So Paul says in verses 15-16 "for we are unto God a sweet savour of Christ, in them that are saved, and in them that perish: to the one we are the savour of death unto death; and to the other the savour of life unto life."

BACKGROUND

The first and second books of Corinthians were written by the Apostle Paul around 56 A.D. Corinth was a port city and wealthy commercial center. Located on the narrow isthmus between the Aegean and Adriatic seas. Ships wanting to avoid the dangerous trip around the southern tip of Greece were dragged across this isthmus. The city boasted an outdoor theater that accommodated 20,000 people and athletic games second only to the Olympics. Corinth was made up of a Greek, Roman, and Oriental population. It also contained the great temple of Aphrodite with its 1,000 prostitutes.

The reputation of Corinth was linked with wealth and immorality. When Plato referred to a prostitute, he used the expression "Corinthian girl." The playwright Philetaerus (Athenaeus 13.559a) titled a burlesque play Ho Korinthiastes, which may be translated "the lecher." A lecher is a man or woman given to uncontrollable lust. The city of Corinth centered around the 1,000 prostitutes. For this reason a proverb warned "not for every man is the voyage to Corinthians."

The spirit of the world was very influential in the Corinthian church than the Spirit of God, despite the splendid gifts given by the Holy Spirit. The church of Corinth was known for divisions, misunderstanding of the ministry of the Holy Spirit, and a lack of growth. The believers were still conducting themselves as babes in

Christ. There was incest, marriage problems, and disagreement with those who wanted celibacy as a lifestyle. Finally there were problems with self-discipline and self-control.

IN DEPTH

1. Triumph in Love (2 Corinthians 2:4-6)

Paul's letter to the Corinthians has come to be known as the "sorrowful [or severe] letter." His aim was to avoid being pained by them when he finally did pay another personal visit (v. 3a). Paul had not been able to bring himself to writing this letter without much mental anguish and distress; and he was often in tears as he wrote it. He knew that the words in his letter would hurt. Although the letter had to be painful, the spirit in which it was written showed his heart-felt affection. In this letter, the word "love" is given the strongest possible emphasis by its position in the Greek. The expression "more abundantly unto you" indicates that Paul had a very special love for the Corinthians.

Paul made his third trip to Corinth during the winter of A.D. 56-57 (Acts 20:2-3). After this painful visit, an insult was directed against Paul or one of his representatives, perhaps by a visitor to Corinth or a Corinthian who may have objected to Paul's disciplinary methods. Paul responds to the Corinthians in love and discounts the sorrow caused by the unfortunate episode. Paul's response may be rendered, "If anyone has caused pain, he caused pain not so much to me as to all or you." The Corinthians apparently failed to make the connection between a challenge to Paul's authority and their own spiritual well-being. They had regarded this as a personal problem requiring no action on their part, a view which Paul had dispelled in his letter and which they now realized was incorrect. Paul's love for the Corinthians kept him from giving up. "Love never fails" (1 Corinthians 13:8). Where there is love, there is always the burden to see others enjoy the very best. Many times pastors weep over wayward Christians. Yet God honored Paul's tears and worked in the church so that sin was put away.

2. Triumph in Forgiveness (vv. 7-12)

The discipline had been issued by the church of

Corinth "as a whole" towards the offender. Paul had reason to believe that their pendulum might swing too far (cf. 7:11). "Forgive him and take him back" says the apostle. "If you don't, Satan will overburden him with too much sorrow."

How often Christians confess their sins and yet fail to believe that God will forgive and forget. There is an abnormal sorrow that is not really true repentance; it is remorse, the sorrow of the world. After denying Christ, Peter showed repentance; his was a godly sorrow that led him back to Christ. After betraying Christ, Judas showed remorse; his was a hopeless sorrow, a sorrow of the world, that led him away from Christ to suicide. Satan wants us to believe that we cannot be forgiven. If Satan can accuse us of sin and discourage us with our past failures, he will rob us of our joy and usefulness to Christ. If God forgives us of sin, we must forgive others, too (Ephesians 4:32).

3. Triumph in Witnessing (vv. 13-17)

Paul uses the account of his trip from Ephesus to Philippi as an example. What had started out as trouble ended up as triumph! How often this happens in the Christian life. The women came to the tomb that Easter morning burdened with disappointment, only to find that a great victory had been won. Paul came to Troas and could not find Titus, but he did find a "tremendous opportunity" to preach the Gospel. In every place of trial there is also a door of opportunity.

However, service is no substitute for peace. Paul longed to see Titus and get word about the church at Corinth. He left Troas and made his way to Macedonia (probably Philippi), bypassing Corinth completely. At Philippi, he met Titus and received the good news that the offender had been disciplined, the majority of the church supported Paul, and things were looking better. This so encouraged Paul that he broke into a song of praise.

The picture in verses 14-17 was familiar to every Roman but is unfamiliar to twentieth-century Christians. Whenever a victorious general returned home from battle, Rome gave him a public parade, not unlike our modern ticker-tape parades. This parade was filled with pomp and glory, and a great deal of incense was burned in honor of the hero. During the celebration, soldiers and officers would enjoy glory and praise, but slaves and captives would end up in the arena to die fighting the wild beasts. For the victors the incense held the aroma of life and joy; but for the captives, the incense was a reminder of their coming death.

In the "Christian parade" that Paul describes, Jesus Christ is the Victor. Through His death on the cross, He has conquered every foe. Christians ride in the procession with Him, sharing His victory (1 Corinthians 15:57). The

Christian, however, carries the incense (sweet savour of Christ) in this procession as the Spirit spreads the knowledge of Christ in and through our lives. This savour, or perfume, means life to other believers, but to the unbeliever headed for eternal condemnation, it means death.

Paul presents a beautiful and challenging picture. What a tremendous responsibility it is to introduce people to life, or to have them reject Christ and go off to death! Being a Christian is a serious responsibility, for our lives are leading people either to heaven or hell. No wonder Paul exclaims, "Who is sufficient for these things?" (v. 16). How can a Christian possess all that is needed to be the best Christian possible, the best witness, the best soldier? Paul answers the question in 3:5: "Our sufficiency is of God." Paul uses this word "sufficient" several times in the letter of 2 Corinthians. Christ is sufficient for our spiritual needs (3:4-6), our material needs (9:8), and our physical needs (12:7-10).

In verse 17, Paul returns to the accusation that his word could not be trusted. Unfortunately, even today there are religious leaders who "make merchandise" of (or corrupt, v. 17) the Word of God, who are insincere and deceptive. The word "corrupt" carries the idea of "peddling" the Gospel, using the ministry only as a means of making a living rather than building the church of Jesus Christ. A form of this Greek word was used to describe an innkeeper or peddler, and carries the idea of doing business just to make a profit. Paul's ministry was not a business; it was a burden. He was not serving men; he was serving Christ. He was sincere in method, message, and motive. He realized that God's eye was upon him and that Christ's glory was at stake.

In these two chapters, we have seen that Paul's ministry was full of suffering and sorrow, yet he experienced triumph and joy in Christ. Let us remember that "our sufficiency is of God" (2 Corinthians 3:5).

SEARCH THE SCRIPTURES

1. How does Paul describe his emotions as he writes a letter to the church of Corinth? (2 Corinthians 2:4)

2. What did Paul instruct the church to do so that their brother would not suffer excessively? (v. 7)

3. When we show love and forgiveness to one another, what are we preventing Satan from doing? (vv. 8-11)

4. Who leads our great procession of life in Christ and spreads the knowledge of Himself as we go? (v. 14)

5. Since we are an aroma of Christ when we share His Gospel there are two different fragrances that can be smelled, what are they? (v. 16)

DISCUSS THE MEANING

1. Paul says that all believers are to God an aroma of Christ to those who are lost and dying. Have you ever thought about how effective you were as an aroma of Christ to those who are lost in our world?

2. Discuss areas in your life that you can change or improve to be a more effective aroma to God of Christ.

LESSON IN OUR SOCIETY

The inner city Union Baptist Church was experiencing a decline in membership that threatened its existence. People were not driving back into the inner city to attend church. One day, the church had a meeting and decided that they would go out into the community, knock on doors, and share the Gospel with all who would receive it. The majority of the members were scared; they had never shared their faith before.

Finally, the day arrived and the members reluctantly showed up. They were divided into groups of two's and three's and off they went. As they left, their faces showed fear of rejection, and lack of confidence in themselves and in God. A few hours passed, and finally the first group returned. They were beaming as they shared what had transpired that morning. Each group that followed them had similar stories of how God had reached the people and how God gave them confidence and courage to share the Good News of Jesus Christ. The church developed a evangelism team and each week thereafter they boldly went into their community to share the Gospel to the lost.

Despite their fears, how did the church triumph as the members went out to share in the community? God cares about the crime, the drugs, and those who are lost without Him, but He needs vessels to work through. Are you available to Him? Is your church available to Him? Can the church really make a difference today in our communities?

MAKE IT HAPPEN

Have you ever been faced with fears of rejection, discrimination, being misunderstood, loneliness, and feelings of inadequacy? Write down your feelings and ask God to help you deal with each one for His glory. Ask God to show you ways that you can grow and become triumphant in these areas.

FOLLOW THE SPIRIT

What God wants me to do:

_____

_____

REMEMBER YOUR THOUGHTS

Special insights you have learned:

_____

_____

MORE LIGHT ON THE TEXT
2 CORINTHIANS 2:4-17

2:4 For out of much affliction and anguish of heart I wrote unto you with many tears; not that ye should be grieved, but that ye might know the love which I have more abundantly unto you.

Paul had hurt them by the letter he sent (7:8), and he had been made aware of it. Paul had lost confidence in them because of all the division which he addressed in his first letter to them (immorality, fights about the gifts of the Spirit, issues concerning the Lord's Supper and the resurrection, etc.). To understand verse 4, one has to study also 7:8 where the first letter in mentioned. Paul sent the letter to show them his love rather than to grieve them. Second Corinthians 10-13 may be that letter.

5 But if any have caused grief, he hath not grieved me, but in part, that I may not overcharge you all.

Paul realizes that an injury had been done to the Corinthians, and as their pastor he is responsible to clear the cloud. His apostleship had been an insult to some. But any injury done to the congregation is also done to its pastor. Likewise any attacks launched against Paul's apostleship are equally done against the church in Corinth. But the congregation had failed to rally in support of Paul thus to reprimand the offender who had caused Paul the pain of trying to discredit his apostleship. So Paul was forced to write a harsh letter, so called the letter of tears, to see how they stood, whether they faithfully accepted his authority or not. The letter was a sort of disciplinary action against the Corinthians who failed to take action against the offender.

6 Sufficient to such a man is this punishment, which was inflicted of many.

Paul's letter had been effective in bringing the congregation to their senses. The letter had caused them the pain which led them to reprimand or even excommunicate the offender (7:8). The offender may have been one who slept with his father's wife (1 Corinthians 5). A penalty was imposed on the offender either by excluding him from the Lord's Supper or other churchly activities. But the offender was still in touch with others. So Paul is calling for a tougher disciplinary action (1 Corinthians 5:1-5).

7 So that contrariwise ye ought rather to forgive him, and comfort him, lest perhaps such a one should be swallowed up with overmuch sorrow. 8 Wherefore I beseech you that ye would confirm your love toward him.

Paul appeals for clemency for the offender. The reason for this is that the offender has reached the point of possibly committing suicide. The term used is *katapothe*, meaning to be consumed. The NIV uses "overwhelmed." Paul considers that it is necessary to halt the disciplinary action against the offender. Love and forgiveness must be the guiding factors. The Corinthians will need to reassure him of their love as Christians. The isolation has been enough to bring the offender to their mercy. The injury meant to hurt Paul has instead hurt the offender. Love, the supreme Christian virtue, must be exercised for the offender (1 Corinthians 13).

9 For to this end also did I write, that I might know the proof of you, whether ye be obedient in all things.

In disciplining the offender, the Corinthians proved that they were still obedient to the Apostle Paul. They acknowledged him as their leader by doing what he asked them to do. This is in line with Jesus' teaching that a house divided within cannot stand. Their actions showed obedience to their leader and to the supreme head of the church, Jesus our Lord.

10 To whom ye forgive any thing, I forgive also: for if I forgave any thing, to whom I forgave it, for your sakes forgave I it in the person of Christ,

Paul gives the Corinthians an example by offering forgiveness himself. In Matthew 19:21-22, Peter asked Jesus, "How many times must I forgive my brother, even seven times?" Jesus answered by directing his disciples to give unending forgiveness to those who wrong them ("seventy times seven"). Paul sets the example for his congregation; he forgives, they forgive. This is also to be obedient to the Lord Jesus Christ who has taught us to forgive.

11 Lest Satan should get an advantage of us: for we are not ignorant of his devices.

Satan causes the damage in the divided community. To be sympathetic to the offender, in terms of joining him, would bring total disaster to the congregation. The offender was already overwhelmed by isolation. The Corinthians had to forgive the offender before Satan got the "better of them." They know that Satan may take advantage of the situation to cause them further damage. There is no cheap grace, so the offender has paid the price for his sin. The offender must come to genuine repentance, so that his sin can be blotted.

12 Furthermore, when I came to Troas to preach Christ's gospel, and a door was opened unto me of the Lord, 13 I had no rest in my spirit, because I found not Titus, my brother: but tak-

ing my leave of them, I went from thence into Macedonia.

Paul had dispatched Titus to Corinth to see how this letter had been received (cf. Acts 16:8-11). Paul cares for those he founded in Christ, even for one who had wronged him and the congregation. He was also concerned for Titus whom he called a "brother" in Christ. It is important how Christians treat each other. Paul had failed to pay them a visit as he had planned before. Now he must spare them the pain by sending Titus to them. Paul really cared for their well being, and for the "peace in their spirit" or "peace of (mind and) of the flesh."

14 Now thanks be unto God which always causeth us to triumph in Christ, and maketh manifest the savour of his knowledge by us in every place. 15 For we are unto God a sweet savour of Christ, in them that are saved, and in them that perish: 16 To the one we are the savour of death unto death; and to the other, the savour of life unto life. And who is sufficient for these things?

Here we see the character of Paul as an apostle. He praises God because of the triumph, indeed the victory in Christ (*Thriambeounti emas en to Christo*). God leads His people to triumphal procession (*Thriambeounti*). Like a victorious emperor displaying the captives of war and all the booty, Paul succeeds in bringing the torn congregation together. He had been publicly ridiculed and regarded by some as a failure (1 Corinthians 4:9-13). Every Christian can rejoice like Paul but only upon winning a war against the evil one. His preaching has become a sweet smell, a fragrance which has spread over its effect like a liturgical incensing for those who practice it.

His workers, too, were a fragrance for God. A fragrance like Christ Himself. The messengers of God who preach the Gospel and bear fruit are the sweet smell offered to God. An apostle, a pastor, a preacher is one bound and committed to the Gospel in its totality. The Gospel does appeal to many but to those who are predestined to destruction it serves no purpose (cf. 1 Corinthians 1:18; Philippians 2:18; 1 Peter 2:7). So the fragrance of the Gospel of Christ turns out to be an *osme*, "a fume," because they are "lost."

They are going to *thanatos* "death," indeed to their destruction. Those who have responded to Paul's message have soared *ek zoes eis zoen*, "from one level of life to another." They have life in Christ, eternal life (Romans 6:23). So Paul asks, "Who then is equipped" for this life? What is

needed of every Christian is *ikanoten*, "competence," "capability," or "adequacy" (cf. 3:5, 6). We are to be examples to others acting as human beings bearing God's divine message as we spread its fragrance (aroma) to the world.

17 For we are not as many, which corrupt the word of God: but as of sincerity, but as of God, in the sight of God speak we in Christ.

Paul challenges the "hucksters" or "peddlers" who "adulterate" the Gospel for profit. They water down the Gospel or commercialize it like some televangelists of today. Paul distances himself from such people, so should every faithful pastor. There are many who may dilute the sharp edge of the Gospel just because they do not want to annoy someone, probably, a big contributor. There were preachers in Corinth who were adulterating the Gospel for cash (11:7-10; 12:13). This is a disastrous practice. We have to seek that which comes from God and proclaim it (4:13-5:10; 5:14-7:1). One has to be a person of *eilekrineia* "sincerity" whose word can be trusted.

DAILY BIBLE READING

M: God Consoles Us in Our Afflictions
2 Corinthians 1:1-11

T: Sealed by God's Spirit
2 Corinthians 1:12-22

W: Love Prevails over Pain and Conflict
2 Corinthians 1:23—2:4

T: Christian Forgiveness for the Offender
2 Corinthians 2:5-11

F: The Gospel: The Fragrance of Life
2 Corinthians 2:12-17

S: Good News Written on Human Hearts
2 Corinthians 3:1-11

S: Freed and Transformed by the Spirit
2 Corinthians 3:12-18

TEACHING TIPS

May 14
Bible Study Guide 11

1. Words You Should Know

A. Troubled. (2 Corinthians 4:8) Greek *thlipsis*—hard-pressed, pressure, hardship.

B. Perplexed. (4:8) Greek *aporoumenioi*—despairing; *exaporoumenoi* means total despairing.

2. Teacher Preparation

A. Prepare for this quarter by reading the QUARTER-AT-A-GLANCE to overview the unit.

B. Now focus on Lesson 11. First read the DEVOTIONAL READING, then the BACKGROUND SCRIPTURE.

C. Carefully study the FOCAL VERSES. Read them at least three times using a different version each time.

D. Read the commentary in the IN DEPTH and MORE LIGHT ON THE TEXT sections, then study the TEACHING PLAN.

E. Materials needed: Bible, a board or newsprint, and a clay pot.

3. Starting the Lesson

A. Before the students arrive, place the clay pot on display for all to see.

B. After the students are seated and settled, take time to explain the process by which the clay pot was made: The potter begins with a lump of clay and then molds and fashions it into the kind of vessel he wants it to be. He kneads and works it with his hands. He tears it apart and presses it together again. He wets it and then dries it. He finally turns it upon a wheel, planes and smooths it, dries it in the sun, and bakes it in the oven. He finally turns it out of his workshop, a finished vessel to his honor and fit for his use.

C. Lead the class in a discussion of how God, as the potter, shapes us and molds us into the vessel He chooses for us to be.

D. Have someone read the IN FOCUS story. Then lead the class in prayer focusing on the LESSON AIM.

4. Getting unto the Lesson

A. To help students understand the context of today's lesson, read the BACKGROUND and THE PEOPLE, PLACES, AND TIMES information.

B. Then ask for three volunteers to read the FOCAL VERSES. After the students have read each segment, ask the corresponding SEARCH THE SCRIPTURES questions.

5. Relating the Lesson to Life

A. Direct the students to the DISCUSS THE MEANING questions, and encourage discussion and debate. This will help them realize how the lesson personally applies to them.

B. Next read the LESSON IN OUR SOCIETY article and allow for discussion. This will help the students see how the lesson applies to our modern-day society.

6. Arousing Action

A. Ask the students to read the MAKE IT HAPPEN suggestions silently. Then ask for a show of hands of any who agree to put the suggestion into practice this week. Call on individuals to explain how they plan to carry out the suggestion.

B. Close the class in prayer, thanking God for giving meaning to our lives.

TRIALS AND TRIUMPHS OF CHRISTIAN MINISTRY

Bible Background • 2 CORINTHIANS 4
Printed Text • 2 CORINTHIANS 4:5-18
Devotional Reading • 2 CORINTHIANS 6:1-10

LESSON AIM

By the end of the lesson, students will understand that growth and maturity only come through trials and struggles, and that the pains of life are given by God not to destroy us but to cause us to grow deeper and fuller in our faith.

KEEP IN MIND

"We are troubled on every side, yet not distressed; we are perplexed, but not in despair; Persecuted, but not forsaken; cast down, but not destroyed" (2 Corinthians 4:8-9).

FOCAL VERSES

2 CORINTHIANS 4:5 For we preach not ourselves, but Christ Jesus the Lord; and ourselves your servants for Jesus' sake.

6 For God, who commanded the light to shine out of darkness, hath shined in our hearts, to give the light of the knowledge of the glory of God in the face of Jesus Christ.

7 But we have this treasure in earthen vessels, that the excellency of the power may be of God, and not of us.

8 We are troubled on every side, yet not distressed; we are perplexed, but not in despair;

9 Persecuted, but not forsaken; cast down, but not destroyed;

10 Always bearing about in the body the dying of the Lord Jesus, that the life also of Jesus might be made manifest in our body.

11 For we which live are always being delivered unto death for Jesus' sake, that the life also of Jesus might be made manifest in our mortal flesh.

12 So then death worketh in us, but life in you.

LESSON OVERVIEW

LESSON AIM
KEEP IN MIND
FOCAL VERSES
IN FOCUS
THE PEOPLE, PLACES, AND TIMES
BACKGROUND
AT-A-GLANCE
IN DEPTH
SEARCH THE SCRIPTURES
DISCUSS THE MEANING
LESSON IN OUR SOCIETY
MAKE IT HAPPEN
FOLLOW THE SPIRIT
REMEMBER YOUR THOUGHTS
MORE LIGHT ON THE TEXT
DAILY BIBLE READING

13 We having the same spirit of faith, according as it is written, I believed, and therefore have I spoken; we also believe, and therefore speak;

14 Knowing that he which raised up the Lord Jesus shall raise up us also by Jesus, and shall present us with you.

15 For all things are for your sakes, that the abundant grace might through the thanksgiving of many redound to the glory of God.

16 For which cause we faint not; but though our outward man perish, yet the inward man is renewed day by day.

17 For our light affliction, which is but for a moment, worketh for us a far more exceeding and eternal weight of glory;

18 While we look not at the things which are seen, but at the things which are not seen: for the things which are seen are temporal; but the things which are not seen are eternal.

IN FOCUS

The story is told long ago in the days of sailing ships, a terrible storm arose and a ship was lost in a deserted area. Only one crewman survived, washed up on a small uninhabited island. In his desperation, the castaway daily prayed to God for help and deliverance from his solitary existence. Each day, he looked for a passing ship and saw nothing. Eventually, he managed to build a crude hut, in which he stored the few things he had recovered from the wreck and those things he had made to help him.

One day, as the sailor was returning from his daily search

MAY 14TH

for food, he saw a column of smoke. As he ran to it, he saw his hut in flames. All was lost. Now not only was he alone, but he had nothing to help him in his struggle for survival. Stunned and nearly overcome with grief and despair, he fell into a deep depression and spent a nearly sleepless night wondering what was to become of him and questioning whether life itself was even worth the effort.

The next morning, he rose early and went down to the sea. There, to his amazement, he saw a ship floating offshore and a small boat rowing toward him. When the stranded man met the ship's captain, he asked him how he had known to send help. The captain replied, "Why we saw your smoke signal yesterday, but by the time we drew close the tide was against us. So we had to wait until now to come and get you."

Don't despair when calamity strikes for God is always able to bring a blessing out of what seems to be a curse. In our lesson today, Paul faced calamities of all kind, but he was confident God was bringing victory and triumph in his life instead of sorrow.

THE PEOPLE, PLACES, AND TIMES

TREASURES IN EARTHEN VESSELS. The art of pottery making is one of the most common and most ancient of all crafts. Earthen vessels were an abundant commodity that extended from boiling caldrons, baskets, and water pots. The message of salvation is great and glorious. The one who receives this treasure is a mere common person. Thus, a great treasure is found in a common vessel.

BACKGROUND

The church of Corinth still battled with discouraging gossip. Much of this was caused by the activity of false apostles in the church and the passivity of the Christians. In the face of sharp accusations, Paul found it necessary to defend himself before people who should have trusted him implicitly. Paul had already addressed some of the attacks against him, but he felt forced to do so again.

AT-A-GLANCE

1. **Light in the Midst of Darkness**
(2 Corinthians 4:5-7)
2. **Life in the Midst of Death**
(vv. 8-12)
3. **Renewal in the Midst of Decay**
(vv. 13-18)

Some at Corinth were accusing Paul of being insincere in his ministry. "Paul is in it for what he can get out of it!" was their accusation. In this chapter, Paul gives the evidence that proves his ministry is sincere.

Why would Paul keep on preaching, with all the dangers and toils involved, if he were not sincere? A man with lesser motives, or a less spiritual view of the ministry, would have given up long ago. Paul looked upon his ministry as a stewardship: God gave it to him, and God also gave him strength to continue and not faint.

IN DEPTH

1. Light in the Midst of Darkness
(2 Corinthians 4:5-7)

If Paul wanted to get a following for himself and make money, then he should have preached himself and not Christ. Yet he would not preach himself; he sought only to honor Christ. Christ was the focus of Paul's message and the object of his concern. In 1 Corinthians 33:1-9, Paul presents himself as a servant of God and a slave for Jesus' sake. No, there can be no light if we exalt men; God alone can cause the light to shine out of the darkness.

Here Paul refers back to Genesis 1:1-5 where God brought light at creation and from this brought life and blessing. This had been Paul's experience on the Damascus road, when a light from heaven flashed around him" (Acts 9:3). Confronted with the risen Lord, he became a new creation. The lost sinner's heart is like that original earth: formless and empty and dark. The Spirit broods over the heart. The Word comes and brings light—the light of the glorious Gospel. The sinner then becomes a new creation, and starts to bring forth fruit for the glory of God. The light in believers' lives is the knowledge of God's salvation, a glory issuing from and seen in the face of Christ and reflected by Paul (cf. 3:18). When people were in the darkness of sin, they had no knowledge of God, no experience of His life and salvation (Ephesians 4:18).

The message of salvation and the results it produces are glorious and divine. By contrast, the bearer of the message is a mere mortal person. The contrast is like a great treasure contained in common jars of clay. "Yes I have a treasure," Paul admits, "but it is in an earthen vessel. I don't want to be seen; I'm just the vessel. The most important thing is that Christ is seen and that Christ gets the glory." It is too bad when Christian workers make the vessel more important than the treasure of the Gospel. God intended this sharp contrast so that no one would question the source of the Gospel and its all-surpassing power. Salvation is the work of God not men (cf. 1 Corinthians 2:5; 3:7).

2. Life in the Midst of Death (vv. 8-12)

In his earlier letter, Paul had compared himself and his fellow apostles to "men condemned to die in the arena" (1 Corinthians 4:9). The metaphors employed here describe the demands of the ministry by contrasting human helplessness on one hand with divine enablement on the other. The contrast includes physical (1 Corinthians 1:8-9, 6:5, 9) as well as psychological affliction (cf. 6:4, 8; 7:5-6). "Hard pressed" is related to troubles and strong pressures. "Perplexed and in despair" means to be in total despair or total hopelessness.

In Paul's letter, he referred to his own life as a demonstration of this humiliation, a constant reminder that through human weakness the power of God is seen to greatest effect (2 Corinthians 12:9-10). In his own body he carried around the death of Jesus; that is, he suffered intensely for Jesus and bore physical scars resulting from wounds inflicted by beatings and a stoning because of his testimony for Jesus' sake (1 Corinthians 4:11; 2 Corinthians 6:5; 9; 11:23). He was always being given over to death; that is, he constantly faced death (2 Corinthians 1:9).

If Paul was out for personal gain, as they said, then why did he suffer so much? The man who compromises the Word of God will not suffer; men will welcome him and honor him. But people were abusing Paul, rejecting him, and making life difficult for him. They were treating him the way men treated Christ.

Paul's willingness to suffer for Christ is one of the greatest proofs of his sincerity as a servant of God. Paul was willing to face suffering and death for Jesus' sake and for the sake of the churches. The experiences that brought death to him meant life for the believers as he suffered to bring the Word to them. The false teachers knew nothing of suffering or sacrifice. All through this letter, Paul points to his scars as the credentials of his ministry. In Galatians 6:17 he said, "I bear in my body the marks (brands) of the Lord Jesus!" "All things are for your sakes!" What an unselfish spirit! Paul was willing to go anywhere, willing to endure anything, if it brought glory to God and good to the church. He had the Spirit of faith; he knew that his sufferings would mean blessings.

The life of Jesus was also revealed in Paul's body, that is, it was evident that he was alive spiritually (cf. 4:16). By means of these experiences, his transformation into Christ-likeness advanced (2 Corinthians 3:18). Paul saw the death that was happening to him through his sufferings (2 Corinthians 4:10-11) was actually a means of causing spiritual life to be at work in others as well as himself.

Paul quotes from Psalm 116 where the psalmist referred to "the anguish of the grave" (v. 3), but he affirmed his confidence that God would deliver him "from death" (v. 8). That same confidence was Paul's so like the psalmist he could declare, "I believed." The second part of the quotation, "therefore I have spoken," is from the psalmist's words about his own suffering: "therefore I said I am greatly afflicted." Paul did not quote these last words from Psalm 116:10.

3. Renewal in the Midst of Decay (vv. 16-18)

Because of the mighty power of God in Paul's life, he did not lose heart or give up. While his earthly mortality was increasingly evident, outwardly he was wasting away (2 Corinthians 1:8-9; 4:8-12). But his heavenly destiny was also increasingly evident (vv. 17-18). While physically he grew weaker, spiritually he experienced the renewing work of the Holy Spirit day by day (Romans 12:2; Colossians 3:10). He was becoming increasingly like Christ (2 Corinthians 3:18), a prelude to what eternal life will be (cf. Romans 8:23; 1 John 3:2).

Part of the means used by God in this transforming, renewing process is suffering (cf. 1 Peter 4:1,13-14). Paul compared the sufferings he had experienced, severe as they were, to light and momentary troubles, pressures, and hardships. They were nothing in view of the eternal glory that would be his when he would be in Jesus' presence and would be like Him (1 Corinthians 15:49). All of his heavy continuous burdens were in his words, "light," "light in weight, easy to bear," and "momentary." Though, as he wrote in 2 Corinthians 1:8, his hardships were "far beyond his ability to endure," yet Paul in the same moment says his coming glory far outweighs all hardships.

These verses bring wonderful assurance to the believer in times of suffering. Though the outward man is perishing day by day, the inward man, the spiritual man, is being renewed day by day (2 Corinthians 3:18). Paul is here weighing his sufferings on God's scales. He discovers that his sufferings are light when compared to the weight of glory God has stored up for him. His days and years of trial are nothing compared to the eternity of bliss that awaits him. How important it is for us to live "with eternity's values in view." Life takes on new meaning when we see things through God's eyes.

Second Corinthians 4:18 is a paradox to the unbeliever, but a precious truth to the Christian. We live by faith, not by sight. It is faith that enables the Christian to see things that cannot be seen (Hebrew 11:1-3); this faith comes from the Word of God (Romans 10:17). The things that the world lives and dies for are temporal, passing; the things of the Lord last forever. The world thinks we are crazy because we dare to believe God's Word and live according to His will. We pass up the "things" that men covet because our hearts are set on higher values.

It is important that we have a sincere Christian life and ministry. Our motives must be pure. Our methods must be scriptural. We must be true to the Word of God. Paul had this kind of a ministry, and so should we.

SEARCH THE SCRIPTURES

1. What was the message that Paul preached to the Corinthian church? (2 Corinthians 4:5)

2. What is the treasure in earthen vessels? (v. 7)

3. What did Paul mean when he used the analogy of troubled but not distressed, perplexed but not in despair, persecuted but not forsaken, and cast down but not destroyed? (vv. 8-9)

4. What do the afflictions that we face today actually do for us? (v. 17)

5. What are the things seen and the things which are not seen according to Paul? (v. 18)

DISCUSS THE MEANING

1. What would you be like today if you had no pressures, struggles, and afflictions in this world? Do you think a life like this would have meaning and purpose for you?

2. What are struggles and pressures really doing for you? Can you rejoice in the unseen (eternal) benefits?

LESSON IN OUR SOCIETY

Adversities can serve a definite purpose in our lives. C.S. Lewis in his book *The Problem with Pain* says "God whispers to us in our pleasures, speaks in our conscience, and shouts in our pain. It is his megaphone to rouse a deaf world."

Think of our society today. Most of the world's achievements have come though hardship and pain, including most professions, inventions, personal accomplishments, relationships, parenting, great leaders and church ministries.

Take time and talk about how pain has been a driving force even in your life. There is truth to the saying "No pain no gain."

MAKE IT HAPPEN

While we still do not like pain in our lives, we must see the value that it plays. Think of someone who is going through tough times. Using the lesson today, think of ways you could encourage them.

Spend time this week praying that God would give you the right words to uplift and motivate others.

FOLLOW THE SPIRIT

What God wants me to do:

_____

_____

REMEMBER YOUR THOUGHTS

Special insights you have learned:

_____

_____

MORE LIGHT ON THE TEXT
CORINTHIANS 4:5-18

4:5 For we preach not ourselves, but Christ Jesus the Lord; and ourselves your servants for Jesus' sake.

Paul sees the Gospel as alighting the hearts of believers, since it is not ourselves that we proclaim but Jesus Christ as Lord. There were others who were preaching themselves and their past achievements. Those who were bogged up in history. Those who tend to present their credentials, "I am Rev. Dr. so and so . . . and I have published . . ." ending in self praise. Some rely on their letters of recommendation (3:1) like politicians who seek endorsements from big names, companies, and newspapers during campaigns. Letters that bear their praise but leave out the praise of Jesus Christ as Lord. In 2 Corinthians 5:12, Paul even says that they pride in outward show and not in "inward worth."

Paul makes it clear that our job as pastors or servants in any capacity is to proclaim Jesus Christ and Him crucified. A preacher must preach Christ rather than parade visible evidence of past achievements, thus claiming superiority. Paul sees himself and all that serve the Lord as "servants for Christ's sake." Some had tried with some success to discredit Paul's apostleship and promote themselves as spiritual lords and masters of the community (11:20). But within the church there is no place for distorted leadership. The apostle, pastor, or preacher is called to be a servant—to work for Christ in the service of God and for humanity. Christ did not please Himself but became a servant of all (Romans 15:3, 8).

6 For God, who commanded the light to shine out of darkness, hath shined in our hearts, to

give the light of the knowledge of the glory of God in the face of Jesus Christ.

So, the Gospel is a divine illumination that enlightens human hearts. Like the creation which God made out of chaos of darkness, so is the Gospel which shines into the darkness of human souls. The Gospel light consists of "knowledge of the glory of God in the face of Christ." God's glory is not unapproachable as it was in the Old Testament. The revelation of God to humanity makes God known. Although God's glory was before associated with particular places like the temple (1 Kings 8:10ff), or certain times and events (Exodus 24:15-18), now it is

exhibited in the face of Jesus Christ through His glorious Gospel.

So Christ's face is made to be a recollection of the old order established by Moses. The Israelites saw a glow on Moses' face that reflected his intimate relationship with God. We Christians behold with unveiled faces the glory of God through Christ who is the image of God. No one has seen God, not even Moses. "But God's only Son, He who is nearest to the Father's hand has made Him known" (John 1:18).

7 But we have this treasure in earthen vessels,

that the excellency of the power may be of God, and not of us.

Again Paul says, "our power comes from God." The treasure of the Gospel which is preached is contained in mere "earthen ware" jars, i.e., fragile human agents who are not angels. There is a vast disparity between the message and its messenger. It's God's will that the divine message is spread by fragile human beings so that its unparalleled power may be seen to come from God and not from men. No human power can transform the human heart, but God's power can. God's power can deliver men and women from captivity to vices and sin, and bring them into freedom to walk in the newness of life (2 Corinthians 3:1-3; cf. 1 Corinthians 6:9-11). No human vessel can do that but God's divine transformative power can do it.

8 We are troubled on every side, yet not distressed; we are perplexed, but not in despair; 9 Persecuted, but not forsaken; cast down, but not destroyed;

Those who preach the Gospel bear the transcendent power of God through the Gospel. Preachers may look weak but are rescued and sustained by the power outside of themselves. Paul notes, "We are hard pressed but never cornered, bewildered, but never at our wits end . . . ." Those who preach the Gospel must be ready for persecution (Matthew 10:17-22). They will have to bear their cross and may even loose their lives for the sake of the Gospel (Matthew 10:28-32, 38-39). The continuing struggle against Satan must not be given up. The source of bearing God's witness is through God's own power.

10 Always bearing about in the body the dying of the Lord Jesus, that the life also of Jesus might be made manifest in our body. 11 For we which live are always being delivered unto death for Jesus' sake, that the life also of Jesus might be made manifest in our mortal flesh.

Paul then contrasts human weakness and divine power by comparing the life and death of Christ. Paul and his team were undergoing trials for the sake of Jesus. They were exposed to the danger of dying. Their escapes were like resurrections or being born again. Persecution and the escape from it is compared to a resurrection for the troubled preachers. The lives of preachers are continually being restored despite the opposition they face. God redeems His servants, and in their weakness He grants them His power. So the same power that enabled the dying and rising of Christ is being realized in Paul's life.

In our suffering, Christians are also integrated. In bap-

tism we die to sin and are raised to serve God in the power of the Spirit (Romans 6:1-11; 7:4-6; cf. Galatians 2:19ff; 2 Corinthians 5:14ff). The believer relies on the hope of the resurrection upon which death will be proven to have no power (Romans 6:5, 6). The believer must continually die in order to be raised in the resurrection with Christ. This can be done through charismatic gifts (10:10) and signs and wonders (12:11f; 11:23ff).

12 So then death worketh in us, but life in you.

Paul's suffering was like suffering with Christ in order to be raised with Him. He was loyal to his call even under these costly circumstances. Paul had literally surrendered his life for Christ's sake and for the Gospel. The greater measure of Paul's suffering is his dying and rising with Christ. He will be led to new life for what he believes. So Paul can say "Death is at work in us, but life in you." All Christians can thus say, we die in order to live. But Paul can also say, he dies that Christians may live.

13 We having the same spirit of faith, according as it is written, I believed, and therefore have I spoken; we also believe, and therefore speak;

Paul and his associates did suffer, but the power of God that raised Jesus from the dead energized them back to the work of witnessing for Christ. Basing on Psalm 116:10, Paul declares "I believe, therefore I speak." He believes that God delivers from death and hence speaks of it. Paul believed that God raised Jesus from the dead (1 Corinthians 15) and thus bore witness of the Gospel based on that belief. He knew that he too would be raised from deadly peril (1:8-10) and led to triumph (2:14). God delivered him from the sufferings and sustained him in the ministry. Pastors, evangelist, missionaries must first believe what they preach just like the psalmist and Paul in order for them to draw others to the same faith. The faith in God who delivers from death.

14 Knowing that he which raised up the Lord Jesus shall raise up us also by Jesus, and shall present us with you.

Belief leads to hope. Knowing that "he who raised Jesus to life," and who continually rescues us, even now, from death, "will with Jesus raise us too," to share with Him eternal life after triumphing over death (Romans 6:9). He will bring believers into His presence with those believers from every time. It is in Christ in whom we believe that God will bring us to share with Him in the eternal life. Through Christ all will be brought before God's presence after triumphing over death (Romans 6:9). So, there is an indivisible nexus between belief in the resurrection of Jesus and belief in the final resurrection. Deny the resurrection and you are destined to destruction. Believe the resurrection and affirm life.

15 For all things are for your sakes, that the abundant grace might through the thanksgiving of many redound to the glory of God.

Paul's efforts were not in vain. The Corinthians have also come to triumph because they too have endured. His work has paid off. Paul had suffered for the Corinthians that they might be saved. Pastor must suffer for their flocks on behalf of the Gospel. Paul suffered for the Corinthians and the Corinthians were committed to his care. So must church workers endure the pains for the sake of the numbers who will share in the abounding grace of God. They will sing a chorus of thanksgiving that rises to God's glory. So Paul's suffering has born God's grace for the Corinthians. They have received the salvation for which every believer praises God. They have had *charis pleonasasa*, "increasing grace" which enables them not only to endure but also to praise God. Paul's suffering and preaching is because of his desire that people be saved. There is no better grace than that. Paul desires that men and women who never glorified God nor gave Him thanks would turn to God and glorify Him in growing numbers (Romans 1:2-10; 3:16).

16 For which cause we faint not; but though our outward man perish, yet the inward man is renewed day by day.

God's mighty power is shown through human fragile vessels. Humanity that decays and the mortal labor on behalf of the Gospel is taking its toll on them. But "day by day" they are "inwardly renewed." The experience of daily renewal, a recycling, inspires the sure and certain hope of the resurrection life (vv. 10ff). Though the outer body may look weak, Christians are renewed by the power of God. The outer person can be equated with *ho palaios hemon anthropos*, "the old personality," (Romans 6:6; Colossians 3:9; Ephesians 4:22) which is an ethical/moral concept applying to the old nature of humanity, i.e., the sinful nature or the unregenerated nature. The inner person is being renewed day after day. The old wastes away but the new survives forever. The eternal weight of glory awaits a believer (cf. Romans 8:18-25). Paul connects suffering in this age and glory in the next life with Jesus. It is for us who believe to enter that glory. The purpose of God cannot be thwarted away by the present evil. The end time is good for those who love Him (Romans 8:28).

17 For our light affliction, which is but for a moment, worketh for us a far more exceeding and eternal weight of glory; 18 While we look not at the things which are seen, but at the things which are not seen: for the things which are seen are temporal; but the things which are not seen are eternal.

Our present troubles are real and short-lived. Trouble fades into insignificance, but eternal weight of glory awaits a believer (cf. Romans 8:18-25). Paul connects suffering in this age and the glory in the next life with Jesus. And that life is for us that believe. We therefore fix our eyes "not on the things that are seen but . . . the unseen." Christians see persecution, suffering, trouble, but look forward for the things unseen (*proskaria*) which have been prepared by God for those who love Him. So, Paul's apostleship was authenticated by God's act of power and glory. God has prepared the *aionion*, coming "age," for those who love Him. Therefore, Christians should not focus only on the present success but must fix their hope, indeed their gaze, to the glory that God has prepared for them. It is a hope based on Christ's resurrection.

DAILY BIBLE READING

M: God's Light Shines in our Hearts
2 Corinthians 4:1-7

T: God Raised Jesus and Will Raise Us
2 Corinthians 4:8-15

W: We Walk and Live by Faith
2 Corinthians 4:16—5:10

T: Reconciled to be Reconcilers
2 Corinthians 5:11-21

F: Open Wide Your Hearts
2 Corinthians 6:1-11

S: We Are Temples of the Living God
2 Corinthians 6:14—7:1

S: Paul's Joy at the Corinthian's Repentance
2 Corinthians 7:2—13

TEACHING TIPS

May 21
Bible Study Guide 12

1. Words You Should Know

A. Exhort. (2 Corinthians 9:5)—To urge by words or advice; to warn earnestly.

B. Purposeth in his heart. (v. 7)—Not being motivated by thoughts of what others will say.

2. Teacher Preparation

A. Prepare for this quarter by first reading the UNIT INTRODUCTION. Use the QUARTER-AT-A-GLANCE to overview the unit.

B. Now focus on Lesson 12. First read the DEVOTIONAL READING, then the BACKGROUND SCRIPTURE.

C. Carefully study the FOCAL VERSES. Read them at least three times using a different version each time.

D. Read the commentary in the IN DEPTH and MORE LIGHT ON THE TEXT section.

E. Materials needed: Bible, a board or newsprint, and an offering plate.

3. Starting the Lesson

A. Before the students arrive place the offering plate out where all can see. You may want to put a few coins in it so that they will clearly understand what it is.

B. After the students are seated and settled, ask someone to read the IN FOCUS story. Then lead the class in prayer focusing on the LESSON AIM.

4. Getting into the Lesson

A. Hold up the offering plate, and ask the class to tell what it is used for and what it means to them. Ask them to describe the general attitude of people towards giving in the church.

B. To help the students understand the context of today's lesson, read the BACKGROUND and THE PEOPLE, PLACES, AND TIMES information.

C. Read the FOCAL VERSES according to the AT-A-GLANCE outline. After reading each segment, ask the corresponding SEARCH THE SCRIPTURES questions.

5. Relating the Lesson to Life

A. Take a "heart poll." Ask for a show of hands of those who really struggle with giving with the right motive from the heart. Discuss the reasons giving may not be a cheerful experience (some reasons may be: more bills than money, poor budget, lack of faith, etc.).

B. Direct the students to the DISCUSS THE MEANING questions and encourage discussion. This will help them realize how the lesson personally applies to them.

C. Next read the LESSON IN OUR SOCIETY article and allow time for discussion. This will help the students see how the lesson applies to modern-day life.

6. Arousing Action

A. Ask the students to read the MAKE IT HAPPEN suggestion silently. Then ask for a show of hands of any who agree to put the suggestion into practice this week.

B. Close the class in prayer, thanking God for giving meaning to our lives and gratitude in our hearts.

THE COLLECTION FOR JERUSALEM CHRISTIANS

Bible Background • 2 CORINTHIANS 9
Printed Text • 2 CORINTHIANS 9:1-13
Devotional Reading • 2 CORINTHIANS 8:1-15

LESSON AIM

By the end of the lesson, students will fully understand the joys of giving which blesses them, others, and brings glory to God. They will also realize that the more they give, the more they become a blessing.

KEEP IN MIND

"Every man according as he purposeth in his heart, so let him give; not grudgingly, or of necessity; for God loveth a cheerful giver" (2 Corinthians 9:7).

FOCAL VERSES

2 CORINTHIANS 9:1 For as touching the ministering to the saints, it is superfluous to me to write to you:

2 For I know the forwardness of your mind, for which I boast of you to them of Macedonia, that Acaia was ready a year ago; and your zeal hath provoked very many.

3 Yet have I sent the brethren, lest our boasting of you should be in vain in this behalf; that, as I said, ye may be ready:

4 Lest haply if they of Macedonia come with me, and find you unprepared, we (that we say not, ye) should be ashamed in this same confident boasting.

5 Therefore I thought it necessary to exhort the brethren, that they would go before unto you, and make up beforehand your bounty, whereof ye had notice before, that the same might be ready, as a matter of bounty, and not as of covetousness.

6 But this I say, He which soweth sparingly shall reap also sparingly; and he which soweth bountifully shall reap also

LESSON OVERVIEW

LESSON AIM
KEEP IN MIND
FOCAL VERSES
IN FOCUS
THE PEOPLE, PLACES, AND
TIMES
BACKGROUND
AT-A-GLANCE
IN DEPTH
SEARCH THE SCRIPTURES
DISCUSS THE MEANING
LESSON IN OUR SOCIETY
MAKE IT HAPPEN
FOLLOW THE SPIRIT
REMEMBER YOUR THOUGHTS
MORE LIGHT ON THE TEXT
DAILY BIBLE READINGS

bountifully.

7 Every man according as he purposeth in his heart, so let him give; not grudgingly, or of necessity: for God loveth a cheerful giver.

8 And God is able to make all grace abound toward you; that ye, always having all sufficiency in all things, may abound to every good work:

9 (As it is written, He hath dispersed abroad; he hath given to the poor: his righteousness remaineth for ever.

10 Now he that ministereth seed to the sower both minister bread for your food, and multiply your seed sown, and increase the fruits of your righteousness;)

11 Being enriched in every thing to all bountifulness, which causeth through us thanksgiving to God.

12 For the administration of this service not only supplieth the want of the saints, but is abundant also by many thanksgivings unto God;

13 Whiles by the experiment of this ministration they glorify God for your professed subjection unto the gospel of Christ, and for your liberal distribution unto them, and unto all men;

IN FOCUS

According to the Associated Press in October 1994, Harvard University Law School announced it had just received the largest cash gift ever given to a law school—a cool 13 million dollars.

The donors were Gustave and Rita Hauser. What was it that inspired such generosity? Romance and gratitude. Back in 1955, Gustave and Rita met at the law school. The

MAY 21st

day after final exams in 1956, they married. They went on to become highly successful in business. Hauser, who is chairman and CEO of Hauser Communications and formerly the head of the Warner Bros. cable unit, was one of the pioneers of cable television and a developer of the Nickelodeon channel. Gustave Hauser never did practice law. It seemed his deep gratitude to Harvard was because of its role as matchmaker. Said Hauser at a ceremony announcing the donation, "The school had a unique role in bringing us together."

When we are given much, and are mature enough to be grateful, we naturally want to give back much. God gave us His only Son, Jesus Christ. It is no wonder, then, that we find great joy in giving back to God our time, energy, abilities, and money. We owe God everything.

THE PEOPLE, PLACES, AND TIMES

MACEDONIA. A large and celebrated country lying north of Greece and south of the Balkans. This region has a mountainous interior and a hardy population. Under it noted kings, Philip and Alexander, its fertile plains and extensive seaboard exercised a surprising influence over the history of the world.

SOWER. The operation of sowing with the hand is a simple procedure. The sower held the vessel or basket containing the seed in his left hand, while with his right he scattered the seed. The sowing season began in October and continued to the end of February; wheat being sown before, and barley after in the beginning of January.

BACKGROUND

In 2 Corinthians 9, Paul turns to the subject of gracious giving. For several years, Paul had been organizing a collection for the poor in Jerusalem. When the Corinthians heard about this collection, they asked Paul if they could have a part in it. Paul never received any money from them, so he instructed Titus to look into the matter (2 Corinthians 8:6).

Titus went to Corinth and found the Corinthians in need of an encouraging word which Paul delivers in chapters 8 and 9. It was Titus' work and that of unnamed assistants (8:23; cf. Acts 20:1-4), climaxed by Paul's visit (Acts 20:3) which brought the collection in Corinth to a successful conclusion (Romans 15:26; Acts 24:17).

The encouraging word to the Corinthians in chapters 8 and 9 both deal with the Christian and giving. Chapter 8 deals with the principles of Christian giving. In chapter 9, Paul deals with the promises that we can claim if we are faithful in our giving to God. These two chapters present giving as a Christian grace, a blessing, not as a legal obligation that burdens people. If giving is difficult for a Christian, then there is something wrong with his or her heart!

IN DEPTH

1. Giving Brings Blessings to Others (2 Corinthians 9:1-5)

In 2 Corinthians 8:1-5 Paul used the churches of Macedonia as examples to encourage the Corinthians. Now he uses the Corinthians as an encouragement to the churches of Macedonia! Christians ought to be an encouragement to one another. Paul had been "boasting to others of the generosity of the church at Corinth (8:24), and as a result the churches in Macedonia

gave. However, apart from promises the Corinthian church had not yet given. Paul wanted to make sure that the Corinthians did not embarrass him. He knew they had readiness of mind and were willing and anxious to share in the missionary offering, but he wanted to remind them just the same.

"Your enthusiasm has stirred most of them to action" (v. 2, NIV) What a testimony! Unfortunately, some Christians provoke people in the wrong way. Hebrews 10:24 urges us to provoke one another to good works, and this is what the Corinthians were doing. A year before, they had urged Paul to take up this missionary offering and had pledged their support. The apostle has used their zeal as an encouragement to the other churches, and now he reminds them of their promise. He seems to be saying, "If you fail to do your share, you will discourage other Christians and hurt the whole offering."

Paul called this offering "a bounty," that is, a blessing. He wanted them to look upon it as an opportunity to be a blessing and get a blessing, and not as a yoke on their necks. How often people misunderstand the true blessing of giving! Giving is a blessing to others, both to those who receive (v. 12—it supplied their want) and to those who share.

When a Christian is faithful in giving, he or she is blessing others and encouraging other Christians to be obedient to the Word.

2. Giving Brings Blessings to Ourselves (vv. 6-8)

In the grace of God, Christians are rewarded in three ways for their generosity: 1) the givers are enriched (vv. 6-10); 2) the receivers needs are met (vv. 11-12); and 3) God, the source of all blessing, is praised (vv. 13-15).

Paul uses an agricultural principle here to illustrate his point. The farmer that sows bountifully will reap bountifully (Proverbs 11:24, Luke 6:38, and Galatians 6:7-8). "Bountifully" here is the same word as "bounty" in verse 5. To sow bountifully means to "sow with blessing" and to reap bountifully means to "reap with blessing." God is faithful to bless us when we are faithful to obey.

Verse 7 is often misapplied. Paul is not talking here about how much we give as much as how we give. He told them how much to give in 8:12-15; it was to be in proportion to what they had. But for a believer to give grudgingly, or out of a sense of obligation, is to miss the blessing of giving. Giving must be from the heart, and God loves a cheerful giver. Some Christians take this verse to mean that it matters not how much we give as long as we give cheerfully what we have purposed in our hearts. Absolutely not! A cheerful heart is not the substitute for an obedient heart.

Our hearts should be both faithful and cheerful, because we give the right gift with the right motive.

Note the word "all" in verse 8: "all grace, always, all sufficiency; all things; every good work." This is God's promise to those who obey Him. This word "sufficiency" is found again in 3:5 and 12:9. God is faithful to supply what we need spiritually (2:6), materially (9:8), and physically (12:9). God meets our needs, not just for our own enjoyment, but that we might be able to serve Him and help others.

We are abound "to every good work" (v. 8). Paul exhorts Christians to go to work that they might be able to help others (Ephesians 4:28). Here he refers to Psalm 112:9 and Isaiah 55:10 to prove that God blesses the person who is faithful in giving. God supplies seed so that sowers might make bread for food and also have more seed for sowing.

Humanly speaking, the person who gives should be the person who loses; but such not the case. "It is more blessed to give than to receive" (Acts 20:35) . "Give and it shall be given unto you" (Luke 6:38). This does not mean that we should bargain with God or look at our giving as a means of purchasing God's blessing. We should look upon giving as an opportunity to show our love for God and our trust in His Word.

3. Giving Brings Glory to God (vv. 9-13)

Paul now produces scriptural proof for the truth that the giver shall be provided for as a result of his giving to others. Paul quoted from Psalm 112:9 where the psalmist says that the righteous man, who desires to express his righteousness in beneficence, will never lack the means of doing it. Righteousness is used here for "almsgiving" (cf. Matthew 6:1).

Many times Paul reminds the Corinthians of their spiritual riches in Christ (1 Corinthians 1:5; 4:8; 2 Corinthians 8:9 and 9:11). God enriches us, we enrich others, and God receives the thanksgiving and glory. The more one gives to others, the more he is enriched, and can be generous on every occasion. Such a generous spirit towards others results in more and more people giving thanks to God.

Paul points out that the distribution of this offering would not only bring help to the saints, but it would bring glory to God. The Jews receiving this offering would glorify God: 1) because the givers showed obedience to God's Word and 2) because this liberal offering helped them and others. The recipients in turn would pray for the churches and love them the more.

There was of course, a very practical thought behind this offering. Paul was anxious to bind the Gentile churches he had founded to the hearts of the Jewish Christians. This offering would prove that Paul was not an enemy of the Jews, and that there was a unity in the church regardless of racial, national, or ethnic distinction.

One cannot read these two chapters without gaining a new attitude toward giving. In the Christian life, there is no such thing as "material" and "spiritual." All that we have comes from God, and all that we have must be used for spiritual ends. Paul teaches that giving is not a burden but a blessing. He show us that true Christian giving enriches the life and opens the fountains of God's blessings. Giving is a grace (8:1, 6-7, 9, 19; 9:8, 14), and the Christian who understands something of grace will understand how to give.

SEARCH THE SCRIPTURES

1. What was Paul doing to those in Macedonia regarding the Corinthians? (2 Corinthians 9:2)

2. What happens to those who sow sparingly and to those who sows bountifully? (v. 6)

3. How should every man give? (v. 7)

4. How much grace is God able to make abound towards you? (v. 8)

5. When we experience the bountiful blessings of God, what does it cause us to do? (v. 11)

DISCUSS THE MEANING

1. It has been said that people can tell a lot about you by the things you buy and the causes to which you give. What things in your life bring you the most satisfaction?

2. Many times when we think of giving, we think of money. However, there are many other things we can give from our lives that would allow someone else to be blessed. Name other things we can give.

LESSON IN OUR SOCIETY

A well-known philanthropist was asked, "How is it that you give away so much, and yet have so much left? "I suppose it's like this," he replied, "I shovel out, and God shovels in, and he has a bigger shovel than I do!"

Our attitude towards giving should be like the philanthropist. We should want to give by the shovels, to bless the lives of all those around. We should look forward to giving

generously in our churches to strengthen the body of believers. We should not give because someone is watching or out of force.

What is the overall spirit of giving in your church? What is the spirit of giving for you? Think of ways the spirit of giving can cause your church to become more generous, bountiful, and pleasing to God.

MAKE IT HAPPEN

Make a list of ways you can glorify God in your personal giving. Beginning with yourself, think of ways you can cause your spirit of giving to be felt by those around you. Pray and ask God to give you boldness to carry out your plan.

FOLLOW THE SPIRIT

What God wants me to do:

_____

_____

REMEMBER YOUR THOUGHTS

Special insights you have learned:

_____

_____

MORE LIGHT ON THE TEXT
2 CORINTHIANS 9:1-13

9:1 For as touching the ministering to the saints, it is superfluous to me to write to you: 2 For I know the forwardness of your mind, for which I boast of you to them of Macedonia, that Acaia was ready a year ago; and your zeal hath provoked very many.

The Corinthians, like everybody in the province of Achaia, are doing a special collection for the hunger-stricken Jerusalem Christians (called *hagioi*, or "saints" in this text). Paul says that he need not write to them for he knows their zeal to give.

The term *prothymia* means "eagerness" or "willingness" to give liberally. For this reason Paul has been "boasting" (*kauchesmai*) about his communities giving in order to save the needy. Their zeal was remarkable.

But Paul has nevertheless been embarrassed because they did not stick to their pledge. In other words, the *kauchesma* or "boasting" has been turned to shame. A year had passed without the accomplishment of their pledge (8:10). The Achaian Macedonians had accomplished what they had pledged, but not the Corinthians whose social status was much higher. To promote a healthy rivalry, or a spirit of competition, Paul encourages the Corinthians to avoid being shamed, and thus saving also the apostle's face.

3 Yet have I sent the brethren, lest our boasting of you should be in vain in this behalf; that, as I said, ye may be ready: 4 Lest haply if they of Macedonia come with me, and find you unprepared, we (that we say not, ye) should be ashamed in this same confident boasting.

The reason for sending brothers before Paul and the team from Macedonia is to try to save both the Corinthians and himself from shame. Because of the credibility of the Corinthians as Christians, Paul is not trying to acquire money by obligating them but by reminding them of their pledge. The Corinthians might have grown indifferent in this project. It happens many times that when there is no spokesperson (or lobbyist) things tend to cool down. Now Paul's boast has become an empty boast (9:5). Paul needed the Corinthians to fulfill their pledge. They should have their collection ready by the time of Paul and his team's arrival. So Paul had to send three brothers to "stir up" (*erethizein*) the people so that they might not be ashamed when the delegation comes. "So that our pride in you might not be proven in vain."

5 Therefore I thought it necessary to exhort the brethren, that they would go before unto you, and make up beforehand your bounty, whereof ye had notice before, that the same might be ready, as a matter of bounty, and not as of covetousness.

Paul calls for a real gift, a voluntary one (*eulogia*). The verb *eulogeo* is "to bless," so *eulogia* is a "blessing." The gift must be freely given to be a blessing rather than money being wrung out of them. So, Paul exhorts them to make the contribution a "blessing" (cf. 2 Kings 5:15, like Naaman's present to Elisha). Their gift should be spiritual and generous whole-hearted giving.

6 But this I say, He which soweth sparingly shall reap also sparingly; and he which soweth bountifully shall reap also bountifully.

Paul now uses a metaphor to explain his point. The scantier the seeds sown, the scantier the harvest. Generous giving is a means of blessing the recipients. The grace of God which compels us from within to give voluntarily is what becomes a blessing to the recipients. God is glorified when giving is from the heart. One who keeps sowing as a regular business also keeps harvesting (cf. Matthew 13:3). It

is a Christian duty to keep sowing. Although Christian sowing is in fact scattering the seed like the parable of the sower, the hope is that harvest is coming. So, it is foolish to withhold seeds and expect to get a good harvest. The source of giving is not the size of our purse, but the heart (cf. Mark 12:4ff). The poor widow in Mark gave more than everybody else. He who trusts in riches falls. He who waters is also watered. Whoever trusts in his/her sowing will reap. Jesus teaches that one who offers a cup of water to one of the little ones does in fact quench Christ Himself (Matthew 10:41-42; Luke 6:38). Feeding the hungry, dressing the naked, quenching the thirsty, sheltering the homeless, welcoming the stranger are expression of giving (Matthew 25:34ff; Proverbs 19:17). Goodness brings its own reward.

7 Every man according as he purposeth in his heart, so let him give; not grudgingly, or of necessity: for God loveth a cheerful giver.

The true measure of Christian giving is the freedom one exercises in his or her heart. Once one purposes in the heart there is no obligation to giving a tithe or a quota scheme of one's earning, one has to give because he is charitable person without grieving as though he/she has lost something. Grudging or forced giving is to discouraged. A good example of bad givers are Ananias and his wife Sapphira (Acts 5:1ff). They tried to cheat God when they sold their field and withheld some of the money. They were struck dead. It is the intent that counts. One who parts with one's belongings willingly, possesses more in the long run. God made His grace abound to all. So it is wrong to fabricate anything before God, because God knows the giver's heart. Givers must be cheerful, *ilaron gar doten agapa ho Theos*, "For God loves a cheerful giver."

8 And God is able to make all grace abound toward you; that ye, always having all sufficiency in all things, may abound to every good work:

The true measure of liberal giving is by realizing God's grace in our lives. Giving involves spiritual satisfaction. What God did for the Macedonians, He is able to do for everyone. God's grace is always abundant and it enriches (8:10). God's grace is sufficient and it is up to the spiritual person to give back. As the Book of Acts says, "It is more blessed to give than to receive" (cf. 1 Corinthians 15:58). The more we give to God, the more we regain.

9 (As it is written, He hath dispersed abroad; he hath given to the poor: his righteousness remaineth for ever.

Paul cites Psalm 112:9 which commends a man who

fears the Lord and delights in His commandments. Surely, giving to the needy is fulfilling God's law. Scattering abroad is an illustration of a sower who is not a miser but scatters generously. His heart cannot be pinched with poverty. Christian giving imitates such a giver. It is denying oneself things that people take for granted in living a civilized giving. God has a whole set of divine grace to offer to a liberal giver. Far from philanthropy, a Christian is moved by God's love. In Deuteronomy 15:7-11 (cf. Leviticus 25:35), the commandment requires believers to open their hands to a brother who is in need and to the poor of the land. Christians have received the supreme gift of God's Son's redeeming grace. Because they received freely, they are require to give freely (Matthew 10:8). One whose giving is motivated by the love of God is considered a righteous giver (cf. Matthew 6:1). A righteous person will not acquire a false reputation, for God watches in secret and discerns the heart.

10 Now he that ministereth seed to the sower both minister bread for your food, and multiply your seed sown, and increase the fruits of your righteousness;)

The grace of God helps the sower and the seed that is sown. The same grace causes growth and hence good harvest. From the land that is tilled through the seed that is sown into it, to the growth and harvest of the fruit, all is done by God (cf. Isaiah 55:10). Interestingly, one person sows another eats. We, who buy food from a grocery store, do not till the land, but we do eat the fruit that we have not toiled for. Seeds may look small and insignificant but the potential is inside. A single seed contains a germ of the whole tree which bears a lot of fruit. The growth and transformation of the seed is enabled by God. So is cheerful giving. God gives us gifts of grace; education, money, riches, homes, etc., which we should use to help the needy. For it is God who makes the miracle.

11 Being enriched in every thing to all bountifulness, which causeth through us thanksgiving to God. 12 For the administration of this service not only supplieth the want of the saints, but is abundant also by many thanksgivings unto God;

Christian giving is an outward expression of a generous heart. In things that are necessary, God allows Christians to seek no more than their needs. Thanksgiving to God bubbles out from one who

gives and one who receives. There is a spiritual gratification for both parties. For thanks is given to God not only for the harvest but also for the original seed. So liberality is public service. Contributing to fund a student's studies or even being an organ donor is part of Christian giving. It is an outreach of generosity which is unlimited. Giving fills the one that lacks the necessities of life. In so doing, God is given glory by the recipient and the giver.

13 Whiles by the experiment of this ministration they glorify God for your professed subjection unto the gospel of Christ, and for your liberal distribution unto them.

The collection becomes proof of the Macedonian's and the Corinthian's Christian commitment to their fellow Christians in Jerusalem. This help which comes during the time of need, given by the Gentiles who were before not recognized by the Jews is proof that the church of Christ is one. Hence the church shares one Baptism, one Lord, one Father of our Lord Jesus Christ, and one Holy Spirit. So the local church must regard itself as part of the universal church (cf. Ephesians 2:1ff). True faith is demonstrated by works, as the epistle of James states.

DAILY BIBLE READING

M: Exceeding Generosity
2 Corinthians 8:1-7

T: Show Your Love by Your Giving
2 Corinthians 8:8-15

W: A Generous Gift Glorifies God
2 Corinthians 8:16-24

T: God Loves and Blesses Cheerful Givers
2 Corinthians 9:1-9

F: Generous Giving Brings Joy to All
2 Corinthians 9:10-15

S: A Collection for Jerusalem Christians
2 Corinthians 16:1-9

S: Paul Intends to Visit Roman Christians
Roman 15:22-29

TEACHING TIPS

May 28
Bible Study Guide 13

1. Words You Should Know

A. Examine yourselves. (2 Corinthians 13:5)—
To consider ones own conduct with regards to justification of Christ. Were they Christians? Did they demonstrate they were in the faith?

B. Reprobates. (2 Corinthians 13:5)—Counterfeit; not passing the test; abandoned to a depraved lifestyle.

C. Be Perfect. (2 Corinthians 13:11)—Greek *Katartisin*— Aim for perfection.

Consider your conduct. Are you a Christian or not? Do you demonstrate that you are in the faith and that Christ is in you by your obedience to His will? Do what is right or be subject to God's discipline.

2. Teacher Preparation

A. Prepare for this quarter by first reading the UNIT INTRODUCTION and the QUARTER-AT-A-GLANCE to overview the unit.

B. Now focus on Lesson 13. First read the KEEP IN MIND verse. Then read the BACKGROUND SCRIPTURE.

C. Carefully study the FOCAL VERSES. Read them at least three times using a different version each time.

D. Read the commentary in the MORE LIGHT ON THE TEXT section

3. Starting the Lesson

A. Before the students arrive, write the AT-A-GLANCE outline on the board along with the word "faith."

B. After the students are seated and settled, ask someone to read the IN FOCUS story. Then lead the class in prayer focusing on the LESSON AIM.

4. Getting into the Lesson

A. Pass out the index cards and have the class describe their faith by using words like: strong, sure, growing, weak, and doubtful.

B. Read the BACKGROUND and THE PEOPLE, PLACES, AND TIMES information.

C. Then ask three volunteers to read the FOCAL VERSES according to the AT-A-GLANCE outline. After the students have read each segment, ask the corresponding SEARCH THE SCRIPTURES questions.

D. Divide the class into three groups, and assign each group a section of IN DEPTH commentary. Ask them to read and discuss it. Then select a spokesperson to share the highlights of their section with the class. Allow about 10 minutes for group discussion.

5. Relating the Lesson to Life

A. Call the class back together and have the spokespersons from each group present their highlights to the class.

B. Direct the students to the DISCUSS THE MEANING questions, and encourage discussion and debate. This will help them realize how the lesson personally applies to them.

C. Next read the LESSON IN OUR SOCIETY article and allow time for discussion. This will help the student see how the lesson applies to our modern-day society.

6. Arousing Action

A. Ask the students to look at the cards they wrote on at the beginning of class. Have those who wish to share with the class do so.

B. Have the class read the MAKE IT HAPPEN suggestion silently. Then ask for a show of hands of any who agree to put the suggestion to practice this week. Have some students share how they will carry out the suggestions.

C. Close in prayer, thanking God for helping us with our faith.

MAY 28TH

369

LIVING IN THE FAITH

Bible Background • 2 CORINTHIANS 13:1-13
Printed Text • 2 CORINTHIANS 13:1-13
Devotional Reading • ACTS 4:32-37

LESSON AIM

By the end of the lesson, students will be more aware of their own personal level of faith in God. They will examine their own lives to determine if there are areas that are controlled by fear or failure, and make a change to walk by faith.

KEEP IN MIND

"Examine yourselves, whether ye be in the faith; prove your own selves. Know ye not your own selves, how that Jesus Christ is in you, except ye be reprobates?" (2 Corinthians 13:5)

FOCAL VERSES

2 CORINTHIANS 13:1 This is the third time I am coming to you. In the mouth of two or three witnesses shall every word be established.

2 I told you before, and foretell you, as if I were present, the second time; and being absent now I write to them which heretofore have sinned, and to all other, that, if I come again, I will not spare:

3 Since ye seek a proof of Christ speaking in me, which to you ward is not weak, but is mighty in you.

4 For though he was crucified through weakness, yet he liveth by the power of God. For we also are weak in him, but we shall live with him by the power of God toward you.

5 Examine yourselves, whether ye be in the faith; prove your own selves. Know ye not your own selves, how that Jesus Christ is in you, except ye be reprobates?

6 But I trust that ye shall know that we are not reprobates.

7 Now I pray to God that ye do no evil; not that we should appear approved, but that ye should do that which is honest, though we be as reprobates.

LESSON OVERVIEW

LESSON AIM
KEEP IN MIND
FOCAL VERSES
IN FOCUS
THE PEOPLE, PLACES, AND TIMES
BACKGROUND
AT-A-GLANCE
IN DEPTH
SEARCH THE SCRIPTURES
DISCUSS THE MEANING
LESSON IN OUR SOCIETY
MAKE IT HAPPEN
FOLLOW THE SPIRIT
REMEMBER YOUR THOUGHTS
MORE LIGHT ON THE TEXT
DAILY BIBLE READINGS

8 For we can do nothing against the truth, but for the truth.

9 For we are glad, when we are weak, and ye are strong: and this also we wish, even your perfection.

10 Therefore I write these things being absent, lest being present I should use sharpness, according to the power which the Lord hath given me to edification, and not to destruction.

11 Finally, brethren, farewell. Be perfect, be of good comfort, be of one mind, live in peace; and the God of love and peace shall be with you.

12 Greet one another with an holy kiss.

13 All the saints salute you.

IN FOCUS

Faith is worthless in itself. If faith is not properly founded, it can lead to nothing other than disaster.

One night cars sped along the main highway between Jackson and Vicksburg, Mississippi. The drivers placed their faith in their cars and in the bridges over the streams. They passed over some bridges at 50 or 60 miles per hour. Everything was lovely, the concrete spans stood firm over the rivers and bayous, and the cars went on their way. Suddenly, the twin headlights in front of a truck melted into the road and disappeared. The driver of the truck caught only a glimpse of a black gap in the concrete before he too plunged into the stream below. Breaking glass, he succeeded in freeing himself. He swam ashore, but before he could reach the highway, other cars zoomed smoothly up to the gap and vanished. Frantically, he tried to flag three others. The drivers ignored the dripping, scarecrow figure and sped on into the void. Each time there was a single booming splash, sometimes followed by a few hoarse shouts and screams.

All the drivers had faith in a bridge that was out. There is only one bridge across the gulf of death. Christ has said, "No man cometh unto the Father, but by me" (John 14:6). Woe to the man who attempts any other highway. His faith will carry him to a Christless eternity and not to heaven. Faith must have a proper foundation Christ.

THE PEOPLE, PLACES, AND TIMES
MOUTH OF TWO OR THREE WITNESSES.
A witness is someone who has personal knowledge of some incident. Witnesses are also called upon to furnish proof or evidence, if necessary. This person gives evidence before a judicial body.

In civil contracts, documentary evidence was required and carefully preserved to seal a transaction. The law was very careful to provide and enforce this requirement for every infraction and all transactions bearing on them. With respect to evidence, at least two witnesses are required to establish any capital charge (Numbers 35:30; Deuteronomy 17:6; John 8:17; 2 Corinthians 13:1).

REPROBATES. Counterfeit, not passing the test. Condemned by degree or judgment of God, also abandoned to depraved lifestyle. A reprobate person puts God out of his mind. God's responding judgment is abandonment (Romans 1:24, 26).

HOLY KISS. Kissing the lips by way of affectionate salutation was customary among near relatives of both sexes, in both patriarchal and later times (Genesis 29:11). Between individuals of the same sex, and in a limited degree between those of different sexes, the kiss on the cheek was a mark of respect or an act of salutation customary in the East and even in Europe.

In the Christian church, the kiss of charity was practiced not only as a friendly salutation, but as an act symbolical of Christian love and brotherhood.

BACKGROUND
The last four chapters of 2 Corinthians which formed the closing section of the "painful" letter are much different from the first ten. In the first ten chapters, the storm clouds have clearly lifted. All is easy and happy. The apostle is full of confidence. The Corinthians have been fully tested and not found wanting. Joy, comfort, and relief are the marks of these opening chapters. In contrast, doubt and hesitation characterize the last four chapters.

The opening words of 2 Corinthians 10, "Now I Paul myself beseech you by the meekness and gentleness of Christ," seem to speak with special emphasis. And Paul has a motive for so doing. He does not want the Corinthians to imagine that, now that they have death with the offenders in the church, there is no danger of further lapses on their part. He has opened his heart to them in gratitude for their loyalty; but the seeds of disunion may still be slumbering in many hearts, ready to break into life again at the next onslaught of the false apostles, whose efforts are uncompromising and untiring. There must be no living in a fool's paradise, unaware of the danger lying ahead. The Corinthians must make up their minds whether Paul is really their apostle or not. There must no longer be any kind of hesitation about this. Their apostle by divine commission is going to visit them once again, claiming the allegiance that is his due. It is natural that before he brings the letter to a close, which is to pave the way for that visit, he should once again mention his apostolic authority and show his superiority to false apostles.

In 2 Corinthians 13, Paul closes the letter with several admonitions to the church.

IN DEPTH
1. Living in the Power of God (2 Corinthians 13:1-5)
In 2 Corinthians 12, Paul mentioned his third visit, and now he repeats that admonition. He refers to the Old Testament law that two or three witnesses are needed to settle the truth of a matter (Deuteronomy 19:15), as though his third visit were God's final opportunity for the church to make matters right. He had told them before, and was now reminding them, that this visit would mean unsparing judgment to those who were guilty of sin. His boldness in dealing with sin would be proof enough that he was not a weakling (2 Corinthians 10:10; 11:6).

His statement in verse 4 is interesting. In His death, Christ seemed to reveal weakness; but His resurrection revealed the power of God. In his previous visit, Paul seemingly showed weakness as he served; this next visit would be different. The paradox of Christ was the paradox of Paul. With God's power at His disposal, Christ followed the course of weakness to the cross (Matthew 26:53). In the resurrection, the magnitude of that untapped power was displayed (Ephesians 1:19-21). On this side of the grave, Paul followed the path of weakness but as in Jesus' life, a glimmer of God's power showed through. Paul wanted this power to be used for constructive rather than punitive purposes. There are times when we show God's power in us by our apparent weakness; there are other times when we must serve through the power of God. Paul's thorn in the flesh experience is an example of being "weak" in Him yet living by the power of God.

Had the Christians obeyed the Word of God, they would have spared themselves and Paul a great deal of agony. It is when Christians ignore or oppose the Word of God that they bring trouble upon themselves, others, and the church. How many pastors have gone through Gethsemane because of Christians who refuse to listen to God's Word.

2. Living in the Faith of God (vv. 6-9)

The Corinthians were spending a great deal of time examining Paul; now it was time they examined themselves. Socrates said, "The unexamined life is not worth living." A true Christian experience will bear examination. "Are you even in the faith?" asked Paul. "Are you truly saved?" Every believer must prove his or her faith; no one can tell others whether or not they are born again.

A true Christian has Christ in him. The word "reprobate" means "counterfeit." The word literally means "not passing the test." His enemies had charged Paul with being a counterfeit (a false apostle), a charge that he denied in verse 6. He begged the Corinthians to turn away from evil living and speaking, not simply that they might prove that Paul was a true apostle, but for their own good. If they repented, he would not have to prove his apostleship by coming to discipline them. He was willing to set aside this privilege for their sakes. Paul would rather risk his reputation to see them helped spiritually, than have them continue in sin and force him to exercise his apostolic authority.

Peter warns pastors that they should not exercise lordship over the church (1 Peter 5:ff), and here Paul is manifesting that same humble spirit. The warning of discipline is never to exalt the pastor, but always to lead the offender to the place of repentance.

As a conclusion to this warning (2 Corinthians 12:20-21; 13:5-7), this prayer for restoration of their ways was certainly fitting. Then Paul could be spared the pain of disciplining those he loved (cf. 2:2), and instead he could work with them with joy (1:24) and help to building them up (13:10).

In this day of satanic counterfeits, it is important that professing Christians know that they are saved. Remember the warnings in Matthew 7:15-29 and the startling truths of 2 Corinthians 11:13-15.

In verse 8, Paul is not suggesting that there is no way to oppose the truth. Satan certainly opposes the truth with his lies, and people are more prone to believe his lies than they are to believe God's truth! Paul is saying that the repentance of the Corinthians would be "that which is honest" (v. 7) and according to the Word of God. Since they would be obeying the truth, Paul could do nothing against them in terms of judging sin or disciplining the offenders. He himself did not want anything other than the truth in the church at Corinth.

In fact, Paul goes on to say that he would be glad to make this next visit another demonstration of his weakness (1 Corinthians 2:1-5) if it meant that they would be living in the power of God. His aim was their perfection, their spiritual maturity in Christ. There were babes in Christ, carnal and worldly, and needed to mature. "I want to build you up, not tear you down," he assured them. "This is why I am writing such a stern letter. I want you to start heeding God's Word and making matters right in the church. If you do, I'll not have to speak with sharpness when I come."

3. Living in the Peace of God (vv. 10-13)

Did the Corinthians respond positively to Paul's warning? Yes. Paul based the expansion of his ministry in other areas on the condition that the problems in Corinth were resolved (10:15-16). He followed the writing of this letter with a visit which lasted three months, during which time he wrote the letter, to the Romans. In that letter, he wrote "Now . . . there is no more place for me to work in these regions" (Romans 15:23, NIV). His appeal had been heeded. The Corinthians were now obedient.

Notice the love that flows from these final words in chapter 13. He calls all of the Corinthian Christians brethren, and makes no distinction between those who attacked him and those who supported him. "Farewell" (v. 11) means "rejoice." Paul has written with tears (2:1-5), yet he found it in his heart to "rejoice evermore" and "in everything give thanks."

"Be perfect" is another admonition to grow up in the faith (see v. 9). If they were mature Christians, then the blessing Paul closes with in verses 11-13 would be their portion. There would be comfort, unity, peace, and fellowship with one another and with God.

The "holy kiss"(v. 12) was an oriental custom among believers; a modern version might read (as J.B. Phillips puts it), "shake hands all around" (PH).

The saints of Macedonia, with whom Paul was staying at the time he wrote 2 Corinthians sent their unified greetings as well.

SEARCH THE SCRIPTURES

1. What had Paul previously and in advance warned the church of Corinth? (2 Corinthians 13:2)

2. What was one reason Jesus was crucified, and one reason Jesus lives? (v. 4)

3. How did Paul tell the church of Corinth to determine whether they were in the faith? (v. 5).

4. Why did Paul rejoice when he was weak and the church was strong? (v. 9)

5. What last instructions did Paul give the church? (vv. 11-12)

DISCUSS THE MEANING

1. How do we examine ourselves to see if we are in the faith? Would the way we live be a strong indication of our faith in God? What are some other things to consider?

2. Why is it so important for us to know whether we are in the faith or not?

LESSON IN OUR SOCIETY

The Impala is a brown, black, and white antelope that lives in the region of southern Africa and north to Angola and Kenya. The male has slender, lyre-shaped horns. The African Impala can jump to a height of over 10 feet and cover a distance of greater than 30 feet. Yet these magnificent creatures can be kept in an enclosure in any zoo with a 3-foot wall. The animals will not jump if they cannot see where their feet will fall.

As believers, we have great power and great potential through the Lord Jesus. But we often allow past failures, present failures, and fearful circumstances to keep us from becoming all we can be.

Can you relate to the Impala? Are there walls in your life that have been built that are keeping you in? Do you lack faith to believe God is able to give you what you need? Faith is the ability to trust what we cannot see, and with faith we are freed from the flimsy enclosures of life and the entrapments of fear.

MAKE IT HAPPEN

Take a few minutes and think of things in your life that are keeping you from experiencing all God wants for you in the Christian life. Write them down. Make these things the basis of personal prayer, asking God to help you in these areas.

FOLLOW THE SPIRIT

What God wants me to do:

_____

_____

REMEBER YOU THOUGHTS

Special insights you have learned:

_____

_____

MORE LIGHT ON THE TEXT
2 CORINTHIANS 13:1-13

13:1 This is the third time I am coming to you. In the mouth of two or three witnesses shall every word be established. 2 I told you before, and foretell you, as if I were present, the second time; and being absent now I write to them which heretofore have sinned, and to all other, that, if I come again, I will not spare:

Having visited the Corinthians twice, Paul is coming for the third time. Pastoral work is incomplete if pastors do not do pastoral visitations. But Paul, as their spiritual father, will chasten them if the situation demands it. Paul will do everything in strict justice as approved by Christ. He will deal with the issues according to God's law sanctioned in Christ. His visit will be the final one but it will put the sinners in their place.

3 Since ye seek a proof of Christ speaking in me, which to you ward is not weak, but is mighty in you.

Paul as their pastor has decided to be strict and to take strict measures against sinners in Corinth. There were those who sought proof (*dokime*) of Paul's apostleship. Paul had endured abuse for the sake of Christ. But when the genuineness of his apostleship is called into question, Paul cannot endure that. He cannot be silenced. For in challenging Paul, they are challenging the Lord Himself who commissioned Paul (1:1) by the will of God. So Paul threatens to come with a rod.

Congregations do make accusations and rebellion

against their ministers. Paul has called on God to help. This does not mean that pastors should not be criticized. Criticism must always be just. In the Old Testament, Korah rebelled against Moses who was appointed by God to lead Israel (Numbers 16:28). Paul reminds the Corinthians that he is an apostle, sent by Christ and by God's grace. Paul is not working for Satan. God has already given them different spiritual provisions (1 Corinthians 12) which came to them through Paul's preaching. So they have that proof already.

4 For though he was crucified through weakness, yet he liveth by the power of God. For we also are weak in him, but we shall live with him by the power of God toward you.

It is Christ's power that transforms the Corinthian's lives. But Christ was crucified in weakness, *asthenaia*. Christ who is the Prince of Life (Acts 3:15) died on the cross in total humiliation (Philippians 2:8). Yet the cross, which was a supreme spectacle of weakness and human degradation, is the source of power unto to salvation for believers. His resurrection is the manifestation of God's power (1 Corinthians 2:3). The instrument of weakness became the instrument of power (1:18; 4:7ff; 6:4ff; 11:23ff; 12:5ff). Christ Himself endured the sufferings of our weakness so that the believer who is united with Christ in His death will also participate in His glorious resurrection (Romans 6:3ff; Philippians 3:10). So Paul can live to say that he is Christ's apostle even in his weakness. Christ who died as though weak was raised to the majestic glory as King of kings and Lord of lords. He will appear in glory (Revelation 19:11).

5 Examine yourselves, whether ye be in the faith; prove your own selves. Know ye not your own selves, how that Jesus Christ is in you, except ye be reprobates?

Now that they can prove that God through Christ is working in Paul, it is time that the Corinthians also prove to Paul whether Christ in them. They should turn their attention to themselves. They must confirm to themselves that they have faith in Christ. Each Christian has to do his or her own self-examination.

The Corinthians must be restored (v. 9) to their former faith. They must be up-built if they have lost their foundation. Through Paul's ministry, they came to faith. Now they must prove their faith to Paul. If they know that Christ dwells in them then they should also know that Paul is Christ's apostle. This could be done either through voluntary confession by individual members or though the disciplining of individual members of the church. They have to scrutinize themselves instead of scrutinizing Paul. Upon self-examination, the Corinthians will discern whether they have faith or not. So Paul hopes that they will start walking in the way of Christ.

6 But I trust that ye shall know that we are not reprobates. 7 Now I pray to God that ye do no evil; not that we should appear approved, but that ye should do that which is honest, though we be as reprobates.

The troublemakers have been stirring the Corinthians to demand proof of Paul's discipleship. They have been questioning his apostolic authority. Paul chastens the Corinthians as their father not because he hates them, but because he loves them. He requires that they shape up for the better. Paul is convinced that, as his children, they will come to power through weakness. They will be convinced of their inadequate proof against Paul.

8 For we can do nothing against the truth, but for the truth. 9 For we are glad, when we are weak, and ye are strong: and this also we wish, even your perfection.

In a pastoral manner, yet partially ridiculing them, Paul desires that they be strong in faith rather than weak. But he and his co-workers considers himself weak. The irony is that the Corinthians are even weaker and need to be strong.

Pastors should not abuse power, neither should they swayed by the wave of disobedient Christians. Misconduct in the congregation must be dealt with cleverly in order to avoid schism. Using Paul's example, pastors must not shrink from imposing discipline when circumstances demand it. But authority must not degenerate into authoritarianism. A pastor must conform to the to the teaching of Christ who is the head of the church. When Christians become strong in faith, the pastor has something to rejoice about. Discipline should always be for pastoral eminence not for status quo. Paul, therefore, longs that there should be harmony that bears fruit among members. When the Christians are perfected (*katartisis*) as the body of Christ, its members will function efficiently.

10 Therefore I write these things being absent, lest being present I should use sharpness, according to the power which the Lord hath given me to edification, and not to destruction.

Paul is accused of being bold and terrifying when he writes but weak when he is present. So, he answers the charge by saying that he does not need to act with sharpness when he comes for he has already exercised his authority by letter. When he comes he will act pastorally. His sharpness is that the church may become a spiritual entity (12:19). He has been given this authority by the Lord (10:8). While he was challenged by his opponents to come for a confrontation to impress the secular world, he will act as a pastor. But he will still discipline the church (12:20). However, as a pastor, he will act in gentleness rather than severity. With a rod of love and a spirit of humility, he will pastor them.

11 Finally, brethren, farewell. Be perfect, be of good comfort, be of one mind, live in peace; and the God of love and peace shall be with you.

Paul concludes his letter with affectionate words to the brethren and with exhortation. The term *chairete* may also be translated "farewell." But in most cases it is translated "rejoice." Indeed Paul wants them to rejoice in the Lord (Philippians 3:1; 4:4ff). Joy should be a mark of every Christian community. *Katartizesthe*, "be perfect," means to be sanctified to righteousness. If all are sanctified they will live in harmony. *Parakaleisthe* means "be comforted." Paul prays that the Corinthians should embrace God's comforting (cf. 3:1ff). In other translations, it is to "be admonished" (RSV), or to "heed to his appeal." *To auto phroneite* means "be of the same mind." Christians, though they hold different opinions as individuals, they should always come to agreement based on the Word of God, to be in one concord. They should respect each other. In so doing they will be united in what is essential, namely, love so that the teaching of Christ may unify them as parts of the body of Christ.

They should fix their eyes on the Lord and promote peace. Christian warfare is an enemy of souls and is instigated by the power of darkness. The plan of God is that love and peace should abide in believers. God alone can grant the qualities.

12 Greet one another with an holy kiss. 13 All the saints salute you.

Saluting one another with a holy kiss can happen only if they live in harmony and have affection for each other. They can then kiss and embrace in joy. This will not be a mere show like some churches do during Sunday service. It is deep commitment to each other or each other's affairs. A "holy kiss" is a childlike kiss, pure and sincere. It is a symbol of mutual respect and mutual love. It is a token of reconciliation and confidence through Christ. Their unity will prove to be part of the larger unity where there are no divisions. They will be part of the body of Christ.

Finally, Paul brings greeting of all the saints, i.e., fellow Christians, with whom they are united in Christ even though many in Macedonia had never seen them. Together they are one in the body of Christ, in unity with other saints of the Christian family wherever they are. These will be gathered during the final consummation in glory (Revelation 7:9ff).

NOTES

INTRODUCTION TO THE JUNE 2000 QUARTER

GENERAL INTRODUCTION

Units for Our Inspiration

The study for this quarter is based on four letters traditionally referred to as Paul's prison letters: Philippians, Ephesians, Colossians, and Philemon.

The Quarter at-a-Glance

NEW LIFE IN CHRIST

UNIT 1. LIVING IN CHRIST

The theme for Unit 1, "Living in Christ," contains four sessions that focus on Paul's letter to the church at Philippi. "Living In Christ," "Having The Mind of Christ," Pressing On In Christ," and "Rejoicing In Christ" are put forth as major themes.

LESSON 1: **June 4 Living Is Christ**
Philippians 1:12-26

This lesson responds to the question, What does it mean "to live is Christ?" The content is derived from Paul's conversation about his life in Christ. Here we learn that in spite of imprisonments, Paul was able to influence others to speak the Word of God courageously and fearlessly. We see this principle of living a Christ-centered life even in the fact that Paul believed that whether he was released or killed, his life would magnify Christ and serve God's purpose. Paul desired to be with Christ, yet he believed that the Philippians needed him. Thus moving Paul to visit the Philippians and rejoice in their spiritual growth.

For the Christian, living is Christ. If our life concerns are centered on the person and power of Christ, then life itself is Christ. For life to be Christ means that even when we face unfortunate circumstances we still do so with hope. Living is Christ means that we must deal with negative feelings about the congregation and pastors whom we may think evangelize with a spirit of rivalry, competition, and improper motives. This "Living Is Christ" principle addresses our struggle with life and death from the perspective of being

with Christ at all times, calling us to a bold expression of faith in Him. Hopefully, as you study you will begin to see that as a believer "to live or to die is Christ," because you are complete in Christ.

LESSON 2: **June 11 Having the Mind of Christ**
Philippians 2:1-13

The key of this lesson is having the mind of Christ. In the biblical passage for this lesson we find that Paul said his joy would be complete when the believers demonstrated unity in Christ and esteemed others better than themselves. For this unity to occur the Philippians must follow the example of Christ in humility, obedience, and service. In this we find that our salvation does not permit us to be lifted up and to refuse to live responsibly. Indeed the passage indicates that salvation is both God's work in the believer and a personal humble response to God, who enables the believer to please God.

The fundamental question that this lesson seeks to answer in light of the text is, "What is genuine humility?" How does one maintain this attitude of humility that reflects the person of Christ in a world where people tend so easily to think of themselves more highly than others? Even in Philippi some Christians were overly concerned with their own interests and thus created an atmosphere replete with problems and conflict. But one who walks in the humility of Christ should find it less difficult to make sacrifices that are congruent with the will of God, with no claim of return or reward. In short, this lesson should help you seek to be more humble following the example of the Lord Jesus Christ.

LESSON 3: **June 18 Pressing On in Christ**
Philippians 3:7-21

In a world where the pressure to give up on commitments abound, this lesson encourages us to continue pressing on. The Scriptural passage provides the example of the Apostle Paul as one who considered that knowing Christ surpasses everything of worth to him. To gain Christ, he gladly suffered the loss of all things. He was willing to press on until he attained the same glory that the Lord had attained through His suffering, death and resurrection. Paul spoke of sharing Christ's suffering and the power of His Resurrection in order to attain eternal life. This pressing on to reach the goal of God's call in Christ, Paul maintained, requires forgetting past failures and pressing toward the future with Christ as a guide.

This lesson also calls us to strive to be Christlike in our character. This means that we must develop confidence in what God can do with us even with our limited abilities. This pressing or striving to be Christlike does not mean we can live a life of good works without Christ. It must be a striving informed by the very God whom we seek. This lesson calls us to experience the power of Christ's Resurrection as a dynamic power operating in our lives. All of us as Christians have one goal to which we ought to work and that is conforming to the image God's Son. Our role model, after whom we pattern our lives, is the Lord Jesus Christ.

LESSON 4: June 25 Rejoicing in Christ
Philippians 4:4-18

The aim of this lesson is to encourage you to live in the joy of the Lord always. Within the text we find that joy, gentleness, refusing to worry, and diligent prayer are connected to the presence of God's peace. Paul, in this passage, encourages his readers to set their minds on positive, life-enriching attitudes. Paul exemplifies this attitude by clearly expressing joy for the concern the Philippians showed him. In fact, it is in the expression of this joy that he tells the Philippians how he learned to be content with what he had. Paul's joy came from recognizing his spiritual partnership with the Philippians and affirming Christ as his ultimate strength.

UNIT 2. CALLED TO BE A NEW HUMANITY

The theme for Unit 2, "Called to Be a New Humanity," is based on Ephesians wherein Christians are called to spiritual blessings, oneness in Christ, use of spiritual gifts, responsible living, and to stand firm as participants in the new community.

LESSON 5: July 2 Called to Spiritual Blessings in Christ
Ephesians 1:1-14

This lesson deals with the fact that God has blessed us in Christ with every spiritual blessing in the heavenly places. Ephesians deals specifically with the spiritual provision of God for believers. God has provided for the leaders gifts to build up the church for the work to which we are called. Just as God calls leaders according to His will, God chose us as believers to praise Him and do His divine will. But more than choosing us through Christ, God has, because of Christ, offered us redemption, forgiveness, and the riches of God's grace. With this knowledge you will enter deeper into the wisdom and knowledge of God, who has revealed the mystery of the divine will through Jesus Christ.

This lesson calls you to claim your spiritual blessings. As you study, you will gain insight that when you undergo change, your search for meaning and purpose must be grounded in the Christ through whom God's eternal riches have become yours. When you have feelings of personal deprivation and think that no one appreciates the tasks you have accomplished, think again. God appreciates you and in fact has provided heavenly blessing to show you that you are appreciated.

LESSON 6: July 9 Called to Oneness in Christ
Ephesians 2:8-22

The biblical content of this lesson focuses on the process whereby those who have been outside God's covenant are now inside of God's covenant, united by salvation through Christ. According to Paul, in order for the Ephesians to be united as one they must realize their salvation is not of their own making, but of pure grace that flows from the heart of God and revealed in Jesus Christ. Because salvation is not of their own effort, there is no need to prove they are better than one another, or separate themselves thinking their separation gives them better access to God. Their main motivation must be the love of God through Jesus Christ. Here, believers are reminded that just as Christ broke the barrier of hostility between the Ephesians, He is able to break whatever animosity may be serving as barriers to Christian fellowship.

Within this lesson the students learn that Christian action does not depend on recognition or reward, but on the free grace God shows. This lesson calls us, as Christians, to strive to eliminate feelings of estrangement and alienation in our fellowship and in our community, and help us have a sense of belonging to those things based in Christ. This then, should lead us to a commitment in Christian action for the purpose of helping others. Finally the lesson calls us to become a people of reconciliation and justice and mercy.

LESSON 7: July 16 Called to Use Your Spiritual Gifts
Ephesians 4:1-16

This lesson is meant to encourage you to use your spiritual gifts. You will again be reminded that each of us was given exactly the right amount of grace and gifts we need to build up the church the way God desires. You will learn that as Christ conquered sin and death by descending into the grave, rising from the dead, and ascending into heaven, He gave different spiritual gifts to build up the church in unity and maturity. Your gift is given to you to promote the church's growth in love.

This lesson is directed to let you know that you have claim to your own ministry based on the gifts with which Christ has endowed you. In this world of discord and strife, there must be a reason for life. God has enabled you with gifts that can help you to cooperate with others to accomplish goals of leading this world to wholeness. As a Christian your desire to live a full and worthwhile life can only be accomplished if you are attuned to the gifts within you and rely on the power of the Lord. This lesson calls you to discover your gifts and to use them. If you do not know your gifts, and worst of all, if you do not use them, the church of the Lord is poorer because of it.

LESSON 8: July 23 Called to Responsible Living
Ephesians 5:1-5, 21-29; 6:1-4

We as believers are called to responsible living. One way in which we can learn to be responsible Christians according to the passage for today's lesson, is to imitate God in our behavior. In this passage, Paul says that impure actions and improper speech are unacceptable behavior for believers, but a grateful spirit is edifying to the kingdom of God and reflects responsibility. He then proceeds to insist that this responsibility is reflected in the submission of wives to their husbands, as the church is subject to Christ, and in the love of husbands for their wives, in the same spirit that Christ yielded Himself to establish the church. Paul further said children are to submit themselves to their parents in obedience, and parents are to guide and discipline their children in the Lord.

In this lesson we are encouraged to claim our responsibilities both familial and communal. As Christians, many of us have gifts and experiences in areas wherein others can benefit from our efforts. Part of our responsibility as believers is to exemplify respect and concern for others over selfish desires and goals.

LESSON 9: July 30 Called to Stand Firm
Ephesians 6:10-24

What is a Christian called to do in a shifting world where everything grounded is shifting and principles change like the surf of the sea? Paul's response in the passage for today's study is, "Be strong in the Lord and in the strength of his power" (Ephesians 6:10). In this passage, Paul told the Ephesians that believers who get their strength and power from God battle against spiritual enemies, rather than physical ones.

In this lesson you are encouraged to claim your power base. God wants you to be confident and to use the resources and abilities that have been given to you through the Spirit to cope with life's conditions. Christians will face oppressive powers in the world. Too many, too often seek sources of security in the armor of the world. But here in this lesson, you will learn that you have a source of power that is greater than what the world can offer. God has given you the provision to defeat all the enemies of your soul. Be strong, not in your own power, but in the power of the Lord, Who made heaven and earth.

UNIT 3. CHRIST ABOVE ALL

The theme for Unit 3, "Christ Above All," centers on Paul's letter to the church at Colossae with emphasis on the supremacy, completeness and righteousness of Christ. Paul's personal letter to Philemon concerning his relationship with Onesimus concludes the study for the quarter.

LESSON 10: August 6 The Supremacy of Christ
Colossians 1:15-28

Every believer should know that Jesus Christ is Supreme. The biblical content of this lesson emphasizes the fact that Jesus Christ is the eternal image of God in Whom all things were created and through Whom all things are held together. Based on the fundamental grounding of all things in Him, Jesus Christ is logically the head of the church. This pre-eminence is also underscored by the fact that He is the first-born from the dead. Not only is Jesus Christ preeminent in the world, but He is also full manifestation of the Godhead. He is God in human form. Finally, the passage affirms the preeminence of the Messiah with regards to the redemptive process of the world, for it has pleased God to reconcile the world through Him. After having told them in whom they have believed, Paul exhorted the Colossians to remain established and steadfast in the faith.

This lesson affirms the Christian principle that Jesus Christ is the source of life. So if you are looking for purpose that holds life together, you can find it in Jesus alone. If you have been given the grace to become the head of a group or institution, you need to know that gifts are derived from Christ, Who is the head of all things. There is no other Lord nor being in this world that can compare with the excellency of Jesus, the Son of God. If you want to succeed in spite of difficult circumstances, then this incomparable Christ is your key.

LESSON 11: **August 13 A Complete Life in Christ**
Colossians 2:6-19

This lesson calls to your attention the fact that you have been given a complete life in Christ. We study that Paul exhorts the Colossians to live their lives in Christ and to remain faithful to him. The lack of a sense of completeness often leads people to go searching for vain ideas that they hope will make them complete. But here we study how believers were cautioned against allowing themselves to be deceived by philosophies that are contrary to Christ's teachings. He then proceeds to let them know that Christ is the head of every ruler and authority, and that everything needed for a full religious life can be found in Him. If they were seeking forgiveness, God's forgiveness is offered through Christ's death and Resurrection, which bring new life.

Those who have Christ are called to acknowledge God's great care and as a result should have a thankful spirit that is contagious. Your understanding that you have life in Christ protects you from being fooled by the false philosophies of this world. You are so fully provided for by the power of God that you cannot help but believe in the renewal of human possibilities through divine dynamics. This lesson is meant to lead you to accept the fact that God gives you fullness of life.

LESSON 12: **August 20 The Way to Righteousness**
Colossians 3:1-3, 5-17

In this lesson we study Paul's understanding of the way to righteousness Jesus Christ. Here we see that Paul told the Colossians how life in Christ means lifting the conduct of life to a higher level, for they were one with Christ. We present the idea that Christians must put aside sinful behavior and live as new creations in Christ. The way to living fully in the righteousness of God is to practice love, which produces harmony and thus allows the peace of Christ to rule in the hearts of Christians. Paul teaches this love will cause us to forgive each other, as Jesus Christ has forgiven us and to live with compassion, kindness, humility, meekness, and patience. We know that we are walking in the way of righteousness when instead of bickering and complaining we teach and admonish each other in wisdom and sing praises to God. Paul exhorted that whatever the Colossians said or did should be in the name of Jesus and in gratitude to God. This lesson concerns the need to seek a higher purpose in life. Our attraction must be to lifestyles that are not deceitful or harmful to the way of Christ. Again, this means that we must have a forgiving spirit.

LESSON 13: **August 27 Welcoming Others in Christ**
Philemon 4-21

In this lesson we study the letter that Paul wrote to his dear friend Philemon. In this letter, Paul expressed thanks to God upon hearing of Philemon's love for all Christians and his faith in the Lord Jesus. Paul asked Philemon to welcome Onesimus back as a brother, rather than as a slave, even as he would welcome Paul. Paul offered to right any wrong and repay any debt owed by Onesimus. Paul was confident that Philemon would do as expected and give reason for Paul to rejoice in the Lord Jesus. All this leads to fact that Philemon serves as an example of our call to welcome others in the name of Christ.

In this lesson you are being called to express the grace of life by believing, as Paul did, in the power of the prayer you offer for others whom you seek to convince to do right. Through this lesson you will gain insight into the depth of joy experienced when we bring love and joy to others. Also, as you study this lesson you will be committed to stand up for others during difficult times in their lives.

Spiritual Keys To Transformative Leadership:
Becoming the Leader Who Changes Lives

The challenges and issues of today's generation call for transformative leaders—men and women who lead in such a way as to have a transformative effect on people. Transformative leaders are men and women who help other people fulfill a higher calling and unleash their latent potential. Transformative leaders are people who help groups and organizations achieve a kingdom mission. Transformative leadership is spiritual leadership. Transformative leadership changes lives.

There was a time when many people thought that only certain people could lead. The fact of the matter is that God planted a leadership seed into humankind when he gave Adam and Eve dominion over the Earth. Sinful humans perverted the practice of leadership by exchanging God's process for their own process of domination and subjugation. With the ushering in of the Kingdom of God, the express rule and reign of God through Jesus Christ, comes a restored view and expectation of kingdom agency or leadership that transforms.

God is raising up women and men across the world who are effecting change in our communities, businesses and churches. God is raising up women and men who are helping to birth another generation of faithful ones. God is raising up women and men to intercede and to deliver families, friends, communities and nations from the grip of Satan. God is raising up men and women who have been called to lead, who can garner support, and work with other leaders to achieve God-inspired results. In short, God is raising up transformative leaders.

The challenges faced by people in this age, young and old alike, require that we touch the core of their issues. Church leaders—educators, administrators, servants—must be transformative. Today's leaders must apply the life-changing power of the God's Word to today's issues. As we look at the challenges people face today, we can see that in order to effectively reach them, our approach and method will have to be different from what we used yesterday. Church leaders are finding that while tradition has its place, today's leaders have to listen to what God is saying to us about this new generation of believers (and non-believers), and how we can effectuate His purpose in their lives.

Author Fred Smith says in his book *Learning to Lead 2,* "The right concept of leadership is vital. And without a solid concept of leadership, you have a faulty leadership." As leaders in the service of the Lord, we must have the right concept of what it is we are called to do, and why. We must ask ourselves pertinent questions such as: What is a leader? What are the assumptions we make about leadership, and the places in which we lead? Tansformative Leadership provides us with a model of leadership that is necessary for the 21st century

Many of us grow up believing that leadership is merely about a position, the Sunday School superintendent, the pastor, the Usher Board president. Transformative leaders realize that spiritual leadership is a process—it's doing God-ordained things to effectuate change in the lives of people. It is a process whereby leaders motivate others to be and do their best, accomplish goals, and realize their divine destiny. For instance, a significant leader in the church is the Sunday School teacher. The Sunday School teacher who sees herself as a transformative leader realizes that her aim and purpose are to shape, mold, and stimulate thoughts, beliefs,

Dr. Jeanne Porter and Evangelist Samira E. Robinson

and attitudes about the Lord. She is to bring forth truth and thus lead her students out of the darkness of misinformation. The lessons taught, while universal, hold a unique meaning in each Sunday School class. The teacher sets the tone for the class, and based on the level of study, spirituality and Biblical knowledge of her students, she influences and impacts youth and adults in positive or not so positive ways.

There are old models of leadership styles, secular in nature, that we have followed that have undoubtedly run their course. Often these models reflect a worldly agenda instead of God's purpose. A review of the traditional versus the transformative leadership model allows us to compare the thrust, and resulting outcomes, of each model. Traditional leadership has a history of viewing the leadership role as a call to dominate or control, and a number of overt and covert methods are used to get what we want. Transformative leadership realizes that leadership is a call to service, first to God and then to the people. Secular leadership often focuses on certain techniques and tactics to get a job done. Transformative leadership relies on God's prompting and leading. The secular leadership model emphasizes taking charge, and often the leader takes pride in his or her abilities. The Transformative Leadership model is activated on one's faith in his or her position in Christ and the call of God in their lives. The secular leadership model is often defined by what the world system says is important. The Transformative Leadership model comes from God's Word and is defined by God.

Based on the Transformative Leadership model, church leaders must adapt an approach to leadership that reflects their faith in God and desire to please Him. Church leaders who desire to be transformative leaders will have to acclimate themselves to utilizing Biblical principles with a revelatory understanding of the needs of today's Sunday School student. The goal must not be to simply get our message to them, but to learn what their message is. What is troubling them? What are their goals? What do they want to be when they grow up? What gifts has God given them, and what skills do they have? Transformative leaders must work at knowing the answers to these questions. That is not to say that one has to know the personal history and be personally involved with each student. But, one should be concerned enough to go beyond the surface, to the depths of caring about each person. It is then that our message will be heard loud and clear. Today's generation encompasses those often referred to as the "unchurched" and those who were raised in church but have not applied the Word to their lives. The transformative leader is in tune with the heart of God, and the heart of the student.

There are nine spiritual keys to transformative leadership that when grasped will take you to the next level in your spiritual growth and fulfillment of your purpose as a leader. These principles help you function more effectively in your calling to help others. The principles are:

1. Understand who you are as a person. The transformative leader must understand who he or she is as a person—who God has created him or her to be versus who society has constructed him or her to be. Leadership is personal. It is about the individual—the unique person who God has created, not the generic label that society has attempted to construct. The leader is a person first, not a role model. Remember that God blesses people with gifts, not roles or positions. The transformative leader will carry his or her God-given special mark.

2. Discover and tap into your purpose. God designed each person with a specific purpose in mind. We are His workmanship (Ephesians 2:10) or His special creation. Every new product comes from the manufacturer or maker with instructions. Each person should imagine that he or she is new product. What would the instructions describing your purpose and function read? What have you been created to do? You are a distinct creation and a model of excellence. What are the unique features, gifts, talents and abilities with which you have been equipped? Until you can get in touch with this purpose, you will flounder or be less than effective as a leader.

3. Determine the proper place for your leadership. Placement is very important to God. Like Esther, Joseph, Paul, and Daniel, God strategically situates his leaders in places to fulfill his purposes in the lives of people. He assigns us to work in churches, businesses, service agencies, professional service agencies, and the community. Too often people get frustrated with where they are, and fail to see the working of God—that He has strategically placed him or her. As you pray about placement, ask God where He wants you to offer your gifts, and where you can be of the best service for kingdom building.

4. Accept God's preparations for you. Even as Jesus

went through extensive preparation for His public ministry, so will every leader go through a preparation phase. Before every harvest, there is a season of sowing. For every walk, there is a toddle. In Jesus' preparation we see isolation and testing—out of which came clarified purpose. A transformative leader must accept God's mode of preparation for them. God prepares leaders in His timeframe. The leader's preparation includes formal and informal lessons that come from living. Every experience, trial, and triumph is part of the preparation process.

5. Develop the process that is inline with who you are and where God has placed you. Transformative leaders must develop the process that is inline with who they are and where God has placed them. The process refers to the way in which the leader accomplishes his or her goals, tasks and objectives. The process depends upon the people with whom you are in a leadership relationship, the tasks or things that need to be accomplished, and the steps you take to do it based on your leadership style.

6. Utilize the power that you have been given. Transformative leaders must practice using the power that God has given them. Traditionally leaders have relied upon power that comes from holding a formal position or title. These leaders operated under the theory, "I get you to do what I want because I'm the boss and I can reward or punish you." Other traditional leaders persuade people using charisma, charm or personality. God is calling for leaders to rely on the dynamic power of the Holy Spirit to guide the leader, grant the leader wisdom to envision possibilities for their organization or department, and to enable leaders to work with people to get results.

7. Follow the plan that God has laid out for you. Transformative leaders follow the plan the Lord has laid out for them. In Jeremiah 29:11, God told the nation of Israel, "I know the plans that I have for you. They are plans of peace and not of evil" (NLT). His plan was to give Israel a future and hope. God has laid out plans for nations as well as for individuals. He has the master plan and the task of the Transformative Leader is to tap into the Master's plan for their lives and their organization or group. They do not introduce their own agendas, but go where God says to go and do what He says do.

8. Love the people God has given you. Transformative leaders love and accept the people God has given them. They do not seek out others with whom they would rather work. The transformative leader resists treating students like needy people and interacts with them as treasures of God entrusted to the leader. The transformative leader learns wisely to utilize the gifts of the people who have been assigned to him or her. Too often traditional leaders blame their staffs for the leader's own inadequacies. Worse yet, these traditional leaders perpetually look for people who can produce for them, instead of learning how to cultivate the resources they already have to get a maximum yield.

9. Develop proficiencies that facilitate spiritual transformation. Transformative leaders develop proficiencies or skills that facilitate spiritual transformation. They realize that God works on the inside and that divine purpose starts in the heart of every believer and works its way out. They practice integrity and work on self-improvement, building on their skills and talents.

This Transformative Leadership model embodies the concept of collaborative leadership, which in actuality many organizations, and corporations are beginning to use because they now realize that the traditional model has lost its effectiveness. They adapt the new model because they feel the winds of change in society and do not want to be left behind. Corporations and businesses fully intend to be successful in this new millennium. The church, the Body of Christ on Earth, must not fall behind but rather set the standard for others to follow, especially when the foundational paradigm supporting collaborative leadership is spiritual and relational.

People need transformative leadership. In this fast-paced and morally—impoverished society, our church and community members need leaders to be dynamic individuals who are willing to accept change and use new ways to reach and teach them. They hunger and thirst for church leaders who are grounded in the Word of God and His divine purpose. It is our challenge, our call and our repsonsibility to become the leaders that God has ordained—transformative leaders or leaders who change lives for the kingdom of God.

1 Adapted from the Dr. Porter's *Leading Ladies: Leadership Development Seminar Series.* Produced by TransPorter Communications.

2 Fred Smith, *"Learning to Lead,"* *Christianity Today,* Inc./Word, Inc., 1986. Distributed by Word Books; p. 24.

THEMATIC ESSAY

NEW LIFE IN CHRIST

You are free falling your way through your life. You allow yourself to give in to the endless possibilities that the night sky seems to hold. You close your eyes as if making a wish, and you cascade soundlessly into the welcoming arms of the sky, a grin forming on your face. Your nostrils and lungs hungrily drink in the air as if it is rocket fuel. You are captivated by what appears to be the power of flight. The air threads through your hair like the fingers of a loved one braiding it. You tumble and twirl through the air like an acrobat. You dance to the whistle of the wind. It seems that the air has allowed you to live your dreams of being an acrobat and a dancer. The wind seems to whisper, "What else do you wish to be?" The reply "An Olympic swimmer," barely passes from your lips when you find yourself closing your eyes and diving headlong into the air. You can even imagine yourself penetrating the cool water. Yet when you open your eyes, you realize that you are not really in a calm pool of water. You see before you what appears to be the never ending darkness of the night sky. For the first time, you realize that the night sky is a starless one. The once warm air that seemed to support your every acrobatic maneuver and dance step has grown cold. You scramble upward, trying to swim upstream like a salmon trying to spawn, but you cannot. Your fingers claw the unforgiving air as you spiral downward ever faster. You grow numb from the chill in the air, and your body folds upward like an umbrella when strong winds get beneath it. You plummet like a piece of lint being sucked into a vacuum. You are a lifeless pile of limbs and bones with a mind that at times dimly recalls that it ever functioned. The last image that your mind holds clearly is the vision of yourself as a child, praying to God for help on a test in school.

The next sensation that you feel is your head dribbling like a basketball on asphalt. Has the Earth risen up to meet you and break your fall? You struggle to open your eyelids, which feel as though they have been sealed shut for a long, long slumber. You realize that you are lying on your back. You feel sharp pains surge through the small of your back and buttocks as you breathe raw breaths that make your lungs ache. Your blood pulses through your body so hard that you can almost visualize it surging through your veins. You relish these sensations because they make you remember that you are alive. God has spared you.

Your free fall journey into chaos and evil has been ended by the steady, firm, certain hand of God. The hand catches you and does not let you go. Your landing was intentionally rough perhaps because God wants you to know for certain that you are still alive. You sense the awesome power of the hand of God, the power to turn you back into dust. Yet, at the same time, you sense that this hand has caught you for the purpose of transforming your life. The firmness of the hand makes you know that God will be the foundation of your life. When you realize that God can be the rock on which you anchor your life, a warm sensation overtakes you. The warm tenderness of God's hand allows you to know what forgiveness feels like. You savor the feeling of being redeemed as you lie cradled in the secure hand of your redeemer. You imagine that you must resemble a baby who feels safe and loved nestled in the warmth of its mother's womb. Like a baby, you are aware that you must emerge from the cradle. You must reenter the same temptation-filled world that seduced you into a free fall dance with evil. The memory of that world and your misdeeds within it cause you to shiver and snuggle deeper into the hand of God. As you embrace Him and His goodness, a warm calm descends upon you, and you realize that God will be with you always and He will support you as you learn to walk in His ways.

The first step in learning how to walk in God's ways is to share with other people how He has trans-

Debra Branker Harrod

formed your life. Unpack your memories of your life of evil. Recall the vivid details of your sinful escapades to breathe life and dimension into your portrait of the past. Remember what it felt like to be the willing architect of a life guided by wickedness. Recall feeling dazed and happy at the thought of your own limitless power. Recall your fear and your guilt when you discovered that you had placed your faith in your own selfish desires and the fragile air and not the will of God. Remember your anguish, despair, resignation and sorrow at the thought of the beautiful life that you had dreamed but not yet lived. Make peace with your life of wickedness by making it into a cautionary tale for others. Let your past stand as a warning for how not to live. Then tell others about how the love of God saved you. Describe how you remembered that you were a child of God. Describe the moment that you sensed that God loved you unconditionally. Mention that once you felt God's forgiveness that you could forgive yourself for straying from Him. Mention that you felt as though you had finally found your way home. Joyously describe your thoughts on how you will use your God-given skills and talents to help others find a new life in Christ.

Studying the Bible can help you to clarify how you will use your talents, skills and your life to serve and honor the Lord. This is the second step in learning how to walk in the ways of the Lord. By closely and often reading, pondering and discussing the Scripture, the Holy Spirit will reveal the meaning of the Word to you. You can then use your talents and skills to share your God-given understanding of the Bible with other people. For example, a person who possesses musical talent studies the Bible and shares his/her understanding of the text through an original song or an original musical. An individual with writing talent who examines the Bible communicates his/her God-given revelations through a play, a book, song lyrics, a poem or a story. In addition to pursuing all opportunities to share our knowledge of the Bible with others, God expects us to apply that knowledge to our daily living. This is the third step in learning how to pursue a new life in Christ. God wants us to live our lives according to His doctrines. He sets out the rules for how humans should live on Earth in the Bible, and His Son Jesus Christ modeled how we should live when He dwelled on Earth among us.

Walking in the ways of the Lord is like "going through the narrow gate" (Matthew 7:13, TEV). It is a disciplined life of faith and sacrifice in which we diligently try to live in accord with God's many teachings. These teachings on right and wrong when viewed as a whole form a rigid path for us to follow so that we might one day reap the gift of eternal life with God. Jesus paints a portrait of "the few people who find the narrow gate to life and the hard way that leads to it" in the Sermon on the Mount (Matthew 7:14, TEV). He refers to "the few" as "spiritually poor, mournful, humble, those whose greatest desire is to do what God requires, merciful, pure in heart, those who work for peace and those who are persecuted because they do what God requires"(Matthew 5:3-10, TEV).

"Those who know that they are spiritually poor" recognize that they will not always do what God calls them to do. Humans are not perfect;, we are not God and at times we will fail to share the Word of God with others. For example, shortly before Jesus was arrested, tried, convicted, tortured and crucified, the disciple Peter assured Jesus that he would remain faithful to him saying, "Lord I am ready to go to prison with you and to die with you" (Luke 22:33, TEV). Yet, as Jesus prophesied, Peter claimed not to know the Son of God three times. Peter was dismayed at his inability to remain faithful to the Lord until the end and "wept bitterly" over his failings (Luke 22:62, TEV). Yet, the Lord forgave a repentant Peter for turning away from Him and He forgives us when we deny Him too. God understands and expects that we will falter at times. Yet, He does not want our inability to be perfect servants to stop us from serving Him. He wants us to recognize our imperfections and serve Him anyway.

In acknowledging that we are God's servants, we acknowledge that we are subject to His will. Jesus said "happy are those who mourn" because mourning is a way of accepting God's will. It is a way of accepting what has come to pass. All things that occur in life are the result of God's will and when we mourn and recognize our losses, we are not contesting but accepting what God has deemed a necessary action or turn of events. We allow our lives to be ordered by what God thinks is best. We submit to Him, and we trust that what God has done, He has done for the greater good.

When we truly accept that we are imperfect servants of our Lord and that our lives will be used to realize His larger vision, we find contentment in our humble status. We do not pursue or expect material wealth, power or praise on Earth as compensation for doing God's bidding. We are aware that "we cannot serve both God and money" (Matthew 6:24, TEV). We seek only to spend our lives telling of the spiritual fulfillment that comes with belief in the Lord, and He provides us with food, shelter, clothing and the richness of His Spirit so that we might spread His Word. Jesus said, "...do not worry about the food and drink you need in order to stay alive, or about clothes on your body...Instead be concerned above everything else with the Kingdom of God and with what He requires of you, and He will provide you with all other things" (Matthew 6: 25,33, TEV).

God requires that "our greatest desire" be to teach the sick, the poor, the wicked and the homeless of the world about the love of God, just as Jesus Christ did during His time on Earth (Matthew 9:10, TEV). Heeding the call to reveal the Holy Spirit to those that society has forgotten or left behind is an act of mercy. In so doing, we confront the harsh reality that our world considers some people expendable or lacking in purpose and casts them off. Those of us who are called do not look the other way at those that society shuns, pretending that they are not there. Instead, we acknowledge and celebrate the fact that by the grace of God they are alive and we acknowledge their station in life, however low it may be. We feel compassion for the downtrodden and seek to relieve their suffering because God's love and compassion rescued us from a wayward life of misery and keeps us from revisiting that existence. When teaching the downtrodden about God, we can draw upon our talents and skills in order to help them to grasp who He is and how and why to follow Him. We can also speak about the depth of meaning and purpose that God gives our lives so that they can understand why we believe in Him. Jesus taught people about God by telling parables to describe His principles. He also taught them about the power of faith in God when He healed the sick. When we introduce the sick, the poor and the homeless to the Lord, we initiate a healing process. The presence of the Holy Spirit in their lives works to restore their spirits and their flesh so that they too can be messengers of God.

It is only if we are "pure in heart" that the Spirit of the Lord can be revealed to others through us. At their core, the pure in heart possess an eternal adoration of God. This devotion to God radiates from their souls and informs every act of Christian service that they undertake. They are the Lord's authentic disciples. Jesus indicates that prior to the Final Judgment that "many false prophets will appear and fool many people" (Matthew 24:11, TEV). Only those who have a steadfast belief in God can truly reveal His Spirit to other people and offer them peace. Those who are truly called allow God to work through them to settle the troubled hearts and turbulent lives of unbelievers in the hope that they will believe. People who choose to accept God as their Saviour realize peace of mind when they order their lives in accordance with His teachings. They then become God's newest authentic disciples. The Lord's true and faithful messengers love Him so much that they would be willing to risk persecution at the hands of unbelievers in order to spread His Word. Such individuals are willing to endure physical and psychological torture and poverty for God. They would even surrender their flesh to death in order to remain true to God, the Creator, and to their purpose in life, which is to extend the gifts of discipleship and eternal salvation to all.

Those who would give up everything for the Lord realize that, because they are cloaked in the warmth and love of His Spirit, they possess all that they will ever need. The love of the Lord is adornment enough for them. These authentic disciples seize every chance to tell others of their past lives of wickedness in order to dissuade them from pursuing such lives. They eagerly study the Bible and apply the knowledge that God reveals to them in their ministries. Their simple, humble lives are examples of how one can strive to live according to God's doctrines. After a lifetime of sharing, study and pious living, God allows them to glimpse the simple beauty of the narrow gate and a path to it. The gate seems to beckon them forward. Stars illuminate the path as it winds its way upward through a very familiar-looking night sky into the heavens. As the chosen ones stride toward the narrow gate, they sense the palms of God beneath the path, supporting it. They recall how His hands radiated warmth and tenderness when they lay like babes within His palms waiting to transform the world. They remember how His palms formed the granite-like foundation for their lives even when they had fallen from grace. They savor the tender love of God, which emanates from His strong hands now, and they thank Him for this new life.

Helping Christians Understand and Survive Abuse

It is imperative that pastors present a theology relevant to the life experiences of the church, including sexual abuse, and remain true to the resurrection power of the gospel. The presuppositions of forgiveness, grace and culpability, integral to a Christian understanding are critical for the treatment of an abuse survivor. An acceptable psychological model for the church must be faith based and embrace three essential Christian understandings for the psychological community and the Christian community to be essentially compatible. They are: (1) the Christian notions of forgiveness, (2) grace and (3) culpability. These three notions address the two essential counseling questions of: (A) how does our yesterday affect our today and tomorrow and (B) who is to blame for the pains of our lives. Christianity offers some unambiguous arguments with prevailing psychological presuppositions on these notions. Biblical theology is based on faith which engages the paradox. This paradox is seen in central themes such as it is in giving that we receive and it is in dying that we live. Things are not what they seem. Rather, they are what our God through our faith deem them to be. Within Christendom faith is the engine that powers the believer and grants access to the riches and resources of God. Without faith it is impossible to please God. Without faith it is impossible to reach the repository of one's psychological strength or to receive forgiveness and grace or to comprehend culpability. Therefore, counseling that is endorsed by the Christian community must be faith based.

Turning to the notion of forgiveness one must understand that the Christian imperative to forgive predicates one's being forgiven, on one's ability to forgive (forgive us our debts as we forgive our debtors). Therefore, to the extent that a sense of our own wrong doing is the source of mental anxiety and psychological disorder, Christianity suggests, forgiveness is the antidote. A Christian-based psychological paradigm encourages one to seek through God forgiveness for and from one's self first and for and from others second. This, easily imagined in simple acting out, must also be true in the more difficult matters of sexual misconduct. This presupposition of Christianity suggests that the survivor of sexual abuse must appropriate the wellspring of empowering hope through the portal of forgiveness, first for and from themselves and then for their attacker. Forgiveness is the key to possessing the power to resolve the attack, abuse or rape. The act of forgiving moves the one attacked from the position of powerless victim to that of proactive survivor. This is the key that empowers the abused to begin their own healing. Pastors can oversimplify the process. There is no excuse for pastors to say to the sexually abused you must forgive, pray and then call the counseling session a success. Still, faith-based forgiveness is a fundamental goal of Christian counseling. Often misunderstandings on forgiving between the psychological community and the parish pose unnecessary hindrances to the progression of mental health.

Secondly is the notion of grace. The Old Testament notion of grace is rooted in the Hebrew notion of *hesed*. *Hesed* is understood as steadfast loving kindness. It is the fuel that empowers one who is carrying another's burden one mile, as well as the strength and will to volunteer to walk the second mile. God's *hesed* or grace is the love which extends from the Divine to us, independent of our actions or circumstances. This love is also independent of the actions or circumstances that are imposed on us by others. This love is even beyond the wonderful and nurturing love of family, it is the power which controls the universe. It is the transdimensional energy that is alone capable of making us whole when our lives have been shattered by the horror of sexual abuse or the vulgarity of evil circumstance. The basis of Christian thought is born from the idea of God's unmatched, unending, and unequaled love. God loves each of us so much that He gave His only Son to die for us on the

Brian K. Woodson, Sr.

Cross of Calvary. Those who receive this love should see and understand the vicissitudes of life through much different lenses than those who have separated themselves from this love or are otherwise unaware of it. To believe in the love of God and seek to experience it in its divine fullness from the Christian point of view is critical. Psychological care given to Christians from a Christian presupposition must believe in this kind of God love. Only then can the final and most difficult notion be embraced.

The most important notion in a Christian's understanding of sexual abuse is culpability. I cannot count the times that members have, with tears staining their Christian cheeks, searched in hope of understanding why. Why didn't my mother protect me? Why wasn't my father around to keep me safe? Who is to blame for the horror that has happened? In such times many pastors and leaders create devils and demons to blame for the travesties of sexual abuse. But I argue that such action is ultimately dishonest. Pastors should not construct some theological curtain that relies on a difference between God allowing something to happen and God authoring that same something. If you stand by and watch something horrible happen when you have the power, authority and opportunity to prevent it, you are an accessory to the act. In fact, if you have all power and all authority to prevent a horror and you choose to do nothing, you are totally responsible for the act. God is either God or God is not. God is either ultimately and completely in control or He is not God. This may be hard for a pastor to swallow but the one who has been abused, raped or molested understands somewhere in their psyche that God is somehow a player in the confusing horror. These thoughts lead the God-fearing sufferer of abuse towards blaming themselves and victimization. Their logic is clear, "If God is all I believe God to be and this horror has happened to me, I must be at fault." But it is base to believe a 10-year-old child contributes to his or her abuse. No one contributes to her abuse. To believe that the perpetrator is wholly at fault is simply to disguise God. The perpetrator is a stick in the hand of God. A stick that God will throw in the fire when God chooses. To blame the perpetrator is only to raise the question again, "Who is in control?" If the perpetrator is at fault why didn't God protect the innocent? It is a theological quagmire to assign our horrors to the devil and our good times to God. It is un-Christian to believe that human agency is autonomous to the power and prerogative of God. This leaves only the paradox; God who loves ultimately authors the vulgarity of abuse.

I realize that I may lose many here, but let me preface how this notion of God's culpability fits Christian faith with words to regulate our theology: Holocaust, Diaspora, the flood, Calvary, slavery—all horrors occurring under the watching and controlling eye of God. The paradigmatic figure of God's culpability is Job. Yet he is not alone. The Bible is full of persons who were raped. There is Esther, a woman objectified and raped, Bathsheba who was raped and widowed, Ruth who was prostituted, Tamar who was raped and left shamed and forgotten, Hagar, Bilhah, Zipah, and Dinah. The list could continue. Do I advocate tolerance or diminish the vulgarity of sexual abuse? Not only no, but absolutely not! Everything must be done to prevent, cease and protect our congregations, communities and families from sexual abuse. Survivors and victims of sexual abuse sit invisibly on church pews every Sunday. Pulpits that are silent on their experiences are wounds in our community and snags in the fabric of our faith. The point I hope to make is that God has demonstrated the Divine prerogative to act as God is pleased to act, autonomous to the will of women or men and outside of both their power and understanding. But there is a way to view this notion of God's culpability within the paradigm of the aforementioned *Hesed* and forgiveness of God. Pastors must be able to bring understanding and order into, what is an unimaginable swirl of confusion.

So, why would God allow innocent children, unyielding youth or wonderful men and women to be raped or abused? Why would God sacrifice the sanity and fray the faith of so many families? The answer is found in the essence of Christianity. The answer is the focal point of the Christian Gospel; the answer is the Cross of Christ. Christians stake their lives and faith on the belief that God sent the only begotten Son to die for us. Christians believe that the ultimate expression of God's love for them is the death of Christ on the Cross. For Christians, it is this death which ultimately and paradoxically gives us the eternal and abundant life. But view the death of Christ from the Cross and you hear Jesus ask the question central to every soul that has suffered from the garden through the flood. View the death of Christ from the nails being driven into innocence and you can see the holy event through the eyes of those burdened and beaten by the Holocaust, slavery, child abuse or rape since time began. In fact, Jesus, in the same position as any other sufferer of injustice and malevolence, asks the same question; "My God, my God, why have you forsaken me?"

If rape is a crime of power (and it is), then the Cross

of Calvary was a rape of Christ (and it was). Look again at Calvary, Christ was innocent of any wrong. Christ was a healer of other's hurts who did nothing but good. Christ was obedient to the Father. Christ was aware of the Father's control and will. Yet, Christ was beaten, stripped, impaled and left naked on the Cross. Even his crucified body was pierced with a spear. Look at the abusive acts of the crucifixion again, what was it like? Christ was raped. And this same Christ says to each of his children, "pick up your cross and go through what I have gone through." Christ did not merely suffer so we do not have to, Christ suffered to show us how to go through. The culpability of God rests first in the Christian reality that God sent the Son to the cross and and hell, then we are to understand that Christ requires those that follow him to bear the same burden. Could it be that God would select some of us to suffer for the sake of others? Definitely! The fact that God selected Christ and the possibility that God had so chosen some of us would indeed be a travesty were it the end of the story. Instead, the triumph of Christ and the essence of the Gospel is not the defeat of the cross but the victory of the resurrection!

The triumph of Christ is that the Cross was not a defeat nor the defining moment of Christ's existence. Rather it is the victory over the victimization of the Cross which defines Christ and the power of the Christian Gospel! Christ was not a victim of Calvary. Christ is the victor over Calvary! Christ has survived Calvary. The Roman crosses are gone. The Roman soldiers are gone. The false accusers are gone. The power of death is gone. But Christ remains and reigns! The power over death is not won by dying but dying and raising oneself up again. Jesus declared no one takes my life, I lay it down. And if I lay it down I will pick it up again! God allows us to die so that we might gain the power of life that dwells, through God, within us. God allows us to be chained that we might find the power to free ourselves! The travesties of life are opportunities to triumph. The path to heaven leads straight through hell.

The Christ story suggests that the only ones who spend eternity in hell are those who cannot find within themselves the strength to keep moving after hell has surrounded, confounded and overwhelmed them. Victims of abuse continue to suffer. The damage done in the past, though sometimes repressed, is repeated in the present whenever we allow ourselves to be defined by people, problems or circumstances outside of us. Our thoughts which prevent us from objectifying the past and personalizing the future leave us powerlessness, breathing life into the memories of abuse and the abuser. But, the survivor moves forward from hell empowered by knowledge and caution. Emboldened by the life they hold on to.

The Christian counselor's perspective on the crosses of our lives must be embedded in the resurrection of power of the Gospel. Why does God write travesty into the fabric of our lives? For the same reason God sent God's only child to the rape of Calvary, resurrection! Why does this make sense? God chose the only one strong enough to bear the burden of sin and damnation and He would bear it on behalf of others. Christ suffered more so others may suffer less. We suffer for those who cannot suffer. God chooses some to bear excessive burdens for those who can carry none. Those who survive are empowered, those who survive are our saviours. There are many survivors of abuse in the Bible but there are no victims. And therein lies the essence of the paradox; "troubled but not distressed, perplexed but not in despair, persecuted but not forsaken, cast down but not destroyed" (2 Corinthians 4:8-9). Our experiences do not define us, our character does. Nothing and no one outside of us control us. We must employ prayers which reorder our yesterdays. We must engage the strength to deal with today. We must find the power within us to order our tomorrows. This is the Christian foundation from which healing grows.

Pastors must realize the prevalence of sexual abuse and publicly and repeatedly address the need for care. As pastors we must educate ourselves and our staffs to minister to sexually abused members of our congregations. Our churches and our pulpits must become centers for prevention, intervention and healing. That we all may survive and that no one is left a victim. We have, through God, access to a greater power than the horror of the past. A power that connects us to the risen Christ who can never be crucified again. It is imperative that pastors present a theology relevant to the life experience of the community including sexual abuse and remain true to the resurrection power of the gospel. The presuppositions of forgiveness, grace and culpability, integral to a Christian's understanding is critical for the treatment of an abuse survivor. They are the litmus test for the synergy between the church and the psychiatrist's office. The pastor must be a bridge of safe passage between a Christian congregation and the psychiatric care community. This community must respect the faith system integral to Christendom and incorporate its paradigm into the care of Christian clients.

BERNICE JOHNSON

The music of the Black church inspired the civil rights protests of the sixties and sustained African Americans when they were thrown into prison. The music gave voice to the faith in Jesus Christ that empowered the Black community and transformed the movement.

Bernice Johnson's father was a minister and so she heard church music from her childhood. Since their church had no piano until she was eleven years old, her early music was *a capella* and her instruments were her hands and her feet. When Bernice was in prison, she was asked by fellow protesters to sing a song. She was accustomed to community singing, not solos, but she began to sing, "This Little Light of Mine, I'm Going to Let It Shine." Although she had sung this song all her life, suddenly it was different. She sang, "All in the street, I'm going to let it shine," and "All in the jailhouse, I'm going to let it shine."

Then she sang, "Over My Head, I See Freedom in the Air." Again the song was different, because of the context in which it was sung. The freedom songs rang out and those in the jails were encouraged. The freedom songs rang out and those in the meetings were ready to march.

In 1962 SNCC (Student Nonviolent Coordinating Committee) established the Freedom Singers with Bernice Johnson, Cordell Reagon, Rutha Mae Harris, and Charles Neblett. These four singers traveled throughout the country inspiring people and raising funds for the movement.

Cordell Reagon, one of the four Freedom Singers, had come to Albany Georgia as a SNCC worker. He later became the husband of Bernice Johnson. Bernice Johnson's singing resulted in a national conference and a three-volume recording called, "Voices of the Civil Rights Movement." Later she sang in the group "Sweet Honey in the Rock" and served as a musicologist for the Smithsonian Institution.

Albany, Georgia, the home of Bernice Johnson, was a small community with many opportunities for African Americans as farmers and small business entrepeneurs. But even though almost half of the residents of Albany were Black, very few had been allowed to register to vote.

Albany was also the home of Albany State College, an all-Black school. Early in the year of 1961 Bernice Johnson, as part of the NAACP Youth Council, protested the harassment of Black female students by White male residents of the town. As a result of the protest all the members of

Albany's student government were suspended.

Little by little Johnson and others were catching the scent of freedom in the air. In the fall of that year two SNCC workers came to town to test the 1960 Supreme Court ruling that segregation of bus and train terminals was illegal for interstate commerce. The police quickly ordered Cordell Reagon and Charles Sherrod out of the "White only" waiting room. They promptly left, but more Albany residents were awakening to freedom's call.

The NAACP, SNCC, and several other African American organizations began competing over the methods and means of achieving civil rights, but soon they joined together to form the Albany Movement. The people gathered together in a church for their first meeting and sang, "We Shall Overcome." They listened to speeches by students who had been arrested at the bus station and when the five students went to trial, they came together to kneel on the sidewalk and pray for the students' release.

Two days later more students marched to the bus terminal and were arrested. And with this second wave, people again marched to the courthouse steps to pray for the release of the students. People were drawing on their commitment to the Lord to come together and support one another in the fight for freedom. Two hundred people who marched to pray at the courthouse were tossed into jail. Slater King, who was the vice-president of the Albany Movement, was in prison with the other Albany protesters. It was at this time that he asked Bernice Johnson, his fellow prisoner, to sing a song.

Even the White police recognized the effectiveness of the music and would sometimes ask the protesters to stop singing. But the singers knew that their word was being heard and they felt the joy. Bernice Johnson said, "There is a way in which those songs kept us from being touched by people who would want us not to be who we were becoming." But it was not a song anymore. People clapped, the feet were going and you could hear the music for blocks away. Your ears were not enough, your eyes were not enough, your body was not enough, and you could not block it. You just had to open up and let go and be moved by the music to another space (Williams 1987, 164-177).

Williams, Juan, 1987. *Eyes on the Prize*. New York: Penquin Books.

TEACHING TIPS

June 4
Bible Study Guide 1

1. Words You Should Know

A. Praetorian Guards (1:13, RSV, NAS)—Roman imperial bodyguards or troops which were assigned to the governors of various Roman provinces.

2. Teacher Preparation

Read the background Scripture of today's lesson. Find other resources which will teach you more about the early Christian church.

3. Starting the Lesson

A. Give each class member a slip of paper and ask them to answer the following questions as honestly as possible: (1) What is the most important thing in the world to you? (2) If you could only be remembered for one thing, what would it be? (3) If you had just been told that you may die in the near future, what would you do?

B. Instruct them not to write their names on the papers and pass them to you. Read a few of their answers aloud and discuss them.

C. Read today's IN FOCUS story about Carl and Brenda. Lead the class in a discussion about how it is often easy for Christians to talk about having faith in Christ no matter what; however, when faced with a life-threatening situation, our faith may be challenged.

4. Getting into the Lesson

A. Collect some information about the various responses and stages of people who are terminally ill. How do they respond? What are their coping mechanisms. Elizabeth Kubler Ross developed what is now a widely-accepted analysis of the five states of grief. See if you can locate them and share them with the class.

B. Compare these stages with Paul's temperament as he awaited his jail sentence. Help class members to develop a deep appreciation for how difficult it is for most people to be joyous when facing death.

5. Relating the Lesson to Life

A. Review the information about prisons and the Roman Empire in today's THE PEOPLE, PLACES AND TIMES section. How might things be different if Paul were imprisoned in a modern American jail? Did the Roman government make circumstances more difficult for Paul?

B. Give students an opportunity to answer the questions in SEARCH THE SCRIPTURES.

C. Today's DISCUSS THE MEANING highlights Paul's deep spirituality, which enabled him to rejoice in suffering. Discuss why Paul, the Philippian Christians, as well as most believers, gain strength through trials and suffering.

D. The LESSON IN OUR SOCIETY focuses on the value we place on life and death. Discuss why even Christians generally cannot rejoice in death, either their own or someone else's.

Debate whether this is a natural human response or the distorted thinking of our culture.

6. Arousing Action

A. Ask class members to think about ways in which they have matured spiritually since they accepted Christ. Has their spiritual growth caused them to have more trust in Him concerning their future?

B. Allow members time to think about what they would do if they were told they didn't have long to live, as directed in MAKE IT HAPPEN. You may want to give each class member a pencil and paper.

C. Give class members an opportunity to complete FOLLOW THE SPIRIT and REMEMBER YOUR THOUGHTS.

WORSHIP GUIDE

For the Superintendent or Teacher
Theme: Living In Christ
Theme Song: Pass Me Not
Scripture: 1 Peter 1:3-9
Song: I Surrender All
Meditation: Lord, help me to entrust my life to your hands. Grant me the faith to have confidence in you, especially during times of uncertainty.

LIVING IS CHRIST

Bible Background • PHILIPPIANS 1:12-30
Printed Text • PHILIPPIANS 1:12-26
Devotional Reading • 1 PETER 1:3-9

LESSON AIM

After studying today's lesson, students should realize that we live for Christ in all that we do, not for ourselves. Therefore, no matter what our fate, Christ must be glorified through it.

KEEP IN MIND

"For to me to live is Christ, and to die is gain" (Philippians 1:21).

FOCAL VERSES

PHILIPPIANS 1:12 But I would ye should understand, brethren, that the things which happened unto me have fallen out rather unto the furtherance of the gospel;

13 So that my bonds in Christ are manifest in all the palace, and in all other places;

14 And many of the brethren in the Lord, waxing confident by my bonds, are much more bold to speak the word without fear.

15 Some indeed preach Christ even of envy and strife; and some also of good will:

16 The one preach Christ of contention, not sincerely, supposing to add affliction to my bonds:

17 But the other of love, knowing that I am set for the defence of the gospel.

18 What then? notwithstanding, every way, whether in pretence, or in truth, Christ is preached; and I therein do rejoice, yea, and will rejoice.

19 For I know that this shall turn to my salvation through your prayer, and the supply of the Spirit of Jesus Christ,

20 According to my earnest expectation and my hope, that in nothing I shall be ashamed, but that with all boldness, as always, so now also Christ shall be magnified in my body,

LESSON OVERVIEW

LESSON AIM
KEEP IN MIND
FOCAL VERSES
IN FOCUS
THE PEOPLE, PLACES, AND TIMES
BACKGROUND
AT-A-GLANCE
IN DEPTH
SEARCH THE SCRIPTURES
DISCUSS THE MEANING
LESSON IN OUR SOCIETY
MAKE IT HAPPEN
FOLLOW THE SPIRIT
REMEMBER YOUR THOUGHTS
MORE LIGHT ON THE TEXT
DAILY BIBLE READINGS

whether it be by life, or by death.

21 For to me to live is Christ, and to die is gain.

22 But if I live in the flesh, this is the fruit of my labour: yet what I shall choose I wot not.

23 For I am in a strait betwixt two, having a desire to depart, and to be with Christ; which is far better:

24 Nevertheless to abide in the flesh is more needful for you.

25 And having this confidence, I know that I shall abide and continue with you all for your furtherance and joy of faith;

26 That your rejoicing may be more abundant in Jesus Christ for me by my coming to you again.

IN FOCUS

Carl and Brenda drove home from the doctor's office in silence. They both had a hundred thoughts passing through their heads. The doctor had actually said the "Big C" word—cancer. If he was to live at all, Carl would have to undergo surgery and extensive chemotherapy. They would have to break the news to their children and grandchildren. Carl would also have to tell the church.

"Well," Carl finally broke their silence, "this will certainly put my faith to the test. Now I must live what I have preached for so long."

"Baby, don't try do deny what you are really feeling about this, not for my sake, not for the children's, and not for the church's sake either," Brenda responded.

"It's not that," Carl said. "I know that people will be watching me. It's important to me that I will be able to praise the Lord throughout this ordeal, whether it means life or death. If I can't, I'll end up feeling like my entire life, not to mention my faith, has been just a front."

THE PEOPLE, PLACES, AND TIMES

PRISON. During the time that the New Testament was written, persons could be imprisoned for nonpayment of debt (Matthew 5:25-26), political insurrection and criminal acts (Luke 23:19, 25), and for certain religious practices (Acts 8:3).

The Apostle Paul was often in prison. On one occasion, he and Silas were placed under the charge of a lone jailer, who put them in an inner cell and placed their feet in stocks (Acts 16:23-24). The inner cell was probably for maximum security or solitary confinement.

In Jerusalem, Paul was detained in a Roman barracks (Acts 23:12-18). In Caesarea, Paul's confinement did allow him some freedom, and he was allowed to have visitors (Acts 23:35). As he awaited trial in Rome, Paul was guarded constantly under a type of house arrest (Acts 28:16-17, 30). While there, he met his own expenses, and was free to receive visitors and preach the gospel.

Based on information from *Holman Bible Dictionary*, Trent Butler, general editor, Nashville: Broadman & Holman Publishers, 1991, pp. 1138, 1139.

ROMAN EMPIRE. In the early days of the Christian movement, several emperors ruled the empire. Most of Paul's ministry is believed to have occurred under the reign of Gaius (Caligula, A.D. 37-41) and his aging uncle Claudius (A.D. 41-54). Claudius reportedly expelled some Jews from Rome because they were creating disturbances with their efforts to spread the Gospel.

It is believed that both Paul and Peter were martyred during Nero's reign (A.D. 54-68), perhaps in connection with the burning of Rome in A.D. 64, an event for which Nero blamed Christians.

Based on information from *Holman Bible Dictionary*, Trent Butler, general editor, Nashville: Broadman & Holman Publishers, 1991, pp. 1207-1209.

BACKGROUND

It is interesting how some people can devote themselves to encouraging others in the midst of their own struggle. Many terminally-ill children, instead of feeling sorry for themselves, have been a source of encouragement for the families they leave behind.

Paul was encouraging to his Christian family. Even as he sat in prison, his letter was full of love, encouragement, and instruction for those who were carrying on the work. It is very likely that his co-laborers in Christ were feeling worse about Paul's imprisonment than he was.

Paul probably recognized that his release from prison was unlikely. As he contemplated his fate, however, Paul did not lose faith in God. He did not become bitter or angry about his circumstances. He did not cease the work to which he had been called. Through good times and trials, Paul remained faithful to his Master and his task.

AT-A-GLANCE

**1. Paul Preaches From Prison
(Philippians 1:12-14)
2. A New Effort (vv. 15-18)
3. A Certain Victory (vv. 19-26)**

IN DEPTH

1. Paul Preaches From Prison (Philippians 1:12-14)

Many people, throughout history, have been imprisoned (or otherwise annihilated) in an effort to silence them. This strategy often backfires, however, as the person's voice is made stronger because of their inaccessibility. When Nelson Mandela was thrown in jail, it was believed that he would die in obscurity, all but forgotten by his people. His imprisonment had just the opposite effect, however. Mandela's popularity grew with each passing year.

As Paul sat in a Roman prison, his message continued to be heard, only in a different format. His jailers thought they would silence his message of Christ by placing him in jail. Unknowingly, they gave him a new pulpit to preach his message. Their efforts to silence the gospel actually caused it to spread further (v. 12).

Everyone, including the Praetorian guards, came to know that Paul's imprisonment was for the cause of Christ. He was not a criminal. Paul was thrown in jail because of his relationship with Christ.

Apparently, Paul's imprisonment has a powerful effect on other Christians. Instead of being frightened into silence, as one might expect, they began to speak out with more boldness. Naturally, they realized the seriousness of Paul's predicament. Nevertheless, they continued to spread the gospel, without regard to consequences.

Paul did not want believers to fall into uncertainty and despair. With Paul being in jail, they could have easily slipped into a state of fear, being unsure about the future. Although Christians profess faith in good times and bad, very often we are confounded when our effort to do ministry for Christ meets opposition. Somehow we feel that as long as we are doing His will, nothing and no one should stand in our way. On the contrary, Jesus told us it is when we do God's will that we should expect opposition.

Paul's faith was sure. He knew that nothing could impede the spread of the Gospel, even prison walls!

2. A New Effort (vv. 15-18)

Paul's confinement led to many new efforts to spread the Gospel. No one particular movement could do the work. Some followers were stronger because Paul was in jail. Perhaps they felt they had to fill in the gap left by Paul's absence.

Paul calls into question the motives of those who were preaching about Christ. Some were preaching out of "envy and strife" (v. 15), while others were preaching out of genuine good will. Some may have been jealous of the attention Paul was receiving even though he was in jail.

This very well may have been the case in Rome where Christianity had been established prior to Paul's coming. His presence there may have posed a threat to the Christian leaders who were already there. Some were likely vying for Paul's leadership role within the Christian community, assuming he would not be released. His rivals must have felt that their success would cause Paul to become jealous, perhaps adding to his troubles. Instead, he rejoiced that others were spreading the Gospel, regardless of their motives.

Paul recognized that the Gospel is powerful enough to transcend human pettiness. If this were not so, the spread of the Gospel would have stopped at Calvary. There is no human who is truly worthy to preach the Gospel. It is human nature to be affected by envy, strife, egotism, narcissism, and partisanship. From the pulpit, all kinds of motives fuel the Sunday morning sermon. Still, the Gospel is preached, as people come to Christ.

Paul's solution was to continue making the Gospel known and rejoice that it comes through a multitude of means. The Good News cannot be held hostage to human imperfection. No one can alter its wonderful saving power. Not even the worst example of Christianity can take away the power of the Gospel. Paul's message has many implications for the Christian community today.

3. A Certain Victory (vv. 19-26)

Paul was confident that his experience both being jailed and harassed by rival Christians would lead to victory. He wrote confidently of "salvation" as a result of his circumstances. Some translations refer to Paul's "deliverance." He was most likely referring to salvation in its fullest sense. The idea is that full redemption would be realized through Christ.

The apostle was sure of his dependency on Christ for the impending victory. He quoted Job 13:16 (Septuagint) where Job looked confidently to his ultimate vindication. There is no indication, however, that Paul believed he would be released from prison, nor did he appear to be concerned about it. Paul's primary concern was not with life or death, as determined by the outcome of his trial. He appears to have been chiefly concerned with his own constitution, that he would not be afflicted with any manner of shame. Instead, he hoped for Christ to be magnified (v. 20). Paul was not looking to be a hero. He was willing to meet his fate, whether life or death, so that all could see how much Christ meant to him.

Paul stood at the crossroads between life and death. The apostle found favor in either outcome. Paul had no desire to escape death in favor of life. He viewed death as an entrance into the greater realm of a life already filled with greatness. To Paul, life was Christ, and Christ was life. Christ gave Paul's life meaning, and apart from Him life held no meaning or purpose. Death, therefore, did not mean loss, but gain. He knew that death was not final. Rather, it was an extension of his marching orders as a soldier in the army of the Lord. The life he knew in Christ would only become more magnificent through death.

Conversely, if Paul's life was spared, he viewed it as an invitation to do more fruitful work for the kingdom. His only interest in release from jail was that it would allow him to continue his ministry. He could preach the Gospel a while longer. He could continue to encourage the churches who had become so dear to him. Through life, he could continue to live and do more for Christ.

For years Paul had been working in the trenches as a missionary, spreading the Gospel and encouraging and guiding the faithful. His hard work was just beginning to show results. Like a farmer who has been tending to trees hoping they will bear fruit, Paul is longing to see evidence of the harvest. He desires to stay because there is so much to be done.

The two options the apostle faced did cause some divided feelings. Understandably, Paul was pulled between his two options. Not that he viewed either as negative. Instead, in his heart he longed to be with Christ. His was not a morbid desire, however. Paul probably envisioned a life with Christ too wonderful for the human spirit to totally conceive.

On the other hand, he wanted to be of service to his fellow Christians. He viewed the continuance of life as being necessary only for the sake of the Philippians (v. 24). Paul was willing for his life to be used in whatever way the Lord deemed necessary. The Philippians were openly proud of Paul, whom they, in a sense, regarded as their own special apostle. Paul lovingly reminded them that Christ, not he, must remain the subject of their boasting. If he was to return to them, they should rejoice in the works of Jesus Christ, not the apostle Paul.

The apostle Paul's ability to have hope, even in the most hopeless of circumstances, came from his own experience of being granted new life after his former life had passed on. The boldness he possessed came from his certainty that Christ would be honored by him, whether through his life or his death.

SEARCH THE SCRIPTURES

1. According to Paul, what was the real benefit of his imprisonment? (v. 12).

2. How was the cause of Christ made known through Paul's confinement? (v. 13)

3. What affect did Paul's imprisonment have on many of his fellow Christians? (v. 14)

4. For what motives were some preaching the Gospel? (vv. 15-17)

5. Why were motives unimportant in preaching the Gospel? (v. 18)

6. What outcome did Paul expect from his experience? (v. 19)

7. What was Paul's primary concern? (v. 20)

8. What caused Paul to be torn between whether to live or die? (vv. 21-24)

9. For what reason did Paul want to remain alive? (v. 25)

10. Of what benefit would his continued life be to the Philippians? (v. 26)

DISCUSS THE MEANING

1. Paul had reached a high spiritual point which caused him to rejoice, whether the outcome of his trial meant life or death. How did he reach such a point of spiritual maturity?

2. Why were some of the Christians strengthened by Paul's imprisonment? Why did they not become fearful that the same thing might happen to them?

LESSON IN OUR SOCIETY

The Book of Ecclesiastes (7:1) says that the day of death is better than the day of birth. It also has been versed that we should rejoice at death and mourn at birth.

Every Christian professes belief in eternal life. Yet, very often, when we think of death, we become fearful. There remains some uncertainty about our fate. Perhaps this is because we do not feel certain about our salvation. Some may doubt Christ's promise.

Our enslaved ancestors sang often of heaven—of the streets paved with gold, the pearly gates, where the Sabbath would have no end. They longed for the day when "trouble will be no more" and every person would live in freedom and equality. Perhaps because there has been general improvement in our social and economic standing, many of us now appear to place more value on life on earth than eternal life. No matter what attainments life holds, it can never compare to the future glory of life with Christ Jesus.

As Christians, we must rejoice in our assurance of eternal life, and leave the matter of "when" to our higher Authority in heaven.

MAKE IT HAPPEN

If you were told today that you may not live much longer, what preparation would you make to insure that Christ would be glorified through your experience from passing from life to death?

FOLLOW THE SPIRIT

What God wants me to do:

_____

_____

REMEMBER YOUR THOUGHTS

Special insights you learned:

_____

_____

MORE LIGHT ON THE TEXT
PHILIPPIANS 1:12-26

The first 11 verses of the book of Philippians can be divided into three sections. The first is the "Greeting," which follows, as in most Pauline letters, the conventional pattern of letter-writing of the day, 'A to B, greeting', with theological undertone (vv. 1-2). The second section (vv. 3-7) is "Thanksgiving" and "Confidence" in God for the Philippian church. The third section, (vv. 8-11) contains Paul's fourfold "Prayer" for blessing:

a) That they may abound in love, knowledge and judgment (discernment);

b) That they may be able to approve or discern things that are excellent or best;

c) That they may remain sincere and blameless till the coming of the Lord; and

d) That they be filled with the fruit of righteousness, through Christ, to the glory and praise of God. After these, Paul now goes to the main body of his letter.

In the foregoing section noted above, Paul started (v. 8) by reminding the church that he was praying for them, and listed the specific things he was praying (see a-d above). He goes on in verses 12-26 to tell them his circumstances, i.e., his imprisonment because of the Gospel and the effect it has on the spreading of the good news. Contrary to expectation, he says, his imprisonment has helped to enhance the Gospel rather than retarding it. Christ is being proclaimed without hindrance, and he expresses hope for his release from prison.

1:12 But I would ye should understand, brethren, that the things which happened unto me have fallen out rather unto the furtherance of the gospel;

This opening clause, "But I would ye should understand, brethren," means literally, "I want you to know, brothers." This is similar in meaning, although worded differently, in Colossians 2:1, "For I would that ye knew . . ." and 1 Corinthian 11:3: "But I would have you know, " It is equivalent in meaning to Paul's unique expression in other epistles, "I (or we) would not have you ignorant, brethren," (Romans 1:13; cf. also 1 Corinthians 10:1; 12:1; 2 Corinthians 1:8; 1 Thessalonians 4:13). This clause in its various forms calls the attention of the addressees that something important is about to follow. Paul wants them to be aware of his situation what is happening to him, and how it is affecting the Gospel. Paul refers to the Philippians as "brothers," Greek *adelphos*, a word of endearment Paul uses often to describe his relationship with other Christians. By virtue of Christ redemptive activity and the work of the Holy Spirit, "as many as received him, to them gave he power to become the sons of God, even to them that believe on his name" (John 1:12), and therefore all believers belong to the same heavenly Father. Hence, they are brothers and sisters. This word "brethren" appears seven times in this epistle, which shows how deep Paul's affection is for the church at Philippi. What is it that Paul wants to make them be aware of? It is not so much the suffering that he is going through in the Roman prison, as the effect of that suffering. Rather than being a hindrance to the gospel, Paul's imprisonment has become a "blessing in disguise," it has led to the advancement of the Gospel. What Satan and the Roman and Jewish authorities had thought would be an obstacle to the spreading of the Gospel has turned to be a catalyst to its growth.

The Bible is full of stories in which God uses "bad" or "tragic" circumstances and situations to bring glory to Himself. Joseph's slavery into Egypt became God's providential act of blessing and deliverance to Israel (Jacob) and his children (Genesis 37:23,24; 50:20). Job's unspeakable tragedy helped him gain more knowledge of and insight to the mysteries of God's wisdom, power and authority over all creation than before (Job 1&2; 19:25-27; 42:5,6). Our victory over Satan, sin, and death is a direct result of Christ's suffering and death on the cross. For this, every believer would proudly join Paul in exclaiming, "Be it far from me that I should boast except in the cross of our Lord Jesus Christ, by whom the world has been crucified to me, and I to the world" (Galatians 6:14). The persecution of the early church, including the stoning of Stephen (Acts 7) and then Paul's own conversion (Acts 9), forced the early Christians to scatter, and providentially, led to the spreading of the Gospel to other parts of the world. It fulfilled Christ's prophecy in Acts 1:8. Paul's imprisonment confirms his words to the Roman church, "All things work together for good to them that love God, to them who are the called according to his purpose" (Romans 8:28). Instead of being an obstacle to the Gospel, it became a stepping-stone for spreading the Good News.

13 So that my bonds in Christ are manifest in all the palace, and in all other places; 14 And many of the brethren in the Lord, waxing confident by my bonds, are much more bold to speak the word without fear.

Paul explains in verses 13 and 14 the manner in which the progress of the Gospel has been achieved. First, his imprisonment has had great impact "in all the palace, and in all other places." The phrase "my bonds in Christ" means his imprisonment because of his faith in Christ. The news of his imprisonment for the sake of Christ has spread all over the "palace," therefore the Gospel became wildly known. The Greek word translated "palace" here is *praitorion*, pronounced **prahee-to'-ree-on,** which means "governor's court-room. It referred to "headquarters" of the Roman camp or the tent of the commander-in-chief. Here it simply means the residence of the governor or procurator of the province (cf. Matthew 27:27) or the soldiers barracks. Paul was under constant guard at the *praitorion* (cf. Acts 28:16,20) and soldiers had shifts watching him. Therefore, many soldiers were exposed to him. It is probable that as soldiers went in and out of the *praitorion*, they

talked to others about the apostle and the reason for his imprisonment—that he was imprisoned for Christ (lit. "in Christ"). They must have told, not only that he was imprisoned because of Christ, but also the spirit by which he bore the imprisonment. They must have watched his patience, heard him talk to his visitors, or to his scribes to whom he dictated his letters, and watched with wonder Paul's attitude and positive disposition even while in chains. The guards probably were so impressed by what they saw, heard, and felt about Paul, that they told others—from one guard to another, to their families, to Caesar's household (cf. 4:22) until the news spread all over the palace "and in all other places." "In all other places" means the whole region or province. The news here is not so much Paul's imprisonment, but the cause that is Christ. Therefore through Paul's suffering, the Gospel and the cause of Christ became "the talk of the town" within the whole region.

Second, his imprisonment not only had impact on the soldiers and all over the province, it had an effect on the "brethren in the Lord." It spurred them to action in the proclaiming of the Gospel. We can hear Paul rejoicing as he writes this epistle that the believers (brothers in the Lord) are rather being encouraged and becoming bolder in telling the good news than being intimidated by his suffering. "Brothers" (brethren) here definitely refers to the congregation in Rome to whom Paul addressed the Epistle to the Romans. The church in Rome consisted largely of Gentile and Jewish converts, to whom Paul preached (Acts 28:20ff.) while in Rome. What does Paul mean in v. 14 with emphasis on "much more bold"? Does it mean a change of attitude from cowardice to boldness? Or does it mean that the brethren's boldness increased? From the tone of this letter, the statement seems to imply that the brethren were at first intimidated and afraid to make known the Gospel (v. 28).

Things are now changing. They are now gaining some courage and boldness to tell the story of Christ and His redemption without fear. This new courage is acquired through Paul's attitude and resolute faith and courage in Christ even through trial and suffering. The positive effect of Paul's imprisonment and its impact in the spreading of the Gospel in the region must have contributed to their boldness and courage in evangelism. Amazed with Paul's attitude and the wide spread of the Gospel in the whole region, they became bold and compelled to preach without being afraid anymore. In addition, they saw the sustaining grace of God working in Paul's life (4:13) both during his trial and in his trip to Rome as a prisoner (Acts 23:11; 27:23). All these helped them to build courage in the evangelistic task.

15 Some indeed preach Christ even of envy and strife; and some also of good will: 16 The one preach Christ of contention, not sincerely, supposing to add affliction to my bonds: 17 But the other of love, knowing that I am set for the defense of the gospel.

Paul's imprisonment has yielded positive results: a) the Gospel is being made known all over the region including the official residence of the governor; b) many of the brothers are now preaching the Good News of the Gospel with boldness. However, Paul separates these preachers into two groups according to their motives. The first group, he says, preaches out of a wrong motive "of envy and strife." This group is prompted by "envy" (Greek *phthonos*), i.e., jealousy or ill will, and "strife," *eris* i.e., rivalry, or wrangling or contention. Paul goes on to illustrate in the next verse how this group's preaching is motivated by evil. They "preach Christ out of contention, not sincerely," i.e., not with a clean motive, but rather with an ulterior motive "to add affliction to my bonds." The word "contention" translates the Greek *eritheia*, pronounced **er-ith-i'-ah,** which means, in simple terms, selfishness, a desire to put oneself forward. Who were these "brothers" who were preaching out of contention and selfish ambition with the intention of adding to Paul's "affliction"? The word translated "affliction" here is the Greek *thlipsis* (**thlip'-sis**), also translated burdened (2 Corinthians 8:13); affliction (Mark 4:17; 13:19; Acts 7:10-11; 2 Corinthians 2:4; 4:17; 6:4; etc); tribulation (Matthew 13:21; 24:21, 29; Mark 13:24; John 16:33; Acts 14:22; etc.); persecution (Acts 11:19); and trouble (1 Corinthians 7:28).

How are they adding to Paul's suffering? Paul does not seem as much concerned with these people and their evil plans as to the positive result of their preaching, as we shall see in verse 18. He does not intend to occupy himself or boggle his audience's mind with much negativity. He, therefore, leaves us with no answer. However, scholars have advanced a number of proposals as to who these people were. Among these proposals is that certain preachers in Rome have attained some prominence before Paul's arrival there. His presence in Rome and the spreading of his fame and the Gospel throughout the region (vv. 13-14) are beginning to affect their prestige. Their names seem to be relegated to the background not mentioned as often as before. Hence, they became envious and contentious; thus, their motive for preaching the gospel is affected. Bear in mind that they were preaching the true Gospel with positive results, but their intention and motive were bad. Paul, later in this book, exhorts the Philippians to be one in the mind of Christ, not putting oneself forward or being selfish

(Philippians 2:3). James denounces selfishness or self-promoting "in your heart" (James 3:14). How their preaching is affecting or worsening Paul's situation is open to speculation (see Gerald F. Hawthorne, *Philippians: Word Biblical Commentary*, vol. 43, Waco, Texas: Word Books Pub., 1983, pp. 37-8, for a detailed discussion on this matter).

The second group preaches out of pure motive "of good will," (v. 15b) and "love." This is evident from the following, "knowing that I am set for the defense of the gospel" (v. 17). This group is motivated out of "good will" prompted by love for Paul and the Gospel, which he proclaimed. These people do not feel indignant about Paul because of his fame that is spreading around the region. Their focus was not on themselves as opposed to the aforementioned group. They heralded Christ, out of love for Christ, and the Gospel, out of concern for Paul and his tribulation— a love which Paul prayed for: "And this I pray, that your love may abound still more and more in knowledge and all discernment" (Philippians 1:9-11). The clause "knowing that I am set for the defense of the gospel," means that they are also motivated by the fact that Paul has been "set" (*keimai*), i.e., destined, appointed for the defense of. This refers either to the immediate trial he is about to face for the sake of the gospel, or that his call or ministry is for the defense *apologia* (**ap-ol-og-ee'-ah**) of the Gospel for which he was imprisoned.

18 What then? notwithstanding, every way, whether in pretence, or in truth, Christ is preached; and I therein do rejoice, yea, and will rejoice.

Rather than moaning over the selfish motivated preaching of the first group aimed at increasing his burden and suffering, and rather than dwelling in self-pity and attracting sympathy for such unchristian behavior towards him, Paul focuses on the end result of their preaching. He says, "What then?" or "What does it matter?" It is another way of saying it "does not matter" the motives, what matters is the result of their preaching, which turned to be positive. Whether they were preaching to hurt him or not, is not the main concern. The most important concern is whether the Gospel is advanced or not. The answer is clear from the following statement "notwithstanding, every way, whether in pretense, or in truth, Christ is preached." What matters to Paul is not what the people are doing to him, but rather what they are doing for the Gospel. From here, we can learn one truth, that is the Lord will work out His desired purpose through the Gospel irrespective of how it is preached, or the motive of the preachers. This is true even today. How many preachers today maintain their integrity in the Gospel without other motives—whether financially motivated, or out of envy to out-do others? How many churches split because of selfish preachers who do not like to be under somebody? Tragically, there are many. And yet people are converted and the Gospel is advanced. This is possible since motive cannot be seen by the listeners. Those who listened to them (the contentious and selfish preachers) did not know what Paul knew about them. They could not see the bad motive. To Paul, it does not matter. What matters is that in "every way" whether in pretense, as by those with selfish motive, or "in truth," as by those who preach with sincere hearts to glorify the Lord, "Christ is preached." "Pretense," *prophasis* (**prof'-as-is**), is the same word used to describe the prayers of the scribes (Mark 12:40, cf. Acts 27:30), an outward show, cloke or pretext. It is the opposite of sincerity. "I therein do rejoice, yea, and will rejoice," Paul says. What gives Paul joy is that the Gospel is preached.

19 For I know that this shall turn to my salvation through your prayer, and the supply of the Spirit of Jesus Christ,

In this section, Paul expresses his confidence in the prayer of the brethren and optimism that he would be set free. This also makes him rejoice. The preposition "for," *gar*, connects the preceding statement with the following assurance of his deliverance. Paul's use of *eido* (**i'-do**), to see, to perceive with the eyes or by any of the senses. It has the sense of certainty and confidence that all will turn out well for him in the end (Romans 8:28). The result will be his deliverance. Paul's knowledge here, I feel, does not mean that he had information of his possible deliverance, but rather he had personal conviction that, through the prayers of the people and the work of the Holy Spirit, he would be set free from prison.

Hawthorne (p. 39) observes the direct similarity in Greek construction here: "this will turn out for my deliverance" (NIV, RSV) with Job's statement (Job 13:16 LXX). Paul probably sees his situation as similar to Job, and since Job was vindicated, Paul is convinced that he would be saved and vindicated. Hence, he says, "I know that this shall turn to my salvation." Although Paul uses "salvation" in the eschatological sense of being saved at the last day, his use of "salvation," *soteria* (**so-tay-ree'-ah**), refers to a possible immediate release from the Roman jail. Trusting the ever faithfulness of God, exemplified by God's deliverance of Job, coupled with the prayer of the saints and the working of the Holy Spirit, Paul is convinced that he would be set free.

20 According to my earnest expectation and my hope, that in nothing I shall be ashamed, but that with all boldness, as always, so now also Christ shall be magnified in my body, whether it be by life, or by death.

This conviction is expressed in his "earnest expectation and my hope" based on the confidence he has in Christ. He has two convictions. The first is that whatever happens he would not be ashamed. The Spirit will not let him down. Writing to the Romans, Paul says that he is not ashamed of the Gospel of Christ. The idea here is that although he is looking forward to his release from prison, the Spirit will not allow him an "easy way" out of his misery by denying Christ, for example. The second conviction, contrary to the first, is that he would wax bold in proclaiming the Gospel, as he has always done, but more so now. The meaning is clear, "Christ shall be magnified" in his person literally "body," *soma*, which means his entire personality. Paul will continue to preach the Gospel and endure in hardship, "whether it be by life," if he is released from prison, "or by death," if he is executed. His goal is that Christ would be magnified through it all. In either circumstance, he would remain faithful to the end so that Christ's name would be lifted. This, in practical terms, is a show of courage, deep resolute conviction, and resignation to the service of the Lord Jesus.

21 For to me to live is Christ, and to die is gain. 22 But if I live in the flesh, this is the fruit of my labour: yet what I shall choose I wot not. 23 For I am in a strait betwixt two, having a desire to depart, and to be with Christ; which is far better:

This conviction and courage is demonstrated in his total resignation to whatever comes his way as expressed in verses 21-24. The use of the phrase "for to me" (*gar emoi*) is purposely put here for emphasis to draw our attention to Paul's personal conviction regarding life and death. Paul gives new meaning to both "life" and "death." To him "living is Christ," which means, among other interpretations, "life means Christ." The essence of living is embodied in Christ Jesus; the fulfillment of life is only to be found in Christ. His very existence is in Christ whatever he does is inspired through his resolute relationship with Christ, and for Christ. To him life would be meaningless and not worth living without Christ (Romans 14:7-9). He owes his existence to Christ. He dedicates his whole being to Christ and His cause to love and obey Him in everything and at all times, and to trust Him in all circumstances. His resolution to live for Christ does not mean a life free from problems and difficulties. On the contrary, it means living for Christ and preaching the gospel in spite of problems and difficulties imprisonment (1:7, 13,16), afflictions (1:16; 4:14), suffering (1:29; 3:10), struggles (1:30), including all types of tribulation, both physical and emotional (2 Corinthians 11:23-27). It is a resolution to "Follow Jesus, no turning back" as one chorus says. Paul's life and ministry were not easy. They were characterized by unimaginable problems and sufferings as we can see from these and other accounts of his life.

On the one hand, for Paul to go on living means leading a dedicated and fruitful life for Christ, (vv. 21a, 22a), and on the other hand, for Paul "to die is gain" (v. 21b). He knows that death means an immediate transformation of a new life into the presence of Christ. Why does he make this comment? Was it out of frustration in life? Was he overwhelmed with all the sufferings he has to endure?

The suggestion that Paul was so overburdened with suffering, that his life became so heavy for him to bear that he was forced to say, "To die is gain," does not sound right. This would mean that he was giving up in life, that it would be better for him to die than live, that he was expressing frustration in life as a dejected man expecting sympathy from his audience. No. This contradicts the Paul we have encountered from the beginning of this epistle. Rather the Paul we have been dealing with is the same Paul who, in spite of his imprisonment, is able to express his joy, his thanks and his confidence in the Lord (vv. 3, 4, 6). Paul's statement is based on a number of things:

Probably he is reacting to the attitude of the brethren who are preaching out of envy and strife whose purpose is "to add affliction to my bonds" (vv. 15,16). These people, it seems, would rather see Paul condemned to death in prison than overshadow them. To them Paul would say, "For to me to live is Christ" in spite of their plans, but if "I am condemned to die," he tends to say, it "is gain," for it will mean being in the presence of Christ the Lord.

Paul is so engrossed in the Gospel and in the reality of eternity that living means working and living for Christ, and dying is even more profitable since he would be with his Lord forever. This is the hope of every believer. Paul is so confident of the reality of heaven and the assurance of resurrection that he says, "If in this life only we have hope in Christ, we are of all men most miserable" (1 Corinthians 15:19). This assurance is found in the fact of Christ's own resurrection, the firstfruit of them that slept (v. 20).

The next reason is related to the first two. Here Paul is expressing his total resignation to the Lord. Whatever comes his way, whether death or life, i.e., vindication from the prison, as we have already mentioned above, he has resigned his life and will to the will of the Lord Jesus Christ.

Therefore, it makes no difference what happens to him, death or life. Should he be acquitted, his life spared and prolonged on earth here, this would mean "fruit of my labour." That is, he would continue to labour for Christ, bearing fruit. Souls would be won; believers would be encouraged, and more churches established. This would afford him more opportunities to proclaim the Gospel, and Christ magnified (v. 20). The phrase "yet what I shall choose I wot not" shows a man in great dilemma to choose between two things, which are of equal value and importance. Here he faces a difficult choice. He does not know which one to choose. Either to "live in the flesh," which would mean more fruit borne and Christ glorified further, or to die, which would mean going into eternity and living forever with his Lord. Paul expresses this dilemma further in the next verse (v. 23) thus, "For I am in a strait betwixt two." This expression, "For I am in a strait," is a translation of the Greek, *sunecho* (**soon-ekh'-o**), which means to hold together, i.e., to compress. Metaphorically used here with the idea of being under pressure and constraint. It is used for a strait that forces a ship into a narrow channel with no way out. Paul pictures his position here as one "sandwiched" between two strong opinions, either as strong as a rock, and there seems to be no way to escape.

Paul's situation here is analogous to an African young man that reaches the age of marriage, the most important stage of his life. Traditionally, it is an honor for parents to choose and marry for their children, especially their first sons. As an African, he is taught to obey his parents, respect, and honor them. His father finds a beautiful young lady from their community and marries her for him without his son's knowledge. However, his son finds another girl in school he loves and would like to marry. Both ladies are beautiful. The son is now faced with a difficulty, either to take his father's choice as a sign of obedience, respect and honor, or to marry the one of his own choice. Paul finds himself in such a dilemma here. While the African young man (a non-Christian) can solve his dilemma by marrying both of them (this is one of the ways many Africans, especially some educated Igbos, became polygamous), Paul does not have such liberty to choose one. However, his desire "to die to be with the Lord" (v. 23), which he seems to prefer, is just a dream because life and death belongs to his Master.

Paul is hard-pressed, or hemmed in, by these difficult choices. On the one hand, his "desire (is) to depart, and to be with Christ; which is far better" (*pollo mallon kreisson*, literally "far far better"). That is, it is more advantageous to Paul because that would mean, "going home" to be with the Lord. It seems that Paul's strong yearning is to depart so that he would be with the Lord. He knows for sure where he would be when he departs from this earthly life—straight with the Lord. His soul does not go into nothingness when he dies, rather it at once enjoys fellowship with his Lord Jesus Christ. This is far better than remaining in the sin-ridden cosmos. Addressing the Romans Paul writes, "For I reckon that the sufferings of this present time are not worthy to be compared with the glory which shall be revealed in us" (Romans 8:18). To the Corinthians also he says, "We are confident, I say, and willing rather to be absent from the body, and to be present with the Lord" (2 Corinthians 5:8). Expressing his readiness "to be offered" and resolute confidence to meet the Lord soon, he says to Timothy, "I have fought a good fight, I have finished my course, I have kept the faith: Henceforth there is laid up for me a crown of righteousness, which the Lord, the righteous judge, shall give me at that day: and not to me only, but unto all them also that love his appearing" (2 Timothy 4: 6, 7-8).

That is why his departure is far better for him. Therefore, his personal preference, subjectively speaking, is to depart and be with Christ.

24 Nevertheless to abide in the flesh is more needful for you. 25 And having this confidence, I know that I shall abide and continue with you all for your furtherance and joy of faith; 26 That your rejoicing may be more abundant in Jesus Christ for me by my coming to you again.

On the other hand, Paul also desires to remain in the flesh for the Philippians' sakes. His love for the church is so strong, and he knows that they would definitely need him for ministration, that he desires to remain, i.e., "to abide in the flesh," even though he would face more persecution and suffering in the flesh. It would also mean more fruit (v. 22) and glory (v. 20) for the Lord. He never allowed his subjective dream to override his objective desire. Rather he places the need of others above his own desire and aspiration. The use of the particle, "nevertheless" (Greek, *de*, pronounced **deh**), which can be translated, moreover, or notwithstanding, shows clearly Paul's unselfish consideration of others' needs, this time the Philippians church, above his own need and wishes. Why does he prefer to remain in the flesh for their sake? The answer can be inferred from chapters 3:1-3, 19, and 4:2, where Paul writes about apparent needs and problems facing the church. To Paul, the need to address these problems and offer further

pastoral care to the believers in Philippi weigh heavier than his own personal desire.

This unselfish desire and self denial is further expressed in verses 25 and 26. Here Paul expresses his confidence for his release as he writes, "having this confidence, I know that I shall abide and continue with you all." Paul speaks here with absolute assurance that he would be released from prison. His release would only be useful for "your furtherance and joy of faith," that is, for their spiritual growth, which produces joy. "Your furtherance," *prokope* (**prok-op-ay'**) or progress, means spiritual growth: in love (1:9), in knowledge (1:9), in fruitfulness (1:11), and in obedience (2:12). Such growth will give them joy in their worship and relationship with the Lord i.e., in the faith. His release would also increase their rejoicing in the Lord Jesus Christ on his behalf. His presence with them would definitely increase their faith and dedication in the Lord. They would realize the grace of God working through Paul's vindication from prison. The phrase "my coming to you again," implies that Paul had visited the church before (cf. Acts 16:11-40; 2 Corinthians 8:1-5; Acts 20:5). According to historical sources, Paul's wish was granted; he was released from prison and he visited the church in Philippi.

DAILY BIBLE READING

M: Paul's Prayer for the Philippians
Philippians 1:1-11
T: Prison Bars Cannot Imprison the Gospel
Philippians 1:12-18
W: Paul Exalts Christ in Life or Death
Philippians 1:18-26
T: Stand Firm in Suffering
Philippians 1:27-30
F: We Have a Living Hope in Christ
1 Peter 1:3-9
S: A Call to Holy Living
1 Peter 1:17-25
S: Living Stones of the Living Stone
1 Peter 2:1-10

June 11
Bible Study Guide 2

1. Words You Should Know

A. Bowels (2:1)—King James translation for a word meaning affection or tenderness.

B. Esteem (v. 3)—Having respect or high regard for.

2. Teacher Preparation

Read the background Scripture of today's lesson. After you have studied the lesson, make a list of qualities that you believe are Christlike.

3. Starting the Lesson

A. Before class begins, think of two or three possible dilemmas which call for a decision to be made, such as deciding whether to report a neighbor who embezzled money from his job. Then ask the question, "What would Jesus do?" Discuss the proper approach to each dilemma, using the mind of Christ as the standard.

B. Read today's IN FOCUS story about Rev. Watkins' dilemma. Lead the class in a discussion about how it is often easy for even the most devoted Christian to get caught up in selfish desires which may cloud thinking and affect decision-making.

4. Getting into the Lesson

Collect some information about congregations, denominations, and religious groups that have been weakened by controversy, disagreement and infighting. As you discuss the lesson, talk honestly about how conflict can destroy a congregation or organization if there is no peaceful and Christlike resolution. Talk about some of the results of unresolved conflict, such as church and denominational splits. Just prior to the Civil War, many denominations split into two camps north and south. Although many have reunited, some remain separated because they cannot agree.

5. Relating the Lesson to Life

A. Review the information about libation and the city of Philippi in today's THE PEOPLE, PLACES AND TIMES article. What caused Paul to compare himself and his sacrifice to libation? How did Paul come to have such closeness with the Philippians?

B. Give students an opportunity to answer the questions in SEARCH THE SCRIPTURES.

C. Today's DISCUSS THE MEANING highlights Paul's experience with the Philippians. Talk about the spiritual development of Paul, which enabled him to be humble in service to the Master.

D. The LESSON IN OUR SOCIETY focuses on the value we place on arrogance or self-absorbed personalities. Emphasize the fact that such persons often rise to fame or notoriety, but seldom enjoy enduring renown.

6. Arousing Action

A. Ask class members to think about persons, both famous and local, who once thought highly of themselves and their accomplishments, only later to be humbled by some of life's experiences. How did the person's life change? Was he/she able to overcome the adversity? Did the experience make him/her a better or stronger person?

B. From the instructions given in the MAKE IT HAPPEN section, create a personality profile of your church, based on the various responses of class members. Try to create a composite of your church on which everyone can agree. You may want to give each class member a pencil and paper.

C. Give class members and opportunity to complete FOLLOW THE SPIRIT and REMEMBER YOUR THOUGHTS.

WORSHIP GUIDE

For the Superintendent or Teacher
Theme: Having the Mind of Christ
Theme Song: More About Jesus
Scripture: 2 Peter 3:8-18
Song: Lead Me, Guide Me
Meditation: May I strive with all my might to elevate my thoughts so that I may attain the mind of Christ.

HAVING THE MIND OF CHRIST

Bible Background • PHILIPPIANS 2:1-18
Printed Text • PHILIPPIANS 2:1-13
Devotional Reading • 2 PETER 3:8-18

LESSON AIM

After studying today's lesson, students should understand the importance of laying aside personal wants and desires which may conflict with the good of the body of Christ and His kingdom.

KEEP IN MIND

"Let this mind be in you, which was also in Christ Jesus" (Philippians 2:5).

FOCAL VERSES

PHILIPPIANS 2:1 If there be therefore any consolation in Christ, if any comfort of love, if any fellowship of the Spirit, if any bowels and mercies,

2 Fulfil ye my joy, that ye be like minded, having the same love, being of one accord, of one mind.

3 Let nothing be done through strife or vainglory; but in lowliness of mind let each esteem other better than themselves.

4 Look not every man on his own things, but every man also on the things of others.

5 Let this mind be in you, which was also in Christ Jesus:

6 Who, being in the form of God, thought it not robbery to be equal with God: **7** But made himself of no reputation, and took upon him the form of a servant, and was made in the likeness of men:

8 And being found in fashion as a man, he humbled himself, and became obedient unto death, even the death of the cross.

9 Wherefore God also hath highly exalted him, and given him a name which is above every name:

10 That at the name of Jesus every knee should bow, of

LESSON OVERVIEW

LESSON AIM
KEEP IN MIND
FOCAL VERSES
IN FOCUS
THE PEOPLE, PLACES, AND TIMES
BACKGROUND
AT-A-GLANCE
IN DEPTH
SEARCH THE SCRIPTURES
DISCUSS THE MEANING
LESSON IN OUR SOCIETY
MAKE IT HAPPEN
FOLLOW THE SPIRIT
REMEMBER YOUR THOUGHTS
MORE LIGHT ON THE TEXT
DAILY BIBLE READINGS

things in heaven, and things in earth, and things under the earth;
11 And that every tongue should confess that Jesus Christ is Lord, to the glory of God the Father.
12 Wherefore, my beloved, as ye have always obeyed, not as in my presence only, but now much more in my absence, work out your own salvation with fear and trembling.
13 For it is God which worketh in you both to will and to do of his good pleasure.

IN FOCUS

Rev. Watkins just couldn't understand why Sister Jenkins had such opposition to the new facility the church was about to purchase. In the past, she had been such a loyal supporter of the church's program. The church was going through with the plan anyway, and Rev. Watkins knew he could not always have the support of every church member, but it still bothered him. He prayed for understanding and insight, hoping that it would make him a better pastor.

His prayer was answered a couple of weeks later when he went to visit Mother Turner, a longtime member of the church who was not able to get to church very often. Without mentioning Sister Jenkins' name, he talked with Mother Turner about his concern and asked her to pray for him and the church in general.

"Pastor," Mother Turner said, "I don't get out much, but I do keep up with what's going on at my church. I know Myrtle Jenkins has been raising sand about the new building. It's long been time you knew why. She's had her mind set on opening a day care center and she wants to use space at the church to save money. She can't use the new church because of the way it's set up."

"So that's it," Pastor Watkins shook his head. "All that fuss was about what's good for her, not what's good for the church."

THE PEOPLE, PLACES, AND TIMES

LIBATION. A drink offering; the act of pouring liquid, usually wine, as a sacrifice to a god. Libation was a part of the Hebrew ritual of sacrifice, which became systematized following the Exodus. Libation was a part of the consecration of the altar of the Temple, which included the offering of two lambs and a grain offering and a libation of wine. This sacrifice was carried out daily for one week.

Based on information from *Holman Bible Dictionary*, Trent Butler, general editor, Nashville: Broadman & Holman Publishers, 1991, pp. 1218, 1219.

PHILIPPI. A city which was located in the Roman province of Macedonia where Paul did a great deal of missionary work.

Paul's first visit to Philippi took place during his second missionary journey, an outgrowth of his Macedonian vision. He and a group of companions sailed from Troas to Neapolis, located on Macedonia's eastern shore. After they docked, the group traveled a few miles inland to Philippi. It was at Philippi that Paul was miraculously delivered from bondage and the jailer was converted. Upon discovering that Paul was a Roman citizen, the magistrates there became nervous. They pleaded with Paul to leave both the jail and the city.

Based on information from *Holman Bible Dictionary*, Trent Butler, general editor, Nashville: Broadman & Holman Publishers, 1991, pp. 1105, 1106.

BACKGROUND

Chapter two begins Paul's second appeal to the Philippians. Apparently division was brewing within the Philippian congregation. Co-workers in the church had become openly divided. Paul had already had the experience of seeing a church riddled with controversy and dissension.

The biggest battle facing the church at Philippi was their internal battle, not any external forces. In the previous lesson, Paul stated his refusal to let external circumstances control his attitudes (Philippians 1:12-18). The congregation could ill afford to let internal strife afflict their witness for Christ.

Paul spoke of his imprisonment in terms of its affect on the Philippian mission. He told them that his imprisonment has special significance to them because of the nature of their relationship to the apostle. The church was full of kindness and loyalty, but their status is threatened by the dangers of dissension.

AT-A-GLANCE

**1. Paul Exhorts the Philippians
(Philippians 2:1-11)
2. Paul Issues Another Exhortation
(vv. 12-13)**

IN DEPTH

1. Paul Exhorts the Philippians
(Philippians 2:1-11)

From the previous chapter, Paul was faced with the delicate task of rebuking the congregation he had just praised. He sought to enlist the Philippians' loyalty and faithfulness against the divisions that had arisen within the church.

The concern at Philippi was not so much about instruction in right and wrong as encouragement and guidance in the right will or spirit. Paul's appeal is for unity and self-denial as exemplified in Christ. Paul was not calling for the Philippians to despise themselves. He was calling for a refusal to let personal interests or advantage govern the course of one's life. He knew that the success of his appeal was dependent upon the degree to which the Philippians abided in the spirit of Christ. If they were united in His bond, they would seek the unity and self-denial that is essential to the Christian's existence.

If they could do this, Paul's joy would be complete in that they would be like-minded, with the same love and of one accord. Many times people misinterpret the meaning of this phrase, thinking that it means there must never be a difference of opinion. It does mean that the body is committed to support the work of the church and that the will of God is fulfilled, regardless of personal opinion.

Love would provide the incentive for the desired goal of unity, humility, and for others. Love (agape) is to do good for another, regardless of the cost to self. Paul fully understood the importance of self-effacement, or self-denial. More often than anything else, it is often self who gets in the way and causes conflict. It is impossible for Christian unity to exist in an atmosphere of self-centeredness.

Paul was concerned that the Philippians give themselves over to a mindset which is governed by Christ. That mind was already present within them because they were in Christ Jesus. Paul's admonition was that they activate (or reactivate) this already present mind among themselves.

Paul wanted to address those in Philippi who were given to self-exaltation. He wanted them to have a true image of humility, as demonstrated in the life of Jesus Christ. In Christ, the perfect example of self-effacement can be found, having voluntarily given up His divinity for humanity. Being in the form of God, Christ "made himself of no reputation" (v.7). Being in human form, Christ humbled himself and became obedient to the Father, even to His death on the cross.

For this reason, the Father has exalted Jesus and given Him the name that is above every name. It is at the name of Jesus that every knee shall bow in heaven, on earth, and under the earth and every tongue shall confess that Jesus Christ is Lord of all.

2. Paul Issues Another Exhortation (vv. 12-13)

In his third exhortation, Paul encouraged the Philippians to work out their salvation, which has already been granted through faith in Jesus. Paul wanted them to do what is right. Their actions were not to be dependent on Paul's presence. Rather, they were to continue doing good whether Paul was granted life or sentenced to death.

Paul was not suggesting that their salvation lay in their own hands. He did not tell them to work "for" their salvation, which cannot be earned, because it is a gift. Instead he instructed them to work "out" the salvation which had already been given to them. Salvation is the work of the Lord, from beginning to end. Paul's challenge to the church was to work on her spiritual well-being, continuing to trod the same pattern of obedience, until the disease which threatened the body of Christ no longer existed.

This same pattern has been applied to other pursuits, such as fitness training. When the body is threatened with poor health, due to lack of activity, a plan of action is undertaken. An exercise plan begins. The first few weeks may prove discouraging, as the only yield may be pain and sore muscles. But the only way to achieve health and fitness is to continue the exercise regimen. Eventually, the body will yield itself to being toned and trained.

Within the body of Christ, the task is so monumental, that it must be approached with "fear and trembling." Paul's suggestion is not that they possess cowardly fear or mistrust. Instead his call was for awe and reverence in the presence of God. The Philippians, like any Christian community of faith, could ill afford take the issue of salvation lightly.

Ultimately, the Philippian Christians would accomplish their task only because the Lord was at work in them. For any human being to think that he/she can attain humility such as that expressed in Christ is folly. It is through the power of God alone that self-centeredness is toppled and self-effacement is embraced.

SEARCH THE SCRIPTURES

1. According to Paul, what would make his joy complete? (v. 2).

2. For what motives did Paul admonish the Philippian believers to service? (v. 3)

3. After whom did Paul advise them to model themselves? (v. 5)

4. What role did Christ choose for Himself? (v. 7)

5. To what extent did God exalt Christ? (vv. 9-11)

6. Why did Paul advise concerning the Philippians' obedience? (v. 12)

7. What was Paul's suggestion concerning their salvation? (v. 12)

8. What disposition did Paul encourage the Philippians to have concerning their Christian service? (vv. 14-15)

9. Why was this important to Paul? (v. 16)

10. To what did Paul compare himself and his sacrifice? (v. 17)

DISCUSS THE MEANING

1. Would the Philippians have regarded each other differently if Paul had been able to dwell among them and spend time with them?

2. Paul offered himself as an example to be followed. Think back over Paul's life and experiences. What were some factors which might have instilled humility in him?

LESSON IN OUR SOCIETY

Humility is not valued or praised very much in our society. Among the rich and famous, those who have given themselves to humility and service seem to garner little attention. Conversely, those who have earned a "bad boy" reputation for arrogance or self-absorption often become media darlings.

This is all the more reason that the Christian community must understand "who we are and whose we are." Our calling, as disciples, is to follow our leader and fashion ourselves to be like Christ as much as we can.

Our efforts to do this will rarely earn us human praise. It will, however, be pleasing in the eyes of the Lord.

MAKE IT HAPPEN

Churches tend to have personalities, just like people. In spite of their troubles at the time Paul wrote his letter, the Philippian congregation seemed to have a loving spirit, with an inclination toward obedience. Paul encouraged them to move forward based on the assets they already possessed.

What assets/gifts/talents do you already possess which can be polished and enhanced to make you of greater benefit to the work of God's kingdom? Ask yourself if you are willing to be used in this manner. If so, what steps must you take to "work through" your salvation? Are you willing to, as Paul did, offer yourself as a sacrifice, for the benefit of fellow Christians and those who have yet to come to know Christ?

FOLLOW THE SPIRIT

What God wants me to do:

_____

_____

REMEMBER YOUR THOUGHTS

Special insights you learned:

_____

_____

MORE LIGHT ON THE TEXT
PHILIPPIANS 2:1-13

Although chapter 2 begins a new section, it is definitely connected to and a continuation of the preceding thought in the closing section of chapter 1. There Paul exhorts and wishes that the Philippians "stand fast in one spirit, with one mind striving together for the faith of the gospel" (v. 27), that they be resolutely united in their faith even in the face of suffering from their adversaries (vv. 28-29). This indicates that the Philippian church was going through persecution. In the present section, Paul reiterates the necessity for unity and appeals for individual humility, which is the quality that will foster true oneness. The first four verses deal with Paul's appeal to them by various considerations, to live in unity and in the spirit of the Gospel, loving one another, and each preferring another to oneself.

2:1 If there be therefore any consolation in Christ, if any comfort of love, if any fellowship of the Spirit, if any bowels and mercies,

Paul starts with a cluster of clauses each introduced with the particle "if," which generally expresses conditional clauses. To translate the particle "if" *ei*, here as conditional

would convey a wrong idea expressing doubt to what he is saying. On the contrary, the use of "if" here is to be considered as strong affirmation. This group of "if" clauses can be viewed in a number of ways. The first way would be "as there is consolation in Christ, as there is comfort of love" etc. The second consideration would be to word them as rhetorical questions: "Have you experienced consolation in Christ; have you received some comfort of love" and so on. Of course, the answer would be affirmative. Then "fulfil ye my joy" etc. The third way to view this cluster of directives would be to see them as affirmative of Paul's expectation of them. Hence they can be rendered thus, "since you have experienced the consolation" or "you have experienced the consolation in Christ, haven't you?" and so on. The fourth consideration is by using the "if" clause, but conveying the same affirmation: "if you (indeed)" or "if really you have." In each of these alternative renderings, Paul conveys the idea that the church at Philippi has attained some spiritual experience, and so they should demonstrate such by living out the principles of Christian life: love, unity, and humility.

The first word used in this cluster of clauses is "consolation," or "comfort," from the Greek word *paraklesis*, pronounced **par-ak'-lay-sis,** also translated "encouragement" or "exhortation." *Paraklesis* is derived from *paraklein* often used by Paul for the exhortation he gives to the churches through the Word of God (Romans 12:1; 15:30; 16:17; 1 Corinthians 1:10; 4:16; 16:15; Ephesians 4:1; etc.). The second word, *paramuthion* (**par-am-oo'-thee-on**), used only here in the New Testament, (cf. *paramoothia*, 1 Corinthians 14:3), is closely related to the first. It conveys the idea of "one coming close to another's side to speak," generally in a friendly manner. Thus, it is translated "comfort" (KJV) and "consolation" (NAS). The word *agape* (translated "of love") is a subjective genitive, which means that the "consolation" is generated by love—Paul's or God's love.

The next word, used in the third clause, is "fellowship," from *koinonia* (pronounced **koy-nohn-ee'-ah),** translated generally as partnership, communion, or communication or association, with the idea of close intimacy or union. *Koinonia* is therefore that close relationship or fellowship that exists between believers, which is based on love and as a result of their corporate and individual union with Christ. The phrase "fellowship of the Spirit" would then mean that fellowship that comes through the indwelling presence of the Holy Spirit in both the church and individual lives of the members. Here Paul is saying to the Philippians, "If you belong to that community brought into existence by the

Holy Spirit, and enjoy any fellowship with one another as a result, then live accordingly" (Hawthorne, p. 66).

In the final clause, Paul uses two words, "bowels," and "mercies." The first word translated, "bowels," is the Greek noun *splagchnon* (pronounced **splangkh'-non**), which means intestines (the heart, lungs, liver, etc.). Bowels were regarded as the seat of the more violent passions, such as anger and love. To the Hebrews, it is the seat of more tender affections, especially kindness, benevolence, compassion. It is usually used figuratively by Paul to express an inward or deep affection, pity or sympathy (1:8; cf. Colossians 3:12; Philemon 7,12, 20). The second word used here by Paul is *oiktirmoi*, the plural form of *oiktirmos* (**oyk-tir-mos'**), meaning "mercies." It appears only five times in the New Testament and is synonymous in meaning with "bowels," and almost exclusively used by Paul to describe such feelings as pity, compassion, and kindness. Both words can then be translated as "affection and compassion" (NAS).

The question is, whose affection and compassion are being referred here, and to whom are they directed? It has been suggested that they refer to the feeling of emotions exhibited either by the Philippians towards one another, or toward Paul; or the feelings of Paul for the Philippians (Hawthorne, 67). However, both words are generally employed by Paul to describe God's tender mercies (Romans 12:1; 2 Corinthians 1:3), and God's compassion (1:8; Colossians 3:12; cf. Luke 1:78). It is then most probable that Paul has in mind here the divine affection and compassion towards the Philippians. Therefore, it seems Paul is saying, "If you have experienced the tender mercies and compassion of the Lord, then respond accordingly, or demonstrate it by living it out in your lives." In summary of this verse, we quote Hendriksen:

"The main thrust of what the apostle is saying is this: If then you receive any help or encouragement or comfort from your vital union with Christ, and if the love of Christ toward you does at all provide you with an incentive for action; if, moreover, you are at all rejoicing in the marvelous Spirit-fellowship, and if you have any experience of the tender mercy and compassion of Christ, then prove your gratitude for all this by loving your brothers and sisters . . . ." (pp. 98-99).

2 Fulfil ye my joy, that ye be likeminded, having the same love, being of one accord, of one mind.

The beginning clause of verse 2 "Fulfil ye my joy" or "make my joy complete" can easily be mistaken as the cli-

max of the preceding fourfold rhetorical clauses of verse 1. If read in such a manner it would give a wrong idea of Paul's main concern, which is for the Philippians to strive for unity and humility, rather than his own feelings. Indeed, what would make Paul's joy complete is if they were united in love and in mind with humility, without selfishness, but caring for one another.

Earlier in chapter 1 (vv. 4, 5) Paul has expressed the joy the Philippians had brought to him, in spite of his affliction, through their "fellowship in the gospel from the first day." The joy will be complete if they will "be like-minded" (v. 2a), "having the same love" (v. 2b), "being of one accord" (2c), and "of one mind" (2d). It is interesting to note how these short clauses correspond with the preceding cluster of clauses of verse 1. "That ye be likeminded" (v. 2a) (*hina*, to auto, *phronete*) and "of one mind"(v. 2c) (*to hen phronountes*) are identical, and emphasize Paul's main concern for the Philippian church, which is unity of mind. Paul's frequent use of the word *phroneo* (lit. "think") in this book reflects his concern for proper Christian attitude, singleness of purpose and mental concentration, which is a catalyst for spiritual growth and holiness. Paul applies this word in various contexts throughout this book (1:7, 2:2; 4:2) and in his other letters. For example, *phroneo* is translated "think" (1:7; Romans 12:3; 1 Corinthians 4:6; 13:11); "be minded" (Galatians 5:10; Philippians 3:15); "like-minded and same mind" (2:5; 3:16,19; 4:2; Romans 8:5; 12:16; 15:5; 2 Corinthians 13:11; etc.). It conveys the general idea of being of the same mind or cherishing the same views and being harmonious in their dealings. What does Paul's use of this word mean in this passage or other passages? Does it means that everyone should have or agree on the same thing all the time without individual or independent opinion? The answer is in the negative. Rather Paul's choice of the verb *phroneo* seems to convey the idea of spiritual unity or oneness, an inward attitude of mind submitted to the authority of the Holy Spirit, which overrides personal or individual and selfish desires or opinions. It is the recognition of diverse ideas and opinions, but holding fast to that which brings unity within the body of Christ.

The second and third clauses, "having the same love" and "being of one accord" seem to reinforce his concern expressed by the two clauses as have been explained above. Both of these clauses serve as an explanation of being "like-minded" and "of one mind." Here Paul seems to be repetitive in expressing his concern for unity. "Having the same love" speaks of mutual love for one another. Love is the cord that binds friends, families, fellowships, and churches together. It is a simple thing to understand that any body or group that lacks love lacks unity. Therefore, mutual love, such as demonstrated by Christ's sacrificial death for the church, should pervade every Christian community (cf. 2 Thessalonians 1:3; 1 John 3:16). The greatest problem facing the Church today is the need for unity which, unfortunately, is lacking in the body of Christ. This lack of unity is caused by the Church's inability to deal in appropriate ways with the apparent diversity of ideas and opinions within the church, and its inability to separate unity and uniformity.

Although the Bible advocates unity among believers, it does not insist on uniformity, neither does it nullify individuality. We do not have to agree in everything or do things in the same way as others. That will take away from the uniqueness and individuality of a person or group of persons, a liberty God grants us. However, we should not allow this liberty to be an obstacle to the unity and oneness of Christ's body. This is a troubling problem in most churches. We rather allow our own individual, or "our church's," ideas and doctrines to override the Master's teaching and purpose for His body. We allow trivial matters to overshadow more important matters —the preaching of the Gospel of Jesus Christ and the expansion of God's kingdom. This attitude breeds discord and hatred within the body. Hence, Paul uses this seeming redundancy of expression to drive home his earnest desire for the church i.e., unity with the intention to awaken hearts of the Philippian Church to the importance of his exhortation.

3 Let nothing be done through strife or vainglory; but in lowliness of mind let each esteem other better than themselves. 4 Look not every man on his own things, but every man also on the things of others.

Verses 3 and 4 are an expansion of the central thought in the previous verses, the exhortation for unity and oneness. Here Paul employs two sets of exhortations using negative tones and each followed by a positive clause introduced by the conjunction "but" (*alla*), followed by an appeal for humility, the overarching concern of the section. Paul is cognizant of the existence of individual ideas and opinions within the membership of Christ's body, hence he admonishes them that they should not allow selfish desire and personal ego encroach in the unity of the church. Firstly, Paul says imperatively, "Let nothing be done through strife or vainglory," i.e., "do not oppose each other, or one another by acting selfishly, for personal gain or self vainglory or pride." In other words, do not hold strongly to your own individual ideas just for personal gratification and egotism, Paul seems to say. One of the common things that can split

a church or break the body of Christ is the inability of certain members to humbly let go of their own selfish desires or ambition for the good of the church. The result of being adamant to such selfishness is obvious, it is a detriment to peace and unity, and does not show love. Individualism or partisanship is an enemy to unity. By employing the word *eritheia* ("strife" or "contention") Paul is probably alluding to his earlier description of those who preach the Gospel out of selfish and impure motive (1:16). Instead, Paul says, "But in lowliness of mind let each esteem other better than themselves." Here Paul points out the fact that humility is the key to unity, that pride and "big headedness" breed strife and contention. To maintain peace and unity in the body of Christ, Paul says, we should shift our attention away from ourselves, but rather esteem others better than ourselves.

The next set of admonitions with a negative tone is "look not every man on his own things," followed by the positive exhortation using *alla*, "but" (let) "every man also [look] on the things of others." The overarching concern here is selfishness, or lack of concern, on the affairs of other people. Individualism is a disease, a "cancer," which easily renders the church powerless and eventually kills the body of Christ. This disease is as much alive and common in our churches today as it was in the ancient churches, perhaps moreso. This lack of concern, or selfishness, or being uninterested in the affairs and welfare of others, shows the absence of the love that Paul spoke of in verse 2, love he also described in 1 Corinthians 13:5 as one that does not seek its own. Writing earlier in the same book Paul says, "Let no one seek his own, but each one the other's wellbeing" (1 Corinthians 10:24, NKJV), and he cites himself as an example of unselfishness for them to follow (10:33). The Bible gives other examples of those who put the well-being of others above their own, e.g., Abraham and Lot (Genesis 13:9); Joseph and his brethren (Genesis 50:21); Moses (Numbers 11:29); Jonathan and David (1 Samuel 18:4); and Daniel (Daniel 5:17). The supreme example of unselfishness is Christ. Writing of Him to the Corinthians Paul says, "For ye know the grace of our Lord Jesus Christ, that, though he was rich, yet for your sakes he became poor, that ye through his poverty might be rich" (2 Corinthians 8:9). Therefore, Paul writes here that they, and indeed the whole Christian community, should not be selfish and unconcerned of one another's welfare, but rather be interested and ready to "bear ye one another's burdens," which constitutes fulfilling "the law of Christ" (Galatians 6:2, KJV). Therefore, the spirit of humility and unselfish ambition, coupled with an attitude of care for others in the community of believers and oneness with love as the binding cord, are the characteristics that foster unity and peace within the body.

The next section (vv. 5-11) expresses dramatically the supreme example of the spirit of humility, the unselfish self-abasement of Christ, which caps Paul's exhortation in the preceding verses. Here Paul calls on the church to follow Christ's example. This section constitutes the most important part of Philippians. It is one of the most interesting portions of the Bible which deals, in a moving and dramatic way, with the work and mission of Christ and His ultimate exaltation. It is also one of the most difficult passages in the Bible to interpret. The poetic structure and pattern of the passage have compelled many scholars to say that it was an early Christian hymn about Christ Jesus. Its composer remains a mystery. However, scholars are divided on who the composer was. Some suggest that its author might have been some unidentified Christian writer before Paul's time, but Paul adapted it to illustrate his point. Others argue that Paul was its composer. Whether or not Paul was the composer is not as important as the message Paul tries to convey to the Philippians through it; that is, humility.

5 Let this mind be in you, which was also in Christ Jesus:

Paul begins by urging the Philippians to "let this mind be in you," the same type of mind "which was also (found) in Christ Jesus." Hitherto, Paul has been exhorting the church to lead a life of humility, self-sacrifice, and love with one another (vv. 1-4). The phrase "let this mind be in you" therefore points backwards to the type of Christian living Paul has been advocating for the Philippians to live; it also links us to the illustration of Christ's example of humility and sacrificial living and death. Verse 5 therefore serves as a transition between Paul's exhortation to the church (vv. 2-4) and his illustration of Christ's own life (especially vv. 6-9). The Greek verb used here is *phroneo* (used also in v. 2) is translated "let this mind (or attitude) be in you."

Simply put, Paul says, "Have this frame of mind in you, which was also in Christ Jesus." This type of attitude that Paul has been explaining and hoping for the Philippians to have in verses 2-4 corresponds with that attitude displayed by Christ in verses 6-9. Elsewhere in his epistles, Paul uses the life and death of Christ as a pattern for Christians to follow (e.g., Romans 15:1-7; 1 Corinthians 10:31-11:1; 2 Corinthians 8:6-9; 1 Thessalonians 1:6, etc.). Other passages that convey the same idea of following or imitating Christ's example include the following: Matthew 11:29; John 13:12-17; 13:34; 21:19; 1 Peter 2:20-23; 1 John 2:6). It

should be noted here that there are limits to what examples of Christ we, as Christians, can follow. We cannot follow His redemptive acts, the sacrificial suffering and death on the cross for man's salvation and for satisfying divine justice are Christ's prerogatives. Any other person cannot copy it. What we can copy is the spirit that is basic to these acts: His love, humility, and servitude to others. These are the attitudes or disposition "which was also in Christ Jesus."

6 Who, being in the form of God, thought it not robbery to be equal with God:

After the transition (v. 5), the main body of the "Christ-hymn" begins. The pronoun "who" (Greek *hos*) links and identifies this historical Jesus (v. 5) with the preexistent Christ before His incarnation. It has been observed that the use of this relative pronoun is consistent with the beginning of other "hymn-like" passages in the New Testament (cf. Colossians 1:15; 1 Timothy 3:16; Hebrews 1:3, etc.). "Who" modifies Christ Jesus whose attitude we are to emulate and introduces us to the Christ who preexisted. It also describes to us what took place in that eternity.

In eternity, Christ was "in the form of God" (Greek *en morphe theou*). The use of *morphe* or "form" constitutes a theological difficulty. The author did not tell us outright that Christ was God, but that He was in the form of God. The word *morphe* has the idea of external appearance, an outward form that strikes the vision, a word used only here, verse 7, and Mark 16:12. What does Paul, or the writer of the hymn, if it was really written by another author, mean by saying that Christ was in the form of God, instead of saying that Christ was God? Does he mean that Christ was "the form of God" as in the husband being "the image and glory of God?" (1 Corinthians 11:7). I think the answer to this latter question is in the negative since he did not say, "Christ was the form of God," but "in the form of God." It would then convey the idea that the form of God was the sphere in which Christ existed. These interpretations would contradict the biblically accepted doctrine of the divinity of Christ as God who existed from eternity (cf. Isaiah 7:14; Micah 5:2; John 1:1-3; Hebrews 1:8 and Revelations 1:8-11). Saying that Christ existed in the form of God is probably a subtle way of affirming the divine nature of Christ, that he possessed the very nature of God, without saying plainly that Christ was God. The reason for this is ever hidden in the mind of the author and it will be extremely difficult to discern. For different interpretations of this rather difficult phrase, see Hawthorne (pp. 81-84).

The next clause "thought it not robbery to be equal with God" seems to corroborate the above interpretation. The expression of Christ's equality with God here is confirmed by and is consistent with John's account in the following scripture: "In the beginning was the Word, and the Word was with God, and the Word was God" (John 1:1). In John 10:30 Jesus said to His audience and disciples, "I and my Father are one." Writing to the Colossians concerning Christ, Paul says, "Who is the image of the invisible God, the firstborn of every creature" (Colossians 1:15). These clearly point to the divinity of Christ and His equality with God. The word "robbery" (Greek *harpagmos*, pronounced **har-pag-mos'**) means to plunder; or the act of seizing. Here it is best interpreted that although He was equal with God in His divine nature, yet He did not think of this equality as something to be seized upon or to be held fast or held onto. That means that Christ possessed the divine nature and was by all accounts equal with God and had the right to hold tight to it and use it to His own advantage. To be in the form of God or possessing the divine nature, and for that matter being equal with God, looking with human eyes is a position of honor, respect and pride with many advantages, a position no "sensible" person would want to give up. Contrary to this human evaluation, Christ did not see His equality with the Father as a position to greedily and selfishly held onto and used to one's own advantage, but as "giving and spending oneself out" for the benefit of others. This is made clearer in the following verses.

7 But made himself of no reputation, and took upon him the form of a servant, and was made in the likeness of men:

With the use of the conjunction "but" (Greek *alla*), Paul clearly states the thought of rather than holding tight to His divine nature and equality with God, Christ "made himself of no reputation" (*kenoo*), i.e., to empty out, or to drain. *Kenoo* is also translated "make void" (Romans 4:14; 1 Corinthians 9:15); make no effect (1 Corinthians 1:17); and be in vain (2 Corinthian 9:3). Here it is best translated that Christ emptied or drained "Himself." The use of the reflexive pronoun "himself" (*haeautou*) in the sentence is emphatic, and suggests that the act of emptying by Christ was voluntary. The natural question is: Of what did Christ empty Himself? Scholars have proposed a number of suggestions. A thorough study of Christ's life on earth would indicate, that although He was, by all intent and purpose, still God, He functioned as an ordinary human. He took on temporarily the human nature. Therefore, we can say that He emptied Himself of:

1. His equality with God (vv. 6-7; John 8:58; 1 Corinthians 11:3)

2. His God-form, the Spiritual "body," which he possessed in eternity and took on the human form (cf. 3:21; Matthew 1:18-25; Luke 1:35; 24:37-40; Zechariah 13:6; John 1:14; Romans 8:3, etc.)

3. His immortality (1 Corinthians 15:4; Psalm 16:10; 1 Peter 2:24; 3:18)

4. The glory He had with the Father before the foundation of the world (John 12:23; 17:5; Matthew 16:27)

5. His authority in heaven and earth for all He did on earth He attributed it to the Father, and this was given back to Him after the resurrection (Matthew 28:18; Ephesians 1:20-23; 1 Peter 3:22)

6. His divine attributes and power; as a human, He could not perform miracles until the Holy Spirit came in fullness (John 2:11; 3:34; Isaiah 11:1-2; 42:1; 61:1-2; Luke 3:21-22; 4:16-21, etc.)

Some would object that "if Christ Jesus actually gave up His favorable relation to the divine law, riches, glory and independent exercise of authority," as Hendriksen put it, "How could He still be God?" The answer lies in His human functionality. While on earth, although He was and is and ever remains God, the Son laid aside all these things (while retaining His divine nature) and functioned as a human, as He assumed the human form (v. 7b).

An illustration or two will suffice. One is not a pastor just because he preaches every Sunday, neither is one an accountant because he deals with figures, or a doctor because he prescribes medicines and heals people. One is a pastor, an accountant, or a doctor by training or qualification, although he or she may not function in that capacity at a given time. He or she can function as a janitor and yet he is still a pastor by ordination or qualification. A qualified doctor who has no job in his or her field of training, but is working in a different field is still a doctor by profession, but not by employment. In a world of unemployment, one can take up an employment for a purpose, to meet his financial obligations. Such employment could be temporal. With Christ, He was never divested of His divine nature in His incarnation, but He "poured out himself," laying aside all the divine attributes and functioned as a human in order to reach the world.

That He retained His divinity can be seen in His teachings and miracles, which testified to His deity and dumbfounded His critics, e.g., the miracle at Cana of Galilee (John 2:1-11). Amazed at the authority and power at which Christ taught and healed disease, the scribes and Pharisees questioned Him: "By what authority doest thou these things? and who gave thee this authority?" (Matthew 21:23). He taught them as one having authority, and not as the scribes (Matthew 7:29). He affirmed His divinity to His disciples when He taught them and said, "If ye had known me, ye should have known my Father also: and from henceforth ye know him, and have seen him. Philip saith unto him, Lord, shew us the Father, and it sufficeth us. Jesus saith unto him, Have I been so long time with you, and yet hast thou not known me, Philip? he that hath seen me hath seen the Father; and how sayest thou then, Shew us the Father?" (John 14:7-9, cf. 10:30).

When the devil took Him to Temple Mount and asked Him to cast Himself down from the pinnacle of the temple during His temptation, Jesus invoked His divinity saying, "Thou shalt not tempt the Lord thy God" (Matthew 4:7).

He not only emptied Himself, but He "took upon him the form of a servant, and was made in the likeness of men." Here again, as in the emptying, He voluntarily took "the form of a slave." We notice the use of *mophe*, "form," with the same meaning as in verse 6 used here. Taking the form of a "servant" (*doulos*), slave or bond-man, does not mean that He adopted external appearance of a slave, neither does it mean that He pretended to be a slave, nor does it infer that He disguised Himself as a servant. Rather it means that he adopted or "accepted"(Greek *lambano*, the disposition), the characteristics and attributes of a slave. He became a slave and assumed all the characteristics and functions of a slave.

The word *doulos*, usually translated "servant" (KJV, NIV, and Beck), "bond servant" (NASB), and "slave," has a negative connotation in its literary sense one under bondage and authority of another. For example, for the Attic Greek, freedom was a highly priced possession, and slavery was a debasing, contemptible term in Greek thought. By implication, the *doulos* belonged to his master or lord, which means a repeal of one's autonomy and freedom. He was seen as the property of the household secured to do all the housework.

Figuratively used, the word can, at least in part, lose the sense of compulsion and have a more positive meaning. It may mean dependence, not as an enforced loss of one's self, but as an independent self-realization. For example, *doulos* can be used to designate man's relationship to God. To some interpreters, "slave" as applied to Christ should be understood this way, especially in light of Isaiah's suffering Servant passages (cf. Isaiah 52:13-53:12). Christ "taking the form of a servant" means that He exactly played the part of a servant of God.

Doulos appears frequently in the New Testament (ca. 124 times), mainly in the Gospels in Matthew about 30 times and in Luke about 26 times and in Pauline literature about 30 times. The "servant" or "slave" is always in absolute obedience to his master (cf. Matthew 8:9); he also has some responsibility in the master's house (Matthew 24:45ff.). The New Testament does not seem to have a problem about slaves and masters in the society, rather Paul gives some advice for mutual relationships between slaves and their masters (see 1 Corinthians 7:20f.; Ephesians 6:5ff.; Colossians 3:22; 1 Timothy 6:1f.). Therefore, in the Roman period of the first century, slavery was a common and an acceptable way of life in society. It was hardly questioned. The slave had no freedom of his own, nor any personal choice or will, but was in bondage to the will of and claim of his master. To whom was Christ servant? To God, or to mankind? The answer can be inferred from the incident in John 13 where Christ put Himself in the place of the servant and washed the feet of His disciples, which is a dramatized call to serve one another. Thus Paul's designation of Christ as *doulos*, as Hawthorne (p. 87) writes, emphasizes the fact that in the incarnation Christ entered the stream of human life as a slave, that is, as a person without advantage, with no rights or privileges of His own for the express purpose of placing Himself completely to the service of all mankind (cf. Mark 10:45; Luke 22:27). For in serving people He was serving God, and in taking the role of a slave toward others, He was acting in obedience to the will of God.

In that dramatized call for service to others, Jesus said to His disciples, "Know ye what I have done to you? Ye call me Master and Lord: and ye say well; for so I am. If I then, your Lord and Master, have washed your feet; ye also ought to wash one another's feet. For I have given you an example that ye should do as I have done to you" (John 13:12-15, KJV). This is exactly Paul's point here for the Philippians and to us all: "Follow the example of your Lord" (cf. v. 5).

Paul continues, Christ not only took on the form of a servant, He "was made in the likeness of men." The verb "was made," *ginomai* (**ghin'-om-ahee**), gives the idea of coming into existence or to become; it is also used of men appearing in public. Here Christ is said to come into existence "in the likeness of man," which speaks of His incarnation as human. The word "likeness" (Greek *homoioma*, pronounced **hom-oy'-o-mah**) does not mean that "Christ only appeared to be a man," or that He seemed to be a man in resemblance. Rather the word should be understood as made after the likeness, image or "similarity" or "identity" that amounts to equality. The idea here is that Christ in all respects, both in appearance and vulnerability,

death, even the death of the cross.

In verse 8 Paul continues to describe the thought of Christ's humility as shown not only by His assuming human form and the role of a servant, but by humbling Himself to such a degree of acceptance and subjecting Himself to the most humiliating type of death—death on the cross. This, Paul seems to convey, is the lowest step of humility. Paul writes "being found in fashion as a man," which means that He was perceived or recognized (Greek *heurisko*) in every respect as an ordinary human. As if assuming the form and the role of a servant and the likeness and nature of a human being were not enough, He also "humbled himself" to the point that "he became obedient (to God, even) unto death." His obedience has no limits, the statement implies. Furthermore, Paul emphasizes the lowest extent that Christ went in His humility and obedience to God when he adds "even the death of the cross." This act is voluntary and in absolute obedience to the will of God. Jesus says (referring to His life), "No man taketh it from me, but I lay it down of myself. I have power to lay it down, and I have power to take it again. This commandment have I received of my Father" (John 10:18). No one on earth could have gone so low, and He could not have gone lower. That was the lowest!

Death by crucifixion is said to have come from the Persians and developed by the Romans. It was the most humiliating and cruel form of capital punishment, reserved only for the worst criminals, such as robbers, murderers, and sometimes slaves. Both Jews and Romans abhorred this type of death. For the Jew, death by crucifixion not only brought shame and pain, it was considered accursed by God (cf. Deuteronomy 21:22-23; 1 Corinthians 1:23; Galatians 3:13; cf. Hebrews 12:2). The equivalent of this

was like other human beings. He was born by woman just as other men, and grew up as others. He was genuinely human. The historical accounts of the Gospels, especially the Synoptic Gospels, attest to this fact (Luke 2:52; John 1:14; see also Romans 8:3; Galatians 4:4; Colossians 1:22). The author of Hebrews speaks of Him saying, "For we have not an high priest which cannot be touched with the feeling of our infirmities; but was in all points tempted like as we are, yet without sin" (Hebrews 4:15; see also 2:17; 5:7-8; 1 John 4:2-3). The use and meaning of "form" or "likeness" in this passage cannot be equated with Daniel's vision of "one like the Son of man" (Daniel 7:13). Such an equation will diminish or contradict the reality of Christ's humanness in His incarnation on earth, for His human nature was as real as other human beings, except that it was not sinful as the others.

8 And being found in fashion as a man, he humbled himself, and became obedient unto

type of death in our modern society is the firing squad for criminals, such as robbers, or those who have committed treason against the nation. This is usually done in an open field, not only to deter people in the future from engaging in such "criminal" acts, but also as a way of shaming and humiliating the people. Hundreds and thousands of people (some quite innocent) have been slaughtered in this way in many dictatorial countries, such as Nigeria, in the recent years.

Here Paul reaches the lowest point in this theme and call for humility to the Philippians, which he started in verse 5. He says in effect that Christ, who was in every conceivable way God (in His pre-existence) and was equal with God (an equality, which He did not think it necessary to hold tightly) emptied and humbled Himself by assuming the role and attributes of a slave, that He came in the likeness of a mortal being, and surrendered Himself totally in obedience to God, even to the point of dying not an ordinary death, but a criminal's death—a death on the cross. We know this was for the benefit and service to mankind. The underlying thought in verses 5-8 is that if Christ humbled Himself and went so low as to die, the Philippians, and indeed all believers, should constantly endeavor to be willing to follow their master's example of humility, and strive to achieve the spirit of oneness among themselves.

9 Wherefore God also hath highly exalted him, and given him a name which is above every name:

While the foregoing section dealt with the total debasement of Christ to the lowest depth of humiliation, this section (vv. 9-11) deals with His unprecedented exaltation to the highest point of honor. While the last segment dealt with Christ's voluntary self-humiliation, this section deals with God exalting Him. In the former, Christ is the actor, the subject of the verbs; in the latter, God is the actor and the subject of the verbs, while Christ is the object.

The section starts with a double conjunction in the Greek, *dio kai* (lit. "and, that is why"). The use of this combination tends to be stronger than using only "therefore" (*dio*); it indicates the certainty of the inference. They can be translated as "and, therefore" or consequently, therefore" or "because of this, therefore" referring back to the self-humiliation of Christ described in the last section and the resulting consequence of His exaltation. It can be restated thus: "Because He humbled Himself to the lowest point of death, even death on the cross, consequently 'God also hath highly exalted him' to the highest point of honor. He humbled Himself, therefore He was exalted, which follows the

natural and divine order of things as taught by Christ Himself. The same rule which He laid down for others is applicable to Him and to the Philippians, and indeed to all Christians of all times. This rule, stated in its various forms throughout the Scripture, simply says, "Namely that in the divine order of things self-humbling leads inevitably to exaltation" (see Hawthorne p. 90).

"Christ taught his disciples saying . . .whosoever will save his life shall lose it: and whosoever will lose his life . . . shall find it . . . what is a man profited, if he shall gain the whole world, and lose his own soul? or what shall a man give in exchange for his soul?" (Matthew 16:25-26). Also, "Whosoever shall exalt himself shall be abased; and he that shall humble himself shall be exalted" (Matthew 23:12; Luke 14:11; 18:14). In answer to His disciple's inquiry regarding who is the greatest in the kingdom of God, Jesus says, "Whosoever . . . shall humble himself as this little child, the same is greatest in the kingdom of heaven" (Matthew 18:4). Jesus, as we have indicated above in the last section, not only taught this principle, He demonstrated it through His act of washing His disciples' feet (John 13:3-17). Peter and James echoed this same teaching in their epistles when they wrote: "Humble yourselves therefore under the mighty hand of God, that he may exalt you in due time" (1 Peter 5:6); "Humble yourselves in the sight of the Lord, and he shall lift you up" (James 4:10).

The Greek word used for Christ's exaltation and translated here as "highly exalted him" by most translations is *huperupsoo*, pronounced **hoop-er-oop-so'-o.** It is found only here in the New Testament. It means to exalt to the highest rank and power, as in the military or highest office, or to be elevated to the highest position. Here Christ is exalted beyond measure, to a point after which there is nothing higher. *Huperupsoo*, indeed literally means "to super-exalt." The use of this rare word confirms the idea that He who humbled Himself to the lowest depth is now raised to the highest heights. The same Greek word is used in the Old Testament (LXX) to describe Yahweh being "exalted far above all gods" (Psalm 97:9) (see Hawthorne, p. 91).

This super exaltation of Christ is historically verifiable in His resurrection and ascension, just as His self-humiliation is historically verifiable in His death and burial. Chirst's exaltation is further described by the writer of Hebrews, who says that He "passed into the heavens" (Hebrews 4:14), that He was "separated from sinners," and exalted above the heavens (Hebrews 7:26, NAS). Paul says, "He that descended is the same also that ascended up far above all heavens, that he might fill all things" (Ephesians. 4:10).

Christ's super-exaltation means that He received the

place of honor and majesty and is accordingly "seated at the right hand of God's throne" (Mark 16:19; Acts 2:33; 5:31; Romans 8:34; Hebrews 1:3), "far above all rule and authority and power and dominion and every name that is named not only in this age but also in that which is to come" (Ephesians 1:20-22) (see Hendriksen, p. 114).

Paul further describes this glorious elevation of Christ by adding that God gave "Him a name which is above every name." This statement serves as a reinforcement of the first and describes the magnitude of Christ's exaltation. He was "given," *charizomai* (**khar-id'-zom-ahee**), i.e., God bestowed on him "a (the) name" (*to onoma*) "which is above [*huper*] every name." The idea here is that just as He is exalted to the highest position, so He is granted or bestowed the greatest name that surpasses every thinkable name.

In the ancient or Jewish tradition, name-giving is more than merely a means of identity, label, or distinguishing one person from another. Rather, a name usually carries a relational, spiritual or historical significance; it also, in many instances, reflects the person's character, inner being, and the true nature of the individual. A name in the Jewish tradition could also reveal God's activity directed for an individual. For example, God changed "Abram" to "Abraham" because He was about to make Abraham "father of many nations," which is the meaning of the new name (Genesis 17:5ff.). Names are also given to reflect an important historical event. The angel of the Lord told Jacob after wrestling with him, "Thy name shall be called no more Jacob, but Israel: for as a prince hast thou power with God and with men, and hast prevailed" (Genesis 32:28). The angel told Mary that Jesus would be called "Emmanuel," which is "God is with us" and reflects Christ as God who came in the flesh. Jesus said to Simon Peter, "Thou art Simon the son of Jona: thou shalt be called Cephas," meaning a stone, which reflected the strong and outspoken nature of the apostle Peter (John 1:42).

This tradition is reminiscent of the African tradition, particularly to the Igbo tribe of Nigeria. They value a "good" name more than riches. The Igbo cannot give a name without meaning or historical significance. For example, the name "Alajemba," which means "perseverance," is given to the present writer based on an historical event that happened to the family. There are many other biblical and historical examples, but these will suffice. Could you think of other examples from the Bible? Do you know the meaning or history behind your own name? Does it reflect in any way your nature or character?

We can therefore deduce from these that God not only *echarisato*, i.e., "graciously bestowed" on Christ the name

that is above every other name to distinguish Him from all other beings, but He bestowed on Him the name that reflects His exalted nature, a title that coincides with a new position. This name is "Lord," *kurios* (v. 11), which means then that Christ not only carries both the title and the character of "Lord," he is Lord. It is important to note that the root meaning of the term *kurios* is used in Old Testament (LXX) to translate the personal name of God, YAHWEH, a name which denotes rulership and authority. This, therefore, means that God installed Christ to the same position, which rightly belongs to God Himself; He is now equal with God, equality and honor. He (Christ) refused to arrogate Himself or grasp with pride (v. 6). He now possesses the sovereign authority and rules over the entire universe. After His resurrection Jesus declared, "All power is given unto me in heaven and in earth" (Matthew 28:18; see also Ephesians 1:20-21).

10 That at the name of Jesus every knee should bow, of things in heaven, and things in earth, and things under the earth;

Paul gives us a two-part purpose for Christ's exaltation and bestowal of the highest name. The first part, introduced by "that," Greek *hina*, which means so that, or in order that, is that "at the name of Jesus every knee should bow." This clause does not say that "at the name, Jesus" every knee should bow, but rather "at the name of Jesus," i.e., the name that now belongs to Jesus or the name that He now bears. That name is *kurios* as we have discussed above. It is now bestowed to the historical Jesus, who humbled Himself to the lowest depth, who took up the role of a slave, who became human in time and space. He was crucified and died the most shameful death on the cross—the same Jesus who was rejected of all men, but whom God has made both Christ and Lord (Acts 2:36). He, who was obedient even to death, is to be obeyed and worshiped.

The bowing of the knee is almost universally used as a sign of reverence to someone of higher stature or authority, such as kings and chiefs. In most African traditions, subjects bow or kneel down and, in some cases, especially in the Yoruba tribe of Nigeria, lie flat on the floor or ground when they approach or see their village "Oba" (chiefs or kings), whether in the Oba's palaces or on the street. This is a way of paying homage or respect to the one in authority. The closest to this in the Western world is to stand at attention or salute when a soldier sees a superior officer. Military officers also accord this respect to the president or prime minister of their countries. "Bending of the knee" is also a symbol of worship. God says in Isaiah 45:23, "Unto me every knee shall bow, every tongue shall swear" and that such worship is reserved for Himself only (Exodus 20:5). Here this honor is now applied to Jesus, who has been accorded the highest name ever imagined, the name *Lord*. Therefore, all must fall on their knees before Christ in worship.

Paul goes on to declare the magnitude and sphere of the homage to Christ with a series of adjectives, "of things in heaven, and things in earth, and things under the earth." This shows that the worship of Christ is universal in nature. In other words, all creation is to worship Him. This would definitely include angels, humans, spirits, and demons, including all principalities and powers (Colossians 1:16, 20; 2:15), all would ultimately join in an act of worship to Christ. They would bow on their knees before Christ in awe and adoration. In his revelation, using the same universal phraseology, the apostle John says that he saw and heard:

"Every creature which is in heaven, and on the earth, and under the earth, and such as are in the sea, and all that are in them, saying, Blessing, and honour, and glory, and power, be unto him that sitteth upon the throne, and unto the Lamb for ever and ever" (Revelation 5:13).

11 And that every tongue should confess that Jesus Christ is Lord, to the glory of God the Father.

The second of the two-part of God's purpose in exalting Christ and giving Him the highest name above every other name, "that every tongue should confess that Jesus Christ is Lord." Here the writer reaches the climax of the "hymn" and gives us, as we previously indicated, the name that is above other names "Lord." The phrase "should confess" is the Greek *exomologeo* (**ex-om-ol-og-eh'-o**), which is to acknowledge openly and joyfully, the Lordship of Christ. The idea here is to affirm and celebrate Jesus as Lord, to praise and honor Him. Who is to "acknowledge Christ as Lord? Paul says every "tongue" (*glossa*), which literally means language, but used here to indicate the universality of the confession i.e., "everyone," "all," or "all peoples." *Glossa*, or "tongue," is often used in the Scriptures as a synonym for "tribe, people or nation" (Isaiah 66:18; Daniel 3:4,7; Revelation 5:9; 7:9; 10:11). Therefore, this confession is not limited to the church, but that every intelligent being within the sphere of God's creation will, in fact, admit that Jesus is Lord. Paul concludes this hymn by saying that the acknowledgment of Jesus as Lord is "to the glory of God the Father." The exaltation of Christ to the highest possible, and the giving of the highest name ever imaginable, and the proclamation of Christ as Lord by all peoples, has one

ultimate goal, i.e., the glory of the Father. Thus when the Son is glorified, the Father is also glorified (John 13:31-32; 14:13; 17:1).

Paul calls the Philippians to follow the example of Christ's humility, for that is the true road to personal exaltation, and to the glory of God. Here the formula is clear, "The surest way up is by stepping down, the surest way to gain for oneself is by giving up oneself, the surest way to life is by death, the surest way to win the praise of God is by steadfastly serving others" (Hawthorne, p. 95).

12 Wherefore, my beloved, as ye have always obeyed, not as in my presence only, but now much more in my absence, work out your own salvation with fear and trembling.

After giving the synopsis of the total work and the mission and the ultimate exaltation of Christ as an example of godly humility and its reward, Paul now returns to his exhortation. By using the conjunction *hoste*, "wherefore," "therefore," or "well then," Paul joins the new section with the preceding section, which actually started from 1:27 and includes 2:6-11. Here the apostle addresses the Philippian brethren as "my beloved," *agapetos*, people highly esteemed, or people dear to him "my dearly loved ones." This goes to verify the close relationship between Paul and the church at Philippi. This use of the adjective is also probably intended to appeal to their emotion, and the seriousness of the appeal for their obedience to what he is calling them to do. Here Paul probably uses some tact, which he continues in the clause immediately following even "as ye have always obeyed, not as in my presence only, but now much more in my absence." While Paul acknowledges their obedience when he was with them, he cautions that his presence should not be their motivating factor for obedience. Rather they should obey whether he was present with them or not, and indeed equally obey in his absence, even more so in his absence.

Apart from applying some tact to appeal to their emotion, Paul is also reminding them how they had responded in the past to the Gospel, which he had preached to them (cf. Acts 16:14, 32-33), and now calls on them to continue in that vent. Earlier on, Paul has written, "Only let your conversation be as it becometh the gospel of Christ: that whether I come and see you, or else be absent, I may hear of your affairs, that ye stand fast in one spirit, with one mind striving together for the faith of the gospel" (1:27). They are to remain consistent in their faith through obedience to the gospel, in spite of the suffering they are going through. They are to "work out your own salvation with fear and trembling," as Paul urges them. To "work out" is a translation of the Greek *katergazomai* (**kat-er-gad'-zom-ahee**), which is to accomplish. It has the idea of bringing to completion what has been started. As someone wrote, it means that the Philippians are to "go on until the work of salvation is fully and finally wrought out" in them. The phrase "work out your salvation" does not mean that the Philippians, or we for that matter, can effect our own salvation. This will definitely contradict the very meaning of salvation and Paul's teaching on the subject found in his other writings (cf. John 15:4f; 1 Corinthians 15:10; Ephesians 2:5,8). "Work your salvation" here then means that they are to live their lives to reflect the experience of salvation which has been wrought in them. Salvation, which is a gift from God, is not to be accepted with complacency, but it should be worked out, or maintained in a spirit of reverence and fear. How do they work out their salvation? The answer is clear from the first part of this verse, by consistent obedience whether in Paul's presence or in his absence.

Another way of looking at this command is to bear in mind that Paul was addressing the whole church as a corporate body and not the individual Philippians. The use of the verb *katergazesthe* ("work out") and the pronoun *heauton* ("your own"), both in the plural, substantiates this claim. This brings us to the consideration of the word "salvation." Apart from the spiritual welfare or safety of the soul, "salvation" (*soteria*) also means health and the physical well-being of the body (Mark 3:4; Acts 4:9; 14:9; 27:34). It seems that from 2:3-4, the entire church had become spiritually ill, and therefore, Paul now charges them to take every necessary step to restore itself to health. The church is "to work at its spiritual well-being until its well-being is complete, until health is fully established, until every trace of spiritual disease selfishness, dissension, and so on is gone" (Hawthorne, 99).

Whichever of the two options above he has in mind here, Paul is calling on both the church as a corporate body and the church on an individual basis to live out their salvation, or "to continue to work out" their salvation with fear and trembling. When we receive Christ as Lord and Saviour, we establish a relationship with Him and the Father. It does not end there, it is rather the beginning. The relationship should be maintained and worked on until the consummation of time. This is comparable to the marriage relationship, or friendship. Just as marriage is a process that grows with each party daily working together through communication, mutual respect and love for each in order to maintain it so that it lasts, so is our relationship with the Father established through salvation. We are to work together with the Holy Spirit to maintain the relationship. This is to be done "with fear and trembling." "Fear and trembling," *phobos kai tromos*, does not mean "alarm" or "dismay" or being afraid, quivering in the face of danger, rather it means with reverence, respect and awe.

13 For it is God which worketh in you both to will and to do of his good pleasure.

Although Paul urges the Philippians to exert some effort to maintain their salvation and their relationship with the Father he has good news for them. God gives them the enabling. Our will to obey God and our willingness to please Him are through God's initiative and prompting. Here Paul confirms the fact that it takes two—God and man. God does not force His will on man. Will God continue to work on man when man refuses to allow Him? There is a built-in power in man to do the will of God, but using this power depends on man. One who does not use this power to work out his salvation will be held accountable. This power is open and available to all, but not all use it (John 3:16-20; Mark 16:15-16; 1 John 1:9; Revelation 22:17).

DAILY BIBLE READING

M: Imitate Christ's Humility in Your Lives
Philippians 2:1-11
T: Rejoice in One Another's Faithfulness
Philippians 2:12-18
W: Timothy, a Faithful Servant of Christ
Philippians 2:19-24
T: Welcome Epaphroditus in Christ
Philippians 2:25-30
F: Repay Evil with a Blessing
1 Peter 3:8-12
S: Suffering for Doing Right
1 Peter 3:13-22
S: You are Participants in God's Nature
2 Peter 1:1-11

TEACHING TIPS

June 18
Bible Study Guide 3

1. Words You Should Know

A. Dung (3:8)—Waste or excrement, having no value.

B. Conversation (v. 20)— King James translation for the place of residence. Other versions translate as "citizenship."

C. Vile (v. 21)—Evil or undesirable.

2. Teacher Preparation

A. Read the background Scripture of today's lesson. Study more about running track or about professional runners and find out some particulars that they must do to prepare for an event and to safeguard against hazards or injury.

B. Use a chalkboard or tear sheet and write the words "World" and "Christ" in two separate columns. Ask the class to name some distinct worldly values and some distinctly Christian values. Discuss how these values are in direct opposition to one another.

3. Starting the Lesson

Read today's IN FOCUS story about Grady and Anita. Ask class members to share how their priorities have changed since they became Christians and since they became adults with responsibilities. Ask older class members to share how their priorities have changed with advancing years.

4. Getting into the Lesson

Draw a picture of a runner on a track. Use a tear sheet, poster board or another large sheet of paper. Ask class members to think about their race toward the prize as Christians. Ask them to place themselves on the track in their Christian walk. Solicit comments and testimonies about running the race for the prize.

5. Relating the Lesson to Life

A. Review the information about Libertines and the tribe of Benjamin in today's THE PEOPLE, PLACES AND TIMES article. In what ways might the Libertine mindset have threatened the stability of the early church?

B. Give students an opportunity to answer the questions in SEARCH THE SCRIPTURES.

C. Today's DISCUSS THE MEANING highlights the enemies of the Cross and sharing in Christ's suffering. Discuss how modern day Christians can still share in His suffering.

D. The LESSON IN OUR SOCIETY focuses priorities we have in goal-setting. Talk about the many things which often serve as distractions to achieving our true goal as citizens of heaven.

6. Arousing Action

A. Ask class members to think of someone who they believe has all of their priorities mixed up. What has the person done to call his/her priorities into question? Remind class members that it is generally very easy to look at others and determine what changes they should make in order that their lives might be better. It is also generally difficult for us to make those determinations in our own lives.

B. Based on the instructions given in the MAKE IT HAPPEN section, give class members an opportunity to consider their personal life priorities. Pass out pencils and paper so they can write down their priorities they should have in life.

C. Give class members time to complete FOLLOW THE SPIRIT and REMEMBER YOUR THOUGHTS.

PRESSING ON IN CHRIST

Bible Background • PHILIPPIANS 3
Printed Text • PHILIPPIANS 3:7-21
Devotional Reading • HEBREWS 10:19-25, 32-36

LESSON AIM

After studying today's lesson, students should realize that every believer's goal is to pursue the path of our heavenly home and cast aside the things which are in opposition to the Kingdom.

KEEP IN MIND

"I press toward the mark for the prize of the high calling of God in Christ Jesus" (Philippians 3:14).

FOCAL VERSES

PHILIPPIANS 3:7 But what things were gain to me, those I counted loss for Christ.

8 Yea doubtless, and I count all things but loss for the excellency of the knowledge of Christ Jesus my Lord: for whom I have suffered the loss of all things, and do count them but dung, that I may win Christ,

9 And be found in him, not having mine own righteousness, which is of the law, but that which is through the faith of Christ, the righteousness which is of God by faith:

10 That I may know him, and the power of his resurrection, and the fellowship of his sufferings, being made conformable unto his death;

11 If by any means I might attain unto the resurrection of the dead.

12 Not as though I had already attained, either were already perfect: but I follow after, if that I may apprehend that for which also I am apprehended of Christ Jesus.

13 Brethren, I count not myself to have apprehended: but this one thing I do, forgetting those things which are behind, and reaching forth unto those things which are before,

14 I press toward the mark for the prize of the high call-

LESSON OVERVIEW

LESSON AIM
KEEP IN MIND
FOCAL VERSES
IN FOCUS
THE PEOPLE, PLACES, AND TIMES
BACKGROUND
AT-A-GLANCE
IN DEPTH
SEARCH THE SCRIPTURES
DISCUSS THE MEANING
LESSON IN OUR SOCIETY
MAKE IT HAPPEN
FOLLOW THE SPIRIT
REMEMBER YOUR THOUGHTS
MORE LIGHT ON THE TEXT
DAILY BIBLE READINGS

---

ing of God in Christ Jesus.

15 Let us therefore, as many as be perfect, be thus minded: and if in any thing ye be otherwise minded, God shall reveal even this unto you.

16 Nevertheless, whereto we have already attained, let us walk by the same rule, let us mind the same thing.

17 Brethren, be followers together of me, and mark them which walk so as ye have us for an ensample.

18 (For many walk, of whom I have told you often, and now tell you even weeping, that they are the enemies of the cross of Christ:

19 Whose end is destruction, whose God is their belly, and whose glory is in their shame, who mind earthly things.)

20 For our conversation is in heaven; from whence also we look for the Saviour, the Lord Jesus Christ:

21 Who shall change our vile body, that it may be fashioned like unto his glorious body, according to the working whereby he is able even to subdue all things unto himself.

IN FOCUS

Grady really enjoyed going to his college class reunion. He'd seen a couple of his fraternity brothers, and a few guys who were on the football team with him.

"Baby, that was my world ten years ago," he told his wife, Anita. "The frat, the football team, and partying were what I lived for in those days. And, if I say so myself, I was quite popular with the girls, too."

"I know what you mean," Anita chimed in. "Isn't it funny how your priorities change, especially after you marry and have children. I remember that all I wanted was to look good in a pair of jeans and have a date on Saturday night."

"I know," added Grady. "Having you and Nicole in my life mean more to me than I ever thought anything could."

THE PEOPLE, PLACES, AND TIMES

LIBERTINE. These persons who were a part of the early Christian church believed they were essentially a soul or spirit. The body was only a temporary house, having no long-term value or significance. They held a dual view of life: spiritual matter is good and physical matter is evil or worthless.

The beliefs of the libertines were countered by the ascetics, who believed that the body was evil and tried to suppress it. Conversely, the libertines believed that the body was insignificant, therefore claiming the freedom to do with it as they pleased.

Based on information from *The Broadman Bible Commentary* Vol. 11, Clifford J. Allen, general editor, Nashville: Broadman Press, 1971, p. 210.

BENJAMIN. The tribe of Benjamin occupies the smallest territory of any of the 12 Hebrew tribes. In spite of its size, however, the tribe played a significant role in Israel's history. Saul, the first ruler of Israel, was a Benjamite.

During the latter period of the judges, Benjamin practically disappeared from history when they mistreated a Levite and his concubine (Judges 19 20).

Based on information from *Holman Bible Dictionary*, Trent Butler, general editor, Nashville: Broadman & Holman Publishers, 1991, p. 165.

BACKGROUND

In chapter three, Paul warned the Philippians about the dangers of a distorted religion. He railed against the problem of having confidence in the flesh, versus the knowledge of Christ. With fatherly concern for the congregation, Paul warned them about persons who could lead them astray.

He was concerned about persons who trusted more in themselves and their accomplishments. None, however, had reason to boast, according to Paul. For he himself had as much reason as anyone else. Paul had a background that was impressive by any standard, but especially by Hebrew standards. He understood from personal experience what it meant to have all the prized religious values, virtues, and achievements, only to discover that it was not the ultimate objective.

Paul was born out of the tribe of Benjamin, and was circumcised on the eighth day, according to the Law. Paul was a Hebrew born of Hebrews. He was from the tribe which

had remained loyal to the Davidic line during the reign of Rehoboam (1 Kings 12:12). He was trained and educated as a Pharisee and he used that knowledge to persecute the church. If anyone had reason to place confidence in their own ability and knowledge, it was Paul.

IN DEPTH

1. All Gain Is Through Christ (Philippians 3:7-11)

If ever a person had reason to have confidence in himself and his intellectual abilities, it was Paul. Yet, even though Paul had impeccable credentials which gave him standing in the Jewish hierarchy, he gave it all up when he encountered the Master.

One can only give up that which one has and one cannot give up what one does not have. Paul was able to speak with authority concerning the worthlessness of something which he once valued highly.

Paul told the Philippians about his own heritage and accomplishments (vv. 5-6). Concerning his heritage, there were four gains, which he now counted as loss for Christ's sake. First, he was circumcised on the eighth day, which meant he was born a Jew, not a proselyte. Second, he was "of the stock of Israel," meaning he was pure Hebrew, not of mixed descent as were many in Palestine during that day. Third, Paul was from the tribe of Benjamin, which had remained loyal to the Davidic line when the kingdom divided. Fourth, he was a "Hebrew of the Hebrews," a phrase commonly used to designate those who had retained the national language. Though settled in a Greek city, Paul's family had continued to speak the Hebrew tongue.

Concerning his expertise in the Law, Paul was a Pharisee, part of a strict sect whose life pursuit was to obey the law in every detail. In his pursuit of righteousness, Paul was no exception. So devoted was he to his way of life that he gladly and eagerly and probably with a great sense of arrogance and superiority persecuted those in the church.

Obviously a man of great intellectual ability, Paul came to realize that no legalistic training or adherence could save anyone. Paul did not give up things which were considered evil or worthless. He willingly walked away from a treasured lifestyle, held in high esteem by his family and community. What he now counted as loss was not a former state of wickedness, but of goodness. Yet whatever advantages Paul had in his former life were nothing in light of the salvation he was now granted through the saving knowledge of Christ Jesus. Now Paul considered his former treasures to be worthless, like dung (excrement).

Paul's surrender of legalism and self-righteousness did not cause him to go to the other extreme of libertinism. He did not understand freedom from legalism to translate lawlessness. As it was when he was a Pharisee, righteousness remained his consuming goal. Now, however, he pursued righteousness from God, found through faith in Christ, not the self-righteousness of his previous life. Righteousness is not a human achievement, it is the work of God in one who has the openness of faith to receive Jesus Christ as Lord and Savior.

In order to know Christ, Paul gave up the life he once held so dear. His former life became all the more meaningless with the recognition that human effort is useless in attaining the righteousness that God requires. Therefore, our righteousness can only come through our faith in Christ. Paul wanted to know Christ and the power of His resurrection.

In order to live with Christ, we must die with Him. We cannot go back to the cross of Golgotha; however, the Christ who was victorious there can come to us and allow us to be conformed to Him and His ways. In life, we can have partial knowledge of His existence. That knowledge will be made complete in the resurrection from the dead.

2. Warning Against False Perfection (vv. 12-16)

After warning them about placing confidence in the self, Paul proceeded to warn the Philippians about the dangers of false perfectionism. Although Paul strived with all that he has to attain this righteousness, he made no claim to having already achieved it. He emphatically rejected any claim to perfection. He knew from personal experience the dangers of legalism and its tendency to produce a false sense of righteousness.

Apparently some at the Philippian church had deluded themselves with the notion that they were perfect. Paul emphasized that resurrection from the dead was not the only goal ahead. Even the goal that may be achieved in this life still lay ahead. Paul was still running the race. He could not slow his pace, to do so would be like a runner stopping short of the finish line.

Paul does not consider his past achievements to be sufficient. He cannot rest on past accomplishments. The race is unfinished. He must continue to strive to fulfill the call of God which is given through Christ Jesus. Paul's goal is to attain the goal which Christ has set for him.

Though unattained, perfection is his goal. Admittedly, it is a goal that one never seems to be able to grasp. Still Paul is willing to continue to press toward the goal. He has begun the race, and is committed to finishing the course. The work he has done so far has been good, but it is not over. As determined as Paul is to finish, he has not yet completed the race. Therefore, he cannot afford to be slack in his efforts. In the meantime, he is concerned with avoiding the illusion of having actually attained the goal.

Since Christ grasped or took hold of Paul, he, in turn, wanted to grab hold of the perfection which is Christ's goal for him. Conversion itself represents the beginning, not the completion of the goal. Salvation has both a beginning and a goal, but it is a process, a lifetime achievement. The King James translation to the word *perfect* in verse 15 appears to be a direct contradiction to Paul's insistence that he is not perfect. What Paul meant here was that the mental attitude described in the previous sentences is the perfect attitude and willingness to admit shortcomings, open to correction, and willing to be recreated In Christ Jesus. Those who possess this perfect attitude are those who hold true to what they have attained.

The Philippians were admonished to remain true to this point of view so that they could make further progress. They must neither forget the goal, nor suffer under the illusion that they have already attained it. Just as there was a danger in assuming perfection had been attained, Paul was well aware, and equally concerned, about those who treated the goal with total disregard.

3. Commitment to Perfection (vv. 17-21)

Having stressed the significance of perfection as the goal for discipleship, and having warned against the presumption that perfection has already been attained, Paul turned his attention to the danger of giving up all efforts to attain perfection. Again, Paul offered himself as an example for the Philippians to follow. He begs fellow Christians to join in imitating him (and perhaps others like him) as a follower of Jesus Christ. He also advised them to pay attention to this example.

It may appear as though Paul was again doing what he had advised against, placing confidence in the self. His only cause for boasting, however, was in Christ. He made no claims of personal virtue or achievement. His offer of himself as an example was with regard to his commitment to the call. The Philippians were challenged to join his example in commitment to the goal of perfection while making no boast of achieving it.

The identity of those who are "enemies of the cross of Christ" is not really clear. They may have been Philippians or persons who resided elsewhere. Most likely, the term refers to persons within the church, not Jews or Judaizers. The apostle's tears reflect his sorrow over the damage those persons may do to the church or to others.

But the damage done by these enemies will not go unpunished. Their "end is destruction." The term "their god is the belly" probably refers to the wanton behavior which was characteristic of the libertines. The term "belly" may point to their gluttony, drunkenness, or a preoccupation with physical and material things.

During Paul's day, some in the church viewed themselves as spiritual persons, having special knowledge of God and being above sin. The essence of their being was spirit; therefore, the body held no worth and did not need to be preserved. The result was shameless behavior that was in direct opposition to the goal they were to pursue.

Finally, Paul reminded the Philippians of their true calling as heavenly citizens. As such, they must conduct their lives according to the standards of His kingdom. Therefore, they were to eagerly anticipate the return of their Savior who, having all power, would bring about resurrection and transformation in them all. Just as Christ, in His raised body passed from earth to heaven, so the resurrection bodies of believers outfitted them for their heavenly home.

SEARCH THE SCRIPTURES

1. Why did Paul now count the things of his former life as loss ? (v. 8)

2. From what source did Paul receive his righteousness? (v. 9)

3. Why did Paul wish to share in Christ's suffering and the power of His resurrection? (vv. 10-11)

4. Why did Paul continue to pursue the goal of perfection? (v. 12)

5. What was Paul committed to doing, even though he had not yet attained the goal? (v. 13)

6. Toward what prize did Paul press on? (v. 14)

7. What was Paul's advice to perfect (mature) believers? (vv. 15-17)

8. Who did Paul suggest as a model to follow? (v. 17)

9. What would happen to the enemies of Christ? (v. 19)

10. What would Christ do for those who were focused on the heavenly prize? (v. 21)

DISCUSS THE MEANING

1. In what ways could persons who possessed libertine beliefs be enemies of the cross on which Christ suffered and died?

2. In what way can believers share in Christ's suffering, as Paul said of himself?

LESSON IN OUR SOCIETY

It is difficult to get through life without setting goals. Far too often in our society, however, the goal of making a heavenly home gets pushed into the background. The pursuit of careers, homes, cars, and other material goods begin to consume us, often without conscious consent.

If we developed the constant state of mind to regard ourselves first as citizens of heaven, perhaps some of the zeal with which we pursue material goals would dissipate and give way to heavenly goals.

Jesus cautioned us not to put up our treasures in places where moths eat and thieves break in and steal (Matthew 6:19-20). The material things of this world are under the control of whims of this world. Therefore, the goal of heaven is the only one which will last through all things.

MAKE IT HAPPEN

In what ways have you pushed your heavenly goal aside, giving way to earthly or material pursuits. If your life has gotten out of balance in terms of where you have placed your priorities, make a list of some steps you can take to shift the balance correctly. List, in ranking order, the priorities your life should have, according to what pleases God.

FOLLOW THE SPIRIT

What God wants me to do:

_____

_____

REMEMBER YOUR THOUGHTS

Special insights you learned:

_____

_____

MORE LIGHT ON THE TEXT
PHILIPPIANS 3:7-21

With the use of "finally" in the opening verse of chapter 3, Paul seems to indicate that he was coming to the end of his letter to the Philippians. However, in content Paul is focusing on a different aspect of the Philippians' situation and addresses it. Here he warns them against Judaizers, who he says put much "confidence in the flesh" rather than in Christ. He gives himself as an example of one who had by all measure reached to the height of fame in the religion of Judaism, and is more qualified both through birth and religious rites and tradition than any other. As to preserving the law and tradition, he was zealous about persecuting the very church that he is now preserving and building with his suffering. The extent of his involvement is best described in his own words: "Circumcised the eighth day, of the stock of Israel, of the tribe of Benjamin, an Hebrew of the Hebrews; as touching the law, a Pharisee; Concerning zeal, persecuting the church; touching the righteousness which is in the law, blameless" (Philippians 3:5-6).

3:7 But what things were gain to me, those I counted loss for Christ. 8 Yea doubtless, and I count all things but loss for the excellency of the knowledge of Christ Jesus my Lord: for whom I have suffered the loss of all things, and do count them but dung, that I may win Christ,

The Pharisees were a sect of self-righteous and zealous Jews who held to the letters of their interpretation of the law and to their own traditions without minding whether they nullify the word of God or not. They were the most privileged and highly "respected" and "honored" people in the temple worship. They held strongly, for example, to the physical circumcision of the flesh and equated righteousness to the keeping of the laws and the Jewish tradition. To reach that height, one must definitely be a Jew, "free born," not a proselyte, an ardent keeper of the law, and "blameless" in all aspects of the religion. To attain to the position of a Pharisee therefore, is a very rigorous undertaking, which requires much learning and knowledge of the law. The position also comes with great advantages and privileges. Pharisaic position was the highest dream and aspiration of every Jewish young man. Paul, as we have seen in the first six verses, had reached that high echelon. Indeed, as to meeting every requirement of Judaism, being of pure stock, and of the fanatical zeal, he had no equal (Acts 7:58; 8:1-3; 9:1-2; Galatians 1:13-14; 2 Corinthians 11:22).

All the things, which were to his advantage, the honor and respect, which he possessed as a Pharisee, he counted loss for Christ, Paul says. Here Paul is saying that all the positions and aspirations, which every Jewish young man dreamed of and are thought to be "gain," *kerdos* (**ker'-dos**), and which he has already attained, are now *zermia*,

"loss," worthless, or valueless to him. *Zermia* here has the idea of loss as related to trade or business enterprise where one incurs a loss. The loss is voluntary, where one for something better and bigger purposely decides to inflict a loss, for example, throwing merchandise overboard to lighten a sinking ship (Acts 27:10; 21) in order to save lives. The word "counted" Paul uses here is the Greek *hegeomai* (**hayg-eh'-om-ahee**), which means to consider, esteem or deem. Paul applies the language of business, as we have intimated above, and considers as loss all the things of his past before the Damascus encounter that he thought were gain.

Paul considered everything loss "for Christ," i.e., for the sake of having a relationship with Christ "knowing Christ" (v. 8). "For Christ" should be understood as for the purpose of gaining Christ, rather than "for Christ" as if Christ were to benefit from the loss. Paul's encounter with the living Christ on the Damascus road altered his perspective and mindset in life. He reassessed his priorities in life between having all the worldly glory and position and being ignorant in the riches of knowing Christ on one hand, and knowing Christ as Lord and gaining life eternal on the other hand. This reminds us of Christ's teaching and instruction to the rich ruler who asked what he had to do in order to inherit eternal life. Christ told him that in addition to keeping the law, he should sell all his possessions and distribute it to the poor, and then "come and follow me" (Matthew 19:21).

The thought of preferring to know Christ rather than having worldly possessions and positions, or basking in his past personal achievements is carried further and indeed reemphasized in verse 8. Paul writes, "Yea doubtless, and I count all things but loss for the excellency of the knowledge of Christ Jesus my Lord." "Yea doubtless," *alla menounge* (**men-oon'-geh**), adds strength to what he has previously said. This phrase can be interpreted as "indeed" or "surely" or definitely. Paul moves from the perfect tense to present, which means that he still regards as loss all those things, which he counted as loss the moment of his conversion on the road to Damascus. He counts "all things," including all the achievements enumerated in verses 5 and 6 and everything which he deemed would be hindrances, liabilities, or would stand in the way of achieving his ultimate goal of knowing Christ, "to be loss." Why does he consider all things as loss? Because of "the excellency of the knowledge Christ Jesus." The word "excellency" is the Greek *huperecho* (**hoop-er-ekh'-o**), which has the idea of superiority, to excel, better or supreme. Here Paul evaluates his past privileges, family, religious heritage, achievements, rise to fame as a Pharisee, power, position, etc. and finds them worthless compared with his new privilege of knowing Christ. In fact, for Paul knowing Christ is superior and supremely more valuable than all other things.

The Greek noun *gnosis*, which translates "knowledge," has a broad range of meanings both in the Old and New Testament times (see Hawthorne, p. 138). However, the knowledge Paul refers to here is more than an acquisition of facts or an intellectual knowledge, but rather experiential. It is more than intellectual cognizance of the truth about Jesus Christ, but a personal and intimate relationship with the "Christ Jesus my Lord." It is having a personal encounter with Christ, which involves more than one's thought and reasoning, but primarily one's heart. This knowledge alters one's attitude and perspective in life, and rearranges one's priorities and views of the world system. It altered Paul's perception of Christ as a radical Jew, whose teaching must be resisted, to that of one who must be loved, served, revered, obeyed, and recognized as Lord. This knowledge therefore surpasses everything so much that because of its ultimate value, Paul sees everything in his life, which before were "gain" to him, as loss.

Paul did not only consider all things loss in order to have personal knowledge of Christ, he indeed incurred the loss of everything. He says, "For whom I have suffered the loss (*zemioo*) of all things," which means to sustain damage, or to receive injury. Here Paul's quest to know Christ cost him everything, including the highest position, which he had attained within Judaism and so on. Therefore, the loss is real, rather than an ordinary cliche or empty boast. We deduce from the tense here "I have suffered" (past passive), that the "loss" occurred at a specific time. This seems to suggest that the Jewish authorities probably stripped him of all his Pharisaic privileges and advantages the very moment he declared his allegiance to Christ following his encounter with the Lord on the Damascus road. He not only "considered" them loss in the past, Paul says he still does "count them but dung" in the present. There is no regret at all. To him these things he formerly cherished are now "dung," *skubalon* (**skoo'-bal-on**), a strong word that describes Paul's attitude towards those things, compared to what he has now gained, "the knowledge of Christ." *Skubalon* here means garbage or refuse or what is thrown to the dogs. It is used to describe any refuse such as the excrement of animals, or things that are worthless and detestable. In order that he might "win (*kerdaino*, or gain) Christ," Paul says, all former things had become garbage, worthless and useless to him.

9 And be found in him, not having mine own righteousness, which is of the law, but that which is through the faith of Christ, the righteousness which is of God by faith:

Another reason for counting all things "dung" is that he might "be found in him (Christ), not having mine own righteousness, which is of the law." Prior to his conversion, Paul attained the high position by personal achievement, by keeping the law, which is the measuring stick for righteousness in Judaism. This type of self-righteousness gives rise to and is characterized by pride and arrogance (Romans 10:1-3), and contradicts the work of Christ. To him, self-righteousness (Pharisaic righteousness), which is based on what one could do, has no more value. Christ said to His disciples, "Except your righteousness shall exceed the righteousness of the scribes and Pharisees, ye shall in no case enter into the kingdom of heaven" (Matthew 5:20). Instead of depending on his own righteousness, now Paul relies on the "righteousness" (*dikaiosunen*) "which is through . . . Christ," based not on personal merit (Isaiah 61: 10), but on the finished work of Christ, appropriated by faith only.

"Righteousness," *dikaiosunen* (Hebrew, *sedeq*), and "justification" with its verb "to justify" were used in both Jewish and Greek communities as judicial terms, whereby a judge would either justify or condemn one. To justify is therefore to vindicate or to declare one right. In the Jewish religion, the criterion for being justified before God was for one to keep the Law of Moses. This amounted to being "good" or doing "good" works in order to earn God's favorable verdict. However, Paul had realized after his dramatic encounter with the Lord that by the deeds of the law there shall no flesh be justified in His sight (Romans 3:20).

This understanding conforms to the Old Testament affirmation that no human can attain God's standards of holiness by doing good work. Without exception, humans are too sinful by nature to do enough good to receive God's approval (cf. Psalm 14:1-3; 53:1-3; 143:2). The only criterion for righteousness before God is by "faith" through Christ. "Faith" here simply means "trust" (Genesis 15:6), having confidence in and accepting God's work of grace through the life and death of Christ. It is not my faithfulness but Christ's faithfulness and loyalty to the Father. Faith is saying, "My approval before God is not dependent on my own merit, the good I can do, or how much law I observe; it is rather dependent on what God has done through Christ on the cross and I accept it." Therefore, Paul's desire is that his approval before God be dependent on his relationship with God through faith in Christ. Paul says that God's righteousness comes through Christ (1 Corinthians

1:30) and it is by faith (Romans 3:22-26; 4:1ff; 9:30-31). Consequently, faith in Christ further explains what Paul means by "be found in him," i.e., being united with Christ by trusting and receiving what he has done for all.

10 That I may know him, and the power of his resurrection, and the fellowship of his sufferings, being made conformable unto his death;

Paul further declares another goal for considering all his personal advantages and everything else as "dung." That is to "know him (Christ), the power of his resurrection, the fellowship of suffering, and to be made conformable unto his death. To "know Christ" as verse 8 implies, not intellectually, but experientially, having an intimate relationship, as in the sexual intimacy between husband and wife (Matthew 1:25; Genesis 4:1). Before his encounter with Christ on the road to Damascus, Paul had the intellectual knowledge of him, but on that special day, he encountered the Lord in a unique way. A special and intimate relationship was inaugurated between him and Christ, which is another dimension of knowing Christ. Hence, he called him "Lord" (Acts 9:5). The idea here is that of an ongoing relationship with Christ—not a one-time knowledge of him, i.e., to develop a deeper relationship with the living Christ. The only obstacle was his past glory and personal advantages. These personal achievements are now rubbish, filthy and stinky garbage to him.

Paul qualifies this intimate knowledge of Christ with a cluster of other phrases. The first is "and the power of his resurrection." What does Paul have in mind by this phrase? It seems to me that Paul is saying that he wants also "to know," i.e., to experience the efficacy of the power in Christ's resurrection. The knowledge here is not separate from his knowing Christ. He wishes to experience the transforming, life-changing power with which Christ has been endowed through His resurrection power by which we are accepted as righteous in God's sight. Christ's resurrection from the dead signifies that God has accepted the ransom He paid on our behalf (Matthew 20:28; Acts 20:28; 1 Peter 1:18) and therefore we are justified (Romans 4:25; 8:1, 16; 1 Corinthians 15:17).

The second phrase is "and the fellowship of his sufferings." It means that Paul's wishes were not only to know Christ and experience the power in His resurrection, but to experience Christ by "sharing" in Christ sufferings. This phrase poses some interpretive problems. What does Paul mean by sharing or participating in the sufferings of Christ? Does he refer to His physical suffering: the beatings, stoning, hunger, the shipwreck, the imprisonment, etc.? (Acts 9:15-16; 22:15). It may include all those, but it does not in any way imply that his own sufferings complement or complete Christ's suffering or as if his own physical suffering augmented Christ's afflictions (Colossians 1:24). Just as to know Christ and the power of His resurrection is an inward spiritual experience, to know Christ in the fellowship of His suffering is equally a spiritual experience expressed in terms of dying with Him (Romans 6:8; Galatians 2:19-20). Indeed, it does not seem that Paul here is wishing to know Christ by experiencing the physical suffering of martyrdom as some may interpret it. Rather it is "to know Christ who suffered and died for him" (cf. 1 Peter 3:18; 4:1), and to know that Paul also suffered and died in Christ (spiritually), to be resurrected in Him through Christ's redemptive act.

Participating in the suffering does not imply inflicting personal suffering on oneself, as in self-mutilating, or exposing oneself purposely to danger or persecution in the name of Christ. When Paul says, "I am crucified with Christ," it is does not mean literal crucifixion as some religious fanatics practice. Each year on Good Friday, some so-called Christians torture and mutilate themselves, and even literally crucify someone on the cross as a sign of suffering with Christ. This is quite unbiblical and a misinterpretation of the Scriptures. Paul's view of partaking in the suffering of Christ is a total resolve to live for Christ and to serve Him in all circumstances, it is an intensive desire to be like Him in holiness. It means dying to sin (Romans 7:9-25), and dying to self, which Jesus himself spoke (Mark 8:34f). With such desire and longing for complete knowledge of Christ, Paul is able to endure all physical suffering that comes his way because of his belief in and defense of the Gospel of Christ (2 Corinthians 4:7-12; Galatians 6:17; Colossians 1:24).

The last in this cluster of phrases, "being made conformable unto his death," tends to confirm Paul's longing for holiness. To "conform," a Greek word *summorphizomai* (**soom-mor-feed'-zo-mahee**), appears once in the New Testament. It is to grant or invest in the same form, to share the likeness of, or to take on the same form. The language and idea here call to mind Paul's language in his epistle to the Romans 6: 4-11. "For if we have been planted together in the likeness of his death, we shall be also in the likeness of his resurrection: . . . Now if we be dead with Christ, we believe that we shall also live with him" (Romans 6:5-8). This implies union with Christ and participation in the unique attributes of Christ, which include His humility and His unselfish love for all, which led to His sacrificial death (2:5ff), His righteousness, which through His death has been imparted to all believers. Indeed, Paul describes the

believer's spiritual union with Christ metaphorically in the following ways: suffered with Christ (Romans 8:17), is crucified with Him (Romans 6:6), died with Him (Romans 6:8; 2 Timothy 2:11), and buried with Him (Romans 6:4; Colossians 2:12). Just as Christ did not remain dead and buried in the grave, but is made alive, the believer is made alive with Him (Colossians 2:13), raised with Him (Colossians 2:12; 3:1), is made joint-heir and glorified with Him (Romans 8:17). Just as He has been enthroned, the believer is enthroned with Him (Colossians 3:1; Revelation 20:4), and will reign with Him forever (2 Timothy 2:12; Revelation 20:4).

Paul, by the efficacy of Christ's death on the cross, is already dead to sin at the instance of his conversion on the road to Damascus. This was past experience. However, he strives to make the effects of this death a daily reality through his life-style and the conscious choices he makes daily, renouncing self with its desires and all that do not conform to the image and likeness of Christ. It means denying self and taking up the cross daily, and following Christ (Luke 9:23). Although, "being made conformable unto his (Christ) death," refers primarily to spiritual union and identification with Christ's suffering, the physical suffering and death of the Christian is not ruled out, but rather is included in the expression. Paul's personal experience, as recorded in his second letter to the Corinthian church (4:7-12), confirms the fact: "Always bearing about in the body the dying of the Lord Jesus, that the life also of Jesus might

be made manifest in our body. For we which live are always delivered unto death for Jesus' sake, that the life also of Jesus might be made manifest in our mortal flesh" (vv.10-11).

11 If by any means I might attain unto the resurrection of the dead.

A superficial and isolated reading of verse 11 would tend to show that Paul was expressing doubt, or is uncertain of his attaining the eschatological resurrection of all believers. Paul never lacked assurance of his salvation or his relationship as a child of God (Romans 8:15-17; Galatians 4:6f), but often celebrates that assurance (2 Timothy 1:12; 4:7,8). Therefore, this verse is to be read in context with the preceding thoughts expressed in the foregoing verses where Paul strives to live a life reflective of the life and likeness of his Saviour Christ Jesus. That is, he endeavors to lead a life that conforms to the life, death, and resurrection of Christ. This is evidenced in his resolve to gladly forego all things—the advantages, and the privileges of his previous life as a Pharisee. These things mattered so much to him in the past, but have now become as dung (vv. 7-8). These he does with the goal of attaining unto the resurrection of the dead. The use of this conditional clause, "if by any means " *ei pos* (**i poce**), if somehow, is rather Paul's humble way of saying that salvation is not by good deeds, but depends totally on God's gracious gift from beginning to end. This humility ascertains that salvation is not a consequence of our good works, or personal efforts, or our attempt to live holy. That is, the future resurrection cannot be presumed based on personal efforts, neither is God's mercy to be assumed or taken for granted because we are Christian. However, there is no room for complacency. Paul recognizes this and looks forward, with great expectation and hope, with enduring faith, to the future bodily resurrection of the dead.

12 Not as though I had already attained, either were already perfect: but I follow after, if that I may apprehend that for which also I am apprehended of Christ Jesus.

Now Paul makes it clear that the attainment of the resurrection is futuristic, something he sets his eyes on, but has not achieved yet. It tends to expel the notion that the resurrection of all believers is only spiritual, totally and completely achieved the moment one receives Christ as Lord. It also goes on to confirm that realization of the resurrection is not what we assume we own, irrespective of the life we live. Rather the attainment of the resurrection is something to be maintained and strived for after receiving Christ. Paul definitely must have had this in mind when he urged the church to "work out your own salvation with fear and trembling" (2:12; cf. 1 Corinthians 9:27; 10:12-14; Hebrews 10: 26-37; 1 Peter 2:20-22).

Here Paul says that he has not yet "attained," *lambano* (**lam-ban-o**), that is to lay hold on, to take, or to receive, as in receiving a prize. The prize is the resurrection from the dead, which is still to come. He has not yet reached his goal, neither is he "already perfect." The word translated "perfect" is the Greek *teleioo* (**tel-i-o'-o**), also translated as fulfill (Luke 2:43; John 19:28); finish (John 4:34; 5:36; Acts 20:24; etc.). It has the idea of completing a given task, or to consummate. What kind of perfection does Paul refer to here? Is it perfection as in character i.e., Christian perfection? Alternatively, is it perfection in finishing his course? It has been suggested that there were in Philippi those who thought they had reached the goal of Christian perfection. Therefore, Paul wants to let them know that he neither thinks of himself as "having arrived," or reached his goal, nor does he see himself as perfect, sinless or holy. This does not imply that Paul was lacking in spiritual experience or that he was deficient morally, or still cleaving to his old nature, but it is another demonstration of his humility, whereby he sees all his life as the work of God's grace.

It means also that the task is not yet complete. The race is not over yet. There is still a course to finish in order to reach the set goal. Hence he says, "But I follow after, if that I may apprehend that for which also I am apprehended of Christ Jesus." To "follow after," *dioko*, i.e., to run swiftly in

order to catch a person or thing, to run after someone. It is also translated, to press on, figuratively used of one that runs swiftly in a race, as in the Olympics, in order to reach the goal and win a prize. There is a definite sense of urgency, eagerness, and effort exerted here. Why is he pressing so hard? So that "I may apprehend, *katalambano* (**kat-al-am-ban'-o** i.e., obtain, attain, lay hold on) that for which also" Christ Jesus "apprehended" (*katalambano*) "me" i.e., laid hold on him. This has the sense of being seized or taking possession of. Paul intimates that Christ had a definite purpose for taking possession of him. What is the purpose? The first is probably his call to ministry. Christ told Ananias following his encounter with Paul on the Damascus road, "he is a chosen vessel unto me, to bear my name before the Gentiles, and kings, and the children of Israel. . . for I will shew him how great things he must suffer for my name's sake" (Acts 9:15-16; cf. 22:15, 21; 26:15-18). The second is the gift of eternal life, the high calling of God (v. 14), "a crown of righteousness, which the Lord, the righteous judge, shall give me at that day: and not to me only, but unto all them also that love his appearing" (2 Timothy 4:8). With these objectives before him, Paul presses on to reach the goal.

13 Brethren, I count not myself to have apprehended: but this one thing I do, forgetting those things which are behind, and reaching forth unto those things which are before, 14 I press toward the mark for the prize of the high calling of God in Christ Jesus.

The content of verses 13 and 14 is more than tautology or mere repetition of what Paul has already stated, but adds emphasis, pointing to the seriousness, and the importance of the matter with loving emotion. It seems that Paul, by adding "brethren" (*adelphos*, a word of endearment) is invoking his close relationship with the church, and showing a deep concern that they understand the truth he is writing them. The use of the word shows that he is deeply moved; that he is speaking the truth and would not lie to them. They are to listen to him and take his word for it rather than listen to those Judaizers (v. 1-3) who probably claim that they have already reached perfection here and now. Again, Paul does not consider himself to have "arrived," or to have taken hold of the goal, or reached the finishing line (using again an athletic metaphor). Although Paul has totally given up everything for the cause of Christ, has renounced his Pharisaic opportunities and advantages, and has identified himself with Christ both in His suffering and in His death, yet Paul does not claim that he has reached perfection. However, there is "one thing I do," he says, and that is "forgetting those things which are behind, and reaching forth unto those things which are before." Paul is focused on the race before him, not allowing any distraction from his past to impede his concentration on his bid for the prize. Here is the three things Paul does:

1. He forgets the past: the ground he has covered, or the hurdles he has scaled in the race. A good athlete does not look back when running. That could result in a loss of speed, direction and, more often than not, the race itself (1 Corinthians 9:24-27). Jesus cautioned, "No man, having put his hand to the plough, and looking back, is fit for the kingdom of God" (Luke 9:62). Literally speaking, Paul would not allow his past achievements (vv. 5-7), or his failures through persecuting the church (v. 6; Acts 9:1ff.) to hinder him from the race. Forgetting those events means that he deliberately and mentally obliterates them from his mind. How easy it is for our past sins to deprive us of the joy and hope of our salvation. This is the one common weapon Satan uses against the Christian, accusing him before the throne. But we have assurance in the finished work of Christ (Romans 8:33-39).

2. He "reaches forth": *epekteinomai* (**ep-ek-ti'-nom-ahee**) means to stretch oneself. That means straining every nerve and muscle, and sparing no energy; using every ounce of his strength in order to reach the goal. It is like running the race of one's life as if life itself depends totally on it, indeed. This is the attitude of every good competitive athlete. He does whatever is legally possible in order to win.

3. He presses on towards the mark: the finish line, where every athlete's eyes and mind are focused from start to finish. The sense here is perseverance and consistency motivated by the ultimate goal and prize, which Paul refers to as "the high calling of God in Christ Jesus."

Sports today are a very lucrative business, which come with a handsome reward. Apart from the gold, silver or bronze medals which athletes win in a race, they are rewarded with millions of dollars in product endorsements and TV commercials. Many take up acting careers and other endeavors that make millions of dollars for them. It is therefore not only the various medals or the wreath of leaves, or flowers which they receive at the podium, but the lasting benefit that follows it. No wonder they train and persevere to win. These rewards are earthly, perishable, and temporary. For Paul, the reward or prize is priceless, imperishable (1 Corinthians 9:25), it is the high calling of God in Christ Jesus, the upward call to life everlasting. "In Christ" here means that Christ is the sphere through which the

invaluable prize is appropriated. There are differences between the earthly and the heavenly races. In the earthly race, the prize is perishable; in the heavenly race, the prize is imperishable (1 Corinthians 9:25). In the earthly race, only one person wins the first prize (1 Corinthians 9:24); in the heavenly race, everyone who loves the appearing of Christ is a winner (2 Timothy 4:8). On earth the fastest wins, while in heaven the winner becomes whoever remains on the course, in spite of the time one begins or ends, or at what pace the race is run.

15 Let us therefore, as many as be perfect, be thus minded: and if in any thing ye be otherwise minded, God shall reveal even this unto you. 16 Nevertheless, whereto we have already attained, let us walk by the same rule, let us mind the same thing.

Using the first person plural, himself included, Paul calls on every believer to do likewise, to think in the same terms with the same spiritual ambition and goal. He longs that they also strive earnestly and persevere consistently to the end in order to attain the same prize. "Let us therefore" is language of appeal; and Paul, including himself, shows again the spirit of humility, which pervades this book, which he exemplifies throughout. He puts himself on the same level with the Philippians as his brethren (vv. 13, 17), and now as those who are "perfect." The word perfect, *teleios* (**tel'-i-os**), the noun form of *teleioo* (v. 12), does not mean sinlessness, or complete in ethical goodness. Rather it means perfect as in mature, or full grown in the knowledge of Christ, not children but those who have been thoroughly instructed and experienced in the ways of Christ (1 Corinthians 2:6; 14:20; Ephesians 4:13; Colossians 1:28; etc.).

Paul urges them "to be thus minded," *phronoe* (see 2:2-5), that is, to set their minds on the same things as he does, to imitate his example, on the things which are behind and stretch or pursue forward towards the mark for the prize. He then commits them to divine revelation and instruction. He says, "If in any thing ye be otherwise minded, God shall reveal even this unto you." That means if any of you is in doubt of anything or not sure of your understanding of Christianity, or still has doubts about the Jewish ordinances, God will "reveal" the truth to you. Reveal is the Greek word, *apokalupto* (**ap-ok-al-oop'-to**), to take off the cover, i.e., disclose what was before unknown. The particle *plen* (v. 16), translated "nevertheless" here, which also means besides, moreover, or in any case, is used as a break in the sentence in order to emphasize an important truth. Here

Paul urges them (including himself) to let their conduct be consistent with the level of understanding to which they have attained. Whatever level that may be, Paul says, "Let us walk by the same rule, let us mind the same thing," stressing the importance of harmony and mutual cooperation, in spite of individual opinions on things. The phrase "let us walk," Greek *stoicheo* (**stoy-kheh'-o**), to march in a row or in orderly ranks as in the military, to keep in line. That means to conform to the standards, or laid down principles, which God has established.

17 Brethren, be followers together of me, and mark them which walk so as ye have us for an ensample.

For the third time here in this chapter Paul refers to the Philippians as "brothers" (cf. vv. 1, 13). He calls on them to "be followers together of me," i.e., they should imitate him. The Greek used only here in the New Testament is *summimetes* (**soom-mim-ay-tace'**) literally fellow-imitator, or a co-imitator. It has the same use of the Greek word *mimtes* in Ephesians 5:1 where Paul calls on the church to imitate God as children do their parents, and in 1 Corinthians 11:1 he appeals to the believers in Corinth to imitate him as he imitates Christ. Here he calls on them to join together as a community of believers to imitate the examples he has set before them. The call for joint-imitation signifies Paul's emphasis on corporate life and harmony in doing things together.

Paul urges them not only to imitate him, but also to "mark them, which walk so as ye have us for an ensample." The Greek word *skopeo* is the verb "mark" (**skop-eh'-o,**), and is translated to observe, to contemplate, to fix one's eyes upon, or to direct one's attention to. It has the same idea of focusing on the finishing line or mark (v. 14) on which the athlete fixes his eyes as he runs. Paul does not think himself as the only example, or as a unique person who is the ultimate model for Christian living. There are others as well whose lives are consistent with the Christian principles. Their daily lives and conduct model the Christian faith and therefore are worthy of emulation. On these, Paul says, they should fix their eyes. Probably these were some of the Christians who were within their community such as Epaphroditus (vv. 2:25-30) and Timothy whom he promised to send shortly (vv. 2:19-24). They, and Paul, have set an "example," *tupos* (cf. 1 Corinthians 10:6, 11; 1 Thessalonians 1:7; etc.), or "pattern" (Titus 2:7; Hebrews 8:5), for the rest to imitate, rather than focusing their eyes on those who walk contrary to the Christian principles.

18 (For many walk, of whom I have told you often, and now tell you even weeping, that they are the enemies of the cross of Christ: 19 Whose end is destruction, whose God is their belly, and whose glory is in their shame, who mind earthly things.)

With the use of the conjunction *gar*, "for," Paul readily gives us the reason for his urgent appeal to his Philippian friends ("brethren") to imitate him and to closely follow in the steps of some of the leaders like himself who have set good examples. The reason is that there are many "enemies of the cross of Christ" who probably pretend to be Christians but walk contrary to Christian principles. These are definitely teachers whose attitudes and the consequences of their conduct Paul describes thus:

1. They are *the* enemies of the Cross of Christ. Probably they are those who oppose Christ, or whose lives contradict the essence of the Cross and the real meaning of Christianity. Their lives and conduct defame the Cross and defeat the purpose of the death of Christ on the Cross.

2. Their end is destruction, Paul says. They would not go without consequences for their actions, for "their end will be according to their works" (2 Corinthians 11:15), and "death" will be the "fruit" of their wicked lives (Romans 6:21) and the "wages" for their sin (Romans 6:23). The destruction is not immediate, nor would they cease to exist here and now. This is eschatological, an "everlasting" punishment (Matthew 25:46), and "everlasting destruction" meant for "those that know not God, and that obey not the Gospel of our Lord Jesus Christ (2 Thessalonians 1:8-9, NIV).

3. Their God is their belly. "Belly," the Greek word *koilia* (**koy-lee'-ah**), the womb, abdomen or the stomach, is figuratively used here. It means they are gluttonous and unable to control their appetites. These people work not to glorify God, but for their belly (Romans 16:18) and for self-gravitation, what they can gain. Probably these are likened to some present day preachers who preach with the motive of enriching themselves instead of enriching people through the preaching of the Cross and converting people to Christ. They use all sorts of gimmicks and tricks to extort money from innocent adherents for their own good and pleasure, thereby deceiving many. Isaiah calls them "greedy dogs which can never have enough" (Isaiah 56:10-12; cf. Ezekiel 13:19).

4. Their glory is in their shame. That is, they take pride in that which they should be ashamed of. They boast in their evil deeds. Not only do they devise and carry out evil designs, they parade themselves on their conceit.

5. They set their minds on earthly things rather than on heavenly things i.e., they are carnal, therefore, they focus their desire, attention, and energy on things of the flesh (Romans 8:5). Since they are carnally minded they become enemies against God (Romans 8:7), they "are the enemies of the cross of Christ." In his letter to Colosse, Paul supplies us with the earthly things on which they set their minds, namely: fornication, uncleanness, inordinate affection, evil concupiscence, and covetousness, which is idolatry, anger, wrath, malice, blasphemy, filthy communication (Colossians 3:2, 5, 8).

Paul warns them against such people, as he has often done, but with much emotion and pain to the point of weeping. This highlights the importance of the warning and the seriousness of the evil these people perpetrate against the Cross and Gospel of Christ. Surely, Paul's agony stems from his love for the Philippian brethren but with great concern for the plight of those who delight in defaming the Cross. These people are probably the Judaizers who would not accept the Gospel message of the Cross, but opposed the truth and denied it by rejecting Jesus as the Christ the Messiah. Paul is able to vividly describe them because he had been in their position, he had firsthand experience of their opposition to the Gospel and their determination to wipe out the truth of the Cross.

20 For our conversation is in heaven; from whence also we look for the Saviour, the Lord Jesus Christ: 21 Who shall change our vile body, that it may be fashioned like unto his glorious body, according to the working whereby he is able even to subdue all things unto himself.

After passionately warning the church and describing these enemies of the cross, whose minds are set on earthly and carnal things. Paul gives the reason for the warning (vv.18-19) and why the church should imitate him and his colleagues (v. 17). The preposition *gar*, "for," introduces the reason, i.e., "our conversation," *politeuma* (**pol-it'-yoo-mah**), i.e., homeland or citizenship, referred as commonwealth, "is in heaven." By virtue of their redemptive relationship with the risen Lord, Paul reminds the Philippians, whose earthly citizenship with all its privileges were under the Roman empire, that they now belong to a new homeland, the heavenly commonwealth or state. Although they enjoyed the freedom as Roman citizens, their real home is heaven for they have been born from above. It implies, therefore, that they focus their minds on things above and not on things below as the false teachers described above (vv. 18-19) do. Paul qualifies this "new" home as a place

where "we look for the Saviour, the Lord Jesus Christ." The use of "to look for," *apekdechomai* (**ap-ek-dekh'-om-ahee**), means to expect fully, or to eagerly and expectantly wait. The word is used eight times in the New Testament and six of them by Paul (3:20; Romans 8:19, 23, 25; 1 Corinthians 1:7; Galatians 5:5). It speaks of the believers' persistent expectation of the return of the Lord Jesus Christ the hope of every Christian. John says, "Every one who has this hope set on him purifies himself even as he is pure" (1 John 3:3). "Who" here (v. 21) refers to Christ Jesus. He "shall change our vile body." "Change" is *metaschematizo* (**met-askh-ay-mat-id'-zo**) i.e., transform, or transfigure, or refashion all believers. The word "vile body," Greek *tapeinosis* (**tap-i'-no-sis**), describes the lowly nature, the humiliated state of man. It refers to the degenerated sinful state of the human nature as opposed to glorious, immortal and sinless nature of the Creator. This vile body will be refashioned "like unto his glorious body," for we shall all be changed from mortality to immortality; from natural body to spiritual body; from corruptible to incorruptible; from humiliation to glory and power (v. 21; 1 Corinthians 15:53-58). The same power that made all things originally will also transform the resurrection body in a moment (1 Corinthians 15:51) and will subdue all things again to God (1 Corinthians 15:24-28; Hebrews 2:9-18).

DAILY BIBLE READING

M: Don't Be Led Astray!
Philippians 3:1-6
T: The Ultimate Richness: Knowing Jesus Christ
Philippians 3:7-11
W: Press on Toward the Goal
Philippians 3:12-16
T: Our Ctizenship Is IN Heaven
Philippians 3:17—4:1
F: Encourage one Another IN Christ Jesus
Hebrews 10:19-25
S: Hold Fast Your Confidence IN Christ
Hebrews 10:26-39
S: Live a Disciplined Christian Life
Hebrews 12:1-13

TEACHING TIPS

June 25
Bible Study Guide 4

1. Words You Should Know

A. Moderation (v. 5)—King James translation of a word meaning "gentleness" or "forebearance," as translated in other versions.

B. Supplication (v. 6)—To make a humble or earnest request or plea; to pray with humility.

C. Abased (v. 12)—King James translation of a word meaning to be in need; without.

2. Teacher Preparation

Read the background Scripture of today's lesson. Reflect on some personal difficulties you have endured.

3. Starting the Lesson

A. Use a chalkboard or tear sheet and write the words "World" and "Christ" in two separate columns. Ask the class to name some distinct worldly values and some distinctly Christian values. Discuss how these values are in direct opposition to one another.

B. Read today's IN FOCUS story about the writer's grandmother. Ask: Is the ability to look for the best in a situation something that develops as a person grows spiritually, or is it a basic personality trait that one is born with?

4. Getting into the Lesson

Talk about a recent issue that created conflict in your city, community, or even your church. Are there some people, even Christians, still harboring bad feelings? Have some people tried to see good in the situation?

5. Relating the Lesson to Life

A. Review the information about Epaphroditus and Macedonia in today's THE PEOPLE, PLACES AND TIMES article. In what ways might the Libertine mindset have threatened the stability of the early church? Discuss the role Christian friends and supporters in ministry can have in helping us to rejoice, even in difficult times.

B. Give students an opportunity to answer the questions in SEARCH THE SCRIPTURES.

C. Today's DISCUSS THE MEANING highlights the role of the Philippian church in Paul's ministry. Discuss how

helping others may often yield greater blessings for the one who gave the help, not the one who was helped.

D. The LESSON IN OUR SOCIETY focuses on the need for Christians to take a stand for Christ's sake, even if the stand does not have popular appeal. Discuss why many people today, Christians included, are not willing to stand for something that is unpopular.

June 18th

6. Arousing Action

A. Ask members to share what they believe to be some of the more helpful or generous churches in their communities that are known for their programs and other forms of missions support. Evaluate how you believe those churches came to be ones that extend themselves to help and encourage those in need.

B. Based on the instructions given in the MAKE IT HAPPEN section, give class members an opportunity to evaluate and consider the personality of your church. Perceptions of the church may vary. Try to create an atmosphere in which class members feel comfortable talking about the pluses and minuses of your church.

C. Give class members an opportunity to complete FOLLOW THE SPIRIT and REMEMBER YOUR THOUGHTS.

431

REJOICING IN CHRIST

Bible Background • PHILIPPIANS 4:4-20
Printed Text • PHILIPPIANS 4:4-18
Devotional Reading • 1 THESSALONIANS 1:2-10

LESSON AIM

After studying today's lesson, class members should recognize the importance of keeping our minds focused on things that are good so that we do not sow seeds of discontent in our hearts.

KEEP IN MIND

"Rejoice in the Lord always: and again I say, Rejoice" (Philippians 4:4).

FOCAL VERSES

PHILIPPIANS 4:4 Rejoice in the Lord always: and again I say, Rejoice.

5 Let your moderation be known unto all men. The Lord is at hand.

6 Be careful for nothing; but in every thing by prayer and supplication with thanksgiving let your requests be made known unto God.

7 And the peace of God, which passeth all understanding, shall keep your hearts and minds through Christ Jesus.

8 Finally, brethren, whatsoever things are true, whatsoever things are honest, whatsoever things are just, whatsoever things are pure, whatsoever things are lovely, whatsoever things are of good report; if there be any virtue, and if there be any praise, think on these things.

9 Those things, which ye have both learned, and received, and heard, and seen in me, do: and the God of peace shall be with you.

10 But I rejoiced in the Lord greatly, that now at the last your care of me hath flourished again; wherein ye were also careful, but ye lacked opportunity.

11 Not that I speak in respect of want: for I have learned, in whatsoever state I am, therewith to be content.

12 I know both how to be abased, and I know how to

LESSON OVERVIEW

LESSON AIM
KEEP IN MIND
FOCAL VERSES
IN FOCUS
THE PEOPLE, PLACES, AND TIMES
BACKGROUND
AT-A-GLANCE
IN DEPTH
SEARCH THE SCRIPTURES
DISCUSS THE MEANING
LESSON IN OUR SOCIETY
MAKE IT HAPPEN
FOLLOW THE SPIRIT
REMEMBER YOUR THOUGHTS
MORE LIGHT ON THE TEXT
DAILY BIBLE READINGS

abound: every where and in all things I am instructed both to be full and to be hungry, both to abound and to suffer need.

13 I can do all things through Christ which strengtheneth me.

14 Notwithstanding ye have well done, that ye did communicate with my affliction.

15 Now ye Philippians know also, that in the beginning of the gospel, when I departed from Macedonia, no church communicated with me as concerning giving and receiving, but ye only.

16 For even in Thessalonica ye sent once and again unto my necessity.

17 Not because I desire a gift: but I desire fruit that may abound to your account.

18 But I have all, and abound: I am full, having received of Epaphroditus the things which were sent from you, an odour of a sweet smell, a sacrifice acceptable, well pleasing to God.

IN FOCUS

My grandmother, Mama Clara, smiled as my cousin Marjorie complained about a problem at their little church, located in a rural community outside Atlanta. As president of the usher board, she felt caught in the middle of a situation. One member of the usher board, she felt, was being petty and manipulative.

After she related the events to me, I asked Mama Clara (who was then still an usher herself at age 94) how she felt about the situation.

Before she could answer, Marjorie interjected, "Oh, you know Mama," she replied with loving sarcasm. "She's always looking for the good in everybody! She just said, 'Well, maybe she didn't mean it like that.'"

I had to laugh myself because it is, indeed, my grand-mother's way to find the good in every situation, a rare quality among people. It is probably the single-most quali-ty which has earned her a loving place in the hearts of so many people.

THE PEOPLE, PLACES, AND TIMES

EPAPHRODITUS. A common name within the first century Greek-speaking world meaning, "favored by Aphrodite or Venus." He was a friend and co-laborer with Paul (Philippians 2:25). Epaphroditus delivered a gift to Paul from the Philippian church while he was still in prison. While he was with Paul, Epaphroditus became very ill. After he recovered, Paul sent him back to Philippi, urging the church to welcome him with gladness.

Based on information from *Holman Bible Dictionary*, Trent Butler, general editor, Nashville: Broadman & Holman Publishers, 1991, p. 421.

MACEDONIA. Archeological research indicates that Macedonia was settled as early as 1500 B.C., probably by Thracian and Illyrian tribes. The Gospel came to Macedonia through Paul's preaching. He and his comrades sailed to Neapolis, an important port city of Macedonia. Paul also did missionary work in Thessalonica, the capital of Macedonia.

Based on information from *Holman Bible Dictionary*, Trent Butler, general editor, Nashville: Broadman & Holman Publishers, 1991, p. 908.

BACKGROUND

At the beginning of chapter four, Paul goes into detail about a problem he has been alluding to throughout the let-ter. He first laid a careful foundation before approaching the problem directly. He had hinted at grumblings within the body and exhorted them to be of one mind and in full accord.

He specifically addressed the problem of Euodia and Syntyche, two co-laborers who had fallen into discord with one another. But their lack of fellowship with one another was not just confined to the two of them. It was having an effect on the entire congregation.

Paul held the Philippian congregation in his heart with such fondness, it probably pained him deeply to know that they were teetering on the edge of conflict and disharmo-ny. They had proven themselves to be giving and loving. Paul did not want to see that spirit destroyed. With fatherly love, he exhorts them to keep their minds focused on good, not giving undue attention to negative and counterproduc-tive feelings and actions.

The Philippian church was special. They had the poten-tial to do even greater things. Paul knew what would hap-pen if they distracted themselves with negative thoughts, thus giving the devil a chance to move in and destroy the loving spirit which made them so strong.

AT-A-GLANCE

**1. Rejoice in the Lord
(Philippians 4:4-7)
2. Think on Good Things
(vv. 8-9)
3. Contentment in All Situations
(vv. 10-18)**

IN DEPTH

1. Rejoice in the Lord (Philippians 4:4-7)

As Paul continued his letter, he continued to press for self-examination. He did not want those in the Philippian church deluding themselves about their own goodness.

Basically, Paul's letter has a joyous undertone, but the let-ter does deal with some unpleasant matters, such as anxiety, discord, and disunity. The apostle wanted the Philippians to know there was no time to waste with such issues. Those who had fallen into a state of anxiety or disharmony need-ed to examine themselves and be willing to do what was necessary to replace anxiety with the peace of God.

The early Christians believed that the Lord would soon return. Paul did not want believers to be distracted with petty, negative concerns. The joy which accompanies acceptance of Jesus Christ as Lord and Savior should be manifest in believers so that it may be seen by others.

Since they awaited His eminent return, they had no rea-son to be anxious. They should focus all their attention on being prepared for the great event. Paul did not want believers to be consumed or distracted by earthly things.

This does not mean we should treat earthly matters as unimportant. Every Christian has a responsibility to be a good steward of the things of this life. But having anxiety over these things is destructive. It is faithless and fruitless.

Paul said that the safeguard against anxiety is prayer with thanksgiving, living in a state of gratitude for life and for all of the blessings God has to give. When we find our-selves in need, however, we should take our requests to God, through prayer and supplication. The apostle recog-nized the importance of thanksgiving and practiced it in order to deepen his own commitment. The more grateful he was, the more eager he became to regard his life as belonging to Christ.

Paul's use of the word "requests" suggests that we cannot demand from God; we request. Because we have faith in Him, we may simply make a request, knowing that He will do what is best for all concerned.

When we are able to entrust our needs to God through faith, we obtain peace. Through our faith and trust in Him, we receive the peace which He possesses, as we open ourselves to God in thanksgiving and supplication.

The word "guard" is a military term. God's peace protects (guards) us against all threats. This is not to say that this peace will not be challenged under threat, but it will be enjoyed in the midst of war with evil.

2. Think on Good Things (vv. 8-9)

Paul mentioned several virtues which are to be an integral part of the Christian mind: whatsoever is true, honest, just, pure, lovely, and of good report. The Christian mind should be occupied with thoughts that are good.

The apostle was not suggesting, however, that we live in a state of denial about the very real hurts and injustices which are present in this world. It is important to acknowledge the reality of bad circumstances and the pain that they inevitably bring. The term "walking wounded" has often been used to describe persons who hold onto pain and negative feelings, while trying to demonstrate a peaceful countenance outwardly. In order to truly heal and forgive, however, we must first acknowledge the painful feelings. At that point, we can strive to move beyond them to think on that which is "of good report."

The Greek word translated as "think" means "to calculate," or "to reckon carefully." We must weigh carefully and seriously the cost of making a part of our everyday lives the virtues that Paul listed in verse 8.

But thinking on good things is not enough. We must think about them in such a way that we commit them to action. Paul did not stress the gift of salvation to the neglect of its demands. Christianity also means both action and practice.

Paul knew there was discord brewing within the body. He also knew that if they dwelled on those feelings, the situation would only grow worse, not better. Christ Himself warned in Matthew 15:19: "For out of the heart proceeds evil thoughts, murders, adulteries, fornications, thefts, false witness, blasphemies." Paul wanted the Philippians to eliminate any evil thoughts so that they would not be tempted to do evil deeds against one another.

Yet again, Paul offered himself as the example of how to commit faith into action. He showed, in both word and deed, that Christianity is not simply a series of rules; it is a way of life. Once Christ appeared to him, Paul gave up his former life and began to plow the mission field for His sake. He put his faith into action, without regard to what others might have said about him.

Throughout his ministry, Paul demonstrated a dual purpose in his ministry. Not only did he impart knowledge to the Christian community through teaching, but he consistently served as a living human example of faith put into practice.

3. Contentment in All Situations (vv. 10-18)

Paul rejoiced that the Philippians' "care" for him had begun to "flourish" once again. Paul did not mean to infer that they had been neglectful of him or his needs. They had only lacked opportunity. Possibly the Philippians wanted to give to Paul earlier, but lacked sufficient resources. Probably, however, communication with Paul was cut off, leaving them with no knowledge of his whereabouts. Paul had endured a number of imprisonments, shipwrecks and other incidents. More than likely, they were always concerned about him, but had only recently the opportunity to demonstrate that concern.

After expressing his appreciation, Paul turned to the matter of his own sufficiency and his source of strength. He obviously wanted to assure the Philippians of both his gratitude and independence. Through his varied experiences, Paul has learned to be content "in whatsoever state."

When he wrote this letter, Paul was an old man, at a time of life when he probably realized that he brought nothing into this world and would take nothing with him. Paul was able to look back over his life and determine what was of real importance.

Paul had endured persecution, imprisonment, and various states of danger and distress. Through all his ups and downs, the Lord had provided for him and he was able to endure. Probably because he was now older, his level of trust in the Lord was at its highest. Knowing that he was always cradled in the arms of the Master, Paul had learned to content himself in all circumstances. In Christ, Paul discovered the source of his strength. Christ had empowered him to both endure and prosper.

The Philippian church had proven themselves to be both friend and supporter of Paul through difficult times. They were willing to help him when no one else would, not even other churches. They had helped him materially, but they had done something more. The Philippian congregation had entered into fellowship with Paul, sharing in his suffering by becoming a partner with him.

Paul sought nothing from them, yet they extended themselves to him anyway. He was not seeking a gift. Rather he sought to add fruit to their account. Paul used terms that were common to the commercial field to describe what happened. The word translated as fruit can be understood as "credit" or "interest." Paul's desire was that spiritual gain would be added to their "account." Whether he wanted to receive was not important. What was important was their desire to give and to aid in the spreading of the Gospel.

Because of their generosity of spirit, Paul had received far more than he needed, but not just in material gifts. The Philippians had become as an "odor of a sweet smell" to Paul, and one which was pleasing to God. Through their gifts, they had extended themselves in sacrificial service, demonstrating the essence of the "mind of Christ."

Paul was certain that God would supply their every need, just as they had so willingly given of themselves to supply Paul's needs. Because of their generosity, they would be blessed. Most likely, Paul had in mind blessings of the spirit as well as material blessings. God would bless them with peace and harmony among themselves. He would enable them to experience fulfillment and His immeasurable "riches in glory by Christ Jesus."

SEARCH THE SCRIPTURES

1. In what manner should we make our requests known to God? (Philippians 4:4)

2. What things, according to Paul, lead to God's peace? (vv. 4-7)

3. As Christians, in what direction should our minds be set? (v. 8)

4. What did Paul suggest that the Philippians do? (v. 9)

5. For what reason had the Philippians given Paul to rejoice? (v. 10)

6. How had Paul learned to adjust to life's circumstances? (v. 11)

7. By what power was Paul confident he could do all things? (v. 13)

8. Who shared in Paul's ministry from the beginning? (v. 15)

9. Who received the benefit of the Philippians' gifts to Paul? (vv. 15-17)

10. What did Paul believe God would do for the Philippians? (v. 18)

DISCUSS THE MEANING

1. The Philippian church was generously supportive of Paul from the beginning. Why were they willing to partner with Paul when other churches were not?

2. How did the Philippians' partnership with Paul benefit their own congregation?

LESSON IN OUR SOCIETY

Paul stuck to his mission of spreading the Gospel no matter what. He learned to rejoice in the Lord no matter what his outward circumstances. He remained loyal to Christ and loyal to his commitment to serve Him.

Likewise, the Philippian church was willing to be a partner with Paul and stand by him through good times and bad. That level of commitment is a rare find, even within the Christian community. Paul was an unpopular figure among many circles, but apparently that didn't matter to the Philippians.

Today's Christians, and the churches where we worship, must be committed to what is right, even when that commitment links us to unpopular persons or positions. We cannot simply follow Christ when times are good and plentiful. Instead, we must hold fast to what Paul taught in Philippians 4:13, "I can do all things through Christ which strengtheneth me."

MAKE IT HAPPEN

Paul's letter to the Philippians, as well as some portions of the Book of Revelations, help us to understand that churches have personalities, just like people.

Make a personality profile of your church. What are its strengths and weaknesses? How did those strengths/weaknesses develop? Has the personality of the church changed from what it once was? What persons and/or factors (either past or present) contribute greatly to the shape of the church's personality?

FOLLOW THE SPIRIT

What God wants me to do:

_____ _____

_____

REMEMBER YOUR THOUGHTS

Special insights you learned:

_____

_____

MORE LIGHT ON THE TEXT
PHILIPPIANS 4:4-18

Paul begins the concluding chapter of his letter to Philippians with the conjunction *hoste*, "therefore" or "so then," which indicates a connection with the proceeding thought of the last chapter. There, Paul has stated that the true believers' homeland or citizenship is in heaven and not on earth, where we await for the glorious return of the Lord Jesus, where we will be changed and transformed in the likeness of His glorious body. "So then," i.e., "with this in mind," Paul urges them, using intimate, loving and endearing adjectives, to stand firm in the Lord, letting nothing sway them from their firm grip on the Lord (v. 1). He then entreats two of the members (women), who probably had some misunderstanding, to resolve their problem and to "be of the same mind in the Lord." He also solicits the help of a third party, whom he called "yoke-fellow," to assist these gospel-women to reconcile their differences.

4:4 Rejoice in the Lord always: and again I say, Rejoice.

After briefly addressing the situation between the two women, Euodia and Syntyche, Paul seems to return to the thought of verse 1 in which he calls on the Philippians to stand firm in the Lord. With an imperative, as if commanding the Philippians, Paul says to them, "Rejoice in the Lord always: and again, I say, Rejoice." It sounds as if Paul is telling them that the best way to stand firm in the Lord is to "rejoice in the Lord always;" that joy is the foundation for a firm grip on the Lord; the cord by which we hold onto the Lord. That means that the Philippian church should let the joy of the Lord reign within them; they should let joy be the force that controls them in every circumstance and situation of their lives.

The verb "rejoice" is the translation of the Greek word *chairo* (**khah'-ee-ro**), which means to be cheerful, i.e., calmly happy, or be glad to be well or thrive. It was used as a form of salutation in the ancient Greek as "Hail!" It also was used as an opening and closing salutation in letter writing. Hence, it has been suggested that Paul's usage of the word here could be both as a farewell "parting benediction" as well as an exhortation to be cheerful. *Chairo* is from the noun *chara*, or joy, cheerfulness, calm, or delight. Joy is defined as a "positive attitude or pleasant emotion." It is an attitude and state of pleasure, contentment, cheerfulness, and gladness. Joy is used in a variety of ways in the Bible to describe the disposition of different people. For example, the wicked are said to experience joy in their triumphs over the righteous (1 Corinthians 13:6; Revelation 11:10).

However, the joy which God's people have is holy and pure; it rises above circumstances and centers on the very character of God. The psalmist, for example, rejoices over God's righteousness (Psalms 71:14-16), salvation (21:1; 71:23) and mercy (31:7). He rejoices also over God's creation (148:5), His word (119:14, 162), and His faithfulness (33:1-6). The acts and characteristics of God motivate a lasting and indelible joy in the inner being of the child of God. This type of joy, which is required of the saints, is the product or fruit of the Holy Spirit of God (Galatians 5:22). It looks beyond the present to the future salvation of all believers (Romans 5:2; 8:18; 1 Peter. 1:4,6). This kind of joy is different from sheer happiness, which is prompted or dictated in most cases by situations, events or mood.

Oftentimes happiness lasts for the moment and is short lived. The joy Paul is referring to is neither dependent on the circumstances at hand, nor is it dependent on the present mood of the individual. It is always present, even in the midst of sorrow (1 Corinthians 12:26; 2 Corinthians. 6:10; 7:4). Hence, Paul exhorts them to rejoice always in the Lord. To the ordinary person, even a Christian, Paul's appeal here does not seem to make sense. How can one rejoice "always," under all circumstances, no matter how trying? Do we have to rejoice even in difficult times when dear ones are suffering or sick, when we lose dear ones, or when one is facing persecution or possible death? To urge the church to rejoice always is paradoxical, to say the least.

Paul must have sensed the questions, and has envisaged the reaction of the Philippians when they read this letter, so he repeats himself "and again I say rejoice." He says in effect, "It is no misprint or mistake. I know and mean what I am saying: Rejoice!" Here is Paul, in prison under the strict guard of the Roman *praitorion* (see commentary on 1:13-41), unsure of his future outcome, whether he would be freed or not (1:20-23), whose friends are also suffering (1:29-30), yet he rejoices and urges others to do the same. Here is a perfect example that circumstances alone do not determine and should not dictate the disposition of a person's heart and mind, that a Christian can be joyful inwardly even when outwardly everything looks dark and dreary. The wise man says, "A merry heart doeth good like a medicine: but a broken spirit drieth the bones" (Proverbs 17:22).

Paul, in this exhortation, gives us the nature of the "rejoicing" or the joy—not an abstract joy that has no foundation—but rather it is a joy that is found in Christ the Lord. It is made possible by virtue of our oneness and relationship with the Lord; it is the fruit that is harvested because of our union with Him through the working of the Holy Spirit (Galatians 5:22). For Paul, there are many reasons for joy (see Hendriksen, p. 193), and it is not unnatural or irrational for him to call, or for a better word, "persuade" the Philippians to rejoice in the Lord always. He calls on them to cultivate the spirit of joy.

It is important to understand this joy. Although it is indescribable, it is full of glory, majestic, and affective. It is the type of joy that is communicable and infectious; it sustains even the most sorrowful, and the most heartbroken. It was what sustained our African slave fathers in the tobacco farms. They were brutally treated, tortured, and forced into hard labor by their taskmasters. Theirs was never a happy situation, nor did it call for merriment. It was, indeed, an inhumane and deplorable situation, and yet it was at these farms that most of the "Negro Spirituals" were composed and sung.

We recall that it was at Philippi that Paul and Silas were tortured and humiliated and thrown into jail because of the Gospel during Paul's "Second Missionary Journey." According to Luke's account they were put into the inner cell, their feet fastened in the stocks. Rather than moaning and lamenting their situation, or blaming anyone for their calamity, they burst out into prayer and praise to the Lord. Their chains loosened. Other lives were affected. The jailer and members of his household were converted. Thus, the Philippian church was established (Acts 16:19ff.). Paul was therefore speaking from personal experience, which was familiar to the Philippians. No wonder he calls on them to rejoice in the Lord.

5 Let your moderation be known unto all men. The Lord is at hand.

They are not only to rejoice, but that joy must be reflected through their lives with Christian character. This Christian quality should be evident in such a degree that others, not only fellow Christians, will be able to see and recognize it in them. The word "moderation" is the Greek word *epieikes* (**ep-ee-i-kace'**), translated in various ways as mildness, kindness, gentleness, sweet reasonableness, magnanimity, (see Hendriksen, p. 193) and patience. Most scholars have concluded that there is not a single word in the English language that would fully express the meaning of the Greek word *epieikes*. It, however, appears in a number of places in the New Testament (1 Timothy 3:3; Titus 3:2; James 3:17;1 Peter 2:18). It is the Christian quality, which keeps a person from insisting on his full rights, but considers and respects others, an attitude that was found in Christ Jesus (2 Corinthians 10:1). It is found in a heart that is reserved in joyful gratitude to the Lord, a heart of peace and tranquillity.

After urging them to show their inward Christian gentleness outwardly, Paul interjects with the phrase, "The Lord is at hand (or near)." What does Paul mean by this phase? There are two possible interpretations. The first could be that the Lord is present with them, and therefore aware of their conduct, and concerned about their attitude. He watches over us. The second possibility is that the return of the Lord is near. The Bible speaks extensively of the Second Coming of the Lord. Every true child of God looks forward to the glorious return of our Saviour and Lord. It is the hope of everyone who believes. He is coming to reward the faithful and punish the wicked, "to heal all ills and to right all wrongs." It is therefore, not only a reason for sanctification (letting our moderation be evident to all), but also a motivation for joy and rejoicing even in the presence of difficulties and afflictions (Romans 5:2-5; 8:18ff; Galatians 5:5). It is probable that Paul, by using this rare Greek word *eggus* (**eng-goos'**), includes both ideas here. The Lord, whose second return is imminent, is the same who came and dwelt among us and who is with us in Spirit (John 14:12; 16-18; 16:12-13; Romans 8:9-11; 2 Corinthians 3:17-18).

6 Be careful for nothing; but in every thing by prayer and supplication with thanksgiving let your requests be made known unto God.

Paul continues with another imperative, "Be careful for nothing," which means "do not worry about anything." The verb "careful," *merimnao* (**mer-im-nah'-o**), used here in a negative connotation, is also translated anxious, to be anxious about something. But it has a positive and favorable undertone in 2:20, "have care" where Timothy shows a genuine concern for the welfare of the Philippians (cf. 1 Corinthians 7:32-34; 12:25). Here Paul echoes the teachings of Christ as recorded in the Gospels (Matthew 6:25-34; Luke 12:11, 22-26). Jesus says not to entertain worry, or be overly concerned about things, such as food, housing, clothing, or any other necessities of life. He assures us that our Father in heaven is aware of these needs and that He will supply them. Therefore, says Jesus, "Seek ye first the kingdom of God and its righteousness" and God will take care of the rest. That is the cure for anxiety.

Likewise, in a different way but with the same idea, Paul says that the cure for anxiety is prayer. He continues, "but in every thing by prayer and supplication with thanksgiving let your requests be made known unto God." Paul is quite aware of the persecution the Philippians were facing (cf. 1:28), with himself in a Roman prison. He is, therefore, not making light of the situation. Rather he is letting them know that it is of no use for one to carry one's burdens by oneself, but to bring them to the One who is greater than all their problems, and lay them before Him. He will take care of all things that worry us (cf. Psalm 55:22; 1 Peter 5:7; 1 Corinthians 7:32).

We notice that Paul says in "every thing," i.e., in all things, no exception, they include all aspects of human needs: physical, material, spiritual, emotional, and psychological they should be brought to the Lord. Using three synonyms: "prayer," *proseuche* (**pros-yoo-khay'**), "petition/supplication," *deesis* (**deh'-ay-sis**), and "request/petition," *aitema* (**ah'-ee-tay-mah**), Paul strongly urges the Philippians to tell the Lord their story in order to release themselves from anxiety. In effect, Paul says with "prayer and more prayer" we should let God know what we need by talking with Him, directing our plea to Him, and making our requests known to Him. He is the One who created us, knows us, can hear us, understand and care for us better than any one else; He is the One who can give rest to a heavy heart and soul (Matthew 11:28-29).

Notice again how this prayer is to be made with "thanksgiving," that is, with a heart of gratitude towards God (cf. 1:12-18; 2:17-18). Praying with thanksgiving is not mentally denying the reality and true nature of our situation (shutting them out of our memory); it is recognizing and accepting their presence. Instead of seeing them as problems and obstacles, we see them as opportunities and stepping stones through which God works out His purpose. It is thanking God for them, and handing them over to Him with a grateful heart. It is realizing the power and efficacy of God's grace to deal with our problem, and then surrendering everything with confidence into His care. Andrae Crouch once sang something like this, "If there is no problem, how can I know that He's gonna solve it?" This may not be a direct quote, but the idea is clear. Problems exist because there are solutions. "If there is no testing, there will be no testimony," said another preacher. We may not be happy with what we are going through, but we can be thankful to God for realizing that He is able to take care of it. With this we can rejoice (v. 4) and be thankful to God always.

7 And the peace of God, which passeth all understanding, shall keep your hearts and minds through Christ Jesus.

The result of all this is: "the peace of God." The conjunction "and" (Greek, *kai*) can also be translated "then." We notice that Paul has used imperatives in the immediate preceding three verses to exhort the Philippians, "Rejoice always in the Lord . . . Let their moderation be known . . . Be careful for nothing; but by prayer . . . let your request be made known to God," without any conjunction (vv. 4-6). So "and" joins them to the thought that follows. That is, if they keep these "commands" already mentioned, "then" they will experience or inherit the "peace of God," not in a conditional sense, but as a result of consequence. What does Paul mean by the phrase "peace of God?" Does he mean the peace with God that believers have the moment we receive our sins forgiven and are justified before Him by faith in Christ Jesus? Alternatively, is Paul referring to "the peace of God," the inner peace of the soul that comes from God, peace that is founded in His presence and promises to us?

"The peace of God" probably refers moreso to the tranquillity that is characteristic of and is resident in God Himself, which believers can share with and inherit from Him. The word "peace" is a translation of the Greek *eirene*, pronounced **i-ray'-nay,** with the idea of quietness, rest or prosperity. It is used to describe the state of tranquillity between nations, the harmony, and concord between individuals. It also has the sense of security and calmness of the soul based on the assurance and confidence that God "who hath begun a good work in you will perform it until the day of Jesus Christ" (1:6); that He "is able to do exceeding abundantly above all that we ask or think, according to the power that worketh in us" (Ephesians 3:20). It is the conviction that "He that spared not his own Son, but delivered him up for us all, how shall he not with him also freely give us all things?" (Romans 8:32). It is a reflection on the goodness and faithfulness of God.

Paul says that this "peace of God," which appears only here and in Colossians 3:15, passes "all understanding." That means this divine peace is above or beyond human intelligence; the human "understanding," *nous*, cannot fully comprehend it. The *nous* comprises the faculties of perceiving, understanding and those of feeling or determining, the intellectual faculty. The idea here parallels Paul's assertion in Ephesians 3:18-19, where he says that Christ's love surpasses all knowledge, that believers will never be able to measure the breadth, length, height, and depth of the love of Christ to them. Just as the love of Christ is unfathomable by the human mind, so is the "peace of God." The believer by nature cannot fully grasp the beauty of this gift from God. It is indescribable! It is beyond all human imagination.

This indescribable peace has a definite and important function: it "shall keep *[phrourein]* your hearts and minds through Christ Jesus," Paul says. The verb *phrourein*, or

phroureo (**froo-reh'-o**), is a military term, which means to mount a guard as a sentinel, to protect. The picture here is that of a detachment of soldiers standing on guard over a city to protect it from hostile invasion, or to prevent the inhabitants of a besieged city from flight. The Philippians at Paul's time were familiar with the presence of Roman garrisons; thus they would understand and appreciate Paul's use of this metaphor. That is, "God's peace, like a garrison of soldiers, will keep guard over our thoughts and feelings so that they will be as safe against the assault of worry and fear as any fortress" (see Hawthorne, p. 185).

Paul's use of the "heart," *kardia*, and mind, *noema*, refers to the total being of the believer, his thoughts, feelings, affections, desires, and passion. The peace of God will garrison the Philippians' (indeed all believers') thought-life "through Christ Jesus," Paul says. It is another way of saying that this peace is reserved only for those who are in Christ Jesus; it is for those that have established a relationship with Christ through His redemption. In other words, this peace is made available to them because of their union with Lord Jesus on the basis of the death and resurrection of Christ.

8 Finally, brethren, whatsoever things are true, whatsoever things are honest, whatsoever things are just, whatsoever things are pure, whatsoever things are lovely, whatsoever things are of good report; if there be any virtue, and if there be any praise, think on these things. 9 Those things, which ye have both learned, and received, and heard, and seen in me, do: and the God of peace shall be with you.

In verses 8 and 9, Paul urges the church to live by Christian virtues and integrity. Using the same word "finally" (*loipon*) again (3:1), which also can mean beside or furthermore, i.e., in addition to, or moreover. It also probably signifies that Paul is now concluding his letter. Whatever the rendering of *loipon*, with the combination of Paul's favorite endearment reference to the Philippians "brethren" (*adelphos*, singular; 1:12; 3:1), this indicates how important is the exhortation that follows and how serious they must take it. It is Paul's special way of calling their attention to something of grave importance to him and of great benefit to the people whom he loved very much.

Here he says that they should occupy their minds with thoughts of things or virtues that are consistent with Christian living. It seems to me that Paul is saying to the Philippians, "Instead of allowing the worries of this world to overtake you or instead of focusing on your problems [v. 6a], you should rather meditate on those things that enhances a Christian. This is possible through prayer [v. 6b], and the resultant peace of God will guard your hearts and minds [v. 7] from focusing on or allowing problems to deny you of such a Christian life." What are those things they should meditate on? Paul sets for six things:

1. Things that are true, *alethes*, i.e., things that are in harmony with the Gospel and eternal truth. True here is the opposite of falsehood (Ephesians 4:25), put here probably because of the false teachers described as "enemies of the cross" (3:18-19). They are to hold to and meditate on the truth that sets people free (John 8:32), the eternal truth in creation and revelation (2 Timothy 2:15; 3:16-17).

2. Things that are honest, *semnos*, i.e., all that is grave, decent, and honorable (1 Timothy 3:8-11; Titus 2:2). This speaks of personal integrity, whatever becomes you as men and women of honor and as Christians.

3. Things that are just or righteous, *dikaios*, i.e., all that is in harmony with justice, uprightness or righteousness in God's sight (Romans 3:24-31; 8:4; 2 Peter 1:4-10). Things that are acceptable to God.

4. Things that are pure, *hagnos*, i.e., all that is chaste and holy in reference to the body and soul, a pure and spotless life, clean and modest (Romans 12:1-2; 1 Corinthians 3:16-17; 2 Corinthians 7:1).

5. Things that are lovely, *prosphiles*, i.e., all that is good and pleasing in itself and has usefulness to blessing others. It has to do with our conduct or conversation and has the idea of kindness towards others (1 Corinthians 13:4-8; Galatians 5:22-23).

6. Things that are of good report, *euphemos*, i.e., whatever things are reputable, and in harmony with the best for public good and benefit (Romans 13:1-10; 2 Peter 1:4-10).

Paul concludes the list, "If there be any virtue, and if there be any praise, think on these things." Paul's use of "if" and "any" tends to signify inclusiveness; he does not want anything left out of the list, and he seems to leave the Philippians to add to the list any other Christian virtue he may have omitted. In others words, Paul is saying if there are other "virtues" or other things that are praiseworthy, that merit praise or are approved of by God, they are to "think on those things" as well.

The word "think," *logizomai* (**log-id'-zom-ahee**), has a number of translations in English: to meditate on, to ponder, or to compute. It also has the idea of esteeming or judging and to take account of, etc. That means that the Philippians are to esteem highly those characteristics listed above, plus other virtues not listed, as part of Christian living. They are not only to consider, or ponder over them, they are to follow them up with action. How can they follow them up? By following his examples. There are four ways by which the Philippians have witnessed Paul's life that would stimulate them to action.

Firstly, Paul insists that they hold fast to those things which they have "learned," *emathete*, through Paul's and others' teaching. "Those things" include the list in verse 8 and probably more that are not listed. Paul told the Ephesians: "I kept back nothing that was profitable unto you, but have shewed you, and have taught you publicly, and from house to house, testifying both to the Jews, and also to the Greeks, repentance toward God, and faith toward our Lord Jesus Christ" (Acts 20:20-21).

Secondly, they must act on or put into practice the things they have "received," *paralambano*, from Paul. The word *paralambano* in this context refers more to the receiving of something (tradition) transmitted with the purpose of passing on to others, most probably by oral transmission. Paul, in effect, is saying that he not only passed on to the Philippians things that he received through revelation, but also those elements of Christian tradition that had been handed down to him through the teaching of others (1 Corinthians 15:1-5). He expects the Philippians not only to receive it, believe it, act upon it, but also to pass it on to others (see Hawthorne, p. 189), just as he is doing even through this letter.

Thirdly, they are to act on the things they have "heard," *ekousate* (plural) from the verb *akouo*, to perceive through the ear what has been announced. What they have "heard," does not seem to refer to what Paul taught them, or the tradition he had passed on to them, for that would be repeating himself. It probably refers to what they have heard spoken about Paul, his character, and the type of person he was, his lifestyle, which he also had modeled to them.

Fourthly, they are also to do what they have "seen" in Paul. Here Paul is saying that our life should be consistent with our teaching. We cannot teach or preach one thing and do another, Paul seems to say. Thus he tells them to act not only on what they have learned through his teaching, the Christian tradition he has handed down to them, or what they heard others say about him, but to put to practice the very type of life they have seen and witnessed in him. One wonders how many of us, preachers today, who can boldly and unashamedly like Paul say to our audience "Look to me. Follow my example or imitate me" (3:17; 1 Corinthians 11:1) and "what you have seen in me do." I remember vividly growing up as a child in the village where the common cliche of most preachers in our local Methodist Church was "do as I say, and not as I do." Although it was a humble way of telling us that "none is righteous" not even the preacher, only Christ and God, it, however, gave me a great concern and left me with questions about Christianity and the essence of the preaching.

Contrary to the contemporary preachers, Paul is neither embarrassed nor arrogant to call on the people to follow or imitate him. Imitating Paul does not necessarily involve living a holy or perfect life (he constantly has disclaimed that 3:12), but by living a worry-free life, a life of prayer guarded by the peace of God (vv. 6-7). It is living a life filled with thoughts of things that are true, good, lovely and honest, and acting on them. Then the "God of peace" will be with them. The phrase, "God of peace" (*ho theos tees eireenees*) means that God is the author, originator, or the source of peace. It could also mean that God is characterized by peace.

In verse 7, Paul says that the peace of God will guard their minds, here (v. 9) he says the very "God of peace," i.e., God Himself, will be with them. Paul, whose life had constantly been bombarded with all kinds of problems and difficulties (cf. 2 Corinthians 11:23-33), found solace in the "God of peace" experientially. Thus, he can write the same phrase to others who are experiencing similar and various kinds of difficulties. Hence he constantly prays, "The God of peace be with you" (Romans 15:33; 16:20; 1 Corinthians 14:33; 2 Corinthians 13:11; 1 Thessalonians 5:23; 2 Thessalonians 3:16, etc.).

After the exhortation, Paul turns to another purpose for writing this epistle to the church at Philippi, something domestic. That is to express his gratitude for their generosity and care for his welfare by material giving through Epaproditus (v. 18).

10 But I rejoiced in the Lord greatly, that now at the last your care of me hath flourished again; wherein ye were also careful, but ye lacked opportunity.

The word translated "but" by most translations, which begins this section, is the Greek particle *de* with various renderings, which include now, moreover, and, and also. Here I feel the proper translation is "now then" because it seems that Paul, after dealing with other topics, now comes to the final point of his letter. He is acknowledging the gift the church had sent to him, that it has arrived and been received with thanks. Paul has alluded to their generosity earlier in the letter at which time he expressed his thanks to God on their behalf (1:3,5). After dealing with doctrinal matters that needed great attention, Paul comes back to talk about the gift in detail. A number of reasons have been proposed why Paul delayed the issue until now (see Hawthorne, p. 194). The most rational reason, I feel, is that Paul left it to the end as an appendix to the whole letter, not, however, in any sense of minimizing its importance.

After saying "finally" twice (3:1; 4:8) he adds the issue, as if saying "lest I forget" or as if saying to the people, "I must not forget to thank you for the gift you sent." Whatever the reason may be, Paul tells the church how grateful and joyful he felt upon receiving such a gift from them. He expresses his gratitude by "rejoicing in the Lord greatly." The word "greatly," *megalos* (**meg-al'-oce**), shows the immensity of his joy, a word that is found only here in the New Testament. However, the expression "great joy" is found elsewhere in the New Testament, e.g., Matthew 2:10 (cf. also Luke 2:10; 24:52; Acts 8:8; 15:3). We notice that this joy is "in the Lord," towards God rather than towards the Philippians. He is thankful to God (cf. 1:3), which shows the depth of his feeling and the genuineness of the gratitude.

To say that he rejoices "in the Lord" signifies not only his union with the Lord, but that, "Every good gift and every perfect gift is from above, and cometh down from the Father of lights, with whom is no variableness, neither shadow of turning" (James 1:17). Why is Paul immensely joyful in the Lord? The answer is clear, "That now at the last your care of me hath flourished again." It was not the gift per se, but the attitude of the people in giving, their concern for him, their thoughtfulness towards him. However, this loving concern is expressed in the gift. The sentence here suggests that for some reason the Philippians, for a time, ceased to help or support Paul in a practical or material way, but now their care for him has been revitalized; it has come to life again.

The verb used here, "flourish," means to blossom again, to spring to life again, as plants and flowers spring into life after the winter. Paul uses it metaphorically here to describe the coming to life of their care for him, the joy that it brought to him is similar to the joy that comes in the springtime when we see the fresh flowers and the green leaves coming to life. This seeming drought in their care, Paul recognizes, is not intentional on their part, for indeed they were concerned, but rather they "lacked the opportunity" to show it. The reason for this lack of opportunity is open to speculation.

11 Not that I speak in respect of want: for I have learned, in whatsoever state I am, therewith to be content. 12 I know both how to be abased, and I know how to abound: every where and in all things I am instructed both to be full and to be hungry, both to abound and to suffer need. 13 I can do all things through Christ, which strengtheneth me.

In order to avoid misinterpretation of his intention in expressing his gratitude, Paul quickly adds a disclaimer: "Not that I speak in respect of want." Here Paul is saying in effect that his praise of them for what they have done for him is not a crafty way of saying that he needed more from them, or a subtle way of begging for more charity. His joy must not be construed as based on the material things he received from them, however essential they might be. Rather it is based on his relationship with the Lord. On the contrary, Paul says no matter what circumstances he finds himself, "I have learned . . . to be content." "Content," *autarkes*, means to be satisfied, or self-sufficient or independent of external circumstances. Here Paul is saying that circumstances do not dictate his mood.

It should be noted that Paul's sufficiency is relative, and dependent on his relationship with the Lord. Paul definitely has "learned" this through personal experience (2 Corinthians 11:23-29), and this has molded him to rely constantly on the Lord. Through these experiences, Paul has known what it means "to be abased," *tapeinoo*, i.e., to make low, to bring low or to reduce to a lower level. Symbolically, it means to bring into a humble condition, to humble (Matthew 18:4; 2 Corinthians 12:21) or to abase oneself by humble living. It is the same word used for Christ's self-humbling (2:8). He, therefore, knows how to cope both with riches and with poverty, i.e., in lean times, and in times of plenty how to abound.

Moreover, he continues, "Every where and in all things I am instructed both to be full and to be hungry, both to abound and to suffer need." Here Paul calls to mind his pre-conversion experience as a prominent Pharisee with a bright future. He had all things at his command, all authority, and material things. Yet he lacked the greatest thing— the peace that comes from knowing Christ. Even after his conversion there were moments of refreshing experiences when his physical needs were met (Acts 16:15; 20:11; 28:2). From these experiences Paul has been schooled that "after the drought there is always the rain" as the adage goes. Hence, he is content in all circumstances, in hunger, in want, in plenty, and when he is filled. It does not make any difference to him. He always has that peace of the soul that

emanates from knowing Christ as Lord. This is made clear in verse 13 in these words: "I can do all things through Christ, which strengtheneth me."

Contrary to the secular world view that places man at the center and the master of his own destiny, Paul attributes this soul-sufficiency to Christ as the person who taught him, and who is constantly teaching him, the secret of contentment. Here Paul says that his sufficiency is rooted in the Lord Jesus, for He empowers him and gives him the grace to cope with whatever life brings his way. What does Paul mean "I can do all things"? Does it refer to "all things," *panta*, in general or "all things" with particular reference to the circumstances described in verses 11 and 12? Although *panta* means all things, I agree with Hawthorne that it can be translated within the context. Paul could not have moved from particular to general. Therefore, if one can supply the article *ta panta* to read "all these things," then Paul seems to say "I am able to do all these things, i.e., to handle or cope with every situation that comes my way because of Christ's enabling."

Christ is the one that sustains us in all circumstances. He is the great help in time of need, the great Comforter, and the One who would carry us through all stormy circumstances. That is why Paul was able to write, "Therefore I take pleasure in infirmities, in reproaches, in necessities, in persecutions, in distresses for Christ's sake: for when I am weak, then am I strong" (2 Corinthians 12:10).

14 Notwithstanding ye have well done, that ye did communicate with my affliction. 15 Now ye Philippians know also, that in the beginning of the gospel, when I departed from Macedonia, no church communicated with me as concerning giving and receiving, but ye only. 16 For even in Thessalonica ye sent once and again unto my necessity.

Paul returns now to complete his note of thanks for the gifts he received from the Philippians, a note of thanks he began in verse 10. He begins it with "notwithstanding," *plen*, i.e., nevertheless, yet, or even so. With this Paul does two things. On the one hand, he stresses for the Philippians the fact that he could have survived without their contribution, and on the other hand, he does not want to leave the impression that he did not appreciate their generosity toward him. He did not want them to misconstrue his insistence on contentment and independence as a sign of indifference to the gift and love that they showed him. Indeed, he is very pleased with their gift. Hence, he says, "Notwithstanding ye have well done, that ye did communicate with my affliction." They have done a very noble thing to share in his suffering. Paul goes on to commend them further and gratefully acknowledges that the present gift was a continuation of a series of ways they have shared with him in the Gospel. They have done this since "the beginning of the gospel," that means from the time when the church at Philippi was established. He mentions a specific period when he was forced to depart out of Macedonia (cf. Acts 17:14), when "no church communicated with me as concerning giving and receiving, but ye only." The Philippians also rushed material aid to Paul when they learned of his troubles in Thessalonica. This aid helped him continue his work in other places, e.g., Athens and Corinth (cf. 2 Corinthians 11:8-9).

17 Not because I desire a gift: but I desire fruit that may abound to your account. 18 But I have all, and abound: I am full, having received of Epaphroditus the things which were sent from you, an odour of a sweet smell, a sacrifice acceptable, wellpleasing to God.

Paul comes back repeatedly to make clear his motive for his recommendation and show of appreciation for their gift to him and care for him. First, Paul's motive is negatively stated, "Not because I desire a gift." Paul is very conscious of how the people might take it, or how his critics would interpret his motive. Second, and more importantly, Paul's desire and main motive is positively stated that the Philippians' benevolence, as fruit, would be an increase to their heavenly account. Here Paul applies agricultural and business terms: "fruit" and "account." The gift is both "fruit," probably referring to the kindness as fruit of the Holy Spirit (Galatians 5:22-23), and an investment that pays dividends. Here Paul gives a clear indication that each man's work on earth means an investment into the heavenly account (Psalm 144:3; Hebrews 13:17; 1 Peter 4:5).

Mankind is either storing up wrath by his evil deeds in the heavenly record (Romans 2:5) or is storing up reward (Romans 14:1-12; 1 Corinthians 3:11-15; 2 Corinthians 5:10; etc.). The Bible teaches that every good or evil deed, a cup of water given or refused, and every motive and intention of the heart will be judged accordingly (Matthew 6:1-18; 10:41-42; 16:27; Luke 6:23,35; 1 Corinthians 3:8-15; 9:17). The wise man says, "The liberal soul shall be made fat: and he that watereth shall be watered also himself" (Proverbs 11:25), and "He that hath pity upon the poor lendeth unto the Lord; and that which he hath given will he pay him again" (Proverbs 19:17).

Emphasizing the fact that he is not asking for more gifts

from the Philippians, Paul continues, "I have all, and abound: I am full." That means that he has all that he needs and has no desire to expect more from them. He says that he is amply supplied, "having received of Epaphroditus the things which were sent" to him from the Philippian church. The content of this gift is not revealed. It is only speculative to suggest money, reading material, or clothing (cf. 2 Timothy 4:14). Whatever the contents are, Paul describes them as "an odour of a sweet smell, a sacrifice acceptable and well-pleasing to God." Here Paul calls to mind the Old Testament Sacrificial motif. The gift is comparable to the offering of Abel (Genesis 4:4), of Noah (Genesis 8:21), and of the type required by the God of Israel (Leviticus 1:9,13,17). It is also comparable to the believer's dedicated life to God (2 Corinthians 2:15-16), just as Christ did, though in a unique way (Ephesians 5:2). Although the gift was to Paul, it is a sacrifice to God, and its acceptability depends on the motive of the giver. Paul credits them with the proper spirit, which is an attitude of faith, love, and thankfulness to God. Just as Hendriksen concludes, "He (Paul) acknowledges that their deed was not merely an act of sympathy shown to a friend in need but a genuine offering presented to God to promote his cause, and thus to Paul as God's representative! That made the deed so grand and beautiful" (p. 209).

DAILY BIBLE READING

M: Rejoice, and Be Gentle with One Another
Philippians 4:2-7
T: Keeping On in Christ
Philippians 4:8-14
W: Paul's Thanks for the Philippian Church
Philippians 4:15-23
T: Life Among the Early Believers
Acts 2:43-47
F: Paul's Thanks for the Thessalonian Church
1 Thessalonians 1:1-10
S: Lives Pleasing to God
1 Thessalonians 4:1-12
S: Faithfulness Brings Great Joy
3 John 1-8

TEACHING TIPS

July 2
Bible Study Guide 5

1. Words You Should Know

A. Predestinated (v. 5) (or predestination)—Meaning God's work in establishing salvation for us without our prior knowledge.

B. Redemption (v. 7)—To pay the price necessary to secure the release of a convicted criminal and the process involved.

C. Dispensation (v. 8)—A position or area of responsibility for which a person has responsibility for the administration of God's plan of salvation.

2. Teacher Preparation

Read the background Scripture for today's lesson. Find other resources which will teach you more about Christian doctrine, based on the teachings of the Apostle Paul.

3. Starting the Lesson

A. Ask students to ponder the following situation: Suppose a law was passed which required you to renounce Christ in order for you to keep the material things you now have. What would you do? Would you simply pretend to renounce the Saviour in order to keep the things you own? Do you know of any persons who could readily give up Christ to keep their material wealth? How would your life be different if you could not acknowledge your belief in Christ? Would you still feel blessed?

B. Allow students to answer these questions as a group, discussing the impact these circumstances would have upon their daily lives.

C. Read the IN FOCUS story about Karen and Earlene. Discuss why people who place their primary value on material blessings are often left feeling empty and unhappy. Why are people who have peace within themselves often envied?

4. Getting into the Lesson

Gather some articles or brief accounts of rich and/or famous people who gave up the pursuit of worldly fame or wealth as a primary goal in order to find God. Ask class members to share some examples, too. Some examples might include Meadowlark Lemon, Gloria Gaynor, Vanity, Deion Sanders, or Donna Summer.

How do such persons count their lives as more meaningful today?

5. Relating the Lesson to Life

A. Review the information in THE PEOPLE, PLACES AND TIMES article. Discuss why the Ephesians may have needed instruction from Paul concerning spiritual blessings, as they were living in the prospering seaport town of Ephesus where material wealth abounded.

B. Give students an opportunity to answer the questions in SEARCH THE SCRIPTURES.

C. DISCUSS THE MEANING highlights the differences between material blessings and spiritual blessings. Talk about why it is often easier for people to focus on the things we can see. Also discuss how our desire for spiritual blessings often grows deeper as we grow older, and as we mature in Christ.

D. The LESSON IN OUR SOCIETY focuses how we often pursue wealth instead of the things which bless us on the inside. Discuss why Jesus warned against pursuing things which can deteriorate or be stolen instead of treasures which cannot be taken away.

6. Arousing Action

A. Ask class members to think about adverse circumstances which eventually became spiritual blessings. Ask for volunteers to share their experiences with spiritual blessings.

B. Allow members time to think about the things that were most important to them 10 or 20 years ago as they list their spiritual blessings as instructed in MAKE IT HAPPEN.

C. Give the class time to dothe FOLLOW THE SPIRIT and REMEMBER YOUR THOUGHTS sections.

CALLED TO SPIRITUAL BLESSINGS IN CHRIST

Bible Background • Ephesians 1
Printed Text • Ephesians 1:1-14
Devotional Reading • Romans 1:8-17

KEEP IN MIND

"Blessed be the God and Father of our Lord Jesus Christ, who hath blessed us with all spiritual blessings in heavenly places in Christ" (Ephesians 1:3).

FOCAL VERSES

EPHESIANS 1:1 Paul, an apostle of Jesus Christ by the will of God, to the saints which are at Ephesus, and to the faithful in Christ Jesus:

2 Grace be to you, and peace, from God our Father, and from the Lord Jesus Christ.

3 Blessed be the God and Father of our Lord Jesus Christ, who hath blessed us with all spiritual blessings in heavenly places in Christ:

4 According as he hath chosen us in him before the foundation of the world, that we should be holy and without blame before him in love:

5 Having predestinated us unto the adoption of children by Jesus Christ to himself, according to the good pleasure of his will,

6 To the praise of the glory of his grace, wherein he hath made us accepted in the beloved.

7 In whom we have redemption through his blood, the forgiveness of sins, according to the riches of his grace;

8 Wherein he hath abounded toward us in all wisdom and prudence;

9 Having made known unto us the mystery of his will, according to his good pleasure which he hath purposed in himself:

10 That in the dispensation of the fulness of times he might gather together in one all things in Christ, both which are in heaven, and which are on earth; even in him:

LESSON OVERVIEW

LESSON AIM
KEEP IN MIND
FOCAL VERSES
IN FOCUS
THE PEOPLE, PLACES, AND TIMES
BACKGROUND
AT-A-GLANCE
IN DEPTH
SEARCH THE SCRIPTURES
DISCUSS THE MEANING
LESSON IN OUR SOCIETY
MAKE IT HAPPEN
FOLLOW THE SPIRIT
REMEMBER YOUR THOUGHTS
MORE LIGHT ON THE TEXT
DAILY BIBLE READINGS

11 In whom also we have obtained an inheritance, being predestinated according to the purpose of him who worketh all things after the counsel of his own will:

12 That we should be to the praise of his glory, who first trusted in Christ.

13 In whom ye also trusted, after that ye heard the word of truth, the gospel of your salvation: in whom also after that ye believed, ye were sealed with that holy Spirit of promise,

14 Which is the earnest of our inheritance until the redemption of the purchased possession, unto the praise of his glory.

IN FOCUS

Karen's mind drifted off as she sat listening to her Sunday School teacher. She had glanced across the room at Earlene, a woman who intrigued Karen.

Earlene always seemed so peaceful and content with herself, even though she'd had a lot of problems to confront—a husband who'd left her with three small children and no money, a mother who was terminally ill, a lifestyle that was only meager, and a car that could never be counted on to start.

By contrast, Karen and Reggie had every advantage a person could want: a huge home in a trendy suburban neighborhood, two beautiful children, expensive European cars, high-level professional jobs, designer clothes—they were the envy of many people.

Even with all that stuff, Karen lived on the verge of tears. The worst blow came last week when Reggie moved in the spare bedroom. It seemed strange that Karen would envy

Earlene, but Karen sure wanted that inner peace she seemed to have.

THE PEOPLE, PLACES, AND TIMES

REDEMPTION. Paying the price required in order to ensure the release of a convicted criminal. In the early use of the words "redemption," "redeem," or "redeemer" related to legal and commercial matters.

In the Old Testament, the Hebrew word *padah* was used to express the idea of redemption of a person or other living being. Another word *kipper*, or "cover," was used extensively in religious contexts. It is a derivative of the word used in "Yom Kippur," the Jewish Day of Atonement, which is probably the most sacred of all of their holy days.

In the New Testament, all redemption centers around Jesus Christ. He bought the Church with His blood, and lay down His life for His sheep. The New Testament redemption is explained as a sacrifice made through substitution and a demonstration of divine love and righteousness.

Based on information from *Holman Bible Dictionary*, Trent Butler, general editor. Nashville: Broadman & Holman Publishers, 1991, pp. 1170, 1171.

EPHESUS. A seaport town, this city was one of the largest and most impressive of the ancient world. The Romans took control of the city in 189 B.C. Under Roman rule, Ephesus thrived. During the time of Paul's ministry, Ephesus was probably the fourth largest city in the world, having an estimated population of 250,000.

Ephesus was the designated capital of the Roman province of Asia. Ruins of the ancient city revealed the existence of a theater with a seating capacity of 24,000, a library, gymnasiums, a civic center, public baths, and several streets containing private residences. Today, the Turkish town of Seljuk occupies that region.

Based on information from *Holman Bible Dictionary*, pp. 424-428.

BACKGROUND

Paul wrote the letter to the church at Ephesus from a jail cell in Rome, just as he wrote three other epistles while incarcerated: Philippians, Philemon, and Colossians.

Amazingly, Paul wrote to the church at Ephesus about unity—being one in the body of Christ. He begins with a praise doxology on spiritual blessings in Christ. This he did from jail, not some high and lofty place where it's easy to be joyous.

Although it is addressed to the Ephesian church, Paul's letter is applicable to the whole Church.

The Book of Ephesians has been referred to as the "church epistle." At the very beginning, Paul explains an important part of what it means to be a member of the Christian church. He refers to those at the Ephesian church as *saints*. Although it may seem strange to many in the modern church, by Paul's definition, every Christian is a saint. Just as Israel was a holy nation, a nation of "saints," Christians are conferred with the status of saint as members of the "new Israel."

It is perhaps for this reason that Paul places particular emphasis on the unity of the body of Christ throughout the Book of Ephesians.

AT·A·GLANCE

1. Paul's Authority (Ephesians 1:1-2)
2. God Chose Us (vv. 3-6)
3. God's Plan Finished through Christ (vv. 7-10)
4. The Ministry of the Holy Spirit (vv. 11-14)

IN DEPTH

1. Paul's Authority (Ephesians 1:1-2)

Paul begins his letter to the Ephesians by stating his authority through his apostleship. This gave him a God-given authority within the life of the churches. He was appointed by the risen Lord, who made the apostles His representatives, assigned to the task of helping Him lay the foundations of His Church.

The word "apostle" is used to refer to one who has been sent to accomplish a mission, usually meaning the Twelve Jesus commissioned. The term is sometimes used to refer to one who has seen the risen Lord. Paul qualifies his apostleship as not of his own doing. It is the will of God. Paul named himself among the apostles on the basis of his having seen the risen Saviour. Paul did not doubt that his experience was real. At the time of his Damascus Road experience, Paul received a commission. The Lord appointed him to be His servant and missionary to the Gentiles.

His letter is addressed to the "saints" and the "faithful" in Christ Jesus. In the Book of Ephesians, Paul uses these terms in some form 35 times. Both words are rooted in Old Testament usage. Israel was called to be a holy people, faithful in service to the Lord.

"Grace" and "peace" are familiar components of Paul's

prayers. Both Paul's usage of the words and the sequence of the words are important. Grace is God's loving extension of Himself to bring persons back to Him. This was done through His Son, Jesus.

The peace that we receive is the first benefit of our new relationship in Christ.

2. God Chose Us (vv. 3-6)

In Paul's day, there were many, many gods. The pagan world had their own stories about miracles and covenants, many of which paralleled biblical stories. In his opening, Paul clarifies the identity of the God whom they serve.

Paul continues his letter with a doxology in praise of God as the Father of our Lord and Saviour. All spiritual benefits are given to the church which exists and draws its life from its Head. Paul's confidence is rooted in this oneness of Christ with His people.

It is this same God who gives all spiritual gifts to His people. Paul's use of the word "spiritual" to describe God's blessings serves to rectify certain Old Testament thoughts concerning what it means to be blessed by God. In the Old Testament, God's blessings were generally equated with material reward; things that could not be seen or measured were not counted as blessings.

Paul had suffered so much, it would have been easy for his Jewish counterparts to interpret his suffering to mean that he had not been blessed by God. Unlike material blessings, spiritual blessings may come even in the midst of physical suffering. A spiritual blessing is not merely a state of mind. It may come in many forms, such as through the blessing of loving relationships. The phrase "in the heavenly places" probably refers to the highest sense of spiritual blessings. The words "in Christ," or some variant, are used over 30 times in the Book of Ephesians. The phrase carries in it a multitude of meanings. On the one hand, it expresses the realm where God makes His purpose known and effects His will. It also expresses the relationship between Christ and His body of believers, whom He fills with His presence and power. Those who believe in Him share in His glorious life and receive through Him spiritual life.

It can seem overwhelming when we sit back and reflect on the fact that God has chosen us or predestined that we would be saved. One may even ask, "Why me?" God has been compared to a movie director, choosing one actor for a particular role. However, we cannot afford to look at the assurance that we are chosen as an excuse for pride or gloating. Being chosen by God carries with it certain responsibilities, which include being "holy and without blame before him in love." Love is the motive for all that

God does. It led Him to create a plan which would offer salvation to all of humanity.

The plan of salvation we are given by His grace is cause for celebration! He has not given sparingly, but freely. God withholds nothing from His people. He has given to us mightily through His Son, Jesus, whom He loves.

God has adopted each of us. That means that everything that He has, whether it be the cattle on the hills or His glorious throne, everything that the Father has belongs to us. Before we were adopted, we were not God's spiritual children. But God has provided us with an eternal (permanent) home.

3. God's Plan Finished through Christ (vv. 7-10)

The words of John Newton's hymn "Amazing Grace" are truly accurate. When the former slave trader took inventory of the wretched state of his soul, he came to understand grace. Grace had brought him safely to the point of recognizing his pitiful existence, and grace would continue to take him beyond his present state. God's grace is truly amazing!

It is by His grace that we have been redeemed through the blood of Christ. By His grace, through the shed blood of Jesus Christ we also receive forgiveness for our sins.

It has always been God's will that we would be with Him. Sin separates us from Him. Sin is also costly. The only way to be reunited with Him was that someone would have to pay the price. The word "redemption" refers to a sense of having become re-acquired through purchase. We already belong to God by virtue of the fact that He created us. Since we were separated from our Creator by sin, He made a way to unite us with Him once again.

But redemption and forgiveness are only a part of His work. He has given us His grace with all wisdom and understanding. Not only has He given us wisdom, He has lavished it upon us. Nothing is held back in His giving. We serve a generous God.

The Cross is the ground where forgiveness takes place. It is essential to our salvation. But forgiveness for our sins is simply the beginning of our experience with the spiritual blessings God bestows. God has also blessed us to know the "mystery" of His will. This mystery is not a riddle to solve; nor is it knowledge reserved for only a few, as the term was often used in Paul's day. The apostle uses the word to refer to a part of God's will which was once unrevealed. But now He has blessed us to know that which was previously unknown.

The Greek word translated "dispensation" means "house rule." Dispensation refers to God's placement of all of history to fulfill His plan of salvation. God's plan, or "house rule" never changes, but His plan has had distinct phases in history. The death of His beloved Son on the cross signals the completion of that plan. Paul likely uses the term to refer to the time when God will establish His eternal kingdom.

4. The Ministry of the Holy Spirit (vv. 11-14)

God took action to save us in order that we would praise Him, having recognized the greatness of His glory. In verse 12, Paul addresses the mystery with regard to its affect on Jewish believers. He speaks of himself and other believing Jews as those who "first trusted in Christ." The Gospel was first preached to the Jews, who most flatly rejected it. But a godly remnant believed in Jesus as the Messiah. Paul was among that number.

Verse 13 is directed toward Gentile believers, as indicated by the switch of pronouns from "we" to "ye."

Unlike the Hebrew community, the Gentiles had previously had no promise on which to stand. They were not the chosen of God. They had not been prepared for the coming of the Saviour by generations of hope. Paul makes it clear that the promise of salvation is guaranteed for them, too. The evidence of that guarantee being the presence of the Holy Spirit. What greater security can be provided? God's seal is upon us, claiming us as His. That claim is guaranteed by the presence of the Holy Spirit.

It always has been God's will to offer salvation to all of His people. The Holy Spirit serves as an installment on the inheritance we will receive; He is our seal, or guarantee. Interestingly, the Greek word for "seal" was also used to refer to an engagement ring. The Holy Spirit is our evidence of a greater promise to be fulfilled. God guarantees that all believers will receive an eternal home in heaven. Our inheritance is sealed.

SEARCH THE SCRIPTURES

1. Why did Paul identify himself as an apostle? (v. 12)

2. What blessings did Paul attribute to God in this portion of his letter to the Ephesians? (v. 3)

3. Why did God choose us? (v. 4)

4. Why did He predestine us? (v. 5)

5. What blessings has God given us freely? (v. 6)

6. What blessings do we have through Christ? (v. 7)

7. What has God made known to us? (v. 9)

8. When will the dispensation these things occur? (v. 10)

9. What provision did God include for us in His plan? (v. 11)

10. How have we, as believers, been marked? (v. 13)

11. What serves as a guarantee of our inheritance? (v. 14)

DISCUSS THE MEANING

1. Why do you think Paul had to help the Ephesians understand the significance of spiritual blessings?

2. Why are spiritual blessings sometimes more difficult for human beings to appreciate? Why is it often easier for people to get excited about material blessings?

LESSON IN OUR SOCIETY

There is a story about a statue of Buddha which sat in front of a store in China which was frequented by tourists. On the Buddha's stomach was written: "If you want wealth and riches, rub here." On his head was written: "If you want knowledge and wisdom, rub here." The writing on the statue's stomach was nearly worn away, but the writing on its head was very much intact.

In spite of Jesus' teachings about where to store our treasures (Matthew 6:19-21), we seem to focus more on material goods. Very often, spiritual blessings become important only when the pursuit of material wealth leaves us feeling empty. The lives of many of the rich and famous have helped us to see that "money isn't everything."

The only things that can bring us real peace and joy are the things that bring us closer to our Lord.

MAKE IT HAPPEN

Make a list of what you consider to be your most important blessings, things which have enabled you to draw closer to God. How many times have adversities been the "blessings" which paved the way for spiritual growth?

FOLLOW THE SPIRIT

What God wants me to do:

_____

_____

REMEMBER YOUR THOUGHTS

Special insights you learned:

_____

_____

MORE LIGHT ON THE TEXT
EPHESIANS 1:1-14

The first section of Ephesians (1:1-2:10) describes a new life God has given us in Christ Jesus. It clearly can be divided into two parts. The first part (1:3-14) consists of praise in which Paul worships God for blessing us in Christ with every imaginable blessing. In the second part (1:15-2:10) consisting of prayer, Paul asks God to open our eyes that we might apprehend the full reality of this blessing.

1:1 Paul, an apostle of Jesus Christ by the will of God, to the saints which are at Ephesus, and to the faithful in Christ Jesus: 2 Grace be to you, and peace, from God our Father, and from the Lord Jesus Christ.

Conforming to the convention of letter writing of his day, the author begins this letter by identifying himself as Paul. He qualifies himself as "an apostle of Jesus Christ by the will of God." The word "apostle" is derived from the Greek *apostolos*, which means "one sent forth with orders, a delegate, or a messenger." It carries the idea of an ambassadorship in which the one sent represents the sender. From the background of the Old Testament and the Rabbinic Judaism, the term designates someone who is specially chosen and sent out with authority to teach. Here Paul says that he is an apostle of Jesus Christ, thereby claiming the title and authority that Jesus had given to the Twelve (Luke 6:12-13). His apostleship is neither through the appointment of the church, he claims, nor by personal choice or volunteerism, but rather by the will of God.

Therefore, he derived his ministry through (Greek *dia*) the will of God and was commissioned by Jesus Christ. By identifying his person and title, Paul tacitly declares his authority and authenticity as one with the stamp of approval both from God the Father and from the Lord Jesus Christ. The approval of the author authenticates the letter, a letter whose content must be adhered to as coming directly from the Lord Jesus Christ. The letter therefore bears a stamp of authority from Jesus Himself whose ambassadorial authority has been conferred on Paul.

After introducing himself as Christ's own apostle (with equal authority and "rights" with the Twelve) according to the will of God, Paul now names the recipients of this letter, the Ephesian church. He uses a number of titles and adverbs to describe them. First, he calls them saints, from the Greek word *hagioi* (the plural of *hagiois*), which means "holy or the holy one." In its verb form, the word means "to set apart," and the plural noun is translated "set apart ones." *Hagiois* in the Old Testament translates the Hebrew

word *qodesh*, which in its various derivations speaks of holiness, consecration, etc., and the setting apart of something or some person to God (cf. Exodus 2:9, 27, 37, 44; 38:41; Zephaniah 1:7). Israel is called a holy nation only because of God's covenant relationship with them (they have been set apart to belong to Him, Exodus 19:5-6; Leviticus 11:44-45) and not because they are morally pure or innocent. This is applied to the whole Christian community. Here, Paul refers to the whole membership of the Ephesian congregation rather than to a few spiritual elite within the church.

Second, Paul describes them as the faithful, a word that translates from the Greek, *pitos*. It means "trusting" or having faith in the active tense. It gives the idea of being trustworthy or faithful in the transaction of business, the execution of commands, or discharge of duties. Here, and in most passages of the New Testament, it refers to all who have become convinced that Jesus is the Messiah and the author of salvation, and who are generally referred to in the Christian circles as believers.

Third, these believers are in Christ Jesus (*en Christos*). That means that they are engrafted in Christ. This term appears almost exclusively in Pauline writings (c. 64 times) and six times in Ephesians. Paul expresses here the essence of the believer's redemption and relationship with Christ (cf. 1 Corinthians 1:30-31). The question that often arises within the community of scholars is what the phrase "in Christ" means. There are two possible understandings. One being where the word in (*en*) Christ is used in locative sense, and the other where Christ is the source, cause and power of the Christian life (*en* used in instrument). When one believes in Christ, one is united in Him spiritually. Therefore, through Him, the believer lives and moves within the orbit of His will.

Fourth, the saints who are faithfully united in Christ are at Ephesus. This specifies the location of the addressees of the epistle, the city of Ephesus. In the time of the apostles, Ephesus, originally a Greek colony, was a busy commercial port and the capital of the Roman province of Asia. Ephesus was also the headquarters of the cult worship of the goddess Diana (also called Artemis), whose magnificent temple became one of the Seven Wonders of the World (Acts 19:27). Ephesus was one of the cities where the success of Paul's ministry threatened the sale of the silver models of Diana. Consequently, the silversmith stirred up public revolt against him (Acts 19:23ff).

Verse two offers the conventional greeting that characterizes all Pauline letters, "Grace be to you, and peace" (Romans 1:7; 1 Corinthians 1:3; Philippians.1:2, etc.), a form of the contemporary Hebrew and Greek greetings, with Christian flavor. In this opening salutation is the adumbration of the message of the Book of Ephesians. For grace (Greek *charis*), usually defined unmerited favor, indicates God's free, saving initiative in redemption, which He wrought through His Son Jesus Christ. Peace (Greek *eirene* or *shalom* in Hebrew) describes a state of spiritual tranquillity and harmony which a believer enjoys when he or she accepts Christ Jesus as the Lord. It is the result of what the Lord has taken the initiative to do, i.e., to reconcile man to Himself and to one another in the new society He has built through the blood of His Son.

This is the focus of the Book of Ephesians. Grace (found 12 times) and peace (found 7 times) are the key words of the book. Both are used in various forms in the epistle to describe the essence and nature of the Gospel of Christ. In Ephesians 6:15 for example, the Good News is called the "the gospel of peace." In 2:14, Jesus "is our peace" for He has "made peace" through His Cross, and "preached peace" to both the Jews and Gentiles (2:15,17). Therefore His people are "to maintain the unity of the spirit in the bond of peace" (4:3). It is by grace, God's free and undeserved mercy to man, that we are saved (2:5, 7, 8) and through grace that we are gifted for service (4:7; 3:2, 7). In verse 2, Paul wishes his readers the continued unmerited favor of God's mercy and the peaceful tranquillity that emanates from both God our Father, and from the Lord Jesus Christ.

The next 12 verses of this chapter constitute praise and thanksgiving for all the spiritual blessings which the Lord in Christ Jesus has blessed us with (vv. 3-14). It is believed that the original Greek of these 12 verses constitute a single complex sentence. Here is record of the numbers of ways God has blessed those who put their faith in Him.

3 Blessed be the God and Father of our Lord Jesus Christ, who hath blessed us with all spiritual blessings in heavenly places in Christ:

Paul begins by eulogizing the Lord for blessing us with every imaginable blessing in Christ. The word translated "blessed" here (and 40 times in the New Testament) is the Greek word *eulogetos* from the verb *eulogeo*, and it means to praise, or to invoke blessings. It has the idea of speaking well about someone or something and giving a celebration of praise for a favor. In his eulogy for the blessing, Paul innately gives a notation of the Trinity. Here we notice that the source of the blessing is the God and Father of our Lord Jesus Christ, who in verse 2 is our Father as well. The medium of the blessing is God the Son, for it is in Christ, by

virtue of our union with Him, and through Him, that God has blessed us. The nature of this blessing is spiritual, "every spiritual blessing," which may also mean every blessing of the Holy Spirit.

Paul then adds the clause "in heavenly places," the first of the five occasions he uses the expression in Ephesians (1:20; 2:6; etc.). This expression is also unique to Ephesians. What does it mean? The expression does not seem to imply a geographical location, hence it is translated "in the heavenlies." Heavenly places certainly does not mean the sky, but the unseen spiritual realm in which the principalities and power operate (3:10; 6:12). It is also the sphere in which Christ reigns supreme with His people in glory (v. 20; 2:6).

It is interesting to note the description of this blessing where we are blessed with all spiritual blessings, meaning every type of, or as one puts it, every conceivable blessing. When we become believers in Christ, God pours out on us every imaginable blessing of the Holy Spirit. He does not withhold anything from us. These gifts become ours the moment we receive Christ, however, we still have to grow and mature in the image of His Son. The growth and maturity are made possible only by the gift (blessing) of the Holy Spirit.

What are these spiritual blessings, with which God has blessed us in Christ? Paul outlines them in a three-fold period: The past, we "were chosen" before the foundation of the world (v. 4); the present, "we are adopted" in Christ (v. 7); and the future, "we will be unified in Christ" in the fullness of time (v. 12).

4 According as he hath chosen us in him before the foundation of the world, that we should be holy and without blame before him in love: 5 Having predestinated us unto the adoption of children by Jesus Christ to himself, according to the good pleasure of his will,

Paul takes our minds back to eternity, before the foundation of the world, before creation, before time when only God existed. In that eternity, God proposed in His mind to do something that would affect humanity on one hand and His Son on the other. That is, even before we existed, God put us in His plan to unite us with Christ; He chose us in Him.

The verb "to choose" used here *eklegomai* (from *eklego*) is in the perfect tense, which gives the sense of a completed assignment. He chose us to be "holy and without blame before him in love." This statement is very rich theologically. Paul is saying here that God decided before time to make us holy people, people without blame (without spot or wrinkle) totally based on the work of Christ and motivated by His divine love. Thus, holiness is defined through the love of God for His own people. Here is a defense for the proponents of the doctrine of election. We make conscious choices when we accept Christ as our Lord only because in eternity God chose us. Our decision to follow Jesus is just the result of the choice God already made on our behalf before time began. This is the work of grace. It is God's love at work, and therefore there is no room for arrogance or boasting. God declared to Israel that He chose them neither because there was anything special about them, nor anything special they have done above the other nations. He chose them simply because he loved them (Deuteronomy 7:7-8).

Using a different intimate term, adoption, Paul continues to outline the work, which God wrought for us in Christ in eternity. He predestinated us unto the adoption of children. Predestine (Greek *proorizo*) means "to predetermine, to decide beforehand." It means, again reaching into the far past of eternity, God in His infinite nature predetermined to adopt (*huiothesia*) us as His children (Romans 8:15; 23; 9:4; Galatians 4:5). The decision of our adoption into the household of God in Christ was a foregone conclusion, being pre-determined by God before anything happened.

Adoption of children is a common occurrence in our society. People adopt because of various reasons. Some spouses adopt out of necessity because they cannot have their own through natural means. Some adopt out of concern for the welfare of suffering children, especially in troubled areas of the world. Whatever the reason people have for adopting, they have to make that decision even before they see or meet the potential child to be adopted. The child has nothing to do with it.

This is the picture presented here in relation to our adoption. God determined in His heart to adopt us into His fold. The choice is His and we have nothing to do, but to accept the offer. While human beings adopt children for various reasons, God's adoption of us is only motivated out of His love for us, and it is made available through Jesus Christ and according to the good pleasure of His will. Again, this is the work of grace. His good pleasure (Greek *eudokia*) means in His "perfect delight" or "personal satisfaction" and a demonstration of His love.

All this is done before the creation. Our adoption or conversion, we can deduce from this passage, is preplanned and pre-determined by God, according to His will and for His pleasure. It is not a last-minute idea of God, but an ageless strategy by which God determined to save His people.

6 To the praise of the glory of his grace, wherein he hath made us accepted in the beloved.

"To the praise of His glory of grace," is to be understood as to His praise or to his glory. As such, it is a repetition which serves to emphasize the fact that our adoption as God's children is entirely of God, and not of ourselves. It, therefore, invokes our praise for such grace wherein, i.e., by which "he hath made us accepted in the beloved." Here, Paul stresses again the grace through which we receive the gift, and the medium through which it is made possible—the Beloved. The word "beloved" here clearly means Jesus. Although used by Paul to describe fellow Christians, the word applies to Jesus here and in all three accounts of the baptism of Christ in the Gospels (Matthew 3:17; Mark 1:11; Luke 3:22).

7 In whom we have redemption through his blood, the forgiveness of sins, according to the riches of his grace; 8 Wherein he hath abounded toward us in all wisdom and prudence;

The phrase "in whom we have redemption through his blood" definitely confirms who the "beloved" is (modified by whom) Jesus Christ the one whose blood has bought our redemption. This phrase is found also in Colossians 1:14. The word translated "redemption" is the Greek word *apolutrosis*, which means "deliverance procured by the payment of a price." The word is closely associated with "ransom" (*lytron*) found in Mark 10:45, and applied generally to the ransom of slaves. Redemption here is equated with forgiveness, and means that we are rescued from the just judgment of God because of the price God paid, i.e., the blood of Christ. This is done according to the riches of His grace, or according to the richness or abundance of His grace "which He lavished upon us" (v. 8a, NASB). Therefore, the election and adoption are a past eternal privilege made available to us, which are realized through redemption and the forgiveness of sins, a reality we presently enjoy now. All this is made possible through the outpouring of the richness of His grace, which he has lavished on us, demonstrated by the blood of His Son Jesus Christ.

9 Having made known unto us the mystery of his will, according to his good pleasure which he hath purposed in himself: 10 That in the dispensation of the fulness of times he might gather together in one all things in Christ, both which are in heaven, and which are on earth; even in him:

Verse 8b seems to go with verse 9 and starts with "in all

wisdom and prudence." God has not only chosen us in Christ in eternity and has given us the privilege of sonship as a present reality by redeeming and forgiving us, He has also "made known unto us the mystery of his will" for the future. The mystery (Greek *musterion*) means "a hidden thing, a secret, or a hidden purpose, yet to be revealed." Therefore, Paul writes that God, in wisdom and insight had revealed to us His hidden purpose, which He set forth in Christ. What is the secret, which God through wisdom and prudence has revealed to us? The answer is found in chapter 3. It is the engrafting of the Gentiles into God's covenant relationship, and making them stand on equal terms with the Jews in His new society. The present unification of Jews and Gentiles is a token, or foretaste, of the future unity that will be consummated at the fullness of time.

While the unity of the present ethnicity is a shadow of God's proposed plan, the actual plan is that at the fulfilled time, "when time merges into eternity again" (John R.W. Stott), God will unify all things in Him (Christ), things in heaven and things on earth. That means everything both in heaven and on earth will be gathered under the headship of Christ. "To gather" is the Greek word *anakephalaiomai*, which means "to condense" or "sum up." The only place where the word is used is Romans 13:9, where the commandments are summed up in the sentence, "Thou shalt love thy neighbour as thyself." The notion of unifying all things under Christ is found in verse 22, in which Paul writes that God has made Christ the head of all things. As we shall see later in the book, Christ is already the head of the church, which is His body, but at the fullness of time both the whole church (i.e., the church universal) and the created cosmos (universe) will be united under headship of Christ.

11 In whom also we have obtained an inheritance, being predestinated according to the purpose of him who worketh all things after the counsel of his own will: 12 That we should be to the praise of his glory, who first trusted in Christ. 13 In whom ye also trusted, after that ye heard the word of truth, the gospel of your salvation: in whom also after that ye believed, ye were sealed with that holy Spirit of promise, 14 Which is the earnest of our inheritance until the redemption of the purchased possession, unto the praise of his glory.

After outlining the spiritual blessings which God has blessed His people with in Christ, Paul adds that the blessings are equally available both to Jews and Gentiles. Using

the first person pronoun plural (we) and referring to the Jews, Paul says they have obtained an inheritance being the first to trust in Christ according to the will of God. Using the second person pronoun plural (you), Paul writes to the Gentile believers. Although "latecomers," as it were, to believe, they are equally accessible to the promise because of their trust in Him after hearing the Gospel, and are sealed with that Holy Spirit of promise which is the earnest (guarantee) of our inheritance.

Here, Paul begins his theme of reconciling the Jews and Gentiles in Christ, a theme he develops further in the second part of chapter two. The repeated use of the prepositional phrase "in him" (vv. 11, 13) emphasizes that Christ is the one who brings about reconciliation, and the union with Him is what makes all God's people one. All the inheritance and spiritual blessings, past, present, and the future which are made accessible and guaranteed by the seal of the Holy Spirit to both the Jews and Gentiles in Christ Jesus, are for the praise and glory of God (vv. 6, 11, 14). The realization of such blessing and inheritance ought to cause one to shout out in praise and live in constant adoration and glory to the Almighty.

DAILY BIBLE READING

M: God Has Blessed Us in Christ
Ephesians 1:1-6
T: God's Grace Lavished on Us in Christ
Ephesians 1:7-14
W: Paul's Prayer for the Ephesian Christians
Ephesians 1:15-23
T: Called to Belong to Jesus Christ
Romans 1:1-7
F: The Gospel: God's Power for Salvation
Romans 1:8-17
S: Bear the Fruit of the Spirit
Galatians 5:16-26
S: Bear One Another's Burdens
Galatians 6:1-10

TEACHING TIPS

July 9
Bible Study Guide 6

1. Words You Should Know

A. Bowels (Ephesians 2:1)—King James translation for a word meaning "affection" or "tenderness."

B. Esteem (2:3)—Having respect or high regard for someone or something.

2. Teacher Preparation

A. Read the background Scripture for the lesson. After you have studied the lesson, write your own definition of God's grace.

B. Before class begins, think of two or three famous persons who are well known for their self-glorification. Ask class members how they feel about such persons. Should we boast about our accomplishments here on earth? Are there times when it is necessary to boast? Are there times when it is harmful to boast?

3. Starting the Lesson

Read the IN FOCUS story about Carl and Regina. Lead the class in a discussion of the difficulty of blending two previously independent groups, whether they be families, churches, or social groups. What are some ways which help foster a sense of unity and harmony?

4. Getting into the Lesson

A. Pose the following question to your class: "What would you say to God if He asked you, 'Why should I let you into heaven?'"

B. Some class members may try to give reasons why they should gain entrance into eternal paradise. After giving class members sufficient time to respond, remind them that eternal life is granted to us only by the grace of God. Read John 3:16 aloud. Spend some time talking about the goodness and generosity of God in giving us His Son and the gift of eternal life.

5. Relating the Lesson to Life

A. Review the information about the Temple at Jerusalem and circumcision in THE PEOPLE, PLACES, AND TIMES article. What traditions or rituals exist in your church which may cause division if abolished or overlooked?

B. DISCUSS THE MEANING deals with the importance of being good disciples and being attendant to our responsibilities. Discuss, with compassion, why the Jewish Christians must have had difficulty giving up their traditions.

C. The LESSON IN OUR SOCIETY focuses on the tendency of some believers to create disharmony within the fellowship based on rituals or doctrines. Why is it important for Christians to devote our time and attention to creating harmony, not discord.

6. Arousing Action

A. Ask class members to take an honest assessment of themselves. Ask each to consider if he or she has ever looked down on another Christian or church member because that person was a new believer or new member like the Jews looked down upon the Gentiles.

January 9TH

B. From the instructions given in the MAKE IT HAPPEN section, create a "job description" for a good disciple, one who is a devoted worker in good standing.

C. Give class members an opportunity to complete FOLLOW THE SPIRIT and REMEMBER YOUR THOUGHTS.

WORSHIP GUIDE

For the Superintendent or Teacher
Theme: Called to Oneness in Christ
Theme Song: "Come We that Love the Lord"
Scripture: John 17:1-11, 20-23
Song: "Pass Me Not, O Gentle Saviour"
Meditation: Lord, thank You for the gift of salvation. I thank You for not waiting me to earn my salvation. Instead, You have given it to me freely out of Your love for me.

453

CALLED TO ONENESS IN CHRIST

Bible Background • EPHESIANS 2
Printed Text • EPHESIANS 2:8-22
Devotional Reading • JOHN 17:1-11, 20-23

LESSON AIM

After studying today's lesson, students should develop a greater appreciation for the fact that salvation is God's gift to all people.

KEEP IN MIND

"Now therefore ye are no more strangers and foreigners, but fellow citizens with the saints, and of the household of God" (Ephesians 2:19).

FOCAL VERSES

EPHESIANS 2:8 For by grace are ye saved through faith; and that not of yourselves: it is the gift of God:

9 Not of works, lest any man should boast.

10 For we are his workmanship, created in Christ Jesus unto good works, which God hath before ordained that we should walk in them.

11 Wherefore remember, that ye being in time past Gentiles in the flesh, who are called Uncircumcision by that which is called the Circumcision in the flesh made by hands;

12 That at that time ye were without Christ, being aliens from the commonwealth of Israel, and strangers from the covenants of promise, having no hope, and without God in the world:

13 But now in Christ Jesus ye who sometimes were far off are made nigh by the blood of Christ.

14 For he is our peace, who hath made both one, and hath broken down the middle wall of partition between us;

15 Having abolished in his flesh the enmity, even the law of commandments contained in ordinances; for to make in himself of twain one new man, so making peace;

16 And that he might reconcile both unto God in one

LESSON OVERVIEW
LESSON AIM
KEEP IN MIND
FOCAL VERSES
IN FOCUS
THE PEOPLE, PLACES, AND TIMES
BACKGROUND
AT-A-GLANCE
IN DEPTH
SEARCH THE SCRIPTURES
DISCUSS THE MEANING
LESSON IN OUR SOCIETY
MAKE IT HAPPEN
FOLLOW THE SPIRIT
REMEMBER YOUR THOUGHTS
MORE LIGHT ON THE TEXT
DAILY BIBLE READINGS

body by the cross, having slain the enmity thereby:

17 And came and preached peace to you which were afar off, and to them that were nigh.

18 For through him we both have access by one Spirit unto the Father.

19 Now therefore ye are no more strangers and foreigners, but fellowcitizens with the saints, and of the household of God;

20 And are built upon the foundation of the apostles and prophets, Jesus Christ himself being the chief corner stone;

21 In whom all the building fitly framed together groweth unto an holy temple in the Lord:

22 In whom ye also are builded together for an habitation of God through the Spirit.

IN FOCUS

Carl and Regina held such high hopes when they married. They could never have known that blending two families together would prove to be so difficult.

Regina's children were crazy about Carl, but they seemed to resent the things he did for his children when they came to stay on the weekends. Regina felt that Carl probably was doing too much for them, trying to make up for not being with them all the time.

Last weekend was the worst! Carl and Regina had to referee what was about to become World War III. Their two daughters were arguing about what to watch on the "big screen" television. Regina's daughter, Nicole, screamed at Carl's daughter Kari, "I don't care what you want! You're not really a part of this family, anyway. Your daddy lives with me!"

Carl and Regina had to explain to their children that,

even though Carl's children weren't there all the time, they were both an equal and important part of their family.

THE PEOPLE, PLACES, AND TIMES

THE TEMPLE. The Temple at Jerusalem was made up of many courts. Paul focuses on the outer court, but there were really about four different courts. The outer court was where the Gentiles had to stay. A lot of money exchanging or selling took place in the outer court. Next, there was the court of the Jewish women. The women could only go as far as this court. Even today the men can go further into the temple, and the women still have to stay out and apart. Next, is the court of the Israelites where the Israelite men would go and offer up sacrifices. The inner court is called the "Holy of Holies." No one could go into that court but the high priest; even he could go in only once a year. Before he could enter, he had to undergo a cleansing ritual. The Holy of Holies is the place where God dwelled. It was separated from the rest of the temple by a curtain. The Gospels report that when Jesus was crucified, the curtain was torn.

Based on information from *Growing Up to the Head*, by Dr. George O. McCalep. Lithonia: Orman Press, 1997, pp. 87-88.

CIRCUMCISION. The act of removing the foreskin of the male sex organ. In ancient Israel, this act was performed as a ritual on children of natives, servants, and aliens on the eighth day after birth. In the Jewish faith, it was an external symbol of one's total and complete allegiance and devotion to Yahweh. Initially, circumcision was performed by the father using a flint knife. In later times, specialists were employed among the Jewish people to carry out the act.

Controversy arose in the early church as to whether Gentile converts to Christianity needed to be circumcised (Acts 15:15). First century A.D. Jews frowned upon non-circumcision among Christians. The Apostle Paul played a crucial role in settling the dispute. He determined that physical circumcision was not essential to Christian faith and fellowship. Circumcision of the heart through repentance and faith were the only requirements of the faith for non-Jewish Christians.

Based on information from *Holman Bible Dictionary*, Trent Butler, general editor. Nashville: Broadman & Holman Publishers, 1991, p. 262.

BACKGROUND

Many barriers divided the Jews and the Gentiles in the ancient world. Paul devotes much of his attention in this portion of the letter to the essential oneness of the church.

For the Jews, Paul did away with the law as a requirement for salvation. Christ is the fulfillment of the law, making it complete. Salvation cannot be earned through works, nor by strict adherence to the law. Nevertheless, we are not absolved of our responsibility to do what is right. No one had the right to boast about personal goodness. Salvation by grace, through faith does lead to good works. There was no need for Jews and Gentiles to be divided based on Mosaic Law. Jesus Christ is the Peace of all believers. Therefore, there is no need for division and discord.

By lessening the significance of ethnic and cultural identity, both Jews and Gentiles gained something far better and greater.

AT-A-GLANCE

1. **Being in Christ (Ephesians 2:8-10)**
2. **The Gentile's Status (vv. 11-13)**
3. **Jew and Gentiles Together (vv. 14-18)**
4. **One Church, One Foundation (vv. 19-22)**

IN DEPTH

1. Being in Christ (Ephesians 2:8-10)

Paul sums up the entire process of salvation by his use of the perfect tense verb form. In versions other than King James, the rendering is "you have been saved." In other words, nothing about imperfect humankind can interfere or take away from God's divine purpose. That means we cannot do anything to affect our salvation. God has already taken care of our salvation.

It is grace, through faith, which saves us. Salvation is not based on worth—we are not, nor can we ever become worthy. We cannot save ourselves through good works. If so, we might be tempted to boast about our goodness. Paul's use of the word "boast" which signifies more than simply proud assertiveness. Here the word implies having confidence in one's own spiritual competence to bring about salvation. God's grace is a privilege we all have access to because He loves us. We have to grow up enough spiritually to understand that there are some things we cannot control or change and that those things are covered by grace.

If we could work our way into heaven, God would owe it to us. God owes us nothing. Salvation is His gift of love. He has already given it to us, even though we don't deserve it. According to God's plan, faith leads to salvation, which directs us to do good works, which moves us toward our heavenly reward. We can make no claims of personal righteousness. Our righteousness is nothing. Isaiah says our righteousness is like filthy rags before God (Isaiah 64:6).

Doris Akers wrote a popular song entitled, "You Can't Beat God Giving." The song is generally sung during the offertory period. But God's giving extends far beyond caring for our physical needs. We cannot beat God's giving in love, in service, in good works, or in grace. No matter how much good we have done, God has done more for us than we ever can for Him.

Our good works are the fruit of our salvation. We do not do good things to become saved . . . we do good works because we are saved. Because we believe in Him, we are still called upon to obey Him. To obey Christ, by definition leads us to do good works. The fact that we do these works, however, is no basis for making personal claims of our own goodness or ability to save ourselves.

God is the divine Architect who has created a blueprint for our lives. He has sketched His plan for our lives. It is up to us, however, to find His will and obey it. We do not have to work out a plan for our lives. God has already done that for us. If we do His will, then good works will certainly follow.

2. The Gentile's Status (vv. 11-13)

Paul reminds his readers that before they were converted, they were Gentiles by birth and therefore considered outcasts by the Jews. They were despised by the Jews, indicated by the fact that they were called the *Uncircumcision*.

The Jews regarded their circumcised state with snobbery, as they were God's chosen people. They referred to themselves as the *Circumcision*. Paul corrects their sense of superiority by clearly stating that their circumcision was by human effort and therefore merely a physical act. What was really important, he told them, was circumcision of the heart.

While the Jews held on to a false sense of superiority about their status as the chosen, the Gentiles were without a Saviour altogether. The Messiah was promised to the Jews, not the Gentiles, even though Isaiah foretold that the blessing would flow to all nations. Christ was sent, "to the lost sheep of the house of Israel" (Matthew 15:24).

The Gentiles were "aliens from the commonwealth of Israel" (v. 12). They did not belong among God's chosen. They were strangers to His promise since all of God's covenants had promised blessings to the Jews. For all practical purposes, the Gentiles stood on the outside looking in without hope.

But because of God's love, the former establishment was done away with. When the Gentiles receive Jesus Christ as Lord and Saviour, God places them in Christ and accepts them through Him. Jesus Christ has broken down the barriers which separate all people.

Jesus enabled the Gentiles to be brought near to God. Until the time of Christ, the world was divided into two camps: Jews and Gentiles. Now the Saviour had introduced a third state: His Church, which united all believers in Him as one.

3. Jew and Gentiles Together (vv. 14-18)

In the first part of chapter two, Paul traced the salvation of both Jews and Gentiles. The two groups held different perceptions of what it means to be saved.

Here, Paul moves forward to dissolve their nationalistic and cultural biases to create unity in Christ and explain the necessity for unity. Through His shed blood, Christ broke down "the middle wall of partition between us." The barriers which divided Jews and Gentiles are now gone. Where there were two, there is now one. There is but one Christ for both the mighty and powerful and the lowly and powerless. For every race and culture, there is only one Saviour.

Paul describes Christ as our Peace. When Christ came to us, He preached "peace" to those near and far. In this instance, those who were near were the Jews. They had already received a promise. Those who were afar were the Gentiles, those who had no covenant with God; they held no assurance of His presence or promise. This being the case, it is not difficult to understand why the Jews held a certain snobbery concerning their status as God's chosen.

Peace was needed to unify two groups which were alienated from each other. As our Peace, Christ has created a new race, free from the limitations of imposed human bondage such as culture, race, gender, education, social, or economic standing. All believers now have access to the presence of God at any time. This was in stark contrast to the Old Testament, when only the high priest could go into the Holy of Holies, the place where God dwelled.

At the same time that Jesus was being crucified, the curtain of the temple which separated humanity from the Holy of Holies was split wide open. The curtain was laid apart, giving free accessibility for all believers through the great Intercessor Himself, Jesus Christ, to the Father. Because of Christ, we also now know God as Father, something foreign to the covenant of the Old Testament. Through prayer, all believers in Christ have equal access to the Father. In fact, all three Persons of the Trinity are directly involved in the prayers of even the most humble believer. We pray to the Father, approaching Him through our Lord, Jesus Christ, in the power of the Holy Spirit.

4. One Church, One Foundation (vv. 19-22)

Paul often uses the words "now therefore" when making a conclusion. He concluded that the Gentiles were in no way inferior to the Jews. Christ did away with all of that. The apostle lists some of the many great benefits available to all believing Gentiles, as they are no longer strangers and foreigners. Never again will they be looked upon as less than others or as outsiders. Now they are fellow citizens and equal heirs to the inheritance. Christians of Jewish ancestry have no advantage over the believing Gentiles. All believers are first-class citizens in the kingdom of heaven.

As they are now a part of the Church, they have become stones, or building blocks in the construction of a holy temple. This new temple will also have a foundation, with Christ as the "chief cornerstone" which bonds the temple together. This new temple, the Church, is built on the foundation of the apostles and prophets of the New Testament. The apostles and prophets are not the foundation; Christ is the foundation. The foundation was laid in what the apostles and prophets taught about the Person and work of Jesus Christ.

Christ is more than the foundation of the Church, however; He is also the chief cornerstone, joining the two walls that were once separated: Jews and Gentiles. In this new temple that Christ has created, everyone will have an equal place.

When Jesus created a new covenant between God and humankind, He made a new being, one body, the Church. He did not raise Gentiles up to be even with Jews. Instead, He melted them all down and raised up a new being: one person, one body, one baptism, one Spirit.

Paul compares the Church to a building or structure, using terms that are familiar in construction. The Church is also a living organism which takes its shape at the guidance of the Holy Spirit. Like any other structure or living thing, the Church must be tended to, and maintained to operate as Christ intended. God expects the church to grow. The church must continue to bring new stones to be fitted into the building. The added stones will be all types, shapes, and sizes. Some will be so dirty we may not want to touch them. Our job as workers is not to judge the fitness of the stones. Our job is simply to bring them to the Church, to continue to add to the magnificent structure God has already built.

SEARCH THE SCRIPTURES

1. By what action are we saved? (v. 8)

2. Why can't our works count in terms of our salvation? (v. 9)

3. What did God ordain that we do? (v. 10)

4. What were the Gentiles called? (v. 11)

5. How did the Jews refer to themselves? (v. 11)

6. How were the Gentiles looked upon? (v. 12)

7. How were those who were far away from the promise of the Messiah drawn near to Him? (v. 13)

8. What barrier did Christ break down? (v. 14)

9. For what reason did Christ make one new man? (vv. 15-16)

10. What did Christ preach? (v. 17)

11. What do we have because of Christ? (v. 18)

12. What is Christ in relation to the Church as a building? (v. 20)

DISCUSS THE MEANING

1. Since it is our responsibility to care for the Church of Christ and to continue to bring new stones, in what ways have we neglected our duties, both to the universal Church and in the local church?

2. There were great barriers separating Jews and Gentiles in the early church. Why was it so difficult, especially for the Jews, to let go of long-held traditions in favor of unity among all believers in the Church?

LESSON IN OUR SOCIETY

No matter how plainly the Bible reads, there are some believers who are determined to create barriers within the Church. Many arguments and divisions have arisen over issues of doctrine. Some religions have attacked other Christians as being unsaved because they do not adhere to certain particulars.

In the early church, the issue of circumcision was no less significant to many from the Jewish faith. Paul reminded them that the matter was a human act, and therefore, could only hold a limited purpose in the faith. He placed emphasis, instead, on unity within the Body.

All believers should be careful in our attempt not to ostracize others and create division based on human preferences. Christ desires that we engage ourselves in activities which draw us closer to Him and to one another.

MAKE IT HAPPEN

Think about your status in your home, in your church, on your job, and in the community. Why is it important that you have good standing in all of these areas? Do you work hard and devote yourself to maintaining your status as a spouse or parent? As an employee, manager, or business owner? As a church member? As a member of your community?

Now think about your status as a child of God. Do you devote yourself equally to maintaining your status as a follower of Christ (not merely a church member)? Do you try to hold yourself responsible to do what Christ desires of you?

Think of at least one action or step you can take to show

that it is important to you to continue to live as a disciple "in good standing."

FOLLOW THE SPIRIT
What God wants me to do:

_____

_____

_____

REMEMBER YOUR THOUGHTS
Special insights you learned:

_____

_____

_____

MORE LIGHT ON THE TEXT
EPHESIANS 2:8-22

After the eulogy for the unspeakable blessings, which God has blessed His people, Paul prays that God will open our eyes to fully understand the magnitude of the blessing. He asks that God might reveal to us the hope and richness of our calling (1:18-19); the greatness of God's power and authority which He has given to the Church (1:20-23); and the efficacy of the death and resurrection of Jesus Christ (2:1-10). In the first 7 verses of this chapter, Paul graphically describes the deplorable human condition without God. Without Him all humanity is dead in sin, enslaved to sin, and condemned (vv. 1-3); but God has made us alive in Christ and saved us because of the richness of His mercy. He has made us to sit together in heavenly places in Christ Jesus (vv. 4-7).

2:8 For by grace are ye saved through faith; and that not of yourselves: it is the gift of God: 9 Not of works, lest any man should boast. 10 For we are his workmanship, created in Christ Jesus unto good works, which God hath before ordained that we should walk in them.

After stating the gloomy condition of humanity and that God has provided His Son as the remedy, Paul now declares how and why God reversed the former condition and makes us alive by His mercy, Then Paul makes a very important assertion, which has formed the bedrock of the Christian doctrine of salvation. In verses 8-10, are the three most important and foundational words of the Christian Gospel: "saved" (salvation), "grace," and "faith." These three words describe God's work of redemption through Christ. That is, our salvation is accomplished only through the grace of God, and that it is a gift, which can be received through faith.

We have learned in the last study that grace (Greek *charis*) is God's free and unmerited favor or undeserved mercy towards mankind. The verb translated "saved" is the

Greek word *sozo*, which means "to rescue from danger or destruction; deliver from the punishment," etc. Faith (Greek *pistis*) is the reliance and trust in the truthfulness of God's promises. The same Greek word is also used for "belief" (to believe) and has the idea of the trustworthiness of the finished work of Christ. So our salvation (deliverance from sin and its consequences) is the result of the work of God's grace (God's free and undeserved mercy) towards us, which is a gift that we receive by faith (humble trust and reliance on the trustworthiness of God).

After the positive statement, Paul is quick to add two negatives as caution and to strengthen the fact that our salvation is based only on grace and faith. First, "and that not of yourselves (i.e., this is not your own doing), it is the gift of God" (v. 8b). Second, "not of works (i.e., not because of work) lest any man should boast" (v. 9). There are two opinions about the meaning of the article "that" (Greek *touto*) in the form of the two negatives. Some believe that it refers to the word "faith" (i.e., "for by grace are ye saved through faith," and even saving faith is the gift of God).

This should be carefully noted by all, especially evangelicals, who oftentimes arrogate ourselves on the false assumption that faith is our personal contribution to the transaction of salvation. In other words, it is an assertion that God supplies the grace and we contribute the faith. This erroneous assumption is common, especially when we testify of our conversion or miracles we have experienced. However, the Bible teaches that faith, too, is a gracious gift from God (Acts 18:27; Philippians 1:29).

The second understanding of the use of the article "that" is that it refers to the whole sentence of verse 8. It then can be reworded thus: "It is by the grace of God you people have been saved through faith, and all this experience . . . is God's free gift to you." The argument for this option is that the use of the article in Greek, *touto* (that), is in neuter; while faith is in the feminine gender and both cannot go together. Therefore, *touto* refers to the whole preceding statement. Salvation is obtained neither by human achievement (not of yourselves) nor as a reward for good deeds one has done (not of works). Because salvation is not a thing one merits by personal achievement, there is therefore no room for boasting. It is important to note Paul's use of the second person plural "ye" (you) in verse 8 referring to the Gentile Christians (cf. 11), and his switch to "we" including him and the Jewish brethren (v. 10).

As if he does not want to leave his audience with a wrong idea about good works (good deeds) or any possible misunderstanding, Paul comes up with another affirmation, "we are his (God's) workmanship, created in Christ." The emphasis is on the pronoun "his," which speaks of possession or ownership. The word "workmanship" is the Greek word *poiema*, meaning "a product," a thing that is made or created (*ktisthentes*) in Christ Jesus. The reference here is not the natural birth of creation, but the spiritual rebirth or recreation as implied in verse 5. Salvation is God's re-creative act whereby, we who were once dead in sin are made alive, once slaves to sin are delivered, and once condemned to death—are now rescued. This describes what God has done through Christ. We are now new creatures in Christ (2 Corinthians 5:17-18). Jesus describes it in two ways: as being born again and being born of the Spirit, which are the only criteria for entering the kingdom of God (John 3:3-6).

We are not only God's works of art, receiving salvation in Christ; we are crafted in Christ Jesus to do good works. Again, this should be made clear in light of apparent misunderstanding between believers. There is no contradiction between this verse and the previous two (vv. 8, 9). Salvation is all of God without any human effort or contribution and therefore nothing to boast about; however, we are saved to do good works. In other words, good works are not the grounds or means of salvation, but are an indispensable and integral element of salvation.

The author then describes these elements (good works) of the new birth in Christ as actions which God from eternity had prepared (before ordained) that we should walk them. "To walk" is a Hebrew expression for "manner of life," or a lifestyle for living. The "good works" expressed here does not mean a type of philanthropic work, although that is not ruled out. Indeed, charitable work is an important element in the Christian walk which is often neglected or underrated. Our love and concern for the welfare of others should flow out of our newly created nature in Christ. It is part of our responsibility as Christians to have concern for people in need.

However, the main idea of "good works" that God from eternity had prepared for us to walk in, is living a changed moral life of obedience to the commandments of God, a life that pleases Him. While in the past, we walked in trespasses and sins (2:1) in obedience to the devil; now we walk in "good works" that God beforehand had planned for us in Christ Jesus. This change in lifestyle is made possible only by the grace of God through faith (God's gracious gift of faith) in Christ Jesus (i.e., through our union with Christ). It is not by the good works we have done, but, so that we can do the good works God has intended for us in Christ before the foundation of the world.

11 Wherefore remember, that ye being in time past Gentiles in the flesh, who are called Uncircumcision by that which is called the Circumcision in the flesh made by hands;

Paul, for the first time, identifies those whom he is addressing in verse 11—the Gentiles. He reminds them who they were before they received Christ. He uses different terms to describe their position before their union with Christ. First, they were "Gentiles in the flesh." That is to say that they were *ethnos*, i.e., heathen, non-Jewish nations by birth, whom the Jews (the Circumcision) disrespectfully called the Uncircumcision. God had instructed Abraham in Genesis to circumcise every male child in his household, including his servants (Genesis 17:11). This practice became a visible, physical sign of the covenant between the Lord and His people. Any Jewish male who was not circumcised was to be cut off from his people (Genesis 17:14) and regarded as a covenant-breaker (Exodus 22:48).

The Jewish people took great pride in circumcision, and it became a badge of their spiritual and national superiority. Devout Jews, in recognition of God's continuing covenant with Israel, faithfully practiced circumcision in the New Testament period. Both John the Baptist (Luke 1:59) and Jesus (Luke 2:21) were circumcised in accordance with the Jewish rite. The practice raised a spirit of exclusivity and resentment between Jews and Gentiles, and later brought discord into the fellowship of the first century Church (Acts 15:1ff; see Paul's letter to Galatians). An exaggerated importance had been placed on the rite, and each side called the other names. Paul (especially in Galatians) seems to de-emphasize this physical rite, and he says that the so-called Jewish circumcision is only in the flesh (a purely physical mark) and something made by human hands, rather than spiritual.

Here, Paul, in essence, says that the true motive behind the circumcision of the flesh is a circumcision of the heart that is spiritual rather than physical. That kind of circumcision is needed and available to both Jews and Gentiles alike (Romans 2:28-29; Colossians 2:11-13). Writing to the Philippian Christians (both Jews and Gentiles), Paul says, "For we are the true circumcision, who worship in the Spirit of God and glory in Christ Jesus and put no confidence in the flesh" (Philippians 3:3, NAS).

12 That at that time ye were without Christ, being aliens from the commonwealth of Israel, and strangers from the covenants of promise, having no hope, and without God in the world:

Apart from being scornfully labeled as the uncircumcision by the so-called Circumcision, Paul calls their attention to their spiritual and physical alienation. First, they are to remember that during that time ("in the time past," v. 11) they were alienated from Christ ("ye were without Christ"). The word "Christ" is probably used here in the general sense of *Messiah*, which means they did not share in the Jews' Messianic hope for the future. This Messianic hope is included in the Jews' privileges which Paul lists in Romans 9:4-5. Since the Gentiles are alienated from the Messiah who is the promised one and the hope of the Jews, they are also alienated or separated from the commonwealth of Israel, and therefore strangers from (and to) the covenants of promise. The word "commonwealth" (Greek *politeia*) means "citizenship." Therefore, Gentiles, by the fact of their birth, are deprived of the privileges of Israel (Romans 9:4-5) and excluded in the participation of their national rights, hopes, and promise. We know from the Old Testament this covenant is the very heart of Israel's relationship with God, in which God solemnly pledges to be Israel's God and they are called His people (Leviticus 26:12). To partake in the covenant relationship, one must be born a Jewish, circumcised male. Gentiles are excluded from this Old Testament covenant.

As people separated from the Messianic hope (without Christ), estranged from the commonwealth of Israel and its privileges, and excluded from the covenant of promise as God's people, the Gentiles have "no hope, and are without God in the world." It is like a chain reaction. One thing leads to another. The ultimate result is that they are without God and, as such, hopeless in the world. This describes their position in their disbelief before they became Christians. It is evident by their lifestyle in which they "walked according to the course of this world, according to the prince of the power of the air, the spirit that now worketh in the children of disobedience" (2:2). They had no knowledge of the true God (Psalm 147:20), neither have they fellowship with him.

This was the position of all of us before we received Christ, we were outside the covenant promise of God, and without hope. However, the death and resurrection of Christ changed it all. We have, through Christ, been accepted into God's new family as adopted children (1:5, 6) with all the privileges that pertain to sonship, and now have God as our Father. We can approach God with confidence through the Spirit, and therefore, we hope to be with Him forever. In verse 18, Paul explains that through Christ we have access to God, the Father. Paul therefore calls on non-Jewish believers to remember the past (v. 11.), in order to appreciate the present, and have hope for the future.

13 But now in Christ Jesus ye who sometimes were far off are made nigh by the blood of Christ. 14 For he is our peace, who hath made both one, and hath broken down the middle wall of partition between us;

After describing the apparently gloomy and hopeless situation of the Gentiles before they became Christians, Paul now moves to the present positive state brought about by their new relationship in Christ. He says, "you who once

were far off have been brought near." That means that they are no more aliens and strangers to the promises and covenant of God; they are no more regarded as people without God and without hope (v. 12). They now have the same close relationship with God, which was formerly reserved for Israel alone. Israel and God are said to be near each other. "Far off" describes how separated the Gentiles were from God compared with His nearness to Israel. Moses, declaring the uniqueness of Israel's relationship with God, says, "For what great nation is there that has God so near to it, as the LORD our God is to us. . ." (Deuteronomy 4:7, NKJV).

The psalmist calls them "the people who are near to him" (Psalms 148:14). The separation or alienation of the Gentiles from God and from Israel is symbolized in the construction of the Temple in Jerusalem. There were partitions between the outer and inner courts. The Gentiles were only allowed entrance to the outer court; hence, its name was Court of the Gentiles. The inner court, which was closer to the court of the priests and the Holy of Holies (representing the presence of God), was reserved for those of the Jewish race. It is said that notices displayed in different languages stated that death was the punishment for any non-Jew caught entering the inner court. This segregation figuratively and literally represented the far off position of the Gentiles from God.

However, God also promised to bring peace to all people both far and near (Isaiah 57:19). Paul says that there is now a change in the position of Gentile believers; they are now brought near. This is done in Christ Jesus. Through Christ and because of their new relationship with Him, Gentiles are brought into the fold. They are now no longer left out, but are now engrafted into the new family of God. The method used to bring about this change is the blood of Christ. The reference to the blood of Christ (also mentioned in vv. 7, 16) signifies the sacrificial and atoning death of Christ on the Cross, through which all believers are reconciled to God and to each other, Jews and Gentiles alike.

The Gentiles who, by their belief in and through the sacrificial death of Christ, have become members of the people of God together with the Jews who have accepted Jesus as their Messiah. Apart from symbolizing alienation from God and Israel, the partition was also a symbol of hostility between the Jews and the Gentiles. The Cross is the uniting force that binds the two sides into one community.

Paul makes the unification of the two groups clear in the next verse through a profound declaration: He is our peace. The use of the pronoun "he" (*autos*) is emphatic, which means "He Himself" or "He and He alone" is our peace. This echoes the prophecy of Isaiah (9:6) where Christ is given the title "Prince of Peace" because of His mission on earth. Christ is peace personified because only through

Him and Him alone are believers reconciled to God and each other He has made both one. Not only has He unified the two sides into one entity, He has also broken down the middle wall of partition which separates them. As we have mentioned above, this probably refers to the literal partitioning wall that separates the courts in the temple.

15 Having abolished in his flesh the enmity, even the law of commandments contained in ordinances; for to make in himself of twain one new man, so making peace;

In addition to the separating walls of the temple, the Jews always endeavored to live separate from the rest of the world, and always wanted a river or wall between them and their Gentile neighbors. Their laws and customs also separated them from the rest of the world, as the physical walls in the temple. These were symbols of hostility between the two. Christ, through His sacrificial death, abolished the Law of Moses with its rituals, provided a new covenant that is inclusive for both Jews and Gentiles, and made them one. He brings everyone to the same level.

This breakdown is literally demonstrated in the renting from top to bottom of the temple veil indicating that the way into the Holy of Holies is left open and accessible to all. The abolition of the law raises some questions. What does Paul mean by abolishing the law in relation to Christ's words in Matthew 5:17? There, Christ teaches that He has come not to abolish, but rather to fulfill the law. Is it then a contradiction of Scriptures? In what sense was either used? The difference, as someone has suggested, seems to lie in the two types of laws: the moral law and the ceremonial law. Christ requires from His followers a more radical obedience to the moral law as compared with the Pharisees' own standards (Matthew 5:18ff.). Paul refers to Christ's abolishment of the ceremonial law, which includes the physical ritual of circumcision (v. 11), rather than the spiritual circumcision of the heart.

Also included are some of the dietary regulations in Colossians 2:11, 16-21. These constitute barriers between the Jews and the Gentiles which Jesus abolished through His death on the cross, thereby making peace between them. The unification of all believers (the Church) in Christ, as we shall see later in the book, include the abolition of the gender, social, and racial distinctions, which are present and cause hatred among different peoples of the earth. The change does not mean amalgamation of all races into one, or change of skin color, or physical and surgical gender change. It refers to change of attitude towards one another and the acceptance of one another as equals in the sight of God and within the society. When we have achieved this attitude, which unfortunately is still rare within Christendom, the peace that Christ died for on the Cross will be realized.

16 And that he might reconcile both unto God in one body by the cross, having slain the enmity thereby: 17 And came and preached peace to you which were afar off, and to them that were nigh.

Verses 16 and 17 speak to the same theme using different terms. These terms further describe what Christ has done through His blood. He has reconciled both (Jews and Gentiles) unto God in one body, by the cross. In verse 15, we see that the Law which brought about the enmity is abolished (*kartageo*), i.e., done away with, rendered idle, or destroyed; but in verse 16 the enmity, which is caused by the Law is slain (*apokteino*), i.e., inflicted a mortal death, or killed. The result speaks of total annihilation. In the one single act of sacrifice on the cross, Christ first abolished the law, which for centuries has separated humanity from each other and from their Creator. Second, He created a new humanity where everyone is equal to each other, and thereby making peace (figuratively, slaying the enmity) between them. Third, by this act of sacrifice, Christ reconciled this new society to God, their Creator. In many of Paul's writings, reconciliation is associated with the Cross (Romans 5:6-11; 2 Corinthians 5:17-21; Colossians 1:21-22).

Continuing the theme of Christ's activity in bringing near those far away, and reconciling the two entities, uniting them into "one new man" by abolishing the law, Paul describes this same activity in a different way in verse 17. While in verse 14, Christ "is our peace" personified (i.e., the object of peace), here he preaches "peace to you which were afar of" (the Gentiles vv. 11-13), as well as "to them that were nigh" (the Jews). "He came and preached peace" probably refers to Christ's earthly mission and the ministry of the early Church.

The word "preached" (*euaggelizo*) is the same Greek word translated "preach the good news" in Luke (4:17ff.), in which Jesus announced His mission in fulfillment of Isaiah's prophecy (cf. Isaiah 61:1-2). Here, Paul says that Jesus came and declared the Good News of peace to those who are afar and those nigh. Those "far off" would include the poor, the sick, the tax collectors, and sinners. He ministered to Gentiles as well, e.g., the Samaritan woman, the Roman centurion, the Samaritan leper, and the Syrophoenician woman. Apart from Christ's ministry, the preaching of the Good News by disciples might also be referred to here as if Christ preached through them. (2 Corinthians 5:20).

18 For through him we both have access by one Spirit unto the Father. 19 Now therefore ye are no more strangers and foreigners, but fellow citizens with the saints, and of the household of God;

Verses 18 and 19 tell us the effect of Christ's preaching. Through Him, Jews and Gentiles are now reconciled to one another and both to God. Consequently, by Him they both can approach God, the Father in one Spirit. It is noteworthy to recognize a deliberate reference to the Trinity here, which proves the separate and distinctiveness of the three persons in the Godhead (cf. 1 John 5:7). The word "access" (*prosagoge*) speaks of the freedom we have to approach God as our Father with boldness and assurance that we are acceptable to Him and that we shall not be turned down.

Paul writes in Romans 5:2, "By whom also we have access by faith into this grace wherein we stand, and rejoice in hope of the glory of God." The access we have is because of the reconciliatory activity of Christ, which resulted in our being at peace with God. This activity, Paul calls "justification" using the court language in Romans (5:1), but here in verse 17 he calls it proclaiming the Good News, using an evangelistic language. Both result in peace with God, whom Paul also calls the Father. The Spirit activates the free approach to the Father; therefore, He regards us equally as His sons and daughters.

To the Galatians (4:6), Paul writes "And because ye are sons, God hath sent forth the Spirit of his Son into your hearts, crying, Abba, Father." Being sons, we are no more bound or barred by fear from approaching God (Romans 8:15). This relationship with our heavenly Father is comparable to our relationship with our earthly parents (vis-a-vis sons and daughters), whom we can freely approach and have access to any time, unless there was a serious relationship breakdown in the family. In such a situation, access to the parents is difficult or impossible until the situation is resolved and peace restored. This was the case between us (both Jews and Gentiles) and God in the past, but through Christ and by the Holy Spirit, the barrier is now removed. Moreover, we are now members of the same family, with the same rights and privileges, belonging to the same citizenship.

There is in verse 19a a shift in Paul's use of metaphors, from the comparison of the membership of a family unit to the metaphor of citizenship—nationhood. In verse 12 the Gentiles are said to be outside of the commonwealth (*politeia*) of Israel, and strangers without hope and without God. Now they are no more strangers (*xenos*) and foreigners (*paroikos*); both terms are synonymous, meaning "one who lives in a place without the right of citizenship." When Israel alone claimed the right of being the people of God, all Gentile nations were excluded from their number. They were regarded and treated as strangers and foreigners. They were not allowed to integrate into the community of God's people. They remained as resident aliens. It is the equivalent of aliens residing in the USA or Canada who have no citizen's rights whatsoever.

As a foreigner, one is denied access to jobs, medical priv-ileges, or voting rights; if one is a foreign student, he or she is charged almost double the tuition charged for students who are citizens. There are many other privileges one enjoys as U.S. or Canadian citizens. The same applies in other countries as well. However, when one becomes an U.S. or Canadian citizen by choice, all the privileges are made accessible (at least theoretically) to him or her. Here, Paul reminds the Gentiles that through Christ, they have become fellow citizens (*sumpolitai*) with the saints, which means with Israel (1:1) in God's own kingdom. Paul again moves back to the use of the more intimate metaphor, the family portrait, to which he alluded in verse 18 (cf. 1:5; 3:14-15; 4:6). They become members of God's household, which is the Church, the body of Christ (5:23), God's new community.

20 And are built upon the foundation of the apostles and prophets, Jesus Christ himself being the chief corner stone;

Paul now moves from speaking of the Church as God's family, or community to referring to it as a building (house) whose foundation is laid upon the apostles and prophets. The apostles and prophets are the foundation (Greek *themelios*) on which the Church is built. Some commentators feel that the language here seems to indicate the letter was written following a considerable length of time after the earliest Christians, and not during the time of the Apostle Paul. With this feature, they question Paul's authorship of the book. To support this argument, they feel that the statement here is inconsistent with Paul's declaration in 1 Corinthians 3:11, which says, "No one can lay any foundation other than the one already laid, which is Jesus Christ" (NIV).

There is no argument that Christ is the true foundation of the Church, however, we believe that by virtue of their ministry and work in founding the early Church, the disciples can equally be regarded as the foundation of the Church. The apostle refers to Christ here as the builder, and it therefore sounds logical that he refers to the apostles and prophets as the foundation, which Christ has laid. Jesus Christ called the apostles and gifted the prophets charging them to bear the Good News to all nations (Matthew 28:19-20). The word "apostles" refers to the Twelve disciples (see our discussion on the word *apostolos* in the last study) and includes Paul himself. Some scholars feel that the word "prophet" here refers to the Old Testament prophets. However, in other passages Paul places the offices of apostles and prophets side by side as God's gift to the Church (3:5; 4:11; 1 Corinthians 12:28, 29).

Christ is not only the builder, He is also the chief cornerstone (*akrogoniaios*). Peter refers to Christ also as the cornerstone (1 Peter 2:6), using the same Greek word. The stability of a house or building depends on its foundation.

Therefore, the most important part of a building is its foundation. A house without a solid foundation would not stand the test of time. Christ's parable of the two builders in the Beatitudes emphasizes the need for a strong foundation laid on a rock. Here, Paul says that Jesus is the chief (the main) cornerstone that holds together the whole building and keeps the rest of the foundation in place, while the apostles and prophets are parts of the foundation. What does Paul mean by referring to the apostles and prophets as foundation on which Christ has built his church? This is a question for group discussion.

21 In whom all the building fitly framed together groweth unto an holy temple in the Lord:22 In whom ye also are builded together for an habitation of God through the Spirit.

Paul goes on to elaborate on the structural make up of the building. As we have seen, the structural stability of a building depends on its foundation, and so the stability of the Church is dependent upon none other than the One who is both builder and the chief cornerstone that is Christ. Jesus says to Peter, and to the rest of the disciples, "Upon this rock I will build my church; and the gates of hell shall not prevail against it" (Matthew 16:18), referring to Peter's earlier confession that Jesus was "Christ, Son of the living God" (Matthew 16:16).

A building does not stop at the foundation. It needs some fittings and other structures before it can be called a building. Paul moves his picture of the whole structure to the individual stones that are used to erect a building. Peter also uses the picture of a building or temple to describe the Church. In the same picture where he refers to Christ as the chief cornerstone (1 Peter 2:6), he describes the individual members as "living stones . . . being built into a spiritual house to be a holy priesthood" (1 Peter 2:4-5). Paul's picture here also sees the members of the Church as the stones, which the master builder (Christ) craftily and meticulously fits together upon the chief foundation (Christ) into a magnificent edifice unto a holy temple in the Lord.

The phrase "whom ye also are builded" refers to the Gentile Christians. The temple as we know represents the dwelling place and presence of God. We have also noted earlier that the temple was exclusively reserved only for the Jews. Gentiles were forbidden to enter the temple. Here, Paul assures them that not only are they now admitted into the temple (they have access unto the Father), but they are also parts of the temple of God. This is based on their union in Christ Jesus, who Himself is the cornerstone. One of the functions of the cornerstone is to hold and stabilize two corner walls together. As the spiritual cornerstone, Christ binds Jews and Gentiles together into a whole new building in God. Without the cornerstone, the building will crumble.

The purpose of the temple in the Old Testament, as we have intimated above, was for a dwelling place for God. This new temple serves the same purpose, namely for God's habitation (*katoiketerion*, i.e., dwelling place). We know from Scriptures that God is so great that even the whole earth cannot contain Him—not even Solomon's magnificent temple, nor the one rebuilt by Herod. God does not dwell in man-made houses (1 Kings 8:27; Acts 7:48-49; 17:24), nor in homes built with earthly materials. He nonetheless manifested His glory and presence in the temple.

However, He also makes His abode in the hearts of men. Paul, in other places, refers to Christians as temples of the living God (1 Corinthians 3:16-19; 6:16; 2 Corinthians 6:16), where God dwells by the Holy Spirit. Instead of the Old Testament temple in which God manifested His presence through His glory, the Church (the individual Christian, the local church, and the universal Church) becomes the New Testament temple in which God manifests Himself through the Holy Spirit. Again, we see a clear reference to the Trinity. For a concluding summary of this passage, I would recommend John R. W. Stott's "Conclusion" from *God's New Society, The Message of Ephesians,* Downers Grove: Inter Varsity Press, 979, pp. 110-1120.

DAILY BIBLE READING

M: Saved and Made Alive by Grace
Ephesians 2:1-10
T: One Body in Jesus Christ
Ephesians 2:11-16
W: God Dwells in You
Ephesians 2:17-22
T: Jesus Commits Disciples to God's Care John 17:1-6
F: Jesus Prays for the Disciples' Protection John 17:7-13
S: Jesus Prays for the Disciples' Unity John 17:14-21
S: May God's Love Be in Christ's Disciples John 17:22-26

TEACHING TIPS

July 16
Bible Study Guide 7

1. Words You Should Know

A. Beseech (4:2)— King James translation of a word meaning "beg" as translated in other versions.

B. Captivity Captive (4:8)—Other versions translate, "led captives in his train," (NIV) and "led a host of captives" (RSV). The term is used to indicate Christ's victory over Satan and his troops.

C. Perfecting (4:12)—To build up or uplift.

2. Teacher Preparation

A. Read the background Scripture for the lesson. Reflect on some of the ways you have matured spiritually as you have walked with the Lord.

B. Read the IN FOCUS story about Stephen and Deacon Matthews.

3. Starting the Lesson

A. Discuss how spiritual growth enables us to handle situations differently as we mature in Christ. Ask the question: "How do we become aware of our spiritual gifts?" Using a chalkboard or large sheet of paper and markers, write down class members' responses. Encourage them to share from personal experience. Ask each of them to share the nature of his/her spiritual gift(s).

B. Ask someone to share an experience wherein he/she was able to handle a situation in a Christlike manner because he/she had grown spiritually.

4. Getting into the Lesson

Ask the class to help you create a list of the spiritual gifts in your church. Then create another list containing ways that those gifts help to uplift Christ's Church. Discuss what happens when we do not use our spiritual gifts to help build up the church.

5. Relating the Lesson to Life

A. Review the information about spiritual gifts and the New Testament definition of peace in THE PEOPLE, PLACES, AND TIMES article. Ask these questions: "How do we know when we have peace? Why did Christ design it so that all believers would have at least one spiritual gift?"

B. Give students an opportunity to answer the questions in SEARCH THE SCRIPTURES.

C. DISCUSS THE MEANING highlights the tendency of some Christians to forget the Source of their spiritual gift(s). Discuss how the gifts Paul named in verse 11 help to build both the local church and the body of Christ today.

D. The LESSON IN OUR SOCIETY focuses on the potential danger of Christians thinking of themselves as having "arrived" or graduated from Christian discipleship. What happens to people who have fallen into this mode of thinking?

6. Arousing Action

A. Create an "evaluation" sheet for your church concerning its adherence to those things Christ intended His church to be. Include such statements as:

1. Enables members to use their gifts for the good of the church and the believer.

2. Constantly seeking ways to grow and become more of what Christ intended.

3. Dedicated to teaching and uplifting new believers.

4. Uses the gifts named in Ephesians 4:11 for the betterment of all believers.

You may also include other statements. Then ask class members to evaluate each statement on a scale of 1 to 10: 1—poor, 10—excellent. Use this time to see how different class members view their church. Use discretion and sensitivity during this discussion so that no person or ministry feels personally attacked. Focus on the positive benefits of assessing your church's strengths and weaknesses.

B. Based on the instructions given in the MAKE IT HAPPEN section, give class members an opportunity to evaluate their personal openness and willingness to be led by the Spirit to learn new things in Christ. Ask them to think of ways they fall short.

C. Give class members an opportunity to complete the FOLLOW THE SPIRIT and REMEMBER YOUR THOUGHTS sections.

WORSHIP GUIDE

For the Superintendent or Teacher
Theme: Called to Use Your Spiritual Gifts
Theme Song: "This Little Light of Mine"
Scripture: Ephesians 3:14-21
Song: "Here Am I, Send Me"
Meditation: Lord, lead me to do the work that You would have me to do. Guide me in the proper use of my gifts so that I may use them to build up Your Church and Your people.

CALLED TO USE YOUR SPIRITUAL GIFTS

Bible Background • EPHESIANS 4:1-16
Printed Text • EPHESIANS 4:1-16
Devotional Reading • EPHESIANS 3:14-21

LESSON AIM

After studying today's lesson, students should gain a greater understanding of God's purpose for the Church and that every believer has an important responsibility therein.

KEEP IN MIND

"But unto every one of us is given grace according to the measure of the gift of Christ" (Ephesians 4:7).

FOCAL VERSES

EPHESIANS 4:1 I therefore, the prisoner of the Lord, beseech you that ye walk worthy of the vocation wherewith ye are called,

2 With all lowliness and meekness, with longsuffering, forbearing one another in love;

3 Endeavouring to keep the unity of the Spirit in the bond of peace.

4 There is one body, and one Spirit, even as ye are called in one hope of your calling;

5 One Lord, one faith, one baptism,

6 One God and Father of all, who is above all, and through all, and in you all.

7 But unto every one of us is given grace according to the measure of the gift of Christ.

8 Wherefore he saith, When he ascended up on high, he led captivity captive, and gave gifts unto men.

9 (Now that he ascended, what is it but that he also descended first into the lower parts of the earth?

10 He that descended is the same also that ascended up far above all heavens, that he might fill all things.)

11 And he gave some, apostles; and some, prophets; and some, evangelists; and some, pastors and teachers;

12 For the perfecting of the saints, for the work of the ministry, for the edifying of the body of Christ:

13 Till we all come in the unity of the faith, and of the knowledge of the Son of God, unto a perfect man, unto the measure of the stature of the fulness of Christ:

14 That we henceforth be no more children, tossed to and fro, and carried about with every wind of doctrine, by the sleight of men, and cunning craftiness, whereby they lie in wait to deceive;

15 But speaking the truth in love, may grow up into him in all things, which is the head, even Christ:

16 From whom the whole body fitly joined together and compacted by that which every joint supplieth, according to the effectual working in the measure of every part, maketh increase of the body unto the edifying of itself in love.

JULY 16TH

IN FOCUS

Stephen said a quick prayer of thanksgiving to God that he was able to walk away from Deacon Matthews without an argument. He was a fine deacon, but as he advanced in age, his temperament was also becoming more disagreeable.

Still, he had great respect for Deacon Matthews. But Stephen and many of the younger members of the church sought some changes in the ministries of the church, and even its business practices. Some members were frustrated because they wanted to use their gifts within the church in a more meaningful way.

Stephen laughed to himself, "I'm 42 years old, but 'Deac' still looks at me as one of the young folks in the church."

Deacon Matthews said that he saw no need for changes.

The church had operated just fine for 137 years, and it would continue to do so.

That's when Stephen said his prayer. He knew there was a time when he would have exploded all over the elderly deacon for being so short-sighted. "By the grace of God," he thought, "I am maturing in Christ."

THE PEOPLE, PLACES, AND TIMES

PEACE. The word is defined as a general feeling of well-being and/or fulfillment given by God and dependent upon God's presence.

In the New Testament, the Greek word *eirânâ* corresponds to the familiar Hebrew term for peace, *shalom*. This word also represents restoration, reconciliation to the Father, and, in the fullest sense, salvation. The Gospel is "the good news of peace" (Ephesians 6:15; Acts 10:36). God has made this peace a reality in Jesus Christ, who is "our peace." We are justified through Him, (Romans 5:1), reconciled through His blood (Colossians 1:20), and made one in Him (Ephesians 2:14).

Based on information from *The Broadman Bible Commentary* Vol. 11, Clifford J. Allen, general editor, Nashville: Broadman Press, 1971, p. 1086.

GIFTS. Spiritual gifts are the skills and abilities given to all believers by the Father through His Spirit. These gifts are for the purpose of enabling Christians to carry out His plan.

Jesus promised His disciples that they also would receive the gift of the Spirit, who will guide them (Mark 13:11; Luke 11:13).

His promise was fulfilled on the Day of Pentecost (Acts 2:1-47). The Spirit was given to every believer. Paul's epistles reveal that this continued in all the churches. Every believer has a spiritual gift (1 Corinthians 12:4-7). No New Testament writer has ever suggested that some believers may be without gifts.

Spiritual gifts are for the benefit of the body of believers, not just for individual benefit or pleasure. The greatest gift, which Paul said every believer should possess, is love (1 Corinthians 12:31 13:1)

Based on information from *Holman Bible Dictionary*, Trent Butler, general editor Nashville: Broadman & Holman Publishers, 1991, pp. 1300-1301.

BACKGROUND

In previous portions of his letter to the church at Ephesus, Paul laid the foundation concerning Christ and His Church. Now he switches his focus to a more practical

purpose, setting out guidelines for his readers concerning Christian conduct. But first, he decides to give them an overview of the Church's place in the world.

Paul called for the Ephesians to be true to who they are called to be in Christ and provides for them several reasons: (1) their responsibility to be one in the body; (2) the call for unity does not mean that they should strive for a type of dull sameness; (3) the church is a living organism, made up of living beings who are expected to grow, according to their use of the gifts Christ has given them; (4) Christ desires that the Church reach maturity and that the people of the Church be prepared to exercise their gifts; and (5) as the Church grows, its members should take on the nature and character of its Head, Christ Jesus.

AT-A-GLANCE

1. The Church's Calling to Unity (Ephesians 4:1-6)
2. The Church's Gifts (vv. 7-12)
3. The Road to Maturity (vv. 13-16)

IN DEPTH

1. The Church's Calling to Unity (Ephesians 4:1-6)

Paul considered himself a prisoner for the Lord, not to the Lord. Always positioning himself as the example, he issued a plea to the Ephesian Christians to "walk worthy" of the "vocation" or to live in a manner which is consistent with their high calling from God. The Christian's call is the divine summons which was answered at the time of conversion. Our calling is not a hobby or a pastime. It is our life's achievement, our duty.

The word "walk" is a literal translation of a Hebrew idiom for everyday conduct. The word "worthy" makes the connection between God's plan for us and our acceptance of that plan, as demonstrated in the way we live.

Paul had previously cautioned against boasting concerning good works. Now he advises them to live out their calling with humility. He did not want them to become arrogant about their godly living. They were also to exercise patience toward the faults and failings of others, or even different personality types and temperaments. We are to genuinely have patience for one another with love.

The reason for possessing these qualities "lowliness, and meekness, with longsuffering, forbearing" is for the purpose of unity within the body of Christ. When Christ established the Church, He abolished the greatest dividing line within humanity—the barrier which separated Jews and Gentiles. Now it was the responsibility of the early church members to try with all earnestness to avoid creating human divisions among God's unified people.

Arguments and dissension threaten to destroy the "bond of peace" within the body of Christ. There is but one Spirit in the Church; nothing can destroy that unity. However, bickering and quarrels can destroy the peace which binds the members of the body of Christ. A healthy formula for keeping the unity is threefold: (a) unity in those things which are essential to the faith; (b) liberty in those matters which are non-essential or not absolute; and (c) charity in all circumstances.

Every believer must realize that he or she has the potential to be a "peace-breaker." Self assessment is essential to maintaining unity and keeping the peace. Instead of highlighting differences, believers should look to the elements which form the basis of Christian unity: one body . . . one Spirit . . . one hope . . . one Lord . . . one faith . . . one baptism . . . one God and Father of all.

In spite of the vast number of Christian churches all around the world, there is only one *body* of believers. The same *Spirit* who dwells in every believer also dwells in the body of Christ. There is but one *hope* in which every believer has placed his or her trust.

Our *one Lord* is the Saviour who shed His blood for our sins. We all share a common *faith* in that one Lord and Saviour. There is one *baptism* by which we profess our faith in Christ. The *one God and Father* who is supreme above all.

2. The Church's Gifts (vv. 7-12)

The unity of the Church must be balanced by its odd twin, diversity. Unity is often confused with uniformity. The Christian Church is communal, where every member makes a contribution. Each member of the body of Christ has been given *grace*, or a particular gift or role to fulfill. No two members are alike. No member should try to imitate the other's gifts. In other letters, Paul outlines the necessity for giving equal value to the gifts of every believer.

By His grace, He has given these gifts as He sees fit. The risen Lord bestowed these gifts by first sending His most excellent gift, the Holy Spirit. Paul quotes Psalm 68:18 as a prophecy that the Messiah would ascend to heaven and conquer His foes and lead them captive. As a reward for His victory, He would receive gifts for humankind.

In verse 9, Paul wanted to show that the prophecy could have referred only to Christ. If Jesus ascended into heaven, He must have first come down from heaven. Some have interpreted "lower parts of the earth" to mean that Christ descended into hell. The Gospel of Luke, however, indicates that His spirit went to heaven when He died (Luke 23:43, 46). The prophecy of Psalm 68:18 was fulfilled by the birth, death, and burial of Jesus.

The ascended Christ is the Giver of all gifts. He is the Source of all blessings. He fills all things. In giving us gifts, Christ has a specific purpose in sight. All of God's saints are to be equipped with the gifts necessary to discharge their duties as Christians in the world. Paul proceeds to explain the nature of some of these most gracious gifts.

Apostles were those persons directly commissioned by the Lord to preach the Word and plant churches. They were those who had seen the risen Christ. *Prophets* were the spokespersons for God. They received revelations directly from the Lord, by the aid of the Holy Spirit, and passed them on to the church. These prophets are not to be confused with the prophets of the Old Testament.

Evangelists are those who preach the Good News. They have been divinely equipped to go out into the world and lead persons to Christ. *Pastors* are those who serve as God's undershepherds, caring for the sheep of His flock. It is their responsibility to guide and feed the flock. The New Testament gives the impression of a number of pastors at a local church instead of one (Acts 20:17, 28; 1 Peter 5:1-2).

Teachers are persons divinely gifted to teach and explain the Bible and what it means. An evangelist preaches the Gospel. A Bible teacher endeavors to fit a passage into the context and into everyday life.

The purpose of all these gifts is for "the perfecting (or equipping) of the saints . . . the work of the ministry . . . edifying the body of Christ." These gifts enable us to serve the Lord, thereby building up the body of Christ. These gifts should always be used to empower others to do even greater deeds for the sake of the kingdom.

3. The Road to Maturity (vv. 13-16)

At this point, Paul may have anticipated the question, "How long will this process of growing continue?" In verse 13, Paul explains that this will go on "till we all come in the unity of the faith . . . of the knowledge of the Son of God."

Possibly nothing can prepare the human mind for the unity that exists in the afterlife. As long as we live, no matter how hard we try, we will have innumerable differences. This will continue until the time when we are able to see Him as He truly is and to know as we are known. At that time the "unity of the faith" will occur. Until then, there will be room for growth. When we come to a position of full knowledge, we enter the state of "perfect man." The word perfect, used in the King James Version, is translated "complete." Our Christian journey is completed only when we come to the place of full knowledge of Christ and unity of our faith.

Verses 15-16 describe the growth process in the body of Christ. As we continue toward spiritual maturity, some things will become apparent. We are no longer juvenile, or "children" who are "tossed to and fro, and carried about with every wind of doctrine." As we grow to be more like Him, we grow in our knowledge of Him. Our understanding is solid and sure. No one can just come along and persuade us to change our beliefs.

America was appalled at the Heaven's Gate cult suicides in 1997. As news of what happened spread, so did news of their beliefs and practices. Many people wondered how middle-aged men and women could be persuaded to participate in such a bizarre and fatal ritual. It must be remembered that, although these men and women were all adults, they were lacked "knowledge of the Son of God," even Jesus Christ. Therefore they did not realize the spiritual maturity Paul addresses here.

All disciples are called upon to grow. Discipleship is a process. It is not a course of study from which we will earn a diploma and never revisit again. There is always room for growth, for training, for new understanding and for enlightenment. As we grow in Christ, so do our challenges. The longer we live, if we are achieving spiritual maturity, we learn to lean on Jesus even more, trusting in His promises and His providence.

When we encounter brothers and sister who have gone astray in their thinking and beliefs, we are commanded to speak "the truth in love," helping each other to grow toward the Head, which is Christ Jesus. He is both the goal of our growth and the Source of our growth. As the Church receives its life from Him who supplies all of our needs, quite naturally, growth comes from Him, too. But Paul adds that the Church grows "toward" Christ as we grow "in" Christ.

The body of Christ is comprised of many members who, although different in very obvious ways, are part of one body, His Church. His action joins together the whole body through His work in and through every joint which He supplies. Each member of the body of Christ fulfills his or her responsibilities for the edification of the entire body. When this happens, the body of Christ grows in "love" because the proper and necessary environment has been created.

With human nature being that which it is, the very fact that the Church is able to function is itself evidence of a miracle. Amid all the diversity of the Christian Church, there exists a fellowship and unity, a singleness of purpose which outweighs any divisions and factions created by human interference.

SEARCH THE SCRIPTURES

1. What did Paul "beseech" the Ephesian Christians to do? (v. 1)

2. What reasons does Paul give them for exhibiting characteristics such as lowliness and meekness? (v. 3)

3. What are the seven things we all share as one body? (vv. 4-6)

4. How are we given grace? (v. 7)

5. What did Christ do when He ascended to heaven? (v. 8)

6. What gifts did Christ leave to some? (v. 11)

7. Give reasons why you think these persons have been so gifted. (vv. 12-13)

8. What did Paul want us to guard against? (v. 14)

9. What should be our goal as we guard against these things? (v. 15)

10. How is the body of Christ put together through Him? (v. 16)

DISCUSS THE MEANING

1. Some Christians tend to forget that their talents and abilities are spiritual gifts from God. In what ways do believers begin to take credit for themselves?

2. In verse 11, Paul named a number of gifts which are to be used to benefit the body of Christ. How do the people with these gifts serve the Christian church today?

LESSON IN OUR SOCIETY

There is a real danger among Christians to look at ourselves as having "arrived" as far as our spiritual growth is concerned. We can never fully know God in this life; therefore, Christian discipleship is not a course of study to be completed. It is a process which causes us to change and grow continuously, if we yield ourselves to the guidance of the Holy Spirit.

As the old saying goes, we are "never too old to learn" in matters concerning the kingdom. The oldest, most seasoned Christian, can still learn about God's love from a newborn baby.

A true sign of Christian maturity is knowing that there is still more to be known.

MAKE IT HAPPEN

Are there ways that you stunt your own spiritual growth because you are not willing to lend yourself to new challenges that are presented to you. Do you ever think, "I'm too old to be learning how to do that now" or "I've lived long enough to know what I'm talking about."

Think about an area of your life where you may be inhibiting your spiritual development, thereby building a wedge between you and the Father.

FOLLOW THE SPIRIT
What God wants me to do:

_____

_____

REMEMBER YOUR THOUGHTS
Special insights you learned:

_____

_____

MORE LIGHT ON THE TEXT
EPHESIANS 4:1-16
In the first three chapters of this book, Paul has been revealing God's eternal purpose for mankind, i.e., the creation of a brand new society through the death and resurrection of His Son Jesus Christ. Christ's sacrificial death and resurrection now unite the formerly fractured humanity into one community. The Gentiles who were hitherto alienated from God and from the citizenship of God's people are now reconciled both to God and to the people of God. After explaining God's creation of a new society, Paul now turns to exhorting the inhabitants on how they should live and act in their brand new society. This exhortation covers the rest of the book (Ephesians 4:1—6:24).

4:1 I therefore, the prisoner of the Lord, beseech you that ye walk worthy of the vocation wherewith ye are called.
Paul has finished praying for them that God through Christ might dwell richly in their hearts so that they would be able to fully comprehend the magnitude of God's love for them in Christ. He starts the new section with an appeal for them to live a Christ-filled life. Using an emphatic first person pronoun "I" (*ego*), Paul begins his appeal by reintroducing himself, as in 3:1, as the prisoner of the Lord. This probably is to assert his apostolic authority. The use of the conjunction "therefore" (*oun*) adds the emphatic nature of the *ego*. The phrase can then be reworded in view of this (i.e., in view of the things God has done through history): I, a prisoner of the Lord appeal to you. The phrase "the prisoner (*desmios*, i.e., captive) of the Lord" means probably that Paul was both a prisoner of Jesus in loyal and loving obedience as an apostle, and a prisoner for Christ in custody for his loyalty to the Gospel of Christ as one under arrest. Both

his authority as an apostle and his personal conviction as a man under house arrest, seem to motivate his appeal to them.

He writes, "I . . . beseech you that ye walk worthy of the vocation wherewith ye are called." We have noted in previous studies that to walk is an idiomatic way of saying to lead a life, conduct oneself or behave (2:2). Paul urges them to conduct their lives in such manner that would match their calling, i.e., their commitment in Christ. Since the Christian life is a response to God's call in one's life, one then has to comport oneself in a way that would show the commitment. God's call is expressed in different ways in the following passages of the book: He "called" them in Ephesians 1:18; "chose" them in 1:4; "adopted" them in 1:5; and "accepted" them in 1:6.

What is the nature of this vocation to which they have been called? There are major characteristics of this call: first, they are called into one single family—into "one new man" (2:15). This emphasizes unity, which occupies Paul's thought in chapters 1-3 and in the passage under review (Ephesians 4:1-16). Second, they are called into a holy family, separate and distinct from the world, and the emphasis here is the purity of the Church (Ephesians 1:17—5:21).

This passage and John 17 are two classic passages that show how fundamental the unity of the church is in the mind of Christ and the first century apostles. Christ's death, as we have earlier noted, is the vehicle through which both those "afar off and . . . them that were nigh" had been brought into one household of God (Ephesians 2:17-19). All through the centuries in the history of the Church, there have been emphases and efforts made to unite the Church. The formation of the World Council of Churches is one of the efforts, the United Church of Canada, is an amalgamation of three denominations in an effort to bring unity.

It seems the more we try to unify the church, the more it eludes us. This writer believes that the Church is getting more fragmented in our present age than ever before, because we talk more of unity in the Church than putting forth effort to achieving it. We fail to practice unity. We spend (more appropriately, waste) immeasurable time and money having conferences, seminars, and workshops which theorize about unity rather than putting our efforts in unifying the Church. Our generation, a generation which has seen more conferences, seminars, and teachings on unity than any other, is still plagued by racial and social segregation. The Church is drifting further apart instead of coming together. Why? This question will remain unanswered until the Church gets hold of this Scripture passage, hopefully soon and before the advent of the Head of the Church.

2 With all lowliness and meekness, with long-suffering, forbearing one another in love;

Paul gives five characteristics of the life worthy of our calling: lowliness, meekness, longsuffering (patience), mutual forbearance, and love. The unity of the Church, Paul seems to imply, starts with individuals and with the keeping of moral qualities. Earlier in 3:17, Paul prays to God that "Christ may dwell in (our) hearts by faith, that (we may be) rooted and grounded in love." Love, he implies, is the soil in which we must grow and the foundation in which we must build a unified church. It is, as we sing in one of our choruses, the cord that binds (or should bind) the Church together.

To maintain unity in the Church, we are to walk in lowliness (Greek *tapeinophrosune* i.e., humility), which was a debasing quality and unacceptable virtue in their contemporary society, especially among the Greek world. The word is better-translated "lowliness of mind," a state of mind which recognizes the worth and values of others. The same mind was in Christ that He emptied Himself and took the form of a servant even unto death (Philippians 2:3-8).

In this passage, Paul urges the Philippian congregation to imitate the same virtue. Here, Paul says that humility is essential to unity. This is apparent in our daily living. We get along easier with those who respect us than those who treat us with disdain. We have disharmony in our churches today because of pride, which are both individually and cooperatively exhibited (racially motivated) in our churches. False superiority is one of the greatest evils in our society. False superiority caused a lot of turmoil earlier in the century, and is still causing problems among the races in our society today. The Church on one hand must continue to denounce this movement, and on the other hand promote racial unity within the body.

This attitude of superiority is evidenced by the fact that for a black pastor, for example, to succeed in ministry, he or she usually has to minister to a black community only.. How many white churches in the US or Canada have black pastors as part of their teaching staff? Or, how many white people comfortably attend black churches in our society? Until recently, Black people were openly segregated against in most white churches of the south, e.g., the Southern Baptist congregations. They were not allowed to attend white churches. This practice has been officially abolished. However, we have yet to see it implemented. It is therefore then not surprising that unity continues to elude the Church in this century in spite of the numerous conferences and seminars on building unity.

We are to walk in meekness (*prautes*) or gentleness. In

Matthew Henry's commentary on this passage, he defines meekness as: "That excellent disposition of the (mind) which makes men unwilling to provoke others and not easily to be provoked or offended with their infirmities. It is opposed," he says, "to angry resentments and peevishness." Meekness can be defined as the demonstration of power under control. It has the idea of the disposition of one, who though has the right or authority, decides not to lay claim on it both before God or others. It seems that humility and meekness go together. Both are found in Christ Jesus (Matthew 11:29). Paul instructs Timothy to teach others with gentleness and meekness of mind (2 Timothy 2:24-25).

The next two characteristics that will foster unity in the body of Christ also seem to go together, long-suffering (*makrothumia*) (patience) and forbearance (endurance, i.e., not seeking revenge or being aggravated by others). A virtue God shows to us through Christ. Forbearing one another (*anechomai*) has the idea of putting up with, or to endure and bear with someone's mistakes or attitude. It speaks of being tolerant towards others; a mutual understanding between people.

These four characteristics, as we have already discussed, are anchored in love, and they form the basis and foundation for unity in the Church. Without these four, based in love, unity will continue to slip away from the Church. Love here can then mean a consideration of other people's welfare and the "willingness to act for their good rather than our own" as one writer puts it. Paul writes, "Put on therefore, as the elect of God, holy and beloved, bowels of mercies, kindness, humbleness of mind, meekness, long-suffering; Forbearing one another, and forgiving one another, if any man have a quarrel against any: even as Christ forgave you, so also do ye" (Colossians 3:12-13).

3 Endeavoring to keep the unity of the Spirit in the bond of peace.

In verse 3, Paul identifies the nature of the unity as the unity of the Spirit. He urges the Church to endeavor (Greek *spoudazo*) to keep the unity of the Spirit in the bond of peace. The word *spoudazo*, translated in different ways in the New Testament (e.g., "diligent" Titus 3:12; 2 Peter 3:14; "do diligence" 2 Timothy 4:9), is emphatic. It means "to spare no effort" or, as we idiomatically express, to leave no stone unturned in order to keep (preserve) the unity of the Spirit. In other words, we should do our utmost to preserve the unity.

What does Paul mean by the unity of the Spirit? There are two possible answers. First, some translate it to mean the spiritual harmony of the Christian, using the small letter "s" for spirit. In this translation, the words "heart" or "soul" can substitute for "spirit." The idea then is that Christian unity is in the heart; it does not lie in one set of thoughts, nor in one form and mode of worship, but in one heart and one mind. The second and more accepted meaning is the unity which the Spirit creates or gives. This unity starts within the individual hearts of its members. To preserve this unity therefore depends on both individual and cooperative efforts of all members of the body of Christ and starts with the heart attitudes. These heart attitudes are exhibited through the foregoing qualities we have mentioned above (v. 2), and they include the fruit of the Spirit as listed in Galatians 5:22-23.

This unity created by the Spirit (of God) is the unification of Jews and Gentiles into one community of believers, God's new society, which Paul has endeavored to explain in the first three chapters. The phrase "in the bond of peace" means that peace serves as the cord which holds unity together. Peace, which is a fruit of the Spirit, is essential in the preservation of Church unity. The absence of peace in any body or organization, whether secular or religious, or in the family causes disintegration and dysfunctionality to that body or entity.

Quarrels and divisions weaken or destroy any congenial groups and demobilize them. They also serve as destructive machines for unity of the Spirit in the Church, and weaken the body in accomplishing the purpose for which it is established. Therefore, the bond of peace is the strength of the body that energizes any organization or family, both spiritual and physical, into action. Where there is lack of peace, there is no unity and the work of Christ suffers. Does this apply only to the local church? On the other hand, does it apply to the universal Church as well? This writer believes that it applies more so to the latter. If it does, then one wonders why we have many denominations in our Christian community.

What type of disposition was present in the minds of the protagonists of the various groups when they created the denominations? How far did they apply the disposition of humility, gentleness, patience, forbearance, and love as they fragmented the body of Christ? How long will we allow personal preferences in methodology and church polity to continue to cut the cord of unity and perpetuate the disintegration of the body of Christ, and thereby hinder the function for which the body was created? Do we all have to agree on one mode of worship, one type of church government, or credal formulae to allow the unity of the Spirit within the body of Christ? These and other questions need to be addressed by all. Paul seems to answer some of these questions in the verses which follow.

4 There is one body, and one Spirit, even as ye are called in one hope of your calling; 5 One Lord, one faith, one baptism, 6 One God and Father of all, who is above all, and through all, and in you all.

To Paul, there is no room for disunity among the Christian community; it is unthinkable as far as he is concerned. He uses a number of adjectives and metaphors to emphasize the oneness of the Church. In these three verses, Paul declares implicitly that the unity of the Church arises from the unity of the Godhead, making deliberate insinuation about the Trinity. First, the Church is *one* body because there is *one* Spirit that created it. Earlier in 1:23, Paul calls the Church the body of Christ, which comprises the Jews and Gentiles. The unity of this body is due to the work of the Holy Spirit who also indwells it.

Writing to the Corinthians in 1 Corinthians 12:13, he says, "For by one Spirit we are all baptized into one body, whether we be Jews or Gentiles, whether we be bond or free; and have all been made to drink into one Spirit." The one Spirit unifies the body and works through it. A body is made of many parts with various functions: the feet, the hands, the ears and eyes, the mouth, and all are joined to the head. The Church, with its parts, is joined to the Head—Christ by the Holy Spirit—to function as one body. The Church is called into one hope, which refers to the present reality and the future benefit of life everlasting. We learned in 1:14 that the Holy Spirit is the seal that is our present guarantee of the fullness of life everlasting that awaits us beyond the grave. The Holy Spirit sustains this hope in the present earthly life of the Christian.

Second, the reality of the Christian calling and hope is founded on the one Lord, Jesus Christ who is the object of our faith (one faith), in whom all Christians hold their belief, and in whom we all are baptized. One faith refers both to the Gospel, which embodies the doctrine of the Christian faith and the gift of faith whereby all Christians are saved (cf. 2:8-10). One baptism is the sacramental covenant through which we profess our faith when we believe in the atoning death and resurrection of Christ for pardon of our sins. By being baptized in the name of the Father, Son, and Holy Spirit, we declare our union with the one Lord and Saviour Jesus Christ.

Third, the Church is described as one family in which every believer belongs, because there is only one God who is the Father of all, who is above all, and through all, and in you all. This cluster of phrases describes the greatness and magnitude of this one God who all Christians have in common as Father. The God, whom the Jews acclaim as "One" in opposition to the Gentile's many gods, is now the Father of all, both Jew and Gentile Christians. All of humanity is now under the same family, all believers are now children of God because of their relationship or union in Christ (John 1:12). Paul identifies God as "our Father" (1:2), a name and relationship we all share together with Jesus. This Father God is "above all" (i.e., over things). This refers to the sovereign, supreme, and transcendent nature of God. He is "through all," which probably speaks of active participation in the activities of His creation, in the human lives in particular. He is "in you all" with particular reference to the church at Ephesus, which comprises the Jewish and the Gentile believers, and it also refers indeed to the Church universal. In the lives of all believers, God makes His dwelling place through Christ and in the person of the Holy Spirit. Here is an echo of 1 Corinthians 3:16; 6:19. "God in you (us) all" also means that He is active in our lives; He works through and in us, and guides and protects us, both individually and cooperatively as Christ's body.

7 But unto every one of us is given grace according to the measure of the gift of Christ. 8 Wherefore he saith, When he ascended up on high, he led captivity captive, and gave gifts unto men.

After expounding the unity and oneness of the Church, Paul turns our attention to the diversity of gifts. In the last three verses (4-6), Paul insists that all churches of every age and everywhere, irrespective of their nationality, social, or racial origin have few things that unify them. They have one Lord and one Spirit, one faith and one baptism, which are in the Lord Jesus Christ, and one Father God—who is in charge of all things. Although, there is unity of belief and purpose, there is also diversity and uniqueness of gifts and functionality.

We also note Paul's change from "all" meaning "us all" (v. 6) to "every one" (i.e., each one) of us (v. 7). Here, Paul communicates that unity does not constitute uniformity. Through God's artistic prowess in nature, we can appreciate His sense of artistry and beauty. This artistry and beauty are also exhibited in the variety of gifts God gives to individuals for the benefit of the united body. Paul begins the section with the conjunction "but," which suggests that in spite of the unity (oneness in the body), there is room for individuality of each member as well. This is evident in the giving of gifts. To each one of us, Paul says, "is given grace according to the measure of the gift of Christ." The word for "grace" (*charis*) used here is not the grace which we encountered in 2:5, 8 by which sinners receive forgiveness; it is rather *charismata* or "gifts" which equip God's people for service. This gift, Paul says, is given according to the mea-

sure (degree) of the gift of Christ. The measure seems to imply generosity (cf. Romans 8:32; Luke 6:38; cp. John 3:34). Paul identifies the Giver of the gift as Christ.

Paul then quotes a verse of Scripture to confirm his emphasis on the gift through Christ, a reference from Psalm 68:18. There is some difficulty and debate about the appropriate use of language in the two versions (here, and in Psalm 68), which we are not obliged to indulge ourselves; for a better treatment of this prolem, we refer the reader to John Stott's book *God's New Society*, Downers Grove: InterVarsity Press, 1979, pp. 156-157). The sentence, "When he ascended up on high, he led captivity captive, and gave gifts unto men," refers to Christ's ascension to the right hand of the Father as Conqueror over death, defeating Satan and his agents. He liberated those who were bound and took them like captives into heaven. From there He gives gifts to the Church, which might refer to the bestowing of gifts of the Holy Spirit on the Day of Pentecost.

9 (Now that he ascended, what is it but that he also descended first into the lower parts of the earth? 10 He that descended is the same also that ascended up far above all heavens, that he might fill all things.)

Verses 9-10 in parentheses serve as support and elaboration of Christ's ascension. Here, Paul seems to apply the principle of apologetics. He argues, as in defense of the death, resurrection, and ascension of Christ, that for Christ to ascend into heaven, He must have descended. Paul has alluded to the same idea in Ephesians 1:20-22 where he writes that "God made him to sit at his right hand in the heavenly places far above all principality and power . . ." Paul explains this further in Philippians:

"Who, being in the form of God, thought it not robbery to be equal with God: But made himself of no reputation, and took upon him the form of a servant, and was made in the likeness of men: And being found in fashion as a man, he humbled himself, and became obedient unto death, even the death of the cross. Wherefore God also hath highly exalted him, and given him a name which is above every name: That at the name of Jesus every knee should bow, of things in heaven, and things in earth, and things under the earth;" (Philippians 2:6-10).

Verse 10 insists that the one who descended is the same that ascended far above everything else, that He might fill all things. The phrase "fill all things" (*pleroo*) means "to accomplish" or "fulfill" all things. It seems to speak about completing His mission. The purpose of His ascension into heaven is then to free Him to accomplish fully the purpose for which He descended. One of which is the distribution of gifts to the Church by the Holy Spirit.

11 And he gave some, apostles; and some, prophets; and some, evangelists; and some, pastors and teachers; 12 For the perfecting of the saints, for the work of the ministry, for the edifying of the body of Christ:

The gift that the ascended Christ gives to the Church is the gift of the Holy Spirit, whom the Lord promised His disciples He would send after His glorification (John. 7:39), and confirmed before His ascension into heaven (Acts. 1:8). The Holy Spirit then equips the Church with special abilities which He bestows on each member for the benefit of all. We must call to mind a variety of gifts Paul lists in Romans 12 and 1 Corinthians 12, where a more extensive list of gifts for the building of the Church is given. Here, Paul lists five administrative offices given to the church: apostles, prophets, evangelists, pastors, and teachers.

The word "apostle" (*apostolos*) is used in three ways in the New Testament. First as in John 13:16, it means "the ones sent." In this case, it applies to every individual Christian, for we are all sent as ambassadors of Christ to proclaim Him to the world. Second, there were apostles of the church (2 Corinthians 8:23), who were sent out by the church as messengers and missionaries. Third, there were the small groups with special designation as apostles, consisting of the Twelve (including Matthias), Paul and James, the brother of Jesus, and a few others. They were eyewitnesses to the risen Lord, chosen and authorized by Christ (Acts 1:21, 22; 10:40-41; 1 Corinthians 9:1; 15:8-9). This later designation is probably the sense in which Paul uses the word here. Some of these apostles were still alive during the time of the writing of Ephesians. Therefore, when used in this sense of the word, there are no apostles today.

The next gift is the prophets (*prophetes*) with special ability from God to give guidance to the Christian community and to declare the will of God (e.g., Acts 13:1-4). Next are the evangelists (*euaggelistes*), preachers or those who proclaim the Gospel (e.g., Philip, Acts 21:8; and Timothy, 2 Timothy 4:5). The verb form is however used to describe the spreading of the Good News. Then we have the pastors (*poimen*) or shepherds, who are also teachers who give instructions. Some argue that pastors and teachers are two names for the same ministry. It is possible that they are two separate ministries since we have some Christian teachers who are not pastors. However all five relate to one form of teaching or the other, and they are set in the church to fulfill certain purposes and functions.

These functions are twofold. One is to equip (for perfecting) the saints for the work of ministry and the other is for building up (edifying of) the body of Christ. The King James Version suggests three functions rather than two: 1) perfecting of the saints; 2) doing the work of a minister; and 3) edifying (building up) of the body. The latter option seems to suggest that the ministry in the Church is reserved for special people rather than the whole body of Christ.

The word translated "perfecting" is the Greek word *katartismos*, which means "to equip, to prepare, or to make ready." Therefore, the apostles, prophets, evangelists, pastors, and teachers' function is to prepare God's people (the saints) or equip them for work of ministry (*diakonia*) or service. They are endowed with the grace of God in order to prepare people to do the work of service within the church community. They are "equippers" who furnish others in the church with necessary tools for the ministry. Paul gives a model of church functionality in which the pastor aims at encouraging all members through teaching and exhortation to use their talents, skills, and gifts for the benefit of all. Paul defines the concept of church building, in which each person takes active part.

The second function of the people endowed with the special gifts is to edify or build up the body of Christ. The word used here in the King James Version is "edifying" (*oikodome*), with an architectural undertone. It means building a house, but used figuratively here referring to building up the church of Christ. We have been called to build one another up in the Lord in love. What does this task include? It seems to include adding to the number, integrating newcomers into the life of the church, and instructing them to become instruments to be used of God in the Church. Building up the body would include encouraging one another, maintaining peaceful coexistence within the body, and preventing alienation and division within the body. This is expanded further in the later verses of this chapter. The goal of these functions are stated in next verse.

13 Till we all come in the unity of the faith, and of the knowledge of the Son of God, unto a perfect man, unto the measure of the stature of the fulness of Christ: 14 That we henceforth be no more children, tossed to and fro, and carried about with every wind of doctrine, by the sleight of men, and cunning craftiness, whereby they lie in wait to deceive;

While the major twofold function and purpose of the gifts are to equip God's people for the work of the ministry and for building up the body, the ultimate goal is fourfold. We are to continue to grow until we attain a complete unity of the faith (cf. v. 3, unity of the Spirit). Paul's intent here is to be understood as speaking of Jews and Gentiles being knit together in faith, i.e., in the belief of the Gospel of Christ (v. 5). The ministry of all members will help the Church grow and to come to the full knowledge of the Son of God, Christ Jesus. The apostle has already mentioned our knowledge of God (1:17), now the focus is on the knowledge of Christ. Here, the word "unity" modifies both faith and knowledge. The aspiration of all Christians should be to attain this unity, which is based on our united understanding of who Christ is. The Church is called to unity, and this is made possible only by our spiritual knowledge of who Christ is and why He died.

The full unity and knowledge of the Son of God leads to maturity—unto a perfect man. "Perfect" (*teleios*) here refers to that which has reached age of maturity or adulthood, rather than moral perfection. The proof of maturity is the unity the Church attains on the basis of its knowledge of Christ. Although, some interpret this as individual maturity in Christ, which is also a New Testament concept, the maturity here refers to the whole body of Christ. Paul, in Ephesians 2:15, refers to the Church God created as "one new man." Just as newborns grow into adulthood, the Church also grows into maturity evidenced by their oneness in unity and knowledge of Christ.

This matured manhood or "perfect man" is measured according to Christ's standards, "unto the measure of the stature of the fulness of Christ." In verse 7, Christ is the measure of God's grace. Here He is the measure or the yardstick of all maturity. Although the concept of growth into maturity is corporate, yet the maturity of the Church depends on the growth of individual members. Using the analogy of the physical body which requires the proportional and normal growth of each part to be a healthy body, individual members need to grow accordingly to the measure of grace each person possesses in order to maintain a healthy Church. When we reach such maturity that is rooted in the knowledge of the Gospel of Christ, we then will not be tossed about with every type of teaching.

Children have the tendency to be easily deceived, or easily attracted to new things, but when they grow to adulthood that tendency diminishes. Maturity in the knowledge of Christ will protect the Church from being swerved around. We have been called upon to be like children in humility and innocence, but adults in knowledge and understanding (Matthew 18:3; 1 Corinthians 14:20). Paul uses the picture of a boat in a rough sea being tossed to and fro (*kludonizomenoi*, i.e., tossed here and there) by the waves and carried about (*periphero-*

menoi), which means to be "driven around" or "carried around" by every wind of doctrine. Such people cannot make up their mind but change from one opinion to another, according to the last teaching or the last books they read, or information they received. There is no stability in their thoughts.

Such people are easy prey to the sleight and cunning craftiness of men, whereby they lie in wait to deceive. The sleight (*kubeia*) literally means "dice playing" and is used metaphorically here to describe the deception, trickery, and manipulation of unscrupulous men who take advantage of people's ignorance. Paul is literally describing what has been happening in our time, especially from the late 1970's until now. We have seen the Gospel used in different ways and forms by preachers and occult leaders to deceive and manipulate people to enrich themselves. Many innocent and well-meaning people have even lost their lives in mass suicide in the name of religion, and many more have been bankrupted through the cunning of many preachers who use a variety of methods to defraud others.

All this adversity occurs because of the lack of the full knowledge of the Son of God, which is the result of improper or lack of instruction. When these "lacks" are present, the ignorant are vulnerable to the gimmicks and cunning of the men who are out to deceive and manipulate their unsuspecting prey. That is why Paul calls for both corporate and individual maturity of the Church, which results from proper use of the various gifts, that is, for the common benefit of all members of the body.

15 But speaking the truth in love, may grow up into him in all things, which is the head, even Christ:

Paul moves from the mark of immaturity, which is doctrinal instability, to the qualities of mature (perfect) Christianity, which will promote unity and peace within the body. These qualities are seemingly a rare combination—truth and love. Nonetheless, these two are essential in the life of the body of Christ. They lead to growth in the Church. It is important for the Christian to hold firm and be loyal to the truth on the one hand, and to have loving concern for others' welfare on the other. Many of us seem to hold so firm to the truth that we sometimes become very harsh in our treatment of other people who seem to have violated it.

Is it possible to be devoted to the truth and at the same speak lovingly to the people who violate it? Where can we draw the line in tolerating those who oppose the truth, without compromising the truth? Paul says it is possible to be loyal to the truth, and also show loving concern to others who do not share in it as well. Jesus is described as "full of grace and truth" (John 1:17), and His dealings with others who are sinners, were seasoned with love. There is nothing more prone to dividing the Church or causing rifts between people than being so dogmatic in one's belief that others are offended. It breeds hatred. The main problem, as Paul identifies here, is the question of communication. How do we communicate the truth so that unity can be maintained? Paul says: Speak the truth in love. This statement also carries the idea that we should be truthful and genuine to one another as opposed to the insincerity and cunning of those described in verse 14, whose goal is to deceive others for their own selfish gain. We should lead transparent and honest lives in our dealings with members of the body. Such sincere lives will help the body to "grow up into him in all things" (i.e., "grow up in all (aspects) into Him," v. 15, NAS), "which is the head, even Christ." Growing up in all things in Him is tantamount to maturing so much spiritually as to becoming like Christ, the head of the body. We are to be deeply rooted in Him in all things so that we exhibit Christ-likeness in our lives—in knowledge, love, and faith and in our relationship with all members of the body.

16 From whom the whole body fitly joined together and compacted by that which every joint supplieth, according to the effectual working in the measure of every part, maketh increase of the body unto the edifying of itself in love.
Paul then employs biological metaphors, using the human anatomy, to describe the Church's relationship with Christ. He compares the natural body and Christ's mystical body, the Church. As the body has many component parts, which are joined fittingly together by different ligaments to the head, and each part works corporately with other parts, so it is with the Church. The Church has many members with various functions, joined fittingly together by the Holy Spirit unto Christ, the Head. The Holy Spirit has endowed every member with various gifts and skills, each member should then work corporately with every other member in love.

Only when every member works properly and each person contributes his or her own share, can the body maintain unity and growth in maturity; the body will work as a single unit. Conversely, there will be disruption in proper function of the body when there is lack of coordination of any part with others, or when one decides to function in isolation. For the body to grow and function properly, there needs to be harmony and obedience to the head through whom the whole body derives its strength and life. Just as Paul opened this section with a call to "walk worthy of the vocation wherewith ye are called . . . in love" (vv. 1-2), he ends it by reminding us to function in love so as to build up one another.

The circulatory supply of blood to different parts of the body is essential for the growth and maintenance of a healthy body whether in animals or humans. Blood gives life to the body. Consequently, love is essential for the proper function of the Church; love is the life-blood that keeps the Church alive and united. When mutual love is lacking in the Church, the head (Christ) is severed from the body. He is not present there any longer. The body dies. Love is the important trait that controls the functionality of all parts of the Church body in relation to one another (vv. 2, 15, 16; 5:2). Paul tells the Corinthians that love is the most important gift of all, even greater than faith and hope (1 Corinthians 13), and the use of all other gifts should be based in love. Yes, even speaking the truth (v. 15).

DAILY BIBLE READING

M: Gentiles Are Fellow Heirs in Christ
Ephesians 3:1-6

T: Gentiles Receive the Gospel's Riches
Ephesians 3:7-13

W: Paul Prays for the Ephesian Christians
Ephesians 3:14-21

T: Unity in the Body of Christ
Ephesians 4:1-10

F: Grow to Maturity in Christ Jesus
Ephesians 4:11-16

S: Live in Righteousness and Holiness
Ephesians 4:17-24

S: Live a New Life in Christ
Ephesians 4:25-32

TEACHING TIPS

July 23
Bible Study Guide 8

1. Words You Should Know

A. Covetousness (5:3)—In this context, Paul warns against desiring what belongs to someone else or gratifying oneself at all costs.

B. Convenient (v. 4)—King James translation for a word meaning "inappropriate." Other versions translate as "out of place" (NIV) or "not fitting" (RSV).

C. Admonition (6:4)—Instruction.

2. Teacher Preparation

Read the background Scripture for the lesson. Study more about marriage and the roles of men and women during Paul's time and the social and governmental institutions which ruled over them.

3. Starting the Lesson

A. Ask class members: "What does the Bible say about how we should behave as followers of Christ? As Christian husbands and wives? As Christian parents and children?" Use this discussion time to discover class members' understanding of proper Christian conduct.

B.. Read the IN FOCUS story about David and Louise. Discuss the difficulties of raising children to live as Children of God and the difficulties of trying to find a spouse, friend, etc., who conducts themselves as true followers of Christ, as Paul has mandated that we ought to do.

4. Getting into the Lesson

Ask class members why they believe submission has been given a "bad name" in contemporary society. How has the biblical mandate for submission out of love been maligned, especially submission of wives toward husbands? Has equal attention been given to the responsibility of husbands toward their wives? Also ask them to share whether they believe Paul's instructions are realistic for marriage in the 21st century.

5. Relating the Lesson to Life

A. Review the information about marriage and children/family in THE PEOPLE, PLACES, AND TIMES article. In what ways have roles changed in marriage and family relationships. What impact have these changes had on the modern-day family?

B. Give students an opportunity to answer the questions in SEARCH THE SCRIPTURES.

C. DISCUSS THE MEANING emphasizes what it means to *walk in love* and what impact, if any, the cultural and religious norms of that time had on Paul's view of marriage.

D. The LESSON IN OUR SOCIETY addresses the significance of relationships based on the model given to us by Christ. The breakdown of institutions in our current society may well be the result of neutral, or perhaps in some cases, hostile attitudes toward biblical codes of conduct for Christians.

6. Arousing Action

A. Ask class members to form three groups. The first group should write a job description for a true follower of Christ based on Paul's message in Ephesians 5:1-4. The second group should write a job description for a married couple, including the responsibilities of both husbands and wives based on 5:21-29. The third group should write a job description for children and parents based on 6:1-4. Allow each of the three groups to share their results.

B. Based on the instructions given in the MAKE IT HAPPEN section, give class members an opportunity to consider areas of their lives wherein they have not conducted themselves as Paul directed. Pass out pencils and paper, if necessary. You may ask for volunteers to share the results of their personal assessments. Lead the class in a time of prayer, asking the Lord to strengthen each member as he or she endeavors to behave in a way that is pleasing to God.

C. Give class members an opportunity to complete FOLLOW THE SPIRIT and REMEMBER YOUR THOUGHTS.

CALLED TO RESPONSIBLE LIVING

Bible Background • EPHESIANS 5—6:4
Printed Text • EPHESIANS 5:1-5, 21-29; 6:1-4
Devotional Reading • EPHESIANS 5:6-20

LESSON AIM

After studying today's lesson, class members should gain a greater understanding of the proper conduct for Christians in the world, in the church, and in the home.

KEEP IN MIND

"Submitting yourselves one to another in the fear of God" (Ephesians 5:21).

FOCAL VERSES

EPHESIANS 5:1 Be ye therefore followers of God, as dear children;

2 And walk in love, as Christ also hath loved us, and hath given himself for us an offering and a sacrifice to God for a sweet smelling savour.

3 But fornication, and all uncleanness, or covetousness, let it not be once named among you, as becometh saints;

4 Neither filthiness, nor foolish talking, nor jesting, which are not convenient: but rather giving of thanks.

5 For this ye know, that no whoremonger, nor unclean person, nor covetous man, who is an idolater, hath any inheritance in the kingdom of Christ and of God.

21 Submitting yourselves one to another in the fear of God.

22 Wives, submit yourselves unto your own husbands, as unto the Lord.

23 For the husband is the head of the wife, even as Christ is the head of the church: and he is the saviour of the body.

24 Therefore as the church is subject unto Christ, so let the wives be to their own husbands in every thing.

25 Husbands, love your wives, even as Christ also loved the church, and gave himself for it;

26 That he might sanctify and cleanse it with the washing of water by the word,

27 That he might present it to himself a glorious church, not having spot, or wrinkle, or any such thing; but that it should be holy and without blemish.

28 So ought men to love their wives as their own bodies. He that loveth his wife loveth himself.

29 For no man ever yet hated his own flesh; but nourisheth and cherisheth it, even as the Lord the church:

6:1 Children, obey your parents in the Lord: for this is right.

2 Honour thy father and mother; which is the first commandment with promise;

3 That it may be well with thee, and thou mayest live long on the earth.

4 And, ye fathers, provoke not your children to wrath: but bring them up in the nurture and admonition of the Lord.

IN FOCUS

David and Louise were sitting in the den when their son, 18-year-old Christopher, came in and sat with them. He was really frustrated about how to handle himself in relationships. He and his girlfriend, Shari, had just had a huge argument, and he was upset. "I'm tired of being the Super Mr. Nice Guy," he said.

The couple sympathized with their son. He was struggling to hold on to the Christian values they taught him to live by, while at the same time finding his place in the world.

"Son," David spoke up, "I know you like Shari a lot. Your

mother and I like her, too. But do you think it's wise to continue spending time with someone who doesn't respect or appreciate your values?"

"Well," Christopher lowered his head, "I guess not. But it's just getting really hard to find Christian friends who are not doing everything that non-Christians are doing."

David and Louise nodded sympathetically. At that moment, neither had the heart to tell him that the struggle probably wouldn't get much easier as he got older.

THE PEOPLE, PLACES, AND TIMES

MARRIAGE. A monogamous relationship in which a man and woman share a lifetime commitment to each other and to God. It is a covenantal agreement. Jesus emphasized that God intends for marriage to be a lifetime commitment (Mark 10:5; Matthew 19:4-9).

With regard to submission in marriage, some hold to the view that the husband, as head of the household, has authority over his wife which has been delegated by God. Others adhere to a more democratic marriage in which both spouses are equal partners in all things. There are still others who advocate mutual submission in love as the ideal for Christian marriage, according to Ephesians 5:21.

Both Paul and Peter regarded submission as a voluntary act within a loving relationship, not forced subjection to an authority, as in a military organization.

Based on information from *Holman Bible Dictionary*, Trent Butler, general editor, Nashville: Broadman & Holman Publishers, 1991, pp. 924-927.

CHILDREN/FAMILY. The Old Testament family had multiple purposes, including reproduction, instruction, care-giving, maintaining traditions, and conveying wisdom. The primary function of the family, however, was to teach religion, thus providing guidelines and instruction which were essential to the prosperity and well-being of the Hebrew family. In the Hebrew context, children were very important to the family and were considered as proof of God's love and blessing (Psalm 127:3). Fathers held absolute authority and control over their children.

Based on information from *Holman Bible Dictionary*, pp. 475-477.

BACKGROUND

From this point to the conclusion of Paul's letter to the Ephesians, he makes a plea for the responsible use of freedom in Christ. Christian liberty was not, as some thought, a license to continue in sin. God had already given the gift of salvation, but He still called for right living among His

people. Christian freedom makes believers a slave of Christ which, therefore, calls for the ongoing production of the fruit of His Spirit. Paul knew that the freedom Christ offers is more challenging than living according to the law. He was concerned that some believers might be tempted to revert to living according to the Law of Moses, where there was neither indecision nor doubt. When some question did arise, the religious authorities provided a definitive answer.

Because they were no longer under the law, the early-believers had questions about how to relate to one another in Christ. Paul provided clear guidelines for responsible Christian living.

Christians are to offer a lifestyle which is a ray of hope to this dark world. Ours should be a way of living and conducting ourselves which honors the Lord we serve. Both in our homes and in dealing with the world, those of us who are part of the body of Christ must honor Him in our daily living.

AT-A-GLANCE

1. **The Nature of True Love**
   (Ephesians 5:1-5)
2. **Conduct in Marriage (vv. 21-29)**
3. **Parent-Child Relationships**
   (Ephesians 6:1-4)

IN DEPTH

1. The Nature of True Love (Ephesians 5:1-5)

Paul issued a summons to imitate God, in the manner of a child. Paul has explained God's example of forgiveness through His Son, Jesus (4:32). Now Paul says, "In light of what God has done by example, go ye and do likewise." The phrase "followers of God" (translated as "imitators" in other versions) paints a vivid picture of Paul's intention.

To be a follower or imitator in the manner of a child can be likened to a child playing dress up. Children, in all sincerity and desire, work to make themselves up in the image of their parents. Most children learn the values of their family and the traits and behaviors that are expected from those who are significant members of that family.

Another way to be like our Father is to "walk in love." This means that we give of ourselves in service to others, just as Jesus did. He loves us and He proved His love by willingly giving up His life for us.

Sacrifices and burnt offerings were a familiar part of the

Jewish religion. The sacrifice made by Christ was superior to any other such offering. His was "a sweetsmelling savour," found pleasing to His Father.

Paul understood the importance of the church maintaining a strong identity in the world. This would be done, in great part, by its members leading pure lives, not given to the immoral practices which were accepted as normal by the Greco-Roman society.

Perhaps because they, and Paul himself, were accustomed to the specifics covered under the law, he gave them specific examples of the kind of behavior that should be shunned. There are some things that a Christian should not be found doing, including "fornication, and all uncleanness or covetousness." In this context, the term "covetousness" is associated with adultery. Paul warns against desiring what belongs to someone else, gratifying oneself at all costs.

Not only our actions, but even the very words we say must be guarded. "Filthiness, foolish talking , jesting, which are not convenient" are all inappropriate conduct for Christians. Paul did not condemn being lighthearted or having good-humored fun. But conversations and actions which are beyond the boundaries of appropriate behavior are off limits for believers. The Christian's conversation should be decent and worthy of the Saviour we follow. A healthy alternative to bad talk, Paul says, is "giving thanks."

One who defiles his or her body has no place in God's Kingdom. God does forgive sin. That does not mean, however, that He is indifferent to sin. We are to conduct ourselves like persons who seek to enter the heavenly realm. True faith is demonstrated by the choices we make in our daily living.

2. Conduct in Marriage (vv. 21-29)

Belief in Christ Jesus does not abolish our earthly relationships. In fact, we often come closer to Him according to how we conduct ourselves in our relationships as spouses, parents, children, co-workers, and so forth.

Prior to verse 21, Paul advises believers to be filled with the Spirit. One indicator of that infilling is mutual submission "in the fear of God." True worship of Christ enables believers to submit to one another out of love.

Earthly living calls for order and structure, in society as well as in the home. Paul applied the concept of mutual submission to the Christian family relationships between husband-wife and parent-child. In both cases, self-giving is prescribed. Paul instructed wives to submit themselves to their husbands. The submission Paul calls for is voluntary, not the result of a husband's demands or overbearing nature.

Paul is not suggesting in verse 23 that a wife unconditionally submit herself to her husband as she does to the Lord. That would be placing the husband in an unhealthy role bordering on idolatry. No wife is expected to submit to her husband if it would require her to compromise her loyalty to Christ. Paul's writing here makes the assumption that both spouses are Christians and that the husband may be entrusted with this sacred responsibility. Both husband and wife fall under the headship of Christ. If both follow His example of love and submission, there is no possibility for abuse or neglect.

The Christian wife submits herself to her Christian husband, who places her welfare even above his own. The call for submission is much greater and deeper than that of a wife simply doing as her husband says. Under the Gospel of Christ, submission cannot be separated from love. Love for one another means acceptance of that person.

Out of love and respect comes the husband's selfless giving to the welfare of his wife. Husbands are to yield themselves to wives with the same selfless love that Christ yielded Himself to the cross for the sake of the church. Paul challenges the husband to take Christ's love for the church as the blueprint for his own attitude toward his wife. The husband's role is not aggression or assertion, but sacrifice.

Christ loves His church and through His sacrifice planned for a greater purpose: "that he might sanctify and cleanse," also that he "might present it to himself a glorious church, holy and without blemish." He paid the greatest price to obtain a bride for Himself. With this as a model for the husband, he should enter into the marriage having a greater purpose for his wife and family.

Christ's love for the Church is demonstrated through His work of sanctification. He set the Church apart for cleansing with "the washing of water by the word." Because of His plan, believers are cleansed as we hear the words of Christ and obey them. In John 15:3, Jesus told His disciples, "Now ye are clean through the word which I have spoken unto you."

Verse 27 turns to the ultimate realization of Christ's purpose: when the bride (the Church) will be ready to meet her Husband (Jesus Christ). Just as a bride and groom vow to set themselves and their relationship apart from all others, Christians are set apart by Christ to be His bride through public confession and baptism.

This is the same type of love and concern husbands are expected to show their wives. In the marriage, the two make vows to become one. Within that union, the husband's love for himself and his love for his wife are inseparable. The man who loves his wife is loving himself.

Paul reminds husbands that no man "hateth his own flesh." The husband and wife are one. Therefore, to treat the wife in any way but lovingly, is to harm himself. In the marital relationship when either spouse acts with hate, it has a negative impact on them both. Both spouses should conduct themselves in a manner which builds the marriage and sets it apart from all other human relationships.

3. Parent-Child Relationships (Ephesians 6:1-4)

In chapter 5, Paul taught that the result of being Spirit-filled is mutual submission. Now he turns to the parent-child relationship, urging children to "obey your parents in the Lord." As they obey their parents, children should do so with the same attitude they would have toward obeying the Lord. He reminds them of the commandment to "honour thy father and mother." To honour one's parents includes not only obedience, but respect and love, also.

The promise of long life accompanies the commandment to honor one's parents. Rules are given to children for their own safety and protection. Those who heed their parents' instructions generally grow up to be fruitful, responsible persons who enjoy a good life. Conversely, youthful rebellion and reckless behavior has caused many lives to end prematurely.

The command for a child's obedience places a great responsibility on the parents. It calls for parents to conduct themselves in a manner worthy of being obeyed. Children are a gift from God. For their own safety, protection, and well-being, children need to obey their parents' instructions. Every child desires a strong moral universe which defines the boundaries of right and wrong. Likewise, children thrive and grow in a stable, loving home environment. Under such conditions, discipline is not resented if the children understand that it is being done for their own benefit.

Paul directs his attention to fathers when issuing the challenge and the responsibility for teaching and nurturing children. Both parents have an important role in the growth and development of their children. Harsh parenting can destroy the parent-child bond. Child-rearing is to be done "in the nurture and admonition of the Lord." Parenting should be carried out according to His will.

SEARCH THE SCRIPTURES

1. In what manner should believers follow God? (Ephesians 5:1)

2. How did Christ demonstrate His love? (v. 2)

3. What kinds of behaviors and attitudes should not be named among Christians? (vv. 3-4)

4. How are believers to relate to one another? (v. 21)

5. What is Paul's command to wives? (v. 22)

6. What position did Paul give to the husband? (v. 23)

7. What model did Paul give for Christian subjection? (v. 24)

8. How are husbands to relate to their wives? (v. 25)

9. For what reason did Christ give Himself to the Church? (vv. 26-27)

10. How are children to relate to their parents? (Ephesians 6:1)

11. What promise is given to children who obey their parents? (v. 3)

12. What words of caution did Paul give to fathers? (v. 4)

DISCUSS THE MEANING

1. What does it mean to "walk in love," as Paul instructed in Ephesians 5:2?

2. Were Paul's mandates to husbands and wives heavily influenced by the societal and religious roles held by men and women during his time?

LESSON IN OUR SOCIETY

There have been many attempts to restructure and redefine the biblical mandate for Christian conduct. Perhaps this is the reason for the breakdown of so many human relationships, in the world, in the church, and in the home.

Paul's admonitions concerning Christian conduct is the way to ensure loving, relationships in which all parties are encouraged to become more than they would be apart from that relationship.

Christians today are challenged to separate themselves from what the world offers in terms of human relationships. Our relationships, whether with family, friends, associates, or spouse cannot be sustained on worldly values. Christians must conduct themselves according to the model that Christ has given of His love for us.

MAKE IT HAPPEN

Review the biblical text for today's lesson. Using a pencil and paper, write down those things which you have not followed, either in your Christian conduct or in your marital or family relationships. Have you conducted yourself as Paul has directed? If not, what factors have influenced you to behave otherwise, as a Christian, as a spouse, or as a parent?

FOLLOW THE SPIRIT
What God wants me to do:

_____

_____

_____

REMEMBER YOUR THOUGHTS
Special insights you learned:

_____

_____

MORE LIGHT ON THE TEXT
EPHESIANS 5:1-5, 21-29; 6:1-4

In the following paragraphs, Paul continues his exhortation to the Ephesian believers (and indeed all believers) on how to lead lives of mutual love that are characteristic of the Lord. They are to "be kind to one another, tender-hearted, forgiving each other, just as God in Christ also has forgiven you" (Ephesians 4:32, NASB). This type of life should characterize members of God's new society.

5:1 Be ye therefore followers of God, as dear children; 2 And walk in love, as Christ also hath loved us, and hath given himself for us an offering and a sacrifice to God for a sweet-smelling savour.

This section is a continuation of the last paragraph. The particle "therefore" refers to all that the apostle has been saying, particularly to the last verse. It connects what he had said there with what is contained in the following verses. Since God, for Christ's sake, has forgiven them, Paul says, therefore they are to "be followers" (Greek *mimetes*) or imitators "of God as dear (beloved) children." This is an echo of Christ's admonishment in the Beatitudes (Matthew 5:45, 48) that we are to copy our heavenly Father just as children copy their parents. Paul, in a number of passages in his letters, invites his converts to imitate him as their father in the Lord (cf. 1 Corinthians 4:16; 11:1; 2 Thessalonians 3:7, 9) just as he himself imitates Christ (1 Corinthians 11:1; 1 Thessalonians 1:6).

The same idea is found in Philippians 2:4-5 in which Paul appeals to the Christians to allow the attitude found in Christ to shape their own lives and conduct. An Igbo adage says literally put, "a cow cannot give birth to a goat." It will always give birth to its kind. It is also a com-

mon saying in the Igbo culture that a child must resemble either of her/his parents, if not she/he would be regarded as a bastard. This is the same idea here. As children of God by virtue of our relationship through Christ, we are to conform to His image and likeness, and to His example of mercy, forgiveness, and goodness, which are marks of perfection (Matthew 5:48).

In addition to imitating God as dear children, we are also to follow Christ's example of love, and conduct our lives in the spirit of love. Using an imperative voice, Paul writes, "walk in love, as Christ also hath loved us." As we have already noted in our last lesson and in previous studies, "to walk" (Greek *peripateo*) is an idiomatic way of saying "to lead a life" or "to conduct oneself" or "to behave" (2:2; 4:1). Here, Paul urges believers to conduct their lives in the spirit of love just as Christ exemplified His love for us by giving up Himself. The Greek verb translated "hath given himself" here is *paradidomi*, which means "self-giving" or "surrender." The same word translates "to betray," "to deliver," or "to hand over." It is noteworthy to know the various ways the word *paradidomi* is used in the New Testament to describe the death of Christ. Judas promised to give Him up to the Pharisees; the high priests and Pilate gave Him up. In Romans 8:32a, Paul says that God "spared not his own Son, but delivered him up for us all." Both here and in Galatians 2:20, Paul says that Jesus is the one who gave Himself up as a sacrifice for us.

The greatest demonstration of love is for one to willingly give up oneself (one's life) for another; it is the willingness to renounce self (ego) for the course and good of others. Such love is only seen in Christ. The Bible says that God is love personified (1 John 4:8, 16), and that He loved the world so much that he even gave up His one and only Son (John 3:16); Christ so loved the Church that he gave Himself up for her (v. 25). This sacrificial "giving up" of oneself for others, Paul says is pleasing to God. Paul metaphorically describes it here as "a sweet smelling savour." The language here is reminiscent of the Old Testament practice of animal sacrifices in which God (the gods) is said to enjoy the smell of the burnt offerings (Genesis 8:21; cf. Exodus 29:18; Leviticus 2:9; Ezekiel 20:41). Here we have a poignant truth that warrants our attention, i.e., that sacrificial love for others is an acceptable offering, which pleases God.

3 But fornication, and all uncleanness, or covetousness, let it not be once named among you, as becometh saints;

While Paul in the previous verse encourages sacrificial love for one another in the new society, he discourages selfish lust among the brethren. While on one hand he advocates genuine love, he warns against its perversion on the other. Here, he says that fornication (Greek *porneia*) and all uncleanness (*akathasia* or impurity), covering all aspects of sexual sin which were too common among the Gentiles in the first century, should not even be mentioned among the Lord's people.

Fornication is an illicit sexual behavior among unmarried people, and all impurity includes all other sorts of lust. To them Paul adds covetousness (Greek *pleonexia*), which means "extortion" or "greediness." Coveting here refers to the extortion of somebody else's body for selfish pleasure. The Tenth commandment prohibits the coveting of a neighbor's wife, and Paul includes coveting or greed in the list of immoral practices that are unchristian (Ephesians 4:19; 1 Corinthians 5:10-11; 6:9-10; Colossians 3:5). These, to Paul, are opposed to the life of sacrificial love, which ought to characterize the Children of God (the saints) as exemplified by God. All forms of immoral acts are not only to be avoided by God's people, they are not to be mentioned, not even once, among them. They are to be totally banished from the Christian community.

Why does Paul give such strong warning? There are two important reasons among others. First the Ephesian goddess, Artemis, or Diana, was regarded as goddess of fertility, and so sexual practices were associated with its worship. The next reason, we propose is the erroneous definition of love that people usually seem to have. This is also common in our own generation in which fornication and all sexual practices are wrongfully associated with love. With the use of the conjunction "but," Paul tends to correct the wrong notion. He says all uncleanness, which includes all sexual intercourse and innuendoes outside the context of God-ordained loving marriage, are prohibited among God's people. They should not be mentioned, thought of, or talked about.

4 Neither filthiness, nor foolish talking, nor jesting, which are not convenient: but rather giving of thanks.

Paul goes further. All types of improper speech and conversations and all manner of vulgarity are unacceptable among God's people. They are all unethical and unbecoming among God's new society. Paul classifies these unethical behaviors as filthiness (Greek *aischrotes*, which means "obscenity"), foolish (*morologia* or silly) talks, and jesting (*eutrapelia*, i.e., acting or making jokes or remarks that

goes beyond good taste). These three are manifestations of a dirty mind expressing itself in dirty or obscene conversation. Paul refers to such minds as reprobate, which are characteristic of those without the knowledge of God (Romans 1:28). These types of behavioral deficiencies are out of place, or fitting, he says; instead, their minds should be filled with thanksgiving (*eucharistia*) or gratitude.

In contrast, Paul calls for God-centered attitude among those of God's household evidenced in grateful thanks, rather than the self-centered behavior, which manifests itself in fornication, covetousness, and vulgarity. To Paul, all gifts, including sex are good and God-given and require our gratitude and thanksgiving, rather than joking about them. We need to preserve their sanctity and worth as gifts from a loving Father, rather than degrading them through silly jokes, which are unbecoming among the people of God.

African cultures understand speech embodies spiritual power. Thus, though one may not mean what one says its spiritual impact is nevertheless real. Words are like seeds, if sown they bear fruit according to their essence.

5 For this ye know, that no whoremonger, nor unclean person, nor covetous man, who is an idolater, hath any inheritance in the kingdom of Christ and of God.

Paul moves from the acts of moral decadence to their consequence. Here, Paul gives his readers a strong warning regarding the repercussions of such immoral behavior— those who practice them would be denied inheritance in the kingdom of God. For this ye know, ("for this you can be sure," NIV) emphasizes the certainty of the fact, and it has a ring of conviction in the tone. Paul identifies those immoral people who would be excluded from the kingdom of God. No whoremonger (*pornos*, i.e., fornicator), no unclean person, no covetous man ("man" here is used in the generic sense, rather than gender), which is equivalent to an idolater, Paul seems to imply, will inherit the kingdom of Christ and of God.

At first glance, the phrase "the kingdom of Christ and of God" seems to show that there is a distinction between the kingdom of Christ and that of God. However the definite article is repeated in the Greek rendering, therefore there is no distinction. The kingdom can then be said to belong to Christ who is also God. In Christ's kingdom righteousness reigns, and all unrighteousness would be excluded. What does Paul mean here? How do we apply Paul's teaching? Does it mean that any single immoral thought, speech or deed would disqualify one from the kingdom of God? If that is the case, one wonders who would qualify for admission into God's kingdom.

We believe that any sin committed through the human weakness and vulnerability, but repented and confessed, would receive God's forgiveness. However, the immoral and impure person, who gives up himself or herself into the lifestyle without shame and repentant attitude, one obsessed with immoral lusts, and covetousness, will not share in the kingdom of Christ (1 Corinthians 6:6, 10; Galatians 5:21).

21 Submitting yourselves one to another in the fear of God.

This is a communal principle grounded in the triune nature of God. There is a fundamental connection between the members of the Godhead. They are conjoined in unity and purity. These two are fundamental to a life that is worthy of the calling and fitting to the status of God's people. To maintain the standard, there are down-to-earth practical things required both in the larger family, the Church, and in the human family, the home. The passage (vv. 21-29) deals with two of them: submission and love. Both are essential in maintaining a healthy and peaceful relationship in the home. In verse 21, Paul calls for a mutual and reciprocal submission among the brethren in reverence to God, and immediately turns his attention to the family and addresses the relationship between husband and wife. Verse 21 also serves as a transition between the prior section, which deals with walking and living in the spirit and the one which follows. The use of the present participle "submitting" here, (and in "speaking to yourselves . . . singing and making melody," v. 19, and "giving thanks," v. 20) indicates a continuation of the command to be filled with the Spirit (v. 18). To live a spirit-filled life, one has to submit to authority and to one another in love. This life of submission should begin in the home as Paul indicates.

22 Wives, submit yourselves unto your own husbands, as unto the Lord. 23 For the husband is the head of the wife, even as Christ is the head of the church: and he is the saviour of the body. 24 Therefore as the church is subject unto Christ, so let the wives be to their own husbands in every thing.

In verses 22 to the end of this chapter, Paul prescribes the duties of husbands and wives. To the wives, Paul prescribes the duty of submission, and to the husband, the duty to love his wife. The verb "submit" is a translation of the Greek *hupotasso* that is "to arrange under," or "to subor-

dinate; to obey." This is usually a military term in which soldiers submit to their superiors.

However, in a non-military context it is a voluntary giving up of oneself under the authority and leadership of the other. Here, Paul calls on the wives to submit themselves not in the military sense in which the soldier has no choice, but in a voluntary sense. This is made clear with the phrase, "as unto the Lord," which describes the type of relationship that exists between the Lord and us. The phrase also indicates that the wives' submission to their husbands should be regarded as submission to the Lord because of their relationship to the Lord and in reverence to Him.

Paul advances two reasons for this self-submission of the wives to their husbands. The first is the analogy from creation and indicates that the husband is the head of the wife; the other is from the redemption and indicates that Christ is the head of the Church. The headship of the husband over the wife probably has its origin in the Genesis 2 account where woman was made after man, out of man, and for man, an understanding made clear by Paul in two of his letters (1 Corinthians 11:3-12; 1 Timothy 2:11-13). He adds that man is also born from woman and indicates both man and woman are dependent on each other.

However, the wife's duty of submission is about order creation. Paul compares man's headship over the wife with Christ's headship over the Church. Christ, Paul says, is both the head of the Church, and the Saviour of the body. Paul seems to imply that just as Christ, who is the head of the Church, has a responsibility over the church as its Saviour, so man as the head of the wife has a similar responsibility. The word "saviour" (*soter*) is used in the sense of preserver of the body. As the head of the woman, the man has responsibility to preserve his wife, protect her, and provide for her; he is to be primarily interested in her welfare, just as Christ is for the Church.

The Church's submissive relationship with its head, Christ, is a consequence of His redemptive work; it is reciprocation of what He did for the Church and a demonstration of our love for Him. It will be interesting to note here that Paul does not refer to the husband as the ruler of the wife, but the head. It, therefore, eliminates the tendency to justify an autocratic and domineering attitude of husbands over their wives, which seems to pervade our society.

Verse 24 is a summary of verses 22 and 23. Here, Paul calls on the wives to submit to their husbands in the same way the Church submits to Christ. As already mentioned above, the church's submission to Christ is prompted not necessarily because it is right and demanded by God, but because of His love for us (1 John 4:19). It is voluntary submission that is wholehearted and sincere. Christ never coerces us into submission through intimidation, neither does He force the Church to love Him against its will, rather He invites us gently to come to Him and have relationship with Him.

Moreover, His sacrificial death is the ultimate demonstration of His love for the Church. Consequently, the church voluntarily shows its love for Him by submitting completely to Him in all things. Paul says let the same be true in respect of wives' submission to their husbands, it should be a loving, voluntary submission, in all things, and based on the husbands' love and care for his wife. This is explicitly explained in the verses following. We should be reminded here that Paul is writing on the assumption that his readers are "genuine" Christians. He is describing an ideal Christian home, where life in the Spirit prevails and where Jesus reigns as the ultimate head.

25 Husbands, love your wives, even as Christ also loved the church, and gave himself for it;

After addressing the duties of the wives towards their husbands, Paul turns to the husbands and admonishes them to love their wives in the same way Christ loves the Church. He goes further to describe the magnitude of Christ's love, which is a direct echo of John 3:16 and 1 John 3:16. The husband should love his wife in such a way as to be prepared to die for her. Jesus exhibited this love to the Church. He humbled Himself and came down to earth. He took the form of man. He literally gave up His own life and died the most humiliating and shameful death on the cross, just to redeem the Church. What a love! Only Christ could do that. No wonder He attracts the submission and love that we (true believers) accord Him, for He first loved us. Christ's love has no measure. It is sincere. It is pure and unconditional. It is purposeful. Paul says that while we were sinners and in enmity with Him, He still loved and died in our stead, thereby paying the price for our sin (Romans 5:8, 10).

26 That he might sanctify and cleanse it with the washing of water by the word, 27 That he might present it to himself a glorious church, not having spot, or wrinkle, or any such thing; but that it should be holy and without blemish.

Paul continues to describe the love that Christ has for the church, which He demonstrated by His death. He says that its purpose is to sanctify (*hagiazo*, i.e., to purify or set apart) the Church, and to cleanse it (Greek *katharizo*), which simply put is "to wash" or "to purge." It has the same idea as

the washing of utensils, or healing of lepers. The agents for the cleansing here are clear: water and the Word. The language here is definitely the language of baptism in which the believer is immersed in water. Paul adds that this rite of baptism is by the Word.

What does Paul mean by this? Scholars and denominations are divided in their opinions on the meaning of this portion. Most liberals put great emphasis on water baptism as the means (grace) for salvation that God has provided for the sinner. They believe strongly that the water baptism is an essential element for entry into the kingdom, hence infant baptism is very important. However, evangelicals hold that baptism is only symbolic (though important) or an outward demonstration of what has taken place inwardly in the life of a believer through the Word. They teach that one has to believe, repent from sin, and confess Jesus Christ as Lord before one is baptized in water. Hence, they advocate believers' baptism.

However, Paul's intention here is not to debate the correctness of water baptism, but to state Christ's concern for the Church and the purpose of Christ's death, i.e., to liberate the Church and set her free from the penalty of sin, and present her as a beautiful bride. To this end, Christ gave up His life for her. Paul says that should be the attitude of the husband towards the wife, and ultimately, the husband is to give himself in love for his wife.

28 So ought men to love their wives as their own bodies. He that loveth his wife loveth himself. 29 For no man ever yet hated his own flesh; but nourisheth and cherisheth it, even as the Lord the church:

The second time in this short passage, Paul charges the husband to love his wife (vv. 25, 28), not in the sense of sexual romance and sentimental passion, which often is today equated with genuine love, instead he should love as Christ loved. Paul adds another dimension, which intensifies the importance and degree of love husbands ought to have and that is, they ought to love their wives as their own bodies. Hither to, Paul's appeal for the husbands' love for their wives has been based on Christ's love for His Church, now he turns to self-love. It obvious that everyone has the instinct to care and protect oneself. Paul, therefore, argues that the man, who loves his wife, loves himself because she is part of him not only in the sense of the intimate relationship of sexual union, but in the mystical union of partnership entered together in the act of marriage (vv. 31, 32; Genesis 2:21-25).

We have already noted that the husband is the head of

the wife just as Christ is the head of the Church. Further, we have established that the Church is the body of Christ, as the wife is in essence the body of the husband. With this understanding in place, the husband should indeed love his wife. Since no man, Paul argues, hates his own flesh, but instead nourishes and cherishes it even as Christ does the Church, it follows then that the husband should do the same to his wife. With the same care men have for themselves, they have an equal responsibility to care, nourish and cherish their wives with tender loving care and affection as exemplified by Christ to the Church.

6:1 Children, obey your parents in the Lord: for this is right. 2 Honour thy father and mother; (which is the first commandment with promise;) 3 That it may be well with thee, and thou mayest live long on the earth.

Paul now turns our attention to the relationship between children and their parents; the role of the children and the responsibility of the parents, primarily fathers, to the children. Paul starts with an imperative: "Children, obey your parents . . ." which has the same notion as the general call for submission required of all members of God's new society (5:21). However, the tone here is stronger. To obey (*hupakouo*) is "to heed or conform to a command or authority." It means that children should listen to their parents. Although it has been, and is being abused by parents in recent times, this command is given for the well-being of the child and the family. The idea here is not autocracy in which parents force their selfish will on the children, but is educational whereby parents teach their children. Parents are charged in the Old Testament to instruct their children in the way of the Lord so that it will be well with them.

Children's obedience, it should be clearly noted, does not and should not constitute denial of freedom of expression of the children. Obedience does not mean suppression. There is no place in the Scripture for the saying: "Children are to be seen, but not heard." Paul gives the reason why children ought to obey their parents for (it) is right or righteous (*dikaios*). That means it is both a lawful and appropriate thing to do. It is also beneficial for the children. A child who hearkens to the advice of her or his (Christian) parents will live to be thankful and appreciate them in later years. This writer, because of the abuse by parents who are not under leading of the Spirit, encloses "Christian" in parentheses. Obedience of children is not a Christian phenomenon, but inherent in every human as part of the natural law, which God has written in the hearts of all (Romans 2:14-15). It is a standard behavior in every society.

Parental disobedience is one of the marks of a sinful society whom God has given up to its godlessness (Romans 1:28-30). Apart from being a natural law inscribed in every heart, it is also part of God's revealed law written in tablets of stone and given to Moses. Quoting the fifth commandment in the Decalogue, Paul charges children to honor (*timao*, i.e., to value, to hold in high esteem) their father and mother (Exodus 20:12), and combines it with Deuteronomy 5:16 "That it may be well with thee." Reverence and obedience is vital to the life of the covenant people of God, and part of their reverence to God.

To dishonor parents is to break God's commandment and dishonor God Himself, since parents are God's representatives charged to teach children God's ways. Indeed a very severe penalty (death) is prescribed on anyone who curses, disobeys, or rebels against his parents (Leviticus 20:9; Deuteronomy 21:18-21). However the apostle reminds his audience of the positive consequence of keeping this command and says that it is the first commandment with promise. He goes further to quote the promise of prosperity and long life. (For a detailed treatment, see the September 19, 1999 study.)

4 And, ye fathers, provoke not your children to wrath: but bring them up in the nurture and admonition of the Lord.

In verses 1-3, Paul instructs children to obey their father and mother, thereby establishing the parental authority over the children in the home. However, verse 4 instructs the parents, with special reference to the fathers, on how to exercise that authority. The picture here is as if Paul is speaking to a mixed gathering of parents and children (5:22 6:4), masters and slaves (6:5-9). After speaking to the parents about their respective relationship and responsibility towards each other, he turns to the children and discusses their dutiful respect and obedience to their parents.

He now turns back to the parents, focusing mainly on the fathers and explains how not to abuse the authority God has given to them. Paul paints a picture that seems to contradict the norm of both his day and our contemporary society, where fathers seem (or assume) to have sovereign authority over all members of the family. It is said that a Roman father had such absolute power over his family that he could sell them as slaves, make them work in his fields, even in chains. He could take law into his own hand and punish, as he liked. He could even inflict the death penalty on his own child (John Stott, p. 245).

That is why Paul addresses the fathers particularly, although the admonition applies to mothers also. Paul says,

"And, ye fathers, provoke not your children to wrath." There should be a difference as members of God's new society, in how to treat members of our family, including the children. To provoke (Greek *parorgizo*) means to "rouse to wrath, to exasperate" (Colossians 3:21) i.e., to embitter them or stir up anger. There are a number of ways this could be done: by the misuse of authority and harsh punishment, placing unreasonable demands and expectations upon the children which give no room for mistakes, failing to consider the inexperience and immaturity of children, also by using cruelty, humiliation and suppression, sarcasm and ridicule. Others include neglect and over-protection of children, bitter words and physical hostility, or abuse and unkindness. These are some of the parental (especially paternal) attitudes which arouse resentment and anger in children. A child, brought up in such atmosphere described above, grows up to resent not only the family, but also the society as a whole. A child reaches his or her potential in life by the positive encouragement of loving, caring, and understanding parents. Parents should allow children some room to be themselves and develop their independence, this is good and healthy for them.

Paul does not stop with the negative instruction to parents not to provoke their children to wrath. He supplements it with a positive admonition: "but bring them up in the nurture and admonition of the Lord." The verb "to bring up" (*ektrepho*) means "to nourish" or feed as we do to our bodies (5:29) and is used for the upbringing of children.

God intends for parents to take time and and make the effort to rear and nourish their children with tender care, just as they do with other things including their own bodies, pets, and gardens. As Dr. Lloyd-Jones says, "If people (parents) gave as much thought to the rearing of their children as they do to the rearing of animals and flowers, the situation would be different" (Lloyd Jones, *Life in the Spirit, the Banner of Trust*, Carlisle, p. 290). Unfortunately today, rearing children is often the most neglected area of life. It is often taken for granted and done with lack of purpose, and the results are frightfully obvious.

How then should parents bring up their children? The answer is clear: in the nurture (*paideia*) and admonition (*nouthesia*) of the Lord. The word *paideia* here means "discipline," or "training" in righteousness (2 Timothy 3:16). It has the idea of correcting, punishing or chastening as used in Hebrews 12:11 for both our earthly father and our heavenly Father who disciplines us for our own benefit. Such discipline often is painful at the time, but is later appreciated and produces good fruits (1 Corinthians 11:32; 2 Corinthians 6:9; 2 Timothy 2:25).

The word "admonition," *nouthesia* has the idea of verbal instruction, warning, or encouragement. The motive for discipline and admonition is that the children will grow to know, love, and obey the Lord. The prayer of all Christian parents is to see their children grow naturally to accept the values of Christianity without coercion or threat from the parents, but through Christian discipline and admonition with loving understanding and tender care. One of the greatest mishaps in child rearing is when parents try to discipline their children through frustration mingled with anger and lack of self-control. To discipline others, one must be disciplined. Punishment must not be meted out in anger or rage, but rather with controlled temper. To conclude this passage, we quote Dr. Lloyd-Jones again:

"When you are disciplining a child you should have first controlled yourself. If you try to discipline your child when you are in a temper, it is certain that you will do more harm than good. What right have you to say to your child that he needs discipline when you obviously need it yourself? Self-control, control of temper is an essential pre-requisite in the control of others . . . . So, the very first principle is that we must start with ourselves. We must be certain that we are in control ourselves, that we are cool. Whatever may have happened, whatever the provocation, we must not react with the violence similar to that of the man who is drunk; there must be this personal discipline, this self-control that enables a man to look at the situation objectively and to deal with it in a balanced and controlled manner." (*Life in the Spirit* p. 279)

DAILY BIBLE READING

M: Turn Your Backs on Pagan Ways
Ephesians 5:1-5
T: Live as Children of the Light
Ephesians 5:6-14
W: Serve and Worship with Thanks
Ephesians 5:15-20
T: Words for Christians in Families
Ephesians 5:21-27
F: Love as Christ Loved the Church
Ephesians 5:28-33
S: Treat Everyone with Love and Respect
Ephesians 6:1-9
S: Hear God's Word and Obey
Luke 6:43-49

TEACHING TIPS

July 30
Bible Study Guide 9

1. Words You Should Know

A. Principalities (v. 12)—A territory, province, kingdom or other region.

B. Girt (v. 14)—To strengthen, brace, fortify or prepare.

C. Shod (v. 15)—To have shoes put on one's feet.

2. Teacher Preparation

A. Read the background Scripture for the lesson. Study more about military preparation, particularly that of Roman soldiers during the time of Paul.

B. Bring one or more newspaper articles about someone who has chosen to take a stand on some issue. Allow class members to discuss why they believe the person is justified in taking his/her stand. Ask for a class member to share a time when he/she had to take a stand in favor of or against an issue.

3. Starting the Lesson

Read the IN FOCUS story about Janice. Ask if any class members have ever felt foolish or defeated because they failed to wear the full armor of God.

4. Getting into the Lesson

Ask class members: "Are you ever concerned about your physical safety?" After giving an opportunity for some to respond, ask "What measures have you taken to protect yourself and your family from physical danger?" After hearing responses, ask "Do you ever find yourself concerned about your spiritual safety?" Depending on how class members respond, ask "What do you do to prepare for and protect yourself against spiritual danger?"

5. Relating the Lesson to Life

A. Review the information about Tychicus and armor in THE PEOPLE, PLACES, AND TIMES article. Discuss the ways that God's armor protects us spiritually in much the same way that military armor protects soldiers physically.

B. Give students an opportunity to answer the questions in SEARCH THE SCRIPTURES.

C. DISCUSS THE MEANING addresses the need to make a conscious effort to put on the full armor each day and our ability to recognize true evil as it approaches. Have

we become so accustomed to wrongdoing that we are almost numb to evil deeds?

D. The LESSON IN OUR SOCIETY acknowledges the disparate concern over physical protection versus spiritual protection. Ask class members to share why they feel many people appear to be more concerned about the body than the spirit.

6. Arousing Action

A. Pose the following questions: "Do we sometimes fail to put on the full armor we have been given because Satan is often very successful at disguising what is evil by making it appear to be good? What are some ways that we seem to have been lulled into acceptance of evil because Satan makes it appear acceptable, or even good?"

B. Based on the instructions given in the MAKE IT HAPPEN section, give class members an opportunity to recall and consider the spiritual warfare they have experienced. Ask someone to share how God's armor gave them preparation and protection for the battle which followed.

C. Give class members an opportunity to complete FOLLOW THE SPIRIT and REMEMBER YOUR THOUGHTS.

WORSHIP GUIDE

For the Superintendent or Teacher
Theme: Called to Sand Firm
Theme Song: "Onward Christian Soldiers"
Scripture: John 14:15-27
Song: "Lead Me, Guide Me"
Meditation: Dear Lord, thank You for the armor of protection You have given us. Help me to remain on guard against the devil's schemes.

CALLED TO STAND FIRM

Bible Background • EPHESIANS 6:10-24
Printed Text • EPHESIANS 6:10-24
Devotional Reading • JOHN 14:15-27

LESSON AIM

After studying today's lesson, class members should be familiar with the armor Christians have been given in the fight against evil and know how that armor should be used.

KEEP IN MIND

"Submitting yourselves one to another in the fear of God" (Ephesians 5:21).

FOCAL VERSES

EPHESIANS 6:10 Finally, my brethren, be strong in the Lord, and in the power of his might.

11 Put on the whole armour of God, that ye may be able to stand against the wiles of the devil.

12 For we wrestle not against flesh and blood, but against principalities, against powers, against the rulers of the darkness of this world, against spiritual wickedness in high places.

13 Wherefore take unto you the whole armour of God, that ye may be able to withstand in the evil day, and having done all, to stand.

14 Stand therefore, having your loins girt about with truth, and having on the breastplate of righteousness;

15 And your feet shod with the preparation of the gospel of peace;

16 Above all, taking the shield of faith, wherewith ye shall be able to quench all the fiery darts of the wicked.

17 And take the helmet of salvation, and the sword of the Spirit, which is the word of God:

18 Praying always with all prayer and supplication in the Spirit, and watching thereunto with all perseverance and supplication for all saints;

LESSON OVERVIEW

LESSON AIM
KEEP IN MIND
FOCAL VERSES
IN FOCUS
THE PEOPLE, PLACES, AND TIMES
BACKGROUND
AT-A-GLANCE
IN DEPTH
SEARCH THE SCRIPTURES
DISCUSS THE MEANING
LESSON IN OUR SOCIETY
MAKE IT HAPPEN
FOLLOW THE SPIRIT
REMEMBER YOUR THOUGHTS
MORE LIGHT ON THE TEXT
DAILY BIBLE READINGS

---

19 And for me, that utterance may be given unto me, that I may open my mouth boldly, to make known the mystery of the gospel,

20 For which I am an ambassador in bonds: that therein I may speak boldly, as I ought to speak.

21 But that ye also may know my affairs, and how I do, Tychicus, a beloved brother and faithful minister in the Lord, shall make known to you all things:

22 Whom I have sent unto you for the same purpose, that ye might know our affairs, and that he might comfort your hearts.

23 Peace be to the brethren, and love with faith, from God the Father and the Lord Jesus Christ.

24 Grace be with all them that love our Lord Jesus Christ in sincerity. Amen.

IN FOCUS

Janice sank back into her huge recliner. It was her thinking chair, her favorite spot when times were down. "How did I get into this situation?" she asked. Although she asked the question, Janice herself knew the answer.

Step by step, Janice reviewed her actions and the choices she'd made. "I failed to put on the full armor," she concluded. "I thought I could handle this on my own, but I was up against something far more powerful than me."

At that moment, Janice decided to pray, "Father, forgive me for my arrogance. I thought I was tough enough to take care of this on my own. I was so stubborn I thought I didn't need you. Now I'm sitting here feeling foolish and defeated. Lord, I hope I never again forget to use the armor you have already provided for me."

THE PEOPLE, PLACES, AND TIMES

TYCHICUS. A personal name meaning "fortunate." There are five references to Tychicus in the Bible. Not much is known about this man; however, he was one of the party that traveled with Paul from Greece to Asia (Acts 20:4). He served as Paul's messenger to the Colossian Christians (Colossians 4:7) along with Onesimus, and to the Christians at Ephesus (Ephesians 6:21). He also may have been Paul's messenger to Titus in Crete (Titus 3:12). Tradition holds that Tychicus died a martyr.

Based on information from *Believer's Bible Commentary*, by William MacDonald. Nashville: Thomas Nelson Publishers, 1995, pp. 1953-1954. Also from *Holman Bible Dictionary*, Trent Butler, general editor. Nashville: Broadman & Holman Publishers, 1991, pp. 1376-1377.

ARMOUR. Armor serves primarily as a shield which is worn directly on the body. Since the human body has the greatest potential for fatal damage in the head and chest regions, this was the area of the body most heavily clad.

The helmet was usually made of leather or metal, designed with various shapes depending on the army or army unit, to enable commanders to distinguish one unit from another. In the chaos of hand-to-hand combat, the variations in helmet design also helped soldiers determine whether they were facing an ally or an enemy.

The evolution of the arrow as a weapon of war gave rise to the breastplate constructed of small metal plates sewn to cloth or leather to cover the torso. These scales could number as high as 700 to 1000 per coat. Obviously, these coats were quite heavy and expensive to produce.

Roman soldiers were equipped with metal helmets, protective leather and metal vests, leg armor, shields, swords, and spears.

BACKGROUND

In his closing words to the church at Ephesus, Paul addresses the reality of the church conducting itself in the world. He calls for believers to be steadfast when facing trials and to be prepared for conflict.

Since Paul wrote his letter to the Ephesians from a Roman jail, it is quite possible that he was inspired by the sight of a Roman soldier dressed in full armor. Paul uses the battle motif to help believers understand the true nature of what they can expect from the world. He makes a stirring appeal to the entire family of God as soldiers of Christ.

The Christian life is a form of warfare. Discipleship necessitates struggle with superhuman forms of evil. The armies of Satan are trained and committed to interfering with the work of the Lord. Satan's soldiers work to remove Christ's soldiers from the battlefield. The more effective a believer is in God's kingdom, the more the believer will be attacked by the enemy. Preparedness is the key. God's spiritual armor helps His disciples through these battles.

AT-A-GLANCE

1. Christian Armor for Warfare (Ephesians 6:10-20)
2. Paul's Farewell to the Ephesians (vv. 21-24)

IN DEPTH

1. Christian Armor for Warfare (Ephesians 6:10-20)

Paul makes two exhortations in verse 10; one interprets the other. The three Greek terms he uses: *be strong, power, might,* are all variations of the notion of power. Here Paul lets believers know that God makes armament available to Christian warriors.

Essential to the idea of protection for Christian warriors is the *armor of God*. This phrase could mean either "the armor which God provides" or "the armor which God wears." We are called to align ourselves with God and against the enemy. This can only be done by taking on the armor of God.

Paul paints a stark portrait with his use of words. In the war against evil, the believer must be fortified with nothing less than the armor that God provides. Warfare takes a heavy toll on soldiers. Christian soldiers are to gird themselves so that they may stand against the devil's tools of war.

The best soldiers know their own strengths and weaknesses and guard themselves against vulnerability. Christian soldiers must rely on God's power and might to guard against our weaknesses. We must be *fully* dressed in His armor; one or two pieces of protective wear still leaves us vulnerable in some area or another.

The enemy is Satan, who is described here in one of his major roles as one who engages in trickery or schemes, as indicated by use of the word "wiles." The devil is the enemy of the church and he cannot be viewed in any other context (Revelation 12:10).

As a part of the process of spiritual maturation, Paul does not mince words when depicting the true nature of the Church's struggle in the world. Looking at the struggle of good and evil in its simplest terms, the struggle may be viewed in respect to persons of goodwill pitted against those of evil disposition. However, such a view is too simple. Paul did not want them to confuse evil with ordinary human conflict.

At its deepest level, the struggle is not against human powers, or "flesh and blood." Our battle is against evil that is far more dangerous than what occurs on a human level. Our struggle is "against principalities, against powers, against the rulers of the darkness of this world."

Christians must also be on guard against "spiritual wickedness in high places." These things cannot be overcome with human power, as they are the tools of Satan.

Because we are human, we cannot necessarily distinguish between these things which Paul has cautioned us to avoid. Satan and his armies are often at work in places where we do not suspect, even in the places that do not belong to him. He is at work in the church, constantly trying to tear it down. He is at work in our homes, trying to destroy the bond of love. He and his angels are at work in the hearts of anyone who will give him an opening. Nevertheless, if we have covered ourselves in the full armor, we are protected.

The "evil day" probably refers to any time when the enemy charges against us. It seems as though Satan opposes individuals in waves, advancing and receding. Even after the devil left Jesus in the wilderness, he did so only "for a season," or according to the New International Version, "until an opportune time" (Luke 4:13).

The phrase "having done all" implies the necessity for total preparedness to meet the enemy when evil presses against us. Paul is warning Christian disciples to be alert and prepared, for we never know when the enemy will appear.

Paul then outlines the necessary equipment for a properly-outfitted soldier. The armor is God's. The equipment is more than adequate; however, it is the responsibility of the Christian to use it.

Most likely, as Paul continued writing, he observed a Roman soldier on duty. The soldier's belt is the first thing mentioned; in the case of Christians, it is the belt of truth, or "having your loins girt about with truth." The presence of a belt on a Roman soldier indicated that he was on duty and ready for service. The Romans used a term, *miles accinctus*, meaning that a soldier was "at the ready" with his belt fastened in position.

The imagery of the "breastplate of righteousness" is taken from Isaiah 59:17: "For he put on righteousness as a breastplate, and an helmet of salvation upon his head; and he put on the garments of vengeance for clothing, and was clad with zeal as a cloak." It is the picture of God's servants doing justice in a world of distorted and perverted values.

A good soldier wears the shoes of preparation, which are "the preparation of the gospel of peace." This suggests a readiness to go out with the Good News of peace. Human feet must have shoes for protection when marching into battle. The Christian journey can be long, and sometimes painful. The well-equipped feet of God's soldiers can give fast, efficient service for the kingdom.

Additionally, the "shield of faith" must be carried so that when evil appears, the Christian soldier is protected. The "fiery darts of the wicked" cannot withstand this shield. They will hit the shield and fall harmlessly to the ground.

The "helmet of salvation" is the Christian's assurance of victory, no matter how intense the battle may become. The term is taken from Isaiah 59:17. Here Yahweh wears a helmet as He goes forth to vindicate His oppressed people. For believers, wearing the helmet means using all that Christ offers in His saving work.

The sword of the Spirit, which is the Word of God, is the Christian's helper in spiritual warfare. Using it, we can speak to our circumstances with the truth of God's Word. The Word of God serves as our guide, giving us direction as we walk the Christian journey.

Wearing all of the armor God has provided us, we are still called upon to pray "always with all prayer and supplication in the Spirit." Our prayers should be inspired and led by the Spirit. Formal prayers given without thought or meaning are of little value in the heat of spiritual battle with the agents of Satan. These prayers should be lifted up with *perseverance*. When the battle is particularly intense, it may sometimes appear that Satan is winning. It is especially during those times that we should pray all the more fervently, never giving up on the power of prayer.

Prayers must also be made "for all saints," as they, too, are engaged in spiritual warfare. We should pray for one another during difficult times. Those who are battle weary need the prayers of those who are not currently engaged in battle to fortify and strengthen them.

Paul wrote these words of instruction and encouragement at he sat in a Roman jail. Instead of asking for prayer for his release, Paul asked the Ephesians to pray that he would be made stronger to do even more of the very thing that placed him in jail in the first place! The apostle wanted to continue to "open my mouth boldly, to make known the mystery of the gospel." He held no regrets. He merely wanted the opportunity to broadcast the message to more and more people.

Instead of referring to himself as a prisoner, Paul considered himself an "ambassador in bonds." He is Christ's ambassador, but unlike a court personnel, he does not have the privilege of diplomatic immunity. The apostle continued to look, not at himself, but at the high calling he had been given. He gave himself totally and without question to Christ.

2. Paul's Farewell to the Ephesians (vv. 21-24)

Paul closes his letter with a message of peace. Not knowing his fate, the apostle continued to give a message of hope and encouragement. He was sending Tychicus from Rome to Ephesus to let them know how he was doing. Tychicus's mission was to inform the saints of Paul's welfare and also to encourage them.

His desire for the Ephesian Christians was for peace and love with faith. Love would enable them to worship God and work with one another. Faith would empower them for exploits in the Christian warfare.

In closing, Paul desires grace for "all them that love our Lord Jesus Christ in sincerity." True Christian love is permanent. It may grow weak at times, but it never dies. God's grace protects and preserves His soldiers as they engage in the battles of life.

Based on information from *Holman Bible Dictionary*, 1991, p. 103.

SEARCH THE SCRIPTURES

1. Whose power did Paul admonish the Ephesians to rely upon? (Ephesians 6:10)

2. What protection were the Ephesians to use for themselves? (v. 11)

3. What are the real enemies that Christians face? (v. 12)

4. How would the armor of God protect them? (v. 13)

5. Name the pieces of armor for the Christian soldier. (vv. 14-17)

6. What else are Christian soldiers to do even with the armor of God protecting them? (v. 18)

7. What did Paul ask for himself? (v. 19)

8. How did Paul describe himself? (v. 20)

9. Who did Paul send as a messenger to the Ephesians? (v. 21)

10. What was Paul's closing desire for the Ephesians? (vv. 23-24)

DISCUSS THE MEANING

1. Paul listed the equipment necessary for Christians to be protected in times of spiritual warfare. Should we consciously "clothe" ourselves in this armor daily, or is wearing this armor a product of continuous spiritual growth?

2. Is it sometimes difficult for us to recognize the true nature of evil when it manifests itself in our daily lives?

LESSON IN OUR SOCIETY

Americans appear to be especially concerned with security. Many families own one or more firearms. Still others have electronic security systems and burglar bars to protect themselves. With all of the millions of dollars being spent on physical security, it is ironic that very little time and attention is devoted to our spiritual protection. Imagine how different our world might be if people began to give equal time and attention to spiritual armor.

It would do us well to remember that true security does not come from external invention. It comes from above.

MAKE IT HAPPEN

Think of a time when you have faced an intense spiritual battle. Recall how the armor of God helped to protect and strengthen you during this time. What do you think would have happened if you had not used the armor of the Lord to protect you?

FOLLOW THE SPIRIT

What He wants me to do:

_____

_____

REMEMBER YOUR THOUGHTS

Special insights you learned:

_____

_____

MORE LIGHT ON THE TEXT
EPHESIANS 6:10-24

Paul concludes this letter by dealing with a very serious topic: spiritual warfare, which unfortunately is usually overlooked or downplayed by many churches. He charges the Church to be aware of the type of conflict they are facing in the world, and summons them to prepare for battle. This battle, Paul reminds them, is not simply against humans, but against forces of evil that are not visible to the human eyes; they are not physical but spiritual. Therefore, the battle is spiritual, and as such, it is to be fought and won with spiritual weaponry. Paul describes with precision, in the following passage, the Church's weapons for this inescapable battle. He exhorts them to fully equip themselves with the divine armor in order to overcome.

6:10 Finally, my brethren, be strong in the

Lord, and in the power of his might. 11 Put on the whole armor of God, that ye may be able to stand against the wiles of the devil.

Paul begins by addressing his readers as my brethren, which emphasizes the bond and intimate relationship that exists between him and the Ephesian church. It also calls for their serious attention and intensifies the importance of the subject matter. The word translated "finally" is the Greek word *tou loipou*, literally "in respect of the rest," indicating Paul's final admonition. He urges them to be strong (Greek *endunamoo*, i.e., to empower, to increase in strength) in the Lord and in the power (Greek *kratos*, i.e., vigor or strength) of His might (*ischus*, i.e., ability, power, or strength). Using these synonyms, Paul calls on the church to rely totally on the Lord for the strength and ability to face the onslaught of the enemy that surrounds them. He says in effect that only with a close and steadfast relationship with Lord (the source of all power) will they be able to fight the battle that constantly awaits them in the world.

Jesus told His disciples that without Him, they could do nothing (John 15:1-5), but Paul writes, "I can do everything through him who gives me strength" (Philippians 4:13; cf. 2 Corinthians 12:9-10; 1 Timothy 1:12, NIV). We must totally rely on God's strength and power because He is all-powerful and His might is infinite, as evidenced in creation and in history. By His power and strength, God not only created the heavens and the earth, but He caused the Red Sea and the Jordan River to be driven back, the moon to stand still, the mountains to tremble and the rocks to melt. He raised Christ from the dead (1:20) and made alive those who were dead in trespasses and sins (2:1). In view of these and other deeds, which reveal God's omnipotence in history, Paul exhorts them to hold fast in the Lord, "the one who is able to do exceeding abundantly above all that we ask or think, according to the power that worketh in us" (3:20).

Although we rely totally on the strength and might of God, we must equip ourselves with the whole armor (*panoplia*, i.e., full, total, or complete armor) of God, that ye may be able to stand against the wiles of the devil. We must recall at this point that Paul is writing from prison in Rome and probably guarded by a well-dressed and completely equipped soldier or soldiers. He has a complete picture and image of a soldier in military regalia and readiness for battle. He, therefore, writes to the brethren in Ephesus, and indeed Christians of all times, to be completely dressed and ready for battle. However, the Christian's armor is not like the Roman's, which is physical—it is God's armor, which is spiritual. It is this type of military regalia we use to withstand and overcome the wiles or craftiness of the devil.

There are few things to learn here about the devil. First, it is a fact that demons, evil spirits, Satan, devils, or whatever name given them, exist contrary to the belief of many (Christians) today who say that evil spirits are a myth. However, we must be careful not to give the devil a place he does not deserve by attributing everything adverse that happens to him. We must not be afraid of him as the pagans are, which leads to the worship of Satan and his agents. We must acknowledge their existence as Paul did, but we are not to be afraid of them or to pay them homage.

Second, we must acknowledge that they possess some power, although their power is limited. God's power is unlimited and superior. Although evil spirits exist, we should not expend our energy daily thinking and fighting them at the expense of other areas of ministry as many churches do today. Instead, we must be ready for the enemy at all times by being equipped with God's own armor, which he has made available to us.

Third, we must acknowledge that Satan, the devil, is cunning and crafty, full of fury, and prowls around like a roaring lion looking for someone to devour (1 Peter 5:8, NIV). Having been cast out of heaven, he is full of fury and envy. His hatred is against God, His people, and all they stand for. He has a well-organized army and is out to destroy God's kingdom and to bring with him as many people as possible into hell. Satan's craftiness can be seen throughout Scripture. He mixes falsehood with some truth to make it plausible (Genesis 3:4, 5, 22); quotes Scripture out of context (Matthew 4:6); masquerades as an angel of light (2 Corinthians 11:14); and his subtlety is making people believe that he does not even exist (Acts 20:22). Therefore, we must be properly equipped to fight him, not with human armor but God's, Paul says. The call here is urgent.

12 For we wrestle not against flesh and blood, but against principalities, against powers, against the rulers of the darkness of this world, against spiritual wickedness in high places. 13 Wherefore take unto you the whole armor of God, that ye may be able to withstand in the evil day, and having done all, to stand.

After Paul establishes the fact of the devil's existence and power, and urges his audience to be fully-equipped with God's own armor, Paul now gives them the reason why they should be so equipped. The reason for this urgent call is that we are not fighting against "flesh and blood," i.e., against mere, frail humans (Galatians 1:16), with all their physical and mental weakness (1 Corinthians 15:50;

Matthew 16:17). Rather, we are fighting against all types of forces in all realms of life, both in the heavenlies and the cosmic world. However, the enemy knows how to use humans who avail themselves to his strategies; thereby we are often deceived into thinking that the fight is against another human being.

Paul categorizes these forces, as "principalities and powers" (*exousia* or authorities, cf. Ephesians 1:21), as the "rulers of the darkness of this world," which speaks of those who are in tyrannical control of the world of ignorance and sin. We are also fighting against spiritual forces of "wickedness in high places" (*epouranios*, i.e., heavenly places). Heavenly places here does not refer to the heavenly kingdom where Christ is enthroned at God's right hand (1:20) and the redeemed are seated with Him (2:6), the home of the obedient angels (3:10). It is the region above the earth but below the heaven, referred to as the "domain of the air" (2:2).

Paul, in effect, says that since we are contending against an innumerable host of spiritual forces, we must be fully equipped and put on the full armor of God (v. 11). Paul repeats this call in verse 13. The repetition of this call intensifies its urgency. The word "wrestle" used in verse 12 can be misleading; since wrestling is viewed as a sport, it therefore can erroneously minimize the magnitude of the battle that is facing the Christian.

The explanation is probably that the battle is so intense and violent that it is like hand-to-hand combat. This battle is not like the phony World Wrestling Federation, which is either for entertainment and/or monetary enrichment. The spiritual battle is serious stuff, and therefore requires a complete armament. It is only with such divine armament that we would "be able to withstand in the evil day," or day of evil, that is, in the day of severe trial and temptation and onslaught of the evil one (Psalm 41:2; 49:5). The implication here is that we must always be ready and on guard since we do not know when these crises will occur.

14 Stand therefore, having your loins girt about with truth, and having on the breastplate of righteousness;

To "stand" here and in verse 11 does not imply passivity, where a soldier is pictured standing like a brick wall waiting for Satan's attack. Rather, Paul paints a picture of a soldier equipped and drawn up in battle array, rushing into war making full use of God's weapons of war for attacks and defense. It is then that the soldier would be able stand his ground and resist the evil one, and he (the devil) will flee from him (James 4:7; cf. Matthew 10:22). The picture is that of a soldier who is alert, vigilant, and awake at all times

(night or day), one that is never asleep and never taken unaware by the devil who cunningly likes to attack at odd times. This is the picture of the Christian Paul paints here, a strong and stable Christian who remains firm against the wiles of the devil (v. 11) and even in the day of evil, that is, in a time of crisis or pressure.

In the next five verses, Paul details the six major pieces of the soldier's armor and gives the function of each one of them: the belt, the breastplate, the boots, the shield, the helmet, and the sword. They represent truth, righteousness, and the gospel of peace, faith, salvation, and the Word of God, respectively. All these pieces of spiritual armor equip us to battle against the evil powers.

The first piece of equipment which Paul lists is the belt of truth: "having your loins girt about with truth." The belt or the girdle, usually made of leather, is tied around the waist and used to brace the armor tight against the body. As the soldier buckles the belt, he feels a sense of hidden strength and confidence. I can remember at a very young age watching women fight in the village. The first thing the women would do was to take off their hair scarf or neck piece, tie it around their waist, and confidently beckons the other for a fight. As she waits for the other person to make a move, one could sense her feeling of confidence and inner strength. The belt is also used to hold daggers, swords, and other weapons to give the soldier freedom movement without being impeded when marching.

Paul says that the Christian's belt is truth. The two possible types of truth meant here are (1) the truth, as God's revelation in Christ and the Scripture and (2) truth, as in honesty or integrity. Only the truth can dispel the devil's lies and set us free (John 8:31-36, 43-45). The psalmist says that God requires truth in the inward being (Psalm 51:6), and Paul says that we are to speak the truth in love (Ephesians 4:15, 25). My father advised me at an early age that if I speak the truth the first time, I would not worry to find another lie in future. He said that truth will always prevail, and lies and dishonesty will always be exposed. Honesty and integrity are marks of brevity, he told me, but lies are a sign of cowardice. The opposite of truth is lies and the Bible says that Satan is the father of lies. Therefore we cannot beat him at his own game. Truth is the only thing that will dispel him, because he hates truth.

The second piece of the Christian's weaponry Paul mentions here is the breastplate (Greek *thorax*) of righteousness. A breastplate is described as the armor that covers the body from neck to the thighs. It consists of two parts, one for the back and the other for the front. They protect the vital parts of the body (1 Samuel 17:5, 38; 1 Kings 22:34).

now no condemnation to them, which are in Christ Jesus, who walk not after the flesh, but after the Spirit . . . ." Who shall lay any thing to the charge of God's elect? It is God that justifieth. Who is he that condemneth? It is Christ that died, yea rather, that is risen again, who is even at the right hand of God, who also maketh intercession for us" (Romans 8:1, 33-34). This relationship disarms the devil and offers protection for the Christian.

To successfully ward off the devil's unceasingly slanderous attack, we must maintain that relationship with the Father by using the weapons of righteousness for the right hand and for the left (2 Corinthians 6:7). The righteousness referred to here, as well as in Ephesians 4:24 and 5:9, is a moral righteousness. Just as the Christian is to cultivate truth as means to overcome the deceptions of the devil, he also has to cultivate righteousness (i.e., moral integrity) in order to overcome the devil's slanderous attacks. Without integrity and a clear conscience, one cannot defend himself or herself against the accusations of the devil who accuses the brethren night and day (Revelation 12:10).

Here, Paul says that the equipment for protection is righteousness (Greek *dikaiosune*), which is often translated in Pauline epistles as "justification." This is theologically explained as the process whereby God through Christ puts the sinner in a right relationship with Himself. The most amazing gift for an unjust sinner is to stand before the Almighty and just God not to be condemned but accepted and clothed with God's righteousness through Christ as if he had not sinned. It is the believer's assurance that through Christ, all of our sins are forgiven and the barrier between God and us has been removed (Isaiah 59:1-2). This is the work of grace, which God wrought through the death of His Son Jesus on the Cross.

One of Satan's greatest weapons is slander, to accuse us through our conscience. Therefore, there is no greater defensive weapon for the Christian against the slanderous attack of the devil than the assurance of a right relationship with the Father through His Son (2 Corinthians 5:21). Paul assures the Roman believers of this fact: "There is therefore

15 And your feet shod with the preparation of the gospel of peace;

The next weapon in the apostle's list for warfare is the boot: the preparation of the gospel of peace. The word translated "preparation" is the Greek word *hetoimasia*, which means "readiness, the act of preparedness." Paul says that the Christian should put on the gospel of peace as his army boots. Boots protect soldiers from slipping, and from thorns or objects that can pierce through their feet and thereby hinder them from marching forward into battle. The gospel (good news) of peace is the protective mechanism by which we are shielded from the dangerous gimmicks the devil lays in our path to hinder our walk with the Lord. The more we are ready and prepared to testify about or confess Christ to others, the better we are protected from backsliding and falling into Satan's traps and temptation. This verse is also an allusion to the prophet Isaiah's proclamation, "How beautiful upon the mountains are the feet of him that bringeth good tidings, that publisheth peace; that bringeth good tidings of good, that publisheth salvation; that saith unto Zion, Thy God reigneth!" (Isaiah 52:7 cf. Romans 10:15). The devil hates the Gospel (Good News) of Jesus Christ for it is the power of God unto salvation to everyone that believes (Romans 1:16).

Boots are a vital part of a soldier's armor, and with them securely strapped on the feet, the soldier feels a certain amount of confidence and is ready for action. Without boots, the soldier will be ill-equipped and unprepared for battle.

16 Above all, taking the shield of faith, wherewith ye shall be able to quench all the fiery darts of the wicked.

The fourth weapon is the shield of faith, which we must take above all (*en pasin*) in the sense that it is an indispensable part of the whole armor, rather than the most important part. It can be rendered: besides all these, take also the shield of faith. "Shield" here is the Greek word *thureos*, which was a large oblong, four-cornered shield, which covered the whole body, rather than the small round one that covered only a smaller part of the body. The *thureos* is specially designed to ward off all types of dangerous darts or missiles thrown, such as the arrows, javelins, spears, or stones that were used then.

The fiery darts also probably refer to the combustible arrowheads that set fire to the enemy's fortifications, boats, or houses, or to shields that were made of wood. In order to quench the fiery darts, the shields are covered with metals. What are the fiery darts of the devil as they relate to the Christian warfare? They no doubt include the following: evil thoughts, lusts, false guilt, sinful passions, temptation of various kinds, doubts, and disobedience; rebellion, malice, and fear (cf. 1 Corinthians 10:13-14; 2 Corinthians 10:4-6; James 1:13-15; Romans 6:10, etc.). The devil ceaselessly launches all these deadly fire-tipped flaming darts at us daily, from time to time, in different forms and combinations. There is one weapon to quench or extinguish them: and that is the shield of faith. Proverbs 30:5 says that God is a shield unto them that put their trust in him. Faith here is reliance in and taking hold of the promises of God in the finished work of Christ on the cross (1:20-22). In times of doubts and depression, it is claiming the power of God in times of temptation (Philippians 4:13). With faith, we can move mountains, Jesus told His disciples.

17 And take the helmet of salvation, and the

sword of the Spirit, which is the word of God:

Paul adds two more pieces of warfare equipment to the list: the helmet of salvation, and the sword of the Spirit. We are to take these as weapons to fight the wicked one. Paul calls the helmet "the hope of salvation" in 1 Thessalonians 5:8, while here it is the "helmet of salvation." There seems to be no apparent difference in these passages, since salvation is both a present and a future reality. Hence, salvation is anchored in hope. This metaphor is used in the Old Testament where, as Isaiah writes, the Lord wears the helmet of salvation on His head as He goes to vindicate His people who had been oppressed. Therefore, just as soldiers receive a helmet from their army superiors in charge of supplies, Paul says we are to take (*dechomai*, i.e., to receive or accept) salvation with faith (2:8) as a gift from God. The ancient helmets were cast from iron and brass (1 Samuel 17:5, 38; 2 Chronicles 26:14) and they offered protection for the head like the breastplate provided for the heart. Salvation is also a protective (defensive) gear that assures the Christian of both the present and the future during times of crisis and persecutions. It is the assurance of God's salvation, which He has wrought through Christ in us. It is this assurance that strengthens and carries the Christian to go on fighting without giving up, even in very difficult situations. It is the confidence that what God has begun in him, He will surely bring to completion (Philippians 1:6; cf. Psalm 138:8).

The final weapon that Paul urges the Christian to take is the sword of the Spirit. While all the other five listed are specifically weapons for defense or protection, the sword is the only weapon which can clearly be used for both offense and defense. The word translated "sword" is the Greek word *machaira*, which is said to be a small or short sword as opposed to a large or long one. Therefore, the combat envisaged here is a close one. The Christian's weapon of offense is the sword of the Spirit (i.e., spiritual sword), which Paul identifies immediately as the word (*rhema*, i.e., the spoken word) of God. Jesus promised His disciples that He would fill their lips with words when they are brought before magistrates (Matthew 10:17-20).

The Bible says that the Word of God has some cutting power and is sharper than a double-edged sword (Hebrew 4:12), and so we ought to use it with confidence. The Word of God refers to both the written Word (the Scripture) inspired by the Holy Spirit (1 Timothy 3:16; 2 Peter 1:21) and the spoken word (*rhema*) the confession and testimony which will stand forever (Isaiah 40:8). Jesus applied the Word to fight Satan's temptations in the wilderness of Judea (Luke 4:1-13). John records the victory of the saints against

Satan saying, "And they overcame him by the blood of the Lamb, and by the word of their testimony; and they loved not their lives unto the death" (Revelation 2:11). The Word of God is the greatest weapon with which we can fight the devil and his gimmicks. It is amazing what victory we can have when we apply the Word of God. Through it, we dispel doubts, fears, and guilt; by it Satan is put to flight, and assurance of salvation is secured in our hearts.

The complete armor of God is made available to every Christian: truth as the girdle, righteousness as the breastplate, the Gospel as the boots, faith as the shield, salvation as the helmet, and the Word of God as the Spirit's sword (or the spiritual sword). Since the battle is not against humans, but spirits, we need all the specified weapons without leaving any, so that we can withstand and stand firm against Satan's ceaseless onslaught against us. We must be fully-equipped, always ready for battle.

18 Praying always with all prayer and supplication in the Spirit, and watching thereunto with all perseverance and supplication for all saints; 19 And for me, that utterance may be given unto me, that I may open my mouth boldly, to make known the mystery of the gospel, 20 For which I am an ambassador in bonds: that therein I may speak boldly, as I ought to speak.

After listing all the armor the Christian should put in use to fight against the wiles and wickedness of the devil, Paul explains how to use them by praying. Prayer and the Word are the two most important aspects of Christian living. Without either or both of them, the Christian's life is in jeopardy, and his life may even be at the mercy of Satan and his agents. No soldier of Christ can do anything on his or her own power without seeking strength and blessing from God, the all-powerful Father, even though he or she may have all their weapons. As a believer puts each piece of the armor on and makes use of it, he or she must rely on God through prayer. Hence, Paul says, put on the whole armor, praying and watching (18-20).

Prayer is not a one-time exercise, but is to be done always (at all times), that is, constantly or habitually with all variety of prayers being "all prayer and supplication." The phrase "all prayer" (*proseuche*) probably includes both public and private, church and family prayer. It will consist of supplication (*deesis*) i.e., petitioning; making a special request or seeking favor for some special necessity from God. It speaks of being specific instead of general in prayer. It should be done at all times (always), as we have already intimated, and it should be done in the spirit through the Holy Spirit who

makes intercession for us even when we do not know how and what to pray (Romans 8:26, 27, 34).

Paul calls on us to be alert (*agrupneo*, i.e., to watch, be attentive) as we pray and with perseverance (*proskarteresis*) and as we make supplication for the saints. This means we must be persistent and resolute in our prayer, not only for ourselves, but also for all members of the family of God in which we now belong. We shall not only be alert and watchful of Satan's strategies, we should be alert to know or be aware of the needs of others so that we can pray objectively, instead of rambling away without tangible things to pray for as we intercede for others.

Paul now, for the first time in the entire letter, makes a request for himself. He asks that when prayer is made on behalf of all the saints, they should remember him in a special way in their prayers. His request is clear, simple, and noble. It echoes his request in Colossians 4:2, 3, that he be endued with power and boldness so that he could continue to make known the mystery of the Gospel. Paul's request is two-fold.

First, that God might give him the utterance (*logos*, i.e., the word) or the correct message when he opens his mouth to speak (Matthew 10:19); and second, that God might give him the courage at all times to deliver the message in a proper manner (Acts 4:13). The request and prayer are important to him since it is because of the Gospel, he says, "for which I am an ambassador in chains; that in it I may speak boldly, as I ought to speak" (v. 20, NKJV). What is that mystery of the Gospel? That through Christ, there is full salvation for everyone who comes to Him in faith, both Jews and Gentile, and it is free. That through Christ the barrier of hostility, which formerly existed between the two (Jews and Gentiles) has now been removed and they are now one in God's new family (Ephesians 3:3-7, 9; cf. Romans 16:25; Colossians 1:26, 26; 2:2, etc.). The Gospel is the mystery, which God through Christ made known, and Paul, though imprisoned at the time in a Roman jail is an ambassador charged to proclaim this Good News.

21 But that ye also may know my affairs, and how I do, Tychicus, a beloved brother and faithful minister in the Lord, shall make known to you all things: 22 Whom I have sent unto you for the same purpose, that ye might know our affairs, and that he might comfort your hearts.

Verses 21-24 conclude Paul's letter to the church at Ephesus with a personal word of encouragement and benediction. It is suggested that Paul wrote this concluding portion of the letter personally, while a scribe to whom he dictated the contents wrote the rest of the book. He did the same at the conclusion of his letters to Galatians (6:11), the Corinthians (1 Corinthians 16:21) the Thessalonians (2 Thessalonians 3:17), and the Colossians (4:18).

It is also generally assumed that Tychicus, whom Paul mentions and highly recommends here, is the scribe and the bearer of the letter to the Ephesians, as well as the Colossians' and Philemon's letters. Tychicus was a native of Asia (Acts 20:4), probably an Ephesian who had been with Paul and his companions during Paul's Roman imprisonment (2 Timothy 4:12). It is this young man that Paul entrusts to deliver the letter, together with the letter to the Colossians (Colossians 4:7-8).

Here, Paul calls him a beloved brother and faithful minister in the Lord. This indicates the complete confidence Paul has in him. He relies on him to both deliver the letter and to give firsthand information regarding the personal welfare of Paul and other colleagues. Indicating his purpose for sending Tychicus, Paul says "that ye also may know my affairs, and how I do, Tychicus . . . shall make known to you all things" (v. 21). Indeed, Paul says, I have sent to you for this very purpose, that you may know our affairs, and that he may comfort your hearts (v. 22, NKJV).

This seems to explain the apparent and unusual absence of Paul's personal messages and greetings at the end of the letter. The third reason for sending Tychicus personally is that he might comfort (*parakaleo* i.e., encourage) the hearts of the believers. Although a letter is an important and vital means of communication, receiving a personal visit and hearing firsthand news or personal words of encouragement would strengthen the Church more than a letter.

In summary, the three major means through which we can enrich and edify one another in the Lord's new society are: a) Prayer (see Paul's prayer for them in Ephesians, chapters 1 and 3, and his request that they pray for him in Ephesians 6:19-20); b) Correspondence (letters through ordinary old fashioned mail or the modern electronic mailing [E-mail] system); and c) Personal visits. Paul employs these methods in this letter to the Ephesians.

23 Peace be to the brethren, and love with faith, from God the Father and the Lord Jesus Christ. 24 Grace be with all them that love our Lord Jesus Christ in sincerity. Amen.

In accordance with the contemporary custom in the ancient world of ending letters to wish good health and happiness for the readers, Paul ends this letter with a wish. He Christianized his opening and final greeting with a wish for God's blessings of peace, love, faith, and grace, all from both God the Father and the Lord Jesus Christ, to the church. These themes pervade the whole Ephesian epistle (cf. for peace, 8 times: 1:2; 2:14, 15, 17; 4:3; 6:15; for love, 14 times: 1:15; 4:2, 15, 16; 5:25, 25, 33, etc.; for faith, 8 times: 1:15; 2:8; 3:12, 17; 4:5, 13; 6:16, 23; and for grace, 12 times: 1:2, 6, 7; 2:5, 7, 8; 3:2, 7, 8; 4:7, 29; 6:24).

Peace, love, and faith are the qualities also needed in the church today. *Peace* is the state of harmonious living, while *love* is the source and outflow of peace and they constitute unity even in the presence of diversity. Love here includes God's love for the Church demonstrated through the sacrificial death of Christ on the Cross, and the believers love for God and for one another in the body. This is made possible through faith (trust in God), and it's a gift of God (2:8) made available by God's grace. Paul wishes or prays that the grace of God be the reward for those who love the Lord with all their heart, i.e., with sincere hearts.

DAILY BIBLE READING

M: Be Strong in the Lord
Ephesians 6:10-15
T: Pray Always in the Lord's Spirit
Ephesians 6:16-20
W: Grace, Peace, and Love from God
Ephesians 6:21-24
T: God's Spirit Will Strengthen You
John 14:15-27
F: Abide in Christ and Bear Fruit
John 15:1-11
S: We Are Chosen by Christ
John 15:12-27
S: Your Pain Will Turn to Rejoicing
John 16:16-24

TEACHING TIPS

August 6
Bible Study Guide 10

1. Words You Should Know

A. Fullness (Colossians 1:19)—Greek *pleroma* the totality of supernatural, divine powers and attributes.

B. Reconcile (1:20)—Greek *apokatalasai* to change from hostility or enmity to friendship. The word implies intensive force, to change completely, to change so as to remove all enmity.

C. Holy (1:22)—Greek *hagios* set apart and made useful. Taking on something of God's character and dedicating one's self for the Lord's use.

2 Teacher Preparation

A. Begin by reading all of Colossians chapter one. Read it in a couple of different translations.

B. Answer the questions in the SEARCH THE SCRIPTURES and DISCUSS THE MEANING sections.

C. Materials needed: Bible, paper and pencils for each student, and a board or newsprint.

3. Starting the Lesson

A. Before class begins, assign the SEARCH THE SCRIPTURES and DISCUSS THE MEANING questions to several students. Tell them you will call on them when the class reaches that part of the lesson.

B. Read IN FOCUS. Ask if anyone has some difficulties they are facing right now, and allow a few students to share or, if it's a small class, go around the whole group and have each person mention something.

C. Pray for the lesson, keeping in mind the Lesson Aim, but also pray for the situations mentioned.

4. Getting into the Lesson

A. To help the students understand the history of the Church, take turns reading the BACKGROUND and THE PEOPLE, PLACES, AND TIMES.

B. Read each section of the Scripture lesson according to the AT-A-GLANCE outline. Call on the students to answer the questions from SEARCH THE SCRIPTURES and DISCUSS THE MEANING during the particular sections.

5. Relating the Lesson to Life

A. Have a student read LESSON IN OUR SOCIETY.

B. Go right into the questions in the MAKE IT HAPPEN section. Have each student make a list and briefly discuss their discoveries.

C. Break off into groups of two and three, and pray about the situations on each person's paper.

6. Arousing Action

A. After prayer, have as many students as you can say what changes they plan to make in the way they think, their attitudes, or their behaviors.

B. Challenge the students to do the DAILY BIBLE READINGS and come next week prepared to share something they have learned.

THE SUPREMACY OF CHRIST

Bible Background • COLOSSIANS 1
Printed Text • COLOSSIANS 1:15-28
Devotional Reading • JOHN 1:1-5, 9-18

LESSON AIM

By the end of this lesson, the students should be able to explain Jesus' superiority over creation, and His headship in the church, and realize that Jesus has the ability to help them in their personal situations and difficulties. They should also understand why our response should then be to allow Him Lordship over our life.

KEEP IN MIND

"For it pleased the Father that in him should all fullness dwell; And, having made peace through the blood of his cross, by him to reconcile all things unto himself; by him, I say, whether they be things in earth, or things in heaven" (Colossians 1:19-20).

FOCAL VERSES

COLOSSIANS 1:15 Who is the image of the invisible God, the firstborn of every creature:

16 For by him were all things created, that are in heaven, and that are in earth, visible and invisible, whether they be thrones, or dominions, or principalities, or powers: all things were created by him, and for him:

17 And he is before all things, and by him all things consist.

18 And he is the head of the body, the church: who is the beginning, the firstborn from the dead; that in all things he might have the preeminence.

19 For it pleased the Father that in him should all fullness dwell;

20 And, having made peace through the blood of his cross, by him to reconcile all things unto himself; by him, I say, whether they be things in earth, or things in heaven.

21 And you, that were sometime alienated and enemies

LESSON OVERVIEW

LESSON AIM
KEEP IN MIND
FOCAL VERSES
IN FOCUS
THE PEOPLE, PLACES, AND TIMES
BACKGROUND
AT-A-GLANCE
IN DEPTH
SEARCH THE SCRIPTURES
DISCUSS THE MEANING
LESSON IN OUR SOCIETY
MAKE IT HAPPEN
FOLLOW THE SPIRIT
REMEMBER YOUR THOUGHTS
MORE LIGHT ON THE TEXT
DAILY BIBLE READINGS

---

in your mind by wicked works, yet now hath be reconciled

22 In the body of his flesh through death, to present you holy and unblameable and unreproveable in his sight:

23 If ye continue in the faith grounded and settled, and be not moved away from the hope of the gospel, which ye have heard, and which was preached to every creature which is under heaven; whereof I Paul am made a minister;

24 Who now rejoice in my sufferings for you, and fill up that which is behind of the afflictions of Christ in my flesh for his body's sake, which is the church:

25 Whereof I am made a minister, according to the dispensation of God which is given to me for you, to fulfill the word of God;

26 Even the mystery which hath been hid from ages and from generations, but now is made manifest to his saints:

27 To whom God would make known what is the riches of the glory of this mystery amount the Gentiles; which is Christ in you, the hope of glory:

28 Whom we preach, warning every man, and teaching every man in all wisdom; that we may present every man perfect in Christ Jesus.

IN FOCUS

"I can't believe this," Mary said in a disgusting tone. She threw her keys down on the kitchen table and frantically searched through her wallet for her Auto Club card. "I've got to make this job interview TODAY!" she said the words out loud as if shouting it into the air would make it become a reality.

"Can someone come by this morning?" Mary pleaded

with the clerk at the auto repair shop. "My car won't start."

"Sorry, we are swamped this morning," the clerk replied. "Anyway, when I put your card number in the computer, it shows you are behind in your motor club payments. We will not be able to help you again until you pay your bill."

The tears began to trickle down Mary's cheek, smearing her freshly applied makeup. "Oh Lord, how can I get a job if I don't have a car to get there? How can I get a better car if I don't have a job? My life is such a mess."

As Mary sat there with her head down on the table, a little tune came to mind, "He's got the whole world in His hand, He's got the whole world in His hands."

Mary had heard that song since she was a child, but today it seemed to communicate a whole new meaning. The Lord had the entire universe inside the palms of His hands. He was keeping it all together. Surely He would help her with the messy situations in her life.

As Mary got up from the table, the tune was still quietly playing in her mind. She washed her face and prayed that somehow the Lord would work out the missed interview. She then boldly dialed the number to make another appointment.

This week's lesson gives believers a bigger picture of who Jesus is and His position in the world. Hopefully, as our view of Him increases, our perception or our personal problems will decrease.

THE PEOPLE, PLACES, AND TIMES

EPAPHARAS. Christianity came to Colossae through the work of Epapharas. He, himself, was converted and rooted in the faith by Paul during Paul's stay in Ephesus. Epaphras had established the faith in Colossae. Paul was not the founder of these congregations and never paid them a visit. Paul commended Epaphras for his excellent work.

BACKGROUND

A heretical (false teaching) movement had started in Colossae. Before any real damage could be done, Epaphras reported the errors that were circulating among the congregation to Paul. Epaphras was the founder of the church in Colossae under Paul's direction. However, Paul was imprisoned at the time, probably somewhere in Rome. Paul responded by sending Tychicus with this epistle to the Colossians. Paul wrote the epistle to crush the false teaching that had arisen.

The identity of the heretics was not clear. It could have been members in the congregation pretending to be Christians or non-members from the outside, like the Judiazers, who attempted to invalidate Paul's teaching. The Colossian heretics may also have been native Jews, not members of the Colossian church, who added fancy ideas to Epaphras' teaching and fought to win members for their peculiar beliefs.

Through this brief but powerful writing, Paul took care of the erroneous ideas completely. The theme of the letter focuses on Christ's superiority. The false teachers in Colossae were attempting to reduce the significance of Christ's authority and work. Paul, therefore, set forth his case about Christ and His elevated position.

AT-A-GLANCE

1. Christ Reigns Supreme in Creation (Colossians 1:15-17)
2. Christ Reigns Supreme in the Church (v. 18)
3. Christ Reigns Supreme in Redemption (vv. 19-23)
4. Christ Reigns Supreme in Paul's Ministry (vv. 24-28)

IN DEPTH

1. Christ Reigns Supreme in Creation (Colossians 1:15-17)

In the earlier verses of Colossians chapter 1, Paul gives many statements and compliments to the Colossian church. Starting in verse 15, however his focus changes and "Christ" takes center stage. Christ has already been addressed as "the Son of the Father's love" and the "King of the kingdom," earlier in the chapter (1:13). Paul continues to lift Jesus up. He gives a long report about Jesus' person, His position, and His work. These teachings about Jesus Christ are not new to the Colossians but they are restated in order to combat the erroneous teachings that were being spread.

The first thing Paul emphasizes about Christ is that He is all God and all man. When we look at Jesus, we see who God is. This concept is difficult to comprehend because it is beyond human understanding. How can two natures, God's divine nature, and man's nature dwell in one man? Yet, Jesus claimed to be, and is, both God and man (John 1:1, 14). Paul used the word "image" to express Christ's exact likeness of God. Like the image in the reflection of a mirror, the nature and being of God are perfectly revealed in Christ.

The second major characteristic that Paul points out is that "He is the first-born Son, superior to all created things." Being the firstborn could mean the first child to come out of the mother's womb, or it could mean the one who is given first place (heir) of honor or authority in the family even though he or she was not the first in the child-birth lineage. Solomon was not David's first son, but he was given the first-born position as heir to the throne when David died. In the Colossians passage both meanings were represented. Christ, in time, was before all creation; He is also over it in rank and dignity.

There was an ancient custom whereby the firstborn in a family was given rights and privileges not shared by the other offspring. He was his father's representative and heir, and the one to whom the management of the household was committed. Following this interpretation, we understand the passage to teach that Christ is His Father's representative and heir. He has the management of everything, here on earth and in heaven.

Since Christ was the Creator of the universe, therefore, He is firstborn or Lord over all creation. Creation was "through" Christ; God spoke the words and gave the instructions, Jesus was the Agent through whom it actually came into being. Because Christ is the reason all things exist, all things which exist are to contribute to His glory. The universe is His footstool, His throne. All things in heaven and here on earth, visible and invisible, angelic hierarchy, or whatever supernatural powers that be, were made by Christ. He is their Lord. Christ is before all things in time and all things hold together because of Him. He sustains all of creation. The world would be in complete chaos if it were not for Jesus.

2. Christ Reigns Supreme in the Church (v. 18)

Paul goes on to further point out Christ's supremacy by saying "he is the head of the body, the Church." He is the source of the Church's life. He guides and governs the Church. Christ and Christ alone is its Chief, its Leader.

The word "church" simply means assembly or congregation. Paul was making reference to all Christians everywhere, not just the individuals assembled in a church building.

The Church is a gigantic, living, moving organism by which Christ carries out His purposes and performs His work. The Church is composed of members joined vitally to one another. God gives gifts to each Christian, and then places His people in His Church that they might serve Him

where they are needed. Through His Word, Jesus Christ nourishes and cleanses the Church.

The body of Christ cannot function without Christ, their Head. He gives instructions and holds the body together. The believers carry out His mission and His purposes. It is often quoted, "Jesus had no eyes but our eyes, no feet but our feet, no hands but our hands." One member cannot accomplish much in the way of winning the world without the other.

Christ is not only the head of the Church, He is the first-born from the dead. This does not mean He was the first to be raised from the dead because He was not. Christ is the first to be permanently resurrected from the dead, the first to be clothed with immortality; the first to obtain and declare His victory over death. For without His resurrection, there would be no resurrection for others. Christ is the origin and source of the life of the Church.

Paul summarized his teaching in one statement, "So that in everything he [Christ] might have the supremacy" (v. 17). Jesus alone has the first place among all and over all—the sole head of all things.

The false teachers of Colossae were attempting to communicate to the people that Jesus Christ was only one of many ways to God. However, the Scriptures are quite clear. Jesus emphatically said, "I am the way, the truth, and the light, no one comes to the Father **except by Me**" (John 14:6, emphasis mine). Jesus is the *only* entrance into heaven and the *only* way to know God.

3. Christ Reigns Supreme in Redemption (vv. 19-23)

Paul makes two more strong statements about Christ before he ends this section. First, "all the fullness of God dwells in Christ," All of who God is has a permanent home in Christ. The sum total, not a portion, but all of God's divine power and characteristics rest in Jesus.

The fact that God would put all that He is inside Jesus proves that Jesus is God, and because He is God, He is able to do what no mere man could ever do—reconcile lost sinners to a holy God. The second strong statement Paul made is that, "Through the Son, God decided to bring the whole uinverse back to himself. God made peace through his Son's blood on the cross and so brought back to himself all things, both on earth and in heaven" (1:20, Good News).

The Father willed that all fullness should dwell in Christ. He also willed to reconcile all things to Himself through Christ—changing the condition of man from separation from God to harmony with God.

Before the Colossians became believers, they were enemies of God, strangers and distant from Him. This hostility towards God affected their thoughts, disposition, and attitude toward God which resulted in evil (doing things against God) behavior.

Paul finally states that God reconciled the Colossians by Christ's death. Paul is alluding to and possibly answering the Colossian heretics. They said reconciliation to God could be accomplished by spiritual or angelic beings. They attached little or no value to the work of Christ. Paul stressed the importance of Christ's death. The result of Christ's reconciliatory work was to present the Colossians "holy in His sight, without blemish and free from accusation." By Christ's death, believers can be brought into God's presence, no longer stained by sin and bearing the burden of guilt, but now blameless—without blemish and free from accusation.

In the Jewish tradition, an animal sacrifice was required by the temple priest to make as a blood offering to "cover" the sins of the people. "Blameless" is a word suggesting that the animals to be sacrificed were to be without blemish or flaw. Paul was not thinking about our personal conduct but about our position in Christ. There has never been, nor will there ever be, a Christian life that is without blemish in actual conduct. But Christians' identification with Christ is such that His righteousness and His standing before God renders us free from any accusations. Believers are set apart and now fit for God's use.

Some conclude Paul was implying that one can lose their salvation when he said, "if ye continue in the faith" (v. 23). But what Paul was attempting to convey was that as the Colossians continued in their faith, this would prove that they truly were believers and that a genuine conversion did take place within their hearts.

In Paul's closing words, he alluded to the teaching the Colossians received from Epaphras, the "Message that was originally preached to them." This message had been heard in all the major cities in that day. Paul, himself, had become a servant of this great Gospel. He is letting the congregation know that the same message preached to them by Epaphras and the message of the Gospel that he proclaimed was the same.

4. Christ Reigns Supreme in Paul's Ministry (vv. 24-28)

Paul now turns his attention to his ministry. He expounds not so much on who he is as a person but the office he now filled. Paul talked about his suffering first of all. He assured the Colossians that his misfortunes were "for you" and "for the sake of His [Christ's] body." Paul's bonds

and imprisonment had been incurred in the course of bringing the Gospel to the Gentiles, to which class the Colossians belonged. Paul's suffering, therefore, was for their sake, in the sense that they shared in the benefit of the ministry that brought on those sufferings. Paul's sufferings are for today's believers as well. If Paul had not suffered and spent time in prison, some of these letters may not have been written.

Paul's sufferings are identified with the afflictions of Christ. The body of Christ is built up by repeated acts of self-denial in individuals from each generation. They present the work which Christ began and completed by their unselfish sacrifices, by presenting their own bodies as a living sacrifice for the Gospel of Christ. Christ's personal suffering is over but His sufferings in His people continue. A Christian should never suffer as a thief or as an evil-doer, but it is an honor to suffer as a Christian. There is a special blessing and reward reserved for the faithful believer who suffers for the sake of Christ (Matthew 5:10-12).

Paul does not hesitate to state that his sufferings are an occasion to rejoice. Paul endured great physical and emotional pain as a result of his ministry, and yet he saw the positive in what he experienced. He was able to find the silver lining when dark clouds encircled. He knew suffering was a part of what he needed to experience in his ministry.

Paul could have escaped some of his suffering if he had stopped his ministry to the Gentiles. But he could not abandon his calling just for personal safety and comfort. He was made a minister by God. He had been given a mission that had to be fulfilled, it was not a matter of choice. Paul was called to communicate the Word of God. God commissioned him to preach the Word fully and to not compromise any truth.

Paul's calling had to do with what is called the "mystery." To us today, a mystery is something eerie and perhaps frightening. But in the Bible it meant "hidden in the past and now revealed by the Holy Spirit."

God called Israel to be His own people. He promised them a King who would one day establish a glorious kingdom and fulfill the many promises made to Abraham and David. The Old Testament prophets wrote about a Messiah who would suffer and a Messiah who would reign. They could not explain or did not fully understand that this Messiah had to suffer.

When Jesus came to earth, He was rejected by His people and crucified. He rose again and returned to heaven. This mystery that was not fully explained by the Old Testament prophets is now fully revealed. The mystery is that today God is uniting Jews and Gentiles in the Church.

When the Church is completed, then Jesus will return and take His people to heaven.

Paul concluded by clarifying the difference between his ministry and that of the false teachers'. The false teachers exalted themselves and their great belief systems, but Paul preached Christ. They preached a system of teaching, but Paul preached a Person. The false teachers preached philosophy and the empty traditions of men, but Paul proclaimed the living, powerful, ever-present, ever-working Jesus Christ on the believers' behalf. The false teachers had a list of rules and regulations, but Paul presented the grace and mercy of God through Jesus Christ. What a difference in ministries!

Paul preached and strongly warned the people. He warned them about accepting the lies of the enemy. Paul considered himself a spiritual father to the local churches and it was his duty to warn his children. But Paul was also a teacher of the truth. It is not enough to warn people; we must also teach them positive truths of the Word of God. The believers in Colossae needed to know that all the treasures of wisdom and knowledge are in Christ. Wisdom is the right use of knowledge. True spiritual wisdom is found only in Jesus.

Paul's mission was to present every believer "perfect in Christ." Paul used the term to mean "complete, mature in Christ." This is the goal of all his preaching, his warning, and his teachings. Paul would know his mission was accomplished if their hearts were encouraged or comforted. They were to be knit together in love. The mature Christian loves the brethren and seeks to be a peacemaker, not a troublemaker. He is a part of the spiritual unity in the church. An immature person is selfish and causes division. These were the goals for which Paul was struggling and suffering.

SEARCH THE SCRIPTURES

1. List as many facts as you can about Christ and creation. (Colossians 1:15-18)

2. Explain the two definitions of first-born and how Jesus fits them both. (v. 18)

3. Explain how it is possible for sinful man to be reconciled to a holy God. (vv. 20-23)

4. Why did Paul suffer? What was his attitude about his suffering? (v. 24)

5. What was Paul's goal for every believer? What does it mean to be perfect? (v. 28)

DISCUSS THE MEANING

1. How do the facts presented about Christ prove His supremacy over everything?

2. What does Christ's reconciling mankind to God through His death on the Cross mean to us today?

3. Why was Paul able to rejoice in suffering?

4. Compare Paul's ministry with the ministry God has called you to do.

LESSON IN OUR SOCIETY

The assistant director of a local crisis pregnancy center had this to say about her clients. "I talk to young women all the time who call or come in and talk about the difficulties in their lives. When I ask them what they have tried to better themselves and their situations, many of them talk about getting a better job, better education, and job training skills. Some even mention getting out of a bad relationship. Very rarely does anyone mention turning to God as a solution."

We live in a society that habitually ignores God. And yet, God desires us to make friends with Him through His Son Jesus, so He can personally be our guide and help us through the difficulties of life. Most people overlook the Almighty God entirely.

MAKE IT HAPPEN

Make a list of personal difficulties and the way you have handled them in the past. Make another list of challenges you are facing presently. What changes are you going to make in your outlook? Attitude? Actions?

FOLLOW THE SPIRIT

What God wants me to do:

_____

_____

REMEMBER YOUR THOUGHTS

Special insight you learned:

_____

_____

MORE LIGHT ON THE TEXT
COLOSSIANS 1:15-28

The supremacy of Christ is one of the three major themes of the book of Colossians, which Paul develops extensively in these verses (1:15-28). Here Paul deals with the glory, the pre-eminence, and the pre-existence of Christ who is the head of the church.

This Christ, Paul says, is the direct image and likeness of the invisible God, and the creator of all things and the head of the church. The emphasis on the theme of Christ's supremacy and His relationship to the Father, e.g. His role in creation, and His relationship to the Church is purposely aimed at refuting the false claims of certain heretics in the Colossian churches. It is aimed, as well, at strengthening the faith of the brethren in the body of Christ, the Church, in relation to their worship of the true image of the Father, rather than the created beings.

1:15 Who is the image of the invisible God, the firstborn of every creature:

The word "who" in verse 13 refers to the dear (beloved) Son into whose kingdom the Church has been translated, and in whom we have redemption through His blood, even the forgiveness of sins (v. 14). The phrase, "the image of the invisible God," is therefore a description of Jesus Christ, the Son of God. "Image" (Greek *eikon*) can be translated as the "likeness, or representation," and most applicable, "the replica of an object." Genesis 1:27 says that man was created in the image of God, which speaks of moral and natural faculties, rather than physical or likeness. Here the word is used to describe the bodily and spiritual likeness of the Son to the Father in every aspect, in power and authority.

Hebrews 1:3 describes the "express image of his person, and upholding all things by the word of his power, when he had by himself purged our sins, sat down on the right hand of the Majesty on high." John confesses that Jesus is the glory of the Father (1:14). To Philip and the other disciples, Jesus says, "He that hath seen me hath seen the Father" (John 14:9, KJV). The picture here is more than the picture of a son's resemblance of his father. It is much more than that. Christ's image of the Father can only be fully understood on the basis of Christ's preexistence. John says that Christ was in the beginning, that He was with God, and that He was, in fact, God (John 1:1). Christ's incarnation is therefore a revelation of the invisible God (John 1:18; cf. John 10:30, 38; Revelation 3:14).

Christ is not only the image of the Father, but also the first-born of every creature, Paul contends. This aspect of Paul's concept of Christ poses some definite theological and doctrinal problems. The major problem is in the meaning of "first-born" (*prototokos*), and how it relates to and is used of Christ here. The word is used in a number of passages in the New Testament (Matthew 1:25; Luke 2:7; Romans 8:29; Hebrews 11:28). It means literally "the first one to be born into a family," and is applied to Jesus as the first-born of His earthly family. It also applies to Him as the first-born into the family of God. However, the problem is whether the word means that Christ is a part of creation, or whether,

in other words, He is a created being as other creatures.

How do we understand this concept of Christ as contained here? Looking at the phrase in isolation and out of context will make one tend to see Christ as a created being and parallel to Romans 8:29. Nonetheless, the context makes it clear that Christ is both the Agent and Creator of all creation. It then places Him above it, and causes us to understand "first-born" in the sense of "supreme and sovereign" rather than as "born before." Christ's sovereignty over all creation is further made clear in John 1:3 and Hebrews 1:2. The deity of Christ supports this concept.

16 For by him were all things created, that are in heaven, and that are in earth, visible and invisible, whether they be thrones, or dominions, or principalities, or powers: all things were created by him, and for him:

The deity and pre-eminence of Jesus Christ is brought in focus by His creative activity, as we read in verse 16. The verse establishes two important things about Christ, as we have already mentioned in the previous verse. The first is that Christ is the agent of all creation, all things were created by Him. The second is that all things belong to Him; all things were created for Him. The statement clarifies and substantiates the fact we have established in verse 15, i.e., the first-born *prototokos* does not include Christ in the creation. This is supported by the conjunction "for" (*hoti*).

The person we know as the historical Jesus, the only begotten of the Father, existed as an equal member of the Godhead, as the Creator of all things. Since all things are created by and through Him and are in Him, He cannot Himself be all things. "All things" includes both earthly and heavenly things, visible and invisible things, all have their beginning and existence in Christ, Paul contends. Nothing would exist without the sovereignty of Christ, whether visible or invisible. Everything derives its existence in Him. The "visible things" refer to the cosmic things, the earthly, material things which includes humans; and the "invisible things" probably refer to spirit beings like angelic agencies.

The New Testament uses different words to describe these invisible created beings, but Paul applies four here: thrones, dominions, principalities, and powers. Paul asserts, as in Ephesians 1:21, 22, the existence of the angelic beings, both good and fallen angels, and that they are able to exert some influence for good or for evil (1 Timothy 5:21; Ephesians 6:12).

However, Paul contends that they have neither power nor existence apart from Christ. The good angels can contribute absolutely nothing towards man's salvation, and the bad (evil) angels cannot separate believers from the love of Christ (Romans 8:35-39). The mention of these four groups of angelic beings, though viewed by humans as superior beings (as wrongly taught by false teachers), are only mere creatures; having been created by and for Christ, and are subject to Him.

17 And he is before all things, and by him all things consist.

If all things were created by Him, for Him and they exist in Him, it then follows that He preceded all things in time, and in Him all things consist (or are held together). Both statements go further to underline the supremacy of Christ over all creation. The first statement, "he is before all things" means that He is from eternity. He is timeless. Indeed, there was no time when He did not exist. This firmly establishes the pre-existence of Christ, as is contained in a number of New Testament passages, including John 1:1; 8:58; 17:5; 2 Corinthians 8:9; Philippians 2:6; Revelations 22:13.

The book of Revelation refers to Christ as the Alpha and Omega, the Beginning and End, the First and Last, and the prophet Micah says that He is from everlasting (5:2). The second statement, "by him all things consist," (or "in Him all things hold together," NAS) signifies that the continuity and coherence of all creation are centered in Him and under His direction, and thus speaks of His pre-eminence. Nothing, as we have already established, could exist without Him, for in Him is life. Paul, defending the Gospel at Mars Hill, says to the Athenians, "For in him we live, and move, and have our being; as certain also of your own poets have said, For we are also his offspring" (Acts 17:28, KJV).

Not only is He the creator of all things (v. 16), He upholds and sustains all things, which translates as the Greek word *sunistao*. It also has the idea of "to set in the place, to put together, or to unite parts into one whole." Probably, Paul has in mind the orderliness of the universe and the harmony of the cosmic world. Although the world seems to be in chaos on the surface: wars, people killing each other, kids killing kids, theft, and all sorts of evil, and yet beneath this seemingly chaotic nature of the world is order and plan. The sun comes up in the day and the moon at the night, the rain comes in its season, and the winter at its time.

Even the globe itself is held in balance in the vacuum, with an unseen gravitational force, it rotates ceaselessly on its axis. Rivers run constantly into the ocean and the ocean is never filled. There is order in the universe. It is neither chance nor fate, nor for that matter the law of nature that keeps these things in place, and makes them function as some would claim. Rather, Paul says that all things are held in Him and by Him, who is the express image of the Father and the Creator of all things all, declaring the supremacy and power of Christ (Revelations 4-5).

This section has been considered by many scholars as a hymn which was sung in worship in ancient time, but adapted by Paul here to clarify the pre-existence, pre-eminence, and superiority of Christ over all things, both in heaven and earth. It defines Christ's position in the nature of things in the created world and places Him in His rightful position in relation to the Father as the true representation.

18 And he is the head of the body, the church: who is the beginning, the firstborn from the dead; that in all things he might have the preeminence.

Hitherto, Paul has been describing the Christ's pre-eminence in the realm of creation. He now refocuses our attention to Christ's relation to the Church and deals with it in the sphere of redemption. He says that Christ is the head of the Church, an assertion he also has made elsewhere; namely, Ephesians (1:22, 23; 4:15) and later in the second chapter of this book (Colossians 2:19). In some of his previous letters, Paul refers to the Church as the body of Christ, but the application is in relationship to the members with one another.

For example, in 1 Corinthians 10 and 12 (especially vv. 12-31) and Romans 12:5, Paul describes the Church as one body with many parts and functionality, just as the human body has different parts hands, feet, eyes, ears and each has different functions. In other words, in the one organism of the Church there are gifts, talents, skills, and functions distributed among the believers, and each believer uses his or her gift for the benefit of the entire body. In these passages, Paul never expressly refers to Christ as the Head of the church. However, the idea is implied, for a body cannot exist without a head. He also had written in 1 Corinthians 11:3 that "the head of every man is Christ." If Christ is the head of every man, it then follows that He is the Head of the Church.

Nevertheless, Paul's main emphasis to the Colossians is about Christ's pre-eminence and relationship with the Church. In his letter to the Ephesians, Paul compares the headship of Christ to the Church with the headship of the husband to his wife (5:23ff), and the main function of the head in relation to the body is for sustenance and growth (Colossians 2:19; Ephesians 4:15-16). The importance of the head to a body is obvious. A body without a head is a dead body. One can survive and lead a fruitful life with any part of the body missing such as the eyes, legs, hands, etc., but has anyone ever seen a body moving without a head?

Consequently, a church without Christ is a dead church and cannot function. Christ is not only the organic Head of the Church, He is also its ruling head in the sense of guidance and exercising authority, which is implied in the Ephesian passages (1:20-23; 5:23-24). Going back to the analogy of the physical body, science clearly shows that the functionality of all other parts of the body is located in the head and contained in the brain. The brain controls and harmonizes all movements and functions of all parts of the body by receiving, interpreting, transmitting, and distributing impulses from both the outside world and inside the body to all parts of the body.

Paul continues to explain the place of Christ within the Church by describing Him as "the beginning, the firstborn from the dead." The word translated "the beginning" is the Greek word *archà* which has a variety of meanings such as: "the origin by which everything begins, the first person in series, the leader in rank," etc. All these are applicable to Christ. However, the inclination here, in view of the statement that Christ is the first-born from the dead, speaking of resurrection, is that He is the first person among the dead who would resurrect.

The resurrection of the body is the hope, joy, and assurance of all who believe in Christ (3:1-17; 1 Peter 1:3ff). Christ is therefore the first among the many, the one that has inaugurated the principle, and causes the glorified physical resurrection of believers. He is both the author and sustainer of life and death; He has authority over life and death (Romans 8:29; 1 Corinthians 15:20; Hebrews 2:14,15; Revelations 1:5); He has the key to death and Hades. He assures His disciples, concerning His resurrection, "because I live, ye shall live also" (John 14:19).

Paul writes to Timothy that "by the appearing of our Saviour Jesus Christ, hath abolished death, and hath brought life and immortality to light through the Gospel" (2 Timothy 1:10). It is to be noted that Paul uses the same word first-born here that he used in verse 15, which speaks of both the aspect of creation (the old) and parallels Christ's relationship to the Church, the new creation. The new creation came into existence on the same principle as the old. All this tied together in the goal of supremacy i.e., that in all things He might have the preeminence (Greek *proteuo*, i.e.," to be first in rank, influence, and importance among all creatures").

19 For it pleased the Father that in him should all fulness dwell;

This high position of the Son is according to the Father's design and for His pleasure and it translates into the embodiment of the fullness of God in the Son.

Here, Paul says that God is delighted to have His fullness (*pleroma*) resident in Christ. *Pleroma* or "fullness" is used in a number passages in the New Testament with two basic meanings: 1) something that fills or completes, such as a patch (Matthew 9:16) or love (Romans 13:10); 2) fullness or the state of being filled, such as the completed number of saved Gentiles (Romans 11:25) or the "full measure" of Christ's blessing (Romans 15:29, NIV). First Corinthians (10:26) speaks of the earth's fullness, and Galatians (4:4) talks about the fullness of the time. In Ephesians 1:10, Paul writes about God's sovereign appointment of events in both space and time.

The use of *pleroma* in Romans 11:12 refers to the completion of God's plan for the nation of Israel. Paul, in verse 19, says that the Lord Jesus Christ possesses the complete fullness of God, which probably include God's divine nature and attributes (cf. Colossians 1:15; Hebrews 1:3). It also says later in Colossians that "In Him (Christ) dwells all the fullness of the Godhead bodily" (Colossians 2:9). The phrase, "all the fullness of God" (Ephesians 3:19) is used by Paul to show that Christ embodies the love of God.

In Ephesians 4:13, the fullness of Christ refers to that state of Christian maturity in which believers are "no longer tossed back and forth and carried about with every wind of doctrine and by the cunning and craftiness of men in their deceitful scheming" (Ephesians 4:14). The Father's delight in the Son was evident even before the beginning of time (Psalms 2:7-8; cf. John. 17:5; Ephesians 1:9) and manifested itself repeatedly in Christ's earthly ministry (Matthew 3:17; 17:5; John 12:28).

Therefore, the fullness of God, His essence, nature, glory, and attributes, and in accordance with God's own delightful pleasure from eternity, is made complete and resident in Christ, who is the Creator and Redeemer, and in whom all things are held together. The incarnate Christ is the total and exclusive revelation of God, and "if you have seen me," He says, "you have seen the Father."

20 And, having made peace through the blood of his cross, by him to reconcile all things unto himself; by him, I say, whether they be things in earth, or things in heaven.

Paul now turns our attention to the work of this exalted Son of God, in whom all the embodiment of the Godhead dwells the reconciliation of all things through Him to Himself. The conjunction "and" (*kai*) denotes a continuation of the thought in verse 19 of God's pleasure in both having His fullness dwell in Christ, and making peace through the blood of Christ by the process of reconciliation to Himself of all things.

Although Paul has stated in verse 17 that in Christ all things hold together, here he recognizes that there is still considerable disharmony in creation, hence the necessity for reconciliation and peace. Just as He is the agent through whom all things are created (v. 16), Jesus is also the agent through whom all things are reconciled (v. 20). In both cases, "all things" means the same. The verb "reconcile" is a translation of the Greek verb *apokatallasso*, which literally means "to bring back a former state of harmony."

To understand this, one has to go back to the creation story in Genesis, where sin ruined the universe and destroyed the harmony that existed between God and His creation (particularly man and God), and between one creature and the other. The only obstacle that separates man and God is sin (Isaiah 59:1-2) thereby causing enmity between them, but through the Cross the obstacle has been removed in principle, the work of reconciliation is accomplished (Ephesians 2:11-18; Romans 5:8-10), and peace is restored (Romans 5:1). The demands of the law have been met (Romans 3:25; Galatians 3:13) and harmony restored.

The method of this reconciliation and peace is of great importance through the blood of Christ that is the atoning sacrifice of the Son of God on Calvary. The importance of this process to the apostle Paul is quite evident in the number of occasions he speaks of the blood of Christ in many portions of his letters (Romans 3:25; 5:9; 1 Corinthians 11:25; Ephesians 1:7; etc.). It is unavoidable at this point not to mention the motive behind this process i.e., the love of God for His creatures (John. 3:16) and His delightful pleasure (Colossians 1:19). A number of questions arise from this verse. What does Paul mean by to "reconcile all things whether they be things in earth, or things in heaven"? What do they include? Does it include angelic beings: good and bad angels? Does "all things" include other lower animals? These questions are left here for consideration and discussion.

21 And you, that were sometime alienated and enemies in your mind by wicked works, yet now hath he reconciled 22 In the body of his flesh through death, to present you holy and unblameable and unreproveable in his sight:

After stating in general the reconciliation, which God

has effected through the death of His Son on the Cross, to all things both on earth and in heaven, Paul now returns to the particular. Here he, seemingly with joy, testifies that the Colossians are also the recipients of this amazing gift of reconciliation. He reminds them of the changes that have occurred in their lives, which demonstrate the blessing of reconciliation. He begins by reminding them of their former state in relation to God using similar words and expressing the same idea as in his epistle to the Ephesians (2:12,13; 4:18): "And you, that were sometime alienated and enemies in your mind by wicked works."

Here too, he is probably referring particularly to the Gentiles as in the Ephesian passage. This state of alienation, Paul tends to says is not due simply to ignorance or the inherited sin in general, but because of their own sin, which he describes as wicked works. The sin of the Gentiles is the rejection of God and the worship of other gods and idols. Even when God through conscience, natural revelation, and history had made Himself known, they through wicked works had suppressed the truth in their hearts (mind), and worshiped and served the creature rather than the Creator (Romans 1:18-25). Such inexcusable wickedness, which by nature is the condition of the sinner, warrants God's wrath (Romans 1:18), and so Paul refers to them as the children of wrath (Ephesians 2:3).

All this is now in the past. They are now reconciled. The relationship with God is now restored. Through the death of Christ on the Cross, which Paul expresses here thus: "In the body of his flesh (physical body) through death," those who were once estranged and separated, alienated from the commonwealth of Israel, and foreigners to the family of God are now returned and accepted into God's household and have become citizens.

Like the prodigal son (Luke 15:11-24), they have

returned to God their Father. This reconciliation is only made possible by the death of Christ, the only possible means through the sovereign grace of God in which the sinner is restored to his former state of harmony enjoyed with the Father before the fall. What is the purpose for the reconciliation? Paul is quick to answer: "to present you holy and unblamable and unreproveable in his sight." The idea behind this statement is the Old Testament presentation of the sacrifice.

"Holy" is used in the sense of "sacred, cleansed from sin and separated unto God;" "unblameable" (*amomos*) carries the idea of "unblemished," or "without fault;" and "unreproveable" (*anegkletos*) has the idea of "blameless" or "irreproachable," in the sense of not open to any charge. This must definitely be viewed eschatologically and refers to the return of Christ at the fullness of time. This idea is made clear in the next statement, "if ye continue in the faith grounded and settled," which sets the condition for the glorious presentation of the righteous at the return of the Lord.

23 If ye continue in the faith grounded and settled, and be not moved away from the hope of the gospel, which ye have heard, and which was preached to every creature which is under heaven; whereof I Paul am made a minister;

To be part of God's eschatological plan for man requires stability in faith, or a firm grip on the Gospe,l which requires perseverance based totally on the grace of God from the start to finish. No one can continue if their faith is based on his or her own strength apart from the grace of God, which He has made available through faith (John 15:15; Philippians 2:12-13). This however does not nullify human responsibility, rather God's grace gives us the strength to persevere.

Paul continues this conditional clause by stating the same thing negatively, "and be not moved away from the hope of the gospel, which ye have heard." Paul warns the Colossian church against relapse into their former state. They are not to move from the hope, i.e., the Good News of eternal life, the essence and purpose of the reconciliation, which they have heard through the preaching of the Word. The Gospel, Paul tends to clarify here, is not exclusive to a few, neither is it confined to a special group of people or race, but rather it is preached (and available) to every creature that is under heaven (Matthew 28:19; Mark 16:15). This type of Gospel is what he has been called to preach "to which I Paul am made a minister" (cf. 1 Corinthians 15:9: Ephesians 3:8: 1 Timothy 1:15-17).

24 Who now rejoice in my sufferings for you, and fill up that which is behind of the afflictions of Christ in my flesh for his body's sake, which is the church:

Paul continues the personal reference he made in verse 23 and says that he now rejoices in suffering on their behalf or for their sake. The word "now" refers to the present situation Paul finds himself in sufferings and afflictions, which he has to endure in prison (cf. 4:10, 18; Ephesians 3:1; 4:1; Philemon 1, 9, 23). It is has been established that Paul was at that moment writing from a Roman jail, serving time for preaching the Gospel. Instead of complaining and agonizing in self-pity, Paul rejoices. He regards the hardship which he had to endure in preaching the Gospel as being in a sense on behalf of the Church. "For you" (i.e., "for your sake") here can be rephrased as "for your benefit," in the sense that such enduring hardship and suffering will strengthen the faith of the Colossians, and indeed the whole Christian Church in every age (cf. also 2:1).

His present personal sufferings and hardship is not only aimed at benefitting the Colossian church, but to "fill up in my flesh what is lacking in the afflictions of Christ, for the sake of His body, which is the church" (NKJV). This statement poses some problem, and has attracted a number of scholarly debates and interpretations. In what sense does Paul apply this statement in view of the meaning of the verb "to fill"? The verb "fill up" (*antanapleroo*) used here suggests the supply or the supplement to a deficiency from whatever source. In what sense is Paul thinking of deficiency in the suffering or affliction of Christ, which he now is filling?

Paul definitely is not thinking that Christ's sacrificial death as a redemptive act was inadequate and needed supplementing. It seems to me that Paul is saying that he is contributing his own share in the suffering of Christ, in a sense as it were Christ is still suffering through him. In other words, Paul's present suffering is therefore an extension of the sufferings of Christ in which all believers are called upon to partake (Matthew 10:25; Mark 13:13; John 15:18-21; 2 Corinthians 1:5, 10; etc.). Paul's suffering, however, is being borne for the sake (i.e., for the benefit) of the glorious body of Christ, which is the Church. Paul's thought here probably means that his endurance of sufferings and afflictions would be a testimony in the Church and through it, the body would be firmly established in faith.

25 Wherefore I am made a minister, according to the dispensation of God which is given to me for you, to fulfil the word of God; 26 Even the

mystery which hath been hid from ages and from generations, but now is made manifest to his saints: 27 To whom God would make known what is the riches of the glory of this mystery among the Gentiles; which is Christ in you, the hope of glory:

Paul has indicated in the previous verse that he rejoices in his suffering because it is for the benefit of the church. He continues that it is for that purpose he is "made a minister, according to the dispensation of God which is given to me for you." The word "minister" (Greek *diakonos*) means "a servant" and is a term Paul uses quite often. He is also a divinely appointed steward or administrator (dispensation or *oikonomia*) for their benefit to fulfill the Word of God; that is to proclaim the Gospel of Christ in its fullness (Romans 15:29) to every race and culture (v. 25).

The Gospel Paul is called to proclaim was a mystery hitherto hidden for ages and generations, now revealed to the saints. "Mystery" (Greek *musterion*) is defined as "a hidden or secret thing not obvious to the understanding," but later revealed to humans. The word is used about 28 times in New Testament, three times in the Gospels (Matthew 13:11; Mark 4:11; Luke 8:10), four times in Revelation (1:20; 10:7; 17:5,7), and 21 times in the Pauline writings (cf. Romans 11:25; 16:25; 1 Corinthians 2:1; 2:7; Ephesians 1:9; 3:3, 4; 5:32, etc.)

What mystery has God revealed to the saints, which He had hidden from ages past? It is the knowledge of Christ made to the Gentile world, which places them on the same footing with the Jews, and makes both equal partakers of the Gospel of Christ, and members of the same body, the church (cf. Ephesians 2:14-22; 3:1-7; 1 Corinthians 12:13). Simply put, the mystery is Christ Himself in all His glorious riches dwelling in the hearts and minds of the Gentiles through the Spirit.

This Christ, Paul proceeds, is in you, (Gentiles), which is "the hope of glory," i.e., the glorious hope of all believers. As we have noted in the previous lessons, the mystery of the Gospel is that through Christ's life, death and resurrection the middle wall that had separated the Jews and Gentiles, that alienated the Gentiles both from God's family and from the commonwealth of God's people, has been completely removed (Ephesians 2:14). They have been reconciled to God and to each other (2 Corinthians 5:17). They are now members of the same family of God. The revelation of this mystery also gives the Gentiles a glorious hope, which is eschatological nature (Romans 8:11). Since Christ is now dwelling richly in them, they are now given the privilege to become the Children of God and to be with Him

forever, both in this world and in eternity, never to be separated again. This eternal salvation is the glorious hope (*elpis*) or joyful and confident expectation of every believer. This forms the object of Paul's calling and ministry and stewardship.

28 Whom we preach, warning every man, and teaching every man in all wisdom; that we may present every man perfect in Christ Jesus:

The subject of Paul's ministry is Christ, which is also the subject of every preacher. "Whom," definitely refers to Christ. Paul identifies three methods for his ministry. First, by preaching (*kataggello*), that is through public proclamation, or declaration of the Gospel with an idea of evangelism (1 Corinthians 9:14; 2:1). Second, by warning (*noutheteo*) or gentle admonition or exhortation. Third, through teaching or instruction (*didasko*), all these are based on the wisdom from God. Here we observe that all teachings, preaching, and exhortation should be based, not in human wisdom, but "in demonstration of the Spirit and of power: That your faith should not stand in the wisdom of men, but in the power of God" (1 Corinthians 2:4-5).

DAILY BIBLE READING

M: Paul Gives Thanks for the Colossians
Colossians 1:1-8
T: Paul Prays for the Colossian Christians
Colossians 1:9-14
W: The Fullness of God Dwelled in Christ
Colossians 1:15-20
T: God's Mystery Revealed to the Saints
Colossians 1:21-29
F: Jesus Christ: God's Word and Light
John 1:1-9
S: God's Word Lived Among Us
John 1:10-18
S: Christ Is Superior Even to Angels
Hebrews 1:1-14

TEACHING TIPS

August 13
Bible Study Guide 11

1. Words You Should Know

A. Rooted (Colossians 2:7)—Greek *errizomenoi* a once for all experience.

B. Built-up (2:7)—Greek *epoikodomoumenoi* a continual process.

2. Teacher Preparation

A. Read the FOCAL VERSES in a study Bible. Take time to read the additional notes surrounding this passage in the study Bible.

B. Read the entire lesson for this Bible study. Answer the questions from the SEARCH THE SCRIPTURES and DISCUSS THE MEANING sections.

C. Don't forget to play around with the acrostic in the MAKE IT HAPPEN section.

D. You will need: Bibles, board or newsprint, and pencils and paper for each student.

3. Starting the Lesson

A. List the words from SEARCH THE SCRIPTURES and challenge the students to find the meanings. Have a prize for the one who completes the task first.

Aswers: 1. roots (v. 7) 2. traditions of men (v. 8) 3. fullness of the Godhead (v. 9) 4. baptism (v. 12) 5. physical circumcise (v. 13) 6. spiritual circumcise (v. 13) 7. beguile (v. 18)

B. Read the LESSON AIM and have one or two students pray about it.

C. Put the AT-A-GLANCE outline on the board. Review what will be covered in the lesson using the outline.

D. Have two or three students take turns reading IN FOCUS.

4. Getting into the Lesson

A. Break the class up into three groups. Write words down from the terms in the Words You Should Know section above. Give one group a Bible dictionary and let them look up the words. Ask a group to read the BACKGROUND and another group to read THE PEOPLE, PLACES, AND TIMES sections of the lesson. Tell them to summarize the information and be ready to give a brief report. Allow each group to report.

B. Read through IN DEPTH and intersperse the questions from the DISCUSS THE MEANING section.

5. Relating the Lesson to Life

A. Read LESSON IN OUR SOCIETY and allow time for discussion.

B. If someone in the class has had a personal experience with one of the groups mentioned, allow them to share. Or you may ask someone you know in the church or someone from your community to do so. But be sure they are now free from the group and trusting Christ for their freedom or they may confuse your class.

6. Arousing Action

A. Work on the acrostic as a class or have the three groups reconvene and work on it; then present their answers to the class.

B. Don't overlook the FOLLOW THE SPIRIT section of the lesson. Have your students give at least a sentence or two about what they feel God wants them to do as a result of the lesson.

C. As you challenge them to do the DAILY BIBLE READINGS, ask if anyone has any insights to share from the readings last week.

A COMPLETE LIFE IN CHRIST

Bible Background • COLOSSIANS 2:6-19
Printed Text • COLOSSIANS 2:16-19
Devotional Reading • ROMANS 8:31-39

LESSON AIM

By the end of this lesson, each student should understand how important it is to grow and mature as a Christian, to not get entangled in false doctrines, and to be motivated to teach and stand firm in the truth about Christ.

KEEP IN MIND

"As ye have therefore received Christ Jesus the Lord, so walk ye in him: Rooted and built up in him, and stablished in the faith, as ye have been taught, abounding therein with thanksgiving" (Colossians 2:6-7).

FOCAL VERSES

COLOSSIANS 2:6 As ye have therefore received Christ Jesus the Lord, so walk ye in him:

7 Rooted and built up in him, and stablished in the faith, as ye have been taught, abounding therein with thanksgiving.

8 Beware lest any man spoil you through philosophy and vain deceit, after the tradition of men, after the rudiments of the world, and not after Christ.

9 For in him dwelleth all the fulness of the Godhead bodily.

10 And ye are complete in him, which is the head of all principality and power:

11 In whom also ye are circumcised with the circumcision made without hands, in putting off the body of the sins of the flesh by the circumcision of Christ:

12 Buried with him in baptism, wherein also ye are risen with him through the faith of the operation of God, who hath raised him from the dead.

13 And you, being dead in your sins and the uncircum-

cision of your flesh, hath he quickened together with him, having forgiven you all trespasses;

14 Blotting out the handwriting of ordinances that was against us, which was contary to us, and took it out of the way, nailing it to his cross;

15 And having spoiled principalities and powers, he made a shew of them openly, triumphing over them in it.

16 Let no man therefore judge you in meat, or in drink, or in respect of an holyday, or of the new moon, or of the sabbath days:

17 Which are a shadow of things to come; but the body is of Christ.

18 Let no man beguile you of your reward in a voluntary humility and worshipping of angels, intruding into those things which he hath not seen, vainly puffed up by his fleshly mind,

19 And not holding the Head, from which all the body by joints and bands having nourishment ministered, and knit together, increaseth with the increase of God.

IN FOCUS

At one time, Islam only reached the United States through religion courses, but today Islamic mosques are continually springing up in urban areas. Many African Americans, especially males, are deciding to convert. One of the main reasons is because they believe Christianity is the "white man's religion."

This is why Carl Ellis, a minister from Chattanooga, Tennessee established a ministry called "Project Joseph" (PJ). Ellis' desire is to meet the challenge of Islamic growth in the black community. Ellis says, "These men have rational needs

AUGUST 13TH

that the traditional church has not addressed. To many African Americans, God is a white European deity. But Muslims project God as a non-white deity; so with Islam, young men find spirituality with ethnicity."

With seminars and dialogues, Ellis and his colleges are trying to show black Muslims and potential converts that the Gospel of Jesus literally addresses their concerns about racism, oppression, and poverty. PJ seminars train Christians to share the Gospel with Muslims. PJ volunteers also take the opportunity, when invited in by a mosque leader, to present various topics from a Christian perspective. Since PJ was organized in 1991, the team has seen significant changes. Ellis is calling Christians in America to view the growth of Islam as a serious challenge.

This week's lesson helps to prepare us to meet the challenges often presented to us by false teachers.

THE PEOPLE, PLACES, AND TIMES

CIRCUMCISION. A cutting of the foreskin of the penis. It was a physical operation; yet, it had spiritual significance. The trouble was that the Jewish people depended on the physical and not the spiritual. A mere physical operation could never convey spiritual grace. God warned His people, thought the Old Testament, to turn from their sins and experience a spiritual circumcision of the heart. People make the same mistake today when they depend on some religious ritual to save them—such as baptism or the Lord's Supper.

It was not necessary for the believer to submit to circumcision because he had already experienced a spiritual circumcision through his identification with Jesus. The Jewish circumcision included external surgery on a part of the body, performed by human hands, with no spiritual help, having nothing to do with conquering sin.

SABBATH. Jewish tradition required that all Jews keep the Sabbath. In the Old Testament, the Sabbath was originated by God Himself; on the seventh day of creation, God rested. He was establishing a pattern for us: work and then set aside time to rest and enjoy that which we have worked on and for. By the time this responsibility had moved to the New Testament many specific laws had been attached to it. The Jew was almost paralyzed on the Sabbath. The religious leaders were quick to give correction if some activity was done on the Sabbath that was not according to the law. This law, like many others, had several man-made attachments that God never intended, which resulted in bondage to the people. They emphasized keeping the law more than worshiping and serving God.

The law was the shadow and Christ is the reality. The law was the introduction to the play, but Christ is the main story and the play itself. It would be foolish for a person sitting in the middle of a play to say "let's go back, I want to hear the introduction again." In the same way, Paul was warning the Colossians not to go backwards.

BACKGROUND

Paul's letter to the Colossian church was basically to fight the heretical ideas some false teachers were attempting to communicate. Their doctrine was a mixture of Oriental mysticism, Jewish legalism, and a smattering of philosophy and Christian teaching. The Jewish legalism was probably the major influence. Human nature thrives on "religious duties." The flesh is weak when it comes to doing spiritual things, but it is very strong when it comes to practicing religious rules and regulations. The person's ego is fed making a person content in self-righteousness.

The Gentiles in Colossae were never under the Law of Moses; that law was given only to Israel. It was strange that now that they were Christians they would want to submit themselves to Jewish legalism.

The false teachers in Colossae were claiming a deeper spiritual life for all who would practice the law. Outwardly, their practices seemed to be spiritual; but in actuality these practices accomplished nothing spiritual.

AT-A-GLANCE

1. Grow! (Colossians 2:6-8)
2. Beware! (vv. 8-10)
3. Freedom! (vv. 11-15)
4. Enjoy! (vv. 16-17)

IN DEPTH

1. Grow! (Colossians 2:6-8)

Paul drew several word pictures in order for the believers at Colossae to understand how crucial it was that they grow and make spiritual progress. A mature Christian is less likely to be deceived by false teaching.

The first word picture Paul described in verse 6, deals with the believers' Christian journey. Paul illustrates it as a pilgrimage. The false teachers wanted to introduce "worldly truths" that they felt were needed for Christian growth and maturity. But Paul says, No! You started with Christ and you must continue with Christ. You started with faith now continue in faith. Many Christians are convinced they cannot save themselves but then start working at being good enough to keep their salvation. Since Christ did the saving work, a Christian's responsibility is now to walk in Him, to become firmly rooted in Him, and be established in faith as we are instructed by God's Word. Then, as a Christian grows in Christ, their attitude should be one of gratitude. Carrying out these responsibilities should be a believer's response to God as a result of their salvation. They should not be thinking, "I am doing these things to earn or keep my salvation."

The next word picture is agricultural. "Rooted" was a word used in farming activities; it meant once and for all having been stabilized. Christians are not to be like dust blown about by every wind of doctrine (Ephesians 4:14). Nor are they to be constantly moved from soil to soil. Once believers are rooted by faith in Christ, there is no need to change the soil. The roots draw up the nourishment so that the tree can grow. The roots also give strength and stability.

Another word used in this passage is the word "built." The word picture used in the last part of verse 7 has to do with building: "being built up." When an individual puts his trust in Christ for salvation, then a Christian grows in God's grace, not their own effort. To make spiritual progress means to keep adding to the temple, to the glory of God.

Paul also points out in verse 7 that the Word of God builds and strengthens the Christian. Epaphras had faithfully taught the Colossian believers the truth of the Word. But the false teachers were undermining the doctrine. Today Christians who study the Word become established in the truth. Satan has a difficult time deceiving the Bible-taught believer.

The last word picture Paul paints is that of a river. The word "abounding" suggests a river overflowing its banks. Our first experience in the Lord is a drink of the water of life by faith. The Lord places within us a well of living water which should become a river that grows deeper and deeper. We are to become mighty rivers not just trickles of shallow water.

The last thing Paul mentioned was thanksgiving. A thankful spirit is the hallmark of Christian maturity. Paul challenges the Colossians to examine themselves in these areas. A mature Christian will not be easily swayed by false teaching.

2. Beware! (vv. 8-10)

Paul warned the Colossian believers, "Beware lest any man carry you off as a captive." The false teacher did not go out and win the lost; they kidnapped the converts from churches. Those who have been ensnared by cults or false teachers are usually ignorant of the truths in the Word of God. They become fascinated by the philosophy and empty delusion of the false teachers. When a person does not know the doctrines of the Christian faith, he can easily be captured by false religions.

This philosophy of the false teachers is "hollow and deceptive" (v. 8, NIV). It is the tradition (which is handed down) of men and not the truth of God's Word. The question should always be asked, "Where did this practice we are engaging in as an individual, family, or a church originate? Is it from God? Does it have a scriptural basis?" In the time of the Colossian church, the religious leaders had traditions, and they were very zealous to obey and protect them. Even Paul, himself had been zealous concerning traditions, before he met the Lord (Galatians 1:14).

Unfortunately, many of the practices in our churches are NOT biblically based. Many times, our man-made traditions are usually more important to us than the God-given doctrines of the Scripture. It is not wrong to have church traditions that remind us of our godly heritage. However, we must be careful not to make these traditions equal to the Word of God.

The false teachers believed that the angels and the heavenly bodies influenced peoples lives. It is similar to modern-day astrology in which some believe the heavenly bodies can help them determine the course of their own personal lives and decisions.

Paul warned the Colossians about "new moon" and other religious practices determined by the calendar. This kind of teaching about demons and angels was not a part of the true Christian doctrine. If anything, such teachings were satanic. This warning should be sufficient to steer Christians today totally away from horoscopes, astrological charts, Ouija boards, and other spiritualistic practices. The Christian who dabbles in those kinds of activities is asking for trouble.

The false teachers in Colossae were not asking the Christians to forsake Christ, but only add to His teaching some of *their* interesting ideas. Paul challenges that thought by asking, "All fullness is in Christ, and you have been made full in Him. Why, then, would you need anything else?" (Colossians 2:9-10, paraphased).

Paul spoke about the "fullness" in Colossians 1:19. It means the sum total of all that God is, including all His attributes and His being. All of God's fullness dwelt or resided in Jesus. Now the remarkable thing, Paul goes on to say, is that every believer shares that fullness. "And you are complete in Him" (Colossians 2:10). When a person is born into God's family, he is born complete in Christ. Nothing needs to be added to Christ because He already is the very fullness of God. Our spiritual life needs nutrition not addition.

3. Freedom! (vv. 11-15)

Some of the false teachers were trying to convince the Colossians that they were to practice circumcision and obey the Old Testament law. They were not saying that these practices would save them like the Judiazers were attempting to say in other cities; these false teachers were simply saying that it would help the believers become more spiritual. If they were circumcised, watched their diets, and observed the holy days, then they would become part of the "spiritual elite" in the church.

Paul made it clear that the Christian is not subject in any way to the Old Testament legal system. Nor can it do him any good spiritually. Jesus Christ alone is sufficient for every spiritual need. For all of God's fullness is in Him. Paul said strongly that it was not only unnecessary for believers to get involved in any kind of legalism, but it was sinful.

Paul went further in giving teaching about circumcision. It was a sign of God's covenant with the Jewish people (Genesis 17:9-14). However, spiritual circumcision in Christ was internal—involving the heart; the procedure is done without any human hands, and enables the believer now to overcome sin.

Paul used the illustration of baptism. The New Testament word "baptize" has both a literal and a figurative meaning. The literal meaning is "to dip" or "to immerse." The figurative meaning is "to be identified with." For example, the Jewish nation was "baptized into Moses" when it went through the Red Sea (1 Corinthians 10:1-2). There was no water involved in this baptism, because they went over on dry land. It simply means the people were now identified with Moses.

When a person is saved, he is immediately baptized by the Spirit into the body of Christ (1 Corinthians 12:12-13) and is identified with the Head, Jesus Christ. This identification means that whatever happened to Christ also happened to us. When He died, we died with Him. When He was buried, we were buried. When He arose again, we arose with Him. All of this took place "through the faith of the operation of God" (v. 12). It was the power of God that changed us, not the power of water.

Since we are identified with Christ, what more do we need? God has forgiven our sins, and we stand perfect before Him (v. 13). Jesus also freed us from the law. Jesus not only took our sins to the Cross, but He also took the law to the Cross. There was no way God's children could ever keep all of the law. God never gave the Ten Commandments to the Gentiles; however, the righteous demands of the law and God's holy standard were "written in their hearts" (Romans 2:12-16).

When Jesus died on the Cross, He shed His blood for sinners. He canceled the huge debt that was against sinners because of their disobedience to God's holy law. In biblical days, financial records were often kept on parchment, and the writing could be washed off. This is the picture Paul painted.

Jesus canceled the sin debt and we are no longer under its dominion or condemnation. We are not under the law but under grace (Romans 6:14). However, this does not mean we are free to do whatever we please. We are now walking in accordance to the Holy Spirit's direction. He now gives instructions as to what to do and also gives us the power to do it.

As a result of Christ's work on the Cross, believers also now have victory over Satan. Christ "disarmed the powers and authorities" (Colossians 2:15, NIV) stripping Satan and his army of whatever weapons they held. Satan cannot harm the believer who will not harm himself. It is when we cease to watch and pray that Satan can use his weapons against us. Jesus "made a public spectacle" of the enemy (v. 15). He exposed Satan's deceit and vileness. In His death, resurrection, and ascension, Christ vindicated God and vanquished the devil. The final thing Jesus did to Satan was to triumph over him. Jesus took Satan's territory like a general who takes captives and ground when he wins a major battle. We have victory over the devil. We need not worry about the elemental forces that govern the planets and influence men's lives. The satanic armies of principalities and powers are defeated and disgraced! As we claim the victory of Christ, use the equipment he has provided for us (Ephesians 6:10), and trust God. We are free from Satan's influence.

4. Enjoy! (vv. 16-17)

Paul has already warned the Colossians about the false teachers. In this section of his letter, Paul gives three warnings for believers to heed if they are to enjoy the fullness in Jesus Christ.

First of all, Paul exhorts, "let no one judge you." This warning exposes the danger of the legalism of the false teachers in Colossae. The basis for our freedom is the Person and work of Jesus Christ. All the fullness of the Godhead dwells bodily in Him. On the cross, He canceled the debt and the dominion of the law. As believers, we are under grace, not under law.

The person who judges a believer because he or she is not living under Jewish laws is really judging Jesus Christ. He is saying that Christ did not finish the work of salvation on the cross, and that we must add something to it. He is also saying that Jesus Christ is not sufficient for the spiritual need of the Christian.

Paul said trying to keep the law was the bondage of legalism (v. 16); controversy surrounded the regulations having to do with foods, partaking or abstaining. Under the Old Testament laws, certain foods were clean or unclean. But Jesus made it clear that, of itself, food was neutral. It was what came out of the heart that made a person spiritual or unspiritual. Peter was reminded of this lesson again when he was on the house top in Joppa (Acts 10:9) and when he was rebuked in Antioch by Paul. Food does not bring us closer to God. It is likely that God's instructions about foods given through Moses had physical reasons behind them as well as spiritual. This point that Paul brings up is a different matter. If a man feels he is healthier for abstaining from certain foods, then he should abstain and care for his body. But he should not judge others who can eat that food, nor should he make it a test of spiritual living (Romans 14-15).

Another law that the Jews were commanded to keep involved the weekly Sabbath. None of this needed to be observed under the new dispensation and God's requirements. The Jews also had their feast days and special celebrations. Their religion was tied to the calendar. This did not mean that the Old Testament law has no ministry to New Testament Christians. The law still reveals the holiness of God. And it is still good if man uses it properly (1 Timothy 1:8). The law reveals sin and warns of the consequence of sin, but it has no power to prevent sin or redeem the sinner, only grace can do that.

Paul warns, "let no man beguile you of your reward" (vv. 18-19). "Beguile" meant "to declare unworthy of a prize." The umpire disqualifies the contestant because he has not obeyed the rules. The contestant does not cease to be a citizen of the land, but he does not get a prize. A Christian who fails to obey God's directions does not lose his salvation. But he does lose the approval of the Lord and the rewards He has promised to those who are faithful.

God has promised rewards to those who serve Him. He does not owe us anything. We ought to be so grateful that He has saved us from judgment that we would serve Him whether or not we receive a reward. Most of God's servants probably obey Him out of love and devotion and never think about rewards. Just as there are degrees of punishment in hell (Matthew 23:14), so there will be degrees of glory in heaven—even though all believers will be like Christ in their glorified bodies.

The false teachers in Colossae had visions and made contact with angels. People have a natural fascination with religious mysticism; learning mysteries, being initiated into the inner secrets, and having contact with the spirit world all seem exciting. But these practices are condemned by God.

It also opens an individual up to all kinds of demonic activity. No Christian needs an initiation ceremony to get into the presence of God. We may have "boldness to enter into the holiest by the blood of Jesus" (Hebrews 10:19). We may "come boldly unto the throne of grace" (Hebrews 4:16). And as for worshiping angels, they are our servants. The angels are "ministering spirits, set forth to minister for them who shall be heirs of salvation" (Hebrews 1:14).

The false teacher would say, "I am not good enough to come directly to God, so I will start with one of His angels." Trying to reach God through anyone or anything other than His Son, Jesus Christ, is idolatry. Jesus Christ is the one and only mediator between God and man (John 14:6). The person who worships through angels or saints now in heaven, does not prove his humility, for he is not submitting to the Word of God.

We are all to minister to one another in the body of Christ, just as in our human body, we minister to each other (1 Corinthians 12:14). If a believer does not draw on the spiritual nourishment that comes from Christ and other Christians, he becomes weak. The false teachers were not holding to the Head, and therefore they were spiritually undernourished; but they thought they were spiritual experts. Imagine thinking yourself a giant when in reality you are a dwarf.

The false teachers were anxious only to increase their numbers. However, the spiritual body of the Church grows by the nurturing from Christ, not by just adding numbers of people.

SEARCH THE SCRIPTURES

Fill in the blanks with the terms for the definitions below.

1. _____ cutting of the body
2. _____ once and for all grounded firm
3. _____ declare unworthy of a prize
4. _____ the sum total of all God is
5. _____ a heart change; now identifying with Christ
6. _____ something handed down; not necessarily biblical
7. _____ to dip or immerse

DISCUSS THE MEANING

1. Why was it essential for the Colossian believers to be rooted and built up in the faith? Why is it essential for us today?

2. How can traditions of men interfere with our true worship of God? In what ways are we guilty of this in our local congregations?

3. Discuss some of the modern-day cults and organizations that may be mixing Christianity with Satanic practices. What is our response to these kinds of groups?

LESSON IN OUR SOCIETY

Our society is filled with people who have various belief systems. The media floods our minds with interesting ideas and thoughts. Various groups have fascinating practices that sometimes draw people in because they want to be able to perform the same kind of mystical activities or at least benefit from those who are engaging in such activity. Even in the church, some of the teaching can be very confusing. It can sometimes seem difficult to know the difference between truth and lies. However, only God's Word contains the light of truth.

MAKE IT HAPPEN

Paul strongly encouraged the church in Colossae to grow and mature in Christ. This was a safeguard against cultist activity.

Take time to fill out this acrostic to help Christians understand how to grow and stand firm in Christ.

G

R

O

W

Example: Go to God in prayer. Read your Bible. Obey the Holy Spirit. Walk close with God.

FOLLOW THE SPIRIT

What God wants me to do:

_____

_____

REMEMBER YOUR THOUGHTS

Special insight you learned:

_____

_____

MORE LIGHT ON THE TEXT
COLOSSIANS 2:6-19

The last chapter ends with the purpose of Paul's labor and striving, and that is to be able to present every man perfect in Christ with all the might given him by the mighty power of God that works in Him (1:28-29). The next seven verses express Paul's anxiety concerning the state of the Church, and his wishes that the members might be united in love, having a fuller understanding of the mystery of the Father and of Christ. This anxiety is based, as we shall see later in this study, on the heresy being perpetrated by false teachers. He warns the Church and urges them to remain faithful in Christ (vv. 1-7).

2:6 As ye have therefore received Christ Jesus the Lord, so walk ye in him: 7 Rooted and built up in him, and stablished in the faith, as ye have been taught, abounding therein with thanksgiving.

We should remind ourselves that this is a letter of encouragement to the church at Colosse to remain steadfast in their belief in spite of the dangers that are threatening the church. The exhortation is made evident in verses 6 and 7. In verse 6, Paul encourages the members of the Colossian church to continue leading a life that is consistent with their belief in Christ. The phrase "received" (*paralambano*) or "accepted" Christ describes the new relationship that takes place when a person comes to the knowledge of Christ. His way of life changes. Paul is saying here, "just as you have accepted Christ as Lord into your lives, continue to live in Him," i.e., cling to Him (Ephesians 3:11; Philippians 2:11).

To Paul, receiving or accepting Christ is just the beginning, the follow-up is to live in Him through our lifestyle, conduct, and faithfulness. In other words, the secret of victorious living is holding faithfully to the teachings and beliefs of the Gospel one has received which is anchored in the Lord Jesus Christ. This is made clear in verse 7 by the use of four descriptive and metaphoric participles, namely "rooted," "built up," "established," and "abounding" in thanksgiving.

The first is probably borrowed from a building metaphor. "Rooted" (*rhizoo*) has the idea being firmly grounded, as the root of a plant or tree or the foundation of a building helps stabilize the house (cf. Jeremiah 24:6; Ephesians 4:15, 16). The words "built up" translates in the Greek, *epoikodomeo*, which has the idea of the continuing construction of a building of which the foundation has been laid. It is figuratively used here to describe the believer's constant increase in relationship with and knowledge of Christ. Paul describes this in another place as "growing in the knowledge of God" (Colossians 1:10, NIV). No building can stand without a firm foundation, and a foundation without a building is worthless.

When both take place, then the house would be established (*bebaioo* i.e., stabilized). Such a building will be able to withstand every storm and wind that come against it. It is like building on the rock instead of the sand as Christ portrays in His parable (Matthew 7:24-27). Paul prays for the Ephesians, "That Christ may dwell in your hearts by faith; that ye, being rooted and grounded in love, May be able to comprehend with all saints what is the breadth, and length, and depth, and height; And to know the love of Christ, which passeth knowledge, that ye might be filled with all the fulness of God" (Ephesians 3:17ff, KJV). Therefore the Colossians are to remain constantly deep rooted, increasingly growing, and firmly stabilized in the faith, "as ye have been taught," i.e., in the teaching they have received probably from Epaphras on behalf of the apostles (1:7; cf. 4:12, 13).

To complete this four-fold cycle of victorious living (in Christ) is the exhortation to abound in thanksgiving. Thanksgiving (*eucharistia*) or gratitude has a special place in the theology of Paul. In several of his letters (especially in the opening sections), Paul always expresses his gratitude to God and to Christ, and urges or challenges his readers to give thanks always to God. He calls on the Philippians to pray with thanksgiving (Philippians 4:6); to the Thessalonians to give thanks in everything, "for this is the will of God in Christ Jesus concerning you" (1 Thessalonians 5:18). Now to the Colossians, Paul encourages them "to abound" (*perisseuo*), or better expressed as to super-abound to the point of overflowing with gratitude and thanksgiving. The language here has the picture of a river overflowing its banks during a heavy monsoon rain or heavy flood. It means being saturated with the spirit of gratitude. This type of thanksgiving is spontaneous, and is always expressed by an outburst of praise, worship, and singing. The type that can be found in African American, Black, or African churches, where gratitude to God is expressed, based not on what you have materially, but rather on who you are in Christ and on His blessings of redemption. It comes deep from within. A reflection on

what God in Christ has done leaves one with gratitude resulting in praise, worship, and singing, which is a mark of being filled with the Spirit (Ephesians 5:18b-20). This attitude of thanksgiving, resulting from the firm foundation of the increasing knowledge of Christ, by faith in the Gospel, will protect the believer from all types of threats, deceptions, and falsities. This is explicitly expressed in the following verses.

8 Beware lest any man spoil you through philosophy and vain deceit, after the tradition of men, after the rudiments of the world, and not after Christ.

Paul continues with a strict warning and cautions the Colossians to be careful of the heresy that is going around. These verses (8-10) are directly connected to the previous two. What he has stated positively in verses 6 and 7, namely, that they should continue to live in Christ the Lord, is stated negatively here; the idea being that they should be careful not to be deceived by false teachings that contradict their belief and faith in Christ Jesus as Lord. Verse 8 starts with a warning against either impending or existing heresy, which Paul labels as philosophy and vain deceit.

With this clause, "Beware lest any man spoil you," Paul shows his love and concern for the spiritual well-being of the Colossian brethren. "Beware" (Greek *blepo*) means "to take heed, or look out," as one looks out for impending danger in crossing a busy street, or swimming in a sea inhabited by sharks, or as one being careful when walking through a bush invested with dangerous animals or poisonous reptiles. Here, Paul calls on them to be on their guard lest they be carried away by the enticing words of the false teachers, and restating what he has said earlier in verse 4 in another form: "And this I say, lest any man should beguile you with enticing words."

Verse 8 employs a battle or war term: "spoil" (*sulagogeo*), in which the defeated are carried away captives and their goods are carried away as booty. The word, figuratively used here, generally applies more specifically to the plunder of goods than being carried away captive. In what sense is Paul using this word, which appears only this once in the New Testament? Is he referring to the carrying away of the believers, as captives (i.e., being deceived) by false teachers? Alternatively, is he referring to the plundering of the believers' goods? What are the goods? Either of the two alternatives is possible. The goods are spiritual blessings of salvation and its benefits, which believers enjoy in Christ.

Paul clearly shows the possibility of a man robbing others of Christ, His blessings, and their relationship with the

Lord. How does this statement compare or contrast with Jesus' assurance in John 10:28-29 and that of Paul in Romans 8:35-38? Do these passages or any like them contradict this statement? There is definitely no contradiction. One must fully follow Christ, firmly rooted and grounded (Colossians 2:6-7) in Him, and totally abide (or be engrafted) in Him (John 15) or one can easily be robbed or spoiled of his or her salvation. How can one be spoiled? Paul readily gives us ways this can be done: through philosophy and vain deceit. The word "philosophy" is a direct transliteration of the Greek word *philosophia* (say **fil-os-of-ee'-ah**), which simply means "love or pursuit of wisdom," and is used here only. It is used by Paul to describe the false theology of certain Jewish Christian ascetics, which, according to Thayer's dictionary, "busied itself with refined and speculative enquiries into the nature and classes of angels, into the ritual of the Mosaic law and the regulations of Jewish tradition respecting practical life."

This type of philosophy amounts to empty deceit (i.e., vain deceit). It is futile and deceptive, and amounts to nothing. It is vain (*kenos*, i.e., empty and devoid of truth) and deceitful because it cannot deliver what it promises to those who obey its ordinances (cf. v. 23). It is valueless. Paul insists that this philosophy is contradictory to the teachings of the Gospel based on Christ Jesus. It is after (according to) the traditions of men, i.e., it is based on man-made tradition, which seems to nullify the commandments of God and is condemned by Jesus Christ (Mark 7:8, 9). The teachings are humanistic and worldly rather than spiritual and Christ-centered.

Paul then adds that this type of teaching is according to the rudiments of the world. The word "rudiment" translates the Greek word *stoicheion*, which indicates elements or units that make up a body or unit. For example, the letters of the alphabet are the elements of speech, or the elements that make of the universe. Rudiments are either in the physical or non-physical realm. Peter warns that with the coming of the Lord, the elements will be burned up with heat (Peter 3:10, 12). Here, as in Galatians 4:3 and verse 9, Paul probably refers to the elementary rules and principles of the world system and of the Jewish religion, which tends to seek salvation through personal efforts and human wisdom, rather than through faith in Christ.

Although Christ's death had nullified this belief, some of the enthusiastic Jews tried to combine faith in Christ with the man-made traditions and Pharisaic ordinances. The philosophy based on the rudiments of the world here probably also refers to the study and worship of the heavenly bodies, as we shall see later in this passage. These teachings are opposed and contradictory to Christ, His works, and His teaching; they tend to take men away from Christ, weaken their trust in Him, and limit their relationship with Him.

9 For in him dwelleth all the fulness of the Godhead bodily. 10 And ye are complete in him, which is the head of all principality and power:

The preposition "for" connects the previous verse with the following verse, and refers to the deity and divinity of Christ. Here, Paul makes a bold assertion regarding Christ, His person and work, in relationship to man's redemption. The clause "in him dwelleth all the fulness of the Godhead bodily" has attracted a number of interpretations (see our last study on Colossians 1:19). Paul says in effect that in Christ alone can be found the fullness of God, the real replica, or representation of God in a bodily (*somatikos*) or physical form.

The word "Godhead" (Greek *theotes*) means "Deity." It appears only once here and relates to the Deity of God. Christ is the personal and physical manifestation of all the fullness of God's power and blessings to man. Therefore, God is found not in the philosophies, or in the human traditions of the Jews and Gentiles, nor in the worldly principles or in the rudiments of the world. Christ is the personal incarnate Godhead, the fullness of the Spirit rests on Him and works through Him (Isaiah 11:2; 42:1-7; 61:1-2; John 3:34; etc.).

Peter speaks of Christ when he says, "How God anointed Jesus of Nazareth with the Holy Ghost and with power: who went about doing good, and healing all that were oppressed of the devil; for God was with him" (Acts 10:38). In addition, that through Him is the fullness of redemption from the Deity, by His sacrifice (1 Peter 2:24). In Christ, we have the entire essence of God concentrated in a human bodily form. He is the total and complete embodiment of God, the express image of the invisible God (1:15). Since the fullness of God is resident in Christ, it makes no sense, Paul seems to argue, to look elsewhere for help or salvation.

Hence, we are complete in Him. That means we have reached the Source of all things, we do not need any other. In Him, we have attained the full measure of all things for this life and the one to come. Thus, we need to abide in Him for eternity (John 15:4, 7, 9) rather than in any other power or authority, for out of His fullness have we all received grace (John 1:16). Since Christ is the full bodily expression of the invisible God, with all His attributes, He is therefore the Head of all principality and power. For the meaning of "principality and power," see our discussion on

Colossians 1:16 in our last study (August 06, 2000). Christ is the Head in the sense of possessing supreme authority and control. All powers and principalities are made subject to Him, and He controls all their activities because He is their Creator. The good angels cannot effect salvation for believers, and the bad angels are limited in what they can do to the believer. This idea is reemphasized in verse 15. It is in Christ who is the full manifestation of the Godhead and controls all spiritual beings, that we are complete, i.e., we are fulfilled.

11 In whom also ye are circumcised with the circumcision made without hands, in putting off the body of the sins of the flesh by the circumcision of Christ: 12 Buried with him in baptism, wherein also ye are risen with him through the faith of the operation of God, who hath raised him from the dead.

Speaking of Christ as the head of all principality and power, Paul continues his thesis, in whom also ye are circumcised. Here, Paul introduces the theme of circumcision, which seem to suggest at this point that there is confusion about the subject among the Colossians. Probably among the false teachers were some Jews (Jewish Christians) who were making the ritual of circumcision a condition for salvation as in the Galatian churches (Galatians 5:2-3; cf. Acts 15:1).

Paul assures his audience that they have received the real circumcision, one that is made without hands, "hands" referring to physical or manual cutting off the foreskin, as in the Abrahamic tradition. Rather, the type of circumcision they have received is of Christ, which Paul describes as putting off the body of the sins of the flesh. This type of circumcision surpasses by far the Judaistic ceremonial rite observed and recommended by the heretics; it is spiritual, the work of the Holy Spirit (made without hands) rather than manual. It is inward, of the heart (Romans 2:28-29; Philippians 3:2-3) rather than outward. It is the putting off (*apekdusis,* **ap-ek'-doo-sis**) of the body of the sins of the flesh, i.e., laying aside the evil nature, rather than the removal of the excess foreskin, Paul seems to contend. This refers to the passion by which they received salvation.

Paul describes further the circumcision, which the Colossians have received as "buried with him in baptism, wherein also ye are risen with him through the faith of the operation of God, who hath raised him from the dead." Here, Paul alludes to the ritual of baptism, which is signified by the death and burial and resurrection of Christ. However, Paul is not referring to water baptism, rather to

the baptism into Christ by the work of the Holy Spirit (Romans 6:1-16; 1 Corinthians 12:13; Galatians 3:27). By baptism, we identify with and partake as it were, in the death, burial, and consequent resurrection of Christ. This refers specifically to the spiritual resurrection of the believer from death in trespasses and sin (Ephesians 2:1-9), and not necessarily a magical efficacy of the ritual of water baptism.

Hence, Paul adds that this is done "through the faith of the operation of God, who hath raised him from the dead." Christ's death and resurrection offers us redemption, whereby all our sins are forgiven. This is made effective through the operation of God accentuated by faith; it is not through the operation of the minister in preaching, the sprinkling of, or the immersing in water. This is confirmed further in verse 13.

13 And you, being dead in your sins and the uncircumcision of your flesh, hath he quickened together with him, having forgiven you all trespasses; 14 Blotting out the handwriting of ordinances that was against us, which was contrary to us, and took it out of the way, nailing it to his cross;

This verse is an echo of what Paul writes in Ephesians 2:1, 5, 11 and describes the effect of the work of God in the lives of the believer. It describes the former state of all humans, the Colossians in particular, but specifically as in the Ephesian epistle, to the Gentiles and contrasts it with their present state after the transformation through Christ's death on the cross. This transformation is all the work of God (the subject "he") referred to figuratively here as "quickened." They were all dead in sins (*paraptoma,* also translated trespasses later in the verse), i.e., lawless, and morally debased in their past state, but now quickened together (Greek *suzoopoieo* with him) which speaks of the effect of Christ's sacrificial death on the cross. The word "quickened" is "to make alive," or "to bring to life a thing that was dead," referred in verse 12 as being raised with Him (Christ).

Apart from the eschatological bodily resurrection of all believers at the end time with Christ, the forgiveness of sins is a type of resurrection, symbolized by the historical, physical, and bodily resurrection of Christ, which all believers experience. While the death and burial of Christ symbolize our sinfulness, and our inability to live rightly before Him, His resurrection symbolizes God's forgiveness extended to man and our righteousness before Him. All transgressions indicate the totality or the extent of God's forgiveness. It is all encompassing, all-inclusive. It signifies that He forgives all types of sins through the sacrificial death of Christ. Paul does not seem to be satisfied with his description of the work of God in the preceding two verses using the metaphors, namely "raised from the dead" and "quickened," and the theological jargon "forgiveness from all transgressions."

He employs another metaphor to describe God's work of redemption through Christ. Not only has He (God) quickened us and pardoned our sins, he has blotted out the handwriting of ordinances that was against us, which was contrary to us. The "blotting" (Greek *exaleipho*) means "to wipe out, erase," or "to obliterate something." Using computer language, it means to delete from existence the written document of the law and its rigid regulations which confront and condemn man because of man's inability to keep them. The handwriting (Greek *cheirographon*) of ordinances (Greek *dogma*) refers to the complete Law of Moses. Paul describes the law with its regulations as the enemy when he writes, "Having abolished in his flesh the enmity, even the law of commandments contained in ordinances; for to make in himself of twain one new man, so making peace" (Ephesians 2:15).

He also writes in another place, describing the effect of the law and commandment, "For as many as are of the works of the law are under the curse: for it is written, Cursed is every one that continueth not in all things which are written in the book of the law to do them" (Galatians 3:10). Since no one is ever able to keep the law, both in its moral and ceremonial aspects, God in His mercy has completely deleted it. He annulled the law and its demand when Christ through His death satisfied the demands of the law and bore its curse on Calvary. It has been figuratively nailed to His cross.

What does this imply? Does it mean that moral law has no place in the life of the believer? Or that man is no more morally responsible for his negative actions? What does Christ's statement in Matthew 5:17-18 mean in the light of Paul's statement here? I believe that Paul's intention is to convey the fact that by virtue of Christ's substitutionary sacrificial death on the cross, believers are no longer under the law but under grace (Romans 7:4, 6; 6:14; Galatians 2:19). Our righteousness is not dependent upon what we do, or on our efforts to keep the law, rather it is dependent on who we are now, and on our trust (faith) on and acceptance of the finished work of Christ on the cross on which the law has been nailed. Christ says, "If you love me keep my commandments." Therefore, the abolition of the law does not imply that man's responsi-

bility has been nullified when the law was crucified on the cross. The law that demands that we love the Lord and our neighbor still has eternal relevance (cf. Romans 13:8, 9; Galatians 5:14).

15 And having spoiled principalities and powers, he made a shew of them openly, triumphing over them in it.

One of the greatest weapons of Satan is accusation against God's people. He knows man's inability to keep the law, and so he uses it against him, accusing him before the Father. Therefore, the abolition of the written law, which hitherto has been a snare to man, renders Satan's strategy against man ineffective. Hence, Paul says: "and having spoiled principalities and powers, he made a shew of them openly, triumphing over them in it." The Greek word translated by KJV as "spoiled" is *apekduomai*, which means "to strip off as in pulling off clothes from another." "Principalities and powers," we have noted earlier are Satanic forces who war against man. Here, Paul says that by blotting out the written law and the ordinances which entangle man, Satanic forces have been stripped of their power. They have been rendered impotent and powerless. They cannot hold man (believers) any longer to ransom and bondage because of the law (Romans 7:5-25). They are not only disarmed, but they are also put to open spectacle (*deigmatizo*) and ridicule.

Paul applies military language in which the defeated are disarmed and stripped of their clothes, and humiliated as prisoners of war. This is what Christ did by His death on the cross on the Calvary Mountain. His death means a defeat and open humiliation for Satan and his forces. That is the basis for Paul's argument in Roman 8, where he points out how through the sacrificial death of Christ, the demands of the law were satisfied. There he asks rhetorically, "Who shall lay any thing to the charge of God's elect?" (v. 33), and again, "Who is he that condemneth?" (v. 34). The answer is obvious since the accuser of the brethren has been decidedly defeated (Job 1:9-11; Zechariah 3:1-5; Revelation 12:10). The crucifixion of Christ, which Satan and his human agents meant for a public shame and humiliation for Christ, turned to be for their public defeat and shame (cf. 1:20-22; Acts 2:23; 3:13-18; 5:28; 1 John 3:8). Satan's defeat means victory for believers and so believers need not be afraid.

16 Let no man therefore judge you in meat, or in drink, or in respect of an holy day, or of the new moon, or of the sabbath days: 17 Which are

a shadow of things to come; but the body is of Christ.

On the basis of the defeat of Satan and the condemnation of the written law, Paul calls on the Colossians not to allow themselves to be judged by anyone in regard to their choice of food, drink, and festivals. We recall that Paul has warned them against people who would try to deceive them through enticing words (2:4). He cautions them to beware of (or look out for) those, who, through philosophy and vain deceit, the tradition of men, and the rudiments of the world, try to cheat them of their relationship with Christ (v. 8). Since the law with its rigorous demands has been rendered ineffective, they have been liberated from it

Paul lists five things by which the Christians at Colosse are being judged. The first is about their food—meat (*brosis*)—or what is eaten. This probably refers to the prohibition by the Mosaic law of eating certain unclean animals (Leviticus 11; Deuteronomy 14). The new covenant has annulled this law and permits all kinds of meat to be used as food (Romans 14; 1 Corinthians 8, 10; 1 Timothy 4:1-8).

The second is concerning drink. While the Old Testament law concerning drinking is liberal (Leviticus 10:9; Numbers 6:3; Judges 13:47,14), yet it has strong warnings against the use of strong drinks (Proverbs 20:1; 31:4-7; Isaiah 5:11-13; Amos 6:6). The New Testament admonishes that everything be done in moderation (1 Corinthians 10:31), but strongly condemns all drunkenness. This allows the Christian the liberty to choose what to drink and what not to drink (Luke 21:34; Romans 13:13; 1 Corinthians 6:9-11; Galatians 5:19-21).

The last three can be discussed together. They concern the observances of holy days, new moons, festivals, and Sabbaths, which in the Old Testament were binding upon all men (Leviticus 23; 1 Chronicles 23:21). However, none of these are commanded in the New Testament, and men are free to choose what they prefer to do in any of these issues, especially with regard to the keeping of the Sabbath (Romans 14:5-6; Galatians 4:9-11). The Sabbath as we noted in past studies does not refer to a day of the week, but to a rest, which in Old Testament is a shadow of the rest we now have in Christ Jesus (Matthew 11:28-30; Hebrews 4:3, 10-11; 10:1).

The mention of these restrictions further indicates the presence of the Judaistic aspect of the heresy present in the Colossian church. By placing such stress on these regulations, the heretics tend to deny the sufficiency of Christ for redemption, and try to convince the Colossian believers that strict observance was indubitably indispensable to salvation. In refuting the falsity of this teaching, Paul is quick

to add that such things are a shadow of things to come; but the body is of Christ. Paul seems to say that observance of these ordinances and festivals is like "pursuing the shadow" rather than clinging to the real body, Christ whose shadow is cast in the Old Testament and represented by these observances.

We must agree that the shadow (*skia*) played an important part in the Old Testament in providing a dim outline of the coming reality, but when the real has come, the purpose of the shadow is served. What further purpose could the shadow serve? Nothing, and it should be discarded. Therefore, Paul urges them to hold on to Christ who is the fulfillment and real body. Access to God is now based on Christ, (the body) and the salvation He provides and not on the observance of the law and its man-made regulations. Paul then urges them to hold on tightly to Jesus Christ, which they have received and not to the shadow which is now done away with.

18 Let no man beguile you of your reward in a voluntary humility and worshiping of angels, intruding into those things which he hath not seen, vainly puffed up by his fleshly mind,

Paul continues his warning, this time against angel worship. Again, using an imperative (cf. v. 16), He urges them never to allow any person to rob them of their reward by his voluntary humility and in the worship of angels. A casual reading of this statement might leave the reader with the wrong interpretation. It sounds as if Paul is advocating or promoting worship of angels as sign of humility. One of the teachings of the occult is the worship of angels and invocation of heavenly bodies during worship. To them, it is a sign of humility.

Therefore, Paul's warning here indicates that he is now changing the focus of his argument against Jewish heretics who strongly advocate the keeping of the Mosaic law and ordinances (vv. 16-17), to the occultists who tend to force the Colossians to worship the heavenly bodies through false self abasement. Paul writes: "Let no man beguile you of your reward in a voluntary humility and worshiping of angels." The phrase, "let no man beguile you of your reward" is a translation of the Greek word *katabrabeuo* (pronounced **kat-ab-rab-yoo'-o**), which is the idea of defrauding one of the prize of victory, with a notion of disqualification.

The idea here is that of an athlete being deprived of his prize/award, or disqualified. The "prize" here definitely refers to the prize of salvation, which the Church has inherited, not by works, but by grace. So Paul warns them that they should not allow themselves to be deprived of their salvation by the ritualists who delight (*thelo* translated "voluntary") themselves in humility (*tapeinophrosune* pronounced **tap-I-nof-ros-oo'-nay**). Humility is a priceless virtue, which Paul later in the book admonishes the church to put on as clothes (3:12; cf. Philippians 2:3). However, the humility of the false teachers was only a disguised pride as is made plain in verse 23. This false humility is demonstrated in (their delighting) in the worship of angels.

What relationship has humility with the worship of angels here? The answer in simple, and some commentators agree. Speaking from personal observation and experience, false teachers (and occultists) always try to create the impression that they consider themselves too insignificant and too unworthy to approach God directly and therefore they have to seek contact with the Divine through a medium or media. Hence, they go through the angels. It is like the African traditional (or the so-called animistic) worshiper or priest would consider himself too trivial to approach the Divine, the *Obasi di ne'lu* (God in heaven) directly. Instead, he goes via his dead ancestors who have gone before and are believed to be in the presence of *Nna anyi bi igwe* (our heavenly Father) or the lesser gods, as messengers and mediators.

Passages usually employed by these advocates of falsity and occultists include Psalm 8:4-5, which says, "What is man, that thou art mindful of him? and the son of man, that thou visitest him? For thou hast made him a little lower than the angels, and hast crowned him with glory and honor." To follow this false teaching is tantamount, using the athletic metaphor once more, to the athlete going totally off course, instead staying focused on the track, which is Christ the Lord. Paul continues by referring to the occultist intruding into those things which he hath not seen as being "vainly puffed up by his fleshly mind."

The false teachers referred to here generically with a single pronoun intrude into things they have not seen or experienced. The word "intrude" (Greek *embateuo*) could mean "to dabble (engage superficially) by pretense into things of which they have no knowledge." In other words, the teachers pretend to have a superior knowledge, or have seen something, or received direct revelation from God, perhaps by way of visions and prophecy. Such subjective knowledge, Paul says, results in self-exaltation and pride in the fleshy mind. Their minds are "puffed up" (*phusioo*) i.e., "blown up" or "inflated." This refers to self-pride, which contradicts and exposes their pretensions to take pleasure in humility or self-abasement (v. 18a). The people who pretend to be very humble as earlier reported, now show their true colors: unnecessary pride, and self-aggrandizement, bragging about the things they purport to have seen.

19 And not holding the Head, from which all the body by joints and bands having nourishment ministered, and knit together, increaseth with the increase of God.

The problem with this type of falsehood, is that the perpetrators intrude or take a stand on their own subjective revelation, which results in fleshy pride, rather than taking firm hold of the Head who is Christ. They do not cling to Christ Jesus, failing to realize that Christ is the fullness of God; in Him (Christ) are all the treasures of heaven and wisdom and knowledge; in Him all the sufficiency for salvation and redemption reside (2:3, 9, 10). In Him and from Him, Paul persists, "all the body by joints and bands having nourishment ministered, and knit together, increaseth with the increase of God."

Using the human physiology as a metaphor as he did in 1:18, Paul develops further the imagery of the Church as dependent on Christ the Head. Here, Paul refers to both the unity and growth of the Church under Christ, where as in the physical body all the parts are joined together with ligaments, and get their nutrition for health and edification. Here is a remarkable picture of how essential unity under Christ is for a healthy Church.

DAILY BIBLE READING

M: Paul Commends the Colossian Christians
Colossians 2:1-5
T: God Dwells Fully in Jesus Christ
Colossians 2:6-10
W: Dead to the Flesh, Alive in Christ
Colossians 2:11-16
T: Hold Fast to Christ, Our Head
Colossians 2:17-23
F: Jesus: Mediator of a New Covenant
Hebrews 8:1-7
S: The Blood of Christ Purifies Us
Hebrews 9:11-15
S: Christ Perfected those Who Are Sanctified
Hebrews 10:11-18

TEACHING TIPS

August 20
Bible Study Guide 12

1. Words You Should Know

A. Seek (Colossians 3:1)—Greek *zeteite*—to set the heart on.

B. Anger (3:8)—Greek *orge*—an emotion displaying instant displeasure and indignation.

C. Rage (3:8)—Greek *thymos*—sudden and passionate outburst of feeling.

D. Malice (3:8)—Greek *kakia*—general feeling of badness, a vicious disposition, prompting one to do harm to another.

2. Teacher Preparation

A. Read the FOCAL VERSES. Do the exercise in the MAKE IT HAPPEN section. Using a Bible dictionary, define the words in both columns briefly.

B. Read through the entire lesson and ask God to give you insight and creative skills to make this lesson clear and practical.

C. Material needed: Bibles, board or newsprint, and pencil and paper for each student. *Optional:* A paper doll set.

3. Starting the Lesson

A. If you have the paper doll set, use it as an opening illustration. Show how easily the doll can change from one outfit to another. She can be dressed for one occasion and then another fairly simply. Make the point that in this lesson we are going to talk about taking off the old and putting on the new; shedding our old life and starting a whole new life in Christ. Have a brief discussion about whether this is as easy as changing the paper doll's outfit from one to another? Why or why not?

B. Have the class read the LESSON AIM in unison and then pray about it.

C. Put the AT-A-GLANCE outline on the board.

D. Read IN FOCUS and the FOCAL VERSES.

4. Getting into the Lesson

A. Allow the students time to silently read the BACKGROUND information and THE PEOPLE, PLACES, AND TIMES section.

B. Read through IN DEPTH and fill in the blanks for SEARCH THE SCRIPTURES.

5. Relating the Lesson to Life

A. Discuss the answers to the DISCUSS THE MEANING questions.

B. Leave time for a brief discussion of LESSON IN OUR SOCIETY. Ask if students agree or disagree.

6. Arousing Action

A. Give the students pencils and paper, and challenge them to make the two lists. Help them with definitions from your study of the words.

B. It is important to help the students understand that the old life had already been discarded when they became Christians. It is a matter now of living in our new clothes. This is a job for our Lord and Saviour Jesus Christ.

C. Encourage the students to read the DAILY BIBLE READINGS for help in walking in our new life in Christ.

THE WAY TO RIGHTEOUSNESS

Bible Background • COLOSSIANS 3:1-17
Printed Text • COLOSSIANS 3:1-3, 5-17
Devotional Reading • MARK 12:28-34

LESSON AIM

By the end of this lesson, students should understand how to be Christ's representative in their daily lives and desire to do so.

KEEP IN MIND

"And whatsoever ye do in word or deed, do all in the name of the Lord Jesus, giving thanks to God and the Father by him" (Colossians 3:17).

FOCAL VERSES

COLOSSIANS 3:1 If ye then be risen with Christ, seek those things which are above, where Christ sitteth on the right hand of God.

2 Set your affection on things above, not on things on the earth.

3 For ye are dead, and your life is hid with Christ in God.

5 Mortify therefore your members which are upon the earth; fornication, uncleanness, inordinate affection, evil concupiscence, and covetousness, which is idolatry:

6 For which things' sake the wrath of God cometh on the children of disobedience:

7 In the which ye also walked some time, when ye lived in them.

8 But now ye also put off all these; anger, wrath, malice, blasphemy, filthy communication out of your mouth.

9 Lie not one to another, seeing that ye have put off the old man with his deeds;

10 And have put on the new man, which is renewed in knowledge after the image of him that created him:

11 Where there is neither Greek nor Jew, circumcision nor uncircumcision, Barbarian, Scythian, bond nor free: but Christ is all, and in all.

12 Put on therefore, as the elect of God, holy and

LESSON OVERVIEW

LESSON AIM
KEEP IN MIND
FOCAL VERSES
IN FOCUS
THE PEOPLE, PLACES, AND TIMES
BACKGROUND
AT-A-GLANCE
IN DEPTH
SEARCH THE SCRIPTURES
DISCUSS THE MEANING
LESSON IN OUR SOCIETY
MAKE IT HAPPEN
FOLLOW THE SPIRIT
REMEMBER YOUR THOUGHTS
MORE LIGHT ON THE TEXT
DAILY BIBLE READINGS

beloved, bowels of mercies, kindness, humbleness of mind, meekness, long suffering;

13 Forbearing one another, and forgiving one another, if any man have a quarrel against any: even as Christ forgave you, so also do ye.

14 And above all these things put on charity, which is the bond of perfectness.

15 And let the peace of God rule in your hearts, to the which also ye are called in one body; and be ye thankful.

16 Let the word of Christ dwell in you richly in all wisdom; teaching and admonishing one another in psalms and hymns and spiritual songs, singing with grace in your hearts to the Lord.

17 And whatsoever ye do in word or deed, do all in the name of the Lord Jesus, giving thanks to God and the Father by him.

IN FOCUS

Most creatures in the animal kingdom shed something periodically. The most commonly known example concerns snakes. Most of us have gone to a museum and have seen a snakeskin that has been shed and abandoned by the snake. It usually is hard and shaped like the snake. If the snake decided to go back into that skin, it would probably have a difficult time. Once the skin is discarded, it becomes hard and it is not suitable for the snake anymore.

We can imagine a similar situation with a butterfly trying to go back into its cocoon. It would no doubt damage its beautiful wings trying to get back into the opening of the cocoon. The butterfly no longer fits. Dogs and cats that shed usually leave their hair all over the place. It would be odd and foolish for a pet owner to gather up the hair and then attempt to attach it back on the dog or cat. That hair is dead and discarded; it no longer belongs on the animal.

In our lesson today, Paul is exhorting the church at Colossae to take off the old life and put on the new one in Christ. Just like the above examples, the old life is no longer appealing or fits our new life in Christ.

THE PEOPLE, PLACES, AND TIMES

BARBARIANS. The inhabited (earth) was used for the world inhabited by Greeks in contrast to those lands unsettled. In the Old Testament, the word indicated the inhabited world in contrast to the wilderness where the nomads roam. The term refers to all foreign people who were non-Greek and unable to speak the Greek language. Because of this, they were considered uncultured.

SCYTHIAN. A native of Scythia, the climax of barbarism, a savage. The Greeks despised the Jews; a barbarian scorned a Scythian. They were the lowest of the low.

BACKGROUND

In the final two chapters of Colossians, Paul challenges the Colossians to make practical application of the doctrines he had been preaching. Paul believed Christians should not just know the truth and be able to defend it, but truth must be lived out in their daily lives as well.

The pagan religions of Paul's day said little or nothing about personal morality. A worshiper could bow before an idol, put his offering on the altar, and go back to live the same old life of sin; what a person believed had no direct relationship with how he behaved. No one would attempt to correct the person for his behavior.

The Christian faith brought a whole new concept into the pagan society. Faith in Christ meant being united to Him. If Christians share His life, they must follow His example. If Christ lives in the believer, the believer cannot continue in sin.

Paul concluded his letter to the Colossians with some specific instructions about Christian conduct.

AT-A-GLANCE

1. Seek Things Above
   (Colossians 3:1-3)
2. New Life in Christ (vv. 5-9)
3. Renewal Procedures (vv. 10-11)
4. Walking New (vv. 12-17)

IN DEPTH

1. Seek Things Above (Colossians 3:1-3)

The first thing Paul encouraged the Colossians to do was to, on a continual basis, seek heavenly things. "To set their heart on things above" meant to set their interest on Christ-centered things. One's attitudes, ambitions, and whole outlook on life are molded by Christ's relation to the believer and that allegiance to Him takes precedence over all other allegiances.

The description of Christ as "seated at the right hand of God" is another implied reminder to those who were seeking to diminish Christ's role as mediator. The right hand of God is a place of supreme privilege and divine authority.

In other words, Paul said the Christian should not just seek to go to heaven but set his mind on the things above. Give God, and the things of God, a large central place in one's thought life. One cannot withdraw from daily activities. But everything a believer does should be seen from the back-drop of eternity.

Paul warned the Colossians to watch their interaction with earthly things: wealth, worldly honor, power, pleasures, and the like. They are not evil in and of themselves, but if they take the Christian's heart and mind away from God, they are not good.

Since Christians have died with Christ, all that is alien to Christ should be alien to them. Because Christ is in us and we are in Christ and Christ is in God, we are all wrapped up together. The focus of a Christian is now totally different from anything they have ever experienced before.

2. New Life in Christ (vv. 5-9)

Paul speaks forthrightly about the demands of the new life and our urgent need to repress all the degrading tendencies of the old nature. The old life is dead. The believer had to let it die. We are not simply to suppress or control evil acts and attitudes; we are to wipe them out completely. Exterminate the old way of life. The action is to be undertaken decisively, with a sense of urgency. It suggests a vigorous, painful act of personal determination. Paul is calling for a slaying of evil passions, desires, and practices that root themselves in our bodies.

Paul goes on to list sins. "Impurity" is not just physical impurity but uncleanness in thought, word, and act. "Lust" which essentially means "a feeling or experience that is an uncontrolled desire." "Greed" is a compound word form whose root meaning suggests "a desire to have more, a ruthless desire for and seeking after material things." This attitude is identified with idolatry because it puts self-interest and other things in place of God.

Paul warned that God's judgment will fall on the disobedient. He reminded the Colossians that this is the way they used to live. This ungodly life belongs to the past and that the Christian should be done with it.

Paul firmly encourages this past life concept in verse 8. The phrase "But now" marks a new beginning. Christians are to rid themselves, or take off, the filth of the past. He specifically names anger, ill feelings, rage (a sudden and passionate outburst of feelings), malice (a vicious disposition, a spirit that encourages one to injure one's neighbor), and slander (insulting talk against one's fellow man). Filthy language is "bad or abusive speech, foul-mouth abuse." The sin of falsehood is singled out. Lying is giving separate treatment and given a strong exhortation: STOP LYING!

The Christian is to have a totally new life change in which he has put off the old self with its practices, habits, or characteristics and put on the new. This is like the resurrection of Christ. He pulled off, then left the grave clothes behind. Those clothes represent the old life with its sinful deeds. Christians now have a new life in Christ, the old deeds and desires must be put off.

3. Renewal Procedures (vv. 10-11)

Paul talked about becoming a new creature in Christ and taking off the old self, but how can that be done? Bad habits and ungodly conduct is not simply going to fall away like dirty clothes.

Paul used the word "knowledge" to explain how a person changes. Not knowledge of more rules and laws; but the knowledge of Christ. Our minds must be renewed. As believers grow in knowledge of the Word of God, when we learn, read, and study His Word (the Bible), God's Spirit changes us. God transforms Christians by washing old thoughts out of our minds and replacing them with new ones.

Paul gives an example of this kind of mind change when he speaks about human distinctions and differences. In Christ, there are no nationalities (Greek nor Jew), religious differences (circumcised or non-circumcised), or no cultural differences (Barbarian or Scythian).

The Greeks considered all non-Greeks to be barbarians and the Scythians were the lowest barbarians of all. Yet, in Jesus Christ, a person's cultural status has no advantage or disadvantage. Neither does economic or political statutes (bond or free). A slave should try to obtain freedom, but if he does not, that does not make him less in Christ's sight. All of these kinds of distinctions belong to the old man and the old way of thinking.

4. Walking New (vv. 12-17)

Christians are chosen of God, set apart by and for God, and loved by God. These are privileges God gave to His people in the Old Testament. Now they are made available to Christians as well. Because God gave these blessings to His people, Paul encourages them to now walk in compassion (a tenderness expressed toward the suffering); in kindness; goodness and graciousness (a sweet disposition); in humility (thinking lowly of oneself); in gentleness (delicate consideration for the rights and feelings of others); and in patience (self-restraint that allows one to bear injury and insult without resorting to retaliation). Also, bearing with and forgiving each other (a "putting up" with things we don't like). The final word is "love." Love is unconditional giving and caring that goes beyond the call of duty.

Peace is another important article of clothing Paul exhorts the believer to put on. Not just peace among each other, but peace of mind. A calm mind that is not ruffled by difficulties and confusion. As usual, Paul weaves an attitude of thanksgiving into this section of the letter. Thankfulness to God and to our fellow man promotes inward and outward peace.

The Colossians are told to allow the Word of God, the Gospel, and the messages about Christ to be a rich treasure for them. Allow it to become so deeply planted that it controls the individual's thinking, attitudes, and actions. When God's Word is deep down in our hearts, Christ's presence causes us to conduct ourselves in a wise manner, influenced by God's insight and instruction. God's Word dwelling in our heart will also cause us to sing psalms from the Old Testament, and hymns and spiritual songs based on the New Testament truths.

Paul concludes with "do all in the name of the Lord Jesus." We are to always act as Christ's representatives. Christ is to live through God's children, those who have trusted in Him for their salvation and are eternally thankful for it.

SEARCH THE SCRIPTURES

1. _____ things which are _____ (Colossians 3:1).

2. Mortify your _____, fornication, _____, inordinate affection, evil _____, and covetousness, which is _____ (3:5).

3. _____ not to one another (3:9).

4. _____ one another, and _____ one another, even as _____ forgave you (3:13).

5. And whosoever you do, do _____ in the _____ of _____ (3:17).

DISCUSS THE MEANING

1. How do we constantly "seek things above" when we have to live and participate in daily activities here on earth?

2. How do we get rid of old habits and lifestyles and put on new ones that Christ wants to give?

3. Why are forgiveness and love two key elements in a life that pleases God?

4. How can an attitude of thanksgiving help us in our relationship with God and with people?

LESSON IN OUR SOCIETY

In our society today, telling lies is as common as drinking a glass of water. If the truth is going to hurt, make you feel uncomfortable, ruin your reputation, get you in trouble, or cause you to pay out some money—lie! Children learn dishonesty early as they watch their parents or other adults conveniently worm their way out of tough situations with out-and-out lies or half-truths. In the midst of this kind of society, the Christian is exhorted to TELL THE TRUTH. Telling lies to one another is considered part of our old life and it must be discarded.

MAKE IT HAPPEN

Old Life	New Life
Earthly interest	Heavenly interest
Sexual immorality	Compassion

Complete these two lists using the characteristics from Colossians 3:1-19. Remember you cannot change yourself or your ways. It is only as you lift up these areas of your life to God and sincerely ask Him to change you in His own timing and in His own way, that you will see some positive and lasting changes in your life.

FOLLOW THE SPIRIT

What God wants me to do:

_____

_____

REMEMBER YOUR THOUGHTS

Special insight you learned:

_____

_____

MORE LIGHT ON THE TEXT
COLOSSIANS 3:1-3, 5-17

In the last section of the last chapter (2:20ff), Paul challenges the Colossians to live as liberated people. Using a rhetorical question, Paul speaks to their conscience and questions their stability in Christ. He reasons with them by asking why they, who have been liberated from the rudiments of the world and ordinances of the Mosaic law through their relationship with Christ, should get themselves entangled again in the same process from which they had been liberated. Indulgence in such rigidity, although may appear good, is profitless and of no value because it is only fleshy indulgence, and not spiritual.

3:1 If ye then be risen with Christ, seek those things which are above, where Christ sitteth on the right hand of God. 2 Set your affection on things above, not on things on the earth. 3 For ye are dead, and your life is hid with Christ in God.

In the third chapter, Paul calls on the believers to be consistent in their lifestyle and in conformity with the truth that they have been raised with Christ, and therefore, they should live accordingly. The paragraph is both a parallel to and a continuation of the thought in the last section. Both of them are introduced with the "if" clause. The first, "if ye be dead with Christ from the rudiments of the world" (2:20), is linked with the second, "If ye then be risen with Christ" (3:1).

In the former section, the thought is expressed negatively, while here the emphasis is positively expressed. Both are a continuation of the thought Paul has expressed earlier in Colossians 2:12,13. It is important to note the contrast between the preceding section (2:20ff) and this. In Colossians 2:20ff, Paul says if you are dead from the rudiments of the world, then act like one who is dead. The idea is obvious. A dead man is no longer conscious of his surroundings, and the things around him have no influence on him; he is not tied to the world around him. Therefore, Paul asked the question why believers would try to relapse to paganism, the bondage of the law, and ceremonial rituals, which profit nothing, when they have been liberated from these very things through the death of Christ.

Here, Paul says, "If you be risen with Christ" then act like a living man. There seems to be an allusion to baptism here. The use of the conditional particle "if" (*ei*) does not infer that Paul was doubting their present spiritual disposition, rather he is reasoning based on their present relationship with Christ, and affirming their belief in the Lord. The phrase, "if ye then be risen with Christ" can be reworded thus: "since or in as much as you have been risen with Christ, seek those things which are above." The verb "seek" (*zeteo*) implies "to strive after with perseverance, to strongly desire for something." The idea here is to hunger after or to crave for something as one craves for one's favorite food. It is seeking constantly with much perseverance in order to obtain the desired object or treasure, such as the valuable pearls in the Lord's parable of the kingdom Christ (cf. Matthew 13:45-46).

The emphasis is not in the seeking, but rather in the object sought; it is not in the discovery, but in the obtaining of it. Jesus taught his followers to "seek first the kingdom of God, and his righteousness; and all these things shall be added unto you" (Matthew 6:3). What are those things which are above that Paul urges them to crave for? They are spiritual values at the disposal of the exalted Lord, which He freely gives to those who diligently seek Him (Matthew 7:7; 1 Corinthians 12:1; Ephesians 1:3). These spiritual values include those mentioned in verse 12 and following, as we shall soon discover later in this study.

The phrase "where Christ sitteth on the right hand of God" seems to give a note of assurance to the believers, and ties in with the first phrase, "you have been raised with Christ." Since the exalted Lord, with whom they have been raised is now sitting at the right hand of God, they can be assured to obtain all the things they seek. The psalmist says, "Thou wilt shew me the path of life: in thy presence is fulness of joy; at thy right hand there are pleasures for evermore" (Psalm 16:11; 17:14-15). The historical ascension and exaltation of the Lord Jesus into the right of God, is one of the bulwarks of the Christian faith and doctrine. It is the basis for our living, the fountain and foundation of our heritage and hope. This hope was foretold in the Old Testament (Psalm 8; 68:18), interpreted in Hebrews 2:1-8, and explained in Ephesians 4:7-8. The Bible is filled with the theme of Christ's exalted majesty sitting on the right hand of God in glory. We feel compelled to give a partial but important list of a few of the passages that deal with the theme for private study: Psalm 110:1; Matthew 22:44; 26:64; Mark 12:36; 14:62; 16:19; Luke 20:42; 22:69; Acts 2:34; 17:55; Romans 8:34; Ephesians 1:20; 4:10; Hebrews 1:3, 13; 8:1; 10:12; 12:2; and 1 Peter 3:21, 22.

In verse 2, Paul continues the theme from verse 1. He changes from "seeking the things above" to "set your affection on things above" and adds emphasis to admonition of the previous verse. "Set your affection" (mind) is the translation of the Greek, phroneo. It means "to direct one's mind to a thing, to strive for," as we have noted above. It is to occupy the mind with the spiritual things, rather than carnal things. This is a practical way of overcoming evil and temptation. Setting our affection on things above is Paul's other way of saying, "clothe yourselves with the Lord Jesus Christ, and do not think about how to gratify the desires of the sinful nature" (Romans 13:14, NIV), and "Walk in the Spirit, and ye shall not fulfil the lust of the flesh" (Galatians 5:16).

To the Philippians, Paul writes:

"Finally, brethren, whatsoever things are true, whatsoever things are honest, whatsoever things are just, whatsoever things are pure, whatsoever things are lovely, whatsoever things are of good report; if there be any virtue, and if there be any praise, think on these things. Those things, which ye have both learned, and received, and heard, and seen in me, do: and the God of peace shall be with you" (Philippians 4:8-9; also see our June 25, 2000 discussion, and vv. 12-17 below).

When we set our minds and thoughts on heavenly things, or occupy ourselves with the things that pertain to righteousness, then we wouldn't have room for the things on the earth, which Paul describes as flesh, carnal, and worldly. We are counseled to love, or be engrossed with heavenly things, rather than the earthly things, which the worldly always tends to crave. Verse 3 answers the obvious question: Why should they seek or set their affection on the things above, and not the things on the earth? Paul's answer is: For ye (gar i.e., because you) are dead (or you died), and your life is hid with Christ in God.

As we have already explained earlier, Paul is saying here that the Colossians, by virtue of their new relationship with the Lord, are now dead to sin, and sin has no more effect on or control (dominion) over their lives (Romans 6:14). If they are dead and buried to sin, then their old self has been crucified with Christ on the cross. It is no longer they that live, rather it is Christ who lives in them (Galatians 5:20). On one hand they are dead, and on the other, they still live (since they have been raised with Christ (v. 1), and now are in Christ. Their life is now bound in Christ.

Paul uses the word "hid" (hidden) with Christ in God. The Greek word used here is krupto, which means "to conceal," or "to hide under something or somebody." That means people do not see them, but Christ that lives in them. How? Through their lifestyle, attitude, and behavior, as we shall see in the remaining part of this passage. It is what Christ means by being "salt" and "light in the world" (Matthew 5:13, 14). Paul says we are the epistles that people read (2 Corinthians 3:2-3).

To "be hid with Christ" is also to be engrafted in Christ through the Spirit; a thought well-developed in the parable of the vine and the branches in John 15. When we receive Christ as Lord and Saviour, our life not only reflects the life of Christ to the world, our life is concealed from the world both from worldliness and the world's system of evil. We are shielded from sin and temptation, which buffet us daily. Since the Son is in the Father and the Father in the Son (John 1:18; 10:30; 17:21; 1 Corinthians 3:23; Colossians 1:15), consequently Paul is justified in saying, "your life is hid with Christ in God" (John 3:16; 10:28; Romans 8:31-39).

The Lord assured the Israelites of His everlasting, protecting presence with them when He says, "Behold, I have graven thee upon the palms of my hands; thy walls are continually before me" (Isaiah 49:16). This assurance is as relevant to us (all believers) today as it was to the Jews in the days of the prophet Isaiah and his peers. Nothing can penetrate the firm grip of God's hands to harm the people whose lives are hid with Christ in God.

Paul moves from the idea that our lives are hid with Christ in God (v. 3), to the fact that Christ Himself is now our life (v. 4), which indicates even a closer relationship. This idea is expressed in different ways in the following passages of Scripture which every Bible student is invited to study: John 14:19; 2 Corinthians 3:18; 4:10; Galatians 1:15-16; 2:20; 4:19; Philippians 1:21. Since we are united with Him in Spirit, it then follows that at His Second Advent, we will appear with Him in glory.

5 Mortify therefore your members which are upon the earth; fornication, uncleanness, inordinate affection, evil concupiscence, and covetousness, which is idolatry: 6 For which things' sake the wrath of God cometh on the children of disobedience:

In view of the foregoing paragraph (being united with Christ and the hope of appearing with Him in glory when He comes), Paul calls the Colossians to "mortify therefore your members which are upon the earth." The word "mortify," imperatively used here, is the active verb *nekrosate* in the Greek from *nekroo* (pronounced **nek-ro'-o,**) which means "put to death, to slay or to kill." The same verb is used only on two other occasions in the New Testament (Romans 4:19; Hebrews 11:12), which relate to Abraham and Sarah in connection with the promise of Isaac. The same meaning and idea is expressed in the use of another Greek verb *thanatoo*, translated "mortify" (Romans 8:13); "kill" (Romans 8:36; 2 Corinthians 6:9); and "put to death" (Matthew 26:59; 27:1; Mark 14:55: 1 Peter 3:18). Here, "mortify" is used metaphorically. It suggests that action should be taken and some effort exerted in order to deal a deadly blow to the sinful habits.

The seeming paradox between verse 3, "Ye are dead " and verse 5, "Put to death therefore your members" is obvi-

ous. A rash judgment of the two would conclude that the apostle is contradicting himself here. On one hand, Paul is saying that the Colossians are already dead, and on the other hand, he is asking them to put to death their members. Understanding and reconciling the two seemingly contradictory statements has never been an easy task among scholars. We can best explain this by an understanding of concepts of grace and working faith. The moment one acknowledges that he (he, his is used here in a generic sense not gender) is a sinner, confesses his sin, and accepts the gift of salvation offered by grace through faith, he is forgiven of his sins. Then and there, he is dead to sin (Romans 6:2, 11; 1 Peter 2:24), to the law (Romans 7:4; Galatians 2:19), and to the rudiments of this world (2:20), in principle. At that moment, all of the baggage of the old man are still there and needs to be dealt with. That is the beginning. A transformation process of the inner man begins, and this is the work of the Spirit.

However, the Holy Spirit does not work in a vacuum, neither does he force himself on any person. He works in a heart totally yielded to the Lord, and solicits our cooperation. As He works in us by convicting us of all the sinful practices, and we start to obey Him, we begin to unload all the baggage of sin, which easily besets us. We begin to live Christ-like lives and all the worldly rudiments begin to dissipate. Our attitude changes, and a new way of life and behavior begins. A change in character becomes noticeable, our desires, passions, and aspirations change. We begin "to seek and set (our) affection on things above, not on things on the earth" (vv. 1-2). This process is called sanctification, the work of the Holy Spirit. However, a conscious and deliberate involvement of self is needed and this is the working faith. Paul says to the Philippians to "work out your own salvation with fear and trembling" (Philppians 2:12). Paul calls it putting to death "your members which are upon the earth."

What members need to be slaughtered? "Fornication" (*porneia*) includes all manner of illicit sexual relationships, or sexual intercourse. Fornication embraces all types of sexual immorality, including adultery by married people (Matthew 5:32; 19:9; 1 Corinthians 7:2; 10:8, etc.), incest (1 Corinthians 5:1; 10:8), etc. Fornication does not apply only to single people, as some teach, but to all sorts of sexual perversion. "Uncleanness" (*akatharsia*) is used in a moral sense to describe whatever is opposite of purity, which include thoughts and motives.

Here the emphasis seems to lie on sexual immorality, which probably includes all forms of sexual seduction, homosexuality and sodomy, etc. (Matthew 23:27; Romans

1:21-23; 6:19; 2 Corinthians 12:21; Ephesians 4:19; 5:3; 1 Thessalonians 2:3; 4:7; 2 Peter 2; Jude 2). "Inordinate affection" (*pathos*) describes the unnatural, unrestrained, and out of control passion and lust for anything (1 Thessalonians 4:5). It is called "vile affections" in Romans 1:26 where Paul writes concerning the practice and result of apostasy: "For this cause God gave them up unto vile affections: for even their women did change the natural use into that which is against nature." This refers to lesbianism, the unnatural sexual relationships between women. "Evil concupiscence" (*kakos* translated evil, *epithumia* translated concupiscence), which is any strong or vehement desire associated mainly with evil and depraved lusts (Luke 22:15; Philippians 1:23; 1 Thessalonians 2:17; John 8:44; Ephesians 2:3). Here again it has the connotation of illicit sexual immorality. "Covetousness" (*pleonexia*) is a greedy desire to have more or to have what belongs to another person.

The first four sins mentioned here (also listed in 1 Thessalonians 4:3-7 and Romans 1:24-29) all have sexual undertones. The fifth one, covetousness or greed or selfish desire, seems to be the underlining evil that summarizes the rest of the vices. It is based on selfishness, which focuses on self (ego), leads to the worship of self rather than God, and eventually replaces the Lordship of Christ with self. For this reason, Paul adds, it is idolatry.

Here, we run into some difficulty, i.e., why are these vices called your members? A number of suggestions have been given in an attempt to solve the puzzle. They include one by John Calvin, which states that these vices are called "members because they adhere so closely to us," (see William Hendriksen, *New Testament Commentary: Exposition of Colossians and Philemon*, Grand Rapids: Baker Book House, 1964, p. 145). "Member" is a translation of the Greek word *melos*, which means "limb or a member of the human body." It is used figuratively here to describe some of the sins, which, as it were, have become attached to the human body as limbs are attached. They have become such a part of our body that we have become used to them, as an inherent part of our being. Isn't it what our sin is to us? Paul, in other places of his epistles, has made us synonymous with sin. He says there is no one born of the lineage of Adam who does not sin.

The metaphorical use of the "members" (parts) of the body is reminiscent of Christ's teaching in the Sermon on the Mount. Jesus says:

"And if thy right eye offend thee, pluck it out, and cast it from thee: for it is profitable for thee that one of thy members should perish, and not that thy whole body should be cast into hell. And if thy right hand offend thee, cut it off, and cast it from thee: for it is profitable for thee that one of

thy members should perish, and not that thy whole body should be cast into hell" (Matthew 5:29-30).

Paul seems to convey the same idea here. He calls on the Colossians, not only to mutilate the vices which have formed part of their being, but to kill them out rightly. Having listed the evils, Paul reminds and warns the Colossians of the consequences of indulging in them. These sins attract or invoke the wrath of God against those who indulge themselves in them, i.e., the children of disobedience. God's wrath (*orge*) or displeasure refers to the coming judgment day (cf. Romans 2:5-11; Ephesians 5:6; 2 Thessalonians 1:8-10; cf. vv. 6-7 with Ephesians 2:2-3).

7 In the which ye also walked some time, when ye lived in them. 8 But now ye also put off all these; anger, wrath, malice, blasphemy, filthy communication out of your mouth. 9 Lie not one to another, seeing that ye have put off the old man with his deeds;

In verses 7 and 8, Paul compares their former lifestyle with their present disposition as those who have been raised with Christ. In their state without Christ, they walked and lived in those vices, but now they have been regenerated through the death of Christ. Therefore, those vices should be done away with, both in their behavior, and the way they live. Paul now uses a different metaphor from the one used in verse 5. Instead of putting to death, he urges them to put off as in putting off worn-out garments, or garments that no longer fit. "Put off" translates into the Greek as *apotithemi* (say **ap-ot-eeth'-ay-mee**), which means "to put away, to cast off." The idea here is more serious than the language seems to convey. It is "to discard, never to be worn again." Last Christmas, my wife and I bought some dresses for our daughters to wear to church. They woke me up early yesterday with a number of those dresses, some of them are old and do not fit, and some are "out of fashion." They decided not to wear them again. This is the idea Paul tries to convey here, the same idea that he included in his letter to the Ephesians churches (Ephesians 4:22).

The phrase, "but now ye also put off all these," means in addition to the listed vices that need to be mortified (v. 5), you must discard as worn-out, unfit and unwanted garments, the following vices listed here: anger, wrath, malice, blasphemy, and filthy communication. Here again is a list of five vices relating to our attitude towards and relationship with others that the Colossians were to put off as discarded garments.

"Anger" (*orge*) is sometimes translated "wrath," and both words are used interchangeably. *Unger's Bible Dictionary*

chrologia), Paul refers to the use of bad or foul language or vile conversation, the same idea Paul expressed in Ephesians 4:29 and 5:4. Lying must also be discarded, Paul says to them. He puts it imperatively, "Lie not one to another, as if it was a command from above," i.e., do not lie to one another. It carries the same idea as in the preceding verse, and included in the things they needed to put off. In Ephesians 4:25, Paul says, "Wherefore putting away lying, speak every man truth with his neighbor: for we are members one of another." The same reason is implicit here: Since you we are members of the same body, do not lie (*pseudomai*, pronounced **psyoo'-dom-ahee**). In other words, don't attempt to deceive one

describes anger as, "The emotion of instant displeasure and indignation arising from the feeling of injury done or intended;" and "wrath" represents more of an abiding and settled habit of the mind (`*ira inveterata*`), with the purpose of revenge. Paul also includes "malice" (*kakia*, badness or wickedness) in the list of things Colossians ought to discard. It is interesting how these sins are related. Extended anger develops into wrath, and when wrath is not dealt with it develops into malice. The Igbos of West Africa call them *iwe, onuma*, and *ekworo*, respectively. When anger is allowed to develop into a grudge, and a grudge becomes hatred, it is sin. That is why Paul says in Ephesians, "Be ye angry, and sin not: let not the sun go down upon your wrath: Neither give place to the devil" (Ephesians 4:26-27).

In addition to the three vices which deal with people's attitude and disposition against others are two others that are related to the use of the tongue: blasphemy and filthy communication. The first three start from inside the heart, and manifest themselves outwardly through the mouth in the way of blasphemy (slander) and foul or abusive language. The word "blasphemy" is a direct derivation of the Greek *blasphemia* (pronounced **blas-fay-me'-ah**), which means evil speaking. Although it is usually used exclusively in reference to evil speaking against God (Matthew 12:31), it also refers to speaking evil or slander against humans (cf. Ephesians 4:31). By "filthy communication" (Greek *ais-*

another by falsehood. "Lie not one to another" may also be rendered, "do not continue to lie to one another" in other words, put an end to the habit of lying which is associated with the old nature.

The reason is explicitly clear: "seeing that ye have put off the old man with his deeds. For, if any man be in Christ, he is a new creature: old things are passed away; behold, all things are become new," Paul writes in 2 Corinthians 5:17. The "old man" is a term Paul often uses to describe man's sinful state before he came to Christ. The old man Paul says has been crucified with Christ (Romans 6:6; Ephesians 4:22) the moment we accept Jesus as Lord and Saviour, symbolized by the baptism (Colossians 2:11-12). With the old man dead, we become new creatures in the Lord. All the vices mentioned above, which belong to the old nature (old man) are now alien to the new nature. The "old man" here probably also means Satan with his deeds, referred to also as the old Adam, as compared with the new man or the new Adam, which is Christ Jesus.

10 And have put on the new man, which is renewed in knowledge after the image of him that created him:

Continuing the clothing motif, Paul instructs the Colossians to "put on the new man." We notice here that the putting off of the old man (v. 8) is precisely, though oppositely, matched with the putting on of the new man here. This is a reminder that there is no middle ground—either be clothed with the old man, or be dressed in the new man, which is renewed in the knowledge of Christ. When we discard the old clothes, we must put on new ones; there is nothing like "nudity" in relation to the things of God. This does echo Christ's statement that no one can serve two masters and confirms the cliche that you can't be on the fence. The word for "put on" is the Greek word *enduo*, which means "to clothe with." Christ used the same word when He asked His disciples to wait in Jerusalem until they be "endued with power from on high" (Luke 24:49). To "put on the new man" is to wear as garments the new nature, which results from our spiritual union with Christ through His death and resurrection (2 Corinthians 5:17).

The "new man," Paul continues "is renewed in knowledge after the image of him that created him." The phrase "is renewed" (Greek *anakainoo*) gives the idea of growth and changing from the former corrupt state into a new kind of life. The language here indicates a progressive and ongoing change, and therefore the phrase is better translated "being changed" (NIV, NASB). Writing to the Corinthians, Paul says, "Therefore we do not lose heart, but though our outer man is decaying, yet our inner man is being renewed day by day" (2 Corinthians 4:16, NASB). It is obvious that this renewal is the work of the Holy Spirit, a process with a definite goal in mind: "in knowledge," i.e., in the full knowledge of God, which is patterned according to the "image of him that created him." This knowledge, which surpasses the knowledge of the false teachers (2:2, 3, 18), is renewed to the likeness of Christ who is also the creator of all things. This progressive change takes place in the heart, and is experienced as we become intimately closer with our Redeemer.

The idea Paul portrays here is comparable to earthly relationships. The closer we get to people, the more we get to know them, and we progressively begin to think, and sometimes even behave, like them. Most times children pattern their life, behavior, and desires either after their father or their mother, or their best friend, people who have great influence in their lives, their school teachers, or after their heroes. Sometimes they mimic their hero's way of talking or doing things. The best example is in the husband-wife relationship. As couples get closer together in long-term relationships, they get to know each other's thoughts and behaviors, and they begin to make the same choices and oftentimes behave alike. They pattern each other's way of life. Sometimes they complete each other's

sentences during a conversation.

When a Christian receives Christ, he begins a new relationship. As he gets deeper with Christ relationally, his life changes, his thought process changes, he makes new choices patterned according to Christ's. That is what Paul meant when he said to the Galatians, "For as many of you as have been baptized into Christ have put on Christ" (Galatians 3:27). Therefore, the standard of the renewal or the new man is God's image. God's very own likeness that is the Creator of this new man in the believers' hearts and lives, just as He created Adam in His own image (Genesis 1:26, 27). Paul writes, "we have borne the image of the earthy (the old Adam), we shall also bear the image of the heavenly" (1 Corinthian 15:49) referring to the new Adam the Spiritual Adam who is Christ.

The next idea we can glean from Scripture is that God's original plan of creating man in His image was for man to have the full knowledge, patterned according to God's moral and spiritual likeness. Man lost it at the Garden of Eden through Adam's sin, which we inherited. Now He renews man after the original pattern and gives him the true knowledge through the new Adam, Christ Jesus (cf. 2 Timothy 1:7; 2 Peter 1:3-13).

11 Where there is neither Greek nor Jew, circumcision nor uncircumcision, Barbarian, Scythian, bond nor free: but Christ is all, and in all.

This progressive transformation into the image of the divine does not distinguish between racial, religious, cultural, and social boundaries. Paul says here that in Christ, all types of people whether Jews, which he describes as "circumcision," Greeks (or Gentiles) who were regarded as uncircumcision, or slaves and free, including barbarians, are equal. The introduction of this theme at this point indicates that Paul is aware of such scandal in his time. The partition between the Greek and Jew was practically unbreakable, especially from the Jewish end. The Jews who were circumcised would look down on the Greeks/Gentiles, the uncircumcised, as inferior and would not acknowledge them. The word "Barbarians" (Greek *barbaros*) refers to all foreigners who were non-Greeks and ignorant of the Greek language. The Greek regarded them as the lower class in the society. Barbarians were also regarded as uncultured, crude, and rough. Hence the term "barbaric" behavior or attitude. Scythians (*Skuthes*), meaning "rude or rough," were said to be the lowest class of barbarians. They were inhabitants of Scythia, probably the modern-day Russia. Compared with more civilized nations of the then known world, such as Rome, Scythians were seen as the wildest of barbarians.

Things have not changed much, have they? Class discrimination, racial bigotry, social, sex or gender superiority, and chauvinism in our society has not changed. No. Not even in the church. The caste system is still alive and practiced widely in India; tribal and national superiority is still evident in many Africans countries; the western world still regards other nations as inferior, hence they coined the phrase "third world countries." We use this term so freely in our churches today as if it is divinely-inspired from Scripture. The people of the United States arrogate themselves as the leaders of the world, thereby looking down on all other nations. Paul condemns all these attitudes and allows no room for such discrimination within the society of his time. How much less should this occur within the community of believers it should not even be mentioned. One would wonder how Paul would react if he were to visit our congregations today?

One of the major problems that the church faces today, though many deny its existence or they close their eyes against it, is hypocrisy. We preach one thing and practice the opposite. We preach unity and equality, but in practice, there is clear evidence of class, racial, and gender discrimination within the body. It took over a century for one of the Baptist denominations in the southern states to realize that segregating African Americans or dark skinned persons from church worship is bad. As few as five years ago, blacks were not allowed to worship in "white churches."

This writer visited a friend and his family in Texas in 1983. For the Sunday morning service, they drove past a number of churches to another district to attend a "black church." I asked him why he had to travel such a long distance to worship when there were a number of churches along the way.. His reply was, "They would not allow us in. They will ask us to leave because this is not a black church." They went to the black church, not by choice, but because of the social disease that has plagued the society, and in fact the church, for centuries.

Similarly, women are subtly but evidently regarded as second class. The battle against women's ordination is still raging in many denominations today. Looking beyond color, accent, gender in hiring ministers is still a thing of the future in our Christian circles. Paul concludes his theme by saying in effect that discrimination is divinely unconstitutional. It is devilish. It's not from God.

Paul sums it up thus, "but Christ is all, and in all." That means Christ is all that matters. He lives in all believers, whether Greek or Jew, Barbarian or Scythian, slave or free-man. He does not discriminate based on race, cultural or social background, or upbringing; His Spirit works in every heart yielded to Him, renewing and progressively transforming them daily in knowledge after the image of the one who created him (v. 10).

12 Put on therefore, as the elect of God, holy and beloved, bowels of mercies, kindness, humbleness of mind, meekness, longsuffering;

Paul returns to the theme of "putting on" he started in verse 10, with the same clothing motif, "Put on therefore, as the elect of God." The use of the conjunction, "therefore" (oun) should be noted. It reflects the preceding thoughts (vv. 8-11). The idea here would mean "since you have put off the old man, and have put on the new man, which is being constantly and progressively renewed in knowledge of the image of God, in principle, then act it out in practice." Paul qualifies them with a cluster of three adjectives to describe who they become when they receive Christ.

First they are "the elect of God," or Greek *eklektos* pronounced **ek-lek-tos'**, which means "the chosen one of God." Paul implicitly advances the theology of salvation based on God's choice or election. Christians are called "chosen or elect" of God. Second, they are holy, *hagios*, pronounced **hag'-ee-os.** It means "set apart ones, special or sacred or saints." All true believers are holy in the sight of God. This holiness is based not on their goodness, or righteousness, but rather based on the righteousness of Christ that is imputed to them (1 Corinthians 3:17; Ephesians 1:4; 2:21; 3:5; 5:27; Colossians 1:22; 1 Thessalonians 5:27; 1 Peter 1:15-16; 2:5, 9, etc.). Paul calls them holy here because of God's election or choice, rather than their moral purity or perfection.

Since the Colossians are the elect of God, they are special and holy before Him, consequently they are God's "beloved." This word completes the cluster of adjectives Paul employs here to qualify them and their relationship with God. "Beloved" is *agapao* from the word love or *agape*. Here, the Colossians are the objects of God's love. "Beloved" is another word that the New Testament (especially Paul) uses quite frequently to describe all Christians (cf. Romans 1:7; 2 Corinthians 7:1; 1 Thessalonians 1:4; 2 Thessalonians 2:13; 1 John 3:2; 4:1, 7, 11). The words "chosen," "holy," and "beloved," drawn from the Old Testament, describe the covenant relationship between Israel and the *YAHWEH*. Paul here affirms the Colossians' special position before God, a special position which they and all Christians now share with the ancient covenant people of Israel (see 1 Peter 2:9; Isaiah 5:1; Hosea 2:23; cf. Romans 9:25).

After affirming who they are because of their relationship with God through Christ, Paul now enumerates the qualities expected of them, the things they are to put on. They are to put on bowels of mercies, kindness, humbleness of mind, meekness, and longsuffering. It is to be noted how the list here counteracts the vices in verse 8, which they are to put off. While the list in verse 8 consist of vices that harm people, the list here implies a desire to care for the well-being of others. While the former is self-oriented, the latter is centered on others. It is interesting, as well, to note how these qualities are paired and overlap. The first pair is "bowels of mercies" and "kindness." "Bowels of mercies" is figuratively used here, and describes the spirit of compassion to be resident in the heart of God's elect.

The word "bowel" (Greek *splagchnon*, say **splangkh'**) refers to the intestines, which sometimes is also used for heart, lungs, liver, etc. "Bowel" is another word for stomach or the abdomen. Used figuratively as here it means, "pity" "sympathy," or "an inward affection." Bowels were regarded as the seat of more violent passions of both anger and love. For the Hebrew, it is the seat of tender affections, kindness, compassion, benevolence, which are usually associated with the heart hence the phrase tenderhearted. "Bowels" *splagchnon* and "mercies" *oiktirmos*, which means "compassion" or "pity," go together. It can literally be translated as "bowels in which compassion resides."

One cannot avoid noticing the similarity in both the meaning and expression of "bowels of mercies" with the West African Igbo language *afo oma*. When one is described as full of compassion, the Igbos would say: *O juru na afo oma* or *O juru na obi oma*, the latter meaning his heart is full of compassion. Just as the Hebrews refer to the bowels as the seat of tender affections, kindness, compassion, etc., the Igbos express the same—the belly or stomach is where the same qualities reside.

The next word "kindness" *chrestotes*, (pronounced **khray-stot'-ace**) is essentially synonymous with bowels of mercies and expresses moral goodness and compassion. The Igbos would call it *obi oma*, which is equivalent to the English expression "good heart." When we say that someone has a good heart, it means that he is kind, just as the Igbos would say: *O were obi oma*. Both express, as one puts it, a yearning with the deep-felt affection of Christ. A few biblical examples will suffice: Joseph's reaction on seeing Benjamin (Genesis 43:30) or in revealing himself to his brothers (Genesis 45:1:4); in the New Testament, the parable of the Good Samaritan (Luke 10:25ff); Barnabas (Acts 15:37); and Paul and his colleagues (1 Thessalonians 2:7-12). Jesus is compassion and kindness par excellence

(Matthew 9:36; 14:14; 15:32; 20:34; Mark 1:41; 6:34; 8:2; Luke 7:13, etc.).

The next set of qualities the Colossians are asked to wear as garments are "humbleness of mind" (humility or lowliness) Greek *tapeinophrosune* (say, **tap-I-nof-ros-oo'-nay**) and "meekness" *prautes* (say **prah-oo'-tace**). Both of these convey the spirit of gentleness and modesty. Humility is a virtue that is despised in the heathen world and is in opposition to pride, but to the Christian, it is an honorable quality to strive for, a quality Christ exhibited throughout His earthly ministry (Philippians 2:3ff). There is however false humility, which Paul despises (see Last Sunday's discussion on Colossians 2:18; cf. 2:23). Jesus says to His audience, "Come unto me, all ye that labor and are heavy laden, and I will give you rest. Take my yoke upon you, and learn of me; for I am meek and lowly in heart: and ye shall find rest unto your souls" (Matthew 11:28-29). The centurion (Luke 7:1-10) and the praying publican (Luke 18:13) are also good examples of true humility. Moses is a perfect example of meekness (Numbers 12:3). The Bible says that God opposes and demotes the proud, but blesses and exalts the humble.

Another quality to strive for that Paul mentions is "longsuffering" (*makrothumia*, pronounced **mak-roth-oo-mee'-ah**), which is patience, i.e., "slowness in avenging wrongs." It characterizes a person who refuses to yield to passion and rage in the face of wrongs done to him, a person who has self-control. An example of longsuffering is seen in Hosea who, rather than rejecting his unfaithful wife, redeems her and restores her to her former place of honor (Hosea 1:2-3; 3:1-3). The Bible attributes longsuffering not only to man (2 Corinthians 6:6; Galatians 5:22; Ephesians 4:2; 2 Timothy 4:2), but to God (Romans 2:4; 9:22), and to Christ (1 Timothy 1:16), as well. It is one of the fruits of the Spirit along with kindness, meekness (Galatian 5:22; Romans 15:5). "Patience" is almost exclusively associated with our relationship with other people. However, it is applied to self in relation to our attitude to the world system and life as a whole. One needs patience to succeed in life. Impatience breeds discontent, leads to evil of all types, and can ruin one's life. We need patience for example when driving on the road in order to save lives, and in our families to maintain healthy relationships.

13 Forbearing one another, and forgiving one another, if any man have a quarrel against any: even as Christ forgave you, so also do ye.

In close association with the five virtues listed above is a pair of activities required of all believers: forbearing one another and forgiving one another. The first, "forbearing," translates into the Greek word *anechomai* (say **an-ekh'-om-ahee**) which means "to hold oneself up against, to bear with or to endure." It has the idea of tolerance or to put up with something negative. Paul urges the Ephesians to bear one another in love (4:2) and he exemplified this through his suffering (1 Corinthians 4:12). James cites Job as another good example of endurance (cf. James 5:11). Paul adds the second activity, "forgiving one another," and gives a scenario of what can constitute forgiveness, "if any man have a quarrel against any," that we should follow the supreme example of Christ. For discussion on Christ's forgiveness, see Bible Study Guide 11 (regarding Colossians 2:13). Christ taught His disciples to pray, "And forgive us our debts, as we forgive our debtors" (Matthew 6:12), and He sets no limit to the numbers of times we are to forgive one another (Matthew 18:22). An unforgiving spirit has divine repercussion as Christ demonstrated in the parable of the unjust servant and says, "So likewise shall my heavenly Father do also unto you, if ye from your hearts forgive not every one his brother their trespasses" (Matthew 18:35; cf. Mark 11:25).

Furthermore, the Lord underscored these qualities with His own example when while on the cross He prayed, "Father, forgive them; for they know not what they do" (Luke 23:34). Likewise, being stoned Stephen prayed, "Lord, lay not this sin to their charge" (Acts 7:60). He was following the example of Christ. All virtues are manifested in Christ's life: a heart of compassion, humility, meekness, longsuffering, endurance or forbearance, and forgiveness. When a believer manifests these virtues, he has truly put on Christ (Romans 13:14).

14 And above all these things put on charity, which is the bond of perfectness. 15 And let the peace of God rule in your hearts, to the which also ye are called in one body; and be ye thankful.

To Paul, and indeed to the disciples, including John and Peter (1 Peter 4:8) love is supreme—a cord that binds together all the other virtues (1 Corinthians 13). It heads the list of the fruits of the Spirit in Galatians 5:22. As someone puts it, "love is the lubricant that enables the other virtues to function smoothly" (Galatians 5:6,13). Love is the essence of living. This fact is made clear in Colossians 3:14.

What does Paul mean by the statement, "And above all these things put on charity?" This probably means, in addition to these, also put on charity or love. Paul has the picture of an overall, or an outer or over-garment, a coat or jacket. That is after putting on the eight virtues above, one

is to put on the outer cloak as the bond of perfectness or as a girdle. "Perfectness," (Greek *teleiotes* say, **tel-I-ot'-ace**) means "completeness," and "bond" (Greek *sundesmos* pronounced **soon'-des-mos**) and is like a joint tie or ligament by which things are bound together, especially uniting the members of the human body together. Simply put, it is the uniting principle of all things. It covers all, unites all, and binds all together as one. Alternatively, "above all these things" would be read as, "more importantly to all these things put on love," which underscores the principle in the 1 Corinthian 13. Paul insists in that passage that whatever we do without love is worthless. Therefore, love should be the basis or the motivating force that guides our actions and activities. Jesus issued a new commandment to His disciples to love one another (John 13:34; 1 Thessalonians 4:9). In effect, Paul says that love for one another is what will strengthen and unite the body of Christ and lead the people of God to desired spiritual attainment, not human knowledge or philosophy such as the false teachers advocate, not the obedience to human (Jewish) regulations.

Paul continues with the theme of unity and says, "And let the peace of God rule in your hearts." The conjunction "and" (Greek *kai*) means "in addition to" or "also," with reference to the virtues mentioned above, with love as the crowning virtue. Where love, mercy, etc. exist there is peace both in the individual heart, which is a condition of rest and contentment, and peace within the body. This peace is derived from the fact that we are forgiven of our sins and redeemed from its slavery. It is the assurance that our Redeemer will fulfill all that He has promises to His own; that He will not fail those that surrender their lives to Him.

Paul wrote to Philippians, "And the peace of God, which passeth all understanding, shall keep your hearts and minds through Christ Jesus" (Philippians 4:7). This peace does not only bring harmony within the individual hearts, it brings harmony and oneness within the corporate body of Christ. "Let the peace of God rule in your hearts" literally means we should allow the peace (*eirene*) of Christ (*Christos*), the Anointed One, to rule (*brabeuo*) or be the umpire or arbitrator who directs or controls our hearts. The peace of Christ ("of God," KJV) means either "the peace that Christ gives" or "the peace that belongs to Christ." A grateful heart produces a peaceful mind. Conversely, an ungrateful heart produces grudges and disharmony within oneself and overflows to others, breeding discord and quarreling within the body of Christ.

16 Let the word of Christ dwell in you richly in all wisdom; teaching and admonishing one

another in psalms and hymns and spiritual songs, singing with grace in your hearts to the Lord.

In the previous verse, it is the peace of Christ that is to rule in your hearts. Paul admonishes the Colossians to "let the word of Christ dwell in you richly in all wisdom." It is not only the peace of Christ being the umpire of our hearts, but the word of Christ should dwell (Greek *enoikeo*, pronounced **en-oy-keh'-o**), inhabit or make its residence within our hearts as well. The word "dwell" is used figuratively with the idea of influencing one's life and activities. While the peace of Christ would control our lives, His Word is to influence our activities, and both should make their inhabitation within our hearts.

The word "richly" (Greek *plousios*, pronounced **ploo-see'-oce**) means "abundantly" and conveys the idea that either the Word of Christ will dwell in abundance in our hearts, or it will dwell in our hearts richly in all wisdom. In any case, the Word of Christ dwelling within our hearts would produce all the wisdom we need in life. It will influence and govern our thoughts, deeds, and our motivations; it would help us to make good and rational decisions in life. This will be made possible if we obey the Word of God (Matthew 13:9), hide it in our hearts (Psalm 119:11), and handle it rightly (2 Timothy 2:15). The word "richly" occurs three other times in the New Testament (1 Timothy 6:17; Titus 3:6; 2 Peter 1:11) each describing, as it does here, the richness of God's provision and blessings for man.

The phrase "teaching and admonishing one another" expresses the same thought as in 1:28 where the apostle relates what he and his fellow believers are doing. Here, he asks the Colossians to do the same. When they are abundantly equipped with all wisdom through the Word of Christ, they would be able to teach and admonish (Greek *noutheteo* pronounced **noo-thet-eh'-o**), i.e., warn, caution or reprove another gently through psalms and hymns and spiritual songs. Paul underscores the purpose of worship songs and singing: for edifying the body, encouraging one another, and for the praise and honor of God. Paul includes the various type of singing: psalms, hymns and spiritual songs (see also Ephesians 5:19). It is not easy to distinguish the three. However, "psalms" probably refers to the Old Testament Psalms. For a detailed discussion and better understanding of the differences, see Hendriksen (pp. 162-163).

17 And whatsoever ye do in word or deed, do all in the name of the Lord Jesus, giving thanks to God and the Father by him.

Paul summarizes this paragraph with a priceless fundamental philosophy of Christian living, i.e., our dealings, both in speech or actions should be Christ-focused. Everything we do, including our day-to-day activities and relationships and our teaching and admonishing of one another (v. 16), must done in the name of the Lord Jesus Christ, with gratitude to God the Father. "Do all in the name of the Lord Jesus" has a cluster of possible but inclusive meanings. It means "in relation to His revealed will," "in our relation with Him" and "in subjection to His authority and power," and "for His own glory" as opposed to our own. To crown it all Paul adds, "giving thanks to God and the Father by him." That is in appreciation for what God has accomplished for us on the basis of Christ's redemptive and atoning sacrifice, whereby we sinners receive forgiveness and are accepted by God the Father as dear sons and daughters. This statement (v. 17) focuses on motives. Our lives, in word (what we say and how we say it) and deed (our actions both to self and to others), are to be motivated by the love of Christ in us, with the purpose of honoring and glorifying His name. It should be done in appreciation of what God has done for us through Christ. Our lives and activities must be governed by the "peace of Christ" in our hearts (v. 15), influenced by the Word of Christ dwelling richly in wisdom (v. 16), and motivated by our relationship with Christ, and with eternity in view.

DAILY BIBLE READING

Who Are Sanctified
Hebrews 10:11-18
M: Revealed with Christ in Glory
Colossians 2:1-5
T: God Dwells Fully in Jesus Christ
Colossians 2:6-10
W: Dead to the Flesh, Alive in Christ
Colossians 2:11-16
T: Hold Fast to Christ, Our Head
Colossians 2:17-23
F: Jesus: Mediator of a New Covenant
Hebrews 8:1-7
S: The Blood of Christ Purifies Us
Hebrews 9:11-15
S: Christ Perfected Thos

TEACHING TIPS

August 27
Bible Study Guide 13

1. Words You Should Know

A. Aged (Philemon 9)—Greek *presbytes*—old age, usually carries with it the connotation of authority. Here the emphasis is on the apostle's aged and feeble condition.

B. Partner (17)—Greek *koinonos*—fellowship, business associate.

C. Welcome (17)— Greek *proslabou*—to receive kindly, always positive, as into a circle of friends; or embrace as a helper.

2. Teacher Preparation

A. Read the entire book of Philemon in one sitting. Mark any parts of it that are unfamiliar to you.

B. Read the IN DEPTH commentary and check the BACKGROUND and THE PEOPLE, PLACES, AND TIMES for some of the verses you had questions about. If you still have questions, read the MORE LIGHT ON THE TEXT section of this lesson and refer to a good study Bible for more explanation.

C. Materials Needed: Bibles, board or newsprint, pencil and paper.

3. Starting the Lesson

A. Have each student write down the AT-A-GLANCE outline. Read the LESSON AIM together. Challenge each one to formulate a one sentence prayer to begin the class.

B. Read IN FOCUS and have a brief discussion about whether this is happening in your church or in your home or neighborhood. Could there possibly be people who are hurting like May while we are unaware of it?

4. Getting into the Lesson

A. Assign three students to talk about the main three characters in the lesson (just the basic facts about Paul, Onesimus, and Philemon). Use THE

PEOPLE, PLACES, AND TIMES and BACKGROUND sections for information.

B. Read the FOCAL VERSES and IN DEPTH with each section separately. Generate discussion with the SEARCH THE SCRIPTURES and DISCUSS THE MEANING questions from each section.

5. Relating the Lesson to Life

A. Ask the students to expand the list of comments in LESSON IN OUR SOCIETY.

B. What are some of the self-centered comments we use in Christian circles?

6. Arousing Action

A. Read the MAKE IT HAPPEN section and have the class break up into groups of twos or threes. Have each group decided how they will make a commitment to do something differently in this area.

B. Allow each group time for prayer.

WELCOMING OTHERS IN CHRIST

Bible Background • PHILEMON
Printed Text • PHILEMON 4-21
Devotional Reading • JAMES 2:1-13

LESSON AIM

By the time the students complete this lesson, they should know the historical account of Paul, Philemon, and Onesimus; they should be motivated to seek the Lord about ways they can demonstrate the love of Christ by unselfish attitudes and actions.

KEEP IN MIND

"That the communication of thy faith may become effectual by the acknowledging of every good thing which is in you in Christ Jesus" (Philemon 6).

FOCAL VERSES

PHILEMON 4 I thank my God, making mention of thee always in my prayers,

5 Hearing of thy love and faith, which thou hast toward the Lord Jesus, and toward all saints;

6 That the communication of thy faith may become effectual by the acknowledging of every good thing which is in you in Christ Jesus.

7 For we have great joy and consolation in thy love, because the bowels of the saints are refreshed by thee, brother.

8 Wherefore, though I might be much bold in Christ to enjoin thee that which is convenient,

9 Yet for love's sake I rather beseech thee, being such a one as Paul the aged, and now also a prisoner of Jesus Christ.

10 I beseech thee for my son Onesimus, who I have begotten in my bonds:

11 Which in time past was to thee unprofitable, but now profitable to thee and to me:

12 Whom I have sent again: thou therefore receive him,

LESSON OVERVIEW

LESSON AIM
KEEP IN MIND
FOCAL VERSES
IN FOCUS
THE PEOPLE, PLACES, AND TIMES
BACKGROUND
AT-A-GLANCE
IN DEPTH
SEARCH THE SCRIPTURES
DISCUSS THE MEANING
LESSON IN OUR SOCIETY
MAKE IT HAPPEN
FOLLOW THE SPIRIT
REMEMBER YOUR THOUGHTS
MORE LIGHT ON THE TEXT
DAILY BIBLE READINGS
TEACHING TIPS
WORSHIP GUIDE

that is, mine own bowels:

13 Whom I would have retained with me, that in thy stead he might have ministered unto me in the bonds of the gospel:

14 But without thy mind would I do nothing; that thy benefit should not be as it were of necessity, but willingly.

15 For perhaps he therefore departed for a season, that thou shouldest receive him for ever;

16 Not now as a servant, but above a servant, a brother beloved, specially to me, but how much more unto thee, both in the flesh, and in the Lord?

17 If thou count me therefore a partner, receive him as myself.

18 If he hath wronged thee, or oweth thee ought, put that on mine account;

19 I Paul have written it with mine own hand, I will repay it: albeit I do not say to thee how thou owest unto me even thine own self besides.

20 Yea, brother, let me have joy of thee in the Lord: refresheth my bowels in the Lord.

21 Having confidence in thy obedience I wrote unto thee, knowing that thou wilt also do more than I say.

IN FOCUS

May lost both of her parents in a car accident as a child and a widowed aunt raised her. She had completed college and had become a very successful business woman. In spite of her career status and financial comforts, May felt an emptiness in her heart.

May's aunt had a bad experience with the church and refused to attend after the death of her husband. She did not teach May anything about Jesus or the Bible.

One Sunday, after the death of her aunt, May decided to visit the local church in her neighborhood. "Maybe here," she thought, "I can find the answer to the ache in my heart. And maybe here I can find some meaningful relationships." Even though May was surrounded by people everyday on her job, she was considered the big boss. People were professional and friendly, but she really did not have any close relationships except with her aunt.

May attended the church on her block for several months. She liked the music, and when the pastor taught from the Bible, her heart stirred as it never had before. But the people in the church were distant. In all the weeks May attended, not one person had attempted to get to know her. After a while May stopped attending.

It is rare that any of us will ever have an experience like Philemon welcoming back a runaway slave as a brother in Christ. Yet God may be calling us to befriend a person like May. Jesus may be calling you to expand the welcome sign in your heart and reach out to someone in need.

THE PEOPLE, PLACES, AND TIMES

PHILEMON. A Christian slave owner who lived in Lycus Valley of Asia Minor. He was a man of wealth and general importance. He had been introduced to Christ by Paul, probably in Ephesus. He may have lived in Ephesus for a time or been there on business and heard the Gospel from the apostle. The church at Colossae used Philemon's home as their headquarters.

ONESIMUS. A runaway slave that belonged to Philemon. He ran to Rome and somehow came in contact with Paul. He was converted and became attached to Paul. Paul wanted to keep him as a fellow worker, but the first thing that Paul had to do was encourage Onesimus to get his past life in order. Paul sent Onesimus back to Philemon with this letter asking Philemon to receive him as a fellow Christian brother, not as a slave.

TYCHICUS. A messenger for Paul. Paul sent Onesimus back to Philemon under the protection of Tychicus with this personal letter. It was not safe to send Onesimus alone because slave catchers might have captured him.

BACKGROUND

Onesimus's status was the lowest that one could reach in the ancient world. As a runaway slave, he was protected by no laws, and he was therefore subject to all kinds of harsh abuse. Fugitive slaves usually went to large cities, remote parts of a Roman state, or into unsettled areas. At this time,

their capture and return was largely an informal arrangement between the owner and provincial administrator. They were frequently beaten unmercifully or given unreasonable tasks. Their life expectancy was very short.

Paul put Philemon in a precarious position indeed. In pleading for forgiveness and restitution of Onesimus without a punishment that was obvious to all, he was confronting the social economic order head on. Paul's request for clemency for Onesimus defied Roman tradition.

Paul moved a step beyond and asked not only for Onesimus' freedom but for Onesimus to be sent back to Paul. Paul wanted his help in the ministry. Scripture does not let us know if Philemon agreed, but other history books indicate that Onesimus did return to Paul and eventually took a high position in Paul's ministry.

This kind of action that Paul was requesting was very uncommon and unusual for slaves and masters. Paul made his request based on Christian principle and a God centered perspective, not on the laws of the land. By this plea, Paul is also giving new dignity to the slave class.

AT-A-GLANCE

1. Paul's Praise (Philemon 4-7)
2. Paul's Plea (vv. 8-16)
3. Paul Offers to Pay Indeptedness (vv. 17-21)

IN DEPTH

1. Paul's Praise (Philemon 4-7)

Paul started this letter by saying that he thanked God always when he remembered Philemon in his prayers. Paul gives thanks for Philemon in his prayers because he has heard of Philemon's love toward all the saints and of his love and faith toward Christ Jesus.

Paul's information concerning the faith and love of Philemon has probably come to him from Epaphras. We learn from Colossians 1:7-8 and 4:12-13 that Epaphras is the minister at Colossae who has come to Paul in Rome, apparently for advice on how to deal with the Colossian heresy. At the time of Paul's writing he is a prisoner at Rome.

It is believed Philemon often hosted the church in Colossae. Philemon did not just convert to Christ and enjoy the blessings of his salvation. He went to work helping others come to know Christ and to grow in Him. Paul's prayer is that Philemon's expression of faith through his ministry to others will lead him into the realization of the riches of grace which are available in Christ Jesus.

Paul returned to his opening thought as he continues to encourage Philemon's ministry there in Colossae. Philemon was a man of some wealth, and he had used his wealth to minister to the needs of his brothers in Christ. As he has given himself to this ministry, he has been deepened in his love of Christ, and his faith in Christ as his Lord and Saviour has been strengthened.

2. Paul's Plea (vv. 8-16)

Paul wanted to ask Philemon for mercy for Onesimus, one of Philemon's runaway slaves. He does not intend to tell Philemon exactly what he must do, preferring rather to leave this to Philemon's own sense of what the situation requires. He hoped that Philemon would receive Onesimus as a brother in Christ. Paul seemed to hint that he would be very much pleased if Philemon would see fit to send Onesimus back to Rome to continue his work with Paul there.

Paul had authority over Philemon as an apostle of Christ. He had the authority to command Onesimus' release and to order Onesimus back to help him. Philemon would have had to obey. But he did not want to use his authority. He wanted Philemon to do voluntarily from love that which Paul thought he ought to do. There were times when those who are in authority have to command, but a much stronger position is established when they can call forth the obedience that is given freely as an expression of love.

Paul referred to two things about himself: his age and his imprisonment for the sake of the Gospel of Christ Jesus. Paul is about 60 years old now. It is as if he were attempting to pull Philemon close to him in tenderness and love. "Philemon, listen carefully and closely to me. I'm an old man in chains." He was about to share his heart and appeal to the heart of Philemon.

The first mention of Onesimus is in verse 10. Paul called Onesimus his child, whose father he had become in his imprisonment. This means of course that Onesimus has become a Christian through the witness of Paul. Onesimus has grown in the Christian faith. Onesimus is now a child of God, no longer is he just a runaway slave. The word "Onesimus" in the Greek means "useful." Paul said, he who has been useless has now become useful. At last Onesimus is living up to his name.

It does not take much imagination to go behind verse 12 to the emotional scene in which Paul and Onesimus decide that Onesimus as a slave must go back to his master. It must have been a very hard decision for Paul and for Onesimus. But the man who has given himself in full surrender to Jesus Christ must do what he can to make right the wrongs that happened in his past.

Paul does not give explanation or reasons why he thinks slavery is right or wrong when Christians are involved. In the world in which they live, it was accepted. Paul exhorted, on several occasions, that a believer was to always conduct himself in a godly manner, no matter what the situation. The apostles consistently urged the Christians who were slaves to be obedient to their masters and to seek to behave themselves in such a way that they would adorn the doctrine of God their Saviour. They also exhorted the masters to be fair and kind to their slaves.

Onesimus was very dear to Paul. He is not simply the one he is sending back. Paul adds that he is sending him back who is my very heart (v. 12, paraphrased). The apostle has been speaking as an educated man of the classical world. But now after he has cited a number of reasons for allowing Onesimus to remain with him, he goes further and urges Philemon to make his decision out of Christian love rather than obligation.

If Onesimus was so dear to Paul, who was a prisoner, that he wanted the comfort of his help, how could Philemon refuse Paul's plea for him? Also observe Paul's sensitive regard for Philemon's personality. The contrast between, "for a time and forever" shows Paul's conviction that the hand of God was at work in the whole situation. It also shows his tact: instead of bluntly referring to Onesimus as a runaway, he speaks of his temporary separation from Philemon as a prelude to permanent reunion with him.

In similar fashion, he contrasts "slave," a temporal and demeaning condition, with "brother," an eternal relationship in the Lord. Paul asks Philemon to receive Onesimus as he would receive Paul himself.

3. Paul Offers to Pay Indebtedness (vv. 17-21)

Paul also involves himself in Onesimus' financial obligations. This is an astonishing statement. Money is often where people draw a line. They will help a person out in every way except financially. But Paul took on that burden as well. Onesimus had, no doubt, robbed his master. This was a common act of runaway slaves. It may be that Onesimus had confessed this to Paul. Or the loss may have been the result of the departure of a highly skilled slave from whose activities produced great income.

The subject is still the indebtedness of Onesimus. Now Paul said that he wrote these words himself. As in our society, hand written statements or obligations carried greater weight and legal validity. Paul gave Philemon what is equivalent to a promissory note.

Paul shifted abruptly to another thought as he concluded the book. In a way, Paul is saying, all Christians are slaves like Onesimus. We all owed God a sin debt we could not pay, and the Saviour took care of it for us. Paul is reminding Philemon of this fact as he continues to plead on behalf of Onesimus.

Paul told Philemon to refresh his heart with this favor, as he has been willing to do in his ministry with many others. Paul has not commanded that Philemon do anything, but he is counting on the fact that he will be obedient to the love and mercy of Christ.

SEARCH THE SCRIPTURES

True or False.

1. Paul exhorted Philemon about having slaves.

2. Paul was a young man at the writing of this letter (v. 9).

3. Paul wanted Onesimus to be punished for running away (vv. 15-16).

4. Paul expected Onesimus to work and repay what was stolen from Philemon (v. 18).

5. Paul was doubtful that Philemon would agree to his request (v. 21).

DISCUSS THE MEANING

1. Why did Paul compliment and encourage Philemon with all those words before he even mentioned Onesimus?

2. What were the relationships like in this passage, and why were they important?

3. How is the love, kindness, and compassion of Paul demonstrated in this letter? How does this coincide with what Christ has done for us?

4. Why was Paul so confident Philemon would answer his request?

LESSON IN OUR SOCIETY

We live in a selfish, self-centered world. It is popular to hear,

"People will step on their own mother to get ahead."

"What's in this for me?"

"Get all you can get."

"What about me?"

Having one's mind on self is a natural thing to do. Reaching out and going beyond the call of duty to help another person, with no thought of self or what we are going to get in return, is a rare attitude.

However, the Church will continue to prosper and increase as we strive to live by the Word of God reaching out to others with the love God has placed within us.

MAKE IT HAPPEN

As you look at how Paul put his neck on the line for Onesimus and then asked Philemon to make a sacrifice for him, consider how your actions compare. When was the last time you went an extra mile for someone? It is not always a pleasant experience, and we may get very little in return. Many of us have been hurt when we have gone "all out" to help someone else, so we are afraid or angry about doing it again. But Paul appealed to Philemon's Christianity. We should take action because the love of God constrains us, not because it seems like it's going to turn out all right.

FOLLOW THE SPIRIT

What God wants me to do:

_____

_____

REMEMBER YOUR THOUGHTS

Special insight you learned:

_____

_____

MORE LIGHT ON THE TEXT
PHILEMON 4-21

The epistle to Philemon is one of four letters that Paul addresses primarily to individuals. The other three are to Timothy (two letters) and Titus. The focus of the Letter to Philemon is forgiveness and restoration of a wayward servant who wronged his master and ran away. Here, Paul tactfully points out how slaves are to be treated in accordance to the rule of Christ. The next, but less obvious, reason is to make lodging arrangements, for him after his release from prison in Philemon's house. After the customary opening address consistent with the contemporary style of his day (vv. 1-3), Paul goes directly to the body of this letter.

4 I thank my God, making mention of thee always in my prayers, 5 Hearing of thy love and faith, which thou hast toward the Lord Jesus, and toward all saints;

This segment starts with Paul's expression of thanksgiving and prayer to God in behalf of Philemon, and his joy for the many good things he heard about him. Paul must have received good reports probably from Epaphras, a leader in the Colossian church (Colossian 4:12, 13), who was now with Paul (v. 23), regarding the condition of the Colossian church. Included in this report was a special mention of Philemon's faith in and work for the Lord, his love, generosity, and hospitality for the brethren and how he was using his house for the spread of the Gospel. Thus, Paul writes to Philemon in appreciation for the good things that he heard about him. A few things also need to be noted regarding this letter. First, Paul writes, "I thank my God," expressing his gratitude first to God for the good work. Paul shows that any good a man does is directly through God's enabling. In us is nothing good at all. All is God's grace given because of our relationship through His Son, and the Spirit who works in us. Therefore, all praise and honor should go to God.

Second, we notice the personal possessive pronoun Paul uses to describe his relationship with the Lord "my God." It draws our attention to Paul's awareness of his personal and intimate relationship with God. He can claim this personal ownership of the Lord because of his unfeigned faith in Christ. This faith is demonstrated by his own suffering, which is evident through his imprisonment even at the very moment he was writing the letter. When we have such close relationship with the Lord, we can claim Him as "my God." Paul used this phrase often in his epistles (Romans 1:8; 1 Corinthians 1:4; 14:8; 2 Corinthians 12: 21; Philippians 1:3; 4:19). Jesus called the Father "My God," showing the same intimate relationship with the Lord God (Matthew 27:46; Mark 15:34; John 20:17, 28). This term of endearment is carried over from the Old Testament, especially in the Psalms.

The third thing we need to take note of is Paul's habit of praying for others. We see repeatedly how he prays for others (cf. 1 Corinthians 1:4; Philippians 1:4; Colossians 1:3; 1 Thessalonians 1:2). The word "always" is characteristic of this habit. "Always" (Greek *pantote*) means "at all times" and conveys the idea of regularity. This means that Paul has formed the habit of mentioning Philemon and the churches to God and interceding on their behalf. "In my prayer" definitely means that in his private devotion, he always brings his readers before God in prayer, giving thanks to God for them.

Paul now gives the reason why he gives thanks to God in verse 5, i.e., because of the report of Philemon's "love and faith . . . toward the Lord Jesus, and toward all saints." Here we run into difficulty in interpretation. Is the phrase "love and faith" associated with the Lord Jesus alone, or

does it include the saint as well? It makes better sense to talk about love *toward* the saints, than speaking of *faith* towards the saints. Both words can be applied to the Lord Jesus. However, it makes more sense to go with the NIV translation of this clause "because I hear about your faith in the Lord Jesus and your love for all the saints." This type of structure is substantiated in Paul's other writings (Ephesians 1:15; Colossians 1:4).

6 That the communication of thy faith may become effectual by the acknowledging of every good thing which is in you in Christ Jesus.

We must, at this point, acknowledge the difficulty of interpreting verse 6. Nonetheless, it links with Paul's prayer for Philemon in verse 4, because it gives the content of the prayer and in the preceding verse 5 as well. In the latter verse, Paul mentions Philemon's love towards all saints. This love, which is a "communication"of his faith, is demonstrated in his willingness to share his goods with others. "Communication" is translated from the Greek word *koinonia* (say **koy-nohn-ee'-ah**) which also means "partnership, participation, fellowship or association." It conveys the idea of the share, which one has in anything, a joint contribution. It is translated "communion" (1 Corinthians 10:16; 2 Corinthians 6:14; 13:14;); "communicate" (Philemon 6; Hebrews 13:16); "fellowship" (Acts 2:42; 1 Corinthians 1:9; 2 Corinthians 8:4; Galatians 2:9, etc.); "contribution" (Romans 15:26); and "distribution" (2 Corinthians 9:13).

Based on the context of this book, Philemon undoubtedly must have made some valuable contributions towards the welfare of the community. Paul is therefore appealing to him to demonstrate the same liberality towards Onesimus, by showing mercy and restoring him. This thought pervades the rest of the letter (vv. 8-21) and seems to underlie the statement here (see Hendriksen pp. 214-215 for detailed treatment of this difficult verse). The closest interpretation is that Paul was praying that the many good things (the generosity and hospitality), which Philemon had shown to the saints may become effectual, Greek *energes* (**en-er-gace'**), active or powerful, in bringing others to the acknowledgment (*epignosis*) of every good thing (*agathos*, i.e., good nature), which is in you (preferably in us, *hemin*, say **hay-meen'**) in Christ. This means in a layman's sense that through Philemon's practical good works, which he had done for the saints and the anticipated work he is about to do, he may bring others to acknowledge the good things we can do in Christ. The goal is to bring people to the knowledge of Christ and to strengthen their faith in Him.

7 For we have great joy and consolation in thy love, because the bowels of the saints are refreshed by thee, brother.

Paul continues by expressing how joyous he was and the comfort he had derived from Philemon's benevolence to the poor in the past, which gave him hope for what he was about to present to him. Verse 7 is, of course, also linked with verse 4 and shows further why Paul is thankful to God. As we have already mentioned, it has been reported that Philemon on several occasions in the past had been generous to others, especially those in need, although not specifically stated, particularly to the slaves. So it is with great joy (*chara*) that Paul writes to express his appreciation for the love Philemon has shown to the poor and needy in the little community.

With this in mind, Paul has the "consolation" (*paraklesis*), i.e., the solace or comfort to plead for more, with particular reference to Onesimus. It is believed to be safe here to translate "consolation" as "confidence." In which case, the report of Philemon's act of kindness in the past gives Paul the confidence and inner solace to present the request he is about to make to Philemon. As seen in the latter part of this verse, Paul writes "because the bowels (hearts) of the saints are refreshed by thee, brother." Paul's use of "brother" *adephos* (**ad-el-fos'**) shows how deeply Paul loved Philemon, how highly he esteemed him, and the extent of confidence and trust he has placed on him. The word is frequently used in the New Testament to address fellow believers in Christ, in the sense which Paul applies it here (cf. 20).

8 Wherefore, though I might be much bold in Christ to enjoin thee that which is convenient, 9 Yet for love's sake I rather beseech thee, being such an one as Paul the aged, and now also a prisoner of Jesus Christ.

After expressing his appreciation to Philemon and the confidence he has in him, Paul comes to the main purpose of this letter. He starts with the conjunction "wherefore" (Greek *dio*) or "therefore," which implies, "since you are the type of person who loves to show kindness and delights in refreshing the hearts of people, I appeal to you." Although, Paul writes that in Christ he has the freedom to order Philemon to do what he is about to ask, he would for love's sake, rather appeal to him. Paul is conscious of his apostolic authority, which on several occasions he invoked in matters of faith and conduct in the church, but he prefers not to invoke it here (cf. Romans 1:1; 1 Corinthians 5:3, 4; 9:1; 2 Corinthians 10:13, 14; 12:12; Galatians 1:1; 2 Timothy 1:1, 11; 4:1; Titus 1:1). This title is obviously and probably deliberately omitted in the opening address in view of the nature of this letter.

Although Paul does not explicitly appeal to his authority as an apostle, the idea is implicitly and tactfully presented. If it were not so, he would not have mentioned it (cf. v. 19). Paul's brief reference to his position "in Christ" is meant to go through Philemon's mind as he considers the appeal Paul is about to make. Paul did not want to use it as the motivating force for his plea, rather he appeals to the most dynamic and motivating power that can change any circumstance—love. In a gentle, but tactful and persuasive way, Paul appeals to his age and suffering, "Yet for love's sake I rather beseech thee, being such an one as Paul the aged, and now also a prisoner of Jesus Christ." The Greek word used for "the aged" is *presbutes*, which also translates as "old man" (Luke 1:18; Titus 2:2), or "an ambassador."

Paul's age at this time is unknown. At the first mention of Paul during the stoning of Stephen, his projected age was 25 years old. Some scholars argue that if he were about 25 years old then, he would not have been more than 56 or 60 years when he wrote the letter. To us today, especially to the western world, that would not constitute old age. We ought to realize that the average life span then was shorter than it is now, and that Paul had probably aged faster than his years due to numerous sufferings and afflictions (cf. 2 Corinthians 11:23-33; cf. Galatians 6:17; 2 Corinthians 12:7).

Suffering, stress, affliction, and poverty are some of the catalysts to aging. A look at the world around us would reveal this fact. People who live in most African countries, the "ghettos" where African Americans are subjected in our inner cities, in South American countries, and the so-called "third-world countries," often age faster than their counterparts in the developed countries. That being the case, we can rightly translate *presbute* as "old man." However, the possibility of rendering the phrase "an ambassador" is evident from Paul's use of the word in other passages of the Bible (Ephesians 6:20). However the former is a better translation on the basis of Paul's tone of the appeal and sympathy he planned to create in Philemon's mind. Definitely, with such a powerful appeal to his conscience, Philemon could not refuse such a plea coming from an old man (a senior citizen in the Lord), who is now also suffering as a prisoner of Jesus Christ.

10 I beseech thee for my son Onesimus, whom I have begotten in my bonds: 11 Which in time past was to thee unprofitable, but now profitable to thee and to me: 12 Whom I have sent again: thou therefore receive him, that is, mine own bowels:

After appealing to Philemon's good nature and love towards others, (4-7, 9a) and to his own age and personal suffering as a prisoner of Christ (9b), Paul presents his request, which is the ultimate reason for the letter. Paul writes, "I beseech thee for my son Onesimus." Paul states that he is appealing on behalf of Onesimus who he qualifies as his son. The Greek verb Paul uses is *parakaleo* pronounced **par-ak-al-eh'-o,** from which the noun form *paraklesis* is derived. It is generally translated "to beg, beseech, pray, or entreat someone for a favor." Paul is asking Philemon for a favor, which is the acceptance of the runaway slave Onesimus.

We notice the affection Paul has for this wayward slave who, probably through Paul's teaching and counseling while in the Roman jail, is now converted to Christianity. He calls him "my son" or more appropriately "my child" (*teknon*) an offspring, child, son, or daughter. The word is used affectionately with close relationship of people such as patrons, teachers, employers, and helpers for their pupils or apprentices. In the New Testament, pupils or disciples are called children of their teachers, because the teachers, by their instruction, nourish the minds of their pupils and mold their characters. This is Paul's idea when he used the word here.

In the Old Testament, the people of Israel are referred to as the Children of God who were especially dear to Him. In Pauline writings, all that are led by the Spirit are thus closely related to God. Paul clarifies how Onesimus

has come to be known as his child, "whom I have begotten in my bonds." This throws more light on how and when Onesimus became converted in a Roman prison while Paul was under arrest. This onetime fugitive, upon arriving in Rome finds refuge under the apostle, and under his ministry becomes not only his son in the Lord, but also a faithful and beloved brother (Colossians 4:9).

Paul continues his description of the subject of his appeal: "Which in time past was to thee unprofitable, but now profitable to thee and to me." This is a recommendation and a reference for Onesimus to Philemon. "In the past," i.e., while he was with Philemon and before he came to Paul, Onesimus was "unprofitable" to Philemon, but after being with Paul and experiencing spiritual rebirth, he becomes profitable not only to Paul but also to Philemon.

There is a definite play on words here as we study the meaning of his name "Onesimus." The Greek *Onesimos* (direct transliterated into English) is pronounced **on-ay'-sim-os,** and is directly synonymous with the Greek word *euchrestos* (say **yoo'-khrays-tos**), which means "profitable, useful, or meet for use." This is opposite of *achrestos* (**akh'-race-tos**), which means "unprofitable or useless" and describes Onesimus, who never lived up to his name in times past. Paul seems to say, your former good-for-nothing slave who robbed you and ran away, now lives up to his name and is useful to me and to you. I am sending him back to you and I recommend that you receive him back (v. 12). The phrase, "that is, mine own bowels" describes further how dear and affectionate Onesimus was to Paul. He was dear to his very own heart, very much attached to him. How could Philemon reject this heartfelt recommendation from a person such as Paul the apostle.

13 Whom I would have retained with me, that in thy stead he might have ministered unto me in the bonds of the gospel: 14 But without thy mind would I do nothing; that thy benefit should not be as it were of necessity, but willingly.

In this verse, Paul seems to insinuate that he is reluctantly sending Onesimus back to his master. That he rather would have retained him in order that Onesimus would render to him, the service Philemon would have given him were he with him in prison. Paul continues tactfully emphasizing the great change that has taken place in the life of Onesimus. Paul finds him so changed that he would have kept him with himself, in fact he thought of that, it seems.

But he realized that it was not his to make the decision regarding Onesimus. Paul is assuming, based on his knowledge of Philemon and how generous he was, that

Philemon would have serviced Paul himself, but distance prevented him from doing so. Had Philemon known the circumstance, he would have been glad to substitute Onesimus' services for his own. Paul knew that he could not act on assumption. That would have been an improper abuse of his authority. So he writes: "But without thy mind (*gnome*, i.e., consent) would I do nothing; that thy benefit should not be as it were of necessity, but willingly." If Paul had requested to retain Onesimus in Rome as his helper, Philemon would have consented, but he did not. Instead, Paul says that he did not want to take advantage of Philemon's generosity, or indirectly force Philemon to give him a benefit by keeping his servant. Rather he wanted him to exercise the freedom to do what he wanted with his own servant.

15 For perhaps he therefore departed for a season, that thou shouldest receive him for ever; 16 Not now as a servant, but above a servant, a brother beloved, specially to me, but how much more unto thee, both in the flesh, and in the Lord?

Verses 15 and 16 support the premise that Paul's intention was not to get Onesimus back, but rather to emphasize the new Onesimus and recommend him back to his master. Paul argues here that Onesimus' departure from his master was not a mistake (although it was at that time) rather, it was God's providential act. God uses evil circumstances to perfect His will and plan. Is Paul's life story not a perfect example of God turning evil to good? Joseph told his brothers that their selling him to slavery in Egypt was an act of God to preserve their lives (Genesis 45:5). God used the evil deeds of Onesimus to bring about some good—salvation.

Paul says that Onesimus departed for a short time in order that he would have him forever. He departed as an unfaithful slave, to return as faithful; he departed as unprofitable and is returning as profitable; he departed a slave, but is returning as a brother in the Lord. Receive thus! Paul seems to say. He is no more a mere slave, but "a brother beloved." Paul was not advocating the abolition of servitude or that Philemon should set him free, rather Paul is saying that Onesimus, because of his conversion has joined the brotherhood of believers, and therefore should be treated thus. He is more than a slave, he is a beloved brother, Paul adds, "specially to me, but how much more unto thee, both in the flesh, and in the Lord." Using logic, Paul says Onesimus' relationship with him, though only spiritual, is like "a beloved brother" to him. However, Philemon's relationship with Onesimus is more than a spiritual one, they are both brothers in the flesh (both Colossians), and brothers in the Lord (both believers now). If he is so special and dear to Paul, how much more would he be to Philemon?

17 If thou count me therefore a partner, receive him as myself. 18 If he hath wronged thee, or oweth thee ought, put that on mine account; 19 I Paul have written it with mine own hand, I will repay it: albeit I do not say to thee how thou owest unto me even thine own self besides.

All Paul has been doing through the preceding verses is preparing the ground to present his heartfelt plea on behalf of Onesimus. A plea he presented so passionately and yet persuasively that it would be difficult to refuse. Paul is becoming very personal now and applying more tact as he goes on. He writes, "If thou count me therefore a partner, receive him as (you would receive) myself." Of course there is doubt that Philemon regarded Paul as a partner. "If thou count me. . . as a partner" cannot be treated as a conditional clause, but rather an affirmative. It means "since I know you regard me a partner, accept Onesimus, as you would receive me." The word "partner" used here (Greek *koinonos*) means more than a friend, but a comrade or companion, one who shares in the worship of Jesus. Paul puts Onesimus on the same level as himself, and requests that Philemon treats Onesimus in the way he would treat him.

Moreover, Paul pleads to be credited for any wrong Onesimus had done against Philemon or any debt he owed. The mention of this debt here shows either that Onesimus had told Paul that he had committed a theft, or that Paul suspected such. The latter would account for the use of "if" in verse 18. It seems that he was not sure, but wanted to cover every ground. However, what is certain is that by running away, Onesimus had caused his master the loss of his services. Such a debt would be the hindrance to reestablishing a proper, Christian relationship between master and returning servant, and therefore must be removed.

Hence, Paul offers to take up the debt whether the wrong he had committed or any material debt owed it should be credited to him. The phrase, "put that on mine account," *ellogeo* (**el-log-eh'-o**) means "to reckon in, impute, or put on account." Paul, in effect, is prepared to bear any due punishment and to pay back any material goods Onesimus had taken away from his master. Isn't that what Christ did on the cross for Paul and for us all? God saw our inability to pay for our sin, He therefore imputed our sins to Christ to reconcile us with Himself (cf. Romans

4:7-8; 2 Corinthians 5:19). Paul knew that Onesimus was incapable of paying Philemon back, he therefore offered himself. Paul is following the example Christ set for us. Paul's offer to compensate for the loss, which Philemon might have suffered, is a sincere and serious one and must be accepted and treated as such. Using the language of commerce, Paul says, "charge that to my account." The sincerity and seriousness of this offer is evident in the next verse, verse 19.

Paul continues, affirming his pledge and assuring Philemon of the promise, and says "I, Paul have written it with mine own hand, I will repay it." In other words, Paul is saying, "here is my signature as assurance of my pledge. I will (surely) repay it the whole thing." The word "repay" is the Greek word *apotino* (pronounced **ap-ot-ee'-no**) i.e., "to pay in full." The statement has been interpreted by many to mean that Paul wrote the letter in its entirety. This is hard to prove, though it is possible. We can only speculate based on 2 Thessalonians 3:17, that the closing salutation (and perhaps all of vv. 18-25) was written by the apostle himself. Paul's signature serves not only as an assurance conveying the seriousness of his pledge to Philemon, it demonstrates the intensity of his love for Onesimus.

The next clause is most probably intended as humor, to soften the apparent tension and seriousness of the matter: "Albeit I do not say to thee how thou owest unto me even thine own self besides." Paul says, "I don't need to remind you how much you owe me, even your very own life." The speculation here is that perhaps Philemon had been converted directly through Paul's ministry, or indirectly through the Epaphras who in turn is indebted to Paul. Whatever the case may be, Paul is making use of his liberty as a believer, a senior citizen to Philemon (v. 9), and his intimacy and friendship with the master as co-laborers and partners of the Gospel, to the fullest here.

20 Yea, brother, let me have joy of thee in the Lord: refresh my bowels in the Lord.

As in verse 8, Paul's personal intimacy with Philemon is reflected here with the term "brother," which expresses their spiritual relationship with each other. Paul continues to identify himself with Onesimus. He says, "let me have joy of thee in the Lord." "Joy" here can mean "favor" or "pleasure." If his request is granted, it will give him pleasure and peace. This pleasure or joy is dependent on Philemon. What favor is Paul asking for? It is obvious. That Philemon might receive Onesimus. In other words, Paul is saying to Philemon, that any favor he grants to Onesimus is to be seen as being granted to Paul himself, such will give him

pleasure, and "will refresh my bowels in the Lord," Paul concludes. For an explanation of this clause, see verse 7 above. Paul, in effect, is saying that he should be included among those for whom Philemon had refreshed their heart in the Lord.

21 Having confidence in thy obedience I wrote unto thee, knowing that thou wilt also do more than I say.

Finally, Paul expresses the confidence that Philemon would definitely do the right thing. Paul seems to say that he would not have wasted his time if he were not certain that Philemon would comply with his request. He tends to entertain no doubt that Philemon would act favorably to his plea, and even more. This confidence is a reflection of the relationship they had established as brothers in the Lord. Such a confidence, trusting relationship ought to exist among the household of God everywhere. Here, Paul is so sure of Philemon's faith in the Lord and integrity that he has great confidence in him. Can we be trusted in such a way? Are we so reliable that people place their confidence in us?

DAILY BIBLE READING

M: Paul Gives Thanks for Philemon
Philemon 1-7

T: Paul Expresses His Love for Onesimus
Philemon 8-12

W: Paul Intercedes for Onesimus
Philemon 13-18

T: Paul's Challenge to Philemon
Philemon 19-25

F: Don't Let Fine Clothes Deceive You!
James 2:1-7

S: Show Mercy, and Love All People
James 2:8-13

S: Have True Faith; Do Good Works
James 2:14-26

NOTES